Written, updated and revised by the Editors at FL Memo

FL Memo Limited

Important Disclaimer

This publication is sold on the understanding that the information provided within it is for guidance only, and that the publisher is not in business to provide legal or accounting advice or other professional services. Readers entering into transactions on the basis of, or otherwise relying on, such information should seek the services of a competent professional adviser.

While every care has been taken to ensure the accuracy of the contents, the editors and the publishers cannot accept responsibility for any loss occasioned to any person acting or refraining to act as a result of any statement in it.

ISBN: 978-0-9575083-1-6

FL MEMO LTD
185 Park Street
Bankside
London SE1 9DY

Telephone (020) 7803 4666, Fax (020) 7803 4699
Email: flm@flmemo.co.uk
Website: www.flmemo.co.uk

© 2013 FL Memo Limited
All rights reserved. No part of this work covered by the publisher's copyright may be reproduced or copied in any form or by any means without a written permission from the publisher.
British Library Cataloguing in Publication Data.
A catalogue record for this book is available from the British Library.

Employment

2013

Your book is fully updated online. Make sure you have your login details!

Your key benefits

Memo Online – a regularly updated service that features the entire contents of the book:

- fully searchable and always up to date giving you peace of mind

- store information, create notes and set up alerts to suit your own needs

Multi-user version – enabling more than one person to access the service at the same time (option available on request at www.flmemo.co.uk/requestlogin.php)

Email updates – alerting you to the latest news and fully integrated in the online service

News and Action Plans – notifying you of proposed new developments, complete with analysis and comment, handy Action Plans and ready to use documents

Indicator has joined forces with FL Memo

Visit us at **www.flmemo.co.uk**

Abbreviations

Acas	Advisory Conciliation and Arbitration Service	**EWHC**	England and Wales High Court decision
Admin	Administrative Court, High Court	**HC**	High Court
Art(s)	Article(s)	**HSWA 1974**	Health and Safety at Work etc. Act 1974
ASPP	Additional statutory paternity pay		
BIS	Department for Business, Innovation and Skills	**ICR**	Industrial Cases Reports
		ITEPA 2003	Income Tax (Earnings and Pensions) Act 2003
CA	Court of Appeal	**IRLR**	Industrial Relations Law Reports
CC	County Court		
ChD	Chancery Division, High Court	**NICs**	National Insurance Contributions
CJEU	Court of Justice of the European Union	**NMWA 1998**	National Minimum Wage Act 1998
cl(s)	Clause(s)	**PAYE**	Pay as you earn
CS	Court of Session	**para(s)**	Paragraph(s)
DG Code	Acas Code on discipline and grievance	**PILON**	Pay in lieu of notice
DP Code	Information Commissioner's Office Code on employment practices	**QB**	Queen's Bench Division, High Court
		reg(s)	Regulation(s)
DPA 1998	Data Protection Act 1998	**s(s)**	Section(s)
DWP	Department for Work and Pensions	**SAP**	Statutory adoption pay
EA 2002	Employment Act 2002	**SC**	Supreme Court
EA 2008	Employment Act 2008	**Sch**	Schedule
EAT	Employment Appeal Tribunal	**SI**	Statutory Instrument
EEA	European Economic Area	**SMP**	Statutory maternity pay
EHRC	Equality and Human Rights Commission	**SNB**	Special negotiating body
		SPP	Statutory paternity pay
EqA 2006	Equality Act 2006	**SRP**	Statutory redundancy pay
EqA 2010	Equality Act 2010	**SSCBA 1992**	Social Security Contributions and Benefits Act 1992
Equal Pay Code	Equality and Human Rights Commission Code on equal pay		
Equality Code	Equality and Human Rights Commission Code on employment	**SSP**	Statutory sick pay
		TULRCA 1992	Trade Union and Labour Relations (Consolidation) Act 1992
ERA 1996	Employment Rights Act 1996		
EReIA 1999	Employment Relations Act 1999	**TUPE**	Transfer of Undertakings (Protection of Employment) Regulations
EReIA 2004	Employment Relations Act 2004		
ET	Employment Tribunal	**UKEAT**	Employment Appeal Tribunal decision
EU	European Union		
EWC	European works council	**UKSC**	Supreme Court decision
EWCA Civ	England and Wales Court of Appeal (Civil Division) decision	**VAT**	Value Added Tax

All references in *Employment Memo* are to paragraphs.

1: Types of employment relationship	1
Employees and workers	10
Employee or self-employed?	30
2: Pre-employment	500
Recruitment and selection	510
Offer and appointment	700
Right to work	750
3: Starting employment	900
Induction	910
Probation	940
4: Continuity of employment	1000
Employment with same employer	1010
Change of employer	1035
Calculating period of continuous employment	1040
Qualifying periods	1080
5: Employment contract, variation and breach	1100
Formation	1110
Terms	1150
Information to be provided in writing	1400
Staff handbook	1480
Varying terms and conditions	1600
Breach of contract	1700
6: Flexible working	1800
Types of flexible working	1810
Working at home	1820
Part-time workers	1870
Fixed-term contracts	1950
Agency workers	2040
7: Directors	2100
8: Assignments	2200
Prerequisites for assignment	2210
Assignment abroad	2230

9: Company information and confidentiality	2300
Intellectual property rights	2310
Confidential information and confidentiality	2400
Restraints and restrictive covenants	2500
Whistleblowing	2700
10: Remuneration	2800
Pay	2805
Tax	3100
Pensions	3400
11: Time on	3600
Working time	3605
Sunday trading	3800
12: Time off	3900
Time off during working hours	3910
Annual leave	4000
13: Sickness, injury and absence	4100
Statutory sick pay	4110
Occupational sick pay	4170
Permanent health insurance	4200
Management of sickness	4210
14: Rights of parents and carers	4400
Maternity rights	4410
Adoption rights	4520
Paternity rights	4570
Parental leave	4620
Right to request flexible working	4690
Time off to care for dependants	4740
Remedies	4760
15: Health and safety	4800
Duties	4810
Means of protection	4860
Specific issues	5010
Remedies and enforcement	5130
16: Equality at work	5200
Discrimination	5210
Equal pay	5650
Enforcement and remedies	5700
Best practice	5800
17: Data protection and privacy	5900
Data protection	5910
Monitoring and surveillance	6150
Email and internet issues	6260
Right to privacy	6285
18: Training and performance	6300
Training	6310
Time to train applications	6400
Evaluation, guidelines and benchmarking	6450

19: Discipline and grievance	6500
Discipline	6530
Grievance procedures	6730
Right to be accompanied	6780
20: Payroll and NIC	6800
PAYE	6810
NICs in relation to employment	6925
21: Trade unions, collective bargaining and industrial action	7100
Trade unions	7115
Recognition and derecognition	7200
Collective bargaining	7360
Strikes and other industrial action	7400
Individual rights	7560
22: Information and consultation in the workplace	7658
Domestic information and consultation	7655
European works councils	7785
23: Lay-off and short-time working	7850
Guarantee payments	7860
Redundancy payments	7875
24: Transfer of the business	7900
Which transfers are covered?	7910
Effect	7950
Information and consultation obligations	8060
25: Ending employment	8100
Termination of employment	8105
Unfair dismissal	8380
Redundancy	8730
Employee rights on insolvency	9040
26: Handling disputes and alternative resolution	9100
Handling potential litigious disputes	9110
Resolving employment disputes	9200
27: Employment claims	9400
Jurisdiction and time limits	9410
Tribunal claims	9500
Claims in the civil courts	9850
Appendix	9900
Model statement of particulars	9900
Model contract of employment for general staff	9910
Model discipline and grievance policy	9915
Main social benefits	9920

Index (p. 1055)

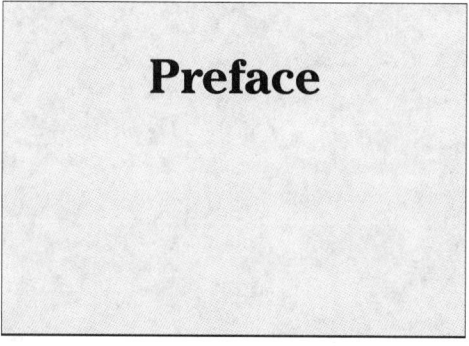

Preface

Employment Memo 2013 is a well-established handbook providing **practical guidance** and **dynamic and fast moving commentary** on employment law and practice. It is accessible and easy to navigate, while retaining depth of coverage on a wide range of employment issues.

Employment Memo 2013 has been **revised and updated** to include all of the recent developments and will continue to provide a reliable source of information throughout the current year using:
– an **online updating facility**, giving detailed updates to individual paragraphs reflecting the latest developments;
– an **online version of the handbook**. The online Memo also **includes tables** of acts, statutory instruments and cases. All online updates are automatically incorporated into the text of the online version;
– **online newsletters**, which highlight and explore new developments; and
– **email alerts** to all updates and newsletters.

Employment Memo 2013 and its updating service will **cover**:
– changes to rates and awards;
– changes to the vetting and barring system, and the planned creation of an online checking service of criminal record checks for employers;
– planned legislative changes to parental leave, whistleblowing protection, collective consultation, and equality law;
– planned new rules and procedure for tribunal claims, and proposals to introduce fees for bringing a claim;
– the planned introduction of "employee-shareholder" contracts;
– proposals to make changes to compensatory tribunal awards and for the introduction of "protected conversations"; and
– new material on reservists, apprenticeships, immigration rules, health and safety reporting requirements, working time, TUPE, redundancy, and much more…

Employment Memo 2013 primarily covers the **law applying to** England and Wales. While reference is made in this edition to the legal systems in Scotland and Northern Ireland, specialist advice should be sought in respect of these jurisdictions. Public sector employment and those working at sea are also largely outside the scope of this handbook.

This handbook is intended to reflect **law and practice as at** 1 February 2013.

FL Memo Ltd
February 2013

CHAPTER 1

Types of employment relationship

OUTLINE	¶¶
SECTION 1 **Employees and workers** 10	SECTION 2 **Employee or self-employed?** 30
Employees................................ 11	Mutuality, control and personal performance 35
Workers................................... 13	Not in business for own account............ 50

This chapter sets out the distinction between employees and self-employed workers, and the distinction between the latter and those that are in business for their own account, who can be termed self-employed persons. The "classic" working relationship is that of employer-employee where an employee works for his employer under a contract of employment. Further, the most common employment arrangement is that of **full-time permanent employment** and this is the standard relationship used in this book unless otherwise stated.

An increasing number of staff have flexible work arrangements, for example working part-time, on fixed-term contracts or through an agency. The legal, contractual and practical issues involved are discussed in chapter 6.

Directors are office-holders and may also be employees. If they are shareholders this may affect their employment status (see ¶43). Their role as directors is discussed in chapter 7.

There are also special rules relating to **apprentices**, **trainees** and **young persons**. The special rules relating to these groups are discussed outside this chapter in the specific topics as follows:

Type of worker	Para
Apprentices	¶6351
National minimum wage	¶2865
Trainees	¶6350
Working time	¶3615
Young persons	¶4970
Government-backed training initiatives	¶6370
Health and safety	¶4970
Right to time off to study	¶6330
Working time	¶3720

SECTION 1

Employees and workers

10 Traditionally, UK law focused on the relationship between employer and employee. As a result, the main employment rights **apply to employees** only (i.e. those who work under a contract of employment) and those who are employed under other contracts are excluded. However, largely as a result of the implementation of EC Directives into UK law, some newer employment rights **apply to** a larger group called **workers**. Generally, the term "workers" includes employees and other persons employed under other contracts for personal service but excludes those who are in business for their own account and are providing these services to a client or customer.

> *MEMO POINTS* The Government has consulted on **proposals** to introduce a new type of employment contract called "**employee-shareholder**" **contracts**. This contract would give employees shares in the business they work for that will be exempt from capital gains tax up to £50,000 (although subject to income tax and NICs under the normal rules that apply for shares acquired by reason of employment) in exchange for giving up certain employment rights. These rights would be the right not to be unfairly dismissed, redundancy rights, the right to request flexible working, the right to request time off for training, and employees would be required to give 16, instead of 8, weeks' notice to return early from maternity/adoption leave and 16, instead of 6, weeks' notice to return early from additional paternity leave. Employers would have the option of inserting more generous employment conditions into the employment contract if they want to, but the thrust of the proposals is to lessen employee rights to enable greater fluidity and ease in hiring and firing employees.
>
> The Government's response to the consultation has clarified that companies must satisfy themselves that the shares to be given are worth at least £2,000 or the employee can assert that their employee-shareholder status is not valid and that they therefore retain the usual employment rights enjoyed by employees. There will be no restrictions on the type of shares issued although they must be fully paid up and individuals must give no consideration for them other than agreeing to be employee shareholders. Any forfeiture and buy-back provisions will be contractual rather than statutory.
>
> Companies of any size will be able to use this new kind of contract, although the intention is for this new type of arrangement to be mainly used by small and medium-sized companies. Non UK-registered companies will also be allowed to use employee shareholder status. Subsidiaries will be permitted to issue parent company shares. Whilst the new employee-shareholder status will be voluntary, the existing rules regarding eligibility for job-seeker's allowance will remain, meaning those in receipt of the benefit will lose their benefits if they unreasonably reject a job offer made on this basis.
>
> Further developments will be covered by our updating service.

Employees

11 The Employment Rights Act gives a **standard definition** as follows (s 230(1) ERA 1996):

"an "employee" means an individual who has entered into or works under (or, where the employment has ceased, worked under) a contract of employment."

A **contract of employment** is defined as a contract of service or apprenticeship, whether express (orally or in writing) or implied (s 230(2) ERA 1996).

Slightly different definitions can be found in other Acts and regulations such as health and safety legislation, business transfer regulations, trade union law and statutory maternity, adoption, paternity and sick pay regulations. How each of these definitions differs from the standard definition is discussed in the relevant topics.

> *MEMO POINTS* Employees can be simultaneously employed by two **different employers at the same time** if they are compatible (*Prison Officers Association and ors v Gough and anor* [2009] UKEAT 0405_09_1712). For example, where the employer releases an employee from their duties to carry out their functions as a union official and during this time they are paid by the union for their work as an official and are subject to the union's control.

The **main employee statutory rights** are shown in the table below; some of which are only activated when the employee has been continuously employed for the requisite **qualifying period** (¶1080). In addition, employees are **also entitled** to the rights of workers (see below).

Employee's right to:	Para.
Continuity of employment on transfer of undertaking	¶7974
Equality for fixed-term employees	¶1950
Guarantee payments	¶7860
Itemised pay statements	¶2985
Maternity, adoption and paternity rights	¶4400
Minimum period of notice	¶8131
Not suffer unlawful deductions	¶3050
Parental rights	¶4620
Pay during medical suspension	¶4985
Redundancy rights	¶8730
Request flexible working	¶4690
Sick pay	¶4110
Time off during work hours	¶3910
Not be unfairly dismissed	¶8380
Written statement of main terms	¶1405
Written statement of reasons for dismissal	¶8310

Workers

A person is a worker when he is either:
– an **employee** working under a contract of employment; or
– working under a contract (other than a contract of employment) and is offering his personal service to another party to the contract, who is not his client or customer, in return for remuneration. Such a contract is often called a "contract for personal services". Such workers can be referred to as **non-employee workers**.

Worker or business undertaking? Those who are self-employed and are in business to provide a client or customer with professional or other services are not workers. They are considered to be sufficiently at arm's length and in an **independent position** to look after themselves, for example a consultant running a consultancy practice or a freelancer who is working for many companies.

However, self-employed contractors/freelancers, subcontractors, home and casual workers who are in a **subordinate and dependent position** and are not providing their services in a client or professional relationship will be workers. Both the Court of Appeal and the EAT have previously suggested that labour-only/semi-skilled subcontractors were good examples of those who would be unlikely to be carrying on a business undertaking and therefore likely to be within the classification of workers, and the EAT has found that such a labour-only subcontractor is a worker for the purposes of the Working Time Regulations, even in a situation where the parties have signed a contract including a clause permitting delegation of the work (*Byrne Brothers (Formwork) Ltd v Baird* [2002] IRLR 96, EAT; *Wright v Redrow Homes (Yorkshire) Ltd* [2004] ICR 1126, CA; *Redrow Homes (Yorkshire) Ltd v Buckborough and anor* [2009] IRLR 34, EAT). However, this will not apply if the clause permitting delegation of work is unfettered (*MPG Contracts Ltd v England* [2009] UKEAT 0488_08_0805; *Premier Groundworks Ltd v Jozsa* [2009] UKEAT 0494_08_1703; *Archer-Hoblin Contractors Ltd v MacGettingan* [2009] UKEAT 0037_09_0307).

EXAMPLE
Workers under Working Time Regulations
1. In *Byrne Brothers (Formwork) Ltd v Baird*, a subcontractor, who signed a contract which allowed him to delegate only if he was unable to provide his services and only with express prior approval of

his contractor, was nevertheless found to be a worker under a contract to provide services personally and not in business for his own account. Consequently, the subcontractor was entitled to holiday pay.

2. In *Redrow Homes (Yorkshire) Ltd v Buckborough and anor*, a labour-only subcontractor who signed a contract which allowed him to delegate his work was found to be a worker under a contract to provide services personally. The delegation clause was a sham in that neither party intended it to take effect, and so did not prevent him being a worker and entitled to holiday pay.

Not workers under Working Time Regulations
In *MPG Contracts Ltd v England*, a father and son worked as partitioning and ceiling erectors under an agreement with a contractor. The agreement included a term allowing them to subcontract their work, provided that they gave the contractor enough information to satisfy itself that the subcontractor was competent. The contractor could refuse to accept an unsuitable substitute. The father and son claimed that they were entitled to holiday pay as workers. The EAT held that the option to veto unqualified subcontractors did not represent a real limitation on the power to subcontract, so the contract was not one to provide services personally and therefore the claimants were not workers.

Highly qualified professionals who work as independent contractors, but who do not market their skills to the world at large, have also been held to be workers: regardless of the type of contractor/subcontractor the test is always whether the contractor/subcontractor is providing his services in a client or professional relationship or not (*The Hospital Medical Group v Westwood* [2012] EWCA Civ 1005).

EXAMPLE In *The Hospital Medical Group Ltd v Westwood*, a GP, W, who worked one day per week as an independent consultant performing cosmetic procedures at a clinic owned by the Hospital Medical Group (HMG), was found to be a worker by the tribunal. Consequently, they had jurisdiction to entertain W's complaints of unlawful deductions from wages, accrued holiday pay and age discrimination. HMG appealed to the EAT and then to the Court of Appeal on the basis that W was engaged in a profession or business undertaking on his own account, and therefore should not have been held to be a worker. The EAT and the Court of Appeal dismissed HMG's appeals. Under his contract for services with HMG, W was engaged personally to carry out the work; he had no right to delegate work to others. He performed the cosmetic procedures exclusively on behalf of HMG, at their premises, using their equipment, and he was recruited by HMG to work as an integral part of their operations. Crucially, he only performed cosmetic surgery on patients introduced to him by HMG and the work was wholly separate from his work as a GP. The fact he did not offer his services as a cosmetic surgeon to the world at large meant that HMG was not a client or customer of his profession or business and W was, as a result, a worker.

16 This analysis is based on the **definition** given by legislation as follows (s 230(3) ERA 1996):
"a worker (except in the phrases "shop worker" and "betting worker") means an individual who has entered into or works under (or, where the employment has ceased, worked under):
a. a contract of employment, or
b. any other contract, whether express or implied and (if it is express) whether oral or in writing, whereby the individual undertakes to do or perform personally any work or services for another party to the contract whose status is not by virtue of the contract that of a client or customer of any profession or business undertaking carried on by the individual;
and any reference to a worker's contract shall be construed accordingly."
There are similar legislative provisions for other worker rights, for example worker rights under trade union law, national minimum wage and working time regulations.

17 The **main worker statutory rights** are shown in the table below. There are **no qualifying periods** that need to be achieved before the worker can benefit from these rights.

Worker's right to:	Para.
Breaks and rest periods	¶3710
Equal pay	¶5650
Equality for part-time workers	¶1870
Health and safety rights	¶4800
National minimum wage	¶2865

Worker's right to:	Para.
Not be discriminated against on grounds of age, disability, gender reassignment, marriage and civil partnership, race, religion or belief, sex or sexual orientation	¶5200
Paid annual leave	¶4000
Not suffer detriment for inadmissible reason	¶8393
Be accompanied at discipline and grievance hearings	¶6780
Trade union activities	¶7100
Whistleblowing rights	¶2700

SECTION 2

Employee or self-employed?

The distinction between those in employment and those who are self-employed is significant for employment and tax law purposes.

Those who are self-employed have less stringent **tax** rules on the deductibility of expenses, benefit from cash flow advantages, and pay less in **social security contributions** (NIC). However, employees have more statutory **rights** than the self-employed and their contracts of employment often give contractual benefits (e.g. contractual sick pay) which are not normally applicable to those who are self-employed.

> MEMO POINTS 1. Contractors who **supply their services through** an intermediary service company, often called a **personal service company**, are taxed as if they are employees of that company. See *Tax Memo* for further details.
> 2. **Agency workers** have a general employment relationship with their agencies. Further, in certain circumstances, it may be possible for an agency worker to be an employee of either the agency or the client (end-user). See ¶¶2042+ for further details.

It is usually clear whether a person is employed or self-employed. However, there are circumstances where it is not clear or it is in dispute. Such **disputes** usually occur when one party is trying to enforce his legal rights, for example the employee claims he has been unfairly dismissed and the employer asserts that he is self-employed and therefore not entitled to make a claim. Typically, disagreement as to status arises where there is no written contract between the parties or where there is a written contract but the parties disagree as to its interpretation or effect.

Disputes may also occur where HMRC disagree with the type of tax and NIC that are being paid.

Further, the **consequences** of treating an individual as self-employed when he is actually employed are likely to fall on the employer, who may be **liable to account for** the **PAYE** (¶6810) and **NIC** (¶6925) that should have been deducted over the course of the employment (although, if certain conditions are met, HMRC can set off any tax paid directly by the employee under self-assessment against an employer's liability for failure to deduct PAYE). Alternatively, HMRC may not impose a retrospective charge and in such cases will only require the employer to commence deduction of PAYE/NIC.

In situations where there is doubt over whether an individual is employed or self-employed, it is therefore in the employer's interests to ensure that the individual is making the appropriate tax/NIC payments under the self-employment regime.

Case law gives guidance on how to distinguish between those in employment and those who are self-employed and the following **tests** have to be satisfied for there to be an employment relationship:
– there must be mutuality of obligation, sufficient control and the work must be personally performed; and
– the worker must not be in business for his own account.

33 In determining status, a court or tribunal will investigate allegations that the written contract does not represent the actual terms agreed to **determine the actual nature** of the relationship between the parties (*Autoclenz Ltd v Belcher and ors* [2011] UKSC 41, *Protectacoat Firthglow Ltd v Miklos Szilagyi* [2009] IRLR 365, CA). This will include evidence of how the parties conducted themselves and what their expectations of each other were. Evidence of how the parties conducted themselves in practice may be so persuasive that an inference can be drawn that it reflects the true obligations of the parties. However, the mere fact that the parties conducted themselves in a particular way does not of itself mean that that conduct accurately reflects the legal rights and obligations. For example, there could be a legal right to provide a substitute worker (see below) and the fact that such right was never exercised in practice does not mean that it was not a genuine right.

Mutuality, control and personal performance

35 In an employment relationship, both parties must be under an irreducible minimum of obligation. This must amount to one party providing work usually for remuneration and exercising sufficient control over the other party who must personally perform the work required (*Montgomery v Johnson Underwood Ltd* [2001] IRLR 269, CA). An **absence** of mutual obligations on both parties will defeat the creation of the contract of employment (*Wilson v Circular Distributors Ltd* [2006] IRLR 38, EAT).

> MEMO POINTS The Court of Appeal in *Montgomery v Johnson Underwood Ltd* noted that as the nature and manner of carrying out employment develops, so will the courts' view as to the nature and extent of mutual obligation and control. Therefore, what will amount to mutuality of obligation and sufficient control may change in the future.

36 **Mutuality of obligation** It is important to consider the **nature** of the mutuality of obligations in order to determine whether a contract of employment has been formed. The focus must be as to whether there is *some* obligation on an individual to perform work and *some* obligation on the employer to pay for it. The fact that an individual might have the right to refuse work and the employer might have the right to withhold it will not deprive the relationship of its mutuality of obligations provided an "irreducible minimum" of obligation on either party exists. Where there is an obligation on the employer to provide work for (and pay) the employee and an obligation on the employee to accept it, this will indicate the existence of a contract of employment, i.e. the "work/wage" bargain (*Cotswold Developments Construction Ltd v Williams* [2006] IRLR 181, EAT).

So long as the **remuneration** is provided by the employer it does not matter if it is not paid directly but through some other arrangement made by the employer. In other words, a person who would otherwise be the employee's employer does not cease to be his employer simply by arranging for wages to be paid via a third party (*Cable and Wireless v Muscat* [2006] ICR 975, CA).

37 With regard to **permanent employees**, it is usually clear that there is an obligation on the employer to provide work and on the employee to work.

The obligation may be less clear with regard to non-permanent staff who are **casual or seasonal**. To ascertain the status of a casual staff member, it must be determined if he is employed for the **specific periods** he works. If he has separate contracts of employment for each of these periods, he will be an employee from the start to end of each period worked.

When a casual staff member has a series of **specific contracts** of employment, he is continuously employed for the duration of each contract and will be able to rely on the main statutory rights once the necessary qualifying periods of employment have been achieved. However, periods of non-employment will usually break his continuity of employment unless the statutory continuity rules are satisfied (¶1010). It may, therefore, be difficult for casual staff to obtain the necessary qualifying periods with regard to rights for which long periods are required (principally the rights not to be unfairly dismissed and to redundancy payments).

> **EXAMPLE**
> **Mutuality of obligation**
> In *Cornwall County Council v Prater* [2006] ICR 731, CA, a teacher who was engaged by a Council to work as a home tutor under a number of engagements over a 10-year period was deemed to be an employee who was continuously employed over that period. During each of the individual engagements, the teacher was obliged to perform work for which the Council was obliged to pay her. However, at the end of each engagement, the Council was under no obligation to offer a further assignment to her and she was not obliged to accept any of the engagements (though in practice she never refused an offer of work). The Court of Appeal found that there was sufficient mutuality of obligation existing between the parties in respect of each individual engagement and it was irrelevant that the Council was not obliged to provide any further engagement at the end of each assignment.
>
> **No mutuality of obligation**
> In *Little v BMI Chiltern Hospital* [2009] UKEAT 0021_09_2404, a hospital porter worked under an agreement which indicated that he was an independent contractor and would work "as and when" required for an hourly rate. In practice, from time to time, he would be sent home during a shift if he was not needed. Having first found that the written agreement represented the parties' true intentions, the EAT went on to hold that there was no mutuality of obligation between the parties and therefore no contract of employment.

38 In certain circumstances, the courts have held that there may be a general contract of employment if the casual worker has a long-standing relationship with the employer which is so regular and constant that it creates an irreducible minimum of obligation on each party (*Nethermere (St Neots) Ltd v Gardiner and Taverna* [1984] IRLR 240, CA). Such a contract is often called an "**umbrella**" or "**global**" contract of employment and whether such a contract is created will depend on all the circumstances. If there is an umbrella contract, subject to the statutory continuity rules, continuity is presumed to run from the beginning of the first assignment and there will be no gaps in the employment relationship or breaks in continuity when the employee is not working between assignments.

Court decisions in recent years, though, have appeared to move away from identifying such umbrella contracts, especially if a casual staff member is only paid when work is available, is not obliged to accept work and does not work when there is none (*Consistent Group Ltd v Kalwak and ors* [2008] IRLR 505, CA; *Carmichael v National Power plc* [2000] IRLR 43, HL; *Clark v Oxfordshire Health Authority* [1998] IRLR 125, CA; *Bunce v Postworth Limited t/a Skyblue* [2005] IRLR 557, CA). However, this has not prevented the courts from finding that umbrella contracts still exist where appropriate (*Pulse Healthcare Ltd v Carewatch Care Services Ltd and ors* [2012] UKEAT 0123_12_0608, [2012] UKEAT 0123_12_2007), and the existence of such a contract will not be negated because the parties entered into it as a matter of convenience (*St Ives Plymouth Ltd v Haggerty* [2008] UKEAT 0107_08_2205).

> **EXAMPLE**
> **No umbrella contract**
> 1. In *Clark v Oxfordshire Health Authority*, the Court of Appeal held there was no umbrella contract where C, a staff nurse who worked for the Authority, was only offered employment at one of the Authority's hospitals when it was available. Although C worked regularly for over 3 years, there were gaps when she did not work. When C worked she was paid hourly and subject to PAYE and NIC deductions. However, she was not entitled to guaranteed or continuous work, she received no payment during periods she was not working and she was not entitled to holiday or sick leave.
> 2. In *Vernon v Event Management Catering Ltd* [2007] UKEAT 0161_07_0207, an employee, V, was employed on a series of casual contracts. It was held that there was no umbrella or global contract because in the periods when V was not at work there were no mutual obligations which could keep the contract alive. V was, however, able to rely on the continuity of employment rules (¶1014) to obtain the necessary qualifying periods to bring his various claims, principally one for unfair dismissal. This was possible as he had worked for his employer for at least 1 day every week from the start of his employment in February 2003 to the end of his employment in June 2006.
>
> **Umbrella contract**
> 1. In *Pulse Healthcare Ltd v Carewatch Care Services Ltd and ors*, the EAT found that a group of carers working on purportedly zero hours contracts were in fact employees employed under umbrella contracts. The "zero hours" element of their contracts did not reflect the true employment relationship and the significant points in establishing their employee status were that: they all worked on a critical

> care package for a severely disabled patient whose care could not have been satisfied by ad hoc arrangements; there were repeated references in their contracts to "employment"; they worked a set amount of hours each month despite the terms of their written contracts; one claimant had been suspended for a period and paid in full during this time, as would have been the case in a normal employment relationship; the carers were subject to control and discipline, had to provide personal service, were provided with uniforms and equipment, and were paid on a PAYE basis; and there was no reason to think that there were any gaps in employment.
>
> 2. In *St Ives Plymouth Ltd v Haggerty*, the EAT held that there was an umbrella contract of employment covering a bank worker who was frequently offered and accepted work over a period of years and who was in the habit of giving advance notice of when she would be available for work. The fact that the mutuality of obligation had arisen from the commercial practicalities, i.e. that the arrangement suited both parties, did not stand in the way of a legal obligation arising.

39 The principle of mutuality of obligation is also relevant to establishing the status of **volunteers**. A volunteer will not be an employee if he receives no pay other than the reimbursement of expenses actually incurred and is not obliged to attend work or be provided with work. The existence of required standards and guidelines if the volunteer does attend work does not create mutuality of obligation (*Melhuish v Redbridge Citizens Advice Bureau* [2005] IRLR 419, EAT).

40 **Sufficient control of employer** The employer must have sufficient control over an employee for there to be an irreducible minimum of obligation (*Ready-Mixed Concrete (South East) Ltd v Minister of Pensions and National Insurance* [1968] 2 QB 497, as supported by recent decisions). In general, an employer can tell an employee what to do, and also how and when to do it, and in such circumstances it is clear that the employer has sufficient control.

The courts have noted that in many kinds of employment, direct supervision and control by an employer is absent, for example highly-skilled employees may have little day-to-day control exercised on them, and in such circumstances the courts will look to see if there is a "sufficient **framework of control**", i.e. overall control (*Montgomery v Johnson Underwood Ltd* [2001] IRLR 269, CA).

41 Control can be exercised indirectly as long as there is a sufficient degree of **actual** control (*Motorola Ltd v (1) Davidson and (2) Melville Craig Group Ltd* [2001] IRLR 4, EAT). Further, if there is a sufficient degree of control, it is irrelevant that another party may have similar or greater powers of control.

So, for example, agencies have been found to be the employers of agency workers even where other companies (the clients or end-users), which have been supplied with the agency workers, have exercised day-to-day control over them (see ¶¶2042+).

42 However, if there is **no contract of any kind** between the worker and the client it is irrelevant whether there is sufficient control as there cannot be an employment relationship (*Hewlett Packard Ltd v O'Murphy* [2001] UKEAT 612_01_2609; *Esso Petroleum Ltd v (1) Jarvis and (2) Brentivine* [2002] UKEAT 0831_00_1801).

> EXAMPLE In *Hewlett Packard Ltd v O'Murphy*, a computer specialist (O'Murphy) was an employee of a company he had set up (Circle Technology (CT)). He provided services to Hewlett Packard (HP) continuously for a number of years as part of a team and was integrated into the workforce. His work was provided through CT (who paid his remuneration) under a contract with an employment agency, which had a separate agreement with HP to provide computer services. HP terminated this agreement when HP considered that O'Murphy was incapable of efficiently performing the work expected of him. The EAT held that as there was no contract of any kind between O'Murphy and HP (except for a confidentiality agreement that had been agreed between O'Murphy and HP), there was no employment relationship between them.

43 It can be problematic for a **controlling shareholder** to be an employee of the company in which he holds his interest, as he may be able, by virtue of his shareholding, to control whether or not he is dismissed. His dual role may also give rise to a conflict of interests. However, these potential problems do not necessarily mean that there will not be a contract of employment between a company and its controlling shareholder, and the Court of Appeal has confirmed that there is nothing to prevent a controlling shareholder being an employee of a company if the facts support that conclusion (*Secretary of State for Business, Enterprise and Regulatory Reform v Neufeld and anor* [2009] IRLR 475, CA, which endorsed most of the elements of the guidance given in *Clark v (1) Clark Construction Initiatives Ltd and (2) Utility Consulting Services Ltd* [2008] IRLR 364, EAT, subject to certain remarks). The **entrepreneurial character** of the shareholder, his role in building the company up, and the fact that he derives a profit from its success do not prevent a finding that there is a contract in place. Likewise, the fact that the individual takes **loans** from the company or **guarantees** its debts could exceptionally have some relevance in analysing the true nature of the relationship, but in most cases such matters are unlikely to carry any weight.

Although the **service agreement** is a significant factor, it is not determinative and all the relevant factors must be considered in determining whether or not he is an employee (*Gladwell v Secretary of State for Trade and Industry* [2007] ICR 264, EAT). The courts will look at the reality of the situation, as they did in *Bunting v Hertel (UK) Ltd*, where the EAT held that there was no actual employment relationship despite what, on the surface, may have seemed to be one (*Bunting v Hertel (UK) Ltd* [2000] UKEAT 1453_99_1702).

The existence of a **written contract** does not place the **burden of proof** that it is not genuine on the party seeking to deny it. It will be for the party asserting the existence of an employment contract to prove it; and the mere production of what purports to be a written service agreement may by itself be insufficient to prove the case sought to be made and the production of additional evidence to prove its true nature may be required (*Secretary of State for Business, Enterprise and Regulatory Reform v Neufeld and anor*). Further, the **conduct of the parties**:
- in accordance with the contract is a strong pointer towards a valid contract of employment; and
- inconsistent with the contract, or the omission of certain key areas usually dealt with in an employment contract, are potentially important factors pointing away from employment.

On the other hand, the **lack of a written contract** should not, by itself, be taken to be an indicator that the contract is not a genuine one, although it can be an important consideration.

EXAMPLE

Controlling shareholder is an employee
1. In *Sellars Arenascene Ltd v Connolly* [2001] IRLR 222, CA, C was a majority shareholder of Arenascene (through his majority holding of its parent company). He was the managing director and chairman though he did not have sole control of the board. He had a written contract of employment with express provisions for his duties, hours of work and holidays. The Court confirmed that C was an employee.
2. In *Secretary of State for Business, Enterprise and Regulatory Reform v Neufeld and anor*, the CA found that a 90% shareholder who had a long history of taking an active sales role in the business was an employee, notwithstanding the fact that he had lent money to the company and guaranteed its debts.
3. In *Nesbitt and anor v Secretary of State for Trade and Industry* [2007] IRLR 847, EAT, a married couple owned 51.99% and 48% respectively of the shares in the company for which they worked. Aside from the facts of their share ownership, the EAT held that all the other facts of the case indicated that the husband and wife were employees: they had bona fide employment contracts, they received remuneration by way of salary, and they behaved like employees. It followed that they were indeed employees.

Controlling shareholder is not an employee
1. In *Bunting v Hertel (UK) Ltd*, the two shares in a company, PMS, were held by B and another on trust for B's family. Neither trustee had a casting vote. B was also the sole director and so had effective control. PB, his wife, was the company secretary. Neither B nor PB had a written contract of employment though they both received a salary from which tax and NIC were deducted. The EAT held that B and PB were not employees.
2. In *Morrison v ODS Business Services Ltd and anor* [2007] UKEAT 0618_06_2106, a shareholder held 50.1% of the shares in a company. He set his own salary and determined the day-to-day running of the company. Although ostensibly the shareholder took advice from other directors, in practice, he was not subject to any disciplinary procedures. The EAT found that he was not an employee.

45 **Personal performance** A person must perform his contract personally (*Ready-Mixed Concrete (South East) Ltd v Minister of Pensions and National Insurance* [1968] 2 QB 497). However, personal performance does not necessarily always indicate that an individual is employed.

46 Where a person can **choose to perform** his contract by sending someone else in his place, he will not satisfy this requirement. In such circumstances, the person need never perform the contract personally and therefore cannot be employed (*Express and Echo Publications Ltd v Tanton* [1999] IRLR 367, CA; *Premier Groundworks Ltd v Jozsa* [2009] UKEAT 0494_08_1703).

However, **substitution** is acceptable if the right to delegate is restricted to circumstances where a person is **unable to perform** (as opposed to choosing not to perform) his duties (*Macfarlane v Glasgow City Council* [2001] IRLR 7, EAT; *James v Redcats (Brands) Ltd* [2007] IRLR 296, EAT).

EXAMPLE
Found to be self-employed
In *Express and Echo Publications Ltd v Tanton*, a driver was made redundant and re-hired. A clause in the new contract provided that "in the event that the contractor is unable or unwilling to perform services personally, he shall arrange at his own expense entirely for another suitable person to perform the services." From time to time the driver did in fact provide a substitute driver. Consequently, the Court accepted that the driver had been re-hired as a self-employed contractor.

Found to be employee
1. In *James v Redcats (Brands) Ltd*, when a motorcycle courier could not attend work, for example when she was on holiday, she would find a substitute. The EAT was willing to treat the courier's use of a substitute while she was on holiday as an example of a substitution provided while the worker was "unable" rather than unwilling to perform her duties. In consequence, the EAT accepted that the courier was an employee.
2. In *Macfarlane v Glasgow City Council*, M, a gymnastics instructor, could arrange for a replacement from a register of coaches maintained by the Council if she was unable to take a class. The replacements were paid directly by the council. The EAT held that such agreed substitution was not contrary to personal performance. It followed that M was an employee.

Not in business for own account

50 For a person to be employed he must show that he is not in business for his own account (*Market Investigations Ltd v Minister of Social Security* [1969] 2 QB 173; affirmed by *Lee v Chung* [1990] IRLR 236, PC).

51 **All the circumstances** should be considered. Further, it has been held that (*Lee v Chung* [1990] IRLR 236, PC):
– there is **no exhaustive list** of the factors that are relevant and that considering factors cannot be done by way of a mechanical exercise of running through items on a checklist to see whether they are present or not; and
– there are **no strict rules** as to the relative weight of the various factors and the weight should be determined in relation to each individual case.

The object of the test is to **paint a picture from the accumulation of detail** and it is a matter of evaluation of the overall effect, which is not necessarily the same as the sum of the individual factors (*Hall (Inspector of Taxes) v Lorimer* [1994] IRLR 171, CA).

52 Though there is no exhaustive list, the courts have identified a number of **important factors** that indicate employee status (*Stevenson Jordan and Harrison Ltd v MacDonald and Evans* [1952] 1 TLR 101, CA; *Lee v Chung* [1990] IRLR 236, PC).
These are posed as questions:

Affirmative answers **indicate employment**:
1. Is it the parties' intention that there should be an employment relationship (see ¶53)?
2. Do the terms of any contract or agreement (including the "label" applied by the parties themselves) indicate an employment relationship?
3. Is the person an integral part of the employer's business?
4. Is the person receiving any benefits?
5. Does the person get paid annual leave?

6. Is the person subject to the employer's disciplinary rules and procedures?
7. Does the employer pay him using the PAYE scheme with tax and NIC deducted?

Affirmative answers **indicate self-employment**:
1. Is the person using his own equipment or tools?
2. Is the person responsible for hiring his own helpers if needed?
3. Does the person take any degree of financial risk and has he opportunity to profit from his work?
4. Is the person effectively selling his services and expertise over and above having the required expertise and skill to perform his work?

If there is **no documentation** regarding the working relationship between the parties, then it is essential that all evidence which is relevant to the possible formation of an oral or implied contract of service is considered (*Franks v Reuters Ltd and anor* [2003] IRLR 423, CA).

> EXAMPLE **Self-employed**
> 1. In *Bacica v Muir* [2005] UKEAT 0004_05_2009, the following facts clearly pointed towards the individual being self-employed:
> – he worked under the Construction Industry Scheme (CIS) Regulations under which tax was deducted from his earnings at 18% and he was responsible for his own NICs;
> – he had his profit and loss accounts prepared by an accountant and submitted to HMRC;
> – he was able to, and in fact performed, work for others;
> – he received payment at a rate which included an allowance to cover his overheads; and
> – he did not receive any payment if he did not work.
> 2. In *McGregor v Edinburgh Leisure* [2007] UKEAT 0027_07_2908, a worker was employed as a fitness instructor on a contract which described her status as that of a self-employed coach. She provided her own music and compact discs and paid for her performance licence. The local council paid for her work clothing and partially subsidised some, but not all, of the training courses she attended. The worker was offered a contract of service, but at a lower rate of pay, which she rejected. The EAT held that she was not an employee.
> 3. In *Kovats v TFO Management LLP and the Family Group of Companies* [2009] UKEAT 0357_08_2104, the EAT considered whether a member of a Limited Liability Partnership could be an employee. In September 2004 the claimant agreed to become a member of an LLP on terms that he was initially to receive a fixed distribution of profits, which was to be replaced by a percentage share in profits when the business was making enough money. In April 2007 the other members voted to remove him from the partnership. He claimed that he was an employee of the LLP and that he had been unfairly dismissed. The EAT upheld the decision that he was a partner, not an employee, and therefore he could not claim unfair dismissal. In the case of an LLP, the first question to ask is whether a member of the LLP is a partner in the business. If so, he cannot be an employee. If not, the next question is whether he is an employee using the normal tests of employment and self-employment. In this case the facts suggested that he was a true partner in the business:
> – he had signed written agreements indicating that the parties intended it to be a partnership;
> – he paid tax and NIC as a partner;
> – while he had not contributed capital to the business, he had taken a large pay cut to join the business and had contributed to the business by his efforts;
> – he had acted as an owner manager of the business and had entered into commitments on its behalf; and
> – the success of the business depended on his efforts.

Intention of the parties As will be seen below, the parties' intention as to their status is a **factor** in determining whether there is an employment relationship. It is not necessary for the parties to have intended to misrepresent the true nature of the relationship to a third party for the courts to look behind the parties' intentions and labels to determine the true relationship, and there is no need to show that the parties did not intend their written agreement to reflect their true agreement for it to be regarded as a sham (*Autoclenz Ltd v Belcher and ors* [2011] UKSC 41, *Protectacoat Firthglow Ltd v Miklos Szilagyi* [2009] IRLR 365, CA). To this end, the general rules of construction will apply with regard to construing the agreement between the parties (¶1118). These have been specifically applied as follows:

If the relationship between the parties is ambiguous, any **clearly stated intention** as to what they consider their relationship to be is a factor that will go towards indicating their position (*Massey v Crown Life Insurance Co Ltd* [1978] IRLR 31, CA). However, **all the circumstances** will be considered, and the courts will look behind the parties' intention and labels to determine

53

the true relationship (*Autoclenz Ltd v Belcher and ors, Young and Woods Ltd v West* [1980] IRLR 201, CA). Therefore, where factors indicate that there is an employment relationship, or they are neutral with regard to this, a label to the contrary attributed by the parties, although important, cannot necessarily be treated as being a decisive factor (*Dacas v Brook Street Bureau (UK) Ltd* [2004] IRLR 358, CA). Likewise, even where an agreement contains an "entire agreement" clause, the tribunal is entitled to look at both the written agreement and at the parties' conduct and how they operated their agreement in practice (*Royal National Lifeboat Institution v Bushaway* [2005] UKEAT 0719_04_2204). What the parties think or say about their relationship is not conclusive; the issue will be **determined objectively** (*Cable and Wireless v Muscat* [2006] ICR 975, CA).

EXAMPLE
1. In *Autoclenz Ltd v Belcher and ors*, workers provided car valeting services under contract to Autoclenz for a single client. In 2007 they all signed agreements which expressly said that they could provide substitutes, and could refuse work. However, the evidence was that, in practice, those clauses were never used nor were they ever intended to be used. The Supreme Court confirmed that where there is a written agreement there is no need to show that the parties did not intend it to reflect their true agreement for it to be regarded as a sham. In an employment case the actual legal obligations of the parties should be determined from all the evidence including any written terms and the parties' conduct, and in this case the workers were employees.
2. In *Launahurst Ltd v Larner* [2010] EWCA Civ 334, the claimant worked for a double glazing company under a contract, which he signed 9 years into the working relationship, which purported to set out the whole of the agreement between the parties and described him as a self-employed sub-contractor. The Court of Appeal found that neither party had put forward any evidence indicating that this agreement was a sham and looking at the totality of the facts held that the claimant was indeed self-employed.
3. In *Ahsan v Westmead Business Group Ltd* [2010] UKEAT 0480_09_0604, the claimant started work on the basis that he was an employee, although he had wanted to work as a consultant. After his contract was terminated by the employer, the parties exchanged emails agreeing to treat the arrangement as a self-employed one. The EAT held that the tribunal had been wrong to treat those post-termination emails as evidence that the relationship between the parties was a self-employed one and found that, looking at the documents and the way the parties conducted themselves before the arrangement ended, the claimant was an employee.

54 Where the intention of the parties has **not been clearly stated**, the other terms of the contract may give an indication of intent. The courts will look at the written contractual documents to see if the terms as a whole truly reflect the parties' intention at the time these documents were entered into and then whether this position has changed and, if so, how and when (*Secretary of State for Education and Employment v Bearman* [1998] UKEAT 1201_97_0604). If there are any other circumstances relating to the parties' intention and the terms of the contract, such as any oral agreements/exchanges and conduct as well as any other supporting documentation, the courts will consider all these factors in determining the position between the parties (*Kettle v Ministry of Defence HQ Defence Dental Service* [2007] UKEAT 0308_06_3101).

55 Where the parties make an **honest mistake** made in good faith about the nature of their working relationship and treat it as one of self-employment, this will not, **in the absence of misrepresentation**, make the contract illegal and in such a case the workers can later assert that they are employees and claim unfair dismissal (*Enfield Technical Services Ltd v Payne; Grace v BF Components Ltd* [2008] ICR 1423, CA; *Young and Woods Ltd v West* [1980] IRLR 201, CA). See ¶1307 for more details.

CHAPTER 2

Pre-employment

OUTLINE

SECTION 1	**Recruitment and selection** ... 510		
I	Recruitment policies and planning ... 520		
A	Company recruitment policy ... 520		
B	Human resource planning ... 525		
	Objectives ... 526		
	The HRP process ... 527		
C	Government assistance ... 535		
	Work Programme ... 535		
II	Equal opportunities ... 540		
	Discrimination on grounds of a protected characteristic ... 543		
	Discrimination on trade union grounds ... 551		
III	Recruitment procedure ... 570		
A	Profiling ... 575		
1	Job descriptions ... 575		
2	Person specification ... 577		
	Qualifications and requirements ... 579		
	Occupational requirement ... 580		
B	Recruitment methods ... 585		
C	Job adverts ... 590		
	Equal treatment ... 591		
	Contractual status ... 596		
D	Applications ... 600		
1	Application forms ... 607		
2	Disability issues ... 611		
3	Criminal convictions ... 612		
	Spent convictions ... 613		
	Criminal record and other checks ... 619		
4	Health questionnaires ... 625		
IV	Selection ... 630		
A	Short-listing for interview ... 630		
B	Selection methods ... 640		
1	Interviews ... 643		
2	Selection tests ... 647		
3	Role plays, exercises and assessment centres ... 653		
C	Arranging and preparing for interviews ... 660		
D	Conducting interviews ... 665		
E	The decision ... 670		
V	Monitoring and data protection ... 675		
SECTION 2	**Offer and appointment** ... 700		
A	Pre-conditions to employment ... 702		
	Confirmation of qualifications ... 703		
	References ... 704		
	Medicals ... 706		
	Restraints on taking up employment ... 709		
B	Appointment ... 710		
SECTION 3	**Right to work** ... 750		
A	Who has the right to work? ... 760		
	British citizens ... 760		
	Commonwealth citizens ... 762		
	EEA and Swiss nationals ... 765		
	Other nationals ... 768		
B	Right to work checks ... 780		

The **recruitment and selection** of the right candidates is of vital importance to employers. Legal issues also impinge on this process. The employer must not discriminate against candidates on the grounds of age, disability, gender reassignment, marriage and civil partnership, pregnancy and maternity, race, religion or belief, sex or sexual orientation. He must also comply with the data protection rules. Once a successful applicant has been identified, the employer can make the applicant an **offer** of employment which may be subject to certain conditions, for example, receipt of references, passing of a medical, or evidence that the individual can work legally in the UK.

500

501 Employers can only employ an individual who has an automatic right or permission to live and work in the UK and an employer will commit a criminal offence if he employs a person who does not meet this criterion. However, if an individual does not fall within one of these groups, the employer may be able to sponsor them to work in the UK under Tier 2 of the points-based immigration system (¶771).

SECTION 1

Recruitment and selection

510 Getting the right size and composition of workforce is a crucial **employment planning** decision. Getting it wrong may mean bearing the costs of overstaffing or redundancies, or having insufficient employees to meet demand, which may result in lost sales opportunities and revenue. There may be fluctuating staffing requirements throughout the year, or even on a weekly or daily basis.

The recruitment process is important in **selecting** the right applicant for the job. If an unsuitable applicant is appointed the employer will have to invest management time (including extra training and more supervision) to deal with the situation, which may involve a higher absence rate, staff turnover and low morale. The employer may also need to invoke disciplinary procedures for poor performance. If the employee is dismissed, the employer may face an unfair dismissal claim.

> MEMO POINTS Acas has published a useful guide on recruitment and induction, which can be obtained on its website by following this link: flmemo.co.uk/em510

511 The recruitment and selection **process** involves identifying the qualifications and experience required for the particular vacancy, formulating a job description, deciding whether and where to advertise, implementing appropriate selection and interviewing processes and keeping records of each stage.

The employer should take steps to ensure that the process is **non-discriminatory** or he may face a discrimination claim, which could lead to a substantial award of damages being made against him. The process should also be **monitored** on a regular basis to ensure that it is up to date and that it complies with relevant legislation, in particular, in relation to equal opportunities. The information generated during the process must be handled in accordance with **data protection** obligations.

I. Recruitment policies and planning

A. Company recruitment policy

520 Company size rather than sector tends to determine company policy on recruitment. A company may need to recruit a new employee because it is **expanding**, or in order to **replace** an employee who has left.

If there is a **vacancy**, the employer should consider whether it requires a full-time or part-time employee, and whether the appointment should be on a temporary, fixed-term or permanent basis. The job duties and the terms and conditions (including the level of remuneration) should be reviewed and updated where necessary.

The employer should consider whether **existing staff** could be **redeployed** as part of their career development, or in order to avoid or minimise possible redundancies elsewhere in the company.

The company's recruitment policy may be affected by the process of human resource planning, discussed below.

B. Human resource planning

An organisation's staff (i.e. its human resources) is one of the resources necessary to meet its business objectives. Human Resource Management is, therefore, important to the success of a business, with Human Resource Planning (HRP) being an essential element of good management.

HRP varies considerably from one organisation to another. Many organisations do not plan ahead or have regard to future needs, but recruit as the need to fill current vacancies arises, while others rely on complex statistical analysis to forecast business requirements. HRP is often equated with **Manpower Planning**, which, in essence, is concerned with simply forecasting the quantity (and to some extent quality) of the workforce with a view to matching supply to demand. HRP certainly includes Manpower Planning but, in some organisations, HRP goes further and embraces organisational culture, attitudes, employee development, employee behaviour and commitment, organisational development, motivation, training and development and establishing best work methods.

HRP may be less important in relatively stable organisations with little technological innovation, fairly constant demand, low labour turnover and a ready supply of suitable labour. However, the following factors may result in a **need for HRP**:
– demography (i.e. the fact that labour supply changes on a national and regional basis);
– market change, whether growth or decline;
– organisational culture change;
– company development such as site relocation, business acquisitions;
– statutory change (for example, new employment laws);
– Government initiatives and plans for education and training; and
– new technology.

HRP may have the following **benefits**:
– anticipating and responding to changes in demand for labour;
– attracting and retaining the required number of employees with appropriate skills;
– achieving the best possible utilisation of staff;
– tailoring training and development to ensure effective performance in current roles and staff development for future roles at the same or higher levels;
– reducing reliance on external recruitment;
– promoting equal opportunities and diversity within the workforce; and
– assisting the process of monitoring, influencing and controlling labour costs.

525

Objectives

HRP is essentially **concerned with** delivering:
– the **right quantity and quality of people** (i.e. the correct numbers of staff offering the desired mix of skills and the levels of outlook, attitude and motivation necessary for the organisation to achieve its objectives);
– at the **right place** (so that the right mix of people and skills is available at each different location, including, for example, planning for opening of a new facility, partial or total closure of a location or transferring key tasks between locations);
– at the **right cost** (to fit in with overall organisational strategy in terms of funds available, relativities, competitiveness, reward strategy and, especially in a production environment, unit labour cost); and
– at the **right time** (taking into account the hours and patterns of work, including responding to the various peaks and troughs in demand for the organisation's products or services, across shifts, weeks, months, seasons or even years).

526

The HRP process

527 HRP requires the collection, collation and analysis of information in order to identify and anticipate the organisation's staffing requirements. The process can be **computerised** (both off-the-shelf and tailored software packages are available) and spreadsheet packages can assist statistical analysis. Where subjective judgements are required, data may need to be analysed **manually**.

528 **Forecasting demand for and supply of labour**   The first step is to forecast the organisation's **demand for labour** (at one or more points in time, usually from 1 to 5 years ahead) as follows:
– gather information such as details of business plans, management expectations, forecasts, productivity and current technology;
– assess current labour requirements including skills, numbers, and location; and
– forecast labour requirements by assessing future needs, taking into account as many relevant factors as possible, including market changes (both product-related and customer-led change, different delivery patterns, changes to product shelf life and product life cycles), the need for new skills, increased or reduced numbers of current skills, reflecting increased or reduced capacities, changes in productivity and technological developments.

The next stage is to forecast the **supply of labour** as follows:
– gather information relating to the organisation including existing staff numbers, skills, likely turnover, age profile;
– consider how many staff may be due for retirement (though, as there is no longer a default retirement age, be careful not to make assumptions about retirement ages that could be discriminatory (¶5600+)), retention factors, stability, reward strategy, recruitment strategy, and training plans;
– gather information external to the organisation including, where relevant, data on the local labour market, other external environmental factors which may impact upon the business, possible changes and trends in labour supply; and
– forecast likely availability of labour, taking into account, where relevant, the skills mix and any factors regarding location.

529 **Gap between supply and demand**   A **comparison** of forecast demand with forecast supply establishes whether there is a potential gap (i.e. over-supply, under-supply or a combination of both across different skills, levels or locations). The employer should then seek to establish the cause(s) of the gap.

Possible **causes of a shortage of labour** include:
– high staff turnover;
– recruitment difficulties arising from, for example, the perceived negative aspects of the job, the image of the organisation or the industry in which it operates, location, lack of reward, poor advertising campaigns, or inefficient recruitment processes;
– lack of suitable skills;
– lack of internal or external mobility (i.e. reluctance to relocate);
– restrictive policies;
– financial constraints preventing improvements to attraction, retention, training and development or reward;
– high absence levels; and
– seasonal fluctuations in demand.

Possible **causes of a surplus of labour** include:
– falling demand for labour (following less demand for the organisation's products or services, a shift in demand for specific skills, or the introduction of new technology/productivity improvements);
– organisational structure (resulting in limited promotional opportunities);
– restrictive policies (for example, a collective agreement to avoid compulsory redundancy);
– financial constraints; and
– seasonal fluctuations in demand.

530 **Reducing the impact**   Once the employer has established the cause of the gap, he can take appropriate action to reduce the impact. Sometimes the reasons for a gap may be outside his control (for example, national skills shortages). However, a **review of the following**

areas (and implementation of appropriate action) may, individually or in combination, close specific gaps:
– recruitment practices (for example, the methods of recruitment, the media used to advertise, the style and content of the advert with specific regard to the actual target audience, the response time to applications). A **proactive recruitment strategy** will assist effective HRP, in that it responds to and attempts to reconcile both the short and longer-term staffing needs. This may result in the recruitment of staff with potential for training and development, or recruiting on a short-term basis in the knowledge that labour reductions will be required within a period of time;
– reward structures;
– organisational image;
– induction process;
– management of absence;
– job redesign;
– policies and agreements;
– productivity;
– working practices/re-allocation of duties;
– flexible working patterns (for example, introducing or extending shift working);
– alternatives to full-time permanent staff (for example, part-time staff, temporary/agency staff, job share, short-term contracts, interim placements, outsourcing and homeworking);
– organisational culture (including management style, communication, policies and procedures, recognition of contribution and performance, employee participation/involvement, training and development, and reward strategy);
– training and development (to improve current and future job performance, productivity, the ability to fill skills shortages, career progression, staff turnover and recruitment);
– job security and redundancy; and
– planning to avoid redundancy.

C. Government assistance

Work Programme

As part of the Work Programme (previously called New Deal) scheme, the employer commonly receives **funding** and **training** subsidies to minimise the costs of recruiting employees. In return, employers are expected to keep on such employees after the scheme is completed. More details on these schemes are provided in chapter 18. **535**

II. Equal opportunities

The company should aim to promote equality of opportunity during the recruitment and selection process. As a result of this, many employers have an **equal opportunities policy**, which, like all good practice policies, they should take care to observe. See ¶5800 for a discussion regarding best practice principles. **540**

Several **codes of practice** offer guidance for employers to help them to avoid discrimination. The codes emphasise the close link between equal opportunities and good employment practice, and that promoting equal opportunities should lead to better work relationships and better use of human resources. **541**

The codes deal in general terms and employers will need to adapt the guidelines in a way appropriate to the size and structure of their organisation. Small businesses, for example, may not be able to carry out all of the detailed recommendations and will require simpler procedures than those in larger organisations.

542 In certain limited circumstances, it is lawful to discriminate in a job for which the age, disability, gender reassignment, marriage and civil partnership, pregnancy and maternity, race, religion or belief, sex or sexual orientation of the worker is an **occupational requirement** (¶580; see also chapter 16 for further details).

Discrimination on grounds of a protected characteristic

543 For a full discussion of discrimination, see chapter 16.

It is unlawful for an employer to discriminate against prospective employees on the grounds of age, disability, gender reassignment, marriage and civil partnership, pregnancy and maternity, race, religion or belief, sex or sexual orientation:
a. in the **arrangements made** for the purpose of determining who should be offered employment. For example:
– the job description;
– the person specification;
– the job advert;
– the application form;
– not being short-listed for interview (*V Saunders v Richmond upon Thames Borough Council* [1977] IRLR 362, EAT);
– the selection process, including the location and timing of interviews, assessment techniques, interviewing (for example, the appointment of a biased interviewer (*Brennan v J H Dewhurst Ltd* [1983] IRLR 357, EAT)) and selection criteria; or
– the final selection;
b. by **refusing or deliberately omitting to offer** employment. For example:
– refusing to consider an application (*Owen & Briggs v James* [1982] IRLR 502, CA) or to interview (*Panesar v The Nestle Co Ltd* [1980] IRLR 64, CA); or
– telling an applicant that the vacancy has been filled when it has not (*Johnson v Timber Tailors (Midlands) Ltd* [1978] IRLR 146, IT); or
c. in the **terms** on which employment is offered (see section 2). For example, part-time work, domestic leave, company cars and benefits for dependants should be available to both male and female employees in the same or not materially different circumstances.

> MEMO POINTS Selection arrangements are **one-off acts** (not continuing acts) for the purpose of compliance with time limits for discrimination claims (¶9460).

544 If an employee or applicant has suffered discriminatory treatment, he will be entitled to a **remedy** (¶5700).

> MEMO POINTS If an **unsuccessful job applicant** proves facts from which the tribunal could conclude, in the absence of an adequate explanation, that the prospective employer has (or is to be treated as having) committed an unlawful act of discrimination, the **burden of proof** shifts to the prospective employer to prove that no discrimination occurred (¶¶5730+). The recruiting employer is not under a positive obligation to disclose information about the short-listing/selection procedure to rejected candidates. However, if an employer refuses to grant access to information about the recruitment process, this refusal can be one fact considered, amongst all of the facts, in deciding whether this burden of proof has shifted (*Meister v Speech Design Carrier Systems GmbH (C-415/10)* [2012] EUECJ C-415/10). In practical terms, requests for information about the successful candidate are currently usually made using the questionnaire procedure (¶¶548, 5711) and an employer facing this kind of request is usually best advised to provide at least redacted information (assuming of course no discrimination has occurred) as opposed to making a complete refusal.

545 Discrimination may be direct or indirect. It may also take the form of victimisation (a form of direct discrimination) or harassment.

> EXAMPLE
> **Direct discrimination**
> Refusal to consider a woman for a lorry driver's job because of her sex.
>
> **Indirect discrimination**
> 1. Requiring all job applicants to have previously been employed by the Armed Forces (fewer women than men would be eligible to apply).
> 2. Imposing a mobility requirement (it may be more difficult for women to comply).

3. Unjustifiably restricting applications to those living in a certain geographical area (if the area is not ethnically or religiously well balanced this may indirectly discriminate on racial/religious grounds).

546 In the case of a **disabled person**, unlawful discrimination occurs (in addition to victimisation and harassment) when:
– because of a person's disability, the employer treats that disabled person less favourably than he treats or would treat a person not having that disability (¶5500). It is not possible for an employer to justify such less favourable treatment;
– for a reason which arises from a person's disability, the employer treats that person less favourably than he treats or would treat others to whom the reason does not or would not apply, and he cannot justify the less favourable treatment (¶5510); or
– the employer fails to comply with the duty to make reasonable adjustments in relation to the disabled person.

EXAMPLE An employer rejects a suitable disabled applicant, A, because he thinks her wheelchair will get in the way in the office. He appoints applicant B, who is no more suitable for the job but who does not use a wheelchair. A has therefore been treated less favourably than B for a reason arising from her disability (i.e. the fact that she uses a wheelchair), which did not apply to B. Unless the employer can demonstrate that this treatment falls within the scope of the lawful treatment permitted by the Equality Act 2010, he will have unlawfully discriminated against A.

547 There is no requirement to treat a disabled person more favourably than other applicants, but employers are obliged to make **reasonable adjustments** to working conditions or the workplace so that the disabled person is not at a substantial disadvantage. The disabled person may be able to offer suggestions as to what adjustments may assist. Less favourable treatment is justified if the disabled person cannot do the job concerned, and no adjustment which would enable the person to do the job is practicable.

EXAMPLE An applicant for a typing job, C, has arthritis in her hands and is, on the face of it, not the best person for the job as her typing speed is too slow. However, if a reasonable adjustment could be made, such as an adapted keyboard, to overcome C's speed problems, the employer would be obliged to make the adjustment and reconsider her application in the light of that adjustment.

548 **Discrimination questionnaires** In order to decide if he has sufficient **grounds to bring a discrimination claim**, a job applicant can serve a questionnaire on the employer asking for **information about** the successful applicant (for example, details of their sex, skills, qualifications and experience) and the recruitment process (for example, how many men and how many women applied, the sex or race of all those interviewed, their qualifications and experience). For further discussion of discrimination questionnaires, see ¶5711.

549 **Positive action** It is permissible to adopt positive measures **to encourage applications** from potential employees who, on the grounds of their age, disability, gender reassignment, marriage and civil partnership, pregnancy and maternity, race, religion or belief, sex or sexual orientation, have been under-represented in particular work (see chapter 16). However, applications from all relevant individuals, regardless of whether they have any of the characteristics listed above, should also be sought, as withholding information from one group in an attempt to encourage applications from another group would be unlawful.

Discrimination in selection to achieve a "racial balance" or, for example, an equal number of male and female employees is not allowed. Selection must ultimately be based on merit.

Discrimination on trade union grounds

551 It is unlawful to refuse employment on the grounds of membership or non-membership of a trade union (s 137 TULRCA 1992) (¶7563). It is also unlawful for employers, employment agencies and others to compile, supply or use a blacklist of trade union members or activists for discriminatory purposes such as employment vetting (¶7565).

III. Recruitment procedure

570 It is advisable for both a member of human resources and the line manager or supervisor to be involved in the entire recruitment and selection process, including the short-listing for interview, the interview itself and the final selection. In small companies, there may not be a separate human resources function and it will therefore fall to the line manager or supervisor to carry out the recruitment process.

A. Profiling

1. Job descriptions

575 The first step in the recruitment process is to give careful consideration to the vacant position, identifying the main purpose of the job, the key tasks involved and the responsibilities of the job holder. A member of human resources should work closely with the line manager or supervisor for the job to ensure proper identification and accuracy.

This information will form the basis of a job description, which should be **broadly drafted** (especially in the case of senior employees) as it will define the scope of the employee's contractual duties. If the scope is sufficiently broad, the employer should be able to move the employee to other duties without the need to obtain his consent to a variation of contract (¶1600).

The job description usually **deals with** the following:
– job title;
– main purpose of job;
– main duties and responsibilities;
– to whom the job holder will report; and
– for whom the job holder will be responsible.

In order to avoid an inference of discrimination, the job title must be neutral in terms of age, disability, gender reassignment, marriage and civil partnership, pregnancy and maternity, race, religion or belief, sex or sexual orientation, unless an occupational requirement applies (¶580; see also chapter 16 for further details).

2. Person specification

577 The next step is to consider the qualifications, skills and experience required by the job holder, with the line manager again taking a major role.

There should be a direct and precise connection between the person specification and the job description to ensure that the focus is on the applicant's ability to do the job rather than unrelated personal characteristics.

The **criteria** of this person specification may include:
– relevant qualifications, knowledge and attainments (any qualifications specified should not disadvantage people at different ages: an employer who wants to specify certain qualifications should ensure that such requirements are justifiable and indicate that he will consider equivalent or similar level alternative qualifications);
– the type of experience required (it is advisable to avoid reference to length of experience since this might be discriminatory on the grounds of age against younger applicants who have the skills required but have not had an opportunity to demonstrate them over an extended period);

– special skills or aptitudes (e.g. oral, written or manual skills); and
– disposition (e.g. reliability) or circumstances (e.g. has a current driving licence, owns a car), where these are a justifiable requirement for the job.

The specification should make clear those criteria which are "essential", and those which would be merely "desirable", and more weight should be given to the essential elements.

Employers in the **finance sector** must comply with regulations on staff recruitment and development (Financial Services and Markets Act 2000), which apply to all employees. In the context of recruitment, the employer must ensure that the applicant is competent, in particular, by relating the applicant's skills and knowledge to that required for the particular job, taking reasonable steps to obtain information about the applicant's previous activities and training, and identifying whether further training is required. The employer must also ensure that references are taken from suitable sources. **578**

Qualifications and requirements

The employer should consider whether any requirements specified in the person specification might be indirectly discriminatory. Even a quality described as "desirable" as opposed to "essential" may constitute a discriminatory requirement if it is clear that it was a deciding factor in the selection process (*Falkirk Council v Whyte* [1997] IRLR 560, EAT). **579**

For example, in order to avoid the most common discrimination claims, the employer should take the following action:

Liability	Employer action
Sex discrimination	– avoid prescribing requirements that effectively inhibit applications from one sex or from married people or civil partners – avoid requiring excessive continuous service, as this may indirectly discriminate against women
Racial discrimination	– avoid prescribing requirements such as length of residence or experience in the UK – where a particular qualification is required, make it clear that a fully comparable qualification obtained overseas is as acceptable as a UK qualification – avoid requiring a standard of English higher than that needed to safely and effectively perform the job
Disability discrimination	– avoid unnecessary requirements in job specifications – be able to justify imposing any health requirements – be able to show that any qualifications required are relevant and significant in terms of the particular job and the particular applicant and that there is no reasonable adjustment (for example, the reassignment of the duties to which the qualification relates) which would change this
Religion or belief discrimination	– avoid unnecessary requirements that the applicant needs to follow a particular faith
Sexual orientation discrimination	– avoid offering benefits packages which are available to married employees only, without also offering the same benefits to civil partners
Age discrimination	– avoid using upper age limits or age ranges in job adverts, or phrases which imply age restrictions, such as "young graduate", "mature person" or "energetic" – ensure that the levels of experience and qualifications required are necessary to the position – do not make assumptions based on age, for example that young people lack supervisory experience, or that older people do not have IT skills

Occupational requirements

It is permissible, in relation to certain jobs, to impose a requirement that applicants have a particular quality related to a particular protected characteristic (i.e. age, disability, gender **580** reassignment, marriage and civil partnership, pregnancy and maternity, race, religion or belief, sex or sexual orientation), where holding that protected characteristic is an occupational requirement for that job. If an occupational requirement has been identified for a particular job, the position should be reviewed from time to time to see whether it is still applicable. For further details on occupational requirements, see ¶¶5290, 5402, 5620.

B. Recruitment methods

585 A vacancy can be publicised in a range of ways, and more than one method is often used (see table).

To avoid discrimination, employers need to give some thought as to which method(s) to use. Not advertising, or advertising in certain publications with a narrow readership, or using particular recruitment methods may restrict the groups of applicants who can apply. In order to avoid claims of **indirect discrimination**, the employer should place adverts in publications that will reach individuals who have any of the protected characteristics listed at ¶543, including in particular both sexes and a wide age range, and will not unjustifiably exclude or disproportionately reduce the numbers of applicants from a particular racial group, religion or belief. People of different age groups, for example, may use different methods of looking for a job: younger people are more likely to use careers services, job centres, newspapers or the internet, while many older people prefer to rely on community and business networks.

In cases of **positive action**, it is permissible for job adverts to be placed specifically to reach members of under-represented groups (for example, through the use of ethnic minority press, as well as other newspapers), and for employment agencies and careers offices in areas where these groups are concentrated to be used.

In general, recruitment by **word of mouth** or on **personal recommendation** is not recommended, as it may give rise to a claim of discrimination (for example, on grounds of sex or race). However, the courts have recognised that recruitment to **highly specific posts** such as personal confidential advisers might be limited to individuals well-known to the person they are serving (*Coker v Lord Chancellor* [2002] IRLR 80, CA).

Method	Description	Comment
Word of mouth	Informal and cost-effective, relying on introduction of applicants through existing employees or an employers' network.	If used by itself, will usually give smaller selection of suitable applicants. Should be avoided where, for example, workforce is wholly or predominantly white or black (and labour market is multi-racial), or where workforce is predominantly of one sex.
Internal recruitment	More formal than word of mouth. Relies on internal promotion (may use company intranet).	Exploits and develops existing employees' skills and training, benefiting both company and individual employees. Likely to boost motivation within workforce if employees can progress their careers within the company.
National newspapers	Expensive. Appropriate if large response is desirable or for more senior vacancies.	Likely to reach a wide and diverse readership.
Local newspapers and radio	Suitable for less specialised jobs. Can be used to target groups in a particular local area.	

Method	Description	Comment
Trade and specialist journals	Less expensive than national press. Targets applicants for specialist and professional vacancies.	
Employment/ recruitment agencies	Often specialise in particular type of work or industry (e.g. secretarial, IT), with job seekers registered with them. "Executive search" companies or "head-hunters" exist for higher management or specialist applicants, who are often approached directly.	See memo points. Can deal with all or part of recruitment process. Employer should check agency's equal opportunities policy to ensure recruitment methods conform to legal requirements and employer's own practice. Both agency and employer have responsibility to ensure that recruitment process operates fairly. Agencies have specific responsibilities as suppliers of job applicants to prospective employers, in addition to own responsibilities as employers of agency staff.
The internet	Increasingly used as means of recruitment, particularly for graduate-level and technical jobs. Some companies include job vacancies on own website. Employment agencies increasingly use the internet. In some cases, applications may be made directly via email.	Many unskilled workers do not have access and so unlikely to be suitable means of recruitment of such staff.
Jobcentres	Provide free nationwide recruitment and advisory service, displaying employers' vacancies and referring potential applicants. Administer some Government training programmes. Disability Employment Advisers (DEAs), supported by local Disability Service Teams, can assist in recruitment of disabled applicants, and advise on practical and financial help available (particularly where employer obliged to make reasonable adjustments).	See memo points. Jobcentres, schools, colleges and careers offices may have a specific, narrow source of applicants (e.g. single sex schools).
Local schools, colleges, careers services	Regular contact with local schools and colleges will ensure that employer's needs with respect to particular skills and abilities are known, and work experience or "shadowing" schemes can be useful to both students and employer. Careers services can give employers information on suitable school leavers under 18.	
Training and Enterprise Councils (Local Enterprise Councils in Scotland)	Provide general information on local labour market and skills balance available. Operate recruitment service and may put forward trained workers, and tailor further training to employer's needs.	

MEMO POINTS When recruiting through employment agencies, job centres, careers offices, schools and other third parties, it is unlawful for employers to give **instructions to discriminate**, for example by indicating that certain groups will or will not be preferred, and/or to bring **pressure** on them **to discriminate** against members of a particular age, disability, gender reassignment, marriage and civil partnership, pregnancy and maternity, race, religion or belief, sex or sexual orientation. It is also unlawful for a person to knowingly **help another to discriminate** on the grounds of disability. If an employment agency, for example, refused to consider an application from a disabled person on the instructions of the employer, the agency could be liable for aiding the company.

C. Job adverts

590 Adverts should be designed and **presented** so as to attract the right sort of applicant for the job. They should therefore be tailored to the level of the target audience, and consistent with the **company image**, using the company logo (if there is one) as appropriate. It may be advisable to require that all job adverts are authorised by human resources or a senior line manager before they are issued.

If the employer becomes aware that a particular applicant's **disability** places the applicant at a substantial disadvantage, the employer will be required, as part of his obligation to disabled applicants to make reasonable adjustments, to provide information about jobs in **alternative formats** (for example, large print, in Braille, by email or computer disk). What is reasonable will depend on the circumstances (including the time available before the new employee is needed and the ease with which the applicant's request can be met) (¶5552).

The advert should be based on the **objective analysis** that was carried out to devise the job description and person specification. It should be concise and easily understood, clear as to what the job is, specific with respect to the qualifications, experience, skills and abilities needed, and should avoid generalisations such as "attractive salary" or "appropriate qualifications".

Adverts for **internal recruitment** should contain the same information as those used externally, and vice versa.

Equal treatment

591 **Pay rates** must comply with legislation on equal pay (¶5650).

592 The employer must avoid **discriminatory wording**, and should ensure that he advertises in such a way that encourages applications from individuals of all protected characteristics i.e. age, disability, gender reassignment, marriage and civil partnership, pregnancy and maternity, race, religion or belief, sex or sexual orientation. The advertisement also must not indicate that the employer will refuse employment to an applicant on the grounds that the applicant is a **member** or a **non-member** of a **trade union** (s 137(3) TULRCA 1992). The employer may also be liable for discrimination if, in the advert, he has set **requirements or criteria** for the job that are indirectly discriminatory. For further details, see ¶5807.

593 In addition to the availability of individual remedies, if an advert indicates an intention to discriminate, the Equality and Human Rights Commission can **enforce** the provisions relating to discriminatory wording by issuing a non-discrimination notice and seeking a restraining injunction from the civil courts. See ¶5790 for further details.

595 The advert can include a **statement of commitment to equal opportunities**. Some organisations are accredited with the "double tick" symbol by Jobcentre Plus, which they can use in their adverts as a sign of public commitment to good practice in the employment and retention of disabled people.

Contractual status

596 Employers should ensure that any **description of benefits and salary** included in the advert corresponds to the terms and conditions of employment set out in the offer letter and/or contract of employment for the successful applicant. Any **discrepancy** could give rise to legal action, although adverts are normally not part of the employment contract. The wording of the advert is usually taken to be no more than an indication of the terms that would apply if the applicant were engaged. If, therefore, an employee accepts a written job offer that contains terms different to those of the advert, the employee cannot normally rely on the advert as evidence of contractual terms.

However, where the terms are in writing but are ambiguous, giving rise to a **dispute as to the interpretation** of the contract, the tribunal can consider the wording of the advert in order to ascertain the intentions of the employer at that time (*Pedersen v The Mayor and Burgesses of the London Borough of Camden* [1981] IRLR 173, CA).

If the applicant is engaged but the job offer is not put in writing (and there are no written terms and conditions of employment), the employee may be able to rely on the advert as proof of his terms.

D. Applications

600 A job advert usually asks applicants to send in their **CV** (curriculum vitae) (with a covering letter), or to complete an **application form**. Either method can be adapted to an **online** process. Each has its advantages, as the following table shows:

Application form	CV
Uniform format makes it easier to compare one application with another.	Although reviewing CVs may be more time-consuming for the employer, using a CV is likely to make the recruitment process shorter and less complicated.
Employers can ensure that all the required information is provided.	CVs may not provide the information required.
Applicants may be put off from applying because forms are time-consuming to complete and may be intimidating.	CVs are less time-consuming for employees as, once they are compiled, they can be used for multiple applications.
Applicants may find the form inadequate as they are unable to control the information given.	Applicants can control the information provided, focusing on their strengths.
Applicants have less scope to lie, as the form sets out the information to be provided, can state that references and qualifications will be checked, and that information must be current and accurate (and warn that inaccuracy will be serious misconduct possibly leading to dismissal).	Some applicants may leave gaps on their CV, distort facts or even tell lies (e.g. stating they have worked for a particular employer when they have not).

601 If possible, applications should be **acknowledged** promptly, and the timetable for short-listing, interviewing and appointment given. If an online application process is used, this can be automatically generated. Some organisations may state that if nothing further is heard by a particular date, the applicant can conclude that he has been unsuccessful. Other organisations will send out a formal notification that the applicant has not been short-listed for interview.

602 To reduce the risk of an appointment based on **inaccurate information**, either in the CV or in the application form, the employer may want to:
a. ask applicants to produce original examination certificates (making this a pre-condition of employment, where necessary), take copies, and contact the institutions for further confirmation if in doubt;

b. in the interview:
- ask searching questions about their qualifications; and
- investigate gaps evident from the CV and go through the applicant's employment history;

c. review any psychological tests (¶650) used; and

d. take up references.

Where employers intend to scrutinise candidates closely they should **take care** to ensure that they do not jump to suspicions on discriminatory grounds, or adopt practices that discriminate between candidates on grounds of age, disability, gender reassignment, marriage and civil partnership, pregnancy and maternity, race, religion or belief, sex or sexual orientation.

603 Some statements are unlikely to give rise to **legal liability** because they are "sales talk", for example, broad statements such as "team player". However, fraudulent or negligent misrepresentations or mis-statements made by an applicant that are relied on by the employer, causing him to suffer loss as a result, may entitle the employer to damages. The **employer's loss** in these circumstances may include costs associated with having to start the recruitment process again, for example advertising or employment agency fees. However, in practice, it is not likely to be cost-effective to bring an action for damages against an employee.

604 If the employee has not been truthful, the employer will only be justified in **dismissing** the employee if the deception is relevant to the particular employment and/or any terms of the contract. The employer's verification of information provided by the applicant is dealt with at ¶680 below.

1. Application forms

607 Companies may have a standard application form, or a series of application forms for different departments or different types of employee. As for the job advert, the application form should **focus** on the skills and abilities required to do the job, as identified in the job description and the person specification.

The employer should consider allowing applicants to apply in ways other than completing an application form (for example, typewritten, by telephone or by email), as the **format** of the form might place a disabled applicant (for example blind or partially sighted applicants, or those with dyslexia) at a disadvantage.

The **standard of completion** can be a guide to the applicant's suitability, if writing and presentation skills are essential to the job. Reliance on this factor may, however, lead to a disability discrimination claim. Application forms should not require a higher standard of English than is required to do the job, as this may discriminate against those whose first language is not English.

608 The application form can include a question as to whether the applicant will need permission or **sponsorship** to work in the UK. The employer will need to check at some stage during the recruitment process whether the applicant can lawfully work in the UK (¶750). In order to avoid racial discrimination, the question must be asked of all applicants and not just those whom the employer suspects (for example, because they have a "foreign-sounding" name) may need permission to work in the UK.

609 The application form should state whether **references** will be required. References are discussed further at ¶704.

2. Disability issues

611 The application form can include a question asking whether the applicant is disabled and, if so, whether the individual will require any adjustments (both during the selection process and in order to do the job in question), and what these might be. Employers should take all reasonable steps to find out whether or not a person has a disability that is likely to place the person at a substantial disadvantage. If an employer's agent or employee (for example, a member of human resources, a line manager, or company doctor) knows of the applicant's disability and its disadvantageous effect, the employer will have "constructive" knowledge of it, and the duty to make reasonable adjustments will apply. Special rules apply where employers want to ask further pre-employment questions about applicants' health, which are addressed at ¶¶625+.

3. Criminal convictions

An employer **may need to know** about his employee's criminal convictions where, for example, there is an obligation to disclose such information on registration forms for regulatory authorities. For some posts this information may be relevant as it may reflect on the individual's character and suitability for the job. If this information is required by the employer a question as to whether the applicant has any criminal convictions should be included on the application form.

Unless the employer has **expressly asked** for information on past convictions, no action can be taken against an employee for failure to disclose convictions which are not spent.

Where an applicant answers a question about previous convictions **dishonestly**, for example by failing to reveal when asked that he has been convicted of an offence and the offence is unspent, the applicant may be committing a criminal deception (s 16 Theft Act 1968).

612

> EXAMPLE In *R v Patel* [2007] ICR 571, CA, an applicant, P, applied for a civilian job with the police, stating "no" on her application form in answer to the question "have you ever been convicted of an offence?". Nine years previously, following a court hearing, she had, however, been made subject to an order for a conditional discharge. Following her job application, P was charged with the criminal offence of obtaining a pecuniary advantage by deception. The Court of Appeal held that, as a matter of definition, an order for a conditional discharge was not a conviction. P had never been convicted of an offence. Accordingly, she had not made a false representation, and the case against her was dismissed.

Spent convictions

If questions about past convictions are raised on an application form or at a job interview, prospective employees are **not generally obliged to reveal** convictions that are "spent" (Rehabilitation of Offenders Act 1974, as amended). Convictions become spent after a certain period of time has elapsed from the date of conviction (the "rehabilitation period"), depending on the nature of the sentence imposed.

613

Sentence	Rehabilitation period
Imprisonment, custody or detention for life or detention at Her Majesty's pleasure	Never rehabilitated
Imprisonment, youth custody, detention in a young offender institution, or corrective training for a term exceeding 30 months	Never rehabilitated
Imprisonment, youth custody, detention in a young offender institution, or corrective training for between 6 and 30 months	10 years (5 years if offender under 18 when convicted)
Imprisonment or youth custody for 6 months or less	7 years (3 years if offender under 18 when convicted)
Probation (for convictions on/after 3 February 1995), fines	5 years (2 years if offender under 18 when convicted)
Probation (for convictions before 3 February 1995), conditional discharge, binding over, care or supervision order	1 year or the duration of the order/bond, if longer
Absolute discharge	6 months
Disqualification from driving	Period of disqualification

MEMO POINTS 1. A **suspended sentence** is treated as one that has taken effect (the rehabilitation period is the same as for the full sentence). If an offender is sentenced for several offences, the rehabilitation period will depend on the time actually served. For example, if two prison terms of 6 months are served **concurrently**, the rehabilitation period is 7 years. If they are served **consecutively**, the rehabilitation period is 10 years.
2. The Government **plans to reduce** the amount of time before convictions become spent. The relevant legislation (Legal Aid, Sentencing and Punishment of Offenders Act 2012) has been published and has received royal assent, but it is not yet in force. We will keep you informed of any developments with our updating service.

617 A "**rehabilitated person**" must be treated as a person who has not committed or been charged with or convicted of the offence in question, and must not be prejudiced in any way by virtue of that conviction or its non-disclosure (s 4 Rehabilitation of Offenders Act 1974). The implications are as follows:

Rejecting applicant	**Spent** conviction (or failure to disclose) not grounds for rejecting applicant or employee from any office, profession, occupation or employment. Convictions that are **not spent** (or where an **exception** applies) can be good reason for rejection.
Dismissal	**Spent** conviction (or failure to disclose) not grounds for dismissal, even if occupation/employment is sensitive (it is generally accepted that a dismissal on these grounds will be **automatically unfair** (¶8390)) (*Property Guards Ltd v Taylor and Kershaw* [1982] IRLR 175, EAT). Concealing convictions that are **not spent** when applying for a job (or where an **exception** applies and full disclosure not given as required) can provide fair reason for dismissal (*Torr v British Railways Board* [1977] IRLR 184, EAT).
Providing reference	If employer/ex-employer refers to **spent** conviction in reference, employee may sue for defamation. Defence of justification may be available, unless revelation made with malice.

618 **Exceptions – when spent convictions must be disclosed** Employees in certain **occupations** and professions are obliged to disclose any spent convictions (Rehabilitation of Offenders Act 1974 (Exceptions) Order SI 1975/1023, as amended). Most of the exceptions relate to the administration of justice, private security, national security, social and health services with patient contact (in particular, those with access to vulnerable groups such as the infirm, elderly, mentally ill and young people under the age of 18), specific areas of the financial sector, certain professions (doctors, lawyers, accountants, pharmacists) and taxi drivers. There is a further exception for any office or employment concerned with the provision of accommodation, care, leisure and recreational facilities, schooling, social services, supervision or training to persons under 18, where the holder of the office or employment would have access in the course of his normal duties to such persons, or where the normal duties are carried out wholly or partly on the premises where such provision takes place.

The **application form** should clearly state whether the job is being treated as an exception. An applicant to whom an exception applies must disclose spent convictions if the question asked **relates** either **to** the applicant himself or, where relevant, to a person who lives in the same household, and the provision of the services mentioned would normally take place in that household.

Criminal record and other checks

619 The employer may need to find out whether the applicant has current (and, in certain circumstances, spent) convictions, such as where the **position involves a specified position of trust**. Until December 2012, such applications were made to the Criminal Records Bureau (CRB), which, along with the Independent Safeguarding Authority (ISA), was responsible for the administration of the **Vetting and Barring Scheme** (Safeguarding Vulnerable Groups Act 2006). This scheme governs how criminal records are shared and accessed by individuals and organisations (in particular, how information should be shared between organisations and how the criminal backgrounds of individuals wishing to work with children and vulnerable adults can be applied for), and also the circumstances surrounding the barring of individuals from working with children and vulnerable adults. However, the CRB and the ISA have now merged to form a single **Disclosure and Barring Service** (DBS). The DBS covers all of the CRB's and the ISA's former functions. Much has remained the same since the merger, though the DBS does have **plans** to introduce an **online checking system** for criminal records checks, as well as a new system of **portable criminal records checks** (where individuals will be able to re-use previous checks that were taken out for other organisations, provided that they pay a small fee and sign up for an update service). Any developments on these points will be covered by our updating service.

For more information on how the vetting and barring scheme operates, including changes to certain aspects of the scheme that came into force in September 2012, see flmemo.co.uk/em619a. For more general information on criminal records and other checks, see the DBS website at flmemo.co.uk/em619b.

Employers who knowingly permit a barred individual to engage in regulated activity face a maximum **penalty** of up to 6 months in prison plus a fine. It is also a criminal offence for a barred individual to seek or undertake work with children or vulnerable adults.

> MEMO POINTS 1. The Vetting and Barring Scheme (VBS) replaces the **three previous lists** of those who are barred from working with children or vulnerable adults (information held under Section 142 of the Education Act 2002 (List 99), the Protection Of Children Act (POCA) list, and the Protection Of Vulnerable Adults (POVA) list) with two barred lists: one for those who are barred from engaging in regulated activity with children, and one for those barred from engaging in regulated activity with vulnerable adults.
> 2. In **Scotland**, applications are made to Disclosure Scotland.
> 3. **Employers in the education sector** are required to carry out checks against the employment of sexual offenders (s 142 Education Act 2002).
> 4. There are also restrictions on employing individuals with criminal records in the **private security industry** (s 7 Private Security Industry Act 2001).

There are **three levels of checks** on the criminal records of individuals (Police Act 1997):   **620**

1. **Enhanced DBS Certificate (enhanced disclosure)**. This check is appropriate for sensitive jobs that come within the exceptions of the Rehabilitation of Offenders Act 1974 (Exceptions) Order (SI 1975/1023, as amended) and includes checks on those working in a regulated activity as defined in the Safeguarding Vulnerable Groups Act (SVGA). It is also used when certain licences are applied for (e.g. gaming and lottery licences) and for judicial appointments. The Certificate will record all convictions (including spent convictions), cautions, reprimands and warnings or state that there are none, and may also include information provided by the local police. It will also show if the individual is barred from working with children and other vulnerable groups.

2. **DBS Certificate (standard disclosure)**. This check is appropriate for jobs that come within the exceptions of the Rehabilitation of Offenders Act 1974 (Exceptions) Order (SI 1975/1023, as amended) where there is a position of trust, for example positions within the security industry and financial services. The Certificate records details of all convictions (including spent convictions), cautions, reprimands and warnings, or will state that there are none. Local police forces will not be involved in the checking procedure. The standard disclosure does not show if the individual is barred from working with children and other vulnerable groups.

3. **Criminal Conviction Certificate (basic disclosure) (not yet implemented) in England and Wales but currently available from Disclosure Scotland for any UK resident**. When implemented, this check will be appropriate for most employers. It will disclose details of recorded offences (other than spent convictions) over the previous 6-year period or state that there are none. Unlike enhanced and standard disclosures, an individual will be able to apply directly to the DBS and a basic disclosure will only be issued to the individual.

> MEMO POINTS With regard to information provided during an enhanced criminal record check, the **police do not owe a duty of care** to individuals (Desmond v The Chief Constable of Nottinghamshire Police [2011] EWCA Civ 3). In this case, the appellant had been arrested on suspicion of indecent assault. He was not charged but two police records were made in relation to this event and information that was not entirely accurate was disclosed by the police under an enhanced criminal record check. It was held that no duty is owed by the police to applicants to take reasonable care in

responding to requests from the CRB (which is now part of the DBS), largely because they are fulfilling a statutory duty which does not envisage a remedy in compensation or damages for its breach, and there is nothing from which a common law duty of care can be discerned. From a public policy perspective, it was also important that the statutory purpose of providing the information required by an enhanced criminal records check was the protection of vulnerable young people and this should not be compromised.

621 **Applications** for enhanced and standard disclosures must be **signed by** the individual on whom the check is being made and countersigned by an organisation registered with the DBS. This may be the recruiting organisation, but if an employer does not want to register he can use another registered organisation (known as an umbrella body) to sign on his behalf. The registered organisation must also **confirm the identity** of the individual by checking and verifying documentary proof of their identity and address. The identity checking guidelines were strengthened in 2012 with the aim of making it more difficult for individuals to conceal their criminal records. Individuals undergoing criminal record checks now need to produce documents that have been acquired through undergoing stringent identity verification with the document issuer, for example the Identity and Passport Service or the Driver and Vehicle Licensing Agency. The full guidelines are available here: flmemo.co.uk/em621

The original disclosure will then be **issued to** the individual and a **copy sent** to the registered entity. In relation to enhanced disclosures, local police forces can also disclose further information directly to the registered entity where such information cannot be included in the certificate itself because its disclosure may hamper detection or prevention of crime.

622 **Registration** As detailed above, only organisations which are registered with the DBS are entitled to countersign an application for a standard or an enhanced check.

Those registering must sign up to the DBS' **Code of practice** which requires that all disclosure material is kept confidential and used fairly. The Code requires the registered entity to have a written policy on the **handling and storage of disclosure material** to ensure that information obtained is kept securely and only for as long as is necessary, usually not more than 6 months, before being disposed of. Organisations must also have a written policy on the **recruitment of ex-offenders** with a view to avoiding unfair discrimination, and **must also**:
a. ensure that application forms for positions where a standard or enhanced disclosure will be requested:
– inform applicants that such a request will be made for successful applicants; and
– state that a criminal record will not necessarily be a bar to obtaining the position (or include this statement in accompanying material);
b. discuss with the applicant any matters revealed before withdrawing an offer of employment;
c. make applicants who are subject to disclosure aware of the DBS Code and make a copy available on request; and
d. give guidance on the recruitment of ex-offenders to those involved in the selection process.

The DBS can **refuse to issue** standard and enhanced disclosures if it suspects that the DBS Code is not being adhered to.

It is a **criminal offence** for employees of registered bodies/recipients of standard and enhanced disclosures to disclose information contained in the certificates other than in the course of their duties.

623 The requirements for registration do not apply where **basic checks** are made. However, as basic disclosure will involve sensitive personal data, the data protection principles will apply (¶5951).

624 **Fees** There is a one-off fee of £300 when an organisation **registers** with the DBS to enable it to receive enhanced or standard disclosures. This includes the cost of the lead countersignatory. There is also a one-off fee of £5 for each additional countersignatory.

The fee payable by a registered body for **each disclosure** is as follows: £36 for an enhanced disclosure and £26 for a standard disclosure, although this fee is waived in the case of volunteers. Organisations can ask the applicants to pay them for the disclosure.

4. Health questionnaires

625 The applicant could be asked to complete a health questionnaire as a **supplement to the application form**. This is common where the job involves driving work and in industries where there is an exposure to certain chemicals. The degree of detail requested on a health questionnaire will depend on the **nature of the job** and the sort of medical conditions that may affect the applicant's ability to carry out that job. Advice can be obtained from the local Employment Medical Advisory Service, which is part of the Health and Safety Executive. Sometimes a health questionnaire is required for **pension or insurance purposes**. A health questionnaire could also form the basis of the health assessment required under the Working Time Regulations for **night workers** (¶3701).

> MEMO POINTS   It may be appropriate with manual jobs in **certain industries**, such as oil or construction, to require an employee to remain in **excellent health** throughout his employment and in such cases the employer should state this as an express term of the contract. If an employer subsequently dismisses an employee on this term, the employer will need to show that the requirement was reasonable and that he was justified and acted reasonably in relying on it.

626 Only information that really needs to be known should be obtained and employers requiring health questionnaires to be completed must ensure that they comply with the data protection **sensitive data condition** (¶5951). This means that, in general, employers should only use health questionnaires if the applicant has freely given his explicit consent, or where it is necessary for the protection of health and safety, to prevent discrimination on the grounds of disability or to satisfy other legal obligations. Medical information should be **obtained separately** and kept separate from the application form. Information about an applicant's health which has been collected for occupational or insurance purposes should not be made available to the employer unless this is necessary to administer the scheme.

The health questionnaire should be treated as **confidential**, and it is advisable that steps are taken to ensure that only the employer's medical adviser sees the completed form.

The employer should **rely on** his medical adviser's professional opinion as to whether the applicant is fit to do the job, or whether a medical examination is required (¶706).

627 **Equality provisions** have been introduced restricting the use of health questionnaires or asking questions about health or disability during recruitment, i.e. before an offer of employment is made (s60 EqA 2010). Questions about absence records also fall within the provisions. Questions are only permitted for limited purposes, including:
– to find out whether reasonable adjustments need to be made during the recruitment process;
– to establish whether the applicant will be able to carry out an essential part of the job;
– to monitor diversity;
– to take positive action in respect of disabled people; or
– where there is the requirement that the job holder has a disability, to establish that the applicant has a disability.

Employees asked health questions which they consider should not have been asked may complain to the EHRC, who can investigate and take enforcement action. There is no freestanding right to make a claim in the employment tribunal but if a prohibited health question has been asked the burden of proof will pass to the employer to prove that he did not discriminate on the basis of the answer.

If the answers reveal that the applicant is **disabled**, the employer will be under a statutory duty to make reasonable adjustments (¶5530).

> MEMO POINTS   When asking questions to establish whether an applicant can perform an essential part of a job the employer must first take into account any reasonable adjustments which could be made.

628 If a prospective employee has **deliberately concealed** a condition (for example a history of mental illness), the employer may be able to terminate the contract if he goes on to employ him, especially if the condition recurs. In such circumstances, the employer must ensure that he dismisses the employee for reason of this deception (using his disciplinary procedure) and not for reason of the employee's illness. It is useful to state on any medical questionnaire that any deliberate concealment or deception will be treated as a matter of gross misconduct which could lead to the dismissal of the employee. The employer will then be on firm ground if he finds out the employee has made a serious concealment or deception and he dismisses the employee, after following his disciplinary procedure, on the ground of gross misconduct. However, if the concealment has no impact on the employee's work and is a condition that will not recur, the employer must act carefully and reasonably and ascertain the reason why the employee concealed his condition before disciplining him.

Employers should ensure that any such **questionnaire** is **well drafted**. It may not be possible to argue that an employee has deliberately concealed a condition if he has truthfully answered a poorly drafted questionnaire, which has been framed in such a way that the answers given may not reveal the whole picture.

EXAMPLE In *Cheltenham Borough Council v Laird* [2009] IRLR 621, HC, a lengthy, complex and expensive case, a council claimed damages for misrepresentation from its former managing director. The claim was based on the fact that when she completed the pre-employment health questionnaire required by the Council, she failed to reveal earlier episodes of work-related stress and depression. However, the questions had been framed in such a way that the truthful answers she gave did not reveal the whole picture. In particular there was no general "sweep up" question asking if there were any other matters which might affect the Council's decision. While the High Court found that satisfactory completion of the questionnaire was a condition of the employment, the answers given were not fraudulent, and so the claim failed.
Comment: The poor drafting of the health questionnaire meant that the employee could answer all the questions asked without revealing three previous episodes of depression. Had the questionnaire been better targeted, the Council might have been awarded very significant damages. However, it is doubtful whether the employee would have been able to pay the damages in practice.

629 **References** are another good way of ascertaining a prospective employee's attendance record and many employees specifically ask appropriate referees what kind of attendance and sickness record a prospective employee has, though be aware that any absences that could be for reasons relating to pregnancy or a disability should be considered with caution, particularly with regard to whether any reasonable adjustments would be possible to improve attendance, in order to avoid discrimination.

IV. Selection

A. Short-listing for interview

630 In some companies, **human resources staff** will be involved in the sifting of application forms and the short-listing of applicants to be invited to the next stage of the selection process, commonly an interview. To avoid any possibility of bias, it is preferable for two or more selectors (including a member of human resources and the direct line manager or supervisor of the vacant post) to be involved in this process.

631 Selectors should be **trained** to ensure that they are aware of their legal obligations (in particular, to avoid discrimination) and that they should base their decisions on objective **selection criteria** which are founded on the key skills and experience identified in the job description and person specification (and not on prejudices and stereotypes (*Horsey v Dyfed County Council* [1982] IRLR 395, EAT)).

632 It is good practice for the selectors who do an initial review for interview selection not to see unnecessary **personal details**, as this reduces the risk of discrimination on irrelevant, unlawful grounds. In smaller organisations it may not be possible for the sifting and selection processes to be separated.

Where certain **qualifications** have been validly stipulated, the selectors should short-list those applicants who have the appropriate qualifications (or overseas equivalents). If an applicant has alternative evidence of the necessary level of competence, the employer may be able to waive the requirement for the particular qualification stipulated.

If, having selected on the basis of qualifications, there are too many applicants to interview, the selectors should consider the relevance of the applicants' **work experience**, keeping a note of the criteria applied. It is advisable not to specify the length of service required, rather focus on the type of experience, in order to avoid falling foul of the age discrimination legislation.

If the employer knows that an applicant is disabled and is likely to be at a substantial disadvantage because of the employer's arrangements or premises, he should consider whether a **reasonable adjustment** may bring the disabled person within the number of applicants to be considered for the position even though he would not otherwise be selected because of that disadvantage. If the selectors **need more information** to be able to make that judgement, they should put the disabled person on the short-list for interview if that is the normal method of seeking additional information on applicants.

All applications should be processed in exactly the same way, and there should not be separate lists of male and female or married and single applicants. Decisions about short-listing should not be made until the closing date for applications.

B. Selection methods

The selection process can involve a number of **different approaches** including:
– interviews;
– practical tests;
– psychometric tests;
– role plays;
– team exercises; and
– assessment centres.

Which approach is adopted will depend on the needs and seniority of the job, the skills of the recruiter and the resources and objectives of the company. More senior or specialised jobs may require more detailed and sophisticated techniques to test the applicant's skills and personal characteristics. In any case, the employer should ensure that the process does not discriminate on grounds of age, disability, gender reassignment, marriage and civil partnership, pregnancy and maternity, race, religion or belief, sex or sexual orientation, but is specifically related to the job requirements.

1. Interviews

The interview is the most common method of selection. It has two main purposes: to assess the applicant's suitability, and to give him information about the job and the company.

Assessing the applicant's suitability The interview should be organised in such a way as to promote **fair treatment** of all applicants. It may be helpful to have a written interview procedure specifying the manner in which interviews should be conducted. For example, this could specify the number of interviewers (such as a human resources specialist, together with the line manager), and the types of questions that can and cannot be asked. This will help to ensure that there is a consistent form to the interviews, and that the required information is obtained from each applicant.

In addition to receiving training in their legal obligations, interviewers should be trained in interviewing techniques.

Interviews can vary in the **degree of formality**, depending on the nature of the job and the type of company. The interview may be conducted one-to-one, by a series of one-to-one interviews, or by panels of two or more people.

Panel interviews tend to be more formal but may be helpful in bringing a range of ages, racial backgrounds and both male/female presence so as to reduce the risk of unlawful discrimination. The number of panel members should ideally be kept to a maximum of three or four, unless there is a pressing reason for exceeding these numbers. Members of the panel may have particular areas of expertise, which they can concentrate on with the applicant. However, the applicant may feel outnumbered and less relaxed, and it may be difficult to achieve a rapport with large numbers present. The environment can be made less intimidating by avoiding formal surroundings, such as a boardroom, and formal layouts (e.g. sitting the applicant opposite a long line of panel members behind a formal table). Panel interviews need to be chaired by one member so that they are well structured and not subject to random interruptions from the various panel members.

Sometimes a member of human resources will conduct an **initial screening interview** in order to pre-select applicants for general suitability and competence. The disadvantage of this approach is that the applicant may be inconvenienced by being asked to attend on more than one occasion, and there is a danger of repetition in sequential interviews. Following a screening interview, there may be a **first interview** (either panel or one-to-one) involving the line manager or supervisor for the vacant position. This stage may identify a few suitable applicants, who may be invited to return for a **second interview**. A second interview may be used to undertake a more detailed analysis of the strengths and weaknesses of the remaining applicants. At this stage, more senior members of the company may be involved in the interview in order to make a final selection. The various stages of the interview process described above may be condensed in smaller organisations.

645 **Providing information to the applicant** Employers should recognise that interviews also give applicants the opportunity to find out about the company, the job, the salary and other employment terms. The interviewer should be equipped to answer these questions. A badly prepared interviewer can create an unfavourable impression of the company and may deter suitable applicants.

2. Selection tests

647 Selection tests can be used as an aid to measure an applicant's **practical ability**, or **personality traits** and **intelligence**. The employer should give careful thought as to whether or not to use tests, and they should not be used (particularly in the case of personality tests) in isolation, but rather in conjunction with other selection techniques.

If tests are used, they should be specifically related to the job and/or career requirements, should measure an applicant's actual or inherent ability to do or train for the work or career against objective criteria, and the employer should have a policy about using tests, storing results and giving feedback to applicants. They should be administered by people who are trained and competent to do so, and applicants should be given an explanation of the nature and purpose of the tests before they are taken. The results should be confidential to the selectors and the applicant.

Tests should be gender **neutral**. Tests should also not contain irrelevant questions or exercises on matters which may indirectly discriminate against applicants of particular nationalities or from particular racial backgrounds.

Routine testing of all applicants may discriminate against particular individuals or place them at a substantial disadvantage. If it does, the tests themselves or the way the results are assessed may need to be revised to take account of **disabled applicants** unless the nature and form of the test are necessary to assess a matter relevant to the job. If an applicant's disability inhibits his performance, it may be a reasonable adjustment to accept a lower "pass rate". Whether this is acceptable will depend on how closely the test is related to the requirements of the job, and what adjustments the employer would have to make if the disabled applicant were appointed.

> EXAMPLE
> 1. A man with dyslexia, E, applies for a job that involves writing letters within fairly long deadlines. He can generally write letters very well but has difficulty doing so in stressful situations. At the interview, applicants must do a test of their letter-writing ability immediately on arrival and within a short time, putting E at a substantial disadvantage compared to other applicants. A reasonable adjustment would be for the employer to allow E more time to settle in and longer to write the test.
> 2. A disabled applicant, F, takes the numeracy test set by the employer for prospective employees and does not achieve the stipulated level. If the job requires a high level of numeracy, it may be reasonable to reject F. If, however, little numerical work is required and F is otherwise suitable, it is likely to be a reasonable adjustment for the employer to waive the requirement.
> 3. In *Project Management Institute v Latif* [2007] UKEAT 0028_07_1005, a qualifications body failed to make reasonable adjustments in relation to arrangements for a candidate to sit a computer-based exam. L, who is registered blind, tried repeatedly to get PMI to reconsider its position regarding adjustments to its exam procedure. PMI provided relevant literature to L, allowed her more time to sit the exam and paid for and arranged a reader. However, they refused to entertain L's requests for specialist software to be installed on the computer at the exam centre.

648 Tests should be subject to regular **review** to ensure that they remain relevant and free from any unjustifiable bias, either in content or in the scoring mechanism.

649 **Practical tests** If the job involves practical skills (e.g. typing, shorthand, or manual skills), tests can be used before or at the time of the interview to measure an applicant's ability. The test must not be discriminatory and must strictly relate to the actual requirements of the job.

650 **Psychometric and psychological tests** These tests set out to measure personality traits and intelligence, in particular reasoning, problem solving, decision making, interpersonal skills and confidence.

The use of such tests is not widespread and is sometimes considered controversial. Guides on their use are available (for example, from the Institute of Personnel and Development).

The data protection implications of using **automated processes** in the selection process are discussed below.

3. Role plays, exercises and assessment centres

653 Larger companies may use assessment centres to put applicants (often senior management or fast-track graduates) through interviews, tests, and individual and group exercises. These may take place in a residential setting over a few days. The exercises may include presentations, role plays and team events. This method is the most time-consuming, but can give an accurate indication of likely job performance. The identification of the skills required to do the job and the choice of exercises to test those skills will be critical to the effectiveness of this method.

C. Arranging and preparing for interviews

660 **Travel expenses** Employers may wish to indicate whether the company will pay an applicant's reasonable travel expenses in the letter inviting the applicant for interview, making it clear whether it will reimburse first or second class travel and/or what mileage rate will be applied to car travel. It may be appropriate to offer a subsistence payment (either actual expenditure incurred based on receipts submitted, or a notional allowance).

661 **Evidence of qualifications** The letter should also indicate what the applicant should bring with him to the interview, such as evidence of his qualifications.

662 **Disabled applicants** The statutory duty to make **reasonable adjustments** in relation to disabled applicants applies where the **employer knows**, or could reasonably be expected to know, that the disabled person in question is or may be an applicant for the post, or that a particular applicant has a disability which is likely to place him at a disadvantage, for example, where the application form has revealed that an applicant has a disability.

If the employer is **not aware** in advance of an applicant's disability and the need to make reasonable adjustments to the arrangements, he should nevertheless seek to do so as soon as he learns of the disability and the disadvantage. What may reasonably be required in these circumstances may be less extensive than if advance notice had been given.

Reasonable adjustments might include the following:
- rearranging the time of the interview;
- accommodating a hearing-impaired applicant by ensuring that the interviewer faces the applicant, is well lit, speaks clearly and is prepared to repeat questions, or by providing a hearing loop or signer;
- paying additional expenses to meet any special requirements, for example travelling expenses for a support worker or reasonable cost of travel by taxi, rather than by bus or train, if this will eliminate any substantial disadvantage to which the arrangements would otherwise put the disabled applicant; and
- allowing the applicant with a learning impairment to bring a friend or relative to assist when answering questions that are not part of tests.

For further details, see ¶5530.

663 **Interviewer preparation** The interviewer should re-read the application form, job and person specifications, and identify areas to develop further in the interview. The interviewer should plan questions, considering whether to ask only a few questions in order to encourage the applicant to talk at length on certain areas, and/or to structure a series of short questions covering several different topics. If there is to be a panel interview or a series of interviews, the topics to be covered by each member of the panel or each separate interviewer should be agreed.

The interviewer should consider, in advance, what information the applicant might ask for, and be ready to answer questions about the company and the job.

D. Conducting interviews

665 It may be useful for the applicant to be given a **tour of the company** or relevant department and to meet employees with whom he would be working. This will be of particular interest to applicants who are new to the job market (e.g. school leavers), and will also give the employer an opportunity to assess the applicant's interaction with other employees.

The interviewer should **begin the interview** by introducing himself and any other interviewers. He should give some background information about the company and the job. The applicant could be made to feel at ease by beginning with straightforward questions. As the interview progresses, it is more productive to avoid questions that merely call for a "yes" or "no" answer. The interviewer should ensure that all the relevant areas are covered. As the applicant speaks, the interviewer should listen, making notes on important points. If possible, there should be no interruptions (for example, incoming telephone calls).

The interview should be **scheduled** to last a certain time, and the interviewer should try to keep within the time allowed, leaving enough time for the applicant to raise any questions he may have. Applicants should be told when they are likely to know the **outcome** of the interview.

Interview questions Unless they have been specifically asked, applicants are not obliged to offer information to prospective employers. It is up to the interviewer to elicit the information required by the employer.

666

The interviewer does not have to ask all applicants the same questions, particularly if there are certain areas relevant to one particular application, for example gaps in an applicant's employment. However, interviewers should be aware of the need to ask **job-related questions**, focusing mainly on the job requirements, and should not ask questions that might indicate an intention to discriminate on the grounds of age, disability, gender reassignment, marriage and civil partnership, pregnancy and maternity, race, religion or belief, sex or sexual orientation. For example, women should not be singled out and asked about their childcare arrangements. If questions are to be asked about matters that could be regarded as discriminatory (for example, **domestic circumstances**), it would be advisable to ask the same questions of all applicants. Questions about marriage plans or family intentions should not be asked, as they could be construed as showing bias against women.

Questions about an applicant's **background, character and private life** may infringe his right to privacy under human rights legislation (Human Rights Act 1998).

It is also advisable for the interviewer to ascertain when the applicant would be able to start the new job. If the applicant is currently employed, he will have to give **notice of termination** to his current employer. This may affect whether the employer decides to offer employment to a particular applicant. It is a commercial decision for the employer whether he is prepared to wait for the applicant to be free to start the new job. It may be possible for the applicant to negotiate a shorter period of notice with his current employer.

The interviewer could ask about a disabled applicant's **disability** if it is, or may be, relevant to the person's ability to do the job, after a reasonable adjustment if necessary. Indeed, this information may be required to assess what adjustments should be made. It should not, however, be used to discriminate against the applicant and discriminatory questions should be avoided.

> EXAMPLE A disabled applicant, G, is asked in an interview whether he may require extra leave because of his impairment. The need for extra time off work may be a substantial factor relevant to the person's ability to do the job and so the question is unlikely to be discriminatory.

Promises Interviewers should take care not to make any promises during the interview that conflict with the employer's standard terms and conditions of employment unless these have been approved in advance. Oral promises have been enforced where the interviewer had authority to make them, even where these conflict with signed contract terms.

667

If any unusual agreement is reached during the interview, it is advisable to record it in writing and amend the offer letter and/or contract of employment as appropriate.

E. The decision

Interviewers should record their assessment of each applicant against the agreed selection criteria. In reaching a final decision, the interviewers should compare their results, taking into account the relative weighting of the criteria. Ideally, assessments of an applicant should be written up as soon as possible after the interview to assist in the decision making process and also to monitor the fairness of the process.

670

The decision should be made as soon as possible after the interview, test or assessment. A scoring system or assessment based on the selection criteria should allow a speedy comparison of results.

Notes of the scores and reasons for decisions should be kept.

671 If an applicant meets the required standard, the appointment process can begin. All applicants should be **informed of the outcome** as soon as possible, or informed of any delay. Rejection letters should be short and to the point. Employers are not obliged to give **reasons** why a particular applicant was unsuccessful. If reasons are given, the employer must ensure that they are accurate, because if the recruitment or selection process is subject to legal challenge, the rejection letter may have to be disclosed. If there is any discrepancy between the rejection letter and the evidence before the tribunal as to the real reason for rejection, the employer's defence to any claim will be weakened.

V. Monitoring and data protection

Monitoring and review

675 Monitoring applications can help to ascertain how people found out about the vacancy, and therefore how **advertising** can be used to best effect in the future.

Application forms should be reviewed periodically to ensure that they comply with legal requirements, and that they cover all the information needed to decide which applicants to short-list for interview.

The recruitment process should also be monitored as part of the company's **equal opportunities programme** so that the profile of applicants can be identified in order to ascertain whether there are any barriers to the recruitment of particular groups. For these purposes, **personal details** such as sex, marital status, ethnic origin or date of birth should be requested in a distinct part of the form that can be separated and reintroduced at the end of the recruitment process. It should be clear that this information is for monitoring purposes only and need only be provided on a voluntary basis.

Data protection

676 Data protection principles are discussed in chapter 17. The application of these principles to recruitment and selection is discussed below and is based on the Recruitment and Selection Part of the Information Commissioner's Employment Practices Code (part 1 DP Code).

Employers are also advised to follow the DP Code's general recommendations with regard to data management (¶6000).

An applicant can ask for **access** to interview notes (and other personal data) if these form part of a set of information about him, for example if they are filed together with the application form and references or, in the case of an existing employee, in his personnel file (¶5980).

677 **Managing data protection** Those involved in the recruitment and selection process should be **trained** so that they understand their own responsibility for data protection compliance, and serious data protection breaches should be a **disciplinary offence**.

Employers should also only request data about an applicant that is **relevant** to the recruitment and selection process.

678 **Advertising** Applicants should be informed of the name of the organisation to which their information will be provided and how it will be used, unless this is self-evident (normally the case with adverts for specific jobs, where the employer's name is on the advert). If the link between the requested information and its potential use is unclear, an explanation must be given.

If a **recruitment agency** is used, it must identify itself when placing an advert on behalf of an employer and explain how an applicant's personal data will be used and disclosed (unless this is self-evident). If the information may be used in connection with future vacancies, this should be clearly stated in the advert. The advert need not identify the employer.

The agency can pass the information to the employer provided the applicant understands that it will do so. If the employer is to receive the information about the applicant, the applicant must be informed of the employer's identity and how the information will be used, unless this is self-evident.

If the employer wishes to remain anonymous at the early stages of the recruitment process, the agency may send information on an anonymous basis about an applicant to him. Once the employer wishes to receive personally identifiable information about the applicant so that the application can be pursued further, the employer must then be identified to that applicant.

Applications Again, the application form should state to whom the information is being provided and how it will be used, unless this is self-evident (normally the case with applications for specific jobs). If the employer receives an **unsolicited application**, he need only provide the above explanation if the application is to be retained and the use of the information or period of retention would not be self-evident to the applicant.

679

Any information requested should be **relevant** to the recruitment decision to be made (or to a related purpose, such as equal opportunities monitoring), and should be proportionate (in terms of its **extent and nature**) to the position. Certain questions will be relevant to some positions and not others, and the application form should be tailored accordingly. There should be a clear statement on the application or surrounding documents which explains what information might be required about the applicant in addition to the information directly supplied by him. This should also state from whom this information will be sought.

Information about **criminal convictions** should only be requested if the role justifies such a request, in which case the form should clearly state that spent convictions do not have to be declared, unless an exemption applies (¶618).

The form should explain what checks may be made to **verify** the information provided (see below), including details of any further sources of information about the applicant.

If **sensitive data** is requested, special conditions must be satisfied (¶5951). Only sensitive data questions that have to be asked at the initial application stage should be requested.

The employer should provide a **secure method for sending** applications. If applications are to be sent by post or by fax, access to them once received should be limited. If applications are made online, the employer should ensure a secure method of transmission (for example, by using encryption-based software). Once received, the application must be **securely stored**.

> MEMO POINTS In the context of recruitment and selection, **sensitive data** may include:
> – relevant criminal convictions to assess suitability for certain types of employment;
> – information about disabled applicants to ensure reasonable adjustments are made during the recruitment and selection process; and
> – information about racial or ethnic origin and/or sexual orientation to ensure that the processes are non-discriminatory.

Verification An employer may need to **check the information provided** by a job applicant. In most cases this can be done on the production of documentary evidence, such as original certificates of educational qualifications, by the applicant. In some cases, however, the employer may need to obtain third party verification, such as following up references from previous employers or checking financial references. In such cases employers should:
– fully **explain to the applicant** how the checks will be carried out. This should be done as soon as is reasonably practicable in the recruitment process. If external sources are to be used to check information, this should be explained to the applicant; and
– **obtain a signed consent** from the applicant if they need to get documents or information from a third party (for example, confirmation of qualifications) unless consent has been indicated in some other way, for example the applicant has already written to the third party

680

confirming that the information can be sent to the employer. Employers should not force applicants to use their subject access rights to obtain **records from another organisation** (i.e. making it a condition of getting the job) unless they are under an obligation to require the collection and verification of any criminal records (¶619) and this is sought from the Disclosure and Barring Service (DBS). Generally, where DBS disclosure is requested this should be confined, as far as practicable, to the applicant that the employer intends to appoint.

If the checks produce **discrepancies**, the applicant should be given the **opportunity to explain**.

Verification should be limited to the checking of information specifically requested in the application form or during the recruitment process and should be proportionate to the requirements of the positions being applied for.

682 **Short-listing** Personal data should be **used consistently** and all short-list methods should be checked with sources of good practice such as the Equality and Human Rights Commission.

Tests based on the **interpretation of scientific evidence** (for example, psychological tests) should only be used and interpreted by individuals who have been properly trained.

683 **Interviews** The collection of personal data at interview, their recording, storage and use are subject to data protection principles (for example, all notes should be destroyed after a reasonable time taking into account the employer's need to protect himself from any potential discrimination claim). These should, therefore, be relevant to, and necessary for, the recruitment process (or defending any challenge to that process). Interviewers should be made aware that interviewees may have a right to request access to their interview notes, and they (or those in contact with the applicants) should be taught how to deal with such requests.

684 **Pre-employment vetting** Enquiries to third parties about the applicant's background and circumstances should be confined to situations where there are particular and significant risks to the employer, clients, customers or others (for example, government workers with access to classified information, employees who work with children or certain vulnerable adults) and where there is no less intrusive and reasonably practicable alternative.

The **extent and nature** of information sought must be justified by the position and proportionate to the risks faced (the aim should be to obtain **specific information**, as opposed to a general intelligence gathering exercise). If sensitive data is collected, special conditions must be satisfied (¶5951). Wherever practicable the relevant information should be obtained directly from the applicant and, if necessary, then verified.

The applicant should be **informed** early in the process that vetting is to take place and how it will be done. The vetting itself should be **carried out** at an appropriate point in the recruitment process and comprehensive vetting should only be conducted on a successful applicant.

An approach should only be made to **sources** likely to provide the required information. If it is necessary to obtain **documents or information from a third party**, the applicant's consent should be obtained. The applicant's family and close associates should only be approached in exceptional cases.

Information from **unreliable sources** should be discounted. The applicant should be permitted to make representations in relation to **adverse information** that will affect the decision to appoint.

If **information** is obtained **about a third party**, that party should (so far as practicable) be made aware of that fact.

685 **Retention of recruitment records** All personal data obtained during the recruitment process should be **securely stored or destroyed**. The employer must carefully consider which information from the application form should be **transferred to the ongoing employment**

record (irrelevant information should be deleted). For example, information about the applicant's former salary should not be kept.

There must be a clear business **need for keeping** any recruitment **records**. No recruitment record should be held beyond the statutory limitation period for bringing a claim which may have arisen out of the recruitment process (¶9452) unless, again, there is a clear business reason for exceeding this period. In such cases, anonymising the recruitment information should be considered. **Information obtained by vetting** should be destroyed as soon as possible, or in any case within 6 months. A record of the result of the vetting or verification may be retained. With regard to criminal convictions disclosure from the Disclosure and Barring Service, such information should be deleted after verification unless the information is relevant to the ongoing relationship.

If information about **unsuccessful applicants** is to be kept on file for future vacancies, they should be informed and given the opportunity to have such information removed (the application form itself can allow the applicant to indicate his wishes).

SECTION 2

Offer and appointment

Once a successful applicant has been identified, the employer can make him an **offer** of employment. Consideration should be given to whether this offer should be subject to any **conditions**, for example receipt of references, passing a medical or evidence that the individual can work legally in the UK. It may be necessary to apply for a work permit for some applicants from overseas. **700**

It is advisable that the **appointment** of the successful applicant is documented. The essential terms should be communicated in an **offer letter**, which may be accompanied by a more detailed written contract of employment. In either case, the applicant should signify his acceptance of the offer in writing. Once an unconditional offer of employment is accepted or any conditions have been satisfied, a binding contract of employment will come into existence. **701**

A. Pre-conditions to employment

Employers who unlawfully employ illegal migrant workers will be subject to civil penalties. It is also a criminal offence for an employer to employ a person aged 16 or over who does not have the **right to live and work in the UK**. The employer should, therefore, obtain **documentary proof** of such a right from successful applicants. If this has not been established, the employment should be made conditional on proof being produced to the employer's satisfaction. **702**

If an applicant does not have the right to work in the UK, the employer could consider if **sponsorship** under Tier 2 of the points-based immigration system is possible (¶771).

These issues are discussed in section 3 below.

Other pre-conditions are discussed immediately below.

Confirmation of qualifications

The job may require the holder to have particular qualifications, registrations, training or licences, and the applicant should be asked to provide proof that he has the necessary qualifications etc, perhaps by bringing the appropriate documentation to the interview. If **703** the employer is to make the check himself, the applicant should be informed, and copies of the relevant checks and responses should be kept on file (subject to the data protection obligations discussed in ¶676).

References

704 It is common to specify that one of the referees should be the applicant's current employer, which may cause problems if the latter is not aware that his employee is looking for a new job. It may, therefore, be helpful for the application form to state whether references will be taken up and at what stage of the recruitment process (for example, prior to the interview or after an offer has been made). It is advisable for the company to require references "**satisfactory to the employer**", i.e. a subjective test. If the employer asks for "satisfactory references", there may be scope for dispute as to whether the references provided are in fact satisfactory.

When **taking up references** the prospective employer should:
– consider why he needs a reference and what he wants to find out (for example, dates of previous employment, position held, attendance and conduct);
– specify his needs carefully, perhaps using a list of structured questions, relevant to an assessment of the applicant's abilities (a copy of the job description could be sent to the referee);
– decide who in the organisation would be best placed to provide a reference and how best to approach the referee; and
– recognise that roles may be reversed and that he may be asked to provide a reference in the future.

The prospective employer should obtain the **applicant's permission** to contact his referee, either in the application form itself or at a later stage in the selection process. References can be obtained over the telephone, but a **written reference** gives the referee time to think and compose a structured response.

The prospective employer should use the reference provided to **supplement his own view** of the applicant, as formed from the application form and the performance at interview. It is unwise to rely solely on references, as they may be biased.

When checking references, the prospective employer should take care not to disclose to prospective employees any **confidential information** received from the referee.

To **avoid any allegation of discrimination**, the process of checking references should be consistent. For example, it will not be discriminatory to refuse to appoint a candidate who cannot provide a reference, if the employer requires that all offers are subject to suitable references (*Jatto v Messrs Godloves Solicitors and ors* [2007] UKEAT 0300_07_2610).

An applicant can **request access** to references **received by** the prospective employer (¶5980). Where an applicant worker has requested to see a reference received by his prospective/new employer which enables a third party to be identified, the employer must make a judgement as to what information is reasonable to withhold (part 2.9.3 DP Code).

EXAMPLE In *Jatto v Messrs Godloves Solicitors and ors*, a black solicitor was offered a post with a firm on condition that he supplied satisfactory references. One of the solicitor's previous employers refused to give a reference, for the reason that any reference would be unfavourable. The firm therefore withdrew the appointment. As the firm had been consistent in requiring all candidates to supply references there had been no less favourable treatment, and no discrimination.

705 When **giving a reference**, an employer owes a **duty of care** to the subject of that reference (the employee), and the latter will be able to sue the employer for damages if he suffers loss as a result of the employer's negligent preparation of the reference (¶8324). An employee also has the right not to suffer a detrimental act or omission (¶8327). As a result, many employers limit references to factual matters such as the employee's dates of employment and job title, which may be of limited value to prospective employers.

The employer should (part 2.9.1-2 DP Code):
– set out a company policy which states who can give references, in what circumstances, and the policy that applies to the granting of access to them. Anyone who is likely to become a referee should be aware of the policy;

– not provide confidential references about a worker unless sure that this is the worker's wish; and
– establish at the time the worker's employment ends whether or not he wants references to be provided to future employers or others.

Medicals

Where relevant, the recruitment process should make it clear that any job offer is subject to passing a medical. However, a medical should only be required where it is necessary for the prospective job. Particular reference should be made to the guidance in the Information about Workers' Health Part of the Information Commissioner's Employment Practices Code (part 4 DP Code). Employers must ensure that the testing is a **necessary and justified measure** to:
– determine whether the applicant is fit or likely to remain fit to carry out the job in question;
– meet any legal requirements for testing; or
– ascertain eligibility for a pension or insurance scheme.

The employer must obtain the applicant's **informed and freely given consent** to a medical examination or testing (unless another sensitive data condition has been complied with (¶5951)), particularly if it involves invasive checks such as blood tests. To be informed, the applicant must fully understand the nature of the tests and how the information obtained through testing will be used.

If a **medical report** is sought (whether from an applicant's doctor or specialist direct to an employer, or to the employer's medical adviser), the applicant's **consent** must be obtained, and the applicant has a **right to see** the report (Access to Medical Reports Act 1988). However, if the medical is conducted by the company doctor, the employer will not be bound by these requirements.

706

An employer should avoid requiring a medical check for **disabled applicants** and not others, as this is likely to constitute unlawful discrimination unless the employer has objective justification, which may be the case where the disability is relevant to the job (for example, a job requiring lifting or carrying where the applicant's condition affects these abilities) or due to the environment in which the job is done. Where there is a **specific condition**, the employer must ensure that he obtains the medical report from the most appropriate authority (for example, in *Paul v National Probation Service*, the employer erred in obtaining and relying on information given by the applicant's GP instead of the applicant's consultant, who had specialist knowledge of his condition (*Paul v National Probation Service* [2004] IRLR 190, EAT)). The employer can take into account medical evidence that shows that the disability affects the person's ability to do the work when deciding whether to appoint a particular applicant. However, where a report highlights potential problems that might affect whether the employer employs the applicant, the employer must **discuss** things further with the applicant and he is under a duty to take reasonable steps **to adjust** the job on offer (*Paul v National Probation Service*).

707

Similarly, **older applicants** should not be singled out simply because of their age, and employers should not make assumptions about the capability or medical fitness of applicants based purely on age.

Restraints on taking up employment

The employer should ascertain the applicant's **current notice period**. If the applicant leaves his current employment to take up the new post without giving the proper notice, the new employer may be liable for inducing a breach of contract.

709

The employer should also establish whether the applicant is restricted in taking up new employment by **restrictive covenants** in his current contract of employment. If so, the employer should review the contract and decide whether the restrictions affect his decision to make an offer.

If it is not possible to clarify this before making an offer, the offer could be conditional on the contract being produced and the employer being satisfied that the applicant's ability to

B. Appointment

710 The legal requirements for a valid contract are discussed in detail at ¶1111. Care needs to be taken to ensure that a **binding contract** is not formed between the employer and a successful applicant before it is intended to be.

In some cases, the offer of employment will be **conditional** on certain requirements being satisfied (see above). It is advisable for the employee not to resign his current employment until he is satisfied that all such conditions will be met. Once all conditions are satisfied, the employer could write again to the successful applicant to confirm that the offer of employment is now unconditional. If this is accepted, there will be a binding contract of employment.

If there are no conditions to be met (or all conditions have already been satisfied), the employer may send an **unconditional offer** letter to the employee. If this is **accepted**, there will be a binding contract of employment. The employer may wish to require acceptance within a certain time, so there is a definite time within which he must leave the offer open before turning to another applicant.

711 **Offer letter** Although an offer can be oral, it is advisable for it to be made in writing. The offer letter will contain a formal offer of the job, and will set out the essential terms and conditions of employment. These should be consistent with the details of the job that were given in the job advert, and should cover the following:
– job title;
– any pre-conditions to the offer;
– whether the employment is subject to a probationary period;
– main terms, namely salary, hours, benefits, pension arrangements, holiday entitlement, place of employment; and
– start date and arrangements for the first day.

The offer letter could form the **statutory statement of written particulars**, in which case it must contain all the necessary information (¶1420). To avoid any confusion over the terms offered and accepted, the employer may wish to set out the terms in a **written contract of employment**, a copy of which the new employee is asked to sign and return. The contract could be enclosed with the offer letter, and should contain, and where necessary expand, on the essential terms contained in the offer letter.

712 It is advisable for the offer to require **acceptance** in writing. Note that acceptance is effective as soon as a letter of acceptance is posted.

713 **Terms** The employer should take care not to discriminate in the terms on which employment is offered. In the case of **disabled employees**, the employer must consider whether any reasonable adjustments need to be made to the terms and conditions which would otherwise apply, for example changing working hours so that a disabled employee who has difficulty using public transport during rush hours can avoid those times.

714 Sometimes employers give "**golden hellos**" to new employees, which can involve substantial bonuses being paid on joining the company. Policy in this area should be developed with care, lest the employer breach his equal pay duties (¶5650).

715 **Relocation assistance and cultural acclimatisation** is particularly beneficial when dealing with international transfers and people relocating their home in order to start employment.

For employees relocating from overseas, the initial months of employment might also include language tuition and assistance on finding accommodation and appropriate schooling for children.

Pre-contractual negotiations In some cases, the successful applicant may not be willing to accept the terms offered. The employer may be prepared to negotiate, in particular, where there are no other suitable applicants and the employer does not wish to start the recruitment process again. The employer should avoid negotiating different terms where these would create discrepancies between that applicant and existing employees, in terms of existing reward structures and terms and conditions of employment. This may leave the employer vulnerable to **discrimination or equal pay** claims.

716

If negotiations do take place, the **outcome** should be recorded in writing, for example as an amendment to the written contract of employment, or as part of a revised offer letter. The latter may be more appropriate where the arrangement agreed is temporary.

If the employer is **not prepared to amend** the terms of his offer, either from the outset or at the conclusion of negotiations, he should write to the applicant stating this fact and either repeating the original offer (perhaps giving the applicant a certain period in which to respond before the offer lapses), or withdrawing that offer altogether.

Withdrawing an offer If a **pre-condition** to employment is **not satisfied** (for example, satisfactory references are not received), the employer may wish to withdraw the offer of employment. He should do so formally by letter, taking care that he has reasonable grounds to do so (for example, a reasonable belief that the unsatisfactory reference received is valid). Legally, a withdrawal is not effective until it is communicated to (i.e. received by) the applicant.

717

Once an **unconditional offer** is **accepted** (or a conditional offer is accepted and the conditions have been satisfied), it cannot be withdrawn as a valid contract exists. This is so even though the date when the employee is due to start work may be delayed. The **employer** should therefore not make an offer until he is sure that he wants to go ahead. If the employer attempts to withdraw the offer after it has been accepted, he could face a claim for breach of contract, and possibly also unfair dismissal and/or discrimination. If the **employee** changes his mind after accepting the offer, this will also amount to a breach of contract, entitling the employer to compensation. In practice, it is unusual for the employer to sue the employee for his losses (for example, the additional recruitment costs in finding a replacement).

SECTION 3

Right to work

An employer can only employ an individual who has permission to live and work in the UK. Individuals fall into different categories for immigration purposes, depending on their citizenship or nationality. Certain individuals can **automatically live and work** in the UK, for example as a result of their ancestry, while others may be given **permission to work**, for example due to their high level of skills. If an individual does not fall within one of these groups, the employer could consider whether **sponsorship** under Tier 2 of the points-based immigration system is possible (¶771).

750

> MEMO POINTS 1. The **UK Border Agency**, which is part of the Home Office (HO), is responsible for immigration control. It also considers applications for permission to stay, citizenship and asylum. For further details, see flmemo.co.uk/em750a
> 2. **UKvisas** manages visa clearance to the UK. For further details, see flmemo.co.uk/em750b. The website also gives details of other websites which give specific information on local visa application centres.
> Alternatively, online applications can be made at flmemo.co.uk/em750c

3. The **Immigration Rules** are the outline rules for most immigration to the UK. An up-to-date consolidated version of the Immigration Rules can be found on the UK Border Agency website at flmemo.co.uk/em750d

4. Where an employee lacks permission to work in the UK, an employer may lawfully **dismiss** him. Further, where an employer has a mistaken but genuine belief that an employee lacks permission to work in the UK, so that it would be unlawful to keep the employee in employment, this will be a fair reason to dismiss him (¶8545).

A. Who has the right to work?

British citizens

760 British citizens are exempt from immigration control (i.e. they can **automatically settle and work** in the UK). British citizenship may be conferred by **birth** or by **descent**. Citizenship may also be acquired by **naturalisation** by meeting certain requirements (including a residence requirement of 5 years or 3 years if married to a British citizen) or **registration** (principally for children, for example children born or living in the UK whose parents were not British citizens or settled in the UK when they were born).

Commonwealth citizens

762 A Commonwealth citizen, like any other national, may be a British citizen by descent (see above). Some Commonwealth citizens have a "**right of abode**" in the UK and, if so, they have the right to the same treatment as a British citizen in the UK, although they cannot hold a British passport and have no free movement rights in the EU. These are:
– Commonwealth citizens born or legally adopted outside the UK before 1 January 1983 with a parent who had UK citizenship as a result of being born in the UK; or
– female Commonwealth citizens who married a male with the right of abode in the UK before 1 January 1983.

> MEMO POINTS **Commonwealth countries** are Antigua and Barbuda, Australia, the Bahamas, Bangladesh, Barbados, Belize, Botswana, Brunei Darussalam, Cameroon, Canada, Cyprus, Dominica, Fiji Islands (suspended from the Councils of the Commonwealth in December 2006), the Gambia, Ghana, Grenada, Guyana, India, Jamaica, Kenya, Kiribati, Lesotho, Malawi, Malaysia, Maldives, Malta, Mauritius, Mozambique, Namibia, Nauru (Special Member), New Zealand, Nigeria, Pakistan, Papua New Guinea, Saint Kitts and Nevis, Saint Lucia, Saint Vincent and the Grenadines, Samoa, Seychelles, Sierra Leone, Singapore, Solomon Islands, South Africa, Sri Lanka, Swaziland, Tonga, Trinidad and Tobago, Tuvalu, Uganda, the United Kingdom, United Republic of Tanzania, Vanuatu and Zambia. Zimbabwe withdrew from the Commonwealth in December 2003.

763 Commonwealth citizens **without a right of abode** require leave to enter the United Kingdom.

EEA and Swiss nationals

765 In general, EEA nationals have an **automatic right to work** or look for work, study, or establish themselves in business in any of the EEA countries (Immigration (European Economic Area) Regulations SI 2000/2326). These rights are called the **rights of free movement** under EU law. For further details, see flmemo.co.uk/em765a

It is generally unlawful to discriminate on grounds of nationality between citizens of the EU, for example by offering British employees compassionate leave while withholding the same benefit from other EU citizens who are employees of the same organisation.

Citizens of the A8 **accession states** whose membership of the EU dates from 2004 (the Czech Republic, Estonia, Hungary, Latvia, Lithuania, Poland, Slovakia and Slovenia) previously had to register under the worker registration scheme before being able to take up new employment in the UK but as of 1 May 2011, they have the same rights as other EEA nationals.

Bulgaria and **Romania** joined the EU and the EEA on 1 January 2007. Workers from these countries will normally need to apply for permission before they start to work. For more information about employing workers from Bulgaria and Romania, see flmemo.co.uk/em765b

> *MEMO POINTS* 1. The following countries are part of the EEA: Austria, Belgium, Bulgaria, Cyprus, Czech Republic, Denmark, Estonia, Finland, France, Germany, Greece, Hungary, Iceland, the Republic of Ireland, Italy, Latvia, Liechtenstein, Lithuania, Luxembourg, Malta, the Netherlands, Norway, Poland, Portugal, Romania, Slovakia, Slovenia, Spain, Sweden and the United Kingdom.
> 2. **Irish nationals** are EEA nationals but in practice they are treated as having settled status in the UK.
> 3. Switzerland is not in the EEA but **Swiss nationals** have the same right of free movement as EEA nationals.

An EEA national has a right **to admission** to the UK and **residence for 3 months** if he produces on arrival in the UK a valid national identity card or passport (regs 11-13 Immigration (European Economic Area) Regulations SI 2006/1003). **766**

Subject to the restrictions on the employment in the UK of citizens of states which have joined the EU since 2007, as set out at ¶765 above, the right of residence is **extended indefinitely** where the relevant EEA national remains in employment, self-employment, full-time education, or is economically self-sufficient (reg 14 SI 2006/1003).

> *MEMO POINTS* 1. There are particular provisions for an EEA national who is unemployed but continues to seek employment (reg 6(2) SI 2006/1003).
> 2. An EEA national may be denied entry to the UK or residence under various grounds, including public policy, public security and public health.

An EEA national has a right to **permanent** residence where he has resided continuously in the UK for 5 years or has retired (reg 15 SI 2006/1003). **767**

Other nationals

If the individual does not fall within one of the groups discussed above, he will require leave (permission) to enter or remain in the UK (i.e. there is **no automatic right** to enter and work). **768**

In addition to leave to enter, **entry clearance** (visas or entry certificates for non-visa nationals) may be required. This depends on the individual's **nationality** (visa nationals always require entry clearance) and the **purpose of entry**. Other than for visitors, entry clearance is now also treated as a **grant of leave to enter**, and all entry clearances state the length of the permission to enter and other conditions applicable to the individual.

Entry clearance, leave to enter and leave to remain are all subject to a number of **general criteria** (for example, an application may be refused if the person's presence is considered "not conducive to the public good"). In addition, entry will be refused if the individual does not satisfy the criteria **specific to the relevant category** of entry.

Indefinite leave An individual with indefinite leave (commonly called **permanent residence** and also known as "**settlement**") can live and **work** in the UK **without restriction** on the length of his stay or the type of work he can do. Settlement is usually acquired after a certain period of limited leave. **770**

Applicants for indefinite leave to remain are required to show that they have a sufficient knowledge of the English language and life in the UK in order to qualify for settlement.

Limited leave In most cases, leave to enter the UK is initially granted for a **limited period** and may also be subject to additional **restrictions** (for example, relating to the type or amount of work that can be done). Limited leave usually needs to be **extended** at least once before indefinite leave is granted, in which case **leave to remain** (granted by the Home Office in the UK) will be required. **771**

With regard to the **work-based categories**, most have been replaced by a points-based system (PBS). Tier 2, relating to **skilled workers**, replaced the work permit scheme. Tier 5 covers **temporary workers** entering the United Kingdom for a short period and is now the most appropriate route for interns. Employers wishing to bring non-EEA migrants to the UK under these tiers need to be a **licensed sponsor**. Sponsors are responsible for issuing certificates of sponsorship to migrants and ensuring that their sponsor obligations are fulfilled. Migrants can use the certificate of sponsorship to apply for entry clearance. Immigration rules are detailed and can change regularly. For further details, see flmemo.co.uk771a and flmemo.co.uk771b. For policy guidance for sponsors, see flmemo.co.uk771c

> MEMO POINTS **Identity cards for foreign nationals** (biometric residence permits) are being phased in and by 2015 it is expected that 90% of nationals from outside the EEA and Switzerland will have a card. As well as being an immigration document for foreign nationals, this identity card allows them to prove their right to live in the UK and to work, study or access public services. Readers should note that identity cards for foreign nationals, administered by the UK Border Agency, is a separate scheme to the national identity cards scheme which has been axed.

Visitors

776 Visitors are **not allowed** to do paid or unpaid work, study, produce goods or provide services in the UK or sell goods and services to members of the public. Further, visits are not allowed for more than 6 months at a time, unless the visitor applies for an extension.

However, a **business visitor** is **permitted** to do business that is directly linked to his employment or business abroad, including:
– going to meetings with United Kingdom businesses or negotiating and entering into contracts with them;
– going to trade fairs, conferences and classroom training; and
– if he is a sports person or entertainer, attending a trial or audition or a personal appearance which does not involve a performance.

Asylum seekers and refugees

777 New asylum seekers are prohibited from working in the UK. However, asylum seekers who have not had an initial decision on their asylum claim within a year can apply to the Home Office for permission to work (EU Directive 2005/85; *R (on the applications of ZO (Somalia) and ors) v Secretary of State for the Home Department* [2010] UKSC 36). Failed asylum seekers cannot work, even if they had previously been given permission to do so. Where, however, an asylum seeker has successfully obtained refugee status or leave to enter or remain, the individual will have a right to work as part of the conditions of his status.

B. Right to work checks

780 Employers who **unlawfully employ illegal migrant workers** will be subject to a system of **civil penalties** (s 15(2) Immigration, Asylum and Nationality Act 2006; Immigration, Asylum and Nationality Act 2006 (Commencement No. 8 and Transitional and Saving Provisions) Order SI 2008/310).

The UK Border Agency has responsibility for issuing warnings and civil penalties. The amount of a penalty will vary in proportion to:
– the number of warnings that an employer has received;
– the extent to which the employer has previously reported suspected illegal workers to the UK Border Agency; and
– the extent to which the employer has co-operated with the UK Border Agency.

The **maximum fine** is £10,000 per illegal worker employed (Immigration (Employment of Adults Subject to Immigration Control) (Maximum Penalty) Order SI 2008/132). It is also a **criminal offence** for an employer to knowingly employ an illegal migrant worker. The offence carries a maximum 2-year prison sentence and/or an unlimited fine (s 21 Immigration, Asylum and Nationality Act 2006). There are also criminal offences under the Accession (Immigration and Worker Registration)

Regulations 2006 regarding employers who employ an unregistered Bulgarian or Romanian worker. The offences carry a maximum fine of £5,000 per illegal worker employed.

Employers are required to undertake specified **document checks** (¶¶781-3) at the point of recruitment (Immigration (Restriction on Employment) Order SI 2007/3290). Where a full check has been conducted, the employer will be entitled to a **statutory excuse** and no penalty will be payable.

> MEMO POINTS   There are two statutory **Codes of Practice**: Civil Penalties for Employers, and Guidance for Employers on the Avoidance of Unlawful Discrimination in Employment Practice While Seeking to Prevent Illegal Working. The UK Border Agency has also published comprehensive guidance for employers on preventing illegal working, which is available from their website.

781

To avoid liability for the civil penalty, the employer should obtain **suitable documentation** from successful candidates (¶¶782-3). Further, the employer must (reg 6 SI 2007/3290):
– take all reasonable steps to check that the documentation is valid;
– check any photograph given in the documentation and satisfy himself that it is a picture of the applicant;
– check any birthdate given in the documentation and the birthdate of the applicant;
– take all other reasonable steps to check that the applicant is the owner of the documentation; and
– check that the documentation meets the legal requirements and that it applies to the applicant.

A **copy** of the documentation must be kept on file for 2 years. In the case of a **passport** or other **travel document**, the front page and any page containing specified information (including the holder's personal details, the holder's photograph, signature, the date of expiry and any information indicating the holder has an entitlement to enter or remain in the UK and undertake the work in question) must be copied in a format which cannot subsequently be altered. All **other documents** must be photocopied or scanned in their entirety.

782

Satisfactory **documentary proof** falls into **two groups**. If reasonable steps are taken to check the validity of a document or documents from the first group ("**List A**"), the statutory excuse will have been established for the duration of the employment and **no further checks** will be required.

The **first group** consists of (Sch SI 2007/3290 as amended):
1. A passport showing that the holder, or a person named in the passport as the child of the holder, is a British citizen or a citizen of the United Kingdom and Colonies having the right of abode in the United Kingdom.
2. A national identity card or a passport which has the effect of identifying the holder, or a person named in the passport as the child of the holder, as a national of the European Economic Area or Switzerland.
3. A residence permit, registration certificate or document certifying or indicating permanent residence issued by the Home Office or the UK Border Agency to a national of a European Economic Area country or Switzerland.
4. A permanent residence card issued by the Home Office or the UK Border Agency to the family member of a national of a European Economic Area country or Switzerland.
5. A Biometric Immigration Document issued by the UK Border Agency to the holder which indicates that the person named in it is allowed to stay indefinitely in the United Kingdom, or has no time limit on their stay in the United Kingdom.
6. A passport or other travel document endorsed to show that the holder is exempt from immigration control, is allowed to stay indefinitely in the United Kingdom, has the right of abode in the United Kingdom, or has no time limit on their stay in the United Kingdom.
7. An Immigration Status Document issued by the Home Office or the UK Border Agency to the holder with an endorsement indicating that the person named in it is allowed to stay indefinitely in the United Kingdom or has no time limit on their stay in the United Kingdom, when produced in combination with an official document issued by a Government agency or a previous employer giving the person's permanent National Insurance number and their name.

8. A full birth certificate issued in the United Kingdom which includes the name(s) of at least one of the holder's parents, when produced in combination with an official document issued by a Government agency or a previous employer giving the person's permanent National Insurance number and their name.
9. A full adoption certificate issued in the United Kingdom which includes the name(s) of at least one of the holder's adoptive parents when produced in combination with an official document issued by a Government agency or a previous employer giving the person's permanent National Insurance number and their name.
10. A birth certificate issued in the Channel Islands, the Isle of Man or Ireland, when produced in combination with an official document issued by a Government agency or a previous employer giving the person's permanent National Insurance number and their name.
11. An adoption certificate issued in the Channel Islands, the Isle of Man or Ireland, when produced in combination with an official document issued by a Government agency or a previous employer giving the person's permanent National Insurance number and their name.
12. A certificate of registration or naturalisation as a British citizen, when produced in combination with an official document issued by a Government agency or a previous employer giving the person's permanent National Insurance number and their name.
13. A letter issued by the Home Office or the UK Border Agency to the holder which indicates that the person named in it is allowed to stay indefinitely in the United Kingdom when produced in combination with an official document issued by a Government agency or a previous employer giving the person's permanent National Insurance number and their name.

MEMO POINTS The provision of a **National Insurance number** in isolation is never sufficient for the purpose of establishing a statutory excuse. The National Insurance number can only be used for this purpose when presented in combination with other documents, as set out above.

783 Each time that a document or combination of documents from the second group ("**List B**") is provided, the employer must note the date on which he carried out the original document check. In order to retain his excuse against a penalty for employing that individual, the employer must carry out a follow-up check at least once every **12 months** after the initial check.

The **second group** consists of (Sch SI 2007/3290):
1. A passport or travel document endorsed to show that the holder is allowed to stay in the United Kingdom and is allowed to do the type of work in question, provided that it does not require the issue of a work permit.
2. A Biometric Immigration Document issued by the UK Border Agency to the holder which indicates that the person named in it can stay in the United Kingdom and is allowed to do the work in question.
3. A work permit or other approval to take employment issued by the Home Office or the UK Border Agency when produced in combination with either a passport or another travel document endorsed to show the holder is allowed to stay in the United Kingdom and is allowed to do the work in question, or a letter issued by the Home Office or the UK Border Agency to the holder or the employer or prospective employer confirming the same.
4. A certificate of application issued by the Home Office or the UK Border Agency to or for a family member of a national of a European Economic Area country or Switzerland stating that the holder is permitted to take employment, which is less than 6 months old when produced in combination with evidence of verification by the UK Border Agency Employer Checking Service.
5. A residence card or document issued by the Home Office or the UK Border Agency to a family member of a national of a European Economic Area country or Switzerland.
6. An application registration card issued by the Home Office or the UK Border Agency stating that the holder is permitted to take employment, when produced in combination with evidence of verification by the UK Border Agency Employer Checking Service.
7. An immigration status document issued by the Home Office or the UK Border Agency to the holder with an endorsement indicating that the person named in it can stay in the United Kingdom, and is allowed to do the type of work in question, when produced in combination

with an official document issued by a Government agency or a previous employer giving the person's permanent National Insurance number and their name.

8. A letter issued by the Home Office or the UK Border Agency to the holder or the employer or prospective employer which indicates that the person named in it can stay in the United Kingdom and is allowed to do the work in question when produced in combination with an official document issued by a Government agency or a previous employer giving the person's permanent National Insurance number and their name.

MEMO POINTS 1. The provision of a **National Insurance number** in isolation is never sufficient for the purpose of establishing a statutory excuse. The National Insurance number can only be used for this purpose when presented in combination with other documents, as set out above.
2. Where an employer is required to carry out a **follow-up** check, this will involve asking the employee to produce a valid original document, or documents, from either List A or List B, and copying it/them for his records. If a document, or documents, from List A are subsequently presented and reasonable steps are taken to check the validity of the document or documents, the statutory excuse will have been established for the remainder of the employment and no further checks will be required.

This is an area of law which is changing rapidly. Accordingly, where employers have any doubt as to whether documents are genuine or sufficient to prove an employee's entitlement to work in the UK, they are encouraged to access the UK Border Agency's **Employer Checking Service**. To use the service the employer should email the form at flmemo.co.uk/em784a to Employerchecking@ukba.gsi.gov.uk. Further information and support is provided through the UK Border Agency's Sponsorship and Employers' Helpline (0300 123 4699) and online at flmemo.co.uk/em784b

784

Racial discrimination issues

In order to avoid racial discrimination claims, the employer should treat all applicants in the **same way** at each stage of the recruitment process, in particular by:
– not making assumptions about an applicant's immigration status on the basis of his colour, race, nationality or ethnic or national origins. An employer who rejects a job applicant simply because he assumes that the person has no right to work in the UK may well be committing unlawful racial discrimination. For example, an employer who rejected the application of a person he (incorrectly) assumed did not have the right to work in the UK was found guilty of indirect racial discrimination (*Grampian Health Board v Cole*, EAT case 470/85);
– informing all applicants that the successful applicant will be asked to produce the required documents. For example, an employer who offered a job applicant a lecturing post, subject to verification of her right to work in the UK without a permit, was found to have discriminated against the applicant on racial grounds because the employer had only asked her (and no other applicant) to produce evidence of her right to work in the UK (*Karimjee v University of Newcastle-upon-Tyne*, EAT case 545/84);
– treating the documents that constitute documentary proof in accordance with List A and List B as of equal value;
– not enquiring about an applicant's immigration status, apart from asking him to produce proof as required by the Immigration Rules;
– not assuming that an applicant is an illegal worker if he cannot produce proof of his right to work (the employer should refer the applicant to a Citizens Advice Bureau or the Immigration and Nationality Enquiry Bureau for advice and keep the position open for as long as possible); and
– not adopting a policy of automatically filtering out applications for training posts from any applicants who needed permission to work in the UK as this has been found to have indirectly discriminated against non-EEA nationals (*Osborne Clarke Services v Purohit* [2009] IRLR 341, EAT). In this case, the employer attempted to justify the discrimination on the grounds of the difficulty of obtaining a work permit. However, the EAT held that there was no evidence to support this defence as the employer had not made any enquiries about the possibility of obtaining work permits for trainees nor ever attempted to obtain one. In 2008, the system for issuing such work permits was replaced by Tier 2 of a points-based system (PBS) (see ¶771); however, the same principles relating to discrimination apply.

785

> **MEMO POINTS** Further details can be found in Code of Practice: Guidance for Employers on the Avoidance of Unlawful Discrimination in Employment Practice While Seeking to Prevent Illegal Working.

786 Although it is advisable that all applicants are treated the same way, the EAT has decided in favour of an employer who applied a **different policy** in respect of evidence of leave to enter or remain in the UK to job applicants from outside the EU as against those from inside the EU. The EAT held that, although this was discriminatory on the grounds of race, as it was permitted by the Asylum and Immigration Act 1996 it was protected from a discrimination claim under the then Race Relations Act 1976 (i.e. that an act of discrimination will not be unlawful if done under statutory authority) (*Olatokun v Ikon Office Solutions* [2004] UKEAT 0074_04_1005).

CHAPTER 3

Starting employment

OUTLINE	¶¶
SECTION 1 **Induction** 910	SECTION 2 **Probation** 940
1 Form and duration .... 915 2 Key points of induction programme ...... 925 3 Special cases 930	1 Rights and obligations during probation 945 2 Completion 950

Most employers have an **induction programme** so that new employees can settle into their new jobs easily and effectively. In particular, certain groups, for example school or college leavers and disabled employees, may require extra help and guidance. To ensure that an induction programme is working well, it may be useful to have a **review** of it with employees after they have been in their jobs for a certain period in order to ensure that the process was successful or identify any problems.

In these initial stages, most employers will also make the employment conditional on the satisfactory completion of a **probationary period** to ensure that new employees are able to perform their duties.

900

SECTION 1

Induction

Induction is important from a **human resource management** perspective. The focus of induction is good practice, rather than legal compliance. Induction programmes aim to ensure that **new recruits** settle into the company quickly and easily so that they can become effective employees as soon as possible. An effective induction process can encourage closer identification with and knowledge of the company and thus can also help to reduce staff turnover.

910

Employees moving from one part of the company to another also need induction training, but this will be more limited than for a new recruit, focusing on the new aspects of their changed role.

911

1. Form and duration

Form

Induction can take the following forms, which may be used on their own or in combination:
– one-to-one briefings from the line manager or a member of human resources;
– group briefings with other new staff; and/or
– receipt of a copy of the staff handbook.

915

Which forms are appropriate will **depend on** the nature of the job, the size of the company, its business sector, strategy, business values and beliefs. If there are trade union or other employee representatives, it may be useful to consult with them when planning an induction programme.

The **degree of formality** may vary, as may the amount of specific training involved. In many companies, the induction programme is carried out informally by the new recruit's line manager on a day-to-day basis. If a number of recruits join at the same time, group induction sessions could be used to cover issues of general application.

In some companies, a **"mentor" or "buddy" system** may be used, so that the new recruit has a more experienced employee to approach with day-to-day queries or problems.

916 Whichever form of induction is used, it is advisable to follow a structured approach. A **written checklist** can be provided to the employee of the topics to be covered in the induction, who will deal with them and when. This checklist is usually compiled by the human resources department in consultation with other people involved in the programme, including the appropriate line manager/supervisor, trade union and/or employee representatives, safety representatives and training officers.

The induction programme may include a large amount of information, and it is important that the programme is carefully structured to avoid "information overload".

Timing and duration

920 It is useful for the induction programme to take place at the beginning of the new recruit's employment, as it can be more difficult to schedule induction sessions once the employee is established in his new job. The induction process can extend over several days or even weeks.

Special plans may need to be made for **shift and night workers**.

2. Key points of induction programme

Reception

925 In order to make a good first impression, the new recruit should be made to feel welcome, and the employer should make **arrangements for his arrival**, including:
– designating someone to meet him on arrival;
– carrying out necessary personnel checks (for example, copy of P45, NI number, proof of entitlement to work in the UK); and
– putting in place any necessary security arrangements (for example, providing the new recruit with a security pass).

Information

926 The employee should be informed/reminded of the following:
– **company information**, i.e. an overview of the company's organisation, its history, products, services, markets, clients, and future plans and aspirations. A member of human resources may be charged with this task, and reference could be made to the staff handbook, which commonly contains such information;
– **the job**, i.e. what it entails, how the department/work area fits into the company structure, what standards are expected, how performance is assessed, who the employee will be working with, and who he reports to. His line manager, supervisor or department head may be best placed to provide this information, and introduce him to immediate work colleagues and others with whom he will come into contact;
– **the terms and conditions of employment**, including hours, holiday entitlement and notice provisions. Details will be found in the statement of particulars (¶1400) or written contract of employment (¶1127), and also the staff handbook (¶1480). The human resources officer is likely to be responsible for supplying this information;

– **pay details**, including the pay date and method. This should be set out in the statement of particulars or the written contract, and the human resources officer should be able to answer any further queries;
– **company rules and codes of conduct**, such as dress codes. These are often set out in the staff handbook, to which the employee could be referred;
– **security arrangements**, in respect of access to the workplace, document control, use and storage of equipment, and personal items at work;
– **health and safety**, including applicable health and safety rules, emergency procedures, and any special hazards or requirements (see chapter 15). Any health and safety training (which may be required to train employees in the skills and knowledge needed to do their jobs) should be identified during the recruitment process and addressed again during the induction programme. If necessary, the employer should carry out a risk assessment (¶4976). The company's health and safety adviser may be involved in this part of the induction programme, and the employee should also be introduced to the workplace safety representative;
– **data protection rights**, including the nature and source of any information kept about the employee (see chapter 17);
– **company policies** (e.g. equal opportunities, bullying and harassment) and **procedures** (e.g. those relating to discipline, grievance, and absence). These are often set out in the staff handbook (see ¶1480 for further information);
– **training (formal and informal) and employee development**, including an explanation of any formal appraisal/performance management systems (see chapter 18). The induction stage may be an appropriate time to assess the employee's training requirements and formulate a personal training plan. This stage may be led by the company's training officer, if it has one;
– **benefits and facilities**, including explanation and further information, where necessary. For example, information on any private medical insurance cover should be provided, as should information on any employee incentive schemes;
– **employee representation**, including information on trade union membership and consultation procedures (see chapter 21). The employee should be introduced to any trade union or employee representatives, who should be given the opportunity to explain their role; and
– **layout of the office/department**, including a tour of the offices so that the new recruit can see where he is working, and where he can find the toilets, first aid, cafeteria etc.

3. Special cases

The employer should be sensitive to the fact that starting work may be more difficult for particular employees, including school leavers, people returning to work after a career break, those changing career direction or arriving from overseas, disabled employees and members of ethnic or religious minority groups.

School and college leavers Health and safety training is particularly important in the case of young new recruits who may have little or no experience of workplace environments, thus making them more vulnerable to accidents. Employers must take these factors into consideration and take extra steps to make such recruits aware of potential risks.

Employers have specific duties to young workers under health and safety legislation to assess risks to workers under 18 before they start work, and to address specific factors in a **risk assessment** (¶4976).

Employees returning from a career break or changing direction New recruits may have been out of the workplace for some time in order to care for children, change direction in their careers, or spend some time working abroad. The employer needs to be sensitive to the fact that such employees may feel apprehensive about their return, and may feel out of touch with recent developments in their area of work. He must therefore ensure that such employees obtain the necessary **training and experience** to enable them to feel confident in their new jobs.

933 **Disabled employees** Disabled employees may face problems in terms of access, equipment, or support from colleagues. Advice for employers on how to provide for such employees is available from Disability Employment Advisers, supported by Disability Service Teams via local Jobcentres. Considerable financial assistance may be available to the employer under Government programmes such as **Access to Work** to assist him in adapting his premises or investing in equipment in order to comply with his duty to make **reasonable adjustments** (¶5530).

934 **Minority groups** In general, new recruits who are members of an ethnic or religious minority group should follow the same induction programme as other new recruits. However, the employer should be sensitive to any **cultural or religious issues or customs** that may impact on the programme (for advice on best practice, see ¶¶5800+).

SECTION 2

Probation

940 The employer may wish to engage a new employee **subject to the satisfactory completion** of a probationary period. If so, the employer should make this clear, and should also state (preferably in the offer letter and/or contract of employment):
– the **duration** and whether the employer reserves the right to extend where there are doubts as to the probationer's performance;
– whether any particular **terms** will **not apply** during the probationary period; and
– whether any **terms** are **varied** (for example, termination on shorter notice than after the employment is confirmed, or a requirement that all accrued holiday entitlement be taken prior to the end of the probationary period).
The employee's **statutory rights** cannot be disapplied (¶9203).

> MEMO POINTS 1. A probationary period **may also be useful following** a change of job, retraining, or where a new working pattern such as job sharing is requested. If it is appropriate, it should be made clear when offering the new post or changed terms that it is subject to successful completion of a probationary period.
> 2. Employers often operate a **shorter disciplinary process** during a probationary period to make it easier to dismiss an employee who is not performing well. However, unless this is made clear by the contract/staff handbook, any failure to follow the full disciplinary process can lead to an inference of unlawful discrimination (shifting the burden of proof to the employer to prove that no discrimination occurred).

1. Rights and obligations during probation

945 **Probationer's rights** Apart from any express statements of non-application or variation of contractual terms, a probationer has the **same rights and obligations** as other employees. He will start to accrue continuous employment at the beginning of the probationary period. He has the same right to a statement of particulars, and may, for example, in common with any other employee in a similar situation, bring a claim of discrimination on grounds of age, disability, gender reassignment, marriage and civil partnership, pregnancy and maternity, race, religion or belief, sex or sexual orientation.

946 **Employer obligations** During the probationary period, the employer is obliged, by an implied term, to take reasonable steps to **appraise** the employee, giving guidance by advice or warning where necessary in order to ensure that the required level of competence is achieved (*White v London Transport Executive* [1981] IRLR 261, EAT).

While there is no implied term to train probationers, or to support, assist, or offer guidance to them specifically during the probationary period, any **contractual training terms** (i.e.

relating to the provision of adequate training and/or agreements on training) highlighted in the recruitment or induction stage will usually be most appropriate during the probationary period.

2. Completion

At the end of the probationary period, the probationer's performance should be reviewed. The outcome of the review will depend on whether the employer is satisfied with the probationer's performance, still has doubts about him or has decided that he is not suitable. The employer's assessment should take into account any appraisals of performance during the course of the probation and any other relevant factors.

Confirmation If the **employer is satisfied** that the probationer is suitable, the employment should be confirmed and the probationary period will come to an end.

Extension If there are doubts as to the probationer's suitability, the probationary period can be extended if the employer has expressly **reserved the right** to do so and has exercised this right in time. Employers do not have an implied right to extend an employee's probationary period so that they can carry out an appraisal/review within a reasonable time after the period has elapsed (*Przybylska v Modus Telecom Ltd* [2007] UKEAT 0566_06_0602). If the employer has **not expressly reserved the right** to extend the probationary period, he will need the agreement of the employee at the review stage to do so. The probationary period should not be extended unnecessarily, and should only be done where the employer has genuinely been unable to come to a decision in the initial probationary period.

Where the probationary period is **not extended**, the employee will be taken to have completed his probation once his probationary period has ended.

> EXAMPLE In *Przybylska v Modus Telecom Ltd*, P's employer held P's probationary review after the end of her probationary period. P failed the assessment and was dismissed with 1 week's notice (her probationary notice period). The EAT held that P was in fact entitled to 3 months' notice (P's notice period once out of probation) as P's employer had not exercised its contractual right to extend P's probationary period to take account of the fact that it had not yet been able to hold her review. Accordingly, P was no longer in her probationary period when she was dismissed, entitling her to 3 months' notice.

Dismissal If the employer concludes that the probationer has **not met the required standard**, the employer can dismiss him but must be careful not to do so for a discriminatory or other inadmissable reason (see memo point below).

> MEMO POINTS The probationer may be qualified to bring an **unfair dismissal** claim if he has been **continuously employed** for 2 years (1 year if he started his employment before 6 April 2012) or earlier if he is dismissed for an inadmissible reason, such as trade union activities or membership.
> To **defend** a claim, the employer must have a statutory fair reason for the dismissal (for example, capability or conduct), and must also act fairly in dismissing the employee. It is not automatically fair to dismiss a probationer, rather the employee's probationary status will be one factor that the tribunal will take into account in reaching its decision on the fairness of the dismissal.
> In reaching its decision, the employment tribunal will apply the **statutory test** applicable to all employees, i.e. it will ask whether the employer acted reasonably in all the circumstances (including the size and administrative resources of his undertaking) in treating the reason for the dismissal as a fair reason for dismissal (¶¶8437+). Consequently, the following **considerations** should be taken into account:
> – whether the employer observed the implied term to maintain appraisal of the probationer throughout the period of probation, giving guidance by advice or warning when such is likely to be useful or fair; and
> – whether an appropriate officer/manager made an honest effort to determine whether the probationer came up to the required standard, having informed himself of the appraisals made by

supervising officers/managers and any other facts recorded about the probationer (*Post Office v P A Mughal* [1977] IRLR 178, EAT).
Moreover, employers should ensure that they follow the Acas code on discipline and grievances at work. Failure to do so may increase the compensation awarded to the employee if he is successful in bringing a tribunal claim for unfair dismissal. See chapter 19 for further details.

CHAPTER 4

Continuity of employment

OUTLINE	¶¶
SECTION 1 **Employment with same employer** 1010	SECTION 3 **Calculating period of continuous employment** 1040
General rule 1010	
Special cases 1013	1 Start date 1045
	2 Relevant end date 1055
SECTION 2 **Change of employer** 1035	SECTION 4 **Qualifying periods** .. 1080

1000 Some employment rights are **only activated** after certain periods of continuous employment (called qualifying periods), for example the right to bring a claim of unfair dismissal or the right to a redundancy payment. The length of continuous employment is also used to **calculate** the amount of a statutory award, such as a redundancy payment.

The **basic rule** is that there is continuity of employment from the start of employment until that particular employment ends. Breaks in the contract of employment with the same employer or changing employment will break continuity except in certain circumstances.

1001 With regard to **statutory rights**, a period of continuous employment cannot be modified by contractual agreement (*Collison v British Broadcasting Corporation* [1998] IRLR 238, EAT; *Morris v Walsh Western UK Ltd* [1997] UKEAT 148_97_1804).

However, if an employee is entitled to **contractual rights** based on the length of his employment, although the parties may choose to rely on the continuity rules to calculate this period, they are free to alter them if they agree to do so (*Secretary of State for Employment v Globe Elastic Thread Co Ltd* [1979] IRLR 327, EAT). For example, with regard to calculating a contractual redundancy payment, an employer may agree to count a period that would not be continuous under the continuity rules or to add an extra period.

SECTION 1

Employment with same employer

General rule

1010 Where an employee is employed under a contract of employment and at least part of his time satisfies the requirements for continuity, there is a **presumption of continuity** (s 210(5) ERA 1996). This presumption can be rebutted by evidence from either party. Where an employee has asserted continuity based on this presumption, the burden of proof will be on his employer to prove that continuity had actually been broken (*Nicoll v Nocorrode Ltd* [1981] IRLR 163, EAT).

This presumption does not apply if the contract becomes **illegal** (*Hyland v J H Barker (North-West) Ltd* [1985] IRLR 403, EAT).

MEMO POINTS   Contractual illegality is further discussed at ¶1305.

1011 Continuity will be preserved even if the employee is **not required to perform** any work.

Special cases

1013 The following rules apply to **successive contracts of employment** with the same employer:

1014 **Gap between two contracts – less than 1 week**   Any week during the **whole or part** of which the employee is under a contract of employment counts in computing continuity (s 212(1) ERA 1996).

If the employee's contract is terminated and restarted or a different contract is commenced with the same employer at a later date, the gap between the two contracts will not break continuity, regardless of what the employee did during it, as long as **at least 1 day in each week** is under a contract of employment with that employer (*Sweeney v J & S Henderson (Concessions) Ltd* [1999] IRLR 306, EAT (Scotland)).

> EXAMPLE   In *Sweeney v J & S Henderson (Concessions) Ltd*, EAT (Scotland), S resigned on Saturday, 15 February, and immediately took up another employment. He regretted that decision and was re-employed by his original employer on Friday, 21 February. The EAT held that continuity was not broken during this break in employment with regard to his original employer, as he was employed by him during the week ending 15 February and for part of the following week (21 February).

1015 Such gaps can occur where:
– the employee moves from one type of work to another;
– the employee moves from one site or department to another; or
– the terms of the contract of employment change.

> EXAMPLE
> **Different type of work**
> In *Tipper v Roofdec Ltd* [1989] IRLR 419, EAT, T, a lorry driver, was dismissed on Friday, 22 May, as a consequence of a 12-month driving ban. His employer found him alternative employment clearing a site, which he began on the following Monday. The EAT held that continuity was preserved and the fact that the first employment was frustrated (i.e. no longer possible because of the driving ban) was irrelevant.
>
> **Different department**
> In *Wood v York City Council* [1978] IRLR 228, CA, W changed jobs within the Council who employed him by resigning from one job to take up another position in a different department. The CA held that continuity was preserved.

1017 **Gap between two contracts – greater than 1 week**   Gaps between two contracts which are greater than a whole week will break continuity unless they fall under one of the following special circumstances where the employee was (s 212(3), (4) ERA 1996):
1. absent from work on account of a temporary cessation of work;
2. absent from work in circumstances such that, by arrangement or custom, he is regarded as continuing in the employment; or
3. incapable of work as a result of illness or injury (limited to 26 weeks).

As long as **each week** where there is no contract of employment satisfies one of these special circumstances it is irrelevant why the previous contract came to an end. These special circumstances are further discussed as follows:

1018 1. There will be a **temporary cessation** or suspension of normal working when the employer is unable to provide work and the employee is laid off, for example when there is a shortage of supplies or orders. The courts have held that temporary means a relatively short time and, in determining this, all the relevant circumstances, particularly the length of the period of non-employment in relation to the period of employment as a whole, will be taken into consideration (*Flack and others v Kodak Ltd* [1986] IRLR 255, CA).

The **intention** of an employer to re-employ the employee at a later date does not in itself indicate that the cessation of work was temporary, though it is a factor that will be taken into consideration (*Sillars v Charringtons Fuels Ltd* [1989] IRLR 152, CA).

> EXAMPLE
> 1. In *Flack and others v Kodak Ltd*, the Court of Appeal held that employees in a photo-finishing department, who had been employed intermittently over a number of years, depending on work requirements, did have their continuity of employment preserved in their non-employment periods.
> 2. In *Ford v Warwickshire County Council* [1983] IRLR 126, HL, the House of Lords held that the weeks between the summer and autumn school terms where there was no contract of employment was a temporary cessation of work and continuity was preserved.
> 3. In *Cornwall County Council v Prater* [2006] ICR 731, CA, a teacher engaged by a Council to work as a home tutor under successive contracts, to teach different children individually who were unable to attend school, was held to be continuously employed by her employer. Any gaps between periods of work were temporary cessations and therefore did not break her continuity of employment.

1019 2. If, by **arrangement or custom**, the employee is regarded by the employer as continuing in employment, even though there is no contract of employment for those weeks (because the employee is between fixed-term contracts or has a break between contracts of employment), continuity is preserved.

An "arrangement or custom" requires that, in advance of the break, there was agreement between the parties that they regarded the relationship as continuing despite the termination of the contract of employment (*Booth v United States of America* [1998] UKEAT 1389_97_0408). A guarantee of re-engagement is not, in itself, sufficient for there to be an arrangement for continuity of employment between the parties (*Curr v Marks & Spencer plc* [2003] IRLR 74, CA). For there to be no break in continuity, both parties must **mutually acknowledge** that their employment relationship continues despite the employee's break from work, **before** the period itself takes place. This cannot be retrospectively done on re-employment.

> MEMO POINTS This does not apply with regard to **contractual entitlements** as the parties can **retrospectively agree** to treat such a period as continuous.

1020 This rule need not be relied on where the employer allows the employee to take unpaid leave and the **contract** of employment **subsists**, as continuity will not be broken in any event. If, though, the contract has been **terminated**, this exception has to be complied with for continuity of employment to be preserved.

1021 3. In exceptional circumstances, the weeks where there is no contract of employment and the **employee is ill** or injured will not break continuity when the employee is re-employed. This is limited to a non-contractual period of 26 weeks.

Continuity will be preserved for the period between termination or suspension and re-employment if during this period the employee was **not able to work** due to his illness or injury. For example, continuity will not be broken if an employee leaves his employment due to ill health but is re-hired when he recovers if this happens within 26 weeks. It is not relevant that the employee may be **capable of some other work** during this period (*Pearson v Kent County Council* [1993] IRLR 165, CA; *Kennaugh v Lloyd-Jones t/a Cheshire Tree Surgeons* [2008] UKEAT 1135_07_1807). He can also **temporarily work** for another employer during this period as long as he remains unable to do the work that he would have done for his employer if he still had a contract (*Donnelly v Kelvin International Services* [1992] IRLR 496, EAT).

1024 **Redundancy and re-employment within 4 weeks** If an employee has been made redundant and starts **suitable alternative employment** within 4 weeks of termination of the original contract, his continuity will be preserved (s 138 ERA 1996). However, a gap of more than 4 weeks will break continuity.

1025 Further, the receipt of a **genuine redundancy payment** will break continuity for the purposes of future redundancy payments only if the employee is later reinstated or re-engaged unless he is re-employed on the condition that the redundancy payment is repaid (s 214 ERA 1996; Employment Protection (Continuity of Employment) Regulations SI 1996/3147; and *Secretary of State for Trade and Industry v Lassman* [2000] IRLR 411, CA). This prevents the employee being entitled to another statutory redundancy payment for this first period if he is made redundant again.

Where such, or part of such, a payment is purely contractual or ex gratia, then this requirement to repay to retain continuity does not apply to the non-statutory part (*Rowan v Machinery Installations (South Wales) Ltd* [1981] IRLR 122, EAT).

1027 **Reinstatement and re-engagement** Continuity will also be preserved between when an employee was dismissed and when his internal appeal (using his employer's contractual internal appeal procedures) was upheld and reinstatement ordered (*London Probation Board v Kirkpatrick* [2005] UKEAT 0544_04_1002). The EAT held that in these circumstances it was not necessary for this to have been specifically agreed at the time the employee was dismissed. The EAT went on to comment that even if agreement was required in such circumstances, this could be implied as reinstatement was one of the possible outcomes of a successful appeal.

Reinstatement and re-engagement orders by the court as a result of a successful unfair dismissal claim require the employer to take the employee back in either the same or a similar role and in such cases continuity will be preserved (¶¶8681, 8682). The position is the same in respect of an agreement to re-engage or reinstate an employee under a compromise agreement or following the intervention of an Acas conciliation officer.

SECTION 2

Change of employer

Although periods of continuous employment normally relate to employment by the same employer, there are **special circumstances** where a change of employer does not break continuity (s 218 ERA 1996).

1035

Type of change	Reference (ERA 1996)
Whole or part of trade, business, or undertaking is **transferred** from one person to another [1]	s 218(2)
Employer dies and employee is taken into employment of personal representatives or trustees [2]	s 218(4)
Change in partners, personal representatives or trustees [3]	s 218(5)
Employee moves to another employer who, at that time, is an **associated employer** [4]	ss 218(6), 231
Act (local or public) changes a contract of employment resulting in the original **body corporate employer** being replaced by some other body corporate [5]	s 218(3)
Health service employee is employed by another health service employer [6]	s 218(8)-(9)
Employee of maintained school is employed by same local education authority, or governing body of school controlled by same local education authority	s 218(7)

1. If a part is transferred it does not need to be self-contained, though the transfer must make some sense as a **transfer of business** and it must not solely be a transfer of assets (*Melon v Hector Powe Ltd* [1980] IRLR 477, HL). The sale must put the new owner in possession of a going concern (or one that has the potential of being a going concern if it is not one at the time of transfer, for example where the transfer relates to an insolvent company (*Teeside Times Ltd v Drury* [1980] IRLR 72, CA)). The burden of proof is on the employee to show that the transfer satisfied these conditions and this will be a question of fact. However, a tribunal will not put an over-strict burden of proof on the employee, who may have little knowledge of the company's financial dealings (though a tribunal may nevertheless require more than the employee stating that it was business as usual under the new owner). The courts have also held that the time of transfer is not limited to a precise date but can be spread over a longer period during which the process of transfer takes place, any part of which is sufficient for the employee to be in the transferor's employment (*Clark & Tokeley Ltd v Oakes* [1998] IRLR 577, CA). If the question of the time of transfer is disputed, it will be a question of fact that the tribunal will determine on looking at the evidence.

It should be noted that such transfers are also **usually governed** by the specific rules regarding transfers of undertakings (**TUPE** rules), which provide for the transfer of employee contracts to the transferee and the preservation of continuity (¶7974). However, **where TUPE does not apply**, continuity of employment may nevertheless be preserved under these rules as the right to continuity under ERA 1996 is a distinct and separate right.

2. Where an **employee is a personal representative**, he can contract with himself in his different capacities (*Rowley Holmes & Co v Barber* [1977] ICR 387, EAT).

3. Continuity of employment can be preserved where the **number of partners** in the partnership is **reduced to one** (*Stevens and anor v Bower* [2004] IRLR 957, CA). The Court of Appeal commented in this case that continuity could also be preserved under the exception relating to transfer of undertaking (see note 1, above) though it considered the change in partners, personal representative or trustees exception preferable in such circumstances.

4. Any two **employers are associated** if one is a company in which the other has **direct or indirect control**, or both are directly or indirectly controlled by a third person who need not necessarily be a company. Whether there is control depends on who has effective control (i.e. usually those who have the majority shareholding or board control). Effective control can extend to a company owned equally between two brothers which was held to be associated with the brothers' partnership (*Tice v Cartwright* [1999] ICR 769, EAT). The fact that an employer is in **voluntary liquidation** does not mean that control has moved from the majority shareholder to the liquidator for these purposes (*Da Silva Junior v Composite Mouldings and Design Ltd* [2008] UKEAT 0241_08_1808). For example, the voluntary liquidation of an employer and the setting up of a second company with the same majority shareholder employing the same employees will not break continuity of employment.

The **definition of company** in this context encompasses partnerships consisting of limited companies (*Pinkney v Sandpiper Drilling Ltd* [1989] IRLR 425, EAT) and foreign companies (*Hancill v Marcon Engineering Ltd* [1990] IRLR 51, EAT).

5. For continuity to be preserved, the employee must have been **transferred from one body corporate** to another as part of the statutory scheme to which the Act relates. This may include privatisations of public companies (*Gale v Northern General Hospital NHS Trust* [1994] IRLR 292, CA).

6. Continuity only occurs where there is **relevant employment**. This is **defined** as employment in which persons are engaged while undergoing professional training that involves their being employed successively by a number of different health service employers.

SECTION 3
Calculating period of continuous employment

1040 The period of continuous employment is assessed on how many successive weeks are continuous, and is, therefore, determined on a **week-by-week basis** running from Sunday to Saturday.

Consequently, there is continuous employment if each **consecutive week** after the first week of continuity satisfies the requirements for continuity (see sections 1 and 2 above) (s 210(4) ERA 1996). If not, the week(s) in question will **break the continuity** and a new period of continuous employment will start at the beginning of the first week that next satisfies the requirements. For example, if the employee changes employment, continuity will usually be broken and a new period will start when he begins his new employment.

In relation to a specific statutory right, award or payment, the **relevant period of employment** is calculated by identifying the start date and the end date (i.e. the date when the employment ends or the date necessary for the entitlement of the right). Depending on the right, this is determined in complete calendar months or years of service.

> EXAMPLE Employee A has worked for the same employer since 1 January 2002. On 31 December 2011 he is made redundant but is re-employed on 1 March 2012. This breaks continuity and his new period of continuous employment is calculated from when he restarted his employment. If he is made redundant again, he will only be entitled to a redundancy payment based on this new start date.
> However, if A had been re-hired within 4 weeks of being made redundant, continuity would have been preserved, see ¶1024.

1. Start date

1045 Continuous employment starts on the first day of employment (s 211(1) ERA 1996). This is the start date **as stated in** the employee's contract of employment and may be different from the actual start date (*General of The Salvation Army v Dewsbury* [1984] IRLR 222, EAT).

> EXAMPLE In *General of The Salvation Army v Dewsbury*, D's contract of employment commenced on 1 May 1982 though the first date she actually worked was 4 May as 1-3 May was a bank holiday weekend. However, her period of continuous employment was held to have started on 1 May.

1046 In special circumstances, the start date may be **moved back** (so increasing the period of continuous employment) if a change of contract does not break continuity. In such cases, it will be calculated as starting from the **beginning of the original employment**.

1047 Conversely, the start date will be subsequently **brought forward** (so reducing the period of continuous employment by a corresponding number of days) if the employee **takes part** in a **strike** or **lockout** (ss 211(3), 216 ERA 1996). If there is a strike and the employee does not take part, there will be no deduction to his period of continuity.

In such cases, the number of days between the last working day before the strike/lockout and the date when work was resumed (including non-working days) will be deducted from his start date. These days are calculated in relation to the workforce, or part of workforce, that is striking/taking part in a lockout. Therefore, if an employee has a rest day at the beginning of the strike, that day is still deductible. Likewise, if he restarts work before the end of the strike any such days are still deducted. On the other hand, if an employer requires the employee to recommence work at a date after the strike has ended, any such days of non-work are not deducted.

> EXAMPLE Employees B, C and D work a 5-day week from Monday to Friday.
> Employee B has a rest day on Monday, the day a strike by the workforce starts. The strike ends on that Thursday, and work is resumed by the workforce on Friday. However, Employee C is told

by his employer not to come back to work until the following Monday. Finally, Employee D returned to work on Wednesday, a day before the strike ended.
All the employees will have 6 days deducted (from Saturday before the strike through to the Thursday the strike ended) even though they all worked a different number of days for different reasons.

MEMO POINTS   It is possible to read the legislation as giving a double jeopardy by way of a double deduction which would occur by 1) discounting any weeks that do not count (i.e. where during each week or part of each week the employee takes part in a strike) and 2) bringing forward the start date as shown above. However, it is unlikely that this was the intention of the legislation.

Similarly, a period during which the employee leaves work on **deployment** with the **volunteer reserve forces** will not count towards continuous employment, provided the employee recommences work within 6 months of finishing serving in the armed forces (s 217 ERA 1996). The employee's start date will be treated as postponed by the number of days between the last day of his previous period of employment and the first day of the period of employment beginning in the 6 month period (s 217(2) ERA 1996).

1048

Further, for the purpose of continuity with regard to **redundancy payments** only, employees **working overseas** who are not paying NIC will have their start date brought forward by 7 days for every week so worked (ss 211(3), 215 ERA 1996).

2. Relevant end date

The end date is determined to ascertain whether an employee has the sufficient length of continuous employment (i.e. qualifying period) necessary to activate a statutory right or to calculate a statutory payment. The relevant end date is, therefore, either the end date of the qualifying period or the termination date of the contract.

1055

As the different periods needed for each right to be activated are expressed in either a set number of **calendar months or years**, so are the relevant lengths of continuity (s 210 ERA 1996).

1056

EXAMPLE   Employee E was employed on 1 January and Employee G was employed on 1 February. The right to minimum notice is activated after 1 month of continuous employment. E will have the right to minimum notice after 1 calendar month which will be from 1 February and G will have the right from 1 March. As January always has more days than February it can be seen that G has actually obtained the right after having been employed for a fewer number of days.
Rights based on a calendar year follow the same pattern. Therefore, in a leap year a new employee will have to be employed for an extra day to obtain the rights that his colleagues who did not start in a leap year obtain after a calendar year.

If the employee has been dismissed, the relevant end date is the date on which the termination takes effect, called the **effective date of termination** (EDT) (¶8340) (s 97(1) ERA 1996). This is the date on which:
– the notice expires (if the contract is terminated by notice); or
– where termination is given without notice, the date that should have been given for expiry of the statutory notice to which the employee is entitled. This can result in a gap between when the employee stopped working and when the termination takes effect. The fact that an employee stopped working prior to the effective date of termination is irrelevant in calculating the period of employment.

1057

MEMO POINTS   The fact that statutory notice (¶8131), to which the employee is entitled but has not been given, is added on and thus the EDT may fall on a later date than the actual date of dismissal often catches out employers who seek to terminate without notice shortly before an employee accrues his qualifying service for the purposes of unfair dismissal rights.

However, if there is a **continuation order** the contract remains in force from the EDT or settlement of the case to determine for any purpose (for example, the amount of a basic award or statutory redundancy payment) the employee's period of continuous employment (¶8704).

1058

SECTION 4

Qualifying periods

1080 As already noted, many of the main statutory rights will depend on whether or not the necessary qualifying periods of continuous employment have been achieved.

The following table is a summary of those that have qualifying periods and the lengths needed. Other statutory rights do not require a qualifying period and can be brought on the first day of service and, in some cases, even before the employment has begun (for example, where discrimination in relation to recruitment is claimed).

Right/complaint	Length of qualifying period
Guarantee payments during lay-off Minimum period of notice Pay during medical suspension Written evidence of terms	1 month
Collective consultation provisions in relation to short-term employees (i.e. those employed for a fixed term of 3 months or less, or for a specific purpose not expected to last for more than 3 months)	3 months
Adoption leave and pay Paternity/additional paternity leave and pay Maternity pay (no qualifying period to take maternity leave) Right to request flexible working (parents of young children and carers of certain adults)	26 weeks
Parental leave Unfair dismissal for those starting employment before 6 April 2012 [1] Written reasons for dismissal for those starting employment before 6 April 2012 [2]	1 year
Redundancy payments Time off to look for work when under notice of redundancy Unfair dismissal for those starting employment on or after 6 April 2012 [1] Written reasons for dismissal for those starting employment on or after 6 April 2012 [2]	2 years
Notes: 1. No qualifying period if automatically unfair, see ¶¶8393-4, and 1 month in relation to dismissals on medical grounds in consequence of certain health and safety requirements or recommendations, see ¶4985. 2. No qualifying period if dismissed while pregnant or on maternity leave or adoption leave, see ¶8310.	

EXAMPLE Employee I starts his job on 1 January 2005 and works continuously until 31 July 2012 when he is made redundant.
Redundancy payments are payable after 2 years' continuous employment and are calculated on the number of whole years of continuous employment. I has the 2 years' continuous employment necessary to entitle him to a redundancy payment and his length of employment with regard to the calculation of the redundancy payment itself is 7 whole years.

CHAPTER 5

Employment contract, variation and breach

OUTLINE

| | ¶¶ |

SECTION 1 **Formation** 1110

A Legal requirements 1111
1 Legal capacity 1111
2 Binding contracts 1112
3 Certainty 1120
B Form 1125

SECTION 2 **Terms** 1150

I Express terms 1155
II Specific terms implied by the courts .. 1170
1 Obvious terms 1172
2 Business efficacy 1174
3 Conduct of the parties 1176
4 Custom in that trade, industry or area . 1178
5 Employer custom and practice 1180
III Terms implied by statute 1185
IV Terms implied by common law as characteristic of the employment relationship 1195
A Employee duties 1200
1 Service 1200
2 Competence 1202
3 Due diligence and care 1205
4 Obedience 1208
5 Fidelity 1213
  a No competition 1215
  b Honesty 1216
  c Account for profits 1217
  d Other duties 1218
6 Confidentiality 1223
7 Notice 1226
B Employer duties 1230
1 Payment of agreed wages 1230
2 Provision of work 1233
3 Health and safety 1237
4 Grievance 1239

5 Reasonableness and mutual trust and confidence 1241
6 Indemnity for costs 1255
7 References 1257
8 Notice 1260
V Other terms 1270
A From collective agreements 1270
B From workforce agreements 1293
C Work rules 1295
VI Unenforceable terms 1305
A Illegal terms and terms contrary to public policy 1305
B Other unenforceable terms 1330
  Discriminatory terms 1330
  No contracting out 1335
  Unfair Contract Terms Act 1977 (UCTA) . 1340
  Terms in restraint of trade 1355
  Terms restricting right to take industrial action 1360

SECTION 3 **Information to be provided in writing** 1400

1 Obligation to provide written particulars .. 1405
2 Contents 1420
3 Changes to written particulars 1450
4 Enforcement and remedies 1460

SECTION 4 **Staff handbook** 1480

SECTION 5 **Varying terms and conditions** 1600

A Contractual right to vary 1615
1 Scope of existing terms 1616
2 Express right 1618
  Flexibility/variation clauses 1618
3 Implied right 1630

B	Mutual agreement	1635	A	Constructive dismissal	1715
1	Express agreement	1638	B	Damages	1725
2	Implied agreement	1640	C	Other remedies	1730
C	Unilateral variation by the employer	1645		Action for arrears of salary/other payments	1730
1	Breach of contract	1650		Injunctions	1732
2	Imposition of new contract	1652		Declarations	1740
3	Dismissal and re-engagement	1655	II	**Employer remedies**	1750
4	Liability for unfair dismissal	1665	A	Dismissal without notice	1755
5	Redundancy issues	1675	B	Damages	1760
			C	Other remedies	1770
SECTION 6	**Breach of contract**	1700		Injunctions	1771
I	**Employee remedies**	1710		Account for profits	1775

1100 Once a successful candidate has accepted a job offer and any pre-conditions are satisfied, the employment can be confirmed. This chapter focuses on the formation and terms of contracts of employment, as opposed to contracts for services (where a person does work for or provides services to another as part of his own business). The distinction between employment and self-employment is discussed at ¶30.

> MEMO POINTS The Government has consulted on **proposals** to introduce a new type of employment contract called "**employee-shareholder**" **contracts**. This contract would give employees shares in the business they work for that will be exempt from capital gains tax up to £50,000 (although subject to income tax and NICs under the normal rules that apply for shares acquired by reason of employment) in exchange for giving up certain employment rights. These rights would be the right not to be unfairly dismissed, redundancy rights, the right to request flexible working, the right to request time off for training, and employees would be required to give 16, instead of 8, weeks' notice to return early from maternity/adoption leave and 16, instead of 6, weeks' notice to return early from additional paternity leave. Employers would have the option of inserting more generous employment conditions into the employment contract if they want to, but the thrust of the proposals is to lessen employee rights to enable greater fluidity and ease in hiring and firing employees.
> The Government's response to the consultation has clarified that companies must satisfy themselves that the shares to be given are worth at least £2,000 or the employee can assert that their employee-shareholder status is not valid and that they therefore retain the usual employment rights enjoyed by employees. There will be no restrictions on the type of shares issued although they must be fully paid up and individuals must give no consideration for them other than agreeing to be employee shareholders. Any forfeiture and buy-back provisions will be contractual rather than statutory.
> Companies of any size will be able to use this new kind of contract, although the intention is for this new type of arrangement to be mainly used by small and medium-sized companies. Non UK-registered companies will also be allowed to use employee shareholder status. Subsidiaries will be permitted to issue parent company shares. Whilst the new employee-shareholder status will be voluntary, the existing rules regarding eligibility for job-seeker's allowance will remain, meaning those in receipt of the benefit will lose their benefits if they unreasonably reject a job offer made on this basis.
> Further developments will be covered by our updating service.

1101 A contract of employment is a type of contract. It must, therefore, meet the **formal requirements** that apply to all legally binding contracts, including offer and acceptance, consideration and an intention to enter into a legally binding agreement (¶1110).

1102 A contract of employment is usually a written document. However, its **form** may vary significantly, ranging from a short oral agreement to a detailed written contract and can be a combination of written and oral agreements, though a written agreement is clearly the most certain form to use, and the least likely to lead to disputes (¶1125).

The contract may be made up of both express and implied terms (¶1150). **Express terms** may be contained in a document called the contract of employment (see the model contract of employment at ¶9910) or may be incorporated by reference to other documents, for example collective agreements between the employer and a recognised, independent trade union. Not all terms will be enforceable – those which are illegal (e.g. those which defraud HMRC) will be void.

1103

Some terms are **implied** into all contracts as characteristic of the employment relationship, such as the employee's duty to give personal service, and the employer's duty to pay for work done. When the contract is silent, the courts may imply specific terms on the basis that the parties can be taken to have intended those terms to apply. Statute may also intervene to impose further obligations on the parties and further protections for the employee, such as the statutory minimum notice periods.

There is no statutory requirement to have a written contract, but the employer is obliged to provide **certain information** about the terms of employment to the employee **in writing** (¶1400; see also the model statement of particulars at ¶9900).

1104

Contractual terms may also be set out in a **staff handbook**, which can also contain non-contractual **policies and procedures** (¶1480).

1105

During the course of the employment, the employer or the employee may wish to **change** the contractual terms (or a change may be imposed, for example, by a change in the law) (¶1600).

1106

The **breach** of a contractual term, by either party, will entitle the innocent party to a remedy for breach of contract. If the breach is sufficiently serious or fundamental, it may entitle the innocent party to terminate the contract, i.e. permit the employer to summarily dismiss the employee, or the employee to treat himself as constructively dismissed (¶1700).

1107

SECTION 1

Formation

It is compulsory for details of certain terms to be provided to the employee in writing (¶1405). However, in order to avoid ambiguity and prevent disputes, it is advisable for all of the terms of the contract of employment to be in writing, preferably in a document that is signed by both the employer and the employee (see the model contract of employment at ¶9910). If terms are agreed orally, it is advisable that these should be confirmed soon afterwards in writing.

1110

It is **common practice** for the terms and conditions specific to each employee to be set out in a written contract of employment, with further terms of general application to the workforce to be set out in a staff handbook, which may also include policies and procedures that, although relevant to the employment relationship, do not form part of the contract of employment between employer and employee (¶1480).

A. Legal requirements

1. Legal capacity

Parties to a contract must have legal capacity to enter into it. There are legal restrictions on the ability of minors, the mentally impaired and drunk people to enter into binding contracts.

1111

An ordinary contract of employment with a **minor** is usually valid at common law. However, there are statutory restrictions which may apply to make the contract totally illegal (¶4970).

Local authorities are empowered to regulate the employment of minors in their jurisdiction and so restrictions may vary from area to area.

2. Binding contracts

1112 As for all legally binding contracts, an employment contract must comprise four elements: an offer (i.e. of employment); acceptance of that offer; consideration (i.e. something provided by one party in return for the other party's contribution to the contract); and intention to enter into a legally binding agreement.

Offer and acceptance

1113 An offer of employment is commonly made to a successful candidate by way of an offer letter (¶711), which may give outline terms and conditions of the employment offered and also details of any conditions which must be satisfied for the employment to be confirmed (for example, providing acceptable references, obtaining a work permit or passing a medical). Once a potential employee has accepted an offer of employment and any conditions have been satisfied, a binding contract of employment comes into existence.

1114 Any **change** to the agreed terms will be a variation (¶1600).

1115 If either party wishes to **terminate** the contract, it will have to do so in accordance with the terms of the contract (i.e. by giving the other party the applicable period of notice and complying with any other terms relating to termination), even if the employee has not yet started work. If it does not, this will amount to a breach of contract (¶1650) entitling the innocent party to compensation for the breach, although in practice, it is unusual for the employer to recover his losses (for example, additional recruitment costs in finding a replacement) from the employee in these circumstances.

Consideration

1116 The consideration is normally salary or wages in return for work, but it can take other **forms**, for example share options, provision of accommodation or other benefits.

Where there is no consideration for the work done, as is usually the case for **volunteer workers**, there is unlikely to be a binding employment agreement. Where a volunteer receives an expenses payment, which is limited to reimbursement for actual costs incurred (for example, travel expenses for the actual cost of getting to/from the place of work), the volunteer will not be working in a manner consistent with a binding employment contract (*Melhuish v Redbridge Citizens Advice Bureau* [2005] IRLR 419, EAT). If there is no such limitation on expenses, this may provide sufficient consideration for employment.

If an agreement is **executed as a deed**, there is no need for consideration.

Where the employer wants to **vary the employment contract** (¶1600) by asking the employee to agree to a change, that agreement should be supported by consideration. Sometimes the offer of continued employment on the new terms will be sufficient consideration to support an agreed change.

Intention to enter into a legally binding agreement

1117 For the parties to enter into a legally binding agreement, they must intend to do so.

1118 **General principles of construction** The court or tribunal must ask itself "what was the agreement between the parties?" (*Autoclenz Ltd v Belcher and ors* [2011] UKSC 41). If there is a dispute as to the parties' intentions, the court or tribunal will construe the contract applying the general principles set out below (*Davies v Hotpoint Ltd* [1994] UKEAT 751_93_0906).

The original written agreement should be read as a whole and objectively in the context of its factual matrix, genesis and aim (*Prenn v Simmonds* [1971] 1 WLR 1381, HL), together with any documents containing or confirming the particulars of the contract, to ascertain the parties' intention in relation to the terms of the contract **at the time the agreement was reached**. What the parties privately intended or expected (either before or after the contract was agreed) may be evidence of what, objectively discerned, was actually agreed between the parties but ultimately what matters is only what was agreed. The relative bargaining power of the parties must be taken into account in deciding whether the terms of any written agreement in truth represent what was agreed and the true agreement will be gleaned from all the circumstances, of which the written agreement may only be a part (*Autoclenz Ltd v Belcher and ors* [2011] UKSC 41).

The tribunal should adopt a construction which gives effect to all the words of the contract and, if possible, **avoid** a construction which makes contractual words ineffective or produces absurd consequences.

An employee will be deemed to have actual knowledge of the terms of a contract he has **signed** and, consequently, has no recourse if he later discovers that one of the terms is more onerous than he expected (*Peninsula Business Services Ltd v Sweeney* [2004] IRLR 49, EAT). However, the parties cannot be presumed to have taken on a "one-sided bargain" unless there are clear words which make this plain (*Brand v Compro Computer Services Ltd* [2005] IRLR 196, CA).

The parties' **subsequent conduct** is not generally admissible in construing the original agreement, but will, however, be relevant to show that the original contract has been varied, whether by the addition of a new term or the variation of an existing one (*Wickman Machine Tool Sales Ltd v L Schuler AG* [1974] AC 235, HL; *Hooper v British Railways Board* [1988] IRLR 517, CA). However, a **practice in place before and after** an agreement is entered into may assist in resolving a contractual ambiguity in that agreement, as it is part of the factual matrix against which the agreement should be construed (*Dunlop Tyres Ltd v Blows* [2001] IRLR 629, CA).

EXAMPLE

1. In *Pedersen v The Mayor and Burgesses of the London Borough of Camden* [1981] IRLR 173, CA, P responded to a **job advertisement** that indicated that the primary duties of the post were as a bar steward, with catering assistant duties as a subsidiary matter. The offer letter indicated that P would be assigned catering duties when not required at the bar. The Court held that the offer letter contained the terms of P's contract, but that it could also look at the advertisement (even though it was not part of the contract) to ascertain Camden's exact intentions in relation to the scope of the job duties. In the light of the advert and the letter, the Court agreed that the parties had intended P's duties to be primarily as a bar steward and that a move entirely to catering duties was a breach of contract.

2. In *Hooper v British Railways Board*, H's contract (which incorporated a BRB Council minute) stated that if declared unfit by BRB's medical officer, he would be paid his basic salary until he resumed work. The Court held that a **subsequent BRB Council minute** (which stated that any such payment would only be made on a short-term basis) could not be relied on by BRB as evidence of its intention as to the original terms. Further, BRB had not shown that H had accepted the subsequent minute as a variation to the original agreement.

3. In *Dunlop Tyres Ltd v Blows*, the contractual terms of a collective agreement were ambiguous as to payments for public holidays. However, a **30-year old practice** of paying employees triple time for working such holidays which existed before and continued after the agreement was acceptable to resolve the ambiguity.

4. In *Judge v Crown Leisure Ltd* [2005] IRLR 823, EAT, a conversation at CLL's Christmas party at which a manager **expressed a general intention** of raising an employee's salary "in due course" did not amount to a legally enforceable variation of the employee's contract since the EAT found there was no intention to create legal relations at the Christmas party and the manager's remarks were merely words of comfort. A different result might have ensued had the comments not been general or aspirational in nature.

5. In *Autoclenz Ltd v Belcher and ors*, despite the fact that there was an express substitution clause in the contracts of car valeters, the Supreme Court found that this did not reflect the true agreement of the parties, which was one requiring personal service by the employees in question.

3. Certainty

1120

In addition, the terms of a contract must be sufficiently certain for the courts and tribunals to be able to interpret them. Therefore, an agreement to agree terms at a later date is likely to be unenforceable.

B. Form

1125 If the formal legal requirements are met, there will be a binding contract, the form of which can be **oral, written** or a **combination of both**.

1126 **Oral contracts** A short conversation during which the employer offers a job on certain outline terms (for example, a salary of X amount with X days' paid holiday per year) that is accepted by the employee will, subject to the parties' intention (see above), be a binding contract. There is clearly more scope for dispute as to the terms of the contract in the case of oral agreements.

1127 **Written contracts** The employment terms may be found in a single document or, more commonly, in a range of written documents, including documents specific to the employee and those common to all staff, the most important of which are set out in the following table:

Offer letter accepted by employee	¶711
Signed contract	¶¶1110, 9910
Staff handbook	¶1480
Codes (e.g. of conduct)/rules (e.g. dealing rules)	¶1480
Applicable collective agreements	¶7367

A written contract can be entered into or varied by email.

Unless where the parties have intended that all the employment terms and conditions are to be only found in one document, the identification of, for example, policies and procedures as part of the contract is a matter of fact.

> EXAMPLE In *O'Flynn v Airlinks the Airport Coach Co Ltd* [2002] UKEAT 0269_01_1503, there was no evidence that only one document was to contain the contract terms. Therefore, whether the employer's drugs and alcohol policy formed part of the employee's contract of employment was a finding of fact, taking into account the immediacy of the implementation of the policy, the employee's knowledge of the policy and its consequences and the fact that she had not objected to it.

1128 **Combination of both** The contract may be partly oral and partly in writing. For example, if the employer tells the employee at the time he is selected that he will be entitled to a company car and the parties then sign a written contract that does not deal with this entitlement, the contract between the parties may (depending on the authority of the promisor and the wording of the written document) comprise the oral promise of the company car in addition to the terms contained in the written document.

SECTION 2

Terms

1150 As a contract of employment can be formed by a variety of methods, including a brief oral exchange, it often falls to the courts and tribunals to attempt to identify what the terms and conditions are.

Terms may be **express**, for example, by oral or written agreement between the parties. Such terms can be incorporated into the contract from another source, for example, those that are agreed through collective bargaining with trade unions or those contained in the staff handbook. If there is an express term, that term will normally prevail, unless the court or tribunal decides that it does not reflect the true agreement of the parties. Some express terms will be void as being illegal or contrary to public policy (e.g. those which defraud HMRC or are for an immoral purpose).

Where the contract is silent, the courts will look to see whether a specific term should be **implied**, for example, by virtue of custom and practice or to include a term identified by the courts over time as characteristic of the employment relationship.

In some cases, statute will impose certain obligations or minimum standards which will override an express term (e.g. the right to statutory minimum notice).

I. Express terms

Terms can be expressly agreed by the parties, either orally or in writing. Written terms may be found in a range of documents (¶1127). If the employer has complied with the obligation to provide written particulars, these will provide evidence of the employment terms and, if signed and accepted by both parties as such, will be contractual terms (¶1405). **1155**

An express term will normally prevail over a **conflicting implied term**, and courts are unwilling to imply terms that would contradict express terms unless the express term does not reflect the true agreement reached by the parties or is a sham (*Stevedoring & Haulage Services Ltd v Fuller* [2001] IRLR 627, CA; *Autoclenz Ltd v Belcher and ors* [2011] UKSC 41). Further, where a written employment contract states that it sets out the "whole agreement" between the parties, the courts are unwilling to imply any other terms. However, an express term will be **overridden by the law** in certain circumstances (¶1185), for example the equality clause implied by the equality legislation (¶5650). **1156**

> EXAMPLE
> 1. In *Stevedoring & Haulage Services Ltd v Fuller*, F's contract stated that the company was not obliged to provide work for him, and that he was not obliged to accept any work offered. The Court declined to imply obligations to offer and accept a reasonable amount of work (¶¶1200, 1233) as this would clearly contradict the express terms.
> 2. In *Autoclenz Ltd v Belcher and ors*, an express substitution clause was found not to reflect the true agreement of the parties, which was one requiring personal service.

See ¶9910 for a model contract of employment. **1157**

II. Specific terms implied by the courts

In the absence of an express term, the courts may have to decide if it is possible to imply a particular term, on the basis that the parties can be **taken to have agreed** it. The court's role is not to determine what the parties should have agreed but what the **parties' intention** when entering the agreement must have been (¶1117). A court will not invent terms where they are neither expressly nor impliedly agreed and will not imply a term just because it is reasonable. **1170**

Where the parties' intentions can be ascertained entirely from documents, the meaning and effect of the contract is a question of law. However, where the parties' intentions have to be determined not only from documents but also from oral communications and conduct, the terms of the contract are a question of fact for the tribunal. The court will examine the facts, and whether or not a term may be implied from those facts is a question of law, rather than a question of fact (*Carmichael v National Power plc* [2000] IRLR 43, HL). This distinction is relevant as only a question of law may be appealed to a higher court, although it is an error of law if an employment tribunal makes a finding of fact which is perverse or clearly wrong.

1. Obvious terms

1172 A term may be implied if it is so obvious that the parties **must have intended** it and both their responses to the suggestion of "an officious bystander" that a particular provision be included in their contract would have been "Oh, of course" (*Shirlaw v Southern Foundries (1926) Ltd* [1939] 2 All ER 113, HC (affirmed by the Court of Appeal); *Deeley v British Rail Engineering Ltd* [1980] IRLR 147, CA).

> EXAMPLE In *Ali and ors v Christian Salvesen Food Services Ltd* [1997] ICR 25, CA, the Court declined to imply a term that the employees' annualised hours contracts should be pro-rated in relation to overtime payments stated to be payable once the annual target was reached. The contracts had been carefully negotiated by union representatives, which led the Court to conclude that the question of pro-rating had deliberately not been dealt with. It was therefore not obvious that a pro-rating term had been agreed.

2. Business efficacy

1174 A term may be implied if it is necessary to give the contract business efficacy, i.e. to make the contract work (*Liverpool City Council v Irwin* [1977] AC 239, HL). An implied term of this kind should be **no wider than is necessary** to give the contract business efficacy and must be **sufficiently precise** (*Marshall v Alexander Sloan & Co Ltd* [1981] IRLR 264, EAT; *Lake v Essex County Council* [1979] IRLR 241, CA).

> EXAMPLE
> 1. If the contract is silent on the need for flexibility in relation to the **place of work**, the courts may imply a mobility clause on the grounds that it is essential to make the contract work, as was decided in *Courtaulds Northern Spinning Ltd v Sibson and TGWU* [1988] IRLR 305, CA, in relation to a **heavy goods vehicle driver**. However, where mobility is not essential to the contract, the court will not imply such a clause, as was decided in *Aparau v Iceland Frozen Foods plc* 1995] UKEAT 196_93_0910, in relation to a **cashier** working for a supermarket chain.
> 2. In *Morley v Heritage plc* [1993] IRLR 400, CA, the Court refused to imply a term into M's contract entitling him to a **payment in lieu of accrued but untaken holiday** on the termination of his employment on the grounds that it was not needed to give business efficacy to the contract. Note that the Working Time Regulations now provide for such a payment to be made (¶4025).
> 3. In *Aspden v Webbs Poultry and Meat Group (Holdings) Ltd* [1996] IRLR 521, QBD and in *Villella v MFI Furniture Centres Ltd* [1999] IRLR 468, QBD, the High Court implied a term that the employer would not terminate the employment in circumstances which would deprive the employee of his **contractual permanent health insurance benefit** (¶4200). If the employer was able to terminate in those circumstances, the contractual terms relating to company sick pay and permanent health insurance benefit would not work.
> 4. The Court will imply a term to the effect that an employer must take reasonable steps to bring to the employee's notice the existence of a particular term (for example, **enhanced pension entitlement**), where the employee must take some action in order to take advantage of that term and where the employee cannot otherwise be expected to be aware of the term unless it is drawn to his attention (*Scally v Southern Health and Social Services Board* [1991] IRLR 522, HL). Note, though, that having taken such reasonable steps, there will be no implied duty on the employer to ensure that the information is actually communicated to the employee (*Ibekwe v London General Transport Services Ltd* [2003] IRLR 697, CA).

> MEMO POINTS The EAT has held that in an exceptional case the tribunal was entitled to hold that it was justifiable for the employer to require the employee to **work temporarily at a different location** notwithstanding that the employee's express contractual terms only provided for her working at her workplace. In this case, L, a teacher, was on sick leave after claiming she had been bullied and harassed by her head teacher (*Luke v Stoke on Trent City Council* [2007] IRLR 305, EAT). An independent investigator hired by her employer to investigate her 33 complaints dismissed all but one of them. L did not accept the report's conclusions, but accepted the report's proposed plan of the use of a mediator to assist her return. Her employer, however, considered that this plan would not work until L had accepted the report's conclusions and as a result deferred her return until the matter had been resolved and requested that in the interim she should do a similar job at a different location. The EAT held that the tribunal was entitled to find that despite the fact there was no express term to support this temporary change in location, a term requiring this could be implied given that the requirement to work was justified and the temporary alternative location was suitable and the employee would suffer no detriment with regard to her benefits or status in doing so.

However, it should be noted that while the Court of Appeal also found for the employer, it did so on different grounds (*Luke v Stoke on Trent City Council* [2007] IRLR 777, CA). The Court was reluctant to express a concluded view as to whether the EAT's analysis of the law had been correct. On the facts, it found that there was no need to imply any term into the contract.

3. Conduct of the parties

1176 A court may imply a term based on the conduct of the parties **at the time of the agreement**, provided that, although nothing was said, it is clear the parties intended that term to apply. **Subsequent conduct** is less reliable as evidence of the original agreement, as it may in fact evidence a variation to that agreement (¶1600).

4. Custom in that trade, industry or area

1178 A term may be implied if it is customary in that trade, industry or area, on the basis that the parties must be taken to have agreed such a term. The custom must be "reasonable, notorious and certain", i.e. fair, well known (although not necessarily to every single employee working in that trade, industry or area) and precise (*Sagar v H Ridehalgh & Son Ltd* [1931] 1 Ch 310, CA; *Bond v CAV Ltd* [1983] IRLR 360, QBD).

> EXAMPLE In *Sagar v H Ridehalgh & Son Ltd*, the Court accepted that the practice in the Lancashire weaving industry of **deducting wages** for poor workmanship was an implied term of employment. The practice had been in operation for over 30 years, was generally well known and followed in at least 85% of other mills in the area.

5. Employer custom and practice

1180 A term may be implied by virtue of the custom and practice of the particular employer (*Duke v Reliance Systems* [1982] IRLR 347, EAT). **Factors** determining whether this is possible include whether the relevant policy has been drawn to the attention of the employees and whether the practice has been followed without exception for a substantial period of time. However, with regard to **discretionary benefits**, it does not necessarily follow that the fact that a benefit has been granted for a number of years will always be deemed to have created an implied term (*Campbell v Union Carbide Ltd* [2002] UKEAT 0341_01_1503).

> EXAMPLE
> 1. In *Quinn v Calder Industrial Materials Ltd* [1996] IRLR 126, EAT (applied in *Albion Automotive Ltd v Walker* [2002] EWCA Civ 946) and *Pellowe v Pendragon plc* [1998] UKEAT 804_98_0110, the employers provided management with guidelines on **enhanced redundancy payments**. In *Quinn v Calder Industrial Materials Ltd*, these were followed on the four occasions between 1987 and 1994 that redundancies were made, and in *Pellowe v Pendragon plc* the formula had been followed for over 20 years. In both cases, despite their awareness of past payments, the management manual had **not** been **communicated directly to employees**. In *Quinn v Calder Industrial Materials Ltd*, the EAT noted that payment of the enhanced terms was not automatic but required a **management decision on each occasion**. The EAT in each case could not therefore infer that the parties intended the enhanced redundancy terms to be contractual.
> 2. In *Campbell v Union Carbide Ltd*, above, the EAT emphasised that the fact that the employer had made **discretionary ill-health payments** for a number of years did not in itself demonstrate the employer's intention that such payments were contractual, rather that he made such payments for the sake of good industrial relations.
> 3. In *Cook v Diageo* [2005] UKEAT 0070_04_3003, a reference in a collective agreement and employees' terms and conditions to **"occasional" holidays** did not oblige the employer to fix such holidays by reference to local public holidays, although this had usually been the case in the past. There was nothing to demonstrate that the intention of the parties to the collective agreement was to create a contractual obligation that the occasional days would always be on local public holidays. The employer's actions had therefore not undergone the passage from policy to contractual obligation.

III. Terms implied by statute

1185 Parties are generally free to agree terms and conditions, and any expressly agreed terms will normally prevail unless the law intervenes to **override** and/or **vary** any contradictory or inconsistent express terms. For example, the **equality clause** overrides any terms which are less advantageous than those applying to a member of the opposite sex doing the same or like work, work rated as equivalent or work of equal value (¶5655), and the **statutory minimum notice period** will prevail where the contract is silent or less favourable (¶8131).

1186 Statute also intervenes to **imply certain rights** and minimum standards in favour of the employee, some of which are subject to qualifying periods of service (¶1080).

Any dismissal of an employee who is seeking to assert his statutory rights is automatically unfair (¶8395).

The most important implied statutory rights are:

Right	¶¶
Written statement of main terms	¶1405
Not to be discriminated against on grounds of age, disability, gender reassignment, marriage and civil partnership, pregnancy and maternity, race, religion or belief, sex or sexual orientation	Chapter 16 (¶5200)
Equal pay	¶5650
National minimum wage	¶2865
Not to suffer unlawful deductions from wages	¶3050
Guarantee payments	¶7860
Itemised pay statement	¶2985
Sick pay	¶4110
Parents' and carers' rights including maternity, paternity, adoption and parental leave and the right to request flexible working	Chapter 14 (¶4400)
Payments during medical suspension	¶4985
Safe place of work	¶4816
Breaks and rest periods	¶3710
Paid annual leave	¶4000
Time off in certain circumstances	¶3910
Trade union membership and activities	¶7560
Right to be accompanied at disciplinary and grievance hearings	¶6780
Continuity of employment on transfer of undertaking	¶7974
Minimum period of notice	¶8131
Redundancy rights	¶8730
Unfair dismissal rights	¶8380
Written statement of reasons for dismissal	¶8310

IV. Terms implied by common law as characteristic of the employment relationship

1195 The courts have identified certain terms which they regard as characteristic of the employment relationship and which they will therefore imply into all contracts of employment. These "common law" terms deal with the parties' respective **rights and duties**.

MEMO POINTS As such terms are characteristic of employment relationships, the presence or absence of these implied rights and duties may serve to indicate the status of the worker, i.e. whether he is an employee or is self-employed (¶30).

1196 In practice, many of these implied rights and duties are **made express**. For example, the employer may wish to extend the protection of his confidential information by express agreement, or may wish to bring certain duties to the employee's attention so that he is clearly made aware of them.

1197 The most important implied duties are:

Employee duties [1]	¶¶
Service	¶1200
Competence	¶1202
Due diligence and care	¶1205
Obedience	¶1208
Fidelity – not to compete against employer or solicit employer's customers – behave honestly – account for profits – notify employer of misdeeds of other staff – disclose information received from third parties – inventions and copyright to belong to employer – work according to reasonable interpretation of contract	¶1213 ¶1215 ¶1216 ¶1217 ¶1218 ¶1219 ¶1220 ¶1221
Confidentiality	¶1223
Notice	¶1226

1. **Directors** are subject to additional duties (¶2133), including their fiduciary duties to the company (¶2139).

Employer duties	¶¶
Payment of agreed wages	¶1230
Payment of contractual sick pay for reasonable period where contract silent as to duration	¶1231
Provision of work in certain circumstances	¶1233
Care for employee's health and safety	¶1237
Provision of grievance procedure	¶1239
Reasonableness and mutual trust and confidence	¶1241
Indemnity for costs	¶1255
References (if provided, must be accurate and compiled with reasonable care)	¶1257
Notice	¶1260

A. Employee duties

1. Service

1200 The employee must give **personal service** (i.e. he must not delegate or assign his duties) (*Ready-Mixed Concrete (South East) Ltd v Minister of Pensions and National Insurance* [1968] 2 QB 497). This means that he must be **ready and willing to work** (*Henthorn and Taylor v Central Electricity Generating Board* [1980] IRLR 361, CA). Sickness absence will not breach this duty (*O'Grady v M Saper Ltd* [1940] 2 KB 469), but participating in a strike may do so, as the employee cannot be said to be ready and willing to work (*W Simmons v Hoover Ltd* [1976] IRLR 266, EAT).

See ¶3007 on the employer's right to deduct some or all of the employee's wages if he refuses to work.

2. Competence

1202 It is also an implied term that the employee will be **reasonably competent** to do the job.

There is an implied term that an employer will take reasonable steps to maintain an appraisal of an employee during a **probationary period** (¶946).

1203 **Incompetence** will be a breach of contract (¶1700). Depending on the seriousness of the breach, the employer may be entitled summarily to dismiss the employee. Less serious cases will require careful management by the employer and, if necessary, implementation of disciplinary procedures (¶6555).

> MEMO POINTS **Incapability** (which includes incompetence) is a statutory fair reason for dismissal, which will enable the employer to defend a claim of unfair dismissal as long as he has acted reasonably in treating the incapability as a sufficient reason for dismissal (¶8450).

3. Due diligence and care

1205 An employee is obliged to **take reasonable care** in the performance of his duties generally, and in particular, to take care of the employer's property (*Lister v Romford Ice and Cold Storage Co Ltd* [1957] AC 555, HL).

If the employee is negligent, and for example injures a fellow employee, the employer may be **vicariously liable** for his actions (¶¶4825+). This means that legal responsibility is imposed on the employer, even though he might otherwise be free from blame. For the employer to be liable, the employee's negligent act must be committed in the course of his employment. Where it is unclear whether this is the case, the **test** will be whether the act is so closely connected with the employment that it would be fair and just to hold the employer liable (*Lister v Hesley Hall Ltd* [2001] IRLR 472, HL). The employer may also be vicariously liable for **acts of discrimination** committed by employees in the course of their employment (¶4826).

1206 **Negligence** will also be a breach of contract, entitling the employer to sue the employee for damages and, in very serious cases, to dismiss the employee without notice.

> MEMO POINTS Failure to exercise reasonable skill may provide a defence to an unfair dismissal claim if it constitutes one of the statutory fair reasons for dismissal (for example, incapability or misconduct) (¶8450).

4. Obedience

1208 An employee must carry out the **reasonable and lawful instructions** given by or on behalf of the employer, even where the employer is in breach of the duty of trust and confidence (¶1245) by issuing an instruction in bad faith.

Whether an instruction is reasonable will depend on the circumstances (in particular, the nature and scope of the employee's duties) and whether the employee is contractually obliged to comply with it (*Macmillan Inc v Bishopsgate Investment Trust plc* [1993] IRLR 393, ChD). For example, if an employee's contract states that he can be required to take part of his annual leave during the employer's Christmas/New Year shut-down period, it will be reasonable for the employer to require the employee to do so.

An employee is obliged to comply with orders that provide for a **new method of doing his job** (as opposed to doing a different job) (¶1616).

1209 **Disobedience** can amount to a sufficiently serious breach of contract such as to justify summary dismissal (it could also amount to misconduct, which may constitute a statutory fair reason for dismissal (¶8490)).

1210 An employee is not obliged to obey **unreasonable or unlawful instructions**. For example, it is usually reasonable for an employee not to obey an instruction that would put him in danger. However, employees in the fire or police services, for example, may be expected to accept a higher degree of risk as part of their duties.

> EXAMPLE
> 1. In *Morrish v Henlys (Folkestone) Ltd* [1973] IRLR 61, NIRC, M was held to have been unfairly dismissed for refusing to participate in the falsification of the employer's records.
> 2. In *Showboat Entertainment Centre Ltd v Owens* [1984] IRLR 7, EAT, an employee of an amusement arcade was held to have been unfairly dismissed when he was dismissed having refused an order from his employer to discriminate unlawfully against black customers.

1211 If the employer insists on the employee carrying out an instruction that falls **outside the scope of his duties**, the employer will be in breach of contract and the employee may, if the breach is fundamental, be entitled to resign and claim that he has been constructively dismissed (*O'Brien v Associated Fire Alarms Ltd* [1969] 1 All ER 93, CA).

5. Fidelity

1213 The relationship between employer and employee is founded on a continuing bond of trust and confidence (¶1241). This tends, in the case of employees, to manifest itself in the more specific common law duty of fidelity (i.e. "to serve the employer faithfully within the requirements of the contract" (*Ticehurst and Thompson v British Telecommunications plc* [1992] IRLR 219, CA), which encompasses the duty of confidentiality discussed below. The duty of fidelity is implied into every contract of employment (*Robb v Green* [1895] 2 QB 315). It ends with the termination of the employment, apart from the obligation not to use or disclose the employer's trade secrets. The principal aspects of the duty of fidelity are discussed below.

> MEMO POINTS Employees are not subject to the same fiduciary duties as directors. For employees, any fiduciary duties must be accounted for in the contract of employment and cannot be implied merely from the existence of other implied duties, such as the duty of mutual trust and confidence (*Ranson v Customer Systems plc* [2012] EWCA Civ 841). For a discussion on the **fiduciary duties** owed by directors, see ¶¶2139+.

1214 **Breach** of the duty of fidelity can amount to gross misconduct.

> MEMO POINTS A dismissal for breach of the duty of fidelity could amount to a statutory fair reason for dismissal on the ground of the employee's conduct.

a. No competition

1215 The scope of this duty obliges an employee, during his employment, not to compete **with his employer's business**, either by working for competitors of the employer or setting up a competing business, and further not to solicit the employer's customers. After the employment ends there is no implied term that an ex-employee will not compete with his former employer. Express terms in restraint of trade may be used, but may be unenforceable (¶2500).

Employees may **prepare to compete** while they are still employed, for instance by talking to business contacts during a notice period with a view to securing work for a competing future business. They must take care when doing this not to breach the duty of fidelity, which requires an employee to have regard to his employer's interests in various ways as set out below. However, this duty does not require an employee to subordinate his interests to those of his employer (as opposed to a fiduciary duty, which would require for undivided loyalty to the employer's interests (¶¶2139+)). Therefore, from a common law perspective (i.e. without taking any contractual restrictive covenants into account), an employee has a reasonable amount of scope when preparing to compete (*Ranson v Customer Systems plc* [2012] EWCA Civ 841).

b. Honesty

1216 The employee must behave honestly. To determine the extent of the duty and the seriousness of any breach, the nature of the employer, the role of the employee, and the degree of trust required of the employee will be relevant factors. **Financial wrongdoing** amounting to gross misconduct, for example, does not necessarily require deliberate dishonesty or deceit (*Neary and Neary v Dean of Westminster* [1999] IRLR 288, Special Commissioner). **Unauthorised access to a computer** is comparable to dishonesty and may also amount to gross misconduct (*Denco Ltd v Joinson* [1991] ICR 172, EAT).

c. Account for profits

1217 The employee is obliged to account to the employer for "**secret profits**" (*Boston Deep Sea Fishing and Ice Co v Ansell* [1888] 39 ChD 399). This means that the employee "must not make a profit out of his trust; he must not place himself in a position where his duty and his interest may conflict; he may not act for his own benefit or the benefit of a third party without the informed consent of his employer" (*Attorney General v Blake* [2001] IRLR 36, HL). This **includes** taking bribes or "backhanders" but could also include benefits such as free "air miles" or gifts for private use, if the benefit to the employee is more than minimal.

Where the employee's **outside activities do not conflict** with his duty to the employer (as determined by his contractual obligations), he will not be obliged to account for any financial gain unless there is an express provision to that effect (*Nottingham University v Fishel* [2000] IRLR 471, QBD).

> MEMO POINTS Although the employment relationship is not a fiduciary one, equity may impose **fiduciary duties** (including a duty to act in the interests of another) as a result of the specific contractual obligations undertaken. These additional duties may oblige an employee to account for profits where he has benefited from his position (¶2665).

d. Other duties

1218 **Notify misdeeds** There is no general duty either to notify the employer of his own misconduct (*Bell v Lever Bros Ltd* [1932] AC 161, HL, although it has since been observed that *Bell v Lever Bros Ltd* does not provide any authority for the assertion that an employee can never be under a duty to notify his employer of his own misconduct (*Item Software (UK) Ltd v Fassihi* [2004] IRLR 928, CA)), or of misdeeds of other staff.

However, depending on the contract and the circumstances (in particular, whether the employee is so placed in the hierarchy of the workplace as to have a duty to report on the misconduct of superiors and/or subordinates (*Swain v West (Butchers) Ltd* [1936] 3 All ER 261, CA)), an employee may **specifically be obliged** to notify the employer of serious misdeeds by other staff (*Sybron Corporation v Rochem Ltd* [1983] IRLR 253, CA). Directors and senior employees also have a positive duty to disclose breaches of their own fiduciary duty (¶2139) (*Tesco Stores Ltd v Pook and others* [2004] IRLR 618, ChD).

If the duty to disclose does apply, it is no defence that the employee was not specifically asked to volunteer the information (*Sybron Corporation v Rochem Ltd*), or that he would thereby incriminate himself.

> MEMO POINTS Where an employee does report the misdeeds of other staff, he may be protected from detriment or dismissal by the whistleblowing legislation (¶2700).

1219 **Disclose information received from third parties** An employee is under a duty to disclose information received from third parties which relates to the employer's business if received in the course of employment. An employee is not, however, generally obliged to disclose information received outside the course of his employment, even if it is of value to the employer (*Macmillan Inc v Bishopsgate Investment Trust plc* [1993] IRLR 393, ChD).

Inventions and copyright When made in the course of the employment, inventions and copyright normally belong to the employer unless there is agreement to the contrary. Legislation also regulates ownership of intellectual property rights (¶2310). **1220**

Work according to his contract An employee must work according to a reasonable interpretation of his contract. For example, a **work-to-rule** was held to be a breach of contract even though the employees were, strictly speaking, carrying out the express terms of the contract properly and fully (*Secretary of State for Employment v ASLEF (No 2)* [1972] ICR 19, CA). **1221**

Withholding goodwill can also breach the implied term of fidelity and justify withholding pay (¶3009).

6. Confidentiality

During his employment an employee is bound by the common law duty of confidence which prevents him from using or disclosing the employer's confidential information and trade secrets. After the employment ends the implied duty only applies to trade secrets, so express provisions are needed to protect confidential information (¶2500). **1223**

An employer may seek damages or an injunction if the employee has **breached** the implied duty of confidence or an express post-termination restriction (¶2640). **1224**

> MEMO POINTS The dismissal of an employee in order to preserve confidentiality may be fair for statutory purposes, relying on the statutory defence of "some other substantial reason" to defend an unfair dismissal claim (¶8530).

7. Notice

Legislation provides for a minimum notice period (¶8131). An express term may provide for a period of notice equivalent to or greater than the statutory minimum period. **1226**

Where the contract is silent as to the amount of notice required to terminate the employment, it is an implied term that "**reasonable notice**" of termination will be given. This is discussed further at ¶8129.

B. Employer duties

1. Payment of agreed wages

It is an implied term that the employer will pay for the **work done** (¶2817). **1230**

Where the employment contract provides for **sick pay** but is silent on the duration of the obligation to pay, a term may be implied to give effect to the presumed intention of the parties (¶1117). The presumption is that the employer will pay for a **reasonable period** only, which will depend on the term normally applicable in the particular industry as determined, for example, by reference to the relevant national agreement (*Howman & Son v Blyth* [1983] IRLR 139, EAT). **1231**

2. Provision of work

The employer does not have a general implied obligation to provide work, as long as the employee is paid (*Turner v Sawdon & Co* [1901] 2 KB 653). However, the employer may be obliged to provide work if the consideration provided by him is more than merely to pay the agreed **1233** wages, extending to an obligation to permit the employee to do the work (*Langston v AUEW (No 2)* [1973] EWCA Civ 7, NIRC). Whether there is a right to work is a **question of construction** of the particular contract in the light of its surrounding circumstances (*William Hill Organisation Ltd v Tucker* [1998] EWCA Civ 615, CA, approving *Langston v AUEW (Nos 1 and 2)* [1974] IRLR 15, CA and 182, NIRC).

An **obligation to provide work** has been identified in the **following circumstances**:
- where earning capacity depends on working, such as pieceworkers, workers on commission and those who regularly work overtime or nights (*Langston v AUEW (Nos 1 and 2)*);
- workers dependent on publicity, such as actors (*Herbert Clayton and Jack Waller Ltd v Oliver* [1930] AC 209, HL); or
- workers needing regular exercise of their skills (*Langston v AUEW (Nos 1 and 2)*; *William Hill Organisation Ltd v Tucker*).

> EXAMPLE In *William Hill Organisation Ltd v Tucker*, the employee, T, was a senior dealer in the specialised business of spread betting. His contract expressly imposed an obligation on him to work those hours necessary to carry out his duties in a full and professional manner and emphasised that T would have every opportunity to develop his skills. When T resigned without giving the required period of notice, WH wanted to put him on garden leave, although it had no express right to do so. The Court held that T's special skills required frequent exercise, and that the express contractual terms were inconsistent with an implied term allowing him to collect wages without doing any available work. There was, therefore, an obligation to provide work during the employment, including the notice period.

1234 It is advisable for the employer to reserve an express contractual **right to suspend** the employee during the employment, and to put him on "**garden leave**" during the notice period, in order to defeat any argument that there is an implied obligation to provide work. Garden leave is discussed further at ¶2529.

Where the employer has expressly reserved the right to make a **payment in lieu of notice** (¶8145), the employee has no right to work out his notice period (*Marshall (Cambridge) Ltd v Hamblin* [1993] UKEAT 705_91_1512).

3. Health and safety

1237 There is an implied term that employers must take **reasonable care** of their employees' health and safety. The health and safety obligations of the employer both in statute and common law are discussed at ¶4800.

4. Grievance

1239 There is an implied term that an employee's grievances will be **promptly and properly** dealt with. Employee grievances are discussed further in chapter 19.

5. Reasonableness and mutual trust and confidence

1241 There is no general obligation on the employer to act fairly and reasonably (*Western Excavating (ECC) Ltd v Sharp* [1978] IRLR 27, CA), as to imply such a term would be too wide and uncertain (*Post Office v Roberts* [1980] IRLR 347, EAT). Therefore, an employer's unreasonable conduct alone is insufficient to found a claim for constructive dismissal, as a fundamental breach of contract is required in such cases (*Western Excavating (ECC) Ltd v Sharp*).

1242 There is, however, an implied term that an employer will **not exercise** his power under a **contractual provision on unreasonable grounds** or in such a way as to make compliance by the employee increasingly difficult. This means that the employer must exercise:
- an express right to suspend, for example, on reasonable grounds for no longer than is reasonably necessary (*McClory v Post Office* [1993] IRLR 159, ChD);

– an express mobility clause on reasonable grounds, i.e. not "capriciously" (*White v Reflecting Roadstuds Ltd* [1991] IRLR 331, EAT), but for business reasons (*HSBC Bank plc v Drage* [2003] UKEAT 0369_02_0807); and
– discretion in relation to contractual bonuses in a rational manner and in good faith (¶2833).

1243 The courts may also be willing to imply a term to the effect that the employer will take **reasonable care in making statements** in the context of a proposed **business transfer** where (*Hagen and ors v ICI Chemicals & Polymers Ltd* [2002] IRLR 31, QBD):
– the transfer will impact on the future economic interests of his employees;
– the transfer will be unlikely to take place if a significant number of the employees object; and
– the employer has access to information unavailable to the employees which he knows will carry considerable weight with them.

1244 An obligation to treat the employee in a reasonable manner may, however, be implied if it can be identified under another head, such as **business efficacy** (*Aspden v Webbs Poultry and Meat Group (Holdings) Ltd* and *Scally v Southern Health and Social Services Board*; ¶1174).

1245 **Trust and confidence** The courts have also upheld an obligation to treat the employee in a reasonable manner as part of the duty to preserve the relationship of mutual trust and confidence (*Imperial Group Pension Trust Ltd v Imperial Tobacco Ltd* [1991] IRLR 66, ChD). This means that the employer will not, without reasonable and proper cause, **conduct** himself in a manner calculated or **likely to destroy or seriously damage the relationship** of trust and confidence which should exist between him and the employee (*Mahmud v BCCI* [1997] ICR 606, HL; *Woods v WM Car Services (Peterborough) Ltd* [1982] IRLR 413, CA and confirmed in *Baldwin v Brighton and Hove Council* [2007] IRLR 232, EAT). A breach will always be **repudiatory** for the purposes of a claim of constructive dismissal (*Morrow v Safeway Stores plc* [2002] IRLR 9, EAT).

This obligation may not be diminished by factors such as the overall working environment (for example, one in which abusive language is acceptable) or the seniority and remuneration of the employee (*Horkulak v Cantor Fitzgerald International* [2003] IRLR 756, HC, confirmed on appeal [2004] IRLR 942, CA). In this case, the Court rejected the argument that high levels of remuneration entitled an employer to apply different standards of treatment to a city broker compared with other less well-paid employees. However, the High Court more recently held that after a group of employees resigned as a result of a campaign by another to recruit a substantial number to move with him as complete teams, a brokers' firm did not breach the duty of trust and confidence when it, for example, gave presentations on the disadvantages of moving to the new firm, informing them that it would take legal action if they did not serve their notice, and the impact of the suspension of the orchestrator of the move (*Tullett Prebon Plc and ors v BGC Brokers LP and ors* [2010] IRLR 648, QB confirmed by the Court of Appeal ([2010] IRLR 648, QB)). The Court held that the claims of constructive dismissal were in reality a manoeuvre to seek to leave early. Although robust, the firm's conduct was unobjectionable, especially as the brokers were no "shrinking violets". The Court therefore held that there had been no constructive dismissals and enforced the restrictive covenants and garden leave clauses.

> MEMO POINTS The EAT in *Baldwin v Brighton and Hove Council* held that other cases which had suggested that an employer was required to refrain from conduct "calculated and likely to destroy or seriously damage the relationship of trust and confidence" (i.e. cases which imply a two-stage test due to the first "and") were incorrect.

1246 The **employer's conduct** must be **serious** to breach the duty of trust and confidence, and, as stated above, there will be **no breach** if the employer had **reasonable and proper cause** for his actions (*Gogay v Hertfordshire County Council*, above; *Hilton v Shiner Ltd – Builders Merchants* [2001] UKEAT 9_00_2405).

The **test** is an **objective** one and, consequently, it is not necessary for the employee to actually lose confidence for there to be a breach (*Meikle v Nottinghamshire County Council* [2004] IRLR 703, CA). Nor is it necessary for the employer's conduct to be targeted in some way at the employee, nor does the employee have to know of that conduct while he is still employed (*Malik v Bank of Credit and Commerce International SA* [1997] IRLR 462, HL). Further, it is not necessary to show that the employer intended such a breach, and an employer who breaches the term on the basis of a mistake may still be liable (*Transco plc (formerly BG plc) v O'Brien* [2002] IRLR 444, CA).

> **MEMO POINTS** Previously, an EAT case held that the employer's conduct must have been calculated to destroy or seriously damage the employer/employee relationship of trust and confidence (*Abbey National plc v Fairbrother* [2007] IRLR 320, EAT, followed in *GMB v Brown* [2007] UKEAT 0621_06_1610 and also with a slight difference in *Claridge v Daler Rowney* [2008] IRLR 672, EAT). In this case, which concerned a claim for constructive dismissal due to the operation of a grievance procedure, the EAT held that an employer will only breach his implied duty of trust and confidence if his conduct of the grievance procedure as a whole was outside the range of reasonable responses to the grievance presented by the employee. This case was criticised for importing the "range of reasonable responses" test required in unfair dismissal cases (see ¶¶8435, 8505, 6588) to employers' handling of grievances, and other EAT decisions limited this approach to breaches of mutual trust and confidence which are related to the conduct of a grievance procedure (*GAB Robins (UK) Limited v Triggs* [2007] ICR 1424, EAT, appealed to the Court of Appeal though the Court did not consider the issue of the test to be applied; *Parsons v Bristol Street Motors* [2008] UKEAT 0581_07_2802).
>
> However, this unsatisfactory situation where it seemed that the test for constructive dismissal appeared to depend on the context of the breach has been resolved with the Court of Appeal firmly holding that the **range of reasonable responses should not be used** to determine a claim for constructive dismissal (*Buckland v Bournemouth University Higher Education Corp* [2010] IRLR 445, CA).

1247 The obligation is confined to matters arising during the subsistence of the employment relationship, and it does not apply in relation to the **manner of a dismissal** (i.e. the acts immediately surrounding the dismissal) (*Johnson v Unisys Ltd* [2001] IRLR 279, HL). However, if an employer breaches either the implied term of mutual trust and confidence or the duty of care in taking steps in relation to an employee **prior to and leading up to** dismissing the employee such that the employee would be entitled to a contractual or tortious remedy (which existed **independently** of any action in respect **of the fairness of the dismissal**) and the employee had suffered direct financial loss as a result of the employer's conduct, then *Johnson v Unisys Ltd* will not bar such an action (*Eastwood and Williams v Magnox Electric plc* heard jointly with *McCabe v Cornwall County Council and anor* [2004] IRLR 733, HL). In *Eastwood and Williams v Magnox Electric plc* and *McCabe v Cornwall County Council*, the employees brought court proceedings (after bringing successful claims for unfair dismissal in the tribunal) claiming that they had suffered financial loss as a direct result of psychiatric illnesses brought on by their employers' unfair treatment of them in the events prior, and leading up to, their dismissals. The House of Lords considered that, ordinarily (with the exception of suspension), an employer's unfair treatment of an employee in the events leading up to dismissal would not cause financial loss. However, exceptionally, **financial loss** might be suffered and, in such cases, the cause of action preceded and was independent of the subsequent dismissal. Note, however, that any such claim will be subject to the principle of double recovery.

> **EXAMPLE** In *King v University Court of the University of St Andrews* [2002] IRLR 252, CS, the implied term of trust and confidence arising from a provision in the contract of employment entitling the employer to terminate the contract with notice for "good cause shown" was held only to cease **once a decision to dismiss has been made** and consequently subsisted during the employer's investigation and evaluation of disciplinary charges.

1248 The implied term of trust and confidence has been **applied** in a wide variety of circumstances, including the following:

> **EXAMPLE**
> 1. In *Malik v Bank of Credit and Commerce International SA* [1997] IRLR 462, HL, the bank went into liquidation after having operated for some time in a corrupt and dishonest manner. This conduct amounted to a breach of the implied contractual obligation of mutual trust and confidence as the employee's **employment prospects** were tainted by the employer's reputation.
> 2. The term may be breached if the employer exercises an express contractual right, such as a **mobility clause**, in a way that has a particularly onerous impact on the employee. When exercising such a clause, the employer is subject to an implied duty to give reasonable notice, to co-operate with and not frustrate the employee's attempt to perform the contract (*United Bank Ltd v Akhtar* [1989] IRLR 507, EAT), and to communicate fully with the employee (*White v Reflecting Roadstuds Ltd* [1991] IRLR 331, EAT).

3. In *French v Barclays Bank plc* [1998] IRLR 646, CA, the Court found that the employer had breached the implied term by **changing the terms of a bridging loan** made to F when he relocated, as required by the bank, from one branch to another. The housing market had collapsed and F was unable to sell his house at the agreed price. The bank demanded that he accept a lower sum or pay interest on the bridging loan.

4. **Providing** an employee's prospective employer with **a reference** that reveals complaints made about the employee, of which he is unaware, amounts to a breach of the implied term (*TSB Bank plc v Harris* [1999] UKEAT 1145_97_0112).

5. **Sexual harassment** can amount to a breach of the implied term (*Reed and anor v Stedman* [1999] UKEAT 443_97_1102).

6. Dismissing the employee in circumstances which would **deprive** him of his **contractual health benefits**, such as permanent health insurance benefit, may amount to a breach of the implied term (¶1174) (*Aspden v Webbs Poultry and Meat Group (Holdings) Ltd* [1996] IRLR 521, QBD; *Villella v MFI Furniture Centres Ltd* [1999] IRLR 468, QBD).

7. **Suspending** an employee pending the outcome of an investigation into an allegation of child sexual abuse amounted to a breach of the term (*Gogay v Hertfordshire County Council* [2000] IRLR 703, CA).

8. **Offering a particular benefit** (a new contract) to an entire class of employees except for one amounted to a breach of the term (*Transco plc (formerly BG plc) v O'Brien* [2002] IRLR 444, CA).

9. Seeking to **impose new terms and conditions of employment** in an aggressive manner, giving only perfunctory and misleading explanations as to the effect of the new terms, amounted to a breach of the implied term of trust and confidence (*Cantor Fitzgerald International v Bird and others* [2002] IRLR 867, QBD).

10. **Inviting an employee to resign** after the employee failed to improve following a warning for poor performance with the suggestion that the employee would be treated favourably in respect of her compromise/severance package should she tender her resignation (*Billington v Michael Hunter and Sons Ltd* [2003] UKEAT 0578_03_1610).

11. **Failing to notify** an employee of a **vacancy** that had **arisen during her maternity leave** if the vacancy is one for which the employee believed she would have been suitable (*Visa International Service Association v Paul* [2004] IRLR 42, EAT). In this case, it was irrelevant that, had the employee applied, she would not have been short-listed for the position in any event.

12. Sex discrimination coupled with a **refusal of a flexible working request** is capable of being a breach of the term but will not inevitably be so (*Shaw v CCL Ltd* [2008] IRLR 284, EAT).

1249 The duty of trust and confidence does not alter the premise that **neither party** to the contract is **obliged to disclose his breach** of the contract to the other (*Bell v Lever Bros Ltd* [1932] AC 161, HL, although see ¶1218). For example, when entering into compromise agreements (¶9315) with an employee, the employer is not obliged by the duty of trust and confidence to make any disclosure that it has previously acted in breach of that implied term (e.g. by carrying on a dishonest and corrupt business) (*Bank of Credit and Commerce International SA v Ali* [1999] EWHC 846 (Ch)).

1250 The employee will be entitled to **damages** in respect of his financial loss (¶1725).

1251 The **rules of construction** of a contract are unchanged and there is no positive obligation on the courts to construe contracts of employment in a way which furthers mutual trust (*Hill v General Accident Fire & Life Assurance Corporation plc* [1998] IRLR 641, CS).

6. Indemnity for costs

1255 The employer is generally expected to pay for or reimburse costs/expenses incurred by the employee in the **course of his employment**.

7. References

1257 There is **no general implied term entitling** an employee/ex-employee to a reference.

If, however, **one is provided**, the employer owes the employee/ex-employee a duty of care to ensure that it is true, **accurate** and fair (¶¶8324+). In such circumstances, there is an implied term that the reference will be compiled (and the information on which it is based will be verified) with **reasonable care**. If it is not, the employee/ex-employee may have a remedy for negligent misstatement (*Spring v Guardian Assurance plc* [1994] IRLR 460, HL). The employer must also take care not to breach the implied term of **trust and confidence** when providing a reference (¶1241) and ensure that it is not discriminatory.

> MEMO POINTS This duty of care may last for a number of years after the employee has left the employer, for example in a recent case on negligent misstatement the High Court found a former employer liable for information about an ex-employee given 6 years after the end of their employment relationship (*McKie v Swindon College* [2011] EWHC 469 (QB) and again see ¶8324 for more details).

8. Notice

1260 Where the contract is silent as to the amount of notice required to terminate the employment, it is an implied term that **reasonable notice** of termination will be given (¶8129). This may be greater than the statutory minimum in some cases.

1261 Where the employer has reserved the right to make a **payment in lieu of notice**, the employment will terminate immediately if the employer exercises it.

V. Other terms

A. From collective agreements

1270 An employer (or an employer's association) may reach an agreement with a trade union. Such an agreement or certain terms of it may be incorporated into the individual worker's contract. See ¶¶7363+ for the **scope** of such agreements, the **method** of negotiating them, and their legal **enforceability**.

B. From workforce agreements

1293 As well as making agreements with a recognised trade union, an employer can also make agreements with relevant members of the workforce.
A workforce agreement can be **used to**:
– partially exclude, or change the calculation period for, the working time rules (¶¶3660, 3681, 3688, 3699);
– alter or exclude some procedural requirements for annual leave (¶4000);
– make arrangements to implement the parental leave rules (¶4650); or
– extend the validity of fixed-term contracts beyond the 4-year period (¶1985).

C. Work rules

1295 There is a **distinction** between collective agreements (which result from negotiations and agreement between the employer and the trade union) and workforce agreements (which result from agreement between the employer and relevant members of the workforce) and work rules (which are unilateral, made only by the employer) (*Cadoux v Central Regional Council* [1986] IRLR 131, CS). The employer is entitled to introduce work rules for the conduct of his employees within the scope of the contract. A set of **rules, a policy or a code of practice** circulated by the employer (and often included in the staff handbook (¶1480)) may be incorporated into an individual's contract of employment if it can reasonably be inferred from the circumstances that the parties must have intended the rules to become contractual terms. To avoid any uncertainty, it is **good practice** for introductory wording expressly to state whether the provisions are binding or not. See ¶¶1482-3 for further details.

VI. Unenforceable terms

A. Illegal terms and terms contrary to public policy

A contract may be **unenforceable** by the parties if its terms are: 1305
– directly **prohibited by statute** (e.g. the contract may be illegal because the employee is a child (¶4970), or because the employee does not have a legal right to work in the UK (¶750));
– **unlawful** (e.g. to defraud HMRC);
– **contrary to public policy** (e.g. for an immoral purpose, such as the procurement of prostitutes); or
– lawful, but the contract is **performed illegally** (e.g. where the employer in practice makes additional undisclosed cash payments to make up for the amount of tax and national insurance deducted).

> EXAMPLE In *Vakante v Addey and Stanhope School Governing Body* [2005] ICR 231, a claimant, V, was a Croatian national who had resided in the UK since 1992. When his leave to remain expired, he applied for asylum. While V's asylum application was under consideration he was precluded from working in the UK without a permit. V nevertheless obtained employment as a graduate trainee teacher, from which he was dismissed 8 months later. V complained that he had suffered discrimination on racial grounds. The CA held that V was prevented from pursuing his complaints on the ground that they were so closely connected with his conduct in illegally obtaining work that no claim could be brought.

Relevant factors when assessing enforceability

Whether a party can enforce a contract is likely to **depend on** the factors set out below. 1306

Parties' intentions and awareness If the parties intend an otherwise lawful contract to 1307 be **used for unlawful means**, it will be illegal and void (*Tomlinson v Dick Evans U Drive Ltd* [1978] IRLR 77, EAT). Similarly, an employee who **lies** to the Contributions Agency regarding the nature of his work in order to maintain the benefits of self-employed status (even though he is an employee) will taint his contract with illegality and this deceit will prevent him from claiming unfair dismissal (*Soteriou v Ultrachem* [2004] IRLR 870, EAT).

It is irrelevant that the parties did not realise that their actions were illegal (*Salvesen v Simons* [1994] IRLR 52, EAT); "ignorance of the law cannot excuse them" (*Miller v Karlinski* [1945] 62 TLR 85, CA). However, where the parties make an **honest mistake** made in good faith about the nature of their working relationship and treat it as one of self-employment, this will not, **in the absence of misrepresentation**, make the contract illegal and in such a case the workers can later assert that they are employees and claim unfair dismissal (*Enfield Technical Services Ltd v Payne; Grace v BF Components Ltd* [2008] ICR 1423, CA; *Young and Woods Ltd v West* [1980] IRLR 201, CA).

> **EXAMPLE**
> 1. In *Young and Woods Ltd v West*, the Court held that the label applied by the parties as to the classification of the contract was wrong. The contract was, however, not void for illegality as the parties had made an honest mistake. HMRC had a duty to reclaim tax deductions that were granted to Mr West as self-employed, but he was nevertheless entitled to claim unfair dismissal.
> 2. In *Enfield Technical Services Ltd v Payne; Grace v BF Components Ltd*, an engineer suggested to his employer that he should be employed on a contract for services rather than as an employee. HMRC accepted that he was self-employed, with the result that he paid tax at a substantially reduced rate. The engineer was subsequently dismissed and brought a claim of unfair dismissal, which is a remedy only open to employees. The employer argued that if the worker had indeed been an employee, it would follow that he had illegally misrepresented his status to HMRC and the contract should be unenforceable. However, the Court of Appeal held that the contract was enforceable. There is often a fine dividing line between those properly defined as employees and those who are self-employed, and without some misrepresentation or some attempt to conceal the true facts of the relationship the contract was legal as the parties had in good faith thought that the employment status could be legitimately considered to fall into one category, even though in fact it fell into another.

> **MEMO POINTS** Where a scheme's only purpose is to **reduce the amount of deductions** that ought to be paid it will be lawful if it is entered into in good faith, constitutes a proper method of reducing tax and is/will be disclosed to HMRC (*Lightfoot v D & J Sporting Ltd* [1995] UKEAT 739_95_1910).

1309 Participation in the illegality The employee may be unable to enforce the contract if he was a party to or knew of the employer's illegality (*Newland v Simons and Willer (Hairdressers) Ltd* [1981] IRLR 359, EAT; *Bakersfield Entertainment Ltd v Church and Stuart* [2005] UKEAT 0523_05_0411).

Whether the contract is unenforceable will depend on the following factors:
– whether, looked at subjectively, the employee in fact **knew or came to know** of the illegal act (and not whether the employee ought to have known of that illegal act), although in cases of statutory illegality the knowledge of the parties is irrelevant;
– the extent to which the employee **colluded** and actively participated with the employer in allowing the illegality to take place;
– whether the employee **benefits from** the illegality; and
– the **relative conduct** of the parties.

> **EXAMPLE**
> **Unenforceable**
> 1. In *Zarkasi v Anindita and anor* [2012] UKEAT 0400_11_1801, Z, an Indonesian national knowingly assumed a false identity to obtain a passport and tourist visa which enabled her to enter the UK to perform domestic work. The deception was orchestrated by her UK employers, but she was a willing participant. Upon arrival in the UK, Z was expected to sleep on the sofa, paid less than the national minimum wage and was discouraged from going out of the family home. She worked for 2 years before making a number of claims before an employment tribunal (including unfair dismissal). The EAT upheld the tribunal's decision that the contract was illegal and unenforceable.
> **Comment**: It is clear from this decision that the key factor here was the employee's willing participation in the illegal entry to the UK and illegal employment contract; if an individual is truly trafficked and involuntarily adheres to a contract e.g. for fear of violence, different considerations might arise. A victim of trafficking may also be able to bring non-employment claims of false imprisonment, trespass, assault or harassment.
> 2. In *Tomlinson v Dick Evans U Drive Ltd* [1978] IRLR 77, EAT, T knew that no tax was being deducted from the weekly cash payment and she did nothing to complain. She lost her right to a redundancy payment and her protection from unfair dismissal.
>
> **Enforceable**
> 1. In *Wheeler v Quality Deep Ltd (trading as Thai Royale Restaurant)* [2004] EWCA Civ 1085, W, a Thai national waitress working in the UK whose English was poor, was deemed not to have knowledge of the fact that her employer had not deducted tax and NIC from her pay and so she could bring an unfair dismissal claim.
> 2. In *Hall v Woolston Hall Leisure Ltd* [2000] IRLR 578, CA, the Court of Appeal found that H had acquiesced in the illegality only because she was powerless to change the situation. Mere knowledge and acquiescence without more participation were insufficient to bar her from enforcing the contract.
> 3. In *Hewcastle Catering Ltd v Ahmed and Elkamah* [1991] IRLR 473, CA, the employer involved the employees in his scheme to evade VAT. The employees subsequently gave evidence to Customs and Excise (now HMRC), and were dismissed by the employer as a result. Despite their involvement in the

illegality, the Court of Appeal allowed their unfair dismissal claim, in part because they had not benefited from the fraud themselves, and further because their conduct was minor and insignificant compared to the employer's.

4. In *Cannon t/a Barkway Park Golf Club v Sadler* [2001] UKEAT 0385_01_1807, S received a taxable benefit in the form of a car which she did not declare to the Inland Revenue (now HMRC). However, she had not participated in any fraud or dishonesty and there was no scheme intended to defraud the Revenue and so she could bring an unfair dismissal claim.

Infrequent or incidental illegality The **duration or frequency** of the illegality may be relevant. The issue will depend on the particular circumstances, including the amount and frequency of the payments and why they are made. A court will also consider whether the illegality is **merely collateral or incidental** to the employment contract. **1311**

EXAMPLE

1. In *Cannon t/a Barkway Park Golf Club v Sadler* [2001] UKEAT 0385_01_1807, the provision of the car was not central to S's unfair dismissal claim but amounted to a collateral illegality which did not taint the whole contract.

2. In *Annandale Engineering v Samson* [1994] IRLR 59, EAT, the EAT held that an occasional, irregular payment made when the employer's greyhound won a race, and which did not form part of S's regular remuneration (as defined in the contract or implicit in its performance), did not render the whole contract illegal/unenforceable where tax was not deducted.

3. In *McConnell v Bolik* [1979] IRLR 422, EAT, B, without the knowledge of the employer, failed to disclose on his tax return to the Inland Revenue (now HMRC) details of a particular benefit he had received from the employer. B's failure was a matter for him and the Revenue, and did not make the contract of service illegal.

4. In *Coral Leisure Group Ltd v Barnett* [1981] IRLR 204, EAT, B, in the course of his employment, procured and paid for prostitutes for his employer's customers. The EAT held that this immoral purpose was collateral to the contract as B did not enter into the employment with the purpose of doing that unlawful act. B was therefore able to bring a complaint of unfair dismissal.

Consequences of illegality

If **part of a contract is illegal**, the whole arrangement will be affected. The courts will not readily sever an offending term so that the remainder of the contract can be enforced (*Miller v Karlinski* [1945] 62 TLR 85, CA). **1313**

A contract can be illegal **throughout** or for **part of its duration** only. Statutory continuity of employment is not preserved during the period of illegality (¶1010). While a contract is illegal, rights cannot normally be claimed or enforced. For example, the rights to bring an unfair dismissal claim or a claim for a redundancy payment depend on the applicant being an employee working under a valid contract of service (*Tomlinson v Dick Evans U Drive Ltd*; *Bakersfield Entertainment Ltd v Church and Stuart* [2005] UKEAT 0523_05_0411). It may also be possible to **sever the unlawful work** from the lawful if the illegal parts can be treated separately from the legal parts of the contract, so that an applicant may be able to bring a claim in relation to the latter (*Blue Chip Trading Ltd v Helbawi* [2009] IRLR 128, EAT). **1314**

EXAMPLE In *Blue Chip Trading Ltd v Helbawi*, a foreign student worked as a security guard under a visa which restricted his hours of work during term time but not in the holidays. During term time he worked for more hours than permitted by the terms of his student visa. He made a complaint that he had not been paid the minimum wage, which the employer defended by arguing that the contract was an illegal one and therefore unenforceable. The tribunal decided that the whole contract was not illegal and the case should be allowed to proceed. The reasons for the decision were that the employer had failed to check the worker's entitlement to work in the UK, the claimant was not always in breach of the visa conditions and workers should be paid at least minimum wage as a matter of public policy. The EAT overturned the decision, holding that it was incorrect to say that the whole contract was legal in these circumstances. However, it was prepared to treat the two parts of the contract separately, so as to allow the worker to enforce payment of the minimum wage during holiday periods when he had not been in breach of his visa conditions.

1315 Case law indicates that, if a contract is "tainted with illegality", an employee can bring a **discrimination claim** (as such a claim is based in tort, not in contract, and only relies on the contract to establish an employment relationship) (*Leighton v (1) Michael and (2) Charalambous* [1995] UKEAT 992_94_2206), unless the claim is inextricably bound up with the illegal conduct (*Hall v Woolston Hall Leisure Ltd*, see example at ¶1309).

> EXAMPLE
> **Not inextricably bound up with the illegal conduct**
> In *Leighton v (1) Michael and (2) Charalambous*, L was permitted to bring a claim of sexual harassment and victimisation despite the fact that her employers were not deducting income tax or national insurance contributions from her wages, which made her contract illegal.
>
> **Inextricably bound up with the illegal conduct**
> In *Hounga v Allen (née Aboyade-Cole)* [2012] EWCA Civ 609, H dishonestly obtained a visa to gain access to the UK so that she could work illegally as a live-in au pair and housekeeper. She worked for her employing family in the UK for around 18 months before they eventually dismissed her and threw her out of the house. She brought unfair dismissal and race claims against her employing family. The unfair dismissal claim was unsuccessful because of illegality, but the tribunal and EAT allowed her discrimination claim. The Court of Appeal overturned the finding of discrimination. Both H and her employer knew that the employment contract was illegal from its inception; H had been a willing participant in the illegality. The basis for the race discrimination claim was that H's employers had treated her badly because she was an illegal immigrant with no right to work in the UK. Inevitably, therefore, the discrimination claim was inextricably bound up with the illegality. The Court could not condone the illegality by allowing H to rely upon her own illegal actions in support of her discrimination case and her discrimination claim was barred by reason of illegality.

B. Other unenforceable terms

Discriminatory terms

1330 Terms that are discriminatory will be unenforceable against the victim of discrimination and, on application from anyone with an interest in the contract, the county court can order that the term be removed or modified (ss 142, 143 EqA 2010).

No contracting out

1335 An employee or employer cannot usually contract out of any **applicable employment legislation**. However, where a conciliation officer is involved in **settling** certain claims or a valid **compromise** agreement has been signed (in respect of those claims which may be settled this way), contracting out will be permitted in those circumstances (¶9203).

> EXAMPLE The Public Interest Disclosure Act 1998 (the "whistleblowing" legislation which amended the ERA 1996) states that any provision in an agreement, including a contract of employment, will be void so far as it purports to preclude the worker from making a protected disclosure. Therefore, in order to ensure that a confidentiality provision can be enforced, it should expressly state that it does not restrict or limit the worker's right to make such a disclosure.

Unfair Contract Terms Act 1977 (UCTA)

1340 The effect of UCTA is to make certain terms always unenforceable, and certain others subject to a test of reasonableness, and until quite recently case law suggested that UCTA could apply to contracts of employment. However, the Court of Appeal has since held that UCTA does not apply to a contract term regarding an employee's remuneration and considered that previous cases on the application of UCTA to employment contracts were not entirely satisfactory and not binding (*Commerzbank AG v Keen* [2007] IRLR 132, CA). The Court firmly held that an employee does not deal as a consumer with his employer in respect of pay for work. The Court went on to hold that neither does the employee deal with his employer on his employer's written standard terms of business. In this case, the employer's business was banking and employee bonus terms could not be said to be standard terms of the business of banking, they were terms of remuneration of certain employees of the bank. Following this decision it is unlikely that UCTA will apply in relation to any aspect of an employee's contract of employment. Only if, under the contract of employment, the employer supplies services or goods to the employee for his use, could the employee to whom they are supplied for his consumption reasonably be regarded as a consumer of the goods or services supplied and consequently be entitled to the protection afforded by UCTA. Further, it should be noted that the Unfair Terms in Consumer Contracts Regulations, based on the corresponding European Directive, also do not apply to contracts of employment (SI 1999/2083).

Terms in restraint of trade

1355 Terms that impose restrictions on an employee's activities after the termination of his employment will be unenforceable if their main purpose is to prevent competition. The term may be enforceable if it goes no further than is strictly necessary to protect the employer's legitimate business interests, such as confidential information or trade secrets, and goodwill. These issues are discussed in detail at ¶2500.

Terms restricting right to take industrial action

1360 Such terms cannot form part of an individual employee's contract of employment unless certain conditions are satisfied (¶7556).

SECTION 3

Information to be provided in writing

1400 There is no statutory requirement to have a written contract but the employer is obliged to provide certain written particulars of the contract terms to the employee, so that he is **aware of the main terms** of his employment.

1401 It is **common practice** to have a written contract of employment, which includes all the information that the employer is obliged to provide in writing, as well as other, non-obligatory, terms. A model contract of employment for general staff is provided at ¶9910.

There may be **other provisions** relating to the employment, such as codes of practice, or policies and procedures, which may be contained in a staff handbook. These may be contractual terms or may be mere instructions or guidelines as to how the employee should carry out his job (¶1480).

Status of written particulars

1402 The statement of particulars does not constitute the contract of employment (*Robertson and Jackson v British Gas Corporation* [1983] IRLR 302, CA). It does, however, provide strong (but not conclusive) **evidence** of the terms of that contract (*System Floors (UK) Ltd v Daniel* [1981] IRLR 475, EAT). Given that it is the employer who issues the statement, it is harder for him to prove that the statement does not reflect the contractual terms. If, on the other hand, the employee has good evidence of the terms of the contract, the statement is considered to be "persuasive" only, and refutable by the employee's evidence.

---

1. Obligation to provide written particulars

1405 There is no requirement for a contract of employment to be in writing, but the employer **must provide** written details of the main terms and conditions of employment to all employees whose **employment lasts for** at least 1 month (ss 1, 198 ERA 1996). This obligation is commonly referred to as the requirement to provide a "statutory statement" or "written particulars" of terms and conditions of employment.

If, after 1 month's employment, the **employment ends** before the statement is provided, the employee is still entitled to receive one (s 2(6) ERA 1996).

A **model statement** of particulars is provided at ¶9900.

1406 As mentioned above, it is common practice for employers to **include** the obligatory particulars in a written contract, which is signed by both the employer and the employee. This is now expressly permitted by the legislation (s 7A ERA 1996 as inserted by s 37 EA 2002). The particulars may form the **foundation of the contract**, with non-obligatory terms being added as required by the employer or the nature of the job. A model contract is provided at ¶9910.

Some employers, however, find that the statement of particulars is sufficient, in which case it will become a written contract of employment if **both parties agree** that the **stated terms are correct** (for example, by signing the statement to that effect) (*Gascol Conversions Ltd v J W Mercer* [1974] IRLR 155, CA).

The statement does not become a contract by virtue only of the employee's **acknowledgement of receipt** (*System Floors (UK) Ltd v Daniel*) or **mere acquiescence** (*Aparau v Iceland Frozen Foods plc* [1995] UKEAT 196_93_0910). In *Aparau*, A did not sign the statement. She did, however, continue to work according to its terms for more than 12 months without objection. This was not enough for the EAT to find that she had impliedly accepted those terms. The statement did not, therefore, constitute the contract.

1407 Subject to the time limit for provision of the particulars as set out below, employers can give the statement in **instalments** (ss 1(2), 2(4) ERA 1996).

However, certain particulars must be **included in a single document**. These are:
– the identity of the parties;
– the start date and date of continuous employment;
– job title;
– place of work;
– hours of work;
– pay details; and
– holiday entitlement.

1408 For the following particulars, the statement may **refer** the employee to **another document**, as long as this is reasonably accessible, i.e. one which he has reasonable opportunities of reading in the course of his employment, or which is made reasonably accessible to him in some other way, such as the staff handbook, intranet, or the employer's notice/bulletin board, if this is accessible to all employees (s 6 ERA 1996):
– the applicable notice period (for this particular, the employer can refer the employee to the relevant statutory provisions or collective agreement if these are reasonably accessible to him);
– sickness;
– pension;
– disciplinary rules; and
– dismissal and disciplinary procedures (although the written particulars must at least identify (i) the person (by description or otherwise) to whom the employee can apply if he is dissatisfied with any disciplinary decision or decision to dismiss him or if he has a grievance, and (ii) how that application should be made, including details of appeal stages).

Timing

1410 The statement (whether provided in a single document or in instalments) must be provided **within** 2 calendar months of the beginning of the employment (s 1(2) ERA 1996). A contract of employment or letter of engagement given to an employee **before** the beginning of his employment is acceptable (s 7B ERA 1996, as inserted by s 37 EA 2002).

The particulars marked with an asterisk in the table below should be correct as at a specified date not more than 7 days before they are given to the employee (to ensure they are as up to date as possible) (s 1(4) ERA 1996).

If, before the end of the 2-month period, the employee is due to go **overseas to work** for more than 1 month, the statement must be provided before he leaves the UK (s 2(5) ERA 1996). Similarly, if he is posted abroad for more than 1 month during the course of his employment, details of the posting must be provided within 1 month of the change to his employment or prior to the departure, if earlier.

1411

2. Contents

The statutory statement must contain the following particulars:

1420

Particulars	ERA 1996
Identity of the parties	s 1(3)(a)
Start date	s 1(3)(b)
Date continuous employment began (¶1045)	s 1(3)(c)
Job title or brief description of main characteristics of work*	s 1(4)(f)
Applicable notice period (¶8127)*	s 1(4)(e)
Expected duration (temporary employees) or expiry date (fixed-term contracts)	s 1(4)(g)
Place of work or indication that employee may work at various places, a list of those places (where known) and employer's address*	s 1(4)(h)
Hours of work, including terms relating to normal working hours (and overtime)*	s 1(4)(c)
Scale/rate of remuneration and intervals of pay*	s 1(4)(a)(b)
Holiday entitlement, including public holidays, holiday pay and sufficient information to allow precise calculation of entitlement (including on termination)*	s 1(4)(d)(i)
Sickness provisions, including terms relating to incapacity due to sickness or injury, and details of any sick pay provisions*	s 1(4)(d)(ii)
Pension provisions*	s 1(4)(d)(iii)
Contracting out certificate [1]	s 3(5)
Disciplinary rules [2]	s 3(1)(a)
Dismissal, disciplinary and grievance procedures [3]	s 3(1)(aa), (b)
Collective agreements directly affecting terms, and details of parties where employer is not a party	s 1(4)(j)
Work outside UK for more than 1 month, including duration, currency of remuneration, other pay and benefits, and terms relating to return to UK	s 1(4)(k)

* Must be correct as at specified date, which must be no later than 7 days before the date they are provided.
1. Since 6 April 2012, contracting out will no longer be possible through a money-purchase (defined-contribution) occupational pension scheme, a personal pension or a stakeholder pension, and those who are contracted out will be brought back into the S2P. For the time being, contracting out through an occupational salary-related (defined-benefit) scheme will still be allowed. Contracting out is now rare, however, at present, statutory statements should still state whether there is a contracting out certificate in force.
2. These requirements (i.e. the disciplinary rules and the procedures) do not apply to rules, disciplinary decisions, decisions to dismiss, grievances or procedures relating to health or safety at work (s 3(2) ERA 1996, as amended by s 35 EA 2002).
3. With regard to the disciplinary and grievance procedures, the statutory statement must, in all cases, identify to whom and how a grievance or complaint about a disciplinary decision or any decision to dismiss an employee should be made (including details of appeal stages).
Note that the exemption for small employers who employ fewer than 20 employees on the date the employment began has been removed.

The above list of information to be provided is not exhaustive – the statement must contain particulars of all of the **essential elements** of the contract (*Lange v Georg Schünemann GmbH* [2001] IRLR 244, ECJ).

1421

Statement of no terms

1425 The parties are not obliged to agree terms in relation to the statutory statement (*Morley v Heritage plc* [1993] IRLR 400, CA). If, in fact, there are **no terms relating to a required particular** (for example, if the employer does not offer any contractual sick pay above the employee's statutory entitlement), the statement should state this (s 2(1) ERA 1996). Applicable disciplinary rules and disciplinary or grievance procedures must nevertheless be stated.

> EXAMPLE In *Morley v Heritage plc*, M was claiming a payment for untaken holiday accrued at the time of the termination of his employment on the basis that the employer was legally required to provide sufficient detail of any terms relating to **holiday pay** so that any such entitlement could be precisely calculated. The Court held that no such provision need be implied into contracts of employment merely because the legislation recognises that employment contracts can include such a provision. Note that the regulations on working time now provide for such a payment to be made (¶4000).

3. Changes to written particulars

1450 If there are any changes to the statement (for example, a salary increase) the employer must, **within** 1 month of the change, give the employee a **written statement** containing details of the change (s 4 ERA 1996). For those terms where there have been no changes, the new statement may refer back to the previous one, indicating that there has been no change.

The change must be notified in a **single document** (not in instalments) but reference can be made to another reasonably accessible document for the details of the change, as for the original statement (¶1408).

If the change relates to the **name** or **identity of the employer** (where the employee's continuity of employment (¶1010) is preserved), the employer does not need to provide a new statement but must notify the employee in writing of that change and, in the case of a change in the employer's identity, give the date the employee's period of continuous employment began (s 4(6) ERA 1996).

> MEMO POINTS If the change involves a change to any **contractual term**, the employer should obtain the employee's consent (¶1601).

4. Enforcement and remedies

Obtaining a statement of terms

1460 If the employer **fails to provide** a statement, provides an **incomplete** one, or **fails to notify** the employee of a **change**, the employee can apply for a determination (i.e. request a reference from the tribunal) as to what particulars should have been provided (s 11(1) ERA 1996). If the statement provided is incorrect, either the employer or the employee can apply to the tribunal, which can affirm, amend or replace the existing particulars (s 11(2) ERA 1996). If it does, the employer is deemed to have provided the corrected version (s 12 ERA 1996). In both cases, there is no right of damages for an employee under such an action, but the determination may give the employee continuing financial advantages e.g. a right to paid sick leave or a contractual right to overtime.

> MEMO POINTS Where an employee has been dismissed, but he has no other claims that can be brought to a tribunal (for example because he has been employed for under 1 year and therefore cannot bring a claim for unfair dismissal), he cannot seek a declaration of his terms as there is no purpose or benefit in setting out his terms and conditions in such cases (*Scott-Davies v Redgate Medical Services* [2006] UKEAT 0273_06_1108).

1462 **Determining or amending particulars** When determining what particulars are missing or how existing particulars ought to be amended, the tribunal **must decide** whether the term had been agreed orally or by necessary implication (*Mears v Safecar Security Ltd* [1982] IRLR 183, CA). If so, it should be included in the statement. If not, the tribunal is entitled to take account of all the facts and circumstances, in particular the subsequent statements or conduct of the parties and, from that, infer the term necessarily agreed by them.

The tribunal's role is **limited to** identifying and declaring the particulars that ought to have been included, and does not extend to interpreting any ambiguous ones (*Construction Industry Training Board v Leighton* [1978] IRLR 60, EAT). In the absence of both express and implied agreement, the tribunal should not invent a term for the parties (*Fagland v British Telecommunications plc* [1992] IRLR 323, CA).

Remedies

1465 If, **during the course of certain tribunal proceedings** (including unfair dismissal and discrimination claims) in which the employment tribunal finds in favour of the employee, it becomes evident that the employer had **failed to provide**:
– a written statement;
– a complete or accurate statement; or
– notification of a change to the written statement,

at the date the proceedings were begun, the tribunal must award a **minimum award** of 2 weeks' pay to the employee and may, if it considers it just and equitable to do so, increase the award to 4 weeks' pay (s 38 EA 2002). This award will be in addition to any damages in respect of the employee's claim which was the subject of the proceedings.

A week's pay is subject to a **statutory cap** (¶2923). For details of how a week's pay is calculated, see ¶¶2920+.

SECTION 4

Staff handbook

1480 The staff handbook (also known as "employee handbook", "company handbook", or "company manual") is principally a source of **rules** of conduct, employee behaviour, rights and miscellaneous information about the company that are normally **non-contractual**. In addition to non-contractual provisions, the handbook may also contain the **statutory statement of particulars** (¶1400) and **contractual terms** of employment (for example, terms relating to holiday entitlement or a policy which the employer wishes his employees to be legally bound by, such as equal opportunities).

The company's rules, policies and procedures make clear what conduct is acceptable/unacceptable, and ensure that employees' conduct and performance meet minimum standards. Policies can also help the employer to comply with his statutory duties, such as his health and safety obligations, and an effective implementation of these policies may provide a defence to employee claims, such as harassment and discrimination. Breach of these provisions may therefore be treated as a disciplinary/capability issue, with disciplinary action being taken as appropriate (¶6538), unless the provision is contractual (either expressly or through custom and practice, see below) in which case any breach (by either the employer or the employee) will give rise to a claim for breach of contract (¶1700).

MEMO POINTS Rules in staff handbooks are normally non-contractual so that, if the employer does not follow them in every instance, employees cannot litigate on the basis of breach of contract (unless of course the rules have become contractual in any event due to custom and practice). It is therefore important for employers to think carefully as to whether there are any aspects of the staff handbook that they would like to be contractual for any reason (such as to allow them to rely on a breach of contract argument themselves or to highlight their significance over and above other rules) and to clearly identify them as such.

1482 Employers must **make clear** (by an express statement where appropriate) which parts of the handbook are contractually binding (¶1155), as an employer should obtain his employees' consent to vary contractual terms (¶1601), and breach of such terms will entitle the innocent party to a remedy for breach of contract (¶1700). It is important to note that even if a particular provision or policy is labelled by the parties as "non-contractual", it is possible for such a provision or policy to be deemed contractual (through "custom and practice") if it has been followed without exception for a substantial period of time (¶1180).

1483 In the **absence of express wording**, a provision will be contractually binding if it should properly be regarded as conferring a right. If, on the other hand, it should properly be regarded as merely setting out guidelines on good practice (*Wandsworth Borough Council v D'Silva and another* [1998] IRLR 193, CA), it will not be binding.

EXAMPLE

Contractually binding

1. In *Dal v Orr* [1980] IRLR 413, EAT, the EAT found that rules in the employees' handbook gave the employer a contractual right to alter shift systems and hours of work. The employer was therefore not in breach of contract when he did so.
2. In contrast to *Grant v South-West Trains Ltd* (see below), in *Taylor v Secretary of State for Scotland* [2000] IRLR 502, HL, the Court accepted the tribunal's earlier finding that an equal opportunities policy (which included an undertaking not to discriminate on the grounds of age) was contractual as it had been notified by a circular in the same way as changes and additions to contractual terms were notified.
3. In *Keeley v Fosroc International Ltd* [2006] IRLR 961, CA, a clause regarding contractual redundancy pay was set out in a staff handbook as follows "Those employees with 2 or more years' continuous service are entitled to receive an enhanced redundancy payment from the Company, which is paid tax free to a limit of £30,000." In speaking clearly of an entitlement, the Court held that the term should properly be regarded as conferring a right, and it consequently had contractual effect.
4. In *Harlow v Artemis International Corporation Ltd* [2008] IRLR 629, HC, an employee was found to be entitled to an enhanced redundancy payment under a scheme set out in a staff handbook expressly referred to in his original contract of employment as setting out his terms and conditions. Over a period of time, the printed staff handbook was discontinued and material relating to the redundancy scheme migrated to a folder on the company's intranet. Changes were made to the policy wording over time but not specifically consented to by the claimant. The language of the scheme (as amended) did not actually impose an obligation to make an enhanced payment, but the company had done so in practice for many years. The fact that payments made in the latter part of the period were expressed to be ex gratia was not material. The claimant was entitled to an enhanced redundancy payment as a contractual right.

Mere guidelines

1. In *Grant v South-West Trains Ltd* [1998] IRLR 188, QBD, SWT adopted an equal opportunities policy which referred to its "commitment" not to discriminate on grounds of sexual preference and its "aim" to eliminate unfair discrimination. G's contract provided for an opposite sex spouse to receive travel concessions. G's partner was of the same sex and SWT refused to provide travel concessions for her. The Court held that the equal opportunities policy had not been incorporated, but was a statement of policy in "general, idealistic terms, and not of contractual obligations". There was no evidence of an intention to be bound, and the policy imposed no obligations on SWT. The Court also said that the policy could not, in any case, be imported into the contract to override a clear, express provision.
2. In *Wandsworth Borough Council v D'Silva and another* (see above), the council revised its code of practice on staff sickness to introduce tighter absence monitoring procedures and more frequent reviews of long-term absence. The Court held that the language of the code did not provide an appropriate foundation on which to base contractual rights but rather aimed to provide guidance. The sickness procedure was designed to be flexible, and this flexibility was inconsistent with the creation of contractual rights. The employers were therefore entitled unilaterally to amend the code.
3. In *Secretary of State for Employment v ASLEF (No 2)* [1972] ICR 19, CA, the Court held that if the staff handbook, for example, contains numerous sets of rules, the courts might conclude that the rules are instructions as to how the employee should carry out his contractual obligations, rather than being contractual obligations in themselves.

1485 An example of a staff handbook is given in outline at ¶1495 below. The handbook can be used as a source of reference to provide **information on the organisation**, and is an important communication tool, allowing the company to impart a sense of its culture, ethos and goals. As such, the handbook can play an important role in the induction of new employees (¶910), helping them to learn about the company and settle in to their new role. The handbook also serves a practical purpose, informing staff of the benefits, amenities and services available to them.

1486 Some of the **statutory statement of particulars** (for example, sickness provisions and information on pensions (¶1408) can be provided in a reasonably accessible document such as the staff handbook. Further, it may be practical to include **provisions of general application** (such as dismissal, discipline and grievance procedures, sick pay and pensions) in the handbook, with variations (if any) applicable to particular employees or groups of employees set out in their individual contracts or issued as a supplement. However, where terms are particular to one individual (such as salary or individually agreed bonus arrangements), they should be included in the individual's contract of employment.

1487 The handbook may contain **rules, policies and procedures** or these may be issued separately. These should be easily accessible to employees, as it is important that they are known and understood by all members of staff. These rules will vary from organisation to organisation, depending on the particular circumstances. It is advisable for them to be in writing, as there is then less scope for misunderstanding.

1489 **Creating a staff handbook** When compiling a new staff handbook, employers should consider the following:
– consultation;
– design and format;
– issue; and
– updating.

It may be useful to **consult** with:
– trade union and/or employee representatives;
– employees/managers with responsibility for particular areas covered in the handbook; and
– solicitors/the in-house legal department to ensure compliance with the law.

The **language** used should be simple and easy to read. The handbook should be clear and concise, avoiding too much detail. The **presentation** of information should be user-friendly and engaging, with use of diagrams, charts and pictures where appropriate. An index should be included for ease of use. Consideration should be given as to whether it may be necessary to provide **translations** for non-native English speakers.

It is good practice for the staff handbook to be accessible to all staff. As technology advances, it is becoming more common for the handbook to be issued on the company intranet. If the handbook contains the statutory statement of particulars (¶1400), it must be **reasonably accessible** to all staff, which may require a hard copy to be distributed.

It may be useful to provide space in the back cover for supplements or amendments to be added. Loose-leaf formats may prove cost effective in that they can be easily updated. The handbook could include space for employees to make their own notes, either in the margin or at the back of the book.

Before issuing the handbook, the employer may consider asking a number of employees to give **feedback** on content, style and format.

To ensure that all employees can access the handbook, the safest course may be to **issue** a copy to all employees when they join the company. It is advisable for employees to be asked to return a written acknowledgement of receipt.

The handbook will need to be **updated** from time to time to take account of organisational, practical and legal changes. If there are any changes to the statutory statement of particulars, in addition to issuing a new statement detailing the change, the handbook may also need to be revised. If the provision to be varied is contractual, the employee's consent should be obtained, unless the employer has already reserved the right to make such changes (¶1615).

1495 **Example of full staff handbook outline**

Introduction – about the company (history, structure, activities, location, mission statement) – introduction to handbook – contractual status of contents – reserve right to change **Terms and conditions** – hours, overtime, time off in lieu – flexible working – holiday provisions – sickness absence/sick pay – notice periods, lay-off arrangements **Remuneration and benefits** – salary/job banding – expenses – pensions – private medical cover – permanent health insurance – life assurance – accident and travel insurance – company car policy – season ticket loans – eye tests – sports and social – staff canteen – parking – childcare **Core policies and procedures** – family-friendly rights – equality and equal opportunities, including complaints procedure – disciplinary rules – disciplinary procedure – grievance procedure – whistleblowing – sickness absence procedure – data protection	**Other policies and guidelines** – change in personal circumstances – references – time off for trade union activities and duties – time off for public duties (e.g. jury service) – compassionate leave/family emergencies – relationships at work – private telephone calls/correspondence – recording of telephone calls – right of search – timekeeping – dress and appearance – health and safety, fire, security – smoking – drugs/alcohol misuse – personal property – public statements – conflicts of interest/outside employment – gifts – protection of intellectual property – email and internet – social media – software and computer usage – company property – client confidentiality – disclosure – trade union (membership and representation, recognition and collective bargaining) **Regulations** – dealing rules – insider dealing – personal transactions – money laundering – anti-bribery and corruption **Career development** – induction – training – appraisals/performance reviews – transfers/secondments

1498 For further discussion on the **main policies and procedures**, please refer to the specific sections which deal with each topic in detail, in particular:
– equality at work (¶5200);
– discipline and grievance (¶6500);
– dress and appearance (¶5826);
– drugs and alcohol (¶5050);
– email, internet and social media issues (¶6260);
– smoking (¶5080);
– rights of parents and carers (¶4400);
– data protection and monitoring (¶5900); and
– company information and confidentiality (¶2300).

When tailoring the model policies, the following **factors** should be taken into account:
1. In order to have a complete understanding of the applicable legal requirements and obligations, each policy must be read in conjunction with the chapters or sections of the book dealing with each topic in detail. The relevant chapter or section is indicated in the memo points to each policy.
2. It must be clear, either from each policy or the introduction to the staff handbook, which policies are intended to form part of the contract of employment (¶¶1480, 1482).
3. The model policies, in general, reflect the minimum statutory rights. If employers wish to provide enhanced rights (over and above the statutory minimum rights), they should decide whether or not these are to be contractual.

4. It should be stated clearly who is covered by the different policies e.g. employees, workers, freelance staff, agency staff etc. Employers may also intend the policies to differ for different staff e.g. senior management may receive more favourable terms. Any variations between different categories of staff must not be discriminatory either on grounds of a protected characteristic or status e.g. part-time, fixed-term or agency worker.

5. The model policies refer in general terms to "the HR Department" and "Line Manager" etc. The relevant positions or departments should be tailored where appropriate, using positions and job titles rather than the names of individuals.

6. Before adopting any policies, employers should consult with recognised trade unions or worker representatives in advance about the contents of the policies.

7. It is also important for employers to ensure that the policies will be effective in practice. This may entail allocating responsibility for the policies (ideally with a member of senior management) and providing guidance, and appropriate training where required, on the relevant law and the contents and requirements of the policies. Such guidance and training should be given not only to employees but also to HR and supervisory staff, who will be responsible for implementing the policies.

8. After adopting the policies, employers should communicate the policies to all those covered by them, ensure the policies contain the date from which they take effect and obtain an appropriate acknowledgement of receipt (¶1489).

9. Employers should also ensure that the policies are applied regularly and consistently, keeping records of all complaints of wrongdoing/infringements and any action taken.

10. All policies should be reviewed on a regular basis to ensure that they reflect current law and in order to maintain ongoing compliance, but it is best not to specify the date of the next review in the policy itself.

SECTION 5

Varying terms and conditions

1600 A contract of employment is a legally binding agreement (¶1112), which means that the parties are bound by its terms. However, it is likely that over the course of the employment relationship, the terms of the contract may need to change.

1601 **Employees** may seek to vary the contract, for example by requesting a reduction in working hours or a change from full-time to part-time working to accommodate new domestic responsibilities, or asking for a pay rise. In many cases, the employee's only recourse is to seek the employer's agreement. If the employer does not agree, the employee may decide to accept the situation, resign or, where practical, implement the change, in which case he will be in breach of contract, and (depending on the seriousness of the breach) the employer may be justified in dismissing him.

More commonly, **employers** may want to vary the terms of a contract for various reasons, including the need to react to economic circumstances, to respond to changes in the marketplace and/or technological advances, or to reorganise the business to make it more efficient or profitable. In particular, an employer may seek to change terms relating to pay or benefits, working hours or shift patterns, duties or place of work. If the change is one which is favourable to the employee he is unlikely to resist it. If, however, the change is unfavourable, there may be scope for dispute. In such circumstances, the change will be a breach of contract unless the employer has a contractual right to vary the contract, obtains the employee's consent, or terminates the existing contract in accordance with its terms and offers a new one containing the variation. These are discussed below.

1602 Changes may also be triggered by sources outside the employer/employee relationship. **Legislation** can impose changes to contract terms. Certain statutory rights, such as the right to maternity pay and to redundancy payments, are automatically implied in employment contracts. If the statute itself changes, the contract will be automatically changed to give the employee an automatic entitlement to the current right. For example, the employee's entitlement to statutory redundancy pay is automatically increased with statutory changes which increase in line with price movements.

The commercial factors involved in a **transfer of undertakings** may give rise to a desire to harmonise terms and conditions, and special considerations will apply in these circumstances. Variation in the context of a business transfer is discussed in detail at ¶8010.

Changes may be negotiated between the employer and a trade union, resulting in amendments to applicable **collective agreements**. The incorporation of collective agreements is discussed at ¶7367, and, given that amendments to collective agreements must also be incorporated into the individual contract of employment, variations involving collective agreements are also discussed in that section.

1603 The variation may have several **legal implications**. For example, it may infringe legislation on discrimination or equal pay, constitute an unlawful deduction from wages, or give rise to a claim of unfair dismissal. The employer must take care to observe the working time regulations, restrictions on Sunday working, and take into account any health and safety considerations when varying any terms.

1604 The **means of variation** will depend on whether the change relates to a non-contractual provision or a contractual term.

Non-contractual provisions can be varied by the employer at any time, without the need for employee consent. In addition to variations following changes in the law or an applicable collective agreement, **contractual terms** can be varied by any of the following means:
– virtue of a contractual right;
– agreement (either express or implied); or
– the employer unilaterally imposing a change.

1605 If contractual terms have effectively been varied and the variation **relates to** any of the **written particulars** that the employer is obliged to provide (¶1420), the employer must, within 1 month of the change, issue a new statement of particulars giving details of the change. A failure to do so will not affect the variation, but will entitle the employee to a remedy for failure to provide the statutory statement of particulars.

The employer cannot vary contractual terms merely by amending the statement of written particulars, as it is usually only evidence of the terms of the contract, rather than the contract itself. However, if the employee continues to work without protest after receiving the amended statement, this may provide evidence that he has impliedly agreed to the new terms (¶1640).

A. Contractual right to vary

1615 The employer may have a contractual right to vary the contract either because it is sufficiently broadly drafted so that the proposed variation falls within its scope, or because there is an express or implied right in the contract to make that variation.

If the employer has a contractual right to vary, the employee will be in breach of contract if he refuses to comply with the new terms.

1. Scope of existing terms

1616 The terms of the contract can be express, implied (by the courts or by statute), or incorporated (by reference to other documents, such as collective agreements). A proposed change may in fact be within the scope of the existing contract terms, in which case the employer does not need to seek the employee's consent. Whether the change is within the scope will **depend on** the construction of the contract. Case law has shown that the ambit of an employee's contractual obligations, especially in **small companies**, may be wider than the ambit of the duties that he actually performs (*Glitz v Watford Electric Co Ltd* [1979] IRLR 89, EAT).

> EXAMPLE
> 1. In *Cresswell v Board of Inland Revenue* [1984] IRLR 190, ChD, the employees were instructed to transfer from a manual accounting system on to a computerised one. They resisted this **new method of work**, but the Court held that their contracts required them to adapt to new techniques and methods of carrying out work within the scope of their duties.
> 2. In *Glitz v Watford Electric Co Ltd*, G's **job description** in her contract referred to her position as a copy typist/general clerical duties clerk. The employer moved her to operate a duplicator machine and the Court held that such a task fell within the ambit of general clerical duties, given the small number of clerical staff in a small office and the resulting need for flexibility.

2. Express right

Flexibility/variation clauses

1618 The contract of employment may contain an express flexibility/variation clause, i.e. one that gives the employer the right to make unilateral **changes to** a **specific contract term** (for example, the employee's job duties or location) or to the **terms in general**.

A common example of a **specific** flexibility clause is a **mobility clause** that gives the employer the right to move the employee to another location without seeking the employee's consent at the time of the transfer (*Rank Xerox v Churchill* [1988] IRLR 280, EAT). However, an employer should consider whether such a clause could amount to a discriminatory work condition before requiring such a provision in a contract of employment (¶5200).

If the clause gives the employer a **general right** to vary terms unilaterally, the extent of that right will be limited to changes of a minor and non-fundamental nature (*United Associated for the Protection of Trade v Kilburn*, EAT case 787/84). For example, it is common for staff handbooks and/or contracts of employment to reserve the right of the employer to amend without the employees' express consent and as such is a useful tool for making minor amendments to a staff handbook and/or contract of employment. In a recent case, a staff handbook, the relevant parts of which were incorporated into the employees' contracts of employment, stated that the employer reserved the right to "review, revise, amend or replace" the contents of the handbook, and to introduce new policies. The EAT held that these words gave the employer power to change contractual terms including pay rates (*Bateman and ors v Asda Stores Ltd* [2010] IRLR 370, EAT). However, if the employer makes significant changes, the employee may still be able to claim constructive dismissal (¶8230).

1619 If the employer has a contractual right to change terms (for example, where the employer reserves the right in contractual work rules to make changes to them without employee consent), an employee will have no redress if the employer exercises that right, even where benefits are withdrawn as part of that change (*Cadoux v Central Regional Council* [1986] IRLR 131, CS).

1621 **Interpretation** The courts will take a strict approach to the interpretation of flexibility clauses. Careful drafting (in particular, clear language) is crucial for various reasons, including the fact that, as a legal rule of construction, any **ambiguity** is resolved against the person seeking to rely on it. If, therefore, a flexibility clause is unclear, it will be construed against the employer (*Bainbridge v Circuit Foil UK Ltd* [1997] IRLR 305, CA).

Further, the courts will construe the flexibility clause to see if its **scope** extends to cover the circumstances of the particular variation, and they will not readily interpret the contract so as to enable a party to vary contractual provisions with which he is required to comply (*Wandsworth Borough Council v D'Silva and another* [1998] IRLR 193, CA). Therefore, it is advisable that care is taken when drafting the clause to ensure that contemplated changes fall within its scope. For example, if the employer wishes to be able to change the number of hours worked by the employees as part of a right to alter shift patterns, it is advisable to reserve a specific right to do so.

> **EXAMPLE**
> 1. In *National Semiconductor (UK) Ltd v Church*, EAT case 252/97 and *SmithKline Beecham plc v Johnson* [1997] UKEAT 559_96_0702, the EAT held that clauses which gave the employers the right to vary existing shift patterns did not extend to giving them the right to increase or reduce the number of hours worked.
> 2. In *Baynham v Philips Electronics* The Times, 19 July 1995(UK) Ltd,, the employer was contractually obliged to provide healthcare cover to a number of former employees. An express term permitting the employer to vary the contract was held by the High Court to be intended to apply to matters such as changes to duties and job title, and did not permit the employer to withdraw the healthcare after the employment had terminated.
> 3. In *Land Securities Trillium Ltd v Thorney* [2005] IRLR 765, EAT, the EAT held that a clause which stated that the employee would "perform to the best of your abilities…any other duties which may reasonably be required of you and will at all times obey all reasonable instructions given to you" did not give the employer carte blanche to require the employee to undertake any duties they wished her to perform but expressly imposed a requirement of reasonableness on the employer's request.

1623 **Implied limitations** The employer is obliged by an implied term to exercise a flexibility clause on reasonable grounds (¶1242) and, although there is no implied term requiring him to operate the clause in a reasonable manner, he may also be restricted by the implied term of mutual trust and confidence (¶1245), for example where a transfer to other work involves a drop in pay. Business efficacy (¶1174) may also require the employer to give reasonable notice of the exercise of the clause.

> **EXAMPLE**
> **Transfer involving a drop in pay**
> In *White v Reflecting Roadstuds Ltd* [1991] IRLR 331, EAT, *BPCC Purnell Ltd v Webb* [1992] UKEAT 129_90_1305, and *Hussman Manufacturing Ltd v Weir* [1998] IRLR 288, EAT, White, Webb and Weir were transferred to **alternative work**, from **one department to another**, and from the **night-shift to the day-shift** respectively. In *White*, the EAT held that the resulting drop in pay did not breach the duty of trust and confidence, whilst in *Webb* it did because Webb's weekly wages dropped from £305 to £225. In *Weir*, the EAT held that a drop in wages would only breach the implied term in exceptional cases, and Weir's decrease of £17 per week was not such a case.
>
> **Relocation**
> In *United Bank Ltd v Akhtar* [1989] IRLR 507, EAT, A was given very little notice of his **transfer from Leeds to Birmingham** and was not given any relocation allowance, which was at the discretion of the employer. As a matter of business efficacy, the employer's right to exercise the mobility clause was subject to a duty:
> – to give reasonable notice;
> – not to exercise his discretion to provide relocation expenses in such a way as to prevent the employee from performing his contractual duties; and
> – not to act in such a way as to undermine the relationship of mutual trust and confidence.

1625 **Sex discrimination** A mobility clause may be challenged on the grounds that it constitutes sex discrimination, in that it has a disproportionately adverse effect on workers of one of the sexes (often women) compared with workers of the opposite sex. If so, the clause will be indirectly discriminatory and will not be valid unless it can be objectively justified by the employer (¶5310). The Court of Appeal has ruled that a mobility clause was indirectly discriminatory against women since women were more likely than men to be "second earners" and, consequently, would find it harder than men to relocate (*Mende-Hill and the National Union of Civil and Public Servants v British Council* [1995] IRLR 478, CA).

1627 **Redundancy** A mobility or flexibility clause that allows the employer to transfer the employee to other locations or other duties may have an impact in redundancy situations. For example, if work is no longer available at the employee's place of work, the employee may be taken to be redundant and the legal rules regarding redundancy would apply. If the employee can be required to work at other locations, he may attempt to argue that he is not technically redundant if work is available at such locations. However, the courts currently give more weight to where the employee actually worked (as opposed to where he may be required to work), so that if an express mobility clause has not been exercised in practice, it will not affect the redundancy situation.

3. Implied right

1630 The employer may be taken to have an implied right to change contract terms if the change is needed to give the contract **business efficacy** (¶1174) i.e. to make the contract work and, by extension, to ensure that the business (to which the employment relates) continues. The term must be both "necessary" and "obvious". It could involve changes in work practices to take account of changed market conditions, but is unlikely to be able to be used to reduce pay rates.

1631 **Implied mobility clause** A term is often implied that the employee is expected to work **within reasonable daily travelling distance of his home** (*Jones v Associated Tunnelling Co Ltd* [1981] IRLR 477, EAT). Therefore, if the employer moves the employee from one place of work to another (which is, for example, no further from his home than the first), the employer may not need an express right to do so and may not be, therefore, in breach of contract. However, other factors will also be relevant, including whether the move from one location to another may entail a loss of status (for example, the EAT identified a distinction between a central London legal secretary and a suburban one (*Blatchfords Solicitors v Berger* [2000] UKEAT 207_00_1705)).

However, where a mobility clause is not needed to make the contract work, the courts will decline to imply any term as to mobility at all (*Aparau v Iceland Frozen Foods plc* [1995] UKEAT 196_93_0910).

As the scope of implied mobility clauses is uncertain, it is preferable for express mobility clauses to be used if employees may be required to move workplace.

B. Mutual agreement

1635 If there is no right in the contract to vary terms and conditions, the contract, in common with other legal agreements, can be varied by the mutual agreement of the parties to it. This agreement can be **express or implied**.

1636 **Consideration** As with any type of contract, a variation will not be binding if there is no consideration for it. For example, the employer may offer to give the employee an **extra day's holiday** in return for the employee agreeing to work longer hours. If the employer wants to promote the employee to a position with more responsibility, the consideration is usually an **increase in salary**.

In the context of **pay negotiations**, the consideration for the pay rise is the settlement of the pay claim and the continuation of the same employee in the same employment (*Lee v GEC Plessey Telecommunications* [1993] IRLR 383, QBD).

It may be possible to rely on the offer of **continued employment** as the consideration for the agreement to vary the existing terms.

1. Express agreement

1638 The parties can agree **orally or in writing** to a variation to the original contract (note that an agreement by email is likely to amount to an agreement in writing). For example, if an employer wishes to change work practices, he could seek the employee's agreement, possibly in return for a pay increase. If the employee agrees, the contract is amended to take account of the change. Pay rises and promotions are common agreed variations to the original contract. However, both parties must intend to enter into a legally binding agreement for any variation to be enforceable (*Judge v Crown Leisure Ltd* [2005] IRLR 823, EAT) (¶1117).

It is preferable for such an agreement to be in writing, as there is more scope for dispute with oral agreements, in which case it would be a question of evidence as to whether a variation had been agreed (*Simmonds v Dowty Seals Ltd* [1978] IRLR 211, EAT).

Of course, there will be no agreement if the employee was forced to accept the change, for example by threat of dismissal.

2. Implied agreement

1640 Over the course of the employment relationship, certain terms may change without any formal agreement having been reached. For example, new methods of work may be introduced, including the introduction of new machines, or the employee may take on a new task.

Where a change is introduced or imposed by the employer and the **employee continues to work without protest** for a significant period of time whilst being aware of that change, the employee may be taken impliedly to have agreed to the change, and there will be no breach of contract by the employer.

1641 Whether implied agreement can be identified will depend on various factors, including the employee's conduct and the nature of the change. There may be uncertainty as to whether the worker's subsequent conduct is evidence of an affirmation of the new terms. When an employee **makes clear his objection** to work that is being done under new terms of employment imposed by the employer, he will not be taken as having affirmed the contract by continuing to work and to draw pay for a limited period of time (*Henry v London General Transport Services Ltd* [2002] IRLR 472, CA). Likewise, if the employee's **behaviour demonstrates** that he has no intention of returning to work under the circumstances that resulted in a material breach he will not be taken to have affirmed the contract, even if he does not indicate that he is working under protest (*Forbes v Salamis (Marine & Industrial) Ltd* [2004] UKEAT 0085_03_2403). Furthermore, simply drawing sick pay during this period does not indicate that he has affirmed the contract.

However, if the employee does **not make his objection known and complies** with the new terms such compliance will normally show that he has accepted them. Similarly, if an employee indicates that he accepts the new terms and conditions only "**under duress**", this will not be sufficient to constitute working under protest (unless there is sufficient duress in the legal sense to negate the employee's consent) and will not be sufficient to invalidate the variation (*Hepworth Heating Ltd v Akers* [2003] UKEAT 13_02_2101).

1642 However, the fact that an employee has continued to work without protest after the introduction of a varied term does not necessarily mean he has consented to the change. In such circumstances, **great caution** should be exercised before finding an implied acceptance of the new term, especially if the new term does not have **immediate effect** (*Jones v Associated Tunnelling Co Ltd* [1981] IRLR 477, EAT).

> EXAMPLE In *Aparau v Iceland Frozen Foods plc* [1995] UKEAT 196_93_0910, A's employer issued her with new terms and conditions of employment that contained a mobility clause. A did not sign and return the copy, but continued to work under the new conditions for **more than 12 months**. The EAT held that it could not be accepted that A had impliedly accepted the new terms as the clause had **no immediate practical effect**. The effect would only be felt if and when the employer attempted to exercise the mobility clause.

1643 If it can be implied from the employee's conduct that he has **agreed to the variation**, there will be no breach of contract by the employer, so the employee will have no claim for damages, and will not be able to resign and claim constructive dismissal.

> MEMO POINTS It should be noted that the fact that employees have **previously expressly agreed to a variation** of their terms and conditions (for example, the imposition of short-time working) does not mean that there is an ongoing implied agreement to work on varied terms and conditions in the future (*International Packaging Corporation (UK) Ltd v Balfour* [2003] IRLR 11, EAT). An employer cannot therefore make unilateral variations (see below) on this basis.

C. Unilateral variation by the employer

1645 If the employer has no contractual right to vary and the employee is unwilling to agree to a variation, the employer can either abandon his proposed changes or insist on implementing them.

1646 If the employer insists on implementing the changes, he will be in **breach of contract** and this method of introducing a change therefore carries the highest risk of legal liability. The new terms are not legally binding on an employee unless he **accepts** them (either expressly or impliedly, i.e. by not protesting), in which case the change will be agreed and the employer will not be liable for breach of contract.

> EXAMPLE In *Adamas Ltd v Cheung* [2011] UKPC 32, the employee, C, was a shop manager who was moved from one shop to another (less profitable) shop and once there was expected to make certain deliveries. The Privy Council held that C's dismissal had been unjustified (the Mauritian equivalent of a dismissal being unfair) when she was dismissed for refusing to take on this new duty as it was not part of her contractual terms. The fact that she had undertaken the deliveries initially when requested to do so as "a favour" did not negate her subsequent refusal and did not mean she had accepted the variation. Moreover, it was perfectly open to her to reject the variation and continue to work under her original contract (¶1651) and to put the onus on the employer to choose how to respond.

1647 Where the variation involves a reduction in wages or other change to remuneration, the employee may also be able to bring a claim of **unlawful deductions from wages** (¶3050).

1. Breach of contract

1650 Any unilateral change amounts to a breach of contract, which gives the employee the right to a remedy, which may include damages or an injunction, or (in certain circumstances) compensation for unlawful deduction from wages (¶3080). If the variation affects a **large number of employees**, the unions may be involved in seeking redress on their behalf.

It is no defence for the employer to show that he had sound business reasons for imposing the change or that he acted reasonably in the circumstances (although these may be a defence in cases of unfair dismissal (¶1666)). In assessing whether it is reasonable for an employer to dismiss an employee for failure to accept a contractual variation with regard to potential unfair dismissal claims, the correct question is not whether it was reasonable for the employee to accept the new terms, but whether the employer's actions were reasonable (*Garside and Laycock Ltd v Booth* [2011] UKEAT 0003_11_2705), though in reality there would be some overlap between the two issues.

> EXAMPLE In *Garside and Laycock Ltd v Booth*, the EAT held that it was reasonable for an employer to dismiss an employee for failure to accept a contractual variation, which would have resulted in a 5% pay reduction, due to an economic downturn in the business. It was not essential for the employer to show that the survival of the business was at stake: avoiding redundancies and improving profits was a reasonable basis for imposing the variation. The employer had consulted with all affected staff, of which more than 80 had accepted the changes with the claimant being the only one who ultimately refused.

Repudiatory or fundamental breach

1651 Where the breach is fundamental (¶1701), the employee who rejects the change has **several options**:
– he can work under the new terms (whilst making his rejection of them clear to the employer), and seek a remedy for breach of contract (¶1700). Further, if the change involves radically different terms, the courts may consider the employee to have been unfairly dismissed from his old contract (¶1652);

– where practical, he can continue to work under the old terms and refuse to work under the new ones (for example, those relating to hours of work or job duties). If he is dismissed for misconduct in these circumstances, the employee may be able to bring claims of unfair and wrongful dismissal; or
– he can resign and claim that he has been constructively dismissed (¶8230), in which case the employer may be liable for both wrongful and unfair dismissal and will not usually be able to rely on any post-termination obligations or restrictive covenants.

An employer will have a defence to any unfair dismissal claim where he has sound business reasons for imposing the change or he acted reasonably in the circumstances (¶1666).

2. Imposition of new contract

1652 The unilateral imposition of **radically different terms** may be interpreted as a dismissal of the employee from the old contract and the immediate entry into a new contract on different terms. For example, where the variation involves a complete change in the employee's job content and the employee continues to work, he will be treated as having accepted the termination of the old contract and entered into a new contract. This may allow the employee to claim that he has been **unfairly dismissed** from the old contract (*Hogg v Dover College* [1990] ICR 39, EAT). Whether the imposition of a new contract can be identified depends on a careful assessment of the surrounding circumstances, and will be a matter of fact and degree in each case (*London Borough of Southwark v Mungul* [2000] UKEAT 1359_99_0102). If the changes are found not to amount to a withdrawal of the old contract, the court may find that the imposition of new terms amounts to a repudiatory breach which the employee has waived by continuing to work without complaint.

In summary, there are four options open to an employee whose employer unilaterally seeks to impose a major change in contract terms (*Robinson v Tescom Corporation* [2008] UKEAT 0567_07_0303). He may:
– agree to the change;
– refuse to agree and leave it to the employer to decide what steps to take in response to his refusal. For example, if he continues to work under the old terms, refusing to work under the new terms and without protesting or agreeing the change, the employer may dismiss him for misconduct and in such circumstances the employee may be able to bring claims of unfair and wrongful dismissal, although the employer will have a defence to an unfair dismissal claim where he has sound business reasons for imposing the change or acted reasonably in the circumstances (¶1666). Alternatively, the employer may choose to abandon the change;
– if the change is a fundamental one, resign and claim that he has been constructively dismissed; or
– work on under protest and claim damages for breach of contract.

EXAMPLE
1. In *Hogg v Dover College*, the employer introduced new terms giving H lower status, shorter working hours and less pay. The EAT held that he could claim that he had been unfairly dismissed from his old contract.
2. In *Alcan Extrusions v Yates and others* [1996] UKEAT 980_95_0502, Y worked under a shift system that operated from Monday to Saturday morning, and was paid overtime for working at weekends and on bank holidays. The employer fundamentally changed the system by introducing a continuous rolling shift pattern, changing hours of work and including weekends and bank holidays, thereby affecting Y's overtime. Holiday provisions, shift premiums and start-up payments were also changed to Y's detriment. The EAT held that the new terms were so radically different from the old that Y could be said to have been dismissed from the old contract.
3. In *Robinson v Tescom Corporation* [2008] UKEAT 0567_07_0303, the employer sought to impose a unilateral change of terms and conditions on R which would require him to undertake significantly more travel. R responded that he would work on under protest and claim damages for breach of contract. However, he then refused to comply with the new terms and his employer dismissed him for misconduct. The dismissal was found to be fair. He had not successfully exercised his right to

continue working on the new terms but instead had in effect refused to agree to the changes and left the employer to take what action he thought fit.

The **terms of the new contract** will be a matter of construction (*S W Strange Ltd v Mann* [1965] 1 All ER 1069, ChD). The courts will, therefore, attempt to identify the intention of the parties (¶1118).

3. Dismissal and re-engagement

If the employee refuses to agree to a change that the employer is determined to introduce, rather than vary the contract unilaterally the employer could terminate the existing contract and offer a new one that includes the variation. If he gives the appropriate **notice of termination** (¶8120) (and complies with any other contractual obligations relating to the termination of employment), there will be no breach of contract as a result of taking such action, thus avoiding liability for **wrongful dismissal** and constructive dismissal claims. If no notice is given and the employee refuses a reasonable offer of employment on new terms, any award of compensation for wrongful dismissal may be reduced by reason of his **failure to mitigate** his loss (*Marenghi v Western Baths Club* [2001] UKEAT 1508_00_1505) (¶8171).

The notice of termination must be clear and unambiguous. A notice from the employer that he is only willing to continue to employ the employee after a period of notice on revised terms is unlikely to be construed as notice of dismissal and re-engagement (*Burdett-Coutts v Hertfordshire County Council* [1984] IRLR 91, QBD).

> EXAMPLE
>
> **Dismissal and re-engagement**
> In *Rogers v Microblade Ltd* [2009] UKEAT 0041_09_1906, an employer wished to discontinue its night shift and wrote to all night workers giving a month's notice of the change. The claimant objected to the change and was told that if he did not agree his contract would be terminated. The employer then wrote to him enclosing a new contract and made the following statement: "…although your old contract comes to an end on 21 April you are immediately re-engaged under your new contract whenever you sign it." The EAT held that these words had the effect of dismissing the claimant and offering him re-engagement on new terms, rather than being an attempt to vary the old contract.
>
> **No dismissal and re-engagement**
> In *Burdett-Coutts v Hertfordshire County Council*, an employer wished to reduce wages as a way of avoiding redundancies and wrote to those affected. The letter, which gave "detailed notice of the variations in your contract of service" and "formal notice of these changes in your contract of service" was held to be an attempt to vary the terms of the existing contract and not a termination and offer of re-engagement.

If the employee accepts the new contract and starts working under it within a week following the termination of the old contract, **statutory continuity** is preserved (¶1014).

Termination of the existing contract will be a dismissal for unfair dismissal purposes, and qualifying employees will therefore be able to bring an **unfair dismissal** claim (*Banerjee v City and East London Area Health Authority* [1979] IRLR 147, EAT; *St John of God (Care Services) Ltd v Brooks* [1992] IRLR 546, EAT). However, an employee who is offered a new contract on reasonable terms without substantial changes is unlikely to be awarded much (if anything) by way of compensatory award if he succeeds in claiming unfair dismissal. The employee will, however, normally receive the basic award in full (¶8575).

The employee may also be eligible for a **redundancy payment** (¶8990). If twenty or more employees are dismissed, there may be collective redundancy **consultation obligations** (¶8916).

Negotiated settlements If the employer dismisses and re-engages an employee on reasonable terms, the employer could consider offering a **financial inducement**, calculated by reference to the unfair dismissal basic award, to persuade the employee to accept changes in terms of employment. In such circumstances, it is advisable for the employer to **seek a waiver** (in a compromise agreement) of the employee's right to bring an unfair dismissal claim in connection with the variation of his employment terms (¶9322).

4. Liability for unfair dismissal

1665 If the employer dismisses an employee who refuses to agree to a variation, or if the employer imposes a change in fundamental breach of contract causing the employee to resign and claim constructive dismissal, the employee may be able to claim that he has been unfairly dismissed.

1666 **Fair reason** In order to avoid liability for unfair dismissal, the employer must show that he has one of the statutory fair reasons for dismissal. In some cases, **redundancy** may be pleaded, but the most common statutory reason put forward is the catch-all "**some other substantial reason**" (SOSR). This is discussed in detail at ¶8530.

Where the employee claims **constructive dismissal**, the employer must be able to justify the variation that caused the employee to resign and treat himself as dismissed.

1667 **Fair procedure** In addition to having a statutory fair reason, the employer must also be able to show that he acted fairly in all the circumstances in dismissing for the statutory fair reason. See ¶8550 for further discussion.

1668 **Automatic unfair dismissal** It is automatically unfair to dismiss an employee because he brought proceedings against the employer or alleged that the employer had infringed a relevant statutory right. In the context of a variation of employment terms, the employee may have asserted his right not to have unlawful deductions from wages (¶8395).

5. Redundancy issues

1675 The implementation of changes to employees' terms and conditions may give rise to a redundancy situation (¶8745). Redundancy is a **statutory fair reason for dismissal**, and may therefore be a defence to an unfair dismissal claim.

1676 **Individual redundancy** If the employer wishes to **dismiss and re-engage** the employee (¶1655), his offer of employment on revised terms may constitute an offer of suitable alternative employment, in which case an employee who unreasonably refuses the offer would not be entitled to a redundancy payment in respect of the termination of the "old" job. If an employee accepts the new terms, his redundancy entitlement is rolled-over into the new contract as his **continuity of employment** is preserved if he commences the new contract within 4 weeks following the termination of the old contract (¶1024). The employee is allowed a 4-week "**trial period**" in redundancy cases where there is re-engagement on revised terms.

1677 **Collective redundancy** If the employer proposes to impose measures involving the termination of existing contracts in respect of a group of **twenty or more employees** at one establishment within a period of 90 days or less, the dismissals will give rise to a redundancy situation for **collective consultation** purposes (¶8916) where the reason(s) for the dismissal do not relate to the individuals concerned (*GMB v Man Truck and Bus UK Ltd* 2000] UKEAT 971_99_2306). This often occurs where employees are dismissed and re-engaged in order to harmonise terms following the sale of a business subject to the TUPE rules (¶7900). The employer will be obliged to consult trade union representatives or employee representatives, in addition to consulting individually with employees.

SECTION 6

Breach of contract

1700 It is important to distinguish between non-binding provisions and binding contractual terms (¶1112) as the innocent party can only bring a claim for breach of a contract in respect of a **binding contractual term**, whether this is express or implied.

The circumstances giving rise to a breach of contract may also support **other claims** (such as unfair dismissal). Conversely, a dismissal in accordance with the terms of the contract may still be unfair for statutory purposes. Certain **disclosures** of a breach of contract will also bring the employee within the protection of the whistleblowing legislation (¶2700).

1701 The remedies available will depend on whether the breach is fundamental or not. A **fundamental breach** is one that is serious enough to be considered to be a repudiation of the contract. This will depend on the circumstances of the case, but to be fundamental the breach must go to the root of the contract and be incompatible with the continuance of the employment relationship (i.e. the party committing it clearly no longer intends to be bound by the terms of the contract). The innocent party may choose to treat himself as discharged from the duty to perform the contract any further, thus terminating it (although he must do so within a reasonable time of the breach) and entitling him to claim **constructive dismissal** and seek compensation for wrongful dismissal and/or unfair dismissal. Alternatively, he can waive the breach (in which case the contract is "affirmed", i.e. it continues) and bring a claim for **damages**. Other remedies include the equitable remedies of **injunction** and **declaration** of the parties' rights.

1703 The parties can **pre-agree** the **amount of compensation** payable in the event of a breach of contract (most commonly, premature termination) by way of an agreed or liquidated damages clause, thus avoiding the need for legal action. Such a clause will be **enforceable** if it is a genuine pre-estimate of the loss likely to result from the early termination (*Dunlop Pneumatic Tyre Co Ltd v New Garage and Motor Co Ltd* [1915] AC 79, HL, applied in *Murray v Leisureplay plc* [2005] IRLR 946, CA and *CMC Group plc and ors v Zhang* [2006] EWCA Civ 408). If it is not, it may (depending on its construction in light of the contract as a whole and the surrounding circumstances at the time the contract was made) be held to be **unenforceable** as a penalty clause. The pre-agreed amount should, therefore, not be "extravagant and unconscionable" in comparison with the greatest conceivable loss, nor should the same fixed sum be payable for a range of breaches regardless of the amount of loss suffered.

This principle has been applied to a "no-show" clause, i.e. one providing that the employee must pay the employer compensation if he fails to take up employment after accepting an offer. It may be difficult to show significant loss in the case of many recruits, so care should be taken when setting the level of agreed damages to ensure that it is not excessive (*Tullett Prebon Group Ltd v El-Hajjali* [2008] IRLR 760, QB).

EXAMPLE
1. In *Giraud UK Ltd v Smith* [2000] UKEAT 1105_99_1201, S's contract allowed the employer to deduct a sum from his final payment in the event that he failed to give notice and work out his notice period. This was held to be a penalty clause as it was not a genuine pre-estimate of loss, since the employer was not prevented from recovering his actual loss if this was greater than the pre-agreed sum and the employee would still lose the entire sum even if the employer's actual loss was less. The EAT found that the clause was designed to deter employees from leaving without notice, not to compensate the employer for the effects of them doing so.
2. In *Tullett Prebon Group Ltd v El-Hajjali*, the High Court was prepared to enforce a "no-show" clause. A senior specialist in "exotic equities" had accepted an offer of employment with the employer, a brokerage. The contract contained a term that the recruit should pay the employer 50% of his basic pay for the agreed period of his employment and 50% of his signing payment if he failed to start work as agreed. The employer was able to show that it would suffer losses considerably greater than this sum as a result of the breach of contract.

1704 To obtain a remedy, the innocent party should **apply to** the courts or, in some circumstances, depending on the monetary value of the claim, the remedy sought, and whether the breach arises or is outstanding on termination, the employment tribunal (¶¶9425+).

I. Employee remedies

1710 If the employer's breach is **fundamental** (see ¶1715 below for examples), the employee is entitled to resign and claim that he has been constructively dismissed. If he chooses not to (i.e. he waives the breach), or if the breach is **not fundamental**, he can bring an action for damages, arrears of salary or other payment, or bring a statutory claim in respect of wages unlawfully deducted, as appropriate.

Where **damages are not an appropriate remedy** (for example, where working hours are changed with no resulting financial loss), the court may grant a declaration (setting out the employer's obligations) and/or an injunction (requiring him to fulfil those obligations) (*MacRuary v Washington Irvine Ltd*, EAT case 857/93).

> EXAMPLE In *Rigby v Ferodo Ltd* [1987] IRLR 516, HL, the employer's unilateral reduction of the employee's contractual wages was a fundamental breach of contract. R did not accept the breach as repudiation of the contract, but rather **continued working**, indicating nevertheless that the variation was unacceptable to him. He successfully sued for damages for sums due under the contract, i.e. by reference to the level of his wages prior to the employer's unilateral reduction.

1711 Timing of claims Where the employee can present his claim to an **employment tribunal**, he must do so within 3 months of the effective date of termination (¶8340) (or, where there is no such date, within 3 months of the last day on which the employee worked). If the claim is brought in the **High Court or county courts**, it must be presented within 6 years of the date of the breach.

1712 Pre-employment breaches The employee need not have commenced employment in order to bring a breach of contract claim, as if he has **accepted an unconditional offer** of employment there is a valid contract. Therefore, if the employer terminates the contract before the start date, the employee can bring a wrongful dismissal claim (¶8155) (*Sarker v South Tees Acute Hospitals NHS Trust* [1997] IRLR 328, EAT), and possibly a discrimination or unfair dismissal claim (where no period of qualifying service is required, e.g. for reasons relating to pregnancy or trade union membership (¶8390)).

> MEMO POINTS Conditional offers of employment may be terminated before the start date if the conditions are not met e.g. satisfactory references are not forthcoming or a medical examination is not successfully passed.

A. Constructive dismissal

1715 If the employer commits a fundamental breach of contract, the employee is entitled to **treat himself as discharged**, i.e. he may resign and claim that he has been constructively dismissed (¶8230). It does not matter what the employer's **intentions** are: even if he wants the employment contract to continue or does not know that he is in breach, a constructive dismissal can still take place (see ¶8235). An employer who has committed a fundamental breach of contract cannot cure it by his subsequent actions. If the employer takes **steps to put matters right** after a fundamental breach this does invite the employee to affirm the contract, but the employee is under no obligation to do so and does not lose the right to accept the breach and claim constructive dismissal (*Buckland v Bournemouth University Higher*

Education Corp [2010] IRLR 445, CA). Note that, in contrast, an employer can cure a **threatened** breach of contract, for example by finding in favour of an employee at a grievance hearing about the impending breach, and the employee does not have a choice as to whether to accept the cure if it occurs before the breach actually takes place (*Assamoi v Spirit Pub Company (Services) Ltd* [2011] UKEAT 0050_20_3007).

A breach often arises in the context of a **variation** of terms and conditions. Whether a variation amounts to a fundamental breach is a question for the courts. If an employee is to claim that he has been constructively dismissed, he must **choose within a reasonable time** to treat the varied contract as at an end, otherwise he will normally be taken to have affirmed the variation to his terms and conditions (*Western Excavating (ECC) Ltd v Sharp* [1978] IRLR 27, CA; see also ¶8242). For example, an employee cannot ordinarily expect to continue working for very long without losing the option of termination, particularly if he fails to make his position clear at the outset and the employer has offered to make suitable amends. See ¶¶1640+ for the rules on when an employee is taken to have affirmed a varied contract or not.

EXAMPLE **Variation amounting to fundamental breach**
– a deliberate reduction of an employee's pay, whatever the amount of the reduction (*Cantor Fitzgerald International v Callaghan* [1999] IRLR 234, CA);
– a decision to reduce wage levels following the termination of a local collective agreement, despite the fact that the previous collectively agreed rate had been incorporated into the individual's contract (*Gibbons v Associated British Ports* [1985] IRLR 376, QBD);
– a change of job duties (*Genower v Ealing Hammersmith and Hounslow Area Health Authority* [1980] IRLR 297, EAT) or an instruction (not contemplated by the contract) to employees to cease their normal work and carry out other work (*Hughes v London Borough of Southwark* [1988] IRLR 55, QBD);
– a decision to put a salaried employee on short-time working where his contract did not include a right to do so, and neither he nor his union had given their agreement (*Miller v Hamworthy Engineering Ltd* [1986] IRLR 461, CA);
– a proposal (i.e. an anticipatory breach) unilaterally to vary working hours and to serve notice of dismissal if the employee refused to agree (*Greenaway Harrison Ltd v Wiles* [1993] UKEAT 304_92_1506);
– replacement of full-time work by part-time and temporary work (*Hogg v Dover College* [1990] ICR 39, EAT);
– seeking to impose new terms and conditions in an aggressive manner, giving only perfunctory and misleading explanations as to the effect of the new terms (*Cantor Fitzgerald International v Bird and others* [2002] IRLR 867, QBD);
– failure to take reasonable care for the health and safety of the employee (*Marshall Specialist Vehicles Limited v Osborne* [2003] IRLR 672, EAT); and
– a unilateral decision to stop an employee working at home if the employee can establish that he is contractually entitled to work at home and if it impacts significantly on the employee's working practices (*France v Westminster City Council* [2003] UKEAT 0214_02_0905).

1716 The implied term of **trust and confidence** introduces a grey area, in that the application of the term can be wide-ranging. Examples of breaches of the term might include changing non-contractual conditions of employment so that the employee feels less secure about his position, removing support systems (e.g. other employees who assist the employee) so that the employee cannot do his job, changing reporting lines so that it appears that management has lost confidence in the employee or, as in *Blackburn with Darwen Borough Council v Stanley*, an ongoing failure to address an employee's complaints of bullying and harassment (either through a company procedure or otherwise) (*Blackburn with Darwen Borough Council v Stanley* [2005] UKEAT 0429_04_2001). A breach of this implied term will always be fundamental (*Morrow v Safeway Stores plc* [2002] IRLR 9, EAT). However, where both parties are in breach of the term, and the employee commits the first breach, he cannot then succeed in a claim for constructive dismissal. It is immaterial that the employer is not aware of the fact that the employee is already in breach at the time he commits his own breach of contract, so the employee cannot benefit from the employer's ignorance (*RDF Media Group plc v Clements* [2007] EWHC 2892 (QB)).

1717 In some cases, breaches by the employer may have a **cumulative effect**, such that, taken together, they amount to repudiatory conduct breaching the implied obligation of trust and confidence (¶8234).

1718 The employee may be justified in resigning if the employer indicates that he intends to commit a fundamental breach (an "**anticipatory breach**"). This is discussed further at ¶8233.

1719 An employee who has been constructively dismissed may seek **compensation** for wrongful dismissal and/or unfair dismissal. In either case, the calculation of damages will be based on the same approach as would be taken where the employer has actually terminated the employment.

B. Damages

1725 The **aim of any award** of damages is to put the employee into the position he would have been in had the employer performed his obligations in accordance with his contractual or implied terms. Employment **tribunal awards** are subject to a **statutory cap** (¶9428) (the High Court and the county court are not subject to these limits).

An employer can be held liable in damages for breach of **any express or implied term** of the contract of employment. For example, damages may be awarded for breach of the following duties:
- to give the required period of **notice** to terminate the employment;
- to **pay** for work done; and
- to observe the duty of **mutual trust and confidence**.

A termination of employment in breach of contract (most commonly for failure to give the required period of notice) is known as **wrongful dismissal**. See ¶8156+ for details on calculating damages in these circumstances.

> MEMO POINTS The parties can **pre-agree** the **amount of compensation** payable in the event of a breach of contract (most commonly, premature termination) by way of an agreed or liquidated damages clause, thus avoiding the need for legal action (¶1703).

1726 Damages awarded will be linked to any **financial loss** suffered, with no award for injured feelings or distress (*Johnson v Unisys Ltd* [2001] IRLR 279, HL, see also *Dunnachie v Kingston upon Hull City Council* [2004] IRLR 727, HL), as such damages are only recoverable where the object of the breached contract was specifically to provide pleasure, relaxation, or entertainment (*Bliss v South East Thames Regional Health Authority* [1985] IRLR 308, CA). An employee who is dismissed in breach of a contractual disciplinary procedure cannot claim damages for breach of express or implied contractual terms flowing from the manner of their dismissal (*Edwards v Chesterfield Royal Hospital; Botham (FC) v Ministry of Defence* [2011] UKSC 58).

1727 Damages may be recovered for the financial losses associated with **psychiatric illness** suffered as a result of a contractual breach (¶5010).

C. Other remedies

Action for arrears of salary/other payments

1730 As long as he can prove that he worked or was ready and willing to carry out his contractual duties, the employee may have a debt action for arrears of salary if the **employer has withheld payment** of salary (or other sums or benefits) due under the contract (*Miles v Wakefield Metropolitan District Council* [1987] IRLR 193, HL).

> MEMO POINTS 1. The employee may not be entitled to bring an action for arrears if he only gives **partial performance** (¶3007), or the employer **terminates without notice** (the employee's remedy will be damages for wrongful dismissal (see above)) (*Gunton v Richmond-upon-Thames London Borough Council* [1980] IRLR 321, CA).

2. If the breach involves a reduction in wages or other change to remuneration, the employee may alternatively be able to bring a claim of **unlawful deductions from wages** (¶3050).

Injunctions

1732 The High Court and county courts (but not the employment tribunal) have the power to grant injunctions (orders requiring a party to do or not do a particular thing), which is an equitable remedy. As time may be a crucial issue (for example, where the employee is about to be dismissed), the courts can order an interim/interlocutory (i.e. **temporary**) injunction. The circumstances in which injunctions will be granted are discussed in detail below. They will not normally be granted where other remedies are more appropriate (for example, in the case of unpaid wages the employee could make an application for summary judgment in an action for arrears of salary (see above) (*Jakeman v South West Thames Regional Health Authority and London Ambulance Service* [1990] IRLR 62, QBD).

1733 The court can impose **conditions** when granting an injunction, for example that the employee will work in accordance with the employer's instructions (*Wadcock v London Borough of Brent* [1990] IRLR 223, ChD).

1734 The granting of an injunction is subject to the **general rule** that there cannot be specific performance of a contract of employment, i.e. the courts will not order the performance of a contract of employment where this would involve requiring an employee to work for an employer (or force an employer to allow the employee to work for him) when the employer has sought to terminate that employment.

1735 The courts will only grant an injunction in **exceptional circumstances** to enforce a contractual term where there is still mutual trust and confidence between employer and employee. It will only do so if it is clear on the evidence (taking into account the nature of the work, the people with whom the work must be done and the likely effect on the employer and his operations) that the employer still has sufficient confidence in the employee's ability and other necessary attributes for it to be reasonable to make the order, and that it is just in all the circumstances to do so (*Powell v Brent London Borough Council* [1987] IRLR 466, CA). In particular, an injunction may be granted where the parties agree that the employment contract subsists, and should subsist, in some form, such that the provisions to be enforced can be put into effect without requiring any greater degree of contact and mutual co-operation than the parties themselves are prepared to accept (such as the implementation of contractual disciplinary procedures when an employee is on suspension (*Peace v City of Edinburgh Council* [1999] ScotCS 39)).

EXAMPLE
Injunction to stay (i.e. prevent) a dismissal or purported dismissal
1. In *Irani v Southampton and South-West Hampshire Health Authority* [1985] IRLR 203, ChD, an injunction was granted restraining the employer from dismissing the employee before completing a contractual disputes procedure.
2. In *Barros D'Sa v University Hospital Coventry and Warwickshire NHS Trust* [2001] IRLR 691, CA, an injunction was granted to restrain the employer from dismissing the employee where he had acted outside the contractual disciplinary procedure.
3. In *Hill v C A Parsons & Co Ltd* [1971] 3 All ER 1345, CA, an injunction was granted restraining wrongful dismissal in order to enable the employer to resist external pressure from trade unions.
4. In *Anderson v Pringle of Scotland* [1998] IRLR 64, CS, the employer was restrained from dismissing the employee in breach of a contractual redundancy selection procedure.
5. In *Kircher v Hillingdon Primary Care Trust* [2006] EWHC 21 (QB), an interim injunction was granted to restrain the employer of a consultant psychiatrist from relying on its letter of termination or otherwise treating his purported dismissal as an effective termination. The consultant had been subject to a number of allegations concerning his conduct and was subsequently dismissed on the grounds of "irreconcilable differences", without the contractual disciplinary procedure relating to matters of professional conduct being carried out. Without the interim injunction, the High Court held that the employee would not be able to argue at trial that he should be entitled to have the opportunity to clear his name or put the complaints that were made about him before an independent tribunal, as was provided for in his contract. Damages were not an adequate remedy, particularly as there

was a significant risk that this employee would never find alternative employment, at least within the NHS.

6. In *Lew v Board of Trustees on behalf of United Synagogue* [2011] EWHC 1265 (QB), the High Court allowed an interim injunction to continue which precluded an employer from instigating capability or disciplinary procedures pending trial, as there was a real possibility that the capability procedure in question was created solely in order to facilitate a dismissal. The employee's, L's, contract stated that in the event of disciplinary issues arising (which included misconduct or neglect of or breach of any of his duties) a contractual procedure would be followed. This procedure was on the generous side and included the formation of a committee made up by a wide variety of members, the meetings of which L was allowed to attend, and L was also entitled to be accompanied by anybody he chose at these meetings (including a legal representative). L, a Rabbi, had various complaints made against him by members of his congregation and it was decided by an honorary executive committee that there were capability issues to be addressed. It appears that a capability procedure (which was not stated to be contractual and afforded L fewer rights) was created solely to deal with L's situation. It was L's case that the sudden invention of this procedure was part of a plan to end his employment more easily by avoiding the use of the contractual disciplinary procedure (which, the High Court held, was very likely to cover any concerns that the executive committee had) and that the avoidance of this procedure amounted to a breach of contract. The judgment stated that there were serious concerns as to the employer's motives in this case and there was a real possibility that the capability procedure would be used to effect a dismissal that was not truly linked to any genuine capability concerns.

Injunction restraining the suspension of an employee with pay
In *Mezey v South West London and St George's Mental Health NHS Trust* [2007] IRLR 237, HC ([2007] IRLR 244, CA), the High Court granted an interim injunction to restrain an employer from suspending an employee with pay pending the outcome of internal disciplinary proceedings. The Court of Appeal, in supporting the use of the interim injunction in such circumstances, emphasised that suspension changed the status quo from work to no work and, as it inevitably casts a shadow over the employee's competence, there was no reason of principle why a court could not restrain an employer from suspending an employee in the same way that it may stay a dismissal.

Injunction restraining an anticipated breach of contract
In *Peace v City of Edinburgh Council*, P was on disciplinary suspension. The Court granted an injunction restraining an anticipated breach of contract on the basis that it did not compel the resumption of duties, but rather prohibited the employer choosing to implement alternative disciplinary procedures in place of older contractual ones.

Injunction to restrain implementation of an instruction
In *Hughes v London Borough of Southwark* [1988] IRLR 55, QBD, an injunction was granted restraining the employer from implementing an instruction (that the employees should cease their normal work and carry out other work) that the employer was not entitled to give.

Instances of no injunction
1. In *Wishart v National Association of Citizens Advice Bureaux Ltd* [1990] IRLR 393, CA, W accepted an offer of employment which was conditional on receipt of satisfactory references. The Association was not satisfied with the references received and the Court refused to grant an injunction to require it to allow W to start work as W had been rejected on grounds of suitability, thus indicating that the Association would have no confidence in him to do the job.
2. In *Alexander v Standard Telephones & Cables Ltd* [1990] IRLR 55, ChD and *Alexander v Standard Telephones & Cables Ltd (No 2)* [1991] IRLR 286, QBD, the High Court refused to grant an injunction to enforce contractual redundancy procedures based on seniority as the selection had been made on the basis of capability, which indicated that the employer had less confidence in A than in the retained employees. A's remedy was in damages only.

Declarations

1740 An employee can apply to the courts for a declaration of his rights (*Gunton v Richmond-upon-Thames London Borough Council* [1980] IRLR 321, CA). However, a declaration cannot require the employer to act in accordance with the contract (an injunction would be required) but merely states the parties' rights, thus bringing moral pressure on the employer to respect those rights. Many of the cases in which a declaration has been granted involve public sector employers, where the pressure to comply may be greater than for private employers.

II. Employer remedies

1750 In cases of **fundamental** breach, the employer can treat the contract as discharged and dismiss the employee without notice or payment in lieu of notice (known as "summary dismissal"), and can also sue for damages. If the breach is **not fundamental**, the employer will not be justified in dismissing (he will be liable for wrongful dismissal if he does so) (*Wilson v Racher* [1974] IRLR 114, CA). In such cases (or where the employer waives the breach such that the employment continues), his remedy will be in damages or withholding the employee's wages. In very rare cases, he may be entitled to an account of profits.

Again, where **damages are not an appropriate remedy**, the court may grant an injunction (for example, to enforce a restrictive covenant).

1751 **Timing of claims** If the employer is bringing a counterclaim (¶9426) in an **employment tribunal**, he must do so within 6 weeks from receipt of the employee's claim, although the time limit can be extended for such period as the tribunal considers reasonable if it is satisfied that it was not reasonably practicable to present the counterclaim in time. If the claim is brought in the **High Court or county courts**, it must be presented within 6 years of the date of the breach.

A. Dismissal without notice

1755 In cases of fundamental breach, the employer can dismiss the employee without notice (known as **summary dismissal**). Whether a breach is sufficiently serious to be considered repudiatory will depend on **various factors**, including the nature of the employment and the employee's past conduct. **Examples** of fundamental breach include gross misconduct (such as disobedience or dishonesty), serious negligence/incompetence, a serious breach of duty, and going on strike (*W Simmons v Hoover Ltd* [1976] IRLR 266, EAT) (¶1701).

However, a dismissal in the above circumstances may nevertheless be unfair for statutory purposes, for example for failing to follow a fair procedure. In cases of strike where industrial action is protected, dismissal will be automatically unfair in certain circumstances (¶7520).

1756 A further factor is whether the **contract expressly states** that certain conduct will result in summary dismissal. For example, the contract may state that gross misconduct includes acts of discrimination or harassment, theft or dishonesty, fighting or other disorderly behaviour, being under the influence of drugs or alcohol at work, and serious incidents of general misconduct, such as poor time keeping or sub-standard work (¶6538).

> MEMO POINTS If the contract defines the circumstances in which the employer can summarily dismiss the employee, whether or not he was justified in doing so is a question of construction of the contract rather than the application of the common law doctrine of fundamental breach.

B. Damages

1760 An employee can be held liable in damages for breach of **any express or implied term** of the contract of employment. For example, damages may be awarded for breach of the following duties:
– to give the required period of **notice** to terminate the employment;
– **fidelity** (*Sanders v Parry* [1967] 2 All ER 803);

- to give **personal service** (i.e. failure or refusal to perform contractual obligations); and
- to work with **due diligence and care** (*Janata Bank v Ahmed* [1981] IRLR 457, CA).

> EXAMPLE In *Janata Bank v Ahmed*, A was Assistant General Manager in the bank's London branch. The Court confirmed an award of damages of approximately £35,000 in respect of the bank's losses caused by A's negligence, which included authorising an overdraft for £5,000 without making any credit checks.

1761 In the same way as an employee may affirm a breach of contract (¶8242), if an employer **affirms** an employee's breach he will not be able to pursue a claim for damages.

> EXAMPLE In *Cook v MSHK Ltd and ors* [2009] IRLR 838, CA, an employer dismissed an employee, C, and then sought damages for breach of contract and a declaration that the dismissal had been lawful. Prior to C's dismissal, C, whose contract included a 6-month notice period and restrictive covenants, gave notice of resignation and led the employer to believe he would not be engaging in competitive activity (producing dance music) in his new job. This was untrue. The employer checked with the new employer who confirmed that he would in fact be working in a competing field. The employer, having already asked C to move to another area of the building on the ground that it was necessary to protect the confidential information, then disabled C's computer access. C was signed off sick the next day on the basis that he was stressed out by events and the way he was treated. Thereafter, the employer, worried because of C's threat to claim constructive dismissal which, if proven, would release C from his restrictive covenants, made efforts to endeavour to get C to return to work, asking him to attend a medical examination and discussing with him what work it wanted him to do until the expiry of his notice period. In doing so, the employer insisted that "now the dust had settled" and that there would be no unreasonable change to C's status or access to information, although with suitable safeguards. However, after C returned to work the employer launched disciplinary proceedings and dismissed him without notice for gross misconduct. The Court of Appeal held that by indicating that he was required back at work without reservations as to the employer's rights, the employer had affirmed the contract and waived the right to make any claim in respect of C's serious breaches of contract in misleading it about his competitive intentions, which it had been aware of when asking him to return to work. There were, however, other breaches by C, of which the employer was not aware, or in respect of which it had reserved its position when he returned to work, and those parts of the claim for damages were allowed to proceed.

1762 **Actions** for damages against employees **are rare** due to the cost to the employer in terms of personnel time and legal fees, the fact that employees often lack the financial resources to meet any claim, and the detrimental effect such actions may have on industrial relations. Also, it may be more practical for the employer, in the case of an employee refusing to work normally, to withhold wages or salary instead (¶1770).

Calculation

1763 Damages should put the innocent party into the position he would have been in had both parties to the contract performed their obligations in accordance with the contract. If, for example, the employee **fails or refuses to perform his obligations** under the contract, the employer could claim damages on the basis of the cost to him of finding a **replacement employee** less any sum that he would have paid to the employee in breach. It may be more expensive to find a replacement at short notice or on a temporary basis and the employee in breach will be liable for this extra cost (*Richards v Hayward* [1841] EWHC CP 1).

The employer may also be able to claim for any **consequential loss** (e.g. the value of work lost as a result of the employee's non-performance) where the consequences of the breach might reasonably be expected to have been in the contemplation of the parties when they entered into the contract of employment.

Alternatively, the employer may wish to recover the **wasted expenditure** incurred as a result of the employee's breach.

> EXAMPLE In *Anglia Television Ltd v Reed* [1972] 1 QB 60, CA, Anglia had engaged R, an actor, to play the lead role in a film. R subsequently backed out and **refused to perform**. Anglia could not find a substitute and abandoned the production. As it was unable to establish what profit the film might have made, Anglia sued to recover its **wasted expenditure**, including the cost of employing other

staff involved in the production of the film. The Court held that both pre- and post-contractual expenditure was in the reasonable contemplation of the parties at the time the contract was made as being likely to be wasted if R decided to pull out.

1764 If the employee breaches his duty of care, he will be liable not only for loss incurred by the employer in relation to the employer's property, but also for any loss suffered by the employer as a result of **vicarious liability** (i.e. where the employer is obliged to compensate third parties in respect of the actions of his employees) (*Lister v Romford Ice and Cold Storage Co Ltd* [1957] AC 555, HL).

C. Other remedies

1770 An employer is entitled to **withhold the wages** of an employee who is not performing his contractual duties, and may deduct an amount in respect of any **consequential financial loss** incurred as a result of the employee's breach of contract, where this can be identified (¶3006). In any event, the employer must be careful not to make an **unlawful deduction** from wages (¶3050).

Injunctions

1771 As in the case of employee remedies, the equitable remedy of injunction may be available in appropriate circumstances. Again, **interlocutory** injunctions are often sought.

1772 A court will **not grant** an injunction or order specific performance of an obligation in order to compel an employee to work (s 236 TULRCA 1992).

An injunction may, however, be **granted** in the following circumstances:
– to enforce post-termination confidentiality provisions or restrictive covenants, to the extent that enforcement of these provisions is strictly necessary to protect the employer's legitimate business interests; and
– to restrain the employee from working for another employer during the notice period, either by enforcing an express clause prohibiting the employee from working for other employers or the implied duty of fidelity.

Further information on the enforcement of confidentiality obligations and restraints by way of injunction is provided at ¶2645.

Account for profits

1775 In exceptional circumstances, the employee may be compelled to account to the employer for any profit he has made as a result of a breach of contract (regardless of whether the employer has suffered any loss). For further details, see ¶2665.

CHAPTER 6

Flexible working

OUTLINE

SECTION 1 **Types of flexible working**	1810
Request for flexible working	1813
SECTION 2 **Working at home**	1820
Employee considerations	1823
1 Organisation of work	1825
2 Equipment and set-up	1835
Health and safety	1840
3 Confidentiality and company information	1845
Security issues	1847
4 Discrimination	1850
SECTION 3 **Part-time workers**	1870
A Scope	1880
Comparison to comparator	1882
Comparison to previous treatment	1884
B Equal treatment	1887
Request for written statement	1891
Remuneration and benefits	1893
Recruitment	1901
Training	1905
Job-sharing	1907
Indirect sex discrimination	1909
C Change of terms	1915
D Remedies	1920
SECTION 4 **Fixed-term contracts**	1950
A Scope	1960
1 Equal treatment	1964
Request for written statement	1977
2 Successive fixed-term contracts	1980
Request for written statement	1987
B Termination	1990
Dismissal before end of contract	1991
Dismissal at end of contract	1996
Redundancy	2000
C Remedies	2010
SECTION 5 **Agency workers**	2040
A Employment status	2042
B Agency obligations	2052
Discrimination by agencies	2066
C Equal treatment	2070

1800 In recent years, **flexible work arrangements** have become increasingly prevalent in the workplace. Section 1 details the growing number of options available while sections 2-4 focus on the particular issues of homeworking, part-time working and fixed-term working. **Agency work** is also a way to work flexibly and is discussed in section 5.

MEMO POINTS Some groups of people who work flexibly are protected by various statutory schemes, including part-time workers, workers on fixed-term contracts and agency workers. The details of the relevant regulations are discussed in the relevant section below. There is as yet no legislation protecting all those who work flexibly, as a group. The European Commission has, however, been consulting on a package of measures under the title of "flexicurity", which would include a floor of rights to protect all who work flexibly. It is not yet clear whether this consultation will result in new legislation.

SECTION 1

Types of flexible working

1810 A certain amount of flexible working has always occurred, for example, shift-working, fixed-term working and agency working, linked to the employer's particular needs. In recent years, the increase of women at work, instances of both parents working and the growing acknowledgement of the necessity for a "work-life" balance have extended flexible working, which can be of benefit to both the employer and worker.

Many workers find that flexible working helps with home commitments, as well as reducing the time, cost and stress of commuting. Employers also find that flexible working gives them better staff retention and lower workplace overheads. The Department for Business, Innovation and Skills (BIS) **encourages companies** to consider flexible working where appropriate.

1811 The following are **examples** of the wide range of working arrangements now being used:
– **annualised hours**: organising the worker's working time based on the number of hours worked over the year rather than a week;
– **career breaks**: allowing the worker an extended period of unpaid leave. It is important that both parties are clear before the break begins as to whether the employment relationship will continue during the break or not (see ¶1019);
– **compressed hours**: allowing the worker to work his total number of agreed hours over a shorter period, for example, working his weekly hours over four rather than five days;
– **flexitime**: allowing the worker choice about his working hours, usually with some hours within and others outside certain agreed core times;
– **homeworking**: as well as the more traditional full-time working at home for, for example, manual workers and telesales, this is being increasingly used by office workers by dividing their working time between the workplace and home;
– **job-sharing**: typically, two workers working on a part-time basis so that together they can cover a full-time job;
– **matching hours/days to school hours**: allowing workers to be available for their children when they are out of school by adjusting their daily hours of work;
– **shift working**: working in shifts, which is also particularly useful for employers with longer than the standard working day production or service demands;
– **staggered hours**: allowing workers to start and finish their days at work at different times;
– **sabbaticals**: usually given by some large companies in the form of a career break or extended leave with pay as a reward for long service. Sabbaticals are usually allowed to be taken for any reason and are often seen as a way for workers to "recharge their batteries";
– **term-time working**: allowing workers to take unpaid leave during school holidays;
– **voluntary reduced hours**: allowing workers to choose to work fewer hours or become part-time; and
– **zero hour contracts**: workers agreeing to be available for work as and when required though with no particular number of hours or times of work being specified.

Request for flexible working

1813 **Workers who have children** or **care for adults** may have the right to request flexible working (¶¶4690+).

1815 However, there is **no actual legal right** for such a worker or any worker **to change his hours of work**. Whether it is possible depends on the contract, and it will be a matter of negotiation between the worker and the employer (¶1601). If a change of terms is **agreed**, either the contract is varied or a new contract is issued.

1816 Although an employer is not generally obliged to offer flexible work arrangements, a refusal to consider forms of flexible working at the request of a **female worker with childcare responsibilities** may amount to indirect sex discrimination if it cannot be justified on objec-

tive grounds, e.g. on business or administrative grounds (*Robinson v Oddbins Ltd*, EAT case 188/96).
Further, a number of cases have established that an employer insisting on inflexible work practices which make life difficult for working mothers, e.g. an inflexible shift system, may be committing unlawful indirect sex discrimination (*Chief Constable of Avon & Somerset Constabulary v Chew* [2001] UKEAT 503_00_2809; *London Underground Ltd v Edwards (No 2)* [1998] IRLR 364, CA).

An employer faced with a request for flexible working made by a **male worker** should be careful not to deal with the request any less favourably than they would treat a request from a female employee in similar circumstances, as any failure to treat the request in the same way will be direct sex discrimination.

> EXAMPLE On her return from maternity leave, a worker requests to change her work arrangements from full-time to job-share. The employer refuses:
> – citing a clause in the worker's contract of employment which requires her to work from 9am to 5pm and to do additional hours as the job may require;
> – stating that it is too expensive to have the job shared; and
> – stating that the job in question cannot be shared effectively (even though this has not been tried before).
> A tribunal faced with a sex discrimination claim by the worker will have to decide whether the employer had properly considered the request. It is likely to disregard the contractual provisions and will need to decide, on the facts, whether it was commercially and organisationally viable to perform the post on a job-share basis. Even if the post could not be shared, a tribunal will consider whether other flexible work arrangements would have been possible.

SECTION 2

Working at home

1820 Homeworking is an increasingly popular form of flexible working and there are a substantial and increasing number of employees who work fully or partly from home as part of a shift to more flexible working. There are now estimated to be over two million people in the UK who use IT to help them work away from the traditional office environment.

Employers and home workers should **address the following contractual and practical issues**, principally concerning the organisation of work, the equipment and set-up (including health and safety), and confidentiality and company information.

1821 It is advisable that a **move to homeworking** (be it for all or part of the employee's working time) should be done on a trial basis to assess its viability and success. Such a period will be usually for 2-3 months with a review at the mid-point to resolve any issues that may have arisen. During the trial period, it is usual for the employee to have stricter reporting obligations and duties than after a successful completion so that the volume of work being produced at home can be assessed.

Employee considerations

1823 A home worker should consider the following, as there may be:
– differences to his home insurance policies which should be checked;
– tax implications in using his home for business purposes, for example he may become liable for capital gains tax if he moves home;
– planning permission considerations if he wishes to extend his home for business purposes; and
– lease implications in using his home for business purposes and any lease should be checked to ensure it can be used for business purposes without such use affecting the rateable value.

1. Organisation of work

Place of work

1825 The **contract of employment** should state the place of work. If it does not, this must be evidenced in a written statement (¶1405). Therefore, it must be stated (either in the original document or by variation) if the employee is required or permitted to work at home for all or part of his time at work.

Working practices

1827 Employers can introduce more comprehensive **contractual obligations** on the working practices of home workers, for example requiring a home worker to:
- regularly report and communicate with his line manager;
- be contactable at certain periods;
- inform him in an agreed time scale when he is on holiday or sick;
- work certain hours;
- attend the workplace at certain times;
- not have responsibility for childcare at times when he is working;
- allow the employer access to his home to check compliance with the rules/procedures;
- be more formally supervised; and
- keep a record of his time-keeping.

It is necessary to ensure that workers have their statutory daily and weekly **rest periods** and in-work rest breaks, and that they do not exceed the average weekly working time limit unless by written agreement (¶3688). To this extent, requiring the home worker to fill out time sheets will provide the employer with the necessary records to ensure compliance.

1828 To prevent feelings of isolation and a lack of motivation, as much **contact with work colleagues** as possible should be encouraged and the home worker should be regularly informed of any developments or problems in the company. For example, established and regular interaction through electronic networking facilities (email, intranet and online discussions) and by telephone and post are important. Good access to the home worker's line manager is also important and the home worker should be encouraged or required to attend the workplace to facilitate face-to-face discussions and to attend certain company or team meetings. Finally, when at the workplace, innovative organisational practices such as establishing "social club facilities" or "soft seating areas" for informal conversations can further facilitate additional patterns of communication.

1829 How the employer can organise cover, if necessary, when the home worker is **absent** due to sickness or on holiday should be addressed.

2. Equipment and set-up

Equipment

1835 Employers may **supply** home workers with equipment necessary to perform their duties, such as laptops, PCs, scanners, answerphones, separate telephone lines or other equipment. What the home worker needs, how equipment is maintained and how any problems with it are solved should be addressed (for example, who will be available to help the home worker with hardware or software problems at home). The employee should also be given training, if necessary, to ensure he is using the equipment properly.

1836 The employer should ensure that any equipment is sufficiently **insured** as the employee's home insurance may not cover it. In particular, the company **insurance policy** should be checked to see if:
- it needs to be extended; and

– any security measures need to be complied with, for example the need to secure equipment when not in use.

1837 Employers can introduce tighter contractual terms on **expenditure and care** of company property for home workers. If a home telephone or fax machine is being used, there should be a written agreement as to how the business use is paid for, for example itemised bills may be required before payment or the employer may agree to pay a certain percentage of non-itemised bills. It is also useful to state contractually who will bear the **cost of moving** and setting up equipment if a home worker moves home.

1838 The employer should make sure that the home worker is aware of any **email or internet policies** in relation to using the workstation equipment and he should clarify whether the home worker can use equipment provided by the employer for personal purposes outside working hours.

Health and safety

1840 Employers have health and safety obligations (both common law and statutory) (¶4800) with regard to their **employees** even when they are working from home (Workplace (Health, Safety and Welfare) Regulations extend employer liability to a home or part of home that is converted into a workplace (SI 1992/3004)).

It is therefore necessary to ensure that home workers use any company equipment safely and that adequate materials are provided. To this end it may be appropriate to **inspect** the home workstation and how the home worker uses it. At the very least, an **ergonomic questionnaire** should be filled out and signed by home workers to ensure that the rules relating to workstations and VDUs are complied with. Like assessments at the workplace, these inspections should be repeated as appropriate (see in particular the requirements as set out by the Health and Safety (Display Screen Equipment) Regulations (SI 1992/2792 as amended)). Employers should also ensure that there are adequate first aid provisions and that any reportable injuries are reported.

1841 The general statutory duty also applies to anyone who is affected by the home worker's work and consequently extends to **members of the employee's household** and any **visitors** to the home. Therefore, if there are others in the home worker's household that may have access to the equipment (especially if it is in a general living area of the home), it is necessary to ensure that this is not a safety risk. For example, cables should be out of the way and equipment that could cause electrical shocks should be out of reach of young children.

1842 To ensure health and safety compliance, it is useful to have a contractual term that allows for **access to the home** for this purpose either by the employer or a health and safety inspector.

3. Confidentiality and company information

1845 Employees have an implied duty of fidelity and good faith (¶1213) towards their employer. This is further subject to the general duty of confidentiality (¶1223). It is useful to include **contractual terms** to augment, clarify and highlight the employer's right to confidentiality and good faith and it may be appropriate to introduce stricter terms on the confidentiality and non-competition/solicitation covenants. At the very least, employers should emphasise to home workers that the same obligations exist as for those working at the workplace. Employers can reserve a contractual **right of entry** to obtain company information if the home worker breaches these clauses or it is reasonable to expect him to do so.

Security issues

1847 Employers may wish to make it clear contractually that the home worker is responsible for the security of confidential information. Where necessary, the employer should supply the home worker with a lockable filing cabinet for such purposes.

Potential breaches of security can also occur with the use of a laptop or PC in three main ways:
- laptops may be lost or stolen, or the display on the laptop may be seen by other people, for example while travelling on trains;
- unauthorised access to corporate systems may occur due to careless use of passwords and/or phone numbers; and
- information in transit over the internet may be read by a third party unless it is sufficiently encrypted.

Care with the use of laptops and PCs should be emphasised and employers should make employees aware of the risks. As a result of a number of high profile cases of lost/stolen laptops, the Information Commissioner's Office (ICO) recommends that portable and mobile devices, including magnetic media, used to store and transmit personal information, the loss of which could cause damage or distress to individuals, should be protected using approved encryption software which is designed to guard against the compromise of information. The ICO has formed the view that, in future, where such losses occur and where encryption software has not been used to protect the data, regulatory action may be pursued.

4. Discrimination

1850 Employers must ensure that if they offer different terms and conditions to home workers they do not discriminate against them, especially if such workers are **predominately female**. In such cases, a home worker may have an equal pay or sex discrimination claim under the anti-discrimination legislation. Further, if home workers are **predominately part-time**, they may have a claim for equal treatment (under the Part-time Workers Regulations (see ¶1887)).

Potential discrimination can occur with regard to **pay and career development** and employers should ensure that home workers are paid appropriately and that they have an equal opportunity to participate in **training courses** and that they are kept informed of vacancies occurring in the workplace.

SECTION 3

Part-time workers

1870 Employers must ensure that part-time **workers** are **not treated less favourably** than full-time staff (Part-Time Workers (Prevention of Less Favourable Treatment) Regulations SI 2000/1551 (referred to in this section as the regulations) as amended by Part-Time Workers (Prevention of Less Favourable Treatment) Regulations 2000 (Amendment) Regulations SI 2002/2035). Employers and workers cannot contract out of the regulations, and any term (express or implied) in the contract of employment, or in any other contract, which seeks to exclude or limit the operation of any of the regulations, or stop workers from bringing proceedings under them, will be void (reg 9 SI 2002/2035).

> MEMO POINTS The regulations implement the Part-Time Work Directive and, in particular, clauses 1-4 of the framework agreement on ensuring equal treatment. As a result, the courts and tribunals can look at the Directive for guidance when interpreting the regulations (EC Part-Time Work Directive 1997/81).
>
> The Directive also promotes the development of part-time work on a voluntary basis and the flexible organisation of working time to take into account the needs of both employers and workers. The **BIS guidance notes** on part-time workers (The Law and Practice – a detailed guide for employers and part-time workers (referred to in this section as "the guidance notes")) reflect this aspiration as well as giving guidance on regulatory compliance. The guidance notes recommend that more types of job and levels of management should be opened to part-time workers and they give best practice recommendations on how this can be achieved. Although the guidance notes do not have any legal status, a court or tribunal may infer that an employer has breached the regulations if he has not followed the relevant best practice recommendations.

1871 As most part-time work arrangements are undertaken by women who, statistically, often have the prime responsibility for childcare arrangements, if employees suffer less favourable treatment as a result, this may also constitute **indirect sex discrimination** (see ¶5323).

Less favourable treatment with regards to pay between part-time and full-time workers may also give rise to an **equal pay claim** (see ¶5650). Where national legislation sets qualifying periods before part-time workers are entitled to the same rights as their full-time counterparts, such a condition will be contrary to article 157 of the Treaty on the Functioning of the European Union (previously article 141 of the Treaty of Rome) and the Equal Treatment Directive if considerably more women than men are affected by it and the condition cannot be objectively justified (Art 157 EU Treaty on the Functioning of the European Union; EEC Equal Treatment Directive 1976/207; *Elsner-Lakeberg v Land Nordrhein-Westfalen* [2005] IRLR 209, ECJ).

Part-time employees also have a separate right to equal treatment with regard to **pensions** and some may also be entitled to past benefits if they were deprived of them (¶3435).

> MEMO POINTS In *Elsner-Lakeberg v Land Nordrhein-Westfalen*, the Court of Justice of the European Union considered the case of a German worker who was prevented from claiming overtime by way of a regional law under which both part-time and full-time workers would be remunerated for overtime worked only when at least 3 additional hours per month had been completed. This rule was found to be a greater burden on part-time workers than their full-time counterparts and offended the principle of equal pay.

A. Scope

1880 The protection under the regulations is given to all **workers** who are not full-time and are therefore considered to be part-time (regs 1 (2), 2 (2) SI 2000/1551). A full-time worker is defined as one who is paid wholly or in part by reference to the time he works and is identifiable as a full-time worker having regard to the custom and practice of the employer in relation to his other workers under the **same type of contract**.

A part-time worker is only entitled to the protection given under the regulations if either:
– he can compare himself to an **identified comparable full-time worker** (i.e. a comparator); or
– he is entitled to compare his part-time terms and treatment to his **own past full-time terms** and treatment.

> MEMO POINTS The Court of Justice of the European Union has held that a casual worker who worked on demand (i.e. there was no guarantee of particular hours of work) was a worker within the meaning of the Equal Treatment Directive and the Part-Time Work Directive. However, working under such a contract could not in itself amount to indirect sex discrimination or discrimination against part-timers as there was no full-time comparator (i.e. a full-time worker working on demand) (EEC Equal Treatment Directive 1976/207; EC Part-Time Work Directive 1997/81; *Wippel v Peek & Cloppenburg GmbH & Co KG, Case C313/02* [2005] IRLR 211, ECJ).

1881 To determine whether a **comparator** has the same type of contract as a part-time worker, the **different types of contract** are divided into the following four groups. The comparator and part-time worker must belong to the same group (reg 2 (3) SI 2000/1551):
1. employees under a contract that is not a contract of apprenticeship;
2. apprentices;
3. workers who are not employees; or
4. any other type of employment relationship (any other description of worker that it is reasonable for the employer to treat differently from other workers on the ground that workers of that description have a different type of contract). Note that this is a miscellaneous group.

These four groups of different types of contract are mutually exclusive, and the group "any other type of employment relationship" is purely a residual group for "other" descriptions of workers who do not fall into one of the other groups (*Matthews v Kent and Medway Towns Fire Authority and ors* [2006] ICR 365, HL). The question as to whether there is the same type of contract should be approached broadly and a contract cannot be treated as being of a different type just because some terms and conditions are different or because the employer chooses to treat workers of a particular type differently. Any such differences should only be considered when deciding whether the employer was justified in treating the worker less favourably on objective grounds.

Comparison to comparator

1882 A comparator is **defined** in relation to a part-time worker. He is a full-time worker who, at the time of the alleged unequal treatment (reg 2 (4) SI 2000/1551):
– is employed by the **same employer** under the same type of contract and engaged in the **same or broadly similar work** having regard, where relevant, to whether he has a similar level of qualification, skills and experience; and
– works or is based at the **same establishment**. Where there is no full-time worker at that establishment who could be a comparator, he can work or be based at a **different establishment**.

With regard to what amounts to "the same or broadly similar work", factual differences should not be treated as an additional factor, without assessing the extent to which these differences affected the work that the full-time and part-time workers were actually engaged in (i.e. their core activity) (*Matthews v Kent and Medway Towns Fire Authority and ors* [2006] ICR 365, HL). Further, correct weight should be given to the similarities and differences. In this case, concerning part-time firefighters, the tribunal had erred in concentrating on the differences which meant that it had not properly assessed the weight that ought to have been given to the similarities. Particular weight should have been given to the extent to which the work of the full-time and part-time workers was the same and the importance of that work to the enterprise as a whole. To do otherwise would run "the risk of giving too much weight to differences which are the almost inevitable result of one worker working full-time and another working less than full-time." Consequently, the fact that full-time workers performed some extra tasks did not, in itself, prevent their work from being the same or broadly similar.

> MEMO POINTS There must be an actual, not hypothetical, comparator (*Carl v University of Sheffield* [2009] IRLR 616, EAT).

Comparison to previous treatment

1884 In two situations, a part-time worker who used to work full-time can be his own comparator regardless of whether he has a new contract or a variation of his existing contract, as long as the terms are for a decreased number of weekly hours (regs 3(1), 4 SI 2000/1551). This applies to a full-time worker who is either:
– **transferring to part-time work**; or
– **returning part-time after absence** if he was a full-time worker immediately before it, and who continues to work for the same employer within a period of less than 12 months from the first day of absence, and does the same job or a job at the same level. Where the contract continues, any contractual variation made during this absence will be taken as included.

1885 If a **new contract** has been agreed, it need not be the same type of contract. For example, a full-time secretary with a permanent contract could transfer or return as a part-time secretary, with protection under the regulations, on a fixed-term contract if the above conditions were satisfied.

B. Equal treatment

1887 A part-time worker has the right **not be treated less favourably** due to his part-time status than a comparable full-time worker (reg 5 SI 2000/1551):
– with regard to the terms of his contract; or

– by being subjected to any other detriment by any act, or deliberate failure to act, of his employer.

However, the employer has a **defence** if he can justify his treatment on objective grounds (¶1890).

1888 While the part-time work must be the **effective and predominant reason** for the difference in treatment between the part-time worker and a full-time comparator, it need not be the only or sole reason (*Sharma and ors v Manchester City Council* [2008] ICR 623, EAT; *Carl v University of Sheffield* [2009] IRLR 616, EAT not following with regard to this point *Gibson v Scottish Ambulance Service*).

However, a part-time worker is not subject to less favourable treatment where the **real reason** for the difference in treatment between himself and a full-time comparator is not by reason of his status (*Gibson v Scottish Ambulance Service* [2004] UKEAT 0052_04_1612). The EAT in a majority decision held that the appropriate test in such circumstances was the subjective "by reason that" test (as set out by the House of Lords in *Chief Constable of West Yorkshire Police v Khan* (a case on race discrimination) and reinforced by the Court of Appeal in *The Law Society v Bahl* (a case on sex and race discrimination)). The question that must be determined is "why did the alleged discriminator act as he did? What, consciously or unconsciously, was his reason?" Consequently, the reason or motivation for the difference in treatment must be determined to ascertain whether the part-time worker has been treated unequally. In this case, the real reason for the difference in the number of stand-by hours the part-time worker had to do compared to his full-time comparator was held to be an issue of demand in the local area and consequently not because he was a part-time worker.

1889 **Same terms and the pro-rata principle** To ensure that the employer is not treating his part-time workers less favourably, he should offer them the same terms as comparable full-time workers. These terms may be offered on a pro-rata basis, as appropriate, so that the part-time worker can receive or be entitled to such proportion of the pay or benefit as is reasonable in the circumstances having regard to the length of his employment and the terms on which the benefit is offered (reg 5(3) SI 2000/1551).

1890 **Objective justification** Less favourable treatment may be objectively justified by the employer (reg 5(2) SI 2000/1551). If this is the case then there will be no breach of the regulations. What amounts to objective justification will **depend on the circumstances** but employers should ensure that they have **good reason** for treating a part-time worker less favourably. Each case should be decided on its own circumstances with the employer weighing up the costs against the benefits obtained. Objective justification may exist if the less favourable treatment is a **necessary and appropriate means** of achieving a **legitimate business objective**.

Request for written statement

1891 If a part-time worker believes that he is being treated less favourably than a comparable full-time worker he has the right to ask his employer **to give reasons for his less favourable treatment**. He should make his request to his employer in writing, and is entitled to receive a written statement from his employer within 21 days of that request (reg 6 SI 2000/1551).

A written statement is **admissible** as evidence in any proceedings concerning a part-time working claim (¶1920) and if it appears to the tribunal that the employer deliberately, and without reasonable excuse, omitted to provide a written statement, or that the written statement is evasive or equivocal, the tribunal may draw any inference which it considers just and equitable, including an inference that the employer has infringed the right in question.

1892 The right to request a written statement does not apply where the treatment in question consists of the **dismissal of an employee**, as in such cases the employee is entitled to a written statement of reasons for his dismissal (¶8310).

Remuneration and benefits

1893 Part-time workers must receive the same basic **rate of pay** as comparable full-time workers unless a lower hourly rate can be justified on objective grounds (for example, where the pay scheme is performance-related and they can be shown to have a different level of performance, measured in a fair and consistent appraisal system). In general, the same principle applies to **enhanced or special rates** of pay such as bonus pay, shift allowances, night work or weekend work. However, part-time workers do not have an automatic right to **overtime payment** once they work beyond their normal hours until they have reached the normal hours of their comparable full-time workers (reg 5(4) SI 2000/1551).

When comparing wages of part-time workers to full-time workers, the **wages as a whole** should be compared (*James and ors v Great North Eastern Railways* [2005] UKEAT 0496_04_0103). In this case, full-time workers were paid at a higher rate for some of their contractual hours, which meant that overall their rate was higher than their part-time colleagues. Consequently, unless the employer could justify this on objective grounds, this amounted to less favourable treatment.

1894 Part-time workers are entitled to receive a pro-rata level of **benefits** in line with the number of hours they work, unless exclusion can be objectively justified. For example, **share option schemes** may be excluded if the value of the share options is so small for a part-time worker that the potential benefit to him would be less than the likely cost of realising them.

It may be inappropriate to offer certain benefits on a pro-rata basis, for example health insurance or company cars, and employers can exclude such benefits from part-time workers if it can be justified on objective grounds. For example, providing a car to a part-time worker might be at a disproportionate cost to the company or might not meet any real need.

The guidance notes state that in such situations employers might, by way of **best practice**, calculate the financial value of the benefit to a full-time worker and apply that value pro-rata to a part-time worker. Alternatively, if the benefit or allowance was given to a full-time worker, for example every year, then a part-time worker working half the full-time hours might be given the benefit or allowance every 2 years. Likewise, other benefits such as **clothing or travel allowance** or **staff discounts** might also be extended to part-time workers in line with these principles.

1895 Detrimental pay differentials between a part-time worker and his full-time comparator may give rise to a claim under the regulations and/or the equality legislation (¶5650).

> EXAMPLE In *Nimz v Freie und Hansestadt Hamburg* [1991] EUECJ C-184/89, an employer paid a different rate of pay to part-time and full-time workers doing a similar job. He tried to justify the pay differential on the basis that his full-time workers gained experience and developed their skills more quickly than his part-time workers. This argument was rejected by the Court of Justice of the European Union, on the basis that it was generalised. According to the Court, pay practices should depend on the particular circumstances of each case and, in particular, on the relationship between the nature of the duties performed and the experience the employee gained from performing those duties after a certain number of working hours.

1897 **Leave** Part-time workers are **entitled** to statutory annual leave (¶4000). Part-time employees are also entitled to maternity, adoption, paternity and parental leave (¶4400).

If these entitlements have been extended for full-time workers, for example by increased annual leave, part-timers are entitled to the same entitlements on a pro-rata basis.

1899 One long-standing issue concerns whether part-time workers are entitled to leave on **public and bank holidays** under **enhanced contractual leave schemes**, which often give these days as additional holiday on top of a fixed entitlement. Where a worker works part-time on days other than Mondays, it follows that the part-time worker will receive proportionately less annual leave than a full-time worker working five days a week, including Mondays. If a company gives the day off to all staff who ordinarily work on the day of the public/bank holiday but no time off in lieu to any other members of staff, it will probably not be unlawful. For example, a part-time worker who works Monday-Wednesday inclusive would be entitled to bank holiday Mondays off, but a part-time worker who works Wednesday-Friday inclusive would not. The guidance notes suggest that as a matter of **good practice** employers should compensate for the disadvantage suffered by those workers who do not receive particular days off as a result of their working pattern by allowing a pro-rata entitlement of days off in lieu.

Recruitment

Although the regulations do not cover external recruitment, the guidance notes recommend as **best practice** that employers periodically review whether the posts they are offering could be performed by part-time workers. Likewise, if approached by an applicant for a full-time post who wishes to work part-time, employers should give consideration as to whether part-time work arrangements could fulfil the requirements of the post. **1901**

The guidance notes recommend that employers make a **wider range of jobs** available for part-time work and, as **best practice**, employers should seek to maximise the range of posts designated as suitable for part-time working or job-sharing at all levels of the company, including skilled and managerial positions. Companies should recognise that just because a worker works part-time does not mean that he does not want to continue to develop a career and that reducing or blocking his chances to move around the company may demoralise or cause him to look for job opportunities elsewhere. Conversely, allowing part-time workers to apply for other posts ensures that the employers will be able to pick the best person for the job.

Part-time workers should be given equal opportunity to seek **promotion**, indeed part-time staff may be willing to work full-time on promotion if, for example, the extra pay will allow them to afford childcare.

Giving part-time workers less **information on job vacancies** will amount to less favourable treatment and the guidance notes recommend that employers should examine their advertising practices to see if there is anything that might disadvantage part-time workers. For example, part-time workers may not hear about vacancies that are filled by informal management practices such as word of mouth. **1902**

As **best practice**, the guidance notes recommend that employers should periodically review how individuals are provided with information on the availability of part-time and full-time positions. Companies should consider how to make it easier for workers to vary their hours, including transferring between part-time and full-time work, to the benefit of both workers and employers.

The guidance notes recognise that **staff representatives** of formal or informal bodies representing the workforce may find it useful to be kept informed of some or all of the following: **1903**
– overall human resource policy with regard to part-time work and any plans to change it;
– number and location of part-time workers;
– whether any requests to change hours have been refused and, if so, why;
– training opportunities for part-time workers and take up; and
– the steps taken to ensure equal access to promotion.

Training

Employers should be aware that training may be inconvenient to part-time workers, for example a part-time worker with personal commitments may find it difficult to attend. As **best practice**, the guidance notes recommend that the provision of training should be arranged to ensure that it is equally conveniently located and timed for part-time as for full-time workers. Where this is not possible, a range of **other measures** might be considered to support their career development, such as paying part-time workers (at their normal rate of pay) for the hours they attend outside their normal working hours, or offering: **1905**
– an equivalent course from an alternative provider at a more convenient time and place;
– the comparable level and quality of training in another area; or
– other training methods, for example open or distance learning (by correspondence, phone or internet/email) courses.

MEMO POINTS   In certain circumstances, part-time work can be a form of **training in its own right**, for example workers who are on a career break can find periods of part-time work a useful way to keep in touch with developments in their companies and their area of work. Further, employers may find that this not only keeps the services of the worker during a career break but when the worker returns he is immediately able to play a full role in the company.

Job-sharing

1907 Job-sharing arrangements consist of dividing a full-time job between two part-time workers. This division can be made in a number of ways to suit the circumstances, for example, one worker may work mornings, the other afternoons, or each may work 2 and a half days. Sometimes, depending of the type of work involved, it may be appropriate to have a hand-over period when both are working.

Employers often benefit from having two people working on a project, with their combined energy, skills and experience. Depending on the agreement, job-sharers may also provide cover when one is on holiday or sick. As a result, the guidance notes recommend that as **good practice** employers should seriously consider requests for job-sharing. The drawback is that it may be difficult to organise a job-share arrangement due to the need to find two workers who can do the job, are capable of working together and want to work complementary hours. Therefore, the guidance notes recommend that as best practice **larger companies** should keep a database of those interested in entering job-sharing arrangements.

Job-share contracts will often state that in the event one job-share partner **resigns or is dismissed** (for a reason other than redundancy) their "share" of the role will be advertised for a limited period after which, if no appointment has been made, the remaining job-share partner's role will revert to a full-time post.

Indirect sex discrimination

1909 A **provision or policy, recruitment criterion or practice** which requires all persons to work full-time is likely to constitute indirect sex discrimination (¶5323), since more women than men will need to work part-time to balance their work requirements with childcare responsibilities. This is an important aspect to the anti-discrimination legislation since the regulations do not protect persons who want to move into or out of part-time work. Staff in this position, who believe that their employer's policies make it difficult for them to do so, may only complain if they can demonstrate that the provision, criterion or practice has an adverse impact on them as women (or, possibly, men). Cases increasingly recognise that problems associated with part-time working (e.g. lack of career progression, reduced benefits) are predominantly female problems.

Therefore, tribunals and courts will often not require much by way of statistical evidence to be persuaded that an issue of indirect discrimination has arisen (*Greater Manchester Police Authority v Lea* [1990] IRLR 372, EAT).

1910 If an employer's provision, criterion or practice is found to have a detrimental effect on part-time workers, the employer's only **line of defence** is to show that he had an objective reason, not connected with sex, for applying the particular provision etc. For example, there might be good business, commercial or administrative reasons for the difference in treatment. Rarely, however, will it be open to an employer to argue that part-timers are less productive or experienced than their full-time counterparts.

EXAMPLE   An employer has the following promotion criterion: workers must have completed at least 5 years' full-time service before they may be promoted to a managerial post. A female part-time worker has applied for the post, but was not promoted because, although she has worked for the employer for 5 years, she has only worked 3 days a week. Were the employer to try to justify this criterion on the basis that 5 years' full-time work is necessary for workers to gain the necessary experience for a managerial post, that approach would in all probability be regarded as a generalisation. Instead, when evaluating the request for promotion, the employer should examine the nature of the duties performed by the worker and the experience she gained in practice during the time she has actually worked.

C. Change of terms

See ¶¶1813+ for a general discussion on the right to **request flexible working**.

As **best practice**, the guidance notes currently recommend that employers should look seriously at requests to work part-time and, where possible, explore with their workers how this change could be accommodated. Further, employers should also consider establishing a procedure for discussing with workers whether they wish to change from full-time to part-time for any reason.

The guidance notes suggest that it is helpful if employers have a **procedure for handling requests** for part-time work together with discussions focusing on any particular worker's tasks and responsibilities and how a change in hours could fit in.

Questions that may be useful in forming the **basis of a policy** for handling such requests are as follows:
– does a worker need to be present in the post during all working hours? If so, can the post be filled as a job-share and is there a suitable candidate?
– can all the necessary work be done in the hours requested?
– can the job be redefined to make it easier to do part-time?
– is there another job of similar level that the worker could do part-time?
– is the change for a known period?
– how much would it cost to recruit and train a replacement if the worker left?
– what benefits would the company get, for example staff retention, lower wage bill and assurance of staff coverage for peak periods? and
– what would be the effect on the morale and commitment of other staff?

If there is a **request for increasing hours**, questions that may be useful in forming the **basis of a policy** for handling such a request are as follows:
– is there sufficient work for an increase in hours?
– could the extra hours be used to reorganise a number of jobs more efficiently?
– can the company afford the increase in pay? and
– will the increase save money on recruitment?

If it is the **employer** who wishes to change the hours worked to correspond with operational needs, he must nevertheless be careful that he has a good business reason to do so and that he has not indirectly discriminated against the worker.

D. Remedies

A part-time worker can bring a claim to an employment tribunal if his employer has infringed his **right to not be treated less favourably** or if he has suffered a detriment (regs 5, 7-8 SI 2000/1551).

A part-time worker has the right not to be subjected to any detriment by any act, or any deliberate failure to act, by his employer if the reason(s) or ground(s) for the act or omission is that the worker has:
– alleged that the employer has infringed his rights;
– refused (or proposed to refuse) to waive a right;
– brought proceedings against the employer in pursuance of his rights;
– requested a written statement of the reasons for less favourable treatment;
– given evidence or information in connection with proceedings brought by another worker; or
– otherwise done anything further in respect of his rights to the employer or any other person.

The worker has the same right if the detriment or act was because the employer believes or **suspects** that he has done or intends to do any of the above.

If the **allegation**(s) that the employer infringed a worker's rights (or acted or did not act because of his belief or suspicion) is false and not made in good faith, the worker will have no right to claim.

> MEMO POINTS   What amounts to a "**detriment**" is not defined by the regulations, but case law on discrimination has held that it is whether a reasonable worker would feel he has been disadvantaged by reason of his employer's acts (¶5279).

1921 An employer has a **defence** if he can show that the less favourable treatment was justifiable on objective grounds (see ¶1890 for further details).

1925 Any dismissal of an employee will be **automatically unfair** (¶8390) if the reason (or, if more than one, the principal reason) for the dismissal is one of those covered by the right not to suffer a detriment (reg 7 SI 2000/1551).

> MEMO POINTS   Non-employee workers (¶13) who are so dismissed should rely on the right not to suffer a detriment (see above).

Procedure

1927 Complaints must be made **within** 3 months beginning with the date of the act or failure to act or, if it is part of a series of similar acts or failures, the last of them. However, a tribunal may **extend** this period if it considers it just and equitable to do so (¶9475).

1928 If the **claim is successful**, the tribunal can:
– make a declaration;
– order the employer to pay compensation; and
– recommend that the employer take, within a specified period, whatever action it considers reasonable to obviate or reduce the adverse effect on the worker.

If the employer fails, without reasonable justification to comply, the tribunal can make an order for compensation (or increase the amount of compensation if one has already been made).

SECTION 4

Fixed-term contracts

1950 Workers may be contracted to work for a **fixed period only** or to **perform a particular task** with the contract terminating at the end of this period or on the completion of the task. Such contracts are called fixed-term contracts.

1951 **Fixed-term employees** have the **right not to be treated less favourably** than comparable permanent employees (i.e. employees with employment contracts for an indefinite or indeterminate term) of the same employer doing similar work, unless the treatment is objectively justified.

Further, all fixed-term employees are entitled to the main statutory **employment rights** (subject to achieving any necessary qualifying period (¶1080)), for example the right not to be unfairly dismissed, the right to a written statement of the reason for dismissal and the right to statutory redundancy payments. It is also automatically unfair to dismiss those employees who seek to rely on the regulations. A full list of statutory rights can be found at ¶13 with regard to employees and ¶17 with regard to workers.

> EXAMPLE   **Pregnant fixed-term employees** should be treated the same way as any other pregnant employee in terms of their statutory right to time off for antenatal appointments and their right to take maternity leave, and they are entitled to parity of treatment in relation to any benefits that the

employer provides. See ¶1996 with regard to an employee's fixed-term contract coming to an end while she is on maternity leave.

A fixed-term employee may also become a permanent employee if he has served under **successive fixed-term contracts**.

EXAMPLE In *Del Cerro Alonso v Osakidetza-Servicio Vasco de Salud, Case C-307/05* [2008] ICR 145, ECJ, a case concerning the implementation of the Fixed-Term Work Directive, the Court of Justice of the European Union ruled that a provision of a collective agreement operative in the Spanish health service, which provided additional salary benefit to permanent employees only and not to workers employed on fixed-term contracts, discriminated against fixed-term workers.

MEMO POINTS 1. The previous imbalance between the employment rights of fixed-term and permanent employees was addressed by the Fixed-Term Employees (Prevention of Less Favourable Treatment) Regulations which came into force on 1 October 2002 (referred to in this section as "**the regulations**") (SI 2002/2034).
The regulations derive from the Fixed-Term Work Directive which, like the Part-Time Work Directive, extends to protect those with "an employment contract or employment relationship as defined by law, collective agreement or practice in each member state." Note, though, that under the Part-Time Workers (Prevention of Less Favourable Treatment) Regulations (which derive from Part-Time Work Directive) protection is extended to "workers" while under the Fixed-Term Employees (Prevention of Less Favourable Treatment) Regulations protection is only granted to the narrower category of "employees" (EC Fixed-Term Work Directive 1999/70; EC Part-Time Work Directive 1997/81; SI 2000/1551; SI 2002/2034).
2. The **BIS guidance notes**, "Fixed-Term Work: A guide to the regulations", are a useful guide to regulatory compliance. Although the guidance notes do not have any legal status, a court or tribunal may infer that an employer has breached the regulations if he has not followed the relevant best practice recommendations.

Further, employers must ensure that any less favourable treatment does not result in unlawful **indirect sex discrimination** (see ¶5300 for further details).

1952

EXAMPLE In *Whiffen v Milham Ford Girls' School* [2001] IRLR 468, CA, it was the school's redundancy policy to dismiss all fixed-term staff before applying objective selection criteria to the remainder of the school's permanent employees. The Court of Appeal found that such a policy was indirectly discriminatory on the grounds of sex since W was able to demonstrate that a considerably smaller proportion of female staff could comply with the redundancy selection policy criterion that an employee had to be employed on a permanent contract to avoid being dismissed at an early stage in the redundancy process than the proportion of men who could comply with it.

A. Scope

A **fixed-term employee** is defined as a person with a contract of employment which is due to end when a specified (reg 1 (2) SI 2002/2034):
– date is reached;
– event does or does not happen; or
– task has been completed.

1960

Such contracts of employment are referred to as fixed-term contracts. Examples are those who are employed specifically to cover for maternity, parental or paternity leave; employees who do "seasonal" or "casual" work, such as agricultural workers and shop assistants employed during busy periods such as Christmas; employees hired to cover unusual peaks in demand, as in the tourist industry; and employees whose contracts will end on the completion of a specified task, such as installing a computer system.

An employee with a fixed-term contract as defined above will still come under the protection of the regulations even if the contract allows for **termination before the expiry date** by notice to either party (*Allen v National Australia Group Europe Ltd* [2004] UKEAT 0102_03_2907).

1961 **Workers** are **excluded** from the protection afforded by the regulations, as are **apprentices**. Likewise, **students on work experience placements** of 1 year or less that are being undertaken in connection with an undergraduate, post-graduate or teacher training course are also excluded. However, students who take on fixed-term employment during their holidays or gap year are covered by the regulations as long as the job is not part of their course.

1. Equal treatment

1964 A fixed-term employee has the right **not to be treated less favourably** due to his fixed-term status than a comparable permanent employee (reg 3 SI 2002/2034):
– with regard to the terms of his contract; or
– by being subjected to any other detriment by any act, or deliberate failure to act, of his employer.

A **comparable permanent employee** (reg 2(1) SI 2002/2034):
– is a permanent employee employed by the same employer as the fixed-term employee;
– is employed to do the same or broadly similar work of the fixed-term employee having regard, where relevant, to whether they have similar levels of qualifications and skills; and
– works or is based at the same establishment as the fixed-term employee with whom he is being compared. Where there is no comparable permanent employee at that establishment the comparison can be made with a permanent employee working or based at another establishment of the employer.

The employer has a **defence** if he can justify his treatment on objective grounds (¶1970).

1965 The fact that an employee has a fixed-term contract as opposed to a permanent contract cannot, in itself, amount to less favourable treatment (*Department for Work and Pensions v Webley* [2005] IRLR 288, CA).

Some areas where a fixed-term employee may be disadvantaged include qualifying periods of work, or in the conditions for accrual of entitlements or benefits, training opportunities or being considered for permanent employment. The fixed-term employee may also be disadvantaged in other areas, such as pay (*Del Cerro Alonso v Osakidetza-Servicio Vasco de Salud, Case C-307/05* [2008] ICR 145, ECJ) or annual leave. Less favourable treatment can occur, for example, when a fixed-term employee does not get an employment benefit that a comparable permanent employee gets. The benefit may be offered to the comparable permanent employee under his contract of employment or it could be a benefit that is generally available to permanent employees but not to fixed-term employees. The permanent employee may also get non-contractual benefits, such as bonus payments, or he may be given training opportunities which are not offered to fixed-term employees even though all other contract terms are identical. In each case the employer may be treating the fixed-term employee less favourably than the permanent comparable employee.

1966 **Same terms and the pro-rata principle** To ensure that the employer is not treating his fixed-term employees less favourably, he should offer them the same terms as comparable permanent employees. These may be pro-rated as appropriate, so that the fixed-term employee can receive or be entitled to such proportion of the pay or benefit as is reasonable in the circumstances having regard to the length of his employment and the terms on which the benefit is offered (reg 3(5) SI 2002/2034). Therefore if **benefits**, such as annual season tickets, are offered to permanent employees but the duration of the fixed-term contract is for only 6 months, the fixed-term employee could be offered a 6-monthly season ticket under the pro-rating principle. Likewise, if a contract is for 6 months, the employee should receive half of an annual benefit; if the contract is for 4 months, he should receive one third.

1967 The employer must also provide fixed-term employees with the same opportunities for **internal recruitment** as their permanent counterparts and must give them the same information on permanent vacancies within the organisation as they provide to permanent employees. The posting of vacancy notices on a notice board, accessible to all employees, will usually be sufficient to show that this obligation has been met. However, if the employer limits the availability of vacancies to permanent employees this will amount to less favourable treatment.

Fixed-term employees must be offered access to an **occupational pension scheme** on the same basis as permanent employees. Vesting periods (i.e. the qualifying period of work that must be met before an employee becomes a member of the pension scheme) are not required to be pro-rated to accommodate fixed-term employees and the same period should apply to both fixed-term and permanent employees.

1968

The fixed-term employee is not obliged to accept entry into the scheme, even when offered. Where the length of employment is not sufficient to provide any, or provides little, benefit under the scheme, the employee may decide not to join. If this happens the employer is not required to offer alternative pension benefits such as contributing to a private pension scheme unless similar arrangements are offered to comparable permanent employees. Where membership of a pension scheme offers few or no benefits to the fixed-term employee the employer may wish to point this out to him at the time of recruitment.

Given that access to an occupational pension scheme may be of little value to a fixed-term employee, the employer and the fixed-term employee can agree that alternative compensation is provided to the employee instead.

Objective justification Less favourable treatment may be objectively justified by the employer (reg 3(3) SI 2002/2034). If this is the case then there will be no breach of the regulations. What amounts to objective justification will **depend on the circumstances** but employers should ensure that they have **good reason** for treating a fixed-term employee less favourably. Each case should be decided on its own circumstances with the employer weighing up the costs against the benefits obtained.

1970

Objective justification may exist if the less favourable treatment is a **necessary and appropriate means** of achieving a **legitimate business objective**. Equally, the **cost to the employer** in offering a particular benefit may be disproportionate to the benefit actually received by the fixed-term employee and, as a result, the employer may be objectively justified in withholding the benefit. There may, for example, be objective justification for an employer not to offer a fixed-term employee access to the occupational pension scheme where the scheme has a vesting period which exceeds the length of the fixed-term contract, or if the employer makes instead a reasonable level of payment into a stakeholder or private pension scheme of the fixed-term employee.

1971

A further example is given in the BIS guidance notes where there is a fixed-term employee on a contract of 3 months and a comparable permanent employee with a company car. The employer may decide not to offer the car to the fixed-term employee if the cost of doing so is high and the need of the business for the employee to travel can be met in some other way.

Comparison

In order to ensure that fixed-term employees are treated comparably with permanent employees or to ensure that different terms and conditions can be objectively justified, the employer should make a comparison, which can be done either on a term-by-term basis or on a package basis.

1973

The **term-by-term approach** involves taking each individual term and condition and showing that they are identical, or, if appropriate, pro-rated for the fixed-term employee.

1974

The **package approach** involves showing that the overall package of terms and conditions afforded to the fixed-term employee, taken as a whole, is no less favourable than the comparable permanent employee's overall package (reg 4 SI 2002/2034). The employer will be able to balance a less favourable term against a more favourable one, the only limitation being that the overall value of the fixed-term employee's employment package should be at least equal to that of the permanent comparable employee. In using the package approach the employer may be able to objectively justify the absence of a particular benefit from the fixed-term employee's package.

1975

Guidance notes published by BIS suggest that when assessing the **value of benefits** for the purposes of the comparison their objective monetary worth should be used.

> EXAMPLE Employee Y is a permanent employee. As a term of her employment, Y is entitled to an annual gym membership, which is equivalent to a cash value of £400. The gym does not offer membership for shorter periods. Y is absent on maternity leave, and a fixed-term employee Z is appointed for a period of 9 months as her replacement on the same salary. It would be appropriate to offer Z a cash benefit of £300 in lieu of the gym membership.

Request for written statement

1977 If a fixed-term employee believes that he is being treated less favourably than a permanent comparable employee he has the right to ask his employer **to give reasons for his less favourable treatment**. He should make his request to his employer in writing, and is entitled to receive a written statement from his employer within 21 days of that request (reg 5 SI 2002/2034).

A written statement is **admissible** as evidence in any proceedings concerning a fixed-term working claim (¶2010) and if it appears to the tribunal that the employer deliberately, and without reasonable excuse, omitted to provide a written statement, or that the written statement is evasive or equivocal, the tribunal may draw any inference which it considers just and equitable, including an inference that the employer has infringed the right in question.

1978 The right to request a written statement does not apply where the treatment in question consists of the dismissal of an employee as in such cases the employee is entitled to a written statement of reasons for his dismissal (¶8310).

2. Successive fixed-term contracts

Deemed permanent contract

1980 Where a fixed-term employee's contract is **renewed or re-engaged after** at least **4 years of continuous employment**, the renewal or re-engagement will take effect as if the contract were permanent unless the employer can justify the fixed-term status on objective grounds (reg 8 SI 2002/2034).

Whether **successive periods of fixed-term contracts** count towards this period or not will depend on continuity of employment rules and whether there is continuity of employment as a result (see ¶1010 for information on continuity).

> MEMO POINTS The regulations include an exclusion for **apprentices**, **agency workers**, and **those on training schemes** that are **funded by the Government** or an institution of the European Community. Individuals in these groups are not able to apply for a declaration of employee status in reliance on the 4-year rule, and it is highly unlikely that they can rely on time served whilst part of one of these groups to go towards the 4-year rule even if they later apply as regular fixed-term employees: they would need to wait until they have 4 years of service as regular employees (this was confirmed by the Court of Appeal in relation to trainees and is likely to also apply to former apprentices and former agency workers: *Hudson v Department of Work and Pensions* [2012] EWCA Civ 1416).

1981 The permanent contract that arises will be regarded as one of indefinite duration and any clause in the fixed-term contract (that has been converted into the permanent contract) which purports to limit its duration will be void. Consequently, once a fixed-term contract takes effect as a permanent contract the statutory minimum notice period (¶8131) will apply unless a longer period has been agreed.

Where a contract has become permanent, the employer must provide his employee with an **amended statement of particulars** which evidences his new rights within 1 month of his change of status (¶1400).

Objective justification The employer may be able to show objective justification for not recognising the renewal or re-engagement as permanent employment where a further fixed-term contract is (BIS guidance notes):
- required to achieve a legitimate objective, such as a genuine business objective;
- necessary to achieve that objective; and
- an appropriate way to achieve that objective.

If there is objective justification, the employer is not required to accept that the fixed-term employee has become a permanent employee and the contract that is renewed will continue as a fixed-term contract.

> EXAMPLE In *Duncombe and others v Secretary of State for Children, Schools and Families* [2011] UKSC 14, the Supreme Court ruled in favour of the Secretary of State for Children, Schools and Families by finding that it was objectively justified to employ D and other UK teachers to work in European schools on a series of fixed-term contracts totalling a maximum of 9 years. These successive fixed-term contracts did not give rise to permanent employment contracts. There was a rule in place, made by the Board of Governors pursuant to European statutory rules, limiting the period of time individual teachers could hold positions at European schools to 9 years. The Secretary of State could not require the schools to employ teachers for longer than this and the fixed-terms contracts were therefore objectively justified. The teachers' complaint was not against the series of fixed-term contracts comprising the 9-year rule but against the 9-year rule itself.

> MEMO POINTS The Court of Justice of the European Union has ruled that objective reasons under the EC Directive concerning the use of fixed-term contracts must relate to the activity in question and the circumstances in which it was being carried out (*Adeneler and ors v Ellinikos Organismos Galaktos, Case 212/04* [2006] IRLR 716, ECJ; *Secretary of State for Children Schools and Family v Fletcher* [2009] ICR 102, EAT). The question was considered in the context of Greek presidential Decrees which purported to treat renewed contracts as bona fide fixed-term contracts where they were conducted in particular sectors by reason of the nature of those sectors and the nature of the work in them. The Court found that more appropriate factors to consider when evaluating whether there was indeed justification included: the likelihood that contracts of indefinite duration will be the general form of employment, and the purpose of the directive, which was to protect workers. National legislation must refer to "precise and concrete" circumstances and specific tasks. Where an employee seeks to defend the re-employment of individuals on fixed-term contracts, the Court held that they will not be able to justify that re-employment solely by reference to "general and abstract" domestic legislation.

Extension beyond four years Employers and employees may also, by the **use of collective agreements** (¶1270) **or workforce agreements** (¶1293), extend the validity of fixed-term contracts beyond the 4-year period. Such agreements are recognised on the basis that they prevent the abuse of successive fixed-term contracts (reg 8 SI 2002/2034). They may be used where there is a specific recognition or need for successive fixed-term contracts, such as where sports professionals or actors are to be employed over successive seasons. Collective or workforce agreements may vary the limit on successive contracts, upwards or downwards, or limit the use of such contracts by adopting one or more of the following:
- a limit on the total duration of successive fixed-term contracts;
- a limit on the number of successive fixed-term contracts; or
- a list of permissible objective reasons justifying renewals of fixed-term contracts.

Request for written statement

If the **employee believes** that he has **met the condition of successive fixed-term** contracts amounting to 4 years of continuous employment he may make a written request to his employer asking that he confirm, in writing, that his employment is considered as permanent. The employer is **required to respond** within 21 days of the request being made either confirming that the employment is now permanent or giving reasons why the employee remains on a fixed-term contract (reg 9 SI 2002/2034).

Such a written statement is **admissible** as evidence in any proceedings before a court, a tribunal and the Commissioners for HM Revenue and Customs, and if it appears to a court or tribunal in any proceedings that the employer deliberately, and without reasonable excuse, omitted to provide a written statement, or, that the written statement is evasive or equivocal, it may draw any inference which it considers just and equitable.

1988 **Declaration as to status** Where the employer **fails to respond or give a statement** with reasons why the contract remains fixed-term, **or** where the **employee considers** that he is a permanent employee despite the employer maintaining that the employee remains on a fixed-term status, the employee may present an application to the tribunal for a declaration to that effect.

To make an application, the following requirements must have been met (reg 9 (5) SI 2002/2034):
– the employee must have written to the employer requesting confirmation of the status of employment (i.e. whether permanent or not);
– the employer must have failed to respond or given a statement giving reasons why the contract remains fixed-term; and
– the employee must be employed by the employer at the time the application is made.

B. Termination

1990 The termination of a fixed-term contract is **recognised as a dismissal** for the purposes of the fixed-term employee's statutory rights, even if mutually agreed at the start of the contract. **Non-renewal by mutual consent** will not, however, amount to a dismissal.

Dismissal before end of contract

1991 In guaranteeing work for a fixed period, the employer is liable to pay for the whole of that period if the employee is willing and able to perform the work. Therefore, where the fixed-term contract is prematurely terminated by the employer, the employee can claim that he has been **wrongly dismissed** and the employer has a liability to pay him for the remainder of the period. However, if there is a **notice clause** in the fixed-term contract which provides that the contract may be terminated on notice, the employer's liability will only be for pay during that notice period. If, though, the contract has been unfairly terminated he may bring a **claim for unfair dismissal** although, in order to bring a claim for unfair dismissal, the employee must have been employed for at least 1 year (unless the dismissal is for an inadmissible reason (¶¶8390+)).

Where an employee on a fixed-term contract is dismissed prior to the expiry of the fixed term, but an internal appeal overturns the dismissal, the appeal does no more than reinstate the original fixed-term contract. If the appeal takes place after the **expiration of the original fixed term**, the successful appeal does not have the effect of extending the fixed-term contract beyond the expiry date without evidence that it would have been renewed (Prakash v Wolverhampton City Council [2006] UKEAT 0140_06_0109).

1992 If the fixed-term contract is for 3 months or less and does not contain a contractual notice period, the employee is entitled to **1 week's notice** period if the contract is terminated after he has completed 1 month or more of continuous service.

1993 If the employee continues to **work after expiry** (without an express extension or renewal), then, in the absence of a specific notice period, the employment can be terminated by either party giving reasonable notice to the other (¶8129).

Dismissal at end of contract

1996 A fixed-term contract will be expected to automatically terminate at the end of the fixed period and therefore if the contract has run its full term, the fixed-term employee **cannot claim** that he has been **wrongly dismissed**. However, as the expiry of a fixed-term employment contract without renewal is deemed to be a dismissal for the purposes of the employee's statutory rights, he may bring a **claim for unfair dismissal** if the non-renewal is unfair, for example if the employer has not followed the correct procedures by failing to consult with an employee before his fixed-term contract ends, although, in order to bring a claim for unfair dismissal, the employee must have been **continuously employed** for 2 years (1 year if he started his employment before 6 April 2012) (or earlier if he is dismissed for an inadmissible reason, such as trade union activities or membership).

The qualifying period of service for bringing an unfair dismissal claim does not apply if the reason for the dismissal is one that would make it automatically unfair (¶¶8390+), for example, if an employee's fixed-term contract comes to an end while she/he is **on maternity/ adoption/additional paternity leave** and the reason for this non-renewal is related to the employee's pregnancy or because she/he is on maternity/adoption/additional paternity leave. In such circumstances, the dismissal will be automatically unfair as well as discriminatory. If the non-renewal of the contract of an employee on maternity/adoption/additional paternity leave is due to a redundancy situation, the employer should also remember that the employee is entitled to be offered any suitable and appropriate vacancies in preference to others facing the same redundancy situation (¶¶4453+).

Redundancy

2000 Fixed-term employees should not be selected for redundancy merely because they are not permanent employees. If they have been employed for specific tasks or periods, the employer may have objective justification in selecting them for redundancy at the end of their contracts when these specific tasks or periods have been completed. However, an employer should consider including any comparable permanent staff in any redundancy selection pool.

Where the employer has a **redundancy policy** that specifies the criteria to be applied in the redundancy selection process, the same criteria should be applied to both fixed-term and permanent employees, unless different criteria can be objectively justified by the employer.

2001 Fixed-term employees have a **right to statutory redundancy payments** once they have been continuously employed for 2 years or more and they are made redundant at the end of their contracts. Consequently an employer **cannot exclude** fixed-term employees from the statutory redundancy payments scheme. Fixed-term employees may, however, be excluded from any contractual redundancy payment scheme if the exclusion is objectively justified.

2002 Sometimes the employer will provide **extra compensation** to his employees in redundancy situations to compensate them for the unexpected loss of employment, or the employer may provide certain services, such as **outplacement services**, to his employees as part of the redundancy policy. As the fixed-term employee will, generally, have **no expectation of employment** beyond the term of the fixed-term contract, the employer may be objectively justified in excluding him from such benefits.

2003 **Waiver of redundancy rights** Any waiver of redundancy rights contained in a fixed-term employment contract is invalid.

C. Remedies

2010 A fixed-term employee can bring a claim to an employment tribunal if his employer has infringed his right **not to be treated less favourably** than a comparable permanent employee (reg 7 SI 2002/2034). The employer has a **defence** if he can show that the treatment was justifiable on objective grounds (¶1970).

2013 Further, fixed-term employees also have a **right not to be automatically unfairly dismissed** (¶8390) and have a **right not to be subjected to any detriment** (i.e. any detrimental act short of dismissal) by any act, or failure of his employer to act, on one of the below grounds

if the reason, or principal reason, for dismissal or detriment is that the employee (reg 6 SI 2002/2034):
– brought proceedings against his employer under the regulations;
– requested a written statement from the employer (i.e. asking for written justification of less favourable treatment or for a written statement of variation);
– gave evidence or information in connection with such proceedings brought by any employee;
– otherwise did anything under the regulations in relation to the employer or any other person;
– alleged that the employer had infringed the regulations. Any such allegation must be made in good faith;
– refused (or proposed to refuse) to forgo a right conferred by the regulations;
– declined to sign a workforce agreement for the purposes of the regulations; or
– being an employee representative or prospective representative performed any functions or activities as such.

This also applies if the employer dismisses the employee or causes the employee to suffer a detriment because he believes or **suspects** the employee will do or has done any of the above.

If the **allegation**(s) that the employer infringed an employee's rights (or acted or did not act because of his belief or suspicion) is false and not made in good faith, the employee will have no right to claim.

> MEMO POINTS The EAT has given **guidance** as to how the **right not to suffer a detriment** will apply to fixed-term employees and has done so by applying discrimination cases to this area of law (*Coutts and Co plc and anor v Cure and anor* [2004] UKEAT 0395_04_1709). Firstly, claims must be for both less favourable treatment and a detriment (applying the House of Lords' decision in *Chief Constable of West Yorkshire Police v Khan*, a race discrimination case). A detriment will occur when a reasonable employee would or might take the view that he had been disadvantaged in the circumstances in which he had to work (applying the House of Lords' decision in *Shamoon v Chief Constable of the RUC*, a sex discrimination case). The EAT also pointed out that where it can be shown that a detriment was due to the employee's fixed-term status it is irrelevant whether or not the employer also discriminated against other groups not covered by the fixed-term regulations (for instance, other non-permanent employees).
> Secondly, the **3-month limitation period** begins on the date the detriment occurred (applying the Court of Appeal's ruling in *Cast v Croydon College*, a sex discrimination case). In this case, the detrimental act was held to have occurred when the details of the bonuses to be paid were finalised (which included a statement that fixed-term employees would be excluded) and not when the promise of the non-contractual bonus was first made.

Procedure

2014 Complaints must be made **within** 3 months beginning with the date of the act or failure to act or, if it is part of a series of similar acts or failures, the last of them. However, a tribunal may **extend** this period if it considers it just and equitable to do so (¶9475).

Where the employee's claim is in respect of the employer's failure to provide him with the opportunity to secure permanent employment (reg 3(2) SI 2002/2034), the time limit is 3 months from the date that other individuals were informed of the vacancy.

2015 If the **claim is successful**, the tribunal can:
– make a declaration;
– order the employer to pay compensation; and
– recommend that the employer take, within a specified period, whatever action it considers reasonable to obviate or reduce the adverse effect on the employee or order the employer to re-employ the employee if it is practicable and just to do so.

If the employer fails, without reasonable justification, to comply, the tribunal can make an order for compensation (or increase the amount of compensation if one has already been made).

SECTION 5

Agency workers

2040 Agency workers are **often used** by businesses (referred to here as end-users) to help on a short-term basis, either due to an increased workload, or to act as a cover for absent staff. They are hired from **employment businesses** (referred to as agencies for the remainder of this section) who supply them on assignments to work under the end-user's instructions and control. Such workers are often temporary or casual workers of the agency, and they often sign on with one or more agencies to increase their chances of finding regular work.

There is no obligation on the part of an agency worker to accept an assignment, though once he does he is bound by various obligations according to the terms under which he is engaged. In return the agency is obliged to pay the worker for work done in accordance with the assignment. Usually, the end-user pays the agency for the services of the worker and the agency pays the worker directly.

One key question concerns the **employment status** of agency workers. Most often an agency worker negotiates a contract for services between himself and the agency, and there is no written contract linking the agency worker to the end-user. In these circumstances, the agency worker is likely to be treated by a tribunal as a worker and not an employee. To escape this finding, the agency worker will most often seek to show that there was an **implied contract of employment** between himself and either the agency or the end-user.

Where an agency worker shows himself to be an employee, he will benefit from the full range of rights that are available to an employee (¶12); where he cannot show this, his rights are those of a worker (¶17). Various legislative schemes also make particular provision for agency workers, and where this is done, the right is discussed in the relevant chapter, as below:

Agency worker's right to:	¶¶
Data protection	¶5920
National minimum wage	¶2868
Paid annual leave	¶4000
Working time rules	¶3615
Statutory sick pay	¶4123
Be accompanied to disciplinary and grievance hearings	¶6780
Not be discriminated against on the grounds of age, disability, gender reassignment, marriage and civil partnership, pregnancy and maternity, race, religion or belief, sex or sexual orientation	¶5200
Whistleblowing protection	¶2710

MEMO POINTS 1. Employers may also use **recruitment agencies** which, broadly speaking, introduce work-seekers to clients for direct employment by them (¶585). With this arrangement, the work-seeker's contract (either as a worker or employee) will be with the client and not with the agency.
2. The **statutory duties** of an agency to workers and end-users are set out in regulations (Conduct of Employment Agencies and Employment Businesses Regulations SI 2003/3319; SI 2007/3575) and statute (s 55 EqA 2010; s 138 TULRCA 1992).

2041 Right to equal treatment New regulations on agency workers came into force on 1 October 2011 (Agency Workers Regulations SI 2010/93) which gave agency workers, who have been in the **same role with the same end-user for 12 continuous calendar weeks** during one or more assignments, the **same basic working and employment conditions** (including pay and holiday) as if they had been recruited directly by the end-user to do the same job. See section C. at ¶¶2070+ for further details.

MEMO POINTS These implement the Agency Workers Directive on the working conditions of temporary agency workers (EU Temporary (Agency) Workers Directive 2008/104).

A. Employment status

2042 Agency workers have an employment relationship with their agency, usually as a **worker**. In certain circumstances, however, an agency worker may be deemed to be an **employee** of either the agency or the end-user, although not both, as an employee may have only one employer in respect of the same employment (*Cairns v Visteon UK Ltd* [2007] IRLR 175, EAT).

Where an agency worker is an employee, he will potentially receive the benefit of all employee rights (for a full list, see ¶12), including protection against unfair dismissal (¶8380).

2043 In deciding whether an agency worker is an employee or self-employed worker, the tribunal will follow general **common law** principles. In particular it will focus on the two questions of whether there is mutuality of obligation between the agency worker and an ostensible employer, and whether the worker is in business for his own account (¶32). These are factual questions and significant factors will include the intention of the parties, the labelling of the contract, arrangements as to leave and sickness absences, the benefits paid to the agency worker, and so on (a fuller list is provided at ¶52). No single factor is decisive. The courts will look behind the parties' intention and labels to determine the true relationship (*Young and Woods Ltd v West* [1980] IRLR 201, CA).

2045 **Agency/agency worker relationship** Under agency regulations, agencies must agree with the worker the terms that will apply between the worker and the agency (¶2054), which includes setting out the employment status of the agency worker (i.e. whether he is a worker or an employee). Agencies usually hire agency workers under **general terms of engagement**, which typically fall short of being a contract of employment (an employee-employer relationship) as there is a lack of mutuality of obligation (i.e. no obligation on a worker to accept a particular job offer or on the agency to make an offer, ¶37), which is a fundamental requirement for there to be a contract of employment (*Dacas v Brook Street Bureau (UK) Ltd* [2004] IRLR 358, CA; *Bunce v Postworth Limited t/a Skyblue* [2005] IRLR 557, CA).

2046 The tribunals and courts have been unwilling to re-interpret any general contract for services between the worker and the agency. However, in a few cases, the courts have held that there may, however, be a contract of service (i.e. of employment) between the agency worker and the agency in relation to a **specific assignment**, which will last for the duration of the assignment (*McMeechan v Secretary of State for Employment* [1997] IRLR 353, CA).

Such a contract of employment may be oral or implied (*Franks v Reuters Ltd and anor* [2003] IRLR 423, CA).

> EXAMPLE
> **Employee of agency**
> 1. In *McMeechan v Secretary of State for Employment*, above, M had no general agreement with his agency, although for each assignment he had a job sheet that included a standard written statement of terms and conditions. The terms stated that M was a self-employed worker, yet the Court held that M was an employee of the agency when he was on a specific assignment.
> 2. In *Heatherwood and Wexham Park Hospitals NHS Trust v Kulubowila and ors* [2007] UKEAT 0633_06_2903, an agency worker, A, had a contract of employment with an agency, but sought to show that his employment was in fact with the end-user. He claimed that from the first day of his employment he had been controlled and managed by the end-user, and that there had never been any mutuality of obligation between him and the agency. In the absence of a meaningful contract of employment, A argued, it was open to a tribunal to find an implied contract between him and the end-user. The EAT rejected A's arguments, on the basis that a contract of employment will only be implied where this is necessary. A's contractual status could be explained by his contract with the agency. There was no need to find any other implied contract.

Not employee of agency
In *Dacas v Brook Street Bureau (UK) Ltd*, the agency had a written temporary worker agreement with D and was responsible for her discipline and pay, whereas the end-user, Wandsworth Council (WC), had exclusive day-to-day control and could decide when it no longer wanted D. The worker D had been assigned to WC for 6 years until WC asked for her to be withdrawn. The Court held that the agency was not D's employer as it was not obliged to provide D with work and it did not have sufficient control over D.

End-user/agency worker relationship Most often, there will be no agreement setting out the terms or nature of the relationship between the agency worker and the end-user. This is because the end-user will operate his relationship with the agency worker through the agency and his agreement will be with the agency. **2048**

Where an agency worker argues that he is actually an employee of the end-user (usually where the agency worker has worked for a certain period under the direct control of the end-user and has been treated as if he is an employee), a tribunal will have to consider whether there was an **implied contract** between these two parties.

In the high-profile case of *Dacas*, the Court of Appeal held that tribunals should **always consider** the possibility that there might be an implied contract of employment linking the agency worker to the end-user and emphasised that tribunals should look at the reality of the situation, especially in relation to long assignments, to ascertain who actually exercises sufficient control over the worker (*Dacas v Brook Street Bureau (UK) Ltd*, ¶2045 above). In a second Court of Appeal case, the Court described the approach adopted in *Dacas* as "unimpeachable" (*Cable and Wireless v Muscat* [2006] ICR 975, CA and followed in *Franks v Reuters Ltd and anor* [2003] IRLR 423, CA). **2049**

However, a more recent decision of the EAT has narrowed the application of *Dacas* and held that while the tribunal should always consider whether there was an implied contract between the agency worker and the end-user, the result of its investigation will **usually** be **negative** (*James v London Borough of Greenwich* [2007] IRLR 168, EAT affirmed by the Court of Appeal ([2008] IRLR 302, CA) and followed and applied in *Tilson v Alstom Transport* [2010] EWCA Civ 1308; *Muschett v HM Prison Service* [2010] IRLR 451, CA; *Craigie v London Borough of Haringey* [2007] UKEAT 0556_06_1201; *Astbury v Gist Ltd* [2007] UKEAT 0619_06_2803). Consequently, while there should be no assumption that either a contract will or will not be implied, a contract should only be implied where "necessary" to explain the work undertaken by the worker for the end-user. Since most end-users hire agency workers without expressing any preference as to which worker is supplied to them, typically, there will not be sufficient mutuality of obligation between the worker and the end-user for a contract to be required. The significance of length of service was also questionable where there is no mutuality of obligation, length of service will not create an employment contract. Different behaviour or words are required to signal that the agency worker has become an employee at some distinct point after the commencement of the relationship.

EXAMPLE

1. In *Tilson v Alstom Transport*, the claimant's services to the end-user, A, were provided under a quadripartite relationship involving three contractual relationships. First, the claimant, T, had a contract with a contractor limited company, S. The second contract was between S and the agency. Under the terms of what was termed a "contract confirmation note", S provided the services of T to the agency. This included a clause that "Neither the company nor the client shall be entitled to or seek to exercise any supervision, direction or control over the contractor or the operatives in the manner or performance of the project." Finally, there was a third contract between the agency and the end-user, A, which provided individual workers such as T to the end-user.
The Court of Appeal confirmed the EAT decision which held that T was not an employee of the end-user and therefore could not bring an unfair dismissal claim against it. In so holding the Court followed recent case law and emphasised that a contract of employment should only be implied between the worker and the end-user where it is necessary to do so to explain the work undertaken by the worker for the end-user. Here, there was no understanding that there should be such an implied contract (indeed T had rejected offers of employment from the end-user, preferring the existing financial set up). Moreover, the mere fact that there was a significant degree of integration of the worker into the organisation of the end-user was not at all inconsistent with the existence of an agency relationship in which there is no contract between worker and end-user. Further, the

degree of integration was a factor of little, if any, weight when considering whether there is an implied contract. The Court also saw no grounds for the conclusion that even if one clause (in this case the "no control" clause) was known to be false this would make the whole contract ineffective. Even if it was so in this case, the end-user was not a party to that contract, and the Court saw no basis for concluding that its contract with the agency would fall away, or should be construed other than at face value.

2. In *Muschett v HM Prison Service*, the claimant worked as a cleaner at a young offenders' institution for 4 months during 2007. He was supplied by an employment agency under a contract setting out details of the work he was to do. He brought both unfair dismissal and discrimination claims on the basis that he was an employee of the prison service. At the tribunal stage, a finding was made that there was no mutuality of obligation between him and the prison service, and that he could have terminated the arrangement at any time by giving notice to the agency. Applying *James v London Borough of Greenwich*, the Court of Appeal held that there was nothing in the facts of the case which made it necessary to find any implied contract of employment or contract for services between the claimant and the prison service. He was therefore not an employee for the purposes of either unfair dismissal or anti-discrimination legislation.

2050 In deciding whether an agency worker is an employee of the end-user or not, all the circumstances of the case will be considered. **Factors** which have led the courts **to imply** a contract of employment between the agency worker and the end-user include:
– the reality of the relationship between the parties where a business transfer caused the introduction of the agency into the relationship (*Cable and Wireless v Muscat*, above);
– the subsequent taking on of the agency worker as a permanent employee (*Royal National Lifeboat Institution v Bushaway* [2005] UKEAT 0719_04_2204);
– acting as though the agency worker were a wholly integrated member of staff (*National Grid Electricity Transmission Plc v Wood* [2007] UKEAT 0432_07_2410);
– the end-user's day-to-day control of the agency worker (*Dacas v Brook Street Bureau (UK) Ltd*; *Motorola Ltd v (1) Davidson and (2) Melville Craig Group Ltd* [2001] IRLR 4, EAT); and
– lengthy continuous service (although see ¶2049) (*Franks v Reuters Ltd and anor* [2003] IRLR 423, CA; *Dacas v Brook Street Bureau (UK) Ltd*).

Factors which have led the courts **not to imply** a contract of employment include:
– an agency worker's acceptance of terms which were unfavourable compared to those of permanent employees (*James v London Borough of Greenwich*, above);
– a refusal by the end-user to take the agency worker onto a permanent employment contract (*Heatherwood and Wexham Park Hospitals NHS Trust v Kulubowila and ors* [2007] UKEAT 0633_06_2903);
– a lack of obligation on the end-user to give notice to the worker (*Craigie v London Borough of Haringey*, above); and
– an agency worker's willingness to work for different end-users (*James v London Borough of Greenwich* [2007] IRLR 168, EAT, above).

EXAMPLE
Employee of end-user
1. In *Cable and Wireless v Muscat*, E Ltd dismissed M, who was employed as a telecommunications specialist, to reduce its number of employees and immediately re-engaged him as a contractor (via E-N Ltd which was set up by M as a personal service company to receive his pay and car allowance). There followed a TUPE transfer from E Ltd to CW who had taken over E Ltd. CW required contractors to be provided through an agency and as a result E-N Ltd entered into a "contract for services" with an agency so that M could continue to work for CW. The Court of Appeal held that on the facts M was an employee of CW (as it had control over the worker, supplied him with all his equipment and his holidays were arranged to suit CW) and that the business reality was that he remained so despite the change in arrangements and the introduction of the agency into the relationship.
2. In *Royal National Lifeboat Institution v Bushaway*, the tribunal held that the agency worker was an employee of the end-user from the start of her assignment (i.e. when she was taken on as a temporary worker) regardless of the fact that her terms as an agency worker were different to the terms she was given once she was taken on permanently. The EAT went on to comment that an employee's terms of employment may well be very different at different times in his employment and what mattered was whether at any one time they indicate employment or self-employment.

3. In *National Grid Electricity Transmission Plc v Wood*, a chartered accountant and agency worker, W, was appointed following a job interview with the end-user. W had direct face-to-face negotiation of contractual terms and negotiated his pay, length of notice and holidays with the end-user. Further, it was a term of the end-user's contract with the agency that only W could carry out the services required and no substitutes could be applied. The EAT held that the end-user was not treating W as a semi-detached member of staff and was in practice acting as though he were a wholly integrated member of staff. Accordingly, the EAT found that W was an employee of the end-user.

Not employee of end-user
1. In *James v London Borough of Greenwich*, a former council employee was later taken on by the council working in the same team but through the intermediary of an employment agency. She did not receive holiday or sick pay, nor was she subject to the employer's disciplinary and grievance procedure. The contract designated her a self-employed worker. When she was absent, the agency provided substitutes. The evidence was that she was willing to work for other clients of the agency. No contract of employment was found between the council and the worker.
2. In *Craigie v London Borough of Haringey*, a council controlled the day-to-day practicalities of an agency worker's employment. However, the council was under no obligation to provide work for the workers and the worker understood that the council could ask him at any time not to come to work on any particular day. Accordingly, no implied contract of employment was found between the council and the worker.
3. In *Astbury v Bentley Motors* [2007] UKEAT 1844_06_0905, an agency worker applied for a permanent post at a hospital but was unsuccessful. In the meantime, he remained working at the hospital, through an agency, on a contract of unspecified duration. The EAT held that he could not be an employee of the end-user.
4. In *Wood Group Engineering (North Sea) Ltd v Robertson* [2007] UKEAT 0081_06_0607, an agency worker was required to submit time sheets to the agency and to refrain from acting in a manner which could conflict with the agencies' interests. She also had a relationship with the agency which was perfectly well explained by the contractual documents between herself and the agency in which she was identified as a worker of the agency. It followed that she was not an employee of the end-user.
5. In *Heatherwood and Wexham Park Hospitals NHS Trust v Kulubowila and ors*, an engineer was taken on by a hospital on a short-term agency contract. After 2 years in the post, he applied for a permanent position at the hospital but was unsuccessful. The tribunal treated his lack of success in his application for a permanent post as evidence that he was not an employee of the trust.

B. Agency obligations

2052 Irrespective of whether an agency worker is its employee or worker, the agency does have certain obligations to him.

2053 **Pre-employment obligations** Before providing work, the agency must confirm the identity and **qualifications** of the worker (reg 19 SI 2003/3319).

An agency may not supply a worker to an end-user unless it has **checked** that the worker and the end-user are each aware of any legal or professional requirements which apply, including health and safety requirements (reg 20 SI 2003/3319).

When an agency supplies workers to **work with vulnerable groups**, such as children, the infirm or the elderly, the agency is further required to obtain from the worker copies of his professional qualifications, two references and confirmation from the worker that he is not unsuitable to work with vulnerable people (reg 22 SI 2003/3319).

> MEMO POINTS   A relevant **health and safety requirement** would include situations such as where the worker is pregnant or a new mother: in these circumstances, the employer has additional duties to carry out a specific assessment of the workplace in order to protect the worker from specified risks (¶4950), and it would be good practice for the agency to bring this requirement to the attention of an end-user.

2054 The agency must also agree with the worker the **terms** that will apply **between the worker and the agency**. The following terms must be included (regs 14-15 SI 2003/3319):
– the nature of the contract under which the worker is employed (i.e. whether the contract is a contract for services, a contract of apprenticeship or a contract of service);

- an undertaking that the agency will pay him;
- notice of the termination period;
- details of the arrangements for remuneration;
- details of the worker's entitlement to annual leave.

An agency may not enter into a **contract on behalf of** a worker or an end-user without the express authority of that worker or end-user (reg 11 SI 2003/3319).

2057 **Obligations during employment** An agency must not **disclose information** relating to a worker to an end-user without the prior consent of the worker (reg 28(2) SI 2003/3319).

2058 An agency must not **withhold pay** from a worker on the **grounds** that he (regs 6, 12 SI 2003/3319):
- has terminated or proposed to terminate a contract with the agency;
- has not taken up a service offered by the agency;
- cannot prove that he has done the work in a specified time, where the agency has other means to satisfy itself as to whether or not the work was done; or
- has not worked during any period other than the period during which he was employed.

2059 **Fees and charges** An agency must not make it a condition of finding employment for a worker that the worker undergoes **services** for which a fee is charged (reg 5 SI 2003/3319). Examples of a situation where this rule applies would be where an agency provides training in CV writing, photographic services, or the use of protective equipment.

> MEMO POINTS Further restrictions have been placed on agencies charging fees to workers and where a worker uses services for which the agency can charge a fee (for example, by providing **transport or accommodation**). The worker may cancel or withdraw these services without a penalty, subject only to giving 5 days' notice (or 10 days where the service concerns living accommodation) (SI 2007/3575).

2060 Where a worker is able to transfer from a contract for services with an agency to employment with an end-user, the agency may not charge a **transfer fee** to either the worker or the end-user (reg 10 SI 2003/3319).

One exception to the above rule occurs where the contract allows the hirer the option of **hiring** the employee for a specified **period** as an alternative to paying a transfer fee.

A further exception occurs where the worker has only worked with the end-user for a **short period** of time before being taken on by the end-user. In these circumstances, a fee will not be payable in the event that either:
- the worker has been supplied to the end-user for more than 14 weeks since the start of the assignment at the time of the commencement of the agency worker's employment with the end-user; or
- there has been a gap of more than 8 weeks between the ending of the assignment and the commencement of the agency worker's employment with the end-user.

2062 **Industrial disputes** An agency must not supply a worker to perform the duties normally performed by a worker who is taking official industrial action (reg 7 SI 2003/3319).

2064 **Remedies** Actions to enforce the above duties, or to recover fees paid charged in contravention of the above duties, may be brought in the civil courts (reg 30 SI 2003/3319).

Discrimination by agencies

2066 Agencies **must not** discriminate against, harass or victimise a person when providing an employment service (s 55 EqA 2010). This includes the terms on which an agency offers to provide their services and refusing or deliberately omitting to provide their services.

> EXAMPLE In *Brocklebank v Silveira* [2006] UKEAT 0571_05_1101, an agency was held to have discriminated on the ground of sex where it failed to provide a risk assessment to a potential recruit who was pregnant as such a failure was a conscious and therefore deliberate omission.

It also places a duty on providers of employment services to make **reasonable adjustments** for disabled people.

> EXAMPLE An agency that advertises job vacancies on its website will need to ensure that it is checked for accessibility and the agency will need to make reasonable changes where necessary to enable disabled people using a variety of access software to access the advertisements.

Where it is **lawful** for an end-user to **refuse to offer a job** on grounds of age, disability, gender reassignment, marriage and civil partnership, race, religion or belief, sex or sexual orientation (for example, because there is a genuine occupational qualification (¶5242)), an agency will also be allowed to discriminate in relation to that job on the same grounds. In addition, an agency may not be liable if it can prove that (Sch 9, para 5 EqA 2010):
– it had acted in reliance on a statement made to it by the end-user to the effect that it could lawfully refuse to offer employment on grounds of age, disability, gender reassignment, marriage and civil partnership, race, religion or belief, sex or sexual orientation; and
– it was reasonable for it to rely on the end-user's statement.

2067

C. Equal treatment

Agency workers are entitled to (Agency Workers Regulations SI 2010/93 as amended):
1. **from the 1st day of an assessment** (referred to as "day 1" rights):
– access to collective facilities and amenities provided by the end-user (such as a canteen, childcare facilities, etc); and
– information on any job vacancies; and
2. **after 12 weeks in the same job**:
– equal pay and other basic working conditions (annual leave, overtime, etc) as those directly employed; and
– paid time off for antenatal appointments during an assignment (pregnant agency workers).

As a result of these new rights, **end-users** who hire temporary agency workers through a temporary work agency (generally referred to in this section simply as an agency) should ensure equal **access to facilities** where it is reasonable to do so and **provide their agencies** with **up-to-date information** on their terms and conditions to ensure that an agency worker receives the equal treatment after 12 weeks in the same job.

2070

> MEMO POINTS 1. These rights **came into force** on 1 October 2011.
> 2. For these purposes, an **agency** can be a "high street" agency, but also an intermediary, such as an umbrella company or a master or neutral vendor if they are involved in the supply of the agency worker (regs 3-4 SI 2010/93). For example, where an end-user appoints one agency (a master vendor) to manage its recruitment process and uses other recruitment agencies as necessary ("second tier" suppliers) or alternatively appoints a management company (a neutral vendor) which does not supply any workers directly but manages the overall recruitment process and supplies temporary agency workers through others.

Excluded workers Excluded from the new set of rights are workers who (regs 2-4 SI 2010/93):
– find **direct employment** with an employer through an employment agency (i.e. employment agencies who introduce workers to employers for direct or permanent employment);
– find temporary work through an agency but are in business on their own account where the status of the **end-user** is that of a **client or customer** of a profession or business undertaking. A worker will only be excluded if there is a genuine business-to-business relationship and a worker providing services through a limited company is not by itself enough to exclude him unless there is an absence of personal service and mutuality of obligation;
– work on **managed service contracts** (i.e. where a company provides a specific service to a customer, such as catering or cleaning, based on a contract for services) and do not work under the direction and supervision of the host organisation (i.e. the end-user). In such

2071

cases, the managed service contractor, not the end-user, has responsibility for managing and delivering the service rather than just supplying the staff;
– work for **in-house temporary staffing banks** where a company employs its temporary workers directly and they only work for that same business or service; and
– are on **secondment or loan** from one organisation to another.

1. Day 1 rights

2075-1 Agency workers have the right **not to be treated less favourably** than a comparable worker in relation to (regs 12-13 SI 2010/93):
– access to collective facilities and amenities provided by the end-user; and
– information on job vacancies.

A **comparable worker** (regs 12(4), 13(2) SI 2010/93):
– is a permanent worker employed by the same end-user as the agency worker;
– does the same or broadly similar work having regard, where relevant, to whether he has a similar level of qualifications and skills; and
– works at the same location (or in relation to access to collective facilities and amenities, if there is no such person, at another location owned by the end-user).

However, the end-user has a **defence** in relation to access to collective facilities and amenities if he can justify his treatment on objective grounds (¶2075-4).

Access to facilities or amenities

2075-2 Facilities or amenities may **include**:
– a canteen or other similar facilities;
– a workplace crèche;
– transport services (e.g. in this context, local pick up and drop offs, transport between sites, but not company car allowances or season ticket loans);
– toilets/shower facilities;
– staff common room;
– waiting room;
– mother and baby room;
– prayer room;
– food and drinks machines; and
– car parking.

Such facilities will **usually be on-site**. However, if they are provided by the end-user for the use of comparable workers then they should be made available: for example, a canteen that is used on another site (or shared with another company).

The end-user can either provide agency workers with **information about** its **facilities directly**, for example as part of an induction pack or by referring them to relevant parts of a staff handbook, or by providing the information to the agency so that it can pass on the information to the agency worker as part of the information about the assignment.

2075-3 Agency workers are **not entitled** to more favourable access rights than permanent workers, for example, where membership to a crèche involves joining a waiting list, agency workers would be entitled to join the list but do not have an automatic right to a place.

Access to benefits which involve **off-site facilities and amenities** which are not provided by the end-user are also excluded. For example, this would include subsidised access to an off-site gym as part of a benefit package to reward long-term service or loyalty. However, this does not prevent end-users offering these to agency workers if they wish to do so.

2075-4 **Justification for less favourable treatment** Facilities or amenities can be excluded if there is an objective justification for less favourable treatment, i.e. the end-user has a good reason for treating the agency worker less favourably (reg 12(2) SI 2010/93). For example, cost will often be a factor although end-users should be cautious about relying on cost alone to justify different treatment. Other factors may be practical and organisational considerations, for example the childcare facility may be at full capacity. End-users may want to consider whether it is possible or feasible to offer agency workers certain access on a partial basis rather than excluding them altogether.

Information on job vacancies

2075-5

Agency workers should be told where and how to access information on relevant job vacancies including internal promotions, for example via the internet/intranet or on a notice board in a communal area. This right only applies to access to information and does not constrain end-users with regard to requiring certain qualifications or experience or how they treat applications.

> MEMO POINTS This will not apply where there is a genuine "**headcount freeze**" with posts ring-fenced for redeployment purposes to avoid staff redundancies.

2. After 12 weeks in the same job

After an agency worker completes a 12-week qualifying period with the same end-user, in the same role, he will be entitled to have the **same basic terms and conditions** of employment as comparable employees that have been hired directly (reg 5 SI 2010/93). These are (reg 6 SI 2010/93):

2080-1

– key elements of pay;
– duration of working time e.g. if working is limited to a maximum of 48 hours a week;
– night work;
– rest periods;
– rest breaks;
– annual leave; and
– paid time off for antenatal appointments.

A **comparable employee** (reg 5 SI 2010/93):
– is a permanent employee employed by the same end-user as the agency worker;
– does the same or broadly similar work of the agency having regard, where relevant, to whether he has similar levels of qualifications and skills; and
– works or is based at the same establishment as the agency worker with whom he is being compared. Where there is no comparable permanent employee at that establishment the comparison can be made with a permanent employee working or based at another establishment of the employer.

2080-2

> MEMO POINTS For these purposes, only permanent employees can be comparators, compared to day 1 rights where comparators can be comparable workers (see ¶2075-1).

Unlike day 1 rights with regard to access to collective facilities and amenities, the employer **cannot justify unequal treatment** on objective grounds (¶2075-4).

2080-3

a. Calculating the 12-week qualifying period

The 12-week qualifying period is achieved by working in the same job with the same end-user for 12 calendar weeks (reg 7(2) SI 2010/93). The affect that breaks between assignments have on the qualifying period is covered in detail below.

2081-1

A **calendar week** in this context will **comprise** any period of 7 days starting with the first day of an assignment. For example, if an agency worker begins work on a Tuesday all work done up to and including the following Monday will count as 1 calendar week. If the agency worker has done some work in a calendar week that week will be accrued **regardless of how many hours** the worker actually does (reg 7(4) SI 2010/93). Therefore, even if the agency worker is on assignment for only a couple of hours a week, it will still count as a week and he will still be entitled to equal treatment after 12 calendar weeks.

2081-2 MEMO POINTS   The new rights are not retrospective and for agency workers already on assignment when the new rights came into force, their 12-week qualifying period started from 1 October 2011 (reg 7(12) SI 2010/93).

2081-2 An agency worker can qualify regardless of whether he has been **supplied by more than one agency** over one qualifying period.

MEMO POINTS   Agencies should ask new agency workers their employment history in order that any relevant periods can be taken into account to ensure that they are not liable, in whole or part, for any claim of less favourable treatment. While there is no legal obligation on the agency worker to provide information on previous assignments, if an agency worker fails to inform his agency, when asked, that he has worked for an end-user before and then brings a claim, the tribunal may take this into account in making any award.

2081-3 An agency worker can **work for more than one end-user** during a week (or even during a day) resulting in more than one qualifying period running at any one time.

Breaks between assignments

2082-1 Breaks between assignments will often cause the qualifying period to restart. However, as the working patterns of agency workers can be irregular, there are a number of circumstances in which breaks between assignments will not restart or delay the qualifying period (reg 7 SI 2010/93).

2082-2 **Qualifying period restarts**   A gap between assignments or a move to a new assignment will mean that the qualifying period restarts where (reg 8 SI 2010/93):
– an agency worker begins a new assignment with a **new end-user**;
– an agency worker remains with the same end-user but is no longer in the same role. In such cases, the end-user must notify an agency in writing when there is a **new role** that is substantively different, and record details of the job requirements. The agency must provide a description of the new role in writing to the agency worker and should inform them that the qualifying period has been reset (reg 7(3)(a) SI 2010/93); or
– there is a **break** between assignments with the same end-user of **6 weeks or more** (which is not one which "pauses" the qualifying period (¶2082-5)).

New end-user

2082-3 A new end-user for this purpose must be a **different person/legal entity**. Where an end-user has multiple sites, merely moving a worker from one site to another will not usually break continuity (unless it is a substantively different role (see ¶2082-4 on factors which indicate whether a role is substantively different)). Where an end-user is part of a larger group and each company has its own legal identity, then the qualifying period will restart when an agency worker moves between the different legal entities unless the intention behind the move is to deprive the agency worker from receiving equal treatment.

EXAMPLE   **Example from BIS guidance**
A large retail group has various subsidiary companies and requests agency workers via line managers to work across the group. The group acts as the end-user and pays the agency. The qualifying period will not start again if a role is not substantively different and if any break between assignments is less than 6 weeks. Even if the individual companies were separate legal entities and engaged the agency workers directly, if the most likely explanation for the structure of assignments is intended to prevent the agency worker from being entitled to equal treatment this could be subject to anti-avoidance provisions in the Regulations.

Substantive change

2082-4 For a substantive change to a job role with the same end-user, there must be a **genuine and real difference to the role**. For example, it will not be enough if a line manager has merely changed or that an agency worker has transferred between similar administrative functions or moved within a single, relatively small business unit or been given a different pay rate.

Questions which can help determine whether there is a genuine and real difference to a role include:
- are different skills and competences used?
- is the pay rate different?
- is the work in a different location/cost centre?
- is the line manager different?
- are the working hours different?
- does the role require extra training and/or a specific qualification that wasn't needed before? and
- is different equipment involved?

> EXAMPLE **Examples from BIS guidance**
> 1. A warehouse has agency workers to work on a production line and to pack their products for distribution. Simply moving from the production line to a packing role requires little training and uses the majority of the same skills and is therefore likely to be not substantively different. A move between these types of roles would not re-start the qualifying clock without a break between assignments of more than 6 weeks.
> 2. An agency worker has worked on a production line but then moves to an administrative role. This is likely to be considered substantively different and the qualifying period would start again.

Qualifying period "pauses" In some circumstances, a break will merely "pause" the qualifying period and **will continue** to run **again** when the agency worker returns. This **occurs where** a break is (reg 7 SI 2010/93): **2082-5**
a. less than 6 weeks;
b. due to sickness or injury, or performing jury service, for up to 28 weeks. If required to do so by the temporary work agency, the agency worker must provided such written medical evidence of sickness or injury as may reasonably be required;
c. due to taking leave, for example annual leave;
d. due to a regular and planned shutdown of the workplace by the end-user (for example at Christmas); or
e. due to a strike, lock out or other industrial action at the end-user's establishment.
Where there are **different types of consecutive absences** the time taken due to b., c., d. and e. is ignored for the purpose of calculating the length of the break.

> EXAMPLE **Example from BIS guidance**
> An agency worker has a break of 5 weeks between assignments, then is absent for 2 weeks due to sickness. Sickness absence "pauses" the qualifying period, which then resumes when the worker returns to the same role. In these circumstances, the break is longer than 6 weeks but continuity is not broken as the clock pauses after 5 weeks.

Qualifying period continues In some limited circumstances, the qualifying period **continues to run** despite the break (reg 7(6) SI 2010/93). This occurs where the break is due to: **2082-6**
- pregnancy, childbirth or maternity and lasts until the agency worker returns to work or up to 26 weeks after childbirth, whichever is sooner; or
- the agency worker taking maternity leave, adoption leave or paternity leave.
In each of these cases the qualifying period will continue for the originally intended duration of the assignment, or the likely duration of the assignment, whichever is longer.

Anti-avoidance provisions

There are anti-avoidance provisions which address any situation where a **pattern of assignments** emerges that is designed to deliberately deprive an agency worker of their entitlements (reg 9 SI 2010/93). For example, an agency worker completes two or more assignments with the same end-user, where he has already worked for 11 weeks with a 6-week break and then a further 11 weeks with another 6-week break. If the agency worker is then taken on for a third assignment, this could be considered an attempt to avoid the completion of the qualifying period, but it would need to be clear that the attempt was deliberate. **2083-1**

2083-2 **Factors** which would indicate that a pattern of assignments was structured with the intention to deprive the worker of equal treatment rights could be:
– the number of assignments;
– the length of assignments;
– the number of role changes;
– whether the role changes were substantively different; and
– the length of break periods.

In all circumstances, the agency worker must have **completed at least** two assignments or two roles (in substantively different roles which break the qualifying period) with the same end-user, or connected end-users within the same group, in order for the anti-avoidance provisions to become relevant.

b. Basic working and employment conditions

2085-1 The right to equal treatment with regard to comparable employees after 12 weeks' qualifying service only applies to certain working and employment conditions (reg 6 SI 2002/2034):
– **pay** (see ¶2085-2);
– any **enhanced rights** to **rest breaks, night work** and **annual leave** above the statutory minimum. An enhancement can be included as a one-off payment. This payment can be at the end of the assignment or as part of the worker's hourly/daily rate. It should be made clear on the agency worker's payslip if this done; and
– paid time off to attend **antenatal appointments** and antenatal classes with regard to pregnant agency workers when on assignment.

Pay

2085-2 Pay **covers**:
– basic pay based on the annual salary an agency worker would have received if recruited directly (usually converted into an hourly or daily rate, taking into account any pay increments);
– overtime payments and any shift/unsocial hours allowances;
– payment for enhanced contractual rights with regard to rest breaks and annual leave (any entitlement above the statutory minimum);
– bonuses or commission payments directly attributable to the amount of quality of work done. For example, commission payments linked to sales, bonuses payable to those who meet a specific individual performance target;
– any non-contractual bonuses that are paid as a matter of custom and practice (i.e. so regularly paid as to be expected); and
– vouchers or stamps which have a monetary value but are not salary sacrifice schemes, for example lunch vouchers or child care vouchers.

> EXAMPLE **Examples from BIS guidance**
>
> **Where an end-user has pay scales or pay structures**
> An end-user has various pay scales to cover its permanent workforce, including its production line. An agency worker is recruited on the production line and has several years' relevant experience. However, the agency worker is paid at the bottom of the pay scale. Is this equal treatment?
> Yes, if the end-user would have started that worker at the bottom of the pay scale if recruiting him directly. But if the worker's experience would mean starting further up the pay scale if recruited directly, then that is the entitlement.
> Starter grades which apply primarily, or exclusively, to agency workers may not be compliant if not applied generally to direct recruits.
>
> **Where there are no pay scales or structures or comparable permanent employees**
> A company engages an agency worker as a receptionist for the first time. The company does not have anyone doing the same job and does not have pay scales or collective agreements. The agency worker is paid at the same rate before and after the 12-week qualifying period. Is this allowed?

> Yes; there are no pay scales or collective agreements, or a "going rate", so in relation to pay, there are no relevant terms and conditions ordinarily included in the contracts of employment of employees in the end-user. However, if, say, the company gives all its permanent employees 6 weeks' paid annual leave and paid time off for bank and public holidays, the agency worker should be entitled to the same treatment on these points.

MEMO POINTS   One common form of remuneration which is not referred to in the BIS guidance is tips/service charges. These are commonly pooled and divided amongst staff by reference to the number of hours they have worked and if this is the case it seems likely that they are directly attributable to the "amount" of work done by the worker and are therefore "pay" for these purposes. If tips are retained by individual members of staff from customers they have served they relate to the "quality" of work done and will be likely be "pay". Conversely, a simple method of dividing tips equally amongst staff without any reference to the amount or quality of work they have done will likely mean that the payments fall outside these provisions.

2085-3 Some of the payments can require a comparable employee to obtain a **period of qualifying hours or service** before he has a right to the payment and in such cases an agency worker will need to achieve the same period of service or qualifying hours to become eligible. In all cases, the agency worker only has a right to equal treatment in relation to comparable employees in such circumstances and does not have the right to more favourable treatment. For example, where a **personal performance bonus** requires a period of qualifying hours or service and an agency worker will need to achieve the same period of service or qualifying hours to become eligible as would apply to a comparable employee, or if there is an eligibility period of service for all employees of 12 months before receiving a bonus, the agency worker will be entitled to the same treatment after 12 months. Likewise, an agency worker may not be entitled to a payment if he has **finished or left the assignment** unless that is different from how a comparable employee would be treated.

Where a **hybrid bonus scheme** is based initially on company performance or performance of a specific business unit to create a "pot", and then awarded depending on individual performance (levels vary according to performance marking), this kind of scheme is likely to be within the scope of "pay", as it is awarded to directly recruited staff on the basis of performance and so linked to the amount or quality of work done by a worker. However, where it is possible to identify the part of the award linked solely to company performance and the part of the award linked to personal performance, then the agency worker will only be entitled to that part of the award that can be shown to be linked to personal performance.

Although agency workers will be entitled to the performance-related bonus that comparable employees will be entitled to, subject to the same qualifying conditions, the same process for **assessing performance** need not be followed if not appropriate. For example, annual appraisals can cover long-term career development and it would be appropriate for the end-user to modify the assessment process and conduct shorter appraisals for agency workers.

2085-4 Where an end-user gives an **annual pay rise** an agency worker should receive the pay increment that he would have been entitled to if recruited directly to do the same job.

2085-5 **Excluded payments**   Pay does not cover:
– occupational schemes, such as sick pay, maternity, paternity or adoption pay, and occupational pensions (note though agency workers will be covered by the new automatic pension enrolment requirements which are currently being phased in (¶3400));
– bonuses not directly attributable to personal performance, for example a flat rate bonus that is given to all direct employees to encourage loyalty or long-term service or awarded for overall performance of the company or department where there is no recognition of individual contribution;
– discretionary one-off bonuses, as long as they have not become custom and practice;
– advances in pay or loans, for example for season tickets;
– payments or rewards linked to financial participation schemes such as share ownership schemes;
– benefits in kind which do not have a monetary value, for example, reduced-rate mortgages or employer-funded training allowances;

– redundancy and notice pay (this applies in relation to both statutory and any enhanced contractual rights);
– pay for time off for trade union duties; and
– guarantee payments as they apply to directly recruited staff if laid off.

Pay between assignments exemption

2086-1 There is an exemption from the equal treatment provisions on pay where an agency offers an agency worker a permanent contract of employment and pays the agency worker between assignments, i.e. during the periods when he is not working because there are no available suitable assignments (reg 10 SI 2010/93). This means that after 12 weeks in a given job, the agency worker will not be entitled to the same pay as if he had been recruited directly.

2086-2 This exemption only applies to contracts which are **at least 1 hour per week** and will not apply to "zero hours" contracts. Any attempts to structure arrangements in such a way as to circumvent pay between assignments can give rise to a legal challenge, for example if the hours the agency offers differ from the expected hours of work included in the contract.

2086-3 Conditions To qualify for this exemption, the agency worker must have a permanent contract of employment with the agency and agree what he is willing to accept on any particular assignment and the level of pay between these assignments. The agency should explain this to the agency worker so he can make an informed decision as to whether he is willing to agree to forgo this entitlement and enter into a permanent contract with it.

1. The **contract of employment** must set out:
– the minimum pay rates and how they are calculated;
– the location of work and where the agency worker is willing to travel;
– the minimum and maximum expected hours, which must be at least 1 hour a week (e.g. an agency worker may only be available for 2 days per week so a 5-day assignment would not be "reasonable");
– the nature of work the agency worker is willing to undertake; and
– a statement that makes it clear that the agency worker is foregoing entitlements to equal treatment with regards to pay.

2. The agency must take **reasonable steps to find a suitable assignment**.

2087 Pay between assignments There is no requirement to pay the agency worker before the first assignment under the contract has begun. The pay between assignments should be **paid where** there are any complete weeks without a suitable assignment after the end of the first assignment. It will not apply to periods between two short assignments which fall within the same week.

Pay between assignments is **calculated** by reference to what the agency worker was paid on previous assignments and must be the higher of 50% of (reg 11 SI 2010/93):
– the last assignment pay rate (or the highest pay rate and hours earned in the previous 12 weeks in relation to assignments that were longer than 12 weeks); and
– the national minimum wage.

2088 Ending pay between assignments contract If the agency worker refuses a suitable assignment the agency can terminate the contract, subject to the requirement for the agency to give 4 weeks' pay. The 4 weeks' pay must be paid before the contract can end, unless the agency worker resigns. If this obligation has been met during the duration of the contract then it does not have to be paid again at the end of the contract. For example, if a contract has been running for a year and during that year the agency worker has been paid between assignments for at least 4 weeks, no further payment is required at the end of the contract.

Depending on the agency worker's length of service, he may also be entitled to notice (¶8131) and a redundancy payment (¶8990).

3. Information requirements

It is in the interests of all parties to **exchange information** in a timely manner to ensure compliance and a certain level of protection against claims. Further, even after initial information has been given, end-users should inform agencies if there have been any changes to terms and conditions and pay rates which affect agency workers. Likewise, agencies should put in place reminders so they can check with end-users that all the information they have with regard to basic working conditions is up to date.

End-user informing the agency

Regarding facilities and vacancies While day 1 entitlements are the responsibility of the end-user, agencies may find it useful to enquire about facilities and how an end-user provides information on their job vacancies. This, though, is a matter for the agency and end-user to agree.

Regarding basic working and employment conditions An end-user should provide the agency with the following details, if and when an agency worker completes 12 weeks in a given job:
– the level of basic pay (based on the annual salary an agency worker would have received, as if recruited directly), if and when there are overtime payments and shift/unsocial hours allowances or risk payments for hazardous duties;
– types of bonus schemes the end-user operates (and how individual performance is appraised and information on annual pay increments);
– details of any vouchers which have monetary value; and
– annual leave entitlement.

It may be clear at the start of an assignment that it will last for more than 12 weeks and the agency may ask for this information at an early stage or even in advance of the assignment starting. This is a matter between the agency and end-user and no **timescale** has been set out in the regulations.

> MEMO POINTS It is essential that correct end-user information is supplied from one agency to another where there are **intermediaries** involved in the supply of an agency worker, such as master or neutral vendor arrangements or umbrella companies. In the event of a claim, the courts would decide which party was responsible for any breach to the extent that it is responsible for the infringement.

Information which can be obtained by an agency worker

Agency workers are entitled to information relating to their equal treatment entitlements, if they believe their rights have been infringed (reg 16 SI 2010/93). This process depends on what aspect of equal treatment they are requesting information on.

A written statement is **admissible as evidence** in any proceedings concerning an agency worker claim (¶2095-1) and if it appears to the tribunal that the employer deliberately, and without reasonable excuse, omitted to provide a written statement, or that the written statement is evasive or equivocal, the tribunal may draw any inference which it considers just and equitable, including an inference that the employer has infringed the right in question.

> MEMO POINTS It is recommended that agency workers should be **encouraged to talk to the agency** in the first instance as the agency will often be able to resolve difficulties without resorting to formal procedures or to liaise with the end-user to ensure the agency worker receives the information.

Regarding facilities and vacancies In relation to this entitlement, the requirement to provide information lies with the end-user and information can be requested any time after the start of the assignment if the agency worker believes that he may not be receiving equal treatment in relation to these rights. To make a valid request, the agency worker must make the **request in writing**.

The **end-user** should, **within** 28 days of receipt of a written request, **provide** a written statement containing:
- all relevant information relating to the rights of a comparable worker; and
- reasons for the treatment of agency workers and what objective justification the end-user has if treatment is different (¶2075-4).

2090-6 **Regarding basic working and employment conditions** In relation to this entitlement, the agency worker cannot make a formal request for information until the 12 weeks have elapsed. In the first instance, the agency worker must make the request with regard to any aspect of equal treatment that he does not believe he is receiving from the agency. To make a valid request, the agency worker must make the **request in writing**.

The agency should, **within** 28 days of receipt of a written request, **provide** a written statement containing:
- the relevant information relating to basic working and employment conditions e.g. rate of pay, number of weeks of holiday as set out in company handbooks, usual contractual terms etc;
- any relevant information or factors that were considered when determining the basic working and employment conditions, for example, where the agency worker is put on the pay scale, if there is one; and
- where the equal treatment is based on a comparable employee (doing the same or similar work), information describing the terms and conditions applicable to that employee, explaining any difference in treatment, e.g. lower rate of pay based on lower level of qualifications, skills, experience and expertise.

2090-7 If an agency worker has **not received** a written statement from the agency **within** 30 days of making that request, the agency worker can write to the end-user requesting the same information.

4. Enforcement and remedies

Agency worker remedies

2095-1 An agency worker can **bring a claim** to an employment tribunal if the agency or end-user has infringed his right not to be treated less favourably (reg 18 SI 2010/93).

Liability rests with the end-user for failure to provide **day 1 rights**, but the **end-user** has a **defence** to unequal treatment with regard to day 1 rights if he can show that the treatment was justifiable on objective grounds (¶2075-4) (reg 14 SI 2010/93).

For failure to provide **basic working and employment conditions after 12 weeks**, liability can rest with either the agency (or agencies, where more than one is involved in the supply of the agency worker) and/or the end-user (reg 14 SI 2010/93). The **agency** will have a **defence** if it can show that it obtained or took "reasonable steps" to obtain relevant information from the end-user about its basic working and employment conditions and treated the agency worker accordingly. If it can establish this defence then the end-user will become liable for that liability which would have been the agency's. The end-user will be liable for any breach to the extent that it is responsible for the infringement. So, if an end-user failed to provide information to the agency about basic working and employment conditions and the agency worker was not receiving appropriate treatment under the regulations, then the liability could be the sole responsibility of the end-user.

2095-2 Agency workers also have a right not to be **automatically unfairly dismissed** (where they are employees) (¶8390) and a **right not to be subjected to any detriment** by any act, or failure of the agency or end-user to act, on one of the below grounds if the reason, or principal reason, for dismissal or detriment is that the agency worker (reg 17 SI 2010/93):
- brought proceedings under the regulations;
- requested a written statement (i.e. asking for written justification of less favourable treatment);

– gave evidence or information in connection with such proceedings brought by any agency worker;
– otherwise did anything under the regulations in relation to the agency, end-user or any other person;
– alleged that the agency or end-user has infringed the regulations. Any such allegation must be made in good faith;
– refused (or proposed to refuse) to forgo a right conferred by the regulations;
– declined to sign a workforce agreement for the purposes of the regulations; or
– being an employee representative or prospective representative, performed any functions or activities as such.

This also applies if the agency or end-user dismisses the agency worker or causes him to suffer a detriment because he believes or suspects the employee will do or has done any of the above. If the allegation(s) that the agency or end-user infringed an agency worker's rights (or acted or did not act because of his belief or suspicion) is false and not made in good faith, the agency worker will have no right to claim.

Procedure Complaints must be made within 3 months beginning with the date of the breach. However, a tribunal may extend this period if it considers it just and equitable to do so (¶9475).

2095-3

If the claim is successful, the tribunal can:
– make a declaration;
– award compensation; and
– recommend that the end-user and/or agency take, within a specified period, whatever action it considers reasonable to obviate or reduce the adverse effect on the agency worker.

2095-4

The agency worker will be compensated for any loss of earnings related to his entitlements or receive an appropriate level of compensation, for example if he has been denied access to a facility. There is **no maximum award** but there is a **minimum award** of 2 weeks' pay (uncapped) that should be made, regardless of the value of the loss, unless a tribunal finds that the agency worker behaved unreasonably and that it would not be just and equitable to do so as a result of his conduct (reg 18 SI 2010/93). For example, if an agency worker brings a claim and has not told the agency or end-user that he has worked for the end-user before (and was therefore already entitled to equal treatment or qualified before the 12 weeks elapsed), a tribunal can take this into account when deciding the level of compensation in any claim.

Enforcement measures

Where a tribunal decides that a pattern of assignments indicates that there is an intention to deprive a worker of his rights (¶2083-1), the tribunal may make an **award of up to** £5,000.

2095-5

CHAPTER 7

Directors

OUTLINE

A	Appointment and employment	2110	2 Specific duties under companies legislation	2155
1	Service agreements	2115	3 Liabilities	2160
2	Removal and termination	2125	4 Bribery	2175
B	Duties	2133		
1	General duties	2137		

2100 Directors are **office holders** and are therefore officers of the company. They serve on the board of directors, in accordance with the company's constitution.

2101 There are **different categories** of director. These categories include:
– **Executive** directors, who are actively involved in the management of a company. They will usually be employed by it under service agreements which set out the terms relating to their status as both a director and employee of the company.
– **Non-executive** directors, who are not usually actively involved in the management of the company and who normally work on a very part-time basis (often only attending certain board meetings). Their function is often to monitor the management activities of the executive directors and to provide an independent balance on the board.
– **Nominee** directors, who are appointed by a particular shareholder or group of shareholders. They are often found in group companies, where the parent company will nominate one of its own directors to sit on the board of a subsidiary to monitor its activities, and in joint venture companies, where each contributor will appoint a director to ensure that his interests are represented.
– **Alternate** directors, who, if it is permitted in the company's articles, can be appointed by a director to take his place on the board.
– **De facto** directors, who claim or purport to act as directors, but have either not been validly appointed or continue to act as directors after they have been removed from office (they are the opposite of **de jure** directors, who are validly appointed). A tribunal or court may decide that an individual is a de facto director, even if he has not formally been appointed as a director, because of his responsibilities and duties.
– **Shadow** directors, who are individuals in accordance with whose directions or instructions the directors of the company are accustomed to act (but not merely someone whose advice, given in a professional capacity, is acted upon by the directors, for example a solicitor) (s 251 Companies Act 2006).
The above categories are not mutually exclusive (for example, an alternate director could be appointed to stand in for a managing director, who is usually an executive director).
However, all directors, irrespective of their title, are subject to the **same duties and liabilities** arising from their directorships.

2102 A director's tenure of office does not automatically confer employee status on him. However, it is usual for directors who work full-time in managing the company to be **employees** of the company.

MEMO POINTS While an **executive director** will usually be an employee, and a **non-executive director** will not be an employee, this is not always the case. For example, an individual could be an employee of a company but also sit on the board as a non-executive director to represent the employees' interests.

A distinction should also be drawn between a director who is an office holder and a senior employee whose **job title** includes the word "director". For instance, in a large company, the manager responsible for operations in Europe may be called the "European Director" but if he does not sit on the board (or if he does not have influence over the board as a shadow director), he is not a director of the company for these purposes with the particular duties and liabilities that the role entails.

2103 Where directors are employees, they are **bound by** the implied duties of all employees and any express terms in their employment contracts. They also remain subject to additional obligations as directors. This chapter focuses on issues relating to directors as officers of the company.

MEMO POINTS The rules and legislation governing directors (relating to their appointment, conduct, remuneration, removal and termination) are summarised in this chapter; for a more detailed discussion, see *Company Law Memo*.

A. Appointment and employment

2110 It is possible for a director to become an employee of the company and, similarly, for an existing employee to become a director. Alternatively, an individual may be appointed as a director and engaged as an employee at the same time. If a director is required to work full time in return for remuneration, the courts are likely to regard him as an employee, although the decision will be based on the circumstances of each particular case.

It is common, particularly in small companies, for a director to have a **controlling interest in the company's shares**, making him a majority shareholder. He may also be an employee, depending on the facts of the relationship (¶43).

2111 Some people **cannot be directors** without the consent of the court because they are subject to a disqualification order or undertaking preventing them from being a director of a company, or from being concerned or taking part in any way in the promotion, formation or management of a company for a certain period (Company Directors Disqualification Act 1986).

A company's articles of association may also place conditions on who can be a director, e.g. by requiring directors to have certain qualifications or particular experience. However, it is more usual for such qualifications to be a matter of recruitment policy or decided on a case-by-case basis.

2112 Directors are **appointed** either by an ordinary resolution of the shareholders or by a resolution of the board (subject to re-appointment by the shareholders at the next general meeting, if the articles require) (Table A, regs 76-79; Model Articles for private companies limited by shares, art 17; Model Articles for public companies, art 20). Any procedural requirements are normally set out in the articles of association.

A new appointment must be **recorded** to ensure that members of the public can find out who is responsible for running the company. Form AP01 (in the case of an individual director) or Form AP02 (in the case of a corporate director, i.e. a director which is itself a company) must be filed at Companies House within 14 days of the appointment (s 167 Companies Act 2006). Each new director must provide his written consent to his appointment by signing the relevant form (i.e. Form AP01 or AP02, as appropriate). The company's own statutory register of directors must also be updated.

MEMO POINTS 1. When a company is incorporated, the appointment of its **first directors** is recorded in a different way on the incorporation forms (s 12 Companies Act 2006).

2. For **private companies** incorporated on or after **1 October 2007** that adopted Table A, the standard form articles have been amended so that they no longer require directors appointed by the board to retire and be re-appointed by the shareholders at the next AGM (SI 2007/2541).
For **private companies** limited by shares incorporated on or after **1 October 2009** that adopt the Model Articles, directors are not required to retire by rotation.
The Model Articles for **public companies** incorporated on or after **1 October 2009** do still require directors appointed by the board to retire and be re-appointed by the shareholders at the next AGM (Model Articles for public companies, art 21).

1. Service agreements

A director who is an employee of his company has a **contract of employment**, which is often called a service agreement to reflect that he has a higher status than general staff. This agreement may be express or implied and need not be in writing (although, as an employee, certain statutory written particulars of employment must be provided (¶1405)). The agreement may also be subject to **detailed negotiation**, in which case specialist legal advice should be sought when agreeing terms. Reference should also be made to the company's articles of association, which will override any inconsistent term in the service agreement.

2115

The service agreement may deal with the director's **outside interests** and may seek to limit his shareholding in competing companies. The company may also wish to **protect its information** and other business interests by including express clauses on intellectual property, confidentiality, garden leave and post-termination restrictive covenants (¶¶2310, 2400, 2529, 2550).

2116

The terms of the service agreement must be **approved by the board**, unless the power to do so has been delegated to the managing director, for example (Table A, regs 72 and 84; Model Articles for private companies limited by shares, arts 5, 6; Model Articles for public companies, arts 5, 6). When setting the terms, the board (or managing director or other delegate) must act in the best interests of the company. The service agreement must reflect the articles of association because any conflicting provisions in the service agreement will be ineffective.

2117

The company can only enter into a service agreement with its directors where the company's right to terminate by giving notice is not restricted, or for a **period up to** 2 years (s 188 Companies Act 2006). For **longer periods** where the company cannot terminate the agreement by giving notice or it can only do so in certain circumstances, prior shareholder approval must be obtained. This approval can either be given in a general meeting or by written resolution. Without approval, any express term referring to a longer period will be void, and the agreement will be deemed to be terminable on reasonable notice (s 189 Companies Act 2006; ¶8129).

2118

> MEMO POINTS If the service agreement was **entered into before 1 October 2007**, the old rules still apply, requiring shareholder approval of service agreements for a period longer than 5 years where the company's right to terminate is restricted (s 319 Companies Act 1985; para 6 Sch 3 SI 2007/2194). If an agreement was approved by the shareholders before 1 October 2007 but entered into afterwards, the shareholders' resolution will still be effective as long as it complies with the requirements of the Companies Act 2006.

Remuneration

The **fees** of directors, as office holders, are governed by the articles of association and any shareholders' resolutions passed pursuant to them (Table A, reg 82; Model Articles for private companies limited by shares, art 19; Model Articles for public companies, art 23). In practice, this sum is usually incorporated into their salaries as employees.

2119

As an employee, an executive director will receive a **salary** according to the terms of his service agreement. He may also be entitled to a bonus and other benefits, including pension, private health insurance, share options, company car etc. The company may also provide directors' liability insurance cover (¶2173). The total value of the director's salary and benefits may be set by the board, a remuneration committee of the board or by the shareholders. In practice, the board (or a committee of the board) usually agrees a package which the shareholders can approve.

2120 The company's annual accounts must **disclose** specified information about their directors' remuneration. Companies' disclosure obligations are set out in regulations, with one set for small companies and groups and another for large and medium-sized companies and groups (s 412 Companies Act 2006; Small Companies and Groups (Accounts and Directors' Report) Regulations SI 2008/409; Large and Medium-sized Companies and Groups (Accounts and Reports) Regulations SI 2008/410).

All companies are required to disclose (paras 1-3 Sch 3 SI 2008/409; paras 1, 4, 5 Sch 5 SI 2008/410; s 413 Companies Act 2006):
– remuneration paid to directors, including salary bonuses and benefits, money or assets paid or received under long-term incentive schemes, and contributions to pension schemes;
– compensation for loss of office;
– sums paid to third parties in respect of directors' services; and
– details of any advances and credits granted to directors, as well as any guarantees entered into on their behalf.

In addition, medium-sized and large companies have to disclose information about their highest-paid directors' remuneration and any excess retirement benefits of current and former directors (paras 2, 3 Sch 5 SI 2008/410).

Inspection of agreements

2122 Each service agreement (or written memorandum of its terms if the contract is not in writing) must be copied and **kept at** (s 228 Companies Act 2006; reg 3 SI 2008/3006):
– the company's registered office; or
– a single alternative inspection location, also known as the company's "SAIL" (i.e. a place that is situated in the same part of the UK as the company's registered office and has been notified to Companies House as being the company's single alternative inspection location).

Copies of the agreements and memoranda must also be retained for inspection for at least 1 year after they have expired or been terminated.

Shareholders must be allowed to **inspect** the agreements/memoranda free of charge (s 229 Companies Act 2006). If a shareholder requests, the company must provide him with **copies**. The company is allowed to charge a prescribed fee for providing copies, but not for allowing inspection (reg 4 SI 2007/2612).

Private companies are required to make their records available for inspection (by those with a statutory right to inspect them) for at least 2 hours between 9am and 3pm on a working day to a person who has given the required notice to the company (reg 4 SI 2008/3006). Public companies have to make their records available for inspection for at least 2 hours between 9am and 5pm on each working day (reg 5 SI 2008/3006). There is no need for a person wanting to inspect a public company's records to give notice to the company in advance.

> MEMO POINTS If the agreement was **entered into before 1 October 2007**, the old rules still apply (para 13 Sch 3 SI 2007/2194; s 318 CA 1985). They impose similar retention and inspection obligations on the company, although they do not require the agreements and memoranda to be kept for at least 1 year after their termination or expiration. Service agreements that will expire or can be terminated by the company without paying compensation within the next 12 months do not have to be retained. Companies must allow shareholders to inspect these agreements or memoranda, but they are not obliged to provide copies of them on request.

2. Removal and termination

2125 If a director's **employment** is terminated, he will not automatically lose his directorship, as the role of employee and director are separate and distinct. Service agreements often include provisions requiring resignation as a director upon termination and giving the company power of attorney to execute that resignation if the employee refuses to do so. When dismissing an employed director, the company should therefore ensure that the director either resigns, or is removed from, his office as a director. The **grounds for dismissal** should be drafted in broad terms, reflecting the circumstances set out in the articles of association in which the director could lose his office.

MEMO POINTS If a power of attorney is included the service agreement must be executed as a deed.

2126 Service agreements often contain a clause dealing with the **reconstruction or amalgamation** of the company. The object of this clause is to prevent the director from claiming damages for breach of contract where he is offered employment on no less favourable terms with the company's successor following its reorganisation.

2127 The articles of association will deal with the removal of a director as an **office holder**. They usually provide for his office to terminate automatically in certain circumstances (see ¶2128 below). The board itself cannot usually remove a director from office on its own initiative. Regardless of any provision in the articles or in the service agreement, a director can be removed before any applicable term of office expires by ordinary resolution of the shareholders in a general meeting provided the appropriate notice procedures have been complied with (ss 168, 169 Companies Act 2006). A written resolution cannot be used instead because the director has the right to attend the meeting to argue against his removal if he wishes (s 288(2) Companies Act 2006). A director who is also a shareholder may be able to block such a shareholder resolution if the articles provide for enhanced voting rights in these circumstances (*Bushell v Faith* [1970] 1 All ER 53). Such a provision is usually only found in small companies.

If a director is removed from office, he will remain an ordinary **employee** (but not an office holder) of the company unless it is an express or implied term of the service agreement that he must be a director, in which case the employment will also terminate. Alternatively, a director's service agreement may specifically provide that the director's employment will automatically terminate on removal from the board. In such cases, the Court of Appeal has held that such dismissal may be legitimate on the grounds of "some other substantial reason" (¶8530), and, therefore, potentially fair.

Often the directorship and the employment are **inter-dependent**. If this is the case, removal from the board may result in the individual being entitled to damages for wrongful dismissal, if he is not given the required notice of termination of his employment, and possibly for unfair dismissal or redundancy. Contractual provisions allowing the company to call for the director's resignation from office should therefore be exercised with caution. The inclusion of an express provision in the service agreement that the termination of any directorship will not amount to constructive dismissal may assist the company's defence to any such claim.

2128 The articles of association often provide for a director to cease to hold office on the occurrence of **certain specified events** (for example, if he becomes bankrupt, is mentally or physically incapacitated, or is absent from board meetings without permission for more than 6 months) (Table A, reg 81; Model Articles for private companies limited by shares, art 18; Model Articles for public companies, art 22). The employment may be made subject to similar provisions, in which case there would be no breach of the employment contract (and therefore no claim for damages) if it were terminated in those circumstances (*Shindler v Northern Raincoat Co Ltd* [1960] 1 WLR 1038).

MEMO POINTS Statute **automatically terminates** a director's office in certain situations:
– when he is disqualified (s 13 Company Directors Disqualification Act 1986); and
– when he is declared bankrupt (s 11 Company Directors Disqualification Act 1986).

2129 Companies may require some of their directors to **retire by rotation** at each AGM (e.g. Table A, regs 73-75; Model Articles for public companies, art 21). Where the company was incorporated before 1 October 2007 and is governed by standard form Table A articles, this requirement only applies to non-executive directors (Table A, regs 73, 84). The articles can be amended to exclude the requirement for all types of directors. If the requirement does apply, the retiring directors are subject to re-election at the next AGM, giving the shareholders the opportunity to review the composition of the board.

MEMO POINTS Under the Companies Act 2006, **private companies** are no longer required to hold **AGMs**, unless their articles include a specific requirement to do so (para 32 Sch 3 SI 2007/2194). Table A does not include such a requirement, and a provision that something should happen at an

AGM (such as retirement by rotation) does not constitute an obligation to hold an AGM. Therefore, even if a private company's articles include the retirement by rotation provisions, it is unlikely to have to follow them. For private companies incorporated on or after 1 October 2007 that adopt Table A, the retirement by rotation provisions have been removed (regs 13-18 SI 2007/2541). **Public companies**, by contrast, still have to hold AGMs and so these provisions are still relevant.

2130 Although the service agreement commonly provides that the director must not **resign his directorship** without the company's consent, he cannot be restrained from doing so. The company's remedy would be for breach of contract.

Termination payments

2131 Generally speaking, payments made to directors in compensation for loss of office (often referred to as a "**golden handshake**") must be approved by the shareholders (ss 217-219 Companies Act 2006). There are some exceptions to this requirement (ss 220, 221 Companies Act 2006):
– pensions for past services;
– payments made under legal obligations unrelated to the event giving rise to the director's loss of office or retirement, such as wages due to the director. This includes damages for breach of such obligations;
– settlements and compromises relating to termination of the director's office or employment; and
– small payments by the company or its subsidiaries of up to £200.

The shareholders' **approval** can be obtained by ordinary resolution (unless the articles require a higher majority or unanimity) at a general meeting or by written resolution. Failure to obtain approval will result in the payment being held on trust for the benefit of the company and any director who authorised the payment will be jointly and severally liable to indemnify the company for its loss (s 222 Companies Act 2006).

B. Duties

2133 As an **employee**, a director will be subject to common law implied duties (¶1195) and any express duties set out in his service agreement. These should be described in broad terms, reflecting the wide obligations owed by the director to the company. It may be useful for the service agreement to provide that the board can specify his duties from time to time, giving it the flexibility to **vary the duties** as required by changing circumstances. Express provisions relating to the director's duties may be subject to negotiation, particularly if he has other interests (which should not conflict with his duties to the company (¶¶2116, 2138)).

If it is envisaged that another person may be appointed to **act jointly** with the director, an express right should be reserved in the service agreement to prevent the director from claiming that he has been constructively dismissed by virtue of a loss of status.

2134 As an **office holder**, a director owes additional duties to his company, which are imposed by common law and statute. These duties are classed as **general duties** (which used to be imposed by common law only but have now been codified by the Companies Act 2006) and **specific duties** (which are those significant statutory duties and liabilities that directors may find themselves subject to when running their companies). Directors should consider their actions in the light of their duties as a whole, and remember that more than one duty may apply. Usually, the duties **overlap and work together**.

> MEMO POINTS 1. The duties and liabilities discussed below **apply to** all types of directors in both public and private companies.

2. There are also circumstances in which directors will owe duties to **persons other than the company**, such as its employees or other third parties (for example, suppliers, creditors and customers). See *Company Law Memo*.

3. A **listed company** will be subject to more onerous obligations under legislation in certain areas. Listed companies must also comply with their continuing obligations under the rules of the relevant market, for example the Listing Rules of the London Stock Exchange. These contain a number of obligations with regard to the display of directors' contracts and particularisation of directors, their emoluments, dealing in the company's securities, etc. It may be useful for the service agreement expressly to refer to these obligations. Further, the Listing Rules require listed companies to comply with the provisions of the UK Corporate Governance Code. This is referred to as "self-regulation", as the Code has been devised and is policed by the City and companies are required to comply with the Code or explain why they have not. The Code is complemented by the UK Stewardship Code, which provides regulation and guidance over the relationship between the company's board of directors and its institutional investors.

The Department for Business, Innovation and Skills (BIS) has also published for consultation the draft Companies Act 2006 (Strategic Report and Directors' Report) Regulations 2013, which include a requirement for listed companies to state the gender split for directors, managers and employees. The draft regulations revoke the requirement for a company's directors' report to include a business review. In exchange for the business review, companies would be required to produce a standalone strategic report each financial year, separate from the directors' report. The requirements of the new strategic report are broadly the same as those under the old business review. However, quoted companies must disclose the number of persons in the company of each sex who are directors, managers (excluding directors) and employees of the company. It is anticipated that the draft regulations will come into force in October 2013. The draft regulations can be viewed at: flmemo.co.uk/em2134

4. The **takeover of a company** (whether it is listed or not) may be subject to the City Code on Takeovers and Mergers, to which directors must adhere during the process. Directors' service agreements will have to be disclosed and the company will not be able to amend or enter into service agreements during the course of a takeover offer if this would involve an abnormal increase in the director's remuneration or a significant improvement in his terms of service.

5. Companies can also be subject to **regulatory supervision**. Regulatory bodies (e.g. the Financial Services Authority) may have the power to investigate companies' conduct, publish reports on them and impose sanctions, which can affect directors personally as well as their companies.

2135 It is acceptable for a director to rely on other directors and office holders. Where it is reasonable for him to do so, and where the company's articles permit, a director may **delegate** his powers (including appointing an alternate director) and there is no right of action against him for the actions or defaults of properly appointed and supervised delegates.

1. General duties

2137 A director's general duties fall into **three categories**:
– the duty to act within his authority;
– fiduciary duties; and
– the duty to exercise care, skill and diligence in performing his duties and functions.

Directors' "general duties" used to **derive from** common law. However, as part of the reform of company law that has resulted in the Companies Act 2006, these duties have been codified into statute. The codified general duties are to be interpreted and applied in the same way as the common law and equitable rules on which they are based, having regard to the same principles (s 170 Companies Act 2006). Therefore, the pre-existing case law remains relevant. The consequences of breach also follow the common law and equitable rules.

Duty to act within authority

2138 As the company's agents, directors must act within the scope of the **powers delegated** to them. Authority to act, as well as more specific instructions, can be given to a director in a number of ways, most commonly:
– the shareholders usually give the board general authority to exercise all of the company's powers in the articles of association (e.g. Table A, reg 70; Model Articles for private companies limited by shares, art 3; Model Articles for public companies, art 3);

– the shareholders can specifically authorise the board or a particular director to do something by passing a special resolution to that effect;
– the board can delegate any of its powers to an individual director; or
– authority can be implied from the director's position. In the case of ordinary directors, only a limited amount of authority to deal with everyday managerial tasks can be implied (e.g. writing letters or signing cheques on the company's behalf). The level of authority that can be implied in the case of a more senior director (such as the managing director or finance director) will be greater. However, it is better to rely on specifically delegated authority because whether authority is implied always depends on the facts of each case.

If a director's instructions are vague or unclear, or if he has no instructions to act in a given situation, he will discharge this duty by following a reasonable course of action which is in the company's best interests.

Fiduciary duties

2139 Given the position of trust which directors have within the company, directors owe certain fiduciary duties to the company. These duties are distinct from and go further than the duty of fidelity applicable to all employees (¶1213). A director's fiduciary duties include the following:
– **acting within their powers** (s 171 Companies Act 2006). This duty is separate from, but clearly linked to, their duty as agents to act within their authority. It requires directors to act in accordance with the company's constitution and only exercise their powers for the purposes for which they are conferred;
– **promoting the company's success** for the benefit of the shareholders as a whole (s 172 Companies Act 2006). This duty aims to make sure that directors consider the consequences of their decisions on the company, looking at factors such as the employees' interests, the company's business reputation and the environment;
– **exercising independent judgment** (s 173 Companies Act 2006). Generally speaking, this means that directors cannot allow others to influence their decisions or to make decisions for them. However, to make the duty workable, they are allowed to delegate to others and to rely on professional advice where reasonable to do so. The company can also enter into agreements that restrict directors' ability to act independently, for example a shareholders' agreement;
– **avoiding conflicts of interest and duty** (s 175 Companies Act 2006). This includes only using company property and information for lawful purposes. However, a company can decide to allow a director to continue to act despite having a conflict, for example by allowing him to have other, specified, business interests;
– **not to accept benefits from third parties**, i.e. a person other than the company (s 176 CA 2006). This duty applies even if the director has acted honestly in obtaining the benefit. Directors who disclose their benefits and profits may be permitted by the company to retain them; and
– **disclosing interests in** proposed and existing **transactions/arrangements** (ss 177, 182 Companies Act 2006).

2140 Consequently, in relation to **confidentiality and restraints**, a director must not place himself in a position where his personal interests and those of the company conflict. For example, a director will be in breach if he takes for himself the benefit of a contract which he had been ostensibly negotiating on behalf of the company (*Cook v Deeks* [1916] UKPC 10).

A director may be in breach of his fiduciary duties if he takes **preparatory steps**, before leaving, to compete with the company's business after he has resigned (*G Attwood Holdings Ltd and another v Woodward and ors* [2009] EWHC 1083 (Ch); *Berryland Books Ltd v BK Books Ltd and ors* [2009] EWHC 1877 (Ch)).

In contrast to the duty of fidelity, fiduciary duties **may continue** after the fiduciary relationship (i.e. the directorship) ends. In particular, former directors must not take for themselves or another a maturing business opportunity which the company is actively pursuing (*Multi Installations Ltd v Varsani and anor* [2008] EWHC 657 (Ch)), where at least part of their motivation for resigning was to take advantage of that opportunity personally or where the opportunity only arose as a result of their directorship (*Island Export Finance Ltd v Umunna* [1986] BCLC 460, QBD). Further, the directors' duty not to misuse company property and/or information continues after the company has entered liquidation, even though their power to act on the company's behalf ceases (*Condliffe and Hilton v Sheingold* [2007] EWCA Civ 1043).

However, like employees (¶2415), former directors may use their **own skill and knowledge** (including, for example, market information learned during the directorship) for their own benefit and in competition with the company. They may also take advantage of a business opportunity where the initiative has come from the client, rather than the director, and where the prospect of taking this opportunity played no part in the director's decision to resign (*Foster Bryant Surveying Ltd v (1) Bryant and (2) Savernake Property Consultants Ltd* [2007] EWCA Civ 200).

Duty to exercise care, skill and diligence

Directors are obliged to exercise reasonable care, skill and diligence (s 174 Companies Act 2006). The **basis of this duty** arises from the director's assumed responsibility for managing the affairs or property of the company and is not dependent on his service agreement, although an executive director may also have this duty expressly set out there (*Henderson v Merrett Syndicates Ltd* [1995] 2 AC 145, HL). **2141**

A **director is expected to** exercise the care, skill and diligence that would be exercised by a reasonably diligent person with the general knowledge, skill and experience that:
– may reasonably be expected of a person in his position; and
– he actually has. **2142**

The first, objective, limb of the test applies a basic standard that must be reached. For example, any reasonable person would actively participate in management and attend sufficient board meetings to maintain an understanding of the company and how it is being run. The second, subjective, limb ensures that directors are also judged by a higher standard if they possess particular knowledge, skills or experience. For example, it is only fair that if a director is also a qualified accountant, this should be taken into account when judging his competence.

2. Specific duties under companies legislation

Statute imposes many duties on directors, mostly relating to housekeeping matters such as filing and record keeping. Breach usually renders a director liable to a fine but can result in civil and/or criminal liability, depending on the provision in question. The following table gives a **summary** of a director's significant managerial obligations. **2155**

Obligation	Reference
Disclose interest in **contracts** and other transactions with company [1]	ss 177, 182 Companies Act 2006
Obtain shareholder approval for **service agreements over 2 years long**	ss 188, 189 Companies Act 2006
Make disclosures and obtain shareholder approval for **compensation for loss of office**	ss 215-222 Companies Act 2006
Obtain shareholder approval for **substantial property transactions** with company [2]	ss 190-196 Companies Act 2006
Observe **restrictions** on company making loans to, or acting as creditor or giving security for, directors or persons connected with them	ss 197-214 Companies Act 2006
Comply with statutory **accounting requirements**, including production of directors' report [3]	Part 15 Companies Act 2006 and related regulations (SI 2008/409, for small companies and SI 2008/410, for large and medium-sized companies).

Obligation	Reference
Maintain up-to-date accounting **records** and file annual returns with Registrar of Companies	ss 386, 854 Companies Act 2006.

Note:
1. Directors' interests can be disclosed at a board meeting or in writing. The **timing** of the disclosure will determine the type of disclosure being made (i.e. whether it is in relation to an interest in an "existing" or "proposed" transaction). **Non-compliance** usually results in a fine but if the director has also failed to comply with general duties of disclosure, any resulting transactions will be voidable, i.e. can be set aside at the option of the innocent party (*Guinness plc v Saunders* [1990] 2 AC 663, HL).
2. Substantial property transaction means **buying** a non-cash asset exceeding a certain value from, or **selling** such an asset to, the company.
3. In **medium-sized and large companies**, directors must produce an enhanced report, giving more detail about the company's business than in a basic report in a small company. For example, medium-sized and large companies must include information about the action that has been taken to introduce, maintain or develop employee participation (providing employees with information, consulting them and encouraging involvement through employees' share schemes or other means).

3. Liabilities

2160 Directors are responsible for their **own breaches and defaults**. They can be held personally liable in a number of ways, examined below, depending on the breach or default in question. Directors can be relieved from the consequences of liability, if their companies or the court decide that it is appropriate.

Companies are treated as separate legal entities with their own rights and duties. Therefore, a director is not usually held responsible for his **company's debts or defaults**. However, he will incur **personal liability** if he caused the breach by the company (e.g. he caused the company to enter into a contract outside of its powers by acting outside of his own powers) or if he accepts responsibility for the company's obligations (e.g. by giving a personal guarantee for the company's debts). Statute can also hold him personally liable. For example if a director breaches a disqualification order/undertaking by acting as a director or taking on a management role in a company, as well as being liable for failing to comply with the order/undertaking, he can be held liable for any of the company's debts incurred while he was in breach (s 15 Company Directors Disqualification Act 1986).

Statute specifically provides for directors to be held personally liable for their companies' defaults in some cases because it provides a stronger incentive for directors to ensure that they act within the law. For offences under the Companies Acts that impose strict liability on the company, its directors and other officers will be liable if they authorise, permit, participate in or fail to take all reasonable steps to prevent the breach, in the case of an offence under the 2006 Act (s 1121 Companies Act 2006). A corporate officer (i.e. a director of a company which is itself another company) will only commit an offence in respect of the company as an officer in default if one of its own officers is in default (s 1122 Companies Act 2006). If this is the case, both the company and its officer will be liable.

MEMO POINTS This discussion focuses on directors' liability for breaches of their duties to the company or under company law. Directors can also be held personally liable for other breaches, for example relating to **health and safety** (¶¶5185+) or **bribery** (¶¶2175+).

For breach of general duties

2162 Breach of the general duties imposed on directors broadly fall within three categories of **civil claims**: breach of contract, tort (negligence) and breach of fiduciary duties. Different remedies are available for each type of action, and the court will grant a remedy, or remedies, appropriate to the consequences of breach. Usually, the director in breach will be required to compensate the company for any loss it has suffered or to relinquish any benefit he has gained as a result of his breach. If the action is successful, the order will generally be made against the director in question, but the court can also make orders against third parties in appropriate circumstances (e.g. where a third party is in possession of the company's property as a result of the director's breach).

Duty breached	Type of claim	Available remedies
Act within authority	Breach of contract	1. Damages for loss 2. Account for profits received by director/loss to company 3. Injunction 4. Avoid/enforce transaction
1. Act within powers 2. Promote company's success 3. Exercise independent judgment 4. Avoid conflicts of interest and duty 5. Not to accept benefits from third parties	Breach of fiduciary duties	1. Account for profits received by director/loss to company 2. Tracing/restitution 3. Injunction 4. Avoid/enforce transaction
Skill, care and diligence	Tort (negligence)	1. Damages 2. Injunction 3. Avoid/enforce transaction

MEMO POINTS Of course, where a director is also an employee he may also incur liability for **breach of his service agreement**.

Since directors owe these duties to the company, any **court action** against them for breach of duty must be **taken by** the company, not individual shareholders (although third parties may also have a cause of action in respect of certain breaches). It may be difficult for the company to take action against a director if he holds enough shares to prevent the shareholders resolving to commence court proceedings and/or he has enough control of the board to ensure that such a resolution is not acted upon. If this is the case, individual shareholders, or a group of shareholders, can still take action in one of the following ways:
– commence a derivative action (ss 260-264 Companies Act 2006). A derivative action is one taken, on the company's behalf, by an individual shareholder when it should have been taken by the company. This type of action can be commenced against a director for his (actual or proposed) negligence, default, breach of duty or breach of trust;
– take action for unfair prejudice (s 994 Companies Act 2006). The applicant has to show that his interests as a shareholder (or the interests of the shareholders generally) have been damaged due to the way in which the company has been run. It is designed to protect minority shareholders who do not have the power to object to the unfairly prejudicial conduct because their voting power is not strong enough. It can also be relied on in cases of deadlock. The court has a wide power to rectify the situation or to give the applicant a fair exit route from the company; and
– petition for the company to be wound up on the ground that it would be just and equitable to do so (s 122 Insolvency Act 1986). This is a drastic remedy, as it will result in the company being wound up and dissolved. Therefore, it should only be relied on in cases of a complete breakdown in the relationship between the parties.

The kind of actions or omissions that directors can be sued for in the civil courts can also lead to their **disqualification**. For example, a director who has been negligent in his management of the company could be disqualified because he is unfit to hold office (s 6 Company Directors Disqualification Act 1986).

2163

In addition to, or instead of, asking the court to intervene, the company may wish to deal with the issue **without** taking **court action**. For example, the offending director could be removed from office and his employment terminated if the breach is serious enough. If the director entered into a contract or other transaction in breach of his authority, the company can choose to declare it void (alternatively, the company could choose to ratify the contract, as long as it is not illegal in itself).

2164

For breach of specific obligations under companies legislation

Each of the many specific duties imposed on directors by companies legislation carries its own punishment. Usually, a director will be liable to a **fine** but in some cases he may also

2166

be **imprisoned**. The legislation may also deal with the consequences of the director's unlawful actions, for example by providing that a contract or other transaction entered into without the proper authority can be declared void by the company so that the company is not in the unfair position of having to perform obligations under a contract that it did not authorise.

A director can be **disqualified** for breaches of companies legislation, including persistent breach of filing requirements, as well as such breaches being considered in an application to disqualify him because he is generally unfit to hold office (Company Directors Disqualification Act 1986).

When the company is insolvent

2168 If a company is in liquidation, action can be taken against a director in respect of his conduct before and during liquidation, the most important examples of which are:

– **misfeasance**, i.e. misapplying, retaining or becoming otherwise accountable for any money or other property of the company or being guilty of any misfeasance or breach of any fiduciary or other duty in relation to the company (s 212 Insolvency Act 1986);

– **fraudulent trading**, i.e. knowingly carrying on the company's business with the intention of defrauding creditors of the company or of any other person, or for any other fraudulent purpose (s 213 Insolvency Act 1986); and

– **wrongful trading**, i.e. failing to take every reasonable step to minimise the potential loss to the company's creditors when he knew, or ought to have concluded, that there was no reasonable prospect that the company would avoid going into insolvent liquidation (s 214 Insolvency Act 1986).

In all cases, the court can require the director to **contribute to** the company's assets.

When a company enters an insolvency procedure, the insolvency practitioner will examine the transactions entered into by the company prior to insolvency as well as the directors' conduct. A director may be personally liable to make up any **loss suffered** by the company as a result of (ss 238, 239, 244, 423 Insolvency Act 1986 respectively):

– a transaction at an undervalue;
– a preference;
– an extortionate credit transaction; or
– a transaction defrauding creditors.

A director can also be **disqualified** if his conduct renders him unfit or if he appears to have engaged in, or is found guilty of, fraudulent or wrongful trading (ss 4, 6, 10 Company Directors Disqualification Act 1986).

Relief from liability

2170 In some cases, the company (i.e. the shareholders) may waive a director's liability by choosing to **ratify** his actions. It is common for the company to do so, since many breaches (such as failing to act within the director's authority) are merely technical and do not cause the company any harm. The company cannot ratify illegal or fraudulent acts and, if it is insolvent, it cannot ratify a breach of duty since the creditors' interests supersede those of the shareholders. The board can no longer ratify directors' acts (s 239 Companies Act 2006). However, it may be able to relieve a director from liability in other ways by deciding not to sue, or to settle or release such a claim, provided it has the power to control litigation brought on the company's behalf.

> MEMO POINTS The board can still ratify the acts of **other officers or agents** if the act in question would have been within the board's powers.

2171 A director may **escape liability** for negligence, default, breach of duty or breach of trust at the court's discretion if he can show that he acted honestly and reasonably and ought fairly to be excused (s 1157 Companies Act 2006).

2172 A company **can indemnify** its director against liability he incurs personally to a third party and for the costs of successfully defending court proceedings (s 234 Companies Act 2006; e.g. Table A, reg 118; Model Articles for private companies limited by shares, art 52; Model Articles for public companies, art 85). These limited indemnities are called "qualifying third party indemnities" and must be disclosed in the company's accounts and made available for inspection by the shareholders (ss 236-238 Companies Act 2006). A company **cannot** otherwise **indemnify** directors for negligence, default, breach of duty or breach of trust.

A company can, however, provide **liability insurance cover** for its directors in respect of any type of liability, including those for which it cannot indemnify them (s 233 Companies Act 2006). However, for public policy reasons, insurance cannot be obtained in respect of illegal acts such as fraud and dishonesty, or for penalties imposed by the courts. Where directors' and officers' insurance is purchased or maintained in any financial year, this must be disclosed in the directors' report to the company's accounts.

2173

4. Bribery

It is a **criminal offence** to (ss 1, 2, 6, 17 Bribery Act 2010):
– offer, promise or give a bribe to another person to bring about or reward improper performance, or behave in a way which, in itself, constitutes improper performance;
– request, agree to receive, or accept a bribe in return for improper performance; or
– bribe a foreign public official with the intention to obtain or retain business or an advantage in the conduct of business or course of a trade or profession. This may include the intention to persuade the official to exercise his functions as a public official, to use his position (even if he does not have authority to use the position in that way) or to fail to exercise his functions in the usual way.

Improper performance means performance which amounts to a breach of an expectation that a person will act in good faith, impartially or in a position of trust (s 4 Bribery Act 2010). The expectation referred to is what a reasonable person in the UK would expect in relation to the performance of the type of function or activity concerned, and local customs or practices should be disregarded unless permitted or required by the domestic law of the country concerned (s 5 Bribery Act 2010).

2175

> MEMO POINTS 1. The new legislation came **into force on** 1 July 2011 which modernised and consolidated the previous bribery law.
> 2. Other individuals can be liable for the offences of bribery listed above, for example **employees**, company secretaries or shareholders.
> 3. To aid organisations in understanding the Act and developing policies and procedures to prevent bribery, the Ministry of Justice has issued **guidance** notes, which, for example, confirm that **proportionate expenditure** on corporate hospitality will not fall foul of the Act and that standards and norms in a particular industry will be relevant to considering whether expenditure on corporate hospitality and gifts is proportionate. The guidance is available here: flmemo.co.uk/em2175a
> The Serious Fraud Office (SFO) has also recently **revised published guidance** setting out its approach to prosecutions (¶2178) for **facilitation payments** and **hospitality and promotional expenditure,** which explains that:
> – facilitation payments (e.g. giving a government official money to perform an existing duty) are bribes and are illegal under the Act irrespective of their size or frequency;
> – whilst genuine hospitality or promotional or other legitimate business expenditure is an established and important part of doing business, the SFO notes that bribes can be disguised as legitimate business expenditure;
> – self-reporting will not automatically avert prosecution: to be part of a public interest factor tending against prosecution, a self-report must form part of a "genuinely proactive approach" of the corporate management team; and
> – even if it does not prosecute for reported violations, the SFO can prosecute for unreported violations of the law and provide information on them to other bodies (such as foreign police forces).
> The statements can be found here:
> flmemo.co.uk/em2175b
> flmemo.co.uk/em2175c
> flmemo.co.uk/em2175d

2176 Directors and employees can be exposed to, or involved in, bribery in the context of activities connected with the company's business. It does not matter whether the bribe (a financial or other advantage) is paid or received in the UK or elsewhere, directly or through a third party. **Financial or other advantage** is not defined but it may conceivably include cash, acceptance of gifts or extraordinary hospitality and other advantages e.g. promises of promotion. It does not matter whether the person to whom the advantage is offered, promised or given is the same person as the person who is to perform, or has performed, the function or activity concerned. Nor does it matter whether the advantage is given directly or via a third party. This means liability cannot be avoided by giving the bribe to a family member or friend of the person whose improper performance the director or employee intends to secure.

2177 **Companies** can also be liable for **failing to prevent bribery** if a person associated with it (for example, a director or employee) bribes another person on the company's behalf (s 7 Bribery Act 2010). However, a commercial organisation has a **defence** to this offence if it can show that it had in place adequate procedures designed to prevent bribery. It is therefore recommended that, where appropriate, employers have a bribery policy which is communicated to all members of staff and actively enforced.

2178 Those who **commit an offence of bribery** are liable to up to 10 years' imprisonment and/or a fine (s 11 Bribery Act 2010). If a body corporate commits a bribery offence (other than the offence of failure to prevent bribery) with the consent or connivance of a senior officer (e.g. a director, senior manager or company secretary) or a person purporting to act in such a capacity, the individual senior officer (as well as the body corporate) is guilty of the offence (s 14 Bribery Act 2010).

> MEMO POINTS The **first prosecution** under the Bribery Act was of a court employee who offered to influence court proceedings for motoring offences if he was paid £500. He was convicted in October 2011 and sentenced to 4 years' imprisonment.

CHAPTER 8

Assignments

OUTLINE

SECTION 1 **Prerequisites for assignment** 2210		Remuneration..................................... 2236	
		Tax position 2237	
Employee consent 2211		NICs and benefits 2238	
Effect on the terms of employment 2215		Healthcare 2245	
Agreement between the employer and the other undertaking 2222		Pension.. 2250	
	B	Applicable law 2255	
	C	Applicable jurisdiction 2260	
SECTION 2 **Assignment abroad (posting)** 2230	D	Statutory employment rights............ 2275	
A Contractual issues 2235			

2200 An employer may want an employee to work for the **benefit of another undertaking** during the course of his employment, for example if the employee's job is such that it needs to be performed in a different office, or when the employer wants the employee to gain additional experience. This is referred to as an assignment or secondment of the employee. This chapter outlines the issues involved, including the special rules and considerations that apply to assignments abroad.

2201 The terms assignment and secondment are often used interchangeably. However, the term **secondment** is usually used where there is a specific contract between the employer and a third party undertaking and the employee is specifically seconded to support that contract, for example, where an employee is provided to another company to act as a consultant to a specific project.

The term **assignment** may be used both for secondment situations and those where an employee works for an affiliate (i.e. an entity within the same group of companies as the employer), or at a branch office of the employer. This might also be referred to as an intra-group assignment.

Where the assignment is to another country the term **posting** is commonly used, although the term **detachment** is being used more and more frequently. Notwithstanding the use of all these different terms, the concept behind them is identical, i.e. the employee continues to be employed by his employer but the work that he carries out is for the benefit of another undertaking.

2202 This chapter does **not cover** situations that involve the legal assignment of the employee's contract of employment to another entity which results in a **change in the identity of the employer**. Such legal assignments would arise, for example, where all or part of the employer's business is transferred to a third party and, as a consequence, the third party takes over the employment of those employees who support that business. Such transfers are dealt with in chapter 24 on TUPE.

SECTION 1

Prerequisites for assignment

2210 The **period of assignment** may be for a **short term**, for example when the employee is asked to carry out a specific task in a branch office of the employer which only takes a few days, or it may be for a **longer term**, for example when an employee is seconded to the office of a third party to provide technical support on a particular project. In each instance, the employment contract remains in place and the employee **remains employed** by the employer throughout the period of assignment, with the period counting for continuity of service. Furthermore, the expectation is that the employee will return to his original job at the end of the period of assignment.

Employee consent

2211 Before an employer assigns his employee, he needs to find out whether he has the employee's consent to the proposed assignment. Although many employees consider assignment as a positive step in their career progression, there may be instances when the employee does not wish to move from his current position.

2212 Consent will **already exist** if the contract of employment specifically provides for the assignment of an employee as part of his job, for example where a management accountant is employed to assist affiliated companies in setting up their accounting systems. Alternatively, the contract of employment may contain a **mobility clause** under which the employer is entitled to relocate his employee (¶1618). Where there is no express mobility clause, one may be **implied** under the principle of business efficacy if the employee is expected to carry out his work at different locations (¶1631). It is **good practice** for the employer to consult with the employee prior to deciding on any assignment.

When there is **no mobility clause** (either express or implied), the employer must obtain the employee's express consent prior to any assignment as this will amount to a variation of the employment contract.

2213 An employer owes an implied **duty of trust and confidence** to his employees (¶1242). The failure of the employer to act reasonably in matters relating to an assignment could result in a breach of that duty, with the possible outcome that the employee could claim against him for breach of contract (*United Bank Ltd v Akhtar* [1989] IRLR 507, EAT).

Effect on the terms of employment

2215 When **variations** to the employment contract are necessary as a result of the assignment, they must be **agreed** and the employer cannot unilaterally make variations to the terms without the employee's consent (¶1600). Variations to some terms are required by law to be **evidenced in writing** (¶1400), but it is **good practice** for all changes arising from an assignment to be agreed by way of written amendment or variation of the employment contract.

2216 Issues such as the **control and direction** of the employee during the period of assignment will need to be addressed, and the employee will need to know to whom he must report. The employer's **grievance and disciplinary procedures** and **health and safety procedures** may need amendment to accommodate the circumstances of the assignment. The assignment may also affect any employee performance evaluation, if carried out during the period of the assignment, and input from the other undertaking in this should be considered. The employer retains ultimate responsibility for these procedures and should also ensure that an adequate **health and safety policy** applies to any workplace to which the employee is assigned (¶4860). Any working practices of the other undertaking, including those that affect the **hours of work** of the employee, should be taken into account.

2217 The employment contract may need to incorporate **new terms** that are agreed in connection with the assignment, depending on the particular circumstances. They will usually include details of the identity of the other undertaking, and the place of work. Terms covering the financial arrangements, the duration of the assignment, the termination of the assignment and the employee's return at the end of the assignment will need to be considered.

2218 The employee may be given **additional benefits or reimbursement of costs** such as:
– paid **home leave**: if the assignment is to a place far from the employee's home the employer may agree to pay for the employee and his family to return home at regular intervals;
– payment of **housing costs**: if the employee is asked to relocate to a different area from his original workplace location he may incur additional housing costs which the employer may agree to meet in full or subsidise; and
– payment of **school fees**: the relocation may affect an employee's family and the employer may agree to pay for the school fees of the employee's children either in the original workplace location or in the new location.
The employer usually agrees to cover the employee's **costs of travel** to the new place of employment and, if appropriate, the **relocation costs** to the new workplace and his return to the original workplace.

2219 As an assignment is not intended to be permanent, the parties must agree the **duration of the assignment** and, if for a fixed term, the date on which it is to end. The parties should also agree on the terms and conditions of the employee's **return** to the original place of employment, covering issues such as the employee's seniority and the availability of his original job on his return.

2220 Both the employer and the employee should agree in advance their respective rights and responsibilities arising on **early termination** of the assignment because of the following events:
– the employee's acts or omissions;
– the employer's recall of the employee to his original workplace;
– the other undertaking no longer requiring the employee; or
– external circumstances e.g. when there is an event of force majeure (acts of God, war, or similar events beyond the control of the parties which prevent the continuation of the contract).

Agreement between the employer and the other undertaking

2222 It is good practice to evidence in writing any agreement concerning a secondment, especially where the other undertaking is a **third party** but also if it is an intra-group assignment. The agreement should reflect the issues discussed above and, depending on the circumstances of the secondment, the extent of the other undertaking's involvement.

2223 The employer may require the other undertaking to cover the **remuneration and costs** of the employee, including those relating to the additional benefits and costs which are incurred in connection with the secondment. Reimbursement may be either to the employer or directly to the employee.

The parties should also agree in advance which **other costs** are recoverable from the other undertaking and in which circumstances, for example where the secondment is terminated early. If there are associated employer costs that arise on early termination the employer may want to obtain an indemnity to cover them. The cost of arranging and placing **insurance cover** for the benefit of the employer may also be met by the other undertaking.

Finally, the employer may want to include a "hold harmless" and **indemnity clause** in the agreement, whereby the other undertaking will cover him with respect to claims, damages and actions arising from the employee's acts or omissions during the period of secondment.

SECTION 2

Assignment abroad (posting)

2230 There are various situations where an employer may want to assign his employee to work abroad. The employer may be part of a multi-national group with offices throughout the world, or he may provide consultancy services to clients who have offices abroad.

2231 The employer will need to consider the **immigration requirements** of the country of posting and ensure that work visas and similar requirements are met. He will also need to check its **employment laws** to ensure that the posting does not breach them and it may be advisable to obtain the advice of a local lawyer for this purpose.

2232 The same issues of employee consent and how the assignment will have an effect on the employee's contract of employment will apply to a posting as they do to a domestic assignment (¶¶2211, 2215). Issues that specifically apply to postings may be covered in the employer's expatriation handbook while further issues may need to be discussed and agreed between the employer and the employee.

A. Contractual issues

2235 Where the employer frequently posts his employees abroad, some terms and conditions relating to postings may be contained in an **expatriation handbook** or similar document. Therefore, although the employment contract itself may not specifically contain the terms and conditions of posting, the terms in the handbook will apply if specifically incorporated into the employment contract by reference.

Other **terms, personal** to the individual postings, will not be contained in the handbook but will need to be agreed on a case-by-case basis. Agreements regarding some terms are required by law to be evidenced in writing (¶1400) but it is good practice for all terms arising from an assignment to be agreed by way of written amendment or variation of the employment contract.

It is usual for the following issues to be discussed and agreed prior to a posting.

Remuneration

2236 Remuneration will cover:
– any incentive payments to encourage the employee to accept the posting;
– additional benefits relating to relocation costs, home leave, flight costs, housing costs and school fees. These are more likely to be offered and expected in postings abroad and usually form part of the incentive package offered to employees; and
– currency of remuneration, rate of exchange, how and when paid, the place of payment and whether there is an allocation of remuneration between UK sterling and foreign currency.

Tax position

2237 The length of the posting may affect the employee's tax residence status in the UK (¶3370) or he may have to pay tax in the country of posting as well as in the UK. The employer may agree to augment the employee's salary to make up any loss that he suffers from paying higher taxes as a result of his posting.

NICs and benefits

2238 Payment of UK NICs establish an employee's entitlement to certain contribution-based UK state benefits as well as counting towards his state pension accrual (¶6931). Generally, if an employee is temporarily posted abroad, Class 1 NICs may still be paid for a certain period. Continuing payment of UK NICs may also be recognised by the country of posting, exempting the assignee from making social security contributions in the country of posting and entitling him to the state benefits, for example healthcare, of that country (see below for a summary and ¶¶7000+ for a more detailed discussion).

When the posting is to an **EEA state** the employee is expected to contribute towards the social security system of the state in which he is working (EC Regulation 1408/1971; ¶7026).

2240

However, **special circumstances** will **exempt** a UK employee who continues to have Class 1 UK NICs paid on his behalf while he is posted abroad (¶7028). These circumstances exist when the posting is:
– to another EEA state;
– in continuation of his employment;
– for a period expected to be not more than 24 months; and
– not taking the place of someone else who works for the employer.

Consequently, the employee will **not be required** to make social security contributions in the EEA state of posting but may still obtain **certain state benefits**, the most relevant for employees being healthcare cover.

Where the special circumstances exist the employer should apply for a certificate of continuing liability from the National Insurance Contributions Office (NICO) before the employee is posted. This certificate (normally a **Form A1** but in some cases an E101 or E102) when shown in the country of posting, will evidence the employee's exemption from social security contributions in the country of posting.

By exception, in certain circumstances it may be possible to remain liable to home contributions for a period of up to 5 years (¶7029).

> MEMO POINTS 1. For the purposes of this section the term "EEA state" covers the EU member states and the EEA countries (i.e. Austria, Belgium, Bulgaria, Cyprus, the Czech Republic, Denmark, Estonia, Finland, France, Germany, Gibraltar, Greece, Hungary, Iceland, the Republic of Ireland, Italy, Latvia, Liechtenstein, Lithuania, Luxembourg, Malta, the Netherlands, Norway, Poland, Portugal, Romania, Slovakia, Slovenia, Spain, Sweden and the United Kingdom) and Switzerland.
> 2. **Persons regardless of nationality** who are **legally resident** in a member state may also be covered if they move to another member state. These arrangements do not apply to Denmark, Switzerland, Iceland, Liechtenstein and Norway. For third country nationals going to Switzerland, Iceland and Norway as posted workers it will still be possible to apply for a certificate of continuing liability under the terms of reciprocal agreements (see ¶2241).

The same **recognition of continuing liability for UK NICs** applies where the special circumstances set out above exist and the employee is posted to a country which has an appropriate **reciprocal agreement** with the UK (¶¶7035+). The employer must apply for a certificate of continuing liability from NICO before the employee is posted abroad and this will be recognised in the country of posting, exempting him from making contributions towards that country's social security system and, in some cases, allowing him to obtain state benefits within that country. The benefits provided in the country of posting will depend on the scope of the relevant reciprocal agreement.

2241

Where the temporary posting of not more than 24 months is **to another country**, and Class 1 NICs continue to be paid in the UK, the employee will, as seen above, retain his right to UK state benefits on his return to the UK. However, in the absence of a reciprocal agreement between the UK and the country of posting it is unlikely that the employee will be able to claim any state benefits in the country of posting except those that are paid through his UK employer, such as statutory maternity pay or statutory sick pay. However, contributions may also be due in the country of posting (this may lead to a **double charge**), which may entitle the employee to certain state benefits in the country of posting (¶7044).

2242

Healthcare

In the UK, the provision of state healthcare cover under the National Health Service (NHS) is not dependent on a person having made NICs but on his residence in the UK. When an

2245

employee is posted abroad his entitlement to state healthcare cover will depend on the country to which he is posted.

2246 If a UK national is **posted to an EEA state**, the employee and the members of his family will be entitled to the full state healthcare cover of that state. As the level of healthcare provided by each EU member state differs, **some services**, such as the ambulance service, that are provided by the NHS without charge to the patient, may not be included in the state healthcare cover of the state of posting and **must be paid for by the patient**. Additional healthcare cover may need to be taken out privately to cover such extra expenses, and the employer may agree to provide and pay for this. Alternatively the employer might agree to directly reimburse the employee as and when such expenses are incurred.

The employee should apply for a **European Health Insurance Card** (formerly Form E111 and a number of other "E" forms) to cover himself and his family during his posting to another EEA state.

> MEMO POINTS   Gibraltar is not included in the definition of EEA for the specific purpose of healthcare cover. Before commencing a posting there the UK employee should get in touch with the Gibraltar Health Authority to establish whether healthcare cover will be provided or if he will have to pay into the Gibraltar Group Practice Medical Scheme.

2247 If a UK employee is **posted** to a country **outside the EEA**, the extent of healthcare cover provided to him will depend on whether there is an agreement between that country and the UK to provide healthcare cover. This can be checked with the Department for Work and Pensions before the employee is posted.

2248 If the state healthcare cover or the medical facilities of the country of posting is inadequate the employer should consider funding private healthcare cover for the employee and his family during the posting.

2249 **Emergency repatriation**   If the posting is to a country of political instability or if there are inadequate medical facilities the employer may consider obtaining additional insurance protection and emergency return cover.

Pension

2250 The employee's **UK state pension accrual** will not be affected as long as Class 1 NICs are made in the UK for him while he is posted abroad. Should the posting exceed 24 months and the employer is unsuccessful in extending the certificate for continuing liability, contributions can continue to be made in the UK, thereby protecting the employee's pension accrual. Unfortunately, this could result in Class 1 NICs being made in the UK as well as contributions being made in the country of posting. In order to protect his UK state pension accrual the employee has the choice of continuing to make UK NICs as voluntary Class 2 payments.

Employer contributions to a **UK occupational** pension scheme should continue while the employee is posted abroad and the employee can continue to make voluntary contributions to such schemes while posted abroad, subject to HMRC limits.

B. Applicable law

2255 The rights conferred on the parties under the employment contract will be decided and applied by reference to the proper or **applicable law of the contract**, while the right to bring an action before a specific court will depend on whether that court has valid **jurisdiction** over the issue. The law governing the contract and jurisdiction are two separate concepts, and, as a result, the court of jurisdiction may be required to apply the law of another country to the dispute before it (see for example *Simpson v Intralinks* [2012] UKEAT 0593_11_1506, where a

claim heard in the UK was to be decided largely under German law). The parties are usually free to choose the applicable law, but this choice is subject to **certain rules**:
– for contracts concluded on or after 17 December 2009, EC Regulation 593/2008 on the law applicable to contractual obligations (often referred to as Rome I) applies; and
– for contracts concluded before 17 December 2009, the rules are set out in the Rome Convention on the Law Applicable to Contractual Obligations 1980.

The **specific principles** relating to contracts of employment set out below apply to any contract which has a foreign element.

The parties to a contract **may choose** which law will determine their respective rights and obligations under the contract. However, even if the parties agree that the law of a country outside the UK is to govern the contract, a UK employee **cannot be deprived of applicable UK statutory employment rights** (¶2275). This means that where there are elements of the law in question that are governed by UK statutes as well as the laws of the other state, the UK statutory position will prevail.

2256

If the parties have **not chosen any law**, the law governing the contract will be:
– the law of the state "in which, or failing that from which" (Rome I) or "in which" (Rome Convention) the employee habitually carries out his work under the contract, even if he is temporarily employed in another state; or
– if it is not possible to ascertain where he habitually carries out his work, the law of the state in which the place of business through which he was engaged is situated.

2257

The place where the employee **habitually carries out his work** is where he has established the effective centre of his working activities or where he in fact performs the essential part of his duties for his employer. This is ascertained by considering where he has an office, spends most of his working time, organises his work and returns after each business trip abroad.

The above also applies where the employee carries out his duties in **more than one state** (*Rutton v Cross Medical Ltd* [1997] IRLR 249, ECJ). Where the employee works in more than one EEA state but the above factors fail to conclusively establish the habitual place of employment, the habitual place of work may be decided by the length of time that an employee spends in each state and where he has worked the longest (*Weber v Universal Services Ltd* [2002] EUECJ C-37/00).

EXAMPLE
1. The parties have not chosen any law but the UK employee habitually carries out his work in France. French law will apply to the contract.
2. If the same employee is only seconded to France for a short period of time, he will habitually carry out his work in the UK, and UK law will apply to the contract.
3. The employee does the same job for 6 months in France, 11 months in Germany and 5 months in the UK. In the absence of the factors explained above conclusively showing otherwise, the habitual place of work is Germany.

C. Applicable jurisdiction

A court or tribunal in the UK would have jurisdiction over an employment dispute between a UK employee working in the UK and his UK employer. However, where an international element is involved, specific rules apply as to where the claim should be brought, and will depend on where the **employer and the employee are domiciled**.

2260

MEMO POINTS Within the **EU**, the rules of jurisdiction for contracts, including employment contracts, are defined within the European Regulation 44/2001 (the Rules) (EC Regulation 44/2001), often known as Brussels I. This replaces and updates the Brussels Convention (Brussels Convention on Jurisdiction and the Enforcement of Judgments in Civil and Commercial Matters 1968 as amended by the San Sebastian Convention). For Denmark only, the Brussels Convention remains in place. The Rules are adopted into

UK legislation under the Civil Jurisdiction and Judgments Order (Civil Jurisdiction and Judgments Order SI 2001/3929, which also amends the Civil Jurisdiction and Judgments Act 1982).

Similar rules are also recognised in the **EFTA states** (Switzerland, Liechtenstein, Norway and Iceland) and are contained in the Lugano Convention, signed by the EFTA states and also by the EU member states (Lugano Convention on Jurisdiction and the Enforcement of Judgments in Civil and Commercial Matters 1988). Consequently, the principles which decide where an employment claim can validly be brought, by either the employer or the employee, are the same within the EU member states and EFTA, and the judgment of a competent court in any of these states will be recognised in the other states.

Claims within EU

2261 When the employer and the employee are both domiciled in an EU member state, the following will apply, depending on whether it is the employer or the employee who is bringing the claim.

If the **employer makes a claim** against his employee he may only do so in the courts of the member state where the employee is domiciled (art 20 EC Regulation 44/2001; Civil Jurisdiction and Judgments Act 1982 as amended by SI 2001/3929).

An **employee can choose** where to bring a claim against his employer. He can do so in the member state where (art 19 EC Regulation 44/2001; Civil Jurisdiction and Judgments Act 1982 as amended by SI 2001/3929):
- he is domiciled;
- his employer is domiciled/registered; or
- he habitually carries out his work (or where he last worked). If he does not or has not habitually carried out his work in any one country, then he can claim in the state where the business for which he works is situated.

> EXAMPLE
> 1. In *Simpson v Intralinks* [2012] UKEAT 0593_11_1506, the EAT held in favour of an employee, S, who wanted to bring her sex discrimination and equal pay claims in the UK despite the fact that her place of work was in Frankfurt and the fact her employment contract stated that disputes were to be governed by German law and the place of jurisdiction was Frankfurt. However, the EAT held that the UK did have jurisdiction to hear this case, primarily because the employer's registered office was in the UK. Their contractual agreement to use German law was upheld, though on any issues that are mandatory under UK law, UK statutes will take precedence (see ¶2256).
> 2. A habitually carries out his work in the UK but is domiciled in France. He is employed by a French company. He can choose to bring a claim against his employer either in the UK (the place where he habitually works) or in France (his country of domicile). If he did not habitually work in any one country, then he could bring his claim in France, as his employer is situated there.

2262 **Domicile** What constitutes domicile depends on how the **law of the relevant state** defines the term and this will differ between each EU state. When determining whether a party is domiciled in an EU state or not, the court where the claim is brought will apply its internal law to ascertain domicile. If it decides that the party is not domiciled in the state where the claim is placed, the court will apply the law of the state where he might be domiciled to establish whether he is domiciled there or not (art 59 EC Regulation 44/2001).

In the UK, an employee will be domiciled in the UK when he is resident in the UK and the circumstances of his residence indicate that he has a substantial connection with the UK, i.e. if he has been resident in the UK for the last 3 months or more. A company will be domiciled in the UK if it is incorporated in the UK or has its central management or control in the UK (SI 2001/3929).

> EXAMPLE B, a UK national, has been seconded for 3 years to Germany by his UK employer. B has acted in breach of contract and the UK employer wants to claim against him. B is now living in Germany. His UK employer, in deciding where to bring his claim, needs to know whether B is domiciled in the UK or in Germany.
> The courts in the UK cannot hear the claim as B has been living in Germany for more than 3 months and therefore is not considered as domiciled under UK law. Whether B is considered as domiciled in Germany will depend on German law.

Agreed jurisdiction In limited circumstances, an employer and employee may **agree** that a specific court of a member state will have jurisdiction. However, this will only be valid if the agreement is arrived at **after the dispute** has arisen or if it allows the employee to bring proceedings in courts other than those identified above (art 21 EC Regulation 44/2001; Civil Jurisdiction and Judgments Act 1982 as amended by SI 2001/3929).

2264

> EXAMPLE C, a German national, is employed by an American company with an office in the UK under a contract of employment that contains a jurisdiction clause that allows any dispute to be heard in the courts of England and Wales. C is seconded to France and habitually carries out work there. In the event of an employment dispute the employer will not be able to rely on the jurisdiction clause to bring the dispute before the courts of England and Wales, as it was entered into before the dispute arose.

MEMO POINTS   Different rules apply to other types of contract.

Recognition of judgment   **Judgments made** by a competent **court in one EU member state** will be automatically recognised by other EU member states without the need for any special procedure, except for purely formal checks on the documents (EC Regulation 44/2001; SI 2001/3929). **In the UK**, the judgment of a competent court of another EU member state must be registered for enforcement in the part of the UK (i.e. England and Wales, Scotland or Northern Ireland) where it is to be enforced. The procedure of recognition in other EU member states is to have the judgment declared as enforceable in that state.

2265

> EXAMPLE
> 1. A UK employer successfully sues his employee in Germany, on the basis that this is the country of domicile. He can have that judgment recognised in any other EU member state where the employee may reside.
> 2. The UK employee sues his German employer in Germany. During the proceedings the employer relocates to Italy. On obtaining a judgment in his favour, the employee will be able to serve the judgment on the employer in Italy with minimal involvement of the Italian courts.

Claims made in EFTA states

Similar rules are applied where the employer or employee is domiciled in EFTA member states, namely Switzerland, Liechtenstein, Norway and Iceland, and, under the Lugano Convention, judgments made in those states will be recognised in the EU member states (Lugano Convention on Jurisdiction and the Enforcement of Judgments in Civil and Commercial Matters 1988).

2266

Claims made in other states

In the UK, jurisdiction is based on the domicile of the defendant (SI 2001/3929). Where either the employer or the employee is domiciled outside the EU or EFTA, the claimant must find the court where the claim will be properly heard.

2268

If an **employer** in the UK has a claim against an employee now domiciled outside the EU or EFTA, he must find out if the courts of the country in which the employee is domiciled admit the claim and what legal redress he can obtain if he is successful. In many cases, it is impractical to pursue a claim against an employee if he has left the EU/EFTA jurisdiction.

If it is the **employee** who has a claim against an employer who is domiciled outside the EU or EFTA, he may bring his claim before a UK employment tribunal. However, any award made against the employer by the tribunal will be unenforceable if there are no assets or presence within the UK.

Exceptions   In some circumstances an employment claim may be brought in an appropriate court in the UK even if the defendant is not domiciled in the UK. Such proceedings may be issued **with the permission of the court** in England and Wales if the employment contract:
– was made in England;
– was breached in England;
– is subject to English law; and
– specifies that the courts of England and Wales had jurisdiction.

2270

In order to obtain the permission of the court to proceed against a defendant who is not domiciled in the jurisdiction, the claimant has to show that he has a **good arguable case** and that the court is the appropriate forum for the action. If the court agrees to serve the defendant out of the jurisdiction and he fails to make an appearance, the case may be heard against him in his absence.

> MEMO POINTS Similar rules, allowing proceedings against an absent defendant, apply in the courts of Scotland and Northern Ireland.

2271 Courts in the UK can also decide not to hear a claim if they consider that it can be **dealt with more appropriately** by a court of another country (this is also known as the doctrine of "forum non conveniens").

> EXAMPLE D, who lives in New York, is employed by Company X, which is incorporated in New York with its offices there. D is seconded to Company Y to carry courier packages to London. D delivers the packages and then returns to New York with packages from Company Y's branch office. If D brought a claim against Company X for breach of contract in an English and Welsh court, the court would be entitled to invoke the doctrine of forum non conveniens and require that the case be heard in New York as all the relevant parties are resident there.

> MEMO POINTS This doctrine may not be used to deprive an employment tribunal of jurisdiction. It is based on the common law while the tribunal's jurisdiction to hear cases is derived under the statutory law and regulations.

2273 **Recognition of judgment** Even if the claimant is successful and judgment is awarded in his favour by a court in the UK, he will have to translate that judgment into one that can be applied in the country where the defendant is located. As seen above, this is not a difficult process where EFTA and EU member states are concerned, but the enforcement of judgments outside those states can prove to be a complicated process, and its success will depend on whether there is a **reciprocal agreement** between the UK and the other country.

> MEMO POINTS Recognition will be by specific statutory instrument, for example, under the Reciprocal Enforcement of Foreign Judgments (Canada) Order (SI 1987/468), the UK recognises civil and commercial judgments of the Federal Court of certain Canadian provinces as the Canadian courts recognise similar judgments made by courts in the UK.
> It should be noted that there is no bilateral treaty or international convention between the United States and any other country on reciprocal recognition and enforcement of judgments.

D. Statutory employment rights

Enforceability of UK statutory rights

2275 Generally speaking, where an employee has been posted abroad, it is necessary to look at the **territorial jurisdiction** of the relevant legislation from which the UK statutory employment right in question is derived to ascertain whether the employee can bring a claim to protect or enforce this right in the Employment Tribunal. For example, the Employment Rights Act 1996 (which provides, amongst others, the statutory right not to be unfairly dismissed) is silent as to its territorial jurisdiction but the House of Lords, confirming the Court of Appeal, has held that the right not to be unfairly dismissed covers "employment in Great Britain" (*Serco Ltd v Lawson* [2004] IRLR 206, CA as confirmed by *Lawson v Serco Ltd; Botham v Ministry of Defence; Crofts and ors v Veta Ltd and ors* [2006] IRLR 289, HL). In providing **guidance** as to when an employee will be deemed to be in "employment in Great Britain", the House of Lords identified three principal categories of employees in respect of which a question of territorial jurisdiction may arise, and its observations in relation to these employees are often referred to as the *Serco* principles:
1. **Standard case** (**working in Great Britain**): the most relevant factor in determining employment within Britain is whether the employee was actually working in Britain at the

time of his dismissal, rather than what was contemplated at the time his employment contract was entered into (which could have been many years earlier). That is not to say that the terms of the contract and prior contractual relationship should be disregarded and they may, in fact, be relevant as to whether the employee is really working in Britain or whether he is merely on a casual visit.

2. **Peripatetic employees**: the common sense approach of treating the base of a peripatetic employee as, for the purposes of the statute, his place of employment remains valid (as applied in *Todd v British Midland Airways Ltd* [1978] ICR 959, CA). Guidance from that case indicated that the conduct of the parties and the way in which they have been operating the contract are relevant. For the place where the employee carries out the main, even the essential, part of his work not to be his base there must be evidence that this is because his base is demonstrably elsewhere (*Anderson v Stena Drilling PTE Ltd* [2006] UKEAT 0080_04_1708).

3. **Expatriate employees**: the concept of a "base" (as for peripatetic employees) is not helpful in respect of expatriate employees. Although it is unusual for an employee who works and is based abroad to come within the scope of British employment law, there are certain circumstances in which one might. The examples provided in this respect are when an employee is posted abroad by a British employer for the purposes of a business carried on in Britain, and where the employee is working as a representative of a business conducted in Britain (for example, a foreign correspondent on the staff of a British newspaper). This category might also extend to an employee of a British employer who is operating within what amounts for practical purposes to an "extra-territorial British enclave" in a foreign country (for example, an individual working on a military base in Germany). These individuals, in order to come within the scope of ERA 1996, would have to demonstrate "equally strong connections" with Britain and British employment law.

EXAMPLE

1. In *Diggins v Condor Marine Crewing Services Ltd* [2010] IRLR 119, CA, a chief officer employed by a Guernsey-registered company to work on a ship registered in the Bahamas which sailed between Portsmouth and the Channel Islands was entitled to bring an unfair dismissal claim. His base was in Great Britain, and the Court of Appeal held that there was no reason why workers on foreign-registered ships should not be protected, provided they fell within the group of peripatetic workers.

2. In *Dolphin Drilling Personnel Pte Ltd v Winks and Dolphin Drilling Ltd* [2009] UKEAT 0049_08_2104, an employee worked offshore on an oil rig off the coasts of first Mexico and then Nigeria. The rig was owned by a UK company but was registered in Singapore, and he was employed by a Singaporean company. When not working he lived in the UK, and he was paid via a payroll company in the UK. Applying the *Serco* principles, the EAT held that these did not amount to the sort of exceptional circumstances needed to give the tribunal jurisdiction to consider his unfair dismissal claim.

3. In *Hunt v United Airlines* [2008] UKEAT 0575_07_0304, the employee, a US citizen, was based in Paris, working for a US airline. Before she was transferred to London, she went on long-term sick leave and never moved to, or worked from, London. Her sickness absence was managed by the US airline from the US and she was dismissed. The EAT decided that the tribunal did not have jurisdiction to hear her unfair dismissal claim as the employee was never actually based in Britain. The EAT went on to hold that where there is a dispute regarding whether the tribunal has jurisdiction to hear an unfair dismissal claim, the tribunal should look at the factual position at the date of dismissal.

4. In *Anderson v Stena Drilling Pte Ltd* [2006] UKEAT 0080_04_1708, the EAT held that the tribunal had no jurisdiction to hear an unfair dismissal claim brought by A, a Scotsman, who had been working on an offshore rig in the Far Eastern waters. A was held to be neither a peripatetic nor an expatriate employee, as he wholly worked and resided in the Far East and his employer was not registered, and did not carry out any work, in Britain. The fact that the operations of the rig (though not day-to-day management, which remained with the employer) were controlled by a UK sister company based in Scotland and another UK sister company also based in Scotland provided logistical, human resources and payroll support did not alter A's position.

MEMO POINTS Note that there is also the **jurisdictional requirement of employment tribunals** in England, Wales and Scotland that the respondent (i.e. the party defending the claim) (or one of the respondents) resides or carries on business in England, Wales or Scotland (¶9423).

There are also **other examples** of the principle where the employment has such an overwhelmingly closer connection with Britain and with British employment law than with any other system of law that it is right to conclude that Parliament must have intended that the employees should enjoy protection from unfair dismissal (*Duncombe and ors v Secretary of State for Children, Schools and Families (No. 2)* [2011] UKSC 36; *Ministry of Defence v Wallis and anor* [2011] EWCA Civ 231).

> EXAMPLE In *Duncombe and ors v Secretary of State for Children, Schools and Families (No. 2)* [2011] UKSC 36, the Supreme Court ruled in relation to whether D and other UK teachers employed by the British Government to work in European Schools abroad could bring unfair dismissal claims and held that they could do so as they had an overwhelmingly closer connection with Britain and with British employment law than with any other system of law. In particular, the Court's decision was based on the following very special combination of factors:
> – their employer was not only based in Britain, but was the Government of the United Kingdom. This was the closest connection with Great Britain that any employer can have, for it cannot be based anywhere else;
> – they were employed under contracts governed by English law; the terms and conditions were either entirely those of English law or a combination of those of English law and the international institutions for which they worked;
> – they were employed in international enclaves and were there because of commitments undertaken by the British government, having no particular connection with the countries in which they happened to be situated and governed by international agreements between the participating states; and
> – it would be anomalous if a teacher who happened to be employed by the British government to work in the European School in England were to enjoy different protection from the teachers who happened to be employed to work in the same sort of school in other countries.

2277 Lastly, in respect to **employees who work outside Great Britain**, the relevant test for whether a tribunal has jurisdiction is whether the employment relationship has a stronger connection with Great Britain than with the foreign country where the employee works (*Ravat v Halliburton Manufacturing and Services Ltd* [2012] UKSC 1). Where the employee does not work wholly abroad it is not necessary to carry out a comparative exercise to decide whether he has a stronger connection to Great Britain than with the foreign country where the employees sometimes works. Where, as here, the individual lives and/or works partly in Great Britain, all that is required is a sufficiently strong connection to Great Britain (*Clyde & Co LLP and anor v Bates van Winkelhof* [2012] EWCA Civ 1207).

2278 This guidance has been held to **apply to other Acts and regulations** where the territorial scope is not set out.

> EXAMPLE
> 1. In *Clyde & Co LLP and anor v Bates van Winkelhof* [2012] EWCA Civ 1207, the Court of Appeal held that it had jurisdiction to hear the discrimination claims of a member of a limited liability partnership (LLP), B, who worked principally in Tanzania as part of a joint venture with her UK law firm.
> 2. In *Netjets Management Ltd v Central Arbitration Committee and anor* [2012] EWHC 2685 (Admin), the High Court held that Central Arbitration Committee had territorial jurisdiction to hear an application for statutory recognition from an independent trade union in respect of a group of pilots of a GB registered company which operated private business jets in Europe.

2279 As a modification to the guidance, jurisdiction has also been granted to ensure that provisions which contain **directly effective rights** can be enforced by UK courts (*Bleuse v MBT Transport Ltd and anor* [2007] UKEAT 0339_07_2112; *Ministry of Defence v Wallis and anor* [2011] EWCA Civ 231).

> EXAMPLE
> 1. In *Bleuse v MBT Transport Ltd and anor*, concerning a lorry driver, B, who worked mainly in Austria and Germany but had a contract of employment with a company registered in England, the EAT held that B did not fall within the *Serco* principles in relation to his unfair dismissal and unlawful deductions from wages claims (both claims under the Employment Rights Act 1996). B did not have his base in the UK and the mere fact that the employer was a company registered in the UK was not sufficient to establish this as his base. Nor was he a peripatetic employee. However, in relation to B's claim under the Working Time Regulations for unpaid annual leave, the EAT held that this was a directly effective right derived from the European Organisation of Working Time Directive and that the Regulations should be interpreted in such a way to give compatibility. On such an interpretation, the EAT held that the tribunal had jurisdiction to hear B's unpaid annual leave claim and ruled that the *Serco* principles must be modified in relation to the Working Time Regulations so that the directly effective rights contained within it could be enforced.

> 2. In *Ministry of Defence v Wallis and anor*, two wives of army personnel were employed overseas in NATO-run organisations as "locally employed dependants" on terms under which, for example, they were not obliged to pay either local or UK income tax. When their spouses left the forces, they were dismissed. They made claims of breach of contract, unfair dismissal and sex discrimination. It was conceded that the UK courts had jurisdiction to deal with the breach of contract claim, but the employer argued that there was no jurisdiction to hear the other two claims. The Court of Appeal held that:
> – their positions as locally employed dependants of serving personnel were a special connection with Great Britain under the third category of employees protected under the *Serco* principles, giving the tribunal the power to hear the unfair dismissal claim; and
> – directly effective rights under the Equal Treatment Directive gave the tribunal the power to hear the sex discrimination claim even though the Sex Discrimination Act was expressly limited in its territorial scope. This was either by a compatible construction of the Act or by disapplying the territorial limitations given within it that were incompatible with the enforcement in the UK of their rights under the Directive. The Court's preference was with regard to the latter, but noted that the outcome was the same if the construction route was used instead.

Status of UK rights if they apply While the employer and the worker are free to agree to enhance these rights if they apply, they may **not reduce or exclude** them, so even if they agree to choose a law other than the laws of England and Wales, Scotland or Northern Ireland, these UK statutory employment rights will still protect the employee. Therefore, the right of a worker not to be unfairly dismissed under UK statutory employment law cannot be avoided by the parties agreeing, for example, that Japanese law will govern the employment contract.

2280

Enforceability of EU minimum rights

All EU member states must ensure that certain minimum rights apply to workers temporarily posted to that state (EC Posted Workers Directive 1996/71). In such cases, the worker can bring a claim to enforce these rights in the EU member state to which he is temporarily posted as long as he normally works in another EU member state.

2282

The minimum employment rights afforded to posted workers are:
– maximum work periods and minimum rest periods;
– minimum paid annual holidays;
– minimum rates of pay, including overtime rates;
– conditions of hiring out workers, in particular the supply of workers by temporary employment undertakings;
– health, safety and hygiene at work;
– protection for pregnant women, or those who have recently given birth;
– protection of children and young people; and
– non-discrimination.

> MEMO POINTS Member states have the power to extend local **collective agreements** to posted workers and this can affect the level of rights afforded to workers seconded to an EU member state.

CHAPTER 9

Company information and confidentiality

OUTLINE

SECTION 1 **Intellectual property rights**	2310
A Ownership	2330
1 Unregistered rights	2335
2 Registered rights	2340
Patents	2340
Registered designs	2344
B Express terms	2350

SECTION 2 **Confidential information and confidentiality**	2400
A Protection against disclosure	2405
1 During employment	2410
2 Post-employment	2415
B Categorisation of information	2425
1 Confidential	2430
2 Trade secret	2435
C Express terms	2450

SECTION 3 **Restraints and restrictive covenants**	2500
I During employment	2510
A Implied duty	2510
Working for a competitor	2511
Intention to compete	2512
B Express terms	2520
Working for a competitor	2522
Garden leave	2529
II Post-employment	2550
Restraint of trade	2551
A Legitimate business interests	2560
B Scope of covenant	2565
1 Non-compete covenants	2570
Protectable interests	2570
Prohibited area	2575

Specific competitors	2578
Restricted activities	2579
Duration	2580
2 Non-solicitation covenants (customers)	2585
Prohibited customers	2586
Duration	2589
3 Non-dealing covenants	2595
4 Non-solicitation covenants (employees)	2600
Prohibited employees	2601
Duration	2604
5 Indirect restraints	2610
C Other factors affecting enforceability	2615
Context of agreement	2615
Employer's fundamental breach of contract	2616
Garden leave	2619
Payment in respect of restricted period	2620
Transfer of undertakings	2622
D Courts' approach	2630
Interpretation	2630
Unreasonable covenants	2633
III Enforcement and remedies	2640
1 Injunction	2645
Garden leave injunction	2651
Injunction against second employer	2653
2 Damages	2660
Damages against second employer	2661
3 Account for profits	2665

SECTION 4 **Whistleblowing**	2700
Passing on details to industry regulators	2704
A Scope of protection	2710
Qualifying disclosures	2711
Protected disclosures	2715
B Acceptable methods of disclosure	2725
1 Internal disclosure	2730
2 Disclosure to a public authority	2735
3 Public disclosure	2740
C Protection and remedies	2760

2300 The ownership of **intellectual property rights** (IPR) can be an important issue for businesses and individuals who may wish to protect their entitlement to such rights, either legislatively or contractually.

2301 IPR may amount to a trade secret or confidential information, and how and when an employer can protect against disclosure to a third party is often vital to his business. **Confidential information** and **trade secrets**, although not defined by legislation, have been held to include many types of sensitive company information, for example a recipe may be a trade secret or a client list may amount to confidential information. Confidential information and trade secrets obtained during employment (and as a result of it) are **protected against disclosure** to a third party by the implied duty of fidelity during employment, which is often supplemented, clarified and highlighted by express contractual terms. This duty also **prevents** an employee **competing** with his employer's business or soliciting its customers during employment.

However, this duty does not apply **post-employment** (with the exception of disclosures of trade secrets). Therefore, employers who wish to restrict former employees' activities (particularly in the case of senior employees) must do so by way of express contractual terms, known as **restrictive covenants**.

2302 Finally, the protection afforded to an employer (by the implied duty of confidentiality and any express contractual terms) is subject to **whistleblowing** legislation, which protects workers who, due to a sense of public duty, reveal **serious employer misconduct**.

SECTION 1

Intellectual property rights

2310 Intellectual property is created by the intellectual effort of individuals. Businesses and individuals need to consider their intellectual property rights (IPR) to ensure that they **identify and protect** these rights and that they have ownership where appropriate. Where employees may be creating original work or invention, it is also advisable for their contracts of employment to have express terms on IPR.

IPR are split into registered and unregistered rights. Unregistered rights, i.e. copyright, design rights and database rights exist automatically, and no formalities are required to create these rights (Copyright Designs and Patents Act 1988 as amended by the Copyright and Rights in Database Regulations SI 1997/3032). Consequently, employees are likely to be creating such rights on an everyday basis. On the other hand, registered rights, i.e. patents (Patents Act 1977, as amended), registered designs (Registered Designs Act 1949) and trademarks only exist on completion of various procedural steps. Companies should have procedures in place to enable them to recognise when work is or will be created that is capable of registration and to ensure that any such rights are registered should they wish to do so.

> *MEMO POINTS* Trademarks are signs that are capable of being represented graphically and which distinguish goods or services or undertakings from others. Issues of ownership rarely arise in connection with the employer/employee relationship, so are not discussed in this chapter.

Unregistered rights

2311 **Copyright** is a right that automatically **exists** in (ss 1(1), 3, 3A Copyright, Designs and Patents Act 1988):
– original literary, dramatic, musical, or artistic works; the general requirement of originality requires that the work must not be copied but produced using the author's own independent skill. Consequently, this is not a difficult hurdle to clear as long as the work is not a copy;
– sound recordings, films, broadcasts or cable programmes; and
– typographical arrangements of published editions.

Copyright in literary, dramatic or musical works does not exist until the **work is recorded** (whether this is in writing or otherwise).

2312

> EXAMPLE
> 1. A person may deliver a speech without notes and copyright will not exist in that speech unless the speech is recorded at the time of delivery (whether by television or sound recording). However, if he prepares for the speech by writing notes prior to delivery, copyright will exist in the notes as a literary work.
> 2. A musician may have composed a "tune" in his head, but copyright in it as a musical work will not exist unless he records it (for example on a score).

The same piece of work may **create different copyrights**.

2313

> EXAMPLE A marketing director gives an informal presentation to the board as to the future marketing direction of the company. No record/recording is made of the presentation. He did not make notes prior to the presentation and therefore no copyright exists. Later, he prepares a formal report in writing and copyright will exist in the written report (as a literary document). There may also be a publisher's copyright in any published version of the report. He then gives a verbal presentation of the report, which is recorded by means of video equipment for training purposes. He uses the copyright work (the written report) and a further copyright work is created in the film recording.

Design rights protect designs of functional items. A design right automatically **exists** in (s 213(1)-(2) Copyright Designs and Patents Act 1988):
a. an original design (a design is not original if it is commonplace in the relevant design field at the time of its creation. While there is no fixed definition of what the relevant design field is, it is likely to be the area in which those designing that type of design would have been involved); or
b. the design of any aspect of the shape or configuration of an article/thing.

2314

Excluded are (s 213(3) Copyright Designs and Patents Act 1988):
a. methods or principles of construction (it is the design itself and not the method by which it is made that is protected); or
b. features of shape or configuration which:
– enable the article to be connected to or placed around another article so that either article can perform its function. This is the so-called "must fit" exception;
– are dependent on the appearance of another article, which is intended by the designer to form an integral part. This is the "must match" exception; or
– are surface decoration.

Databases are also protected by specific database rights. A database right automatically **exists** in an original database if, by reason of selection or arrangement of the contents of the database, the database constitutes the author's own intellectual creation.

2315

Registered rights

A **patent** may be **granted** to an invention, if it (s 1(1), (3) Patents Act 1977):
– is new;
– involves an inventive step; and
– is capable of industrial application.

2316

However, the invention must **not be**:
– a scientific or mathematical discovery, theory or method;
– a literary, dramatic, musical or artistic work;
– a way of performing a mental act, playing a game or doing business;
– the presentation of information;
– certain computer programs;
– an animal or plant variety;
– a method of medical treatment or diagnosis; or
– anything that is against public policy or morality.

A **design** in respect of an article or set of articles may be **registered** if it is new (s 1(2) Registered Designs Act 1949). It is important to note that for the design to be protected by registration there must be a design and an article to which the design is applied. Design is defined as the

2317

appearance of the whole or a part of a product resulting from the features of, in particular, the lines, contours, colours, shape, texture or materials of the product or its ornamentation.

Excluded are:
a. methods or principles of construction; and
b. features of shape or configuration of an article which are:
– dependent solely on function (i.e. the feature of the shape or configuration can be attributed to or caused by the article's function and there has been no embellishment to those features); or
– dependent upon the appearance of another article which is intended to be an integral part of the article in question (i.e. the two articles must be an integral part of each other and this must have been the intention of the author/designer).

A. Ownership

2330 Individuals or groups of individuals use their intellectual ability to create IPR and innovation is, therefore, **not limited to** individuals who are specifically employed to invent. For example, an employee may be employed to invent or produce literary or musical works; a salesman may write his company's next advertising campaign; and a director may design new packaging for a company product.

It is important to ascertain who is the owner of the right or to whom the right has first been granted. Generally, this will be the **employer** where the employee has created the IPR as part of his employment. It is also possible, in most cases, to **transfer** ownership where required by contractual agreement between the parties, although there are certain formalities that have to be met.

1. Unregistered rights

2335 Where the employee in the **course of his employment** creates the work or right, the **employer** is deemed to be the first owner of the work (subject to an agreement to the contrary) (ss 11(2), 215(3) Copyright Designs and Patents Act 1988; reg 14(2) Copyright and Rights in Databases Regulations SI 1997/3032).

2. Registered rights

Patents

2340 A patent is granted to the **inventor** who is defined as (s 7 Patents Act 1977):
– the actual deviser of the invention;
– any person who is entitled to the invention by law, i.e. deemed to be the inventor (for example, the employer, if his employee creates the invention in the circumstances set out below); or
– any person who has acquired the right to the invention by succession.

There is an assumption that, unless proved to the contrary, anyone applying for a patent is the inventor or somebody entitled to the invention.

2341 The employer will be **deemed to be the inventor** where the employee creates the invention (s 39 Patents Act 1977):
a. in circumstances such that an invention might reasonably be **expected to result** during the course of:
– **normal duties** of the employee, for example if designing or inventing forms part of his duties. It is also considered to be in the course of normal duties if he is required to overcome problems (by way of inventions) as they arise; or
– **duties specifically assigned** to him if outside his normal duties; or

b. in the course of his duties when because of the nature of his duties and responsibilities he had a **special obligation** to further his employer's business, as may be the case with a more senior employee. However, the decision as to whether the invention belongs to the employer will depend not only on the employee's position and status but also his attendant duties.

> EXAMPLE In *LIFFE Administration and Management v Pinkava* [2007] EWCA Civ 217, a manager at the London Futures Exchange was asked to devise a system to enable various electronic trades to be made. The invention he came up with was more radical than anything he had been asked to do. The employer sought a declaration that it was entitled to the confidential information. The Court of Appeal held that while the initial duties of the manager had not included work of this character, the task of devising such a system had been assigned to him, and at that point became part of his normal duties. Further, when deciding whether the invention was made in circumstances such that an invention might be expected to result, the task of the Court was to assess the question objectively. There was no need to imply any additional test that the employer should be deemed to be the patentor only where the patent was similar to what might have been expected to be produced, or where the patent provided a solution to a pre-identified problem. The employer was therefore entitled to the invention.

The invention must be a result of the objectives of the employee's duties. Consequently, any invention that is in reality **coincidental to** the employee's **duties** will not belong to the employer (*Harris' Patent* [1985] RPC 19).

2342

> EXAMPLE In *Helmet Integrated Systems Ltd v Tunnard and ors* [2007] IRLR 126, CA, a salesman designed a helmet in his spare time which he later marketed in competition with the products of his former employer. There was no express term of his contract to forbid such activity, nor was it obvious, given his employment as a salesman rather than a designer, that any other terms of his contract could be read as creating such a duty. Consequently, the Court of Appeal held that the intellectual property in the helmet belonged to the salesman and not to his former employer.

Employee compensation If the employer is deemed to be the inventor, the employee may be entitled to statutory compensation to be paid by his employer where, having taken into regard the size and nature of the employer's undertaking, outstanding benefits are derived from the patented invention (s 40 Patents Act 1977 as amended by s 10 Patents Act 2004).

2343

The **amount** of the award should be a fair share of the benefit that the employer has or might reasonably be expected to derive from the invention or the patent (or from the grant or assignment of any right in the invention, or any right under an application for the patent, to a person connected to the employer) (s 41 Patents Act 1977 as amended by s 10 Patents Act 2004). Employers should therefore ensure that their arrangements for rewarding employee compensation in respect of such benefits reflect these provisions.

Registered designs

The employer will be treated as the first owner of the design where it is created by an employee in the **course of his employment**, or it has been **commissioned** by the employer (s 2 Registered Designs Act 1949). Otherwise, registered designs are granted to the **designer**.

2344

B. Express terms

Where employees may be creating original work or inventions, it is advisable for their contracts of employment to have express terms on IPR, principally to ensure that their employer has ownership. Although the employer will be deemed to be the owner in most cases (as seen above), it is often useful to have an express term to highlight, clarify and augment these rules. This can be seen as a "belt and braces" approach. Employers should seek **legal advice** with regard to any express terms they may wish to introduce into employees' contracts, as the exact wording will depend on the requirements of the business.

2350

SECTION 2

Confidential information and confidentiality

2400 Confidential information and trade secrets obtained during employment (and as a result of it) may be protected against disclosure to a third party by the **implied duty** of fidelity or the express terms of the contract of employment. The **degree of protection** provided by the express term will depend on the type of information and the timing of the disclosure. Employees are free to impart or use trivial information in any way and at any time they please. Unauthorised disclosure of trade secrets is prohibited both during and after employment, while confidential information is only protected against disclosure during employment. **Express contractual terms** can restrict the disclosure of both confidential information and trade secrets during and after employment.

There is no definitive legal **definition** of confidential information or trade secrets, although there is court guidance. Where confidentiality is important to an employer, it is advisable to have a **policy** to identify and categorise the different types of information employees may be given, create or use.

> *MEMO POINTS* **Directors** are also subject to separate duties under company law to, amongst other things, avoid conflicts of interest and promote the company's success (¶¶2139+). Using his company's confidential information for his own benefit or breaching confidentiality obligations could also constitute a breach of the director's duties to the company.

2401 The duty of confidentiality is subject to **whistleblowing** legislation, which protects workers who disclose information to another party in certain circumstances (¶2700). Any express terms which restrict the employee's right to make a protected disclosure are void.

A. Protection against disclosure

2405 In summary, there are three types of information which are protected as follows:

	Protected during employment	Protected post-employment
Trivial information	X	X
Confidential information	✓	X (unless express contractual term)
Trade secrets	✓	✓

1. During employment

Confidential information and trade secrets

2410 During employment, an employee is bound by the **implied duty** of fidelity (see also ¶1213) and he can only use confidential information and trade secrets for the benefit of his employer. An employee will be in breach if he uses or discloses such information for his own benefit (or that of another employer), for example by creating, copying or deliberately memorising lists of the employer's customers to use as a "springboard" to launch himself into business after his employment ends.

The duty applies during and outside working hours (*Hivac Ltd v Park Royal Scientific Instruments Ltd* [1946] 1 All ER 350, CA).

This duty also **applies to employers**, for example with regard to information held as part of personnel records, if the information has the necessary quality of confidence (*Dalgleish v Lothian and Borders Police Board* [1991] IRLR 422, CS). Employers are also bound by their obligations under data protection legislation with regard to personal data (¶5900).

> MEMO POINTS When considering an obligation to observe a duty of confidence with regard to **making confidential information public**, a court will adopt the test of proportionality, asking whether, in regard to the nature of the information and all the relevant circumstances, it is legitimate for the owner of the information to keep it confidential or whether it is in the public interest that the information should be made public, and whether this need is sufficient to outweigh the right of the employee to freedom of expression (*HRH Prince of Wales v Associated Newspapers Ltd* [2006] EWCA Civ 1776). In such cases, the Court held that a duty of confidentiality that has been expressly assumed under a contract will carry more weight, when balanced against the right of freedom of expression, than an implied duty. Even in these circumstances, however, the extent to which a contract will add to the weight of the duty will depend upon the facts of the individual case.

Many employers include **express terms** of confidentiality which can clarify, highlight and supplement this implied duty.

2411

2. Post-employment

Confidential information

When an employee has left employment, he is **entitled to use** confidential information for his benefit (or that of another employer) to the extent that such information has become part of his own **general skill and knowledge** (*Robb v Green* [1895] 2 QB 315). Confidential information will become part of an employee's skill and knowledge if it is inevitable that such information will be carried away in his head (*Roger Bullivant Ltd v Ellis* [1987] IRLR 491, CA).

2415

This does not include confidential information that has been **deliberately memorised**.

> EXAMPLE In *Roger Bullivant Ltd v Ellis*, E took certain documents from RB Ltd, including a card index listing RB's trade contacts which amounted to confidential information, and set up in competition with his former employer. The Court upheld an injunction preventing E from contracting with those people on the list and, as it was unable to distinguish between those people whom E could have lawfully contacted (because they had become part of his general knowledge) and those he could not, the injunction applied to all of them.

Where trade or business contacts are held in the form of an **electronic database** on a company's software, they are confidential information (*Pennwell Publishing (UK) Limited v Ornstien and ors* [2007] IRLR 700, QB).

> EXAMPLE In *Pennwell Publishing (UK) Limited v Ornstien and ors*, a director's electronic database of contacts included both names acquired in the course of the employment and his own personal contacts, including members of the director's family. A High Court judge ruled that where an address list is contained on Outlook or some similar program which is part of the employer's email system, and where the email system is backed up by the employer, the database will belong to the employer. While an employee may periodically check a database and remove from it any personal contacts for his personal use, it may not be copied or removed in its entirety by an employee for use outside employment or after the employment has ended.

Ownership of confidential business contacts stored on social networking sites such as LinkedIn is less clear. Although the employee may spend time at work building up those contacts, under the terms of his contract with LinkedIn he cannot transfer ownership of his profile to any other person, disclose his login details or allow another person to use his account. Thus an employer seeking the transfer of a LinkedIn account may be acting unlawfully by procuring a breach of contract. However, in the only known case to have touched on contacts stored on LinkedIn, an employee was required to give pre-action disclosure of some, but not all, of his contacts (*Hays Specialist Recruitment (Holdings) Ltd and anor v Ions and anor* [2008] EWHC 745 (Ch)).

2416 If an employer wishes to protect against disclosure of confidential information after the employment has ended, he will need an **express term** in the contract of employment.

> MEMO POINTS   It is questionable, however, whether such an express term can survive termination where the person seeking to rely on the term has committed a **repudiatory breach of contract** (*Campbell v Frisbee* [2002] IRLR 728, CA). Note, however, that this case involved a contract for services rather than an employment contract and that no final determination on the issue was required from the Court of Appeal.

Trade secrets

2417 An employer is protected by the **implied duty** of fidelity against a former employee using a trade secret for his own benefit (or that of another employer), even if it has become part of his general knowledge (*Johnson & Bloy (Holdings) Ltd and Johnson & Bloy Ltd v Wolstenholme Rink plc and Fallon* [1987] IRLR 499, CA).

However, as the distinction between trade secrets and confidential information is sometimes not clear (see below), it is often advisable for an employer who wishes to protect against disclosure of a trade secret to have an **express term** to clarify, supplement and augment the implied duty.

B. Categorisation of information

2425 In summary, the **three different types** of information are as follows:

Trivial information	Information of a trivial nature which is easily accessible from public sources, which would not be considered by any reasonable person to be confidential, for example details of registered intellectual property rights published by the UK Intellectual Property Office (previously the Patent Office)
Confidential information	Information which the employee must treat as confidential, either because he is expressly told that it is confidential (unless it is actually trivial) or because of its very nature or character it is obviously confidential
Trade secrets	Specific trade secrets

2426 Just because information can at one time be classed as confidential information or a trade secret, it does not necessarily always remain so. The information may lose its confidential nature due to the **passage of time** or because the information becomes **available to the public** by some other means. Information will be made public if it has been made available to a substantial number of people (*Stephens v Avery* [1988] FSR 510).

1. Confidential

2430 It is usually clear what is confidential information and what is trivial information. The **basic requirements** for information to be confidential are that it must:
– have the necessary quality of confidence; and
– be communicated in circumstances importing an obligation of confidence.

2431 **Quality of confidence**   **Public knowledge** of the information may be relevant when assessing whether the information has the necessary quality of confidence. It is not clear whether **unauthorised and wrongful publication** by the employee or a third party will destroy confidentiality. It has been held that the employee should not escape his duty of confidentiality if he has wrongfully disclosed the information (*Speed Seal Products Ltd v Paddington* [1986] 1 All ER 91, CA), although the information has arguably lost the required quality of confidence.

Information will not be regarded as confidential if it is in the **public interest** for it to be disclosed, i.e. the public's interest in discovering wrongdoing outweighs the individual's right to confidentiality (the so-called "just cause" defence). This may include disclosure of the commission of a crime or a fraud. The disclosure must be made to the most appropriate person or body, and the employee must have reasonable grounds to support his allegations. The whistleblowing legislation may also apply to disclosures made in such circumstances (¶2700).

Circumstances of communication Information is more likely to be confidential if the importance placed by the employer on it (and the need to keep it confidential) is made clear by him. Thus the express terms that the employer seeks to apply, and the degree to which he restricts access to the information, will be relevant. However, confidential information is by its very nature confidential regardless of whether it is **labelled confidential** or not. Therefore, an employee cannot disclose confidential information simply because it is not labelled as such, nor can an employer prevent the use or disclosure of information merely by labelling it as confidential if it is actually trivial.

2432

2. Trade secret

It is often more difficult to ascertain whether confidential information is so highly confidential that it is a trade secret. Unfortunately, in practice, the terms have at times been used interchangeably and the courts have recognised that the distinction is not an easy one (*Thomas Marshall (Exports) Ltd v Guinle* [1978] IRLR 174, ChD). There is no definitive **legal definition of trade secrets**, although the courts do give **guidance** as to how to make the distinction.

2435

Some trade secrets are **readily identifiable** as such, for example, secret processes of manufacture such as chemical formulae (*Amber Size and Chemical Co Ltd v Menzel* [1913] 2 Ch 239), or designs or special methods of construction (*Reid and Sigrist Ltd v Moss Mechanism Ltd* [1932] 49 RPC 461). Trade secrets are not confined to technical information but can include highly confidential information of a non-technical or non-scientific nature (*Lansing Linde Ltd v Kerr* [1991] IRLR 80, CA).

Whether or not information amounts to a trade secret is a **question of degree**. For example, a document that lists the ingredients of a specific food product is clearly more confidential (and may amount to a trade secret) than a list of suppliers for certain raw materials. However, if they are of a sufficiently high degree of confidentiality, customer or supplier lists/requirements and pricing information (such as pricing in tender documents) will also be trade secrets.

2436

Four specific factors (set out below) must be considered when determining whether information is of a sufficiently high degree of confidentiality to amount to a trade secret (*Faccenda Chicken Ltd v Fowler* [1986] IRLR 69, CA; confirmed in *A T Poeton (Gloucester Plating) Ltd v Horton* [2000] ICR 1208, CA). They must all be taken into account, and none is conclusive on its own:

Nature of the employment

A higher duty of confidentiality may be imposed on employees who **habitually handle** confidential information and trade secrets, and would therefore be expected to fully understand the importance of discretion, as opposed to those who only receive such information **occasionally or incidentally** and are not specifically reminded of their duty of confidentiality.

2437

Nature of the information

Information that is highly confidential in nature and of paramount importance is likely to be a trade secret. The employer must make a realistic assessment of the information in question, and the courts are unwilling to overestimate the degree of confidentiality of a document. The **employer's categorisation** of the information cannot determine the issue, and his

2438

description of confidential information as a trade secret will not make it one if the nature of the information is such that it does not actually have a sufficiently high degree of confidentiality.

> **EXAMPLE** **No trade secret**
> 1. In *Lock International plc v Beswick* [1989] IRLR 481, ChD, information such as circuit design or the use of diodes which had been described by the former employer as trade secrets was not, as it was extremely general.
> 2. In *Brooks v Olyslager OMS (UK) Ltd* [1998] IRLR 590, CA, detrimental information about the employer's solvency, ability to carry on business for a period of time and relationship with its holding company was not capable of amounting to a trade secret.

Communication of confidentiality

2439 If the **employer has made it clear** that the information is highly confidential, then it is more likely that the information will amount to a trade secret. Consideration will also be given to the number and types of employees who have **access** to such information. Information is more likely to be a trade secret if it has a limited and restricted distribution.

However, where the **employee is fully aware** of the confidential nature of a particular process or piece of information, the employer's failure to impress the confidentiality on him will not prevent it from being highly confidential, and the matter is often one of common sense (*Lancashire Fires Ltd v SA Lyons & Co Ltd* [1997] IRLR 113, CA).

> **EXAMPLE**
> **Trade secret**
> In *Lancashire Fires Ltd v SA Lyons & Co Ltd*, the employer was a manufacturer of decorative gas fires. The employee was a products manager, involved in the development of new products and the refinement of the manufacturing process. Although the employer had not precisely specified what he considered to be confidential, the mould technology used still amounted to a trade secret as it was highly confidential, and the employer was not required to highlight the exact limits of this confidentiality.
>
> **No trade secret**
> In *Faccenda Chicken Ltd v Fowler*, F was the company's sales manager, with access to sales information which included names, addresses and requirements of customers, delivery routes, dates and times, and prices paid. F left and set up a competing business, making use of the sales information. In the absence of express terms, he was free to use this information as it did not amount to a trade secret, in part because the information was generally known to junior employees and not restricted to senior management, and no express instruction had been given to treat it as confidential.

Isolation from other information

2440 If the information forms part of a wider base of information that is widely known or readily available, it is less likely to possess the necessary high quality of confidentiality to constitute a trade secret. For example, if the information in question is part of other information which is trivial or merely confidential and it cannot be easily isolated, then it is less likely to be a trade secret.

> **EXAMPLE** **No trade secret**
> In *Faccenda Chicken Ltd v Fowler* (see previous example), the pricing information could have amounted to a trade secret, but was not isolated from the rest of the sales information, so F was free to use the information.

C. Express terms

2450 Contracts of employment can contain express terms which prevent disclosures of both confidential information and trade secrets.

2451 The employer can use the contract of employment (or a separate confidentiality policy) to **define** confidential information. Although this label will not make trivial information confidential (or confidential information a trade secret), it serves to emphasise the importance placed by the employer on the information (¶2432), and may make the employee aware of its confidential nature (¶2438). It may be appropriate to have a more detailed analysis of what kinds of information would be confidential in a **supporting policy**.

2452 A provision in an agreement (including a contract of employment) that purports to preclude an employee from making a protected disclosure under the **whistleblowing** legislation is void (¶2700). It is therefore advisable to exclude protected disclosures from the scope of any confidentiality clause.

2453 If the employee will obtain any confidential information of other **group companies**, the contract could require him to enter into direct confidentiality undertakings with those companies.

2454 The company may wish to limit the employee's freedom to **speak to the press**. The contract may require the employee to obtain the Board's consent before doing so. If he fails to obtain consent, this may constitute a breach of the agreement, which, if sufficiently serious, could entitle the company to terminate the employment summarily.

2455 After the employment has ended, the employer may also seek to protect his trade secrets and confidential information by way of a **restrictive covenant** (¶2500). There is some uncertainty as to what class of information can be protected in this way. It has been held that the information need not amount to a trade secret (*Lansing Linde Ltd v Kerr* [1991] IRLR 80, CA, approved in *FSS Travel and Leisure Systems Ltd v Johnson* [1998] IRLR 382, CA), but would extend to such information as warranted legitimate protection (*SBJ Stephenson Ltd v Mandy* [2000] IRLR 233, QBD). This would include information (i) which its owner used in a trade or business; (ii) dissemination of which its owner limited or at least did not encourage or permit on a widespread basis; and (iii) which, if disclosed to a competitor, would be liable to cause real or significant harm to the owner (for example, marketing strategies/other business plans, if these are sufficiently concrete) (*Lansing Linde Ltd v Kerr* [1991] IRLR 80; *Scully UK Ltd v Lee* [1998] IRLR 259, CA).

SECTION 3

Restraints and restrictive covenants

2500 An employee has an **implied duty** not to compete with his employer's business or solicit his customers **during employment**. This is the duty of fidelity, which also prevents employees from disclosing trade secrets and confidential information (¶2400). Employers may also wish to impose **express contractual provisions** to highlight, supplement and extend this implied right.

2501 The implied duty does not apply **post-employment** with the exception of disclosures of trade secrets. Therefore, employers may wish to restrict a former employee's activities (particularly in the case of a senior employee) by way of express contractual terms, known as **restrictive covenants**. Although the implied duty does apply post-employment to trade secrets, as the distinction between trade secrets and confidential information is sometimes not clear (¶2425), it is often advisable to have an express term in relation to trade secrets as well as in relation to any confidential information.

Restrictive covenants must be **agreed with the employee**. This is usually done by including them in the contract of employment. However, if, at the time of termination, there are no existing restrictive covenants, the employee could be asked to agree to enter into such covenants, perhaps as part of a negotiated termination settlement (¶¶9276). There are **different types** of restrictive covenant, including a restriction against competing with the employer's business ("non-compete" covenants), from soliciting or dealing with his customers or clients ("non-solicitation" and "non-dealing" covenants), and from soliciting his employees ("anti-poaching" covenants). Other post-termination provisions may indirectly restrict the employee's activities, for example where outstanding commission will not be paid if he joins a competitor.

> MEMO POINTS 1. **Directors** also owe fiduciary duties to their companies, and the sort of activities addressed by restrictive covenants could also constitute a breach of these duties (¶¶2139+).
> 2. It is important to make sure that any express restrictive covenants are accepted in writing by the employee. Where express restrictive covenants are incorporated into an **unsigned employment contract**, it is questionable whether an employer will be able to rely on them. This will largely depend on whether or not it can be established that the employee impliedly accepted the contract as a whole, and therefore the covenants, by reference to his conduct. For example, in *FW Farnsworth Ltd and another v Lacy and ors* [2012] EWHC 2830 (Ch), the High Court decided that an employee was bound by restrictive covenants in an unsigned employment contract that had been given to him at the time of a promotion. The promotion also gave the employee the opportunity to apply for membership of the company pension scheme and private medical insurance, both of which he availed himself of. The fact that he sought out the new fringe benefits was a significant factor in the decision and simply continuing to work in itself may not have been sufficient to imply acceptance.

2502 As an alternative or supplement to restrictive covenants, employers may seek to put an employee on so-called "**garden leave**" during his notice period, which means the employee does not attend work, and must not take up other employment during the garden leave period (¶2529). To enforce garden leave an express contractual term is required. Further, garden leave is a form of restraint in itself and is subject to the same regime as restrictive covenants. If both are used, care must be taken to ensure that the enforceability of one or both forms is not prejudiced.

2503 Both restraints during employment (including garden leave provisions) and restrictive covenants are subject to the public policy **doctrine of restraint of trade** (¶2551) that ensures that employees retain the ability to earn a living and use their skill and knowledge.

I. During employment

A. Implied duty

2510 The implied duty of fidelity (¶1213) **includes** the duty **not to compete** with the employer's business, either by working for competitors or by setting up a competing business, and encompasses a duty **not to solicit his customers or suppliers** (*Wessex Dairies Ltd v Smith* [1935] 2 KB 80, CA). This duty applies during the period of employment (even outside working hours (*Hivac Ltd v Park Royal Scientific Instruments Ltd* [1946] 1 All ER 350, CA)) unless the employer gives the employee express permission to compete.

In addition to the implied duty of fidelity that they may owe as employees, **directors** are bound by their fiduciary and other duties, which are independent of any contract of employment (¶2138).

Working for a competitor

2511 The implied duty can prevent an employee working for a competitor during his employment if it causes or may cause **significant harm** to his employer's interests, which will depend on the circumstances of the case. Rather than rely on this concept, employers who wish to restrict the activities of employees during their spare time should consider using an express term (¶2520).

EXAMPLE

No breach
In *Nova Plastics Ltd v Froggatt* [1982] IRLR 146, EAT, an odd-job man who did some work for a competitor during his employment was not in breach, as the nature of the work done would not significantly contribute to any competition.

Breach
In *Hivac Ltd v Park Royal Scientific Instruments Ltd*, skilled manual employees of H Ltd worked for H Ltd's sole competitor on Sundays. They could be said to be causing H Ltd significant harm as they were advancing the interests of its only competitor.

Intention to compete

An employee will not breach the implied term of fidelity by merely indicating an intention to set up in competition with his employer at some time in the future. An employee is free to make **preparations** to compete with his employer outside working hours, subject to any express provision. For example, he may set up a company, arrange finance and order equipment and material (*Balston Ltd v Headline Filters Ltd* [1990] FSR 385, ChD), as long as these do not go further than taking **preliminary steps** (which will be a question of degree in each case) (*Lancashire Fires Ltd v SA Lyons & Co Ltd* [1997] IRLR 113, CA – see example below).

2512

However, if an employee goes **beyond the intention to compete** and there are grounds for considering that he is abusing or intends to abuse his confidential position or that he is in actual competition with his employer, he will be in breach of his implied duty. For example, an employee will be in breach if he competes with his employer for the future business of one of his employer's customers.

EXAMPLE

No breach
In *Laughton and Hawley v Bapp Industrial Supplies Ltd* [1986] IRLR 245, EAT, L and H **wrote to their employer's suppliers** requesting product lists, price lists and details of terms, with a view to starting up a competing business several weeks later. Merely indicating an intention to compete in the future was not a breach.

Breach
1. In *Adamson v B & L Cleaning Services Ltd* [1994] UKEAT 712_93_1111, A was a foreman in a firm of contract cleaners. One particular contract was up for renewal and A put his name forward for the tender list and refused to undertake not to submit a **competitive tender while employed** by B & L.
2. In *Marshall v Industrial Systems & Control Ltd* [1992] IRLR 294, EAT, M, the managing director, had formed a **plan** with another key employee to **deprive the employer of his best client** and to persuade another senior employee to join them.
3. In *Lancashire Fires Ltd v SA Lyons & Co Ltd*, above, the employee planned to set up a business in competition with his employer. He entered into an agreement giving him **financial backing, bought equipment and rented premises**, which he renovated in his spare time, installing equipment in readiness for production, going further than mere preliminary steps.
4. In *Wessex Dairies Ltd v Smith* (¶2510), a milkman **solicited customers** on his last day by informing them that he had set up his own business and would be able to supply them with milk after he left his employment.
5. In *Shepherds Investments Ltd and anor v Walter and ors* [2007] IRLR 110, HC, employees **drafted business plans**, prepared financial predictions and cash flow summaries, **contacted** offshore **attorneys** and recruited customers who were currently clients of their employer.

An employee will not be in breach of the implied term by **seeking employment with a competitor**, unless he intends to abuse the employer's confidential information or his position with the employer. A dismissal in these circumstances will only be justified if there are solid grounds for believing that the employee intends to commit such a breach (*Harris & Russell Ltd v Slingsby* [1973] IRLR 221, NIRC; approved in *Laughton and Hawley v Bapp Industrial Supplies Ltd*).

2513

Where an employee learns of **confidential matters relating to competition from a potential new employer**, he is not normally bound to pass this information to his existing employer, as he would then be in breach of confidence to this new employer (*Customer Systems Plc v Ranson and ors* [2011] EWHC 3304 (QB)).

B. Express terms

2520 Express terms may be advisable to clarify, highlight and supplement an employee's implied duty, and much will depend on the employer's specific needs. However, such clauses are subject to the doctrine of restraint of trade (¶2551).

Working for a competitor

2522 Employers can have an express term that **specifically prohibits** employees working for a **competitor** during their employment. However, the courts have held that preventing an employee from working for **anyone else** (i.e. a blanket restriction) is an unreasonable restraint of trade (*William Robinson & Co Ltd v Heuer* [1898] 2 Ch 451, CA; *Symbian Ltd v Christensen* [2001] IRLR 77, CA).

2523 An employer can include a term that the employee must obtain his **consent** before undertaking outside work. In such circumstances, failure to obtain consent would be a breach of contract entitling the employer to damages if he has suffered any loss (¶2660).

2524 In order for the employer to be able to comply with his obligations under the **working time regulations** (¶3605), it is advisable for the contract to oblige the employee to notify him of any hours worked for other employers.

2525 As the implied term does not cover **preparatory activities** (¶2512), the contract could also include an express term restricting such activities during the employment. For example, an express term prohibiting employees from holding a material interest in a company, which might impair their ability to act at all times in the best interests of the employer, may prevent an employee from **setting up an off-the-shelf company** for future competition purposes, even where that company remains dormant during the employment (*Ward Evans Financial Services Ltd v Fox* [2002] IRLR 120, CA).

2527 The employer may wish to ascertain what outside interests the employee has, in particular where these interests may compete with those of the company or prevent him devoting sufficient time to his duties. The agreement should therefore oblige the employee to **disclose** his outside interests.

2528 The company could seek to limit the employee's competing outside interests by **limiting his shareholding** in any competing company to a certain percentage. It may wish to include a different percentage for quoted and unquoted securities.

Garden leave

2529 When the employer or, more commonly, the employee gives notice to terminate the employment (or where the employee intends to leave without giving proper notice), the employer may wish to distance him from confidential information, customer connection and staff, and to stop him going straight to a competitor (or setting up in competition) with such information and knowledge. He could achieve this by putting the employee on "garden leave", which means that he remains employed (and is paid and receives his full contractual benefits) **during the notice period**, but does not attend work or carry out his job duties.

Garden leave may be a useful option where the employer wishes to remove the employee from the business immediately, without incurring the risk of restrictive covenants being held to be unenforceable if the employee is wrongfully dismissed (¶8155), or where there are no restrictive covenants.

2530 It is advisable to have an **express contractual right** to put the employee on garden leave, as otherwise a skilled employee may be able to argue that the employer has an implied duty to provide him with work and the opportunity to exercise his skills (¶1233; *William Hill Organisation Ltd v Tucker* [1998] EWCA Civ 615), in which case the employer's breach of contract in putting the employee on garden leave may entitle the employee to resign and claim constructive dismissal (¶8230) and, in turn, threaten the enforceability of any restrictive covenants. However, where the employee is skilled and has a right to be given work, it may be possible to impose a period of garden leave, even in the absence of an express clause, if the employee has committed such a serious breach of contract that the employer cannot allow him to continue to work (*SG & R Valuation Service Co v Boudrais* [2008] EWHC 1340 (QB); *Standard Life Health Care Ltd v Gorman* [2010] IRLR 233, CA). The employer's obligation to provide work and the employee's duty of fidelity are interdependent obligations.

Note that there may be an obligation to inform any relevant **regulatory body** that the employee is on garden leave and not performing normal duties.

> EXAMPLE
> 1. In *SG & R Valuation Service Co v Boudrais*, senior employees made extensive preparations to take business with them before resigning from their employment. This included collecting client contact details and discussing by email how they could damage their old employer's business after their departure. Although, as skilled senior employees, they had a right to be provided with work whilst they remained employed, they had forfeited this by their own serious breaches of contract.
> 2. In *Standard Life Health Care Ltd v Gorman*, the Court of Appeal upheld an injunction preventing self-employed insurance agents working for a new company during their notice periods. Under their contracts they were tied to a single insurance company, S, and as "commission only" agents, if they did not work they would not be paid. The agents' contracts included 3-month notice periods, but no power entitling S to require them not to work during their notice. While the Court recognised that S would not in normal circumstances be entitled to prevent agents from earning a living by requiring them not to work, it considered that because the employees were themselves in breach of contract by not giving proper notice of termination of contract, it was right to allow the injunction to stand.

2531 Garden leave provisions used to be treated by the courts with greater flexibility than post-termination restrictive covenants. However, case law suggests that they will be subject to the doctrine of restraint of trade and will only be enforceable in the same circumstances as a restrictive covenant (*William Hill Organisation Ltd v Tucker*, above; *Symbian Ltd v Christensen* [2001] IRLR 77, CA). This may affect the **length and scope** of any garden leave injunction granted against a former employee (¶2651).

If the employment is for a **fixed term** (without provision for termination by notice prior to expiry), the facility to impose garden leave for any unexpired part of the fixed term should be limited to a reasonable period of time. In any case, the **garden leave period** should not be excessive, taking into account the nature of the employee's work and his need to exercise his skills regularly in order to maintain them or to preserve his reputation in the market. The garden leave period may, therefore, be shorter than the notice period.

2532 Whether or not there is an express garden leave clause, the courts may grant an injunction to enforce the **duty not to compete** (whether express or implied) during the employment, which arguably continues to bind the employee during the notice period as he remains employed. Blanket restrictions (¶2522) may be limited by the courts to a specific competitor (*Symbian Ltd v Christensen*, above).

> MEMO POINTS It has been suggested that an express garden leave clause operates to terminate the duty of fidelity (and the implied duty not to compete) because it ends the relationship of employer and employee even though the contractual relationship continues. The contract would therefore have to contain an express term preventing the employee from working for a competitor for the duration of the contract of employment (*Symbian Ltd v Christensen*).

2533 If the employee has been on garden leave during all or part of his notice period, it is still possible, depending on the circumstances, to impose **restrictive covenants** as well (¶2550). The period of such covenants need not necessarily be reduced by the period spent on garden leave (*Crédit Suisse Asset Management v Armstrong* [1996] IRLR 450, CA). However, a court may take into account the existence of a garden leave clause in determining the validity of a restrictive covenant. An express set-off will, therefore, probably assist the enforceability of the covenants, and will be appropriate unless the employer is confident that the minimum length of necessary protection is the period of garden leave plus the restricted period of the covenant.

> EXAMPLE In *Crédit Suisse First Boston (Europe) Ltd v Padiachy* [1998] IRLR 504, QBD, P was an equities research analyst. His contract with CSFB contained a non-solicitation covenant (with respect to clients and employees) for 12 months after the termination of his employment and a non-compete covenant for 3 months. After giving notice, P was put on 3 months' garden leave. The court refused to enforce the non-compete covenant taking into account the speed with which the market changes and the 3 months of exclusion from the market during the garden leave period, and also the existence of the non-solicitation covenant.

II. Post-employment

2550 The implied duty (with the exception of disclosures of trade secrets) does not apply after the employment has ended and, in the absence of any express contractual obligation, employees are free to compete with their employers after the termination of their employment. **Fiduciary duties** may extend beyond the end of the fiduciary relationship (¶2510).

Any express contractual terms that restrict a former employee's activities after termination are called **restrictive covenants** and are subject to the restraint of trade doctrine.

Restraint of trade

2551 The doctrine of restraint of trade holds that any contractual term that seeks to restrict an individual's freedom to earn a living and use his skill and knowledge is, in principle, void and unenforceable.

However, such terms may be enforced if it is both reasonable in the interests of the parties, and reasonable in the interests of the public.

2552 To be reasonable in the **interests of the parties**, the **employer** must have a legitimate business interest to protect (see below), and the restraint must be no wider than is necessary to protect that interest (for example, the duration, geographical area and restricted activities of a covenant must be limited to that necessary to achieve the protection required in each particular case). If these tests are satisfied, the courts will then consider the restraint from the **employee's** point of view to assess whether it is fair in the light of the general principle of restraint of trade. The severity of the restraint on the employee will be balanced against the employer's need for protection and is judged on the facts of each case.

The three-stage **process of assessing** the **reasonableness** of such restrictive covenants has been reiterated by the High Court (*T F S Derivatives Ltd v Morgan* [2004] EWHC 3181 (QB)). It is first necessary for the court to decide what the covenant means when properly construed. Having done this, if the court concludes that there is an element of ambiguity and that there are two possible ways in which the covenant can be construed, one of which would make the clause unlawful in restraint of trade, but the other of which would be lawful, the court should adopt the latter on the basis that the parties are deemed to have intended to negotiate a lawful contract which is not contrary to public policy. The second stage is to find evidence that the employer has legitimate business interests which are worthy of protection in respect of the employee's employment. The third stage is for the employer to demonstrate that the covenant is no wider than reasonably necessary to protect those legitimate business interests.

2553 The courts will balance the parties' private interests with the **interests of the public** in maintaining a business environment of healthy competition. For example, an agreement between two employers not to employ each other's staff is likely to be void as an unlawful restraint of trade (*Kores Manufacturing Co Ltd v Kolok Manufacturing Co Ltd* [1958] 2 All ER 65, CA; *Esso Petroleum Ltd v Harper's Garage (Stourport) Ltd* [1967] UKHL 1).

This section will focus on the interests of the parties and, in particular, the tests that the employer must satisfy to achieve a potentially enforceable restraint.

A. Legitimate business interests

The courts will closely examine the **subject of a restraint** in order to decide whether the employer has a real legitimate business interest to protect. Whether he does will depend on the nature of the employer's business, and the employee's position within that business. The **types of interest** that the employer can seek to protect are:
- trade secrets or other confidential information (¶2425 and section 2 above);
- customer/client connection (i.e. goodwill); and
- a stable workforce.

> EXAMPLE
> **Interest**
> In *Dawnay, Day & Co Ltd v de Braconier d'Alphen* [1997] IRLR 442, CA, the Court held that the employer, D, had a legitimate interest in protecting the **customer connection** established by former employees as inter-dealer brokers, as D had incurred considerable expense in establishing and fostering that connection.
>
> **No interest**
> However, in *Cantor Fitzgerald (UK) Ltd v Wallace* [1992] IRLR 215, QBD, the employer sought to enforce a non-compete covenant (to protect goodwill) in respect of W and other former inter-dealer brokers. The Court held that where the true skills and art of a job lie in the **personal qualities** of the person performing it (as was the case with W and the other brokers, whose success depended on their personality and ability to get on with the traders), there is no proprietary right which the employer can claim to protect for himself as part of his business.

The connection of an **employment agency** with the pool of workers available for temporary employment is also capable of being a protectable business interest (*Office Angels Ltd v Rainer-Thomas and O'Connor* [1991] IRLR 214, CA).

B. Scope of covenant

To have a better chance of being enforced, the covenants should be **carefully drafted** to suit the specific circumstances of the employer and each particular employee. The employer should not include every conceivable type of covenant to try and ensure blanket protection. If he did so, a court may conclude that he has not given careful consideration to what protection he really requires.

The **type of restriction** considered reasonable for a particular employee will depend on the nature of his work, in particular, whether he has access to confidential information, and/or has contact with the employer's customers such that they tend to identify him with the business. For example, it would not be appropriate to include a covenant protecting customer connections in the contract of an employee who has no contact with customers.

Different covenants may be suitable in different industries, geographical areas, and in relation to different positions within the same company.

The **reasonableness of a particular covenant** will depend on various factors, including the duration, the geographical area, the scope of the restricted activities, the definition of prohibited customer, and the link between the interest and the restraint. A long restricted period (for example, 2 years) is less likely to be enforced than a shorter period, and it may be necessary to have different restricted periods for different covenants. The various factors do not apply in isolation, but all interrelate. For example, the longer the time, the smaller the geographical area must be, and the narrower the scope of the activities.

1. Non-compete covenants

Protectable interests

2570 Non-compete covenants prohibit the former employee from engaging in a competitive activity. They are, however, viewed very cautiously by the courts and will be unenforceable and will not be upheld if their effect is limited to restricting competition.

2572 They will only be upheld in order to give **adequate protection** to the employer's legitimate interests, and will only be enforced where a non-solicitation or non-dealing covenant would provide inadequate protection (*Office Angels Ltd v Rainer-Thomas and O'Connor* [1991] IRLR 214, CA), for example where the employer's customers, although regular, are not readily identifiable (for example, hairdressing businesses), or where their solicitation by the former employer would be difficult to detect.

The courts have upheld non-compete covenants on two grounds: to protect the employer's confidential information, and customer connection.

2573 **Confidential information** A covenant will only be enforced where:
– it is not possible to protect the confidential information in any other way (for example, because it is difficult to monitor the observance of a confidentiality undertaking or to distinguish between information which is confidential and information which is not (*Lawrence David Ltd v Ashton* [1989] IRLR 22, NICA)); and
– the information is capable of causing real damage in the hands of a competitor (*Thomas v Farr Plc and anor* [2007] ICR 932, CA, ¶2455).

> EXAMPLE In *Thomas v Farr Plc and anor*, the managing director of a firm of insurance brokers left to join a competitor. His previous employers sought to prevent this employment, relying on a clause of his contract that prevented the director from working for a competitor during a period of 12 months. In his previous employment the director had no access to client details. He argued that any information he did have was in the public domain. The Court of Appeal found, however, that he did have access to information regarding growing a business and acquisition strategy, the running of a company, its turnover and its strategies to maximise profitability. After employment this knowledge could not be protected except by a restrictive covenant and would be of real assistance to a competitor. It followed that attempts to limit the use of this information were reasonable.

2574 **Customer connection** The employer must show that the former employee had acquired influence over his customers. However, in order to be a protectable interest, the customer connection must be a proprietary interest of the employer, rather than a result of the personal qualities of the employee (*Dawnay, Day & Co Ltd v de Braconier d'Alphen* [1997] IRLR 442, CA; *Cantor Fitzgerald (UK) Ltd v Wallace* – see example at ¶2560).

Prohibited area

2575 Non-compete covenants are usually drafted as area covenants (i.e. by reference to a "prohibited area"), which can be **defined by reference** to a:
– radius taken from the employer's place of business; or
– territory or region which reflects the scope of the employee's duties or the employer's operations.

In any case, non-compete covenants should only operate in respect of an area where the employer has **legitimate business interests** (*Greer v Sketchley Ltd* [1979] IRLR 445, CA), and there must be a "functional correspondence" with the interest that the employee is seeking to protect (*Office Angels Ltd v Rainer-Thomas and O'Connor* [1991] IRLR 214, CA). This means that there must be a **close link** between the prohibited area and the actual operations of the employer's business, reflecting, for example, the likely distribution of the employer's customers.

The reasonableness of the **geographical extent** of the restriction will depend on the circumstances of each case. In *Lansing Linde Ltd v Kerr*, the employer failed to justify the extension of their covenant to all countries in which the group operated (*Lansing Linde Ltd v Kerr* [1991] IRLR 80, CA). However, in some circumstances a national or even **worldwide** covenant may be justifiable (*Scully UK Ltd v Lee* [1998] IRLR 259, CA).

If **no area is stated**, the covenant will be deemed to be worldwide, and therefore unenforceable in most cases.

> EXAMPLE In *Office Angels Ltd v Rainer-Thomas and O'Connor*, R-T and O'C were a branch manager and a consultant of the employer, an employment agency. The non-compete covenants were limited to a radius of 1,000 metres from the branch at which they worked. Nevertheless, the location of that branch meant that the prohibited area covered most of the City of London. As such, it was too wide, and therefore unenforceable.

If the employer's real concern is to prevent the former employee dealing with his customers, a non-solicitation/non-dealing covenant may be sufficient to protect his interests, particularly where customer contact is not confined to a particular area (for example, where dealings are over the telephone). An area covenant is more likely to be reasonable where the employer's business involves **clients visiting his premises** to receive the service or use the business (e.g. hairdressers, estate agents).

An area covenant will be unenforceable if it is not an effective means of **protecting customer connection** (for example, because the number of customers within that area would be too high, including those with whom the employee had no previous dealings). In such cases, it may be necessary specifically to limit the covenant to customers with whom the employee had dealings during the latter stages of his employment for there to be a valid covenant.

Specific competitors

An alternative to the prohibited area non-compete covenant is to identify specific rival businesses, with which the former employee must not be involved (*Littlewoods Organisation Ltd v Harris* [1977] 1 WLR 1472, CA).

Restricted activities

Non-compete covenants are often criticised on the grounds that they would prohibit the former employee from taking part in activities that would not be harmful to the employer (for example, where he joins a competitor but in a business area that does not compete with the employer, or in a role where his knowledge of the employer's confidential information or customer connection is of no use).

It is advisable, therefore, to limit the scope of the activities to the **particular sector** of the industry in which the employee is involved (*Scully UK Ltd v Lee*, above) and, within that sector, to specify the **exact nature of the occupation(s)** in which the employee is prohibited from working.

> EXAMPLE **Unreasonably wide scope**
> 1. In *Wincanton Ltd v (1) Cranny (2) SDM European Transport Ltd* [2000] IRLR 716, CA, the covenant, contained in a booklet containing standard terms and conditions, prohibited C from working in competition with "any business carried on by the company". This was too wide because it was of a **standard form** and was plainly intended to apply to a wide range of situations.
> 2. In *J A Mont (UK) Ltd v Mills* [1993] IRLR 172, CA, the restriction was unreasonable because it restrained M from working "in **any capacity** whatsoever" and "in **any sector** of the tissue industry".
> 3. In *Marley Tile Co Ltd v Johnson* [1982] IRLR 75, CA, J was restricted from supplying, selling or fixing **products similar to** the employer's. The covenant was too wide because it was not limited to the roofing business and could therefore extend to purposes other than roofing.

Duration

The duration of the covenant will also be critical to its enforceability. However, there are no hard and fast rules for determining whether a particular period is reasonable. Restrictions of more than 1 year would, in most cases, be unreasonable.

> **EXAMPLE** In *Barry Allsuch & Co v Harris*, 4 May 2001, HC, a non-compete covenant prohibiting a former employee from working as an estate agent within a specified area for 2 years was unreasonable. Covenants imposed by other estate agencies in the area were for a maximum of 6 months and there was no evidence to suggest that the longer period was justified.

2581 In the case of restraints protecting **confidential information**, it will depend on the "shelf life" of the information (i.e. how quickly the industry changes), and the length of time for which it will be valuable to the former employee. In the case of restraints protecting **customer connections**, it will depend on the length of time the employer will need to rebuild the relationship with clients following the former employee's departure.

2. Non-solicitation covenants (customers)

2585 These covenants seek to protect the employer's customer connection by preventing the former employee from soliciting the custom of the employer's clients and customers.

Prohibited customers

2586 It may be appropriate to use a **prohibited area** definition in order to clarify the identity of customers who cannot be solicited. However, the covenant may be unenforceable where the class of prohibited customers is very large in number (*Marley Tile Co Ltd v Johnson* – see example at ¶2579).

2587 It is therefore advisable for the pool of prohibited customers to be restricted to those who were customers, and with whom the employee had dealings, within a **specified period** (which should be as short as possible in the circumstances) **prior to the termination date**. The length of this period may depend on the regularity of contact between the former employee and customers. For example, if the former employee would deal with most customers every 6 months, then a period of 6 months might be appropriate.

The courts have, however, upheld non-solicitation covenants where there is **no time limit** on the past period when such dealings took place (*Dentmaster (UK) Ltd v Kent* [1997] IRLR 636, CA), and even where there was **no link** between the former employee and clients (*G W Plowman & Son Ltd v Ash* [1964] 2 All ER 10, CA; *Allan Janes LLP v Johal* [2006] ICR 742, HC). Although this may be justified in the case of very senior employees (for example, a managing director), there is a high risk of the covenant being found to be unreasonable. It is therefore advisable to restrict the scope of the covenant to those clients with whom the former employee had dealt.

2588 It may be appropriate to restrict the covenant to those customers who were still **customers on the termination date**. However, if it is not immediately apparent whether or not a particular individual or company was a customer of the employer on any specified date (for example, because customer contact is typically irregular), such a restriction will not be appropriate.

The covenant should not usually extend to **prospective clients**, i.e. those who became customers after the termination date, as the former employee could have no influence over such customers (*Konski v Peet* [1915] 1 Ch 530). However, where sufficient influence exists, a covenant may be upheld (*International Consulting Services (UK) Ltd v Hart* [2000] IRLR 227, QBD).

> **EXAMPLE** In *International Consulting Services (UK) Ltd v Hart*, the Court upheld a covenant restraining the former employee from soliciting anyone who, during the 12 months immediately prior to the date of termination, was negotiating with the employer for the supply of services and with whom the employee or one of his subordinates had dealt. The word "negotiations" was interpreted as meaning a discussion between the parties about the terms of a contract which both parties have in view and which is a real possibility. The Court found that the former employee had an influential position such that any previous contact might have given him a rapport with the customer, and that he might have had some input into the preparation of a proposal for negotiations.

Duration

2589 The reasonableness of the period chosen will depend on the length of time the employer will need to rebuild the relationship with clients following the former employee's departure.

3. Non-dealing covenants

2595

A covenant prohibiting an employee from dealing with customers also seeks to protect the employer's customer connections, but is more onerous than a non-solicitation covenant. A non-dealing covenant may be enforceable where it is unlikely to be possible to prove that the former employee has solicited or will solicit customers (*PR Consultants Scotland Ltd v Mann* [1996] IRLR 188, CS), or if he may be able to take advantage of the employer's customer connection without actively doing so (for example, where they approach him independently). When deciding whether a covenant is enforceable, an important consideration for the Court will be the nature of the market in which the employee was engaged. The more specialist the market, the more likely it is that a non-dealing covenant will be upheld (*Beckett Investment Management Group Ltd and ors v Glyn Hall and ors* [2007] ICR 1539, CA).

A non-dealing covenant should be **used in conjunction with a non-solicitation covenant** in order to prohibit the former employee from dealing with the employer's customers, regardless of who initiated the approach.

The comments made above in respect of the enforcement of non-solicitation of customers apply equally to non-dealing covenants.

4. Non-solicitation covenants (employees)

2600

The employer may be concerned that the employee may seek to take other members of staff with him when he leaves the company. There is no implied term that will prevent a former employee enticing other staff to leave the employer (although there may be liability for inducing a breach of contract). An express non-solicitation or "anti-poaching" covenant can be used to try to prevent this situation and to protect the employer's interest in a **stable workforce**. In the absence of an express clause, the courts may be prepared to grant an injunction to prevent an employee benefiting from having poached staff (*UBS Wealth Management (UK) Ltd v Vestra Wealth LLP* [2008] EWHC 1974 (QB)).

The employer's need for protection arises because the former employee may seek to exploit the knowledge that he has gained of employees' qualifications, rates of pay and other terms. Although there has been much debate as to whether the employer has a legitimate interest to protect, the courts are increasingly willing to recognise an interest in maintaining a stable, trained workforce where the employer can show an **investment in a complement of skilled staff** (*Dawnay, Day & Co Ltd v de Braconier d'Alphen* [1997] IRLR 442, CA).

> EXAMPLE In *UBS Wealth Management (UK) Ltd v Vestra Wealth LLP*, the High Court granted an interim injunction preventing a new start-up business from making use of a springboard gained by poaching a large number of staff. A senior employee left his employer, a bank, and, it was alleged, carried out a concerted campaign of poaching staff who then approached clients. Although this took place after any covenants he had entered into had expired, the Court was persuaded that on balance the mass defections could not have taken place without there being breaches of the employees' duties of loyalty and fidelity, which he had encouraged.

Prohibited employees

2601

The definition of prohibited employees needs careful consideration. The clause is most likely to be enforceable if it is limited to current employees with a particular level of seniority or expertise. It should not normally cover clerical or secretarial staff, or any staff who are unskilled and could readily be replaced. The employer must therefore consider in each case the **category of employees** the covenant should seek to protect.

The tighter the definition, the greater the prospect of enforceability. For example, a covenant restraining the former employee from soliciting anyone who was, during his employment, "a **director or senior employee**" was upheld (*Dawnay, Day & Co Ltd v de Braconier d'Alphen*, above), as was a covenant restraining the former employee from soliciting anyone working "in a **senior capacity**" (*Alliance Paper Group plc v Prestwich* [1996] IRLR 25, ChD).

Conversely, a covenant restraining the former employee from soliciting "**any employees** of the company" was held to be unenforceable as being unreasonably wide (*Hanover Insurance Brokers Ltd v Shapiro* [1994] IRLR 82, CA). However, a covenant restraining the former employee from soliciting "any individual who was an **employee or director**" was held to be enforceable where the company had invested a great deal in the training of both its broking and support staff, and therefore had a legitimate interest in protecting the stability of the workforce as a whole in the circumstances (*SBJ Stephenson Ltd v Mandy* [2000] IRLR 233, QBD).

2602 It may assist the test of reasonableness if the covenant is linked with the former employee's **exercise of personal influence**, i.e. by defining the prohibited employee as someone with whom the departing employee worked closely. As the departing employee's knowledge or personal influence will decrease with time, this link could be limited to staff with whom the former employee worked closely **during the latter stages** (for example, 6 months) of his employment.

2603 The covenant will be invalid if it includes **new employees** who join the employer after the departing employee has left (*Hanover Insurance Brokers Ltd v Shapiro*, above).

Duration

2604 The reasonableness of the period chosen will depend on the period over which the influence or knowledge of the departing employee is likely to diminish.

5. Indirect restraints

2610 An indirect restraint is a clause which penalises the former employee after the termination, for example, by providing that **outstanding commission** will not be paid if the employee joins a competitor (*Sadler v Imperial Life Assurance Co of Canada Ltd* [1988] IRLR 388, QBD; *Marshall v N M Financial Management Ltd* [1996] IRLR 20, ChD, on appeal [1997] IRLR 449, CA). Such restraints must also go no further than is necessary to protect the employer's legitimate business interests (¶2560).

C. Other factors affecting enforceability

Context of agreement

2615 Restrictive covenants entered into as part of a **business or share sale** (where the person accepting the restriction is the vendor) will be easier to enforce, even if the vendor is also an employee of the business (*Allied Dunbar (Frank Weisinger) Ltd v Weisinger* [1988] IRLR 60, ChD; *Systems Reliability Holdings plc v Smith* [1990] IRLR 377, ChD). The purchaser has an interest in protecting the newly acquired business from any **competing activities of the vendor**, particularly where the sale price included an element for goodwill.

> EXAMPLE In *Allied Dunbar (Frank Weisinger) Ltd v Weisinger*, W was a self-employed sales associate of AD. He had built up a highly successful practice, which was dependent on his personal connections and customer recommendations. W sold his practice to AD, including its goodwill and connections, and agreed to stay on as a consultant for 2 years and to be bound by non-compete and non-solicit covenants for a further 2 years after his consultancy ended. The Court indicated that it would adopt the less stringent approach applying to the protection of the goodwill of a business sold by the covenantor to the covenantee, and that the covenants were therefore enforceable even though W had been engaged as an employee during the intervening 2-year period.

Employer's fundamental breach of contract

2616 It is a general legal principle that a party **may not take advantage of its own breach** of contract. If, therefore, the employer terminates the employment in breach of contract (for example, by not giving the required period of notice), or the employee resigns following the employer's repudiatory breach, the employer will not be entitled to enforce any of the employee's obligations that are stated to continue or take effect after the termination (*General Billposting Co Ltd v Atkinson* [1909] AC 118, HL). A breach of the implied term of trust and confidence (¶1241) will also lead to restrictive covenants being unenforceable.

2617 The employer **cannot circumvent** this principle by **expressly stating** that the restrictive covenants will be enforceable however the employment is terminated, or even where the employer terminates in breach. Restrictions stated to apply after the termination of employment "however that comes about and whether lawful or not" are unenforceable because they are "manifestly wholly unreasonable" (*Living Design (Home Improvements) Ltd v Davidson* [1994] IRLR 69, CS).

Wording such as "terminated for any reason whatsoever" and "irrespective of the cause or manner", which may indicate that the covenant will apply even where the employee is dismissed in breach of contract, has been held to render the entire covenant clause unenforceable (*D v M* [1996] IRLR 192, QBD). It is not likely to be possible to sever the offending wording by applying the blue pencil test (¶2633) so as to leave the rest of the clause to be enforced (*Living Design (Home Improvements) Ltd v Davidson*).

However, it has since been held that the **mere existence of a provision** stating that the covenants will apply following the termination of the employment "howsoever occasioned" or "howsoever arising" will not necessarily make the covenant unreasonable and unenforceable, although if the employer actually terminated in breach, they would be (*Rock Refrigeration Limited v Jones* [1996] IRLR 675, CA).

2618 Where the employer has a contractual right to terminate the employment by making a **payment in lieu of notice**, he will not be in breach of contract if he does so, and can therefore rely on any post-termination restrictions (*Rex Stewart Jeffries Parker Ginsberg Ltd v Parker* [1988] IRLR 483, CA). If the employer makes a payment in lieu of notice where he has no contractual right to do so, this may still amount to a wrongful dismissal unless the employee consents to it. The safest course would therefore be to repeat any post-termination restrictions in settlement documentation (¶9300).

MEMO POINTS If the employee is asked to **reaffirm his post-termination restrictions in the settlement documentation**, then the employer should consider allocating some additional consideration to the obligations to ensure that he will be able to enforce the restrictions at a later date.

Garden leave

2619 A court may take into account the existence of a garden leave clause in determining the validity of a restrictive covenant (¶2529). Employers wishing to include both a garden leave clause and restrictive covenants in a contract should therefore consider including wording which will have the effect of reducing the period of restrictive covenants by the amount of any garden leave served.

Payment in respect of restricted period

2620 The concern underlying the doctrine of restraint is not only to ensure that employees can earn their living, but also to uphold the public interest in competition and the proper use of the employee's skills. **In general**, therefore, it makes no difference to the enforcement of restrictive covenants that the former employee is remunerated during the period of restraint (*J A Mont (UK) Ltd v Mills* [1993] IRLR 172, CA).

However, in **certain circumstances** (for example, where a senior employee receives an additional payment as part of a termination agreement), a payment may be taken into consideration in assessing the reasonableness of a covenant (*Turner v Commonwealth & British Minerals* [2000] IRLR 114, CA).

2621 Payment for goodwill will be relevant to restrictive covenants entered into as part of a **business or share sale**.

Transfer of undertakings

2622 Under the transfer regulations, the rights and obligations of the transferor employer will pass automatically to the transferee employer, and restrictive covenants may, therefore, be enforced by the transferee employer against employees who have transferred to it in certain circumstances (¶7975).

The transferee employer may wish to impose **new covenants** on the transferred employees. However, any variation of terms made in connection with the transfer may be void (¶8010).

D. Courts' approach

Interpretation

2630 As with any binding contractual term, covenants must be **sufficiently certain**. If they are not, they will be void for uncertainty, although the courts are slow to come to that conclusion (*Dawnay, Day & Co Ltd v de Braconier d'Alphen* [1997] IRLR 442, CA).

An employer should avoid drafting "**multiple choice**" restrictions (for example, including a prohibited area by reference to "London, Manchester, Birmingham, England and Wales, the UK"), in the hope that the courts will enforce one of the choices. The risk in this approach is that the clause may be held to be void for uncertainty.

2631 If a contract includes a covenant which is unreasonably wide in its scope, it will normally be held void and of no effect. However, it may be possible to **construe the covenant** as having a more limited application, in which case it may meet the reasonableness requirement. The courts will apply the normal rules of construction, construing the covenant realistically to give effect to the **intention of the parties** (¶1117). They will reject a literal interpretation of the words used if that would contradict the obvious intention of the parties, limit general wording, where necessary, to reflect the assumed purpose of the restraint, and discount remote possibilities in which the covenant could operate unreasonably.

> EXAMPLE
> 1. In *Hanover Insurance Brokers Ltd v Shapiro* (¶2601), S was prohibited from soliciting the insurance broking business of clients of the employer, the parent company and that company's subsidiaries. S argued that the extension to other companies made the clause unreasonably wide. The Court took a flexible approach and decided that, as the parent and other subsidiaries were not involved in insurance broking, the clause could be construed as referring only to the employer.
> 2. In *G W Plowman & Son Ltd v Ash* (¶2587), the employer sought to enforce a covenant restraining A from canvassing customers. Although the covenant did not mention the kind of goods to which it applied, the Court held that it should be construed in the light of the contract as a whole. As the contract did make reference to the employer's products (corn and agricultural merchandise, and animal feed), the clause was limited to those products and was therefore not too wide.
> 3. In *Home Counties Dairies Ltd v Skilton* [1970] 1 All ER 1227, CA, S, a milkman, was restrained from serving or selling milk or dairy produce to, or soliciting orders from, those who had been customers of the employer during the last 6 months of the employment and who had been served by him. The Court discounted the argument that the covenant could cover the situation where both the milkman and the customer moved to another area, in which case the application of the covenant would be unreasonable. Further, the Court rejected a literal reading of the covenant which might have led to the conclusion that S was restrained from becoming a grocer, as this also involved the sale of dairy produce. The covenant had to be considered in the context, concerning the employer's trade as a dairy and the employee's trade as a milkman.

2632 The reasonableness of the covenant is assessed in the light of the facts and circumstances as they were at the time **when the contract was entered into**, although the parties' reasonable expectations are also to be taken into account (*TSC Europe (UK) Ltd v Massey* [1999] IRLR 22, ChD, and *Patsystems Holding Ltd v Neilly* [2012] EWHC 2609 (QB)). For this reason, it is particularly important to keep employees' restrictive covenants under review as their careers change, because what was appropriate at the beginning of an individual's employment may not still be so when it comes to an end.

When the employer seeks to enforce a covenant by way of an injunction, the courts will also assess whether the covenant is reasonable at that time.

Unreasonable covenants

If, having construed a post-termination restriction, a court finds it to be unreasonable, the restriction will be unenforceable in its **entirety**. A court will not rewrite a covenant so as to make it reasonable and, therefore, enforceable, nor will it enforce a restriction in **more limited terms** than those imposed by the restrictive covenant (*J A Mont (UK) Ltd v Mills* [1993] IRLR 172, CA).

If a single clause contains several restrictions (for example, a non-compete and a non-solicitation covenant), the court may decide the enforceability of **each restriction** separately. If one restriction is unreasonable, the courts may be able to sever the unreasonable part without affecting the enforceability of the remaining restriction. **Individual words or phrases** may also be severed in this way, providing that (*Sadler v Imperial Life Assurance Co of Canada Ltd* [1988] IRLR 388, QBD):
- what is left makes independent sense without the need for further changes;
- the remaining terms continue to be supported by adequate consideration; and
- the sense of the agreement is not changed.

This is known as the "**blue pencil test**". This test will be used "where the part so enforceable is clearly severable, and even so only in cases where the excess is of trivial importance, or merely technical, and not a part of the main purport and substance of the clause" (*Beckett Investment Management Group Ltd and ors v Glyn Hall and ors* [2007] ICR 1539, CA; *Mason v Provident Clothing and Supply Co Ltd* [1913] AC 724, HL). For example, a covenant might be drafted to stop a former employee soliciting customers of the employer and other group companies for 3 years after termination. A court might be prepared to sever the reference to other group companies, but it will not change the 3-year period to 1 year in order to make it enforceable. To facilitate the application of the blue pencil test where necessary, it is advisable to deal with each type of restriction in a separate and distinct clause. This should include repeating any common definitions in full in each separate and distinct clause. For example, the High Court has held that the blue pencil test could not be applied to the definition of "Restricted Area" within a non-compete clause as the definition was used in other restrictive covenants within the contract which were agreed by all parties to be valid without any modification (*Francotyp-Postalia Ltd v Whitehead and ors* [2011] EWHC 367 (Ch)).

2633

> EXAMPLE
>
> 1. In *Rex Stewart Jeffries Parker Ginsberg Ltd v Parker* (¶2618), P's contract restrained him from soliciting anyone who to his knowledge "is or has been" during his employment a customer of the company or any associated companies. The Court agreed that there were four distinct restrictions that prohibit the soliciting of:
> - those who had been customers to the date of termination;
> - those who might have become customers after the date of termination;
> - customers of the company; and
> - customers of associated companies.
>
> The second and the last prohibition were unreasonable, and so the judge deleted the reference to "is or" and the part of the clause relating to associated companies, thus limiting the restriction to customers of the company up to the date of termination, making it reasonable and enforceable.
>
> 2. In *Beckett Investment Management Group Ltd and ors v Glyn Hall and ors*, two financial consultants were bound to their employer by contracts that included restrictive covenants. One term held that on leaving employment the consultants should not compete for the business of any client of their employer, nor for the private business of any individual who was an officer, employee or representative of a client. The Court of Appeal held that a restriction which prevented the consultants from canvassing work from individuals who had not been, in their personal dealings, clients of the employer was so wide as to be unreasonable. It severed the offending clause, leaving only the reasonable restriction against competing for the business of actual clients.

2634 Some agreements contain **express wording** stating that if any restriction is found to be void but would be valid if some part of it were deleted, those restrictions will apply with such modifications as may be necessary to make them valid or effective. Such wording has been accepted (*Hinton & Higgs (UK) Ltd v Murphy and Valentine* [1989] IRLR 519, CS), but it has also been considered that such wording did not enable the Court in question to do anything more than the blue pencil test and did not extend the Court's powers to enable them to rewrite the contract (*Living Design (Home Improvements) Ltd v Davidson* [1994] IRLR 69, CS).

III. Enforcement and remedies

2640 An **employee** or **former employee** can apply to the court for a declaration that an express term/covenant is invalid and unenforceable, or for summary judgment against the employer on the grounds that the employer's claim has no real prospect of success.

2641 An **employer** may be justified in **dismissing** an employee for breach of his implied duty of fidelity/express term and the dismissal could amount to a fair dismissal (¶8422). However, it is likely that, at this stage, the damage will have been done so as an enforcement measure it will not be effective other than to serve as a deterrent to other employees.

An employer must also be careful before he takes such action, if he merely believes that an employee is going to breach an implied or express term. In such cases, to justify dismissal, the employer would need strong evidence to show that he knew that the employee was going to disclose confidential information, compete or solicit.

2642 If the former employee has taken **confidential documents** belonging to the employer, the employer can ask the court to order the employee to preserve these documents or to **deliver them up** (*Roger Bullivant Ltd v Ellis* [1987] IRLR 491, CA). In extreme cases, the court may grant a search order, which would permit the employer to enter particular premises in order to **search** for them. Such orders will only be granted sparingly, and there is a heavy evidential burden on the employer to show that there is a grave danger or real possibility that evidence might be destroyed if the order is not granted (*Lock International plc v Beswick* [1989] IRLR 481, ChD).

1. Injunction

2645 In practice, the usual remedy for a threatened or actual breach of an implied or express term/restrictive covenant is an injunction (granted by the High Court and county courts, but not employment tribunals) which prevents the employee or former employee (most usually the former employee) from breaching or further breaching the term/covenant. In many cases the employer requires immediate relief and will apply straight away for an "**interlocutory**" or "**interim**" (i.e. temporary) injunction pending the trial of the action. Where the matter is extremely urgent, the employer can apply to the court without notifying the former employee (an "**ex parte**" application), although notice should usually be given where the employer's interests will not be prejudiced by doing so.

If, unusually, the period of the restrictive covenant enforced by an interlocutory injunction has not expired before the matter comes to trial, the court may grant a **permanent** injunction.

2646 For an injunction to be **granted**, the requirements of the civil court rules and related practice direction must be satisfied (Civil Procedure Rules SI 1998/3121). Previous guidance given by the House of Lords (now the Supreme Court) will probably continue to be relevant (*American Cyanamid Co v Ethicon Ltd* [1975] 1 All ER 504, HL). This requires the employer to show that there are serious issues of law and fact to be tried (i.e. that he has an arguable claim), and if so, that, on the balance of convenience, the injunction should be granted. If the court is in doubt as to the balance of convenience, it will favour maintenance of the status quo.

In making its decision, the **court will consider** whether:
– damages would be an adequate remedy; and
– more harm will be done by granting or refusing to grant an injunction (taking into account the employer's cross-undertaking in damages, see ¶2649).

It will also take account of the right to **freedom of expression** guaranteed by the Human Rights Act 1998 (Human Rights Act 1998).

Damages will probably not be considered an adequate remedy:
– if the former employee does not have the financial means to meet an award;
– if damages are difficult to quantify;
– to restrain the misuse of confidential information; or
– to enforce non-solicitation or non-compete covenants.

EXAMPLE In *Wincanton Ltd v (1) Cranny (2) SDM European Transport Ltd* [2000] IRLR 716, CA, C was restricted by a customer non-solicitation covenant. However, the Court of Appeal refused to grant an injunction because (i) there were only 3 months of the 12-month restriction left to run, such that the balance of convenience lay in C's favour, and (ii) Wincanton, who had been able to quantify their loss by reference to the loss of specific customer contracts, could be **adequately compensated** by way of damages. Wincanton should therefore have concentrated their efforts in securing a speedy trial.

2647 Normally, the **court will not consider** the merits of the parties' case (*American Cyanamid Co v Ethicon Ltd*, followed in *Lawrence David Ltd v Ashton* [1989] IRLR 22, NICA). However, if the grant or refusal of an injunction at the interlocutory stage would in effect **dispose of the action** (for example, because a speedy main hearing is not possible and the action cannot be tried before a restraint has expired or nearly expired), the court may also consider the employer's prospect of success at the main hearing (*NWL Ltd v Woods* [1979] IRLR 478, HL, followed in *D v M* [1996] IRLR 192, QBD). This will result in a more onerous burden on the employer than merely establishing an arguable claim.

2648 An employer seeking an injunction to enforce **confidentiality obligations** must specify in detail the information they claim to be confidential (*Lock International plc v Beswick* [1989] IRLR 481, ChD). The duration or shelf life of the confidential information will be relevant to the court's decision on whether to grant an injunction and for how long. For example, in the case of an employee who has copied client lists for use as a "springboard" to launch into business after his employment ends, the court may grant an injunction so as to neutralise the unfair advantage gained for as long as the information is likely to be commercially sensitive.

2649 Seeking an injunction is **costly**, both financially and in terms of management time. The employer must therefore weigh up the damage to his business against the costs of seeking this remedy. He must be prepared for the following:
– to give a cross-undertaking in damages (i.e. an undertaking to pay damages to the former employee in respect of any loss suffered by him if the court decides at the main hearing that the interlocutory injunction should not have been granted);
– to demonstrate that he could afford such damages;
– to meet his own legal costs, which are likely to be substantial given the amount of work and the speed with which an application must be made; and
– to pay the former employee's legal costs if the employer loses.

If the matter proceeds to a main hearing and the employer is successful, he may be able to recover part of his legal costs from the former employee.

However, one advantage is that a successful application for an interlocutory injunction may actually be, in effect, a final injunction as the former employee may be financially unable to continue fighting the action. Many cases involving negotiations are resolved at this stage.

2650 Given the uncertainties surrounding the enforcement of post-termination restrictions and the cost of seeking an injunction, employers may consider their use and enforcement as a **tactical deterrent**, rather than a weapon of legal protection. If a former employee has breached or is about to breach a covenant, the **threat of legal proceedings** alone (for example, a letter from his former employer's legal representative) may be sufficient to stop him.

Garden leave injunction

2651 If the employee works for a competitor during his notice period while on garden leave, the employer can apply to the court for a garden leave injunction. The court **may grant** an injunction if:
- the employer is not in breach of contract;
- the period of garden leave is not excessive;
- the employer continues to pay the employee's salary and benefits;
- the employer undertakes not to claim damages from the employee if he chooses not to work for him during the notice period; and
- the employer can show that he will suffer serious and unquantifiable damage if the injunction is not granted, in terms of the fostering of the rival business or the confidential information that the employee knows (if the employee has confidential information but this is not relevant to the rival's business, an injunction would not be granted) (*Evening Standard Co Ltd v Henderson* [1987] IRLR 64, CA; *Provident Financial Group plc and Whitegates Estate Agency Ltd v Hayward* [1989] IRLR 84, CA).

2652 The **scope and period** of any injunction granted will be limited to that which is absolutely necessary to protect the employer's legitimate interests (*GFI Group Inc v Eaglestone* [1994] IRLR 119, QBD). In contrast to the enforcement of restrictive covenants, a court may, if necessary, **narrow the scope** of the restriction, for example, by preventing the employee from working for specified competitors or competitors generally, such that he could take up **non-competitive work** during garden leave (*Provident Financial Group plc and Whitegates Estate Agency Ltd v Hayward*; *Symbian Ltd v Christensen* [2001] IRLR 77, CA). The courts will carefully examine the length of the notice period, and will **limit the duration** of the garden leave period where the notice period is excessively long.

> EXAMPLE
> **Period reduced**
> In *GFI Group Inc v Eaglestone*, above, the court refused to grant an injunction restraining E, a foreign exchange options broker, from joining a competitor firm for his entire notice period of 20 weeks, as two other brokers (whose contracts provided for only 4 weeks' notice) had already joined the competitor firm. This meant that, to a certain extent, the damage to GFI's customer connection had already been done, and it was not necessary for the protection of GFI's interests to hold E to the full period of 20 weeks. A shorter period of 13 weeks was held to be sufficient.
>
> **Period not reduced**
> In *Eurobrokers Ltd v Rabey* [1995] IRLR 206, ChD, the court granted an injunction restraining R, a money broker, from joining a rival firm for his notice period, up to a maximum of 6 months. In this case, a significant customer connection had been furthered at the employer's expense, and this goodwill was something that the employer was entitled to protect. The injunction for the full 6 months was necessary given that the potential damage of being deprived of the opportunity to put new traders in place to deal with R's customers was not quantifiable in monetary terms.

Injunction against second employer

2653 Injunctions may also be brought against a second employer who is **inducing a breach**.

> EXAMPLE In *Hivac Ltd v Park Royal Scientific Instruments Ltd* [1946] 1 All ER 350, CA, the Court ordered an injunction against the second employer, who was a competitor, on the basis that the employees of the first employer were in breach of their implied duty of fidelity by working for this second employer on Sundays.

2. Damages

2660 Where the employer has reacted slowly to the former employee's activities, or where financial compensation is a sufficient remedy (such that no injunction is granted), the employer may proceed to a trial of the matter seeking damages for breach of contract or an account for profits (see below). This will be **assessed** on the loss suffered by the employer as a result of the breach and is **calculated** by reference to the profits on contracts or opportunities lost as a result of the former employee's activities. While it is relatively easy to describe that loss, problems often arise in proving that the loss directly resulted from that breach. An employer may also have difficulty quantifying his lost profits.

> EXAMPLE
> **No actual loss**
> In *Nottingham University v Fishel* [2000] IRLR 471, QBD, F was in breach of an express term which required him to obtain consent before undertaking paid work abroad. However, as the university suffered no actual loss, it was not entitled to damages.
>
> **Difficult to quantify loss**
> A company has experienced severe competition from a number of small start-up companies in the same geographical area. One of its sales managers leaves his employment, taking with him confidential product information that was protected by an express contractual provision in his contract of employment. He establishes a further company in competition. His former employer suffers severe financial hardship. However, it may prove difficult to show what loss was a result of that breach and what was due to other non-related causes, i.e. the other start-up companies.

Damages against second employer

2661

If the former employee has gone to work for a competitor, it may be more financially viable to issue proceedings against the second employer for unlawfully interfering with contractual relations, and **inducing** (or aiding and abetting) a **breach** of contract (i.e. by inducing/attempting to induce the employee to breach a restrictive covenant or confidentiality undertaking).

Liability for inducing a breach of contract depends on the former employee having committed an actionable wrong. Further, the second employer must have intended to procure (i.e. bring about) a breach of contract although he does not have to intend to cause loss (*Lumley v Gye* (1853) 2 E & B 216; *OBG Ltd and ors v Allan and others, Douglas and another v Hello! Ltd and others, Mainstream Properties Ltd v Young and others* [2007] IRLR 608, HL). This economic tort is different from another economic tort, the unlawful means tort, where to be liable there must be an intention to cause loss although, conversely, no specific intention to procure a breach of contract is necessary. However, with regard to this intention to cause loss, it is not necessary to show that the dominant intention or purpose was to injure the employer's business, and it is sufficient that the second employer intended to injure the business as a means to an end.

> EXAMPLE In *Tullett Prebon Plc and ors v BGC Brokers LP and ors* [2010] IRLR 648, QB (appeal dismissed by the Court of Appeal reported at [2011] EWCA Civ 131, H, the chief operating officer of a firm of inter-dealer brokers (TP), accepted a new contract with another firm, BGC. He then conducted a campaign to recruit a substantial number of brokers to move with him, as complete teams. A number accepted contracts with the new firm, on the basis that they would start work when they were free to do so. BGC agreed to indemnify the brokers for losses suffered as a result of leaving TP early. When H's activities were discovered, he was suspended from work. The brokers' contracts all included long notice periods, garden leave clauses and restrictive covenants. They each resigned, claiming constructive dismissal based on how they had been treated – for example, being given presentations on the disadvantages of moving to BGC, informing them that TP would take legal action if they did not serve their notice, and the impact of the suspension of H. TP started proceedings against H and BGC, claiming that BGC had induced breaches of contract by TP's employees and for conspiracy to injure TP's business. The individual employees were added to the proceedings and counterclaimed for constructive dismissal. The High Court found that:
> – TP's conduct had not amounted to a breach of trust and confidence, and the resignations were in reality a manoeuvre to seek to leave early. Although robust, TP's conduct was unobjectionable, especially as the brokers were no "shrinking violets". The Court therefore held that there had been no constructive dismissals and enforced the restrictive covenants and garden leave clauses;
> – BGC had induced the brokers to leave early in breach of their contracts by offering to indemnify them; it was sufficient that it did not matter to BGC whether they breached their contracts or not;
> – the claim for conspiracy to injure by unlawful means by TP's business succeeded because the parties acted together to recruit TP's employees, which would necessarily injure the business; and
> – the counterclaim by BGC, that TP had induced breach of contracts by brokers who had agreed to join them but been persuaded to stay, failed because they were entitled to refuse to join BGC because of its behaviour in asking them to leave TP early in breach of their contracts.

> **MEMO POINTS** A second employer may also be liable for breach of the **equitable duty of confidence**, which is independent of the employment contract, if he receives information from a new employee which he knows has been obtained in breach of that employee's previous obligations or duties (*Attorney General v Guardian Newspapers Ltd* [1988] 3 All ER 545 (known as the Spycatcher case)). In this case, the newspaper was held to be in breach of confidence when it published material which it knew was in breach of the writer's (the former secret service agent, Peter Wright) contract with a third party (the Crown).

3. Account for profits

2665 This remedy is available for a breach of **equitable fiduciary** duties, which may nevertheless be imposed in the context of a contract of employment as a result of specific contractual obligations undertaken by the employee which place him in a position where he must act solely in the interests of the employer. It is **assessed** on the profit made by the employee and not the loss suffered by the employer.

> **EXAMPLE** In *Nottingham University v Fishel* [2000] IRLR 471, QBD (see example at ¶2660 above), F, the scientific director of an infertility clinic set up by the university, also carried out private clinic work in the UK and abroad. Junior embryologists from the university worked for him privately. As F directly benefited from his position, he was obliged to account for the profits he made as a result of their work, even though the university had suffered no loss.

> **MEMO POINTS** In exceptional circumstances, this remedy may be available for a **breach of contract** if the employer has a legitimate interest in preventing the employee's profit-making activity (*Attorney General v Blake* [2001] IRLR 36, HL). In this case, B published an autobiography in breach of his contract with the Crown not to disclose information about his work as a former secret service employee.

SECTION 4

Whistleblowing

2700 Legislation protects workers who, out of a sense of public duty, reveal **serious employer misconduct** (ERA 1996 as amended by the Public Interest Disclosure Act 1998. Claims based on the Public Interest Disclosure Act are often referred to as PIDA claims). Such workers are often termed whistleblowers. In these circumstances, whistleblowing takes precedence over and above a worker's private contractual and common law duties of confidentiality to his employer (¶2400). Further, any **contractual term** or any other agreement that **purports to prevent** a worker from making a protected disclosure will be void and, to avoid this, confidentiality clauses should state that such disclosures are allowable (¶2452) (s 43J ERA 1996).

2701 To be protected, a worker must usually make the disclosure to his employer, his legal adviser or to an appropriate public authority and only in certain circumstances or if exceptionally serious will a worker be justified in disclosing the information to the general public or another body. This gives employers, in most cases, an opportunity to resolve the issues internally and, to facilitate this, it is advisable that employers have a **whistleblowing policy**.

2702 In reality, workers may still find themselves with a stark choice, for although they may have legal protection not to be victimised or dismissed, they may feel unable to continue with their employment after making a protected disclosure. However, if they are **victimised or dismissed**, they will be entitled to bring a claim against their employer. Given the highly explosive nature of certain disclosures and the damage they may have on public confidence in a company or organisation, companies/organisations will often want to **settle** any such claims rather than have their "dirty laundry" aired in a tribunal or have sensitive information revealed.

2703 If there is a threat of a public disclosure, an employer may wish to seek an **injunction**, although this will only be given if it is in the public interest. Naturally, once there has been a public disclosure, there is little a company can do other than clean up its act and try to restore public confidence, although many companies and other organisations will try to down-play any such disclosures as much as possible.

Passing on details to industry regulators

2704 Tribunals have the discretion to pass on details of whistleblowing claims to industry regulators, provided the claimant has consented to this on the ET1 claim form (SI 2010/131). The list of designated regulators reflects the list of appropriate public authorities (see memo point to ¶2735).

A. Scope of protection

2710 Whistleblowing protection applies to all **workers** and is specifically extended to include four groups of working individuals as follows (s 43K ERA 1996):
– agency workers (*Croke v Hydro Aluminium Worcester Ltd* [2007] ICR 1303, EAT);
– home workers (where working in a place other than a workplace and includes those who perform the work personally or otherwise);
– trainees (other than those provided by an educational establishment); and
– certain NHS doctors, dentists, ophthalmologists and pharmacists.

The definition of a "worker" in this context is exceptionally wide and may also extend, for example, to employees of sub-contractors working on an employer's behalf e.g. security personnel.

> MEMO POINTS **Excluded** are workers where the "employer" is in fact a client or customer of a profession or business undertaking carried on by them. Also excluded are partners in a partnership and equity members of LLPs (*Clyde & Co LLP and anor v Bates van Winkelhof* [2012] EWCA Civ 1207).

Qualifying disclosures

2711 To qualify for protection, the disclosure must, in the reasonable belief of the worker making the disclosure, show that one or more of the **following events** has happened, is happening or is likely to happen (s 43B ERA 1996):
– criminal offence;
– failure to comply with any legal obligation. This includes a breach of contract (of employment or for services) where there is a breach of a legal obligation of the contract and the disclosure has resulted in the dismissal of the worker (*Parkins v Sodexho Ltd* [2001] UKEAT 1239_00_1701 as applied in *Wilson Odong v Chubb Security Personnel* [2002] UKEAT 0819_02_0411);
– miscarriage of justice;
– danger to health and safety of any individual;
– danger to the environment; or
– deliberate concealment of any of the above.

To qualify, the disclosure must consist of information and **not** mere **allegations** (*Cavendish Munro Professional Risks Management Ltd v Geduld* [2010] IRLR 38, EAT), and must identify, albeit not in strict legal language, which of the above events the worker is relying on (*Fincham v HM Prison Service* [2002] UKEAT 0925_01_1912).

> EXAMPLE In *Cavendish Munro Professional Risks Management Ltd v Geduld*, a dispute arose between two directors of a company on the one hand and a third director, G. G's solicitors wrote to the other directors suggesting that a proposal they had made to backdate a shareholders' agreement was unlawful. The EAT held that this was no more than an allegation and did not qualify for protection.

> MEMO POINTS 1. **Excluded** are disclosures where it is a criminal offence to disclose the information, for example civil servants to the extent that they are bound by the **Official Secrets Act**.

Further, information protected by **legal professional privilege** (or, in Scotland, confidentiality between a client and professional adviser) is also excluded.

2. The Government **intends to remove breaches of** an employee's employment **contract** as a qualifying disclosure under the whistleblowing rules in **April 2013**. Further developments will be covered by our updating service.

2712 The event is called a **relevant failure**. It is immaterial whether the relevant failure reveals a wrongdoing or failure **by** the employer/person for whom the employer is responsible or reveals a wrongdoing or a failure by any other person (*Hibbins v Hesters Way Neighbourhood Project* [2009] ICR 319, EAT).

> EXAMPLE In *BP Plc v Elstone and anor* [2010] IRLR 558, EAT, an employee "blew the whistle" in respect of breaches of health and safety by his employers, P, to managers at a client, BP. P dismissed him, and he started work for BP as a consultant. BP then said that they would not offer him further work, because P told them that they had dismissed the claimant for disclosing confidential information. The EAT held that he was protected from detrimental treatment by BP based on his "blowing the whistle" on his previous employer.

It is also immaterial whether the relevant failure **occurred**, occurs or will occur in the UK or elsewhere, and whether the law applying to it is UK law or the law of another country or territory (s 43(2) ERA 1996).

A disclosure will still qualify even if the **person who receives the information** regarding the relevant failure is **already aware** of the information contained in the disclosure, and in such cases the worker will be deemed to have brought the information to his attention (s 43L(3) ERA 1996).

2713 A worker's **reasonable belief** relates to what he perceived to be the facts and the basis on which he considered it reasonable to rely on them (*Darnton v University of Surrey* [2003] IRLR 133, EAT). It can also relate to his legal knowledge (*Babula v Waltham Forest College* [2007] ICR 1026, CA, overruling *Kraus v Penna plc and anor* [2004] IRLR 260, EAT). Consequently, if the worker mistakenly believes that a legal obligation exists, when in fact it does not, he may still be protected under the legislation if he reasonably believed that a legal obligation existed.

> EXAMPLE In *Babula v Waltham Forest College*, an American citizen was employed as a lecturer at a UK college. He learned from students that his predecessor had divided the class into Islamic and non-Islamic groups, ignoring the latter, and had celebrated the events in New York on 11 September 2001. The lecturer brought this matter to the attention of his employers, suffered what he judged to be various detrimental acts, and resigned. The Tribunal ruled that the most that the previous lecturer could be accused of was incitement to religious hatred, which had not been a crime at the time. It followed that the college was under no legal duty to investigate, and the lecturer's disclosure was not protected. This decision was overturned by the EAT, which held that even if religious incitement had not actually been outlawed at the time, it was reasonable for the lecturer to have believed that it was illegal.

2714 The right does not extend to a worker **threatening to make a disclosure**. Consequently, if an employer threatens or pressurises a worker not to reveal a relevant failure, the worker will not be protected until he actually makes a protected disclosure.

Protected disclosures

2715 Protection is only given to qualifying disclosures that have been **disclosed in an acceptable manner**. This ensures that, except in certain or exceptional circumstances, the worker does try to resolve the matter internally, or through any other appropriate channel, before going public with any qualifying disclosure. Qualifying disclosures that are disclosed in the correct manner are called "protected disclosures".

2716 **Standard** protected disclosures are made to the following (s 43A ERA 1996):
- an employer or appropriate person;
- an appropriate public authority; or
- a legal adviser.

Only in special cases can there be **wider disclosure** to other bodies or persons, most often in the form of publicity.

Regardless of how the disclosure is made it must be made in **good faith**. Consequently, a disclosure which is predominantly motivated by the worker's personal antagonism towards his employer, that is, to "advance a grudge", will not be made in good faith (*Street v Derbyshire Unemployed Workers' Centre* [2004] IRLR 687, CA). Similarly, an employee who brings an "opportunistic" whistleblowing claim in order to strengthen an otherwise weak constructive unfair dismissal claim will not be acting in good faith (*Milne v The Link Asset and Security Co Ltd* [2005] UKEAT 0867_04_2609).

2717

Where there is an allegation that an employee has not made a disclosure in good faith, the **burden of proof** rests on the employer to prove this allegation (*Bachnak v Emerging Markets Partnership (Europe) Ltd* [2006] UKEAT 0288_05_2701). There must be cogent evidence provided to support such an allegation and the more serious the allegation, the more cogent the evidence required (*Lucas v Chichester Diocesan Housing Association Ltd* [2005] UKEAT 0713_04_0702). The allegation must be brought explicitly to the employee's attention in advance of any hearing, for example, in the employer's response to the tribunal claim (¶9520), or in witness statements exchanged before the hearing itself (*Roberts v Valley Rose Ltd t/a Fernbank Nursing Home* [2006] UKEAT 0394_06_3110), and not just in oral submissions made at the tribunal. In considering such an allegation, importance should be placed by the tribunal on the chronology of events leading up to the disclosure, together with the impression given by witnesses.

EXAMPLE
Allegation of bad faith raised only at hearing
In *Lucas v Chichester Diocesan Housing Association Ltd*, an employer sought to discredit an employee who claimed to have brought her allegations in good faith. The suggestion of bad faith was made for the first time in closing submissions at the tribunal hearing, and the employee had no real opportunity to reply.

Allegation of bad faith raised in advance of hearing
In *Roberts v Valley Rose Ltd t/a Fernbank Nursing Home*, an allegation of bad faith was raised briefly in the employer's defence to the claim, and more extensively in a witness statement which was sent to the claimant 5 days in advance of the hearing. The EAT held that the allegation had been properly raised in advance.

The protected act is **limited to the act of disclosure itself**, rather than other conduct, even if it is connected in some way to the disclosure. The statutory whistleblowing provisions do not protect any act which is aimed at establishing the reasonableness of the employee's belief (*Bolton School v Evans* [2007] IRLR 140, CA).

2718

EXAMPLE In *Bolton School v Evans*, a technology teacher informed his school that its computer system was inadequate and would enable students to hack in and gain access to confidential information. When the school failed to address the teacher's concerns, he hacked into the system himself to illustrate the problem. Although he informed the school about his actions, the entire system had to be shut down. The teacher received a written warning and subsequently resigned, claiming detriment (i.e. the written warning) and constructive unfair dismissal on the grounds he made a protected disclosure. The Court of Appeal found in favour of the school. As the disciplinary action taken by the school related to the teacher's actions rather than his disclosure, his actions were not protected.

B. Acceptable methods of disclosure

Disclosures should be made to the employer especially if there is an appropriate internal procedure to facilitate this. Barring this, disclosure can be made to an appropriate public authority or, in certain circumstances and if exceptionally serious, to the public.

2725

If a worker is concerned about the implications of a relevant failure he knows about or suspects, he can seek **legal advice and guidance**. Qualifying disclosures made in such a manner are protected (s 43D ERA 1996). Therefore, if a worker is uncertain as to his rights, whether the information he has is a qualifying disclosure or which, if any, of the following disclosures to make, he can seek legal advice without recourse from his employer. For example, if an employer finds out that a worker has gone to a legal adviser and fears that as a result of the advice the worker will make a public disclosure, it is possible that he may dismiss the worker before he has time to act. In such cases, any qualifying disclosure the worker makes to the adviser is protected and the employer cannot dismiss the worker because of it.

1. Internal disclosure

2730 A qualifying disclosure is protected if it is disclosed to the **employer** (s 43C ERA 1996).

Disclosures **should be made** to the employer, especially if there is an appropriate **whistleblowing policy**, unless another method of disclosure can be justified. Indeed, if there is an adequate policy, it will be difficult for a worker to show that he could have reasonably believed that he would have been victimised for making a disclosure to his employer.

A whistleblowing policy **should cover** how different types of worker can disclose internally or externally to an appropriate person. For example, a different procedure may be appropriate for agency or self-employed workers compared to employees. Further, it may be necessary to vary the person to whom a disclosure should be made, depending on the status of the worker and the type or seriousness of the allegation. For example, a senior manager may require disclosure to a non-executive director if the allegations relate to an alleged malpractice by senior management. If the policy requires disclosure to a person other than the employer, the worker will be treated as if he made the disclosure to his employer. The policy should also make it clear that malpractice in the workplace is a matter that will be taken seriously by the employer and it should seek to encourage employees to discuss any genuine suspicions they have.

Employers must ensure that such policies are **communicated** to their workers so that they are aware of the relevant procedures if they need to make a qualifying disclosure.

Disclosures not relating to employer

2731 Where the worker reasonably believes that the relevant failure relates solely or mainly to:
– the conduct of a person other than his employer; or
– any other matter for which a person other than his employer has legal responsibility,

it should be made to that **other person**.

> EXAMPLE If a supplier is regularly supplying less than the agreed amount to the employer, the worker may make a disclosure to the supplier and gain protection. However, if the worker discovers that the supplier and his employer are defrauding HMRC over supplies then his disclosure will only be protected if it is made to his employer, and disclosure to the supplier alone will not give the worker protection.

2. Disclosure to a public authority

2735 A qualifying disclosure is protected if it is made to an **appropriate** public authority (s 43F ERA 1996). There are a number of regulators, commissioners and watchdogs which have been specified as an appropriate public authority for disclosures within their remits (SI 1999/1549 as amended). For example, the Secretary of State for Business, Innovation and Skills (for disclosures regarding fraud, and other misconduct, in relation to companies, investment businesses, insurance businesses or multi-level marketing schemes (and similar trading schemes); insider dealing; and consumer safety) and the Director of the Serious Fraud Office (for disclosures regarding serious or complex fraud).

To be protected, the worker must also **reasonably believe** that the information falls within the remit of that public authority and that the information disclosed, and any allegations contained in it, are substantially true.

MEMO POINTS The list of these appropriate public authorities and **relevant contact details** can be found at flmemo.co.uk/em2735

3. Public disclosure

In the **following circumstances**, a qualifying disclosure to the public or any other body is protected if, at the time the worker makes the disclosure (s 43G ERA 1996): **2740**
– he reasonably believes that he will be subject to a detriment (i.e. victimised) if he discloses to his employer;
– there is no appropriate public authority and he reasonably believes that it is likely that evidence relating to the relevant failure will be concealed or destroyed if he makes a disclosure to his employer; or
– he has previously made a disclosure of substantially the same information to his employer.

However, the following **conditions** must be satisfied: **2741**
1. the worker must reasonably believe that the information disclosed and any allegations contained in it are substantially true;
2. it must be reasonable in all the circumstances for the worker to disclose in this manner. In determining reasonableness, particular regard is given to:
– the identity of the person to whom the disclosure is made;
– the seriousness of the relevant failure;
– whether the relevant failure is continuing or is likely to occur in the future;
– whether the disclosure is made in breach of a duty of confidentiality owed by the employer to any other person. For example, where a doctor's receptionist believes he has discovered a malpractice and disclosure would breach patients' rights to privacy; and
– any action by the employer or appropriate person that has been taken or should have reasonably been taken where there has been a previous disclosure of substantially the same information. In assessing the reasonableness of the employer's response to the previous disclosure, a tribunal will look at whether the worker complied with any employer policy on whistleblowing; and
3. the disclosure must not be for purposes of personal gain. Therefore, the main motive for selling a story about a relevant failure must not be to make money. This does not preclude the worker receiving money for his information if he can show that his main motivation was that he was acting in the public interest rather than out of self-interest. Naturally, this will be a question of degree and a worker may find it harder to convince a court or tribunal that his motivation was a public duty to see justice done if he sells his story for a large sum of money (for instance to a tabloid newspaper) where there were other ways which would have been just as, or more, effective for disclosing the information.

EXAMPLE In *Smith v Ministry of Defence* ET cases 1401537 and 1401899/04, MOD security guards were dismissed for gross misconduct after they had contacted the press to object to working with a colleague who had been convicted of indecently assaulting a child. The tribunal found that their disclosure to the press was not made "in good faith"; the disclosure was motivated not by concern for children's safety but by their revulsion at having to work with their colleague. They should have used the MOD's whistleblowing procedure or approached the nursery or OFSTED. For a disclosure to the press to have been made in good faith, there must be special features, such as a high degree of urgency or an inability to raise concerns properly through other avenues.

Disclosure of an exceptionally serious nature

If the relevant failure is of an exceptionally serious nature, wider public disclosure can occur at any time (s 43H ERA 1996). What is exceptionally serious is a matter of judgement and the worker will most likely need to show the matter was so serious that it was in the public interest to disclose the information in this manner. Nevertheless the conditions for public **2742** disclosure have to be satisfied, though the requirement of reasonableness will be easier to satisfy on the consideration of all the circumstances. In such situations, particular regard is given to the identity of the person to whom the disclosure is made.

> EXAMPLE In *Collins v The National Trust*, ET case 2507255/05, an employee who was dismissed after he disclosed to the press a report about the risk to the public of a contaminated site was held to have been automatically unfairly dismissed under the statutory whistleblowing provisions.
> The tribunal held that the employee's disclosure was made in good faith, he reasonably believed that the information disclosed was substantially true, it was reasonable in all the circumstances for him to disclose the information to the press and the relevant failures (i.e. the danger to the environment and the health and safety of the public) were of an exceptionally serious nature.

C. Protection and remedies

2760 A protected disclosure must not result in the worker being disciplined and/or dismissed. A worker **cannot be** held in **breach of contract** if he makes a protected disclosure, as it is not a breach of his implied duty of fidelity and any express term that purports to make such a disclosure an express breach is void.

2761 Further, a worker has legal protection from any **detrimental acts or omissions** (i.e. victimisation) by his employer which have occurred as a result of a protected disclosure and any dismissal for a reason connected with a protected disclosure in relation to an employee will be automatically unfair. However, unlike in discrimination cases, the employer is not vicariously liable for acts of victimisation carried out by its employees (*NHS Manchester v Fecitt and ors* [2011] EWCA Civ 1190).

> EXAMPLE In *NHS Manchester v Fecitt and ors*, three nurses raised concerns as to the qualifications of a colleague which amounted to a protected disclosure. Following the disclosure, the claimants suffered poor treatment by some colleagues, including a death threat, and investigations into this treatment were held to have been inadequate. The situation at work became increasingly difficult and rival factions were established, with the claimants' supporters on one side and supporters of the nurse they had complained about on the other. Two of the claimants were redeployed and the other was simply not offered any further work (this was a substantial part of the "detriment" of which the claimants complained). The tribunal held that these detriments occurred as a result of the dysfunctional work situation rather than as a result of the protected disclosures. The Court upheld the tribunal's decision: there is no direct liability for employees who perform acts of victimisation in whistleblowing cases (as there is in discrimination cases) so the employer cannot be held vicariously liable. As the tribunal had been satisfied that there were genuine reasons for the treatment other than the disclosure for the detrimental acts complained of the tribunal's original decision was restored.

> MEMO POINTS The **disclosures** may occur **before the whistleblowing rules came into force** as long as the detrimental act/omission or dismissal occurred when the rules were in force (i.e. after 2 July 1999) (*Miklaszewicz v Stolt Offshore Ltd* [2002] IRLR 344, CS; *Meteorological Office v Edgar* [2001] UKEAT 1448_00_1406). This is because although the disclosure was not protected at the time it was made, it is a protected disclosure, and the employer should know it was protected when he acts as a result of it and causes the employee to suffer a detriment or dismissal.
> This is most likely to occur when there is a long train of events/conduct stretching over a number of years. Naturally, though, as a matter of proof, the longer ago the disclosure is, the harder it may be for the employee to prove that a future act of detriment or dismissal is in relation to it.

2762 The **reason** or principal reason for the detriment or dismissal is a question of fact and may be established by direct evidence or inference. Where the reason for a dismissal is disputed, once the employee has given some evidence in support of his claim that the reason for the employer's actions was because he made a protected disclosure, the burden of proof moves to the employer to prove that his reason or principal reason was not because of the protected disclosure (*Kuzel v Roche Products Ltd* [2008] EWCA Civ 380). If the tribunal is not satisfied that the employer has proved this, it may conclude that the reason put forward by the employee is the true reason. On reviewing all the evidence, it is also open to the tribunal to conclude that another reason not put forward by either party is the actual reason for the treatment. With all types of detriment, what is important is for the tribunal to determine what was in the **employer's mind at the time** of the act or omission (*NHS Manchester v Fecitt and ors* [2011] EWCA Civ 1190).

Right not to suffer a detriment

A worker has the right not to be subject to any detriment by any act, or a deliberate failure to act, on the ground that he made a protected disclosure, for example he has been passed over for promotion (s 47B ERA 1996). The Court of Appeal has held that whistleblowers are protected against such a detriment not only during employment, but also **after the employment has ended** (*Woodward v Abbey National plc* [2006] IRLR 677, CA).

2763

> MEMO POINTS What amounts to a "**detriment**" is not defined by the ERA 1996, but case law on discrimination has held that it is whether a reasonable worker would feel he has been disadvantaged by reason of his employer's acts (¶5279).

If the worker has suffered a detriment he can bring a **claim** to the employment tribunal. The complaint must be **made before** the end of 3 months beginning with the date of the detrimental act/failure to act, or, where the last act was part of a series of similar acts or failures, the date of the last of such acts or omissions.

2766

Whether acts are of a **series of similar acts or failures**, i.e. whether there is significant linkage between the acts, will depend on all the circumstances surrounding the acts, and can only be decided on the basis of evidence (*Arthur v London Eastern Railway Ltd t/a One Stansted Express* [2007] IRLR 58, CA). Once all the facts have been ascertained, the tribunal will decide whether the acts are linked by looking at who caused the detriments and what their intent was in doing so, whether the acts were concerted or organised, and other factual questions of this type.

> EXAMPLE In *Arthur v London Eastern Railway Ltd t/a One Stansted Express*, a rail worker suffered assaults at work on 31 March, 30 May and 4 September 2001. He brought various complaints against his employer and made disclosures. He then claimed to have suffered detriments involving 12 different people continuously between September 2001 and April 2004, when he submitted a complaint to a tribunal. The employer argued that the majority of these complaints were not linked, and occurred long before the 3-month deadline. The tribunal and the EAT did not hear evidence of the complaint, but ruled that it was out of time. The Court of Appeal found that the full claim should have been allowed to come either to a full hearing, or alternatively, if a pre-trial hearing was required, the hearing should have taken evidence as to the claimed linkage between the various events.

If it is not reasonably practicable for the complaint to be brought within 3 months, the **tribunal** can **extend** this period as it considers reasonable (s 48(3) ERA 1996).

If the tribunal finds the complaint well-founded, it can make (ss 48(1A), 49 ERA 1996):
– a **declaration** to that effect; and
– if appropriate, an award of **compensation** to be paid by the employer.

2767

The **amount** of compensation is the amount the tribunal considers just and equitable in all the circumstances, having regard to (s 49(2)(5) ERA 1996):
– the victimisation suffered; and
– any loss which resulted from the victimisation. Loss includes any expenses reasonably incurred or the loss of any benefit because of the victimisation, though the worker has a duty to mitigate his loss as far as possible.

Detriment under the whistleblowing legislation is a form of discrimination and, consequently, the guidelines laid down in *Vento* (*Vento v Chief Constable of West Yorkshire Police (No 2)*, ¶5751) will apply with regard to the level of compensation for injury to feelings (*Virgo Fidelis Senior School v Boyle* [2004] IRLR 268, EAT followed in *Commisioner of Police of the Metropolis v Shaw* [2011] UKEAI 0125_11_2911).

> EXAMPLE In *Commisioner of Police of the Metropolis v Shaw*, an officer in the Metropolitan Police reported dishonest conduct by a colleague. As a result of his complaint, the colleague and his superior officer had him suspended on unfounded disciplinary charges, which were collusively supported

by a more senior officer. The charges were in due course dropped, but the officer was unable to return to his old department and had to move to a new role which he found less congenial and suffered lasting distress and disillusionment at the way he had been treated. His whistleblowing detriment claim was upheld and the Tribunal awarded £37,000 compensation, comprising £17,000 for injury to feelings and £20,000 for aggravated damages. The EAT confirmed that compensation for whistleblowing claims should be assessed on the same basis as awards in discrimination cases, following an earlier EAT authority on this point (*Virgo Fidelis Senior School v Boyle*). However, it went on to hold that the award of £20,000 for aggravated damages was outside the recognised range for such awards. Further, it was also abnormal that an award of aggravated damages should exceed the award for injury to feelings. The Tribunal had made errors in assessing the level of aggravated damages; including focusing entirely on the seriousness of the employer's conduct rather than on the impact on the employee and thus the tribunal had wrongly introduced a punitive element. Aggravated damages are compensatory only and represent an aspect of compensation for injury to feelings rather than a wholly separate head of damages. The overall figure of £37,000 was excessive. The award was reduced to £30,000, of which £7,500 would be identified as aggravated damages.

2768 Where an employee has suffered a detriment and has then resigned claiming **constructive unfair dismissal**, compensation for injury to feelings in respect of the detriment should be assessed up to the date of dismissal (not the point at which the employer's conduct amounts to a breach of contract) (*Melia v Magna Kansei Ltd* [2006] IRLR 117, CA).

If the detrimental act **results in dismissal**, workers who do not have a contract of employment will be entitled to the same level of compensation as if they were an employee who has been unfairly dismissed (see below) (s 49(6) ERA 1996).

The tribunal will take into consideration the extent to which the worker caused or **contributed** to the detriment claimed and will reduce the amount of compensation if it considers that it is just and equitable to do so.

Right not to be unfairly dismissed

2769 Any **dismissal** of an employee due to the making of a protected disclosure will be automatically unfair (s 103A ERA 1996) (¶8390). As a result, no qualifying period of continuous employment is necessary (s 108(3)(ff) ERA 1996). An employee will also be unfairly dismissed, if the reason or principal reason for selecting him for **redundancy** is that he made a protected disclosure (s 105(6A) ERA 1996).

> MEMO POINTS Non-employee workers (¶13) who are so dismissed or so selected for redundancy should rely on the right not to suffer a detriment (see above).

2770 The employee can also claim **interim relief** and this will be given if the tribunal considers it likely that he will succeed at the full hearing (ss 128-129 ERA 1996) (¶8700). If so, the tribunal will order the employer to continue his contract by reinstating him or re-engaging him on similar terms and conditions. "Likely" in the context of whistleblowing claims should be taken to mean that the claimant has a "pretty good" chance of succeeding in the final hearing (*Dandpat v The University of Bath and anor* [2009] UKEAT 0408_09_1011).

2771 The amount of **compensation** that can be awarded, if the complaint is successful, is uncapped (s 124(1A) ERA 1996 as amended by Public Interest Disclosure (Compensation) Regulations SI 1999/1548). Like with unfair dismissals under the general scheme, the manner of the dismissal will not of itself attract compensation (i.e. there is no award for injury to feelings and aggravated damages) (¶8615). This can be contrasted to a claim for detriment short of dismissal where such damages are included (¶2767). As a result an employee may also bring a complaint that he has also been subject to pre-termination detriments as well as having been unfairly dismissed.

CHAPTER 10

Remuneration

OUTLINE

SECTION 1 **Pay**		2805
I	Elements of remuneration	2810
A	Remuneration package	2810
1	Basic pay	2815
2	Overtime	2825
3	Bonuses, incentive payments and commissions	2828
4	Benefits and employee share schemes	2837
B	Other types of payment	2845
II	Level	2860
A	Right to a minimum wage	2865
	Minimum wage rates	2869
1	Calculation of average hourly rate	2870
	a Gross pay in pay reference period	2875
	b Deductions from gross pay	2880
	c Total number of hours worked	2885
2	Compliance	2900
	Records	2900
	Enforcement	2903
3	Remedies	2910
B	A week's pay	2920
	Maximum limits	2923
1	Type of calculation	2930
	a Employees with normal working hours	2935
	b Employees with no normal working hours	2950
2	Calculation date	2955
III	Payment	2980
A	Forms and rate of pay	2980
B	Itemised pay statements	2985
	Remedies	2988
IV	Deductions	3000
A	Lawful deductions	3005
1	Contractual deductions	3005
	Refusal or failure to work	3007
	Withholding of goodwill	3009
	Overpayments	3010
2	Statutory deductions	3015
	a Attachment of earnings	3017
	b Student loan deductions	3030
	c Union subscriptions	3035
B	Unauthorised deductions	3050
1	General rule	3055
2	Deductions not protected	3065
3	Special protection for retail employment	3070
4	Remedies	3080
SECTION 2 **Tax**		3100
I	Earnings	3100
A	Regular earnings	3100
B	Lump sum payments	3115
1	On commencement of employment	3120
2	On variation of duties or earnings	3121
3	On termination	3122
4	Specific provisions	3132
	Redundancy payments	3132
	Payments in lieu of notice	3134
	Garden leave	3137
	Benefits from an employer-financed retirement benefit scheme	3138
	Restrictive covenants	3140
	Outplacement counselling for losing employment	3141
	Unfair dismissal compensation	3143
	Legal costs	3144
II	Benefits and expenses	3145
A	Benefits	3150
1	Non-taxable benefits	3155
2	Taxable benefits	3190
	a Benefits chargeable on all employees	3200
	b Benefits charged on relevant employees only	3215
B	Expenses	3265
1	General principles	3265
2	Tax deductible employment expenses	3278
3	Expenses subject to special rules	3284
	a Travel and subsistence	3285
	b Other expenses	3322

III	Share schemes	3340	Normal retirement date	3412
IV	Employment income taxable in the UK	3370	1 Registered schemes	3420
			2 Unregistered schemes	3425
	a Whether taxable in the UK?	3380	B Employer obligations	3430
	b Treatment of expenses	3390	Duty to members	3430
			Duty to trustees	3432
			Discrimination	3435
SECTION 3 **Pensions**		3400	Data protection compliance	3445
			Information and consultation requirements	3448
I	Occupational pension schemes	3405	C Compliance	3460
A	General principles	3410	Remedies	3461

2800 Remuneration can be made up of the following: basic pay, overtime, bonuses, incentive payments and commissions, benefits, employee share schemes and a pension scheme. Employees may also be entitled to sick pay (see chapter 13) and maternity, adoption or paternity pay (see chapter 14). Further, an employee may be entitled to guaranteed payments for workless days (see chapter 23) and medical suspension payments if prohibited from attending work for health reasons (see chapter 15).

This chapter details what is permissible in the remuneration package, the minimum level of pay, the forms and rate of pay, deductions from pay, and taxation.

MEMO POINTS   HM Revenue and Customs (HMRC) was previously called the Inland Revenue. This chapter refers to HMRC material and with regard to this the following abbreviations are used: SP (Statement of Practice) and ESC (Extra Statutory Concession).

SECTION 1

Pay

2805 Employers and workers are **free to negotiate** and agree terms on remuneration, subject to certain employment rights such as the right to equal pay and the right to be paid at least the national minimum wage (ERA 1996; National Minimum Wage Act 1998; Part-time Workers (Prevention of Less Favourable Treatment) Regulations SI 2000/1551; Part-Time Workers (Prevention of Less Favourable Treatment) Regulations SI 2002/2034; Working Time Regulations SI 1998/1833; EqA 2010).

2806 The employee has an implied **right to be paid** in accordance with his express contractual terms as long as he is ready and willing to work or he is absent due to illness or other unavoidable circumstances. Any **failure to pay** will give rise to a breach of contract. Further, employees have **special protection** against their employer making unauthorised deductions, which includes unlawful deductions and deductions made in an incorrect manner. Only in certain specific circumstances can employers make (for example a contractual term allowing for deduction of wages due to unauthorised absences), or be required to make (for example due to an attachment of earnings order), **lawful deductions** from their employees' remuneration.

2808 Employees and directors must pay **income tax** on their earnings (i.e. tax on the sums that legislation defines as employment income and including certain lump sum payments made on commencement, termination or variation) and on the value of most benefits. Lump sum payments on termination or contract variation that are not earnings (for example compensation for breach of contract on termination) will be taxable under a special provision which allows for certain exceptions, including the exemption of the first £30,000 from tax. The payment of expenses by the employer is also subject to tax but employees/directors will be able to claim a deduction for business expenses that are incurred wholly, exclusively and necessarily in the performance of their duties. Special rules apply to certain expenses, for example travel expenses.

For payroll and NIC issues, see chapter 20.

> MEMO POINTS **Pay** is used here to refer to wages or salary. **Remuneration** is used to denote all employment income (i.e. pay, overtime, bonuses and benefits) and pension rights. For tax purposes, the term "**earnings**" is used to denote all chargeable employment income, which can include additional elements such as certain lump sum payments on commencement, variation or termination of employment.

I. Elements of remuneration

A. Remuneration package

Depending on the type and seniority of the employee and the size and type of his employer's business, his remuneration will **include** one or more of the following:
- basic pay (¶2815);
- overtime (¶2825);
- performance-related additional payments, for example bonuses, incentive payments and commissions (¶2828);
- allowances, for example a daily allowance, London weighting allowance or a standby allowance;
- benefits, for example health cover (¶2837);
- permanent health insurance (¶4200);
- employee share schemes (¶2839); and
- a pension scheme (¶3400).

2810

1. Basic pay

The employee has an implied right to be paid in accordance with his **express contractual terms** as long as he is **ready and willing to work** or he is absent due to illness or other unavoidable circumstances (*Miles v Wakefield Metropolitan District Council* [1987] IRLR 193, HL). As a result, pay can only be validly withheld or deducted if there is a specific term of the contract that allows for the deduction, and the burden of proof will be on the employer to show he is entitled to do so.

2815

> EXAMPLE
> 1. In *Beveridge v KLM UK Ltd* [2000] IRLR 765, EAT, after a long period of sickness absence, B wanted to return to work and produced a doctor's certificate to show she was fit for work. However, KLM refused to take her back until their own doctor was satisfied that she was fit for work. The EAT held that she had an implied right to be paid from when she was willing to work and had been certified as fit to do so.
> 2. In *Miller v Hamworthy Engineering Ltd* [1986] IRLR 461, EAT, M's employer, H, introduced a system of "work sharing" as an alternative to immediate redundancies. This had to be agreed by M's union each time H wanted to decrease the hours of work, in which case M's normal contractual terms on remuneration were waived. The EAT held that M's contractual terms were not waived when the reductions to his working hours were not accepted by his union and he was ready and willing to work under his existing terms.

2816 If, on the other hand, the employee is **not ready and willing to work** or declines to perform part of his job, his employer is entitled to withhold wages for the period in question without terminating his contract of employment and without relying on any right to damages for breach of contract.

> MEMO POINTS In recent years, heavy **snow** fall has made it impossible for some employees to get into their place of work; unless the employer is willing to allow the individual to work from home, or to work unpaid overtime to make up for the missed time, the employer may withhold pay on the basis that the employee did not present himself at work ready and willing to work. Employers can, of course, also choose to continue to pay employees in such circumstances if their employees genuinely cannot attend their place of work.

2817 If the amount of pay is **not expressly stated**, there is an implied term which gives the employee the right to be reasonably remunerated for work done if it can be shown that there was an **intention to pay** (*Way v Latilla* [1937] 3 All ER 759). This is called the "quantum meruit" principle.

This principle has also been used to quantify a contractual right to a **bonus** (*Powell v Braun* [1954] 1 WLR 401).

2818 Employers can include express contractual terms to **increase or decrease pay**. Pay can be validly increased or decreased by **collective bargaining** where the relevant collective agreement is incorporated into the workers' contracts. If the worker wishes to contest that the terms have not been incorporated into his contract, he must make a **clear, prompt and continuing objection** (*Henry v London General Transport Services Ltd* [2002] EWCA Civ 488).

Pay increases

2821 It is useful to expressly state whether **pay reviews** and increases are contractual or discretionary.

Where the **contract is silent**, the courts are reluctant to imply a contractual right to a pay increase and past annual increases do not give rise to such a right (*Murco Petroleum Ltd v Forge* [1978] IRLR 50, EAT).

2822 Most employers **provide salary reviews** on an annual basis with a right to an increase subject to their **discretion**. In such cases, the employee does not have a right to an increase. However, if the employer decides not to exercise his discretion, he must nevertheless ensure that he did not act arbitrarily, capriciously or unfairly in not increasing pay (*F C Gardner Ltd v Beresford Ltd* [1978] IRLR 63, EAT).

2823 Some employers give **contractual automatic increases** depending on length of service, qualifications, age, and banding/grade of the employee. More rarely (and most often with regard to senior employees), employers may provide a contractual right to an annual increase which is linked to inflation and calculated by reference to an appropriate index (such as the retail prices index).

2. Overtime

2825 In the absence of an express or implied contractual term that provides for overtime (paid or unpaid) there is no obligation to work overtime. On the other hand if an employee voluntarily works longer hours in the absence of an express contractual term, he has no general implied right to be paid for the extra hours worked (*Ali v Christian Salvesen Food Services Ltd* [1997] IRLR 17, CA).

> EXAMPLE In *Ali v Christian Salvesen Food Services Ltd*, A was contractually entitled to be paid overtime once he had worked a set number of hours in his pay year. The Court held he was not entitled to paid overtime when he was dismissed during a pay year, as he had not yet reached this number, and the agreement was silent as to what should happen in such circumstances.

2826 It is, therefore, necessary to have an **express contractual term** covering when overtime is allowable and the terms of entitlement. Contractual overtime is usually paid for extra hours or for unsociable working hours and is often expressed as a multiple of the employee's hourly rate, for example one and a half times the hourly rate. However, sometimes **time off in lieu** is given as an alternative and any contractual terms should set this out.

Such terms must at least be evidenced in writing (¶1400).

3. Bonuses, incentive payments and commissions

Commission payments are regular contractual payments which depend on the employee's performance. These may be based on a percentage, for example on a percentage of sales received, or on set amounts, for example a fixed amount per sale. Usually, commission payments are additional to a basic salary and may form a substantial part of the employee's remuneration. Occasionally, the employee's salary may be based solely on commission payments.

2828

Bonuses and incentive payments are usually offered as a reward for performance and/or loyalty, and will usually be in the form of additional payments or awards such as share options.

2829

Bonuses are usually calculated on an individual basis based on the **employee's performance** in the required period (for example, on a yearly basis as a result of an appraisal of his year's work). Alternatively, bonuses can be based on the **company's performance** or the employee's group/department's performance.

In contrast, **incentive schemes** will usually set individual, group or company targets which will need to be achieved in the required period before any payments can be made.

> MEMO POINTS 1. The High Court has held that employees were not in breach of their **implied duty of trust and confidence** or fiduciary duties by not giving up payments negotiated when times were better (*Fish and anor v Dresdner Kleinwort Ltd* [2009] IRLR 1035, HC).
> 2. In a potentially interesting development, the High Court allowed a claim to go to trial on the basis that there was a real prospect of success that there was an **implied term of co-operation** in the claimant's contract of employment that the employer would co-operate in, and not prevent, the employee achieving his bonuses (*Takacs v Barclays Services Jersey Ltd* [2006] IRLR 877, HC). However, it has been reported that this case has been settled out of court. A court decision on these issues will now have to wait for another time.

Employers may wish to state the **terms** as to when any payments will be made, for example that the employee must still be in employment (which may also state without notice of termination having been given on either side) at the date of payment (which can be later than the period to which it relates (usually the company's financial year)). These should be clearly expressed.

2830

> EXAMPLE
> 1. In *Andrew Locke v Candy and Candy Ltd* [2010] EWCA Civ 1350, the employee was dismissed and given 6 months' salary in lieu of notice. This meant that the dismissal occurred a matter of weeks before the employee would have been entitled to receive a guaranteed bonus payment which, according to his employment contract, was only payable if he was employed when it fell due. In a majority 2:1 judgment, it was held that he was not entitled to receive his bonus.
> 2. In *GX Networks Ltd v Greenland* [2010] EWCA Civ 784, an employer ran a sales incentive scheme which included an element of additional reward for salespeople who exceeded their targets. The incentive scheme was contractual and included a power to cap commission on sales above target levels. This power was stated to be exercisable "by exception only". An employee, G, had a particularly successful year and exceeded her target by more than 200%, which would have entitled her to additional commission of £16,503. Rather than increase her target the employer decided to cap her commission on over target sales. G made a claim for the full commission. The Court of Appeal held that the words "by exception only" meant that the power to cap commission could only be used in exceptional circumstances. As the scheme was designed to reward success in making sales, G's good year could not be regarded as exceptional. The power to cap could not therefore be exercised and she was entitled to her full commission.

Such express terms are also important as the courts will not imply such terms, for example the High Court has held that it would not imply a term that the employee must be in employment at the date of payment (*Rutherford v Seymour Pierce Ltd* [2010] IRLR 606, HC). Likewise, it has also held that a term in severance agreements which required employees to act in the best interests of the company, so long as they remained employed, did not create an implied term that they had a duty to give up the payments as being in the best interests of the company when its poor financial position was discovered (*Fish and anor v Dresdner Kleinwort Ltd* [2009] IRLR 1035, HC).

EXAMPLE

1. In *Rutherford v Seymour Pierce Ltd*, a sales manager in the financial services sector was dismissed without notice. He brought proceedings for breach of contract seeking payment of a discretionary bonus in respect of the period up to his dismissal. The payment date for that period fell after the date of his dismissal. The employer resisted the claim, arguing that a term should be implied into the contract that an employee must be employed on the payment date to be entitled to receive the bonus. The High Court rejected this argument: the employer had not established any grounds for implying a term that he was not entitled to a bonus. In particular, it was not an obvious omission, nor necessary to give effect to the agreement, nor was there any evidence that the practice was customary in the City of London. Further, because the employer had not considered giving the claimant a bonus at all, it had not exercised its discretion and the court was therefore free to award such bonus as it thought fit.
2. In *Fish and anor v Dresdner Kleinwort Ltd*, five bankers were dismissed in the wake of the banking crisis. They claimed severance payments and bonuses under the terms of severance agreements which had been agreed as a consequence of the sale of the bank employing them and which the new management subsequently wanted to substantially reduce because of a later realisation of the bank's poor financial position. When they applied for summary judgment for the amounts claimed, the High Court allowed the application:
– holding that a term in each of their severance agreements which required the employees to act in the best interests of the company, so long as they remained employed, did not mean that they had a duty to give up the payments as being in the best interests of the company; and
– rejecting arguments that the employees were in breach of their implied duty of trust and confidence or fiduciary duties by not giving up payments negotiated when times were better.

However, such terms must not be **discriminatory** (*Gus Home Shopping Ltd v Green and McLaughlin* [2001] IRLR 75, EAT; *Caisse Nationale d'Assurance Vieillesse des Travailleurs Salaries v Thibault* [1998] IRLR 399, ECJ).

EXAMPLE

Discriminatory
In *Gus Home Shopping Ltd v Green and McLaughlin*, GHS introduced a discretionary **loyalty bonus** largely contingent on the effective transfer of the department (in which G and M worked) over the preceding 6 months. The EAT held that GHS discriminated against G and M when it disqualified M from receiving a bonus and reduced G's bonus because they were absent on maternity leave/due to a pregnancy-related sickness during this period.

Not discriminatory
However, in *Lewen v Denda* [2000] IRLR 67, a bonus that was calculated by reference to **actual performance** or contributions was not held to be discriminatory in relation to a worker on maternity leave.

2831 Schemes can be **contractual**, i.e. the employee will have a right to the payment/share options as long as he has satisfied any express conditions. In some circumstances employees may wish to negotiate contractual bonuses, sometimes with a guaranteed element, for example a **retention bonus** in a takeover situation.

MEMO POINTS   A claim for unlawful deduction of wages is often the preferred route to bringing a claim for breach of contract as the costs are higher in the civil courts, and a breach of contract claim can only be brought in the employment tribunal if the employment has ended and compensation is capped at £25,000 (¶¶9425+).

2832 However, most employers will normally wish to avoid any obligation to make payments, and will include an express contractual term indicating that the terms of the bonus or incentive payments may be varied. Such schemes are called **discretionary**. If an employer wishes to have the option to withdraw a bonus scheme, he should make this clear in express contractual terms otherwise, as well as incurring potential liability for a breach of contract claim, he may be liable for an unlawful deduction of wages if he does not make a payment (*Kent Management Services Ltd v Butterfield* [1992] IRLR 394, EAT; *Khatri v Cooperatieve Centrale Raiffeisen-Boerenleenbank BA* [2010] IRLR 715, CA). For example, in *Khatri* the effect of wording in a bonus clause which stated that "The Bank maintains the right to review or remove this formula linked bonus arrangement at any time" in a contract which provided for a one-off guaranteed bonus and also a contractually binding continuing performance-related bonus did not allow the employer to withdraw the scheme. The whole context of the scheme will be considered to determine the effect of the term "discretionary", for example, whether the term refers to the whole scheme or merely to a particular aspect of it, such as the amount to be paid (*Small and ors v Boots Co PLC and anor* [2009] IRLR 328, EAT). As well as being **careful as to how** a discretionary bonus **scheme is worded**, the employer must also be careful with regard to any **oral statements** he makes about the scheme. For example, in a recent High Court case concerning over 100 investment bankers, the High Court held that their employing bank was liable to pay their bonuses from a guaranteed minimum bonus pool, even though the level of the pool was guaranteed orally at a staff meeting without any written confirmation being sent to the bankers. The bank later tried to claim that the promise made at the staff meeting was binding in honour only, but the court held it was a contractually binding obligation (*Attrill and ors v Dresdner Kleinwort Ltd and Commerzbank AG* [2012] EWHC 1189). Finally, where the employer wishes a scheme to remain discretionary, he must be careful not to create a contractual entitlement by **custom and practice**; for example, he should state that he is exercising his discretion on each occasion a bonus is awarded.

EXAMPLE In *Hoyland v Asda Stores Ltd* [2006] IRLR 468, CS, the Court of Session held that the bonuses, although labelled "discretionary", were in fact contractual as they were paid on a yearly basis to all employees who met certain standards (the only thing that varied was the amount awarded).

However, the **exercise of any discretion** is not absolute and the employer must not exercise it irrationally or perversely (*Mallone v BPB Industries plc* [2002] IRLR 452, CA; *Clark v Nomura International plc* [2000] IRLR 766). Indeed, the employee is entitled to expect his employer to exercise his discretion **rationally and in good faith** (*Horkulak v Cantor Fitzgerald International* [2004] IRLR 942, CA). This applies to anticipatory as well as actual payments/awards and is part of the implied term of trust and confidence. However, the Court of Appeal has highlighted that it would take an overwhelming case to persuade a court to find that the level of a discretionary bonus payment was in fact irrational or perverse where the employer had a very wide contractual discretion, and where the industry in which the employer operated was subject to fluctuating market and labour conditions (in this case a bank) (*Commerzbank AG v Keen* [2007] IRLR 132, CA). Independent evidence would be needed in such circumstances to support the employee's claim of irrationality with regard to the size of his bonus. The Court emphasised that the only function of a court is to decide on the **legal limits with regard to any contractual discretion** and whether the employer in question had acted within or without these limits. Apart from this, it remains with the employer, not the court, to judge what he should pay his employees.

2833

If the employer **acts irrationally or perversely**, the employee will be able to bring a breach of contract claim. Further, the employee may have the right to claim that he has been constructively dismissed and claim wrongful dismissal (compensation may include an element for the "lost bonus") and unfair dismissal. The employee may also have a discrimination claim under the provisions of the Equality Act 2010 if he has been treated less favourably as a result.

Where a **bonus should have been awarded**, the court will determine what the employee would have received had his employer acted rationally and in good faith taking into account the employee's expectations as to what a reasonable employer would have awarded in the circumstances (*Horkulak v Cantor Fitzgerald International*, above). Where necessary, it will apply the quantum meruit principle (i.e. the right to be reasonably remunerated for work done) to determine the amount of the award if it is not quantified (*Powell v Braun* [1954] 1 WLR 401).

> **EXAMPLE**
>
> **Irrational or perverse exercise of discretion**
> 1. In *Mallone v BPB Industries plc*, under the rules of a share option bonus scheme, executives who ceased employment could, at certain times, still exercise options which had been awarded to them, subject to BPB's discretion to allow only a fraction of the options to be so exercised. The fraction consisted of a denominator of 36 and a numerator which was chosen by BPB. On the day of M's dismissal, BPB determined that this numerator should be zero resulting in the cancellation of his share options.
> This was held to be an irrational exercise of BPB's discretion as the options had been awarded because of good service and there was nothing in the circumstances of M's dismissal that warranted the total removal of his options.
> 2. In *Horkulak v Cantor Fitzgerald International*, H, who held a senior managerial position in a firm of brokers, resigned due to bullying and abusive behaviour which had amounted to a breach of his implied contractual term of trust and confidence. He successfully claimed damages for wrongful dismissal on the basis that had he remained in employment he would have received his discretionary annual bonus given that in the context of his employment in a high-earning and competitive activity his bonus clause was properly viewed as part of his remuneration structure. Further, he was entitled to expect that his employer would have exercised this discretion rationally and in good faith.
>
> **Acting within legal limits of discretion**
> 1. In *Commerzbank AG v Keen*, the employee, a trading manager for a bank, failed in his attempt to obtain damages for breach of contract in respect of alleged underpayments of his discretionary bonus. In this case the Court of Appeal emphasised that the employer had a very wide discretion with regard to the exercise of discretionary bonuses, and the employee had not been able to prove that the payment was irrational or perverse in an area where so much depended on the discretionary judgement of the employer in fluctuating market and labour conditions.
> 2. In *Humphreys v Norilsk Nickel International (UK) Ltd* [2010] EWHC 1867 (QB), bonuses depended on a performance scheme. Employees' performances were graded into six grades, ranging from "unsatisfactory" to "superior". The claimant was an economist, and part of his duties involved forecasting nickel prices. The employer awarded him no bonus, having graded his performance as unsatisfactory because he had inaccurately forecast prices. The employee brought a claim for a bonus, arguing that he should have been graded much higher (as he had been in previous years). The High Court held that the assessment of the employee's performance was a subjective exercise and, so long as the board of directors' decision was not irrational or made in bad faith, it could not be attacked. To claim a bonus, the employee had to show that his performance was good enough to merit a bonus contrary to the employer's assessment.

2834 **Where claims are brought** Once a discretionary bonus is **declared on certain terms**, this creates an obligation to pay it on these terms, and withholding some or all of the bonus will be an unlawful deduction of wages (¶3050) (*Tradition Securities and Futures SA v Mouradian* [2009] EWCA Civ 60). This applies equally to discretionary bonuses granted under contract and those given by custom or by an ad hoc decision (*Farrell Matthews & Weir v Hansen* [2004] UKEAT 0078_04_2610). However, where the claim is for an **unquantifiable loss** suffered, this should be brought as a breach of contract claim and not a quantifiable claim for unlawful deduction of wages (*Coors Brewers Ltd v Adcock and ors* [2007] ICR 983, CA). A **claim for unlawful deduction of wages** (¶3080) is often the preferred route to bringing a **claim for breach of contract** as the costs are higher in the civil courts, and a breach of contract claim can only be brought in the employment tribunal if the employment has ended and compensation is also capped at £25,000 (¶¶9425+).

With regard to **discriminatory terms**, where a bonus scheme is contractual, claims of unequal treatment in relation to it should be brought under the equal pay, as opposed to the sex discrimination, provisions of the Equality Act 2010 (*Hoyland v Asda Stores Ltd* [2006] IRLR 468, CS).

Best practice

2835 In **practical terms**, to ensure that a bonus scheme is fair and transparent, employers should ensure that:
– the terms of the scheme are clear and unambiguous, and set out the factors that will be taken into account in determining awards;

– the same criteria and methods of calculation are used for all employees (or specified groups of employees, for example employees, managers, and directors) covered by the scheme;
– discretionary bonuses are awarded rationally and in good faith, and not irrationally or perversely, i.e. in a manner that no reasonable employer would have done; and
– the terms are non-discriminatory.

4. Benefits and employee share schemes

2837 Employers often provide employees with benefits (called benefits in kind) as well as a basic salary and other cash payments. These may be offered as part of an offer package to entice prospective employees to work for them and to assist in the retention of staff. Certain benefits, such as private healthcare and gym membership, may also aid their employees' health and well-being.

Flexible benefit packages have increased in popularity and are typically **made up of** a set of "core benefits" provided to all staff (e.g. pension, private medical cover), with a menu of add-ons funded from the employee's total package value, for example by sacrificing other benefits (e.g. giving up a day's holiday or accepting a lower grade company car) or from deductions from salary. A points system can be used, whereby the employee is given a certain number of points that he can use to "buy" a range of benefits according to his personal requirements. A flexible benefit package scheme should be **set out** in a policy which deals with the operation and administration of the scheme (e.g. limiting the number of times employees can make changes to their options).

For a comprehensive list of the main types of benefits, see ¶3155 (for non-taxable benefits) and ¶3190 (for taxable benefits).

2838 Such benefits are generally taxable as being a **payment made other than in cash** to an employee or director (or a member of his family or household) as a result of his employment. If and how a benefit is **taxable** will depend on whether he is classed as a relevant or lower paid employee (¶3146).

> MEMO POINTS Entitlement to non-cash benefits continues during periods of maternity, adoption and paternity leave. Current HMRC guidance suggests that benefits provided via salary sacrifice should continue without any sacrifice being made from SMP, SAP or SPP/ASPP.

2839 Employers may also provide employees with **share schemes** which give their employees discounted or free shares in their company, or an option to buy the shares at a reduced rate at a later date. The **taxation** of such schemes depends on the structure of the package and whether it has HMRC approval (¶3340).

B. Other types of payment

Lump sum payments

2845 Employees may also receive lump sum payments on the **commencement, variation or termination** of their contract. Such payments are often made as compensation for the loss or surrender of rights, or instead of notice of termination. Alternatively, a lump sum payment may simply be made to reward an employee for past or future services. For tax issues, see ¶3115.

It is important to be **precise when describing payments**, especially in relation to terminating an individual's employment.

> EXAMPLE In *Publicis Consultants UK Ltd v O'Farrell* [2011] UKEAT 0430_10_2705, the employee in question was entitled to 3 months' notice, but was dismissed with only 4 days' notice. She was paid the equival-

ent of 3 months' salary, which was described in a letter as an "ex gratia payment" and as being "in excess" of her contractual entitlements. In considering her breach of contract claim, the EAT held that the payment truly had been ex gratia and that she was also entitled to her notice monies. The EAT commented that although there was no ambiguity in this case, if there had been it would have been decided in the employee's favour in accordance with the *contra preferentem* rule, as it was the employer who had drafted the letter.

Gratuities

2846 Employees may receive gratuities **from a third party**, for example waiters and waitresses are usually given tips by their customers. The employer may have in place a system whereby these gratuities are pooled in a "tronc" and then distributed between the employees. The troncmaster must deduct PAYE tax and, in some circumstances, NIC will also be due.

Compulsory service charges and gratuities that have been added to a cheque or credit card, or are otherwise distributed by the employer, will need to be administered through payroll and will form part of the employee's earnings upon which PAYE tax and NICs are due.

MEMO POINTS Since 1 October 2009, tips and gratuities cannot form any part of the employee's pay for national minimum wage purposes (¶2875).

Expenses

2847 Employees may also **incur** expenses which will be:
– reimbursed by their employer, either for specific expenses incurred or by way of an expense allowance;
– paid by them without reimbursement; or
– paid by their employer directly.

The payment of expenses by the employer is subject to tax (though expenses incurred by lower paid employees are not usually subject to tax provided they are not excessive) (¶¶3265+). However, the employee will be able to make a claim for business expenses.

Loans

2848 Employers may give their employees an advancement on their wages or loans for specific purposes, for example to go on a course or to buy a season ticket.

It is useful to have a **separate written agreement** for each loan agreement setting out the terms as these are likely to vary depending on the type of loan. Such agreements should include **terms** on:
– the amount of the loan;
– the circumstances in which it becomes repayable; and
– when the deductions are to be made, for example a percentage of the loan in each pay period until the loan is paid off, with the authority to deduct an outstanding amount if the employee leaves before the loan is completely paid off.

2849 The employer may require repayment of all or some of the **cost of a training course** if the employee leaves the company within a set period after completing the course or fails to successfully complete it. However, such costs will only be enforceable in a breach of contract claim if they are a genuine pre-estimate of loss suffered by the employer (in not having a trained employee) and not a penalty clause against the employee (*Neil v Strathclyde Regional Council* [1984] IRLR 14, CS). Whether or not there is a genuine pre-estimate of loss is a question of construction that depends on the terms and circumstances of the contract at the time the contract was made.

2850 In any event, an express clause in the contract or in a separate agreement is necessary for the employer to make a lawful deduction. Further, all loan repayments (other than for the repayment of an advancement of wages) must comply with the statutory protection against unauthorised deductions.

II. Level

2860 Employers and workers are **free to negotiate** and agree terms on pay **subject to the following rights**:
– of workers to be paid a minimum wage (¶¶2865+) and to be paid for statutory annual holiday entitlement (¶¶4000+); and
– of part-time workers not to be treated less favourably than full-time workers (¶¶1870+).

Further, those who are employees have the following **additional rights** to:
– equal pay (¶¶5600+);
– the fact that fixed-term employees should not be treated less favourably than full-time workers (¶¶1950+).
– pay for time off in certain circumstances (¶¶3910+, 3930+);
– statutory sick pay (¶4170);
– statutory maternity pay, statutory adoption pay and statutory paternity pay (¶¶4400+, 4554+, 4600+);
– guarantee payments with regard to workless days (¶¶7860+); and
– medical suspension payments if there is a risk of a health hazard (¶¶4985+).

A. Right to a minimum wage

2865 A worker's average hourly rate **must not be less** than the national minimum wage (NMW) (National Minimum Wage Act 1998 (NMWA 1998); National Minimum Wage Regulations SI 1999/584 (as amended) and referred to in this section as "the regulations").

> MEMO POINTS Where the employee is paid less than the national minimum wage, any basic and compensatory unfair dismissal awards will be based on the national minimum wage (*Paggetti v Cobb* [2002] UKEAT 136_01_2203).

2866 Any **provision** in any agreement (whether a worker's contract or not) is void in so far as it purports to **exclude or limit** the operation of the statutory rules or to preclude a person from bringing proceedings under them (s 49 NMWA 1998). However, agreements prohibiting the bringing or continuance of proceedings are permissible if they are part of a conciliation or valid compromise agreement.

Entitlement

2867 To be entitled, the **worker must** (s 1 NMWA 1998; reg 12 SI 1999/584):
– be above compulsory school leaving age; and
– work, or ordinarily work, in the UK.

2868 A **worker** is **defined widely** (s 54(3) NMWA 1998). All workers other than those who are genuinely self-employed are covered and there are specific provisions to ensure that agency workers and homeworkers are included (ss 34-35 NMWA 1998). An agency worker will be deemed to be a worker of either the agency or the client and this will depend on who pays the worker.

The following categories of workers are **excluded** (SI 1999/584 as amended):
– company directors who are office holders but not employees;
– family members working in the family business or home, so long as they are members of their employer's family (or are treated as such), live in the employer's home and share in the tasks and activities of the family (*Jose v Julio* [2011] UKEAT 0597_10_0812). This applies even where the domestic tasks are not shared out equally amongst the family, because a person receiving free meals and accommodation might be expected to carry out more household

duties. That said, the courts are mindful of this exception being used as a ruse to obtain cheap domestic labour (*Nambalat v Taher and ors* [2012] EWCA Civ 1249);
– residential members of certain religious and other communities;
– share fishermen;
– voluntary workers and volunteers;
– workers on schemes made under Government arrangements who are on state benefits rather than remuneration;
– workers participating in a trial period of work with a prospective employer under Government arrangements for the first 6 weeks;
– workers participating in the EC Youth in Action Programme;
– workers participating in the latest phase of the Leonardo da Vinci Programme;
– workers participating in the European Community Erasmus Programme or Comenius Programme;
– workers who are participating in the Programme Led Apprenticeships scheme in England, Get Ready for Work in Scotland and Steps to Employment in Wales (i.e. where a young person can obtain some work experience before moving onto a full apprenticeship); and
– workers who attend a period of work experience as part of a course of higher or further education, where the work experience placement does not exceed 1 year.

Minimum wage rates

2869 The rates **from 1 October 2012** are as follows (National Minimum Wage (Amendment) Regulations SI 2012/2397 which amends SI 1999/584):

Type of worker	Hourly rate
Standard workers	
16 to 17 years who are no longer of compulsory school age	£3.68
18 to 20 years (the "development rate")	£4.98
21 years and over (the "principal rate")	£6.19
Apprentices	
Apprentices who are in their first year of apprenticeship or under 19 (the "apprenticeship rate")	£2.65
Apprentices who are not in their first year of apprenticeship and are 19 and over	Standard worker rates according to age

> **MEMO POINTS** Many **agricultural workers** may be entitled to a higher rate under agricultural wages regulations.

These rates are likely to increase **from 1 October 2013** and will be covered in our updating service.

1. Calculation of average hourly rate

2870 In order to determine whether a worker has been paid the NMW, it is necessary to calculate his average hourly rate of pay. This is calculated in **three steps** by (reg 14 SI 1999/584):
– taking the worker's gross pay in a pay reference period;
– deducting any amounts in that period that do not count towards NMW; and
– dividing this by the total number of hours which the worker has done in that period.

If a worker's average hourly rate is below the NMW, his wages must be increased to at least the NMW for that period.

a. Gross pay in pay reference period

Gross pay

2875 Gross pay is the **gross amount of included payments** the worker receives (SI 1999/584 as amended by SI 2012/2397).

Included payments	Excluded payments
Pay	Advances of wages/salary or a loan
Bonuses and incentive payments or commissions	Extra/premium payments for overtime and shift working Service charges, tips, gratuities and cover charges [1]
Allowances attributable to worker's productivity	Allowances not attributable to worker's productivity [2]
Accommodation benefit provided by employer up to a maximum of £33.74 per week. The daily rate is £4.82. Payments made for "sleeping-in" at residential accommodation [3]	Benefits in kind (including the amount of any accommodation benefit over £33.74 per week)
Payments by worker for goods and services provided by employer where he is free to choose whether to buy	Payments by worker for goods and services provided by employer where he is required to buy (for example a bank requiring its workers to bank with it)
	Reimbursement of expenses
	Pension payments
	Payments by way of award under a suggestions scheme
	Redundancy payments
	Court/tribunal awards or similar settlements

1. Tips and gratuities paid through the employer's payroll system are no longer included (reg 5 SI 2009/1902).
2. *Aviation and Airport Services Ltd v Bellfield and ors* [2001] UKEAT 194_00_1403; *Laird v AK Stoddart Ltd* [2001] IRLR 591, EAT.
3. *Smith v Oxfordshire Learning Disability NHS Trust* [2009] UKEAT 0176_09_2406.

Pay reference period

2876 The relevant pay reference period is 1 month (reg 10(2) SI 1999/584). Where a worker is paid by reference to a shorter period (for example, weekly or hourly), it is that period. Therefore, workers who are paid monthly, weekly or hourly will have a pay reference period of 1 month, 1 week and 1 hour respectively.

Employers who pay their workers at intervals of more than a month apart, for example quarterly, have to make sure that the workers receive the NMW at least on a monthly basis.

EXAMPLE A 20 year old shop worker, A, is paid solely by commission. He works 40 hours a week and is paid weekly. He should be paid a minimum of £199.20 per week (£4.98 x 40).

	Pay reference period			
	1	2	3	4
Commission earnings	£200	£250	£200	£150
Average hourly rate of pay	£200/40	£250/40	£200/40	£150/40
	= £5.00	= £6.25	= £5.00	= £3.75

> A is paid over the NMW in his first three pay reference periods. However, his employer must increase A's pay in pay reference period 4 by £49.20 (£199.20 – £150).

Calculating gross pay in reference period

2877 The gross pay in a pay reference period is the gross pay **in that period** plus any payments earned in that period which are not paid until the **next period** (for example, where payment for overtime or commission is not calculated or paid until the next pay period) (reg 30 SI 1999/584).

2878 However, if a payment has been earned but is not paid in the period it is earned or in the next period, and is paid in a later **subsequent period**, it must be included in the calculation of gross pay in that subsequent period. Note though, there is a special rule relating to annual bonuses and a proportion of an **annual bonus** can count towards pay allocated to a previous pay period. For example, if an annual bonus is paid in December and the pay reference period is 1 month, a twelfth of the bonus can be allocated to the November pay period for NMW purposes. The rest of the bonus will count towards the NMW in December and does not affect the NMW calculations for January-October.

> MEMO POINTS Payments made in a later pay reference period are taken into account where the worker has to complete a record of the amount of work done before any entitlement to payment arises, and he has failed to submit the relevant record before the fourth working day before the end of that following pay reference period.

b. Deductions from gross pay

2880 For the purposes of NMW, the **following amounts** must be deducted from the gross pay (reg 31 SI 1999/584):
– payments that have been included in an **earlier pay reference period**;
– overtime and shift **premium payments** in so far as they are additional to the normal rate of pay; and
– payments made in respect of periods in which the worker is **absent from work** or is taking part in **industrial action**.
To **calculate the premium element** of an overtime payment, the lowest basic rate that is paid to the worker must be subtracted from the overtime payment.

2881 On the other hand, the following actual deductions made by the employer are **ignored** (reg 33 SI 1999/584):
a. tax and NIC; and
b. any deductions in respect of:
– the worker's conduct for which he is contractually liable;
– the repayment of a loan or recovery of an accidental overpayment; and
– the purchase of shares, options or other securities, or an interest in a partnership.

c. Total number of hours worked

2885 This is calculated by reference to the type of work the worker performed in the relevant pay period. The rules and calculation of hours differ for each type of work, for example certain periods of time may be excluded. Where a period of time is excluded from the calculation of the total hours, any pay that the worker may receive for excluded time is also ignored in calculating the average hourly rate.

There are four different **types of worker** identified for this purpose:
– salaried-hours workers;
– time workers;
– output workers; and

– unmeasured time workers who work unspecified hours or who do not fall into the other categories above.

Salaried-hours and time workers

A worker is a **salaried-hours** worker if he is (reg 4 SI 1999/584):
– paid an annual salary for a set basic number of minimum hours per year; and
– paid in equal instalments, for example 12 monthly or 52 weekly instalments.

A worker is a **time** worker if he (regs 3, 15 SI 1999/584):
– has set hours or times at which he is expected to work but is not paid an annual salary; or
– does piece work or commission work in set hours.

Time that is to be counted for salaried-hours workers and time workers is as follows:

2886

2887

Period of time to be counted	Salaried-hours worker	Time worker
Time required to be at work	✓	✓
Rest breaks	✓	X
Time on standby or on-call at or near the place of work (see ¶2888)	✓	✓
Absences paid at normal rate of pay	✓	X
Absences not paid at normal rate of pay and any absences due to industrial action	X	X
Time spent travelling in connection with work during normal working hours/normal range of hours	✓	✓
Commuting between home and work	X	X
Time spent on training at or away from the place of work during normal working hours	✓	✓

Time on standby or on-call at or near a place of work Determining whether or not time spent on standby or on-call constitutes working time is not a straightforward issue. The starting point is the premise that time spent on standby or on-call at or near a place of work only counts where the **worker is available** "for the purpose of doing work" (*British Nursing Association v Inland Revenue (National Minimum Wage Compliance Team)* [2003] ICR 19, CA). Workers on standby at home are also entitled to NMW for all of the hours they are available for work (for example, answering telephones calls from customers) even if they are free to undertake other activities, such as watching TV or reading when not answering calls (*British Nursing Association v Inland Revenue (National Minimum Wage Compliance Team)* [2003] ICR 19, CA). Where there is no expectation of any availability to do work, such time will not be counted (*Baxter v Titan Aviation Ltd* [2011] UKEAT 0355_10_3008; *Wray v JW Lees and Co (Brewers) Ltd* [2011] UKEAT 0102_11_1407). For example, if an employee is expected to stay clear of but within a reasonable proximity of the workplace and abstain from alcohol in order to be fit for work, for the purposes of being called into the workplace in the event of an emergency, but is otherwise able to pursue normal leisure activities, this would not be classed as being "available for work" and would therefore not count as working time, even though the employee is somewhat restricted in terms of what he can do during his free time. However, if the employee is required to be at his place of work on the off chance that he is needed, then this would count as working time.

A recent EAT case has focused on the concept of **core duties** as a way of determining whether or not a worker's time **on-call at night** counts as working time or not. The judgment stated that if a worker's on-call time does not form a part of their core duties then it does not constitute working time (see *City of Edinburgh Council v Lauder and ors* [2012] UKEAT 0048_11_2003 outlined in example 1 below). It will not always be obvious as to what constitutes core duties (for example, in *Lauder* the workers were required to be available to answer the alarm

2888

in sheltered housing if it went off in the middle of the night. The EAT held that this was not a core duty but the counter-argument has some force in that having someone there to deal with urgent situations in the middle of the night was essential). The concept of core duties is relatively new and hopefully it will be reviewed in forthcoming judgments in order to clarify just how significant an issue it is going to be in determining whether time counts as working time or not.

> EXAMPLE
> **Time counted for NMW purposes**
> 1. In *South Manchester Abbeyfield Society Ltd v Hopkins and anor*, a night-sleeper in a residential care home who had a responsibility throughout the night for those present in the home was entitled to a NMW for those hours.
> 2. In *Scottbridge Construction Ltd v Wright*, a nightwatchman who was paid by reference to the time he worked and was permitted to sleep at the workplace while at work, was entitled to a NMW for all of the hours he was required to be on the premises.
>
> **Time not counted for NMW purposes**
> 1. In *City of Edinburgh Council v Lauder and ors* [2012] UKEAT 0048_11_2003, the EAT held that sheltered housing wardens who worked their core hours between 8.30am and 5.30pm from Monday to Friday were not entitled to NMW for the hours that they were required to be on call between midnight and 8.30am. During these early morning hours an alarm system linked the sheltered housing to the wardens' tied accommodation and if the alarm went off and the wardens were required to attend to a resident they received time off in lieu or overtime payments (though this happened very rarely). Although the wardens were on-call at this time, the EAT held that they were not entitled to receive the NMW because a distinction should be drawn between cases where a worker is required, as part of their core duties, to work during the night and cases where a worker is required to be on-call in addition to their core duties. If a worker is carrying out their core duties at night, the whole period will count as working time for NMW. However, where the night-time work is not the essential nature of the worker's job, the exemption applies so that only time spent awake for the purpose of working counts as working time for NMW.
> 2. In *Wray v JW Lees and Co (Brewers) Ltd*, the employer ran a large number of pubs. The employee was a temporary pub manager and was provided with free accommodation at the pub she was managing for the employer. She had no responsibilities of any kind during this period and was not in breach of her duties if she left the premises for periods during the evening or night, provided she slept there each night. The employee was not entitled to a NMW for sleeping at the premises as there was no expectation of any availability to do work.
> 3. In *Baxter v Titan Aviation Ltd*, the employer was a holiday company. One of its services was to pick up clients going on holiday from their homes and drive them to the airport or other point of departure. The drivers would sometimes be asked to stay overnight in a hotel or B & B in order to be able to pick up passengers in the morning. Typically this would occur where a driver had done a job the previous day with a drop-off point fairly near the next day's pick-up point – or at least nearer to it than if he or another driver had had to come from their base. The time spent in the overnight accommodation was described as "lay-over" time. The claimant, who was one of the drivers, was not entitled to a NMW during such overnight lay-overs as there was no expectation of any availability to do work.

MEMO POINTS Whether or not time spent on standby or on-call would be **working time under the Working Time Regulations** (which set out worker rights in relation to time at work, breaks and statutory annual leave) is irrelevant (*Baxter v Titan Aviation Ltd*). While it is a matter of common sense that in most cases the answers to the question of what hours a worker "works" for the purpose of the National Minimum Wage Regulations and what constitutes "working time" for the purpose of the Working Time Regulations should be the same, the provisions are quite differently structured and worded and have different legislative origins.

Output worker

2889 A worker is an "output worker" if he is paid not for the time that he works, but for the number of pieces of work he produces or the number of tasks (for example sales or deals) he performs (reg 25(1) SI 1999/584). Consequently, his **hours of work are not fixed** by his employer. This is commonly known as "piece work" or "commission work."

The system **to calculate** the total number of hours worked in such cases provides for the determination by the employer of the "**mean hourly output rate**" on an actual or estimated basis (SI 2004/1161 amending SI 1999/584).

The number of hours taken by a worker in producing pieces or performing tasks during the pay reference period will be treated as being 120% of the number of hours that a worker working at the mean hourly output rate would have taken to produce or perform the same number of pieces or tasks.

MEMO POINTS   This system replaced the old system of "fair estimate agreements".

2890 To determine the mean hourly output rate, the employer must conduct a **satisfactory test or estimate** of the speed at which the workers produce the subject piece or perform the subject task (reg 26A SI 1999/584).

To conduct a **test**, the employer can choose a sample of these workers that, in respect of the speed at which the workers work, is representative of them all. To be performed satisfactorily, the chosen group must be tested in working conditions similar to those in which the workers work. The hourly output rate is then calculated by dividing the total number of subject pieces or subject tasks (or the fraction of a piece or task) produced or performed by the tested workers per hour during the period of the test by the number of workers in the group tested.

2891 If necessary, employers can make an **estimate** of the average speed, in terms of pieces or tasks per hour, at which the workers are likely to work. For an estimate to be satisfactory, the employer must test the average speed, in terms of pieces or tasks per hour, at which a sample of workers of the employer work either:
– in similar conditions to produce a piece or perform a task that is reasonably similar to the subject piece or subject task; or
– in different working circumstances but on the same subject piece or subject task.
In both circumstances, the employer must fairly adjust the average speed to take into account any differences that would affect the speed of production or performance.

2892 Having conducted a satisfactory test or made a satisfactory estimate, **subsequent changes** to the workforce will not require a new test or estimate unless the employer has reason to believe that the changes materially affect the mean hourly output rate.

2893 A **written notice** must be given to the worker at any time before the beginning of the pay reference period and must contain (reg 25(2) SI 1999/584):
– statements conveying that the notice is being given to inform the worker that, to secure compliance with NMW legislation, he will be treated with regard to his production of the subject piece or performance of subject task during the pay reference period as working for a certain period of time and, for the purposes of determining this, the employer has conducted a test or made an estimate to ascertain what the mean hourly output rate is;
– the mean hourly output rate and the rate the worker is to be paid for the production of a single subject piece or performance of a single subject task; and
– the telephone number of the NMW helpline, which is identified as such.

Unmeasured time worker

2895 This covers those who work **unspecified hours** and all other workers who do not fall into the other three categories above (reg 6 SI 1999/584). It includes, in particular, work where there are certain tasks to be done but no specified hours or time when they must be done. These workers are most often domestic staff with no set hours, output or annual salary. This group includes live-in care workers (*Walton v Independent Living Organisation Ltd* [2003] ICR 688, CA).

2896 To calculate the total number of hours worked in such cases, the employer and worker can have a "**daily average**" **agreement**. This must be in writing and agreed between them before the start of the pay reference period it covers, setting out the daily average number of hours which the worker is to work in this period (the employer must be able to show that this figure is realistic).

If there is no agreement, the employer must nevertheless ensure that he pays at least the NMW for every hour worked with regard to each pay period.

2. Compliance

Records

2900 Employers are required to **keep** records **for** 3 years (s 9 NMWA 1998; reg 38 SI 1999/584). These must be sufficient to establish that the worker has been paid at least the NMW. The records required must be in a **form** which enables them to be produced in a single document.

2901 If the **worker** has reasonable grounds to believe that he is being or has been remunerated for any pay reference period at a rate which is less than the NMW, he can give **notice** to his employer **requesting** the production of the **relevant records** relating to periods listed in the notice (s 10 NMWA 1998). The worker has a **right to be accompanied** by another person chosen by him if stated in the notice.

The employer must give the worker reasonable notice of the time and **place** at which the relevant records will be produced, which must be:
– the worker's place of work;
– any other place at which it is reasonable, in all the circumstances, for the worker to attend to inspect the relevant records; or
– such other place as may be agreed between the worker and the employer.

2902 The records must be **produced**:
– **before** the end of the period of 14 days following the date of receipt of the production notice; or
– **at such later** time as may be agreed during that period between the worker and the employer.

The worker is entitled to make a **copy** of the records.

Enforcement

2903 HMRC NMW enforcement officers can **require employers** to (s 14 NMWA 1998):
– produce records;
– allow access to premises; and
– provide information in order to determine whether there has been compliance.

NMW enforcement officers can copy any relevant documents and can remove such records in order to do so (s 14(3A) NMWA 1998). If removed they will be returned to the employer as soon as reasonably practicable.

Information so obtained must only be used for the purposes of the NMW rules or for criminal or civil proceedings (s 15 NMWA 1998).

> MEMO POINTS 1. It should be noted that **HMRC** can **disclose information** which comes into their possession in the course of their duties, such as during an employer tax compliance visit (s 39 NMWA 1998). Disclosure in such circumstances is to the Secretary of State who will pass the information on to NMW enforcement officers.
> **Officers** can disclose information obtained from the employer to the worker and vice versa (s 16A NMWA 1998 as inserted by s 44 EReIA 2004).
> 2. In the **agricultural sector**, the relevant officers are called agricultural wages inspectors.

2904 **Notice of underpayment** Where it appears that the employer is paying, or has in the past paid, below the NMW, the enforcement officer can issue notice of underpayment requiring him to comply with the NMW and to:
– **make up the loss suffered** by his worker(s) within 4 weeks (28 days) of the date of service of the notice of underpayment (s 19 NMWA 1998); and
– pay a **financial penalty** of between £100 and £5,000, depending on the amount owing, to the Secretary of State within the 4-week period (s 19A NMWA 1998 as introduced by the EA 2008).

If the employer does not agree with the enforcement notice or any penalty notice, he can **appeal** to an employment tribunal within 4 weeks of its issue (s 19C NMWA 1998). If the tribunal finds that the notice should not have been served, it will rescind the notice. If the tribunal finds that the amount specified is wrong, it will rectify the notice and state what the correct amount should be. Where there is unsatisfactory evidence, the tribunal will do its best to estimate the accurate figure (*Commissioners of Inland Revenue v St Hermans Estate Co Ltd* [2002] UKEAT 0121_01_0205).

> MEMO POINTS 1. A notice of underpayment cannot relate to a **pay reference period** ending more than 6 years before the date of service of the notice (s 19(7) NMWA 1998).
> 2. Enforcement officers can **withdraw and replace** a notice of underpayment (ss 19F-H NMWA 1998).

Failure to comply may result in (ss 19D-E NMWA 1998): **2905**
– with regard to the penalty fine: the enforcement officer bringing county court proceedings against the employer to recover the penalty; and/or
– with regard to non-payment of arrears due to the workers: the enforcement officer bringing employment tribunal or civil court proceedings against the employer on behalf of that employer's workers.

Criminal offences The employer will commit a criminal offence if he: **2906**
– refuses or wilfully neglects to pay NMW;
– fails to keep records or falsifies records; or
– obstructs an enforcement officer or knowingly provides false information.

Offences are triable in either the Crown Court or magistrates' court (s 33 NMWA 1998 as amended by the EA 2008). The fine is unlimited in the Crown Court and subject to a maximum of £5,000 (level 5 on the standard scale) in the magistrates' court.

3. Remedies

Unauthorised deduction from wages claim

A worker can bring a claim for an unauthorised deduction from wages (¶3050) if he is not paid the NMW, if his employer reduces the number of his hours of work in order to offset the extra cost of implementing the NMW (as happened in *Burr v Buckle & Bowen-Jones t/a Industrial Cleaning Services*, ET case 1502147/99) or if his employer changes the payment arrangements without consent to fund the payment of the NMW (*Laird v AK Stoddart Ltd* [2001] IRLR 591, EAT). **2910**

The complaint must be made **within** 3 months from the date the deduction was made (¶3081).

The **burden of proof** is on the employer to establish that the worker has been paid at least the NMW (s 28 NMWA 1998).

> EXAMPLE In *Laird v AK Stoddart Ltd*, L's employer increased L's hourly rate to comply with the NMW by consolidating part of L's attendance allowance into the basic hourly rate. If L had not consented to this change, this would have amounted to an unauthorised and/or unlawful deduction. However, as L had agreed to this variation in his payment arrangements there was no unauthorised and/or unlawful deduction.

Compensation for financial loss Tribunals have the power to order employers to compensate workers for any financial loss sustained as a result of unlawful deduction from wages (s 7 Employment Act 2008). **2911**

Compensation for failure to allow access to records The worker can make a complaint to the employment tribunal if his employer fails to comply with a request for information in respect of a pay period (s 11 NMWA 1998). If the tribunal finds the complaint well-founded, it will: **2912**
– make a declaration to that effect; and
– order the employer to pay the worker an award of 80 times the hourly amount of the relevant NMW.

The complaint must be made **within** 3 months from the date by which the records should have been produced.

Breach of contract claim

2913 Workers may also be able to bring a claim for breach of contract if there is an unlawful deduction (¶1710).

Right not to be dismissed or suffer detriment

2915 Workers also have the right **not to suffer detriment** as a result of their request to be paid the NMW (s 23 NMWA 1998). Any **dismissal** of an employee in such circumstances will also be **automatically unfair** (s 104A ERA 1996).

> MEMO POINTS Non-employee workers who are so dismissed should rely on the right not to suffer a detriment.

B. A week's pay

2920 The **following entitlements and rights** are calculated by reference to a week's pay:
a. statutory redundancy pay;
b. special redundancy pay for lay-offs or short-time working;
c. guarantee payments;
d. guarantee debts on the employer's insolvency;
e. medical suspension payments;
f. paid annual leave;
g. paid time off:
– to perform duties as an employee representative/candidate or as a member/candidate of an SNB, EWC, or information or consultation body;
– to look for new employment under notice of redundancy;
– for a young person to study; and
– for antenatal care; and
h. the following awards:
– unfair dismissal awards (basic, compensatory and additional);
– award due to infringement of the right to written particulars;
– award due to infringement of the right to minimum statutory notice;
– award for employer's failure to allow worker to be accompanied to disciplinary/grievance hearing or hearing regarding flexible working;
– award for employer's failure to consider/correctly consider employee's request for flexible working;
– protective award for employer's failure to consult on redundancy;
– award for employer's failure to consult on training (statutory recognised unions);
– award for employer's failure to comply with employer notification requirements regarding request to work beyond intended retirement date; and
– award for employer's failure (or threat to fail) to allow an employee to be accompanied to a meeting to consider his request to work beyond his intended retirement date.

The broad aim of the rules relating to a week's pay is to **ascertain the minimum amount** to which the employee would be entitled under his contract if he worked a normal week.

The rules give **four different formulae** for calculating a normal week's pay and which formula to use will depend on the type of employee. Once the correct formula is identified, it is applied to the calculation date, which is the date used for calculating a week's pay. This date will vary depending on the entitlement.

2921 Where the employee is paid **less than the national minimum wage**, the calculation of a week's pay should be based on the NMW he should have received and not what he was actually paid (*Paggetti v Cobb* [2002] UKEAT 136_01_2203).

Maximum limits

2923 There is a **statutory cap** on the amount of a week's pay with regard to certain entitlements and rights, the most important of these relating to (s 227 ERA 1996):
– **statutory redundancy payments**; and
– basic awards and additional **awards in unfair dismissal cases**.

The **current maximum** is set at £450 for cases in which the calculation date (¶2955) falls on or after 1 February 2013 (SI 2012/3007).

The following table sets out when the statutory cap applies and maximum limits, and other awards which increased on 1 February 2013:

Entitlement or right	Maximum limit	¶¶
Employer's insolvency: guaranteed debts	£3,600 (arrears of pay) £2,700 (holiday pay)	¶¶9053+
Flexible working: failure to consider/correctly consider employee's request	£3,600	¶4788
Redundancy pay: statutory (SRP)	£13,500	¶9005
Right to be accompanied: disciplinary/grievance hearing/flexible working hearing	£900	¶¶6790, 4788
Trade unions: refusal of employment or employment services of agency on grounds of trade union membership	£74,200	¶7590
Trade unions: employer's unlawful inducement	£3,600	¶¶7573, 7582, 7593
Trade unions (statutorily recognised): employer's failure to consult on training	£900	¶7388
Trade union: unjustified discipline, or unreasonable exclusion or expulsion, by union	£87,700 (maximum) £8,400 (minimum if applicable)	¶¶7143, 7141
Unfair dismissal: basic award	£13,500 (minimum in certain cases: £5,500)	¶¶8575, 8577
Unfair dismissal: compensatory award	£74,200 (no limit where dismissed unfairly or selected for redundancy for reasons connected with health and safety)	¶8587
Unfair dismissal: additional award (failure to re-employ or reinstate employee)	between £11,700 and £23,400	¶¶8689, 7598
Written particulars: employer's failure to provide statement/incomplete or inaccurate statement	£900 or £1,800	¶1465

MEMO POINTS The previous maximum for events giving rise to the entitlement to compensation or other payments between 1 February 2012 and 31 January 2013 was £430 (SI 2011/3006).

2924 **Guarantee payments** have a daily limit of £24.20 for a workless day and are only payable for a maximum of 5 workless days in any 3-month period (i.e. £121.00).

MEMO POINTS From 1 February 2013 (SI 2012/3007).

1. Type of calculation

2930 Each of the four formulae relates to a different type of employee. These **types are as follows**:
– employees with normal working hours (i.e. the hours are constant from week to week);
– regular employees with a flat (i.e. paid by the number of hours they work) or variable (i.e. paid by piece, product or commission) rate;

– shift or rota workers; and
– employees with no normal working hours.

2931 Whichever of the four formulae is used, a week's pay is **calculated by reference** to the employee's pay.

The courts have held that, for these purposes, **pay includes** the employee's wages or salary including any regular bonuses or like payments if the employee is entitled to them (*Mole Mining Ltd v Jenkins* [1972] ICR 282, NIRC; *S and U Stores Ltd v Wilkes* [1974] IRLR 283, NIRC). Ex gratia payments are, therefore, not included.

Pay does **not include** benefits in kind, cash payments by a third party and payment for expenses where they represent a true reimbursement. Additional expense payments may be included, therefore, if it can be shown that the payment represented a profit which exceeded the employee's real expense.

> MEMO POINTS **Agricultural workers** can include benefits in kind where such benefits are included in the minimum wage set by agricultural wages regulations (*W A Armstong & Sons Ltd v Borrill* [2000] ICR 367, EAT).

a. Employees with normal working hours

No variation

2935 If an employee's pay for work done in normal working hours does not vary, a week's pay is the pay due for the **basic hours** the employee is contracted to work. This can include **premium rates** if the normal hours he works attract this higher rate, for example because he is a night-worker. **Regular contractual bonuses or allowances** (except expense allowances) which do not vary with the amount of work done are also included (s 221(2) ERA 1996).

It does not include **discretionary bonuses** (*Canadian Imperial Bank of Commerce v A Beck* [2010] UKEAT 0141_10_2408) or any **commission payments** which are paid over and above basic salary (*Evans v Malley Organisation Ltd t/a First Business Support* [2003] IRLR 156, CA). Likewise, **overtime** pay can only be included if it is obligatory and guaranteed by the contract of employment. Voluntary overtime must be excluded (*Bamsey and others v Albon Engineering and Manufacturing plc* [2004] IRLR 457, CA).

> MEMO POINTS With regard to **statutory annual leave pay** which is based on a week's pay, this inability to include commissions or overtime payments could suggest that the Working Time Regulations do not correctly implement the EC Working Time Directive and it may, therefore, be open for workers employed by public authorities to try to rely on the Directive directly.

2936 A week's pay must be the amount payable under the contract of employment in force on the calculation date (¶2955).

Variation

2937 If there is a variable element with regard to the employee's pay, the following special rules apply.

2938 **Flat or variable rates** If an employee has normal working hours but his pay varies with the amount of work done (for example, under piece rates), or where pay is partly made up of variable productivity bonuses or commissions, then a week's pay is his average hourly rate over a 12 calendar week period times the number of normal weekly working hours (s 221(3) ERA 1996).

2939 The **formula** to calculate the average hourly rate is as follows:

$$\text{average hourly rate} = \frac{\text{pay over the 12 calendar week period}}{\text{total number of hours during this period}}$$

2940 This **12 calendar week period** is **ascertained by** reference to the calculation date (see ¶2955). If the calculation date is on the weekly pay day, the period will end on this date. If not, it will end on the pay day of the previous pay week to ensure that 12 complete calendar weeks are taken into consideration. If the employee's pay period is more than a week, the pay day is deemed to be a Saturday.

2941 Hours worked as **voluntary overtime** are included as part of the total number of hours worked over the 12-week period. However, where pay for such work is higher than pay for the same work done in normal working hours, the pay must be adjusted (i.e. the premium element must be ignored and it is brought down to the level it would have been if the same work had been done in normal working hours) (*British Coal Corporation v Cheesbrough* [1990] ICR 317, HL).

As with the general rule, full pay for overtime hours can be included if it is **obligatory and guaranteed**.

2942 12/13 of any quarterly **bonus**, or 12/52 of any annual bonus, can be included provided the bonuses are not paid specifically for some time outside the 12-week period.

2943 **Any hours** in which the employee was **not working** are not included and consequently any pay for hours not worked, for example under a guaranteed week agreement, is ignored.

Further, **any week** in which no work was done should be replaced by the last previous week when the employee did work, to bring the total number of weeks up to 12.

2944 If the employee has **less than 12 weeks' service**, the parties can look to other factors that might be relevant in ascertaining the average hourly rate, for example the working hours of other employees of the employer and/or the expected pattern of working based on the terms on which the job was offered.

2945 **Shift or rota workers** Where an employee is contracted to work normal hours but on days or at times which differ from week to week or over a longer period, a week's pay is the average weekly working hours times the average hourly rate (see ¶2939) (s 222 ERA 1996).

2946 The **formula** to calculate the average weekly working hours is:

$$\text{average weekly working hours} = \frac{\text{total number of normal working hours during 12 calendar week period (see ¶2940)}}{12}$$

b. Employees with no normal working hours

2950 For an employee with no normal working hours (for example, an employee paid wholly by commission), the amount of a week's pay is the average weekly pay over the 12 calendar week period (s 224 ERA 1996). The EAT has held that employees who worked for notional hours and were required to complete certain tasks each week, irrespective of how long it actually took them to finish, should be treated as having no normal working hours (*Sanderson and anor v Exel Management Services Ltd* [2006] UKEAT 0194_06_1506).

2951 The **formula** to calculate the average weekly pay is:

$$\text{average weekly pay} = \frac{\text{total pay during 12 calendar week period (see ¶2940)}}{12}$$

2. Calculation date

2955 The calculation dates for awards and payments under the following entitlements are as follows (ERA 1996; TULRCA 1992; ERelA 1999; EA 2002; SI 2002/3207; SI 2006/1031).

Entitlement or right subject to the statutory cap for a week's pay	Calculation date	¶¶
Employer's insolvency: guaranteed debts	Usually date employer becomes insolvent	¶9053
Flexible working: failure to consider/correctly consider employee's request	Date of failure in relation to the application or of the decision to reject the application	¶4788
Redundancy pay: statutory (SRP)	In relation to an employee whose contract of employment is terminated by notice, whether given by his employer or by the employee, the date on which the notice expires. In relation to an employee whose contract of employment is terminated without notice, the date on which the termination takes effect. In relation to an employee who is employed under a fixed-term contract which expires without being renewed, the date on which the contract expires.	¶9005
Redundancy pay: statutory (SRP) (lay-off or short-time working)	In relation to a notice of intention to claim or a right to a redundancy payment in pursuance of such a notice, the date on which the last of the 4 or more consecutive weeks before the service of the notice came to an end, or the date on which the last of the series of 6 or more weeks before the service of the notice came to an end.	¶7891
Right to be accompanied: disciplinary/grievance hearing/flexible working hearing	In relation to a failure or threatened failure to allow the worker to be accompanied at the hearing, to allow the companion to address the hearing or confer with the worker, or to postpone the hearing, the date of the failure or threat.	¶¶6790, 4788
Trade unions: refusal of employment or employment services of agency on grounds of trade union membership	Date of refusal	¶7590
Trade unions: employer's unlawful inducement	Date conduct complained of occurred	¶¶7573, 7582, 7593
Trade unions (statutorily recognised): employer's failure to consult on training	Date of failure to consult	¶7388
Trade unions: unjustified discipline, or unreasonable exclusion or expulsion, by union	Date of declaration, or date of refusal or expulsion	¶¶7143, 7141
Unfair dismissal: basic award	The effective date of termination (EDT)	¶¶8575, 8577
Unfair dismissal: compensatory award	The effective date of termination (EDT)	¶8587
Unfair dismissal: additional award (failure to re-employ or reinstate employee)	The date the order should have been complied with	¶¶8689, 7598
Written particulars: employer's failure to provide statement/incomplete or inaccurate statement	Date proceedings were begun	¶1465

III. Payment

A. Forms and rate of pay

2980 Levels and intervals of pay will normally be fixed by **express contractual terms**. Where there is no written contract of employment or where it does not cover these provisions, the employer must provide his employee with a **written statement of particulars** (¶1400).

2981 The **rate of pay** is commonly expressed as:
– a yearly sum for a fixed number of hours per week payable in monthly instalments;
– a sum for a lesser period, for example weekly or daily, for a fixed number of hours payable on a monthly, weekly or daily basis; or
– an hourly rate payable on a weekly, daily or hourly basis.

2982 If there is a **collective agreement** between the employer and a recognised trade union for the purpose of pay bargaining, the contract of employment should provide that the amount to be paid is incorporated into the contract (*Airlie v City of Edinburgh District Council* [1996] IRLR 516, EAT).

2983 Earnings (i.e. basically the tax term for remuneration) are subject to income tax and NIC.

B. Itemised pay statements

2985 An employee is entitled to be given by his employer, at or before the time at which any payment of wages is made to him, a **written** itemised pay statement **containing** (s 8 ERA 1996):
– the gross amount of the wages;
– the amounts of any variable or fixed deductions from that amount;
– the net amount of wages payable; and
– where different parts of the net amount are paid in different ways, the amount and method by which each part payment will be paid.

2986 With regard to **fixed deductions**, the employer need only state the aggregate amount of fixed deductions including the fixed deduction in question, if he has given the employee, at or before the time at which the pay statement is given, a **standing statement of fixed deductions** (s 9 ERA 1996).

The standing statement must be in **writing**, effective at the **date on which the pay statement is given** and must **contain** (in relation to each deduction comprised in the aggregate amount of deductions):
– the amount of the deduction;
– the intervals at which the deduction is to be made; and
– the purpose for which it is made.

A standing statement will be effective at the date on which it is given to the employee and can remain effective for 12 months, after which it will be necessary to re-issue the statement. A **re-issued statement** should be consolidated and must incorporate the particulars of any notices of amendment (see ¶2987). The first re-issue must be **made within** 12 months of when the first standing statement was given and thereafter should be re-issued at intervals of not more than 12 months.

2987 A standing statement can be amended if necessary to add a new deduction, to change the existing deduction or to cancel it. The **notice of amendment** must be given to the employee in writing and must contain the particulars of the amendment.

Remedies

2988 The employee can bring an application to an employment tribunal if the employer **fails to provide** an itemised pay statement (s 11 ERA 1996).

Both the employee and the employer can also bring an application where a question arises over the **particulars of the information** given in a pay or standing statement. Questions cannot relate solely to the accuracy of the amount stated in such particulars, nor can they relate to whether the employment has been, or will be, contracted out of the Second State Pension (formerly referred to as SERPS).

Any application must be **brought** while the employee is employed, or within 3 months of the date on which employment ended (s 11(4) ERA 1996). This time limit can be extended as the tribunal considers reasonable where it accepts that it was not reasonably practicable for the application to have been made in time.

2989 In both cases, the tribunal will **determine** what the itemised pay statement should contain.

The tribunal will also make a **declaration** if the employer has failed to give a pay statement, or if a pay or standing statement does not, in relation to a deduction, contain adequate particulars (s 12(3) ERA 1996). In such cases, if the tribunal further finds that any unnotified deductions have been made during the period of 13 weeks beginning with the date of the application (whether or not the deductions were made in breach of the contract of employment), the tribunal may order the employer to **pay** the employee a sum **up to** the aggregate of the unnotified deductions (s 12(4) ERA 1996).

This has been used by the tribunals to penalise employers for not complying with these legal requirements and it is, therefore, irrelevant whether or not the employee was aware of the deduction and whether the employer was contractually entitled to make the deduction (*Milsom v Leicestershire County Council* [1978] IRLR 433, IT). Alternatively, a tribunal may decide it is only appropriate in the circumstances to award any shortfall between what the employee should have received and what he did in fact receive (as it did in *Scott v Creager* [1979] IRLR 162, EAT).

IV. Deductions

3000 The employer may be able **lawfully** to make a deduction if:
– he has an express contractual right to do so;
– he is obliged to do so by a statutory order; or
– the employee has refused to perform all his duties.

Otherwise, it is **unlawful** and the employee will be able to bring a breach of contract claim. For example, if the employer tries to make a deduction by varying the contractual terms unilaterally by imposing a pay cut. Deductions made with regard to overpayments must also be **valid**. In certain circumstances, the employer may be also estopped from recovering the overpayment.

3001 Further, employees have **special statutory protection** with regard to certain deductions and, within this group, unlawful deductions are unauthorised, as are any deductions made in an incorrect manner. In such cases, an employee can bring a claim in an employment tribunal for the repayment of the unauthorised deduction.

MEMO POINTS All deductions must be adequately **set out** in itemised pay statements.

A. Lawful deductions

1. Contractual deductions

Requirement for right to deduct

The employer has **no implied right** to withhold pay or make deductions and an **express clause** will be needed. **Specific** clauses providing for deductions in specific circumstances, for example for poor performance, stock deficiencies, unauthorised absences, season ticket loans, training costs etc, are usually considered reasonable.

However, a **general** clause allowing the employer to vary pay will not allow him to reduce pay as this is likely to be held unreasonable.

> MEMO POINTS Whether or not an employer has an express clause allowing him to deduct wages for **poor or incomplete performance**, he may alternatively be able to claim damages for breach of contract in respect of that performance. If the breach is sufficiently serious (i.e. it is fundamental), the employer will be entitled to dismiss and consequently stop paying wages. Poor performance should first be dealt with under an appraisal system to find out the causes for it and whether training, support or increased supervision will solve the problem. If not, it may be a disciplinary matter.

Common specific clauses giving the employer the right to deduct from wages are as follows for:
– overpayments of wages or expenses;
– unauthorised absences;
– loans;
– any losses caused by the employee's breach of his duties or by his negligence (for example, damage to company property); and
– any other amount which the employee owes (for example, season ticket loans) from the final salary payment, including any overpaid holiday.

There may also be a **right to suspend** without pay in certain circumstances (for example, until a serious matter has been dealt with by a disciplinary hearing).

Refusal or failure to work

If the employee refuses to work, he is not entitled to his contractual wage. This **includes** situations where the employee is absent from work while in custody or on remand (*Burns v Santander UK Plc* [2011] UKEAT 0500_10_2303).

> EXAMPLE In *Burns v Santander UK Plc*, the EAT held that an employee, B, who was remanded in custody had not been a victim of an "unavoidable impediment" that prevented him from working when he was otherwise ready and willing to perform his contract. Although B had not been convicted of a criminal offence at the time of the non-payment of wages, the fact that the criminal courts felt that he had conducted himself in such a way that he should be remanded in custody was sufficient for the employer to decide that B's impediment was avoidable and that he had contributed to his inability to work. This was confirmed when B was convicted of two of the nine charges made against him.

> MEMO POINTS In recent years, heavy **snow** fall has made it impossible for some employees to get into their place of work; unless the employer is willing to allow the individual to work from home, or to work unpaid overtime to make up for the missed time, the employer may withhold pay on the basis that the employee did not present himself at work ready and willing to work. Employers can, of course, also choose to continue to pay employees in such circumstances if their employees genuinely cannot attend their place of work.

If the employee **refuses to perform all** of his contractual duties, he is not entitled to his full contractual wage and his employer can deduct a sum equal to the proportion of time the employee deliberately refuses or fails to fulfil his contractual duties (*Miles v Wakefield Metropolitan*

District Council [1987] IRLR 193, HL). This is based on the quantum meruit principle (¶2817). However, this does not apply where employees are engaged in **non-strike industrial action** (*Spackman v London Metropolitan University* [2007] IRLR 744, CC). In such instances, they take the risk that, even if they are present for work and undertake some or most of their ordinary duties, the employer is under no obligation to pay them and will not be in breach of contract if he does not do so. If the employees are paid something, it will be more than they are legally entitled to expect. This will be all the more so where the employer has expressly stated that full pay will not be paid to participants of the industrial action, and that any payments made will be substantially less than their normal pay.

> EXAMPLE
> 1. In *Spackman v London Metropolitan University*, S, a lecturer, was unsuccessful in seeking to recover some or all of the 30% deduction to her wages which was made for the period in which she took part in an industrial action short of a strike, even though S claimed that she had performed nearly all of her of her contractual duties.
> 2. In *Cooper and ors v The Isle of Wight College* [2008] IRLR 124, HC, various college employees had been engaged in a single day of strike action. Under their contracts, the employees were entitled to 104 weekend and non-working days and 32 days of annual leave. The employer discounted all these days to calculate that the employees worked 228 days in a year, and deducted 1/228 of the employees' annual wage. The High Court held that the employer had been correct to discount weekend and non-working days in making the calculation, but should not have discounted the employees' annual leave. The correct figure for deductions was 1/260 of the annual wage.

> MEMO POINTS An alternative way of reducing the employee's wages for part-performance is by **setting-off** the loss due to the employee's breach of contract against his wages (*Sim v Rotherham Metropolitan Borough Council* [1986] IRLR 391, HC). However, the end result is the same.

3008 The employer is entitled to **withhold the whole of** the employee's **pay** if he makes it clear that part-performance is not acceptable (*Wiluszynski v London Borough of Tower Hamlets* [1989] IRLR 259, CA).

> EXAMPLE In *Wiluszynski v London Borough of Tower Hamlets*, the Court held that the Council was entitled to withhold the whole of W's wages as it had made it clear to him that his refusal to perform part of his duties (answering councillors' enquiries) was unacceptable. This was so even though this was a very small part of his duties and he had performed the substantial part of his contract.

> MEMO POINTS A refusal to work part of the day is **underperformance** and will allow the employer to discipline accordingly. A sufficiently serious breach may be fundamental allowing the employer to summarily dismiss the employee.

Withholding of goodwill

3009 A withholding of goodwill can breach the implied term of fidelity and justify a withholding of pay (*Ticehurst and Thompson v British Telecommunications plc* [1992] IRLR 219, CA).

> EXAMPLE In *Ticehurst and Thompson v British Telecommunications plc*, T, who had withdrawn her goodwill as part of a concerted action by union members, was not permitted to return to work and was not paid after taking industrial action until the dispute was settled, because she refused to sign an undertaking to work normally in accordance with the terms of her contract of employment. The Court held that she had not proved that she was ready and willing to perform in full her obligations under her contract of employment, and that the withholding of pay was not unlawful.

Overpayments

3010 Recovery will only be possible if the employer can show that the overpayment was due to a mistake in fact (for example, an error in computation). If it is, the deduction will be **valid**. However, if the overpayment was due to a mistake of law (for example, the employer did not realise that he did not legally have to pay the employee for a particular absence) then the deduction will be **invalid**. In such cases, the employee can bring a claim to prevent the deduction or for reimbursement in the civil courts.

Further, an employer may also be prevented (**estopped**) from claiming repayment (called "restitution") if the following conditions are satisfied:
– he has made a representation of fact which led the employee to believe that he was entitled to treat the money as his own;
– the employee must have, in good faith and without notice of the employer's claim, consequently changed his position for the worse where it would be inequitable in all the circumstances to require him to repay some or all of the amount (*Home Office v Ayres* [1992] IRLR 59, EAT; *Lipkin Gorman v Karpnale Ltd* [1991] 3 WLR 10, HL); and
– the payment must not have been primarily caused by the fault of the employee.

3011

2. Statutory deductions

An employer may be **legally required** to make the following deductions which he must pass on to a third party:
– attachment of earnings;
– student loan deductions; and
– trade union subscriptions.

3015

a. Attachment of earnings

The employer may be statutorily bound to make a deduction from his employee's earnings if the courts have made an attachment of earnings order (Attachment of Earnings Act 1971). In such cases, the employer will pass the money deducted to the relevant court office.

3017

Scope

An attachment of earnings order can be made by a court against the employee's earnings in relation to the following, if the employee has **failed**, or is likely to fail, **to pay** the sums due in a satisfactory manner (s 1 Attachment of Earnings Act 1971):
– judgment debts made in the county court or the balance of it if it has been part-paid;
– maintenance orders made in the High Court, county court or magistrates' court;
– fines or compensation orders made in the magistrates' court on the conviction of an offence;
– payments under a legal aid contribution order; or
– payments under a county court administration order.

There are specific regulations in relation to attachment of earnings for failure to pay council tax (¶3028) and for failure to pay child support maintenance by an absent parent (¶3029).

3018

Procedure

When an employer **receives** an attachment of earnings order, he must make the deductions that are set out in it (s 6 Attachment of Earnings Act 1971). The order will state:
– what the employee's **attachable earnings** are;
– what sum is to be deducted from the earnings on each pay day (called **normal deductions**); and
– the earnings from which no deduction can be made (called **protected earnings**).

3019

> MEMO POINTS **Earnings** include (s 24 Attachment of Earnings Act 1971):
> – basic pay;
> – overtime payments;
> – any other fee, bonus, commission or other emolument referable to his employment;
> – statutory sick pay; and
> – company occupational pensions and annuities over the guaranteed minimum pension.
> **Excluded** are:
> – any social security payments, for example statutory maternity pay, pensions or allowances;
> – pensions or allowances payable due to disability; and
> – compensation for loss of office (unless made by pension contribution).

When making a payment under a compromise agreement upon termination it is advisable to seek guidance from the helpline: 0845 4085312 or to apply to the court to declare whether particular sums are "earnings" for these purposes. However, as a general rule, payments upon which tax upon termination is usually payable e.g. accrued holiday and notice pay are subject to the attachment of earnings order whereas genuine compensation payments are not.

3020 The employer must make the stated deductions **on the relevant pay days** subject to the protected earnings limit.

If all or part of the normal deductions **cannot be made on a pay day** because the amount is greater than the difference between the employee's attachable earnings and his protected earnings, the outstanding arrears created on that pay day can be carried forward to the next pay day. This carrying forward of arrears does not apply to orders relating to judgment debts or payments under an administration order.

3021 Where the employer receives **more than one attachment of earnings order** in relation to an employee, he must comply with the orders in date order except that orders relating to judgment debts or payments under administration orders must always be complied with last.

This can only occur when there is an **excess** between the attachable earnings and the protected earnings after the normal deduction is made in accordance with the first order. This excess is then applied to the other attachment orders in the required order.

3022 The deductions must be **shown on** the employee's itemised pay statement.

The employer must also give the employee a **written statement** stating the total amount of the deduction, the intervals at which the deductions are to be made, and the purpose for which it is made (ss 8, 9 ERA 1996). Such statements will be **valid for** 12 months.

If there is a **change to the statement**, for example if there is a deduction or an alteration or cancellation of an existing order, the employer must give written notice to the employee. In such circumstances, the employer should also issue an updated statement.

3023 **Administrative cost** The employer is entitled to make a deduction up to £1 to cover any administrative costs involved in making the deduction (s 7 Attachment of Earnings Act 1971; Attachment of Earnings (Employer's Deduction) Order SI 1991/356). The employer must inform the employee of the deduction in the written statement.

Compliance

3024 The employer must comply **within** 7 days with:
– an attachment of earnings order;
– a variation to it; and
– a notice stopping or discharging the order.

The court may also require the employer to **supply the court** with a signed statement of the employee's earnings and anticipated earnings within a specified period (s 14 Attachment of Earnings Act 1971).

3025 The employer must also **notify the court** that made the order:
– if the employee is no longer employed by him or within 10 days of termination of his employment (s 7 Attachment of Earnings Act 1971); or
– within 7 days of becoming his employer or finding out that the new employee has an attachment of earnings order against him. In such circumstances, the employer must also inform the court in writing and include a statement of the employee's earnings and anticipated earnings (s 15 Attachment of Earnings Act 1971).

3026 **Penalties** If the employer fails to comply with any of the above provisions, he can be subject to **criminal proceedings** in the magistrates' court (s 23 Attachment of Earnings Act 1971). If found guilty, he may be liable to a maximum fine of £500 (level 2 on the standard scale). Alternatively, he may be fined up to £250 in the **High Court or county court**.

Further, if the employer deliberately makes a **false statement**, he may also be liable to imprisonment for up to 14 days.

The employer has a **defence** if he can prove that he (s 23(5) Attachment of Earnings Act 1971):
– took all reasonable steps to comply with the order; or
– did not know and could not reasonably be expected to have known that the debtor was not employed by him, or had stopped working for him, and that he gave notice of this fact as soon as was reasonably practicable when he became aware of the relevant circumstances.

Specific rules

3028 The relevant bill authority (i.e. the district or borough council) can make an attachment of earnings order for the payment of any outstanding **council tax** once it has obtained a liability order from the magistrates' court (reg 37 Council Tax (Administration and Enforcement) Regulations SI 1992/613 as amended). The employer must comply with this order if it relates to one of his employees, and non-compliance is a criminal offence with a maximum fine of £1,000 (level 3 on the standard scale). These rules are very similar to the general rules above.

The amount to be deducted is specified for any given level of net earnings.

> MEMO POINTS **Earnings** has the same meaning as with a general attachment of earnings order. Net earnings are gross earnings after the deduction of income tax, NIC and pension contributions.

3029 The relevant rules relating to the attachment of earnings order in relation to the payment of **child support maintenance** by an absent parent are also very similar to the general rules (Child Support (Collection and Enforcement) Regulations SI 1992/1989 as amended).

b. Student loan deductions

3030 Student loans are available to help students meet their expenses while they are studying and are known as "income-contingent" loans because repayment is related to the borrower's level of income. HMRC are now responsible for collecting repayments, although the loans continue to be administered by the Student Loans Company. In most cases, the employer **collects** student loan repayments by making deductions from the borrower's pay and **passes the amount on** to HMRC.

For when and how much to deduct, see ¶6911.

c. Union subscriptions

3035 There is no legal obligation on an employer to have (or keep) any arrangement for direct deduction of dues, and whether the employer does so will depend on the agreement between the employer and the union.

The employer must have **written permission** from the worker (which must not have been withdrawn) before he can make any deduction from wages for trade union subscriptions. The worker retains the ability to withdraw authorisation at any time. **Notice of withdrawal** must be given in writing and must be received in time for it to be reasonably practicable for the employer to ensure that no deduction is made. There is no time limit on the length of the worker's authorisation (Deregulation (Deduction from Pay of Union Subscriptions) Order SI 1998/1529).

3036 If the worker contracts out of paying into the **political levy**, the employer must make sure that he only deducts the flat subscription fee. In such cases, the worker must give notification in writing that he is exempt from making payments to the political fund, and this amounts to withdrawal of any authorisation to deduct (s 86 TULRCA 1992). The employer cannot refuse to deduct the flat subscription fee if contributions are deducted in respect of other workers.

3037 A union member claiming that the employer has **not complied** with his duties can apply to the county court for a declaration. The complaint must be made within a period of 3 months. The court can order the employer to take steps to comply within a specified time.

B. Unauthorised deductions

3050 Certain deductions that are **not made in compliance** with these rules are unauthorised and consequently reimbursable. The employer also loses his right to the deductions and will not be able to recover them even in the proper manner.

The same rules apply to the right not to have to make **payments to the employer** (s 15 ERA 1996).

3052 The employer cannot include a provision in the worker's contract, or have an agreement with him, which excludes or limits the right of the worker to **contract out** of his right not to suffer an unauthorised deduction, unless certain exceptions apply (¶9333).

1. General rule

First limb

3055 No deduction from a worker's wages **may be made unless** (s 13 ERA 1996):
- it is required or **permitted** by the contract or by statute; or
- the worker has given his **prior written consent**.

Consequently, where an employer unilaterally imposes a variation to employees' contracts (for example, by introducing short-time working), unless he is entitled, either expressly or impliedly, to reduce the wages paid to employees, any reduction of wages as a result will constitute an unlawful deduction of wages (*International Packaging Corporation (UK) Ltd v Balfour* [2003] IRLR 11, EAT).

Where any deductions are to be made pursuant to a contractual provision, a copy of these provisions must be **shown to the worker** or, if not in writing, its effect notified in writing to the worker, prior to any deduction.

3056 **Wages include** (s 27 ERA 1996):
- basic pay;
- any fee, bonus, commission, holiday pay or other emolument referable to his employment, whether payable under his contract or otherwise. Therefore, non-contractual bonuses are included if they can be shown to be normally expected and are treated as wages payable on the day on which payment is made (*Kent Management Services Ltd v Butterfield* [1992] IRLR 394, EAT);
- vouchers, stamps or similar documents which have a fixed value expressed in monetary terms and are capable of being exchanged for money, goods or services (for example, luncheon vouchers);
- statutory sick pay, statutory maternity/adoption/paternity pay, guarantee payments, suspension on medical grounds and suspension on maternity grounds payments;
- payments for paid time off when payment is required by statute;
- pay under a protective award; and
- sums payable due to an order for reinstatement, re-engagement or the continuation of the contract.

Discretionary and **ex gratia payments** are wages if they are for service and are made (or the intention to make them existed) before termination of employment. This includes discretionary bonuses that have been declared on certain terms but not yet paid (be it under contract, by custom or by an ad hoc decision) (*Farrell Matthews & Weir v Hansen* [2004] UKEAT 0078_04_2610). **Commission payments** that become payable after termination are wages as they are made in connection with the employee's employment (*Robertson v Blackstone Franks Investment Management Ltd* [1998] IRLR 376, CA). Likewise **garden leave payments** are wages as the contract subsists during the time the payments are made. **Payments in lieu of notice** are not as they relate to a period after the termination of the employment (*Delaney v Staples* [1992]

IRLR 191, HL). In any event, payments in lieu of notice are also expressly excluded (see below) when they are compensation for loss of office (*Foster Wheeler (London) Ltd v Jackson* [1990] IRLR 412, EAT).

The following payments are **excluded** from the definition of wages and therefore are not protected by these rules:
– all other benefits in kind;
– payments made in respect of expenses;
– pension, allowance or gratuity payments in connection with the worker's retirement or as compensation for loss of office;
– any payments relating to the worker's redundancy; and
– any payments made/received otherwise than in his capacity as a worker.

3057

> MEMO POINTS **Advances** under a loan agreement or advances of wages are also excluded from the definition of wages, but this does not apply in relation to unauthorised deductions of wages, and the employer must not make an unauthorised deduction in respect of such advances.

Second limb

A **deduction** will occur where the total amount of any wages that are paid on a pay day by the employer are **less than the total amount** of wages that are properly payable by him to the worker on that pay day (*Murray v Strathclyde Regional Council* [1992] IRLR 396, EAT). For example, if the worker is paid monthly, a reduction with regard to the first month's payment will be a deduction if it is made against another month's payment. If an employee is **not paid any of his salary** on time, this also constitutes a breach of the employee's statutory right not to have deductions made from his wages (*Elizabeth Claire Care Management Limited v Francis* [2005] IRLR 858, EAT).

3058

If the amount properly payable is **not certain**, then any reduction to a pay packet is not classified as a deduction (*New Century Cleaning Co Ltd v Church* [2000] IRLR 27, CA).

> EXAMPLE Employee A is paid on the last day of each month. A's February pay packet is reduced to take into account a contractual entitlement to deduct pay for certain types of absence which occurred in January and February.
> The reduction in relation to absent days in February is part of the calculation as to what is the total amount of wages properly payable in February and is, therefore, not classified as a deduction. However, the reduction in relation to absent days in January is not part of this calculation and is a deduction.

The protection will not apply to reductions that are made as a result of an **error in the employer's computation** (i.e. the process of counting and calculating) (s 13(4) ERA 1996; *Morgan v West Glamorgan County Council* [1994] UKEAT 560_92_2302).

3059

An error in computation will not include the employer's conscious decision to withhold a payment because he **wrongly believes he has the right** to do so under the contract (*Yemm v British Steel plc* [1993] UKEAT 341_92_1607; *Morgan v West Glamorgan County Council*, above).

> EXAMPLE In *Morgan v West Glamorgan County Council*, the Council demoted M because it believed it could do so. However, the Council did not have a contractual right to do so, and the resultant reduction in M's wages was held not to be an error of computation and was an unauthorised deduction.

2. Deductions not protected

The **following deductions** are not protected if they are (ss 14, 16 ERA 1996):
– to reimburse the employer for an overpayment of wages or expenses;
– made as a result of disciplinary proceedings held due to a statutory provision;
– due to a statutory payment required to be made to a public authority;
– for taking part in a strike or other industrial action;
– to satisfy a tribunal or court order for payment to the employer with the worker's written prior agreement/consent; or
– payments to third persons with the worker's written prior agreement/consent.

3065

> **EXAMPLE** In *Patel v Marquette Partners (UK) Ltd* [2009] IRLR 425, EAT, an employee was due a large bonus from his employer. After receiving a letter from an HMRC officer which said that the bonus would be treated as pay for tax purposes, the employer deducted tax before making payment. The employee complained that this was an unlawful deduction from pay because there had been no formal determination of liability to tax. The EAT upheld the decision of an employment tribunal that it could not consider the claim because such a deduction was not protected. There was no need for there to be a formal determination for a deduction to qualify as a statutory payment to a public authority; the letter from HMRC was sufficient.

3066 If a deduction is made under one of the above exceptions, it is irrelevant whether the deduction is lawful or not for the purposes of the protection given by the rules (*SIP (Industrial Products) Ltd v Swinn* [1994] IRLR 323, EAT).

3. Special protection for retail employment

3070 Special protection covers workers who carry out **retail transactions** directly with the public or are involved with the collection of such amounts and applies with regard to cash shortages and stock deficiencies (s 17 ERA 1996). **Cash shortages** are defined as a deficit arising in relation to amounts received in connection with retail transactions (i.e. the sale or supply of goods or the supply of services (including financial services)). **Stock deficiencies** are defined as deficiencies in stock in relation to retail transactions.

3071 There are **limits** on the amount of any deductions due to cash shortages and stock deficiencies that can be made, and regarding when such deductions can be made (s 18 ERA 1996):
– the employer cannot deduct **more than** one-tenth of the gross amount of wages payable to the worker on each pay day; and
– he must make such a deduction **within** 12 months beginning with the date when the employer discovered or ought reasonably to have discovered the shortage or deficiency.

3072 There are also limits on **payments to the employer** with regard to cash shortages and stock deficiencies as follows (ss 20-21 ERA 1996):
– the employer must notify the worker in writing of his total liability in respect of the shortage or deficiency;
– he cannot require payment of more than one-tenth of the gross amount of wages payable to the worker on each pay day, or the balance of that amount after any of the above deductions; and
– his demand for payment must be in writing and on the pay day. This must not be made earlier than the first pay day on or after notification, and must be made within 12 months beginning with the date when the employer discovered or ought reasonably to have discovered the shortage or deficiency.

The **restriction to one-tenth** of the gross amount of wages does not apply to the final instalment of wages nor to a payment after this as long as it is made within the 12 months set out above (s 22 ERA 1996). After this period the employer cannot receive payments or recover them by bringing proceedings.

3073 If proceedings are brought against a retail worker to recover such sums, any sums for which he is found to be liable to pay must not be recovered at a rate that exceeds these special provisions.

4. Remedies

3080 The worker can **bring a claim** to an employment tribunal that an unauthorised deduction or payment has been made or received (s 23(1) ERA 1996). Retail workers can also bring a claim that a deduction or payment made was over the limit allowed. In deciding whether it has **jurisdiction to hear** a deduction from wages claim, a tribunal must make findings of fact if necessary (*Gill and ors v Ford Motor Co Ltd; Wong and ors v BAE Systems Operations Ltd* [2004]

IRLR 840, EAT). In this case, the tribunal should not have refused to hear such a claim because the employer stated that due to industrial action the wages in question were not protected, as whether the applicant had actually taken part was in dispute. Instead, the tribunal should have considered the evidence to make a finding on the disputed facts to ascertain whether it had jurisdiction to hear the claim.

3081 The **time limit** for bringing a claim is 3 months beginning with the date of payment from which the deduction was made, or the date the payment was received by the employee, whichever is relevant (s 23(2) ERA 1996).

Where there has been an **actual deduction** in breach of contract, the time for the complaint to start to run is the date when that deduction was made, or the date the payment from which the deduction was made was received by the worker. Where all that happens is that the employer pays too little and there is a **shortfall** the same principle applies: time starts to run from the moment when the reduced payment is made (Arora v Rockwell Automation Ltd [2006] UKEAT 0097_06_2104). Further, where there is a **series of deductions or payments**, the time limit runs from the date of the last deduction or payment. However, where there has been a **complete non-payment**, time may start to run in effect at an earlier date; it will start to run at the time when the contractual obligation to make a payment arose (Group 4 Nightspeed Ltd v Gilbert [1996] UKEAT 521_96_2609; Arora v Rockwell Automation Ltd).

The tribunal can **extend** the time limit if it is satisfied that it was not reasonably practicable to have presented the claim in time. In such cases the tribunal will indicate what extension is reasonable (s 23(4) ERA 1996).

3082 Where the tribunal finds that the complaint is well-founded it will (s 24 ERA 1996):
– make a **declaration** to that effect; and
– **order** the employer to pay the worker as appropriate.

If the amount deducted is greater than that which has been held to be lawfully deducted, the tribunal will order the employer to **pay the difference** between the actual amount deducted and the amount which was lawfully deducted (s 25 ERA 1996).

3083 Any sums paid or repaid to the worker as a result of a tribunal claim **cannot be subsequently lawfully deducted** and consequently the employer loses his right to make the deduction for that sum or part of it (Potter v Hunt Contracts Ltd [1992] IRLR 108, EAT). This is a sanction against making unauthorised deductions and in such cases the employer's only course of action would be to bring a common law action against the worker in the county courts.

SECTION 2

Tax

I. Earnings

A. Regular earnings

3100 When an individual who is resident or ordinarily resident in the UK (¶3370) performs the duties of his office or employment wholly in the UK for a UK employer, the individual will be **taxed** on the earnings arising from that office or employment (s 62(2) ITEPA 2003). The amount of earnings subject to tax will be **reduced** to take account of travel and subsistence expenses incurred necessarily, and other expenses incurred wholly, exclusively and necessarily in the performance of the duties of the employment (¶3270).

> MEMO POINTS   For tax purposes, the term "emoluments" has been superseded by the more user-friendly term "earnings" and, consequently, will be referred to as such. Employment income used to be **taxable under Schedule E**.

3101   If HMRC successfully argue that a worker has been incorrectly treated as self-employed, the individual will be **re-categorised** as an employee.

In a re-categorisation it is likely that the **consequences will fall on the employer**, who is liable to account for the income tax and NIC that should have been deducted under PAYE. In addition, penalties and interest may be charged.

There is no automatic recognition of the **tax and NIC paid by the individual** as a self-employed person. However, HMRC may transfer all or part of the PAYE liability from the employer to the employee. When assessing the employer for PAYE, any tax paid by the employee under self-assessment will be taken into account.

3110   **Earnings** can essentially be summarised as a payment in return for acting, or being, an employee. Earnings are **defined as** (s 62 ITEPA 2003):
- any salary, wages or fee;
- any gratuity or other profit or incidental benefit of any kind obtained by the employee if it is in money's worth; or
- anything else that constitutes an emolument of employment.

The **factors** which must be taken into account are:
- whether there is a direct link between the payment and the employment;
- its monetary value; and
- the time when the remuneration is assessed.

Providing the earnings arise from the office or employment, they are assessable for tax whether or not they are **received from** the employer (*Hochstrasser v Mayes* [1960] AC 376, HL).

> MEMO POINTS   1. **Money's worth** is defined as something that is:
> - of direct monetary value to the employee; or
> - capable of being converted into money or something of direct monetary value to the employee.
> 2. Employees are taxable on **commission** received in respect of goods, investments and services sold to third parties during the course of their employment: HMRC SP 4/97. Where the employee is obliged to pass on the commission to another party, wholly, exclusively and necessarily to perform his employment duties, he will be able to claim a deduction for the amount paid.

Payment derived from employment

3111   Not all payments made by employers to employees constitute earnings. Conversely, some payments made by persons other than the employer will constitute earnings. The crucial test is whether the payment is derived from the employment, which essentially includes the situation of a reward for services, rendered either in the past, currently, or in the future, or to encourage the employee generally.

Each case will be addressed on its merits, but as with employment status, a body of case law exists from which the **following tests** have evolved:

Type of payment	Details
Gifts	Recognition of the person, such as gifts on marriage, does not constitute earnings. However, gift vouchers given to employees at Christmas were held to be earnings because the primary reason for the gift was the position of the individuals as employees, with a secondary reason of encouraging future productivity. (The fact that the employees were not contractually entitled to the payment was ignored.)
Prizes	A payment relating to exceptional examination performance was held not to be earnings, as it was paid for personal reasons. However, employees earning more than £8,500 per annum are still assessed.

Type of payment	Details
Compensation	May not be earnings. In the case of a payment made to an employee on the withdrawal of a savings-related share option scheme, it was held that the payment was a recognition of the loss of the right to benefit from the scheme, and not made as a result of employment.
	However, a payment to an employee in return for giving up a benefit was held to be taxable as earnings.
	Where an employer reimburses an employee in respect of bank charges, which have arisen due to a failing on the part of the employer, this will not be earnings.
Inducement	May be earnings if it can be shown that there is a link between the payment and future services.
	A payment may be taxable even where the old employer, or an unrelated third party, makes a payment to induce an individual to take up employment with another employer.
Reasonable expenses	Paid to a teacher attending a course voluntarily have been held not to be earnings.
Payments from someone other than the employer	Generally earnings, including tips to waiters or taxi drivers. For the PAYE treatment, see ¶6812, and for the NIC treatment, see ¶6946.
Payments to a third party	By the employer on behalf of the employee are earnings taxable on the employee. So payment of the employee's health club bill is taxable as earnings.
Payments made in exceptional circumstances	May not be taxable.
Payment anticipated by employee	It is likely that such a payment will be earnings.

Disguised earnings through third parties

3112 New legislation came into force on 6 April 2011 to discourage the use of a number of methods for rewarding employees by using trusts and other vehicles to hold assets (which may include shares or cash) on their behalf (ss 554A-554Z14 ITEPA 2003). This strategy relies on the argument that because of the way the arrangements are structured, the employee has no legal right to the assets, and hence is not taxable on their value.

Arrangements of this kind include:
– Employee Benefit Trusts (EBTs);
– trusts used by quoted companies to hold employee shares; and
– Employer Funded Retirement Benefit Schemes (EFRBS).

The legislation **treats as earnings** benefits or sums derived from certain forms of arrangement involving an employer, an employee and a third party to provide rewards or recognition in connection with the employment, in circumstances such that the benefit or sum would not otherwise be taxed as earnings. To fall within this treatment, the arrangements must include:
– a loan of money or assets to the employee;
– the earmarking (however informally) of money or assets for the subsequent benefit of the employee; or
– a payment of money or transfer of assets to the employee.

HMRC will apply a series of subjective tests to decide whether a particular set of arrangements gives rise to a tax charge.

The **taxable amount** is the higher of:
– the sum of money made available to the employee; and
– the market value of any asset or other benefit provided.

The rules also apply to retirement benefit arrangements other than those made through registered schemes, but not to payments that are taxable as pension income.

MEMO POINTS 1. The provisions are very **widely drawn**, embracing employees and employers irrespective of whether the employment relationship is past, present or future, and includes transactions with persons linked to either the employee or the employer.
2. There are a number of **conditional exclusions** for arrangements involving the provision of taxable benefits such as car schemes and share schemes, and for normal commercial transactions or terms.
3. **Earmarking** can also give rise to a tax charge if it involves action by the employer rather than a third party.
4. **Anti-forestalling provisions** apply from 9 December 2010, to ensure that arrangements made before the legislation was finalised still come within its scope.

Value of remuneration

3113 **Monetary** payments made in the form of cash, cheque or bank transfer are the most common forms of earnings, and are easy to value. By its very nature, **non-monetary** remuneration, such as benefits in kind (¶3150) or shares (¶3340), does not have an immediate cash value, so special valuation rules exist.

If an employee **accepts a reduction** in his pay in return for a benefit in kind, the unreduced pay will still be liable to tax. As an exception, this rule no longer applies when an employer provides a car as a benefit in kind in return for an agreed reduction in pay, as the employee will almost always be taxed on the benefit in kind.

Time of assessment

3114 Monetary earnings are assessed on a receipts basis, irrespective of when the services which relate to the earnings were actually performed (s 15 ITEPA 2003). There are special rules for non-monetary earnings such as benefits in kind, including vouchers.

In most cases it is straightforward to ascertain when earnings are assessable. However, the following rules apply if earnings are paid:
– in a tax year **before commencement** of the employment, when the earnings will be assessed as occurring in the tax year when the employment commences;
– **after cessation** of the employment, such as the case of continuing medical benefit, when the earnings are assessed on a receipts basis; or
– **after death**, when it is likely that the employee's death estate will be assessed to income tax on a receipts basis.

Earnings for **employees** other than directors are treated as received on the earlier of the following dates (s 18(2) ITEPA 2003):
– when the payment of earnings is made; or
– when the employee becomes entitled to the payment.

For directors, the rules are extended so that earnings (whether arising from the directorship or a different role) are treated as received on the earliest of the following dates (s 18(2) ITEPA 2003):
– when the payment of earnings is made;
– when the director becomes entitled to the payment;
– when sums on account of earnings are credited in the company accounts or records (regardless of whether the director has the right to draw the money);
– where the amount of earnings for a period has already been determined, the date on which the period of account ends; or
– where the period of account has already ended, the date when the amount of earnings for a period is determined.

MEMO POINTS It is common for a **general accrual** to be made for directors' bonuses in the draft accounts. For the accrual to be recognised for accounting purposes (and therefore for corporation tax), it is important that the company has at least a constructive obligation at the balance sheet date to pay extra remuneration to the directors, and this should be appropriately minuted as a board resolution. If so, the date of the resolution will be the key date for the directors' receipt of remuneration, unless the directors are also shareholders, when the date of the decision regarding the amount of bonuses will be the operative date.

B. Lump sum payments

3115 In addition to earnings paid in the normal course of employment, payments may also be made in the form of a lump sum on the commencement, termination or variation of employment. Such payments are often made as compensation for the loss or surrender of rights, or for failure to give notice of the termination of employment. Alternatively, a lump sum payment may simply be made to reward an employee for past or future services.

The nature of a lump sum payment will determine whether and how it is taxed.

1. On commencement of employment

3120 The crucial question with respect to payments made on the commencement of employment is whether the payment is a **reward** or an **inducement** for becoming an employee, in anticipation of future services. If this is the case, the payment will be taxed as earnings. In contrast, payments that are shown to be **compensation** for giving up an advantage relating to a previous employment will be free from income tax.

2. On variation of duties or earnings

3121 The same **criteria** as on the cessation of employment apply to lump sum payments paid on the variation of an employment in connection with a change of duties or earnings (¶¶3123+).

3. On termination

3122 Depending on the circumstances, either part or all of a payment may be exempt from tax if it is a valid termination payment (¶3124).

To decide on the tax treatment, HMRC **apply** the following four tests to each element of a termination package in a strict order. If a payment falls within more than one category, it will be taxed under the earliest e.g. a payment which is both earnings and a termination payment is taxed as earnings.

Test	Criteria	Tax treatment
1	Earnings from the employment	Taxable
2	Restrictive covenant	Taxable
3	Benefits from an employer-financed retirement benefit schemes	Taxable
4	Termination payment	Possibly exempt

Taxable as earnings

3123 The general rule is that termination payments are taxable in full as earnings if they arise out of a **contractual liability** or constitute a **reward for past services**.

Exemptions

3124 If a payment is **validly made on termination** and is not chargeable under any other section, the **following types** of exemption are available (s 401 ITEPA 2003):
– a £30,000 tax-free amount;
– payments on death or disability;

– payments to a registered pension scheme; and
– certain payments relating to foreign service.

3125 **Tax-free amount** This is the most common exemption, and the **maximum** exemption for each employment is £30,000 (s 403(1) ITEPA 2003). The exemption is applied first to cash payments and then benefits.

For these purposes **two or more payments** will be treated as deriving from the same employment and therefore eligible for only one £30,000 exemption where the payment is from:
– the same employer; or
– different employments with the same or associated employers (i.e. employers under common control).

If the threshold is **not used up in one tax year**, it can be carried forward and set against payments made in respect of the same employment in future tax years.

3126 **On death or disability** Tax will not be **charged** on any payment or other benefit provided by an employer (s 406 ITEPA 2003):
– in connection with the termination of employment on the death of an employee; or
– on account of injury to, or disability of, an employee.

To qualify under the latter exemption it must be established that either an injury or disability exists, and it was for this reason only that the employer made the payment.

This exemption must be considered at the time of the termination, as a **subsequent medical condition** cannot be cited as the reason for any payment.

> MEMO POINTS For these purposes, the term **disability** covers not only a condition resulting from a sudden affliction but also continuing incapacity to perform the employment duties, arising from deterioration of physical or mental health caused by chronic illness. There must be medical evidence confirming the nature of the disability.

3127 **To a registered pension scheme** Where a lump sum is paid under the provisions of a registered occupational pension scheme, it will be exempt from tax and NIC if the payment (s 407 ITEPA 2003):
– is compensation for either loss of employment or a decrease in earnings due to ill health; or
– has been earned by past service.

> MEMO POINTS Special **employer contributions** to an approved pension scheme (personal or occupational) will be exempt from tax and NIC, if the related benefits are within the scheme rules (s 408 ITEPA 2003). Similarly, tax will not be charged where the employer purchases an **approved annuity** from a life office for an employee.

3128 **Effect of periods of foreign service** A payment may be fully or partially exempt where an employee has undertaken foreign service **during** his employment and makes an appropriate claim within 5 years and 10 months following the tax year (s 413 ITEPA 2003). A period of foreign service is essentially defined as a period when earnings are not liable to UK income tax. The **strict definition** of a period of foreign service is a period when all duties of the employment were undertaken outside the UK and the employee was either:
– UK domiciled but not resident and ordinarily resident in the UK; or
– resident and ordinarily resident in the UK, but non-UK domiciled and working for a foreign employer.

The following table sets out the **criteria** to be satisfied for the payment to be fully exempt:

Period of service up to termination	Period of foreign service
Any duration	At least 75% of the whole period of service
More than 10 years	The last 10 years of service
More than 20 years	At least 50% of the whole period of service, including any 10 of the last 20 years

Where the employee's foreign service **does not meet the criteria** above, the payment will be taxed as follows (s 414 ITEPA 2003):
a. deduct the tax-free sum of £30,000; and
b. apply the following fraction to the remaining amount to calculate the taxable payment.

$$\frac{\text{Foreign service}}{\text{Total service}} \times \text{Amount otherwise chargeable to tax}$$

3129

Reporting requirements

Employers must provide HMRC with a report including **details of** any payments or benefits in excess of £30,000 paid to employees on the termination of employment, unless the payment is purely in cash and form P45 has not already been issued. The report must be submitted by 6 July following the end of the tax year. There is **no requirement** to report a termination package **worth less** than £30,000.

3131

The report should **state** the following (reg 91(3) SI 2003/2682):
– the total package (including estimates where necessary);
– the payments and benefits paid in the year of termination;
– any future payments and benefits to be paid; and
– the total number of years in which the package will be paid with details of any event which would reduce this period.

Employees must be **provided with** the same information as contained within the report (reg 96 SI 2003/2682). The employee should include the termination payment on his tax return, to ensure the correct amount of tax is paid.

<u>MEMO POINTS</u> If an event occurs which causes the **reported payments to change**, a further report should be made by 6 July following the tax year in which the event occurs.

4. Specific provisions

Redundancy payments

Statutory redundancy payments are exempt from income tax. However, such payments will reduce the £30,000 tax-free limit available for valid termination payments (¶3124).

3132

<u>EXAMPLE</u> B was made redundant and received £15,000 of statutory redundancy pay. He was also given his company car (cash equivalent £17,000) as compensation. Although the redundancy pay will not be subject to tax, it will reduce the amount of the exemption available with respect to the car to £15,000 (30,000 – 15,000).
The taxable amount will therefore be £2,000 (17,000 – 15,000).

Many employers pay amounts in **excess** of the statutory amount, and provided the whole amount is a genuine redundancy payment, it will all be taxed as a termination payment, i.e. the first £30,000 will be tax free (¶3124).

3133

This has been held to apply to a payment given to an employee who had "done the right thing" by her employer in resigning, instead of staying on and being made redundant, on the basis that the employer had benchmarked this payment against the employee's potential redundancy package and it was in consequence of or in connection with her termination of employment (*Resolute Management Services Ltd and anor v Revenue and Customs* [2008] UKSPC SPC00710).

<u>MEMO POINTS</u> **Re-employing** an individual after making them redundant may lead HMRC to challenge any package originally taxed as a termination payment.

Payments in lieu of notice

A payment in lieu of notice (PILON) can **include** the following:
– a contractual payment made instead of giving adequate notice;

3134

– a discretionary payment made by the employer instead of giving notice; and
– a payment agreed between the employer and employee at the time of termination with no prior contractual commitment or understanding.

The tax treatment will depend on whether the PILON has been made in relation to a breach of the employment contract. If the **contract** of employment **provides for a PILON** to be made by the employer and the employer pays the employee according to this clause, there is no breach of contract and the payment is taxed as earnings. If, however, the contract of employment does **not provide for a PILON** and the employer fails to give the employee notice, any payment made to the employee for his notice period will be in breach of contract. The payment is deemed to constitute compensation for this breach and will not be treated as earnings.

3135 The tax treatment of PILONs has been subject to much interpretative case law.

If a **contractual PILON** is subject to the **employer's discretion**, the payment will still constitute earnings as there is no breach of contract (*EMI Group Electronics Limited v Coldicott (HM Inspector of Taxes)* [1999] IRLR 630, CA). It may be argued that the employer did **not exercise his discretion** but instead breached the contract and paid compensation (*Cerberus Software Ltd v Rowley* [2001] IRLR 160, CA). In such circumstances, all the factors need to be considered to ascertain whether the employer has exercised his discretion or not.

Where a PILON is made in circumstances **contemplated in the contract**, the payment will be taxable as earnings (*SCA Packaging Ltd v HM Customs & Excise* [2007] EWHC 270 (Ch)). In this case, although the contract did not provide for PILONs, there was a reference to a memorandum of understanding agreed between the employer and the trade union, which contained provisions relating to redundancy, notice periods and PILONs.

While HMRC now accept that it is unlikely that an implied contractual term in relation to PILONs can exist (because it would conflict with the contractual and statutory right to receive a period of notice), it may treat a **non-contractual PILON** as earnings where an employer has **established a practice** of making non-contractual PILONs. However, HMRC acknowledge that a payment made automatically or habitually does not of itself make it earnings; an employer may pay damages in that way. An employer does not make an automatic payment if he makes a genuine **critical assessment** in the making of the payment (i.e. one that essentially seeks to identify adjustments typical of a damages payment). However, the employer may have valid commercial reasons not to make any such adjustments and any such reasons will be taken into account when deciding whether the character of the payment is that of damages.

3136 For any payment to be treated as compensation in breach of contract, it is advisable that **termination occurs before** any payment is agreed (*Richardson (HM Inspector of Taxes) v Delaney* [2001] IRLR 663).

Garden leave

3137 If the employee is on garden leave (¶2529), any payments made during the period will be taxable as earnings and liable to NIC, because the employee is still employed until the end of the notice period, even though he is not attending his place of work.

Benefits from an employer-financed retirement benefit scheme

3138 A payment will be at risk from an HMRC challenge under this provision, and therefore taxable, if the employee is at, or approaching, **retirement age** (determined either by the employment contract or the state pension age). Any payment under an arrangement could be caught, unless the package includes only benefits and no cash.

These provisions do not, however, apply to payments on redundancy, ex gratia payments or payments made because of death, or disability due to ill health or accident.

MEMO POINTS HMRC consider that an **arrangement** exists where the payment flows from any prior formal, or informal, understanding with the employee, or as a result of any system, plan, pattern or policy. Payments made in the following circumstances would be caught under this provision:

– as a result of a decision at a meeting;
– decided upon by a personnel manager who is acting under delegated authority; or
– where it is common practice for an employer to make such a payment to a particular class of employee.

Restrictive covenants

3140

Where an employer makes a payment in respect of a covenant (whether legally valid or not) given by an employee, the intention of which is to restrict his activities or his ability to compete with his employer, the payment will generally be taxable as earnings (s 225 ITEPA 2003). In practice, where restrictive covenants are part of a termination settlement, it is usual for a nominal amount to be allocated to such restrictive covenants in compromise agreements to establish the amount that will be taxed as earnings (¶9276).

Unless the payment is excessive, HMRC will not seek to tax a payment made in respect of a restrictive covenant under a compromise agreement which **reaffirms undertakings** stated in the original employment contract or contains a provision which states that: HMRC SP 3/96
– the agreement is in full and final settlement of the employee's claims; and/or
– the employee agrees not to commence legal proceedings, and to discontinue any which may already be in progress.

Outplacement counselling for losing employment

3141

Where this is **provided by the employer**, the costs incurred (including related travel expenses) are not taxable on the employee, if all of the **following conditions** are met (s 310 ITEPA 2003):
a. the employee must have been employed for a 2-year period ending either when the counselling begins, or when the employment ends;
b. the only or main purpose of the counselling is to enable the employee to adjust to losing his job or find some other method of earning income (including self-employment);
c. the counselling is generally available to employees or a particular class of employee; and
d. the counselling consists of the giving of advice, imparting skills, or providing normal office facilities or equipment.

> MEMO POINTS 1. Any amount attributable to outplacement counselling does **not use up** the £30,000 tax-free amount.
> 2. There is tax relief for the costs of **re-training** provided by the employer in the event of redundancy (¶3160).

Unfair dismissal compensation

3143

Where damages for unfair dismissal are awarded by an employment tribunal, the tax treatment will depend on whether the employee is reinstated.

Where **reinstatement or re-engagement** occurs, there is no termination, and so any arrears of pay are usually taxable as earnings.

Otherwise, any compensatory awards are a valid termination payment.

> MEMO POINTS Compensation awarded in relation to the employer's failure to provide a **written statement** detailing the reasons for dismissal is also a termination payment for tax purposes.

Legal costs

3144

Where an **employer agrees to pay** the employee's legal costs in relation to the **termination of his employment**, this would normally be a taxable benefit for the employee.

However, the employee will be **exempt from tax**, where the dispute is settled (s 413A ITEPA 2003):
a. outside court and all of the following apply;
– the employer pays the solicitor direct;
– the fees paid only relate to the termination of the employee; and
– the fees are paid under a specific term in the settlement agreement; or
b. by a **court order** and payment is made under such an order (even if the payment is made direct to an employee).

If the solicitor finds it necessary to consult with another professional, such as an accountant, whose fees are treated as **disbursements** by the solicitor, then these will also be included within the legal costs which could qualify for exemption.

II. Benefits and expenses

3145 Benefits in kind are assessable on most employees. Usually an employee will also be assessed on expenses incurred by the employer, subject to making a claim for a business expense deduction against earnings.

> *MEMO POINTS* Expenses and benefits must be valued inclusive of VAT where it applies, and are not subject to immediate deduction of income tax through the payroll. Instead, the employer must report all relevant items to HMRC on forms P11D or P9D, and the employee pays tax through his PAYE code for the next year, or through his self-assessment return.

Classification of employees

3146 The rules for benefits in kind and expenses depend on the type of employee, defined as follows (s 216 ITEPA 2003):

Term	Definition	Directors (¶3148)
Relevant employee	An individual who earns £8,500 or more per annum	✓
Lower paid	An individual earning less than £8,500 per annum	X (with a limited exception)

Summaries of the different tax treatment for benefits and expenses depending on the type of employee can be found at ¶3194 and ¶3270 respectively.

3147 To determine whether the **threshold** of £8,500 has been met or exceeded, the following items should be taken into account, on the basis of amounts earned in the tax year (s 218 ITEPA 2003):
– salary;
– all benefits received, whether taxable on all employees or under the provisions relating to relevant employees (including share schemes etc), excluding exempt income;
– any deemed earnings arising from the personal service company provisions; and
– expenses incurred by the employee and reimbursed by the employer (other than when a dispensation (¶6900) is in force).

Deductions may be made for approved pension contributions and contributions under payroll giving schemes. No deduction is made for expenses of employment.

> *MEMO POINTS* 1. If an employee is employed for only **part of the year**, the threshold is compared to the annualised earnings.
> 2. Where a person has **two or more employments** with the same employer, the total income from all employments is aggregated. If the threshold is exceeded, the employee is treated as a relevant employee for all of the employments (s 220 ITEPA 2003).

Directors

3148 As directors are in a position of control, they may be able to influence the level of benefits which they receive and are therefore identified separately (s 67 ITEPA 2003).

A director (including a shadow director, whose instructions the directors usually follow) is **treated as** a relevant employee **unless** he earns less than £8,500 per annum, does not have a material interest (essentially more than 5% of the ordinary share capital of a company) and is either a:
– full-time working director (devoting substantially the whole of his time to the service of the company in a managerial or technical capacity); or
– director of a non-profit making company or charitable organisation.

A. Benefits

3150 A benefit in kind (referred to in this section as a benefit) **is usually** a payment made other than in cash to an employee or director (or a member of his family or household) by reason of his employment. Certain minor benefits which are available to all employees of an employer may be specifically exempted.

The **general test** is whether such a payment is one made in return for acting as, or being, an employee. This means that payments or provisions made by an employer (other than a company) in the normal course of his social relationships will not constitute benefits. It is **not necessary** for the benefit to be **from the employer** for it to be taxable, although it must be provided by virtue of the employment. For example, a car provided to a professional footballer by a car dealer would be an assessable benefit.

Goods and services provided to an employee as a result of his employment will not be assessable if they are for business purposes only. Where there is an **element of private use** or where an **asset is transferred** to the employee an assessable benefit may arise.

3151 A benefit may also arise where a payment is made to a member of an employee's **family or household** as a result of the employment (s 721(5) ITEPA 2003). Family is generally defined as the employee's spouse, parents and children (and their spouses) and dependants. Household has the same definition but also includes servants and guests.

3152 This section identifies various benefits and explains the valuation rules applicable to each type. Exempt benefits are discussed before taxable benefits, and reference should be made first to the table at ¶3155, before consulting the table at ¶3190.

1. Non-taxable benefits

Summary

3155 The following table provides a summary of the benefits which are not taxable on any employee.

General area	Specific benefit	Basic conditions	Legislation reference (ITEPA 2003)	¶¶
Subsistence	Meals and drinks	Provided to all employees on similar terms. Meals made available by an employer who is not the employee's own employer are also exempt.	s 317	¶3157
	Small and seasonal gifts	Being made generally available to all employees on similar terms e.g. Christmas bottle of wine, flowers on birthdays etc	s 210	-
	Luncheon vouchers	Up to 15p per day until 5 April 2013, but exemption abolished after that date	s 89	-
	Homeworking allowance	Up to £208 p.a. automatically exempt. Further amounts possible.	s 316A	¶3326

REMUNERATION

General area	Specific benefit	Basic conditions	Legislation reference (ITEPA 2003)	¶¶
Travel	Workplace parking space	For cars, vans, motorbikes and bicycles	s 237	-
	Mileage allowances	If within certain limits dependent on mileage	s 229	¶3303
	Free transport	Travel, accommodation and subsistence provided during a public transport strike	s 245	-
		Employer-subsidised public bus services	s 243	-
		Work bus provided for journey between home and workplace, including minibuses with at least 9 seats	s 242	-
		Travel by taxi etc between workplace and home for occasional late night working (9pm or later), if the number of late nights is less than 60 nights in a tax year. Appropriate records must be kept.	s 248	-
		Provision of alternative transport when expected car sharing arrangements are not available	s 248	-
		Travel from home to workplace for disabled employees	s 246	-
	Cycling	Cycles and related safety equipment made available to all employees, and used mainly for commuting and/or certain short journeys between work and local amenities. Incidental private use does not disqualify the bicycle.	s 244	-
		Provision of breakfast to cyclists on an unlimited number of designated cycle to work days	SI 2002/205	-
	Use of a heavy goods vehicle	Exceeding 3,500kg fully laden and mainly used for business purposes	s 238	-
Training and counselling	Work-related training	Includes retraining programmes on redundancy	ss 250, 251, 311, 312	¶3159
	Scholarships	Not received by reason of employment	s 211	¶3162
	Welfare counselling	Made available to all employees on similar terms. Not relating to finance (other than debt), tax, legal issues or leisure	SI 2000/2080	-
	Pensions advice	External advice paid for by the employer up to £150 p.a.	SI 2004/3087	-
Provision of equipment	Any work equipment and services	Where private use is not significant	s 316	¶3165
	Provision of single mobile phones (including a car phone)	All private use exempt unless employer pays bill in employee's name	s 319	¶3167

General area	Specific benefit	Basic conditions	Legislation reference (ITEPA 2003)	¶¶
Medical costs	Medical checks	Health screenings and medical check-ups	s 320B	¶3166
	Overseas medical costs	Medical insurance and treatment during foreign visits where performing employment duties	s 325	-
	Eye tests and corrective glasses	Where employee uses VDU, and provision of test and glasses is required by Health and Safety regulations	s 320A	-
Miscellaneous	Childcare	Workplace facilities exempt	s 318	¶3171
		Weekly allowance per employee of direct nursery payment/voucher exempt	s 318A	¶3173
	Parties and functions	Cost up to £150 per head Event must be available to employees generally	s 264	¶3175
	Removal expenses	Up to £8,000 exempt	s 271	¶3177
	Job-related accommodation	Where necessary for better performance of duties, or for security reasons	ss 99, 100	¶3201
	Personal equipment for disabled individuals	Provision of equipment and services to enable duties of employment to be performed	SI 2002/1596	-
	Long-service awards	For at least 20 years of service and not cash	s 323	¶3180
	Sports facilities	Available to all employees but not to the general public. Facilities also made available by an employer who is not the employee's own employer are also exempt.	s 261 SI 2004/3087	-
	Staff suggestion schemes	Open to all employees on equal terms	s 321	¶3182
	Entertaining and gifts from third parties	Cost of gift to donor is £250 or less	s 324	¶3184
	Goods provided at a discount	Provided amount paid by the employee is more than the cost of the goods incurred by the employer	ss 62, 203	-

Provision of meals and canteen facilities

A **benefit does not arise** where employees are provided with canteen facilities, even if the canteen is not in the employer's premises or under his control (s 317 ITEPA 2003). The **basic premise** of the exemption is that all staff of the employer, or at least all at a particular location, are provided with a meal. However, the exemption also applies where:
– meals are provided on a reasonable scale; and
– the employer gives free or subsidised meal vouchers to staff for whom meals are not provided.

However, since 6 April 2011, the provision of subsidised or free canteen food for workers is a **taxable benefit** in circumstances where:
– the availability of the canteen is linked to a salary sacrifice arrangement where the employee has given up some of his gross salary in return for food and drink; or

3157

– there is a flexible benefits scheme in operation, so that the employee has chosen to give up some salary in return for food and drink.

The luncheon voucher scheme is unaffected by these changes (until its abolition with effect from 6 April 2013), as are arrangements where the employer provides a general subsidy for canteen food, to offer food at lower prices to all employees.

MEMO POINTS 1. The exemption also extends to **light refreshments** such as tea and coffee.
2. It is common for employers to provide lunch during **meetings**, which would be taxable unless all employees were to be provided with lunch.
3. No benefit arises where free or subsidised canteen facilities are made available at the **premises of another employer**, who is not the employee's own employer (SI 2004/3087).

Work-related training courses

3159 Where an employee attends training courses paid for by his employer (either directly or via reimbursement), no benefit arises provided the training is related to his current employment (ss 250, 251 ITEPA 2003). In certain cases, this will also be true where it relates to a position with a prospective employer. In addition to the actual training course, this exemption covers any **associated costs** (for example, accommodation, examination fees and registration fees which become payable as a result of achieving a qualification) and **assets provided** for use by the employee during the period of training, or in his employment.

The exemption does **not apply** to entertainment and recreation costs or courses provided as an inducement or reward for services.

3160 Certain benefits provided for employees at a **time of redundancy** are not taxable (s 311 ITEPA 2003). These include training courses (including related travel costs) of up to 2 years' duration, allowing the employee to retrain for a new career. The exemption will apply where the employee's job has already been terminated, or he ceases to be employed within 2 years of the end of the course. **Counselling services** in connection with redundancy are also excluded from the charge to tax (¶3141).

Scholarships

3162 **Generally** income from a scholarship is exempt from tax for the recipient (ss 211-213 ITEPA 2003). However, where an employee, or a member of his family or household, receives a scholarship by reason of employment, it will be taxable on the employee (unless the employer is an individual, and the scholarship is made as a result of a social relationship).

By **exception**, where the employer makes a scholarship available to a member of the employee's family or household, but only as a result of fortuitous circumstances (such as the employee's child wins the scholarship through a public exam), the income will be exempt, providing all of the following conditions are met:
– the scholarship is not provided by reason of employment;
– the funds are provided by a trust fund or a scheme;
– the scholarship is to be held by an individual in full-time education, such as a school or university student; and
– less than 25% of the payments made by the trust are scholarship payments provided by reason of employment.

3163 An employee who receives a scholarship from his employer for undertaking a **full-time educational course** will, by concession, be exempt from tax up to a maximum of £15,480 (for the 2007/08 academic year and later years) (HMRC SP 4/86). If this limit is exceeded the whole amount will become taxable. The exemption does not apply to payments for periods spent at work (whether during college vacations or otherwise).

MEMO POINTS 1. **To qualify** for the exemption, the employee must be enrolled in the educational establishment for at least 1 academic year with an average attendance of not less than 20 weeks per year.
2. The payments are also free of **NIC**.

Provision of equipment and services

Equipment and services provided by an employer will be exempt where they are (s 316 ITEPA 2003):
– **provided at work**, and the employee's private use is not significant (e.g. private emails sent during lunchtime); or
– **intended for home use**, but the sole purpose of doing this is to enable the employee to perform his work duties, and again private use is not significant.

However, if the employer has any intention of rewarding the employee, the exemption does not apply.

Common items which could be covered by this exemption include computers, the provision of broadband, and newer PDAs which are akin to a computer. Cars, boats, aircraft and living accommodation are never covered by the exemption.

> MEMO POINTS HMRC decide whether private use is **not significant** by taking into account the necessity for the employee to have the equipment or services provided in order to carry out his duties. So the time spent on business or private use is of relevance but not of paramount importance.

3165

Medical check-ups

Annual health screenings and medical check-ups provided by an employer are exempt. The benefit can be selectively **provided to** some employees and still be exempt. The exemption is limited to one instance per year per employee.

> MEMO POINTS 1. **Health screenings** are assessments to identify employees who might be at particular risk of ill health.
> 2. A **medical check-up** is a physical examination of an employee by a health professional in order to determine his state of health.

3166

Mobile phones

The provision of a single mobile phone (including a car phone) to an employee for his use only is not a taxable benefit, provided it is supplied under a **contract in the employer's name**. The provision of more than one phone leads to a benefit, although the employee can choose which phone is taxable. The provision of a voucher by the employer to facilitate the employee's use of a single mobile phone is exempt.

If the contract is in the **name of the employee**, and the employer meets the costs of the phone, any private use will be taxable. As the employer is settling a debt of the employee, the payments made should be put through the payroll, which means Class 1 NIC applies.

When a phone is taxable, the benefit is calculated by adding together all the bills received in the tax year, and then deducting any costs for business calls. Basic contract costs are not business related for this purpose.

> MEMO POINTS HMRC accept that a smartphone qualifies as a mobile phone for the purpose of this tax exemption. This applies to smartphones as configured and understood at the start of 2012, and does not imply automatic exemption for future technology. HMRC consider that many modern PDAs will also qualify as smartphones, but any device that is solely a PDA will be regarded as a computer (¶3165).

3167

Childcare

For employees with **parental responsibilities** the following potentially qualify:
– employer-provided childcare facilities; and
– direct payment for childcare by the employer.

Where an employer offers either scheme, it must be open to all employees or to all those working at a specific site where the scheme is offered.

> MEMO POINTS 1. Employers can include childcare as **part of an overall package** which offers the benefit:
> – as an addition to the existing salary;
> – as part of a flexible benefits scheme; or
> – in return for a sacrifice of salary.

3169

2. A **salary sacrifice** is a legally-binding change in the contractual arrangements between the employer and the employee, and most commonly occurs where the employment contract is amended to reduce the employee's entitlement to cash salary in return for a non-cash benefit (such as childcare, pension contribution, or more holiday entitlement). The value of the non-cash benefit may equate to the amount of salary "sacrificed". **To be effective**, a salary sacrifice must be irrevocable and future remuneration must be given up before it is treated as received for the purposes of either NIC or income tax. Employers should ensure that the payslip shows the reduced salary only. A salary sacrifice cannot reduce an employee's remuneration below the national minimum wage. Non-cash benefits provided via salary sacrifice schemes must continue to be provided (at the employer's expense) during periods of maternity, adoption and paternity leave with no deduction being made from the employee's SMP, SAP or SPP/ASPP. In addition, a reduction in salary may impact on other benefits, such as entitlement to state pensions and tax credits. Employers should seek legal advice when setting up sacrificial arrangements.

3171 **Workplace nurseries** To be excluded from taxation (and also NIC), childcare facilities must be housed in non-domestic premises that are **provided** either **by** the employer, or by a group of people including the employer (s 318 ITEPA 2003). The employer must be wholly or partly responsible for managing and financing the provision of childcare facilities. Any care registration requirements for either the staff or the premises must be met.

Childcare may be **provided to** any child under 18 years of age (including a stepchild) of the employee who either lives with the employee or is maintained fully by the employee. Children for whom the employee has parental responsibility are also included, regardless of whether they live with the employee or not.

> MEMO POINTS 1. HMRC have stated that the employer must make a substantial commitment to **funding** the facility, such as guaranteeing to underwrite potential losses or paying a fixed contribution for the long term.
> With respect to **management**, the employer must have close involvement in:
> – appointing and reviewing the performance of the carers;
> – the extent of care provided, and the related conditions; and
> – the allocation of nursery places.
> 2. There are many **commercially marketed schemes** which involve an employee entering into a salary sacrifice arrangement, whereby he gives up an amount of pay equal to the cost of the nursery place that is provided. The employer pays for the nursery place for the employee's child, but also pays an additional annual fee per place. The employer appoints a scheme promoter to act as agent at meetings with the nursery management committee.
> HMRC may attack these arrangements as follows:
> – the salary sacrifice is not effective, so the full salary is taxable;
> – the nursery place is in reality a contract between the employee and nursery, so the amount paid by the employer is taxable as earnings; or
> – the financing and management criteria are not met because the arrangements are a sham.

3173 **Direct payment** For employees who **entered into childcare arrangements on or after 6 April 2011**, the limits on tax and NIC exemption for childcare vouchers and directly-contracted childcare provided through employer-supported schemes are dependant upon the employee's income tax band as follows:

Tax band [1]	Maximum exemption (£ per week)
Basic rate (20 %)	55
Higher rate (40 %)	28
Additional rate (50 %)	22

1. Details of the tax band thresholds can be obtained from HMRC. See *Tax Memo* for more information.

This makes the net value of the relief the same for all taxpayers at £11 per week. Employers are required to estimate the employee's likely annual earnings (including benefits, but excluding potential bonuses or overtime) when making payments.

These limits do not apply to employees who joined the childcare arrangements **before 6 April 2011** and remain in the same employment after that date. For them, the former weekly limit of £55 continues to apply.

The exemption from tax (and NIC) is given against the first earnings for the week per employee, regardless of the number of children involved (ss 318A, 270A ITEPA 2003). So two working parents paying basic rate tax with one child can receive up to £110 tax free per week.

The contract must be between the employer and the childcare provider. Alternatively the employer can provide **vouchers** with the appropriate face value for the employee's income tax band (or, for employees whose childcare arrangements pre-date 6 April 2011, a face value of up to £55 per week) which will also be exempt. The administration costs incurred by the employer are not an assessable benefit for the employee.

For this exemption, a **qualifying child** is a child aged 15 or less, up to 1 September following the child's 15th birthday; and either:
− a child or stepchild of the employee who is maintained (wholly or partly) at the employee's expense; or
− resident with the employee, and for whom the employee has parental responsibility.

MEMO POINTS 1. In this case, a child for whom the employee has parental responsibility, but who **does not live with** the employee, will not qualify.
2. For **disabled children**, the age requirement is extended by a year to 16.
3. Vouchers cannot be exchanged for cash, otherwise tax and NIC become due. So any **refund** made by the nursery to the employee must be routed through the employer.
4. The provision of tax-free childcare may reduce a claim for **tax credits**, in which case HMRC should be notified. Low paid employees who accept vouchers instead of a salary rise are particularly adversely affected, because the corresponding reduction in tax credits outweighs the value of the tax-free childcare and so they are worse off.

The **type** of childcare which qualifies for the exemption includes registered or approved care provided by a:
− registered childminder;
− school or educational establishment;
− school or local authority, for children who are at least 8 years old, in relation to pre- and after-school care; and
− registered nanny in the child's own home.

However, care provided by the employee's partner (married or unmarried) will not qualify. Care provided in the child's house by a relative is also precluded.

MEMO POINTS 1. There are specific **inclusions** for **qualifying childcare** in relation to England, Wales, Scotland, Northern Ireland, and outside the UK.
2. **Nannies** should be registered with OFSTED for their costs to qualify for this exemption.
3. The definition of **relative** includes parents, grandparents, siblings, aunts and uncles.

3174

Parties and functions

There is an exemption which applies to an **annual party** (e.g. a Christmas party), or similar annual event (e.g. a summer barbecue), provided for employees where the cost per head does not exceed £150, and the party is either available to (s 264(3) ITEPA 2003):
− all employees generally; or
− all those working at a specific location, where the employer has more than one location.
This can also be extended to different sections or departments providing the party is available to all staff at the site.

If the employer provides **two or more annual functions**, no charge arises in respect of the events for which the costs per head do not exceed £150 in aggregate. If the aggregate cost per head exceeds £150 per head, then the events within the limit are exempt (choosing the best combination), and the others are taxable.

The **cost of the function** is calculated by adding together all costs, including VAT and transport, and dividing by the number of all attendees (including non-employees). If insufficient numbers attend a function, this could make it taxable rather than exempt. However, an assessable benefit would only be calculated on the proportion of the cost represented by attendees who are employees and members of their family or household.

Where tax arises, the employer should pay it through a PAYE settlement agreement (PSA) (¶6902) to relieve the employee from any liability.

3175

Removal expenses

3177 When an individual relocates due to his employment, removal expenses **up to a maximum** of £8,000 may be paid by the employer without being treated as a benefit, where they consist of (ss 271-289 ITEPA 2003):
– reimbursements from his employer in respect of removal costs; or
– costs directly incurred by the employer.

For these purposes, **relocation includes** the situation where an employee moves:
– in order to take up a new employment;
– as a result of being given a new job within the organisation; or
– where the location of the current employment changes.

The relocation must be **necessitated by** the old residence not being within a reasonable daily travelling distance of the workplace. The new home obviously must be within commutable distance.

> MEMO POINTS   Where **payments exceed £8,000**, the excess will be taxed, although lower paid employees (¶3192) are only assessable on payments made to them in respect of their costs, not on expenses directly incurred by the employer (s 287 ITEPA 2003).

3178 The removal **costs** may include the following (s 272 ITEPA 2003):
– fees in connection with selling the previous residence and acquiring the new one (including stamp taxes and legal costs);
– fees in connection with an abortive acquisition, where the intended new residence is not acquired due to circumstances outside the employee's control, or other reasonable circumstances;
– costs of transporting belongings including insurance, reconnection fees etc;
– costs of replacing equipment which is not suitable for use at the new residence (e.g. replacing a gas cooker with an electric one where the new residence is not connected to the gas supply);
– travel and subsistence costs (e.g. costs incurred in going to view possible properties); and
– bridging loan expenses to the extent that the loan is used to purchase the new residence and does not exceed the proceeds from the sale of the old residence (including loans by the employer).

Generally, qualifying removal costs must be **incurred by** the end of the tax year following the tax year in which the employee relocated, although HMRC have discretion to extend this time limit.

Long service awards

3180 For service in excess of 20 years, awards **consisting of** assets or shares in the employing company valued at up to a maximum of £50 for each year of service (up to 20 years) can be made to staff without a tax charge (s 323(2) ITEPA 2003).

Where the award is made in **cash**, an assessable benefit will arise for all employees. Relevant employees (¶3146) will also be assessable where an award in excess of the maximum is made in the form of an **asset** or other non-cash benefit.

Staff suggestion schemes

3182 Awards may be made to employees under qualifying staff suggestion schemes without a tax charge (ss 321, 322 ITEPA 2003). **To qualify**, a staff suggestion scheme must be open to all employees on equal terms. If the award relates to a specific suggestion, it must relate to the employer's business and be outside an employee's normal duties.

Awards are usually only made when a suggestion is **implemented** and, subject to an overriding maximum of £5,000, they should not exceed:
– 50% of the expected net benefit of implementation in the first year; or
– 10% of the expected net benefit over 5 years.

Where a cash award is non-qualifying it will be assessable on all employees. However, a non-qualifying award which is made in the form of an asset is only assessable on relevant employees (¶3146).

Where a suggestion is **not implemented**, but the employer wants to encourage future suggestions, the maximum award is £25.

> *MEMO POINTS* 1. Suggestions made during **meetings** are considered part of the employee's normal duties.
> 2. Where the award **exceeds** £5,000, the excess is taxable.

Third party gifts and entertaining

3184

Goodwill gifts (such as a bottle of wine from the employer's client) can be received by an employee without an income tax charge where all of the following conditions are met (s 324 ITEPA 2003):
– the cost to the donor is less than £250 (including the cumulative cost of all gifts within the same tax year);
– the gift is the goods themselves, or a voucher to acquire goods;
– the donor is not connected to the employer, or anyone connected with him; and
– the gift is unsolicited and not given in return for the employee's service.

Where **someone other** than the employer **entertains** an employee, including hospitality of any kind, there will be no taxable benefit if all of the following conditions are met (s 265 ITEPA 2003):
– the entertaining was not procured by the employer, or anyone connected with him;
– the person providing the entertainment is not connected with the employer; and
– the hospitality is not provided in return for any services of the employee.

If these **conditions are not met**, the third party must provide the employee with information about the amount of the benefit, which the employee should then include as assessable income on his tax return.

2. Taxable benefits

Summary of common benefits

3190

Benefit	Taxed on		Legislative reference (ITEPA 2003)	¶¶
	Lower paid	Relevant (£8,500+)		
Accommodation	✓	✓	s 102	¶3200
Ancillary expenses and services for accommodation	✗	✓	s 315	¶3218
Vouchers and credit cards	✓	✓	ss 73, 266	¶3208
Permanent health benefits	✓	✓	s 660	¶3211
Medical insurance	✗	✓	s 201	¶3194
Use of assets [1]	✗	✓	s 205	¶3215
Transfer of assets	✓ [2]	✓	s 206	¶3217
Company cars	✗	✓	s 114	¶3221
Car fuel	✗	✓	s 149	¶3229
Company vans	✗	✓	s 154	¶3233
Beneficial loans	✗	✓	s 175	¶3238
Payment of director's PAYE	✗	✓	s 223	¶3247

1. Excluding cars, vans, phones and accommodation.
2. See ¶3192.

Lower paid employees

3192 With the exception of living accommodation and vouchers (which have specific valuation rules), lower paid employees are **principally assessable** only on items that can readily be converted into cash.

This means that, in the absence of specific legislation, lower paid employees are only assessable on items which can be sold. For example, the right to use a car cannot be sold and therefore a lower paid employee would not be assessable. However, a gift of a car would be assessable as the employee could sell the car for cash. The cash equivalent of **an asset transferred** is the second-hand value, i.e. the amount for which the benefit can be sold. No comparison is made with the market value of the asset.

Relevant employees

3194 Relevant employees are **taxed on** every benefit received by reason of employment, such as private medical insurance, prizes, or gym membership, **unless** a specific exemption exists (s 201 ITEPA 2003). Generally, the time at which the benefit becomes **taxable** is **when** it can be enjoyed by the employee, which may be later than the time when the expenditure is incurred by the employer. Where an assessable benefit arises, the cash equivalent of the benefit is included as income of the employee and taxed accordingly.

3195 The **cash equivalent** is generally calculated as follows.

	£
Full cost to provider of benefit	X
Less: employee contribution	(X)
Cash equivalent	X

However, where a **cash alternative** is offered in lieu of the benefit, the value of the benefit will be the amount of cash offered. The exception to this is living accommodation, where the benefit will be valued under the rules in ¶3200 if this provides a higher figure than the amount of cash offered.

> MEMO POINTS Where the benefit consists of the provision of **in-house benefits** arising out of **surplus capacity**, the cash equivalent is usually the marginal cost incurred by the provider of the benefit. For example, in the case of a school educating the sons of teachers for reduced fees, the cost of providing education was not the fees that other parents paid, but the marginal cost to the school in having one extra pupil attend (*Pepper v Hart* [1993] AC 593).

---

a. Benefits chargeable on all employees

Living accommodation

3200 Living accommodation is not specifically **defined** but it is taken to mean all kinds of residential accommodation with the exception of overnight accommodation, a stay in a hotel room or board and lodging.

The provision of living accommodation by reason of employment, other than job-related accommodation, is a **taxable benefit for all employees** whether provided to the employee himself, or a member of his family or household (s 102 ITEPA 2003). Ancillary services provided with the accommodation are only taxable on relevant employees (¶3146).

3201 The provision of living accommodation **is job-related**, and thus non-taxable, where it falls within one of the **following exceptions** (ss 99, 100 ITEPA 2003):
a. where it is necessary for the proper performance of the employee's duties that he should occupy the accommodation e.g. a caretaker;
b. where the accommodation is provided for the better performance of the duties of his employment, and his is one of the kinds of employment where it is customary for employers to provide living accommodation for employees e.g. farm workers; or

c. where, because of a special threat to the employee's security, special security arrangements are in force and he resides in the accommodation as part of those arrangements e.g. the chairman of a company providing politically sensitive and therefore high risk services.

The exemptions outlined in **a.** and **b.** above will not be available to a **director** unless he is a full-time working director either:
- with no material interest in the company; or
- of a non-profit making or charitable company.

> MEMO POINTS 1. Providing accommodation for the **employee's convenience** is not job-related accommodation, and the exemption does not apply.
> 2. A further exemption is available where a **local authority provides** accommodation for an employee on terms which are not more favourable than those made available to non-employees.

Valuation of the benefit Where taxable living accommodation is provided to an employee, the way in which the benefit is valued depends on the cost of providing the property (usually taken to be the rent paid by the employer if it is leased, or its rateable value otherwise), less any rent paid by the employee. All accommodation is subject to the same cash equivalent calculation, but property with a cost to the employer in excess of £75,000 is also subject to an additional charge.

3202

Where the ownership period of the person providing the accommodation exceeds the 6 years before it is first occupied by the employee, cost is substituted by the market value at the date the property is first occupied (including any improvements made between acquisition and first occupation), provided the original costs of purchase and subsequent improvements were in excess of £75,000.

> MEMO POINTS 1. If a **cash alternative** is offered instead of the accommodation, this may affect the value of the taxable benefit.
> 2. **Shared accommodation** is taxed by apportioning the benefit fairly between the employee occupants.

Vouchers, credit tokens and credit cards

When any employee (or a family member) receives **vouchers or credit tokens**, an assessable benefit arises (s 75 ITEPA 2003). A voucher is defined for this purpose as any voucher, stamp or similar document, or token capable of being exchanged for money, goods or services, and includes transport vouchers and cheques. A credit token is something which allows the holder to obtain goods or services on presentation, without actually being surrendered at that time. The most common credit token is a credit card.

3208

Vouchers giving entitlement to the following are specifically **exempt** from the benefit rules:
- parking provision;
- childcare up to the weekly limit (¶3173);
- exempt transport (¶3155);
- subsidised meals;
- third party entertainment and gifts;
- cycles and associated safety equipment;
- one mobile phone;
- annual parties etc;
- sporting and recreational benefits; and
- eye tests and correctional appliances.

Vouchers give rise to a tax liability as if the employee had received a **sum equal** to the cost of providing the voucher. Where a **credit token** is used, the **cash equivalent** is the expense incurred for the provision of the credit token. Where the token can be used on multiple occasions, the value of the benefit at each use is the additional cost to the employer. Initial or annual subscriptions are ignored, as is interest.

For both vouchers and credit tokens, a **deduction** will be made against the taxable benefit for any sum made good by the employee.

> MEMO POINTS 1. If the voucher is used to incur expenses which are **business expenses**, a claim for a deduction can be made.

2. PAYE should be applied if the taxable voucher can be **exchanged for** a readily convertible asset, or the voucher can be exchanged for money. If the employee does not reimburse the employer with the amount of PAYE within 90 days, a further benefit will arise.
3. Concessions are available which allow some **employees of passenger transport undertakings**, such as railway companies, to receive non-taxable travel vouchers.

3209 Strictly, where a **credit card** is made available to any employee by reason of his employment, the employee will be taxed on any cost incurred on the card, including any subscription cost, but not any interest for late payment (s 94 ITEPA 2003).

The following **exceptions** exist, however, when:
– the employer receives HMRC approval that no tax liability will result from purely business use of the credit card; or
– the credit card is used to pay for exempt benefits, such as workplace parking, third party entertainment, incidental overnight costs or other exempt travel expenses.

If the credit card is used to purchase **readily convertible assets**, PAYE should be applied by the employer. If the employee does not reimburse the employer with the amount of PAYE within 90 days, a further benefit will arise.

Permanent health benefits

3211 The **right to receive sick pay** or the prospect of receiving it is not a taxable benefit.

Where the employer pays into a permanent health insurance policy, and the employee **receives benefits** while suffering from ill health, the employee will be taxed on those benefits as if they were earnings. If the policy is not funded by the employer, any benefits will be exempt.

---

b. Benefits charged on relevant employees only

Use of assets

3215 Where assets are made available (other than bicycles, cars or vans) for a relevant employee's private use, the **cash equivalent** of the benefit is based on the annual value of the asset (s 205 ITEPA 2003). The annual value is calculated as 20% of the market value of the asset when first made available to the employee. Any expenses incurred in connection with the provision of the asset are added to the benefit. Where the employer pays rent or a hire charge for the asset and this is greater than the annual value calculated above, the amount paid is substituted.

MEMO POINTS 1. If **two or more employees** have the use of the same asset, a fair apportionment should be made.
2. **Motorbikes** are assessed under these rules and this gives a more favourable result than the provisions for company cars.
3. **Land** is valued on the basis of the rent which might reasonably be expected to be obtained on letting (s 207 ITEPA 2003).

3216 Unless the criteria for limited private use apply (¶3165), the loan of a computer to an employee is taxable. If the employee only makes **business use** of the computer, this does not constitute a benefit in kind. **Mixed use** will mean that the employee is taxable on significant private use, although the employer will be liable for Class 1A NIC on the whole benefit.

MEMO POINTS There is a limited **exemption** for arrangements entered into before 6 April 2006.

3217 Where assets are **transferred** to a **lower paid employee**, the amount of benefit is the second-hand value of the asset (s 206 ITEPA 2003).

Where assets (other than bicycles and some computers) are transferred to a **relevant employee**, a benefit arises which is equal to the higher of the market value at the following times:
– at the time of transfer; or

— when first made available to an employee, if the asset has already been used by the employee, less amounts already taxed (both on the employee in question and other employees (¶3215)).

This amount is then **reduced by** any price paid by the employee.

> MEMO POINTS The benefit which is chargeable on the transfer of a **previously loaned bicycle** (¶3155) (or a **computer** which qualified for exemption while loaned) into an employee's ownership is based on the asset's current market value only. So where the employee buys the asset from the employer at this value, no benefit arises. HMRC operate a simplified procedure for valuing a bicycle transferred to an employee after the end of a loan or salary sacrifice arrangement. This avoids the difficulty of establishing a market value for the machine.

Ancillary services for living accommodation

3218 Ancillary services provided in connection with living accommodation may give rise to an assessable benefit for relevant employees, and **include**:
– heating, lighting or cleaning;
– repairs, maintenance or decoration (excluding structural alterations);
– council tax; and
– furniture or other effects normal for domestic occupation.

The **cash equivalent** of the benefit is generally the cost to the employer (e.g. if the employer provides a cleaner, the cash equivalent of the benefit will be the cleaner's wages and the cost of items such as cleaning materials) (ss 203-205 ITEPA 2003). The **exception** to this rule is where the ancillary service is in the form of an asset (for example a television) which is made available to the employee. In this case the cash equivalent will be valued in accordance with the rules for assets made available for the private use of employees (¶3215).

3219 Where the provision of living accommodation is not taxable because the employee satisfies one of the **exceptions** in ¶3201, the amount assessable in respect of ancillary services is restricted to 10% of the taxable earnings (excluding this benefit) from the employment, and then reduced by any amounts paid by the employee (s 315 ITEPA 2003).

In addition, **council tax** paid by the employer in relation to job-related accommodation is not assessable (s 314 ITEPA 2003).

> MEMO POINTS **Taxable earnings** are defined as remuneration after deducting pension contributions and deductible expenses, including capital allowances.

Company cars

3221 A benefit occurs when a car (often referred to as a company car) is provided, by reason of the employment, and is **available** for private use by a relevant employee (including a member of the employee's family or household) (s 114 ITEPA 2003).

The employer must **report** the provision of a car to an employee within 28 days of the end of the quarter in which the car is first made available.

3222 A car is treated as being available for **private use** unless (s 118 ITEPA 2003):
– such use is prohibited by the employer; and
– no private use actually occurs.

As an exception, the use of a **pool car** which satisfies all of the following conditions is not an assessable benefit (s 167 ITEPA 2003):
– it is made available to, and actually used by, a number of employees and is not usually used by one of them to the exclusion of the others;
– it is not normally kept overnight at or near the home of any of the employees who use it; and
– any private use is incidental to its business use.

3223 A car (including the provision of fuel and other related expenses) made available to a **disabled employee** by an employer will not constitute a benefit where all of the following conditions are satisfied (s 247 ITEPA 2003):
– the car has been specially adapted for the employee's needs (or is an automatic car where required);

– the car is only available for business travel, home to work travel and travel to training, and any other private use is prohibited; and
– no private use actually occurs.

If the vehicle is an **automatic car** provided to a disabled employee, the carbon dioxide emissions figure for an equivalent manual car should be used (s 138 ITEPA 2003). If the list price of the equivalent manual car is lower, that should also be used in the calculation.

Where accessories are added to **convert a car** for a disabled person, the price of such accessories is not a benefit (s 125 ITEPA 2003).

3224 **Accessories** provided for use in the performance of the **duties of the employment** are not assessed as a benefit. The price of **other** accessories (not supplied as standard) which are added when a car is first made available will increase the price of the car. If accessories with an individual price of at least £100 are added later, their full price is included in the price of the car for the tax year in which they are purchased, and in all subsequent years.

> *MEMO POINTS* **Replacement accessories** are normally ignored unless the replacement is superior to the original. In such a case the price of the car is increased by the difference between the price of the new accessory and the price of the original.

3225 **Valuation of the benefit** The **cash equivalent** of the benefit of a car made available for private use by an employee is a percentage of the list price of the car (which cannot exceed 35%), **determined by** the level of the car's carbon dioxide (CO_2) emissions and the date it was first registered. There are no reductions for high business mileage. Additional discounts off the standard charge apply to **dual fuel cars** and there is no assessable benefit on the cost of conversion.

Once the cash equivalent is calculated there is no separate charge on any **other costs** associated with the provision of the car (such as insurance and servicing). The exceptions to this rule are the cost relating to the provision of a chauffeur, which is assessed as a separate benefit under the normal rules (¶3194), and the provision of fuel for private motoring (¶3229).

> *MEMO POINTS* 1. The **price of the car** is the list price, if it has one, or, if not, the notional price, reduced by any capital contributions made by the employee. The price actually paid for the car is irrelevant. The former £80,000 limit on the list price of a car ceased to apply on 6 April 2011.
> The **notional price** is the price which might reasonably be expected to be the list price, if its manufacturer, importer or distributor had published one for an equivalent car sold in the UK in a single open market sale on the day before its first registration.
> 2. Where an employee makes one or more **capital contributions** to the cost of a car, the price of the car is reduced by the amount of the total contributions in that and earlier years, subject to a maximum of £5,000. No such deduction is made if the car's price exceeds £80,000.
> 3. Cars **registered before 1 January 1998** will not have a CO_2 emissions figure and therefore the benefit continues to be based on the engine capacity (whether petrol or diesel).

3227 The cash equivalent will also be **reduced** to take account of any periods of unavailability or any employee contributions, in that order (s 143 ITEPA 2003).

A **period of unavailability** will arise when the car is:
– made available or withdrawn part way through the year; or
– off the road for a period of at least 30 days (which may run into a new tax year).

Any amount **paid by the employee** as a condition of using the car during the tax year reduces the cash equivalent (s 144 ITEPA 2003).

Car fuel

3229 If private fuel is provided for a car by reason of employment, a further benefit arises, unless (s 150 ITEPA 2003):
– the car is a pool car (¶3222);
– the employee is disabled; or
– the fuel is electricity for an electric car, or any energy for a car which cannot in any circumstances emit CO_2 by being driven.

Where fuel is provided for a **non-company** car, the value of the benefit is the cost of providing the fuel. Where private fuel is provided for a **company car** (¶3221), the **cash equivalent** of the benefit is calculated by multiplying a fixed sum (£20,200 increasing to £21,100 from 6 April 2013) by the appropriate percentage determined by the level of the car's carbon dioxide (CO_2).

To **avoid a fuel benefit**, but ensure the employee and employer are not out of pocket, either the employee can **fully reimburse** the employer for private fuel, or the employer can reimburse the employee for business fuel. In either case, careful records of business mileage must be kept. **Partial reimbursement** by the employee will not reduce the fuel benefit. HMRC publish advisory fuel rates for these purposes.

The cash equivalent of the fuel will be **reduced** where (s 152 ITEPA 2003): **3231**
– the cash equivalent of the car benefit is reduced because it is unavailable for use throughout the tax year; and
– free fuel ceases to be available to an employee from any date to the end of the tax year (although if free fuel is provided later in the same tax year, no reduction is due).

Company vans

Where an employer makes a van available for the **private use** of a relevant employee (or a member of his family or household), an assessable benefit arises. A van is defined as any mechanically propelled road vehicle (not exceeding 3,500kg fully laden) which is primarily suited to the conveyance of goods of any description. **3233**

However, an employee who uses a pool van for mainly business purposes and who takes it **home overnight** is not taxed on a benefit where (s 168 ITEPA 2003, Sch 14 Finance Act 2004):
– he only uses the van for commuting; and
– any other private use is insignificant.

If private use is unrestricted, however, there will be a benefit (even where the employee makes a contribution to the costs). HMRC are unlikely to accept that a van is only used for commuting unless the employee has another vehicle available to him for private use e.g. a spouse's vehicle.

> MEMO POINTS   HMRC have published guidance on the interpretation of **insignificant**, which is deemed to take its dictionary meaning of "too small or unimportant to be worth consideration."

The cash equivalent of the benefit is £3,000 (s 155 ITEPA 2003). **3235**

The amount of the cash equivalent is **reduced** where the van is either unavailable (¶3227) or is a shared van. Any payments made by the employee for private use may also be deducted from the cash equivalent.

From 6 April 2010, for a period of 5 years, a vehicle designed primarily for the carriage of goods, and that cannot under any circumstances produce CO_2 emissions, will attract no benefit charge. Where **private fuel** is provided, the employee will be assessed on a benefit of £550 (increasing to £564 from 6 April 2013). To **avoid a fuel benefit**, but ensure both the employee and employer are not out of pocket, either the employee can **fully reimburse** the employer for private fuel, or the employer can reimburse the employee for business fuel. In either case, careful records of business mileage must be kept. **Partial reimbursement** by the employee will not reduce the fuel benefit (s 161 ITEPA 2003).

> MEMO POINTS   A van is a **shared van** for any period throughout which it is made available (but not necessarily used) **simultaneously** to more than one employee of the same employer. In this case, the van benefit (and fuel benefit if any) is reduced on a just and reasonable basis to take account of the sharing.

Beneficial loans

A relevant employee (including his relatives) who receives a cheap loan or credit by reason of his employment will be **liable to tax** on (s 175 ITEPA 2003): **3238**
– the cash equivalent of the cheap interest rate (if this is lower than the official rate of interest); and
– any waiver of the loan (¶3245).

MEMO POINTS 1. An employee will also be taxable on **loans obtained** in the following circumstances:
- the employer guarantees or facilitates a loan;
- low-cost alternative finance arrangements provided by the employer;
- a loan is provided by a shareholder in a close company as a result of the employment; or
- the employer takes over a loan from another person.

2. **Relative** includes the following for the purposes of these rules:
- the employee's spouse or civil partner;
- the parents, children and more remote ancestors or descendants of both spouses;
- the siblings of both spouses; and
- the spouses of all those mentioned above.

3239 The following types of loan are **exempt** from these rules, and so no benefit arises if the loan:
a. is an advance made by an employer to pay for necessary expenses and/or incidental overnight expenses where the amount outstanding does not exceed £1,000 and the advance is spent within 6 months of it being made;
b. is a fixed-term loan with a fixed rate of interest, which, at the time the loan was made, was not less than the official rate of interest;
c. is made as a result of a personal or family relationship;
d. would wholly qualify for tax relief if interest were charged;
e. balance is below £5,000 throughout the tax year (aggregating all loans from the employer, but ignoring any such loans qualifying for tax relief); or
f. is made on a commercial basis by an employer whose business includes the making of loans, provided a substantial proportion of loans are made to the public and the terms received by the employee are comparable to those received by the public at arm's length.

3240 **Valuation of the benefit** The **cash equivalent** of a loan is determined by calculating the difference between the interest paid by the employee and what would have been paid at the official rate of interest, using either the **averaging method** or the **strict method**. The employee should check both methods to see which is the more beneficial for the tax year. HMRC can, however, insist that the strict method is applied.

Loan waivers

3245 Where a loan provided by reason of employment is written off, it is **usually** taxable as regular earnings (¶3100) (s 188 ITEPA 2003). **Otherwise** an assessable benefit will arise for relevant employees, and the **cash equivalent** is the amount of the loan written off.

A loan written off after the **death of the employee** does not lead to an assessable benefit (s 190 ITEPA 2003).

PAYE paid for directors

3247 Where the employer **does not deduct PAYE** from the earnings of an individual in the following circumstances, then the PAYE itself becomes earnings if (s 223 ITEPA 2003):
- the individual has been a director at any time during the tax year;
- the employer pays the PAYE to HMRC; and
- there is no reimbursement to the employer by the director.

For these purposes a director is defined as for a relevant employee (¶3146).

B. Expenses

1. General principles

3265 As a general rule, where an **employer settles an expense**, the employee will be treated as having received earnings upon which he will be taxed, subject to a claim for expenses incurred in relation to the duties of employment, or to a dispensation arranged by the employer (s 72 ITEPA 2003).

Less common is the situation where the employee incurs **expenses which are not reimbursed by the employer**, in which case the employee will be at a disadvantage, having incurred expenses out of taxed income. Again a claim should be made, in order to deduct business expenses against taxable income.

EXAMPLE A receives an annual salary of £30,000 from B Ltd and incurs £1,500 of employment expenses in the tax year.
1. If B Ltd does not reimburse A, he will have a net salary of £28,500 but in the absence of a claim he will still be taxed on income of £30,000.
2. If B Ltd reimburses A, he will (in the absence of a claim) be treated as if he had received earnings of £31,500.
In both cases A will effectively pay tax on £1,500 which he has in fact used to pay expenses.
If the conditions are satisfied, A can submit a claim which will reduce earnings by the amount of the expense:
1. No reimbursement

	£
Salary	30,000
Less: claim	(1,500)
Taxable	28,500

2. Expenses reimbursed

	£
Salary	30,000
Reimbursed expenses	1,500
	31,500
Less: claim	(1,500)
Taxable	30,000

Summary

There are **three ways** in which employment expenses are incurred:
– the employee pays the expenses and is reimbursed by the employer either for specific expenses incurred or by way of an expense allowance;
– the employee pays the expenses without reimbursement; or
– the employer pays the expenses directly.

The **tax treatment** is different for each type of payment, depending on the type of employee, as follows:

Payment method	Lower paid employee	Relevant employee	¶¶
Reimbursement	Not taxable unless excessive	Taxable but may claim deduction	¶3274
No reimbursement	May claim deduction	May claim deduction	¶3276
Employer pays directly	Not taxable	Taxable but may claim deduction	¶3277

3270

Timing

Expenses are **deemed to be incurred** in the same tax year as the earnings they relate to, even if that is a different tax year to when they were paid (s 328 ITEPA 2003).

EXAMPLE B incurred employment expenses on 15 March 2012 which were reimbursed to him on 12 April 2012.
The reimbursed expenses will be assessable in 2012/13 and B will therefore be deemed to have incurred the expenses in 2012/13.

3273

Expenses paid by employee and reimbursed by employer

3274 **Relevant employees** (¶3194) are assessed on any cash payment made to them arising from the employment. The result of this provision is that any expenses paid to an employee (whether as an expense allowance or as reimbursement of expenses incurred) are considered to be earnings (ss 70, 216 ITEPA 2003). For example, an employee who is reimbursed for a train fare incurred on a business trip would be liable to tax and NIC on that amount.

Where the relevant conditions are satisfied (¶3278), a claim may be submitted which will allow the taxpayer to **deduct** a corresponding amount from his taxable income. The net effect is therefore that an employee will not be taxed on genuine business expenses.

In practice, where it can be shown that specific expenses payments will always be covered by such a claim, a **dispensation** (¶6900) can be obtained which will avoid the necessity of completing a P11D and having to make an expense claim.

Employers are obliged to **declare** to HMRC all expenses payments made to employees, unless a dispensation is in place.

> MEMO POINTS Expenses reimbursed to **lower paid employees** are not taxable where the reimbursement is an:
> – exact repayment of expenses incurred in performing the duties of employment;
> – allowance to cover expenses while away from home; or
> – HMRC-agreed scale allowance.
> Any excessive payments, however, may be taxable.

Expenses incurred by employee with no reimbursement

3276 Where the appropriate conditions are satisfied, **any employee** who incurs expenses without reimbursement may claim a deduction against his taxable earnings. HMRC will, however, often query the validity of expenses where there has been no reimbursement by the employer, because in reality an employer would normally provide the necessary tools and equipment for the employee to carry out his duties.

Expenses incurred directly by the employer

3277 For **relevant employees**, expenditure incurred directly by the employer will be assessable as earnings although a corresponding claim for a deduction can be submitted providing the conditions (¶3278) are satisfied.

For **lower paid employees** the direct payment of bills on behalf of an employee will not be taxable unless it is the payment of a monetary liability. For example, the direct payment of a telephone bill (i.e. where the bill is addressed to the employer) is not subject to tax.

---

2. Tax deductible employment expenses

3278 For an expense to be allowable as a deduction:
– qualifying **travel expenses** must have been incurred necessarily in the performance of the duties of the employment;
– **capital allowances** claimed in respect of assets must relate to expenses incurred necessarily in the performance of the duties of the employment (ss 15, 36 CAA 2001); and
– all **other expenses** must have been incurred wholly, exclusively and necessarily in the performance of the duties of the employment (s 336(1) ITEPA 2003).

> MEMO POINTS The amount of a deductible expense is limited to the amount of the earnings from which it is to be deducted.

3279 The phrase **wholly, exclusively and necessarily** is derived from the legislation but each element has been the subject of a great deal of interpretative case law. The general conclusion has been that, where all of the elements apply, the expenses must relate specifically to the employment rather than to the individual who holds the employment. This means that the duties of the employment must require the outlay of the expense, any personal benefit being incidental.

Wholly and exclusively

An expense may be incurred for the **purposes** of the employment but may not wholly and exclusively relate to that employment. For example, if a company decided to install a telephone in the home of an employee so that he could make business calls, the cost of the business calls would be deductible but the line rental would not. This is because the line can be used to make personal calls and is not therefore wholly and exclusively used for the employment.

3280

Necessarily

The requirement for an expense to have been incurred necessarily in the performance of duties **means** that it would not be possible to perform the duties without the expense being incurred. There is no corresponding requirement for self-employed individuals, which is the main reason that it is easier for them to claim a deduction for expenses.

3281

In the performance of duties

The issue of whether an expense is incurred in the performance of duties is primarily a **question of fact**. Further, a distinction must be drawn between expenditure incurred to put the employee in a position to perform his duties efficiently (not deductible) and expenditure incurred as part of those duties (deductible).

3282

3. Expenses subject to special rules

Some expenses in employment do not fall within the general principles outlined above because the conditions for claiming a deduction are different, or because special rules are required for calculating the amount of the expense. These expenses are covered in greater detail as follows:

3284

Expense	¶¶
Travel and subsistence	¶3285
Business entertaining	¶3322
Subscriptions	¶3324
Working at home	¶3326
Payroll giving	¶3328
Capital allowances	¶3329
Employee's liability and indemnity insurance	¶3330

a. Travel and subsistence

Employees are taxed on travel and subsistence expenses incurred by reason of the employment and paid for or provided by the employer (or a third party) either directly or by way of reimbursement (s 337 ITEPA 2003; Booklet 490).

3285

Where the expenses are incurred necessarily in the performance of the duties, the employee will be able to claim a deduction from his earnings.

Qualifying situations

Whether travel and subsistence expenses (referred to for the remainder of this section as travel expenses) are incurred in the **performance of the duties** of the office or employment will depend in part on the nature of the journey. Broadly, a deduction will not be available if the journey represents ordinary commuting or private travel.

3286

A journey directly from the office to a client site for a meeting will be an allowable deduction but the following scenarios are not as clear cut:
- travel between home and workplace;
- travel between home and workplace where home is also a place of work;
- travelling between two employments; and
- travelling between two centres of the same employment.

Each of these scenarios is considered in the following paragraphs.

3287 **Qualifying travel expenses** Qualifying travelling expenses are defined as those incurred in the performance of the duties of the employment which are:
- necessarily incurred in travelling in the performance of those duties; or
- other travelling expenses attributable to the necessary attendance of the employee at any place of work (other than expenses connected with ordinary commuting or private travel).

Ordinary commuting is deemed to be travel between the employee's home and the permanent workplace, where the employee regularly attends to perform his duties of employment (s 338 ITEPA 2003).

Private travel is deemed to be travel from the employee's home to somewhere other than a workplace. The primary purpose of the trip is the key issue. For example, if an employee undertakes a journey in order to carry out employment duties, but he also visits a relative in the same town after work, the journey will not be private travel.

3288 **Travel between home and workplace** As a **general rule** the cost of travel between an employee's home and his normal place of work will not be a deductible expense. However, an **exception** allows employees to claim a deduction for qualifying travelling expenses between home and a temporary workplace.

3289 A **temporary workplace** is a place that the employee attends in the performance of the duties of the employment for the purpose of performing a task of limited duration (s 339 ITEPA 2003). If there is no substantial effect on the journey time or expense normally incurred, travel to such a temporary workplace would still constitute ordinary commuting.

3290 A period of attendance at a workplace for a **limited duration** will be a permanent workplace if the employee attends it for practically all of the period for which he or she is likely to hold that employment.

A workplace will **become permanent** if it is attended (or is likely to be so) for a period of continuous work of more than 24 months during which time 40% or more of the employee's working time is spent there. It is therefore possible for an employee to have more than one permanent workplace at the same time.

Where the workplace is **expected to be temporary**, but then it is decided that the employee will actually be spending more than 24 months there, travel expenses incurred:
- up to the date when the decision is made are deductible; and
- after that date relate to ordinary commuting, and no deduction can be claimed.

> MEMO POINTS 1. Where the period of continuous work is 24 months or less but is likely to represent all of the employee's **remaining period of employment** the workplace cannot be treated as temporary.
> 2. If the employee travels **direct from home to a temporary workplace**, he can claim the full cost as a deduction.
> 3. Where the employee **passes the permanent workplace** on the way to a temporary workplace, but does not stop there, he can claim a deduction for the whole journey from home to the temporary workplace.
> 4. For an **agency worker**, each assignment is treated as a separate employment, and each workplace is therefore a permanent workplace. Where an agency worker **undertakes a number of different jobs on the same day** (e.g. nurses), HMRC will accept a deduction for the cost of travel between different jobs on the same day: Booklet 490. However, there will be no deduction for the cost of travel from home to the first job of the day or to home from the last job of the day.

> EXAMPLE Mr A lives in Town X and works 5 days a week in Town Y. He is not entitled to claim a deduction for the expense of travelling between the two towns.

> Mr A's employer is setting up a new branch, and asks him to spend a proportion of his time in Town Z.
>
> If Mr A is asked to spend:
> 1. 3 days a week in Town Z for a period of 18 months, he can claim a deduction for travel to Town Z, because the period is less than 24 months.
> 2. 1 day a week in Town Z for a period of 26 months, he can claim a deduction for travel to Town Z, because although the period exceeds 24 months, Mr A is spending less than 40% of his time there.
> 3. 3 days a week in Town Z for a period of 26 months, he will not be entitled to a deduction as he will be deemed to have a permanent workplace in both Town Y and Town Z.
> 4. 3 days a week in Town Z for a period of 30 months, but Mr A actually only spends 18 months in Town Z. There is still no deduction, because the initial intention was for Town Z to become a permanent workplace.
> 5. 3 days a week in Town Z for a period of 18 months, which is extended, 1 year later, to a total of 28 months. Mr A can claim a deduction for travel to Town Z for the first year only, until the decision is made to lengthen his working period.

3291 An **exception** to the rules on travelling expenses applies to area-based employees (such as salesmen or estate workers) who will be treated as if their permanent workplace is a specific area (s 339(8) ITEPA 2003). An **area-based employee** is one:
– whose duties are defined by reference to an area (although they may require attendance outside that area);
– who attends various places in that area in the performance of his duties; and
– where none of those places represents a permanent workplace.

Travel from home to the boundaries of the area will not be allowable as a deduction but expenses within the area will be allowable. Where the area-based employee lives within the area all travel within the area will be allowable.

3292 Home is also a workplace Expenses incurred in travelling between home and a place of work may be deductible if the employee is genuinely using his home as a base of operations, and there is an objective requirement for him to perform his employment duties at home. Where an employee works at home for reasons of convenience only, his home does not become a workplace.

3293 Travelling between two employments The cost of travelling between two different employments or between two different employers will not be a deductible expense (s 340 ITEPA 2003).

By exception, expenses incurred by a director or employee when travelling between two companies within a group will be deductible.

3294 Travelling between two centres of employment An employee who is required to attend more than one place of work in the performance of his duties may claim a deduction for the expenses of travelling between two places of work (provided they are both part of the same employment).

Amount of deduction

3300 Where travel expenses qualify for relief, the amount of the deduction is the full cost with no adjustment for the saving that the employee made by not having to travel to his normal workplace.

For these purposes travelling expenses will include:
– fares on train, bus, plane etc;
– vehicle hire charges;
– costs associated with an employee's use of his private car;
– toll fees and car parking; and
– subsistence expenses where an overnight stay is required.

Where expenditure is **not attributable to the business travel** (for example the cost of private telephone calls, laundry and newspapers) it will not qualify as a deduction under these provisions. Instead a fixed sum is allowed for incidental expenses based on the number of nights spent away from home (¶3309).

3301 In most cases the **full cost** will be the actual amount paid, such as the cost of a ticket or of a hotel room. Special rules apply to determine the expense incurred by an employee who uses his own car for business journeys.

3302 A deduction is **only available** for the expenditure actually incurred, so an employee who chooses to take a coach rather than a plane will only receive a deduction for the cost of the coach, even if the employer reimburses the cost of a plane fare. The employee will therefore be taxed on the difference.

Similarly, the fact that travel costs were not the cheapest available will not prevent a claim being allowed for the full amount of the expenditure incurred. For example, the cost of a first class ticket will be allowable even if a standard class ticket was available. However, where the cost of travel and subsistence is **unusually lavish**, HMRC may seek to tax an element of the cost, on the basis that it was provided by way of a reward. For example, if an employee who usually travels standard class and stays in two star hotels flies first class to New York and stays in a five star hotel, an element of the cost of the trip may be deemed to be a reward for past performance.

3303 **Use of employee's own vehicle or bicycle** There is a statutory **exemption** from tax for the following approved mileage allowance payments which are made to an employee in respect of a qualifying vehicle (s 230 ITEPA 2003). The payments must be made by the employer and are not available if the employee is a passenger in the vehicle, or if the vehicle is a company vehicle. Since 6 April 2011, these maximum tax-free amounts are:

Vehicle	Mileage in tax year	Rate per mile
Cars and vans	Up to 10,000 miles	45p
	Excess over 10,000 miles	25p
Motorcycles	No restriction	24p
Bicycles	No restriction	20p

3304 If an employee is entitled to, but **does not receive**, mileage allowance payments as described above, he may be able to claim a deduction from earnings, being:
– the amount of mileage allowance payments to which the employee would have been entitled; less
– any payments which he actually received.

If the employee receives **excess mileage payments**, he will be taxable on the excess, and only this amount should be entered on the employee's P11D and tax return.

3305 A driver who takes **passengers** with him in a car or van will not be taxable on any related payment of up to 5p per passenger per mile paid by his employer. The passenger must also be engaged on business travel for the employer. If no passenger allowance is payable by the employer, the employee cannot claim a deduction.

3306 **Subsistence** Subsistence is not **defined** by the legislation but is taken to be the additional costs of living away from home. If the employee has continuing commitments at home and is obliged to live away from home in order to carry out the duties of his employment, the additional costs will normally be allowed in full. If the employee does not have a permanent residence (e.g. he normally lives in a hotel or club) then a subsistence deduction will not be available.

3307 From 6 April 2009, HMRC have introduced an **advisory system of benchmark scale rates** which all employers can use to make subsistence payments free of tax and NIC to employees.

This **affects** subsistence expenses incurred while travelling on an allowable business journey during the day only, when the following **qualifying conditions** are met:
– the travel is in the performance of an employee's duties or to a temporary place of work;
– the employee is absent from his normal place of work or home for a continuous period in excess of either 5 or 10 hours; and
– the employee incurs a cost of a meal (i.e. food and drink) after starting the journey.
Employers wishing to use the benchmark system must **notify** HMRC by ticking the appropriate statement on form P11DX (¶6901) before starting to use the system.

The following **rates** apply:

Situation [1]	Detail	Rate (£)
Breakfast (irregular early starters only)	The employee leaves home earlier than usual (before 6 am) and pays for breakfast	5
One meal rate	The employee has been away from his home/normal place of work for a period of at least 5 hours and pays for a meal [2]	5
Two meal rate	The employee has been away from his home/normal place of work for a period of at least 10 hours and pays for meals [2]	10
Late evening meal rate (irregular late finishers only)	The employee has to work later than usual (finishing after 8 pm) having worked his normal day, and has to buy a meal which he would usually have at home [3]	15
Note: 1. A **limit** of three meal rates in a 24-hour period applies. 2. Where employees are required to **start early or finish late on a regular basis**, the 5 or 10 hour rates could be paid provided all the other qualifying rules are satisfied. 3. If the employee is **paid an allowance under the 5 or 10 hour rule**, the late meal allowance could still be paid if work finishes after 8 pm and he buys a meal that he would usually have at home, unless he regularly finishes work late.		

An employer may choose to pay **higher rates**, although any excess will be liable to tax and NIC unless a specific agreement is reached with HMRC, or the employer is merely reimbursing the actual cost incurred.

Incidental overnight expenses The expenses which fall under this provision are those considered incidental to the individual's stay away from his usual abode during a qualifying absence from home (ss 240, 241 ITEPA 2003). For example, this might include telephone calls home, laundry or newspapers.

3308

A **qualifying absence** from home is any continuous period during which the individual is obliged to stay away from home for at least 1 night.

Personal incidental expenses are not earnings providing they are below the de minimis **limit** of £5 per night in the UK and £10 per night outside the UK. Where the de minimis limit is exceeded, the whole amount (not just the excess) will become taxable.

MEMO POINTS   Where the expenses of travelling to a particular place would not be deductible, this prohibits any claim for related accommodation expenses. For example, where a salesman makes a visit to relatives on the way to a client, the cost of travel from the office to the relatives' house will not be deductible, and neither will the cost of hotel accommodation nearby.

Where the employee spends **two or more consecutive nights** away, the total expense for the period is compared to the total of the de minimis amounts for the nights spent away. There is no requirement for each night to be looked at in isolation. Where the employer pays the expenses directly and the expenses for a number of employees are aggregated so that separate identification would be difficult, HMRC will accept a reasonable apportionment of the expenses.

3309

Foreign elements

Where an employee who is resident and ordinarily resident in the UK (¶3370) performs the **duties** of his office or employment **wholly overseas**, then a deduction will be allowed for

3310

the cost of travelling to and from any place in the UK at the beginning and end of the employment (s 341 ITEPA 2003).

Such an employee who performs the duties of his employment **partly overseas** can claim a deduction for an unlimited number of visits to the UK provided that (s 370 ITEPA 2003):
– each journey to the UK is made after carrying out duties that can only be performed outside the UK; and
– the journey outwards is undertaken in order to commence or resume such duties.

The deduction is made from taxable earnings but is restricted to the amount borne or reimbursed by the employer.

If the **employer is foreign**, the employee must be UK domiciled to claim a deduction.

3311 Where the employee holds **two or more offices or employments** and the duties of at least one are performed wholly or partly outside the UK, then the cost of travelling from one to another will be deductible from the earnings of the destination employment (s 342 ITEPA 2003).

3312 Where, for the purpose of enabling the employee to perform the duties of the overseas employment, expenses are incurred on **board and lodging** outside the UK, a deduction will be allowed (s 376 ITEPA 2003). Apportionment will apply where the board and lodging is only partly provided to enable the employee to perform his duties.

A deduction will be available if the employer incurs the expense of certain **journeys** by the employee's **spouse or any child** of his, where he is absent from the UK for a continuous period of 60 days or more for the purpose of performing the duties of employment (s 371 ITEPA 2003). The journeys must be made to accompany him at the beginning of the period of absence or to visit him during that period, and there is a limit of two return trips by the same person in any year of assessment.

b. Other expenses

Business entertaining

3322 Expenses incurred in entertaining customers are strictly not wholly, exclusively and necessarily incurred in the performance of the duties of an employment because of the dual function of feeding the employee as well. Often an employer will provide an employee with an allowance to be used for business entertaining purposes (ss 356, 357 ITEPA 2003). **In practice**, HMRC do not seek to tax reimbursed entertaining expenses, gifts or entertaining allowances on the principle that the employer will not be able to claim a deduction for the expenditure, and to tax the employee would create a double charge.

Staff entertaining is a deductible expense, unless the entertaining of non-employees is the main purpose of the expenditure (s 358 ITEPA 2003).

Subscriptions

3324 Two types of subscriptions are **allowable as a deduction** from earnings (ss 343, 344 ITEPA 2003):
– where the performance of the employment duties requires membership of a certain organisation, and it is a condition of employment; or
– where the performance of the duties of the employment is directly affected by the knowledge concerned or involves the exercise of the profession concerned.

The latter type of subscription is only eligible as a deduction if it is approved by HMRC, and a list of approved bodies, which is updated periodically, can be obtained from flmemo.co.uk/em3324

Working at home

3326 No liability to income tax arises where an **employer makes a payment** to an employee in respect of reasonable additional household expenses which the employee incurs while working from home (s 316A ITEPA 2003). There is no wholly, exclusively and necessarily test in this case.

The annual **limit** for such payments is £208 (£4 per week) since 6 April 2012. Amounts **in excess of** this figure can also be paid free of tax, provided the employer has reached prior agreement with HMRC, or he can provide supporting evidence that the payment is in respect of additional household expenses incurred by the employee.

If the **employer does not pay** any homeworking allowance, a deduction will be allowed for reasonable expenses where the employee does not have a permanent office base.

3327

HMRC have clarified that unreimbursed homeworking expenses are only valid as a deduction where the employee's situation fulfils all of the following **conditions** (Tax Bulletin 79):
– the main duties of the employment are carried out at home;
– those duties require specific facilities;
– either the facilities are not available at the employer's premises, or the nature of the duties requires the employee to live so far from the premises that it is unreasonable for him to travel there; and
– at no time before or after the contract is written is the employee able to choose between working at the employer's premises and elsewhere.

In particular, HMRC have stated that no deduction can be claimed for council tax, rent, water rates, mortgage payments or insurance premiums.

However, a £4 per week deduction may be claimed where it is impossible to calculate the value of homeworking costs (which can include light and heat, and telephone), and a further amount will be allowed where evidence is retained. Alternatively, the employer can agree a different rate of average reimbursement with HMRC.

Payroll giving scheme

Employees may be able to make **charitable donations** direct from their salary, where the employer operates an approved payroll giving scheme (s 713 ITEPA 2003). Under the scheme, an employee arranges for a regular amount (with no maximum limit) to be withheld from his salary by his employer, which is allowed as a tax deductible expense against his earnings.

3328

The amounts withheld are then passed by the employer to an approved agent (or charity) for onward distribution to nominated charities.

> MEMO POINTS   1. The employer must deduct the amount from earnings when calculating the **PAYE** (but not NIC) deductions. Therefore the employee obtains tax relief at source, so a donation of £100 will only cost £80 for a basic rate taxpayer, and £60 for a higher rate taxpayer, and £50 for an additional rate taxpayer.
> 2. Employers who **second employees** to charities or educational establishments are entitled to relief for staff costs.

Capital allowances on assets other than cars

Where expenditure is incurred necessarily on **plant and machinery** (other than a car) for use in the performance of the duties of the employment, capital allowances may be claimed.

3329

Employee's liability and indemnity insurance

Where an employee has incurred a liability (to the employer or a third party) as a result of negligence in his capacity as an employee, he will be able to obtain a deduction for the following **types of expense** (s 346 ITEPA 2003):
a. insurance premiums paid to indemnify the employee against liability for his acts or omissions while undertaking his employment duties;
b. payments to settle an uninsured liability for the same acts and omissions as in **a.**; and
c. payments of costs incurred which relate to the liability, such as court fees.

3330

An employee may also claim relief for payments made within the 6 years following the tax year in which a **previous employment** ceases (s 555 ITEPA 2003). Relief is given in the year in which the payment is made, and unused relief cannot be carried forward.

However, no deduction or relief will be due for payments where the main purpose, or one of the main purposes, is to **avoid tax** (s 556A ITEPA 2003).

III. Share schemes

3340 An employee will be chargeable to income tax when, by reason of his employment, he acquires shares in the employer company at a reduced price, either immediately or in the future via an option. The idea is to tax value when it is transferred to the employee.

There are **special HMRC-approved schemes**, with stringent conditions, which allow the employer to make such shares or options available to the employees without a charge to income tax, or with a reduced tax charge. Generally, unapproved schemes are subject to a higher tax charge.

> MEMO POINTS 1. Generally, the recipient of the shares must be **resident or ordinarily resident** in the UK to be chargeable to income tax under these provisions.
> 2. In addition to income tax, share schemes also have implications for **corporation tax**, **PAYE and NIC**, and **capital gains tax**.
> 3. The employer may choose to set up an **employee share trust** in conjunction with a share scheme, which gives an artificial trading market as well as being a vehicle in which to store shares. In addition, when the employee sells the shares to the trust, this will always be treated as a capital disposal, avoiding any possible distribution treatment, which might apply if the company acquired the shares directly. However, such schemes are likely to fall within the rules taxing disguised earnings (¶3112).

3341 The most common type of charge in relation to an **unapproved scheme** is where the employee receives shares for less than market value, when he will be treated as if he had received a loan from the employer. There are many other situations in which a tax charge can arise, however, and readers are referred to *Tax Memo* for further details.

3342 An **approved scheme** allows the employer to make shares or options available to the employees without a charge to income tax or with a reduced tax charge (though the employee will be subject to capital gains tax), providing all the stringent prescribed conditions are met in relation to the following criteria:
- eligible employees;
- type of company;
- restrictions on shares; and
- scheme specific approval requirements.

In addition, **corporation tax relief** for the costs of the scheme should be available to the employer.

The main types of approved schemes are summarised below. Full details can again be found in the *Tax Memo*.

Reporting requirements

3343 The **general rule** is that all reportable events must be reported to HMRC before 7 July following the tax year, whether or not a return has been issued. Online reporting is encouraged.

Some companies may prefer to report events as they happen during the year, although HMRC still retain the right to issue a return.

Reportable events include:
- the acquisition of shares by reason of the employee's or someone else's employment;
- grant of options (a summary only);
- chargeable events in relation to restricted shares or convertible shares;
- artificially enhancing the share value;
- disposal of shares for more than market value;

- discharging of a notional loan;
- receipt of a benefit which gives rise to employment income (i.e. not dividends); and
- exercise, assignment or release of a share option where a benefit is received in money or money's worth.

MEMO POINTS The following **forms** are relevant to each situation:
- ASCOP, form 35;
- EMI, form 40, except for any options in excess of £120,000, when form 42 applies;
- Share Incentive Plan (SIP), form 39;
- SAYE, form 34; and
- any other case, form 42. However, no form 42 is required for new UK companies on the first issue of shares, and subsequent allotments in the early life of the company.

The **obligation to report** is imposed on: 3344
- the employer;
- the person from whom the shares were acquired;
- the person who issued the shares; and
- any host employer (where the actual employer is abroad).

If there is more than one responsible person, the duty to report is not met until one has actually reported.

Failure to report will result in penalty proceedings.

Approved company share option plans

Approved company share option plans (ACSOPs) are **discretionary share option schemes**, which means that the options may be granted to employees on a **selective basis** rather than to the workforce as a whole. 3345

There will generally be no income tax charge on the **grant or exercise** of the options, nor on the subsequent increase in value of the shares (s 518 ITEPA 2003). Capital gains tax on the eventual **disposal** of the shares is usually the only charge to tax for the employee.

MEMO POINTS 1. The general rule is that the **exercise of an option** under an ACSOP will be free from income tax provided the option is exercised at least 3 but no more than 10 years after it was granted to the director or employee (s 524 ITEPA 2003). An income tax charge will not arise on death, or if the employee is a good leaver (individuals who cease employment because of injury, disability, redundancy or retirement) and exercise the option within 6 months of their cessation date.
2. **Exceptionally**, where the subscription price proves to be less than the market value of the shares on the date of the grant, an income tax charge will arise (s 526 ITEPA 2003). For example, a rise in a company's share value at the time of its flotation would give rise to such a charge.

Enterprise management incentives

The enterprise management incentive scheme (EMI) enables small higher risk trading companies to grant qualifying share options with a value up to £250,000 to eligible employees without an income tax charge. 3350

The **grant of an option** will not give rise to an income tax charge (s 529 ITEPA 2003). Capital gains tax on the eventual **disposal** of the shares is usually the only charge to tax for the employee. Options can be granted at a discount and they can be restricted to selected employees.

MEMO POINTS 1. Prior to 16 June 2012, the maximum unrestricted value of shares for which an employee could hold unexercised qualifying options was £120,000 rather than the current limit of £250,000.
2. Special rules apply to the **exercise of an option** where it occurs within 10 years of the date of the grant, and those rules are dependent on whether the option is to acquire the shares at or above the market value (in which case no tax charge will arise on exercise) or below the market value (in which case a tax charge will arise on exercise). Where the option is exercised **more than 10 years** after the date of the grant, the option falls outside the EMI scheme and so the unapproved option rules apply, and a tax charge will arise on exercise.

3. Where a **disqualifying event** occurs **before the exercise of a qualifying option** and that option is not exercised within 40 days of the event, the tax benefits of EMI status are lost (s 532 ITEPA 2003).

Share incentive plans

3355 Share incentive plans (SIPs) **allow** shares worth up to £7,500 per annum to be passed to a trust on behalf of each employee (who is known as the participant) without giving rise to an income tax charge. The shares are then transferred to the employees once a specific period of between 3 and 5 years has elapsed.

The **purpose** of a share incentive plan must be to give employees a continuing stake in the company. A scheme with the purpose of making advantageous salary payments to employees is unlikely to be approved. Share incentive plans are **only appropriate** for quoted companies, as the risks are too great for employees of smaller companies. In addition, there are substantial costs associated with the setting up and running of a SIP.

Broadly, the scheme allows for **four different types of shares**:
a. free shares – awarded to the employee by the employer without payment;
b. partnership shares – acquired by the employee through deductions from his salary;
c. matching shares – offered by the employer if partnership shares are purchased; and
d. dividend shares – purchased with dividends reinvested on behalf of the employee.

The **tax treatment** is different for each type of share within a share incentive plan. The general idea behind a share incentive plan is that an award of shares to an employee will not give rise to an income tax charge providing the shares are left in the plan for at least 3 or 5 years from the date of the award (depending on the type of share awarded). An income tax charge will arise if the shares cease to be subject to the plan too early, but the amount of the charge will depend on the type of share. Capital receipts may also give rise to an income tax charge.

> *MEMO POINTS* The **withdrawal of approval** of a share incentive plan does not affect the operation of the share incentive plan rules in relation to shares already awarded to participants. However, a **disqualifying event** will remove any tax advantages for shares which are subsequently awarded.

Save as you earn option schemes

3360 Save as you earn option schemes (under the concept of savings-related share option schemes and commonly referred to as SAYE schemes) allow directors and employees to acquire shares **using the funds retained in a savings scheme** for a period between 3 and 7 years. The **shares** under an SAYE scheme must be **acquired out of savings** (and interest) with a certified contractual savings scheme which is approved for this purpose by HMRC. The scheme rules must **permit contributions** between a minimum of £10 and a maximum of £250 per month. Simple schemes are **available from** the major banks at no cost to the employer, so long as sufficient contributions are made. However, the SAYE scheme is usually only applicable to larger companies.

Providing the scheme is approved and all of the conditions are met, the **grant of the share** options will be tax free, as will the increase in value of the shares between the grant of the option and its exercise. Interest and bonuses paid in relation to the funds in the scheme are also exempt from tax. On **disposal**, the resulting gain or loss will be subject to capital gains tax.

> *MEMO POINTS* 1. The general rule is that **options** under an SAYE scheme must not be capable of being **exercised** before, or more than 6 months after, the bonus date. The bonus date will be 3, 5 or 7 years after the commencement of the SAYE scheme, and this period must be determined at the time when the option is granted.
> 2. The **acquisition price** must not be manifestly less than 80% of the market value of the shares at the time when the rights are acquired (or at an earlier time that has been agreed in writing with HMRC).

IV. Employment income taxable in the UK

3370 Tax payable on earnings arising from the individual's office or employment is based on the **residence status** of the employee, **where the duties are performed** and the **location of the employer**.

Residence

3372 In the majority of cases the residence of an individual will be a question of fact which will have a simple answer (for example someone has lived in the UK all his life). Residence is more difficult to determine when an individual arrives in, or leaves, the UK. The tests use the number of days spent in the UK to determine residence. However, these cannot be applied in advance, and so provisional criteria are applied for individuals arriving in, or leaving, the UK.

Although an individual will generally be resident for tax purposes in **one country**, it may be possible to be resident in **more than one country**, in which case the relevant double taxation agreement will decide in which country the individual is resident. It is also possible for an individual not to be resident in any country.

> MEMO POINTS 1. The UK has concluded **double taxation agreements** with most countries, which contain a tie-breaker clause for situations where an individual would otherwise be resident in both territories. Where tax is actually suffered in both countries, double taxation relief may be available.
> 2. HMRC have announced that a statutory definition of residence will be introduced with effect from April 2013. Further information will be provided by our updating service.

3373 **183 day test** An individual who is **physically present in the UK** for 183 days in any tax year is resident for that tax year. This rule applies whether the stay is for one continuous period or a succession of visits. As an **exception**, an individual who is resident and ordinarily resident in the UK will be treated as UK resident even where he remains outside the UK for all or part of a year for the purpose only of occasional residence abroad.

3374 **91 day test** Where an individual makes **regular visits** to the UK, he may become UK resident, although he will never be considered resident in a year in which he does not set foot in the UK.

If an individual is present in the UK for an average of 91 days or more per annum over a 4-year period, the individual will become resident in the UK on the first day of the 5th tax year.

For these purposes, the average is taken to be:

$$\frac{\text{Total visits to the UK (in days)}}{\text{Relevant tax years (cumulative days)}} \times 365 = \text{Average annual visits}$$

Ordinary residence

3375 It should be noted that the Government has announced its intention that the concept of ordinary residence will be **abolished** with effect from April 2013.

Ordinary residence is a more general concept and denotes **greater permanence** than residence. An individual may be ordinarily resident for a year despite not setting foot in the UK during that year.

An individual may be resident for a tax year, for example where he is temporarily working in the UK, without becoming ordinarily resident. In contrast, an individual may be ordinarily resident, by virtue of living in the UK throughout his life, but not resident for a number of years because of employment abroad.

If either of the following two **criteria** are satisfied, an individual will be treated as ordinarily resident:

a. he visits the UK and has available accommodation which implies a stay in the country of 3 years of more (i.e. excluding a lease for a period shorter than 3 years); or
b. his visits average 91 days or more per tax year over a 4-year period (the same test as for residence).

Domicile

3377 Domicile is a general concept which is a question of law, and which is **more fundamental and permanent** than residence and ordinary residence. An individual must have a domicile, but cannot have more than one at the same time. Domicile is a **link to** a jurisdiction and is not necessarily the same as place of residence or nationality.

a. Whether taxable in the UK?

3380 The **general rule** (s 15 ITEPA 2003) is that earnings will be taxable on the arising basis if the employee is:
– domiciled (¶3377), resident (¶3372) and ordinarily resident (¶3375) in the UK; or
– not domiciled but resident and ordinarily resident in the UK and his duties are performed (either wholly or partly in the UK) for a UK employer.

Not resident or not ordinarily resident (s 25 ITEPA 2003): This applies to earnings received in the UK by employees who are either not resident or not ordinarily resident in the UK. Where duties are performed partly in the UK and partly abroad, earnings must be apportioned between the two.

Remittance basis (ss 22, 26 ITEPA 2003): This means that income is taxed only when it is remitted to, or received in, the UK. While the money remains outside the UK, there is no UK tax liability. It applies to earnings from work done abroad:
– by employees who are resident but not ordinarily resident in the UK, regardless of whether the work was done wholly or partly abroad; and
– income received by non-domiciled employees of a foreign employer in a year when the remittance basis applies.

> MEMO POINTS Since 6 April 2008 the remittance basis must be claimed on an **annual basis**. The rules in this area are complex and further guidance is given in the *Tax Memo*.

The table below **summarises** the tax treatment:

Status of employee		Residence of employer	Where employee's duties carried out		
			Wholly or partly in the UK		Wholly outside the UK
Residence	Domicile		In the UK	Outside the UK	
Res and ord res in UK	Any	UK	Liable	Liable	Liable
Res and ord res in UK	Foreign	Foreign [1]	Liable	Liable	Liable if remitted to UK
Res but not ord res in UK	Any	Any	Liable	Liable if remitted to UK	Liable if remitted to UK
Not res	Any	Any	Liable	Not liable	Not liable

1. A foreign employer is resident outside the UK. It is possible for a foreign employer to be considered resident outside the UK even where it has a separate permanent establishment in the UK.

Place where duties are carried out

3382 Where an employee carries out his duties is a question of fact. While this is often easy to determine, an employee may sometimes carry out his duties in more than one country. In addition, certain types of occupation require the employee to travel widely, while having a central base of operations. In this case, the central base determines the place where duties are carried out.

> **MEMO POINTS** 1. **Crews** of ships and aircraft are treated as performing overseas duties if the journey does not begin and end in the UK.
> 2. **Mobile UK employees**, such as lorry and coach drivers, will remain UK resident and ordinarily resident, even though it is possible they could numerically fall within the 91 day test.

Duties performed abroad

The **remittance basis** applies to the following employees (s 33 ITEPA 2003): **3384**
– individuals who are resident but not ordinarily resident in the UK, performing duties wholly or partly abroad; and
– non-domiciled individuals performing duties wholly abroad for a foreign employer.

Incidental UK duties will be ignored for this purpose.

Earnings will be taxable when remitted, even where the employment has already ceased, or the earnings relate to a previous year.

> **MEMO POINTS** In order to reduce the UK income tax liability, some **foreign domiciled** employees have entered into employment contracts with both the UK employer and a foreign employer, known as dual contracts. As the earnings relating to overseas duties undertaken for the foreign employer are only taxable in the UK if remitted, these earnings are paid into an overseas bank account, thus escaping UK tax altogether.
> While such contracts have always been subject to enquiry, **HMRC** are taking a harder line, as there is concern that there is often an artificial split of a single job with the motive of saving tax: Tax Bulletin 76. For example, where duties are split based on geography alone, with no evidence of commercial rationale or two distinguishable jobs, this is likely to be challenged on the basis that there is in reality a single employment, with duties both in the UK and abroad. In this case, all earnings will be assessable on a receipts basis, although the foreign earnings will not be subject to PAYE.

Until 5 April 2009, HMRC accepted that apportionment of income applied to an individual who was **resident but not ordinarily resident**, and performed the duties of a single employment both inside and outside the UK. The calculation was based on the number of working days spent inside and outside the UK, where the employee's rights to earnings accrued on a daily basis. It was a question of fact where the substantial duties for each working day were carried out. In some cases this basis was not appropriate, for example where the employment contract specifically allocated earnings to specific duties. This treatment continues to apply from 6 April 2009, but if the employee has a mixed fund, the transfers to the UK should, strictly, be calculated separately (HMRC SP 1/09 and Tax Bulletin 63). **3385**

> **MEMO POINTS** 1. Where part of the income is paid in the UK, the practice of **HMRC** is to accept that a liability will only arise under the remittance basis where the aggregate of the following exceeds the amount of taxable earnings for the year:
> – earnings paid in the UK;
> – benefits enjoyed in the UK; and
> – earnings remitted to the UK.
> 2. Where an employee is not liable to UK tax on some of his earnings, the employer should seek a direction from HMRC that not all earnings are liable to **PAYE**.
> 3. Often the **overseas country** will have a similar system of PAYE, and the employer should ensure he is aware of his legal obligations.
> 4. In some cases, the UK employer may be **deducting both foreign and UK tax** from the employee's earnings, even though the employee will be suffering too much tax. HMRC can authorise an employer to reduce the amount of income tax paid under PAYE by the amount of foreign tax paid, which will alleviate the cash-flow problem for the employee.

b. Treatment of expenses

The tax charge on employment income is based on the full amount of the earnings from the employment subject to authorised deductions. The general rules outlined from ¶3265 and particularly ¶3310 apply. Special rules apply to employment income taxed on a remittance basis and to foreign earnings. **3390**

Duties performed abroad

3392 Where the **remittance basis** applies, a **deduction** may be made **for** (s 353(1)-(3) ITEPA 2003):
– expenses paid for out of those earnings;
– expenses paid on the employee's behalf and included as earnings; and
– any other expenses paid for in the UK in that year of assessment or any earlier year in which the employee was resident in the UK.

The expenses must be of a type that would be deductible if the earnings had been charged under the general rules for the year of assessment in which they were incurred.

Non-UK domiciled employees

3394 An assessment in respect of **foreign earnings** may be reduced by a **deduction for** expenses for payments which (s 355(4)-(6) ITEPA 2003):
– are made out of earnings subject to UK tax;
– are of a type that would normally have reduced the employee's liability to income tax; and
– would not normally fall within the scope of UK law because they were made abroad.

HMRC require **strict proof** that the payment is made out of the earnings concerned, and that the employee does not have sufficient overseas income, that is not chargeable to UK tax, from which to make the payments.

3395 A deduction may also be allowed for **travel expenses** incurred or reimbursed by the employer (so far as it is included in the assessable earnings of the employment) for a period of 5 years beginning with the employee's date of arrival in the UK to perform the duties of the employment (s 373 ITEPA 2003).

However, the deduction will **not be available unless**, on the date of his arrival in the UK to perform the duties, the employee was either:
– not resident in the UK in either of the 2 immediately preceding years of assessment; or
– not in the UK for any purpose at any time in the 2 years ending immediately before the date of arrival.

> *MEMO POINTS* The **allowable expenses** are those provided:
> a. for any journey between the employee's place of usual abode (i.e. outside the UK) and any place in the UK to perform the duties of the employment; or
> b. where the employee is in the UK for the purposes of such an employment for a continuous period of 60 days or more, for any two outward and return journeys per person per year by the employee's spouse and/or child, either to accompany him at the beginning of the period or to visit him during it. In practice the period of 60 days is met if the employee is:
> – working in the UK for at least 2/3rds of his working days; and
> – present in the UK at the beginning and end of the period.

SECTION 3

Pensions

3400 Many employers offer **occupational pension schemes** (OPS) (also known as retirement benefit schemes) by which they can make tax-efficient retirement provision for their employees. An employer who offers such a scheme has certain legal obligations to his employees generally, the members of the scheme and its trustees. Alternatively, some employers will offer to pay into their employees' **personal pension schemes**.

> *MEMO POINTS* 1. The **obligation to provide** a designated **stakeholder pension scheme** has been abolished and replaced with new automatic enrolment requirements which are currently being phased in (¶3402). Consequently, employers will no longer need to provide access to a stakeholder pension scheme to new employees on or after 1 October 2012, even if their auto-enrolment staging date may be some years off. With regard to employees who were contributing to a

designated scheme before 1 October 2012, employers must continue to take and pay contributions from their employees' remuneration until employees ask them to stop or stop paying contributions at a regular interval.

2. The **current pensions regime** has been in force since 6 April 2006, resulting in the tax treatment for all types of approved schemes, including occupational schemes, being amalgamated into the rules for registered schemes. In addition, the tax treatment of unapproved schemes was also changed at this time.

3. **Detailed information** on the tax charges and their various calculations with regard to the different schemes and benefits is beyond the scope of this book and readers should refer to the *Tax Memo*, and contact HMRC with regard to specific issues.

3401

Individuals are also entitled to receive a **state retirement pension** once they have reached the state pension age (currently 60 for women, 65 for men). This is made up of two elements:
– a basic flat rate; and
– the second state pension (S2P). This scheme represents a reform of the state earnings related pension scheme (SERPS). The accrual of benefits under SERPS ceased on 6 April 2002, although future pensions will still take account of any existing rights built up before that date.

Since 6 April 2012, it is no longer possible to **contract-out** of the additional State Pension (S2P) through a money-purchase (defined-contribution) occupational pension scheme, a personal pension or a stakeholder pension, and those who had contracted-out have been brought back into the S2P. For the time being, contracting-out through an occupational salary-related (defined-benefit) scheme is still allowed.

MEMO POINTS The **state pension age** is to be equalised at age 65 between April 2016 and November 2018. The retirement age for both sexes will rise to 66 by October 2020 (Pensions Act 2011).

Obligation for automatic enrolment

Since 1 October 2012, an obligation is being **phased in** for employers to automatically enrol all their eligible employees into a contributory pension scheme (Pensions Act 2008; SI 2010/5; SI 2010/772). The transitional period is over 4 years, starting with the biggest employers (those with a PAYE scheme size of 120,000 or more). Subsequent staging dates, for increasingly smaller employers, are due to occur on the 1st day of each of the following months (excluding December) up to 1 February 2018. Small employers (**those with a PAYE scheme size of fewer than 50**) are due to automatically enrol their staff **from 1 June 2015** onwards depending on the PAYE reference numbers. Staging for new businesses, where PAYE income is first paid after 1 April 2012, will be towards the end of this period.

3402

Employers will be able to **meet this obligation** in any way they choose as long as it is a good quality scheme, but one way will be through a government-sponsored National Employment Savings Trust (NEST), a simple, low-cost scheme with limited fund choice, and initial restrictions on transfers and contribution levels. NESTs will be operated by the NEST Corporation, a not-for-profit trustee body which is regulated by the Pensions Regulator. The **threshold** for automatic enrolment is aligned to the personal allowance for income tax and applies to those who are aged between 22 and state pension age and who work in the UK. To encourage participation, employees' pension contributions will be supplemented by **contributions** from employers (employers' contributions are also due to be phased in from 1% of an eligible employee's qualifying earnings to 3% by October 2018) and tax relief, although employees will be able to opt-out if they choose not to participate.

For more information, see the GOV.UK website at flmemo.co.uk/em3402

I. Occupational pension schemes (OPS)

An OPS can be set up for any number of employees and can include all or some of the employer's workforce. It is usually in a form of a trust with legally appointed trustees and is separate from the employer's business. The trustees can delegate the day-to-day management of the scheme to an administrator who will be named in the scheme documentation and

3405

A. General principles

3410 There are **two main types** of OPS and the level of benefits under each is calculated differently. The first is a **final salary scheme** (also known as a defined benefit scheme) where the employer guarantees a pension which is a fraction of the employee's salary based on the number of years of service. This type of pension is now being phased out by many companies or is being limited to existing employees.

The other main type of scheme is a **money purchase scheme** (also known as a defined contribution scheme), where the benefits under the scheme ultimately depend on the amount that the fund has built up, and the level of contributions made by the employee and the employer. Consequently, there is no set promise or guarantee about the level of benefits that the employee will receive on retirement.

3411 Both types usually offer a **pension** or a pension and a **lump sum** on retirement. Some may also allow for part of the pension to be given up in **exchange** for a lump sum on retirement. The rate of exchange will depend on the scheme's rules and current legislation, and may apply to all members or a certain group/member. It is usually expressed as a ratio and is referred to as the "commutation factor".

Schemes can also give **benefits on death**, for example the payment of a lump sum and/or a pension to the surviving spouse and/or dependants. Indeed, some may be **limited to such payments**. Such benefits will be "death in service" if the employee dies before reaching the normal retirement date (NRD) and/or "death on retirement" payable when the employee dies during retirement. The tax rules will vary depending on the type of benefit.

Normal retirement date

3412 Each scheme should set out the age at which the employee is expected to start to receive his pension, called the normal retirement date (NRD). It is **distinct and independent** from the state pension age, contractual retirement age (CRA) (¶¶8203+) and normal retiring age (NRA) (¶¶8206+), though it may be the same date.

The NRD must be the same for **men and women** as pension is "pay" for the purposes of EU equal pay provisions (*Barber v Guardian Royal Exchange Assurance Group* [1990] IRLR 240, ECJ). However, an employer may have different retirement ages for **different jobs**, provided the disparity is not gender-based.

3413 **Early retirement** Early retirement occurs if the employee leaves his job and takes his retirement benefits before his NRD. This may be offered as an **alternative to redundancy** and the scheme may provide for one or more of the following if there is early retirement:
– immediate payment of the employee's full pension (with no reduction for early payment);
– payment of part of the pension as a lump sum;
– additional years' service for the purpose of calculating pension entitlement; and
– payment of the whole or part of any termination payment into the scheme to increase the pension entitlement.

In general, the statutory tax rules allow an employee to retire early from the age of 55 years, although, with regard to approved schemes, not before this age (unless due to ill health or in a specialised occupation, such as a sportsman).

MEMO POINTS This retirement date raised from 50 to 55 years in April 2010.

Most schemes will provide for early retirement due to **ill health**, commonly granting immediate payment of full pension, perhaps with additional pensionable service added on in order to calculate an enhanced ill health pension. Some schemes apply a tiered system, such that full prospective pensionable service is used for complete incapacity and actual pensionable service is used when the employee can do some work (but not his normal duties).

Some schemes will also allow for commutation on the grounds of **serious ill health**. If so, and the employee's life expectancy is severely shortened, the scheme will commute the whole of his retirement benefit into a lump sum.

Medical evidence is normally required to prove that the employee's ill health prevents him from carrying out his normal employment. Often, the incapacity must be expected or likely to be permanent, with provisions for suspension of pension payments if the employee is able to resume work before reaching pensionable age.

The employer is bound by his duty to act in **good faith** when deciding whether the employee meets any definition of incapacity (*Mihlenstedt v Barclays Bank International Ltd and Barclays Bank plc* [1989] IRLR 522, CA) and the scheme **rules must be construed** in a purposive and practical way (*Derby Daily Telegraph Ltd v The Pensions Ombudsman and Thompson* [1999] IRLR 476, ChD).

> MEMO POINTS   **Personal pensions** can also come into payment early, at a reduced rate, and the employee should check his policy, if necessary.

1. Registered schemes

Schemes must be registered by HMRC to attract the following **tax advantages**:
– relief from income tax and NIC on employee contributions;
– relief from corporation tax on employer contributions;
– relief from income tax on the benefit of any employer contributions (i.e. such payments are not treated as a benefit in kind);
– exemption from income tax and capital gains tax on the income and growth of the scheme's investments; and
– tax-free cash lump sum payments on retirement or death if entitled.

Previously, schemes were **approved** and all schemes which were approved before this date **automatically became registered** unless a specific request was made for the scheme not to be.

Essentially, HMRC will **register** a scheme if:
– employer contributions are paid into the scheme; and
– the money held by the scheme and the benefits paid out of the scheme are in the form of pension benefits and do not exceed set maximum limits.

Contributions

There is **no minimum or maximum restriction** on the amount of contributions, payable either by the member or an employer, although only a certain amount attracts tax relief. The maximum aggregate contribution on which **tax relief** is due is the higher of £3,600 per tax year and 100% of earnings (subject to the annual allowance).

The annual allowance is limited to **£50,000** for 2011/12 and 2012/13 (2010/11: £255,000). Excess contributions are taxed at the "appropriate rate" (effectively, the individual's marginal rate). This is called the annual allowance charge.

> MEMO POINTS   From 2011/12 the annual allowance charge also applies:
> – with some exceptions, in the year that benefits are drawn; and
> – to individuals with enhanced protection of pension rights as at 6 April 2006.

2. Unregistered schemes

Unapproved pension schemes are now known as **employer financed retirement benefit schemes**. There is no facility for such schemes to be registered with HMRC, and no tax advantages therefore apply. Unregistered pension schemes will generally fall within the scope of the new rules for the taxation of disguised earnings (¶3112). This is likely to reduce their effectiveness considerably. Following the decrease in the annual allowance for 2011/12, HMRC will look closely at any situation where it appears that contributions have been switched from a registered pension scheme to an unfunded scheme. Anti-avoidance provisions may apply.

> MEMO POINTS 1. There are two types of unregistered schemes:
> a. a **funded scheme (FURBS)**, where the employer makes arrangements for future benefits by paying into an insurance policy or by setting up a separate trust fund, thereby ringfencing assets purely for the purpose of providing pension benefits; and
> b. an **unfunded scheme**, where the employer promises to pay a pension or other similar benefits in the future, but makes no formal provision beforehand.
> 2. As there were no limits on the benefits provided by unapproved schemes before 6 April 2006, they **were commonly used** to top-up pension provision for executives whose contributions to approved schemes were restricted by the then earnings cap.

Schemes set up after 5 April 2006

3426 For a **funded scheme**, the following apply (s 245 FA 2004):
– employer contributions (and the scheme administration costs) are only deductible when pension benefits are actually paid and taxed on the employee;
– employer contributions are not taxable on the employee nor liable to NIC;
– scheme income and gains are taxed at the rate applicable to trusts;
– the lump sum received at retirement is fully chargeable to income tax;
– lump sum death benefits are liable to both income tax and inheritance tax;
– the value of the fund (even a discretionary fund) forms part of an individual's death estate for the purposes of inheritance tax; and
– no NIC is due on benefits paid if these are within the limits which could be paid out by a registered scheme (which is unlikely).

> MEMO POINTS There is **transitional protection** for pre-April 2006 funded schemes as follows:
> – a proportion of the lump sum which relates to the indexed market value of the fund at 6 April 2006 will be tax free, where either employer contributions or the fund income and gains have already been taxed on the employee. If employer contributions ceased before 6 April 2006, the lump sum will remain completely tax free;
> – benefits will be exempt from NIC if they derive from contributions paid between 1999 and 2006 which were themselves subject to NIC; and
> – lump sum death benefits which were provided under the scheme rules before 6 April 2006 will remain exempt from income tax and inheritance tax. Death benefits relating to post-6 April contributions and funding will be liable to income tax and inheritance tax.

Where an employer guarantees benefits in an **unfunded scheme**, the cost of the guarantee is assessed on the employee as a benefit in kind. The form of the guarantee could be insurance, or asset backing (s 248 FA 2004).

B. Employer obligations

Duty to members

3430 Any powers an employer may have under the rules of an OPS must be exercised in **good faith** and he must treat his employees in a reasonable manner as part of the duty to preserve the relationship of mutual **trust and confidence** (*Imperial Group Pension Trust Ltd v Imperial Tobacco Ltd* [1991] IRLR 66, ChD).

Such powers must be exercised with a view to the efficient running of the scheme, and to preserve his employees' rights and the pension fund. In particular, this creates a contractual obligation to take reasonable steps to bring to the employees' attention the existence of **new or varied beneficial terms** (*Scally v Southern Health and Social Services Board* [1991] IRLR 522, HL).

> **EXAMPLE** In *Scally v Southern Health and Social Services Board*, a collective agreement amended the employees' individual contracts, introducing a beneficial OPS right contingent on the employees taking appropriate action. The employer was held to be under an implied duty to draw this to his employees' attention.

However, there is no implied duty on an employer to make employees aware of their **pension rights** generally, although there is a corresponding duty in tort to take reasonable care in any information he does give, and if the employer negligently misrepresents information to his employees, he will be in breach of his duty of care (*Hagen and ors v ICI Chemicals & Polymers Ltd* [2002] IRLR 31, QBD). The implied duty also does not stretch to requiring the employer to give **financial advice**, for example, that the employee is not choosing the most financially advantageous option when exercising his rights under the scheme (*University of Nottingham v Eyett* [1999] IRLR 87, ChD; *Outram v Academy Plastics* [2000] EWCA Civ 141). If, on the other hand, the employer does give advice, he is under an implied duty to ensure that the **information** is not misleading, inaccurate or negligent.

With regard to employers exercising their **discretionary duties** under a scheme, members must show that the employer has acted perversely and irrationally and that those actions have seriously damaged the relationship between the employer and the scheme members for the employer not to have acted in good faith (*Prudential Staff Pensions Ltd v The Prudential Assurance Company Ltd and ors* [2011] EWHC 960 (Ch)). There is no requirement for general fairness, and an employer can take his own interests into account when making discretionary decisions.

3431

> **EXAMPLE** In *Prudential Staff Pensions Ltd v The Prudential Assurance Company Ltd and ors*, the employer had exercised its discretion to make changes to the increases it made to pensions in payment, and in 2010 it did not award any increase at all (at this time the RPI was negative). Following numerous complaints from members, the trustees applied to the High Court to determine various matters, including whether or not the employer had been in breach of its obligation of good faith in changing its policy on payment increases. The Court found in favour of the employer.

Duty to trustees

Trustees of the scheme who are also employees have the right to take reasonable **paid time off** for training and for the performance of their duties (ss 58-60 ERA 1996). This does not apply to election candidates. Trustees have the right to be remunerated for the work they would have done had they not had the time off (¶3910).

3432

Trustees also have the **right not to suffer a detriment or be dismissed** because of their duties or the performance (or proposed performance) of their duties as trustees (ss 46, 102 ERA 1996).

3433

Discrimination

A detailed discussion of pension-related discrimination is beyond the scope of this book. However, the main principles are discussed below.

3435

Sex discrimination The current inequality between men and women relating to their **state retirement ages** (65 and 60 respectively) is in the process of being removed (with the retirement age increasing for women to 65), and this should be complete by 2018 with a further rise for both sexes to 66 by 2020, although there is speculation that the Government's plans will change and the state retirement age will ultimately be higher than this for both men and women. Note, however, that it is unlawful for employers to discriminate between men and women in respect of **contractual retiring ages** (s 61 EqA 2010) (¶8203).

3436

It is also unlawful to discriminate in respect of access to, and benefits payable under, **occupational pension schemes**. The law relating to this matter has developed in a piecemeal manner.

3437

Article 157 of the Treaty on the Functioning of the European Union (previously article 141 of the Treaty of Rome) requires that men and women must receive equal pay for equal work

3438

(art 157 EU Treaty on the Functioning of the European Union). "Pay" is now deemed to include any benefits paid under an occupational pension scheme (*Barber v Guardian Royal Exchange Assurance Group* [1990] IRLR 240, ECJ). However, any claim relating to **treatment under** (as opposed to access to) an occupational pension scheme which is based on the principle of equal treatment enshrined in *Barber* is restricted to **pensionable service on or after 17 May 1990** (the date of the *Barber* decision).

Following *Barber*, domestic legislation was implemented to provide that all occupational pension schemes would incorporate the "**equal treatment rule**", including any provisions which provide for the benefit of scheme members' dependants (ss 62(1)-(2), 63(1) Pensions Act 1995). Later Court of Justice of the European Union cases further clarified that the principle of equality extends to the trustees of an occupational pension scheme (*Coloroll Pension Trustees Ltd v Russell* [1995] ICR 179, ECJ) and that survivors' benefits are also covered (*Ten Oever v Stichting Bedrijfspensioenfonds voor het Glazenwassers en Schoonmaakbedrijf* [1995] ICR 74, ECJ).

> MEMO POINTS   The Treaty on the Functioning of the European Union has direct effect in the UK and does not require further domestic implementing legislation.

3439 However, in contrast, Court of Justice of the European Union (CJEU) case law has held that the **right to join** an occupational pension scheme is within the scope of art 157 but is not subject to the same time limitation as in *Barber* (*Vroege v NCIV Instituut voor Volkshuisvestuing BV* [1994] IRLR 651, ECJ), although employee contributions would need to be backdated in respect of any period of retrospective membership claimed (*Fisscher v Voorhuis Hengelo BV* [1994] IRLR 662, ECJ).

A long-standing issue of access to occupational pension schemes has involved **part-time workers**, many of whom were previously excluded from access to their employers' occupational pension schemes. It has been held that the exclusion of part-time workers (many of whom were women) from their employers' occupational pension schemes constituted indirect sex discrimination, on the basis that the exclusion adversely affected more women than men. Despite the CJEU decisions in *Vroege* and *Fisscher*, UK domestic legislation did not previously allow claims regarding access to be backdated in respect of pensionable service more than 2 years before the date on which the complaint was presented.

However, following a referral to the CJEU from the House of Lords, this is no longer the case (*Preston v Wolverhampton Healthcare NHS Trust* [2001] IRLR 237, HL), and domestic legislation has been introduced to implement the *Preston* decision (Part-time Workers (Prevention of Less Favourable Treatment) Regulations 2000 (Amendment) Regulations SI 2002/2035).

However, a distinction should be drawn between claims **relating to benefits** payable under, as opposed to access to, an occupational pension scheme, where the time limitation in *Barber* continues to apply (*Quirk v Burton Hospital NHS* [2002] IRLR 353, CA).

> EXAMPLE
> 1. In *Quirk v Burton Hospital NHS*, a male nurse, who would be financially worse off than his female counterparts if he decided to retire early, was held not to have suffered discrimination contrary to the equal pay rights under article 141 of the Treaty of Rome (now article 157 of the Treaty on the Functioning of the European Union), and could not claim equality of treatment in respect of pensionable service prior to 17 May 1990.
> 2. In *Harland and Wolff Pension Trustees Ltd v Aon Consulting Financial Services* [2006] EWHC 1778 (Ch), an employer introduced a valid scheme to take effect from 7 September 1993. For the period between May 1990 and September 1993, the employer treated women's contributions as if they had operated on the same basis as men's. This arrangement was equal between the sexes but disadvantaged women pensioners who had previously enjoyed a more generous arrangement. The High Court has ruled that such a policy is contrary to article 141 of the Treaty of Rome (now article 157 of the Treaty on the Functioning of the European Union).

> MEMO POINTS   Where a new scheme was properly introduced after May 1990, that scheme may lawfully achieve equality between male and female pensioners by reducing the benefits paid to women. This case turned on the rules regarding the "**Barber window**", i.e. the period between the decision of the courts and the introduction of the new scheme.

3440 **Discrimination** against a woman in respect of her access to membership of, or rights to benefits payable under, an occupational pension scheme is unlawful in relation to terms of employment, opportunities for or access to benefits, or subjecting an employee to any detriment (s 61 EqA 2010).

The principle of equality is also incorporated in the **equal pay** legislation (s 6(1B) EPA 1970, as amended by the Pensions Act 1995 and now incorporated into the EqA 2010). This extends the principle of equal treatment to cover any term in the contract relating to a person's membership of, or rights under, an occupational pension scheme, unless the term is one in relation to which the equal treatment rule would be excluded.

3441

With regard to the issue of **time limits** in respect of equal pay claims involving liability under the EPA 1970 (now under the EqA 2010), and article 157 of the Treaty on the Functioning of the European Union (previously article 141 of the Treaty of Rome) for failure to provide equal access to pension benefits where TUPE applies, following the reference to the Court of Justice of the European Union, the House of Lords (now called the Supreme Court) held that such liability remains with the transferor and any claim relating to the pension scheme of the original employer (the transferor) must be brought within 6 months of the end of the employment to which the claim relates, i.e. within 6 months of the date of the transfer (*Powerhouse Retail Ltd and ors v Burroughs and ors* [2006] IRLR 381, HL).

Disability discrimination Every occupational pension scheme is taken to include a non-discriminatory rule in relation to access to, and benefits under, the scheme. Both the trustees and managers of an occupational pension scheme are prohibited from discriminating against or harassing a disabled person in carrying out their functions as trustees and managers (s 61 EqA 2010). In addition, trustees and managers are under a duty to make reasonable adjustments where a provision, criterion or practice (including a scheme rule) applied by or on behalf of the trustees and managers, or any physical features of premises occupied by the trustees and managers, places a disabled person at a substantial disadvantage compared with a non-disabled person. In such circumstances, the trustees and managers are under a duty to make any reasonable adjustments which would prevent the provision, criterion, practice or physical feature from having that effect (s 61(11) EqA 2010). This might include altering the pension scheme rules or the trustees'/managers' premises. There is no defence of justification for failure to make such reasonable adjustments.

3443

See ¶5450 for further details on disability discrimination.

Other discrimination Moreover, all occupational pension schemes are subject to the principle of non-discrimination against any person in relation to access to such schemes, entitlement to benefits under them, the payment of pension contributions, admission to the scheme and the provision of any benefits relating to pensions on the grounds of, as well as sex and disability as previously discussed, **sexual orientation**, **gender reassignment**, **marriage and civil partnership**, **race**, **religion or belief**, and **age**). Individuals who must implement this rule are trustees, pension scheme managers, employers whose employees are, or could be, members of the scheme, and those involved in recruiting employees who are, or could be, scheme members.

3444

See ¶¶5260, 5375, 5600 for further details on anti-discrimination provisions.

MEMO POINTS It is **unlawful** for trustees or managers of an occupational pension scheme or employers in relation to such a scheme **to harass or discriminate** against a member or prospective member of the scheme on the grounds of age (s 61 EqA 2010). In addition, every occupational pension scheme is treated as including a **non-discrimination rule** and trustees and managers have the power to alter schemes to comply with the rule. Certain **age-related rules or practices** in occupational pension schemes are **exempted** from the scope of the regulations, such as using minimum and maximum ages for admission to schemes or entitlement to benefits.

The Court of Justice of the European Union has held that where national law recognises that **life partnerships** place persons of the same sex in a situation comparable to that of spouses, legislation to the effect that the survivor's benefit under an occupational pension scheme does not apply to such partnerships is contrary to the Equal Treatment Framework Directive (*Maruko v Versorgungsanstalt der deutschen Bühnen case C-267/06* [2008] IRLR 450, ECJ). In this case, which was commenced in the German courts, the same sex surviving registered life partner (the German equivalent of a civil partner) of a contributor to an occupational pension scheme claimed that denial of the survivor's benefits under the same conditions as a surviving spouse was discriminatory. The Court of Justice decided that if surviving spouses and surviving life partners were in a comparable situation under the occupational pension scheme, preventing their access to the benefit would be less favourable treatment on grounds of their sexual orientation.

Data protection compliance

3445 The **administrator of the OPS** has the general responsibility for the administration of the scheme, including keeping membership records, corresponding with members, reporting changes to the scheme to the relevant authorities, and providing the scheme's actuary with information. If the employer takes on this responsibility it will usually be through a director or a senior member of his staff, most likely in the human resources department. The **function of the scheme administrator** will extend to the processing of personal and sensitive data of both workers and non-workers, if scheme members include past employees, and, in some cases, spouses and dependants.

> MEMO POINTS The Information Commissioner has also published a Good Practice Note in relation to how **pension trustees** can comply with their obligations under the Data Protection Act 1998 when they **use pension administrators** to help them run a pension scheme.

3446 Where employers have administrative obligations in relation to such schemes or are, in fact, party to a scheme, they must ensure that they comply with the data protection rules (¶5945) (for example, where the data is personal and sensitive (¶5925), explicit consent should be obtained).

Further, as **good practice**, employers should (part 2.4 DP Code):
– remember that they do not have a right of access to personal information required for the administration of an OPS. The information should not be used for general employment purposes. For example, if a worker gives his medical records to the scheme administrator for the purposes of the OPS, these records should not be used by the employer for non-OPS purposes, such as in deciding whether the worker is eligible for sick pay or not. If information is collected on behalf of the insurer, the employer must ensure there is a secure method of collection:
– limit the exchange of information with a scheme provider to the minimum necessary for operation of the scheme; and
– ensure that when a worker joins a scheme it is made clear what, if any, information is passed between the insurer and the employer and how it will be used. Unless told otherwise, workers are entitled to assume that information they give to a doctor, nurse or other health professional will be treated in confidence and not passed to others.

Employers are also advised to follow the DP Code's general **recommendations** with regard to data management (¶6000).

> MEMO POINTS The Data Protection (Processing of Sensitive Personal Data) Order sets out more detailed provisions for processing information in establishing and administering an occupational pension scheme, and the information that is required to determine eligibility for, and benefits payable under, such a scheme (SI 2000/417).

3447 The employer who acts as scheme administrator should also be conscious of data protection compliance when **providing information to others** in connection with the administration of the scheme. Therefore, if the scheme actuary requires information on the age profile of scheme members in order to carry out a valuation of the scheme, any information that could identify individual scheme members should be anonymised before being sent out. The scheme administrators must ensure that they comply with the data protection rules (¶5945) (for example, where the data is personal and sensitive (¶5925), explicit consent should be obtained).

Information and consultation requirements

3448 Certain employers are required to inform and consult with employees before making specified **changes to** their occupational and personal pension schemes (Occupational and Personal Pension Schemes (Consultation by Employers and Miscellaneous Amendment) Regulations SI 2006/349). In line with the Information and Consultation of Employees Regulations (¶¶7655+), these regulations apply to employers with 50 or more employees since 6 April 2008.

In respect of **occupational pension schemes**, the changes about which employers will have to inform and consult are proposals to (reg 8 SI 2006/349 as amended by SI 2010/499):

a. increase the normal pension age for members (or members of a particular description);
b. prevent new members (or members of a particular description) from being admitted to the scheme;
c. prevent the future accrual of benefits under the scheme for or in respect of members (or members of a particular description);
d. remove the liability to make employer contributions towards the scheme in respect of members (or members of a particular description);
e. introduce (where previously not payable) or increase member contributions;
f. change what elements of pay are included within pensionable earnings, or change the proportion, or limit the amount of any element of pay that forms part of pensionable earnings;
g. in respect of money purchase benefits only, reduce employer contributions in respect of members (or members of a particular description); or
h. in respect of non-money purchase benefits for members of the scheme, or in relation to members of a particular description:
– change money purchase benefits;
– change the basis for determining the rate of future accrual of benefits;
– modify the scheme so as to reduce the future accrual rate of benefits; or
– make any other reduction in the rate of future accrual of benefits.

In respect of **personal pension schemes**, the changes about which employers will be required to inform and consult are proposals in respect of members (or members of a particular description) to cease, reduce or increase employer contributions to the scheme (reg 9 SI 2006/349).

C. Compliance

The Pensions Regulator is the **regulatory body** for work-based pension schemes in the UK (Pensions Act 2004). A work-based pension scheme is defined as any scheme that an employer makes available to employees and includes all occupational schemes and any stakeholder and personal pension schemes where employees have direct payment arrangements.

3460

The Pensions Regulator has the **following objectives**:
– to protect the benefits of members of work-based pension schemes;
– to promote good administration of work-based pension schemes; and
– to reduce the risk of situations arising that may lead to claims for compensation from the Pension Protection Fund.

To meet these objectives, the Pensions Regulator has a **wide range of statutory powers**, including:
– the power to issue improvement notices requiring schemes to take specific action;
– the ability to gather information to identify schemes most likely to present a risk to scheme members' benefits;
– increased powers to suspend, prohibit and remove trustees; and
– powers to require those involved with schemes to report suspected breaches of pensions legislation to the Pensions Regulator.

Remedies

An employee will have several options if his employer or trustees do not comply with the:
– statutory pension rules or any other appropriate statutory rules, for example the right to equal pay;

3461

- rules of the scheme; or
- implied duty of good faith or mutual trust and confidence.

3462 Claims **against** the **employer** can be brought in the civil courts as a contractual claim (Harris v Lord Shuttleworth [1994] ICR 991, CA) whereas claims regarding **trustees** should be brought as a tortious action. Alternatively, the employee can bring a claim in the employment tribunal if it arises on, or is outstanding at, the termination of his employment, although this will be limited to the statutory maximum for contractual claims (currently £25,000) (Employment Tribunals Extension of Jurisdiction (England and Wales) Order SI 1994/1623).

3463 The employee can also complain to the **Pension Ombudsman** who can determine claims of maladministration against employers, trustees, or the scheme's managers or administrators. However, the Ombudsman cannot act if the employee has already brought an action in the civil courts or employment tribunal. There is a time limit of 3 years to make a claim, though this can be extended at the Ombudsman's discretion (Personal and Occupational Pension Schemes (Pension Ombudsman) Regulations SI 1996/2475). Decisions can be appealed to the High Court.

CHAPTER 11

Time on

OUTLINE ¶¶

SECTION 1 Working time 3605

    Summary of the application of the rules .. 3608
- **I Scope of regulations** 3615
  - 1 Unmeasured working time 3625
  - 2 Shift workers................................. 3635
  - 3 Workers in certain sectors 3640
  - 4 Flexibility, continuity or other special reasons 3650
  - 5 Collective or workforce agreement 3660
- **II Minimum standards**......................... 3670
  - A General system of average weekly working time..................................... 3680
    - Reference period 3681
    - Calculating average weekly working time 3684
    - Opting out 3688
  - B Night time working........................... 3695
    - Normal hours of night work 3696
    - Work involving special hazards or strain.. 3699
    - Health of night workers 3701

- C Rest periods 3710
  - Daily and weekly rest periods................. 3711
  - In-work rest breaks 3715
  - Compensatory rest............................... 3717
- D Young workers 3720
- **III Records** 3740
- **IV Enforcement and remedies** 3750
  - Summary of enforcement provisions 3751
  - A Criminal offences and penalties........ 3755
  - B Remedies 3760

SECTION 2 Sunday trading 3800

- I Shop employees............................... 3810
  - A Protected employees....................... 3815
  - B Opting in... 3845
  - C Remedies 3860
- II Betting employees........................... 3880

3600   **Time at work** is regulated by legislation and generally concerns all workers (Working Time Regulations SI 1998/1833 as amended). Employers must ensure that the limits on the hours worked and breaks given comply with these regulations. Further, there are stricter obligations with regard to night workers and young workers.

Workers also have the right to paid annual leave and this is discussed in chapter 12.

3601   Further, **shop and betting employees** have special rules relating to them if they work or may be required to work on Sundays (ss 36-43 ERA 1996; Sunday Trading Act 1994).

SECTION 1

Working time

3605   The **minimum regulatory standards** that employers must comply with concern (Working Time Regulations SI 1998/1833 as amended, referred to in this chapter as "the regulations"):
- the average weekly working time and night work;
- daily and weekly rest periods, and in-work rest breaks; and
- annual leave (¶4000).

While employers must ensure compliance, workers are not obliged to make use of their entitlements and an employer cannot force a worker to take an entitlement that is made available to him (subject to health and safety considerations).

3606 Subject to the ability of workers to opt out of the average weekly working time, neither employers nor workers can **contract out** of any of the regulations (regs 4, 5, 35 SI 1998/1833; *Witley & District Men's Club v Mackey* [2001] IRLR 595, EAT). Any term in the contract of employment or in any other contract, express or implied, will be **void** in so far as it seeks to exclude or limit the operation of any of the regulations or where it seeks to stop workers from bringing proceedings under them.

However, a **relevant agreement** can affect the application of the regulations. This is **defined** as any workforce agreement (¶1293) that applies to the worker, any provision of a collective agreement (¶7363) which forms part of a contract between him and his employer, or any other agreement in writing which is legally enforceable as between the worker and his employer (for example, the contract of employment). Unless it is signed by the employee, a written statement giving the statutory particulars relating to the terms and conditions of employment is unlikely to amount to a relevant agreement, as it is usually only evidence of the employment contract (¶1402).

3607 If employers **breach** certain provisions of the regulations they will commit a criminal offence. The courts have imposed a contractual obligation on employers with regard to the average weekly working time which workers will be able to enforce. Workers also have the right to bring a claim against employers in an employment tribunal to protect their working time rights.

> MEMO POINTS   The regulations are the implementation of the European Organisation of Working Time Directive and aspects of the European Protection of Young People at Work Directive (EC Organisation of Working Time Directive 1993/104 and EC Protection of Young People at Work Directive 1994/33 respectively).

Summary of application of the rules

3608 The following tables show when the different regulatory standards apply (for young workers, see ¶3720 and for workers in certain sectors, see ¶3640).

Hours worked	48-hour weekly limit	Night time limit	Daily and weekly rest	In-work breaks	Compensatory rest	Annual leave
Set and determined time under the control of the employer	✓	✓	✓	✓	n/a	✓
Unmeasured time	X	X	X	X	X	✓
Due to distant commuting	✓	X	X	X	✓	✓
Due to foreseeable surge of activity in agriculture, tourism and postal services	✓	X	X	X	✓	✓
Due to unusual and unforeseeable circumstances beyond control of employer	✓	X	X	X	✓	✓
Due to exceptional events which could not reasonably have been avoided by the employer	✓	X	X	X	✓	✓
Due to an accident or the imminent risk of an accident	✓	X	X	X	✓	✓
Due to shift work	✓	✓	X	✓	✓	✓
Due to collective or workforce agreement	✓	X	X	X	✓	✓
✓ = entitlement to right; X = no entitlement to right; n/a = not applicable						

I. Scope of regulations

3615 The legal requirements on working time apply to all **workers** (reg 2(1) SI 1998/1833) and also apply to:

a. agency workers (reg 36 SI 1998/1833). This is regardless of whether the agency worker comes under the general definition of worker or not. In the latter case, the regulations will apply as if there is a contract between the agency worker and whoever pays or is responsible for paying the agency worker in respect of the work (whether that is the agent or the principal); and

b. persons who are **receiving relevant training**, other than under a contract of employment (regs 42, 2(1) SI 1998/1833). Relevant training is **defined** as work experience provided in relation to a training course or programme, training for employment, or both, other than work experience or training:
– where the immediate provider is an educational institution/person whose main business is the provision of training; and
– which is provided on a course run by that institution/person.

Workers may be **totally or partially excluded** from certain rights **if they**:
– have unmeasured or partially unmeasured working time;
– work in shifts; or
– work in air, rail, road, sea, inland waterway and lake transport and sea fishing.

Further, workers can be partially excluded from certain rights **where**:
– it is needed for flexibility, continuity or other special reasons; or
– there is an agreement to do so in a collective or workforce agreement.

These exceptions are covered in detail in the following sections. It should be noted, though, that even if such workers are excluded in whole or in part, an employer cannot require them to work such hours that would result in a breach of the employer's implied duty to take reasonable care for the health of his employees (¶4815) (*Johnstone v Bloomsbury Health Authority* [1991] IRLR 118, CA).

1. Unmeasured working time

3625 Workers are excluded from all the regulations except those regarding annual leave (¶4000) if they have unmeasured working time (reg 20(1) SI 1998/1833). This occurs in the following three circumstances where:

a. the workers have **complete control** over the hours they work. For example, this will include managing executives who need to control their own work time, directors and those in similar positions who have autonomous decision-making powers. It will also include those who decide how and when they work, what is and what is not done, and who determines the time and effort that is devoted to their various tasks and objectives;

b. the workers' time is not monitored or pre-determined by their employers because of **specific characteristics of the activity** in which the workers are engaged. For example, sales representatives who need to visit customers, often over a wide area, will determine themselves the hours worked. Workers who are engaged to complete a particular project or task, for example home piece-workers (i.e. workers who are paid per piece or item produced), may fall within this exception, as their work is not measured by the number of hours; or

c. the workers are **family workers**.

2. Shift workers

3635 In certain circumstances, shift workers' right to **daily and weekly rest periods** may not apply (reg 22 SI 1998/1833). Shift work is defined as any method of organising work in shifts so that workers succeed each other at the same workstations according to a certain pattern. This pattern includes a rotating pattern and may be continuous or discontinuous, with the need for workers to work at different times over a given period of days or weeks.

If a **shift worker changes shift**, or where the work is split up over the day, as may be the case for cleaning staff who have a morning and evening shift, it may not be possible for him to take his full rest entitlements before starting a new shift. If this happens, the entitlement to daily and weekly rest will not apply.

Shift workers who have had their rest entitlements affected will be entitled to **compensatory rest** (¶3717).

3. Workers in certain sectors

3640 This subsection refers to the special series of working time rules that apply to workers in **air, rail, road, sea, inland waterway and lake transport, sea fishing**, and **other work at sea (for example, offshore work in the oil and gas industry)**. In most of these sectors, different rules apply to non-mobile and mobile workers.

> MEMO POINTS 1. These sectors were excluded from the original Directive (EC Working Time Directive 1993/104 which was implemented in the UK by the Working Time Regulations SI 1998/1833) as it was agreed that these sectors required their own special rules. As a result, there are four specific Directives which concern specific groups (EC Aviation Directive 2000/79, EC Seafarers' Directive 1999/63, EC Seafarers' Enforcement Directive 1999/95 and EC Road Transport Directive 2002/15). How these have been implemented is detailed below.
> The European Horizontal Amending Directive has expanded the original Directive to either fully or partially include workers who were previously excluded (non-mobile workers and certain groups of mobile workers working within these sectors) (EC Horizontal Amending Directive 2000/34). This Directive has been implemented in the UK by the Working Time (Amendment) Regulations which amend the original regulations (SI 2003/1684).
> 2. **Doctors in training** are subject to an average weekly working limit of 48 hours (reg 7 Working Time (Amendment) Regulations SI 2003/1684 which adds a new reg 25A SI 1998/1833). There was an exception in relation to certain doctors in training, who are subject instead to an average weekly working limit of 52, instead of 48, hours, but this ended on 31 July 2011 (SI 2009/1567 as amended by SI 2009/2766).
> 3. The **definition of offshore work** includes work performed in the UK sector of the Continental Shelf as well as that performed within the territorial waters of the UK (SI 2006/2389).

Non-mobile workers

3642 Non-mobile workers (for example, administrative/clerical workers) are protected by the regulations in (Working Time (Amendment) Regulations SI 2003/1684):
– road, rail, air, sea, and inland waterway and lake transport;
– sea fishing; and
– other work at sea (for example, offshore work in the oil and gas industry).

Mobile workers

3644 The minimum regulatory standards (¶3605) generally apply to mobile workers although special exemptions and derogations will apply depending on the type of mobile worker. Some mobile workers are covered not by the regulations but by other legislation. For more information, readers are referred to the relevant regulatory/legislative source as set out below.

Mobile workers **protected by the regulations** are as follows:
1. those not covered by the European Road Transport Directive (including all drivers not covered by the EU Community Drivers' Hours Regulation (tachograph rules)) (for example, couriers, drivers of taxis or white vans) (EC Road Transport Directive 2002/15; EU Community Drivers' Hours Regulation 3820/1985);
2. rail transport workers. Special exemptions apply to workers whose activities are intermittent, spent on trains and whose activities are linked to railway transport timetables and ensuring the continuity and regularity of railway traffic. Further, specific regulations apply to workers whose daily shift includes more than 1 hour on train services going through the Channel Tunnel that require at least two network safety requirement certifications (SI 2008/1660);

3. workers in aviation who are not covered by the European Aviation Directive, including those who work in corporate and general aviation as opposed to commercial air transport (EC Aviation Directive 2000/79); and

4. offshore (oil and gas exploration and production) workers. There is a special derogation to allow for the weekly working time limit of 48 hours to be averaged over 52 weeks.

Mobile workers **protected by other legislation** are as follows:

1. those covered by the European Road Transport Directive (i.e. commercial drivers and crews of heavy goods vehicles and public service vehicles), or, in some cases, the AETR (the European agreement concerning the work of crews of vehicles engaged in international road transport), are covered by the Road Transport (Working Time) Regulations (SI 2005/639) which have implemented this Directive (EC Road Transport Directive 2002/15). Special provisions allow for a maximum of 60 hours' work in any single week (subject to compliance with the average weekly working time limit) and night workers are restricted to 10 hours' working time in any 24-hour period;

2. those in civil aviation covered by the European Aviation Directive including all mobile workers in commercial air transport (both flight crew and cabin crew), which has been implemented through the Civil Aviation (Working Time) Regulations (EC Aviation Directive 2000/79; SI 2004/756). Special provisions concern the maximum annual working time of crew members, adequate health and safety protection services and facilities at work along with adequate rest breaks to be given to crew members where work is organised in a certain pattern. Crew members are also entitled to a minimum number of rest days, free from all duties, in every calendar month and year. However, with regard to the right to paid leave, the Regulations do not set out a method of calculating the rate of holiday pay and the Court of Justice of the European Union, following the Supreme Court's referral regarding this point, has held that holiday pay must, in principle, be determined in such a way as to correspond to a worker's normal remuneration. This means that an airline pilot is entitled not only to the maintenance of his basic salary while on annual leave, but also to all monetary components intrinsically linked to the performance of the tasks which he is required to carry out, and all such elements relating to his personal and professional status as a pilot (such as seniority, length of service and professional qualifications) (Williams and ors v British Airways plc [2011] EUECJ C-155/10). Consequently, as with the calculation of the rate of holiday pay with regard to the Working Time Regulations (¶4012), the pilots' flying time allowances should be included in this calculation.

3. seafarers on seagoing ships covered by the European Seafarers' Directive which has been implemented through the Merchant Shipping (Hours of Work) Regulations (EC Seafarers' Directive 1999/63; SI 2002/2125). Special provisions require employers to ensure seafarers have at least the specified minimum hours of rest;

4. those in inland waterway and lake transport covered by the European Horizontal Amendment Directive implemented through the Merchant Shipping (Working Time: Inland Waterways) Regulations (EC Horizontal Amendment Directive 2000/34; SI 2003/3049 (which amends the Merchant Shipping Act 1995)); and

5. sea fishermen covered by the European Horizontal Amendment Directive (EC Horizontal Amendment Directive 2000/34, which has been implemented by SI 2004/1713). Special provisions limit the maximum hours that fishermen may work in a 24-hour or 7-day period by reference to minimum hours of rest. Average working time is limited to 48 hours to be calculated over 52 weeks. Sea fishermen are further entitled to paid annual leave and health assessments.

4. Flexibility, continuity or other special reasons

Where workers fall under certain categories (detailed below), they will be **excluded from** the entitlements regarding (regs 21, 4(5) SI 1998/1833):
- length of night work;
- daily and weekly rest periods; and
- in-work rest breaks.

In these cases, workers still keep their entitlement to annual leave. Employers will also have to make sure workers do not exceed the average weekly working time. In calculating this, the relevant reference period (¶3681) will be any 26-week period.

Workers will only be subject to these limited entitlements where they fall under one of the **following three categories** and they will also be entitled to **compensatory rest** (¶3717):

3652 **1. Distant commuting** Where a worker's place of work and home (or different places of work) are distant from one another, it may be beneficial to let him work more flexible hours (reg 21 (a) SI 1998/1833). Flexibility may be desirable to allow him to work longer hours for a short period to complete a task more quickly, or because continual changes in the location of work make it impractical to set a pattern of work. Such working practices must be by agreement and will be acceptable as long as the average weekly working time is adhered to.

> EXAMPLE Worker A's employer has agreed that A can work flexible hours because he lives far from the workplace. This results in some days being worked without a break so that A can leave before the rush hour.
> Worker B is a site worker and he needs flexible hours as he regularly visits different sites.

3654 **2. Continuity of service or production** Employers may require the need for continuity of service or production as may be the case in (reg 21(b), (c) SI 1998/1833):
a. services relating to the reception, treatment or care provided by:
– hospitals or similar establishments;
– residential institutions; or
– prisons;
b. work at docks or airports;
c. press, radio, television or cinematographic production;
d. postal and telecommunications services;
e. gas, water and electricity production, transmission and distribution, household refuse collection and incineration;
f. industries in which work cannot be interrupted on technical grounds (as may be the case where there is a need to keep machinery running);
g. research and development activities;
h. agriculture; or
i. security and surveillance activities by security guards or caretakers (including any worker who is providing a permanent presence in order to protect property and persons).

When considering whether a derogation from the entitlement to an in-work rest break can be invoked, the need for continuity of service or production must relate to the activities of the workers concerned as opposed to those of the employer (*Gallagher and others v Alpha Catering Services Ltd t/a Alpha Flight Services* [2005] IRLR 102, CA). Without such interpretation, the protection given by the regulations would be vulnerable to abuse by employers who deliberately understaff their workplaces to ensure a need for continuity of service or production is maintained. Moreover, when considering the meaning of "foreseeable surge of activity", this must refer to something more acute than mere fluctuations in activity which take place as a matter of course.

> MEMO POINTS 1. This list is not exhaustive; the above examples are illustrative.
> 2. In a case involving the application of this exemption to the working patterns of river pilots, the EAT has agreed to make a reference to the Court of Justice of the European Union (CJEU) regarding the proper construction and scope of these provisions (*Associated British Ports v Bridgeman* [2012] UKEAT 0425_11_0404). The reference will ask whether the requirement for continuity of service or production has to be established separately with respect to each right from which exemption is sought, or whether the issue of continuity of service or production should be addressed generally and provide an employer with an exemption from all of the listed rights, irrespective of whether they can comply with some of them. The EAT has given the provisional view that the tribunal was right in holding that the correct interpretation is that the need for continuous service or production must be established in respect of each right the employer is seeking exemption from, but we now await the decision of the CJEU. This is an important issue for employers who have relied upon the exemption and assumed that once a need for continuity of service or

production has been established, the employer is exempt from all the listed rights and can provide compensatory rest instead.

3. Special events or circumstances Employers may require greater flexibility with regard to their workers' working hours in the following circumstances:
– a foreseeable surge of activity (as can happen in relation to agriculture, tourism, and postal services);
– an occurrence due to unusual and unforeseeable circumstances beyond the control of the employer;
– exceptional events, the consequences of which could not have been avoided despite the exercise of all due care by the employer; or
– an accident or the imminent risk of an accident.

3656

5. Collective or workforce agreement

A collective agreement or workforce agreement may **modify or exclude** the following aspects of the regulations with regard to particular workers or groups of workers (reg 23 SI 1998/1833):
– length of night work limit;
– daily and weekly rest periods; and
– in-work rest breaks.

3660

Workers who are affected will be entitled to **compensatory rest** (¶3717).

Such workers are still entitled to annual leave. Employers will also have to make sure that workers do not work over the average weekly working time limit. The **relevant reference period** (¶3681) for calculating the average weekly working time can be up to 52 weeks if it is necessary for objective or technical reasons or for reasons concerning the organisation of work.

II. Minimum standards

Limitations are set as to how long a worker can work during a week (the average weekly working time, ¶¶3680+), though workers can opt out by agreement. Workers are also entitled to weekly, daily and in-work rest periods.

3670

Working time is **defined** as when a worker is working at his employer's disposal and is carrying out his employer's activities or duties (reg 2(1) SI 1998/1833). Both these elements must be satisfied for time worked to be regarded as working time. Additional periods can be counted as working time if allowed under a collective or workforce agreement.

3671

For example, time worked that is **paid hourly**, **prescribed hours** of work, work done under **close supervision**, or **expressly or implicitly requested periods** of work will be working time. Implicitly requested periods of work include longer hours worked either because:
– of the requirements of the work, for example, to finish a delivery or meet a deadline; or
– the worker may suffer a detriment, for example be passed over for promotion, if he does not work longer hours.

Where the worker is obliged to be **present and available** at his workplace with a view to providing his professional services, it is regarded as working time.

3672

This includes time spent resting or sleeping **at the workplace** where such facilities are provided, for example providing on-call hospital doctors with beds for use when they are not attending to patients or on-call residential care workers with flats at the workplace to live in and to rest and sleep while on call duty (*Landeshauptstadt Kiel v Norbert Jaeger* [2003] IRLR 804, ECJ; *Dellas and others v Prime Minister and another (C-14/04)* [2006] IRLR 225, ECJ; *MacCartney v Oversley House Management* [2006] IRLR 514, EAT). The fact that this includes some periods of inactivity is irrelevant, though there must be some obligation to be available for work if required.

However, where the worker is **not present at his place of work** but is on call, his time is not regarded as working time if he is free to pursue leisure activities, although if a worker is called to his place of work while on call, his time at his place of work in response is, naturally, working time (Sindicato de Médicos de Asistencia Publica (SIMAP) v Consellería Sanidad Y Consumo de la Generalidad Valenciana [2000] EUECJ C-303/98).

3673 The following table sets out specific activities as examples of what counts towards working time:

Periods included as working time	Periods excluded as working time
Working/business lunch or corporate entertaining	Lunch break
Working at home with prior consent of employer	Taking work home without prior consent
Time spent travelling if it is an essential part of work (for example, a sales representative)	Time spent travelling to and from a place of work
Time on call where the worker is at his place of work or is restricted as to what he can do and cannot pursue leisure activities	Time on call where the worker is otherwise free to pursue leisure activities
Time spent on relevant training (for example, training a machine operator)	Time spent on other training or activities (for example, training and playing football in a company team)

A. General system of average weekly working time

3680 A worker's working time, including overtime, **must not exceed** an average of 48 hours a week (7 days) in any reference period (reg 4(1) SI 1998/1833) unless he has **opted out**, see ¶3688.

> MEMO POINTS A **day** is taken as a period of 24 hours beginning at midnight (reg 2(1) SI 1998/1833).

Reference period

3681 This average is calculated over a reference period. For each worker, this is any 17-week period of work, unless a relevant agreement has pre-defined specific consecutive periods of 17 weeks. Employers, therefore, can require workers to work more than 48 hours a week for some of the weeks within a reference period as long as some of the other weeks are less than 48 hours to compensate and to ensure that the average remains 48 hours or less.

If the worker has worked for less than 17 weeks then the working time is calculated for the period he has worked up to the date of calculation. If he is a **night worker** he will also be subject to the night work limit (see below).

Where there is the need for **flexibility, continuity or other special reasons** (¶3650), the average weekly limit will still apply but it should be noted that the reference period will be any 26-week period.

An **extended reference period** of up to 52 weeks is allowed under a workforce or collective agreement (reg 23 SI 1998/1833).

Calculating average weekly working time

3684 Average weekly working time is calculated by dividing the number of hours worked by the number of weeks in the reference period.

3685 The number of working days taken into account must be days worked and **days of absence** due to sickness, annual leave or maternity, paternity, adoption or parental leave are excluded from the reference period. In effect, this makes little practical difference to the calculation as actual days worked (equal to the number of days of absence) must be added to the reference period by including the appropriate number of worked days immediately after the reference period has ended.

If the reference period is set to start at a specific date by a relevant agreement, the inclusion of extra days immediately after one reference period has ended will not affect the date on which the subsequent reference period starts. Such extra days are counted twice, both in the reference period in which there was absence and in the subsequent reference period.

The **average weekly hours** can be calculated by using the formula:

3686

$$\frac{(A + B)}{C}$$

A is the total number of hours worked **during** the reference period;
B is the total number of hours worked **immediately after** the reference period equal to the number of days missed during that period due to absence;
A + B are the total hours worked; and
C is the number of weeks in the reference period.

MEMO POINTS   This process of averaging means that an employer can require an employee to work more than 48 hours in any given week. However, the maximum weekly hours are practically restricted as a consequence of the employee's separate entitlements to daily and weekly rest periods.

Opting out

Individual workers can voluntarily agree to work **more than the average weekly limit**. The arrangement must be **agreed in writing** and it must allow the worker to terminate it (regs 4, 5 SI 1998/1833). Any such agreement can be for a specified or an indefinite period, and can have a notice period of up to 3 months. If no notice period is specified, only 7 days' written notice will be required to end the agreement. If it is obvious from the outset that the worker may exceed the average weekly limit, the opt-out can be included in the contract of employment.

3688

The Court of Justice of the European Union has emphasised that a worker's **consent** to opting out of the average weekly working time limit "must be given not only individually but also **expressly and freely**" (*Pfeiffer and others v Deutsches Rotes Kreuz, Kreisverband Waldshut eV, Case C397-403/01* [2005] ICR 1307, ECJ). Consequently, employers must ensure that not only do they have a written agreement with each worker who is opting out (which can be included in the worker's contract of employment), but that it is made clear to them that they have the freedom to choose whether or not to opt out. Further, employees must be able to **assert their right to refuse** to work more than the average weekly limit without being punished or suffering some kind of detriment, such as being transferred to a different role with less favourable terms and conditions (*Fuß v Stadt Halle (Social policy)* [2010] EUECJ C-429/09). However, an employer may be justified in imposing an overtime ban on an employee who has refused to sign an opt-out (*Arriva London South Ltd v Nicolaou* [2011] UKEAT 0293_11_2112).

Where an opt-out agreement **covers only part** of a reference period, this must be excluded from the average weekly hours formula (above) and an equivalent period must be added to the end of the reference period. This may occur if the opt-out is for a specified period or if it has been terminated.

MEMO POINTS   There have been various attempts at revising the Working Time Directive, none of which have so far been successful, with the main stumbling block being the proposal to end the opt-out. The European Commission agreed a joint proposal from the European social partners which extended the negotiating period on reviewing the Working Time Directive to 31 December 2012. Any further developments will be covered by our updating service.

B. Night time working

3695 Night time is **defined** as a period of at least 7 hours (which must include the period from midnight to 5am) which is determined by a relevant agreement. If there is no agreement, night time will be from 11pm to 6am (reg 2(1) SI 1998/1833).

A **night worker** is defined as any worker "who, as a normal course, works at least 3 hours of his daily working time during night time, or who is likely, during night time, to work at least such proportion of his annual working time in a collective agreement or a workforce agreement". The term night worker is therefore intended to apply to workers who work at night as part of a regular shift pattern rather than on an occasional or infrequent basis.

Stricter controls operate on **young workers** (¶¶3720+).

Normal hours of night work

3696 A night worker should not exceed an average of 8 hours' work for each 24 hours over the reference period (reg 6 SI 1998/1833). The **reference period** and **extended reference period** are the same as for the average weekly working time (¶3681).

The night working limit is a **separate limit** to the average weekly working time. Employers must ensure that night workers also comply with the weekly average.

3697 **Calculating normal hours of night work** The hours of night work are calculated by dividing the number of a worker's **normal hours** of working time in the reference period by the total number of days in the period, less the number of rest days to which the worker was entitled. This calculation is **based on** normal hours worked (which can include overtime where it is part of the worker's normal hours) and not actual hours worked.

Average night hours can be calculated using the formula:

$$\frac{A}{(B-C)}$$

A is the number of normal working hours during the reference period;
B is the number of days during the reference period; and
C is the number of hours of weekly rest to which a worker is entitled (i.e. 24 hours for each 7 days (¶3712)) divided by 24.

> EXAMPLE A night worker normally works four 12-hour shifts each week.
> Therefore, A is for a 17-week reference period:
> 17 weeks of four shifts of 12 hours
> $17 \times (4 \times 12) = 816$
> B is the number of days during the reference period:
> $17 \times 7 = 119$ days
> There are 17 weekly rest periods of 24 hours to which the worker is entitled during the reference period.
> Therefore, C is:
> $17 \times (24/24) = 17$
> The calculation of the total of hours divided by the number of days a worker could be required to work:
> $816/(119 - 17) = 8$, giving an average of 8 hours in each 24-hour period.

Work involving special hazards or strain

3699 Where a night worker's work involves special hazards or heavy physical or mental strain, there is a limit of 8 hours on the worker's actual daily working time. The **8-hour limit** must be observed in any period of 24 hours during which the night worker performs such work.

A night worker is regarded as being involved in special hazards or heavy physical or mental strain if either:
– the collective or workforce agreement identifies the work as such; or

– it is recognised as such in a risk assessment made by the employer under the Management of Health and Safety at Work Regulations (SI 1999/3242).

Health of night workers

3701 An employer must offer a worker a free health assessment **before assigning him** work that makes him a night worker (reg 7 SI 1998/1833). If the worker has already had a health assessment due to a previous assignment and the employer has no reason to believe that the assessment is no longer valid (because it was a recent assessment and there are no indications of any health problems), the employer will have satisfied this requirement.

3702 Free health assessments must be offered at **regular intervals** as appropriate (reg 7 (6) SI 1998/1833). If a night worker is doing hazardous work or has a medical condition that might be affected by the work then free health assessments should be offered at **shorter intervals** than with regard to other night workers.

Where a registered medical practitioner advises that a worker is **suffering from health problems** which are considered to be connected with the worker working at night and it is possible for the employer to transfer the worker (to work for which the worker is suitable and which allows him to stop being a night worker) then the employer must do so.

C. Rest periods

3710 Workers are **entitled** to weekly, daily and in-work rest periods. Stricter controls operate on employers of young workers (¶¶3720+). **Periods of inactivity** or sleep during working time while workers are **on-call at the workplace** do not count towards their rest periods, particularly if they are not guaranteed a minimum number of hours of continuous rest (¶3672).

Employers should **ensure that their policies** emphasise that workers must take their weekly, daily and in-work rest breaks and that this is a health and safety requirement. Where possible, employers should also check that rest periods have been taken.

> MEMO POINTS BIS guidance notes on working time used to advise employers that while they were required to ensure that workers could take their rest, they were not required to ensure that their workers actually did so. However, BIS removed this reference after the Court of Justice of the European Union ruled that the guidance notes were unlawful on this point and that a more proactive requirement should be given (*Commission of the European Communities v UK, Case C-484/04* [2006] IRLR 888, ECJ).

Daily and weekly rest periods

3711 These are **separate entitlements**. Weekly rest is additional to any paid annual leave to which workers may be entitled.

3712 A worker is entitled to **daily rest** of 11 consecutive hours during a 24-hour period (reg 10 SI 1998/1833).

A worker is entitled to **weekly rest** of an uninterrupted rest period of not less than 24 hours in each 7-day period (reg 11 SI 1998/1833). This may be averaged over a 2-week period so that the worker is entitled to either two uninterrupted rest periods of not less than 24 hours each or one uninterrupted rest period of not less than 48 hours.

> MEMO POINTS The weekly rest period should not include any part of a daily rest period unless this is justified by objective or technical reasons or reasons concerning the organisation of work (reg 11(7) SI 1998/1833); as the daily and weekly rest entitlements are cumulative, a worker should typically have 35 hours' continuous rest (24 + 11) once a week.

In-work rest breaks

3715 A worker is **entitled to** an uninterrupted break of 20 minutes when his daily working time is more than 6 hours (reg 12 SI 1998/1833). It should be a break in working time and should not be taken either at the start or at the end of a working day. It should not overlap with a worker's daily rest period. A worker is not entitled to a rest break for each period of 6 hours which he works and is only entitled to one period of rest for however long he works in excess of 6 hours (*Corps of Commissionaires Management Ltd v Hughes* [2008] UKEAT 0196_08_2210 confirmed by Court of Appeal on a different point).

Workers should know when they are **starting a rest break**. The employer cannot retrospectively deem a period of "downtime" a rest break just because it lasted at least 20 minutes (*Gallagher and others v Alpha Catering Services Ltd t/a Alpha Flight Services* [2005] IRLR 102, CA); nor can a period when an on-call worker happens to go 20 minutes without interruption count as their rest break (*MacCartney v Oversley House Management* [2006] IRLR 514, EAT).

Although rest breaks should be **uninterrupted** where possible, in exceptional circumstances this may not be possible, for example where continuity is essential such as in certain healthcare services. If breaks are **interrupted** in such circumstances, they can still count as rest time if compensatory rest is given (see ¶3717 below) (*Martin v Southern Health and Social Care Trust* [2010] NICA 31).

Where the **pattern of work** is such as to put the health and safety of the worker at risk, employers must make sure that workers are given adequate rest breaks to negate this risk which may exceed those specifically required by the regulations (reg 8 SI 1998/1833). Such circumstances include monotonous work or uninterruptible work, for example, repetitive work on a factory line, or work involving special hazards or heavy physical or mental strain.

Compensatory rest

3717 Where the rest periods or in-work rest breaks do not apply or have been modified (in relation to shift workers (¶3635), those working in conditions that require flexibility, continuity etc (¶3650), those working under a collective or workforce agreement which has modified or excluded certain rights (¶3660) and young workers (¶3720)), the workers concerned must be permitted to take **equivalent periods** of compensatory rest wherever possible (reg 24 SI 1998/1833; *Hughes v The Corps of Commissionaires Management Ltd* [2011] EWCA Civ 1061). Compensatory rest should be provided **within** a reasonable time from when the entitlement to rest was not applied or modified. The daily rest entitlement may be incorporated into the weekly rest entitlement if this is justified by objective or technical reasons or reasons concerning the organisation of work.

> **EXAMPLE** In *Hughes v The Corps of Commissionaires Management Ltd*, a security worker (whose work required a permanent presence (¶3654)) was provided with an area where breaks could be taken but he had to remain on call during these periods. However, importantly, if his break was interrupted he was permitted to start his break again from scratch. The Court of Appeal upheld the EAT's finding that the security worker had been given appropriate rest breaks.

In exceptional cases, **where** it is **not possible** for objective reasons to give compensatory rest, the employer must give the worker such protection as may be appropriate in order to safeguard his health and safety. This can include health checks, or whatever rest can be offered, though rest breaks should be as close as possible to a minimum of 20 minutes in length (*Hughes v The Corps of Commissionaires Management Ltd* [2010] UKEAT 0173_10_2211 confirmed by Court of Appeal on a different point).

D. Young workers

3720 Employers with young workers have **stricter controls** with regard to the night time limit. Young workers are also entitled to longer rest periods and there are restrictions on whether these can be altered or modified.

MEMO POINTS For other **health and safety requirements** which limit the type of work a child or young person can do, see ¶4970.

The **definition** of a young worker is a worker who is 15 to 17 years old and is over compulsory school age (reg 2(1) SI 1998/1833). **3721**

Children of compulsory school age are not workers within the meaning of the regulations (*Addison & another (trading as Brayton News) v Ashby* [2003] ICR 667, EAT). Such children are covered by other regulations (Children (Protection at Work) Regulations SI 1998/276) (¶4970).

Day time limit

Young workers must **not work for more than** 8 hours a day or 40 hours a week **unless** (regs 5A, 27A(1) SI 1998/1833): **3722**
– it is necessary to maintain continuity of service/production or as a response to a surge in demand for a service/product;
– there is no adult available to perform the task; and
– the employer ensures that the training needs of the young worker are not adversely affected.

This cannot be averaged out over a period of time nor can young workers opt out. Employers must also take all reasonable steps to ensure that this limit is complied with (reg 5A(4) SI 1998/1833).

Night time limit

Young workers must **not work at night between** 10pm and 6am, though if their contract of employment specifically provides for work after 10pm this prohibition can be changed to between 11pm and 7am (regs 2, 6A SI 1998/1833). **3724**

However, as **exceptions**, **if it is necessary** to maintain continuity of service/production or as a response to a surge in demand for a service/product, or there is no adult available to perform the task, and the employer ensures that the training needs of the young worker are not adversely affected, young workers are (reg 27A SI 1998/1833): **3725**
a. permitted to work at night if they work in a hospital or similar establishment or are employed in connection with cultural, artistic, sporting or advertising activities; and
b. permitted to work between 10pm and midnight and between 4am and 7am if they are employed in agriculture, retail trading, postal or newspaper deliveries, a catering or bakery business, or a hotel, public house, restaurant, bar or similar establishment.

In such cases, the employer must ensure that the young worker has the opportunity of a **free assessment of his health and capacities** before working such hours.

Further, where in such circumstances young workers are required to work during a period which would otherwise be a rest period or in-work break, they must be **supervised** by an adult worker where such supervision is necessary for their protection and they must be allowed an equivalent period of **compensatory rest** (¶3717).

Daily and weekly rest periods

A young worker is entitled to daily rest of 12 consecutive hours in each 24-hour period during which he works (reg 10(2) SI 1998/1833). **3727**

A young worker is also entitled to weekly rest of 2 days each week which cannot be averaged over a 2-week period (reg 11 SI 1998/1833). This weekly rest may be reduced to 36 hours, where justified by technical or organisational reasons, for example, where such reasons are inherent in the nature of the work or its desired purpose.

The minimum daily and weekly rest periods can be interrupted in the case of activities involving periods of work that are split up over the day or do not last long.

In-work rest breaks

A young worker is entitled to an in-work rest break of 30 minutes when daily working time is more than 4.5 hours (reg 12(4) SI 1998/1833). **3729**

Alterations or modifications to rest periods and in-work breaks

3731 A young worker's entitlement to daily rest periods and in-work rest breaks may be modified or excluded where he has to undertake tasks because there is no adult worker available. In addition, these tasks must (reg 27 SI 1998/1833):
a. need to be performed immediately;
b. be of a temporary nature; and
c. be due to:
– unusual and unforeseeable circumstances beyond the employer's control; or
– exceptional events, the consequences of which could not have been avoided by the employer regardless of whether due care has been taken.

If a young worker is required to work in these conditions, the employer must allow him to take an equivalent period of **compensatory rest** (¶3717) within the following 3 weeks.

III. Records

3740 Employers must keep records which **adequately show** that the average weekly working time and night work limits for workers and the maximum working time and night work provisions for young workers have been complied with in regard to each worker, and all records must be **retained for** 2 years (reg 9 SI 1998/1833). An up-to-date record of any workers who have opted out of the average weekly working time limit will need to be kept by employers, but there is no need to record how many hours they actually work (reg 4(2) SI 1998/1833).

Employers will not be expected to keep a running total of how much time workers work on average each week, and will only be expected to make occasional checks on workers who do standard hours and who are unlikely to reach the average weekly working time limit. However, employers should monitor the hours of workers who appear close to the working time limits to ensure that such workers do not exceed these limits.

Records can be based on time sheets produced by workers or information produced on requiring workers to clock in and out of their places of work. If there are no time sheets or clocking in and out procedures, the normal contractual hours can be used as a guide, with the employer adding any working time done above this, for example, from overtime sheets. Employers might be able to use existing records maintained for other purposes, for example pay, or they may have to make new records.

Employers should require workers to inform them of any hours they work for other employers (as these will count towards the limit on working time) so that they can ensure that the working time limits are complied with.

3741 There is no requirement to keep records to show that the entitlements to **daily** and **weekly rest periods** and **in-work rest breaks** have been complied with. However, as an employee can make a complaint to an employment tribunal if the employer breaches the regulations with regard to these entitlements, it is advisable for both parties to keep adequate records.

Should any disputes arise as to the number of hours worked, it will be a factual and evidential issue which the tribunal or court will decide.

3742 Records of **health assessments** must also be **kept for** 2 years and they must not be disclosed to any person other than to the worker to whom the assessment relates, unless (regs 9, 7(5) SI 1998/1833):
– the worker has given his consent in writing to the disclosure; or
– disclosure is confined to a statement that the assessment shows the worker to be fit for night work.

IV. Enforcement and remedies

3750 Employers will commit a criminal offence and will be subject to penalties if they do not comply with certain rules.

Workers can also ensure that employers comply with certain entitlements and have two enforcement options available to them. The first is from a contractual obligation on employers which will be enforceable in the civil courts. The second is from a regulatory obligation on employers which can be enforced through the employment tribunals.

Workers may also have a specific action in an employment tribunal for unfair dismissal and have the right not to suffer detriment.

Summary of enforcement provisions

3751

Working time provision	Offence/Complaint	Where enforced	Penalty/Remedy
Average weekly working time	Criminal offence	Magistrates' court	Fine
		Crown Court	Fine
	Breach of contract	Civil courts	Declaration of rights Injunction
Night time limit and provisions	Criminal offence	Magistrates' court Crown Court	Fine Fine
Adequate rest breaks during monotonous work			
Records			
Daily and weekly rest periods	Breach of regulations	Employment tribunal	Declaration Compensation
In-work rest breaks			
Compensatory rest			
Annual leave (¶4000)			
Specific protection from unfair dismissal in relation to working time and annual leave (¶4000)	Unfair dismissal	Employment tribunal	Reinstatement Re-engagement Compensation
Right not to suffer detriment for insisting on working time and annual leave (¶4000) rights	Breach of right	Employment tribunal	Declaration Compensation

A. Criminal offences and penalties

3755 The authority **responsible for enforcing** the regulations is the Health and Safety Executive, except where the relevant requirements apply in relation to workers employed in premises for which the local authority has control, in which case responsibility lies with that local authority (reg 28 SI 1998/1833).

An employer will commit an offence on failing to comply with (reg 29 SI 1998/1833):
– average weekly working time and the maximum working time for young workers, both of which he must take all reasonable steps to observe;
– the night time limit and the provisions regarding night work for young workers, both of which he must take all reasonable steps to observe;

- giving compensatory rest where necessary with regard to night time workers and young night time workers;
- the requirement to provide free health assignments for night time workers and young night time workers;
- providing young night time workers with supervision by an adult worker where necessary for their protection;
- his duty to transfer a night time worker to day work on advice from a doctor where it is possible to do so;
- giving adequate rest breaks for workers with monotonous or repetitive work; or
- keeping records.

The penalties are:
- in the **magistrates' court**, a fine not exceeding the statutory maximum; and
- in the **Crown Court**, a fine as decided appropriate by the judge.

B. Remedies

Breach of contract

3760 The regulations impose an implied contractual obligation on employers not to require workers to do more than the **average weekly working time** (*Barber v RJB Mining (UK) Limited* [1999] IRLR 308, QBD). This creates a free-standing legal right under the contract of employment or any other relevant contract and a worker can bring an action against his employer in the **civil courts** for a **declaration of his rights** as happened in *Barber*. Such a declaration meant that the workers were entitled to refuse to continue working until their average working hours came within the specified limit.

However, it should be noted that this remedy is a protection against being required to work excessive hours in the future. It does **not** give rise to a free-standing right to claim **damages**.

> EXAMPLE In *Sayers v Cambridgeshire County Council* [2007] IRLR 29, HC, a senior manager worked 50 to 60 hours a week for many months, and ultimately suffered a breakdown. Before the High Court, she argued that these excessive hours had represented in themselves a harm, for which she should be recompensed by way of damages. The Court considered a variety of routes by which such an action might be founded: by a claim on the Regulations, as an action for a breach of a statutory duty, as a claim by way of the direct effect of the European Working Time Directive, or by reference to other health and safety legislation. None of these different approaches, the Court insisted, could be used as the basis of a claim for damages.

Breach of regulations

3761 Workers can bring a complaint against their employers in an **employment tribunal** for breach of the following entitlements (reg 30 SI 1998/1833):
- daily and weekly rest periods;
- in-work breaks;
- compensatory rest (including compensatory rest with regard to young workers); and
- annual leave.

3762 The worker must **bring** his **complaint within** 3 months starting on the date when:
- it is alleged that the exercise of the right should have been allowed (where the alleged rest period or leave extended over a day, the date on which it should have been permitted to start); or
- a payment should have been made as compensation in relation to an annual leave entitlement.

For example, where the worker should have been given a compensatory rest period, he must bring his claim in relation to it within 3 months from the time it should have been given (*Corps of Commissionaires Management Ltd v Hughes* [2008] UKEAT 0196_08_2210). This period may be extended if considered reasonable by the tribunal, and if the tribunal is satisfied that it was not reasonably practicable for the complaint to be presented before the end of the 3-month period.

Where a **tribunal finds** a **complaint well founded**, it will make a declaration to that effect, and may make an award of compensation (s 18(1) ERA 1996). A tribunal will award whatever it considers to be just and equitable in all the circumstances having regard to:
– the employer's default in refusing to permit the worker to exercise his right; and
– any loss sustained by the worker that is attributable to the matters complained of.

3763

> EXAMPLE In *Miles v Linkage Community Trust* [2008] IRLR 602, EAT, a care worker worked shift patterns which did not allow him the appropriate prescribed daily rest periods. He was required to remain at work for periods of over 48 hours at a time, during which time he was permitted to sleep. This pattern continued for some time before he complained about his working hours. The EAT held that he was entitled to a declaration but no compensation should be awarded, on the grounds that:
> – only the period of default after the employee's request to take his daily rest period had been refused should be taken into account in deciding the degree to which the employer was at fault;
> – the employer had taken advice and not been guilty of bad faith in dealing with the complaint; and
> – the employee had suffered no financial loss.

Right not to suffer detriment

A **worker** can make a complaint for detrimental effect, or deliberate failure to act by his employer, which has occurred as a result of him (s 45A ERA 1996):
a. having refused (or proposing to refuse) to comply with a requirement which his employer imposed (or proposed) in contravention of the regulations;
b. refusing (or proposing to refuse) to forgo a working time or annual leave right;
c. failing to:
– sign a workforce agreement for the purposes of the regulations, or
– enter into, or agree to vary or extend, any other agreement with his employer; or
d. being a representative of members of the workforce for the purposes of workforce agreements, or being a candidate in an election in which any worker elected will become such a representative, and performing (or proposing to perform) any function or activities in his role.

3765

Workers can also suffer a detriment for **alleging an infringement** for any of the above acts or for bringing proceedings against their employers.

It is irrelevant and immaterial whether or not a worker did have the right or whether a right has been infringed. However, all claims must be made in **good faith**.

> MEMO POINTS What amounts to a "**detriment**" is not defined by the ERA 1996, but case law on discrimination has held that it is whether a reasonable worker would feel he has been disadvantaged by reason of his employer's acts (¶5279).

Contractual **changes to accommodate opting back in** are not detrimental if they are necessary to facilitate the reduction of working hours and are not, on weighing up their advantages and disadvantages, substantial or material (*Clamp v Aerial Systems* [2004] UKEAT 0266_04_0610).

3766

> EXAMPLE In *Clamp v Aerial Systems*, an engineer, C, who drove to appointments, had an opted-out working week of 60 hours which was unregulated. When he opted back in, his employer calculated C's hours from the start of his first job to the end of his last job. When he had no first job, his working time now started from a designated spot on the motorway. The EAT held that discounting C's time spent travelling to and from work was not detrimental as it is common ground that time spent travelling to and from a place of work is not working time and in any event his salary was the same as before. Further, requiring him to wait at a designated spot rather than at home had more advantages than disadvantages and meant that he started his working day earlier. Consequently, despite the fact that C could no longer wait at home, this was not a detriment.

> MEMO POINTS The EAT also commented in this case that reducing a worker's pay, if his hours are reduced on opting back in, would not be a detriment as long as the worker's hourly rate of pay remains the same.

Right not to be unfairly dismissed

3769 Any dismissal of an employee will be **automatically unfair** (¶8390) if the reason (or, if more than one, the principal reason) for the dismissal is one of those covered by the right not to suffer a detriment (s 101A ERA 1996).

Where there is a **dispute as to the reasons** for the dismissal, and the employee alleges that the dismissal was on the grounds of his refusal to work more than 48 hours per week or outside any of the other protections set out in the Working Time Regulations, there is no requirement for the employee to have positively asserted his rights, as, for example, by naming the Regulations. All that is required is that the employer must have required the worker to work outside the Regulations, and the worker must in turn have refused to accede to that request (*McLean v Rainbow Homeloans Ltd* [2007] IRLR 14, EAT). To be a refusal it must be explicit, i.e. the refusal must be made known to the employer and cannot be implied by a worker's conduct alone (*Ajayi and anor v Aitch Care Homes (London) Ltd* [2012] UKEAT 0464_11_0302).

> MEMO POINTS Non-employee workers who are so dismissed should rely on the right not to suffer a detriment (see above): compensation is awarded on the same basis as for unfair dismissal.

SECTION 2

Sunday trading

3800 Although Sunday is normally regarded as an ordinary working day, shop and betting employees have **special rules** relating to them if they work, or may be required to work, on Sundays (ss 36-43 ERA 1996; Sunday Trading Act 1994).

Unless a shop or betting employee is employed solely to work on Sundays, he has the **right to opt out** of Sunday working and, if he was such an employee when the various rules came into force, he is automatically protected and cannot be required to work on Sundays. In this section, opted-out employees and those who are automatically protected will be referred to as **protected employees**. If protected, employees can nevertheless opt in and expressly agree to work on Sundays, or on a particular Sunday.

> MEMO POINTS In **Scotland**, shop and betting employees have been protected since 6 April 2004 (Sunday Working (Scotland) Act 2003). Their rights depend solely on whether they have contracted terms regarding Sunday working (¶¶3830+) or not (¶¶3825+).

3801 Within 2 months of becoming a shop or betting employee, the employer must give the employee an **explanatory statement** setting out the employee's rights with regard to Sunday working.

3802 Any contractual term, made either before or after the employee was protected, that **purports to override** his protection is unenforceable (s 37 ERA 1996). If a protected employee has opted in to Sunday working, his contractual terms are varied only to the extent necessary to give effect to any subsequent express agreement to work on Sundays or on a particular Sunday.

3803 There is no statutory right for an employee working on Sundays to receive an enhanced hourly **rate of pay** (s 45 ERA 1996). However, most employers do offer special overtime rates or premiums to encourage employees to work on Sundays and this is legally acceptable. Therefore, a protected shop or betting employee has no remedy if his wage is reduced because, although he does the same hours, he no longer works on Sundays. Likewise, a protected employee has no remedy if the employer does not provide him with any other benefit that is related to Sunday working.

> MEMO POINTS 1. **Small shops**, whose floor areas for the display, sales and serving of goods are not more than 280 square metres, can open freely on Sunday and **larger shops** can open for up to 6 continuous hours between 10am and 6pm (there are exemptions for certain types of large shop).

2. There are no restrictions on Sunday trading in **Scotland**, although shop workers are protected in relation to Sunday working (see the memo point to ¶3800). Northern Ireland, on the other hand, does have similar (but not identical) provisions to those that apply in England and Wales.

I. Shop employees

Definitions

A shop employee is an employee who, under his contract of employment, is or may be required to do shop work (s 232 ERA 1996). Shop work is work in or about a shop that is open for serving customers. This includes sales assistants, check-out operators, shop managers and supervisors, and those working around the shop such as shelf-fillers and security staff. As the rules relate to shops opening on Sundays, those employed, for example shelf-fillers or stock-takers, while the shop is closed are excluded.

3810

> EXAMPLE A, a shelf-filler, works when the shop is closed and is required to work Sunday mornings, 6am until 10am prior to the shop opening at 12 noon. A is not a shop employee.
> His colleague, B, is a cashier and works behind the till when the shop is open including Sundays from noon until 5pm. B is a shop employee.

A **shop** is defined as any premises where a retail trade or business is carried on and includes barbers, hairdressers, hiring of goods (other than for use in the course of a trade or business) and retail auctions. It does not include restaurants or other catering businesses that sell meals, refreshments or alcoholic drinks for consumption, either on the premises or immediately off the premises, or the sale of programmes, catalogues and similar items at a theatre or place of amusement.

3811

Where premises are mainly used for other purposes, only the **part of the premises** which is used wholly or mainly for the purposes of retail trade, or which is used together with a wholesale trade (i.e. the sale, resale or hire of goods for use in the course of a business), is within the definition of a shop.

A. Protected employees

What, if any, protection a shop employee has will depend on when he became a shop employee and his contractual terms (s 36 ERA 1996).

3815

Excluded employees

Where a shop employee's contractual terms state that he is to work solely on Sundays, he has no protective rights with regard to Sunday working and is termed an excluded employee regardless of when he became a shop employee.

3816

1. Shop employees employed on or before 25 August 1994

Regardless of whether there are contractual terms, where a shop employee was employed as a shop worker (but not to work only on Sundays) he will be automatically protected (s 36(2) ERA 1996). It is irrelevant whether or not the employee performed regular or occasional Sunday work before this date.

3820

3821 Where there are contractual terms, an automatically protected employee, as with opted-out employees, has no right to work extra hours if he chooses not to work on Sundays and his pay or any other benefits can be reduced accordingly (¶3803).

2. Shop employees employed after 25 August 1994 with no contractual terms

3825 Where there are no contractual terms requiring or allowing for Sunday working, the shop employee is automatically protected (s 36(3) ERA 1996). He can surrender his protection (i.e. opt in) (¶3845).

3. Shop employees employed after 25 August 1994 with contractual terms

3830 Where there are contractual terms requiring or allowing for Sunday working, the shop employee has the right to be protected (ss 40-41 ERA 1996). If the employee exercises this right, he will have opted out. This right is obtained when the employee gives the employer a written notice called an opting-out notice. The employer must inform the employee of his right to opt out. Even if he opts out, the employee can always opt in again.

Opting out

3831 The opting-out notice must be signed and dated by the employee, stating that he objects to Sunday working. The employee does not need to give any reason as to why he does not wish to work on Sundays.

3832 **Notice can be given** at any time while he is a shop employee and is effective 3 months from the date of the notice. If the **employer does not issue** the required **explanatory statement** (see below) within 2 months of the employee becoming a shop employee, the opting-out notice period is reduced to 1 month.

During this opting-out notice period, the employee can be required to work on Sundays or on a particular Sunday in accordance with his contractual terms.

3833 **Employers' duty to inform of opt-out rights** Before the end of 2 months from when the employee became a shop employee, the employer should give the employee an **explanatory statement** (s 42 ERA 1996). This statement is **legally prescribed as follows**:

"You have become employed as a shop worker and are or can be required under your contract of employment to do the Sunday work your contract provides for.

However, if you wish, you can give notice, as described in the next paragraph, to your employer and you will then have the right not to work in or about a shop on any Sunday on which the shop is open once 3 months have passed from the date on which you gave notice.

Your notice must:
– be in writing;
– be signed and dated by you; and
– say that you object to Sunday working.

For 3 months after you give the notice, your employer can still require you to do all the Sunday work your contract provides for. After the 3 month period has ended, you have the right to complain to an employment tribunal if, because of your refusal to work on Sundays on which the shop is open, your employer:
– dismisses you; or
– does something else detrimental to you, for example, failing to promote you.

Once you have the rights described, you can surrender them only by giving your employer a further notice, signed and dated by you, saying that you wish to work on Sunday or that you do not object to Sunday working and then agreeing with your employer to work on Sundays or on a particular Sunday."

In summary, the statement sets out the employee's statutory rights, in particular: **3834**
a. the right not to work on Sundays after serving an opting-out notice on the employer;
b. when the notice takes effect; and
c. after the opting-out notice period:
– the employee has the right to complain to an employment tribunal if the employer dismisses him or subjects him to a detriment or causes him to suffer a detriment (for example, fails to promote him) because he does not agree to work on Sundays or on a particular Sunday; and
– the employee must give an opting-in notice (¶3845) to surrender his protective rights, if the employee subsequently does not object to Sunday work or wants to work on Sundays.

EXAMPLE On 1 January 2013, in accordance with his contractual terms, A starts work as a shop employee as he is moved from stocking shelves when the shop is closed to working behind the till as a cashier. A is required to work every Sunday in accordance with these terms. His employer must inform A of his legal rights in the prescribed statement by 28 February 2013.
1. A's employer **serves the prescribed form** in early February and in response A gives his employer an opting-out notice on 10 February, which is effective 3 months later. Consequently, from Sunday, 12 May, A cannot be required to work (or any Sunday thereafter as long as he remains a shop employee) unless he opts in to Sunday working. During the 3-month notice period though, A will be obliged to work in accordance with his contractual terms and can therefore be required to work on Sunday.
2. A's employer does **not serve the prescribed form** by 28 February. A is aware of his rights from talking to other employees, and so gives notice to his employer on 1 March that he does not want to work on Sundays. As a result, his protection starts on 1 April, 1 month after he gives notice.

Effect of opting out

If a shop employee chooses to exercise his right to not work on Sundays, he cannot insist on working extra hours on the other days of the week to make up for not working on Sundays (s 38 ERA 1996). This applies even if the contractual terms state a specified number of working hours per week. In such cases, the shop employee's number of specified hours can be reduced if he stops working on Sundays. **3837**

Where it is not apparent from the contractual terms what part of the remuneration payable, or other benefit due, was attributable to working on Sundays, the employer can **reduce the amount of remuneration paid**, or the extent of any other benefit, proportionately (s 39 ERA 1996). **3838**

B. Opting in

A protected employee can surrender his protection and **opt in** to work on Sundays by (ss 36, 41 ERA 1996): **3845**
– giving his employer a written opting-in notice, signed and dated by him, that expressly states that he wishes to work on Sundays or that he does not object to Sunday working; and
– after giving notice, expressly agreeing with his employer to work on Sundays or on a particular Sunday.

A protected employee can, therefore, **modify** his protection, by expressly agreeing to work particular Sundays, for example Sundays in December, or enter into a rotational pattern, for example every fourth Sunday. If the employee limits the Sunday work that he is prepared to do, he will remain protected with regard to general Sunday working.

After opting in, an employee retains his right to **opt out again** on giving an opting-out notice. **3846**

EXAMPLE A, who has opted out of Sunday working, decides that he would like to take advantage of the special rates that his employer has chosen to give for those working on Sundays.

1. A sees his employer and agrees to work on Sundays. A signs and dates a form (to ensure proper compliance, the form has been prepared by the employer for use by employees), which expressly states that he now wishes to work on Sundays and agrees to work on Sundays in general. A is now required to work on Sundays as long as he is a shop employee unless he subsequently opts out.

2. A sees his employer about working on the four Sundays leading up to Christmas. A signs and dates a form (to ensure proper compliance, the form has been prepared by the employer for use by employees), which expressly states that he now does not object to Sunday work and in which he agrees to work on the four Sundays leading up to Christmas. A is now required to work these specified Sundays (but no other Sunday) as long as he is a shop employee unless he subsequently opts out. However, A can further agree in writing to modify his protection and work on Sundays in general or another particular Sunday(s).

C. Remedies

3860 A protected employee must be continuously employed as a shop employee to the appropriate date necessary to apply the relevant protective remedy. For example, where a protected employee is dismissed for not working on Sundays, the appropriate date is the effective date of termination.

If there is a **break** in his continuity of employment **as a shop employee**, the employee will lose his protection. In such situations, the employee has to give an opting-out notice to regain these rights if he is **subsequently required to work** as a shop employee.

Not to suffer a detriment

3861 If a protected employee suffers any detriment, as a result of the employer's act or deliberate failure to act for any of the same reasons as outlined above in the case of dismissal, he can make a complaint to an employment tribunal (s 45 ERA 1996).

> MEMO POINTS   What amounts to a "**detriment**" is not defined by the ERA 1996, but case law on discrimination has held that it is whether a reasonable worker would feel he has been disadvantaged by reason of his employer's acts (¶5279), for example because he has been refused promotion, overtime or training due to these reasons.

Not to be unfairly dismissed

3862 Any dismissal will be **automatically unfair** (¶8390) if a protected employee is dismissed and the reason or the principal reason for the dismissal is that he (s 101 ERA 1996):
– refused (or proposed to refuse) to do shop work on Sundays or on a particular Sunday (this does not apply to employees who refuse to perform any such contractual duties during their opting-out notice period); or
– gave (or proposed to give) an opting-out notice to his employer.

II. Betting employees

3880 Identical rules apply to betting employees, though the date these rules came into force is different (s 36 ERA 1996). Therefore, the level of protection will depend on whether the employee was a betting employee **on or after 2 January 1995** instead of on or after 24 August 1994.

3881 A **betting employee** is an employee who, under his contract of employment, is or may be required to do betting work (s 233 ERA 1996). **Betting work** is work:
– at a track for a bookmaker when the bookmaker is doing work, which consists of or includes dealing with betting transactions; and
– in a licensed betting office when open for use for betting transactions.

A betting transaction includes the collection or payment of winnings on a bet and any transaction in which one or more of the parties are acting as a bookmaker. A bookmaker is a person who, whether on his own account or as an employee or agent, carries on, regularly or occasionally, the business of receiving or negotiating bets or conducting pool betting operations, or holds himself out, or permits himself to be held out, as such a person.

CHAPTER 12

Time off

OUTLINE	¶¶
SECTION 1 **Time off during working hours** 3910	SECTION 2 **Annual leave** 4000
	A Entitlement 4005
I Right to time off 3910	Public and bank holidays 4009
Public officials 3920	Payment in respect of leave 4012
Jury service 3925	Requesting leave 4015
Armed forces reservists 3926	Untaken leave 4018
II Right to remuneration 3930	B Calculation of leave 4020
A Statutory remuneration 3935	A week's leave 4021
B Set off against remuneration 3945	First year of employment 4024
III Remedies 3960	Termination of employment 4025
	C Records 4030
	D Remedies 4040

The law imposes **minimum requirements** on employers entitling employees to: **3900**
– paid or unpaid time off during working hours in certain circumstances, for example for some trade union duties;
– annual leave; and
– family-friendly leave (maternity, adoption, paternity and parental).

Employers can provide **more generous contractual terms** to employees, providing them with enhanced annual leave and paid time off during working hours to attend to non-work duties and obligations.

Employers may also give additional time off for certain personal reasons, which is often called **compassionate leave**. Employers will usually state that the extent and amount of any compassionate leave will be discretionary, though they will often provide guidelines as to when they may grant such leave. Employees do have a statutory right to time off to care for dependants, although this is unpaid and only applies to employees taking time off to deal with unforeseen events with regard to their dependants.

SECTION 1

Time off during working hours

I. Right to time off

The minimum requirements entitling employees to paid or unpaid time off **during working** **3910**
hours are outlined in the table below. Working hours are defined as any time when, in

accordance with the employee's contract of employment, he is required to be at work. These rights are **effective from** the start of employment except for the right to time off under notice of redundancy and parental leave.

The extent of time off depends on the type of right. This is discussed in the relevant subject chapters with the exception of the right to take time off for public duties and for jury service. For the right to take the following types of leave, see chapter 14:
- maternity;
- adoption;
- paternity; and
- parental.

> MEMO POINTS There is also a **right to request time off to undertake relevant training** which currently applies to businesses with 250 or more employees. Such requests need to meet certain conditions in order to qualify for the scheme, for example it needs to be for study or training that is intended to improve an employee's effectiveness at work and the performance of the employer's business. See ¶6400 for further details.

Employee	Purpose of time off		Whether paid A = at appropriate hourly rate (¶3935) B = for work would have done (¶3940) X = no right to paid time off
Companion	Accompany worker to disciplinary or grievance hearing, flexible working hearing, time off to train hearing	¶¶6784, 4722, 6432	B
Employees between 18 and 70 years old	Jury service	¶3925	X
EWC, SNB or information or consultation body member or candidate	Perform duties	¶7855	A
Negotiating representative	Perform duties	¶7706	A
Information and consultation representative	Perform duties	¶7740	A
Pregnant	Antenatal care	¶4411	A
Public official	Certain public duties	¶3920	X
Redundancy: employee representative and candidate in election	Perform duties	¶8931	A
Reservists (armed forces)	Perform duties	¶3926	X
Safety representative and representative of employee safety	Certain health and safety duties	¶4930	B
Trade union member	Certain trade union activities, consulting with ULR	¶7151	X
Trade union representative	Certain trade union duties	¶7151	B
Trustee of occupational pension scheme	Perform duties	¶3432	B
Union learning representative (ULR)	Training and perform duties	¶7151	B
Under notice of redundancy	Look for new employment or training	¶8885	A
With dependants	Care of dependants	¶4740	X
Young person	Study or training	¶6330	A

Public officials

3920 An employee has the right to take time off to perform any duties of his office if he is (s 50 ERA 1996):
– a magistrate (also called a justice of the peace);
– a local councillor;
– a school governor or a member of the managing or governing body of an educational establishment (a member of a school council or board in Scotland);
– a member of a policy authority;
– a member of any statutory tribunal (for example, an employment tribunal);
– a member of the General Teaching Councils for England and Wales;
– a member of the Environment Agency (a member of the Scottish Environment Protection agency, Scottish Water or a Water Customer Consultation Panel in Scotland); and
– a member of the prison independent monitoring boards (a member of the prison visiting committees in Scotland).

3921 The employer must allow the employee a **reasonable amount** of time off taking into account all the circumstances, in particular (s 50(4) ERA 1996; *Riley-Williams v Argos Ltd* [2003] UKEAT 811_02_2905):
– how much time off is required for the performance of the duties of the office or as a member of the body, and how much time off is required for the performance of the particular duty;
– how much time the employee already takes off further to any trade union duties and activities; and
– the circumstances of the employer's business and the effect of the employee's absence on the running of it.

It may be considered reasonable to expect an employee who has **extensive duties** to devote part of his annual leave to the performance of them but this will depend on all the circumstances (*Borders Regional Council v Maule* [1993] IRLR 199, EAT).

If the employee holds **several public offices** he may be expected to organise them so that the time taken off is reasonable.

Jury service

3925 Employees called for jury service are entitled to protection if they take time off work to serve as a juror (ss 43M, 98B ERA 1996; ¶¶3910, 3960+). Jury service is obligatory for individuals between 18 and 70, unless they fall within limited exemptions (Juries Act 1974). They may apply for jury service to be **deferred** to meet work commitments, in which case they should submit a letter of support from their employer with their application. Work commitments will not normally be accepted as a reason to be **excused** from jury service altogether.

There is **no obligation to pay** an employee who is absent for jury service, but if the employee loses pay he may **recover** all or part of his lost **earnings** from HM Court Service by submitting a certificate of lost earnings or other written evidence.

Armed forces reservists

3926 An employee who is a member of one of the Reserve Forces (the Territorial Army, Royal Naval Reserve, Royal Marines Reserve or Royal Auxiliary Air Force) will be expected to attend regular training. **Training commitments** vary between the different Reserve Forces, but in most cases include:
– weekly training: usually at their local reserve centre for around 2.5 hours, one evening a week;
– weekend training: reservists are usually expected to attend a number of training weekends each year; and
– annual training: usually a 15-day continuous training course, or "annual camp", normally within the UK, although some reservists do train overseas.

Reservists are **not legally entitled to time off**, or any additional holiday, to attend Reserve Forces training, and, as the training received is not intended to improve the employee's effectiveness at work nor the performance of the employer's business, they are not entitled to the right to time off to undertake relevant training (¶6400). However, because the employer can indirectly benefit from the many skills a reservist develops e.g. leadership, many employers do choose to allow members of the Reserve Forces additional leave or some paid time off to attend Reserve Forces training. A certain degree of flexibility over when time off is granted might also be necessary, e.g. reservists will have very little control over the timing of the annual camp they must attend.

> **MEMO POINTS** 1. The Ministry of Defence (**MOD**) has an employer notification system which will **inform an employer** when they recruit an armed forces reservist or if an existing employee becomes a reservist (except in Northern Ireland where this does not apply).
> 2. It is a **criminal offence** for an employer to **terminate** a reservist's job solely or mainly because he is a reservist or has a liability to be mobilised (Reserve Forces (Safeguard of Employment) Act 1985). Reservists can be included in a redundancy pool if this is appropriate but any redundancy criteria must not discriminate against reservists on the grounds of their reserve service or mobilisation liability.
> 3. The Government has consulted on the future of the UK's Reserve Forces following its announcement that the numbers of armed forces reserves will more than double by 2020. In summary, the consultation included **proposals** for:
> – tax breaks or other financial incentives, such as a cash award (possibly aimed at SMEs), for employers that are willing to employ and retain more reserve troops;
> – the introduction of a "patriotic employer" kite mark for those employers who are supportive of armed forces reservists;
> – improvements to the mobilisation process so that employers are given more notice before employees are deployed on active service; and
> – possible new legislation to prevent employers discriminating against employees who are in the reserves.
> If the Government achieves its aim of doubling the number of reservists, then over the coming years employers can expect to see an increase in the number of staff becoming reservists. This will be coupled with an increase in the amount of training that they will be required to undertake (mainly in the evening and at weekends, but most will be required to attend up to 16 days of compulsory training a year) and an increased likelihood of deployment. Given the practical difficulties this may cause for employers, it is not surprising that consideration is being given to a form of anti-discrimination protection. Any further developments will be covered by our updating service.

3927 Mobilisation All members of the armed forces reserve are liable to be called-up or mobilised into active duty. Employers have no statutory entitlement to be given **notice** that an employee has been mobilised, but the MOD does aim to give employers at least 28 days' notice that their employee is to be mobilised. The **length of time** for which a reservist may be mobilised varies widely depending upon the MOD's operational needs and the particular skills and training of the reservist. However, reserves are commonly mobilised abroad for between 6 to 12 months. This period may also include some pre-mobilisation training in the UK (usually around 4 weeks) and a period of post-operational tour leave. Depending upon operational needs, a reservist's mobilisation period can be extended or he may be re-mobilised at any time (subject to certain statutory limits).

The employer does not have to pay any **salary** or associated benefits (such as pension or company car) for the **duration of** the mobilised employee's **operational duty**. Reservists are paid service pay by the MOD and, subject to financial caps, can claim financial assistance from the MOD for the difference between their service pay and their civilian pay and for other benefits lost such as loss of health or life insurance and loss of a company car. Employers can claim **financial assistance to cover additional costs** incurred whilst their employee is mobilised, subject again to financial caps. Such additional costs may include, for example, overtime for other employees used to cover the reservist's work or the salary costs of a temporary replacement, but they can only be claimed if they exceed the reservist's usual salary. Employers can also claim financial assistance to cover costs associated with recruiting a temporary replacement or retraining the reservist under certain circumstances upon their return to work.

> **MEMO POINTS** 1. The **cap** on financial assistance that the reservist can claim from the MOD is currently £548 per day (£822 for medical consultants) with an additional £10.70 a day for the loss of a

company car used by a spouse, partner or dependants. The cap on financial assistance that the employer can claim from the MOD is currently £110 per day, normally paid monthly in arrears.

2. Mobilised reservists do **not accrue annual leave** (¶4000) with their primary employer during mobilisation. They are entitled to a pro-rata entitlement for any part of the holiday year they are actually at work. Reservists accrue leave with the MOD whilst they are in full-time service and when they are demobilised they are granted a period of paid post-operational leave.

3. The statutory provisions are ambiguous about whether the employment contract comes to an end or subsists during the period of military service. This is important for the calculation of **continuous service**. The fact that the relevant legislation refers to the reservist's "former employer" implies that the contract comes to an end and is revived upon reinstatement. However, it is arguable that the contact will subsist during mobilisation unless it is expressly brought to an end by either party. For the sake of clarity, employers should reach an agreement with the reservist to either bring the contract to an end (preferably by mutual agreement) or to allow it to subsist. If the contract is brought to an end, reservists will still have the right to reinstatement and their period of continuous service will not be broken, but the period of their military service will not count towards the calculation of continuous employment and the beginning of the period of continuous employment will be brought forward by a period equivalent to the duration of their military service (s211 ERA 1996). If the contract is allowed to subsist throughout the period of military service, contractual rights, except for the right to be remunerated, will continue to apply unless an express agreement is reached to the contrary.

3928 An employer who believes the mobilisation of his reservist employee will cause **serious harm to the business** (or that of an associated employer) has the right to seek **exemption, deferral or revocation** of the mobilisation. Provided the employer's concerns cannot be resolved by the provision of financial assistance by the MOD, serious harm to the business may include:
– financial harm, such as loss of sales, markets, reputation, goodwill;
– impairment of the business's ability to produce goods or provide services; and
– harm to the research and development of new products, service or processes.

Any **application** for exemption, deferral or revocation of the mobilisation must be made within 7 days of the mobilisation notice being served. Late applications can only be considered with the permission of the adjudication officer, whose details are on the mobilisation notice. The employer must write to the adjudication officer giving the reservist's personal details (name, address, payroll and NI numbers) and explain, in as much detail as possible, the nature of the business, the employee's role and duties, any difficulties the employer will have covering those duties or in recruiting a temporary replacement, and the effect and serious harm his absence will have on the business if he is mobilised. The adjudication officer will balance the needs of the business and the potential harm which might be caused to it (or the business of an associated employer) against the MOD's operational needs. An application for exemption, deferral or revocation is more likely to succeed if the reservist has skills that are widely available within Reserve Forces (and thus another reservist could easily be called up in exchange), but has very specialised skills in the employer's workplace (which render it difficult to find a temporary replacement). An employer who is unhappy with the adjudication officer's decision can appeal within 5 working days to a Reserve Forces Appeal Tribunal (RFAT). RFAT decisions are made after a hearing (which usually takes place at the nearest employment tribunal).

3929 **Employee right to re-instatement after mobilisation** When a reservist employee returns from mobilisation, the employer has a legal obligation to reinstate him in the same role and on equally favourable terms and conditions as before he was mobilised. If this is not possible then a suitable alternative should be offered, which is the most favourable occupation on the most favourable terms and conditions which are reasonable and practicable. The **extent** of a reservist's right to be re-employed depends upon on his length of employment prior to mobilisation. If he has less than 13 weeks' continuous service prior to mobilisation, he must be reinstated for at least 13 weeks on his return. Those with between 14 and 51 weeks' continuous service must be reinstated for 26 weeks and those with 52+ weeks' continuous service must be reinstated for at least 52 weeks.

To be eligible for the right to be reinstated, the reservist must **write** to the employer **to state** that he is available to come back to work no later than the third Monday after his last day of full-time service, unless there are extenuating circumstances such as sickness or injury. The reservist must also inform his employer of the date on which he will be available to start back at work and this date must fall within a set time limit, approximately 6 weeks from the last day of full-time service.

If a reservist believes that an employer's response to his application for reinstatement **denies his rights**, or if he is not happy with the offer of alternative employment and has written to his employer stating why there is reasonable cause for him not to accept it, he can make an **application** for assessment **to a Reinstatement Committee**, who can make an order for reinstatement and/or compensation.

II. Right to remuneration

3930 Where there is the right to statutory pay, such statutory remuneration is calculated by one of two systems, depending on the right. A right to statutory pay does not affect any right of an employee to contractual remuneration under his contract of employment.

A. Statutory remuneration

At appropriate hourly rate

3935 Where indicated in the table at ¶3910, an employee who is entitled to take paid time off is remunerated for the period of absence at the appropriate hourly rate.

With regard to the right to take time off when **under notice of redundancy**, employers are entitled to limit payments to 40% of a week's pay (s 53(5) ERA 1999).

3936 **Regular working pattern** The appropriate hourly rate, in relation to an employee, is the amount of a week's pay (¶2920) divided by the number of his normal working hours in the week in which time off has been taken. For time off taken under a notice of redundancy, this is the week in which the notice of dismissal is given.

3937 **Irregular working pattern** Where the number of normal working hours differs from week to week or over a longer period, the appropriate hourly rate is ascertained by dividing the employee's week's pay by his average normal working hours calculated over the period of 12 weeks ending with the last complete week before the day on which the time off is taken (or the notice of dismissal is given).

> EXAMPLE Like E, employee F has also taken time off.
> F, though, has an irregular working pattern. In the 12 weeks before the day on which F started to take time off, he worked a variety of hours: 35, 4 × 40, 32, 3 × 38, 34, 2 × 36 = 447. F's 1 week's pay is also £300.
> The average number of normal working hours is 447 divided by 12 = 37.25
> F's appropriate hourly rate is 300 divided by 37.25 = £8.05

3938 Where the employee has been employed for less than 12 weeks, the appropriate hourly rate is calculated by dividing 1 week's pay by a number, which fairly represents the number of normal working hours in a week. The following must be taken into consideration as appropriate:
– the average number of working hours in a week that the employee could expect to work according to his contract; and
– the average number of normal working hours of other employees engaged in relevant comparable employment with the same employer.

Remuneration for work that would have been done

Where the employee's **remuneration does not vary** with the amount of work done, he is entitled to be paid as if he had worked for the whole of the time off.

If it **does vary**, he must be paid an amount calculated by reference to his average hourly earnings. The average hourly earnings are:
– those of the employee concerned; or
– if no fair estimate can be made of those earnings, the average hourly earnings for work of that description of persons in comparable employment with the same employer or, if there are no such persons, a figure of average hourly earnings which is reasonable in the circumstances.

The employer is required to remunerate the employee for his time off work, which may not be the whole time of the duty or training if it is outside working hours. If part of the activity is **outside working hours** and the employee is given time off in lieu, he will not be entitled to be paid for it (*Hairsine v Kingston upon Hull City Council* [1991] UKEAT 544_89_0907).

> EXAMPLE H, a shop steward, is given permission by his employers to attend a union course. On the day of the first session, which ran from 9am to 4pm, H was rostered to work the late shift between 3pm and 11pm. H went to work after the session ended until 7pm. H will be paid for the 1 hour of the session that he was rostered to work, and for the time he actually worked. H, though, will not be paid for the time he took off (between 7pm and 11pm) because he had attended the course.
> If H had attended a course from 3pm to 11pm, he would have been entitled to be paid for the entire shift. If H's shift had been from 9am to 4pm, he would have been entitled to be paid for the entire shift.

Similarly, part-time workers, who are remunerated for work that would have been done, are only entitled to be paid for the **part-time hours** not worked, even if the duty or training is a full-time event. However, this may be contrary to the right to equal pay under article 157 of the Treaty on the Functioning of the European Union (previously article 141 of the Treaty of Rome), as part-time workers affected are predominantly female compared to a male full-time workforce (art 157 EU Treaty on the Functioning of the European Union; *Arbeiterwohlfahrt der Stadt Berlin eV v Bötel C-360/90* [1992] IRLR 423, ECJ; *Kuratorium für Dialyse und Nierentransplantation eV v Lewar, Case C-457/93* [1996] IRLR 637, ECJ). The EAT has required payment for the whole period in these circumstances (*Davies v Neath Port Talbot County Borough Council* [1999] IRLR 769, EAT).

> EXAMPLE In *Davies v Neath Port Talbot County Borough Council*, the EAT held that a part-time worker was entitled under article 141 (now article 157) to be paid by her employers as if she were a full-time worker when she was given time off to attend a full-time trade union training course on her duties as a health and safety representative. The EAT held the employer must remunerate the employee for the whole of the training. In doing so, the EAT did not follow an earlier EAT decision (*Manor Bakeries Ltd v Nazir* [1996] UKEAT 628_95_0108) which had held that attending a union conference was not work under article 141.

MEMO POINTS As *Davies* is a later EAT decision and is in line with decisions of the Court of Justice of the European Union, it is suggested that this is the course UK law will follow.

B. Set off against remuneration

Any contractual remuneration paid to an employee in respect of a period of time off goes towards discharging any statutory liability of the employer to pay in respect of that period (either at the appropriate hourly rate or by remuneration for work that would have been done).

Similarly, any payment of remuneration that is due under statute in respect of that period goes towards discharging any liability of the employer to pay contractual remuneration for that period.

III. Remedies

Right to remedies

3960 An employee can make a claim in an employment tribunal that his employer has failed to allow him to take time off to which he is entitled or, depending on the type of time off, that the employer has subjected him to a detriment by failing to allow him to take time off to which he is entitled, under any of the provisions listed in the table set out in ¶3961 below. Where an employee had the right to paid time off, he can also claim for the whole or part of any amount to which he is entitled. In all cases, where a tribunal finds a complaint well-founded, the tribunal will make a **declaration** to that effect.

> MEMO POINTS   Unless the employee's contract provides for payment while on **jury service**, failure to pay the employee during jury service will not be treated as a detriment (s 43M(3) ERA 1996).

3961 If the claim is successful, the tribunal can order **compensation** and, where relevant, an **award for payment**.

The following table sets out:
- the type of compensation available on a successful complaint to a tribunal when time off has been refused; and
- the type of award for payment, where relevant, on a successful complaint to a tribunal that the employer has failed to pay the amount of remuneration due.

Right to time off	Complaint Time off refused	Basis of compensation	Complaint Failure to pay amount due	Basis of award	Reference
Antenatal care	✓	2	✓	3	s 57 ERA 1996
Care of dependants	✓	1	n/a	n/a	s 57B ERA 1996
EWC, SNB or information and consultation body members or candidates	✓	2	✓	3	reg 27 SI 1999/3323
Information and consultation representative	✓	2	✓	3	reg 29 SI 2004/3426
Jury service	✓	1	n/a	n/a	s 48 ERA 1996
Negotiating representative	✓	2	✓	3	reg 29 SI 2004/3426
Notice of redundancy	✓	4	✓	4	s 54 ERA 1996
Public official	✓	1	n/a	n/a	s 51 ERA 1996
Redundancy: employee representative and candidate in election	✓	2	✓	3	s 63 ERA 1996
Representative of employee safety	✓	1	✓	3	Sch 2 para 2 SI 1996/1513
Safety representative	✓	1	✓	3	reg 11 SI 1977/500
Training for young persons	✓	2	✓	3	s 63C ERA 1996
Trade union member	✓	1	n/a	n/a	s 170 TULRCA 1992
Trade union official	✓	1	✓	3	ss 168-169 TULRCA 1992
Trustee of occupational pension scheme	✓	1	✓	3	s 60 ERA 1996

Right to time off	Complaint Time off refused	Basis of compensation	Complaint Failure to pay amount due	Basis of award	Reference
Union learning representatives (ULR)	✓	1	✓	3	ss 168A, 169 TULRCA 1992

1. Compensation is awarded according to what tribunal considers just and equitable in all circumstances, having regard to:
– the employer's default in refusing time off, and
– any loss sustained by the employee attributable to the employer's refusal.
With regard to an employer's refusal to allow an employee to take time off for trade union duties, compensation for this failure under TULRCA 1992 is wide enough to encompass cash reparation for the individual for the wrong done to him, independent of any specific loss he may have suffered (*Skiggs v South West Trains Limited* [2005] UKEAT 0763_03_0703).
2. Compensation is equal to remuneration to which the employee would have been entitled.
3. Where the employer has failed to pay the amount due, in whole or in part, he will be ordered to pay the employee this amount.
4. The employer will be ordered to pay:
– remuneration for the time taken off;
– the amount that the employee should have received, or would have received if he had been allowed to take the time off; or
– both.
This is subject, in respect of the period of notice, to a limit of 40% of the employee's week's pay. Any award for payment for time off refused is not set against any contractual remuneration received.

3962 The **time limit** for presenting such claims is 3 months beginning with the date on which it is alleged that the time off should have been permitted or paid. This period can be **extended** by the tribunal, as it considers reasonable, if it is satisfied that it was not reasonably practicable for the complaint to be presented before this date (¶¶9466+).

Automatic unfair dismissal

3965 Employees can make a claim for **automatic unfair dismissal** if they are dismissed in connection with their statutory entitlement to take time off (¶8390).

SECTION 2
Annual leave

4000 Workers are entitled to **paid statutory annual leave** from when they start work (Working Time Regulations SI 1998/1833 as amended, which will be referred to in this section as "the regulations"). Any term in the contract of employment or in any other agreement, express or implied, will be void so far as it seeks to exclude or limit this entitlement or the right to bring a claim under the regulations (reg 35 SI 1998/1833).

A **relevant agreement** can alter or exclude some of the procedural requirements. This is **defined** as any workforce agreement (¶1293) that applies to the worker, any provision of a collective agreement which forms part of a contract between him and his employer, or any other agreement in writing which is legally enforceable as between the worker and his employer (for example, the contract of employment).

> MEMO POINTS An **agency worker** will be treated as being employed by either the agent or the end-user, whichever is responsible for paying him, or, if that cannot be established, by whichever party in fact pays the worker (reg 36 SI 1998/1833).

4001 **Contractual terms**, express or implied by the custom and practice of the industry/employer, can also **enhance** the minimum statutory entitlement by increasing the number of days of paid annual leave and/or allowing for unpaid annual leave. See ¶9910 for a model clause.

A. Entitlement

4005 A worker is currently entitled to **annual statutory leave** of 5.6 weeks (SI 2007/2079, which has added reg 13A SI 1998/1833). This entitlement is **capped at** 28 days.

Employers can, of course, give enhanced contractual rights. The above entitlement is not additional to any **contractual entitlement** and taking contractual paid leave in a particular leave year will count against the worker's statutory entitlement.

4006 **Time** when a worker would **not otherwise be working** can count towards their annual leave entitlement. The case of *Russell and ors v Transocean International Resources Ltd and ors* [2011] UKSC 57 considered this point, and the facts centred on oil and gas industry workers whose shift patterns involved 2 to 3 weeks' **working offshore** followed by 2 to 3 weeks' resting onshore. Part of their free onshore time was designated as annual leave and they were not ordinarily permitted to take holiday during time when they should be offshore working. They brought claims arguing that they should be permitted to take their holiday during "working weeks". The Court confirmed that periods spent resting onshore can count towards that worker's entitlement to annual leave. It is not necessary that holidays must always be taken from time that would otherwise be working time and the employer was entitled to insist that annual leave was taken during the periods when the workers were not working. This principle has a far wider application than just the offshore industry. Many employers, such as those who employ **teachers** and **manufacturing production operatives**, operate shift patterns which designate part of their non-working time as holiday; such systems can continue.

4007 The Court of Justice of the European Union has ruled that a worker on **long-term sick leave** is entitled to statutory annual leave even if he is **absent from work throughout that leave year** (*Stringer and ors v HM Revenue and Customs, Schultz-Hoff v Deutsche Rentenversicherung Bund, Joined Cases C-520/06 and C-350/06* [2009] IRLR 214, ECJ). As to the amount of holiday leave that can be carried over, the Court of Appeal has held that workers on long-term sick leave are **entitled to carry forward** the 4 weeks of leave conferred on them by European legislation and to be paid for this leave on termination, even if they are absent due to illness for an entire leave year and even if they do not request to carry the leave forward in advance of the leave year coming to an end (*NHS Leeds v Larner* [2012] EWCA Civ 1034). Although this judgment related to a public sector employee and referred heavily to European cases based on the Working Time Directive, which is not directly effective in UK law (and therefore cannot be relied upon in the national courts by private sector workers), the Court of Appeal clarified that the national Working Time Regulations can be read in line with the European Directive in relation to the points decided in this case, allowing both private and public sector workers to benefit from this decision. The additional 1.6 weeks of leave conferred by the national regulations need not be carried over unless this is permitted under an individual's contract of employment (*Neidel v Stadt Frankfurt am Main* [2012] EUECJ C-337/10).

While carry-over periods should be allowed to ensure that the worker can have, if need be, rest periods that may be staggered, planned in advance and available in the longer term, there should be a **limit to carrying over** untaken leave (*KHS v Winfried Schulte (Social policy)* [2011] EUECJ C-214/10). Carry-over periods should be substantially longer than the reference periods in respect of which they are granted. On the facts of this case, the carry-over period was limited to 15 months, which was sufficient. Reference was also made to a limit of no more than 18 months.

> MEMO POINTS The Government is consulting on **proposals** to make the necessary amendments to the Working Time Regulations in light of the Court of Justice of the European Union decisions (see memo point to ¶4014). Meanwhile, despite the fact the Regulations do not currently permit carry-over of leave, employers are advised to allow carry-over periods of at least 15 to 18 months, as it is very likely that employment tribunals will interpret the Regulations in line with the decisions of the Court of Justice of the European Union.

4008 If a worker **falls ill before commencing a pre-planned period of holiday**, he is legally entitled to re-schedule that holiday and take it at a later time, if necessary in a later leave year (*Pereda v Madrid Movilidad SA* [2009] IRLR 959, ECJ). The same principles apply if a worker **falls ills during** their **holiday** (*Asociación Nacional de Grandes Empresas de Distribución (ANGED) v Federación de Asociaciones Sindicales (FASGA) and ors* [2012] C-78/11).

> MEMO POINTS The Government is consulting on **proposals** to make the necessary amendments to the Working Time Regulations in light of the Court of Justice of the European Union decisions (see memo point to ¶4014). Meanwhile, despite the fact the Regulations do not currently permit carry-over of leave, employers are best advised to apply these decisions in principle, as it is very likely that employment tribunals will interpret the Regulations in line with the decisions of the Court of Justice of the European Union. As a sensible precaution, employers may wish to amend their ill health reporting procedures to clarify how and when an employee should report an illness arising on holiday and what (if any) medical evidence will be needed.

Public and bank holidays

4009 Christmas Day and Good Friday are common law English and Welsh public holidays whereas bank holidays are set by legislation in the banking industry, which provides for financial dealings to be suspended on these designated days. A bank holiday may also be appointed by Royal Proclamation.

There is no statutory entitlement or general implied right to bank or public holidays with, or indeed without, pay. Therefore, whether these days are leave days will depend on the contract between the employer and the worker, and there will need to be either an **express term** giving a right to some or all designated public and bank holidays (for example, 24 days' holiday, plus 8 days of bank and public holidays) or an implied term due to the custom and practice of the industry/employer. If there is **no contractual right** to a particular public holiday, the worker is not entitled to an additional day's paid leave (*Campbell & Smith Construction Group Ltd v Greenwood* [2001] IRLR 588, EAT).

> EXAMPLE
> 1. In *Campbell & Smith Construction Group Ltd v Greenwood*, G was contractually entitled to a winter holiday of 7 working days in addition to Christmas Day, Boxing Day and New Year's Day. His employer always set 31 December as one of these days. In 1999, the Government appointed 31 December 1999 as an extra bank holiday to mark the Millennium. The EAT held that G was not entitled to an additional day's leave as the date was already part of the 7-day paid leave period.
> 2. In *Cook v Diageo* [2005] UKEAT 0070_04_3003, the reference in a collective agreement and employees' terms and conditions to "occasional" holidays did not mean that the employer was required to fix such holidays by reference to local public holidays (although this had usually been the case). Further, there was nothing to demonstrate that the intention of the parties to the collective agreement was to create a contractual obligation that the occasional days would always be on local public holidays.

4010 Paid leave on bank or public holidays will **count toward** the annual statutory entitlement.

> EXAMPLE On the basis of 6 bank holidays and 2 public holidays per annum and on the basis that the following workers commence their leave year on 1 April and are employed full-time for 5 days a week (therefore, entitling them to 28 days' statutory annual leave):
> – Worker A has a contract giving him 4 weeks of annual leave plus bank and public holidays. He will not be entitled to any further leave.
> – Worker B has a contract giving him 4 weeks of annual leave without bank and public holidays. He will be entitled to 8 additional days to bring his total up to 28 days' statutory annual leave.
> – Worker C has a contract giving him 3 weeks of annual leave plus bank and public holidays. He will be entitled to 5 additional days to bring his total up to 28 days' statutory annual leave.

4011 As the **date of Easter** varies, some April - March leave years may contain two Easters and others none. This can also occur if "birthday" leave years are used (i.e. leave years that start from the employee's birthday or month of birth, which can have the benefit of spreading any end of leave year congestion). Where this arises, an employer should make sure that a worker receives at least their statutory entitlement each year.

Payment in respect of leave

4012 Workers should be paid at their normal rate during holidays, i.e. a worker is entitled to be paid, in respect of any period of annual leave to which he is entitled, at a **rate** of 1 week's pay for each week's leave (reg 16 SI 1998/1833). The Supreme Court, in applying the answers from a referral to the Court of Justice of the European Union (CJEU), has held that tribunals should assess a worker's normal pay as including all monetary components intrinsically linked to the performance of the tasks which he is required to carry out, and all such elements relating to his personal and professional status (such as seniority, length of service and professional qualifications) using an average over a sufficiently representative period (*British Airways Plc v Williams and ors* [2012] UKSC 43). The decision has wide implications for all workers, not merely those in the aviation sector which was before the Supreme Court in this case, since it seems very likely the same approach will be taken to holiday pay under the main Working Time Regulations. Currently, holiday pay is calculated in accordance with the statutory formula for a week's pay (¶¶2920+). In several respects, the statutory formula for a week's pay, and case law previously decided under it, may no longer be correct, particularly in respect of commission and compulsory overtime payments. As a result, employers are advised to include all payments made to a worker in calculating his normal rate.

> MEMO POINTS   It remains unclear whether the principle will extend beyond the 4 weeks' statutory minimum holiday imposed by the Directive, and whether it applies to the additional 1.6 weeks provided for under the main Working Time Regulations. Recent CJEU case law suggests not, but, in practical terms, the distinction may be irrelevant as the complexity of operating two different holiday pay rates will deter most employers from seeking to rely upon that case law.

4013 Employers should pay workers while they are actually on holiday as it is **unlawful to roll up** workers' annual leave payments, i.e. not to pay workers on holiday but to purport to include an element of holiday pay as part of their regular pay when they are working (*Robinson-Steele v R.D. Retail Services Ltd, Clarke v Frank Staddon Ltd, Caulfield and ors v Hanson Clay Products Ltd (formerly Marshall Clay Products), Joined Cases C-131/04 and C-257/04* [2006] IRLR 386, ECJ). The principle behind this prohibition is that rolling up pay may act as a disincentive to take leave due, which would be against the health and safety aims of the Working Time Directive.

> EXAMPLE **Not rolled-up holiday pay**
> In *Gee and ors v Haberdashers' Aske's Boys' School* [2012] ET/3304122/10, 3304123/10 and 3304125/10, an employment tribunal had to consider a claim brought by three visiting music teachers, who **worked during term-time only** at a boys' school. Like other teachers at the school, they were deemed to be on holiday for the remaining 22 weeks of the year. They were paid by reference to an hourly rate which was paid over the 12 months of the year according to their hours of work (as opposed to being paid during the weeks in which they actually work). Over a 10-year period, various discussions took place between the teachers and the school in connection with the teachers' claims that they did not receive holiday pay in respect of the 22 weeks of each year that they are deemed to be on holiday. While accepting that their hourly rate could include an element of holiday pay, they pointed out that their hourly rate of pay had not increased when the Working Time Regulations (which introduced a minimum statutory annual leave and pay) came into force. The school pointed out that they were being treated the same as other teachers and that holiday pay was part of teachers' pay; the hourly rate paid to the teachers had been calculated by dividing the national recommended salary for music teachers by 1265 (i.e. the annual number of hours teachers are expected to work in state schools). The teachers eventually brought claims under the Working Time Regulations and for unlawful deductions from wages. The employment tribunal found in the school's favour and rejected the claims; the teachers' hourly rate of pay included statutory holiday pay. The fact that their pay was tied to the number of hours they worked each term did not make any difference; the rate was derived from a full-time teacher's rate of pay, which included an element of holiday pay, and therefore the pro-rata rate also included an element of holiday pay. The tribunal held that this was not rolled-up holiday pay; they were simply paid in equal instalments for work done over the year.

> MEMO POINTS   Some decisions have tried to soften this approach, at least in relation to activities which occurred before this prohibition, on the principle that any rolled-up contractual pay made in relation to work undertaken will go towards discharging the employer's liability to paid statutory leave (reg 16(5) SI 1998/1833), and if the payments have been made in a transparent and comprehensible manner, the employer will be given credit for any such payments, i.e. he will be able to set off any such payments already made against any future leave payments due at the proper

time (*Lyddon v Englefield Brickwork Ltd* [2008] IRLR 198, EAT). Going forward, though, employers should avoid rolling up pay, i.e. leave should be paid when taken and any untaken leave should be paid in lieu on termination.

Pay in lieu of leave As a **general rule**, the statutory entitlement cannot be replaced in the leave year by a payment in lieu **except** where the employment relationship is terminated (¶4025) (reg 13(9) SI 1998/1833). In such cases, payment in lieu can be given for untaken leave in the leave year that termination occurs. Previously, the Working Time Regulations were interpreted as stating that no payments had to be made for untaken leave with regard to previous leave years on termination. However, the Court of Appeal has stated that where workers are on long-term sick leave and are unable to take their leave, they should be allowed to carry over 4 weeks of their leave (which is the element of statutory annual leave dictated by European legislation), even if they do not make this request before the end of the leave year (*NHS Leeds v Larner* [2012] EWCA Civ 1034). The carry over period is unclear, but employers are advised to allow a carry-over period of between 15 and 18 months until this issue is clarified by proposed amendments to the national legislation (see the memo point below). The additional 1.6 weeks of statutory leave that workers are entitled to under national legislation does not need to be carried over (*Neidel v Stadt Frankfurt am Main* [2012] EUECJ C-337/10).

4014

> MEMO POINTS The Government is consulting on **proposals** to make the necessary amendments to the Working Time Regulations in light of Court of Justice of European Union (CJEU) decisions and is proposing to:
> – restrict the significant elements of the CJEU rulings on carrying over leave due to sickness absence to the EU leave entitlement (4 weeks per year) and not the additional UK entitlement (an additional 1.6 weeks per year, as the UK domestic entitlement is 5.6 weeks per year) and likewise restrict the rescheduling of leave due to sickness absence to the EU leave entitlement (4 weeks per year);
> – allow, as required by the CJEU rulings, the carrying over of annual leave due to maternity, paternity, parental or adoption leave for the full 5.6 weeks entitlement per year; and
> – make other changes to allow employers to "buy out" untaken leave by agreement with regard to the additional UK entitlement (1.6 weeks per year) and require employees to carry over leave on justifiable business grounds also in relation to the additional UK entitlement (1.6 weeks per year).
> Further developments will be covered in our updating service when available.

Requesting leave

It is **standard practice** to allow workers to choose when they take their leave. Many employers, though, do set **certain conditions**, for example that only a certain number of workers may take leave at the same time or that workers may not take more than a certain number of consecutive working days off.

4015

There are **procedural notification** requirements that need to be followed when either the employer or the worker requests leave, though a relevant agreement (¶4000) can exclude these provisions. If excluded, the employer and worker can agree their **own provisions**.

4016

An **employer requesting** a worker to take leave at specified times must give notice to his worker of at least twice the period of leave to be taken (reg 15 SI 1998/1833). Similarly, a **worker requesting** to take leave at specified times must give the same prior notice to his employer. However, the employer's permission is required and employers can refuse their workers the permission to take any leave requested, but if they do so they must notify the workers within a period equivalent to the period of leave.

> EXAMPLE In *Industrial and Commercial Maintenance Limited v Briffa* [2008] UKEAT 0215_08_2207, an employee agreed a contractual term that if he was not required to work during his notice, he would be treated as taking outstanding holiday during his notice period. When he gave his notice, he had 4 days' holiday outstanding and his employer required him to take that during his week's notice. He complained that he had not been given 8 days' notice of these holiday dates, as required by the regulations (see above), and claimed 4 days' holiday pay. The EAT held that the contractual term was a relevant agreement (¶4000) which excluded the procedural notification requirements, so that he was not entitled to any such pay.

4017 Depending on the custom and practice within a sector, the EAT has held that **employers** have a wide **discretion** to insist that leave is only taken at certain times (*Sumsion v BBC (Scotland)* [2007] IRLR 678, EAT). In schools, for example, it is common for teachers to take their leave during the holidays rather than term-time. Mandatory 6-day working is common during certain trades at particular times of the year. So, where a film-maker was employed to work for 6 days a week on a contract of short duration, and the employer required that all leave be taken on Saturdays, the worker was obliged to comply with that instruction.

> MEMO POINTS   While in *Sumsion v BBC (Scotland)*, the EAT allowed an employer very considerable powers to limit the worker's freedom to take leave, the facts of the case were unusual. The worker worked for a relatively short period of time and the leave he accrued in this period was modest. Where an employer imposes leave restrictions which are out of line with custom and practice in a sector, he may be vulnerable to challenge.

Untaken annual leave

4018 As a **general rule**, untaken annual leave is lost at the end of the leave year: an employee may not carry over untaken leave days from one year to the next. However, there may be exceptions where the employees cannot take their leave because they are on maternity/adoption leave (see ¶4442) or are on long-term sick leave (see ¶4007).

With regard to any **contractual entitlement** over and above the statutory entitlement, whether any such days unused can be carried over to the next leave year will depend on the terms of the contract and will often be a matter of employer discretion (¶4007 and ¶4014).

> EXAMPLE   In *Lyons v Mitie Security Ltd* [2010] IRLR 288, CA, a security guard brought a claim for unfair dismissal and for unpaid holiday pay. During his employment he made a number of complaints about matters such as cancelled work bookings and non-payment of holiday pay; these complaints were dealt with at the time they were made. His contract included provisions:
> – requiring him to give 4 weeks' notice if he wished to take holiday "wherever possible";
> – that late applications would be considered on their merits; and
> – that holiday could not be carried forward.
> He made a request for holiday pay shortly before the end of the holiday year, at a time when he had not been scheduled to do any work before the year end. He did not give 4 weeks' notice. The employer refused to pay him the holiday pay because he had not given sufficient notice. He resigned and claimed constructive dismissal. He argued that the Working Time Regulations should be interpreted to mean that an employer could not refuse an employee holiday leave if that meant that he would lose the right to take outstanding holiday at the end of the year. The EAT rejected this, holding that the proper meaning of the regulations was that an employee might lose holiday entitlement as a result of failing to comply with his employer's notification requirements. The EAT accepted that the refusal to pay holiday pay could amount to a "last straw" in this case, given the previous history of grievances (see ¶8234), but sent the case back to a new tribunal to consider whether, on the facts, the employer had been in breach of contract in refusing the employee his holiday pay.

4019 Payment in lieu of leave is generally not allowed, see ¶4014.

B. Calculation of leave

4020 Entitlement to paid leave relates to the **leave year** and this **starts** on the date **provided for in** any relevant agreement (¶4000) (reg 13(2) SI 1998/1833). If there are **no such provisions**: where the worker started work on or before 1 October 1998, the leave year will start on this date and on each subsequent anniversary; and where the worker starts work after 1 October 1998, the leave year will start on the date on which the worker started his employment and on each subsequent anniversary.

Where a worker starts work **part-way through** his **leave year**, his entitlement is proportionate to the amount of the leave year that he works (reg 13(5) SI 1998/1833).

A week's leave

A week's leave is equivalent to the time a worker works in a week.

For example, a worker whose annual leave year commences on 1 July 2011 is entitled to 5.6 weeks' annual leave. It follows that if the worker normally works 5 days a week, he will be entitled to 28 days' annual leave. If, however, he is a **part-time worker** who normally works 2 days a week, he will be entitled to 11.2 days' annual leave.

With regard to the following **atypical** working arrangements:
– if a worker has a **shift pattern** which **does not exactly fit a 7-day week**, his holiday entitlement can be calculated on the basis of the shifts he works. Thus if a worker works four 12-hour shifts followed by 4 days off, his average working week is 3.5 12-hour shifts. The worker's entitlement is the equivalent of $5.6 \times 3.5 = 19.6$ 12-hour shifts;
– if a worker works in **term-times only**, his holiday entitlement can be calculated on the basis of his annualised hours. If a worker works 40 hours a week for 40 weeks of the year, he works a total of 1600 hours over 46.4 weeks of the year (52 weeks – 5.6 weeks) = 34.48 hours a week. The worker's entitlement is 5.6 weeks $\times$ 34.48 hours a week = 193.09 hours' holiday over the year or 4.83 weeks; and
– if a worker works **casual or very irregular hours**, his holiday entitlement can be calculated on the basis of hours worked. The worker is entitled to the equivalent of 12.07% of hours worked (i.e. 5.6 weeks' leave divided by 46.4 weeks (52 weeks – 5.6 weeks) $\times$ 100 = 12.07 %). So if a worker has worked 10 hours in a year, he is entitled to 72.6 minutes' paid holiday.

> MEMO POINTS A recent Court of Justice of the European Union case has held that an employee's entitlement and calculation of holiday pay should be based on when it had been due (*Zentralbetriebsrat der Landeskrankenhaüser Tirols, Case C-486/08* [2010] EUECJ C-486/08). This interpretation is not consistent with the Working Time Regulations as they presently stand, as leave entitlement and pay is currently calculated on when it is taken. Any proposals to amend the regulations to bring them into line with this decision will be covered in future updates. The case itself concerned a worker who changed from working full time to part time during a leave year. The Court of Justice considered a rule of Austrian law which had the effect that the worker lost holiday accrued on the basis of working full time which had not been used up before switching to part time. In such a situation, according to the Court of Justice, the employee would be entitled to take all the days accrued, and not have the number of days reduced pro-rata, and to be paid for those days at the full-time rate, even if they take it while working part time.

Where a worker is entitled to a **proportion** of a full day's statutory leave, the employer may find it easier to round up that proportion to make a half or full day. Part days do not need to be rounded up to the nearest full day (although they cannot be rounded down). Other options include allowing workers to take a full day's leave or paying the worker only for the part owed. Alternatively, the part day could be taken off a day's shift, allowing the worker to leave early or come in late, or the part day could be carried over to the following leave year.

For an **assessment** of a specific worker's entitlement, readers are advised to use the Government-sponsored online calculator from GOV.UK to work out the relevant leave entitlement: flmemo.co.uk/em4023

First year of employment

Workers accrue their entitlement on a **pro-rata basis** during their first year of employment (reg 15A SI 1998/1833). This is calculated in relation to the proportion of the employment year worked. Therefore, the annual entitlement will accrue over the course of the worker's first year of employment at a rate of 1/12 of his entitlement starting on the first day of each month.

Where this calculation does not result in an exact number of days, the figure will be rounded up to the nearest half day. This does not apply for the purposes of calculating a payment in lieu on the termination of employment (see below).

> EXAMPLE Worker H starts full-time work on 1 October 2011. He will accrue his year's entitlement leave at a rate of 2.5 days per month, i.e. 28 divided by 12 = 2.33 rounded up to 2.5. He will accrue his full entitlement by month 11.

Termination of employment

4025 If a worker's employment is terminated, his leave entitlement is proportionate to the part of the leave year that has been worked (reg 14 SI 1998/1833). As a result, a worker is **entitled to** be paid in lieu for any leave accrued but not taken.

The **calculation** of this payment in lieu can be provided for in a relevant agreement (¶4000). This is usually the same rate as normal remuneration but there may be circumstances where, due to the behaviour of the worker, it might be appropriate to allow for this sum to be reduced. However, in such circumstances, the sum payable cannot be nothing otherwise it would breach the regulations, as a contract of employment cannot deny such payment on termination to which the worker was entitled (*Witley & District Men's Club v Mackey* [2001] IRLR 595, EAT).

> EXAMPLE In *Witley & District Men's Club v Mackey*, W was dismissed for **dishonesty** and under his contract such a dismissal rendered that outstanding holiday pay would not be payable on termination. However, the EAT held that this term was contrary to the provisions preventing contracting out of any of the working time regulations.

4026 If the method of calculation is **not set out** in a relevant agreement, the following formula must be used:

$$(A \times B) - C$$

A is the worker's leave entitlement.
B is the proportion of the worker's leave year that had been worked before his effective date of termination.
C is the period of leave taken by the worker between the start of the leave year and the effective date of termination.

> EXAMPLE Worker J works 5 days per week. He starts full-time work on 1 April 2011, which is also the start of his leave year resulting in a 28-day annual entitlement for his 2011-2012 leave year. His employment is terminated 6 months into the leave year (i.e. half the leave year has been worked) during which he has taken 3 days' leave.
> Therefore the employer must pay J the equivalent of 11 days' ((28 × 0.5) − 3) payment in lieu.

4027 Although the regulations do not provide a formula for **calculating a day's leave or a day's pay**, the EAT has held that the daily rate of pay is calculated by dividing the worker's annual salary by the number of working days in the leave year, as opposed to the number of calendar days in the year (*Leisure Leagues UK Ltd v Maconnachie* [2002] IRLR 600, EAT; approved in *Yarrow v Edwards Chartered Accountants* [2007] UKEAT 0116_07_0806). Unless there is clear wording in the contract to the contrary, salaried employees working 5 days per week should be paid 1/260 of their annual salary per day of leave.

> MEMO POINTS There are diverging views as to how a worker's payment in lieu of unused holiday entitlement should be calculated. In the absence of an express contrary provision, some may still hold that the Apportionment Act 1870 will apply so that the rate is calculated on the basis of daily accrual using calendar days (Apportionment Act 1870). On this basis, a day's pay is calculated by dividing annual salary by 365 (*Thames Water Utilities v Reynolds* [1996] IRLR 186, EAT). While this method was confirmed as correct in *Taylor v East Midlands Offender Employment*, the EAT has since held (*Leisure Leagues UK Ltd v Maconnachie*) that the daily rate of pay is calculated by dividing the worker's annual salary by the number of working days in the leave year, as opposed to the number of calendar days in the year. This decision has been approved subsequently by the EAT (*Yarrow v Edwards Chartered Accountants*) and is the most commonly used approach.

4028 Where a worker has taken holidays in **excess of his entitlement**, and if provided for by a relevant agreement (¶4000), his employer can recover the sum equal to the gross salary paid in respect of such holidays from his final payment of wages. However, if there is no relevant agreement, then his employer cannot recoup any "overpayment" made in respect of annual holiday pay (*Hill v Chapell* [2003] IRLR 19, EAT).

C. Records

4030 There is no requirement to keep records to show that the entitlements to paid annual leave have been complied with. However, as a worker can make a complaint to an employment tribunal if the employer breaches the regulations with regard to these entitlements, it is advisable to keep adequate records. Should any disputes arise as to the number of hours/days worked, it will be a factual and evidential issue for the tribunal or court to decide.

D. Remedies

4040 Workers can bring a **complaint** against their employers in an employment tribunal for **breach of their entitlement** to annual leave. The **time limit** for presenting such claims is 3 months beginning with the date on which it is alleged the statutory annual leave entitlement should have been permitted or paid. This period can be **extended** by the tribunal, as it considers reasonable, if it is satisfied that it was not reasonably practicable for the complaint to be presented before this date (¶¶9466+).

Applications to recover unpaid annual leave or pay in lieu can be made under the Working Time Regulations or as a claim for an unlawful deduction of wages (¶¶3055+) (*HM Revenue and Customs v Stringer and ors* [2009] IRLR 677, HL). This means that employees can recover accrued holiday pay for substantial periods if they bring claims under the unlawful deduction of wages provisions, potentially for the whole of their employment, as the provisions allow recovery for a series of deductions as long as the claim is made within 3 months of the last deduction. In contrast, recovery under the Working Time Regulations requires employees to bring claims within 3 months of the date that each payment was due.

4041 Workers also can make a complaint for **any detrimental effect**, or any deliberate failure to act by their employer, which has occurred in connection with this entitlement.

Employees can also bring a claim for **automatic unfair dismissal** (¶8390) if they are dismissed in connection with their entitlement to annual leave. Non-employee workers (¶13) who are so dismissed should rely on the right not to suffer a detriment.

CHAPTER 13

Sickness, injury and absence

OUTLINE

		¶¶
SECTION 1 **Statutory sick pay** ...		4110
A Employed earner		4120
Agency workers		4123
Employees with more than one job		4125
Pregnant employees		4127
Employees absent due to a trade dispute		4132
B Incapacity to work		4135
Extent of incapacity		4138
Night shift workers		4139
Period of incapacity to work (PIW)		4142
C Period of entitlement		4145
Start of entitlement		4145
End of entitlement		4150
1 Linked PIWs		4155
2 Non-linked PIWs		4160
D Rate		4165
SECTION 2 **Occupational sick pay**		4170
SECTION 3 **Permanent health insurance**		4200
SECTION 4 **Management of sickness**		4210
Self-certification and GP "fit" notes		4211
Gathering information about workers' health		4213
Return to work interviews		4217
Policy and procedure		4220
Sickness records		4223
A Disciplinary matters		4230
B Long-term illness		4240
1 Dismissal		4245
Disabled employees		4248
Medical evidence and investigation		4251
Prior consultation		4258
2 Frustration		4270
C Persistent short-term absences		4280

4100 Certain prudent steps can be taken at the **recruitment stage** to ensure that prospective employees will be fit and able to perform their duties, though care must be taken that employers do not discriminate in doing so (¶706). For discrimination issues in relation to the management of sickness, see ¶¶4240+.

See also chapter 15 for the **duties** the employer has with regard to the health and safety of his employees, including employees with stress-related or psychiatric illnesses.

4101 When an employee is unable to work due to sickness, illness or injury (referred to in this chapter as sickness or illness), he is generally entitled to **statutory sick pay (SSP)** paid by his employer. Alternatively, his employer may provide a company scheme giving **occupational sick pay (OSP)** instead of paying SSP. In addition, he may provide **permanent health insurance (PHI)** if the employee continues to be sick or has a serious illness. In managing OSP and in providing information to the insurers of PHI, the employer may require information from the employee as to his health which has data protection implications. **Private healthcare** is a popular and common benefit and cover may be extended to include the employer's spouse and dependant children, commonly at an additional cost to the employee.

MEMO POINTS 1. The provisions relating to SSP are **contained and regulated** by the Social Security Contributions and Benefits Act 1992 (SSCBA 1992) and Statutory Sick Pay (General) Regulations (as amended and referred to in this chapter as "the regulations") (SI 1982/894).

2. HMRC also publish a **help book** on SSP (E14), which can be found at see flmemo.co.uk/em4101. Though it has no legal status it is useful as an indication of the position HMRC take on certain procedural issues as well as outlining the scope and breadth of the regulations.

4102 The Court of Justice of the European Union has ruled that a worker on **long-term sick leave** is entitled to statutory annual leave even if he is **absent from work throughout that leave year** (*Stringer and ors v HM Revenue and Customs, Schultz-Hoff v Deutsche Rentenversicherung Bund, Joined Cases C-520/06 and C-350/06 [2009] IRLR 214, ECJ*). As to the amount that can be carried over, the Court of Appeal has held that workers on long-term sick leave are **entitled to carry forward** the 4 weeks of leave conferred on them by European legislation and to be paid for this leave on termination, even if they are absent due to illness for an entire leave year and even if they do not request to carry the leave forward in advance of the leave year coming to an end (*NHS Leeds v Larner [2012] EWCA Civ 1034*). Although this judgment related to a public sector employee and referred heavily to European cases based on the Working Time Directive, which is not directly effective in UK law (and therefore cannot be relied upon in the national courts by private sector workers), the Court of Appeal clarified that the national Working Time Regulations can be read in line with the European Directive in relation to the points decided in this case, allowing both private and public sector workers to benefit from this decision. The additional 1.6 weeks of leave conferred by the national regulations need not be carried over unless this is permitted under an individual's contract of employment (*Neidel v Stadt Frankfurt am Main [2012] EUECJ C-337/10*).

While carry-over periods should be allowed to ensure that the worker can have, if need be, rest periods that may be staggered, planned in advance and available in the longer term, there should be a **limit to carrying over** untaken leave (*KHS v Winfried Schulte (Social policy) [2011] EUECJ C-214/10*). Carry-over periods should be substantially longer than the reference periods in respect of which they are granted. On the facts of this case, the carry-over period was limited to 15 months, which was sufficient. Reference was also made to a limit of no more than 18 months.

MEMO POINTS   The Government is consulting on **proposals** to make the necessary amendments to the Working Time Regulations in light of the Court of Justice of the European Union decisions (see memo point to ¶4014). Meanwhile, despite the fact that the national Regulations do not currently permit carry-over of leave, employers are advised to allow carry-over periods of at least 15 to 18 months, as it is very likely that employment tribunals will interpret the Regulations in line with the decisions of the Court of Justice of the European Union (not least because of the position taken by the Court of Appeal in *NHS Leeds v Larner* outlined above).

4103 If a worker **falls ill before commencing a pre-planned period of holiday**, he is legally entitled to re-schedule that holiday and take it at a later time, if necessary in a later leave year (*Pereda v Madrid Movilidad SA [2009] IRLR 959, ECJ*). The same principles apply if a worker **falls ills during** their **holiday** (*Asociación Nacional de Grandes Empresas de Distribución (ANGED) v Federación de Asociaciones Sindicales (FASGA) and ors [2012] C-78/11*).

MEMO POINTS   See memo point to ¶4102. As a sensible precaution, employers may wish to amend their ill health reporting procedures to clarify how and when an employee should report an illness arising on holiday and what (if any) medical evidence will be needed.

4104 Where the employee has a **long-term illness** or is **persistently sick**, his employer may be able to **dismiss** him fairly if he has a genuine business reason for doing so. However, employers must be careful not to discriminate against disabled employees.

Alternatively, the employer may choose to offer the employee early retirement on the grounds of ill health. Occupational pension schemes usually provide for this and see ¶3414 for the typical requirements that need to be satisfied before such payments are made. These may grant extra pensionable service to calculate enhanced ill health provisions or tiered benefit (i.e. full prospective pensionable service where the employee is unable to perform any work and actual pensionable service where he is able to do some work though not his usual or previous job).

A dismissal **without good cause** which would deprive the employee of the benefit of an early retirement occupational pension or a PHI scheme may be a breach of the implied term of trust and confidence (see section 3).

In relatively rare situations, an employee's ill health may **frustrate** his employment contract, bringing it to an end, and in such cases there is no dismissal.

4105 **Pregnant employees** have special protection during their pregnancy and maternity leave and any dismissals due to a pregnancy-related illness will amount to direct discrimination (¶5320).

4106 The absence records of employees can be part of valid **redundancy selection criteria** where they are used to measure reliability of future attendance, although certain absences should be ignored; see ¶8836.

SECTION 1

Statutory sick pay (SSP)

4110 Employers **must pay** statutory sick pay (SSP) or at least the equivalent occupational sick pay (OSP) (see section 2), usually **from** the fourth qualifying day, to employees who are employed earners and who are absent due to their incapacity, i.e. sickness (s 151 SSCBA 1992).

Employers are free to choose **whether or not to operate** the following rules of the SSP scheme if they give OSP at or above the SSP rate for each day of SSP entitlement. Employers must **not** make their employees **contribute** directly or indirectly towards SSP (or the equivalent amount of SSP in an OSP scheme).

> MEMO POINTS   Many employers include a contractual provision seeking recovery of sick pay from the employee in the event of a successful personal injury claim against a third party. Such a clause should exclude SSP or it may be rendered void.

4112 SSP is **funded by** the employer. However, if the SSP paid in any tax month **exceeds** 13% of the gross Class 1 primary and secondary contributions payable for that month, the excess may be recovered by reducing the amount of PAYE, NIC and student loan deductions payable to HMRC.

4113 Any **dispute** as to whether SSP is due to an employee will be determined by HMRC and not by an employment tribunal (*Taylor Gordon & Co Ltd (t/a Plan Personnel) v Timmons* [2004] IRLR 180, EAT).

Records

4115 Employers are required to maintain **full records** of the employee's absence from work in order that entitlement to SSP may be checked by HMRC. To aid employers, HMRC have produced an optional "self-certification form", **SC2**, which can be used for employees to certify themselves as sick for the first 7 days of sickness. Also optional is HMRC form **SSP2**, "record sheet", which has been produced to help small businesses operate the SSP scheme.

Employers must complete and give to their employees HMRC form **SSP1** (or their own computerised version) if they are off sick for 4 or more days and are not entitled to SSP, or if their entitlement has stopped during their time off sick. This form will set out why the employee is not entitled to SSP and will enable him to claim appropriate social security benefits.

It is a good idea to keep these records not only to comply with HMRC's requirements, but also to help with the effective management of employee absence in order that employers have a clear picture as to the number and length of absences taken and the reasons given for them (see ¶¶4210+ for guidance on absence management).

4116 Payments of SSP are **subject to PAYE and NIC deductions** and must also be recorded on the deductions working sheet (P11) (¶6842) and on the annual return (P35) (¶6877).

Penalties

4118 Employers who **fail** to **produce** any document or record required under the SSP scheme face an initial penalty of £300 with further penalties of £60 per day for continuing failure. Employers who fail or repeatedly refuse to **make payments** will be liable to a penalty of up to £3,000.

Further, employers who **fraudulently or negligently**:
- make any incorrect payments of SSP;
- produce any incorrect document or record, provide any incorrect information, or make any incorrect return; or
- receive incorrect payments in connection with the recovery of SSP,

will be liable to a fine of up to £3,000.

Penalties may also be charged in relation to errors on returns and documents (¶6881).

> MEMO POINTS   Note that **employees** will face similar penalties if they fraudulently or negligently:
> - make any incorrect statement or declaration in connection with a claim for SSP; or
> - provide any incorrect document or information which has been required to be produced to an HMRC officer.

A. Employed earner

4120 Employed earners, i.e. **employees who pay Class 1 NIC**, qualify for SSP from their **employers who contribute** to their NIC payments if they have **average weekly earnings** of at least the lower earnings limit for NIC for the 8 weeks prior to the period of incapacity to work (PIW) (¶4142).

All employees, regardless of their length of contract, are treated exactly the same for SSP purposes. Consequently, all employees, including those with **contracts of 3 months or less**, will be entitled to SSP provided they satisfy the remaining qualifying conditions.

> MEMO POINTS   To calculate the average weekly earnings, all gross earnings paid in the set period are divided by the number of days, weeks or months, depending on the pay practice, in that set period.

4123 **Agency workers** who are **employed on one contract or a series of contracts** are entitled to claim statutory sick pay (Sch 1 SI 1978/1689). An agency worker is deemed to be an employee for these purposes irrespective of whether he is an employee for other purposes (¶2042).

Agency workers employed on a series of contracts cannot claim SSP from their agency when they are **not employed** to work for a client. When employed, the same rules as above will apply in determining qualification.

If a worker qualifies, his entitlement continues for the duration of the contract or until he is fit for work, regardless of whether the agency is required to provide a **replacement** for the client. Therefore, if the contract is **terminated** purely for the purpose of avoiding SSP, the worker will remain entitled to SSP (reg 4 SI 1982/894).

> MEMO POINTS   It used to be the case that agency workers employed on a contract of specific duration of less than 3 months were not entitled to claim statutory sick pay. However, this was repealed on 27 October 2008 and all agency workers are now entitled to statutory sick pay (SI 2008/2776).

Employees with more than one job

4125 Whether an employee who has more than one job with the same or with different employer(s) qualifies for SSP with regard to one or all of his jobs will depend on whether he is an employed earner for each job.

Where there are two or more concurrent contracts with the same employer (or employers trading in association) and his earnings are in both cases **aggregated for NIC**, the employee must be incapable of work under all his contracts before he is entitled to SSP (regs 20-21 SI 1982/894). For example, an accountant working for associated companies must be unable to perform all his duties under his contracts to qualify, if his earnings are aggregated for NIC.

However, if the contracts are separate and the employee's earnings are **not aggregated for NIC** (usually because he is working for different employers), he will qualify for SSP with regard to the job he is incapable of performing even if he remains capable of performing the other(s). For example, a man could be a manual labourer during the day and work for another employer as a bingo caller in the evening. In such circumstances, he will be able to claim SSP from his daytime employer if he breaks his arm and is unable to perform his duties even though he can still perform his evening job of calling numbers.

Pregnant employees

A pregnant employee does not qualify for SSP during a 39-week period called a **disqualifying period** unless she has suffered a miscarriage or an abortion (s 153(2), (11), (12) SSCBA 1992; reg 3(4)-(5) SI 1982/894). **4127**

If she is **entitled** to statutory maternity pay (**SMP**) or maternity allowance (**MA**), this period will start at the beginning of the week when she is first entitled to either of these payments and will last for the duration of entitlement. **4128**

If she is **not entitled** to SMP or MA and is **receiving SSP**, her disqualifying period will start with the earlier of the following dates:
– the day after the date of birth; or
– the first day she is sick with a pregnancy-related illness on or after the start of the 4th week before the week the baby is due.

If she is not entitled to SMP or MA and is **not receiving SSP**, her disqualifying period will start with the earlier of the following dates:
– the beginning of the week in which the birth occurred; or
– the beginning of the week in which she is first off sick with a pregnancy-related illness if this is on or after the start of the 4th week before the week the baby is due.

SSP will only be payable **after the disqualifying period** has ended. If a period of incapacity to work (PIW) (¶4142) is formed before or during the disqualification period, a new PIW after the disqualifying period must be at least 57 days (i.e. more than 8 weeks) later for SSP to be payable. Otherwise, under the PIW rules, it would be treated as a linked PIW (¶4155). **4129**

Employees absent due to a trade dispute

An employee does not qualify for SSP if at the **beginning of his incapacity** (or the start of his employment contract if later) he is absent because of a trade dispute unless he can show that he had no direct interest in it either on or before the start of his sickness (Sch 11 SSCBA 1992; reg 3 SI 1982/894). He is deemed to be **directly interested** if the outcome of the dispute will be applied across the workforce automatically by the employer due to a collective agreement or because of established custom and practice (*Presho v Insurance Officer* [1984] IRLR 74, HL). **4132**

A trade dispute is **defined** as any dispute between employers and employees, or between employees, which is connected with the employment or non-employment or the terms and conditions of employment of any persons, whether or not they are employed by the employer (s 27 SSCBA 1992).

B. Incapacity to work

To qualify for SSP, an employee must be off sick with a disease or disability that renders him **incapable of performing** any work which he can reasonably be expected to do under his contract (s 151(4) SSCBA 1992). Therefore, if an employee is able to perform contractual work other than his usual duties, he will not qualify. **4135**

If an employee is suffering a **bereavement**, his employer should decide whether to accept the time taken off due to bereavement as sickness, for example due to shock or depression.

Naturally, if there is an extended period of absence and an employee produces a medical certificate stating he is suffering from shock or depression, his employer should treat the time taken off as sickness.

4136 In **exceptional circumstances**, an employee will be **deemed incapable** of work and entitled to receive SSP even though he is actually capable of working. This happens where (reg 2(1) SI 1982/894):
– he is excluded from work on a certificate of a Medical Officer for Environmental Health and is under medical observation because he is a **carrier** of, or has been in contact with, an infectious disease; or
– a doctor states that the employee should not work for **precautionary or convalescent reasons**. For example, a doctor may deem a pregnant woman incapable of work if there is an outbreak of rubella (German measles) at her place of work, to prevent the risk of serious harm to her unborn child.

Extent of incapacity

4138 An employee must be incapable or deemed to be incapable for the **whole** of each of the **working days** he is absent. Therefore, if an employee has done even a short period of work in a working day it will not be treated as a day of incapacity for SSP purposes. If, on the other hand, an employee turned up to work but was unable to start due to incapacity, the day will be treated as a day of incapacity.

Night shift workers

4139 Work done in any shift which **extends over midnight** is treated as having been done entirely on the first of the two days (reg 2(2) SI 1982/894). Therefore, if an employee becomes incapable of work after the end of such a shift, the second day is deemed to be a day of incapacity even though he did some work during that day.

Period of incapacity to work (PIW)

4142 The employee will only qualify for SSP if the days of incapacity create a period of incapacity to work (PIW). A PIW is formed when the employee is **incapable** of work for **4 or more consecutive calendar days**. As a PIW is measured in consecutive calendar days, all days of incapacity count towards determining its length, including weekends, holidays and any other days on which the employee is not expected to work. The PIW ends when the employee's incapacity ends.

Occasional days of incapacity of **up to 3 consecutive calendar days** do not count and cannot create PIWs.

C. Period of entitlement

Start of entitlement

4145 The entitlement starts from the **4th qualifying day of a PIW** and is payable on all qualifying days after that for up to a **maximum** of 28 weeks (i.e. 196 days) (s 151 SSCBA 1992).

SSP is only payable on qualifying days and is calculated on a weekly basis (¶4165). Consequently, the rate for qualifying days is the weekly rate for SSP divided by the number of qualifying days in that week. For example, if the qualifying days are Monday-Friday, the daily rate on these qualifying days will be the weekly rate divided by 5. If there is only 1 qualifying day in the week then the rate for that day will be the full weekly rate.

> *MEMO POINTS* The employee must have normal or average **weekly earnings** (to calculate the average weekly earnings, all gross earnings paid in the set period are divided by the number of

days, weeks or months, depending on the pay practice, in that set period) of at least the lower earnings limit for NIC for the 8 weeks prior to the PIW to be entitled. This needs to be calculated afresh with regard to each PIW if necessary.

There are slightly different rules when a PIW is **linked** with one or more PIWs, i.e. when they are less than 57 days apart from each other (¶4155). Where a new PIW occurs which is **not linked** to previous PIWs, the employee's entitlement will start afresh.

4146

The **first 3 qualifying days** are called **waiting days**.

Qualifying days The employer and employees or their representatives can **choose** which days of the week are qualifying days (s 151(2) SSCBA 1992). These will **normally be** the days of the week on which the employee is contracted to work.

4147

Choosing qualifying days must be by agreement, with at least 1 qualifying day a week (s 151(3) SSCBA 1992). These must not be determined by the actual days an employee is off sick.

If qualifying days **cannot be agreed**, the following rules determine the qualifying day(s) to be:
– the day(s) on which the employee is required to work, and Wednesdays if the contract does not specify a day(s). For example, if the employee is contracted to work Monday to Wednesday every other week, his qualifying days would be Mondays to Wednesdays on the weeks he is required to work and Wednesdays on the weeks he is not; or
– every day of the week except those on which there is agreement that none of the workforce is required to work. For example, if there is no agreement, but the employer and employee agree that Saturday and Sunday are days on which none of the workforce is required to work, the qualifying days will be deemed to be Monday-Friday.

> EXAMPLE Employee D is contracted to work Monday to Friday and these are his qualifying days. D is off sick from Wednesday to the following Tuesday. As the absence lasts longer than 3 consecutive calendar days, he has formed a PIW (¶4142) which runs from that Wednesday to the following Tuesday.
> He has 5 qualifying days within that period: Wednesday, Thursday, Friday and the following Monday and Tuesday. He will be entitled to SSP from the fourth qualifying day and therefore will be entitled to SSP on the Monday and Tuesday he is off sick.
> Employee E is a part-time employee working Monday to Wednesday, which are his qualifying days. E is off sick during the same period and therefore has the same PIW as D.
> However, he only has 3 qualifying days within that period: Wednesday and the following Monday and Tuesday. He will not be entitled to SSP as the first 3 qualifying days are waiting days.
> Employee F, who works from 6pm on Sunday to 9am on Monday, has agreed with his employer that Sunday is his 1 qualifying day in the week.
> He works his shift but is sick on Monday which is his first day of PIW. He returns to work four Sundays later. The PIW lasts for 27 calendar days.
> However, there are only 3 qualifying days in this PIW (the three Sundays he did not work) and as these are waiting days, F does not qualify for SSP.

Where staff work on a **rota system** or have an **unusual working pattern**, the HMRC manual suggests that for simplicity employers should agree with their employees or their employee representatives that the same day(s) in every week is/are a qualifying day(s).

4148

End of entitlement

An employee's entitlement will end on the last qualifying day of his PIW. This will occur **at the earliest** of the following events (s 153(2), (11), (12) SSCBA 1992):
– he recovers and is able to return to work;
– he reaches the maximum entitlement of 28 weeks of SSP;
– he travels outside the EEA (unless he is a mariner, airman or an employee working on the Continental Shelf);
– the contract ends (unless it was terminated by the employer in avoidance of SSP); or
– the employee is pregnant and has reached the disqualifying period.

4150

In all but the first situation, when the employee returns to work, he may be entitled to other state benefits when his SSP ends, for example employment and support allowance or severe disablement allowance. Pregnant employees may be able to claim statutory maternity pay (SMP) or maternity allowance (MA) and/or other state benefits.

1. Linked PIWs

4155 Any two periods of incapacity for work which are **separated by** a period of 8 weeks or less (i.e. **56 clear calendar days or less**) are treated as linked and are regarded as a single period of entitlement. A PIW with a **former employer** does not count.

> EXAMPLE Employee G is off sick from 28 June to 1 July and 27 August to 31 August. G's PIWs are separated by exactly 56 days and are therefore linked.
> Employee H is off sick from 28 June to 1 July and 26 August to 31 August. H's PIWs are separated by less than 56 days and are therefore linked.
> Employee I is off sick from 28 June to 1 July and 28 August to 31 August. I's PIWs are separated by more than 56 days and are therefore not linked (and see ¶4160).

4156 As linked PIWs are regarded as a single period of entitlement, the following rules occur:
1) **Waiting days** are carried forward from a previous linked PIW.

> EXAMPLE Employees J's, K's and L's qualifying days are Monday to Friday. All are sick from Sunday to Friday. Their PIWs run from Sunday to Friday within which there are 5 qualifying days, Monday to Friday.
> J's last PIW was more than 56 days ago and is therefore not linked. Therefore, J's waiting days are Monday to Wednesday and he is entitled to SSP for Thursday and Friday.
> K's PIW is linked to a previous PIW which had occurred 4 weeks previously. This previous PIW was from Tuesday to Friday, K's waiting days were Tuesday to Thursday of that week and he was paid SSP for that Friday. All his waiting days have been served and he is entitled to SSP for Monday to Friday in his new linked PIW.
> L's PIW is linked to a previous PIW which had also occurred 4 weeks previously. This previous PIW was from Friday to Monday and therefore L's waiting days were Friday and Monday. L has 1 waiting day to serve to be entitled to SSP and, therefore, Monday of the new linked PIW will be his final waiting day and he will be entitled to SSP for Tuesday to Friday of that week.

4157 2) The SSP **maximum entitlement** of 28 weeks is spread over the linked period.

> EXAMPLE Employee O has used up 4 weeks of entitlement in a previous PIW. This PIW is linked with a newly formed PIW which is 56 or less days after it. O has 24 weeks of entitlement left which can be paid in this new PIW.

4158 3) If a series of linked **PIWs lasts longer than 3 years**, entitlement to SSP ends after the third year. This will apply regardless of whether the maximum entitlement of 28 weeks has been reached.

> EXAMPLE Employee P has a number of linked PIWs over the last 3 years to 1 July. If P is off sick, creating a new PIW on or before 27 August, the PIWs will be separated by 56 days or less and P's employer is not liable to pay SSP as the entitlement ends after 3 years of linked PIWs.

2. Non-linked PIWs

4160 Where a PIW occurs **over 8 weeks** after the end of the last PIW, it will not be linked to the previous PIW. In such cases, each PIW will be treated as a **separate period of entitlement**. This means that the first 3 qualifying days are waiting days and SSP will not be payable on these days. The maximum entitlement of 28 weeks will start afresh.

> EXAMPLE Employee I is off sick from 28 June to 1 July and 28 August to 31 August. I's PIWs are separated by more than 56 days and are therefore not linked. Therefore, his 3 qualifying days from his first PIW do not count and 28 – 30 August will be his 3 qualifying days for his new period of entitlement.

D. Rate

4165 SSP is **payable at** a fixed weekly rate of £85.85. This is likely to **increase from** 6 April 2013 and any new rate will be covered by our updating service. The daily amount payable depends on the number of qualifying days during the week (¶4147). For example, if the qualifying days are Monday to Friday, the daily rate for being off sick on a qualifying day will be a fifth of the weekly rate. HMRC provide a table in their guides to sick pay, and PAYE and NICs rates and limits (E14 and E12 respectively) setting out the daily rate for all the available combinations of qualifying days, see flmemo.co.uk/em4165a and flmemo.co.uk/em4165b

4167 SSP is **funded by** the employer and, in many cases, the payments cannot be recovered from HMRC. However, if the SSP paid in any tax month exceeds 13% of the gross Class 1 primary and secondary NIC payable for that month, the excess may be recovered by reducing the amount of PAYE, NIC and student loan deductions payable to HMRC.

SECTION 2

Occupational sick pay

4170 Employers can **opt out** of the SSP scheme if they have a company scheme, namely an OSP scheme that matches or exceeds the amount payable under SSP.

4171 Where an employer has contractual terms on incapacity to work due to sickness and/or an OSP scheme, it is advisable that he **sets out** these terms in the **contract of employment**. Where there is no written contract of employment or where it does not cover these provisions, employers must provide employees with a **written statement of particulars** relating to them (¶1400).

4172 Where there is an OSP scheme, the provisions should state how much will be paid, how it will be paid and for how long. An employer can also choose to cover some employees and not others in a scheme, though he must ensure that he does not discriminate against his employees on grounds of age, disability, gender reassignment, marriage and civil partnership, race, religion or belief, sex or sexual orientation in doing so.

A **typical scheme** will give full pay on sickness for a certain period reducing to a percentage of full pay for a following set period with no further sick pay thereafter. Sometimes no OSP will be payable in a probation period and/or the level of entitlement may increase with length of service. If **no duration** is stated, a term may be implied to give effect to the presumed intention of the parties (¶1170). The presumption is that the employer will pay for a reasonable period only, which will depend on the term normally applicable in the particular industry as determined, for example, by reference to the relevant national agreement (*Howman & Son v Blyth* [1983] IRLR 139, EAT).

The scheme should also set out any **conditions** to which it is subject (commonly self-certification for periods of absence up to 7 days, and the production of a medical certificate for longer periods).

> MEMO POINTS Many employers include a contractual provision seeking recovery of sick pay from the employee in the event of a successful personal injury claim against a third party. Such a clause should not exclude SSP or it may be rendered void.

4173 Where an employee is on **long-term sickness absence** as a result of an illness **related to disability**, there is no need to provide for full pay: while not doing so may constitute indirect disability discrimination, this can be justified (*O'Hanlon v Commissioners for HM Revenue and Customs* [2007] IRLR 404, CA).

4175 **Data protection** Employers must ensure that they comply with the data protection rules (¶5945) (for example, where the data is sensitive (¶5925), explicit consent should be obtained).

Further, as **good practice**, employers should (part 4.2 DP Code):
– make workers aware how information relating to their health will be used and who will have access to it. Unless told otherwise, workers are entitled to assume that information they give will be treated in confidence and not passed on to the employer or another third party;
– not compromise the confidentiality of communications between workers and their occupational health professionals, for example if emails can be used as a form of confidential information, this should not be monitored; and
– act in a way that is consistent with the Guidance on Ethics for Occupational Physicians from the Faculty of Occupational Medicine.

Employers are also advised to follow the DP Code's general **recommendations** with regard to data management (¶6000) and its good practice recommendations with regard to information about their workers' health (see ¶4940).

No OSP scheme

4190 If there is no OSP scheme, the employer must ensure that this is stated either in the contract or written particulars. This is especially important if, under the same employer, some employees have access to an OSP and others do not, as failure to specify lack of membership in a contract may result in an **implied right** to any existing scheme (*Mears v Safecar Security Ltd* [1982] IRLR 183, CA). In deciding whether there is such a right, a tribunal will consider all the facts and circumstances to see whether a term can be implied. Relevant circumstances are the knowledge of the parties at the time the contract is made, the nature of the contract and how the parties have behaved since the employee started work. Such a term may also be implied from the custom or practice in the industry.

SECTION 3
Permanent health insurance

4200 Many employers also provide permanent health insurance (PHI), otherwise known as long-term disability cover or even more generally as sickness and accident benefit. PHI usually gives employees the equivalent or a proportion of a salary if they have a long-term illness and cannot return to work, and is nearly always provided by an insurer who will have an agreement with the employer to provide cover to his employees in the event of such illness. Such payments are normally triggered after the employee has been sick for a set period of time and will continue until the employee either recovers from his illness and returns to work or reaches retirement age. See ¶3211 for the tax treatment of permanent health benefits.

4201 To **ensure an employer has no contractual liability** to provide payments if the **insurer refuses or cannot pay** an employee's claim, it should be expressly stated that the benefit is provided in accordance with the terms of the insurer's policy from time to time in force (which may be changed by the insurer without notice to the employee). The employer should also ensure that he has an express clause which gives him the right to change insurers, vary the entitlement or discontinue the scheme. Further, if there are major exemptions to the payment of the benefit (for example the ending of payments if an employee leaves employment), the employer must ensure that the employee is aware of these exemptions, for example the employee should be shown the policy or told to read it, otherwise the employer may be liable for these exemptions (*Villella v MFI Furniture Centres Ltd* [1999] IRLR 468, QBD). It should be noted that the terms of PHI policies will be interpreted in a realistic and practical way (*Walton v Airtours plc and Sunlife Assurance Company of Canada* [2003] IRLR 161, CA).

4202 If the above is not expressly stated, the employer may have a **contractual liability** to the employee. This will depend on what is outlined in any other documents provided to the employee and any other representations made to him. In such circumstances, if there is a contractual liability and the insurer refuses to pay a claim, the employer may have an obligation (as part of his general duty of trust and confidence) to challenge an insurer's assessment of the employee's fitness if the employee has no other means of redress. The duty to challenge will depend on whether the claim is genuine and the employer's view as to whether the claim would be successful (*Marlow v East Thames Housing Group Ltd* [2002] EWHC 1460 (QB)). In certain circumstances, the employer may even be liable for continuing payments if the insurer stops making them (*Jowitt v Pioneer Technology (UK) Ltd* [2002] IRLR 790, EAT, which has been overturned on appeal, but this point remains unaffected).

4203 **Dismissal** of an employee **without good cause** in circumstances which will deprive him of the benefit of a PHI scheme may be a breach of the implied term of trust and confidence (*Aspden v Webbs Poultry and Meat Group (Holdings) Ltd* [1996] IRLR 521, QBD; *Adin v Sedco Forex International Resources Ltd* [1997] IRLR 280, CS) (¶1241). This includes dismissing the employee for specious or arbitrary reasons, for no reason at all or solely with the view of preventing, or bringing to an end, any such payments (*Hill v General Accident Fire & Life Assurance Corporation plc* [1998] IRLR 641, CS).

However, there is no implied term to prevent dismissal if otherwise **justified**, for example if the employee was summarily dismissed for a fundamental breach of contract due to his gross misconduct or if he is made redundant, even if one of the results is that entitlement under a PHI scheme ends.

> EXAMPLE In *Briscoe v Lubrizol Ltd* [2002] IRLR 607, CA, B's misconduct in failing to attend meetings to discuss his long-term absence and failing to respond to requests for contact amounted to a fundamental breach entitling his employers to dismiss B even though there was a PHI scheme.

4204 If an employee has successfully brought a **personal injury** claim against his employer as a result of an injury sustained at work, any insurance payments will be regarded as a contractual benefit and will not be taken into account in the **assessment of damages** (*Lewicki v Brown & Root Wimpey Highland Fabricators Ltd* [1996] IRLR 565, CS).

4206 **Data protection** If an employee becomes unfit for work and makes a claim, the insurer might justifiably approach the employer for a report as to his fitness and to determine whether suitable alternative work is available. This could involve the disclosure of some health information and employers must ensure that they comply with the data protection rules (¶5945) (for example, where the data is sensitive (¶5925), explicit consent should be obtained).

Further, as **good practice**, employers should (part 2.4 DP Code):
– remember that they do not have a right of access to personal information needed by a third party for the administration of employment-related benefits. The information should not be used for general employment purposes. If information is collected on behalf of an insurer, the employer must ensure there is a secure method of collection;
– limit the exchange of information with a scheme provider to the minimum necessary for operation of the scheme; and
– ensure that when a worker joins a scheme it is made clear what, if any, information is passed between the insurer and the employer and how it will be used. Unless told otherwise, workers are entitled to assume that information they give to a doctor, nurse or other health professional will be treated in confidence and not passed to others.

Employers are also advised to follow the DP Code's general **recommendations** with regard to data management (¶6000) and its general good practice recommendations with regard to information about their workers' health (see ¶4940).

Alternative to PHI cover

4208 Some employers who wish to give the benefit of PHI may prefer to give their employees a sum of money to purchase their own PHI cover. Such payments are a taxable benefit.

SECTION 4
Management of sickness

4210 Employers are free to choose the procedure for **monitoring and control** of sickness absence, though they must make employees aware of any company policy and procedural rules. It is important that the procedure is applied consistently, in order that employees know that sickness absence is taken seriously and, more importantly, so that lack of consistency cannot be used to demonstrate discrimination or unfair treatment (particularly where dismissals take place on the basis of sickness absence).

Self-certification and GP "fit" notes

4211 Employers are entitled to ask for **reasonable evidence** of incapacity, for example self-certification or a sick note (now called a "fit note", see below) from the employee's doctor. For SSP purposes, for periods of sickness lasting 4 to 7 days, employers may accept self-certification orally or by letter, or they can use HMRC form SC2 for self-certification or their own equivalent form. After 7 days, employers can ask for reasonable medical evidence from a doctor or other suitably qualified person (e.g. chiropractor). Such a record is strong evidence of incapacity and should usually be accepted as conclusive unless there is **evidence to the contrary**, for example a GP's note states the employee is unable to work due to an ankle injury but he is seen playing football (*Bailey v BP Oil Kent Refinery Ltd* [1980] IRLR 287, CA). At the very least, this example may indicate that the employee was reckless as to trying to make a full and speedy recovery if the note indicated that he should rest his ankle as a recuperative measure.

Generally, if an employee is doing anything **away from work** while he is off sick which suggests that he is not genuinely sick, this is a matter which properly concerns the employer. For example, in *Hutchinson v Enfield Rolling Mills Ltd* [1981] IRLR 318, the employer acted reasonably when he dismissed H who took part in a union demonstration when he was off sick, regardless of the fact that H had a note from his doctor stating that he was suffering from sciatica. See further at ¶4231.

4212 Fit notes In 2010, fit notes replaced GP sick notes. The **format and content** was changed so that, as well as indicating whether a patient is fit or not for work for benefit and sick pay purposes, they allow doctors to indicate if there are any changes to the employee's work environment or job role which could help in achieving an earlier return to work (SI 2010/137). Specifically, the fit note includes an option so that doctors can provide an **assessment** of a patient's fitness for work and doctors can indicate where a patient "may be fit for some work now", giving general details of the functional effect of that individual's condition. If appropriate, they can also suggest one or more common ways which would help the employee return to work, such as a phased return to work, amended duties, altered hours and/or workplace adaptations. For example, where an individual has moderate lower back pain, a doctor may suggest that they will be unable to lift heavy objects and should be given the opportunity to change position or take breaks regularly.

Employers are **not obliged** to make any recommended changes and where such changes cannot be agreed a "may be fit for some work now" fit note will be regarded as an "unfit" fit note for benefit and sick pay purposes and the employee should not return to work until they have further recovered.

> MEMO POINTS **Electronic fit notes** (eMed) were rolled out across GP practices in 2012. There were no changes to the issuing of fit notes and once printed, signed and given to the patient, an electronic fit note is designed to be used in the same way as a handwritten fit note. Electronic fit notes also include a system-generated barcode which is expected to reduce the issue of forged notes. Handwritten notes may still be issued, principally by hospital doctors, doctors conducting home visits, and GPs with older IT systems.

Gathering information about workers' health

Contractual or procedural terms on the right to ask employees to attend an **occupational medical practitioner** (i.e. company doctor) for check-ups or when a medical issue affects their work may prove useful in the management of employee sickness and may highlight a potential problem early on.

Further, if necessary, it may provide an employer with a medical assessment as to the capability of an employee. An occupational health doctor/professional may have a better understanding of the employer's business and the employee's work than the employee's GP. Tribunals often put more weight behind a occupational health report for this reason. Reports could be helpful in instances of:
– short-term absence: is there an underlying cause linking the absences? Could anything be done to help?
– long-term absence: what is the likely length of absence? Could anything be done to reduce it? and
– ill health related to work: is the work or working environment the true cause of the illness? Could anything be done to decrease the impact on the worker?

4213

To ensure that both employer and employee get the maximum benefit from an occupational health report, it is essential to give precise and carefully thought out **instructions** so that the report can help with matters such as temporary cover for the employee's role, reasonable adjustments, whether dismissal is necessary, whether disability may be an issue or whether alternative roles may be suitable. It is also important to make it clear to everyone involved (and also in any relevant policy) that occupational health professionals are not in charge of making the final decision in relation to how the health problem is addressed. It should be made clear that they can suggest adjustments that could be made to improve the health/ability to work of an employee, but that they are not able to determine whether those adjustments are reasonable. Issues that should be addressed in the report, depending on the type of problem, are:
– the cause of the employee's absence. In the case of persistent short-term absence, are there a number of different causes or is there one underlying cause?
– is the employee physically and mentally able to carry out their current role?
– what is preventing them from working, or preventing them from working to their full potential?
– is the cause of the absence something that can be resolved, and if so, is it likely to recur?
– what is the timescale for recovery?
– are there any aspects of the employee's current role that he will not be able to perform?
– are there any changes that could be made to any aspect(s) of the role or working environment that would enable a return to work or assist in improving the condition?
– is there any medical support that could assist the employee?
– details of any measures that are being taken, or have already been taken, to deal with the medical problem;
– does the employee have a physical or mental impairment?
– if the employee does have an impairment, does it have an adverse effect on their ability to carry out day to day activities? and
– if the employee has an impairment that has an adverse effect on their ability to carry out day to day activities, what is the effect and is it substantial and long term?

This is not an exhaustive list and instructions should always be tailored to the situation in question.

4214

Employers must ensure that they comply with the **data protection rules** (in particular the requirements relating to sensitive data (¶5925)) when obtaining, using, handling and retaining information about workers' health. Further, the Data Protection Code sets out core principles and good practice recommendations for employers to follow. See ¶4940 for details.

4215

Return to work interviews

Return to work interviews can be a very **effective tool in managing absence**. They can provide a forum for employees to share any issues that may be contributing to their absence,

4217

such as underlying medical conditions or stress at work, and they can also identify patterns of absence. They enable managers to be more accurate in recording and identifying reasons for absence and also serve as a reminder to workers that absence is noted and managed consistently.

In order that the interviews are most effective, a common approach should be taken by all managers in terms of the consistency of holding the interviews as well as their content. In most circumstances, return to work interviews do not need to be overly long or complex, but a checklist of matters to be addressed and questions to be asked could be a useful tool. Matters to be addressed could include:
– welcoming the worker back;
– reasons for the absence (though care must be taken not to ask disproportionately intrusive medical questions);
– whether anything in the workplace contributed to the absence;
– whether a medical professional was consulted;
– enquiring as to the worker's current fitness to work; and
– whether there is any support that the worker may require in his return to work.

Policy and procedure

4220 Provisions on sickness and sick pay should be supported by a policy and procedure which will usually be found in supporting documentation or the staff handbook (¶¶1480+). A policy and procedure concerning sickness should help ensure that absence is minimised and that the employer deals with his employees fairly and consistently. The latter is especially important if an employer reaches the stage where he wishes to dismiss an employee who has a long-term illness or is persistently ill (¶4245 and ¶4280).

It is advisable that the procedure is **separate** from the employer's disciplinary procedure for all cases of ill health as opposed to misconduct. For example, if the employer wishes to put the employee on guard that his attendance record due to sickness is unacceptable, a caution would be more appropriate than a disciplinary warning. This helps maintain good employment relations, as a warning often carries a suggestion that the employee is required to change or improve his conduct and this may be inappropriate where absence is due to ill health.

The procedure should include **informal and formal discussions/consultations**, though if the employee is **unable to attend** such meetings, the employer should write to see if he would be prepared to deal with the process by correspondence.

4221 Employers should ensure that in making their sickness policy clear and emphasising its importance, they do not encourage workers into **presenteeism**, i.e. causing them to feel obliged to come into work even if they are unwell. This could lead to contagious health problems being spread around the workplace and more significant productivity problems than would have been the case if the worker who was the source of the problem had simply taken the appropriate time off in the first place.

Sickness records

4223 Keeping **accurate** sickness records and **consistently** conducting and making records of return to work interviews are essential tools in managing absence: they allow employers to build an accurate picture of employees' absence patterns which will help in dealing with the underlying causes of, and the appropriate reaction to, both short- and long-term sickness absence. They will help to ensure that decisions are based on facts rather than opinions, and employers will be more able to treat employees consistently where poor health leads to performance, attendance or disability issues.

4224 Sickness records are almost certain to include **sensitive data** (¶5925) and employers must make sure that they comply with the data protection rules (¶5945).

Further, as good practice, employers should (part 2.3 DP Code):
– keep sickness and accident records separate from absence records. Sickness or accident records should not be used for a particular purpose when records of absence can be used instead;

- ensure that the holding and use of sickness and accident records is either with explicit consent or required by health and safety legislation;
- only disclose information from sickness or accident records about a worker's illness, medical condition or injury where there is a legal obligation to do so, where it is necessary for legal proceedings or where the worker has given explicit consent to the disclosure; and
- not make sickness, accident or absence records of individual workers available to other workers, other than to provide managers with information in so far as this is necessary for them to carry out their managerial roles.

Employers are also advised to follow the Data Protection Code's general recommendations with regard to **data management** (¶6000) and its general good practice recommendations with regard to information about their workers' health (see ¶4940).

A. Disciplinary matters

If a prospective employee has **deliberately concealed** a condition, for example a history of mental illness, the contract may be held to be void, especially if the condition recurs. The employer must ensure that in such circumstances he dismisses the employee due to the deception and not his illness. **4230**

If the employee has **deliberately deceived** his employer about his health, be it a deliberate concealment or lie, the employer should use his disciplinary procedure. For example, if an employee rings in sick but was at Wimbledon watching tennis, this may well amount to gross misconduct. This would also be the case if an employee **abuses** his employer's policy on **self-certification** of short-term sickness absence procedure by stating that he was sick when in fact he had been on holiday (as happened in *Bailey v BP Oil Kent Refinery Ltd* [1980] IRLR 287, CA). However, the employer should always investigate whether a holiday, or any other activity that may be causing concern, has actually been recommended by the employee's doctor to aid recuperation. Employers should also consider whether the activity in question is relevant to the employee's sickness: not all illnesses that prevent an individual from carrying out work activities require bed rest. For this reason it is essential that employers carry out a full investigation and follow their disciplinary procedure carefully before making a decision to dismiss. **4231**

EXAMPLE
Dismissal reasonable
In *McCann v Clydebank College* [2010] UKEAT 0061_09_1706, a part-time employee, M, was dismissed after he was caught working in his own business while signed off and receiving sick pay from his employers, C. There was no express rule against working elsewhere while off sick, and C had known that M had other work before his sickness absence began. M argued that:
– he had not been working during hours when he was contracted to work for C; and
– C's investigation methods, which involved putting him under surveillance, were a breach of his right to privacy.
The EAT found that M had not established, on the facts, that he was only working in his own time, and noted that when challenged the employee had not been open about his actions. Further, in any event, where an employer was paying sick pay, it was entitled to object to the employee doing paid work elsewhere, because the employee was able to earn money, and because the other work may delay his recovery. The dismissal was therefore fair in this case, although if the situation had been ambiguous or there had been an innocent misunderstanding, the position might have been different. The allegation regarding the invasion of privacy failed, in part because the decision to dismiss did not depend on the surveillance, and secondly because surveillance was proportionate in this instance.

Dismissal unreasonable
In *Perry v Imperial College Healthcare NHS Trust* [2011] UKEAT 0473_10_2207, an employee on sick leave was unfairly dismissed for misconduct when she carried on with a second part-time job, for which she was still medically fit, without permission from the first employer.

4232 Dismissals on the grounds of conduct may be justified if there has been gross misconduct as a result of **unauthorised absences, malingering** or **persistent, significant and consistent failures** in following the employer's reporting procedures. However, in such circumstances, the employer must ascertain the state of the employee's health to determine if it had any bearing on his actions.

4233 Any failure by the **employer to follow his procedure** will be taken into account, but it should be weighed against all the other circumstances. In *Bailey* (see ¶4231), the employer had failed to comply with the agreed company disciplinary procedure by failing to make contact with the appropriate union official who should have been informed when the dismissal was being contemplated. The Court of Appeal held that although this failure should be taken into account, it should be weighed against all the other circumstances and in these circumstances the dismissal was not unfair. Here, the requirement was not a condition precedent to dismissal but merely that the employer should keep the union official informed of what he was considering so that the official could take such action as he thought fit.

4234 Employers should ensure that they follow the Acas code on discipline and grievances at work. If the employee is successful in bringing a tribunal claim for unfair dismissal, failure to do so may impact on any compensation which may be awarded to the employee.

See chapter 19 for further details on this and also see ¶¶6650+ for dealing with absence.

4235 Although **reasonable adjustments** are only strictly necessary for disabled employees (¶4248), it can be useful to consider making such adjustments for all employees with absence issues that are genuinely related to ill health. Such adjustments could help to demonstrate the general fairness of any subsequent dismissal and also avoid the need to lose otherwise experienced and capable workers. Employers should, however, bear in mind the need for consistency of treatment and should be careful about setting precedents for expensive or problematic adjustments where they are not altogether necessary.

B. Long-term illness

4240 Where an employer is considering the status of an employee who has a long-term illness, he must **investigate** the situation as far as is possible and obtain a medical opinion as to the employee's current and future capability. The employer should discuss the employee's capability with him (once medical evidence has been obtained or after such a request has been refused), so that he is in a better position to make a decision as to whether the employee is likely to return to work, and what the business consequences are for a continued absence.

1. Dismissal

4245 An employer may wish to dismiss an employee who has a long-term illness with **no reasonable expectation of recovery** in an acceptable and reasonable period. Dismissal on the grounds of incapacity is a statutory fair reason for dismissal (¶8450).

In order to avoid liability for unfair dismissal, the employer should ensure that he has undertaken an appropriate medical investigation, consulted with the employee, and considered whether the employee could be employed in some **alternative capacity**. In doing so, he must act reasonably in **all the circumstances**. This includes considering the type of illness, the likely length of continuing absence, and whether recovery is possible within a period that is reasonable and acceptable. This should be balanced against the genuine **business needs of the employer** (*K Spencer v Paragon Wallpapers Ltd* [1976] IRLR 373, EAT). Therefore, it is a balance between the needs of the employer to fill the role and whether he should be expected to wait any longer, and if he should, for how long. As with all unfair dismissal claims, the tribunal will look at whether the employer's response was within the range of reasonable responses that a fair and reasonable employer would make (*Rolls-Royce Ltd v Walpole* [1980] IRLR 343, EAT).

In assessing the fairness of a dismissal, the tribunal can take into account any medical reports obtained by the employer during the notice period (*White v South London Transport Ltd* [1988] ICR 293, EAT).

4246 The fact that an employee has not exhausted his sick pay entitlement will not automatically make his dismissal unfair, as the existence of a contractual sick pay procedure does not indicate that there is a guaranteed period of sickness absence before dismissal will be considered. However, if sick pay is contractual, dismissal before the right to it has ended may be unfair unless the employer has strong evidence that dismissal at that time was justified. Further, automatic dismissal when sick pay entitlement has run out will not necessarily be fair. Note that if dismissal stops or prevents payment under a PHI scheme, this might be in breach of an implied duty (¶1241).

4247 An employee who has been dismissed due to absence on the grounds of sickness has not been discriminated against under the EC disability provisions (*Chacon Navas v Eurest Colectividades SA, case C-13/05* [2007] ICR 1, ECJ). Sickness and disability are two different concepts and cannot be treated in the same way. **Absence due to sickness**, by itself, is not a ground of discrimination. However, although sickness is not, in itself, a disability, employers must consider whether the reason for any sick leave relates to a disability before dismissing an employee on the grounds of incapacity due to such absence(s). If an employee is disabled, the employer is under a duty to make all reasonable adjustments to facilitate the employee's return from sick leave and, if necessary, must also consider whether there is suitable alternative employment (see below). In practice, this will be a helpful approach to take in ensuring that other dismissals relating to sickness absence, regardless of whether disability is involved, are fair.

Disabled employees

4248 If an employee is disabled, his employer must make all **reasonable adjustments** to facilitate his return from long-term sick leave. Further, if necessary, he must also consider whether there is **suitable alternative employment**. If the employer does not do so he will open himself up to a possible disability discrimination claim.

Further, an employer must not treat an employee **less favourably because of the employee's disability** than he treats, or would treat, a person not having that disability (this will amount to "direct discrimination"). An employer must also not treat a disabled person less favourably **because of something arising in consequence of the employee's disability** than he treats, or would treat, another person without that disability (this will amount to "indirect discrimination"), unless he can justify the unfavourable treatment by showing that it was a proportionate means of achieving a legitimate aim. Long-term sickness absence is a common reason for less favourable treatment for a disability-related reason (for example, a dismissal) of a disabled worker. Examples of where an employer's actions in dismissing a worker on long-term sick leave were justified include where a worker was physically incapable of performing the functions of his job due to his disability (*Allen v H Hargrave and Co* [1999] UKEAT 150_99_1405); where the employee was a key worker in a small team whose duties needed to be carried out on a full-time basis and were not suitable for job-sharing or temporary cover; where temporary cover was not considered suitable, reasonable or realistic; where the employee repeatedly stated that she was incapable of returning to work (*NCH Scotland v McHugh* [2006] UKEAT 0010_06_1512); and where an employee was deemed unfit for any duties, even light work, and there was no indication as to when the employee might next be able to work again (here the employer was unable to consider any reasonable adjustments to the employee's working arrangements) (*Joy v Connex South Central* [2002] UKEAT 975_01_1311).

Therefore, before an employer dismisses an employee due to his incapacity, he must consider if the reason for dismissal **relates to a disability**, as, if it does, he must ensure that he does not discriminate against his employee.

> **EXAMPLE** In *H J Heinz Co Ltd v Kenrick* [2000] IRLR 144, EAT, K was frequently off sick. Although his condition was never satisfactorily identified, he told the company's medical adviser that he thought he had chronic fatigue syndrome (CFS). During the last period of absence, K was warned that he was at risk of being dismissed if there was no indication of a likely date for his return. K's doctor could not give a return date. After nearly a year's absence, K was still certified unfit for work and Heinz dismissed him despite the fact that K had asked Heinz to wait until he had seen an immunologist before acting. A diagnosis of CFS was later confirmed.
> Heinz was found liable for disability discrimination, as it should have ascertained whether K was disabled by waiting until he had seen the immunologist. It should then have considered making any reasonable adjustments such as lighter duties or changes to his working hours.

See the disability section in chapter 16 for more details (¶¶5450+).

Medical evidence and investigation

4251 Employers must, as far as they are able, inform themselves of the **true medical position**, and ensure that they are relying on up-to-date medical records, so they can make a rational and informed decision as to whether to dismiss. However, they cannot be expected to be medical experts and the decision to dismiss is not a medical question but one that is answered in the light of the available medical evidence (*East Lindsey District Council v Daubney* [1977] IRLR 181, EAT; *A Links & Co Ltd v Rose* [1991] IRLR 353, CS).

4252 To **obtain medical evidence**, the employer may ask the employee to attend a medical examination by an **occupational health doctor** or adviser. If he does not have a contractual right to do so, the employer must obtain the employee's consent. Furthermore, even where there is a contractual right, it is good practice to obtain the employee's express consent before requiring him to attend a particular examination. In such cases, the employer is not bound by the medical access rules.

Alternatively, if this is not possible or where specialist advice is needed which cannot be provided by any occupational health service, the employer should try to obtain a report from the **employee's own GP**. In such cases, the following **medical access rules** must be complied with (ss 3-5 Access to Medical Reports Act 1988):
– the employee must consent; and
– the employer must inform the employee of his right to withhold his consent, his right to have a copy of the report before his consent is given and his right to amend or correct errors.

Where an employee **refuses to provide unequivocal consent** to his occupational health report/GP/specialist, the employer is entitled to make his decision on the basis of the limited material available to him.

> **EXAMPLE** In *Elmbridge Housing Trust v O'Donoghue* [2004] EWCA Civ 939, O **refused** to provide unequivocal consent to her occupational health report being passed to her employer, EHT, after a **prolonged attempt** by EHT to persuade her otherwise and was deemed to have been fairly dismissed on the grounds of capability after 3 and a half months on sickness absence. The Court held that the dismissal was within EHT's band of reasonable responses given that, without access to the occupational health report, EHT was entitled to conclude that O was incapable on the basis of the limited material available to it.

> **MEMO POINTS** Employers can apply to the county court if a **doctor refuses** to comply with a request for a report (s 8 Access to Medical Reports Act 1988).

4253 It may also be appropriate and necessary to obtain a report from a **specialist** in the relevant field, rather than rely solely on the company doctor and/or the employee's GP (*Crampton v Dacorum Motors Ltd* [1975] IRLR 168, IT). This is especially so when a GP gives an unconfirmed diagnosis or it is one that is required to be made (or is better made) by a specialist. It is important to give well thought out **instructions** in order for the report to be most effective, and issues such as those discussed at ¶4214, in relation to occupational health reports, will be relevant to all specialists, though of course the instructions need to be carefully tailored to the circumstances.

The employee may also be prepared to apply for his actual **health records** made by his doctor in addition to any medical report. These may give a useful insight as to what was being said or reported at the doctor's surgery and ascertaining what drugs the employee is taking (Access to Health Records Act 1990). The doctor can refuse this request if such access would cause harm to the patient (s 4 Access to Health Records Act 1990).

Conflicting reports Where there are conflicting medical reports, the employer may act reasonably if he accepts the less favourable report of an occupational health doctor who knew the nature and importance of the employee's job, particularly with regard to the risks it entailed (in *Singh-Deu v Chloride Metals* [1976] IRLR 56, IT, a paranoid schizophrenic who worked with hazardous materials was fairly dismissed on the medical report of the occupational health doctor despite the fact that a specialist had thought he was capable of resuming work).

Prior consultation

The employer **must consult** with the employee before dismissal unless there are wholly exceptional circumstances, for example to prevent the employee discovering a pessimistic prognosis of which he is unaware (*East Lindsey District Council v Daubney* [1977] IRLR 181, EAT (¶4251); *Eclipse Blinds Ltd v Wright* [1992] IRLR 133, CS). A discussion will enable the situation to be weighed up, bearing in mind the employer's need for work to be done and the employee's need for time to recover his health. Further, discussions and consultations may show facts and circumstances that the employer was unaware of and which may throw new light on to the situation. Alternatively, the employee may wish to seek medical advice on his own account which, when brought to the notice of the employer's medical doctors or advisers, may cause them to change their opinion.

> EXAMPLE In *Eclipse Blinds Ltd v Wright*, W's health had deteriorated and she was often ill and off work. The employer obtained a report from W's doctor which stated that he could not see any possibility of her returning to work in the near future and that her ultimate prognosis was not good.
> As W had told her employer that she thought she was improving and clearly did not know the seriousness of her illness, the director, who took the decision to dismiss her, decided to write to her instead of discussing the situation where it might be difficult to avoid disclosing information about her health. These particular facts led the Court to hold that this was an **exceptional case** where consultation was not required.

In certain cases where the employee has mobility problems, or where it has been difficult to keep in contact with him, a **home visit** may be appropriate. However, the employer should first check with the employee's doctor that the employee is fit to undergo an investigatory process or a welfare visit.

2. Frustration

In relatively rare circumstances, a contract may be brought to an end due to an employee's illness frustrating the contract. In such cases, the contract is **nullified** and the parties cannot choose to keep it alive though they can, naturally, agree to enter into a new contract. If a contract is frustrated, there is no dismissal and, therefore, no possibility of an unfair dismissal claim. Further, the EAT has indicated that a contract may be frustrated even if it contains an ill health termination procedure which has not yet been concluded, as whether the employee has been expressly dismissed is not determinative of whether the contract is frustrated (*Hogan v Cambridgeshire County Council* [1999] UKEAT 382_99_1810).

Frustration only **occurs** when it is no longer practical to regard the contract as continuing and only happens if the employee has been ill for a lengthy period and has no likelihood of return (*Notcutt v Universal Equipment Co (London) Ltd* [1986] IRLR 218, EAT). In particular, a contract cannot be frustrated during the period in which any contractual sick pay is payable if the employee returns to work or is likely to do so (*RA Marshall v Harland & Wolff Ltd* [1972] IRLR 90, NIRC).

4271 The **relevant factors** that a tribunal will take into account are (*Egg Stores (Stamford Hill) Ltd v Leibovici* [1976] IRLR 376, EAT):
– the length of past employment;
– how long it had been expected that the employment would continue;
– the nature of the job;
– the nature of the illness;
– the employer's need for a replacement;
– the risk to the employer of acquiring obligations in respect of redundancy payments or compensation for unfair dismissal to any replacement employee if the employee returns;
– whether wages have continued to be paid;
– the acts and statements of the employer; and
– whether in all the circumstances a reasonable employer could have been expected to wait any longer.

The tribunal will also look at the intention of the parties as their **conduct** may be relevant as evidence to whether the changed circumstances were so fundamental that they went to the root of the contract (*Hogan v Cambridgeshire County Council* [1999] UKEAT 382_99_1810).

EXAMPLE
Frustration
In *Collins v Secretary of State for Trade and Industry* [2000] EAT 1460_99_2203, C, who had worked for many years with a transport company, was signed off work from February 1996 due to a severe injury to his right hand. He received SSP and later incapacity benefit and disability living allowance. He remained "on the books" of his employer, receiving a Christmas voucher and P60s at the end of each tax year showing zero pay. In late 1998/1999 he was offered the choice either to stay on their books or take a redundancy payment. He chose the former. However, the company went into receivership soon afterwards. The EAT held that the contract was frustrated due to his injury and that the Secretary of State therefore was not obliged to pay C's application for a state redundancy payment.

No frustration
In *Jones v Friction Dynamics Ltd (in administration) and ors* [2007] UKEAT 0428_06_2803, J was signed off sick for 6 months in 2001. After that certificate expired J did not return to work, although he was fit to do so. J remained "on the books" of his employer, but did not receive any pay. There was no further contact between J and his employer. The employer company went into administration in 2003 and when the administrator was appointed he wrote to J, dismissing him. The EAT held that J's contract could not have been frustrated as he had been capable of work since late 2001 and that his employment had been terminated by the administrator's letter of dismissal, and not by operation of law. Consequently, J was entitled to a redundancy payment.

4272 However, as frustration could prevent an employee claiming unfair dismissal and/or disability discrimination, and may prevent any permanent health insurance payments, tribunals are reluctant to find a contract has been frustrated (*Williams v Watsons Luxury Coaches Ltd* [1990] IRLR 164, EAT). This is particularly true if the employee was disabled and a reasonable adjustment could have facilitated a return to work or where the contract needs to continue for permanent health insurance payments to be made.

C. Persistent short-term absences

4280 The same considerations as for long-term illnesses apply when dealing with an employee who is persistently off sick with short-term absences, except that a formal medical investigation may not be necessary. Where there are unconnected intermittent periods of absence, the employer is not obliged to make **medical enquiries** as such investigations are rarely fruitful because of the transient nature of the employee's symptoms and complaints (*Lynock v Cereal Packaging Ltd* [1988] IRLR 510, EAT, below). However, any indication that there may be an underlying cause should be investigated in the same way as it would be in relation to long-term absence (¶¶4251+).

> **EXAMPLE** In *International Sports Co Ltd v Thomson* [1980] IRLR 340, EAT, T was off sick for about 25% of the time in the last 18 months of her employment due to a series of minor ailments mostly supported by sick notes. The acceptable level of absence as agreed with her union was 8%. T was issued with four separate warnings (persistent absence was dealt with under the employer's disciplinary procedure) over nearly a year, with the final warning stating that if there was no improvement she would be dismissed. T did not improve and was dismissed. The company had consulted its occupational doctor prior to dismissal who had advised that there was no useful purpose in examining T because she had no illnesses that could be subsequently verified. Further, on examining the sick notes, the occupational doctor could not see any common link between the illnesses. The EAT held that this was reasonable behaviour by the company and that it could not be expected to investigate the illnesses further.

4281 All situations of persistent short-term **absence should be treated** with sympathy, understanding and compassion (*Lynock v Cereal Packaging Ltd* [1988] IRLR 510, EAT). However, if the employee has an unacceptable attendance record and has, despite **cautions**, failed to improve, dismissal may be appropriate and this is capable of constituting a fair reason ("some other substantial reason") for unfair dismissal purposes (¶8530). Cautions should be given using the employer's sickness procedure rather than giving a disciplinary warning unless the absences are not due to genuine sickness. The employer should firstly give a **fair review** of the poor attendance record and the reasons for it and allow the employee an opportunity to make representations before issuing any cautions.

The employee should also be cautioned when he has reached a stage when it has become impossible to continue with his employment, i.e. when a reasonable employer is entitled to say "**enough is enough**". If there is **no adequate improvement**, the employer may be justified in dismissing him (*International Sports Co Ltd v Thomson* [1980] IRLR 340, EAT). In such cases, the employee does not have to be incapacitated at the time of the dismissal (*Lynock v Cereal Packaging Ltd*, above).

4282 Employers should ensure that they follow the Acas code on discipline and grievances at work. If the employee is successful in bringing a tribunal claim for unfair dismissal, failure to do so may impact on any compensation which may be awarded to the employee.

See chapter 19 for further details on this and also see ¶¶6650+ for dealing with absence.

4883 As with long-term illness dismissals, the employer must have sufficient grounds to fairly dismiss the employee and must act reasonably in all the circumstances. As with all unfair dismissal claims, the tribunal will look at whether the employer's response was within the range of reasonable responses of a fair and reasonable employer (*Rolls-Royce Ltd v Walpole* [1980] IRLR 343, EAT). The employer should be clear as to the reason for dismissal because procedural requirements vary according to whether the reason is poor attendance (conduct) or sickness (capacity). The courts have held that, in relation to persistent short-term absences, considerations should include the nature of the illnesses, the likelihood of recurrence, the existence of any underlying sickness that has resulted in the persistent absences, the length of the absences, and the periods of good health in between such absences. These factors should be balanced against the genuine business needs of the employer.

CHAPTER 14

Rights of parents and carers

OUTLINE

	¶¶
SECTION 1 Maternity rights 4410	
A Time off for antenatal care 4411	
B Maternity leave............................. 4420	
1 Starting leave............................. 4423	
Employee notification and evidence 4423	
Employer notification of maternity leave end date 4428	
Automatic commencement 4430	
Prohibition against work for two weeks after birth............................ 4433	
2 Terms and conditions during leave 4435	
3 Contact during leave 4445	
4 Ending leave 4449	
Right to return 4450	
Employer notice of end date 4457	
Employee notice for earlier return 4459	
5 Type of job on return..................... 4465	
Ordinary maternity leave 4469	
Additional maternity leave 4474	
C Maternity pay 4480	
SECTION 2 Adoption rights 4520	
A Adoption leave............................. 4521	
Eligibility 4522	
1 Starting leave............................. 4524	
Employee notification and evidence 4524	
Employer notification of adoption leave end date 4528	
2 Rights during leave and return to work 4530	
Terminated placement 4532	
B Adoption pay 4554	
SECTION 3 Paternity rights 4570	
A Standard paternity leave 4571	
Eligibility 4574	
Employee notice and evidence............ 4576	

	¶¶
Rights during leave and on return 4583	
B Additional paternity leave 4585	
1 Starting leave............................. 4587	
2 Rights during leave and return to work 4595	
C Statutory paternity pay/Additional statutory paternity pay 4600	
SECTION 4 Parental leave 4620	
A Eligibility and minimum standards 4625	
B Procedure................................... 4650	
Fallback scheme............................. 4660	
SECTION 5 Right to request flexible working 4690	
Carers for children 4694	
Carers for adults 4695	
A Making a request 4700	
B Procedure for considering request ... 4710	
Right to be accompanied at a meeting ... 4720	
C Withdrawal of request..................... 4725	
SECTION 6 Time off to care for dependants 4740	
Eligibility 4742	
Notice 4744	
Duration 4746	
SECTION 7 Remedies 4760	
1 Right not to be discriminated against for relying on parents' and carers' rights 4765	
2 Right to remedies for employer failure to give or apply parents' and carers' rights 4780	

4400 Parents and carers are entitled to **special rights at work**.

The structure of statutory parents' and carers' rights follows a broad logic, depending on the nature of the person being cared for, and the relationship between them and the parent or carer. Thus the person with the greatest rights is an expectant mother, who has the right to take paid leave for antenatal care, in addition to periods of paid and unpaid leave following the birth of her child. At the other end of the spectrum is someone who simply cares for a neighbour or friend. Such a person is unlikely to be able to take more than brief periods of unpaid leave.

Some of these rights, including a mother's right to maternity pay, have been in place for many years. Some have been introduced more recently. Parental leave was introduced in 1999, paternity and adoption pay and the right to request flexible working in 2003. The rights of parents, adopters and carers to take paid or unpaid leave were extended by the Work and Families Act 2006. For example, the Maternity and Parental Leave etc and the Paternity and Adoption Leave (Amendment) Regulations 2008 (SI 2008/1966) gave employees on maternity and adoption leave the same rights to their contractual terms and conditions throughout their leave. This significant change has greatly reduced the difference between ordinary and additional leave. More recently, the Additional Paternity Leave Regulations 2010 gave parents of babies due on or after 3 April 2011, and parents who have received notification on or after 3 April 2011 that they have been matched with a child for adoption, a right to additional paternity leave (SI 2010/1055).

> MEMO POINTS 1. The Government has announced **proposals to introduce a new system** of flexible parental leave from 2015 to "encourage fathers to take a greater role in caring for their babies and enable working families to be able to share the leave and pay that is currently only available for the mother". The proposals are:
> – once the early weeks of maternity and paternity leave have ended, parents will be able to share the overall leave allowance between them and leave would be able to be taken in a number of different blocks with both parents being able to take leave at the same time, although employers would be able to ensure that the leave is taken in one continuous period if agreement cannot be reached. Subject to qualifying conditions, working parents will be able to share up to 50 (out of 52) weeks of the leave and 37 (out of 39) weeks of pay that is currently available to the mother;
> – paternity leave will remain at 2 weeks, though the Government will "take powers" to extend paid paternity leave and to make it more flexible at a later date;
> – fathers and partners of pregnant women will be able to take unpaid time off to attend 2 antenatal appointments;
> – from March 2013, unpaid parental leave will be increased from 13 to 18 weeks in order to comply with EU legislation (EU Parental Leave Directive 2010/18), which repeals and replaces the Parental Leave Directive (EU Parental Leave Directive 1996/34), and in 2015 the age limit on unpaid parental leave will increase from 5 years to 18 years, which will allow each parent the right to take up to 18 weeks of unpaid parental leave for each child under 18; and
> – adoption leave and pay will be changed to be more in line with the leave and pay rights that birth parents benefit from: statutory adoption leave would become a day 1 right, statutory adoption pay would be enhanced to 90% of the primary adopter's salary for the first 6 weeks, and working couples who adopt would also be able to opt in to the flexible parental system if they meet the qualifying conditions in the same way that birth parents do. Parents of children born via a surrogate who are able to apply for a parental order will also be eligible for statutory adoption leave and pay and for flexible parental leave and pay, provided they meet the qualifying criteria, as well as unpaid time off to attend two antenatal appointments.
> The Government is also considering making arrangements for working parents who do not meet the qualifying requirements to receive statutory payments. This would not be introduced before 2018 to allow time for development and to ensure the payments fit appropriately with the forthcoming new welfare benefit, Universal Credit (a new single payment for people who are looking for work or who are on a low income), which the Government plans to launch next year to replace income-based Jobseeker's Allowance, income-related Employment and Support Allowance, Income Support, Child Tax Credits Working, Tax Credits, and Housing Benefit.
> Any further developments will be covered by our updating service.
> 2. The Government has also announced **proposals to extend** the right to make a **flexible working request** to all employees with 26 weeks' continuous service, irrespective of the reason for request, from 2014. The statutory procedure for considering requests will be replaced with a new duty upon employers to consider requests in a reasonable manner, within a reasonable period of time. Any further developments will be covered by our updating service.

4401 Subject to satisfying eligibility criteria, new parents are entitled to statutory **paid leave**. With the exception of the first 6 weeks of maternity pay, which are paid at a higher rate (¶4493), statutory maternity pay, maternity allowance, statutory adoption pay and statutory paternity pay are all paid at a **set rate**, which is currently £135.45 per week. This is likely to **increase from** 7 April 2013 and any new rate will be covered by our updating service.

MEMO POINTS With regard to the set rate, if 90% of the **employee's average weekly earnings is lower** than this rate then this amount should be paid.

4402 Employers can choose to give **more favourable contractual or non-contractual terms**, for example longer leave and contractual paid leave. **Composite rights** will be formed of the most favourable elements of any enhanced right and the statutory minimum requirements. The same applies to any statutory procedural requirements and, consequently, if an enhanced term is silent with regard to any procedural matter or has a more onerous requirement, the statutory procedural rules will apply (with the exception of parental leave, which has slightly different rules (¶4650)).

4403 **Terms used** For ease of reference, the following codes are also used:
- ML: maternity leave;
- CML: compulsory maternity leave;
- OML: ordinary maternity leave;
- AML: additional maternity leave;
- SMP: statutory maternity pay;
- AAL: additional adoption leave;
- AL: adoption leave;
- OAL: ordinary adoption leave;
- SAP: statutory adoption pay;
- PAL: paternity leave;
- APAL: additional paternity leave;
- SPP: statutory paternity pay;
- ASPP: additional statutory paternity pay;
- PL: parental leave; and
- KIT: keeping in touch.

SECTION 1

Maternity rights

4410 The following table summarises the main rights of mothers to ordinary and additional leave and to statutory maternity pay.

	ORDINARY MATERNITY LEAVE (OML)	ADDITIONAL MATERNITY LEAVE (AML)	STATUTORY MATERNITY PAY (SMP)
QUALIFICATION FOR RIGHT	All pregnant employees		Earn at least NIC lower earnings limit (¶6955) for 8 weeks up to and including the 15th week before the week the baby is due
QUALIFYING PERIOD	None		26 weeks' continuous employment up to and including qualifying week
DURATION	Up to 26 weeks	Up to 26 weeks from end of OML	Up to 39 weeks

	ORDINARY MATERNITY LEAVE (OML)	ADDITIONAL MATERNITY LEAVE (AML)	STATUTORY MATERNITY PAY (SMP)
RATE OF PAY	n/a		For first 6 weeks: earnings-related rate. Week 7 onwards: set rate.
START DATE	Either can be taken from 11th week before the week the baby is due, or automatic on birth or absence due to pregnancy-related illness during 4 weeks before the week the baby is due	At end of OML	Start of OML
NOTICE TO TAKE	Before end of 15th week before the week the baby is due (employer must respond within 28 days setting out when due back)		28 days before start date, usually satisfied by giving notice to take leave
EVIDENCE FOR ENTITLEMENT	If requested, maternity certificate (MAT B1) or other written document. If so this will also satisfy SMP evidence requirement.		Maternity certificate, but can accept any document, signed by a doctor or midwife, that includes date baby is due
TERMS AND CONDITIONS DURING LEAVE	All terms except remuneration remain the same		n/a
WORKING DURING LEAVE	On agreement, employee can do up to 10 days' work during maternity leave (although not during her compulsory maternity leave period)		n/a
NOTICE TO RETURN	Once on leave, 8 weeks' notice of employee's intention to return unless mother intends to take full 52 weeks of ordinary and additional leave, in which case no notice is required		n/a
JOB ON RETURN	Right to return to same job	Right to return to same job unless not reasonably practical, in which case most suitable employment	n/a
ENFORCEMENT AND REMEDIES	Right not to suffer detriment and right not to be unfairly dismissed in relation to above rights		

A. Time off for antenatal care

4411 Pregnant employees have the right to take paid leave to attend antenatal care (s 55 ERA 1996). The care must be arranged by appointment and on the advice of a GP, midwife or health visitor. The care may take the form of appointments with a nurse or doctor. The guidance notes published by the Department for Business, Innovation and Skills (BIS) suggest that antenatal care is not restricted to medical examinations and could, for example, include relaxation or parenting classes if either was medically advised.

> **MEMO POINTS** The Government has announced **proposals** to extend the right to time off for antenatal care so that fathers and prospective parents of children born via surrogacy will be entitled to unpaid time off to attend two antenatal appointments. Any further developments will be covered by our updating service.

4412 To be eligible for this right, the employee must **inform her employer** that she is pregnant and that she has an antenatal appointment for which she needs time off to attend. For the **second and subsequent appointments** the employer can also ask her to produce:
– a certificate from a GP or midwife or health visitor, stating that the employee is pregnant; and
– an appointment card or some other document showing that the appointment has been made.

> **MEMO POINTS** Evidence usually takes the form of a **maternity certificate** (MAT B1, see ¶4487).

4413 Employers must **not unreasonably refuse** to permit employees to take such time off (s 57 ERA 1996). There may be circumstances where the employer could reasonably refuse time off, for example if the employee could have reasonably made her appointment outside working hours (*Gregory v Tudsbury Ltd* [1982] IRLR 267, IT). However, each case will be decided on its merits and it is unlikely that an employer could reasonably expect an employee to make an appointment outside working hours given that she will probably have little or no control over the appointment times. If she does have some choice, it may be considered reasonable for her to organise them, if she can, at the beginning or end of her working day.

There may also be circumstances where it may be reasonable for the employer to re-arrange the employee's working schedule to make up the time, especially if she is working part-time. However, as this may give rise to a claim for discrimination, unless the employee wants to make up time, it is advisable that the employer does not require it.

4414 Employees have the right to be remunerated for time off at the appropriate hourly rate (s 56 ERA 1996). See ¶3935.

B. Maternity leave

4420 Employees (including apprentices) (reg 2(1) SI 1999/3312) who are pregnant are **entitled** to take up to 26 weeks' ordinary maternity leave and 26 weeks' additional maternity leave, making a total of 52 weeks of maternity leave (ML). The employee can choose when to start her maternity leave as long as she gives adequate notice, unless her maternity leave automatically commences (¶4430). The **earliest** day that leave can begin is the 11th week before the week the baby is due (called the "expected week of confinement" (EWC)) (s 71 ERA 1996; reg 4 SI 1999/3312) and the **latest** day that leave can begin is on the day after birth.

> **EXAMPLE** If Employee A's baby is due on Thursday 28 March 2013, the week the baby is due (the EWC) will start on Sunday 24 March and the earliest A can start her maternity leave is Sunday 6 January 2013. If she chooses to start her leave at this date, her maternity leave will end on Saturday 4 January 2014 (her ordinary maternity leave ending on Saturday 6 July and her additional maternity leave beginning on Sunday 7 July).

> **MEMO POINTS** 1. The **week the baby is due** is defined as the week beginning with midnight between Saturday and Sunday in which it is expected that childbirth will occur.
> 2. The Government has announced **proposals** to introduce a new system of flexible parental leave from 2015. Under the proposals, once the early weeks of maternity and paternity leave have ended, parents will be able to share the overall leave allowance between them and leave would be able to be taken in a number of different blocks with both parents being able to take leave at the same time, although employers would be able to ensure that the leave is taken in one continuous period if agreement cannot be reached. Under the new regime, mothers whose partners also meet eligibility criteria can convert the balance of their maternity leave and pay entitlement to flexible parental leave and pay which they can take concurrently or in turns. With an employer's agreement, flexible parental leave can also be broken into 1 week blocks. Any further developments will be covered by our updating service.

1. Starting leave

Employee notification and evidence

4423 **Notification** The employee must notify her employer, **before** the end of the 15th week before the week the baby is due (reg 4 SI 1999/3312):
- that she is pregnant;
- the week the baby is due; and
- her proposed maternity leave start date.

These requirements can be **given separately**.

4424 In return for the employee notifying her employer, her **employer must reply**, setting out when her full maternity leave will end (¶¶4428, 4457).

4425 **Failure to give notice** Any failure to give adequate notice must be disregarded if it was **not reasonably practicable** for the employee to notify her employer correctly and in time, for example, because she does not realise she is pregnant or she only starts to work for her employer after notification was due (reg 4 SI 1999/3312). In such cases, she should notify her employer as soon as reasonably practicable, i.e. when she finds out she is pregnant or starts employment.

> MEMO POINTS   If it should have been **reasonably practicable**, the employer may be able to insist that the employee postpones her start date to ensure that she gives at least 3 weeks' notice (i.e. the period from the end of the 15th week (the latest date to give notice) to the beginning of the 11th week before the week the baby is due (the earliest date to start leave)).

4426 **Changing start date** The employee can change her start date (reg 4(1A) SI 1999/3312). If she wants to bring her original start date **forward**, she must give at least 28 days' notice before her new start date. If she wants to take her original start date **back**, she must give at least 28 days' notice before the original start date. She can choose to further vary the start date using the same procedure. Each change must be notified in writing if requested.

4427 **Evidence of entitlement** An employee is entitled to maternity leave provided that she notifies her employer of her pregnancy, the expected week of childbirth and the date on which she intends her leave period to start. Her **employer may request** that she produces for the employer's inspection a certificate from a registered medical practitioner or midwife.

> MEMO POINTS   Evidence usually takes the form of a **maternity certificate** (MAT B1, see ¶4487).

Employer notification of maternity leave end date

4428 As a result of an employee's notice (¶4423) of her proposed or varied start date (or of the automatic commencement of her maternity leave), her employer must give her notice of when her full maternity leave (i.e. her ordinary maternity leave and additional maternity leave) will end (reg 7(6) SI 1999/3312).

This document must be sent **within** 28 days of notification unless the employee has notified her employer of a change to her start date, in which case the employer must notify her of the new end date within 28 days of the varied start date.

> MEMO POINTS   If the employer **fails to notify** in time, he will not be able to reprimand his employee for coming back too early or too late (¶4457).

Automatic commencement

4430 Regardless of whether the employee has specified a start date in accordance with the notice requirements above, her maternity leave will automatically commence the **day after** either of the following two situations (reg 6 SI 1999/3312):
1. The employee is **absent** wholly or partly **because of her pregnancy at any time from** the beginning of the 4th week before the week the baby is due. Technically, as the employee

need only be absent because of the pregnancy, she need only be a few minutes late for work due to, for example pregnancy-related fatigue, for this to automatically start maternity leave. However, the BIS guide suggests that short periods including occasional days of absence can be disregarded at the **employer's discretion** if the employee wishes to defer the start of her maternity leave to her chosen date.

Leave due to illness that is **unrelated to pregnancy** (for example, flu) must be treated as sick leave and does not automatically commence maternity leave.

2. The employee has **given birth**.

In both circumstances, the employee must **notify** her employer that she is absent from work wholly or partly because of pregnancy as soon as it is reasonably practicable. The employer must in return give her notice as to when her maternity leave will end.

4431

Prohibition against work for two weeks after birth

Employers must not permit employees to work in the 2 weeks after the date of the birth (s 72 ERA 1996; reg 8 SI 1999/3312). This is called **compulsory maternity leave** (CML). This restriction applies to any type of work and not just attending work at the workplace. For example, an employee must not be permitted to work at home or from the hospital during this period. Any breach will result in the employer being liable for a criminal offence unless the employer can show that he did not require the employee to work and had no intention that she should do so.

4433

CML counts as part of the employee's ordinary maternity leave and the same entitlements and conditions apply. Indeed, as ordinary maternity leave commences automatically on birth in any event (¶4430), CML should not have an impact on maternity leave except for the criminal prohibition on doing any work during this period. The prohibition does not apply during the rest of maternity leave.

Factory workers must not be permitted to work for 4 weeks after the date of birth (s 205 Public Health Act 1936).

> MEMO POINTS Under European proposals to amend EC Directive 1992/85, the period of CML is likely to be increased to 6 weeks. Any further developments will be covered by our updating service.

2. Terms and conditions during leave

The following are the statutory minimum requirements (s 71 ERA 1996; reg 9 SI 1999/3312 and amended by SI 2008/1966). As with every aspect of family-friendly rights, the employer can provide for more favourable contractual or non-contractual terms.

4435

The employee's **contract of employment continues** during leave and she is:
– entitled to the benefit of the express and implied terms and conditions of employment which would have applied if she had not been on leave; and
– bound by any obligations arising under these terms and conditions except for those that require her to work and attend her place of work.

Relevant terms include all matters connected with the employee's employment, whether or not they arise under her contract, **except** for those concerning remuneration. For example, failing to notify an employee of a vacancy that had arisen during her maternity leave will breach the implied term of trust and confidence if the vacancy was one for which the employee would have believed she could apply (it does not matter whether her application would have been successful (*Visa International Service Association v Paul* [2004] IRLR 42, EAT)).

As the contract continues, any period of ordinary leave will count towards the employee's statutory **continuity of employment**. The same applies to any contractual rights that are based on continuity, for example an occupational pension scheme or seniority.

4436

Remuneration during leave An employer is not required to pay an employee her normal remuneration during her maternity leave. Remuneration is defined as wages or salary and includes any **payment related to the employee's performance**, for example bonuses,

4438

commissions or profit-related pay (reg 9(3) SI 1999/3312). In such circumstances, the employee will only be entitled to whatever part of the bonus or commission relates to the time she was at work before she took leave, plus an additional 2 weeks on account of the CML period. She must be paid this pro-rata amount even if it is paid while she is absent (ss 73, 74 EqA 2010).

Any **bonus** which is **not work-related**, i.e. given equally to all staff (or a distinct group of staff of which the employee is a member) and is not related to individual performance, should not be treated as remuneration and must be paid in full.

4439 Remuneration does **not include** all other benefits such as **paid annual leave** over and above the statutory minimum or **benefits in kind**, for example a company car or private health cover. Nor does it cover payments made in lieu of a benefit, for example a car allowance. Consequently, an employee is entitled to these benefits throughout her maternity leave.

> MEMO POINTS   Current HMRC guidance suggests that benefits provided via salary sacrifice should continue at the employer's expense without any sacrifice being made from SMP.

4440 **Pension benefits**   Social security law provides that employer contributions to an occupational pension scheme must be maintained during paid maternity leave (Sch 5 para 5 Social Security Act 1989). If the benefits are based on a percentage of earnings, the employer's payments should continue to be based on a percentage of the employee's full salary rather than a percentage of maternity pay (whether that be statutory or contractual maternity pay), whereas the employee's payments should be based upon the maternity pay actually received.

4442 **Annual leave**   The employee will be entitled to any enhanced **contractual** leave that accrues. Even if there are no enhanced terms, the statutory entitlement to annual leave still accrues.

Annual leave cannot be **taken during** maternity leave.

The Court of Justice of the European Union has confirmed that a worker is entitled to take her annual leave at a time **other than during** her **maternity leave** and has held that this principle should not be adjusted where the woman's maternity leave period coincides with a period of annual leave specified in a collective agreement (e.g. when there is a general shutdown of the workplace) (*Merino Gomez v Continental Industrias del Caucho SA* [2004] IRLR 407, ECJ).

> MEMO POINTS   1. This may cause practical problems where an employee takes maternity leave that stretches over 2 different leave years, since, as a general rule, untaken statutory leave cannot be carried over to the next leave year unless preferential contractual terms apply (¶4018). However, it is **recommended** that employers follow the guidance of the Court and **allow employees to carry over** statutory annual leave where being on maternity leave prevented the employee from taking it during the preceding leave year.
> 2. The Government is consulting on **proposals** to make the necessary amendments to the Working Time Regulations in light of Court of Justice of the European Union (CJEU) decisions and is proposing to:
> – allow, as required by the CJEU rulings, the carrying over of annual leave due to maternity, paternity, parental or adoption leave for the full 5.6 weeks' entitlement per year; and
> – make other changes to allow employers to "buy out" untaken leave by agreement with regard to the additional UK entitlement (1.6 weeks per year) and require employees to carry over leave on justifiable business grounds also in relation to the additional UK entitlement (1.6 weeks per year).
> Further developments will be covered by our updating service when available.

3. Contact during leave

4445 The general rule is that an employee cannot remain on maternity leave during a week in which she works for her employer. Beginning work will bring her leave and pay or allowance to an end.

However, some contact, as set out below, is allowed between employers and employees during the maternity leave period. While the employee is on maternity leave an employer may make **reasonable contact** with her, and an employee may make contact with her employer. What constitutes "reasonable" contact will vary according to the circumstances, including such factors as: the nature of the work and the employee's post, any agreement that the employer and employee might have reached before maternity leave began as to contact; and whether either party needs to communicate important information to the other, such as news of changes at the workplace that might affect the employee on her return.

MEMO POINTS In *Gardner v BBT Thermotechnology UK Ltd*, ET/1307647/07, the claimant was subjected to harassment by the employer when they repeatedly and unreasonably asked her when she intended to return from maternity leave, and threatened disciplinary action if she failed to reply.

Keeping in Touch days An employee's entitlement to maternity leave and pay (or allowance) will not be jeopardised where she **agrees to work for** up to 10 days of her leave, known as Keeping in Touch (KIT) days (reg 9 SI 2006/2014, which adds reg 12A SI 1999/3312; reg 3(3) SI 2006/2379, which adds reg 9A SI 1986/1960; and reg 4(1) SI 2006/2379, which amends reg 2(1)(a) SI 1987/416). **4447**

Work may take the **form** of any activity designed to help the employee keep in touch with her workplace. It is not limited to her usual job and can be used for training or other events, for example attending conferences, undertaking a training activity, or attending a team meeting. It may also be helpful for her to use some KIT days to ease her return to work. Any work carried out on any day shall constitute a day's work (reg 12A(2) SI 1999/3312). In other words, any **part of a day** worked as a KIT day, even as short a period as 30 minutes, will be counted as a whole day.

The work must be by **agreement** between the parties.

As KIT days allow work to be done under the employee's contract of employment, the employee is entitled to be **paid** for the work. The rate of pay is a matter for agreement with the employer, and may be set out in the employment contract or agreed on a case-by-case basis. The employer will need to bear in mind his duties to pay at least the national minimum wage (¶2865) and to ensure that women and men receive equal pay for work of equal value (¶5650).

It should be noted that an employee cannot be required to take up KIT days nor is the employer required to offer them.

MEMO POINTS KIT days must not be worked in the first 2 weeks after giving birth (¶4433).

4. Ending leave

An employee has the right to return to work when her maternity leave has ended. If she does not wish to return to work, she must give notice in accordance with her contract. However, as long as the employee specifies the date on which she wishes to terminate the contract (for example, the date she was due back at work after maternity leave), her maternity leave and entitlement to statutory maternity pay and to accrue annual leave and other benefits continues to up this date. **4449**

Right to return

An employee has the right to return to work when her maternity leave has ended. As long as an employee **returns immediately** after the leave period or has given the requisite notice to return earlier, she has exercised her right to return. **4450**

Where an employee **fails to return** without good reason on the specified date it may be a disciplinary matter. Disciplinary action should not be taken lightly, however. If the employee has a good reason (for example, illness) for not returning on the specified date, any dismissal will be a breach of contract and is also likely to constitute pregnancy-related discrimination (*Halfpenny v IGE Medical Systems Ltd* [1999] IRLR 177, CA).

4451 If the employer does **not allow the employee** to **return** or to return to a job to which she is entitled, the employee is deemed to have been **unfairly dismissed** unless the employer can justify his actions. Further, if the employer proposes a material change in the employee's job as a condition of return, this may also give rise to a claim for **constructive dismissal**. A claim may arise even before the employee is due to return if the employer has made it plain that there is to be a material change (*Nelson v Kingston Cables Distributors Ltd* [1999] UKEAT 662_99_2809).

4453 **Redundancy** Special rules apply where, during leave, it is not practicable by reason of redundancy for the employer to continue to employ the employee under her existing contract of employment (reg 10 SI 1999/3312). In such circumstances, the employer must offer the employee any **suitable and appropriate vacancies** that are available. The employee is entitled to be offered such an alternative before the end of her employment under her existing contract and, if accepted, the new job will take effect immediately on the existing contract's termination. This requirement takes **precedence** over offering suitable vacancies to any other employees who have been selected for redundancy. It is no defence for the employer to argue that such an offer would be economically undesirable (*Community Task Force v Rimmer* [1986] IRLR 203, EAT).

These special rules apply once an employee has been **selected for redundancy**. There should be no special treatment in assessing who should be selected for redundancy (*Eversheds Legal Services Ltd v De Belin* [2011] UKEAT 0352_10_0604).

> EXAMPLE In *Eversheds Legal Services Ltd v De Belin*, the EAT held that a male employee was discriminated against when his female colleague was given a maximum score in one element of a redundancy exercise. The maximum score was given to her on the basis that she was on maternity leave and had no performance records for the relevant period in that element of the scoring matrix. This score was crucial in determining who would be selected for redundancy as the scoring gap between the two employees in question was narrow. The EAT held that awarding a maximum score went beyond what was reasonable and proportionate in the circumstances, and for this aspect of the scoring process the employer should have considered less discriminatory ways to assess performance e.g. the employer could have looked at both employees' performances in the pre-maternity leave period. The male employee had been discriminated against on the grounds of his sex.

> MEMO POINTS Similar provisions requiring preferential treatment in a redundancy situation, in respect of suitable alternative employment, also apply to those on adoption and additional paternity leave. It is unclear how an employer with only one suitable alternative vacancy should act if faced with more than one employee with such a competing right. It is suggested in that situation that the employer might choose to offer the vacancy first to whichever of the employees it is most suitable for.

4454 The **new contract** of employment must be:
– for work that is of a kind which is suitable and appropriate for the employee. Consequently, the employer will have to take into account any added domestic responsibilities the employee may have and an increase in travelling time and additional childcare costs may mean that an alternative job is not suitable; and
– on terms that are not substantially less favourable to the employee as to her capacity, place of work and other terms and conditions.

Alternative employment can be with her employer, his successor, or an associated employer.

4455 If there is a **suitable vacancy** and the employer does not offer it to the employee, the dismissal will be automatically unfair. If there is **no suitable vacancy** in accordance with these special rules, it is open for an employer to dismiss on the grounds of redundancy during a maternity leave period (*Calor Gas Ltd v Bray* [2005] UKEAT 0633_04_1209).

> EXAMPLE In *Simpson v Endsleigh Insurance Services Ltd and ors* [2010] UKEAT 0544_09_2708, an employee, S, worked in one of the employer's retail premises in London as an insurance consultant. While she was on leave, the employer decided to restructure the business, closing all retail outlets and operating from call centres in Cheltenham, Burnley and Northern Ireland. There were vacancies at all of these call centres, but although the employer sent S details, it did not offer her any of them. S claimed that this was a breach of her right to be offered any suitable vacancy if her job became

> redundant while she was away on maternity leave. The EAT held that it was for the employer to decide whether any vacancies were suitable for an employee absent on maternity leave, based on what they knew of the employee's circumstances. In this case the employee had not expressed any significant interest in any jobs outside London, and had not applied for any of the vacancies; in the circumstances it was reasonable to conclude that the vacancies were not suitable. There was therefore no breach of the obligation to offer her a job.

Notice requirements regarding return date

Employer notice of end date As a result of an employee's notice of her proposed or varied start date (or of the automatic commencement of her maternity leave), her **employer** must give her **notice** of when her leave will end (¶4428). **4457**

If the employer **fails** to notify in time, he cannot complain or reprimand his employee for coming back:
− too early (i.e. without giving at least 28 days' notice that she wishes to come back before the end of her leave); or
− too late (i.e. after the leave has ended) where the employee reasonably believed that her leave had not ended, or, where the employer has given less than 28 days' notice, it was not reasonably practicable for the employee to return on that date.

Employee notice for earlier return An employee does not have to give notice of her return where she intends to return immediately after her full leave entitlement ends. **4459**

However, if she wishes to return earlier, she **must give** 8 weeks' notice. Further, if an employee goes on to **change her mind** as to her expected date of return, she will have to give her employer not less than 8 weeks' notice ending with the original date of return (reg 11 SI 1999/3312).

Failure to give proper notice entitles her employer to postpone her return until the notice requirement has been satisfied or her leave entitlement ends, whichever is earlier.

5. Type of job on return

The **type of job** an employee will be entitled to return to will depend on whether she returns after ordinary maternity leave or additional maternity leave. **4465**

It should be noted that employees may wish to return on **different terms**, for example part-time or on a different working pattern. An employee returning from maternity leave has the right to request flexible working (¶4690). It should also be noted that an employer's refusal to permit an employee to return part-time or to a job share may result in indirect discrimination if there was no justification for insisting on full-time work (*Coyle v Georgiou* [2001] UKEAT 535_00_1501; *British Telecommunications plc v Roberts and Longstaffe* [1996] IRLR 601, EAT). **4466**

Ordinary maternity leave

An employee on ordinary maternity leave is **entitled** to return to the same job in which she was employed before her absence (reg 18(1) SI 1999/3312). For these purposes the job must be identical in terms of its (s 235(1) ERA 1996; reg 2 SI 1999/3312): **4469**
− **nature** (in accordance with the contract of employment);
− **capacity** (for example, seniority); and
− **place** of work.

The employee is entitled to return with the same **seniority**, **pension** and **similar rights** that she would have been entitled to if she had not been absent, and on no less favourable terms and conditions (s 71(4), (7) ERA 1996). Therefore, an employee is entitled to any pay increases or other enhanced terms that she would have received had she not been absent.

> **EXAMPLE**
>
> **Same seniority**
> In *Edgell v Lloyd's Register of Shipping* [1977] IRLR 463, IT, before taking maternity leave, E was employed as a bookkeeper with authority to sign cheques and reported to the manager (although these aspects were not part of her contractual job description). On her return, E was offered a post as bookkeeper on the same grade but with no authority to sign cheques and reporting to a supervisor. The changes were held to be administrative resulting from a reorganisation while she was on leave and, therefore, not contractual. As a result, she had been offered the same job with the same seniority.
>
> **Not same seniority**
> In *McFadden v Greater Glasgow Passenger Transport Executive* [1977] IRLR 327, IT, before taking maternity leave, M was employed as an established grade CG3 clerk. When she returned to work, M was told her position had been filled and she was placed in another department as a supernumerary i.e. an unestablished grade CG3 clerk. The tribunal held that M had not been allowed to return to the same job.

4470 Likewise, if a contractual term has been validly **changed to her detriment** during her leave, she will be bound by it (for example, if a collective agreement has changed her contract and reduced the time that can be taken during a lunch break).

4471 If the contract allows for a **range of work** the employee can perform, and the duties within this range are specific, then the employee may be required to do different duties from those that she had prior to her absence on ordinary maternity leave (*Blundell v Governing Body of St Andrew's Catholic Primary School and anor* [2007] ICR 1451, EAT).

> **EXAMPLE** In *Blundell v Governing Body of St Andrew's Catholic Primary School and anor*, a primary school teacher was employed before maternity leave teaching a reception class (pupils aged 4-5). On her return, she was asked to teach a year two class (pupils aged 6-7). Her employer justified this request by saying that it was a settled principle of job allocation in her school that teachers ordinarily changed classes every two years. The EAT agreed that the teacher was employed to teach more widely than merely to a reception class, and in consequence her employer had indeed allowed her to return to the same job.

4472 Where the contract allows for **mobility**, the employer may be able to require her to change her place of work. However, the employer must take into account the burdens which will inevitably exist for the employee simply because she has a young infant making new demands upon her. Offering a job at a different workplace may therefore be unreasonable.

An employer must also be careful that he does not discriminate against her in requiring her to attend a different place of work.

Additional maternity leave

4474 An employee on additional maternity leave has the right to return to the **same job** that she had before leave began **except** where it is no longer reasonably practicable to do so. In such circumstances, she must be given another job which is both suitable and appropriate for her (reg 18(2) SI 1999/3312). For these purposes the job must be identical or a suitable and appropriate alternative in terms of its (s 235(1) ERA 1996; reg 2 SI 1999/3312):
– **nature** (in accordance with the contract of employment);
– **capacity** (for example, seniority); and
– **place** of work.

4475 A **suitable and appropriate job** must be as close as possible to the employment previously held by the employee (*Blundell v Governing Body of St Andrew's Catholic Primary School and anor* [2007] ICR 1451, EAT).

This must be on the same **seniority** and **pension** and with **similar rights** that she would have been entitled to if she had not been absent, and on no less favourable terms and conditions (reg 18A SI 1999/3312 as amended by SI 2008/1966).

> **MEMO POINTS** In *Blundell v Governing Body of St Andrew's Catholic Primary School and anor*, the EAT held that in situations where it was no longer practicable to offer an employee her old job, reference should be made to the nature, content and location of the employee's old job. These factors should all

be construed narrowly. The closer the match, the greater the likelihood that a new job would indeed be suitable and appropriate.

The **onus** will be on the employer to show that it was not reasonably practicable to give the employee the same job back. For example, an employer would have difficulty showing this if he filled the employee's position in her absence because the **temporary replacement** was better at the job. However, if the employer considered all alternative options before making a replacement employee permanent, he may be able to support a claim that it was not reasonably practicable to give the employee her job back.

4476

C. Maternity pay

Eligible employees are **entitled** to a maximum of 39 weeks of SMP (reg 3(2) SI 2006/2379, which amends reg 2(2) SI 1986/1960). An eligible employee is still entitled to statutory pay, even if she is **dismissed** (reg 3 SI 1986/1960) or **decides not to return to work** after the qualifying week before commencing her leave (reg 2(6) SI 1986/1960).

4480

The employee will **not be entitled** to SMP for any week in which she **works during the maternity pay period** (s 165(4) Social Security Contributions and Benefits Act 1992). An employee may, however, work for 10 Keeping in Touch (KIT) days without jeopardising her entitlement to statutory pay (¶4447).

SMP is **paid by** employers who can recover most, and in certain circumstances all, of the amount (¶4495).

> MEMO POINTS 1. Any agreement will be void in so far as it purports to **exclude, limit or modify** any provision of the SMP scheme or require an employee to contribute to any costs incurred by the employer (s 164 SSCBA 1992).
> 2. HMRC also publish a **help book**, "Pay and time off for parents" (E15). Though it has no legal status, it is useful as an indication of the position HMRC take on certain procedural issues as well as outlining the scope and breadth of the regulations.

Eligibility

To qualify for statutory pay (s 164 SSCBA 1992) the employee must fulfil two conditions:
1. be an **employed earner**. That means that she must be an employee or office holder (for example, a director), pay Class 1 NIC and have average weekly earnings (¶4493) of at least the NIC lower earnings limit (£107 per week for 2012/13; £109 for 2013/14); and
2. have **26 weeks' continuous employment** up to and including the **qualifying week** (which is the 15th week before the week the baby is due).

4482

> MEMO POINTS 1. As well as the **general rules of continuity** of employment applying (¶1010), for these purposes continuity of employment is **also preserved with regard to** a whole or part of a week of non-employment (i.e. no contract of employment) if this is due to pregnancy or birth (which is limited to 26 weeks unless the employee returns to work after additional maternity leave or returns as a result of an offer of suitable alternative work) (reg 11 SI 1986/1960).
> 2. Further, the interval between dismissal and re-employment will be counted as continuous employment if an employee is **reinstated or re-engaged** as a result of:
> – an unfair dismissal claim;
> – action by an Acas conciliation officer (before the employee had presented an unfair dismissal claim); or
> – a designated dismissals procedure agreement.
> Where there has been a **stoppage due to a trade dispute**, an employee's continuity will not be broken, but the weeks in which the trade dispute occurred will not count toward calculating her period of continuous employment unless she can prove that she did not have a direct interest in the trade dispute (reg 13 SI 1986/1960).

If an employee is **not entitled to statutory maternity pay**, the employer should complete the HMRC Form SMP1 and give it to the employee. This form sets out why the employee is

4483

not eligible and enables the employee to claim social security benefits. Where an employer does not pay statutory maternity pay, it is **for the employee to secure** other maternity payment.

> MEMO POINTS 1. The **main alternative benefit**, subject to certain qualifying conditions, is **maternity allowance**. To claim maternity allowance a woman needs to:
> – have been employed or self-employed for at least 26 weeks in the 66 weeks before the baby is due, and
> – have average earnings over any 13 weeks in the 66-week period of more than £30 per week.
> Maternity allowance is paid at the **set rate** (¶4401). It cannot start before the 11th week before the week the baby is due.
> It is payable for a maximum of 39 weeks (reg 4(3) SI 2006/2379).
> A claim for maternity allowance should normally be made through the employee's local Jobcentre Plus office.
> 2. Those who are not entitled to get either statutory maternity pay or maternity allowance may be able to get some **employment and support allowance** instead. Some **NI credits** may also be possible for a short period for those who do not qualify for statutory maternity pay, maternity allowance or employment support allowance. Further, a woman may be able to continue to claim **jobseeker's allowance** (JSA) after the beginning of the 11th week before the week the baby is due if she is available for, capable of and actively seeking work. **Income support** from the period beginning 11 weeks before the week the baby is due until 15 weeks after her pregnancy ends and for any time during the pregnancy where the woman is unable to work because of the pregnancy may also be available. Finally, those who or whose partners are getting income support, income-based jobseeker's allowance, pension credit, child tax credit at a rate higher than the family element or working tax credit where a disability or severe disability element is included in the award may be able to get a sure start maternity grant. A guide to maternity benefits (NI17A) gives further information on these benefits and is available from Jobcentre Plus/social security offices and at the Department of Work and Pensions (DWP) website via this link: flmemo.co.uk/em4483

Employee notice and evidence requirements

4485 Employees must give 28 days' **notice** (s 164(4) SSCBA 1992) of their intention to **claim** SMP. If it is **not reasonably practicable** to give notice in time, the employee should do so as soon as it is. Where SMP is to start on the date of birth, or on a set number of days after this date, the employee must give further notice of the actual date as soon as is reasonably practicable.

In practice, most employees will usually give notice of their intention to claim SMP at the same time that they give notice of their intention to take maternity leave (¶4423).

4487 An employee must provide her employer with **medical evidence of the week the baby is due** and the week of actual birth where relevant (reg 22(1) SI 1986/1960). This must be **submitted no later than** the end of the 3rd week of the statutory pay period unless the employer accepts that there was a good reason not to do so. The very latest the evidence can be given is the end of the 13th week. This evidence is usually in the **form** of a maternity certificate (MAT B1) (though the employer can accept other medical evidence) from her GP or midwife. The certificate must **contain** (Statutory Maternity Pay (Medical Evidence) Regulations SI 1987/235):
– the employee's name;
– the week the baby is due or, if the certificate is issued after the birth, the actual date of birth. A birth certificate will also be sufficient evidence of the date and week of actual birth;
– the date of the examination on which the certificate is based;
– the date on which the certificate is signed. This must not be earlier than the 20th week before the week the baby is due; and
– the address of the GP or midwife, his registered number and the expiry date of his registration.

4488 If an employee does **not give adequate notice or evidence**, her employer can refuse to pay statutory pay and if the employer does so the employee will lose her right to it. In such cases, the employer should give the employee the appropriate form setting out why her request for statutory pay has been refused.

Informing employee if not entitled

If an employee is not entitled to SMP, the employer should give his employee the relevant **4490**
Form **SMP1** "Why I cannot pay you SMP".

> MEMO POINTS   The forms are **available from** HMRC, Jobcentre Plus/social security offices and the Department for Work and Pensions.
> The employer can **produce** its own computerised or paper versions as long as it includes the employee's name, address and NI number and the reason why it cannot pay SMP or, if some payments have been made, the reason why the employer is now stopping the payments, the date these payments will stop and how many weeks have been/are to be paid. It is helpful if the employer also includes information on what the employee should do if she disagrees with his decision and who to contact or what to do to find out about other government help and assistance.

Disputes

If there is a dispute, the matter can be referred to HMRC for a formal decision. Any dispute **4491**
as to whether SMP is due to an employee will be determined by HMRC and not by an employment tribunal (*Taylor Gordon & Co Ltd (t/a Plan Personnel) v Timmons* [2004] IRLR 180, EAT).

Rate

SMP must be included in gross pay at the time it is paid. **Contractual payments** to which **4492**
the employee is entitled during this period can be **offset**.

First 6 weeks   The first 6 weeks of statutory pay are paid at 90% of the employee's average **4493**
weekly earnings (the **earnings-related rate**). In relation to **pay rises**, an employee on maternity leave is entitled to be treated the same as other employees who remain at work. The **average weekly earnings** are determined by reference to the 8 weeks up to and including the qualifying week (the **relevant period**). Where an employee is awarded a pay increase (or would have been awarded such an increase had she not been absent on statutory maternity leave) and the pay increase applies to the whole or any part of the period between the beginning of the relevant period and the end of her statutory maternity leave (both her ordinary maternity leave and additional maternity leave), then her average weekly earnings must be calculated as if such an increase applied in each week of her relevant period (reg 21(7) SI 1986/1960 as amended by Statutory Maternity Pay (General) (Amendment) Regulations SI 2005/729, following *Alabaster v (1) Woolwich plc, (2) Secretary of State for Social Security (C-147/02)* [2005] ICR 695, ECJ).

Employers must therefore be careful not to delay any **pay reviews** of employees on maternity leave and must ensure that they review such employees' pay in tandem with other employees. Where staff are offered formal **appraisals**, employers must remember to include those on maternity leave as to do otherwise may give rise to claims of sex discrimination. Pay increases must then be included when calculating the employee's average weekly earnings.

> MEMO POINTS   1. If the **pay increase** has occurred **after the first 6 weeks of maternity leave** (and, consequently, the earnings-related rate has been already calculated and paid), it can only be presumed that the employer must make an additional payment equal to the difference between the revised rate (which takes account of the increased average weekly earnings) and the rate paid at the time.
> The Court of Appeal has held that employees can bring a claim for unpaid back-dated pay increases under the equal pay regime despite the fact that there is no male comparator (*Alabaster v (1) Barclays Bank PLC and (2) The Secretary of State for Social Security* [2005] ICR 1246, CA).
> 2. Under European **proposals** to amend EC Directive 1992/85 this will be increased to full pay for 18 weeks of maternity leave. However, it is proposed that member states can set a ceiling for this pay as long as it is not below the level of sick pay. Further developments will be covered by our updating service.

Following weeks   Statutory pay is payable for the **rest of the statutory pay period** (i.e. 33 **4494**
weeks (¶4480)) at the **set rate** (¶4401).

Recovery

4495 The employer can recover 92% of the statutory pay by reducing the amount of PAYE, NIC and student loan deductions paid to HMRC (SI 1994/1882 as amended).

Small employers are entitled to recover 100% plus an additional amount (3% of the total SMP paid for the tax year) to compensate for the secondary Class 1 NIC payable on SMP. A small employer is one where the total Class 1 NICs for the previous tax year were £45,000 or less (SI 2011/725).

> MEMO POINTS Employers can calculate likely maternity pay, including recovery, from the HMRC site via flmemo.co.uk/em4495

Records

4496 The employer must **keep** records **for** 3 years after the end of the tax year in which the employee's statutory pay ends that show (reg 26 SI 1986/1960):
- the day statutory pay started;
- the number of weeks in that tax year for which SMP was paid and the weekly amount; and
- any week of statutory pay in that tax year where no statutory pay was paid together with the reasons why.

Form SMP2 can be used.

The employer must also keep the employee's evidence of entitlement for the same period.

> MEMO POINTS The forms are **available from** HMRC.
> The employer can **produce** his own computerised or paper version as long as it includes the employee's name, address and NI number, a record of the payment dates and the amount paid, the date the pay period began and a record of any weeks when the statutory pay was not paid together with the reasons why.
> It may also be helpful to record:
> - the week the baby is due and qualifying week;
> - the date of birth;
> - the date the employee told the employer she planned to start her leave;
> - the date she planned to start her leave; and
> - if the employee has changed her start date, when the employer was told of the new date and the new date.

4497 Employers must also be able to show the **correct accounting** of such payments, as appropriate, on the following records:
- deductions working sheet (P11);
- end of year returns (P14); and
- annual return (P35).

Further, the employer should be able to produce for **inspection** by HMRC if required all appropriate wage sheets and all other documents and records which concern the calculation or payment of such statutory payments within 30 days of a notice being issued to that effect (reg 26A SI 1986/1960 as amended by SI 2005/989).

4498 Employers who **fail** to **produce** any document or record required under any of the statutory payment schemes will face an initial penalty of £300 with further penalties of £60 per day for continuing failure. Employers who fail to or repeatedly refuse to **make payments** will be liable to a penalty of up to £3,000 (s 11 EA 2002).

Further, employers who **fraudulently or negligently** make any incorrect payments, produce any incorrect document or record, provide any incorrect information, make any incorrect return or receive incorrect payments in connection with the recovery of such payments **will be liable** to a fine of up to £3,000 (s 12 EA 2002; ss 113A-B Social Security Administration Act 1992).

Penalties may also be charged in relation to errors on returns and documents (¶6881).

SECTION 2

Adoption rights

The following table summarises the main rights of adopters to ordinary and additional leave and statutory adoption pay.

4520

	ORDINARY ADOPTION LEAVE (OAL)	ADDITIONAL ADOPTION LEAVE (AAL)	STATUTORY ADOPTION PAY (SAP)
QUALIFICATION FOR RIGHT	Employees who are adopting; and who have agreed to placement with approved agency		Earn at least NIC lower earnings limit (¶6955) for 8 weeks up to and including week in which they are notified of match for adoption
QUALIFYING PERIOD	26 weeks' continuous employment ending with week in which they are notified of match by approved agency		
DURATION	Up to 26 weeks	Up to 26 weeks from end of OAL	Up to 39 weeks
RATE OF PAY	n/a		Set rate
START DATE	From 14 days before expected placement	At end of OAL	In practice coincides with start of OAL
NOTICE TO TAKE	Within 7 days of notification of adoption, employer must respond within 28 days setting out when due back	No additional requirements	At least 28 days before start date. Usually satisfied by giving notice to take leave
EVIDENCE FOR ENTITLEMENT	If requested, matching certificate or other written document. If so this will also satisfy SAP evidence requirement	No additional requirements	Matching certificate
TERMS AND CONDITIONS DURING LEAVE	All terms except remuneration remain the same		n/a
WORKING DURING LEAVE	On agreement, employee can do up to 10 days' work during adoption leave		n/a
NOTICE TO RETURN	8 weeks' notice of intention to return unless employee intends to take the full 52 weeks of ordinary and additional leave, in which case no notice is required		n/a
JOB ON RETURN	Right to return to same job	Right to return to same job unless not reasonably practical, in which case most suitable employment	n/a
ENFORCEMENT AND REMEDIES	Right not to suffer detriment and right not to be unfairly dismissed in relation to above rights		

A. Adoption leave

All employees (including apprentices) (reg 2(1) SI 2002/2788), i.e. both male and female, who are **notified by an approved adoption agency** of a match with a child or children are entitled

4521

to take adoption leave (AL). In this section, such employees are called adopters. If a couple is **adopting jointly**, they can choose who takes adoption leave. In such cases, the other partner is eligible to take paternity leave.

AL can **begin** from the actual date of the child's placement or from a fixed date which can be up to 14 days before the expected date of placement (regs 16, 18 SI 2002/2788).

Adoption leave may last for **up to** a maximum of 52 weeks (reg 18 SI 2002/2788). The first 26 weeks of the entitlement take the form of ordinary adoption leave (OAL), the second 26 weeks additional adoption leave (AAL).

Only one period of leave can be taken irrespective of whether more than one child is adopted.

Eligibility

4522 To be entitled, the adoptive parent must have (reg 15 SI 2002/2788):
– been **continuously employed** with the employer for at least 26 weeks ending with the week in which he/she is notified of being matched with a child; and
– **notified his/her agency** that he/she agrees to the child being placed with him/her on the expected date of placement.

> MEMO POINTS   1. **Foster parents** who adopt are entitled to adoption leave as long as the child that they fostered is matched with them for adoption by a UK adoption agency. There is no statutory entitlement if adoption is by a court order.
> An employee who becomes a parent through **surrogacy** is not normally entitled to statutory adoption leave. However, once they are a parent, they will be entitled to take parental leave, if eligible, and take time off to care for dependants if necessary.
> There is no statutory entitlement for parents who adopt **step children** by a court order.
> 2. The Government has announced **proposals** to make adoption leave a right which accrues on day one of employment. Any further developments will be covered by our updating service.

---

1. Starting leave

Employee notification and evidence

4524 **Notification**   Employees must notify their employer as to when the child is expected to be placed for adoption and the date on which they want leave to begin (reg 17 SI 2002/2788 as amended by reg 3 SI 2004/923). This must be given no later than 7 days after being notified of having been matched with the child.

4525 **Failure to give adequate notice** must be disregarded if it was **not reasonably practicable** for the employee to notify his/her employer correctly and in time. In such cases, it should be done as soon as it is reasonably practicable.

4526 The employee can **change** his/her **start date** (reg 17(4) SI 2002/2788). Consequently, if he/she wants to vary the date:
– to the date on which the child is **actually placed** for adoption, he/she must give at least 28 days' notice before the expected date of placement; and
– to **another set date**, he/she must give at least 28 days' notice before that date.

He/she can choose to **further vary** the start date using the same procedure. Each change must be notified in writing if requested.

4527 **Evidence of entitlement**   The **employer can request** that:
a. the notice is given in writing; and
b. the employee provides evidence of his/her entitlement. This takes the form of one or more documents from the adoption agency that state:
– the name and address of the agency;
– the date on which the employee was notified that he/she had been matched with the child; and
– the expected date of placement.

Employer notification of adoption leave end date

4528 As a result of an employee's notice (¶4524) of his/her proposed or varied start date, the employer must give notice of when the leave will end (reg 17(7) SI 2002/2788).

This document must be sent **within** 28 days of notification unless the employee has notified his/her employer of a change to his/her start date, in which case the employer must give notice of the new end date within 28 days of the varied start date.

> MEMO POINTS If the employer **fails to notify** in time, he will not be able to take action about his employee coming back too early or too late (¶4457).

2. Rights during leave and return to work

4530 An employee on adoption leave has the **same rights and duties** as an employee on maternity leave concerning:
- terms and conditions (s 75A ERA 1996; reg 19 SI 2002/2788; ¶4435);
- contact with the employer during leave (reg 21A SI 2002/2788; ¶4445);
- ending leave (¶¶4449+);
- type of job after returning from OAL (reg 26(1) SI 2002/2788; ¶4469);
- type of job after returning from AAL (reg 26(3) SI 2002/2788; ¶4474);
- special protection in redundancy situations (reg 23 SI 2002/2788; ¶4453);
- notice to return early (reg 25 SI 2002/2788; ¶4459); and
- dismissal during leave (¶¶4762, 4763).

Terminated placement

4532 If a child's placement is terminated during adoption leave, **special rules** in relation to when adoption leave will end apply if (reg 22 SI 2002/2822):
- the employee has started adoption leave before the placement and the adoption agency has notified the employee that the child will no longer be placed with him/her; or
- the child dies or is returned to the adoption agency during adoption leave.

In such circumstances, unless adoption leave is due to end earlier, it will end 8 weeks after the end of the week during which:
- the employee is notified the adoption will not take place; or
- the child dies or is returned.

B. Adoption pay

4554 SAP runs for a **maximum of** 39 weeks.

Eligibility

4555 As well as satisfying the eligibility criteria above, to qualify for SAP an employee must meet the same earnings criteria as an employee seeking to qualify for SMP (reg 33 SI 2002/2822; ¶4482). The qualifying period is the week in which he/she is notified of a match for adoption.

Employee notice and evidence requirements

4557 An employee must **give notice**, in writing if required, 28 days before he/she wishes his/her statutory pay to start (s 171ZL SSCBA 1992).

4559 An employee must provide his/her employer with **evidence** of the adoption and a declaration that he/she has elected to receive SAP (reg 24 SI 2002/2822). HMRC **Form SC4** "Becoming an adoptive parent" provides a declaration form that can be used. Evidence of adoption

must be from the adoption agency which will provide a letter or a "**matching certificate**: statutory adoption leave and pay". The evidence must **include**:
- the name and address of the agency;
- the name and address of the employee;
- the date on which the employee was notified that he/she had been matched with the child; and
- the expected date of placement (or actual date if it has already occurred).

4560 Where an employee does **not give adequate notice or evidence**, the employer has the power to make the same sanctions as when an employee on SMP fails to give notice or evidence (¶4488).

Informing employee if not entitled

4561 If an employee is not entitled to SAP, the employer should give his employee the relevant **Form SAP1** "Why I cannot pay you SAP".

MEMO POINTS   The forms are **available from** HMRC.
The employer can **produce** his own computerised or paper version as long as it includes the employee's name, address and NI number and the reason why he cannot pay SAP.

Disputes

4562 If there is a dispute, the matter can be referred to HMRC for a formal decision.

Rate, recovery and records

4563 Statutory adoption pay is paid at the set rate (¶4401). It must be included in gross pay at the time it is paid. Contractual payments to which the employee is entitled during this period can be offset.

It follows the same rules as SMP with regard to recovery (¶4495) and records (¶4496).

MEMO POINTS   The Government has announced **proposals** to make SAP mirror SMP in that the first 6 weeks will be paid at 90% of the employee's salary. Any further developments will be covered by our updating service.

SECTION 3

Paternity rights

4570 The following table summarises the main rights of employees to leave and to statutory paternity pay.

	PATERNITY LEAVE (PAL)	ADDITIONAL PATERNITY LEAVE (APAL)	STATUTORY PATERNITY PAY (SPP) ADDITIONAL STATUTORY PATERNITY PAY (ASPP)
QUALIFICATION FOR RIGHT	Employees who are biological father (or mother's or adoptive partner's husband/civil partner/partner) and take leave to care for newborn or to support mother or adoptive parent		Earn at least NIC lower earnings limit (¶6955) for 8 weeks up to and including 15th week before the week the baby is due/the week in which notified of match
QUALIFYING PERIOD	26 weeks' continuous employment by end of 15th week before the week the baby is due/ending with week adoptive partner notified of match		

	PATERNITY LEAVE (PAL)	ADDITIONAL PATERNITY LEAVE (APAL)	STATUTORY PATERNITY PAY (SPP) ADDITIONAL STATUTORY PATERNITY PAY (ASPP)
DURATION	1 or 2 whole weeks	Minimum – 2 whole weeks. Maximum – 26 whole weeks. Latest can end is when their partner's additional maternity or adoption leave would have ended	SPP: 1 or 2 whole weeks ASSP: for period their partner would have been receiving statutory maternity or adoption pay
RATE OF PAY	n/a		Set rate
START DATE	Within 56 days of birth	– 20 or more weeks after birth/child placed for adoption; and – partner has returned to work from statutory maternity or adoption leave	SPP: at start of PAL ASSP: at start of APAL if in period their partner would have been receiving statutory maternity or adoption pay
NOTICE TO TAKE	Before end of 15th week before the week the baby is due/within 7 days of notification of adoption	Not less than 8 weeks before start date	SPP: At least 28 days before start date. Usually satisfied by giving notice to take leave ASSP: As for APAL
EVIDENCE FOR ENTITLEMENT	Self-certificate and declaration by employee	Self-certificate and declarations by employee and partner	As for PAL and APAL
TERMS AND CONDITIONS DURING LEAVE	All terms except remuneration remain the same		n/a
WORKING DURING LEAVE	n/a	On agreement, employee can do up to 10 days' work during additional paternity leave	n/a
NOTICE TO RETURN	n/a	Once on leave, 6 weeks' notice if want to return sooner than end date	n/a
JOB ON RETURN	Right to return to same job	If returning after 26 weeks or less additional paternity leave, right to return is same as for employees on ordinary maternity leave unless it is taken immediately after additional maternity/adoption leave or parental leave of more than 4 weeks (¶4469). Otherwise, same right as for employees on additional maternity leave (¶4474).	n/a
ENFORCEMENT AND REMEDIES	Right not to suffer detriment and right not to be unfairly dismissed in relation to above rights		

A. Standard paternity leave

4571 Eligible employees (including apprentices) are entitled to either 1 or 2 whole weeks' paid paternity leave where they wish to take leave to (regs 2, 4, 8 SI 2002/2788):
- **care** for a newborn or newly adoptive child; or
- **support** the child's mother or adoptive parent.

In addition, there is also a relatively new right to **additional paternity leave** (¶4585). This enables those whose spouses/partners are returning to work early from maternity or adoption leave to take a certain period of leave effectively in their place.

As with every aspect of family-friendly rights, the employer can provide for more favourable contractual or non-contractual terms.

> MEMO POINTS   There is **one entitlement** to paternity leave **per pregnancy (or adoption)** so multiple births or adopting more than one child at the same time will not generate extra paternity leave.

4572 Paternity leave must also **be taken**:
- as either 1 or 2 whole weeks; and
- within 56 days of the date of birth or placement.

The employee can choose whether he/she takes 1 or 2 weeks.

The **earliest start date** is the date of birth or placement.

Eligibility

4574 To be eligible for paternity leave, the employee must (regs 4, 8 SI 2002/2788):
a. have been **continuously employed** for 26 weeks:
– before the end of the 15th week before the week the baby is due, be either the biological father of the child or the mother's husband, civil partner or partner; or
– ending with the week in which the adoptive parent is notified of being matched for adoption, be either married to, or the civil partner or partner of, the adoptive parent; and
b. have or be expected to have **responsibility for the upbringing** of the child where the employee is the child's father. Where the spouse, civil partner or partner of the adoptive parent is not the child's father, the employee must have or be expected to have the main responsibility along with the mother or adoptive parent.

With regard to adoption leave, where a **couple** is adopting jointly, they can choose which one takes adoption leave, leaving the other to take paternity leave if desired.

> MEMO POINTS   A **partner** is a person (of a different or the same sex) who lives with the mother or adoptive parent and the child in an enduring family relationship but is not a relative of the mother or adoptive parent. A relative in this context is a mother's or adoptive parent's parent, grandparent, sister, brother, aunt or uncle. Partners include **civil partners** (SI 2005/2114).
> With regard to taking paternity leave to support a spouse/civil partner/partner who is **adopting from overseas**, this is covered by s 80B ERA 1996; Employment Rights Act 1996 (Application of Section 80B to Adoptions from Overseas) Regulations SI 2003/920; Paternity and Adoption Leave (Adoption from Overseas) Regulations SI 2003/921; Social Security Contributions and Benefits Act 1992 (Application of Parts 12ZA and 12ZB to Adoptions from Overseas) Regulations SI 2003/499; Statutory Paternity Pay (Adoption) and Statutory Adoption Pay (Adoptions from Overseas) Regulations SI 2003/500; Statutory Paternity Pay (Adoption) and Statutory Adoption Pay (Adoptions from Overseas) (Administration) Regulations SI 2003/1192 and Statutory Paternity Pay (Adoption) and Statutory Adoption Pay (Adoptions from Overseas) (No. 2) Regulations SI 2003/1194.
> In such cases, the employee must receive an official notification. For further details, see the legislation listed above and the latest version of the BIS guide on parents adopting a child from overseas. Assistance can also be obtained from the Department of Health Intercountry Adoption Team.

Employee notice and evidence

4576 Employees must **notify** their employer **no later than** the end of the 15th week before the week the baby is due or no later than 7 days after being notified of having been matched with the child (regs 6, 10 SI 2002/2788):

- of the week the baby is due/date which the adoptive parent was notified and the expected date of placement;
- whether 1 or 2 weeks of leave is to be taken; and
- the chosen start date.

In practice, most employers will accept the chosen start date as "on the date of the child's birth" together with the date of the week the baby is due as sufficient.

The employee must give **further notice**, as soon as reasonably practicable, of the actual date of birth or placement. **4577**

Failure to give adequate notice must be disregarded if it was **not reasonably practicable** for the employee to notify his/her employer correctly and in time. In such cases, it must be done as soon as it is reasonably practicable. **4579**

Changing start date: the employee can change the start date (regs 6(4), 10(4) SI 2002/2788). Consequently, if the employee wants to vary the date to: **4580**
- the **date of birth or placement**, the employee must give at least 28 days' notice before the first day of the week the baby is due/the expected date of placement;
- a date that is a **set number of days** after the date of birth or placement, the employee must give at least 28 days' notice before that set number of days taken after the first day of the week the baby is due/the expected date of placement; or
- **another set date**, the employee must give at least 28 days' notice before that date.

He/she can choose to further vary the start date using the same procedure. Each change must be notified in writing if requested.

Evidence of entitlement The **employer can request** that (regs 6(3), 10(3) SI 2002/2788): **4581**
a. the notices are given in writing; and
b. the employee provides a signed declaration as evidence of his/her entitlement. This must state that:
- the employee is taking the leave to care for a newborn or newly adopted child or to support the child's mother or adoptive parent;
- the employee is either the biological father of the child, the mother's or adoptive parent's spouse/civil partner/partner; and
- the employee has or is expected to have the main responsibility (apart from any responsibility of the mother/main adoptive parent) for the child's upbringing.

HMRC provides **model self-certificates and declarations** (Form SC3 (Becoming a parent) and Form SC4 (Becoming an adoptive parent)) which can be used.

Rights during leave and on return

All terms except remuneration remain the same during leave and the employee has the right to return to the same job. **4583**

B. Additional paternity leave

Additional paternity leave entitles **eligible employees** (¶4574; regs 4, 14 SI 2010/1055) whose spouses/partners are returning to work early from maternity or adoption leave to take a certain period of leave effectively in their place. The purpose of the leave must be to care for the child (unlike standard paternity leave, which allows leave to support the child's mother/adopter). **4585**

> MEMO POINTS 1. This is a **relatively new right** and applies to parents of babies due on or after 3 April 2011, or parents who have received notification on or after 3 April 2011 that they have been matched with a child for adoption.
> 2. With regard to taking paternity leave to support a spouse/civil partner/partner who is **adopting from overseas**, this is covered by s 80BB ERA 1996; Employment Rights Act 1996 (Application of Section 80BB to

Adoptions from Overseas) Regulations SI 2010/1058; Additional Paternity Leave (Adoption from Overseas) Regulations SI 2010/1059; Additional Statutory Paternity Pay (Adoptions from Overseas) Regulations SI 2010/1057; and Additional Statutory Paternity Pay (Birth, Adoption and Adoptions from Overseas) (Administration) Regulations SI 2010/154.

3. The Government has announced **proposals** to replace the right to additional paternity leave with a joint right to flexible parental leave and pay from 2015 under which, after the initial period of compulsory maternity leave and paternity leave, mothers whose partners meet certain eligibility requirements can choose to convert any remaining maternity leave and SMP to flexible parental leave and pay, which the parents can take concurrently or divide up into week-long blocks with their employer's agreement. Any further developments will be covered by our updating service.

4586 The employee will only be able to **start** his/her additional leave:
– 20 or more weeks after the child's birth or placement; and
– after his/her partner has returned to work from statutory maternity or adoption leave.

The **minimum** amount of additional paternity leave that can be taken is 2 weeks and the **maximum** period is 26 weeks (regs 5, 15 SI 2010/1055). Additional paternity leave must be taken in multiples of complete weeks and must be taken as one continuous period.

The **latest** that additional leave **can end** is the date on which his/her partner's additional maternity or adoption leave would have ended, i.e. the end of the 52nd week after his/her partner's statutory maternity or adoption leave began.

> MEMO POINTS   In circumstances where the **mother/main adopter dies within 12 months of the child's birth/placement for adoption**, there are various modifications (regs 10-13, 20-23 SI 2010/1055). In such cases, the employee's entitlement may be to a longer period of leave starting earlier than it would otherwise have done and with different notification requirements.

1. Starting leave

Notification and evidence

4587 **Not less than** 8 weeks before their chosen start date, employees must give their employers (regs 6, 16 SI 2010/1055):

1. **written notice** as to their intention to take additional paternity leave which specifies:
– the week which was the baby's expected week of birth and the date of birth or the date on which their partner was notified of having been matched with the adopted child and the date on which they were placed; and
– the requested start date and end date;

2. a **written signed declaration** which states that:
– the employee is taking the leave to care for a newborn or newly adoptive child or to support the child's mother or adoptive parent;
– the employee is either the biological father of the child or the mother's or adoptive parent's spouse/civil partner/partner; and
– the employee has or is expected to have the main responsibility (apart from any responsibility of the mother/main adoptive parent) for the child's upbringing; and

3. a **written declaration by the mother/main adoptive parent** which states:
– their name and address;
– that they have given notice to their employer that they intend to return to work and the date they intend to return to work;
– their NI number;
– that the employee is either the biological father of the child or the mother's or adoptive parent's spouse/civil partner/partner, and that the employee has or is expected to have the main responsibility (apart from any responsibility of the mother/main adoptive parent) for the child's upbringing;
– that the employee is, to the mother's/main adoptive parent's knowledge, the only person exercising the entitlement to additional paternity leave (and pay if applicable) in respect of the newborn/newly adoptive child;
– that the mother/main adoptive parent consents to the employer processing such information as is contained in the declaration; and

– for additional statutory paternity pay purposes if applicable, the start date of their maternity pay/maternity allowance/adoption pay period.

4588 Employers **can request**, within 28 days of receiving the leave notice, a copy of the child's birth certificate/one or more documents issued by the adoption agency which state the name and address of the agency, the date on which the adoptive parent was notified of the match and the expected date of placement, and the name and address of the mother's/main adoptive parent's employer (or, if he/she is self-employed, his/her business address) (regs 6(3), 16(3) SI 2010/1055).

Employees must provide this within 28 days of receiving the request.

Changing date(s), cancelling or withdrawing leave

4590 Before additional paternity leave starts, the employee can change his/her start or end date or cancel his/her leave by giving **written notice** 6 weeks before the new date or the date being cancelled or varied or, if this is not possible, as soon as is reasonably practicable (regs 7, 17 SI 2010/1055). Likewise, if the employee wishes to return earlier than the agreed date (¶4587) once on additional paternity leave, he/she can do so if he/she gives at least 6 weeks' notice (¶4598).

If, after giving leave notice, the employee no longer becomes entitled to additional paternity leave, the employee must give written notice ("withdrawal notice") as soon as reasonably practicable (regs 6, 16 SI 2010/1055). This will apply if the information in the signed declaration no longer applies or if or the mother/main adoptive parent is no longer entitled to maternity/adoption leave, statutory maternity pay/maternity allowance or statutory adoption pay or does not return to work (¶4485).

In all instances, if the employee **fails to give enough written notice**, or to give any notice at all, and if it is not reasonably practicable for the employer to accommodate the change in arrangement, the employer can require the employee to take up to 6 weeks' APAL starting on the date the employee originally requested (or any previously rearranged date) and ending no later than 6 weeks after any written notice to change, cancel or withdraw or until the original agreed end date, whichever is earlier. Likewise, where the employee has given a withdrawal notice after the period of additional paternity leave has begun and where it is not reasonably practicable for the employer to accommodate the change in arrangements, failure to give proper notice entitles the employer to postpone the employee's return until the notice requirement has been satisfied or until the original agreed end date, whichever is earlier.

Employer notification of dates

4592 As a result of an employee's notice (¶4587) or when the employee gives a proposed or varied date(s) (¶4590), the employer must give **written** confirmation of the relevant dates (regs 8, 18 SI 2010/1055).

This document must be sent **within** 28 days of notification unless the employee has notified his/her employer of a change to his/her start or end date, in which case the employer must give notice of the new end date within 28 days of the varied start date. Where the employer requires the employee to take a period of additional paternity leave as set out in ¶4590, the employer must notify the employee of the dates of that leave as soon as reasonably practicable, and in any event before the start of the leave.

---

2. Rights during leave and return to work

Rights during leave

4595 An employee on additional paternity leave has the **same rights and duties** as an employee on maternity leave concerning:
– terms and conditions during leave (reg 27 SI 2010/1055; ¶4435);

- contact with the employer during leave (reg 26 SI 2010/1055; ¶4445);
- ending leave (¶¶4449+);
- special protection in redundancy situations (reg 28 SI 2010/1055; ¶4453); and
- dismissal during leave (¶¶4762, 4763).

Return to work

4596 If the employee is returning after 26 weeks or less additional paternity leave, the employee's right to return is the same as for employees on ordinary maternity leave unless it is taken immediately after additional maternity/adoption leave or parental leave of more than 4 weeks (¶4469) (reg 31 SI 2010/1055). Otherwise, the employee's right to return will be the same as for employees on additional maternity/adoption leave (¶4474).

4598 Employee notice for early return If the employee wishes to return earlier than the agreed date (¶¶4587, 4590) once on additional paternity leave, he/she can do so if he/she **gives at least** 6 weeks' written notice (reg 30 SI 2010/1055).

Failure to give proper notice entitles the employer to postpone his/her return until the notice requirement has been satisfied or until the original agreed end date, whichever is earlier.

Child's death or termination of placement

4599 If a child dies or a placement is terminated during additional paternity leave or after the employee has notified the employer of his/her intention to take additional paternity leave **special rules** apply (reg 24 SI 2010/1055). In such cases, unless the additional paternity leave is due to end earlier, it will end 8 weeks following the week of the child's death or the end of the child's placement.

C. Statutory paternity pay/ Additional statutory paternity pay

4600 An employee is entitled to either 1 or 2 full weeks of statutory paternity pay (SPP), depending on the duration of paternity leave. An employee may also be entitled to additional statutory paternity pay (ASPP) during the time his/her partner would have been receiving statutory maternity or adoption pay (SI 2002/2822; SI 2010/1056).

Eligibility

4601 As well as satisfying the eligibility criteria above, to qualify for statutory paternity pay or additional statutory paternity pay an employee must meet the same earnings criteria as an employee seeking to qualify for SMP (¶4482). The qualifying week is the 15th week before the week the baby is due/the week in which the adoptive parent has been notified of a match for adoption.

Further, to be eligible for additional statutory paternity pay, the mother/main adoptive parent must have at least 2 weeks of his/her SMP/SAP or maternity allowance period unexpired (regs 13, 23 SI 2010/1056).

Employee notice and evidence requirements

4602 Statutory paternity pay Employees must give **notice**, in writing if required, 28 days before they wish their statutory paternity pay to start (s 171ZC SSCBA 1992). In practice, most employees will usually give notice of their intention to claim pay at the same time that they give notice of their intention to take leave.

4603 An employee must **provide** his/her employer with a declaration of his/her family commitment (regs 9, 15 SI 2002/2822). HMRC **Forms SC3** "Becoming a parent" and **SC4** "Becoming an adoptive parent" provide a declaration that can be used. It must be **submitted at least** 28 days before the start of the statutory pay period. If this is **not reasonably practicable**, it must be given as soon as it is, for example HMRC Help Book on pay and time off for adoptive parents notes that sometimes there is very little time between the date the adoption agency informs the employee of a match and the date the child is placed with him/her and in such circumstances late notice must be accepted.

If an employee does **not give adequate notice/evidence**, the employer can refuse to pay statutory pay and if the employer does so the employee will lose his/her right to it. In such cases, the employer should give the employee the appropriate form setting out why the request for statutory pay has been refused.

4604 **Additional statutory paternity pay** The **notice and declaration** requirements are the same as for additional paternity leave. Employees will therefore be giving notice of their intention to claim any pay at the same time that they give notice of their intention to take leave.

Informing employee if not entitled

4605 If an employee is not entitled to statutory paternity pay or additional statutory paternity pay, the employer should give his employee the relevant **Form SPP1** "Why I cannot pay you SPP".

> MEMO POINTS   The forms are **available from** HMRC.
> The employer can **produce** his own computerised or paper version as long as it includes the employee's name, address and NI number and the reason why it cannot pay SPP.

Disputes

4606 If there is a dispute, the matter can be referred to HMRC for a formal decision.

Rate, recovery and records

4608 Statutory paternity pay and additional statutory paternity pay is paid at the set rate (¶4401). It must be included in gross pay at the time it is paid. Contractual payments to which the employee is entitled during this period can be offset.

It follows the same rules as SMP with regard to recovery (¶4495) and records (¶4496).

> MEMO POINTS   There is one small difference regarding the penalties for employers who fraudulently or negligently make any incorrect payments, produce any incorrect document or record, provide any incorrect information, make any incorrect return or receive incorrect payments in connection with the recovery of such payments. While with regard to ASPP the employer will be liable to a fine of up to £3,000 (as for SMP and SAP (¶4498)), this amount is reduced to £300 with regard to SPP.

SECTION 4

Parental leave

4620 All employees (including apprentices) who are parents of children aged under 5 or disabled children under 18 have the right to take unpaid parental leave for the **purpose of caring for a child** for whom they are responsible.

The legislation sets out relatively prescriptive "fallback" standards for the **administration** of parental leave (¶4660), but they do not have to be used and can be varied (¶4650).

In addition to the rights set out in this section, parents also have the right to request flexible working (¶4690). If an employee does not qualify for parental leave, he/she may be entitled in addition to take unpaid time off in the form of care for dependants (¶4740) although this is only designed for short periods.

4621 The following table summarises the employee's entitlement to parental leave.

	PARENTAL LEAVE (PL)
QUALIFICATION FOR RIGHT	Registered fathers and those who have parental responsibility of a child under 5 or a disabled person under 18
QUALIFYING PERIOD	1 year's continuous employment with the employer
DURATION	13 weeks (18 weeks for disabled child) for each child. This is due to increase in March 2013 to 16 weeks and please see our updating service for further developments. Fallback scheme: leave must be taken as whole weeks, maximum of 4 weeks per child per year.
RATE OF PAY	Leave is unpaid
START DATE	Fallback scheme: from when entitled, subject to correct notification
NOTICE TO TAKE	Fallback scheme: at least 21 days before leave
EVIDENCE FOR ENTITLEMENT	Fallback scheme: on request
TERMS AND CONDITIONS DURING LEAVE	Most terms are suspended
WORKING DURING LEAVE	n/a
JOB ON RETURN	If leave is for less than 4 weeks, right is as for employee on OML (¶4469); if returning after more than 4 weeks of PL, or if returning after a period of PL taken immediately after AML or AAL, right is as for employee on AML (¶4474)
ENFORCEMENT AND REMEDIES	Right not to suffer detriment and right not to be unfairly dismissed in relation to above rights

A. Eligibility and minimum standards

4625 To be entitled to parental leave, parents must have completed 1 year's **continuous employment** with their current employer.

The employee's rights to **take the leave last until** the child's 5th birthday or, in the case of adoption, until 5 years have elapsed following placement (reg 15 SI 1999/3312). Parents of disabled children have until their child's 18th birthday to take the full entitlement. A child is disabled for the purposes of this right if he/she is entitled to a disability living allowance.

Employers can offer **more favourable contractual terms** than these minimum standards, for example, by providing longer leave, contractual paid leave, no qualifying period, or making it available to a larger group of staff.

> MEMO POINTS The Government has announced **proposals** to lengthen by, 2015, the period within which parental leave can be taken so that it will not expire until the child's 18th birthday. Any further developments will be covered by our updating service.

4632 **Responsibility for child** An employee has responsibility for a child if he/she has "parental responsibility" (reg 13(2) SI 1999/3312). This requirement covers **mothers**, and also **fathers** who are **married to the mother** at the time of birth. It also includes those who have acquired responsibility as a result of a court order or a formal agreement with the mother, for example, **adoptive parents** who take responsibility when the adoption order is made, and those who have been registered as the father on the birth certificate (this covers **fathers unmarried to the mother** at the time of birth).

4633 As long as parents have parental responsibility they do not have to live with the child to be entitled to take leave. On the other hand, step-parents or foster parents who have not formally obtained parental responsibility will not be entitled to take parental leave.

As a **good practice example**, the BIS guide on parental leave indicates that employers who wish to improve on this right can do so by extending it to employees who have informal responsibility for looking after a child, for example step-parents, foster parents and even grandparents.

Purpose of caring for child The regulations are silent as to what amounts to leave for the purpose of caring for a child but it is likely to include (BIS guide on parental leave):
– spending more time with young children;
– accompanying a child during a hospital stay;
– checking out new schools;
– settling a child into new childcare arrangements; and
– enabling the family to spend more time together, for example by taking the child to see their grandparents.

If an employee takes leave **without a valid reason** this will be a disciplinary matter.

Duration

An employee is **entitled** to 13 weeks' leave in respect of **each child** (reg 14(1) SI 1999/3312) and 18 weeks in respect of a **disabled child** (reg 14(1A) SI 1999/3312). This is due to increase in March 2013 to 16 weeks (to implement Parental Leave Directive (EU Parental Leave Directive 2010/18), which repeals and replaces the Parental Leave Directive (Parental Leave Directive 1996/34)). Please see our updating service for further developments.

This entitlement applies as a total: if an employee has had 4 weeks' leave with a previous employer, he/she will be entitled to 9 weeks' leave with his/her present employer. The BIS guide on parental leave observes that employers can, as good practice, **disregard** leave taken in a previous job.

Terms and conditions

The following are the statutory minimum requirements. As with every aspect of family-friendly rights, the employer can provide for more favourable contractual or non-contractual terms.

Although an employee's contract continues during parental leave, most of its terms and conditions are **suspended**. So for example, there is no entitlement to accrue any contractual **annual leave** during parental leave (unless otherwise agreed), though employees do accrue statutory annual leave.

Some terms will, however, continue to apply. The employee will be **protected** by his/her employer's implied obligation of trust and confidence, as well as any contractual terms and conditions relating to compensation in the event of redundancy; or disciplinary or grievance procedures. The employee will be bound by his/her implied obligation of good faith and by any contractual terms and conditions relating to disclosure of confidential information; or acceptance of gifts or other benefits; or participation in any other business. The employer and the employee will both have a duty to give notice of termination.

The employer can disregard time spent on parental leave as "**service**" for the purposes of determining the employee's seniority and other contractual rights (unless otherwise agreed).

Type of job on return

The type of job an employee will be entitled to return to depends on the length of parental leave or whether it is taken immediately after a period of additional maternity or adoption leave. If the employee's leave is for less than 4 weeks, his/her right is the same as for employees on ordinary maternity leave (¶4469), and if the employee is returning after more than 4 weeks of parental leave, or returning after a period of parental taken immediately after additional maternity leave or additional adoption leave, his/her right is the same as for employees on additional maternity leave (¶4474).

B. Procedure

4650 To give employers enough flexibility in the implementation of parental leave so that it can suit the needs of their business and the workforce, employers may make their own **arrangements** as to how and when parental leave can be taken. If there is **no arrangement** then the fallback scheme (¶4660) will apply.

Arrangements **can be made individually** between the employer and employee through individual agreements. **Alternatively**, arrangements can be incorporated into the employee's contract or operate **by reference to** a:
– collective agreement i.e. a union agreement; or
– workforce agreement i.e. a non-union agreement.

> MEMO POINTS 1. A **collective agreement** is any arrangement made by or on behalf of one or more independent trade unions and one or more employers or employers' associations. See ¶¶7363+.
> 2. A **workforce agreement** is a non-union agreement formed with **relevant members** of the workforce (¶1293; Sch 1 SI 1999/3312). These are **defined** as all the employees except those whose terms and conditions are provided for to any extent in a collective agreement. The agreement must apply to all of the relevant members or to all of the relevant members who belong to a particular group. A particular group could be a group of relevant members who undertake a particular function, work at a particular workplace or belong to a particular department or unit within their employer's business.
> The **agreement must be** (Sch 1 para 1 SI 1999/3312):
> – in writing and signed by the representatives of the workforce or of the particular group except those who are not a relevant member on the date on which the agreement is first made available for signature or if the employer has 20 or fewer employees on this date, the agreement can be signed by a majority of members; and
> – in effect for a specified period of not more than 5 years.
> **Representatives** are employees elected to represent the relevant members of the workforce or particular group. Elections must follow the following rules (Sch 1 para 3 SI 1999/3312):
> – the employer determines the number of representatives;
> – the candidates are relevant members of the workforce or particular group and no eligible member can be unreasonably excluded;
> – all relevant members of the workforce or particular group are entitled to vote and may vote for as many candidates as there are representatives to be elected;
> – the election is, so far as is reasonably practicable, in secret; and
> – the votes are fairly and accurately counted.

4651 Where terms on parental leave have been **agreed individually**, the fallback scheme will still apply if the contract is **silent or less favourable** with regard to some or all of the procedural requirements.

4652 Where arrangements have been incorporated into the employee's contract or operate by reference to **collective or workforce arrangement**, the fallback scheme does not apply and therefore the terms can be **more or less favourable** though they cannot be less favourable than the minimum standards. Consequently, if the arrangement is silent about some or all of the procedural requirements, the only procedural requirement will be that of the common law requirement of reasonableness.

Fallback scheme

4660 Employees must give **notice** (orally or in writing) of their intention to take leave **at least** 21 days before the leave is due to begin (Sch 2 SI 1999/3312). The notice must **specify** the date on which the period of leave is to begin and end.

Where the employee is an expectant father/adoptive parent and the **leave is to begin on the date of birth/placement**, notice must be given at least 21 days before the beginning of the week the baby is due/the beginning of the week of the expected placement and must specify the week the baby is due/the date of expected placement and duration of leave. If it is not reasonably practicable to give 21 days' notice then notice must be given as soon as it is reasonably practicable; this may particularly be the case with regard to adoptive parents as placements can often be given on short notice.

Employees must comply with any **request by their employer** to produce for inspection **evidence** of their entitlement (Sch 2 paras 1-2 SI 1999/3312). Such evidence amounts to that which may reasonably be required to show:
– the employee's responsibility or expected responsibility for the child for whom the employee proposes to take leave;
– the child's date of birth or the date on which they expect a child to be placed with them for adoption; and/or
– the child's entitlement to a disability living allowance, if relevant.

Duration of leave An employee must take parental leave **in blocks of** 1 or more weeks **unless** the child is disabled (Sch 2 para 7 SI 1999/3312). Therefore, the period of leave will be rounded up to the nearest complete week in calculating how much of the employee's entitlement has been used. This method has been criticised by the Court of Appeal, although it confirmed that parental leave must be taken in complete blocks of 1 or more weeks and an employee is not entitled to take less than this (*New Southern Railway Ltd (formerly South Central Trains Ltd) v Rodway* [2005] ICR 1162, CA).

> MEMO POINTS This ruling only concerns the fallback scheme and does not apply if preferential contractual terms allow for leave to be taken in shorter periods. Further, where the need to provide childcare arises unexpectedly, an employee will be able to take time off to deal with this situation under the right to time off to care for dependants.

An employee may **not take more than** 4 weeks of leave in respect of each child during a particular year (Sch 2 para 8 SI 1999/3312). A year is calculated as starting on the date on which the employee **first becomes** entitled to leave with regard to each child, or where his/her entitlement has been interrupted at the end of a period of continuous employment (as when he/she has changed jobs and is working for another employer), on the date on which the employee **most recently became** entitled to take parental leave. Subsequent years will start on the anniversary of that date.

This deters an employee from using parental leave to work part-time after, say, maternity leave. If the employee works for 3 days out of her 5-day week and takes off 2 days a week as parental leave, she can only do this for 4 weeks in any year, and the time off will reduce her remaining entitlement in respect to that child to 9 weeks.

Postponement An employer may **postpone** a period of parental leave unless it relates to an employee taking leave from the date of birth or date of placement (Sch 2 para 6 SI 1999/3312). The employer can postpone leave for **up to** 6 months if he considers that the operation of his business would be unduly disrupted if the leave is taken. This may be the case if, for example, the work is at a seasonal peak, a significant proportion of the workforce will be on parental leave at the same time or the employee's role is such that his/her absence at that particular time would unduly harm the business.

If, because of postponement, the period of leave falls **after the child's 5th birthday**, then the employee is allowed to take it after this date.

The employer must give the employee **notice** in writing of the postponement, including the reasons for it and the new dates, not more than 7 days after the employee's notice was given to him.

There is no requirement to **keep records** though it is advisable to keep a track of how much leave has been taken.

SECTION 5

Right to request flexible working

4690 Employees who **care** for **adults** or **children under 17 years** (or **children under 18 if disabled**), subject to certain qualifying conditions (such as having worked for the employer for 26 weeks continuously prior to making the application), have the right to request a flexible working pattern which must be given serious consideration by their employer (ss 80F-I ERA 1996; Flexible Working (Eligibility, Complaints and Remedies) Regulations SI 2002/3236 as amended by SI 2009/595).

This entitlement does not give employees the right to work flexibly and, if the employer refuses an application, the tribunals cannot force the employer to accept flexible working practices. Rather the right is to a **procedure** that employees can use to facilitate the discussion for and mutual agreement of flexible working practices (Flexible Working (Procedural Requirements) Regulations SI 2002/3207). Consequently, the **initial onus** is on the employee to present a carefully thought-out application well in advance of when he/she would like the change in working pattern to take effect. On receipt of an application, the employer must follow a set procedure with him only refusing a request where there is a clear business reason for doing so.

> MEMO POINTS The Government has announced **proposals** to extend the right to make a flexible working request to all employees with 26 weeks' continuous service, irrespective of the reason for request, from 2014. The statutory procedure for considering requests will be replaced with a new duty upon employers to consider requests in a reasonable manner, within a reasonable period of time although there are no plans to alter the existing business reasons for an employer to refuse a request. The Government also intends to publish a statutory Code of Practice for businesses and proposes that employers should be allowed to take into account employees' individual circumstances when considering conflicting requests. Any further developments will be covered by our updating service.

4691 The following **changes can be requested** (s 80F(1)(a) ERA 1996):
– a change to the hours the employee is required to work;
– a change to the times the employee is required to work; and/or
– a change to the location of work (e.g. working from home).

See ¶1810 for further discussion of flexible working arrangements.

4692 If the request is accepted this will result in a **permanent change** to the employee's contract (unless otherwise agreed, for example a trial period may be initially appropriate to assess viability or to last for a set period).

Consequently, where the request is to care for a child, any changes do not have to be limited to the child's 17th birthday (or 18th if disabled). Likewise, where the request is to care for a sick adult, the changes will not necessarily be limited to the period of that adult's sickness. The exact changes will depend upon what is agreed between the parties.

Where any changes are permanent there is no automatic right to revert back to the former working pattern. Any subsequent reversion or change must be agreed.

Carers for children

4694 The right only applies to employees with **children under 17 years** (or **disabled children under 18**) who (s 80F ERA 1996; reg 3 SI 2002/3236 as amended by SI 2007/2286 and SI 2009/595):
a. have been **continuously employed** for at least 26 weeks;
b. **are** the mother, father, adopter, guardian, special guardian, foster parent or private foster carer of, or a person in whose favour a residence order is in force in respect of, the child, or their spouse, civil partner or partner (including partners of the same sex);
c. have, or are expected to have, **responsibility for the child's upbringing**; and
d. make the request to enable them to **care for the child**.

MEMO POINTS A **partner** is defined as the other member of a couple consisting of (a) a man and a woman who are not married to each other but are living together as if they were husband and wife, or (b) two people of the same sex who are not civil partners of each other but are living together as if they were civil partners.

An **adopter** is defined as a person with whom an adoption agency has decided the child should be placed for adoption, or a person who has given notice of his/her intention to apply for an adoption order.

Carers for adults

Carers of qualifying adults also have the right to request flexible working arrangements where the employee (reg 3B SI 2002/3236 as inserted by SI 2006/3314):
1. has been **continuously employed** for not less than 26 weeks; and
2. is **caring** or expects to be caring for a **person aged 18 or over** who is:
– **married** to, or the partner or civil partner of, the employee;
– a **relative** of the employee; or
– **living at the same address** as the employee.

4695

MEMO POINTS A **relative** in this context is a mother, father, adopter, guardian, special guardian, parent-in-law, step-parent, son, step-son, son-in-law, daughter, step-daughter, daughter-in-law, brother, step-brother, brother-in-law, sister, step-sister, sister-in-law, uncle, aunt or grandparent, and includes adoptive relationships and relationships of the full blood or half blood or, in the case of an adopted person, such of those relationships as would exist but for the adoption.

A. Making a request

Form and content of application The application must be **dated and in writing** and can be by letter, on a form provided by the employer or by email (reg 4 SI 2002/3236).

If an employee has **previously made an application**, he/she must wait a year before making a further application to the same employer.

4700

The application must state (s 80F ERA 1996; reg 4 SI 2002/3236):
– that the **application** is being **made under** the statutory right to request flexible working;
– that the **parent or carer** is responsible for the upbringing for the child (or adult) and that he/she is the mother/father etc (see ¶4694, above). Such self-certification will suffice;
– the **flexible working pattern** applied for and the **date** which he/she would like it to **start**. This date should allow time for the application to be considered and implemented. There is no set time, but the BIS guide on flexible working suggests that employees should expect it to take around 14 weeks or longer if a problem arises;
– **what effect**, if any, the employee thinks the proposed change would have on the employer and explain how, in his/her opinion, it can be dealt with. Employees are not expected to know every factor that might influence their employer's decision but they should show that they have considered the factors that they are aware of; and
– whether a **previous application** has been made to that employer and, if so, when.

4702

EXAMPLE
Examples of possible requests: variation sought
1. A claims processor requests on his application to **compress his hours** from 9am – 5pm Monday to Friday to 8am – 6pm Monday to Thursday. He states that he will still be working the same number of hours a week and will be able to continue to manage his existing caseload. He also states that most claims are received earlier in the week and that Friday is normally the quietest day.
2. A tyre fitter requests on his application that he would like to **start work an hour later** each day. He accepts that this would mean a reduction in his pay and states that he has asked the other fitters working in the branch whether they would be able to manage, and they have no problems with this. Mornings are usually less busy than afternoons, and they believe they would be able to handle any eventualities that may occur.

3. A shop assistant requests on her application to **change her hours** from 8am – 1pm to 10am – 3pm. She states that early mornings tend to be the quietest time and that the other two assistants agree that they will cover this period. She also states that as the lunch period is the busiest time, her new working pattern would result in an increase in the number of customers that could be served.

4. A manager requests on his application that he would like to **work from home** one day a week in order, by avoiding commuting, to care for his young child in the early evening. He states that he has asked other colleagues for their opinions and they have no objection. He also states that as he has a computer with broadband Internet access at home, he can readily stay in contact with the office.

Examples of possible requests: purpose of variation
Where an employee requests flexible working in order to **care** for a **child**, no further explanation will normally be expected. The sort of care-giving activities that **carers** of **adults** are likely to be involved in include:
– help with **personal care** (e.g. dressing, bathing, toileting);
– help with **mobility** (e.g. walking, getting in and out of bed);
– **nursing** tasks (e.g. daily blood checking; changing dressings);
– giving/supervising **medicines**;
– **escorting** to appointments (e.g. general practitioner (GP), hospital, chiropodist);
– **supervision** of the person being looked after;
– **emotional support**;
– keeping **company** with the care recipient;
– practical **household tasks** (e.g. preparing meals, doing shopping, domestic labour); and
– helping with financial matters or **paperwork**.

4703 The BIS guidance on flexible working recommends that employees provide the employer with as much **information** as possible, including evidence of a caring relationship although this is not required by the legislation.

Employees are not required under the flexible working legislation to demonstrate that the child or adult in question requires any **particular level of care**. Nor will employees be required to demonstrate why **they personally** are **needed** to provide that care.

EXAMPLE
1. An employee asking for a change in hours in order to care for her elderly mother will not need to show that her mother is unable to cope alone or that she qualifies for disability living allowance.
2. A father asking for reduced hours in order to care for his child will not be required to demonstrate why the care cannot be provided by the mother or by somebody else.

On the other hand, requests for flexible working can only be made for the purpose of providing care, and not for any other purpose. While an employer is not entitled under the legislation to ask for proof of either parental or caring responsibility, an employer might wish to be satisfied that a request is being made in **good faith**.

4704 BIS also recommends that as best practice employers should acknowledge the application.

Alternatively, if the employee has **failed to provide all of the required information**, the employer should inform the employee of what they have omitted and ask him/her to re-submit the application. The employer is under no legal obligation to consider the application if it is incomplete, but a failure to do so may be indirect sex discrimination (¶¶5300+).

B. Procedure for considering request

4710 **Meeting to hear request** The employer must hold a **meeting** with the employee to discuss the request and how it can be best accommodated **within** 28 days of receipt of the application, unless the employer has already agreed to it in writing, setting out the contract variation agreed to and the date it will take effect (reg 3 SI 2002/3207).

Where the **manager** who would ordinarily consider the application is **absent** due to annual leave or sickness, this **period only starts** to run from the earlier of the manager's return or 28 days after the receipt of the application (reg 13 SI 2002/3207).

The **time and place** of the meeting must be convenient to the employer and the employee (reg 11 SI 2002/3207).

If the employee **more than once fails to attend** a meeting to discuss a request without reasonable cause, the employer can treat the request as withdrawn (¶4725). In such circumstances, the employer must inform the employee in writing that he considers the employee's request to be withdrawn.

> MEMO POINTS The applicant has the **right to be accompanied** at the meeting (¶4720).

Making the decision Employers must **consider** all applications and establish whether the desired work pattern can be accommodated within the needs of the business. The advice from BIS is that employers should consider each application **objectively** on this basis, and not attempt to judge whether one applicant's need for flexible working is greater than another's.   **4711**

If the employer has received a valid request but feels that he **needs additional information** before he can give the request proper consideration, the employer can ask the employee to provide additional information. If the employee unreasonably refuses to provide this additional information, the employer can treat the request as withdrawn (¶4725). In such circumstances, the employer must inform the employee in writing that he considers the employee's request to be withdrawn.

Notification of decision Within 14 days of the meeting, the employer must inform his/her employee in a **written dated form** that he either (regs 4-5 SI 2002/3207):   **4712**
– **agrees** to the request, specifying the variation of contract terms agreed to and the date on which they are to take effect; or
– **rejects** the request, providing clear business grounds why the application cannot be accepted, including sufficient explanation as to why these reasons apply, as well as setting out an appeal procedure.

If a request for flexible working is only **partially accepted** then the employer should offer an appeal in respect of the part of the request which is rejected.

The **business grounds** must relate to one or more of the following grounds (s 80G ERA 1996):   **4713**
– burden of additional costs;
– detrimental effect on ability to meet customer demand;
– inability to re-organise work among existing staff;
– inability to recruit additional staff;
– detrimental impact on quality;
– detrimental impact on performance;
– insufficiency of work during the periods the employee proposes to work; and
– planned structural changes.

The BIS guide on flexible working suggests that an explanation of around two paragraphs will usually be sufficient, although the actual length will depend on the particular circumstances. In particular, it should:
– say why the business ground is relevant and why it cannot be accepted;
– avoid unfamiliar jargon;
– include all relevant and accurate facts; and
– not be overly complex or unnecessarily long.

For example, an appropriate explanation (given as an example by the BIS guide on flexible working) for rejecting a request not to work on a Thursday in a small manufacturing factory might be:

"I am sorry that I cannot grant your request to change the days that you work, but to allow you not to work on a Thursday would have a detrimental effect on the performance of the business.

Thursday is our busiest day of the week, when all staff are required to ensure that the machinists can continue making curtains while stock is received, and finished curtains are packaged ready to be despatched the following morning. You are aware that on a Thursday morning we receive our weekly delivery of fabric. This requires the involvement of all staff to help move the material from the delivery bay into the storeroom, before the newly made curtains can be prepared for despatch the following morning.

As I indicated when we met to discuss the application, if you decide to change the day you would prefer not to work to one earlier in the week, then I would be happy to reconsider your application."

> MEMO POINTS Employers should be careful to ensure that they do not discriminate in refusing a request otherwise a female employee whose request for flexible working is refused may have an indirect sex discrimination claim (¶¶5300+) and a male employee whose request is treated less favourably than a request from a female employee would have been treated may have a direct sex discrimination claim (see ¶¶5240+).

4715 **Appealing a refusal** The employee can appeal against any refusal by giving **written dated notice** within 14 days of the notification of the decision (reg 6 SI 2002/3207). This must set out the grounds of appeal.

> EXAMPLE While there are no restrictions on the grounds for appeal, common grounds for appeal are likely to be that:
> – the employee challenges a fact given by the employer to explain why a business reason applies;
> – a new fact has come to light (like another employee is now prepared to cover the time the employee does not want to work); or
> – the employee proposes an adapted working pattern that accommodates the grounds as set out in the refusal.

4716 If the employer does not accept the grounds of appeal, he should arrange a **meeting to discuss the appeal within** 14 days of receiving the employee's written notification.

The **time and place** of the meeting must be convenient to the employer and the employee (reg 11 SI 2002/3207).

If the employee **more than once fails to attend** a meeting to discuss a request without reasonable cause, the employer can treat the request as withdrawn. In such circumstances, the employer must inform the employee in writing that he considers the employee's request to be withdrawn.

> MEMO POINTS The applicant has the **right to be accompanied** at the appeal (¶4720).

4717 Within 14 days of the appeal meeting, the employer must inform the employee in a **written dated form** that he either:
– **upholds** the appeal, specifying the variation of contract terms agreed to and the date on which they are to take effect; or
– **dismisses** the appeal, stating the grounds for the dismissal including sufficient explanation as to why these grounds apply.

Extension of procedural time limits

4718 Any of the preceding time limits can be extended if the employer and employee agree (reg 12 SI 2002/3207): the employer's time to arrange the meeting or appeal; the employer's time to give a decision after the meeting or appeal; and the employee's time to choose whether to appeal.

In all circumstances, the employer must send a **dated written record** of the agreed extension to the employee stating the process the extension relates to and the date on which the extension ends.

Right to be accompanied at a meeting

4720 The employee has the right to be accompanied to the meeting to discuss the request or the appeal by a colleague, or a trade union representative as long as he also works for the employer (reg 14 SI 2002/3207). The colleague does not have to be an employee as long as he is a worker employed by the same employer as the employee. The employee can ask if a companion from outside the employer's organisation can attend, for example a trade union representative who is not employed by the employer, though the employer is under no obligation to accept such a request. The **role of the companion** is to support the employee and to this end he can address the meeting on behalf of the employee and confer with the employee during it, but cannot answer questions on behalf of the employee.

> MEMO POINTS   There is no statutory right for the companion to be a trade union representative (i.e. a trade union representative regardless of whether he is also employed by the employer) in contrast to the right to be accompanied to discipline or grievance hearings (¶6782).

4721 The employee should **contact his/her companion** as soon as he/she is given the date of the meeting. If the companion is **unable to make** this, the employer must accept an alternative time as proposed by the employee that is convenient for all parties and which takes place within 7 days of the date of the original meeting. If this cannot be achieved, the employee should consider an alternative companion.

4722 Companions are entitled to **paid time off** to act as a companion (reg 14(6) SI 2002/3207) (¶3910).

C. Withdrawal of request

4725 **Employees can withdraw** their application at any time by notifying their employer orally or in writing. In such cases, they cannot make a new application within 12 months of the date on which the application was made (reg 17 SI 2002/3207).

The **employer can also deem** that the **application has been withdrawn if** the employee (¶¶4710, 4711, 4716):
– misses two meetings to discuss the request/appeal without reasonable cause; or
– unreasonably refuses to provide the employer with information necessary for him to be able to consider the application. For example, an office worker may request to work 3 days a week at home but refuses to comply with any checks to ensure that their working space at home satisfies health and safety standards.

4726 The employer must **confirm the withdrawal** of the application in writing (unless already so provided by the employee).

SECTION 6

Time off to care for dependants

4740 This right was created to help employees to take time off to **deal with unforeseen events** regarding their dependants.

An employee can take **unpaid time off** to take whatever action is necessary (s 57A(1) ERA 1996):
– to provide assistance when a dependant falls ill (including mentally ill), gives birth or is injured or assaulted;
– to make arrangements for the care of a dependant who is ill or injured;
– when a dependant dies;
– because of the unexpected disruption or termination of arrangements for the care of a dependant; or
– to deal with an incident involving the employee's child that occurs unexpectedly during school.

4742 **Eligibility** A **dependant** is defined as a spouse, child, parent or person living in the same household as the employee other than those who are employed by the employee or his/her tenants, lodgers or boarders (s 57A(3)-(5) ERA 1996). With regard to the responsibilities of the employee to provide assistance when a dependant falls ill, or to make arrangements for the care of an ill dependant, or because of the disruption of arrangements for the care of a dependant; a dependant can be any person who reasonably relies on the employee for assistance or to make arrangements when such events occur.

> MEMO POINTS The rights to time off to care for dependants are the widest of all the family-friendly rights in that they potentially relate to all dependants including neighbours and friends and not just to employees' children or other relatives.

4744 **Notice** Employees must inform their employer of the reason for their absence as soon as reasonably practicable (s 57A(2) ERA 1996). Unless this cannot be complied with until the employee has returned to work, he/she must also tell his/her employer how long he/she expects to be absent. If the employee does not properly notify his/her employer, he/she loses his/her entitlement under this right (*Qua v John Ford Morrison Solicitors* [2003] ICR 482, EAT) and any unauthorised absences will be a disciplinary matter.

However, given that the right to take time off to care for dependants concerns taking time off to deal with **unexpected difficulties**, all that needs to be communicated is sufficient information for the employer to understand that something has occurred to cause a care arrangement to break down making it necessary for the employee to be urgently absent from work (*Truelove v Safeway Stores plc* [2005] ICR 589, EAT). It may not matter if the employee had advance warning that an unexpected difficulty was going to occur if he/she was not able to make alternative arrangements in time (*Royal Bank of Scotland v Harrison* [2009] ICR 116, EAT). Employers should not require a formal procedure to be used nor should they expect employees to make their application with any formality.

> EXAMPLE In *Royal Bank of Scotland v Harrison*, an employee had some weeks' warning that her usual childminder would not be available for a working day. After she had unsuccessfully tried to make other arrangements for cover, she made a request for time off to care for her children on that day. Her request was refused 2 days before she needed the time off. She took the day off anyway and was given a verbal warning for unauthorised absence. The EAT held that although there was advance warning of the need for leave of absence, it was still an unexpected event and therefore she was entitled to take the time off. The fact of advance knowledge might in some cases mean that it is not necessary for an employee to take time off, but that was not the case here, as she had no other option but to stay at home.

4746 **Duration** The employer must allow the employee a reasonable amount of time off so that he/she can take whatever actions are necessary. What is **necessary** will depend on the particular circumstances of each case, and factors include the nature of the incident that has occurred, the relationship between the employee and the dependant and the extent to which anyone else can provide assistance. For example, where a dependant has died, this includes taking time off to make funeral arrangements, attend the funeral, register the death, apply for probate etc. However, it does not include time off to deal with the emotional effects of bereavement (*Forster v Cartwright Black Solicitors* [2004] IRLR 781, EAT). What is **reasonable** will depend again on the circumstances of the employee and any disruption, inconvenience and cost to the employer must be ignored (*Qua v John Ford Morrison Solicitors* [2003] ICR 482, EAT).

> EXAMPLE Examples of what may be necessary:
> – Employee A taking time off when one of his parents dies to take action that is necessary as a consequence of the death.
> – Employee B attending a problem arising at her child's school.
> – Employee C assisting and making arrangements for an elderly neighbour, who relies on C, after he falls and injures himself.
> – Employee D sorting out alternative care arrangements for his friend, who requires care and relies on D, after his friend's carer does not turn up.

4748 If there is a **significant change in the circumstances** which results in the employee needing to extend the leave to more than what would be reasonable and necessary under the original circumstances, then he/she should re-notify his/her employer as soon as is practicable (*MacCulloch and Wallis Ltd v Moore* [2003] UKEAT 51_02_1102).

SECTION 7

Remedies

Employees have a right not to suffer a detriment, be unfairly dismissed or be less favourably treated as a consequence of exercising their rights to time off, leave and statutory pay. They also have additional specific remedies that will apply to each of these rights. **4760**

It is recommended that an employee who believes that he/she is entitled to make a complaint to a tribunal should **first seek to resolve** it with the employer, for example through a grievance or internal appeals procedure where one exists. Any compensation awarded by a tribunal may be reduced if the employee has not tried to resolve the matter in this way. **4761**

Further, **external dispute resolution** by third party mediation or conciliation, for example by using the services of an Acas conciliation officer, may be more desirable than pursuing an application through the tribunals. In particular, there is a **dispute resolution scheme** for employees to use with regard to complaints regarding the right to request flexible working (ACAS (Flexible Working) Arbitration Scheme (England and Wales) Order SI 2003/694).

Dismissing an employee because she is pregnant or for a reason connected with pregnancy or childbirth, or because he/she is on maternity, adoption or paternity leave, is **automatically unfair** (¶4771). Employees on leave also have a right to return and **failure to allow an employee to return** will amount to an unfair dismissal unless the employer can justify his actions (¶4451). Further special rules apply where, during leave, it is not practicable by reason of **redundancy** for the employer to continue to employ the employee under his/her existing contract of employment (¶4453). **4762**

If an employee is dismissed while pregnant or on maternity or adoption leave, he/she is entitled to a **written statement of reasons for his/her dismissal** (¶8310). Unlike with regard to the general right to a written statement of reasons for dismissal, no period of continuous employment is required and no request for the statement need be made. **4763**

> MEMO POINTS Under European **proposals** to amend EC Directive 1992/85, the duty to provide a written statement of reasons for dismissals will be extended to apply to dismissals up to 6 months after leave. Further developments will be covered by our updating service.

1. Right not to be discriminated against for relying on parents' and carers' rights

Sex discrimination and equal pay

As well as the following rights, it should be noted that an employee may, in certain circumstances, also have a claim for sex discrimination or equal pay (¶¶5261, 5320 and 5650). In particular, pregnant employees and those on maternity leave also have special protection, and any dismissals or detrimental treatment during this period due to a pregnancy or post-birth-related illness will amount to direct discrimination (¶5320). See the memo point to ¶5321 for a discussion as to what protection those undertaking IVF have. **4765**

Right not to suffer a detriment

An employee has the right not to be subjected to any detriment (short of dismissal) by an act or deliberate failure to act because of (ss 47C, 47D ERA 1996; reg 19 SI 1999/3312; reg 28 SI 2002/2788; reg 16 SI 2002/3207; reg 9 SI 2006/2014 which adds reg 20(3)(eee) SI 1999/3312; reg 33 SI 2010/1055): **4767**

– a reason connected with pregnancy or childbirth;
– taking maternity/adoption/paternity (including additional) leave or parental leave;
– time off to care for dependants;
– exercising his/her right to request flexible working;
– being a companion for a colleague at his/her meeting to request flexible working (this applies to workers as well as employees);
– undertaking, considering undertaking or not undertaking work during statutory maternity or adoption leave; or
– undertaking, or refusing to undertake, work on a KIT day.

> MEMO POINTS   What amounts to a "**detriment**" is not defined by the ERA 1996 and regulations, but case law on discrimination has held that it is whether a reasonable worker would feel he has been disadvantaged by reason of his employer's acts (¶5279).

4768 Complaints must be made **within** 3 months beginning with the date of the act or failure to act (or if it is part of a series of similar acts or failures, the last of them) (s 48 ERA 1996). However, a tribunal can **extend** this period if it is satisfied that it was not reasonably practicable for the employee to make the complaint in time.

4769 If the claim is **successful**, the tribunal can (s 49 ERA 1996):
– make a declaration; and/or
– order the employer to pay compensation.

Compensation will be the amount the tribunal considers just and equitable in all the circumstances having regard to the infringement and any loss which is attributable to the act, or failure to act. It will include any expenses reasonably incurred as a consequence and any loss of benefits which the employee might reasonably be expected to have had but for the act or failure to act. If the tribunal finds that the employee caused or contributed to the action, it will reduce the amount of compensation by such proportion as it considers just and equitable in the circumstances.

Automatic unfair dismissal

4771 An employee will be held to be automatically unfairly dismissed where the dismissal is:
a. on the **above grounds** (¶4767); or
b. on the **grounds of** (ss 99, 104C ERA 1996; reg 20 SI 1999/3312; reg 29 SI 2002/2788; reg 34 SI 2010/1055):
– a health and safety provision that could require a maternity suspension; or
– redundancy during maternity/adoption/additional paternity leave if the employer fails to offer any available suitable alternative employment.

> MEMO POINTS   1. For a dismissal to be automatically unfair because of a reason connected with the pregnancy of the employee, the employer must have **knowledge of the pregnancy** or must have believed the employee to be pregnant. It is not enough that the employer should have deduced from the employee's symptoms that she was pregnant (*Ramdoolar v Bycity Ltd* [2004] UKEAT 0236_04_3007). However, the EAT in this case did comment that it may be possible for a dismissal to be automatically unfair where the employer dismissed the employee because the employer had a suspicion that she might be pregnant.
> 2. For a dismissal to be automatically unfair because an employee is taking **paternity leave**, the dismissal has to be "**causally connected**" to the taking of paternity leave (*Atkins v Coyle Personnel plc* [2008] IRLR 420, EAT). In this case, the employee had a heated argument when his manager contacted him during his paternity leave, which culminated in the employer dismissing the employee. The EAT decided that on the facts the dismissal resulted from the argument and not from the taking of paternity leave and consequently the employee had not been automatically unfairly dismissed.

2. Right to remedies for failure to give or apply parents' and carers' rights

4780 An employee has the **right to complain** to a tribunal if the employer has:
– failed to allow the employee time off to attend antenatal appointments, or allowed her to attend such appointments but failed to pay her for such time (ss 57, 57A ERA 1996);

- unreasonably postponed or prevented, or attempted to prevent, a period of requested parental leave (s 80(1) ERA 1996);
- not allowed an employee to be accompanied at a meeting when making a request for flexible working (reg 15 SI 2002/3207); or
- not followed the correct procedure with regard to a request for flexible working, or has rejected the application on a ground that is not a valid business reason or was based on incorrect facts (s 80H ERA 1996).

> **MEMO POINTS** The tribunal has no power to order the employer to comply with a **request for flexible working**. The tribunal is entitled to consider the evidence to assess whether the employer's decision to refuse a request to work flexibly was based on incorrect facts, although it is not permitted to consider whether the employer acted fairly or reasonably in putting forward its rejection of the employee request for flexible working (*Commotion Ltd v Rutty* [2006] ICR 290, EAT). In order for the tribunal to assess whether the facts upon which the employer based his decision were correct or not, the tribunal will examine all the circumstances surrounding the situation in which the request was made. In particular, the tribunal will consider the following (non-exhaustive) factors:
> - could the request have been accepted without disruption?
> - how do other staff feel about the request? and
> - could the time be made up?

4786 Complaints must be made **within** 3 months beginning with the date of the act or failure to act or if it is part of a series of similar acts or failures, the last of them. Complaints regarding flexible working requests must be made within 3 months of either the date when the employee was notified of the final internal appeal decision or the date on which the alleged breach of duty was committed. However, a tribunal may **extend** this period if it is satisfied that it was not reasonably practicable for the employee to make the complaint in time (¶9465).

4788 If the claim is **successful**, the tribunal can:

Protected right	Remedy for breach	Legislative reference
Time off for antenatal care	Order employer to pay employee what she should have received for the period requested	s 57(4) ERA 1996
Time off to care for dependants	Order employer to pay employee such compensation as tribunal considers just and equitable in all the circumstances	s 57B(3)-(4) ERA 1996
Parental leave	Order employer to pay employee such compensation as tribunal considers just and equitable in all the circumstances	s 80(3)-(4) ERA 1996
Flexible working (right to request)	Order employer to reconsider request, or to pay employee such compensation as the tribunal considers just and equitable in all the circumstances, up to a limit of 8 weeks' pay, subject to the statutory cap (¶2923)	s 80I ERA 1996; reg 7 SI 2002/3236
Flexible working (right to be accompanied)	Order compensation of up to 2 weeks' pay, subject to the statutory cap (¶2923)	reg 15 SI 2002/3207

CHAPTER 15

Health and safety

OUTLINE

	¶¶
SECTION 1 Duties 4810	1 Women of child-bearing age and new or expectant mothers 4950
A Reasonable care............... 4815	2 Children and young people 4970
1 Tortious duty 4815	D Pay during medical suspension 4985
Vicarious liability............. 4825	E Insurance requirement 4990
2 Contractual duty 4835	
3 General statutory duties....... 4840	**SECTION 3 Specific issues** 5010
B Strict liability................. 4850	
	A Stress........................ 5010
	Scope for liability 5012
SECTION 2 Means of protection 4860	Employer responsibilities 5025
	B Bullying...................... 5040
	C Drugs and alcohol 5050
A Adequate management system 4860	D Smoking..................... 5080
1 Risk assessments 4865	E Asbestos-related and other single agent claims 5110
2 Further statutory duties....... 4870	
3 Information and training 4875	
4 Reporting requirements 4880	**SECTION 4 Remedies and enforcement** 5130
5 People with health and safety responsibilities 4900	
a Safety advisers and first aiders 4900	A Remedies 5130
b Employee representatives 4910	B Enforcement 5160
B Data protection................ 4940	1 Enforcement notices and prosecutions .. 5165
C Specific duties relating to vulnerable workers 4950	2 Offences..................... 5180

Employers have a number of duties in relation to health and safety at work. These are drawn from three areas of law. Under the common law, the employer owes duties in both **tort** and **contract** to employees and others. There are also extensive **statutory duties** to ensure the health and safety of their workers while at work and others affected by their activities; these comprise a **general** duty (Health and Safety at Work etc Act 1974 (HSWA 1974) as amended; Management of Health and Safety at Work Regulations SI 1999/3242 as amended) and **specific** duties covering working conditions and safety at work. For the rules relating to working time, see ¶¶3600+.

4800

Specific duties dealing with specific issues have developed from the general rules on health and safety. For example, certain **groups** within the working population, such as women of child-bearing age and young people, have additional statutory protection and further legislation has been introduced to provide this. Social and political developments have extended the scope of legislation to cover other health-related issues, including smoking. In recent years, the common law has also developed to deal with emerging **workplace problems** including stress, bullying and injuries caused by asbestos and other single agents.

> MEMO POINTS Practical guidance on the regulations is given by **Approved Codes of Practice** (referred to as HS Codes) issued by the Health and Safety Executive. Where an employer fails to comply with a code, this does not in itself give rise to a liability in criminal or civil law. However, failure to comply may be accepted by the courts as evidence of a breach of the relevant legislation unless the employer can prove that the requirement was met in some equally, or more, effective way. This approach has been confirmed by the Court of Appeal, although it emphasised that such guidance always had to be treated with caution as it did not carry the authority of a judicial decision and may be wrong (*Ellis v Bristol City Council* [2007] EWCA Civ 685).

4801 The **level of duty** owed by employers varies according to the source of the duty. The standard of duty under common law is one of reasonable care. Under **tort**, it is to take reasonable care of the health and safety of employees. Employers also have an **implied contractual duty** to take reasonable care of their employees' health and safety and an implied contractual duty of trust and confidence. Under **health and safety legislation**, the general level of duty is to take such steps as are reasonably practicable to protect health and safety, but in certain cases liability may be strict, i.e. the employer will be liable for breach regardless of how difficult it may be to comply with a duty.

4802 There are two sources of penalty for employers who fail in their health and safety duties. Workers may bring claims for **damages** under the common law, and the health and safety authorities can bring **criminal prosecutions** in respect of statutory offences. Breaches of common law duties will give rise to civil liability in damages if physical or mental injury arises (subject to proof of causation), whereas breach of statutory duties may lead to criminal proceedings and fines, irrespective of whether an individual worker is injured. Further, individual directors and managers can be personally prosecuted and fined, or, in extreme cases, imprisoned, as a result of offences committed by their company or organisation for breaches of statutory rules.

4803 There are also a number of **other** possible related **claims** based on the employment relationship, including:
– constructive dismissal, arising from a breach of mutual trust and confidence;
– unfair dismissal and the right not to suffer a detriment;
– disability discrimination; and
– further statutory claims relating to time off for safety representatives/representatives of employee safety, pay on medical suspension, maternity-related rights and whistleblowing.

4804 Employees and workers also have health and safety duties under tort, contract and statute.

Employees have a **tortious duty** to take reasonable care and an **implied contractual duty** to follow employer instructions and take reasonable care. They may also be bound under **express contractual terms** relating to health and safety. Within the statutory framework, all workers have an **obligation to take reasonable care** for their own safety while at work and for the safety of others who may be affected by their acts or omissions (s 7 HSWA 1974). They also have a **duty to co-operate** with their employer to enable him to comply with his statutory obligations. Workers must not, therefore, work in a dangerous way, or refuse to wear or use necessary protective equipment, as this will amount to a breach of their statutory obligations even if it is only their own safety which is affected. Further, workers have **particular duties** to use equipment and materials in accordance with the training that has been provided and to report any hazardous situations or shortcomings in the employer's arrangements to the employer.

Disciplinary action may be taken against those who are in **breach** of these duties and in certain circumstances a breach may justify dismissal (¶6540). Such behaviour may also reduce the amount of damages that they might be able to obtain as a result of a successful court or tribunal claim.

SECTION 1

Duties

The health and safety obligations of the employer are to be found under the law of tort, contract and statute. There are **two standards** of duty. Under tort, contract, and most statutory provisions the standard is qualified, being either one of reasonable care or what is reasonably practicable. Certain statutory duties impose a higher standard – absolute or strict liability (i.e. where an employer is held responsible even if he is not negligent or at fault, see ¶4850).

Under the principle of vicarious liability, an employer may also be liable for actions of his employees, and others under his control, which cause damage to third parties.

A. Reasonable care

1. Tortious duty

Employers have a common law duty under tort to take **reasonable care** of their employees' safety. What is considered reasonable will depend on the circumstances and what steps the employer took or should have taken to prevent the harm from arising. This is not, therefore, an absolute duty. For example, working in a war zone involves risks that cannot be guarded against even by the exercise of reasonable skill and care for the safety of the employee (*Tarrant v Stuart Ramage* [1995] IRLR 35, QBD). Consequently, where the terms of the employment contract require an employee to perform a task where there is an obvious health risk, the scope of the employer's duty will be narrower than if that term did not exist (*Johnstone v Bloomsbury Health Authority* [1991] IRLR 118, CA). Where an employee runs the risk of **physical danger to himself** (other than when this is a necessary, reasonable and acceptable part of his job) if he continues in employment, the employer is under a duty to dismiss him (*Coxall v Goodyear Great Britain Ltd* [2003] 1 WLR 536, CA).

Further, employers who **occupy premises** must take such care as is reasonable in all the circumstances to ensure the premises are safe. This duty is owed not only to employees but also to **visitors** and, in some cases, **trespassers**.

The courts have recognised that an employer **will have shown reasonable care** by providing his employees with a safe place of work, safe tools and equipment and a safe system of working (*Wilsons and Clyde Coal Co Ltd v English* [1938] AC 57, HL). Generally, an employer will only breach his duty of care if he fails to take **reasonable steps** to prevent the harm, bearing in mind the magnitude of the risk, the gravity of any harm, the costs and practicability of preventing it and any justifications for running the risk.

The employer's duty is owed to **each individual employee** (*Paris v Stepney Borough Council* [1951] AC 367, HL). With regard to this, an employer will not be expected to take extra precautions to protect an employee with an **unusual susceptibility** unless the employer is aware or ought to have been aware of that employee's vulnerability (*Barber v Somerset County Council* [2004] IRLR 475, HL; *Paris v Stepney Borough Council* [1951] AC 367, above). Similarly an employer is entitled to take into account an employee's **particular skill or experience**.

> EXAMPLE In *Pickford v ICI plc* [1998] IRLR 435, HL, the House of Lords found that the employer did not have a legal duty specifically to warn a qualified and experienced senior secretary (who had responsibility to organise and plan her own work) that she should intersperse other work with her typing to avoid risk of Repetitive Strain Injury (RSI). RSI was not reasonably foreseeable in her case. The Court contrasted P's position with that of typists in the accounts department, to whom the employer was obliged to give instructions, warning and advice about the need to take breaks.

4818 Tests which are used to determine whether an employer has been negligent include a comparison with the actions expected of a **reasonable employer**, and whether the injury, loss or damage was **reasonably foreseeable**. For example, the possibility that there may be an explosion when using welding equipment in tanks containing flammable material would be reasonably foreseeable.

Where the damage is **not foreseeable**, for example if the employee's job involves the use of a chemical which is not known to have long-term effects, the employer will not usually be liable for the employee's ill health which occurs as a result of the exposure, if the chemical was used correctly in light of the contemporaneous knowledge.

> EXAMPLE
> **Reasonably foreseeable**
> In *Robb v Salamis (M & I) Ltd* [2007] ICR 175, HL(Sc), a worker was sleeping on a top bunk on an oil platform, woke, and attempted to climb down using a movable ladder which had not been attached properly. He fell and was hurt. No accidents had previously happened on the platform in this way. The House of Lords held, however, that to place a movable ladder next to a bunk bed was to create a risk which, in the ordinary course of human affairs, a reasonable employer should have anticipated.
>
> **Not reasonably foreseeable**
> In *Maguire v (1) Harland & Wolff Plc and (2) Harland & Wolff Holdings Plc* [2005] EWCA Civ 1, it was held the dangers of asbestos poisoning became generally known as a result of an article published in the *Sunday Times* in October 1965. Accordingly, where the wife of a boilermaker had acquired mesothelioma as a result of washing the clothes that her husband had brought home during his employment in a shipyard between 1961 and March 1965, the risk was not foreseeable to the employer given the knowledge at that time and she was unsuccessful in her claim.

4819 The **damage suffered** by the employee, which can be physical injury or financial loss, must be shown to have been **caused by** the employer's negligence and the onus is on the employee to show that the injury or loss was caused by his employer's breach of duty.

> EXAMPLE In *Volex Group plc v Jane Wilson Evans* [2002] EWCA Civ 225, E's claim failed because she had not proved that her illness was caused by the fumes from her employer's machinery.

Vicarious liability

4825 **For employee actions** An employer may be vicariously liable for his employee's acts or omissions and may be held responsible if his **employee injures someone** in the course of employment, even when the employer did not specifically authorise the act that caused the injury. Whether or not the act was in the "**course of employment**" will be determined by looking at the job being done in general terms and not whether the employer authorised each step of the task carried out by the employee (*Fennelly v Connex South Eastern Ltd* [2001] IRLR 390, CA). The correct **approach** is to concentrate on the relative closeness of the connection between the nature of the employment and the employee's wrongdoing, and not whether the acts could be viewed as authorised (or a wrongful and unauthorised mode of doing an authorised act) (*Lister v Hesley Hall Ltd* [2001] IRLR 472, HL; *Dubai Aluminium Co Ltd v Salaam* [2003] IRLR 608, HL followed in *Mattis v Pollock (t/a Flamingo's Nightclub)* [2003] EWCA Civ 887). This point should be taken broadly: what is important is whether the employee's wrongdoing can be closely connected with the employment so that when "looking at the matter in the round" it is just and reasonable to hold the employer vicariously liable (*Bernard v Attorney-General of Jamaica* [2005] IRLR 398, PC). The reality is that there is often a fine line between acts carried out in the course of employment and those that are not and it is important to note that each case will turn on its own facts but the nature of the workplace, the respective roles of the violent employee and the victim, how quickly the violent reaction occurred and where it occurred are all relevant factors to be taken into account in deciding whether the employer should be vicariously liable.

> EXAMPLE
> 1. In *Weddall v Barchester Healthcare Ltd; Wallbank v Wallbank Fox Designs Ltd* [2012] EWCA Civ 25, the Court of Appeal jointly dealt with two cases in which junior employees, having been given reasonable and lawful requests or instructions, were violent towards senior colleagues, and considered whether

the employers were vicariously liable for those acts of violence. The facts of the two cases and the Court's findings in respect of them are as follows:

– W, the deputy manager of a care home, was responsible for arranging replacements for night-shift employees who were absent. One night, he telephoned M, a senior health assistant, and asked if he was willing to work a shift which needed to be covered. M was free to accept or refuse the request. M was drunk when he received the call and was upset because he thought that W was mocking him because of his drunken state. M proceeded to cycle to the care home and, just 20 minutes after receiving the phone call, violently attacked W. In the leading judgment, the Court of Appeal stated that it had no difficulty in upholding the county court judge's decision that M's actions were separate and distinct from his employment. W's request to M to fill an empty shift was simply a pretext for M's violence, which was unconnected with his work as a health assistant. The assault merely happened to occur at the place of work, but was otherwise unconnected with M's employment. As such, the employer was not vicariously liable; and

– WBK was the managing director of a small manufacturing company. There was evidence that it was sometimes difficult to communicate instructions to one of the employees, B. During B's supervision, WBK noticed a gap in the manufacturing process, which was resulting in a loss of fuel. WBK told B to fix the error, but B did not reply. WBK said "Come on", to indicate a willingness to help B. B then put his hand on WBK's face and threw him onto a table. The Court of Appeal found this case more difficult to decide and "not without hesitation" concluded that the employer should be vicariously liable for the spontaneous violence used by B in reaction to the reasonable instruction given to him. While the use of force was not inherent in the nature of B's employment, the instantaneous nature of the reaction and its close relation with the employment in both time and space were relevant factors. Further, recent authorities suggested that what is reasonably incidental to an employee's duties should be viewed broadly. The possibility of friction is inherent in any employment relationship, but particularly one in a factory, and frustrations which lead to a reaction involving some violence are predictable. As such, the employer was vicariously liable.

2. In *Gravil v Redruth Rugby Football Club Ltd and anor* [2008] IRLR 829, CA, a semi-professional rugby player punched another during a match, while the ball was out of play. The punch caused significant injury, for which damages were awarded. The Court of Appeal held that the club for which he was playing was vicariously liable for the injury. The Court's decision was based on the existence of a contract of employment, which included a term that the player should not assault another player, and the fact that the type of incident which led to the assault was a frequent part of the game.

4826 An employer may also be vicariously liable if he fails to protect an employee against **harassment, bullying or victimisation by fellow employees**, particularly when he knows that acts carried out by his employees during their employment may cause physical or mental harm to a fellow employee and does nothing to prevent it when it is in his power to do so (*Waters v Commissioner of Police of the Metropolis* [2000] IRLR 720, HL).

4827 The House of Lords has held that an employer can be vicariously liable for a **breach of a statutory duty imposed only on its employees**; in this case under the Protection from Harassment Act 1997 (legislation originally introduced to give protection from stalkers) (*Majrowski v Guy's and St Thomas's NHS Trust* [2006] ICR 1199, HL) (¶5045). As with all claims under vicarious liability, the employer will only be liable if the acts or omissions occur in the course of employment (i.e. there is sufficient link between the wrongdoing and the employee's duties to make it fair and just to hold the employer vicariously liable).

4829 **For actions of contractors and their employees** An employer may also be vicariously liable for the acts of its contractor's employees where the employer has control over the way in which they work (*Hawley v Luminar Leisure Ltd and ors* [2006] IRLR 817, CA). In such circumstances, the contractor's employees will be "temporary deemed employees" for the purposes of vicarious liability. In this case, the employer, who was the owner of a nightclub, was held to be vicariously liable for an assault carried out by a doorman employed by a security company but over whom the employer had control.

MEMO POINTS 1. As a **practical measure**, if employers want to limit their exposure to such liability, they must ensure that any contractors they hire retain the responsibility for controlling and supervising their employees. Where control and supervision cannot be left to the contractor, employers should ensure that the contractor's employees are properly trained and supervised at all times.

2. **Dual vicarious liability** is possible (i.e. more than one "employer" is liable) if, on the facts of a particular case, the sensible answer to the core question "who was entitled, and in theory

obliged, to control the employee's negligent act so as to prevent it" would be each of two "employers". (*Viasystems (Tyneside) Ltd v Thermal Transfer (Northern) Ltd and ors* [2005] IRLR 983, CA).

2. Contractual duty

4835 There is an implied contractual term that the employer has a duty to take reasonable care which mirrors the duty under tort (*Marshall Specialist Vehicles Limited v Osborne* [2003] IRLR 672, EAT). The employer's duty of care is also covered by the implied term of **trust and confidence**. This obligation is confined to matters arising during the subsistence of the employment relationship, and does not apply in relation to the manner of a dismissal (¶1241).

4836 **Damages** are assessed on the basis of whether the injury was within the reasonable contemplation of the parties at the time the contract was made (the test of "remoteness").

4837 Where the **breach of duty is fundamental**, an employee is entitled to resign and claim constructive dismissal (¶8230). The requirements for establishing liability also mirror the duty under tort (*Marshall Specialist Vehicles Limited v Osborne*, above).

3. General statutory duties

4840 Employers have a general statutory duty to ensure the health and safety of their workers while at work **as far as is reasonably practicable** (s 2 HSWA 1974). The duty extends to risks arising from:
– the work;
– how the employer conducts the undertaking;
– supervision, training, instruction or lack of it;
– the plant, equipment, materials and substances used; and
– the condition of the premises and provision of welfare facilities.

The employer's duty is to take steps to **eliminate identified risks** if it is reasonably practicable to do so. What is reasonably practicable will depend on the circumstances and the degree of risk in a particular job or workplace balanced against the time, trouble, cost and physical difficulty of taking measures to avoid or reduce that risk. In the event of a prosecution, the **burden of proof** will be on the employer to prove that it was not reasonably practicable to have taken additional steps which would have avoided or reduced the risk.

> MEMO POINTS 1. The HS Codes provide **further guidance** on what is reasonably practicable.
> 2. A **challenge** to the formula of reasonable practicability ended with the Court of Justice of the European Union ruling that the test is compatible with European health and safety law (*Commission of the European Communities v UK, Case C-127/05* [2007] ICR 1393, ECJ).

4841 The employer, as an **occupier of premises**, also has a duty to ensure the safety of employees, visitors and, in some cases, trespassers under statute law (Occupiers Liability Acts 1957 and 1984).

Further, where an employer has, to any extent, **control of premises** used as a workplace, or a place where others may use plant and substances provided for their use, statutory health and safety duties to employees also arise with respect to those premises (s 4 HSWA 1974; Workplace (Health, Safety and Welfare) Regulations SI 1992/3004). A person or organisation is in control of premises if they have obligations under a tenancy or contract for the maintenance or repair of premises, or the health and safety of plant or substances to the extent of the contractual duties imposed upon them. These obligations extend to employers who **use premises** as a place of work, or use the machinery or materials there. The obligation on the employer is not absolute but he is expected to take such steps as are reasonable for an employer in his position to take to ensure that, as far as is reasonably practicable, the premises, the plant and machinery are safe (s 4 HSWA 1974).

Where the workers of one employer **work on the premises of another**, the employer in charge of the premises should provide the employer of the visiting staff with comprehensible information on any risks that the host employer's activities may cause to the visiting workers, and the relevant precautions that are required. Further, there is a duty on the host employer to provide both the employer of the visiting workers, and the workers themselves, with details of the staff nominated by the host employer to implement emergency procedures on the premises (reg 11 Management of Health and Safety at Work Regulations SI 1999/3242).

Duty to non-workers Employers also have a statutory duty to take reasonable steps to protect non-workers from risks to their health and safety as a result of the employer's activities, so far as is reasonably practicable (s 3(1) HSWA 1974). Non-workers **include** visitors to an employer's workplace, members of the public affected by the work undertaken, and contractors and their workers undertaking work for the employer.

The duty extends to the provision of information, instruction or training where this is needed to avoid putting non-workers at risk.

4843

Where an employer engages a **contractor** to undertake work on his behalf, or on his premises, the employer has responsibilities in relation to the competence of the contractor to undertake the work safely, and the information provided to the contractor in relation to risks on the employer's premises, or in relation to the work involved. To comply with this duty employers must, therefore, assess the competence of the contractors to be engaged and ensure that they are provided, so far as is reasonably practicable, with sufficient information and, if necessary, instruction and training to reduce the risks (ss 2-3 HSWA 1974; regs 11-12 SI 1999/3242).

4844

There are additional requirements where **large construction contracts** are undertaken, or in the case of any **demolition work**.

4845

B. Strict liability

Compliance with statutory duties will usually be satisfied by taking all reasonable steps. However, with regard to certain risks the employer's liability will be **absolute** and the employer will be liable for any breach irrespective of whether it is reasonably practicable to comply with the duty imposed. For example, there is an absolute obligation on the employer to ensure that work equipment is maintained in an efficient state, in efficient working order and in good repair (Stark v The Post Office [2000] EWCA Civ 64; SI 1998/2306).

4850

EXAMPLE In R v Gateway Foodmarkets Ltd [1997] IRLR 189, CA, the practice at a local depot was to leave a trap door open frequently. R, a worker, fell through the trap door and died. The offence (under s 2 HSWA 1974) was held to be one of strict liability and it was, therefore, irrelevant that the practice was not known or sanctioned by head office.

SECTION 2

Means of protection

A. Adequate management system

Employers have a responsibility not only for the physical standards of health and safety at work, but also for the management system that ensures such standards are established and maintained. The management system for managing health and safety **covers** the way in which health and safety matters are planned, organised, controlled, monitored and reviewed (reg 5 SI 1999/3242).

4860

The health and safety management system must also provide adequate **emergency procedures** (reg 8 SI 1999/3242). Employers have an obligation to establish emergency procedures for the evacuation of the workplace in the event of serious and imminent danger, and to ensure that employees do not return to the workplace until it is safe to do so. The procedures must include arrangements for informing employees of the nature of the hazard which has arisen and the appropriate steps to be taken. There must also be a sufficient number of competent persons to implement these procedures.

MEMO POINTS   The HSE has produced useful guidance entitled "Five steps to risk assessment", which can be found at flmemo.co.uk/em4860.

4861 In **establishing** an adequate management system, the employer should:
– **consult** his safety advisers and other appropriate representatives (¶¶4910+);
– **assess** where there are any risks and take appropriate action where necessary (¶4865). In particular, risk assessments are required to be performed with regard to certain activities and groups (¶¶4956, 4976); and
– **inform and train** employees and others who are working at or visiting his premises.

4862 Employers are required to make a **written record** of these arrangements and these can be incorporated into the overall health and safety policy.

Further, employers are required to produce and, where necessary, update a written **statement of general policy** with respect to health and safety and the organisation and arrangements for implementing it (s 2(3) HSWA 1974). The health and safety policy, therefore, needs to detail, or make reference to, the responsibilities of key members of staff within the organisation and the health and safety procedures and standards that are implemented. It is normally a three part document – Health and Safety Policy Statement, Organisation, and Arrangements. Depending on the complexity and scale of the organisation there may be a number of more detailed procedures which supplement or which together make up the "Arrangements" part of the Policy.

MEMO POINTS   Employers with **four or fewer employees** are exempt from the requirement to write down their health and safety policy.

1. Risk assessments

4865 Employers must assess the risks affecting their employees whilst they are at work and also those risks arising from the work activities affecting non-employees. The risk assessment process is a part of the employer's health and safety management system (SI 1999/3242). The primary purpose of risk assessments is to identify the actions the employer needs to take to comply with legal requirements and, therefore, to ensure that risks are adequately controlled. In addition to this general duty to assess the risks of their activities, employers are required to undertake certain specific types of risk assessment such as those covering manual handling risk, noise and exposure to substances hazardous to health (¶4867).

4866 Significant **findings** of the risk assessment must be recorded.

MEMO POINTS   Employers with **four or fewer employees** do not have to make a written record, although it may be advisable to do so. Recording the risk assessment can be used as evidence to show that a risk assessment was carried out. However, it should be borne in mind that it is also evidence of what was included and what was omitted – weaknesses could be used against the employer in the event of a prosecution or civil claim.

4867 **Specific risk assessments** must be made regarding women of child-bearing age (¶4956) and children and young people (¶4976).

Further, the following specific risk assessments (which are outside the scope of this chapter) must also be made regarding:
– manual handling which involves risk of injury (SI 1992/2793);
– noise (SI 1989/1790);
– personal protective equipment (SI 1992/2966);

- fire safety (SI 2005/1541);
- first aid (assessment of first aid needs) (SI 1981/917); and
- workstations and display screen equipment (SI 1992/2792).

This list is not exhaustive. The risk assessment must identify the hazards arising from the work activity and the action required to control them. Following the risk assessment process, actions must be implemented. Staff must be consulted on the findings of risk assessments.

2. Further statutory duties

Over and above the duty to carry out risk assessments, employers have other duties under the following provisions relating to common risk areas:

Subject matter	Regulation	SI
Provision of a safe workplace	Workplace (Health, Safety and Welfare)	1992/3004
Electrical equipment and processes	Electricity at Work	1989/635
Fire precautions	The Regulatory Reform (Fire Safety) Order	2005/1541
Provision and maintenance of safe plant and equipment	Provision and Use of Work Equipment	1998/2306
The reduction of risk where manual handling operations involve a risk of injury	Manual Handling Operations	1992/2793
The reduction of risk with regard to working at heights	Work at Height	2005/735
Physical working conditions, including ventilation, heating, lighting and welfare issues	Workplace (Health, Safety and Welfare)	1992/3004
Noise	Control of Noise at Work	1989/1790
Vibrations	Control of Vibrations at Work	2005/1093
Display screen equipment	Health and Safety (Display Screen Equipment)	1992/2792
Provision of protective clothing, personal protective equipment (PPE) and safety signs	Personal Protective Equipment at Work	1992/2966
Provision for first aid	Health and Safety (First Aid)	1981/917
Duty to manage asbestos	Control of Asbestos	2012/632
Hazardous substances	Control of Substances Hazardous to Health	2002/2677
Construction site safety and management	Construction (Design and Management)	2007/320

There are also **detailed requirements** relating to specific problems, for example dangerous substances, radiation, lead and the transportation of hazardous materials.

EXAMPLE In *Gravatom Engineering Systems Limited v Parr* [2007] EWCA Civ 967, a case concerning the reduction of risk in manual handling operations, the Court of Appeal considered an employee whose back was injured while working as part of a group of four employees moving large machines in a factory. Preventive measures which the employer could have taken would have included the use of mechanical lifting devices or the use of more personnel in the group. Moreover, the employer had not carried out a risk assessment. The Court held that the employer had not taken all reasonable and practical measures to reduce the risk.

MEMO POINTS **Using hand-held mobile telephones** while driving is a criminal offence (SI 2003/2695). There is an exemption for emergency calls where it is not possible for the driver to stop. Note that employers may be liable if they require their employees to use hand-held phones while driving on business or if they fail to expressly ban such use.

3. Information and training

4875 As well as informing employees with regard to any specific risks, employers must also provide their employees with certain **basic information** concerning their health, safety and welfare at work (Health and Safety Information for Employees Regulations SI 1989/682). This information is contained in a poster and a leaflet approved by the HSE. Employers can comply with their duty either by displaying the poster or by providing employees with a copy of the leaflet.

> MEMO POINTS Employers can obtain copies of the poster and leaflet from HSE Books. The leaflet is also available at flmemo.co.uk/em4875.

4877 An employer has considerable **duties** to provide health and safety training for employees and the management system for health and safety should explain how health and safety training needs will be identified and fulfilled (SI 1999/3242). Employers must, in particular, ensure that the selection of employees takes **account of their capability** in relation to health and safety matters, and that employees receive adequate health and safety training in the following circumstances:
– on being recruited into the employer's undertaking;
– on being exposed to new or increased risks because of a transfer or change of responsibilities, or due to the introduction of new technology; and
– with regard to work equipment or a new or changed system of work.

The requirements for health and safety training **apply at** all levels in an organisation, including senior managers and directors. The content of the health and safety training necessary will vary because while more junior staff may need specific training on particular work equipment or systems of work, senior staff will need training in health and safety responsibilities and the overall management of health and safety.

4. Reporting requirements

4880 Employers must report the following to the relevant health and safety enforcement authority (HSE, local authorities and Office of Rail Regulation) (Reporting of Injuries, Diseases and Dangerous Occurrences Regulations SI 1995/3163 as amended by SI 2012/199) (known as RIDDOR):

a. accidents to employees resulting in a reportable injury on the employer's premises or on other premises if they occur in connection with the work activity or due to work-related violence. **Reportable injuries** are:
– death;
– a specified major injury; and
– an injury resulting in absence from work for more than 7 consecutive days excluding the day of the accident but including any rest days when the employee would have been unfit for work. This used to apply to over-3 day accidents, but this has been increased to over 7 days since 6 April 2012. Over-3 day accidents must be still recorded though and the record made available to the enforcing authority on request;

b. accidents to non-employees where the person dies or they are taken from the scene of an accident to hospital for treatment;

c. occupational diseases; and

d. dangerous occurrences (i.e. near-miss accidents) relating to work that occur on premises under their control.

> MEMO POINTS 1. See the **Health and Safety Executive website** for full details.
> 2. **Road accidents** involving work and **incidents involving gas** have additional reporting requirements.
> 3. There are also a number of reporting requirements administered by other regulators in the **health and social care sector**. These requirements are separate to and distinct from the reporting requirements above. There are also requirements for the reporting of notifiable diseases which apply to medical practitioners and should not be confused with reporting requirements for occupational diseases under RIDDOR.
> 4. In autumn 2012, the HSE consulted on **proposals** to simplify and lessen the current set of obligations in relation to the reporting of injuries, diseases and dangerous occurrences. Proposals included the removal of both the duty on employers to report dangerous occurrences outside

of high-risk sectors/activities and requirements to report most occupational diseases. Under the proposals, the need to report all fatal injuries to workers and to members of the public as a result of a work activity would remain, as would the duty to report major injuries to workers. Further developments will be covered in our updating service.

Procedure

Reports **must be made**:
– without delay in cases of death, major injuries, reportable accidents to non-employees, and dangerous occurrences;
– within 15 days of the incident in cases of over-7 day injuries; and
– as soon as possible when a doctor has notified that an employee is suffering from a reportable occupational disease and has been doing a connected work activity.

Employers can report a reportable incident online or by webform or post. Major injuries and deaths can be reported by telephone if preferred. See the Health and Safety Executive's incident reporting requirements at flmemo.co.uk/em4883 for further details.

Records of reports must be **kept for** 3 years and should contain the following information (reg 7 SI 1995/3163):
– date and time of the accident, dangerous occurrence or disease;
– brief description of the circumstances;
– full name, nature of the injury/disease and occupation of any relevant employee;
– full name, nature of the injury and status, e.g. school pupil, customer, passenger etc, of any injured member of public;
– date on which the event was first reported; and
– method by which the event was reported.

There is no legal requirement as to the **form** records should be in and records may be kept, for example, by:
– keeping copies of report forms in a file;
– recording the details on a computer; or
– maintaining a written log.

It is advisable to keep a copy of the RIDDOR form submitted to the HSE as the employer's record of the accident, incident or disease. Insurers are likely to ask for this in the event of any claim or prosecution arising from the event.

> MEMO POINTS   Employers with 10 or more employees must also keep an **accident book** under the social security regulations (Social Security (Claims and Payments) Regulations SI 1979/628 as amended) and these records will suffice for the purposes of the health and safety regulations above.

4883

4884

---

5. People with health and safety responsibilities

a. Safety advisers and first aiders

Assistance and advice

Employers are required to **appoint** one or more competent persons to provide health and safety assistance and advice (SI 1999/3242). The person(s) selected must be given sufficient training or have the requisite knowledge and experience to assist the employer properly. The actual **level of training and competence** required will depend on the risks in the employer's undertaking and the scope of advice required. The **number** of employees (or consultants) appointed must be adequate, having regard to the size and nature of the organisation and the type of risks involved.

The person(s) appointed can either be an employee or an external body or person, or a combination of both. However, where there is an appropriate employee with adequate competence, there is a legal preference that such an employee is appointed. Where there is insufficient or inadequate assistance within the organisation, then external competent assist-

4900

ance must be sought. In many cases, a range of different types of assistance may be needed, including professional health and safety practitioners and occupational health professionals, such as occupational health physicians or occupational health nurses. In certain circumstances, other disciplines such as safety engineering staff and occupational hygienists may be needed.

4901 Where the employer is undertaking certain types of **specialist activity**, trained and competent staff must be appointed. For example, work with ionising radiation will usually require the appointment of radiation protection supervisors and a specialist radiation protection adviser, and work involving the transport or consigning for transport of hazardous goods will require the appointment of a dangerous goods safety adviser with particular qualifications and training.

Fire safety

4903 Employers must **appoint** one or more competent persons for providing assistance and advice on fire safety matters (SI 2005/1541). The same considerations apply in relation to internal and external appointments (¶4900). The same person may be used for both health and safety and fire safety, provided the adviser is competent in both areas.

Emergencies and first aid

4905 Employers must **assess** the equipment, facilities and numbers of first aiders needed to give first aid at work. In **small, low risk organisations** (SI 1981/917) it may be sufficient to appoint an untrained person to take charge of emergencies and first aid equipment. Two or more employers can share arrangements for first aid provided the cover is adequate and the arrangements are agreed in writing (SI 1981/917).

4906 **Appointed persons** are not required to have any formal training although they will need to know the procedures for calling the emergency services. Untrained appointed persons should not attempt to administer first aid.

First aiders must be adequately trained and hold a **valid certificate of training** issued by a training organisation approved by the HSE. There are two levels of first aid training, Emergency First Aid at Work (EFAW) which involves 6 hours of training and First Aid at Work (FAW) which require at least 18 hours of training. Certificates are valid for 3 years. To extend the FAW qualification the first aider must attend a retraining course and pass the test no later than 28 days after the expiry of the certificate. Retraining can take place up to 3 months before the expiry date of the certificate. If the retraining deadline is missed the full course must be retaken to obtain a new certificate.

> MEMO POINTS **Additional training** will be needed where the employer has special risks, for example work in confined spaces or work with toxic or hazardous substances. Annual refresher training is also strongly recommended.

4907 The HSE publishes guidance on the **typical number** of first aiders required, as shown below. There should be sufficient numbers to cover **periods of holiday** and foreseeable **sickness** absence.

Risk level of operation	Numbers employed at any location	Suggested number of first aid personnel
Lower risk e.g. shops, offices, libraries	Fewer than 50	At least one appointed person
	50-100	At least one first aider
	More than 100	One additional first aider for every 100 employed
Medium risk e.g. light engineering and assembly work, food processing, warehousing	Fewer than 20	At least one appointed person
	20-100	At least one first aider for every 50 employed
	More than 100	One additional first aider for every 100 employed

Risk level of operation	Numbers employed at any location	Suggested number of first aid personnel
Higher risk e.g. most construction sites, slaughterhouses, chemical manufacturers, extensive work with dangerous machinery or sharp instruments	Fewer than 5	At least one appointed person
	5-50	At least one first aider
	More than 50	One additional first aider for every 50 employed
	Where there are hazards for which additional first aid skills are necessary	In addition, at least one first aider trained in the specific emergency action

b. Employee representatives

Employers must **consult** with employees or their representatives on health and safety matters. The requirements differ depending on whether or not there is a recognised trade union representing the employees.

Establishments with recognised trade unions

A recognised trade union has the right to appoint **safety representatives** who are employees of the employer (reg 3 Safety Representatives and Safety Committees Regulations SI 1977/500). An employee appointed as a safety representative must, so far as is reasonably practicable, either have been employed by the employer for the previous 2 years, or have at least 2 years' experience in similar employment. Provided the trade union notifies the employer in writing of the names of the safety representatives appointed and the group or groups of employees they represent, the safety representatives will have the rights and functions detailed below.

Where at least two safety representatives request, in writing, that a **safety committee** be set up, the employer must, in the course of establishing the committee, consult with the safety representatives and representatives of recognised trade unions whose members work at the workplace (reg 9 SI 1977/500). This includes determining the exact composition of the safety committee, details of its membership and terms of reference. The employer must then post a notice, stating the composition of the committee and the workplace(s) covered by it, where it can be easily read by employees. The committee must be set up within 3 months of the written request.

Safety committees should **include** elected representatives and representatives of management, together with other functions such as safety advisers, personnel/HR managers and works engineers. The management representatives should have adequate authority to give proper consideration to views and recommendations of the committee. The number of management representatives should not exceed the number of employee representatives.

Employers must **consult** appointed safety representatives with a view to ensuring the co-operation of employees in promoting and developing health and safety measures at the workplace, and checking the effectiveness of those measures.

The employer must **specifically consult** safety representatives **on the following matters**:
– the introduction of any measure at the workplace which may substantially affect health and safety;
– the arrangements for appointing competent persons;
– any health and safety information the employer is required to provide to employees;
– the planning and introduction of health and safety training; and
– the health and safety consequences of the introduction of new technology to the workplace.

In addition, safety representatives have the following **rights** (regs 4-8 SI 1977/500).

4916 **Investigation** Safety representatives may investigate:
– potential hazards, dangerous occurrences and the causes of accidents at the workplace; and
– health and safety complaints from employees.

4917 **Inspection** Safety representatives may inspect:
– any part of the workplace not inspected in the preceding 3 months, after giving the employer reasonable notice in writing;
– where there has been a substantial change in the conditions of work, or if the HSE has published new information relevant to the hazards of the workplace;
– following a notifiable accident, dangerous occurrence or disease, provided it is safe for the inspection to be carried out and the interests of employees represented might be involved; and
– any document (and take copies) which the employer is legally required to keep under health and safety legislation and which is relevant to the workplace, or the employees represented, except a document consisting of, or relating to, the health record of an identifiable individual.

4919 **In relation to information, representation and training** Safety representatives are entitled to:
– make representations to the employer on general health and safety matters, or arising out of their investigations;
– attend safety committees in the capacity of a safety representative;
– receive information from health and safety inspectors who must provide factual information relating to health and safety in the premises inspected and any action they intend to take; and
– take reasonable time off with pay for health and safety training (¶4930), which is normally provided by the trade union. The employer is entitled to a copy of the syllabus of the relevant course.

4920 Employers are obliged to provide safety representatives with **information** necessary to enable them to fulfil their functions **including**:
– regarding the plans and performance of the undertaking if they affect health and safety;
– technical information about hazards to health and safety and precautions necessary to minimise or eliminate them;
– records kept by the employer on accidents, dangerous occurrences and notifiable diseases;
– results of measurements taken to check the effectiveness of health and safety arrangements (for example noise, ventilation or exposure levels of toxic materials); and
– information on articles or substances issued to home workers.

It does **not include** information:
– where disclosure would be against the interests of national security, or is prohibited from being disclosed by law;
– relating specifically to an individual, unless consent has been obtained for its disclosure;
– where disclosure would cause substantial injury to the employer's undertaking, for reasons other than health, safety or welfare, or such damage to the undertaking of another person where the information was supplied by that other person; and
– obtained by the employer for the purposes of bringing, prosecuting or defending legal proceedings.

4922 **To be provided with facilities and assistance** Employers must provide safety representatives with facilities and assistance that may be required to enable the representatives to fulfil their functions. This would normally include providing information as needed, giving access to relevant parts of the workplace, and facilitating independent investigation of accidents and private discussions with employees.

Establishments/groups of employees without recognised trade unions

4925 Employers who do not have recognised trade unions, or who have groups of employees who are not represented by a trade union, must also **consult employees** on the same matters on which safety representatives must be consulted (see above) (regs 3, 4 Health and Safety (Consultation with Employees) Regulations SI 1996/1513). The consultation must be either with employees directly (for example, in a small workplace), or with elected representatives of employee safety, who have been elected by the workforce, or a group of employees within the workforce. The elected representatives must be employed within the group that elects them and this group can cover multiple sites, if appropriate. Employers can decide on the appropriate groups, numbers of representatives and the frequency of elections.

4926 Representatives of employee safety have **similar functions** to those of a safety representative (¶¶4912+) listed above, with the exception of those relating to investigations, inspections and receiving information from (as opposed to consulting with) health and safety inspectors. Employers must provide such **facilities and assistance** as the representatives may reasonably require for the purposes of carrying out their functions.

4927 Employers must provide representatives of employee safety with such **training** in respect of their statutory functions under the regulations as is reasonable in all the circumstances (reg 7 SI 1996/1513). Employers must meet the **reasonable costs** associated with the training, including travel and subsistence costs.

Time off

4930 Safety representatives and representatives of employee safety have the right to paid time off to attend training and fulfil their functions, and employers must allow candidates for election reasonable paid time off. The **amount** of time off must be what is reasonable in all the circumstances rather than what is "necessary" (*Duthie v Bath and North East Somerset Council* [2003] UKEAT 0561_02_2904). Such employees have the right to be remunerated for time off for the work that would have otherwise been done (¶3940).

> EXAMPLE In *Walker v North Tees & Hartlepool NHS Trust* [2008] UKEAT 0563_07_0307, a safety representative complained that his employer had failed to give him time off to attend courses relevant to his duties. He already regularly had 2.5 days off each week for these duties. On receipt of the request, his manager referred it to personnel without making a decision. A tribunal rejected his claim, on the basis that the employer had not refused to let him have time off. The EAT held that this approach was incorrect: the training requested was reasonable, and so the tribunal should have considered whether he could have attended the course without exceeding his existing time off allowance; if he could not, the time off was necessary, and the claim should succeed.

B. Data protection

4940 Collecting, handling and retaining information about workers' health is intrusive, and in certain circumstances may be highly intrusive. Moreover, workers have a **legitimate expectation** that they can keep information about their personal health private. However, employers may **need or wish to process** health information, for example, the employer may want the worker to:
– fill out a health questionnaire;
– be assessed as to his fitness with regard to a particular job or in relation to certain benefits;
– inform the employer of any disabilities or special needs;
– take an eye test if he is a VDU user;
– if appropriate to his job, have blood tests, etc to ensure he has not been exposed to hazardous substances;

– undergo random alcohol or drugs testing; and/or
– inform the employer of his vaccination and immunisation status and history.

As well as the following specific recommendations in relation to information concerning their workers' health, employers are also advised to follow the DP Code's **general recommendations** with regard to data management (¶6000).

Before processing such information, employers must ensure that they comply with the **data protection principles** (¶5945). For example, where the data is sensitive (¶5925), **consent** must be **explicit and freely given** before any sensitive data is processed **unless** it can be shown that it was necessary:
– to enable the employer to meet his legal obligations, for example a health and safety requirement;
– for medical purposes, for example, for the provision of care or treatment, and undertaken by a health professional or someone who has an equivalent duty of confidentiality; or
– for actual or prospective legal proceedings.

Consent should be specific to the health information required and employers must make sure it covers not only any testing but also any subsequent handling, using and retaining of the results. Blanket consent obtained at the start of employment may not be sufficient.

4941 **To process** any such data, the employer must be clear about its purpose and benefits and that they are justified (part 4.1 DP Code).

Employers must **assess**, preferably by impact assessment (¶6165), whether the benefits from processing such data can justify the intrusion into their workers' privacy or any other adverse impact it may have, unless they are under a legal duty to process the data, for example the duty to monitor for exposure to hazardous materials. The effectiveness of any collection of data must also be considered in ascertaining whether it is a proportionate response to a particular problem. The possible **adverse impacts** to take into consideration include the intrusiveness of the processing, who will see the data, how it may affect the duty of mutual trust and confidence and whether such collection of data is oppressive or demeaning. **Alternatives** should be considered, where possible, to ascertain whether it really is necessary for the data to be collected and, if so, whether a less intrusive method than the one proposed could be used. Employers should be careful not to collect more information than is necessary (part 4.1.5 DP Code). For example, an employer should not seek a worker's consent to the disclosure of all or substantial parts of his GP records unless it is genuinely necessary, but should limit any request to the relevant issues. In addition, if commissioning a medical report on a sick worker, the information requested should focus on the worker's fitness for continued employment rather than medical details.

The business purpose of all testing should be **recorded** with a note stating which sensitive data condition has been satisfied.

4942 Employers must **take into account their obligations** as to how medical information can be securely handled in accordance with the data principles. Employers should ensure that, wherever practicable, only suitably qualified health professionals have **access to medical information** (part 4.1.4 DP Code). Where managers need to access information about a worker's health this should be limited to information that is strictly necessary to establish fitness to work or for his protection at work. Safety representatives should be provided with anonymised information unless workers have given consent to the information being identifiable. Medical information should, unless the general standard of information security is sufficiently high, be kept separately from other personnel information. Employers must always realise that the **interpretation** of any piece of medical information should be left to suitably qualified health professionals. Workers should be made **aware** of how any health information is held and the reasons for it.

Medical examination and testing

4944 Where an employer wishes to carry out medical examination or testing, as **good practice**, he should (part 4.3 DP Code):

a. make sure the rules and standards are clearly set out in a policy if the information to be obtained is to be used to enforce the employer's rules and standards. Workers must be made aware of the policy; and
b. obtain information through medical examination or testing of applicants only where there is a real likelihood of appointing them and the testing is a necessary and justified measure to determine fitness for the job in question, or to meet any legal requirements or determine the worker's eligibility to join a pension or insurance scheme. Applicants should be informed early on in the recruitment process that medical testing may be required. Where possible, less intrusive methods should be used, for example a health questionnaire instead of a medical examination; and
c. obtain information through medical examination or testing only where it is part of an occupational health and safety programme and the procedures are a necessary and justified measure to:
– prevent significant risk to the health and safety of the worker/workers;
– determine a worker's fitness in relation to his specific job;
– determine whether a worker is fit to return to work after having been off sick and, if so, when;
– determine a worker's entitlement to health-related benefits;
– prevent discrimination on the grounds of disability and assess whether reasonable adjustments should be made; or
– comply with any other legal obligations.

Equality provisions have been introduced restricting the use of health questionnaires or asking questions about health or disability during **recruitment**, i.e. before an offer of employment is made (¶¶625+; s60 EqA 2010). Questions are only permitted for limited purposes, including:
– to find out whether reasonable adjustments need to be made during the recruitment process;
– to establish whether the applicant will be able to carry out an essential part of the job;
– to monitor diversity;
– to take positive action in respect of disabled people; or
– where there is a requirement that the job holder has a disability, to establish that the applicant has a disability.

In many instances, **post-job offer**, a pre-start health assessment has replaced pre-employment health assessment where it is necessary and justified to determine fitness for the job in question, or to meet any legal requirements or determine the worker's eligibility to join a pension or insurance scheme.

Parameters should be set as to who should be tested, what precisely should be tested, the frequency of the testing and the consequences of the results. Samples obtained from testing should never be used for **any other purpose** than that for which they were originally obtained unless the worker is informed and his consent obtained. Further, bodily samples should not be covertly obtained as it is highly unlikely that this will ever be justifiable.

Only information that is required for the purpose of the medical examination/testing should be **retained** if it is necessary to do so. All extraneous and irrelevant information should be destroyed.

C. Specific duties relating to vulnerable workers

1. Women of child-bearing age and new or expectant mothers

Although an employer's statutory duties extend to all of his workers regardless of gender, he has **additional obligations** to protect women of **child-bearing age** and new or expectant mothers from certain specified risks (SI 1999/3242). He is required to carry out a specific assessment of health and safety risks for workers in this group and must identify the measures needed to avoid any risks (¶4956).

MEMO POINTS   Child-bearing age is not defined but is generally accepted as the period which falls between puberty and menopause.

4952 The employer also has a **specific duty to prevent** a **new or expectant mother from being exposed to a risk** after she has **notified** him in writing that she is pregnant, has given birth within the previous 6 months or is breast-feeding (reg 16 SI 1999/3242). Where relevant, the employer can require that she produces, within a reasonable period, a written certificate from a registered medical practitioner or midwife confirming that she is pregnant (reg 18 SI 1999/3242). This specific duty will not apply if the employer knows that she is no longer a new or expectant mother or if he cannot establish whether she remains so.

EXAMPLE   In *Day v T Pickles Farms Ltd* [1998] UKEAT 369_98_0111, the worker told her employer that she was pregnant and gave him a medical certificate to say that she was suffering from "hyperemesis gravidarum", which is severe vomiting associated with pregnancy. The EAT held that as there had been written notification, it was for the employer to prove that it was not adequate and did not indicate pregnancy.

Further, the duty to undertake a risk assessment has been held to apply only where the work is of a kind which **may give rise to a risk** to a mother or baby (*O'Neill v Buckinghamshire County Council* [2010] IRLR 384, EAT).

EXAMPLE   In *O'Neill v Buckinghamshire County Council*, a teacher, O, informed her employer that she was pregnant after an investigation into her work performance had begun. Her head teacher made a start on a risk assessment when notified of her pregnancy. The summer holidays then intervened, and both the risk assessment and disciplinary procedure were put to one side. The disciplinary procedure was resumed after the holidays ended but not the risk assessment. The disciplinary procedure was also halted when O went off sick and while off sick she started her maternity leave. After unsuccessfully raising a grievance, O resigned and claimed constructive dismissal. Amongst other things, O claimed that the employer had discriminated against her in failing to complete the risk assessment. The EAT upheld the decision of the tribunal that there was no general obligation to carry out a risk assessment unless:
– the employer has received written notification of the pregnancy;
– the work is of a kind which may give rise to a risk to a mother or baby; and
– the risk arises from working conditions, processes or agents used at work.
In the case of a teacher in a primary school there was no evidence of such a risk.

4953 When an employee has given notice to her employer in writing that she is pregnant or has given birth within the last six months, or is breast-feeding, the **following progressive steps** must be taken until a risk is **removed or reduced to its lowest acceptable level**:
1. **Alter** the worker's **working conditions** or **hours of work** if it is reasonable to do so.
2. **Offer** her **suitable alternative work** (¶8867) if available. A worker can refuse the alternative work, in which case the employer may have to go to step 3 and suspend her for as long as is necessary to protect her or her child. However, if a worker unreasonably refuses suitable alternative work, she will lose her right to remuneration during the period of suspension from her normal duties.
3. **Suspend** her **from work** as long as is necessary to protect her safety or health or that of her child. However, pregnant employees should not be suspended merely because their job presents a remote risk to them or their pregnancy (*New Southern Railway Ltd v Quinn* [2006] ICR 761, EAT). The first two steps must be considered and only if such adjustments are unreasonable or would fail to minimise the risk would suspension be justifiable.

A worker on maternity suspension is entitled to **remuneration** at her full normal rate for as long as the suspension continues. This is calculated by reference to a week's pay (¶2920) in respect of each week of suspension (or proportionately for part of a week). The right to paid suspension does not affect any contractual right to remuneration, though any contractual remuneration will be offset.

A worker's **employment will continue** during maternity suspension and therefore the period will count towards continuity for both statutory and contractual rights. A worker on maternity suspension will start her **maternity leave** on her chosen date or date of childbirth, if earlier. If the period of suspension is likely to apply up to the birth she must give notice when she wishes to start her leave otherwise it may start automatically at the beginning of the 4th week before the week the baby is due (¶4430).

EXAMPLE In *British Airways (European Operation at Gatwick) Ltd v Moore and Botterill* [2000] IRLR 296, EAT, B's removal from flying duties to ground crew did not amount to **suitable alternative work** as the loss of her cabin crew member's flying allowance meant that the ground crew terms were substantially less favourable than her normal terms.

Where a new or expectant mother is engaged in **night work** and the employee provides a medical certificate from a registered medical practitioner or registered midwife stating that for health and safety reasons the employee must not work at certain times as specified in the certificate, the employer must either change her hours of work or suspend the employee for as long as is necessary (reg 17 SI 1999/3242).

4954

Risk assessments

As well as the general duty to assess the risks to the health and safety of their workers, employers must make a risk assessment if there may be a possibility of any of the particular risks below. So, for example, employers should make a specific risk assessment if they have workers of child-bearing age even before a worker becomes or is aware that she is pregnant. On completion, the employer must **provide** all workers of child-bearing age with any comprehensible and relevant information on the risks to their health identified by the assessment (SI 1999/3242). The employer should also give the information to representatives of employee safety and union appointed safety representatives.

4956

There are **particular risks** in relation to new or expectant mothers and their babies where:
– the workers in an undertaking include women of child-bearing age; and
– the work could involve risk to the health and safety of a new or expectant mother due to her condition, or her baby, from any processes or working conditions, or physical, biological or chemical agents, including those specifically listed in EC Directive 1992/85.

4957

MEMO POINTS The specified list of agents, processes and working conditions is non-exhaustive and is set out in full in Annexes I and II of EC Directive 1992/85:
1. **Physical agents** include:
– shocks, vibrations or movement (for example, travelling in off-road vehicles);
– manual handling of loads;
– movements and postures, travel;
– mental and physical fatigue, and other physical burdens (for example fatigue from standing for long periods);
– excessive physical or mental pressure;
– ionising radiation and non-ionising electromagnetic radiation which could cause harm by raising body temperature (for example, by overexposure to radio-frequency radiation);
– extremes of temperature; and
– working in pressurised environments, for example pressurised enclosures and underwater diving.
Emissions from display screen equipment (VDUs) have been found (from research carried out by the former public authority the National Radiological Protection Board) not to present a risk.
2. **Biological agents** include:
– hepatitis B;
– HIV;
– herpes;
– TB;
– syphilis;
– chickenpox;
– typhoid;
– rubella;
– toxoplasmosis;
– cytomegalovirus; and
– chlamydia.
For most workers, the risk of infection is no higher at work than from living in the community, but in certain occupations (for example, laboratory workers, healthcare staff, or those looking after animals and dealing with animal products) exposure to infection is more likely.

Pregnant workers should not be exposed to toxoplasma or rubella virus unless they have adequate immunisation.

3. **Chemical agents** include:
– substances that may have irreversible effects, or that may cause cancer and heritable genetic damage, or harm to an unborn or breast-fed baby;
– carcinogenic agents, mercury and mercury derivatives and antimitotic (cytotoxic) drugs (which may be absorbed by inhalation or through the skin); and
– dangerous chemical agents (which are absorbed through the skin) including certain pesticides, carbon monoxide, and lead and lead derivatives (in so far as they are absorbable).

Pregnant workers and workers who are breast-feeding may not be involved in mining absorbable lead and lead derivatives underground where there is a risk to their health or safety.

4958 If a worker **believes there is a risk** to her or her unborn baby's health or safety which the employer has not considered in the general risk assessment, or where a risk has been identified but the employer will not take preventive action, she should bring the risk to the attention of her employer or employee representative. If the employer discounts the risk and the worker remains concerned, she should discuss the matter with her doctor or get in touch with her local Health and Safety Executive office for advice.

4959 Where an employer **fails to carry out a risk assessment**, it may amount to a detriment entitling a pregnant or breast-feeding worker to claim discrimination. She may also have a negligence claim if there is a demonstrable harm or loss. Failure to carry out a risk assessment in respect of a pregnant woman, who, as a result, suffers a detriment, will also amount to sex discrimination (*Hardman v Mallon t/a Orchard Lodge Nursing Home* [2002] IRLR 516, EAT).

2. Children and young people

4970 Special restrictions apply to the employment and working conditions of children and young persons. A **child** is, unless otherwise specified, a person who is not over the compulsory school age (s 58 Education Act 1944) and a **young person** is a person over compulsory school age but under 18 (s 114(1) Education Act 1944).

> MEMO POINTS The basis for rules and restrictions applying to young persons and children is the Young Workers Directive (EC Directive 1994/33). This has been implemented by:
> – the Children (Protection at Work) Regulations (SI 1998/276);
> – the Health and Safety (Young Persons) Regulations (SI 1997/135) (which amended the then Management of Health and Safety at Work Regulations (now SI 1999/3242)); and
> – the Working Time Regulations (SI 1998/1833).

4971 Employers are prohibited from employing **children** in a factory or industrial undertaking, but children above the age of 13 may be employed in non-industrial undertakings, subject to local authority bylaws. These bylaws restrict the number of hours which children may work and generally require that an application be made to the local authority for the issue of an employment card before the child starts work. Further, all work must be **light**. This is not defined by the appropriate regulations, however, EC Directive 1994/33 defines light work as any work that is not likely to be harmful to a child's safety, health, development, attendance at school or participation in work experience.

4972 Employers can employ **young persons** in a factory or industrial undertaking as well as a non-industrial undertaking. However, they must ensure that young persons are protected at work from any risks to their health or safety which are a consequence of their lack of experience, their absence of awareness of existing or potential risks or the fact that they have not fully matured (reg 13D SI 1999/3242).

4973 It is **prohibited** for an employer to employ a young person in work which:
– is beyond the young person's physical or psychological capacity;
– involves harmful exposure to agents which are toxic or carcinogenic, cause heritable genetic damage, or harm an unborn child, or which in any other way chronically affect human health;
– involves harmful exposure to radiation;

– involves a risk of accidents which, it may reasonably be assumed, cannot be recognised or avoided by the young person, due to insufficient attention to safety or lack of experience or training; or
– involves a risk to health from extreme heat or cold, noise or vibration.

However, work in the above categories is **permitted** if it is necessary for the young person's training, there is supervision by a competent person and any risks are reduced to the lowest level reasonably practicable.

> MEMO POINTS   In addition there are **further specific restrictions** or prohibitions in relation to the following types of work:
> – certain work with lead and ionising radiation; and
> – supervising a vehicle carrying dangerous goods when it is parked.

See also ¶3720 for the **working time restrictions** on young workers.

4974

Risk assessments

As well as the general duty to assess the risks to the health and safety of their workers, employers who employ, or intend to employ, young persons must make a specific risk assessment which particularly takes account of the (SI 1999/3242):
– inexperience, lack of awareness of risks and immaturity of young persons;
– fitting-out and layout of the workplace and workstation;
– nature and degree of exposure to physical, biological and chemical agents;
– form, range and use of work equipment and the way in which it is handled;
– organisation of processes and activities;
– extent of the health and safety training provided; and
– risks from certain types of agents and processes.

4976

Where the employer employs a child, the employer must ensure that the **parents** or guardians of the child are provided with comprehensible and relevant information on the risks identified in the risk assessment, any risks notified to the employer by another employer sharing the workplace and, in both cases, the required control measures.

4977

D. Pay during medical suspension

In certain circumstances, an employer may be required by law to suspend an employee on medical grounds, or a Code of Practice may recommend suspension. If so, provided that the provision is specified in one of the prescribed regulations (s 64(3) ERA 1996), an employee who has to be suspended from his normal work on medical grounds may be **entitled to** payment during his period of suspension (s 64(2) ERA 1996). Suspension simply means that the employee, although still employed by the employer, is not provided with work or does not perform the work he normally performed before the suspension (s 64(5) ERA 1996).

4985

In order to **qualify** for the right to payment during suspension, the employee must have been continuously employed for 1 month (¶1080) and must not be physically or mentally incapable of undertaking work (s 65(3) ERA 1996). Certain categories of employment are excluded from the right. Moreover, an employee may **lose his right** to payment during suspension if his employer has offered to provide him with suitable alternative work during the suspension and the employee has unreasonably refused the work, or if the employee has not complied with reasonable requirements imposed by his employer to ensure that his services are available (s 65(4) ERA 1996). An employee may receive **payment** during a period of medical suspension at the statutory rate for up to 26 weeks. The amount of payment is based on a week's pay for every week of suspension (pro-rated, if necessary) (¶2920).

Employers have additional specific duties with regard to the medical suspension of **women** of child-bearing age and new or expectant mothers (¶¶4953+) and the right to remuneration is not limited to 26 weeks.

4986

E. Insurance requirement

4990 **Employers** carrying on a business in the UK are obliged to maintain **insurance against liability** for bodily injury or disease sustained by employees in the course of their employment in the UK (Employers' Liability (Compulsory Insurance) Regulations SI 1998/2573). They must make a copy of the certificate of insurance **reasonably available** to employees; this may be by displaying a copy at all premises they occupy or by making a copy readily available in some other way, for example on an intranet (Employers' Liability (Compulsory Insurance) (Amendment) Regulations SI 2008/1765).

> MEMO POINTS 1. Employers **do not need** to have employers' liability insurance if they are **only employing** a family member or someone who is based abroad.
> 2. Where employees are **working abroad**, the failure by the employer to provide **personal accident insurance** will not be a breach of his common law or implied duties (*Reid v Rush & Tomkins Group plc* [1989] IRLR 265, CA).
> 3. It is no longer a requirement that a copy of each certificate of insurance should be **retained** for 40 years (SI 2008/1765).

SECTION 3

Specific issues

A. Stress

5010 Stress is not of itself a source of liability for employers, and a degree of work pressure can enhance job performance if it is not excessive. However, an employer may be **liable for damages** for physical or psychiatric illness arising from workplace stress in a tortious or contractual claim.

> MEMO POINTS There are a number of sources of useful information on how to reduce the risk of employees suffering work-related stress. These include:
> – the **Acas stress at work guide**; and
> – the **booklet on work-related stress** for employers and employees published by **BIS** and the **Health and Safety Executive (HSE)**, together with the CBI, TUC, the Forum of Private Business and CEEP UK.

Scope for liability

5012 Workplace stress will only give rise to liability where the relevant conditions are met (*Hartman v South Essex Mental Health and Community Care NHS Trust and other linked appeals* [2005] IRLR 293, CA; *Sutherland (Chairman of the Governors of St Thomas Becket RC High School) v Hatton* [2002] IRLR 263, CA):
– it gives rise to a physical or psychiatric **injury** to health;
– the injury is **attributable** to that workplace stress;
– the injury is caused by a **breach** of the employer's **duty of care**; and
– it is **foreseeable**.

5013 **Guidelines** were given in *Hatton* to assist in deciding whether there will be liability for work-related stress, which are incorporated in the paragraphs below. These have been approved of and followed in subsequent cases and are often referred to as the *Hatton* guidelines. However, they are not intended to cover all the possible circumstances which might arise in such cases and their **relevance to particular facts** should be considered in each case (*Hartman v South Essex Mental Health and Community Care NHS Trust and other linked appeals*, above). In all cases, therefore, it is necessary to identify the steps which the employer both could and should have taken to assess whether there has been a breach of the duty of care.

Breach of duty of care The employer will breach his duty of care if he knows or should have known of the employee's problem or vulnerability and has failed to take **reasonable steps** to try and **prevent the injury** from occurring or recurring. This requires him to take whatever measures are possible and appropriate to try to support and help the employee.

The employer's duty **does not protect** employees from the everyday stresses or anxieties of normal working life which do not cause injury, nor from the normal range of feelings such as anger or resentment.

Foreseeable injury Foreseeability depends on what the employer **knows or ought to know** about the individual employee.

Psychiatric injury is of its nature difficult to foresee. **Factors** likely to be relevant in establishing whether such an injury is foreseeable include:
– the **nature** of the work done by the employee;
– whether the **workload** is much more than is normal for the particular job;
– whether unreasonable **demands** are being made of this employee, considering his capabilities and compared with other employees;
– **signs** that the employee or others are suffering harmful levels of stress;
– complaints or **warnings** from the employee or co-workers; and
– previous **history** of psychiatric problems.

In the absence of such signs, the employer is not expected to foresee any greater susceptibility to injury from work pressures than would be expected from **other employees in the same or similar role** (*Sutherland (Chairman of the Governors of St Thomas Becket RC High School) v Hatton* [2002] IRLR 263, CA). An employer is also entitled to assume that the employee can **withstand the normal pressures** of the job. While an employer knows or ought to know that a decision will cause an employee emotional upset, it does not necessarily follow that he knows or ought to know that the decision will cause the employee to suffer a psychiatric illness such as depression (*Fraser v The State Hospitals Board for Scotland*, 11 July 2000, CS; *Morland v London Borough of Tower Hamlets*, 1 May 2003, High Court). For example, the courts recognise that employers often have to take decisions (for example, in relation to disciplinary issues) which they know are likely to cause anger and anxiety, and generally it is safe for an employer to assume that an employee can **deal with ordinary disciplinary matters** without worrying about how such disciplinary matters will affect the employee's mental health (*Croft v Broadstairs and St Peter's Town Council* [2003] EWCA Civ 676).

While the **nature and extent** of an employee's **job** will be a relevant factor when deciding what is reasonably foreseeable, and while there are some occupations which appear intrinsically stressful, such as the work of traffic police officers who regularly deal with gruesome accidents, the courts have emphasised that it is not the job but the **interaction** between the individual and the job which causes the harm. Even where one employer has foreseen a **particular risk in a particular field of work**, it does not necessarily follow that all others in the same field should have done so as well (*Melville v The Home Office* [2005] IRLR 293, CA). No **job in itself** is intrinsically dangerous to mental health (*Sutherland (Chairman of the Governors of St Thomas Becket RC High School) v Hatton*, above).

The House of Lords has confirmed that it is not necessary to establish that the **actual injury** suffered by the employee was reasonably foreseeable as long as that **kind of harm** was reasonably foreseeable and the injury is not too remote on the grounds of policy or fact (*Corr (Administratrix of the Estate of T Corr, deceased) v IBC Vehicles* [2008] ICR 372, HL). In this case, it was held that the employer was responsible for the suicide of its employee who had become severely depressed following a serious injury at work 6 years previously.

EXAMPLE
Not foreseeable
1. In *Bristol City Council v Deadman* [2007] IRLR 888, CA, a stress claim failed because the damage was not foreseeable. The main breaches by the employer were that:
– it failed to make sure that three members of staff were on a **disciplinary panel**, so that a new hearing had to be called; and

– the employee was told that an **investigation** into a complaint against him was continuing by a letter left on his desk, where he found it on arriving at work.
It was not reasonably foreseeable that these failures would result in psychiatric harm.

2. In *Vahidi v Fairstead House School Trust Ltd* [2005] EWCA Civ 765, V, a school teacher, had her **teaching methods re-organised** as a result of an inspection which had highlighted shortcomings in the school's procedures. She was unhappy about the new arrangements and became depressed resulting in 8 months off work. V **returned to work** when her psychiatrist informed the school that she was well enough to do so. The school, aware of the risk of a relapse, took her back initially on a **part-time** basis and organised **weekly support meetings**. Unfortunately, V still could not cope, suffered depression again and left the school. The Court held that although the relapse was clearly foreseeable, there was no breach as it considered that the school had taken all the reasonable steps it could in supporting V on her return.

Foreseeable

1. In *Daw v Intel Corporation Ltd* [2007] IRLR 355, CA, D, an accountant, became vulnerable to psychological injury in the workplace, partly as a result of two periods of **postnatal depression**. D made twelve **attempts to draw** her supervisors' **attention** to her situation of over-work. Little support was given to the employee beyond the offer of a short-term counselling service. The Court found that the employer was partly responsible for the employee's subsequent breakdown: damages were awarded but with a discount reflecting D's vulnerable personality.

2. In *Dickins v O2 plc* [2009] IRLR 58, CA, the Court of Appeal held that psychiatric injury was foreseeable where the employee had **complained about stress**, had frequently been late for work and had told her line manager that she was at the **end of her tether** and did not think she could carry on much longer without becoming ill.

3. In *Garrod v North Devon NHS Primary Care Trust* [2006] EWHC 850 (QB), G was a health visitor. The work was **stressful** and members of G's team were repeatedly absent from work with long-term illnesses. G herself had a disclosed history of previous breakdowns and had made at least five **attempts to draw** her employer's **attention** to the risk of work-related stress. The High Court held that the employer breached its duty of care as it failed to take precautions against what was a foreseeable risk.

MEMO POINTS Where the employer has acted unreasonably in the **events leading up to dismissal**, but not in the manner of dismissal itself, an employee will be able to claim for damages in respect of psychiatric injury that has been suffered because of the way the disciplinary procedure was conducted up to the actual dismissal (*McCabe v Cornwall County Council and anor* [2004] IRLR 733 heard jointly with *Eastwood and Williams v Magnox Electric plc* [2004] IRLR 733, HL). Compensation is not recoverable at common law for financial loss due to psychiatric injury arising from an employee's **dismissal or the manner of his dismissal** (*Johnson v Unisys Ltd* [2001] IRLR 279, HL; *Dunnachie v Kingston upon Hull City Council* [2004] IRLR 727, HL). However, unfairness in the circumstances of dismissal may give rise to a claim for unfair dismissal (¶8380).

5020 **Cause of injury** The employer will only be liable for **damages** where the breach of duty has **caused or materially contributed to** the harm suffered. It is not enough to show that occupational stress has caused the harm; there must also have been a breach of duty by the employer.

Where there is **contributory negligence**, the general rules of apportionment apply and an employer will only be liable for the proportion of damages which are attributable to his wrongdoing. However, the fact that an employee has not taken time off or seen a doctor before suffering a breakdown will not absolve the employer of liability if the injury is foreseeable (*Dickins v O2 plc* [2009] IRLR 58, CA).

Where the harm suffered has more than one cause, the employer should only pay for that proportion of the harm suffered which is attributable to his wrongdoing, unless the harm is truly indivisible. It is for the employer to raise the question of apportionment. Any assessment of damages will **take into account** any pre-existing condition or vulnerability, the employee's behaviour and the chance that the employee would have succumbed to a stress-related disorder in any event.

Employer responsibilities

5025 **Identifying workplace stress** The employer should be alert to **general** signs of possible workplace stress, such as an abnormal level of sickness or absenteeism in a particular job

or department, particularly where he is aware of an employee who has a specific vulnerability. So far as individual employees are concerned, the employer should be aware of signs **specific** to the employee of impending harm to his health, for example:
- a previous history of mental illness attributable to stress at work;
- abnormal patterns of absence; or
- uncharacteristic behaviour patterns.

5026 It is generally reasonable for an employer to take what his employee tells him at **face value**, unless there are other **indications to the contrary**. This would include the situation where the employee has already had time off for stress. The employer does not generally have to make searching enquiries of the employee or seek permission to make further inquiries of his medical advisers. However, once the employer is aware of an issue, it will be important to seek medical advice and where appropriate to monitor the employee (¶5035).

5027 Employers cannot be expected to have **knowledge of confidential information** to which they do not have access. For example, employers are not expected to know of an employee's vulnerability where the employee has declared it on a health screening questionnaire which was for the sole use of their occupational health service (*Hartman v South Essex Mental Health and Community Care NHS Trust and other linked appeals* [2005] IRLR 293, CA). The Court of Appeal commented in this case that there may be circumstances in which an **occupational health department** has a duty of care to an employee which requires the department to seek the employee's consent for the **disclosure** of the information **to the employer** so that the latter can take proper steps for the welfare of the employee.

5030 **Giving reasonable support** An employer must take reasonable steps to protect the employee from an occurrence or recurrence of the psychiatric illness taking into account the following **factors** (*Barber v Somerset County Council* [2004] IRLR 475, HL; *Young v The Post Office* [2002] IRLR 660, CA):
- the magnitude of the risk;
- the cost of preventing it; and
- the effectiveness, if taken, of such steps.

In a dispute, expert evidence may be needed to establish whether any measures would have made any difference.

The **size** and the **scope of the employer's operation**, its resources and the demands it faces are relevant in deciding what is reasonable; these include the interests of other employees and the need to treat them fairly, for example, in any redistribution of duties.

Although it might be an appropriate course of action in certain circumstances, it will not be a breach of duty to **opt not to dismiss** an employee to protect him from harm where the employee wants to go on working (*Sutherland (Chairman of the Governors of St Thomas Becket RC High School) v Hatton* [2002] IRLR 263, CA; *Vahidi v Fairstead House School Trust Ltd* [2005] EWCA Civ 765).

An employer who offers a **confidential advice service** is less likely to be found in breach of its duty of care. However, the Court of Appeal has emphasised that the weight given to this factor will depend on the facts of the case (*Daw v Intel Corporation Ltd* [2007] IRLR 355, CA; *Dickins v O2 plc* [2009] IRLR 58, CA). By itself, a counselling service may not prove to be sufficient as it may not be able to do anything other than advise the worker and consequently its scope is limited. For example, such a service cannot reduce a worker's workload if this is the cause of the problem. Moreover, a worker cannot be reasonably criticised for not using such a service.

EXAMPLE In *Connor v Surrey County Council* [2010] EWCA Civ 286, a head teacher who became clinically depressed took ill-health retirement after being subjected to bullying and harassment by members of the school's governing body, including unfounded allegations of racism and religious prejudice. The employer was found to be in breach of its duties by failing to consider measures to protect her, such as establishing an interim executive board, sooner. It was therefore liable in negligence for the personal injuries she had suffered.

MEMO POINTS Failure to comply with the **Working Time Regulations** (SI 1998/1833) does not in itself constitute a breach of the employer's duty of care, although an apparent lack of awareness

5035 **Monitoring for stress** There is no general duty to monitor for stress in the absence of knowledge of a specific vulnerability. As a **practical approach**, where there are indications that an employee is showing signs that he is either under great pressure from work or is already suffering stress, the employer should carry out an **assessment** of the causes of these signs and the exact state of the employee's health. If work-related stress is identified, appropriate action, support and monitoring may be required to ensure that the employer does not breach his duty of care. To trigger a duty to take steps, the indications of impending harm to health arising from stress at work must be plain enough for any reasonable employer to realise that he should do something about it.

Where an employer is aware of an employee's problem or vulnerability, there is a more positive requirement to **monitor** the situation **actively** and in such circumstances the employer should not solely rely on the employee informing him of his ongoing condition (*Barber v Somerset County Council* [2004] IRLR 475, HL). Employers will not necessarily be expected to require the employee to undergo intrusive medical assessments (for example a further visit to the employee's psychiatrist) and in such circumstances it is reasonable to rely on the employee's reassurances as to his health (*Vahidi v Fairstead House School Trust Ltd* [2005] EWCA Civ 765).

B. Bullying

5040 Bullying at work may leave the employer liable for damages under four types of claim:
– a **harassment or discrimination claim** on the grounds of age, disability, gender reassignment, marriage or civil partnership, pregnancy and maternity, race, religion or belief, sex or sexual orientation (¶¶5200+);
– a claim in tort for stress causing **psychiatric injury** (¶¶5010+);
– under the **Protection from Harassment Act 1997** (see below); and/or
– a claim for **constructive dismissal** if the bullied employee resigns as a result of the bullying (¶8230).

Employers should therefore try to ensure workplace bullying is prevented by making workers aware of the issue in staff policies and, if it arises, by dealing with it satisfactorily.

> MEMO POINTS The **Acas guide** on bullying and harassment at work offers practical advice to employers to help them prevent bullying and harassment and to deal with any cases that occur, and includes guidelines for the development of policies and procedures.

Claims under the Protection from Harassment Act 1997

5045 This legislation was originally introduced to provide protection from stalkers, but has been held to apply to harassment and bullying at work (*Majrowski v Guy's and St Thomas's NHS Trust* [2006] ICR 1199, HL; *Banks v Ablex Ltd* [2005] ICR 819, CA; *Veakins v Kier Islington Ltd* [2010] IRLR 132, CA). It has also been used to restrain aggressive former employees (*First Global Locums Ltd and ors v Cosias* [2005] IRLR 873, QBD). An employee will be able to **bring a claim** where the wrongdoer has engaged in a course of conduct (i.e. conduct or speech on at least two occasions) which is intentional and which the wrongdoer knew or ought to have known amounted to harassment (*Banks v Ablex Ltd*). The conduct must be oppressive and unacceptable and while malice is not a required element of harassment, its presence will make it easier to establish (*Veakins v Kier Islington Ltd*). To cross the boundary from the regrettable to the unacceptable the gravity of the misconduct must be of an order which would sustain criminal liability (*Majrowski v Guy's and St Thomas's NHS Trust* [2006] ICR 1199, HL; *Conn v City of Sunderland* [2007] EWCA Civ 1492). The case law conflicts as to whether it is necessary to prove that each occasion relied upon can individually, i.e. standing each by itself, amount to harassment (contrast the approach taken in *Iqbal v Dean Manson Solicitors* [2011] EWCA Civ 123 and *Marinello v City Of Edinburgh Council* [2011] ScotCS CSIH_33, both of which indicate that it is not necessary as the test is whether the source of conduct as a whole amounts to harassment, with that taken in *Conn v City of Sunderland*, which indicates that a course of harassment cannot be established if only one incident is sufficiently serious as to be regarded as harassment). Depending on the circumstances, a lengthy gap of over a year between incidents may still amount to a course of action (*Marinello v City Of Edinburgh Council*).

> **EXAMPLE**
> 1. In *Marinello v City Of Edinburgh Council*, the claimant, M, brought a vicarious liability claim against his employer under the Protection from Harassment Act 1979 that two of his superiors, H and K, had subjected him to a course of conduct which amounted to harassment under the Act. M alleged that up to the time he was signed off on long-term sick leave, he had been subjected to almost daily verbal abuse and criticism by H and K. M also alleged that about 17 months later, when walking down a public street while on sick leave, a van veered towards him with its horn sounding and with the driver, H, gesticulating to M with a clenched fist. M brought the claim over 3 years from the incidents before he was signed off on long-term sick leave but less than 3 years after the incident on sick leave. As claims under the Act must be brought within 3 years in Scotland, the issue that the Court of Session had to decide was whether the last incident could be part of the course of action as, if not, the claimant would be out of time to bring his claim. The Court of Session held that in its view an interval in the order of 17 months did not appear so great a gap as to automatically exclude the incident. Further, the fact that the last incident occurred in a public street was of little significance here as M's workplace was frequently a public place when working with offenders on community service and although M was not at work at the time of the last incident he was still in employment in the same department under the supervision of H. As to whether there was a course of conduct that could amount to harassment, the last incident should be considered in relation to the other incidents, and did not need to amount separately to harassment in order to be included. The Court of Session remitted the case for a full hearing so that evidence could be heard and a decision made on the facts as to whether there was a course of conduct that amounted to harassment under the Act.
> 2. In *Conn v City of Sunderland*, a manager, (a) became angry and threatened to punch out a window when an employee refused to inform him of colleagues leaving early; and (b) swore at the employee whilst shaking with rage and threatened to give him "a good hiding". The Court of Appeal overturned a county court's decision that those incidents were a course of conduct amounting to harassment under the PHA. The Court of Appeal held that the manager's conduct during incident a) did not "cross the boundary from the regrettable to the unacceptable", as it was not sufficiently serious to be regarded as criminal. The Court of Appeal held that as a "course of conduct" must involve at least two incidents of harassment, the judgment on liability was overturned.

5046 Claims under this Act **do not need** to relate to a particular characteristic of the victim e.g. race, sex (unlike harassment claims brought under the discrimination provisions of the Equality Act 2010), nor do victims need to show that they have suffered a recognised psychiatric illness (general anxiety or distress will suffice) or that their injury was foreseeable, as is required for personal injury claims. Employees also have 6 years in which to bring civil claims under the Act (3 years in Scotland) compared to 3 months with regard to discrimination claims. The Act therefore gives employees who have been harassed or bullied at work another potential avenue of redress, although it should be noted that the Court of Appeal has remarked that it is rare that workplace conduct would be severe enough to support a claim under the Act (*Veakins v Kier Islington Ltd*).

5047 **Vicarious liability** Employers may also be vicariously liable (¶4825) for a breach of the statutory duty imposed on their employees under this Act if the relevant act or omission occurs during the **course of employment** (*Majrowski v Guy's and St Thomas's NHS Trust* [2006] ICR 1199, HL). In a case concerning bullying by co-workers and junior colleagues, the High Court held that an employer was vicariously liable under the Protection from Harassment Act 1997 for his employees' bullying of a co-worker (*Green v DB Group Services (UK) Ltd* [2006] IRLR 764, HC). The court did not make a separate award in this instance, because the employer was also directly liable for negligence for the psychiatric injury suffered by the bullied employee, as it had not taken adequate steps to try to support and help the employee, and the court awarded the employee damages (of over $800,000) for negligence.

C. Drugs and alcohol

5050 An employer could be **prosecuted** for a breach of health and safety legislation, and could also be **liable in damages**, if employees or third parties are injured as a result of the actions of an employee who is under the influence of drugs or alcohol.

> MEMO POINTS 1. It is a criminal offence for certain workers to be unfit through drugs or alcohol while working on **railways, tramways and other guided transport systems**, and the operators of those systems would also be guilty of an offence unless they had shown all due diligence in trying to prevent the offence being committed (Transport and Works Act 1992).
> 2. **Aircrew, air traffic controllers** and **certain staff on ships** may be prosecuted if they are impaired from carrying out their duties by drink or drugs (Railways and Transport Safety Act 2003).

5051 It is a **criminal offence** for occupiers or managers knowingly to permit people to undertake certain activities on their premises, including producing or supplying controlled drugs, and smoking cannabis (Misuse of Drugs Act 1971).

> MEMO POINTS If the employer or the employee is required to be registered with a **regulatory authority** (for example, in the financial services sector), drug or alcohol abuse may have an effect on these registrations, for example, because the employee must be a "fit and proper person". If an employee is dismissed for, or convicted of, drug-taking, the employer may be required by applicable regulatory rules to notify the relevant regulatory body.

Setting up a policy

5055 It is advisable for an employer to have a drugs and alcohol policy in order to ensure compliance with his health and safety obligations. The policy will also serve to set the standards of behaviour required of employees, and failure to observe these standards will raise disciplinary and performance issues. However, the employer must distinguish between disciplinary issues arising out of drug/alcohol abuse and possession, and medical issues connected with addiction, which should be handled with sensitivity.

5056 If drug-taking or alcohol abuse is a concern, it may be useful to have a specific policy dealing with those issues, in addition to the general disciplinary procedures. The HSE's "Drug Misuse at Work: Guide for Employers" recommends a **four step approach** to introducing a policy on drug misuse:
1. find out if there is a problem;
2. if there is, decide what to do;
3. take action; and
4. monitor the policy in practice.

The same approach could apply to alcohol abuse.

> MEMO POINTS The drug/alcohol misuse policy could form part of the company's overall health and safety policy.

5057 In assessing **whether misuse is a problem**, the employer should:
– review sickness records for any periods of unexplained or frequently taken absence;
– check whether there have been any behavioural changes or unexplained drops in productivity;
– identify any performance or conduct problems; and
– review accident records for any increase in accidents or near misses, or for patterns involving particular employees.

The policy should detail **unacceptable behaviour** and the procedures that will be applied in cases of alcohol or drug abuse. These procedures should be consistent with the **general disciplinary procedures**, which may be triggered by misbehaviour, misconduct or non-attendance due to excessive drinking. The disciplinary rules will often include a definition of **gross misconduct** entitling the employer summarily to dismiss the employee (¶6540). This may include being under the influence of drugs or alcohol at work.

Screening/testing

5060 Screening and drug testing is becoming more common, particularly in relation to safety-critical jobs. Screening may be appropriate as a matter of routine (whether occasionally or on a random basis), or in specific circumstances, such as after an accident. If a company is introducing screening for the first time, the workforce should be consulted (through trade union and/or employee representatives, as appropriate) and its agreement in principle obtained. The use of screening and drug testing as a means of regulating an employee's private conduct could amount to an **infringement of an employee's right to privacy** under the Human Rights Act 1998 if the drug-taking is unlikely to have any impact on public safety or the maintenance of the employer's reputation (*O'Flynn v Airlinks the Airport Coach Co Ltd* [2002] UKEAT 0269_01_1503).

5061 Employers must make sure that they comply with the **data protection rules** in relation to information obtained from drug and alcohol testing, for example explicit consent should be obtained where the data is sensitive (¶5925). For more details, see ¶4940 for the general core principles and good practice recommendations for employers to follow with regard to information about their workers' health, and ¶4944, which sets out specific **good practice recommendations** in relation to medical examination and testing.

Dealing with employees who have addictions

5065 Employers should seek **medical advice** when dealing with an employee with an alcohol or drug-related problem. Addiction to or dependency on alcohol or any other substance is not a disability for the purposes of disability discrimination, so there is no duty to make reasonable adjustments in respect of the addiction alone (¶5464). However, conditions caused by substance abuse, such as liver disease, may themselves amount to a disability. Further, alcoholics and drug addicts may benefit from **counselling or medical treatment**, possibly with sick leave covering any periods of absence. This may be advisable especially where it may be more costly to recruit and train a replacement than to permit an employee time off to get expert help. It may be appropriate to consider **suitable alternative employment** before contemplating dismissing the employee, especially if the employee's normal work is safety-critical. An employee who performs unsatisfactorily at work or shows poor attendance levels having **declined help or treatment**, or who has discontinued treatment before satisfactory completion, will be subject to normal disciplinary procedures.

5066 The employer should **monitor** implementation on a regular basis and consider whether any changes need to be made, and whether employees are aware of the policy and issues raised.

5070 **Unfair dismissal** If the employer considers that there is no choice but to dismiss the employee, the employer's **defence** to an unfair dismissal claim (¶8380) may be strengthened if the employer can show that he followed the company policy on drug/alcohol abuse. If the employer fails to follow company policy, any dismissal may well be unfair, even if the employer acted in accordance with his general disciplinary procedures. In particular, a dismissal may be unfair if no attempt has been made to help an employee with an alcohol or drug dependent condition.

In order for a dismissal to be fair, the employee's conduct must in some way reflect on the employment relationship. An employee's **conduct outside the workplace** is therefore unlikely to amount to grounds for dismissal, unless the employee's day-to-day work was affected or the employer's reputation would be damaged by that employee's conduct.

> **EXAMPLE**
> 1. In *Sinclair v Wandsworth Council* [2007] UKEAT 0145_07_0511, an employer's **alcohol policy** provided for suspension of disciplinary procedures where an employee sought assistance to cure his alcoholism. The employer dismissed an alcoholic employee, but without providing a copy of the alcohol policy to the employee until immediately before the hearing which resulted in his dismissal. The employer also failed to consider any steps the employee could take which might have resulted in disciplinary action being suspended. The EAT found that the employer had not followed a fair procedure and the employee had been unfairly dismissed. In the light of his alcohol problem, it made a reduction in the award for the employee's contributory fault (¶8635).
> 2. In *O'Flynn v Airlinks the Airport Coach Co Ltd*, above, the employer, whose disciplinary policy stated that being under the influence of drugs constituted misconduct, was justified in dismissing an employee who had taken drugs **outside working hours** since the employee could have been affected by her drug-taking while at work.

D. Smoking

Smoking ban

5080 It is unlawful to smoke in a place which is required to be smoke-free (s 7 Health Act 2006; Smoke-free (Premises and Enforcement) Regulations SI 2006/3368).

Further, smoking in smoke-free places or vehicles is not within the scope of the right to privacy or family life under article 8 of the European Convention of Human Rights (*N, R (on the application of) v Secretary of State for Health* [2009] EWCA Civ 795; Human Rights Act 1998; European Convention on Human Rights).

> **MEMO POINTS** The Department of Health maintains a website called "Smokefree England" (see flmemo.co.uk/em5080) which has useful advice on implementing the ban.

5082 **Smoke-free places** All enclosed or substantially enclosed places which are **open to the public** or are "**used as a workplace**" for more than one person must be smoke-free (s 2 Health Act 2006). In deciding whether premises come within this definition, it is necessary to treat each **part of the premises** separately (s 2(3) Health Act 2006). If only part of the premises comes within the definition, then the other parts will not be covered by the ban.

An **enclosed space** is defined as one which has a ceiling or roof, and which (except for doors, windows and passageways) is wholly enclosed (either permanently or temporarily). Workplace toilets come within this definition.

A **substantially enclosed place** is defined as a place with a ceiling or roof where there is an opening in the walls, or an aggregate area of openings in the walls, which is less than half their area. For these purposes, a roof includes any fixed or moveable structure or device which is capable of covering all or part of premises as a roof (for example a retractable canvas awning). This definition is wide enough to include tents, marquees and some shelters on the outside of buildings. Structures that are **not substantially enclosed** will be deemed to be compliant and smoking within them will be lawful.

> **EXAMPLE**
> 1. Where employees have previously been allowed to smoke outside beneath a **smoking shelter**, the issue of whether the continuation of this practice is lawful or unlawful will depend on whether the shelter is a compliant structure (i.e. whether it is not substantially enclosed).
> 2. Enclosed **smoking rooms** will be unlawful.
> 3. An employee smoking in his own **office** will also be unlawful if enclosed.

> **MEMO POINTS** Certain identified spaces are **exempt** from the ban (Smoke-free (Exemptions and Vehicles) Regulations SI 2007/765):
> – prisons;
> – rooms in care homes and hospices;

– private homes (this includes self-contained residential accommodation for temporary or holiday use and any garage, outhouse or other structure for the exclusive use of persons living in the dwelling);
– accommodation for guests and club members in hotels, guest houses, inns, hostels and members' clubs;
– shops of specialist tobacconists; and
– designated rooms in offshore installations.
Venues are to be exempt where an artistic performance requires a person to smoke.

Vehicles Work vehicles and vehicles used by members of the public are also required to be smoke-free (s 5 Health Act 2006). A vehicle is affected by this rule if it is used by members of the public or if it is used as a work vehicle by more than one person, even if those persons use the vehicle at different times or only intermittently (reg 11 Smoke-free (Exemptions and Vehicles) Regulations SI 2007/765).

5085

> EXAMPLE A van driver, smoking alone in his van, commits no offence, but where the vehicle could be used by others or if he could take a companion with him, the driver will commit an offence if he smokes.

> MEMO POINTS The smoke-free law also does not apply to vehicles which are for private use only.

Employer's duties

The employer has a duty to stop persons from smoking in smoke-free premises and vehicles. The employer is also obliged to put up signs indicating that premises are smoke-free.

5090

To stop a person from smoking It is the duty of an employer to stop a person smoking in smoke-free premises (s 8 Health Act 2006).

5092

> MEMO POINTS The employer has a duty not merely to stop smoking by workers, but also by **third parties**, including clients and customers.

Three **defences** are open to the employer (s 8 Health Act 2006):
– that he took reasonable steps to cause the person to stop smoking;
– that he did not know, or could not reasonably be expected to know, that a person was smoking; or
– that on other grounds it was reasonable not to comply with the duty.

5093

To erect a no smoking sign An employer must put up no smoking signs in smoke-free places (s 6 Health Act 2006; SI 2012/1536; SI 2007/287).

5095

No smoking signs are also required in **vehicles**.

5096

Enforcement A system of penalties has been put in place (SI 2007/760; SI 2007/764). Where a **person smokes in a smoke-free place**, he will be subject to a warning or a fine, up to a maximum of £200. Where an **employer fails to prevent a person from smoking** in a smoke-free place, he will be subject to a warning or a fine, up to a maximum of £2,500. Where an **employer fails to display** a required **no smoking sign**, he will be subject to a warning or a fine, up to a maximum of £1,000. Unitary, district and borough councils are responsible for enforcing these rules.

5098

> MEMO POINTS Where an employer fails to prevent a person from smoking, in addition to the criminal penalties listed above, he may potentially be vulnerable to **civil action**, for example if a non-smoker's asthma was aggravated, or a non-smoker acquired lung cancer, while working for him.

Smoking policy

Employers should have a **no smoking policy**, which indicates that smoking is not permitted in the workplace, whether smoking breaks are permitted (and, if so, where they should be taken), whether smoking will be allowed, and the sanctions employees will face if they breach the ban. When drafting a policy, one of the key questions facing the employer is

5100

whether to **prohibit all smoking** in the workplace, **or** whether to continue to **allow** smoking in **certain, designated compliant structures** (i.e. a structure that is not substantially enclosed) and **places** (for example, in a specified area outside the workplace building). If the second option is taken, a compliant structure will be required for this purpose.

Many employers allow smokers to take **smoking breaks** at certain intervals. Sometimes, these are given at the time of statutory rest breaks (¶3715). In some workplaces, however, smokers have been allowed to take breaks on a much more frequent basis. Where such practices have become custom and practice, and an employer orders them to end, an employee may attempt to argue that there was a contractual right to take such breaks. However, in cases preceding the ban, the right to take smoking breaks was considered to be non-contractual at best (*Dryden v Greater Glasgow Health Board* [1992] IRLR 469, EAT). Following the ban, it seems certain that an employee would not be able to rely on any such right.

An employer may also outline in the policy **positive measures** to encourage smokers to stop smoking, for example by agreeing to subsidise nicotine patches or by funding activities designed to help smokers to quit. Given that the employer faces the prospect of criminal penalties for allowing workers or customers to smoke, any policy should be **robust**. The employer should warn workers of disciplinary **sanctions** for smoking in an unauthorised place (see below). By setting out sanctions clearly, the employer protects himself against the possibility of litigation in the event that disciplinary action is taken.

5105 **Disciplining smokers** Where an employer **has** introduced a clear no smoking **policy**, he will be able to discipline workers who breach it. Even where an employer **has not** introduced a **policy**, given the clear criminal prohibition on smoking at work, it is likely that he will be held by a tribunal to be justified in disciplining a worker who smokes unlawfully at work. Any dispute at work is most likely to concern not whether an employer is entitled to sanction a worker who breaks the smoking rules, but the **reasonableness** of an employer's sanction. In a case that preceded the ban, it was held that a single instance of smoking at work was not enough to justify a dismissal on grounds of misconduct (*Marks and Spencer plc v O'Connell* [1996] UKEAT 230_95_0410). The position may be different now that a criminal offence has been introduced, but it is still best practice for employers to implement any prohibition fairly and to use their discretion where appropriate.

Any sanction should also take into account the **circumstances** of each particular **workplace**. For example, it would be reasonable for an employer whose business includes the handling of flammable chemicals to state in its policy that smoking in dangerous areas will be treated as gross misconduct (¶8490), carrying the sanction of immediate dismissal. A lesser sanction would be reasonable, however, for a first time offender caught smoking in a substantially enclosed space outside a commercial office. The policy should make similar distinctions, where they are relevant to the employer's business.

> EXAMPLE In *Marks and Spencer plc v O'Connell*, which concerned an employee working for a company with an absolute no smoking policy, the EAT held that summary dismissal for the single instance of smoking outside a store, where the smoking had taken place at night, during a 12-hour shift, had been unfair because the employer had not considered the individual circumstances of the case.

E. Asbestos-related and other single agent claims

5110 Where the employee has **worked for two or more employers**, has been diagnosed with mesothelioma and the exposure to asbestos which caused the disease might have occurred while working for any of them, each employer may be liable (*Fairchild v Glenhaven Funeral Services Ltd* [2002] UKHL 22). In *Fairchild*, the House of Lords held that where an employee had been negligently exposed to asbestos during the course of employment with more than one employer and his asbestos-induced illness could only have been caused by the employment, it was sufficient to prove that each of the employers had materially increased the risk of injury. Consequently, the employee could recover damages from each employer, even though it was not clear which particular employment had been the actual cause of the illness.

In relation to how **liability** for mesothelioma damages should be awarded, each responsible party will be liable in respect of the **whole of the damage** caused to the employee by the disease, subject to any reduction due to the employee's contributory negligence (s 3 Compensation Act 2006). It is for each responsible party to seek a contribution from each other if necessary and possible. This also applies where there is only one defendant and other causes could be environmental, and provided the defendant's negligence materially increased the risk to the employee, a single defendant could be liable in full even if they were only responsible for low levels of exposure (*Sienkiewicz v Greif* [2011] UKSC 10).

5111

> MEMO POINTS This provides protection for claimants who have contracted mesothelioma as a result of the negligence of multiple employers, one or more of whom is insolvent or untraceable. Where an employee has contracted mesothelioma **as a result of** work for **two or more employers**, all of whom are traceable and solvent, he should **bring an action** against all of them; but where an employee has contracted mesothelioma as a result of work for two or more employers, only one of whom is traceable or solvent, he can bring an action in tort against just the traceable and solvent employer, who can be held liable for the whole of the damages.

SECTION 4

Remedies and enforcement

A. Remedies

Damages Where there is a breach of the employer's duty to take care, a worker will be able to make a claim for damages if the damages suffered were as a result of the breach and were reasonably foreseeable (or are not too remote in relation to a contractual claim, although most claims of personal injury and ill health are usually based on the tort of negligence). A worker can also bring his claim for damages as a **civil claim** arising from his employer's breach of statutory duties relating to health and safety. See section 1 (¶¶4810+) for further details about the employer's liability and the extent of damages recoverable. Where an injury is due, in part, to the worker's own actions, any damages awarded against his employer may be reduced on the basis of such **contributory negligence**.

5130

Damages awarded by the courts are generally covered by the compulsory employer's liability **insurance** that the employer is required to hold.

5132

Time off for safety representatives/representatives of employee safety Such representatives or candidates have the right to complain to an employment tribunal if their employer has **failed to allow** them to take time off to attend training or fulfil their functions or has failed to pay them for such time taken off. The **tribunal can** make an order for compensation or an award for payment where appropriate (¶3960).

5135

Pay during suspension on medical grounds An employee who is suspended on medical grounds has the right to complain to an employment tribunal if his employer **fails to pay him** during the period of suspension (¶4985). The **tribunal can** order the employer to pay the amount due (s 70 ERA 1996).

5137

5139 **Maternity-related rights** An employee who has been suspended by her employer on the grounds that she is pregnant, has given birth or is breast-feeding is entitled to be paid during the period of that suspension (s 68 ERA 1996). If her employer **fails to pay her** she may bring a claim before an employment tribunal and the tribunal can order the employer to pay her the amount that is due to her (s 70 ERA 1996). Furthermore, if her employer has **failed to offer** her alternative work, where it is appropriate to do so prior to her suspension, the tribunal can also award her compensation for the infringement of her rights and for any loss she has sustained as a result.

5141 **Whistleblowing** If an employee is concerned that his employer is failing in his responsibility to his employees' health and safety, or has a reasonable belief that there is a danger to the health and safety of any individual(s), he has **special protection** in certain circumstances if he discloses such facts (¶2700).

5143 **Constructive dismissal** If the employer fails in his duty to take reasonable care, his breach may amount to a **fundamental breach of contract**, allowing the employee to bring a claim for constructive dismissal (¶8230).

5145 **Right not to be unfairly dismissed or suffer a detriment** The following health and safety-related grounds for dismissal are treated as inadmissible reasons for the purpose of **automatic** unfair dismissal (i.e. no qualifying period of service is required) (s 100 ERA 1996):
– the employee was or proposed to be involved in activities relating to preventing or reducing health and safety risks (having been designated by the employer to do so);
– the employee was acting or proposing to act as a health and safety representative or member of a safety committee, either in accordance with statutory arrangement or having been acknowledged by the employer as such;
– the employee took, or proposed to take, part in health and safety consultation or in an election of employee safety representatives (as a candidate or otherwise);
– the employee brought to the employer's attention, by reasonable means, circumstances relating to his work which he reasonably believed were or could be harmful to health and safety (and where there is no health and safety representative or committee at the workplace or it was not reasonably practicable for him to raise the matter through those means). "Reasonable means" does not include unlawful industrial action (*Balfour Kilpatrick Ltd v Acheson and ors* [2003] UKEAT 1412_01_0104);
– the employee left, proposed to leave or refused to return to his workplace, believing there to be serious and imminent danger (from the workplace or other employees) which he could not reasonably be expected to avert; and
– the employee took, or was proposing to take, appropriate steps (determined by reference to all the circumstances, including his knowledge and the facilities and advice available to him at the time) to protect himself or others (not restricted to other employees) from what he reasonably believed to be serious and imminent danger.

> **EXAMPLE**
> 1. In *Harvest Press Ltd v McCaffrey* [1999] UKEAT 488_99_0707, M was dismissed after he left his workplace in the middle of a shift because the abusive behaviour of a fellow worker made him fear for his safety. The EAT held that dangers caused by the behaviour of fellow workers are within the wide scope of the statutory protection.
> 2. In *Oudahar v Esporta Group Ltd* [2011] UKEAT 0566_10_2206, an employee refused to clean an area behind kitchen fryers on the basis that he felt exposed wires due to maintenance work posed a health and safety risk, following which he was suspended and an investigation took place. He was ultimately dismissed both for failing to obey a reasonable instruction and disregard for food hygiene. He stated that he had refused to comply with the instructions solely for health and safety reasons, though the employer disputed that any such reasons had existed. The EAT held that it was irrelevant whether or not the employer believed that there was a health and safety problem: what mattered was whether the employee reasonably and honestly believed there to be a serious and imminent danger.

5146 Employees also have the right not to suffer detrimental actions for the same reason(s) or on the same ground(s) as above (s 44 ERA 1996).

B. Enforcement

Enforcement of health and safety legislation is undertaken by the Health and Safety Executive (HSE) for most industrial premises, or the Environmental Health Department of the local authority for offices not forming part of an industrial site, shops and a range of other premises (The Health and Safety (Enforcing Authority) Regulations SI 1998/494). The HSE is also the enforcement authority in relation to the safety of articles and substances supplied for use at work. Fire safety legislation is enforced by the local fire authority. Enforcement authorities employ **inspectors** who have a wide range of powers, including the power of entry into premises without prior notice. Inspectors can issue enforcement notices, or bring prosecutions, depending on the seriousness of the offence in question.

The HSE has adopted a "**name and shame**" **policy** in relation to health and safety prosecutions. Details of organisations prosecuted under health and safety legislation or in receipt of Improvement and Prohibition Notices are now listed on their website, including in the case of prosecutions, details of penalties imposed (see flmemo.co.uk/em5161). This policy is aimed at enhancing the deterrent effect of prosecution.

1. Enforcement notices and prosecutions

Employers Health and safety and fire inspectors can issue enforcement notices to **employers** for breaches of the health and safety or fire rules. **Failure to comply** with the requirements of any enforcement notice is a serious offence, which can result in an unlimited fine and imprisonment. While the employer on which the notice has been served will be vulnerable to prosecution for the breach of the notice, any director or senior manager who allows or connives with such a breach will also be at risk of personal prosecution.

Health and safety inspectors can issue two types of enforcement notice. Where an inspector is of the opinion that legal requirements are not being met, an **improvement notice** can be served requiring the contravention to be rectified in a specified period of time. This period will be at least 21 days. An **appeal** against the notice can be made to an employment tribunal within 21 days of the issue of the notice, and if an appeal is brought the notice is suspended until the appeal is heard.

Where, however, the inspector is of the opinion that the activities being, or likely to be, undertaken involve a risk of serious personal injury, a **prohibition notice** can be served directing that the activities in question are stopped. A prohibition notice can either take immediate effect, or come into force after a specified period of time. An **appeal** can be brought against the issue of the notice in the same way as described for an improvement notice above, but the notice will still remain in force until the appeal is heard.

Fire safety inspectors can serve **enforcement notices** where the fire authority is of the opinion that there has been a failure to comply with any aspect of workplace fire precautions legislation (reg 30 SI 2005/1541). An **appeal** against the notice can be made to the magistrates' court within 21 days, but the notice will remain in force until the appeal is heard. **Prohibition notices** can also be served where the fire authority is of the opinion that the risk to persons on the premises in the event of fire is so serious that the use of the premises should be prohibited or restricted (reg 31 SI 2005/1541). If the fire authority is of the opinion that the risk is imminent, the notice can take effect immediately. The same **appeal** procedures apply as for health and safety enforcement notices.

Workers Enforcement action may also be taken against workers. When enforcement officers discover a breach of the worker's statutory duty of care (¶4804) they may consider taking action against the individual by way of warning, improvement notice, prohibition notice or prosecution. Prosecution generally only occurs in cases where there is a flagrant disregard of health and safety rules by a properly trained worker.

2. Offences

Offences under health and safety/fire precautions rules

5180 Prosecutions under health and safety and fire precautions legislation can be brought by the relevant enforcement authority in either a magistrates' court or the Crown Court (s 33 HSWA 1974; s 9 Fire Precautions Act 1971).

The **maximum penalties** for the majority of offences are as follows (Health and Safety (Offences) Act 2008):
- magistrates' court: £20,000 fine and/or 6 or 12 months' imprisonment; and
- Crown Court: unlimited fine and/or 2 years' imprisonment.

> MEMO POINTS The Corporate Manslaughter and Health and Safety Offences Causing Death Guideline (February 2010) stipulates that the appropriate fine for a health and safety **offence which is shown to have caused death** should seldom be less than £100,000 and could be hundreds of thousands of pounds. This figure will then be adjusted to take into account factors which aggravate or increase the seriousness of the offence, along with any mitigating factors. The guideline sets out factors likely to be regarded as aggravating or affecting the seriousness of the offence and those likely to afford mitigation. In addition, the court should consider the financial consequences of a fine, including the resources of the company and its ability to pay. For this purpose companies will be expected to provide the court with their published audited accounts for a 3-year period, including the year of the offence.

5181 The courts have held that it is impossible to lay down a tariff or formula, but stated that both mitigating and aggravating factors need to be considered when imposing fines (R v F Howe & Son (Engineers) Ltd [1999] 2 All ER 249, CA).

Mitigating factors include:
- prompt admission of responsibility and a timely plea of guilty;
- steps taken to remedy deficiencies after they were drawn to the defendant's attention; and
- a good safety record.

Aggravating factors include a failure to respond to warnings and where safety has been compromised in order to make a profit.

5182 Each case has to be dealt with according to its own particular circumstances. When setting the level of the fine, the court will balance the need for the fine to be large enough to show managers and shareholders that it was important to provide a safe environment in the workplace with the financial circumstances of the offending company.

5183 Prosecutions will usually only follow an improvement or prohibition notice. The inspectors can, however, choose to prosecute without notice.

5185 **Personal liability of directors** Where an offence under health and safety or fire precautions legislation is committed by a company or other body corporate, it is possible for senior individuals within the organisation to be personally prosecuted (s 37 HSWA 1974; reg 32 SI 2005/1541). This occurs if the offence was committed with the consent or connivance of, or can be attributable to any neglect on the part of, a director, company secretary or senior manager. An example would be where a director of a company failed to ensure that corrective action was taken, knowing that a particular safety problem existed, or if he refused to authorise expenditure on essential health and safety training. An example of connivance would be wilfully turning a blind eye, such as allowing dangerous machinery to be operated while pretending not to know of the practice. The courts have held that this type of offence is only applicable to senior staff who have the power to decide corporate policy and strategy (R v Boal [1992] IRLR 420, CA). With regard to the meaning of neglect, the correct test was not what the director/officer did know but what he should have known (R v P Ltd and anor [2008] ICR 96, CA).

Manslaughter at work

5187 Where an individual is **prosecuted for** gross negligence manslaughter (¶5190), or where a company is prosecuted for corporate manslaughter (¶5192), there **may also be** a prosecution for criminal breaches of the Health and Safety at Work Act (HSWA 1974).

While prosecutions under general health and safety law are **initiated by** the health and safety enforcement authorities, prosecutions for manslaughter are initiated by the Crown Prosecution Service (CPS) following information provided by the police. The HSE, CPS and police services now have a **joint protocol** for the investigation of such accidents. This involves a senior police officer attending the scene of any workplace death to establish if there is any evidence for manslaughter charges, and HSE inspectors passing information to the CPS where such evidence is discovered in the course of an investigation.

> EXAMPLE In *R v British Steel plc* [1995] IRLR 310, CA, the employer was liable for a breach of s 3 HSWA 1974 even though the incident occurred under the supervision of an engineer who was not a member of senior management. This section contained an absolute prohibition and it was not necessary to attribute corporate liability only for acts of the directing mind of the company.

5190 **Individual liability** Any individual, including an employer, a director or a worker, may be prosecuted for **gross negligence manslaughter** where there is sufficient evidence to show that there has been gross negligence on his part. The **test** for gross negligence is an objective one, and the ordinary principles of the law of negligence apply to ascertain whether there has been a breach of duty to the person who has died, i.e. the existence of the duty and the breach of it causing death. There is gross negligence where the conduct of the defendant was so bad in all the circumstances as to amount to a criminal act or omission. It is for the jury to decide whether the conduct qualifies (*R v Adomako* [1995] 1 AC 171, HL).

5192 **Corporate liability** There are **four elements** to the statutory offence of corporate manslaughter:

1. the company must owe a relevant duty of care to the victim (s 2 Corporate Manslaughter and Corporate Homicide Act 2007). This requirement reflects the position under the common law, so that a company owes the duty where it employs a person, where a person is on its land, where it supplies goods or services to a person, when constructing buildings etc, and when it carries out other activities on a commercial basis. There are various "public policy" exceptions, so that public authorities making policy decisions or carrying out policing and law enforcement activities, such as the Ministry of Defence and the emergency, child protection and probation services, do not owe this duty in carrying out their functions. This is not a wholesale exemption under the Act (it does not exempt these bodies from their duties as employers or occupiers of premises), but it does include situations in which it would not be reasonable to hold the body liable for a person's death, such as when an organisation or its representatives administer emergency treatment to a patient or attempt to rescue a person from a burning building;
2. the company must have breached that duty as a result of the way in which its activities were managed or organised (s 1 Corporate Manslaughter and Corporate Homicide Act 2007). A substantial factor in the breach must be the conduct of the company's senior management (i.e. people who play a significant role in the management of all or a substantial part of the company's activities);
3. management failure must have caused the death although it need not have been the only cause (s 1(1)(a) Corporate Manslaughter and Corporate Homicide Act 2007); and
4. management failure must amount to a gross breach of the duty of care (s 1(1)(a) Corporate Manslaughter and Corporate Homicide Act 2007). A breach is "gross" if it falls far below the standard that could have reasonably been expected.

> MEMO POINTS The Corporate Manslaughter and Corporate Homicide Act 2007 came into force on **6 April 2008**, applying to offences committed on or after this date. It abolished the previous common law offence of gross negligence manslaughter in so far as it applied to companies and other organisations (including partnerships) within the Act, replacing it with a statutory offence of corporate manslaughter (corporate homicide in Scotland).

5193 Sanctions under the act include an unlimited **fine**. The Corporate Manslaughter and Health and Safety Offences Causing Death Guideline (February 2010) stipulates that the appropriate fine for a corporate manslaughter offence should seldom be less than £500,000 and could be millions of pounds. This figure will then be adjusted to take into account factors which aggravate or increase the seriousness of the offence, along with any mitigating factors. The guideline sets out factors likely to be regarded as aggravating or affecting the seriousness of the offence and those likely to afford mitigation. In addition, the court should consider the financial consequences of a fine, including the resources of the offending company and its ability to pay. For this purpose companies will be expected to provide the court with their published audited accounts for a 3-year period, including the year of the offence.

In addition, the court has the power to impose a **remedial order** and a **publicity order** on a convicted organisation. Publicity orders may be made with regard to offences committed on or after 15 February 2010 (SI 2010/276). The Corporate Manslaughter and Health and Safety Offences Causing Death Guideline states that a publicity order should be imposed in virtually all cases and should be seen as part of the penalty. A **compensation order** in favour of relatives and dependants of the deceased for bereavement and funeral expenses may also be made (s 130 Powers of Criminal Courts (Sentencing) Act 2000). Compensation orders may also be made as a result of a civil action.

CHAPTER 16

Equality at work

OUTLINE

SECTION 1 **Discrimination**	5210
I Key concepts	5215
1 Scope	5215
2 Liability	5225
Employer	5225
Worker	5233
Other groups/bodies	5236
3 Forms of discrimination	5240
Direct discrimination and subsidiary forms	5240
Indirect discrimination	5245
Harassment	5246
Bullying	5247
II Specific types of discrimination	5250
A Sex and sexual orientation	5260
Associative and perceptive discrimination	5263
1 Direct	5265
a Unlawful	5270
b Lawful	5280
Positive action	5282
Occupational requirement	5290
2 Indirect	5300
a Unlawful	5300
b Justification	5310
3 Application to specific situations	5320
a During pregnancy or maternity leave	5320
b Part-time work	5323
c Marital and civil partnership status	5325
d Gender reassignment	5335
4 Victimisation	5350
5 Harassment	5360
B Racial and religion or belief	5375
Associative and perceptive discrimination	5385
1 Direct	5390
a Unlawful	5390
b Lawful	5397
Positive action	5399
Occupational requirement	5402
2 Indirect	5410
a Unlawful	5410
b Justification	5418
3 Victimisation	5425
4 Harassment	5430
C Disability	5450
Associative and perceptive discrimination	5453
1 Definition of disability	5455
a Physical or mental impairment	5457
b Effect	5469
Substantial and adverse	5470
Long-term	5481
c Normal day-to-day activities	5485
2 Unlawful	5495
a Direct discrimination	5500
b Indirect discrimination	5509
c Discrimination arising from disability	5510
d Failure to make reasonable adjustments	5530
e Victimisation	5565
f Harassment	5570
D Age	5600
1 Direct and indirect	5605
a Unlawful	5610
b Lawful	5614
Justification	5615
Occupational requirement	5620
Positive action	5623
Specific exceptions	5625
2 Victimisation	5640
3 Harassment	5645
SECTION 2 **Equal pay**	5650
1 Scope of protection	5653
Sex equality clause	5655
2 Unlawful	5660
3 Lawful	5680
Material factor defence	5680

SECTION 3 **Enforcement and remedies**	5700	A	Remedies – discrimination	5735
		1	Declaration	5738
I Tribunal claim	5710	2	Compensation	5740
Questionnaires	5711	3	Recommendation	5760
Bringing a claim	5720	B	Remedies – equal pay	5770
Multiple claims	5724	II	Enforcement	5790
Evidence	5725			
Burden of proof	5730	SECTION 4 **Best practice**		5800

5200 Discrimination on the grounds of **age, disability, gender reassignment, marriage and civil partnership, pregnancy and maternity, race, religion or belief, sex or sexual orientation** is prohibited. This is legislated for in the Equality Act 2010 (EqA 2010), which collectively refers to these grounds as "**protected characteristics**".

Where men and women are paid differently for work of equal value, members of either gender may bring a claim under the sex discrimination provisions of the EqA 2010 in certain circumstances, but there is also an additional form of action regarding **equal pay** (also included within the EqA 2010), which is discussed in section 2.

The most common **remedy** for a successful discrimination complaint is compensation and, unlike most other tribunal claims, there is no cap on the amount which may be awarded.

> MEMO POINTS   Discrimination or pay inequality may **also give rise to**:
> – **contractual claims**, including constructive dismissal or unlawful deduction of wages;
> – **common law claims**, for example, psychiatric injury; or
> – **non-discrimination claims** under **other legislation**.

5202 Workers who experience workplace bullying due to the protected characteristics of age, disability, gender reassignment, race, religion or belief, sex or sexual orientation may also bring claims for **harassment**.

5203 The following illustrations of discrimination are discussed outside this chapter:

Illustrations of discrimination in relation to:	¶¶
Pre-employment: advertisements, recruitment and selection procedures	¶¶540 +, 570+
Terms of employment including mobility clauses	¶¶1330, 1625
Training	¶¶6340+
Appraisal and promotion	¶6468
Pensions	¶3435

5205 **Legal framework**   The majority of the EqA 2010 came into force on 1 October 2010 and most of the previous legislation covering the various strands of equality law, including equal pay (collectively referred to as "predecessor legislation"), was repealed. The EqA 2010 **harmonises and consolidates** the patchwork of predecessor legislation to give a single approach to the law relating to discrimination and inequality where appropriate. It incorporates developments in both statute and case law which have taken place since the predecessor legislation was enacted. As the EqA 2010 is primarily a consolidating piece of legislation and much of the law remains the same, most of the case law decided before the EqA 2010 came into force remains relevant. Unless stated otherwise, cases referred to apply to the EqA 2010 just as they did to the predecessor legislation.

Under the EqA 2010, two comprehensive **codes of practice** have been published by the Equality and Human Rights Commission in respect of equality in employment and equal pay. These are referred to in this chapter as the Equality Code and the Equal Pay Code respectively.

> MEMO POINTS 1. The **Equality and Human Rights Commission** (EHRC) came into existence in October 2007, replacing previous separate commissions that dealt with disability rights, racial equality and sex discrimination. The EHRC also has considerable powers to investigate claims of discrimination, to issue employers (or other organisations) with unlawful act notices and to require them to carry out action plans (¶5790).
> The Government intends to reform the powers and scope of the EHRC. These proposed changes to the EHRC can be found in the Enterprise and Regulatory Reform Bill and further developments will be covered by our updating service.
> 2. The **underlying EU legislation** (EC Race Directive 2000/43; EC Employment Framework Directive 2000/78; EC Equal Treatment Amendment Directive 2002/73) continues to be of importance and is implemented by the EqA 2010.
> 3. The Department for Business, Innovation and Skills (BIS) has published for **consultation** the draft Companies Act 2006 (Strategic Report and Directors' Report) Regulations 2013, which include a requirement for **listed companies** to **state the gender split** for directors, managers and employees. The draft regulations revoke the requirement for a company's directors' report to include a business review. In exchange for the business review, companies would be required to produce a standalone strategic report each financial year, separate from the directors' report. The requirements of the new strategic report are broadly the same as those under the old business review. However, quoted companies must disclose the number of persons in the company of each sex who are directors, managers (excluding directors) and employees of the company. It is anticipated that the draft regulations will come into force in October 2013. The draft regulations can be viewed at: flmemo.co.uk/em5205

5206

The EqA 2010 covers the same forms of discrimination (with some changes to definitions) as the predecessor legislation did, and adds two new forms. The **forms** of discrimination which have been **re-enacted** are:
– direct discrimination;
– indirect discrimination;
– in the case of disability, failure to make reasonable adjustments;
– victimisation; and
– harassment.

The two **new forms** of discrimination are:
– **associative discrimination** (treating a person less favourably because of his association with someone with a protected characteristic, for example the carer of a disabled person); and
– **perceptive discrimination** (treating a person less favourably because he is perceived to have a protected characteristic, even if he does not in fact possess that characteristic).

5207

Some elements of the EqA 2010 have **yet to come into force**. This includes a new area of protection: intersectional multiple discrimination claims (commonly referred to as **dual discrimination**). Such a claim would apply where a person has experienced direct discrimination because they have a combination of two of the following protected characteristics: age, disability, gender reassignment, race, religion or belief, sex, and sexual orientation. For example, black women may experience discrimination because of stereotyped attitudes or prejudice which white women and black men in the same circumstances would not encounter. The Government has announced, in a written ministerial statement by the Secretary of State for the Home Department on 15 May 2012, that it also intends to delay the commencement of the dual discrimination and any further developments will be covered by our updating service.

> MEMO POINTS 1. Despite the provisions on dual discrimination not yet being in force, tribunals may be willing to find such discrimination under the ordinary direct discrimination provisions – they were certainly prepared to do so under the predecessor legislation. In *Ministry of Defence v Debique* [2009] UKEAT 0048_09_1210, a tribunal combined two provisions, criteria or practices to find both sex and race discrimination. Upholding the decision, the EAT recognised that discrimination is often a multi-faceted experience which cannot always be compartmentalised.
> 2. Proposals were also in place for various other plans to be enacted under the EqA 2010, such as requiring companies with more than 250 employees to publish gender pay audits, and compelling public bodies to reduce inequalities caused by socioeconomic background. The Government

has announced that these plans will be shelved and the socioeconomic duty may be repealed without having been brought into force. Any further developments will be covered by our updating service.

5208 **Public sector bodies** are now subject to a single equality duty which requires them to take equality issues into account in their decision making and to advance equality of opportunity. Specific duties require them to publish certain information in connection with their compliance with the single equality duty on a regular basis (s 149(1) EqA 2010; SI 2011/2260).

> MEMO POINTS The Government has announced that it also intends to review the scope of the single equality duty. Any further developments will be covered by our updating service.

SECTION 1

Discrimination

5210 To explain the protected characteristics, we have brought together the **key concepts** that apply to them under the EqA 2010 and, where appropriate, the anti-discrimination provisions which previously applied to them.

We have organised the **protected characteristics** set out in the EqA 2010 (and previously covered by separate pieces of legislation) into **four groups**:
– sex (including pregnancy and maternity leave, gender reassignment, and marital and civil partnership status) and sexual orientation;
– race and religion or belief;
– disability; and
– age.

I. Key concepts

1. Scope

5215 The EqA 2010 **covers** job applicants, workers (including agency workers and those working under a contract of apprenticeship) and, in certain circumstances, former workers.

> MEMO POINTS **Arbitrators** are not covered by the equality legislation because they cannot be "employed". The Supreme Court has held that, although they provide a service, they do not act under anyone's influence or direction and exercise an independent role, and are therefore not within the scope of the equality legislation (*Jivraj v Hishwani* [2011] UKSC 40).

While under the predecessor legislation, workers who worked wholly or partly in GB were covered, the EqA 2010 does not specify its **territorial scope**. The decisions relating to the enforceability of other UK statutory rights can be applied in assessing whether a worker working outside Great Britain will be protected (see ¶2275 for a discussion of the relevant case law and *Clyde & Co LLP and anor v Bates van Winkelhof* [2012] EWCA Civ 1207). Case law relating to the predecessor legislation may also be helpful.

Where the courts do not have jurisdiction to hear complaints alleged to have been committed outside GB, details of any such complaints may be allowable as evidence if they are relevant as background to the complaints alleged to have been committed in GB.

> EXAMPLE
> 1. In *Clyde & Co LLP and anor v Bates van Winkelhof*, the Court of Appeal upheld the EAT's decision that a tribunal had jurisdiction to hear discrimination claims brought by a member of a limited liability partnership (LLP), B, who worked principally in Tanzania as part of a joint venture with her UK law

firm. As B had not worked wholly abroad it was not necessary to carry out a comparative exercise to decide whether she had a stronger connection to Great Britain than Tanzania. Where, as here, the individual lives and/or works partly in Great Britain, all that is required is a sufficiently strong connection to Great Britain.

2. In *Tradition Securities and Futures SA and ors v X and ors* [2009] ICR 88, EAT, two employees who worked for a French company, initially in Paris and later in London, alleged that they had been subjected to sex discrimination and harassment in both locations. The EAT held that there was no jurisdiction for an English tribunal to hear allegations in respect of the acts of sex discrimination which took place in Paris. These could not be regarded as part of a continuous act of discrimination with the acts which took place in London. However, evidence of events in Paris could be heard, if the tribunal considered them relevant, as background to the events in London.

5216 **Volunteers** working under a non-contractual volunteer agreement were not covered in case law decided under the predecessor legislation (*X v Mid Sussex Citizens Advice Bureau and anor* [2012] UKSC 59). However, they were if they performed services under a contractual arrangement.

EXAMPLE In *X v Mid Sussex Citizens Advice Bureau and anor*, an HIV-positive volunteer adviser made a claim of disability discrimination after she had been asked to stop volunteering. She had signed a non-contractual volunteer agreement, which was expressly stated not to be binding, and attended 4 to 5 hours a week to provide advice to clients. Quite frequently she did not attend when she was expected, and no complaint was ever made about this, which reflected the non-binding nature of the agreement. The Supreme Court held that she was not entitled to bring a claim because she was neither an employee nor a worker, as on the facts of the case there was no contract between her and the CAB.

5218 **Before employment** **Job applicants** are specifically covered in respect of discrimination in the arrangements made by an employer in determining who should be offered a job, in the terms offered to applicants, and regarding an employer's refusal or deliberate omission to offer an applicant a job (s 39(1) EqA 2010).

EXAMPLE In *Glasgow City Council v McNab* [2007] IRLR 476, EAT (Scotland), an atheist was successful in a claim of discrimination on the grounds of religion or belief where he applied for a post at a Roman Catholic school and was not considered for the position because he was not a Catholic.

MEMO POINTS The recruiting employer is not under a positive obligation to disclose **information about the short-listing/selection procedure** to rejected candidates. However, if an employer refuses to grant access to information about the recruitment process, this refusal can be one fact considered, amongst all of the facts, in deciding whether the burden of proof has shifted to the recruiting employer to prove that no discrimination occurred (¶¶5730+) (*Meister v Speech Design Carrier Systems GmbH (C-415/10)* [2012] EUECJ C-415/10). In practical terms, requests for information about the successful candidate are currently usually made using the questionnaire procedure (¶¶548, 5711) and an employer facing this kind of request is usually best advised to provide at least redacted information (assuming of course no discrimination has occurred) as opposed to making a complete refusal.

5220 **During employment** **Workers** are covered in respect of discrimination which occurs during the employment relationship. An employer must not discriminate in the terms of employment which he affords a worker; in the way in which he affords them opportunities for promotion, transfer or training, or any other benefits, facilities or services, or by refusing or deliberately omitting to afford such access, or by dismissing or subjecting a worker to any other detriment (s 39(2) EqA 2010).

5222 **Post-employment** **Ex-workers** are covered in respect of discrimination and/or harassment after the employment relationship has ended where it **arises out of** and is **closely connected** to that relationship. Common situations in which post-employment discrimination is found include where an employer (*Rhys Harper v Relaxion Group plc, and joined cases*, [2003] UKHL 33):
– refuses to provide references;
– handles an appeal against dismissal in a discriminatory fashion; or
– refuses, in a discriminatory fashion, to reinstate a worker.

Post-employment victimisation may also occur where an employer **fails to pay a compensation award** for discrimination (*Coutinho v Rank Nemo (DMS) Ltd* [2009] IRLR 672, CA).

> MEMO POINTS   A strict reading of the EqA 2010 may suggest that post-employment victimisation is not covered, but the Equalities Office has stated that this was not the Government's intention and that the relevant section should be read alongside the relevant case law. This has proven so in a recent tribunal claim where a tribunal allowed a claimant's post-termination victimisation claim to proceed on the basis that the Act was intended to replace the former equality legislation and could therefore be expected to maintain the status quo unless the Government has expressed a contrary intention, which it has not. Further, the EHRC Statutory Code of Practice suggests that post-termination victimisation is intended to be covered by the Act and the Government Equalities Office has stated that "protection from post-employment victimisation is maintained under the Act read together with the relevant case law (as underpinned by EU directives, including the Equal Treatment Directive)". Taking all of this into account, the judge concluded that he could apply a purposive interpretation to the Act (*Taiwo v Olaigbe and ors* [2012] ET/2389629/11).

2. Liability

Employer

5225 The scope of an employer's liability for a discriminatory act is wide and can cover both his own acts and those of others.

5226 **Employer's acts**   An employer can be directly liable for any unlawful discriminatory acts which he commits.

5227 **Workers' and agents' acts**   An employer will be liable for his workers' acts which are carried out (s 109(1) EqA 2010):
– "in the course of their employment" whether or not they are done with the employer's knowledge or approval; or
– with the authority (express or implied) of the employer.
An employer may also be liable if he aids another person to do a discriminatory act.
In order for an employer to be liable for the discriminatory acts of an **agency worker**, it must be established that the agency worker is either an employee or acting as an agent for the employer (not to be confused with simply being an agency worker) (*Mahood v Irish Centre Housing Limited* [2011] UKEAT 0228_10_2203; *May and Baker Ltd (t/a Sanofi-Aventis Pharma) v Okerago* [2010] UKEAT 0278_09_1702).

> EXAMPLE   In *May and Baker Ltd (t/a Sanofi-Aventis Pharma) v Okerago*, an agency worker supplied to a company made a discriminatory remark to one of its employees. The employee made a complaint of race discrimination and victimisation based on the company's failure to deal with her grievance about the remark. The EAT overturned a finding by an employment tribunal that the company was liable for discrimination. Firstly, the agency worker was not in employment with regard to the company. Secondly, there was no evidence to support a finding that the worker was acting as an agent of the company in making the remark. Finally, the employer's actions could not amount to aiding the discriminatory act, on the grounds that:
> – providing the environment in which the remark was made did not mean that there was any co-operation or collaboration with the agency worker;
> – it is not possible to aid a person to do something which has already been done; and
> – the employer had no knowledge of the discriminatory remark at the time it was made.

> MEMO POINTS   An employer can also be liable for the acts of non-employee **board members** if they are acting as agents. In the case of *Bungay and anor v Saini and ors* [2011] UKEAT 0331_10_2709, two board members were found to be acting as agents of the employer as they had the power to manage the employer's business and they had carried out a discriminatory campaign in the course of their work as board members.

5228 In the "**course of employment**" is to be interpreted in the sense in which the phrase is used in everyday layman's language and, accordingly, is said to include all acts committed **at work**, whether or not these acts are associated with the worker's duties (*Jones v Tower Boot Co Ltd* [1997] IRLR 168, CA). The test is to ask whether there was a sufficient "nexus" between the act and the job. For example, if a worker of a certain ethnic origin is repeatedly subjected to racist and physical abuse by colleagues at work, his employer is likely to be found liable for his other workers' behaviour if the worker complains of racial discrimination.

Even acts committed **outside working hours** and/or the **place of employment** can give rise to liability on the part of the employer if the acts were committed in circumstances connected to the employment. For example, if the acts occurred following a work conference or at an after-work party.

EXAMPLE In *Chief Constable of Lincolnshire Constabulary v Stubbs* [1999] IRLR 81, EAT, inappropriate sexual behaviour by a police officer in a pub after work and at a leaving party was held to be sufficiently work-related to be in the course of the officer's employment.

Lack of knowledge or approval by the employer of the discriminatory act is no defence.

5229

However, the employer may have a **defence** in such circumstances if he can establish that he took such steps as were reasonably practicable to prevent the worker or agent from committing the discriminatory act in question, or acts of that nature (s 109(4) EqA 2010). Steps which the employer has taken before the discriminatory act took place are most relevant and an employer cannot rely only on acts he has taken to remedy the discrimination.

In practice, the question of whether an employer has taken **all practicable steps** to prevent discrimination will depend on the extent to which the employer has implemented best practice in his sector. **Public sector bodies**, for example, have duties to publish equality policies, and to regularly assess (by monitoring and other means) the extent to which their service (including its employment function) promotes equality. The extent to which an employer has implemented best practice can best be judged in light of the **anticipatory duties** of the employer, as discussed in more detail at ¶¶5800+.

Third parties' acts An employer may also be **vicariously liable** for the acts of third parties, for example, clients and independent contractors.

5231

With regard to **harassment**, an employer will be liable for harassment of a worker by a third party if he knows that a third party has harassed the worker on at least two previous occasions, unless he has taken reasonably practicable steps to prevent the harassment (s 40(2) EqA 2010).

With regard to **other third party acts**, an employer will be liable for discriminatory acts where the detrimental act was caused or permitted in circumstances in which he had sufficient control over whether or not the act would happen, and where his failure to take reasonable steps to protect his workers from the discriminatory act was itself for a reason connected to a worker's protected characteristic. In order for an employer to be liable for the direct discrimination claimed, there has to be a failure of the employer which must itself be an act of discrimination (*Pearce v Governing Body of Mayfield School* [2003] IRLR 512, HL).

In practice, employers must exercise good management to protect their staff whenever possible, for example, the employer could ask third parties to adhere to his equal opportunities policy and/or instruct his staff to oversee the conduct of a third party.

MEMO POINTS The Government is **proposing to repeal** the provisions relating to employers' liability for third party harassment under the EqA 2010. The regulations remain active at the time of publication, though the impending change is part of a draft bill called the Enterprise and Regulatory Reform Bill which is proceeding through Parliament. Any further developments will be covered by our updating service.

Worker

Where a discriminatory act is committed during the course of employment, then, in addition to the employer's vicarious liability, **personal liability** can attach to the worker who performed the act (s 110 EqA 2010).

5233

EXAMPLE In *Allaway v Reilly* [2007] UKEAT 0054_06_3105, a worker who was named as a second respondent to a sex discrimination claim attempted to have this part of the claim struck out at a pre-hearing review (¶9580) on the basis that the primary responsibility for acts of discrimination at work lies with the employer. This argument was rejected by both the tribunal and the EAT.

5234 A worker has a **defence** if (s 110(3) EqA 2010):
- he acts in reliance on his employer's statement that he would not be acting unlawfully if he did the specific act; and
- it was reasonable for him so to rely on it.

> EXAMPLE An organisation which has relied on word-of-mouth recruitment tells one of its supervisors to fill a vacancy "in the usual way". This is potentially (indirectly) discriminatory because it excludes persons from a different background for consideration. However, the supervisor may be protected if it was found that he was relying on his employer's instruction. By contrast, if he is ordered to eliminate Asian women from a recruitment exercise, and did so, he would be unable to claim that he reasonably believed this to be a lawful instruction and would not have a defence.

Other groups/bodies

5236 The following groups can also be liable and are discussed in the relevant sections.

Liability of:	¶¶
Trade unions, workers'/employers' organisations	¶7146
Authorities/bodies conferring an authorisation or qualification	¶6345
Providers/arrangers of vocational training	¶6348
Occupational pension scheme trustees/managers	¶3435

3. Forms of discrimination

Direct discrimination and subsidiary forms

5240 Direct discrimination is the most easily recognisable form of discrimination. It **occurs** when a person makes assumptions or judgements about another person based on inappropriate factors (for example, their race, religion, or sexual orientation) and, on such grounds, treats that person less favourably than others. The ambit of direct discrimination is therefore quite wide. As a general rule, all acts of direct discrimination will be unlawful, except in limited circumstances (¶5242). The major **exception** concerns discrimination on grounds of age, for which justification can be a defence (¶5600).

There are **three subsidiary forms** of direct discrimination:
- **victimisation** (treating a person less favourably because he has previously made a complaint or assisted another in bringing a claim against the employer, provided his complaint was well founded and made in good faith);
- **associative** discrimination (treating a person less favourably because of his association with someone with a protected characteristic, for example the carer of a disabled person); and
- **perceptive** discrimination (treating a person less favourably because he is perceived to have a protected characteristic, even if he does not in fact possess that characteristic).

5241 Discrimination after the **employment relationship has ended** is a relatively uncommon form, but can have a significant impact on a former worker's future employment. The most common situation in which it is likely to occur is when a worker has left his employment and his employer has provided him with a discriminatory reference or has refused to provide him with a reference for discriminatory reasons.

5242 In certain circumstances, direct discrimination can be **justified** if there is an **occupational requirement** for a particular position. This concept is examined in more detail alongside the respective protected characteristics throughout the chapter.

5243 **Positive action** by employers is allowed in respect of persons with protected characteristics who (s 158 EqA 2010):
- have needs not shared by others without that protected characteristic;
- are disadvantaged for a reason connected to the protected characteristic; or
- are from under-represented groups;

and allows employers to use proportionate means to:
- meet those needs;
- enable or encourage them to minimise or overcome disadvantages; or
- encourage participation by the under-represented group.

The rationale behind positive action is to address and rectify the fact that some sections of the workforce may be under-represented or have certain disadvantages because of their particular characteristics. A typical example of positive action would be where an organisation advertises its employment vacancies in a wider range of publications than before, and the intended effect of this practice is to encourage applicants from certain backgrounds to apply. For further information on positive action, see ¶¶5282+.

Indirect discrimination

5245 Indirect discrimination **occurs** when an employer applies a policy, provision, criterion or working practice which, although on the face of it is neutral and applicable equally to all workers, in fact inadvertently puts a certain group of workers (for example, women or people of a certain religion) at a disadvantage in comparison to other workers.

In certain circumstances, indirectly discriminatory provisions can be **justified** if the disadvantage suffered is proportionately balanced against the needs of the employer in the successful running of his business.

Harassment

5246 Harassment **occurs** if, on grounds relating to age, disability, race, religion or belief, sex or sexual orientation, a worker is subjected to unwanted conduct from his employer or another worker which has either the effect or purpose of violating his dignity or creating an intimidating, hostile, degrading, humiliating or offensive environment (s 26 EqA 2010). Harassment after the employment relationship has ended, although unusual, can occur.

A claim may also be brought under the Protection from Harassment Act 1997 (¶¶5045+). This legislation was originally introduced to provide protection from stalkers, but has been held to apply to harassment and bullying at work.

Bullying

5247 Bullying is a more general term for unwanted conduct that has a detrimental effect on a worker's health or morale. Sometimes, the **cause or underlying motive** for the bullying is connected to an individual's gender or membership of a particular group under one of the specific types of discrimination, and may well lead to a claim for harassment.

Bullying in the workplace may also result in other potential claims (¶¶5045+).

II. Specific types of discrimination

5250 Discrimination on the grounds of **age, disability, gender reassignment, marriage and civil partnership, pregnancy and maternity, race, religion or belief, sex and sexual orientation** (except in certain circumstances outlined below) is prohibited (EqA 2010).

A. Sex and sexual orientation

5260 Sex and sexual orientation discrimination can be divided into standard direct discrimination, victimisation and associative and perceptive discrimination (all also forms of direct discrimination), indirect discrimination and harassment.

5261 **Sex discrimination** Sex discrimination is **defined** as discrimination based on a person's gender (i.e. the fact that a person is male or female). However, other instances of discrimination which are akin to sex discrimination include discrimination on grounds of:
– pregnancy, childbirth and maternity leave (¶5320);
– marital or civil partnership status (i.e. the fact that a person is married or a civil partner (but not because he/she is single) (¶5325));
– the fact that a person has undergone, is undergoing or intends to undergo gender reassignment (¶5335); and
– flexible working (chapter 6).

Both **female and male workers** are protected in identical terms, except in relation to discrimination on grounds of pregnancy, childbirth, maternity and paternity.

MEMO POINTS **Ministers of religion** are excluded from the protection of the EqA 2010 (Sch 9 para 2 EqA 2010).

5262 **Sexual orientation** Sexual orientation is **defined** as a sexual orientation towards persons of (s 12(1) EqA 2010):
– the same sex;
– the opposite sex; or
– the same sex and the opposite sex.

The **effect** of this definition is to protect not just lesbian and gay workers against discrimination, but also bisexual and (where relevant) heterosexual workers.

EXAMPLE
1. In *Hegarty v The Edge (Soho)*, ET case 2200027/05, a heterosexual woman, H, worked in a bar in Soho. She was informed that the bar was closing and she was redundant with immediate effect. In fact, the bar did not close, but was relaunched with gay bar staff. H's claim of unlawful discrimination was successful.
2. In *Grant v HM Land Registry* [2011] EWCA Civ 769, a gay employee, G, made a complaint of direct discrimination and harassment after he had been "outed" by a manager. He had moved to a branch of the employing organisation from one where he had himself been open about his sexuality. An employment tribunal found that a manager had deliberately set out to make G's sexuality known against his wishes. The EAT and the Court of Appeal found that, on the facts, there had not been enough evidence to support the claim, because the tribunal had failed to take into account the fact that G had been happy to be open about his sexuality at his previous workplace. However, they did comment that deliberately outing an employee against their will could constitute direct discrimination or harassment, where proved.

Associative and perceptive discrimination

5263 A worker is protected against discrimination even if the discrimination is on the grounds of **someone else's sex or sexual orientation** (s 13(1) EqA 2010, as discrimination is defined as being on the grounds of sex or sexual orientation, which is not limited to the claimant's sex or sexual orientation). Consequently, a worker can bring proceedings if he/she objects to instructions given by an employer to discriminate on grounds of sex or sexual orientation, or if the worker is discriminated against because his/her friends are, for example, gay, bisexual or heterosexual, as the case may be.

Moreover, less favourable treatment based on the **employer's or another worker's perception** of an individual's sexual orientation, whether that perception is rightly or wrongly held, is also covered. For example, there could be unlawful discrimination if an individual is treated less favourably because he/she is thought to look gay or is rumoured to be bisexual.

MEMO POINTS The definition of direct discrimination means that associative and perceptive discrimination on the grounds of sex and sexual orientation are covered, but this does **not extend to pregnancy, maternity, marital status or civil partnership.**

1. Direct

5265 Direct discrimination is unlawful, though there are a certain number of situations which can result in lawful discrimination.

a. Unlawful

5270 Direct sex and sexual orientation discrimination occurs where there is "**less favourable treatment**" of an individual, **compared** with the treatment of another person of the opposite sex/of a different sexual orientation. There must be no material difference between the circumstances relating to each case when comparing them (s 23(1) EqA 2010).

For a discussion as to the **scope** of the relevant legislation (i.e. who is protected in terms of the type of worker, geographical scope and time periods), see ¶¶5215+. Moreover, details as to an **employer's liability** for his own discriminatory acts, together with those of his workers and agents, as well as individual **workers' liability** for discrimination, are provided at ¶¶5225+.

Claims in relation to discrimination in employment terms generally and matters of contractual pay are dealt with under different sections of the EqA 2010. Claims relating to terms of employment other than pay are dealt with under s 39 EqA 2010, while terms relating to contractual pay are within the scope of the equality clause implied by s 66 EqA 2010 (s 70(1), s 71(1) EqA 2010).

It is unlawful for a person who has authority over another person to give **instructions** to that person **to discriminate** against a worker on the grounds of sex or sexual orientation (s 111 EqA 2010). The EHRC (see memo point 1 to ¶5205) can also bring proceedings in respect of unlawful instructions to discriminate on the grounds of sex or sexual orientation.

MEMO POINTS Under the EqA 2010, there must be no material difference between the circumstances relating to each case when comparing them (s 23(1) EqA 2010).

5271 The EqA 2010 is silent as to whether the alleged discrimination needs to be **intentional** or not for protection to be provided, but case law decided under the predecessor legislation established that intent was **not relevant** (S: *R v Birmingham City Council, ex parte Equal Opportunities Commission* [1989] IRLR 173, HL; *James v Eastleigh Borough Council* [1990] ICR 554, HL).

EXAMPLE
Examples of direct sex discrimination:
1. In *Corus Hotels Plc v Woodward and anor* [2006] UKEAT 0536_05_1703, a candidate was interviewed for a post as a receptionist, which required working morning and evening shifts. The first question the candidate was asked was whether she had children. As a male candidate would not have been asked the same question, the behaviour constituted direct sex discrimination.
2. In *Eke v Commissioners of Customs and Excise* [1981] IRLR 334, EAT, E complained to her employer that she had been subjected to sexual harassment. Her employer refused to investigate the allegation and it was held that if the refusal to investigate was on grounds of sex, it could amount to a refusal of access to benefits and therefore be directly discriminatory.
3. In *Calder v James Finlay Corporation Ltd* [1989] ICR 157, EAT, the employer offered a non-contractual mortgage subsidy scheme for workers aged 25 and over. All male workers received the subsidy, but no female workers did. This was held to amount to unlawful sex discrimination.

Examples of direct sexual orientation discrimination:
1. In *Brooks v Findlay Industries UK Ltd*, ET case 1304323/2004, an employer directly discriminated where he failed to investigate the behaviour of workers who subjected a gay worker to inappropriate language and behaviour.
2. In *Hubble v Brooks*, ET case 1600381/05, where a man was refused employment as a manager of the pub, on the grounds that he was in a long-term relationship with another man, this was held to be direct discrimination.

5273 **Comparator** A comparator (real or hypothetical) is required in cases of discrimination (s 23 EqA 2010). If there are **material differences** between the worker and his/her comparator, it may not be possible to establish less favourable treatment. The comparator must be a real or hypothetical person who does not share the protected characteristic of the claimant but who is, or is assumed to be, in not materially different circumstances to the claimant.

EXAMPLE In *Nelson v Newry and Mourne District Council* [2009] IRLR 548, NICA, two employees were disciplined for an incident in which A, a female council employee, handed over plants to B, a male employee, at his request. A was given a written warning to be kept on her record for 6 months whereas B's

warning was to remain on his record for 12 months (reduced on appeal from 24 months) and B was treated less favourably during the investigation; he was not given notice of the hearing, was not allowed to be accompanied by a union representative and was not provided with a copy of a complaint from a member of the public regarding the incident. B made a successful complaint of sex discrimination, which was overturned on appeal by the Northern Ireland Court of Appeal. The Court held that the employment tribunal had failed to take into account a number of differences between the cases of A and B which meant that their circumstances were materially different. These included that:
– B had asked for the plants for himself knowing it was against council rules, whereas A was not aware what he planned to do with them;
– B did not immediately admit the offence whereas A was co-operative; and
– A and B were members of different unions so that different procedures applied to them.

5274 However, it is not necessary that a minutely exact actual comparator must be found and where circumstances are **unidentical but not wholly dissimilar**, tribunals are free to consider whether the treatment is less favourable (*Chief Constable of West Yorkshire v Vento* [2001] IRLR 124, EAT, overturned on appeal on the issue of remedies only ([2003] IRLR 102, CA)). Only the **relevant circumstances** of the claimant and the comparator can be taken into account. The relevant circumstances are those which were taken into account by the employer when deciding how to treat the claimant and therefore all the characteristics of the claimant which were relevant to the way he/she was treated must also be found in the comparator (*Pearce v Governing Body of Mayfield School* [2003] IRLR 512 heard with *Macdonald (AP) v Advocate General for Scotland* [2003] IRLR 512, HL).

> EXAMPLE A female worker fails to secure a promotion and complains of sex discrimination. She uses as a comparator a male worker who applied for the same post. The employer argues that the work experience of the two workers is so different as to make comparison of their treatment impossible. For the purpose of establishing an appropriate comparator, however, the relevant circumstances to be taken into account are limited to the fact that both workers applied for the same post. Their level of experience is not a relevant factor. It may, however, be relevant when the employer comes to explain why he offered the promotion to one worker and not the other (i.e. it will help to establish whether or not the complainant has, in fact, been subjected to less favourable treatment).

5275 If a claimant cannot refer to the treatment of an actual comparator, it is appropriate that he/she refers to the treatment of a **hypothetical comparator** (*Balamoody v UK Central Council for Nursing, Midwifery and Health Visiting* [2002] IRLR 288, CA). When a hypothetical comparator is used, the comparison has to be made in the context of the same employment as the claimant's (*Grieg v (1) Community Industry (2) Ahern* [1979] IRLR 158, EAT; see also *Martin v Lancehawk Ltd (t/a European Telecom Solutions)* [2004] UKEAT 0525_03_2203). A tribunal is entitled to use its discretion in determining the **particular circumstances** of a hypothetical comparator and, in doing so, must have regard to the purpose of the legislation, i.e. the elimination of discrimination (*Home Office v Saunders* [2005] UKEAT 0260_05_0711).

Moreover, if a claimant tries to rely on a comparison with an **inappropriate comparator**, then the tribunal may compare him/her with a hypothetical comparator even if the claimant did not present his/her case on this basis (*Balamoody v UK Central Council for Nursing, Midwifery and Health Visiting*, above).

> EXAMPLE
> 1. In *Grieg v (1) Community Industry (2) Ahern*, the claimant, a job applicant, was turned down on the basis that she would have been the only woman in an all-male team. Attempting to defend her sex discrimination claim, the employer argued that her treatment should be compared with that which would have been afforded to a hypothetical male applicant who would have joined a women-only team. This was rejected by the EAT which stated that for the purposes of making a comparison, it was appropriate to compare the treatment of the claimant with that of a male job applicant seeking to do the same job with the same team.
> 2. In *Home Office v Saunders*, a female prison officer was ordered to do a rub-down body search of a male prisoner, which she refused to carry out. There was no actual comparator since prison rules prohibited rub-down searches of female prisoners by male prison officers. However, the correct hypothetical comparator was a male officer conducting such a search of a female prisoner,

despite the prohibition in practice. On this basis, the EAT held that the claimant had been subjected to a detriment and had suffered direct discrimination. It was irrelevant that the circumstances of the hypothetical comparator could not, in reality, have existed.

Less favourable treatment In respect of sex discrimination, **mere unfavourable** or unfair **treatment** will **not be discriminatory** since it cannot be inferred, from the fact that an employer has treated a worker unreasonably, that he would have acted reasonably in respect of another worker in the same circumstances (*Zafar v Glasgow City Council* [1998] ICR 120, HL). Therefore, an employer may act unreasonably, but provided he does not treat members of the opposite sex more favourably, he may escape a claim for direct discrimination.

5276

EXAMPLE In *Kettle v Ward* [2006] UKEAT 0016_06_0811, a male manager who believed that a woman worker was taking an unauthorised break chose to enter the company's female toilets to shout at her. A female manager, the EAT held, with the same robust style, would have shown the same insensitivity towards a male cleaner in the male toilets. It followed that there was no unlawful discrimination.

However, the more unreasonable the treatment, the greater the possibility that the employer's **explanation for his conduct** will be challenged (*Law Society v Bahl* [2003] IRLR 640, EAT, upheld on appeal ([2004] IRLR 799, CA)). The employer's conduct may, moreover, amount to indirect discrimination (¶5300).

The **sex of the claimant** must be at least a significant or important reason for his/her less favourable treatment, but it does not need to be the sole reason.

5277

In cases involving the application of **gender-specific criteria**, the question is whether "but for" the worker's sex, the employer would have acted differently (*James v Eastleigh Borough Council* [1990] ICR 554, HL). However, the EAT has suggested that this test is limited to circumstances in which the less favourable treatment of the claimant by the employer stems from the application of gender-based criteria and where it arises from the selection of the claimant because of his/her gender (*Martin v Lancehawk Ltd (t/a European Telecom Solutions)* [2004] UKEAT 0525_03_2203; *B v A* [2007] IRLR 576, EAT).

In cases which do **not involve** the application of **gender-specific criteria**, a claimant must still demonstrate that the less favourable treatment was taken on the grounds of his/her sex and, to this end, the correct test is to ask the "reason why" the employer acted as he did: was this on the grounds of sex or for some other reason (*Nagarajan v London Regional Transport* [1999] IRLR 572, HL; *Chief Constable of West Yorkshire Police v Khan* [2001] IRLR 830, HL; *Shamoon v Chief Constable of the RUC* [2003] IRLR 285, HL; all considered by *Martin v Lancehawk Ltd (t/a European Telecom Solutions)*).

EXAMPLE
1. In *B v A*, a female worker, B, was dismissed by her male employer A at the end of their sexual relationship and on account of A's feelings towards her of intense sexual jealousy. The EAT was highly critical of the tribunal's reasoning, which had been to operate a "but for" test, asking whether the claimant would have been subject to such discrimination if she was not a woman. This was the wrong test, the EAT held, and the tribunal should rather have asked what the reason was for the employer to act as he did, and whether this was on grounds of sex. With regard to the actual or hypothetical comparator, the EAT held that this should be a worker who was in all respects identical to B except for her gender. In practice, that would be a homosexual man who had conducted a relationship with the employer. Since such a worker would equally have been dismissed by the employer, B could not be said to have suffered any discrimination.
2. In *Johal v Commission for Equality and Human Rights* [2010] UKEAT 0541_09_0207, a complaint of sex discrimination was made by a woman who, as a result of an administrative error, had not been notified of job vacancies which arose while she was on maternity leave. In reaching the conclusion that the employee had not suffered sex discrimination, the EAT emphasised that the correct question to ask was what the reason for the treatment complained of was. In this case, the reason was the administrative error, and not her absence on maternity leave, and so the claim failed.

Dismissing a worker on grounds of his/her sex may constitute less favourable treatment amounting to unlawful discrimination. Where the principal reason for the dismissal is gender-neutral, there will be sex discrimination where the means by which the employer dismissed

5278

5279 a worker are gender-specific, for example, in reliance on the statutory maternity leave provisions (*Lewis Woolf Griptight Ltd v Corfield* [1997] UKEAT 1073_96_2503). In addition, where the employer's conduct is such that it entitles the worker to resign, the discrimination could also give rise to a complaint of constructive dismissal (¶8230).

The test as to whether or not a worker has suffered a **detriment** is whether a reasonable worker would feel he/she had been disadvantaged by reason of his/her employer's acts.

A **single incident** can amount to a detriment (*Bracebridge Engineering Ltd v Darby* [1990] IRLR 3, EAT; *Insitu Cleaning Co Ltd v Heads* [1994] UKEAT 576_92_0505). Where there is a **series of incidents**, each incident should not be considered in isolation but in light of the entirety of the situation (*Driskel v Peninsula Business Services Ltd* [2000] IRLR 151, EAT).

It is **not necessary** to demonstrate that the worker has suffered any substantial **economic** or **physical** loss (*Shamoon v Chief Constable of the RUC* [2001] NICA 23, upheld on appeal at [2003] IRLR 285, HL), but where the loss is modest, this may be reflected in any sum awarded by way of damages.

> EXAMPLE In *Moyhing v Barts and London NHS Trust* [2006] IRLR 860, EAT, Hospital B operated a policy that female student nurses were entitled to carry out intimate procedures on male patients, while male student nurses were only entitled to carry out intimate procedures on female patients in the presence of a female chaperone. Although the loss caused by the detriment was not substantial, the EAT held that this policy directly discriminated against male workers, and therefore was not subject to a defence of justification.

b. Lawful

5280 Sex and sexual orientation discrimination may be **justified** if an employer can demonstrate that special provisions regarding preferential treatment or occupational requirements apply.

Moreover, an employer may be **required to take certain action** to comply with another law, even if this would otherwise amount to unlawful sex discrimination (Sch 22 para 2 EqA 2010), for example, health and safety legislation in relation to pregnant workers (¶¶4950+).

> MEMO POINTS Special rules apply to employers who provide **communal accommodation** (i.e. residential accommodation which includes dormitories or other shared sleeping accommodation which, for reasons of privacy or decency, or because of the nature of the sanitary facilities serving the accommodation, should be used by members of one of the sexes only) (Sch 23 para 3 EqA 2010).

Positive action

5282 There are limited circumstances in which an employer is lawfully permitted to give preferential treatment to persons with a protected characteristic, where such action would otherwise have constituted unlawful discrimination (s 158 EqA 2010). This is otherwise known as positive action, but it should be noted that **positive discrimination is not currently permitted** as such except that it is not unlawful for an employer to treat a disabled person more favourably in comparison to a non-disabled person in relation to making reasonable adjustments, such as implementing a guaranteed interview scheme if minimum criteria are met. For more detailed explanation of the boundaries of positive action, see ¶5243.

Any action that employers take needs to be **supported by evidence** to show that the group of people who had the protected characteristic were either at a disadvantage (e.g. suffering from exclusion or lacking in opportunities and choice), had different needs (e.g. a need for something that, whilst not necessarily unique, is more pressing for that particular group, such as workers over the age of 60 who may be more likely to need IT training) or suffered from low participation (supported by, for example, statistics or evidence based on monitoring, consultation or national surveys), though this evidence does not have to be very detailed or complex (para 12 Equality Code).

The Equality Code gives examples of the types of action that employers might take (para 12 Equality Code):
– setting targets for increased participation;

- providing bursaries for obtaining qualifications in particular professions;
- outreach work such as raising awareness of public appointments within a community;
- reserving places on training courses for people with the protected characteristic;
- targeted networking opportunities;
- working with local schools and FE colleges, inviting students from groups whose participation in the workforce is disproportionately low to spend a day at the company; and
- providing mentoring.

Whether the action is a **proportionate means of achieving** one of the relevant aims will depend, amongst other things, on the seriousness of the relevant disadvantage, the extremity of need or under-representation and the availability of other means of countering them.

Some positive action can be taken in relation to **recruitment and promotion**, though there are strict controls as to how far such action can go (as prescribed by s 159 EqA 2010). This can occur where a person reasonably believes either that individuals sharing a protected characteristic suffer a disadvantage as a result of that characteristic, or that their participation in the area in question is disproportionately low. As with other situations where positive action is allowed:
- some information or **evidence will be required** to indicate that one of those conditions exists, for example looking at the profiles of the workforce in comparison to other comparable employers in the area or sector as a whole, or looking at national data such as labour force surveys for a national or local picture; and
- the action must be a **proportionate means** of achieving the aim of overcoming or minimising the disadvantage or the low participation caused by the protected characteristic. Factors will depend, amongst other things, on the seriousness and extent of the disadvantage or under-representation and the availability of other means to counter it.

Employers must be careful not to automatically or **routinely favour candidates** who share the protected characteristic as it can only be used in cases where there is a "tie-breaker" between two or more candidates of equal merit. This is because positive action in recruitment or promotion does not allow an employer to appoint or promote a less suitable candidate just because that candidate has a protected characteristic that is under-represented or disadvantaged. Both candidates must be as qualified as each other for the role in question and this means taking into account a candidate's overall ability, competence and professional experience together with any relevant formal or academic qualifications, as well as any other qualities required to carry out the particular job.

If a decision has been made to apply positive action, employers should be prepared to objectively justify their decision to an unsuccessful candidate to protect themselves against any claims of positive discrimination.

Sex discrimination An employer may provide to individuals of a particular sex **access to facilities for training** (which would help to fit them for particular work) and encourage individuals of one sex to take advantage of **opportunities for doing particular work**.

Sexual orientation discrimination An employer may provide to individuals of a particular sexual orientation **access to facilities for training** (which would help to fit them for particular work) and encourage individuals of a particular sexual orientation to take advantage of **opportunities for doing particular work**. They may do so where it reasonably appears to the employer that such treatment would prevent, or compensate for, disadvantages linked to sexual orientation suffered by persons of that sexual orientation doing that work or likely to take up that work (reg 26 SI 2003/1661).

Occupational requirement

In limited circumstances, it is **permissible** to require a worker to have or not have a particular protected characteristic **if**:
- it is an occupational requirement; and
- the requirement is a proportionate means of achieving a legitimate aim.

The requirement must not be a sham, and must be connected to the job (para 13.7 Equality Code; Sch 9 para 1 EqA 2010). This may prove to be a lower threshold than the wording used in the predecessor legislation which stated that a requirement had to be genuine and determining. Where an employer seeks to rely on an occupational requirement, the employer must be reasonably satisfied that the claimant (the unsuccessful job applicant) does not meet the requirement.

Where there is an occupational requirement, the types of discrimination permitted are (Sch 9 para 1(2) EqA 2010):
– recruitment: both the arrangements made for arranging how the position is filled (e.g. advertising) and the final decision as to who is offered the position;
– access to training, promotion, transfers or receiving benefits, facilities or services; and
– dismissal.

> EXAMPLE An employer turns down a male job applicant for the position of sales assistant in a women's clothing shop on the basis that the job involves contact with customers in a state of undress in fitting rooms and, thus, being a woman is an occupational requirement. However, this argument will fail if the employer has a sufficient number of female sales assistant workers who can perform the relevant duties (of assisting customers in the fitting rooms).

> MEMO POINTS An additional exception applies where the employment is for the purposes of an **organised religion** and it is necessary to employ a person of a particular sex or sexual orientation to avoid conflicting with the strongly held religious convictions of a significant number of the religion's followers (Sch 9 para 2 EqA 2010).
> Earlier case law on genuine occupational requirements and qualifications may be helpful in assessing whether a particular requirement falls within this exception and is a proportionate means of achieving a legitimate aim.

> EXAMPLE In *Reaney v Hereford Diocesean Board of Finance*, ET case 1602844/06, an interview panel decided that R was the best candidate for a post as a youth officer with the Church of England. R had disclosed on his job application form that he had recently ended a same sex relationship. He was interviewed by the Bishop of Hereford, and was told, in line with the Church's policy, that sexual behaviour outside marriage is inappropriate in a worker of the Church. R gave guarantees to the Bishop that he would not engage in further relationships while employed by the Church. The Bishop did not accept these assurances and a tribunal ruled that he had been unreasonable in not accepting them.

2. Indirect

a. Unlawful

5300 Indirect discrimination occurs where treatment which **appears neutral** and unconnected with sex, marital status, civil partnership status, gender reassignment or sexual orientation, **nevertheless** turns out to have a **disproportionately adverse impact** on members of a particular group sharing a protected characteristic.

Case law decided under the predecessor legislation which established that it was irrelevant whether the alleged discrimination was **intentional** or not is likely to hold true for claims brought under the EqA 2010 (S: *R v Birmingham City Council, ex parte Equal Opportunities Commission* [1989] IRLR 173, HL; *James v Eastleigh Borough Council* [1990] ICR 554, HL).

5301 Indirect discrimination is **defined** as when the employer applies or would apply a provision, criterion or practice to a worker, which (s 19 EqA 2010):
– puts, or would put, members of the same gender/sexual orientation as that worker at a particular disadvantage when compared with the opposite gender/different sexual orientation;
– puts, or would put, that worker at that disadvantage; and
– the employer cannot justify this by showing it to be a proportionate means of achieving a legitimate aim (¶5310).

Indirect discrimination by an employer may often be inadvertent. The phrase "**provision, criterion or practice**" is not defined, but is said to include not only formal conditions and requirements, but also **informal work practices**.

> EXAMPLE In *British Airways v Starmer* [2005] IRLR 862, EAT, a worker applied to her employer to halve her working hours. The employer refused her application and required that she work 75% of full-time hours if she was to work part-time. The employer's actions were held to be indirectly discriminatory. The requirement that she work 75% of full-time hours constituted a "provision, criterion or practice", even though it was claimed to be a one-off discretionary decision.

5302

Examples of indirect sex discrimination where a policy or provision might inadvertently disadvantage more women than men include:
– a change in working hours unilaterally imposed by an employer;
– a contractual provision requiring workers to be available to work their normal contractual hours without variation;
– a requirement on workers to work overtime;
– a requirement that workers be of a certain height;
– a contractual obligation or a practice or culture of workers being expected to undertake long working hours (*London Underground Ltd v Edwards (No 2)* [1998] IRLR 364, CA);
– an unreasonable refusal to allow a worker to work from home;
– a refusal to accept requests to work flexibly for reasons related to childcare;
– a requirement to work without fixed hours but on an "as and when" basis; and
– excluding periods of part-time work, or even counting part-time work on a pro-rata basis, in order to calculate length of service.

5303

A provision, criterion or practice will **not** be **unlawful** if an employer is able to demonstrate that there are sound reasons for the provision, criterion or practice and that it can be justified objectively by demonstrating that it achieves a legitimate aim and that it is a proportionate means of achieving that aim (¶5310). The definition of indirect sex and sexual orientation discrimination therefore recognises that it is not always possible, or necessary, to require detailed statistical analysis to demonstrate that a particular worker has suffered a disadvantage. Indeed, non-statistical evidence could be sought from experts or other witnesses.

5305

However, **statistical evidence** may play a role in providing evidence to tribunals as to whether a provision, criterion or practice causes disadvantage to a particular group of people.

In appropriate cases, especially those which are reflective of social conditions generally, even a very small **marginal difference** can be enough to establish indirect discrimination (*London Underground Ltd v Edwards (No 2)* [1998] IRLR 364, CA). In this case, a female single parent was successful even though only 4.8% of women (compared with 0% men) could not comply with a requirement to work certain shifts. Indeed, the claimant was the only female worker of the company to be adversely affected by the requirement. Tribunals are not restricted to looking at statistical evidence only, but may carry out a **general assessment of the impact** a provision, criterion or practice has on members of both sexes (*London Underground Ltd v Edwards (No 2)*, above; *Chief Constable of Avon & Somerset Constabulary v Chew* [2001] UKEAT 503_00_2809).

5306

> EXAMPLE In *Chief Constable of Avon & Somerset Constabulary v Chew*, the difference between the number of female police officers unable to comply with a shift system compared with male police officers was only 2.26%. The EAT confirmed that, apart from statistical considerations, tribunals are entitled to take into account other factors to find that a disparate effect had been established. The EAT held that the female applicant had suffered indirect sex discrimination.

The **types of factor** which tribunals may consider are (*Chief Constable of Avon & Somerset Constabulary v Chew*, above):
– the make up and overall numbers of the workforce under consideration;
– the point that no or very few members of the other sex were not disadvantaged;
– the effect of a change in numbers of men and women; for example, when the numbers of women were small, a reduction could have a dramatic effect on the proportion who were disadvantaged;

5307

– the history in respect of or relevant to the workforce; and
– the inherent or inherently likely effect of the provision, criterion or practice.

Although these criteria came from a case decided under predecessor legislation, it can reasonably be expected that tribunals will continue to conduct a general assessment of disparate impact, rather than one based purely on percentages and numbers.

b. Justification

5310 In certain circumstances, an employer may be able to justify an indirectly discriminatory provision, criterion or practice if he can demonstrate that the provision, criterion or practice is a **proportionate means** of **achieving a legitimate aim** (s 19(2)(d) EqA 2010).

In general, it would appear that a **legitimate aim** will include economic and administrative objectives which support the employer's business (*Rainey v Greater Glasgow Health Board* [1987] ICR 129, HL) However, the single aim of reducing costs may not be a legitimate aim (para 4.29 Equality Code), nor, it is also suggested, will the greater cost involved in using a less discriminatory approach be proportionate unless there is another good reason for the discriminatory practice (para 4.32 Equality Code).

However, an employer cannot justify an apparently discriminatory practice by applying the "range of reasonable responses" test relied on in unfair dismissal claims (¶8437). While the principle of proportionality requires the tribunal to factor in the reasonable needs of the business, the tribunal must make its own judgment as to whether the relevant practice is **reasonably necessary**, based on a fair and detailed analysis of the business considerations involved (*Hardys & Hansons plc v Lax* [2005] IRLR 726, CA).

3. Application to specific situations

a. During pregnancy or maternity leave

5320 Unfavourable treatment because of pregnancy, illness arising from pregnancy and maternity leave is discrimination which requires no comparator (s 18 EqA 2010). Where the discrimination is because of pregnancy or pregnancy-related illness, the protection is restricted to the period from the start of pregnancy until the end of any maternity leave (or if the worker is not entitled to maternity leave, 2 weeks from the end of the pregnancy). This period is known as "the **protected period**" (s 18(6) EqA 2010). It is also restricted to discrimination in relation to the worker's **own pregnancy**, so that associative discrimination is not covered.

> MEMO POINTS As protected characteristics, it appears that pregnancy and maternity also fall within the scope of **direct sex discrimination** in respect of discrimination **outside the protected period**, which may give **protection from associative discrimination** if claims are brought under this head rather than as pregnancy or maternity discrimination.

5321 **Dismissing** a woman because she is pregnant or **refusing to employ** a woman because she is of child-bearing age on the ground that she might become pregnant is unlawful direct sex discrimination under the EqA 2010, and under the predecessor legislation this was also the case because pregnancy and the capacity to become pregnant are exclusively female characteristics (*Webb v EMO Air Cargo (UK) Ltd*, above).

Unfavourable treatment will also be discriminatory if the pregnancy was the effective and predominant reason for such treatment even if it was not the only or main reason (*O'Neill v Governors of St Thomas More RCNA Upper School and Bedfordshire County Council* [1996] IRLR 372, EAT; *Rees v Apollo Watch Repairs plc* [1996] UKEAT 23_93_0502).

> EXAMPLE The employer hires a temp to cover for a worker on maternity leave. The temp is found to do the job better than the absent worker. If the employer keeps the temp and dismisses the worker on maternity leave, the dismissal will be for a reason connected with pregnancy and, as such, will amount to unlawful sex discrimination. This is because the effective cause of the dismissal

is the worker's absence on maternity leave and, but for this absence, the temp would not have been hired and the worker would not have been dismissed.

MEMO POINTS In cases of sex discrimination involving **IVF treatment**, the Court of Justice of the European Union has held that the earliest date at which pregnancy begins is at the date of implantation (*Mayr v Backerei und Konditorei Gerhard Flockner OHG, case C-506/06* [2008] IRLR 387, ECJ). Consequently, where a woman is dismissed during her IVF treatment, but prior to the transfer of the fertilised ova into her uterus, she is not considered pregnant at the date of dismissal and is not protected under the specific right not to be discriminated against because of pregnancy or maternity leave (i.e. under the EC Pregnant Workers Directive). However, she is protected under the general right not to suffer sex discrimination (under the Equal Treatment Directive) as undergoing IVF treatment only affects women. Unfavourable treatment due to a woman undergoing IVF should be treated as sex discrimination in the same way as discrimination against women because they are likely to become pregnant.

The EAT has commented on the effect of the *Mayr* case and has also held that protection would not cover the entire period of IVF treatment, but only the periods (*Sahota v Home Office and anor* [2009] UKEAT 0342_09_1512):
– between the retrieval of the ova and immediate transfer of fertilised ova into the woman's uterus (i.e. implantation); and
– after implantation.

5322 Where discrimination is on pregnancy/maternity-related grounds and it occurs **during pregnancy or maternity leave**, a comparator (actual or hypothetical) is not required, though a complainant must show that she has been treated "less favourably than is reasonable" (s 18 EqA 2010). Further, under health and safety legislation, in respect of a failure to carry out a risk assessment of a pregnant woman, the woman does not need to demonstrate that she has been treated less favourably than a hypothetical male or non-pregnant woman (*Hardman v Mallon t/a Orchard Lodge Nursing Home* [2002] IRLR 516, EAT).

However, where the discrimination on pregnancy/maternity grounds occurs **after maternity leave**, it may be appropriate to compare the woman's position with that of a man absent on sick leave (*Brown v Rentokil Ltd* [1998] IRLR 445, ECJ).

EXAMPLE In *Ministry of Defence v Williams* [2003] UKEAT 0833_02_0810, a female worker was directly discriminated against when she was unable to attend a training course which clashed with her maternity leave and she was not selected for the course the following year on her return from maternity leave.

MEMO POINTS Pregnant women and those on maternity leave are also protected under the following specific **non-discriminatory claims**:
– the right not to be dismissed for a reason related to their pregnancy or maternity leave under the automatic unfair dismissal legislation (¶8394); and
– the right not to be subjected to any detriment (other than dismissal) for a reason due to their pregnancy, childbirth or maternity leave (¶¶4767, 4771).

b. Part-time work

5323 Since most part-time work arrangements are **undertaken by women** who, statistically, often have the prime responsibility for childcare arrangements, a requirement that all workers work full-time is more likely to disadvantage workers with childcare responsibilities, a larger proportion of whom are likely to be women, and thus fall within the definition of indirect discrimination. Whether such a requirement can be justified, for example, on grounds of administrative efficiency of the organisation or business, will depend on all the facts.

EXAMPLE
Full-time work objectively justified
1. In *Greater Glasgow Health Board v Carey* [1987] IRLR 484, EAT, where the employer was providing health-visit services, the requirement to work full-time was found to be objectively justified on the particular facts of this case.
2. In *Nelson v Chesterfield Law Centre* [1996] UKEAT 1359_95_2606, this same requirement was justified in circumstances where the vacancy in question required the successful applicant to collaborate closely with an existing worker so that a further division of work by way of job sharing was undesirable.

Full-time work not objectively justified
In *Home Office v Holmes* [1984] IRLR 299, EAT, this requirement applied to a civil servant and was held to be unlawful as the employer could not justify the requirement on the basis that the bulk of industry was organised on a full-time work basis.

> **MEMO POINTS** **Part-time workers** are further protected from less favourable treatment under the Part-time Workers (Prevention of Less Favourable Treatment) Regulations (SI 2000/1551); for a detailed discussion on part-time workers, see ¶1870.

c. Marital and civil partnership status

5325 It is unlawful to discriminate, directly or indirectly, against a worker who is **married or a civil partner** of either sex, on the ground that he/she is married or a civil partner under the Civil Partnership Act 2004 (ss 13, 19 EqA 2010).

Discrimination on the basis of marriage to or a civil partnership with a **particular individual** is not covered, for example, colleagues who victimise a worker because her husband is convicted of a sexual offence would not be committing acts of marriage discrimination for which both they and the employer (vicariously) may be liable (*Hawkins v Atex Group Ltd and ors* [2011] UKEAT 0302_11_1303). In so holding, the EAT doubted an earlier EAT decision of *Dunn v The Institute of Cemetery and Crematorium Management* (*Dunn v The Institute of Cemetery and Crematorium Management* [2011] UKEAT 0531_10_0212) in which it was suggested that a woman was protected from discrimination because she is married to a particular man, as opposed to merely being married. There is a clear conflict between these decisions and clarification from a higher court is required. In the meantime, as the later decision was given by the president of the EAT, it seems likely that this decision may be preferred.

> **EXAMPLE**
> 1. In *Hawkins v Atex Group Ltd and ors*, a corporate marketing manager was employed by A Ltd in January 2010. She was married to the chief executive of the company. Five months into her employment she was suspended pending investigation. One of the allegations being investigated was that she had been employed by the company in breach of an express instruction given to her husband not to employ family members beyond the end of 2009. Her husband and daughter, who worked for A Ltd in human resources, were also suspended. Following a disciplinary procedure, all three family members were dismissed. A Ltd had no formal nepotism policy but the board were concerned that the company was being inappropriately run as a family business; having the chief executive's wife in a senior role created a conflict of interest, damaged transparency and had an impact on management morale. The employee brought a marital discrimination claim. A Ltd successfully applied to have the claim struck out on the basis that it had no reasonable prospect of success. H appealed. The EAT upheld the employment judge's decision to strike out the claim: H had no realistic prospect of establishing that A Ltd had been motivated specifically because she was married to the chief executive, rather than because of their close relationship.
> 2. In *Dunn v The Institute of Cemetery and Crematorium Management*, which was brought under the predecessor provisions of the Sex Discrimination Act, the employee was married to a man who was in dispute with her employer. She alleged that she was constructively unfairly dismissed as a result of that relationship; that the employer had treated the couple as a unit and had allowed its dispute with her husband to influence its treatment of her. She pointed to references to him, which the employer had made when dealing with her grievances, and correspondence which demonstrated that the employer thought of them as one joint unit with whom it was in dispute. The EAT held that, although the employer did not discriminate against married people generally, the employee was entitled to claim that her unfavourable treatment was marriage-specific and specific to her particular marriage. A person who is married or who is in a civil partnership is protected against discrimination on the ground of that relationship and on the ground of their relationship to the particular partner. Any less favourable treatment which is marriage-specific is unlawful.

> **MEMO POINTS** Actions which could amount to marital or civil partnership status discrimination may **also result in other types of discrimination**, for example, if a worker can show that he/she was discriminated against on grounds of the employer's gender prejudices (for example, a belief that married female workers have children and cannot give as much to the job as male workers), he/she may have a complaint of sex discrimination (*McLean v Paris Travel Service Ltd* [1976] IRLR 202, IT).

This does not, though, prohibit discrimination against **single persons** (including those who are getting married or becoming a civil partner), **cohabitees, divorced persons or parents** on the ground of their status. It is, therefore, important to note that the statutory provisions give more rights to married persons and civil partners than to others in stable, non-married or civil partnership, relationships.

Direct discrimination

Direct discrimination against a worker who is married or a civil partner occurs if an employer treats him/her **less favourably** than he treats or would treat either a person of the same sex who is unmarried or not a civil partner or a person of the opposite sex who is married or a civil partner (s 13 EqA 2010). The married worker or civil partner alleging discrimination must establish that the alleged discriminatory conduct came about **as a result of his/her status** as a married person or civil partner, although this may not have to be the only reason.

EXAMPLE
1. In *Chief Constable of the Bedfordshire Police v Graham* [2001] UKEAT 1061_00_2609, G was denied a promotion opportunity because had she been promoted she would have been managed by her husband. Her employer tried to justify the refusal on a number of grounds, including that to promote the worker could have resulted in potential managerial and disciplinary problems (persons working for the worker would be reluctant to complain as they would know that the complaint would be handled by her husband). The EAT held that the worker was less favourably treated on grounds of marital status as the major reason to refuse promotion had been because of G's marriage, and thus she had been treated less favourably than a single woman would have been.
2. A council refuses to second a social worker to a two-year course in Maidstone because her husband has just been promoted to a post in London and the council thinks that the worker would stay with her husband rather than return to Wales when her course is finished. This will amount to unlawful sex and marital status discrimination.
3. An employer refuses to allow a worker to attend certain meetings (which she would, given her position in the company, otherwise be entitled to attend) because she has married someone working for a competitor.

MEMO POINTS Marriage and civil partnership status are **excluded from the scope of associative discrimination** (s 13(4) EqA 2010).

The predecessor legislation allowed for an exception permitting discrimination where there was a genuine occupational qualification on the grounds of marital or civil partnership status in relation to a particular job, for example, that the post was one of two to be held by a married couple or a couple who were civil partners. This may now fall within the general exception for **occupational requirements** in the EqA 2010, provided that the application of a requirement to employ a married couple or a couple who are civil partners is a proportionate means of achieving a legitimate aim (Sch 9 para 1 EqA 2010). For a more detailed discussion on occupational requirements generally, see ¶5290.

MEMO POINTS There is a further exception in respect of **organised religions** which can lawfully discriminate in applying a requirement relating to not being married or to not having a civil partner (in addition to a requirement relating to whether a person has a living spouse/civil partner or to how that person has ceased to have a living spouse/civil partner) if such a requirement has been genuinely imposed to comply with the doctrines of that religion or, because of the nature of the employment and context in which it is carried out, so as to avoid conflicting with the strongly held religious convictions of a significant number of the religion's followers (Sch 9 para 2 EqA 2010).

Indirect discrimination

Indirect discrimination is **defined** as when the employer applies to a worker who is married or a civil partner a provision, criterion or practice which applies or would apply equally to all workers who are not married or in a civil partnership, and which (s 19 EqA 2010):
– puts, or would put, persons who are married or in a civil partnership at a particular disadvantage when compared with persons who are not married or in a civil partnership;
– puts a married or civil partner worker at that disadvantage; and
– the employer cannot show it to be a proportionate means of achieving a legitimate aim.

5332 **Justification** An employer may be able to defend his allegedly discriminatory practices, criteria or provisions, if he can show that they are objectively justifiable on grounds other than marital or civil partnership status. Such grounds may relate to the nature of the job at hand, or to business, administrative or organisational reasons. Whether the defence of justification is established is always a matter of fact and will depend on the particular circumstances of each case.

d. Gender reassignment

5335 Gender reassignment is **defined** as a process for the purpose of reassigning the person's sex by changing physiological or other attributes of sex, from the point at which they propose to undergo the process. Medical intervention is not a requirement, but **transvestism** (a person wearing clothes of persons of the opposite sex without the intention of reassigning their sex) is not intended to be covered.

It is unlawful for an employer to treat a worker **less favourably** than he treats or would treat other persons on the ground that the worker has undergone, is undergoing, or intends to undergo gender reassignment (s 7 EqA 2010). The appropriate **comparator**, in such circumstances, is an actual or hypothetical person of the complainant's birth gender who is not intending to undergo, is not undergoing, or has not undergone gender reassignment (*P v S* [1996] IRLR 347, ECJ).

In addition, **pay discrimination** on grounds of gender reassignment is specifically prohibited (s 39 EqA 2010).

> *MEMO POINTS* 1. The Gender Recognition Act, which came into force on 4 April 2005, allows transsexuals who make an appropriate application to obtain **legal recognition** of their **acquired gender** (ss 1-4 Gender Recognition Act 2004). Such applications are determined by a Gender Recognition Panel which issues successful applicants who have demonstrated that they meet the evidential requirements with a gender recognition certificate which is effective from the date of recognition. In summary, the evidential requirements are that the person (s 2 Gender Recognition Act 2004):
> – has or has had gender dysphoria;
> – has lived in his/her acquired gender for 2 years prior to the application; and
> – intends to live permanently in his/her acquired gender.
> 2. The Women and Equality Unit has published **guidance**: "Gender Reassignment – A guide for employers", to assist employers in understanding the relevant law on how to deal with the issues when a worker (or job applicant) is a transsexual person.

5336 **Protection starts** as soon as a worker has indicated that he/she is proposing to undergo the process. This might be by expressly telling those around him/her, by changes in behaviour, or seeking advice or counselling.

5337 The Gender Reassignment Guidance recommends that employers discuss and write an **action plan** with their workers to agree the procedure and steps they wish to follow to handle the process and transition period, in particular if they are to avoid facing discrimination claims. For example, the action plan might include:
– whether the worker is to stay in his/her existing role or be redeployed;
– the expected timescale of the worker's medical and surgical procedures (if known) and any time off he/she requires for medical treatment;
– agreeing a procedure for adhering to or revising an existing dress code;
– the expected point or phase of change of name, personal details and social gender;
– whether the worker wishes to inform his/her line manager, colleagues and clients him/herself, or would prefer this to be done for him/her, and whether training or briefing of colleagues and/or clients is necessary;
– what amendments will need to be made to records and systems;
– agreeing with the worker, if possible, the point at which the use of facilities such as changing rooms and toilets should change from one sex to the other; and
– discussing whether the worker is covered adequately by existing policies on insurance, confidentiality and harassment and, if not, how these may be amended.

5338 The **use of single sex facilities** of the worker's acquired sex should be agreed between the employer and worker. This may be the stage at which the worker begins to present him/herself permanently in his/her acquired sex. It may be reasonable for an employer to require the worker to use unisex facilities for a limited period (for example, disabled toilets), but this is not an acceptable long-term solution. The employer must maintain a flexible approach and keep matters under review (*Croft v Royal Mail Group plc* [2003] IRLR 592, CA).

Since the process of gender reassignment is likely to lead to **absence from work**, there is specific protection for transgender workers from being discriminated against on such grounds (s 16 EqA 2010). Employers cannot treat a transgender worker less favourably than another worker who is absent due to sickness, injury or some other cause. In such circumstances, the appropriate comparator is an actual or hypothetical colleague who is absent on account of illness or injury or, where there is some other comparable absence (for example, compassionate or study leave), a worker who can reasonably be compared with the transgender worker.

5339 Employers may have to take **additional steps** (over and above their existing equal opportunities policies and procedures) to ensure that the worker is not subjected to **harassment or other detriment by colleagues**, agents or other persons over whom the employer exercises the appropriate level of control. For example, it may be necessary to provide staff with general information about gender reassignment and specific information to enable them to understand the situation of the particular worker.

5340 **Occupational requirement** The general exception for occupational requirements applies to cases of gender reassignment (Sch 9 para 1 EqA 2010). See ¶5290 for a general discussion of occupational requirements. However, these exceptions cease to apply in relation to discrimination against a person whose gender has become acquired under the Gender Recognition Act 2004. Therefore, once a person has obtained legal recognition of his/her acquired gender, the occupational requirements exceptions are no longer available to an employer.

> MEMO POINTS   There are two specific occupational requirements relating to **organisations** whose purpose is to **advance or teach a religion or belief** that apply in the case of gender reassignment and permit an employer to require that a worker is not a transsexual to avoid conflict with the strongly held religious convictions of a significant number of the religion's followers or to comply with doctrines of the religion (Sch 9 para 2 EqA 2010). In some denominations, this exception might prevent a person from being employed as a minister (¶5290).

4. Victimisation

5350 Victimisation consists of subjecting a worker or ex-worker to a detriment because that worker has done a protected act. A protected act **covers**:
– bringing proceedings against his/her employer, another worker or a third party;
– giving evidence or information in connection with proceedings brought by another person under the Act;
– taking any other action under or by reference to the Act; or
– making any allegation against his/her employer or any other person which would amount to a contravention of the Act.

This extends to a **threat by the worker** to do any of these things, or a suspicion by the employer that the worker intends to do any of them. A worker is also protected if he is victimised by his employer for his protected acts against a former employer or third party.

A worker will not be protected if the **allegation** made by him/her, or evidence or information given by him/her, was **false** and not made (or given) in good faith (s 27(3) EqA 2010).

> EXAMPLE   In *Corpora Software Limited v Perry* [2008] UKEAT 0039_08_0105, the EAT has held that an employee would be victimised where an employer's grievance procedures were a sham used purely by the employer to protect its position against possible tribunal claims.

> MEMO POINTS   For the purposes of the legislation, proceedings will normally mean tribunal proceedings; but where an **internal grievance or disciplinary matter** ends without coming to

tribunal, the witness may be protected against subsequent victimisation (*National Probation Service for England and Wales (Cumbria Area) v Kirby* [2006] IRLR 508, EAT).

5351 **Detriment** is not defined but essentially means anything that changes the complainant's situation for the worse or puts them at a disadvantage. Examples include being rejected for promotions, not being chosen to represent the employer at external events, excluded from training opportunities or being overlooked for discretionary bonuses or performance related rewards (para 9.8 Equality Code).

5352 It is irrelevant whether the alleged victimisation is **intentional** or not (*Nagarajan v London Regional Transport* [1999] IRLR 572, HL).

5353 There is no longer an absolute need for a **comparator** in victimisation claims. The Equality Code states that "the worker need only show that they have experienced a detriment because they have done a protected act or because the employer believes (rightly or wrongly) that they have done or intended to do a protected act" (para 9.11 Equality Code). However, it will invariably be useful to compare the complainant's treatment with a comparator to help demonstrate why the treatment in question took place. The appropriate comparison is between the treatment given to the worker bringing the complaint of victimisation and the treatment which was or would be given to other workers who had not done a protected act (i.e. brought discrimination proceedings, given evidence or information in connection with discrimination proceedings, taken any other action or made any allegation of discrimination etc.) (*Chief Constable of West Yorkshire Police v Khan* [2001] IRLR 830, HL). The appropriate test is to ask whether the discrimination would have occurred "but for" the original complaint (*St Helens Borough Council v Derbyshire and ors* [2007] IRLR 540, HL).

EXAMPLE In *Visa International Service Association v Paul* [2004] IRLR 42, EAT, in sex discrimination proceedings brought by P, VISA brought a counterclaim against P for repayment of P's enhanced maternity benefit. The EAT held that the counterclaim was a direct result of the proceedings and, consequently, amounted to victimisation since other workers (who had not returned to work and had not brought proceedings against VISA) had not been pursued by VISA for repayment by way of legal proceedings.

5354 Where litigation is under way between an employer and worker, due to the adversarial nature of such proceedings, an employer has some latitude in **encouraging** a worker to **settle**, in a manner which might otherwise amount to victimisation. This latitude includes honest and reasonable attempts to compromise the proceedings, provided that these do not cross the line and become victimisation (*St Helens Borough Council v Derbyshire and ors*, above).

EXAMPLE In *St Helens Borough Council v Derbyshire and ors*, a council responded to a group of female catering staff bringing an equal pay claim by sending a threatening letter to the workers concerned, encouraging them to withdraw their claim, and threatening them and the schoolchildren for whom they cooked with particular consequences if the caterers did not settle. The House of Lords found that the caterers had suffered mental distress: the council's action amounted to victimisation.

5. Harassment

5360 **Sexual** harassment occurs when an employer (including any other person in respect of whose actions an employer will be vicariously liable) engages in any form of conduct related to a protected characteristic, including sex, sexual orientation and gender reassignment, which has the purpose or effect of (s 26(1) EqA 2010):
– violating a worker's dignity; or
– creating an intimidating, hostile, degrading, humiliating or offensive environment for a worker.

In addition, engaging in unwanted sexual conduct with the same purpose or effect will constitute harassment (s 26(2) EqA 2010).

This extends to harassment **related to the sex of another person** or **sexual orientation** or the fact that a person intends to undergo, is undergoing or has undergone **gender reassignment**, and occurs where an employer subjects a worker to unwanted conduct which has the same purpose or effect as above (s 26(1)(a) EqA 2010).

In respect of sex or sexual harassment or gender reassignment harassment, harassment will also occur if an employer, on the grounds of a worker's rejection of, or submission to, any such unwanted conduct, treats that worker less favourably than he would treat him/her had the worker not rejected, or submitted to, the conduct (s 26(1) EqA 2010).

Also covered is harassment on the grounds of **characteristics associated** with sexual orientation (*English v Thomas Sanderson Blinds Ltd* [2009] IRLR 206, CA). The Court remarked that the same interpretation of the legislation would apply to other areas of discrimination such as race and religion.

EXAMPLE

Examples of sexual harassment

1. In *Houlden v Ian Fairburn t/a Foxhall Plant Hire*, ET case 2601288/05, where an employer claimed not to be attracted to an older female employer but used unwanted touching as a means to bully and humiliate her, the employer was found to have harassed the worker.
2. In *Honda Motor Europe v McMillan* [2007] UKEAT 0471_06_2203, where a worker sexually assaulted his colleague at an after-work event, it was no defence to say that the event had been alcoholic, with other workers exchanging lewd comments and drunken banter.
3. In *Nixon v Ross Coates Solicitors and Mr R Coates MBE* [2010] UKEAT 0108_10_0608, gossip spread about the paternity of an employee's baby constituted a course of unwanted conduct and met the definition of harassment. Moreover, the employer's failure to deal adequately with the employee's related grievance was discrimination on the grounds of her pregnancy and sex, and further that she had been constructively dismissed, largely as a result of this treatment.

Following a very lively Christmas party, which led to two different employees of the Respondent being candidates for paternity of the Claimant's baby, the Claimant informed her employer of her pregnancy. News of the pregnancy was then leaked amongst staff against her wishes, and gossip began to spread about the paternity of her baby. She raised a grievance and requested to work at a different office. Her request was refused and she felt that her grievance was not adequately handled. The EAT found in the Claimant's favour. This case is a timely reminder of the need to make the standards of behaviour expected of staff at Christmas parties very clear in advance of the event, and also to deal promptly and effectively with any fallout.

Example of sex harassment where a worker is subjected to less favourable treatment related to his/her sex

The classic situation would be where a male manager enters a woman's toilet to reprimand the female occupant. The woman has not been badly treated because of her sex; but her sex is relevant to the decision of whether this conduct has violated her dignity or created an intimidating, hostile, degrading, humiliating or offensive environment for her.

Example of sex harassment which relates to the sex of a person other than the claimant

The classic situation here would be where a claim for sex harassment is brought by a worker who has not been subjected to the unwanted conduct himself or herself but who witnessed the unwanted conduct and whose dignity is nevertheless violated, or who finds that an intimidating, hostile, degrading, humiliating or offensive environment has been created for him or her.

Examples of sexual orientation harassment

1. In *Gismondi v (1) Council of the City of Durham (2) Tutty*, ET case 2502956/04, an employer was found guilty of constructive unfair dismissal and discrimination on the grounds of sexual orientation after a worker was repeatedly referred to as "gay boy" and subjected to ongoing bullying and harassment by his manager.
2. In *Mann v BH Publishing Ltd*, ET case 2203272/2004, the tribunal found that where a manager repeatedly mimicked the behaviour of a gay worker, this conduct constituted harassment.
3. In *Grant v HM Land Registry* [2011] EWCA Civ 769, a gay employee made a complaint of direct discrimination and harassment after he had been "outed" by a manager. He had moved to a branch of the employing organisation from one where he had himself been open about his sexuality. An employment tribunal found that a manager had deliberately set out to make his sexuality known against his wishes. The EAT and the Court of Appeal found that, on the facts, there had not been enough evidence to support the claim, because the tribunal had failed to take into account the fact that the employee had been happy to be open about his sexuality at his previous workplace. However, they did comment that deliberately outing an employee against their will could constitute direct discrimination or harassment, where proved.

Example of no sexual orientation harassment
In *Thomas Sanderson Blinds Ltd v English* [2011] UKEAT 0316_10_2102, an employee, E, was subjected to sexual innuendo to the effect that he was gay, because he lived in Brighton and had attended boarding school: the perpetrators went as far as writing an article in an internal newspaper portraying him as a gay man. His work colleagues knew, however, that he was heterosexual. The Court of Appeal held that homophobic mockery meted out in the knowledge that the victim is not homosexual could be harassment on the ground of characteristics associated with sexual orientation, in the same way as harassment might occur on the ground of a person's actual sexuality, or their reputed or assumed sexuality. The EAT considered whether such harassment had occurred in this case and concluded that it had not. Although they were less than impressed with E's treatment, they also found that he had engaged in similar conduct and his own behaviour was at times "extremely offensive". He remained good friends throughout his employment with the perpetrators and the original tribunal was correct in finding that the treatment he received could not have had the effect of violating his dignity or creating an intimidating, hostile, degrading, humiliating or offensive environment for him.

5362 Even if the complainant cannot establish that the employer's conduct was **intentional**, the tribunal must consider whether, having regard to all the circumstances, including in particular the perception of the worker concerned, the conduct should reasonably be considered as having that effect (s 26(4) EqA 2010).

The **test** is neither entirely objective nor subjective, since some account needs to be taken of the alleged victim's perception. However, a complainant who **unreasonably takes offence** at an innocent comment would probably not be considered to have been harassed, although if the conduct was repeated after the complainant made his/her feelings known, then the repeat conduct could well constitute unlawful harassment.

5363 An employer may also be **vicariously liable** for acts of harassment committed by his workers, agents, and, in some cases, third parties (¶5231). In this regard, the **use of email** and the **internet** at work is an increasingly common vehicle for harassment of workers by other workers. It is therefore vital for employers to prepare and implement an effective policy on the use of email and the internet to try to ensure that sexist, harassing and offensive communications are not sent and received in their workplaces.

EXAMPLE In *Moonsar v Fiveways Express Transport Ltd* [2004] UKEAT 0476_04_2709, the use of pornography on a workplace computer by male workers in the presence of a female colleague gave rise to a claim for sexual harassment even though the female worker was not shown any of the images and she did not make a complaint at the time regarding the use of pornography. In this case, it was sufficient that the behaviour of the male workers had undermined the female worker's dignity at work for the burden of proof to shift to the employer to disprove that she had suffered any harassment.

5364 If an employer **fails to investigate** a worker's grievance that he/she has been harassed, then this failure might in itself constitute a further act of discrimination if it is due to the complainant's sex, sexual orientation or gender reassignment. However, if the failure to investigate is unrelated to the complainant's sex, then this will not amount to discrimination (*Coyne v Home Office* [2000] EWCA Civ 236).

Third party harassment

5370 An employer will be liable for harassment where he **fails to take reasonable practical steps** to protect workers from harassment by third parties, for example clients and customers, where such harassment is known to have occurred on at least two other occasions (s 40 EqA 2010). Employers will not be liable for conduct beyond their control.

MEMO POINTS The Government is **proposing to repeal** these provisions relating to employers' liability for third party harassment. The regulations remain active at the time of publication, though the impending change is part of a draft bill called the Enterprise and Regulatory Reform Bill which is proceeding through Parliament. Any further developments will be covered by our updating service.

B. Racial and religion or belief

Discrimination on the grounds of race or religion or belief is prohibited. **5375**

Discrimination on the grounds of race, religion or belief is **divided into** direct discrimination (including victimisation), indirect discrimination and harassment. **5380**

Racial discrimination "Race" is **defined** as including **colour, nationality or ethnic or national origins** (s 9(1) EqA 2010). Consequently, the legislation protects people from distinct racial groups who are defined by reference to any of these grounds. Under the predecessor legislation, the definition of "racial grounds" was exhaustive, but this is not the case under the EqA 2010, meaning that there is scope for other "sub-groups" of the definition to be included. For example, there is some speculation that **caste** discrimination could be litigated under the race discrimination umbrella ("caste" is defined in the Explanatory Notes to the EqA 2010 as denoting a hereditary, endogamous community associated with a traditional occupation and ranked accordingly on a perceived scale of ritual purity). **5381**

> MEMO POINTS It is worth noting that despite this possibility, "caste" may also be added as a separate category of "race" in its own right, though this is subject to both an ongoing report that the Government has commissioned as to the extent of the problem of caste discrimination as well as parliamentary consent. Any progress in this regard will be included in our update service.

Prior to the implementation of the EqA 2010, **guidance** on the various aspects of "race" was primarily developed by case law. Much of this case law has been incorporated into the Equality Code (specifically paras 2.36-49 Equality Code). **5382**

Case law decided under the predecessor legislation established that **language**, in itself, is not a racial ground, but it can be a factor in determining a person's racial group (Gwynedd County Council v Jones [1986] ICR 833, EAT). It has also established that preventing someone from using their own language in the workplace can amount to discrimination because language is intrinsically linked to nationality (in Dziedziak v Future Electronics Lts [2012] UKEAT 0270_11_2802, the EAT held that it was direct discrimination to instruct an employee not to speak "in her own language". The line manager chose these words rather than the alternative of asking all employees to speak English, or asking her not to speak Polish: the choice of words was intrinsically linked to her nationality and she had a direct comparator in that employees of other nationalities were not subjected to the same restriction). The Equality Code states that a common language can be a factor in establishing an ethnic group.

A racial group can include more than one colour, ethnic origin or national origin. An individual may, therefore, fall into a number of different racial groups. For example, he may be a national of one country (for example, British), have his national origin in another country (for example, India) and be a member of a distinct ethnic group (for example, Sikh). Depending on the circumstances of the case, the individual may place himself in the appropriate racial group to proceed with his claim (s 9(4) EqA 2010).

A person's "**national origin**" refers to his race, rather than his citizenship (Ealing London Borough Council v Race Relations Board [1971] UKHL 3; Tejani v Superintendent Registrar for the District of Peterborough [1986] IRLR 502, CA). The Equality Code gives the example that many people of Chinese national origin will be citizens of other countries (para 2.44 Equality Code). Persons of "**non-British**" origin could form a single racial group, even if they are of a number of different national origins (s 9(4) EqA 2010). For example, where employment is conditional on residency in the UK, all "non-British" job applicants who cannot meet the requirement may have a claim, whatever their individual national origin (Orphanos v Queen Mary College [1985] IRLR 349, HL).

Everyone has an ethnic origin, but to gain the protection of the EqA 2010 a person must belong to an "**ethnic group**" as defined by the courts. Ethnic group has a wide definition, though the members must have a long shared history and a cultural tradition of their own. They may also share a common language, literature, religion, geographical origin, be a minority or an oppressed group (para 2.40 Equality Code). Case law brought under the predecessor legislation established that ethnic group means a segment of the population distinguished from others by a sufficient combination of shared customs, beliefs, traditions and characteristics derived from a common or presumed common past (*Mandla and anor v Lee and ors* [1983] IRLR 209, HL). This covers Sikhs, Jews, Romany gypsies, Irish travellers, Scottish gypsies, and Scottish travellers (para 2.42 Equality Code).

Rastafarians are a religious, rather than an ethnic group, and were not covered under the predecessor legislation (*Dawkins v Department of the Environment* [1993] IRLR 284, CA) though they are covered by the prohibition against discrimination on the grounds of religion (para 2.53 Equality Code).

MEMO POINTS 1. While discrimination on grounds of nationality is unlawful, employers are nonetheless required to comply with **UK immigration laws** which, in effect, directly discriminate against non-UK citizens (¶750).
2. Employment in the following sectors is excluded from the race provisions: **representative sport and national security** (ss 192, 195 EqA 2010).

5383 **Religion or belief discrimination** "Religion or belief" is **defined** as any religion or any religious or philosophical belief. The definition includes lack of religion and lack of belief (s 10 EqA 2010).

The definition of **religion** is broad and consistent with Article 9 of the ECHR, which protects freedom of thought, conscience and religion. The primary limitation imposed by Article 9 is that the religion must have a clear structure and belief system. Prior to finalising the EqA 2010, there was debate as to whether **cults** should be specifically excluded from the definition of religion, but it was decided that it was too difficult to define a cult, so when in doubt it will be for the relevant court or tribunal to determine the issue on a case by case basis.

To fall within this definition, a **philosophical belief** must (para 2.59 Equality Code):
– be genuinely held;
– not simply be an opinion or viewpoint based on information currently available;
– concern a weighty and substantial aspect of human life and behaviour;
– attain a certain level of cogency, seriousness, cohesion and importance;
– be worthy of respect in a democratic society; and
– be compatible with human dignity and not conflict with the fundamental rights of others.

5384 The following individuals are among those who have been held to be **protected** under case law brought under predecessor legislation:
– a Christian proselytising in a multi-cultural workplace (*Monaghan v Leicester Young Men's Christian Association*, ET case 1901830/04);
– a non-Christian employed by a Christian employer (*Nicholson v The Aspire Trust*, ET case 2601009/04);
– a pagan (*Keeling v (1) Public Information Pillars Ltd, (2) Oakden, and (3) Oakden*, ET case 2600017/06);
– a Muslim in a Hindu-dominated workplace (*Shah v Harish Finance Ltd*, ET case 3302110/04);
– an individual who was wrongly supposed by his employer to be Muslim (*Mayet v HM Customs and Excise*, ET case 2301870/04);
– a Sikh schoolgirl wearing her Kara bangle (*R (on the application of Watkins-Singh) v Governing Body of Aberdare Girls' High School* [2008] EWHC 1865 (Admin)); and
– an individual who genuinely believed that action is urgently needed to address climate change (*Grainger Plc and ors v Nicholson* [2010] IRLR 4, EAT).

EXAMPLE
1. In *Keeling v (1) Public Information Pillars Ltd, (2) Oakden, and (3) Oakden*, an employer told his customers that a pagan worker worshipped the devil and danced naked around a fire. The tribunal accepted evidence from the Pagan Federation, to show that the remarks were inaccurate and amounted to stereotyping.
2. In *R (on the application of Watkins-Singh) v Governing Body of Aberdare Girls' High School*, the High Court held that a schoolgirl had been discriminated against when she had not been allowed to wear her Kara (a bangle which was contrary to the school's dress policy) as, despite not being an actual requirement of being a Sikh, she genuinely believed for reasonable grounds that it was of exceptional importance to her racial identity or her religious belief.

3. In *Grainger Plc and ors v Nicholson*, the EAT held that an employee who claimed that he had been dismissed because he had made protected disclosures about the company's environmental practices and felt compelled to do so because of his belief in climate change could continue with his discrimination claim, because his beliefs had the potential to qualify as a protected philosophical belief, but that to succeed he would have to show, under cross-examination, that his beliefs were genuine and that the protected disclosures he had made were done on the grounds of his beliefs.

The following individuals are among those who have been held **not** to be **protected** under case law brought under predecessor legislation:
- a member of a racist political party (*Baggs v FDA Fudge*, ET case 1400114/05);
- a patriotic American wearing a "Stars and Stripes" badge on his jacket (*Williams v South Central Ltd*, ET case 2306989/03);
- a person who had engaged in religious-inspired acts of charity (*Devine v Home Office*, ET case 2302061/04);
- a justice of the peace who believed that arguments in favour of allowing same sex couples to adopt were inadequately supported by evidence, and who resigned from his post rather than continue with duties during which he might have been required to order same sex adoption (*McClintock v Department of Constitutional Affairs* [2008] IRLR 29, EAT);
- a registrar of Births, Marriages and Deaths who refused to register civil partnerships as she was a committed Christian, and whose employer started disciplinary proceedings against her as a result (*Ladele v London Borough of Islington* [2010] IRLR 211, CA);
- a marriage counsellor who asked to be excused from providing psycho-sexual therapy to same sex couples (although he was prepared to provide other relationship counselling to them) as he was a committed Christian, and who was dismissed when he failed to give unequivocal confirmation that he would work in accordance with the employer's policy of providing services irrespective of clients' personal or group characteristics (*McFarlane v Relate Avon Ltd* [2010] IRLR 196, EAT – Court of Appeal refused leave to appeal at [2010] EWCA Civ B1). It is worth noting that the Equality and Human Rights Commission (EHRC) has submitted an intervention to the European Court of Human Rights (ECHR) for confirmation that the UK courts took the correct approach in both this case and the case of *Ladele* (see above) on the basis that although there is a clear freedom for all individuals in terms of holding beliefs and adhering to a religious ethos, it will almost always be proportionate to refuse to allow those beliefs to be manifested in the work place if they are discriminatory, particularly when a worker serves a public function. Such a refusal will always pursue the legitimate aim of non-discrimination. For further details, see: flmemo.co.uk/em5384, and we will continue to keep you informed via our updating service;
- a social worker who promoted his beliefs as a Christian to service users, and who was dismissed for misconduct as a result (*Chondol v Liverpool City Council* [2009] UKEAT 0298_08_1102); and
- a job applicant who had, in the past, approved of the use of violence to achieve political ends, and was refused employment as a result (*McConkey and anor v Simon Community Northern Ireland* [2009] IRLR 757, HL). This case was decided under the Northern Ireland Fair Employment legislation covering discrimination on the ground of religious belief or political opinion. The wording of this legislation is different to that used in the Employment Equality (Religion or Belief) Regulations, which refer to religious or philosophical belief, but the distinction between beliefs and criminal activity in support of them would be likely to be adopted in the context of this legislation.

EXAMPLE

1. In *Devine v Home Office*, an individual was denied employment at the Home Office on account of work he had done for immigration claimants, while working for the Citizens Advice Bureau. He complained of discrimination, on the basis of his sympathy for underprivileged asylum seekers, which was a manifestation of his belief in the Christian virtue of charity. The Tribunal considered this claim too vague to succeed.
2. In *Chondol v Liverpool City Council*, a social worker was dismissed for misconduct following a number of incidents in which he promoted his beliefs as a Christian to service users. He claimed that he had suffered discrimination on the grounds of his religion. He failed both in the tribunal and before the EAT on the ground that the reason for his dismissal was not his religious belief but that he was

improperly foisting it on clients, contrary to a clear rule of the Council. The EAT held that the tribunal was right to find that the Council would have treated any employee who inappropriately promoted any religious belief or other strong personal view in the same way.

3. In *R (on the application of E) v The Governing Body of JFS and ors* [2010] IRLR 136, SC, the Supreme Court considered whether it was unlawful for a Jewish faith school to refuse to admit a child whose mother had converted to Judaism at a Progressive Synagogue, which meant that the child was not recognised as Jewish by the Office of the Chief Rabbi. The criteria for admission to the school meant that children who were ethnically Jewish were preferred over those who might adhere to the Jewish religion but were not racially Jewish. While the EqA 2006 provided an exemption allowing oversubscribed faith schools to discriminate on the ground of religion in their admissions policies, here the criterion was based on race, not religion, and was unlawful.

Allegiance to a **political party** has previously been held not to be a philosophical belief (see *Baggs v FDA Fudge* above). However, the ECHR has cast some doubt over this in the recent decision of *Redfearn v UK – 47335/06 – HEJUD* [2012] ECHR 1878. This case had been ongoing for quite some time, and had worked its way up to the Court of Appeal before being heard in Europe. R, a worker, was summarily dismissed from his job as a bus driver. The majority of his passengers were Asian and R's dismissal followed his employer's discovery that he had been elected as a councillor for the British National Party which, at the time, restricted its membership to white people only. R did not have the requisite continuous employment to enable him to bring an unfair dismissal claim, so he brought a claim for race discrimination (which has no qualifying period). The Court of Appeal dismissed his claim and held that although racial considerations (i.e. the race of fellow workers and customers and the policy of the BNP on racial matters) were relevant to the employer's decision to dismiss R, the dismissal was not on racial grounds. R then commenced a case in the ECHR claiming that his dismissal was in breach of the European Convention on Human Rights and, in particular, his right to freedom of assembly and association under article 11. The ECHR agreed with R and ruled, by a majority of 4 to 3, that UK legislation is deficient in its lack of protection to employees who are affiliated with political parties. They held that the qualifying period for unfair dismissal (which was 1 year at the time of R's dismissal, but has since been increased to 2 years), prevented R from challenging his dismissal at a domestic level. They noted that this qualifying period was waived for certain claims (such as discrimination) and held that it was incumbent upon the UK to either waive the qualifying period for dismissal claims relating to political opinion or affiliation, or to create a freestanding cause of action that could be brought without a qualifying period. This decision has immediate significance for **public sector workers**, who are able to directly rely on this judgment regardless of whether or not the Government legislates on this matter. Additionally, the Government may legislate for a new standalone form of protection for political opinions or affiliations, or alternatively the tribunals may take a wider view of "philosophical belief" protections already provided under the EqA 2010. We will keep you informed via our updating service of any developments in this area.

Associative and perceptive discrimination

5385 A worker is protected against discrimination even if the discrimination is on the grounds of **someone else's racial group, religion or belief** (s 13(1) EqA 2010), as discrimination is on the grounds of racial group, religion or belief, which is not limited to the claimant's sex or sexual orientation. Consequently, a worker can bring proceedings if he/she objects to instructions given by an employer to discriminate on grounds of racial group, religion or belief or the worker is discriminated against because his/her friends belong to a particular racial group or hold a particular religion or belief.

Moreover, less favourable treatment based on the **employer's perception** of an individual's racial group, religion or belief, whether that perception is rightly or wrongly held, is also covered. For example, there could be unlawful discrimination if an individual is treated less favourably because he is thought to look as if he holds a particular religion or belief.

MEMO POINTS 1. **Direct discrimination** can take place even where the complainant shares the relevant protected characteristic with the discriminator (s 24(1) EqA 2010).

2. In a **high-profile case**, R, a worker, was summarily dismissed from a job working with Asian people following his employer's discovery that he had stood for election as a candidate of the British National Party, which restricts membership to white people only. It held that although racial considerations (i.e. the race of fellow workers and customers and the policy of the BNP on racial matters) were relevant to the employer's decision to dismiss R, the dismissal was not on racial grounds. At the Court of Appeal, R argued that where a worker was dismissed for racist activities, the dismissal was on racial grounds, and therefore unlawful. Such a proposition, the Court of Appeal held, would render the statute absurd (*Redfearn v Secro Ltd (trading as West Yorkshire Transport Service)* [2006] ICR 1367, CA). Please note, this case has since gone to the ECHR on a different point, namely whether R had been denied his human right to freedom of assembly and association under article 11 of the European Convention on Human Rights (¶5384). The ECHR found in his favour, though this should not affect the Court of Appeal decision.

3. A complainant does not need to show **proof of** his **religion or belief** in order to bring a claim since it is sufficient that he has suffered less favourable treatment due to the (incorrect) assumptions made about his religion or belief.

1. Direct

a. Unlawful

Direct racial and religion or belief discrimination occurs where there is "**less favourable treatment**" of an individual because of his/her race or religion or belief, **compared** with the treatment of a person of a different racial group, religion or belief in the same, or not materially different, circumstances (s 13 EqA 2010). It does not matter whether or not the discriminator shares the protected characteristic (s 24(1) EqA 2010).

5390

For a discussion as to the **scope** of the relevant legislation (i.e. who is protected in terms of the type of worker, geographical scope and time periods), see ¶¶5215+. Moreover, details as to an employer's liability for his own discriminatory acts, together with those of his workers and agents, as well as individual workers' liability for discrimination, are provided at ¶¶5225+.

Dismissal on the grounds of any of the protected characteristics includes a constructive dismissal on those grounds (s 39(7)(b) EqA 2010).

In addition, **segregating** a worker on racial grounds will amount to less favourable treatment (s 13(5) EqA 2010) and an employer cannot justify the segregation of workers of different racial groups on the basis that each racial group is provided with equally good (or bad) segregated facilities.

Moreover, it is unlawful for a person who has authority over another person, or in accordance with whose wishes that other person is accustomed to act, to give **instructions** to, or put **pressure** on, another person **to discriminate** against a worker on the grounds of any of the protected characteristics (s 111 EqA 2010). Both the individual who was instructed or pressured to discriminate and the third party (i.e. the individual or group who was discriminated against) can bring proceedings themselves if they are subjected to a detriment as a result of the discriminator's conduct (s 111(5) and (6) EqA 2010).

The EqA 2010 is silent as to whether the alleged discrimination needs to be **intentional** or not, though case law brought under the predecessor legislation established that, in relation to racial discrimination, intention was irrelevant and this is likely to hold true for cases brought under the current legislation (*Seide v Gillette Industries Ltd* [1980] IRLR 427, EAT; *R v Commission for Racial Equality, ex parte Westminster City Council* [1985] 426, CA; *Nagarajan v London Regional Transport* [1999] IRLR 572, HL; *Ahmed v Amnesty International* [2009] IRLR 884, EAT).

5391

EXAMPLE In *Ahmed v Amnesty International*, an employee of northern Sudanese origin who resigned made a complaint of race discrimination against her employer, Amnesty International, after they had refused her application for promotion to a job as a researcher dealing with the Sudan. The reasons for the refusal were that they were concerned that a person of her ethnic origin would be unable to carry out the full duties of the job (which involved travel in the region) without unacceptable risks to her and others' safety, and because her ethnic origins might give the impression of bias. The EAT held that the employer's reasons for the treatment were irrelevant to the question of whether or not there had been direct discrimination. The only issue to be considered was whether the grounds for the treatment were the ethnic origin of the employee, which was that she was Sudanese. The EAT held that they were so she had been directly discriminated against. However, she failed in her constructive dismissal claim, because the employer's conduct in rejecting her application after careful consideration of potentially justifiable reasons had not broken the term of mutual trust and confidence.

5393 **Comparator** In respect of discrimination on the grounds of race and religion or belief, the legal principles regarding the use of a comparator are the same as those set out at ¶¶5273+.

It should be noted that a **hypothetical** comparator used in a race discrimination claim does not need to be a clone of the claimant in every respect (including personality and personal characteristics) except that he is of a different racial origin to the claimant (*Madden v Preferred Technical Group Cha Ltd and anor* [2005] IRLR 46, CA).

It is not necessary to identify a comparator if the case relates to **racial segregation**, as this will always be discriminatory (provided that it takes place as a result of a deliberate act or policy) negating the need for a comparator.

5395 **Less favourable treatment** In respect of religion or belief and racial discrimination, the legal principles relating to less favourable treatment are the same as those for sex discrimination (¶5276) except for one point: where the issue in question is racial segregation, this is unequivocally less favourable treatment.

In racial discrimination claims, tribunals must not simply focus on the worker's specific complaints but should also consider the **wider employment picture** beyond the matters complained of, in order to determine whether racial factors have influenced the employer in subjecting a worker to less favourable treatment (*Rihal v Ealing London Borough Council* [2004] IRLR 642, CA).

Moreover, in determining whether a worker has been treated less favourably, tribunals are not permitted to attribute **specific characteristics** to a particular national or ethnic group without evidence to support such assumptions (*Bradford Hospital NHS Trust v Al-Shabib* [2002] UKEAT 709_01_0710). One of the objects of the EqA 2010 is to ensure that people are treated as individuals and are not assumed to belong to a **stereotype** of a particular racial group, whether or not in reality most members of that group do conform to such a stereotype.

EXAMPLE In *Royal Bank of Scotland plc v Morris* [2011] UKEAT 0436_10_1910, the employee, who was black, was employed by RBS as a software engineer. Tensions developed between him and T, his manager, leading, after a number of incidents, to a meeting with T's line manager. At that meeting, this more senior manager suggested that the employee was alleging that T's conduct was connected with race. The employee denied this and resented the implication that he was "playing the race card". He later went off sick with stress and anxiety. He then lodged a grievance focused mostly on T's conduct (which he did not think was racially motivated) but alluding to the senior manager's comment that his complaint was on racial grounds. The HR team took the view that the race issue was peripheral to the main complaint, i.e. T's conduct, and that as such it could be "parked" while they dealt with that issue. The employee subsequently more clearly articulated that the senior manager had "tried to play the race card in relation to my thinking", but the manager investigating his grievance told him that if he wished to complain about this, he would have to raise a separate grievance. The employee's grievance about T's conduct was eventually rejected and the report did not address the race issue. A few months later, discussions took place about the possibility of the employee returning to work. He stated that he wanted to work away from the section T was managing but RBS informed him that their transfer policy required him to return to work before they could consider transferring him to a new section. He subsequently resigned and brought a claim for race discrimination. The EAT upheld the tribunal's decision that the "race card" comment had been an act of direct race discrimination. The comment was demeaning and based on a stereotype; the tribunal was able to infer that the senior manager would not have treated a white employee complaining about a black colleague in the same way. However, the EAT did overturn the tribunal's decision that the employer's incompetent investigation into the employee's subsequent grievance was also an act of direct race discrimination; there was no evidence that they would have been any more competent in investigating a complaint made by a white employee.
Comment: The EAT commented that if the employee had suggested that his complaint about his manager was one of racial discrimination, or if the circumstances themselves indicated this, an attempt by the manager to clarify this would have been "wholly unobjectionable".

b. Lawful

An employer can **justify** racial and religion or belief discrimination **only if** special provisions regarding preferential treatment or occupational requirements apply.

Moreover, an employer may be **required to take certain action** to comply with another law, even if this would otherwise amount to unlawful racial discrimination (Sch 23 para 1 EqA 2010), for example, where the employer refuses to engage, or dismisses, a worker because he does not have the legal right to work in the UK (¶750).

Positive action

There are limited circumstances in which an employer is permitted to lawfully discriminate in giving preferential treatment to persons having certain protected characteristics, including race and religion or belief, where such action would otherwise have constituted unlawful discrimination (s 158 EqA 2010). This is known as positive action, but it should be noted that the positive action provisions **do not permit positive discrimination** as such. See ¶¶5243 and 5282 for further details.

Occupational requirement

In limited circumstances, an employer may be permitted to lawfully discriminate where an occupational requirement applies (¶5290).

Race **Examples** of occupational requirement that satisfied the test under the predecessor legislation (which was slightly stricter than the current test as it required an occupational requirement to be "genuine and determining") are:
– participation in a dramatic performance or other entertainment for which a person of a particular racial group is required for authenticity (this example is given in the Explanatory Notes to the EqA 2010);
– participation as an artist's or photographic model in the production of a work of art, visual image or sequence of visual images for which a person of a particular racial group is required for authenticity;
– working in a place where food or drink is (whether for payment or not) provided to and consumed by members of the public or a section of the public in a particular setting for which, in that job, a person of that racial group is required for authenticity; or
– the holder of the job provides persons of that racial group with personal services promoting their welfare and those services can most effectively be provided by a person of that racial group.

Religion or belief In relation to religion, there are **additional** occupational requirement **provisions**.

Firstly, where **employment is for the purposes of a particular religion**, the employer is allowed to apply a requirement that the worker is of a particular gender, not a transsexual, or to make a requirement in relation to a person's marriage or civil partnership status or sexual orientation, provided that this is a proportionate way of avoiding conflict with the religion's doctrines, or where, because of the nature and context of the appointment, it is a proportionate means of avoiding conflict with a significant number of the group's followers' strongly held religious convictions. The requirement must be crucial to the post and not just one of several important factors, and it must not be a sham or a pretext (Sch 9 para 2 EqA 2010). This is quite a narrow provision and would include ministers of religion and a small number of lay posts in place to promote and represent the religion. For example, it would be lawful to require a gay catholic priest to be celibate, and the provision may cover a requirement that a gay youth worker who teaches bible classes remains celibate. However, it would not cover a requirement that a church accountant be celibate if he was gay.

Secondly, **employers who have an ethos based on religion or belief** may also lawfully impose a requirement that a position should be held by a worker of a particular religion or belief where, having regard to that ethos and to the nature of the employment, and the context in which it is being carried out, being of a particular religion or belief is an occupational requirement for the job, that it is proportionate to apply such a requirement and the person to whom it is applied does not meet the occupational requirement (Sch 9 para 3 EqA 2010). The Explanatory notes give the following example: "A religious organisation may wish to restrict applicants for the post of head of its organisation to those people that adhere to that faith. This is because to represent the views of that organisation accurately it is felt that the person in charge of that organisation must have an in-depth understanding of the religion's doctrines. This type of discrimination could be lawful. However, other posts that do not require this kind of in-depth understanding, such as administrative posts, should be open to all people regardless of their religion or belief."

2. Indirect

a. Unlawful

5410 Indirect discrimination occurs where treatment which appears plausible and motivated by innocent considerations unconnected with racial grounds or religion or belief nevertheless turns out to have a **disproportionately adverse impact** on members of a particular racial group or religion or belief.

Case law decided under the predecessor legislation established that it was irrelevant whether the alleged discrimination was **intentional** or not, and this is likely to remain so under the EqA 2010 (*Seide v Gillette Industries Ltd* [1980] IRLR 427, EAT; *R v Commission for Racial Equality, ex parte Westminster City Council* [1985] 426, CA).

It is possible for the **same set of facts** to give rise to a claim for both direct and indirect racial discrimination. In practice, this will not normally be the case (*Jaffrey v Department of Environment Transport and Regions* [2002] UKEAT 692_01_0507).

5411 Indirect discrimination is **defined** as a provision, criterion or practice which an employer applies or would apply equally to all workers (or to all workers of a particular group), regardless of whether they possess a particular protected characteristic, which (s 19 EqA 2010):
– puts, or would put, persons with the same protected characteristic as the complainant at a particular disadvantage when compared to other persons;
– puts, or would put, that particular worker at that disadvantage; and
– the employer cannot show to be a proportionate means of achieving a legitimate aim.

The phrase **provision, criterion or practice** includes not only formal conditions and requirements, but can also include **informal work policies**, rules, arrangements, conditions, prerequisites, qualifications, and one-off or discretionary decisions (para 4 Equality Code). For example, lax dress requirements or an expectation that alcohol will be consumed when entertaining clients could amount to a provision, criterion or practice.

> EXAMPLE
> 1. In *Fugler-Macmillan-London Hairstudios Ltd*, ET case 2205090/04, a company which encouraged its workers not to take their leave on Saturdays was found to have indirectly discriminated against a Jewish worker, who was prevented from taking a day's holiday leave on Yom Kippur, one of the most important days in the Jewish calendar.
> 2. In *Bodi v Teletext Ltd*, ET case 3300497/05, a company which failed to promote B, a Muslim, was found to have indirectly discriminated against him, where B was able to show that no Muslim workers had ever been appointed to positions at that grade, and where the company was unable to prove that other candidates had met the selection criteria.
> 3. In *Williams-Drabble v Pathway Care Solutions Ltd and anor*, ET case 2601718/04, a Christian worker whose hours were changed, requiring him to work on Sundays, was successful with an indirect discrimination claim since, while the new rota applied to all staff, it placed that worker at a particular disadvantage. As the employer had neither entered a defence nor attended the tribunal hearing, he had not demonstrated that the rota change was justified as being a proportionate means of achieving a legitimate aim.
> 4. In *Mohmed v West Coast Trains* [2006] UKEAT 0682_05_3008, a Muslim worker was unsuccessful in a discrimination case where he had been instructed to trim his beard to comply with the company dress code. The EAT accepted that such conduct was potentially indirect discrimination, but on

the facts of the case, the employer had made similar requirements of other non-Muslim workers and had not discriminated.

5414 In respect of the test for indirect discrimination, how a condition or requirement is described is less important than how it is **applied in practice**. Hence, a condition may be said to be "desirable" or a "preference", but in practice be applied as a strict condition (*Raval v Department of Health and Social Security and the Civil Service Commission* [1985] IRLR 370, EAT; *Falkirk Council v Whyte* [1997] IRLR 560, EAT).

In order to assess whether a "considerably smaller" proportion of persons within a certain racial group can comply with a condition or requirement, compared to members of other racial groups, a tribunal must **identify a pool** for comparison. This will generally consist of all those to whom the condition or requirement is applied. The pool will then be divided into members of the complainant's racial group and members of other racial groups. To establish whether or not there has been racial discrimination, the "pool" is everyone to whom the requirement or condition could be applied, provided statistics are available. Proper identification of the relevant "pool" of workers is vital and can significantly affect the outcome of any dispute.

Tribunals will then determine the proportion of the complainant's group and the "**control group**" in order to see, in each case, what percentages can and cannot comply with the condition. This exercise can become quite complex especially as, in appropriate cases, tribunals are allowed to take their own knowledge into account, such as the cultural norms in the Indian subcontinent. There is no hard and fast rule as to the required proportions, unlike some other jurisdictions.

EXAMPLE An employer requires good oral English. A job applicant complains that as a Moroccan he is less likely to be able to comply with the requirement than an English person, and produces statistics to prove his point about Moroccans. However, the requirement would not just be applied to Moroccans and he has therefore made his pool for comparison too small.

b. Justification

5418 In respect of all aspects of race and religion or belief, an employer may sometimes be able to justify an indirectly discriminatory provision, criterion, practice, condition or requirement.

5419 An employer can justify an indirectly discriminatory provision, criterion or practice if he can demonstrate that the provision, criterion or practice is a proportionate means of achieving a legitimate aim (s 19(2)(d) EqA 2010).

EXAMPLE
Example of where practice was proportionate
1. In *Azmi v Kirklees Metropolitan Council* [2007] ICR 1154, EAT, a Muslim teaching assistant who wore the full veil (niqab) to teach was unsuccessful with her discrimination claim where the school could show that the veil had an adverse effect on children's ability to learn language skills from her.
2. In *Cherfi v G4S Security Services Ltd* [2011] UKEAT 0379_10_2405 a Muslim security guard was unsuccessful in his claim that he had been indirectly discriminated against because of a workplace policy requiring staff to remain on site throughout their shifts (which prevented him from going to mosque to pray on Friday lunchtimes). There was a prayer room on site and the employee had the option of working on a Saturday or Sunday rather than a Friday, but he refused both of these options. Although the policy placed him at a disadvantage, it was a proportionate means of achieving a legitimate aim because the employer would be in danger of financial penalties or possibly losing its contract with its client if a full number of security staff were not on site at all relevant times

Example of where practice was disproportionate
In *Eusebio and ors v TD Packaging Ltd*, ET case 1402286/04, a factory employed staff from 20 different nationalities and required workers to speak English at all times. This policy was held to discriminate indirectly. On the production line, it could be justified, as in an emergency it would be important for commands or warnings to be given urgently. There could, however, be no justification when requiring workers to speak English in the staff canteen.

3. Victimisation

5425 This occurs when a worker is subjected to **less favourable treatment** than others **because** he has (s 27 EqA 2010):
- brought proceedings against his employer, another worker or a third party;
- given evidence or information in connection with proceedings brought by another person against his employer, another worker or a third party;
- taken any other action under or by reference to these provisions; or
- made any allegation against his employer, another worker or a third party which would amount to a contravention of these provisions.

This extends to a **threat** by the worker to do any of these things or a suspicion by the employer that the worker intends to do any of them. A worker is also protected if he is victimised by his employer for his protected acts against a former employer or third party.

However, a worker will not be protected if the allegation made by him, or evidence or information given by him, was **false** and not made (or given) in good faith (s 27(3) EqA 2010).

> MEMO POINTS In the above definition, proceedings will normally mean tribunal proceedings, but where an internal grievance or disciplinary matter ends without coming to tribunal, the witness may be protected against subsequent victimisation (¶5350).

5427 Case law decided under predecessor legislation established that for victimisation to occur, the employee's protected act must be a **reason** why the employer took the action it did; it is not a "but for" test. The correct test is to ask the "reason why" the employer acted as he did: was this on the ground of the worker having made a protected act or for some other reason? (recently illustrated in *Pasab Ltd t/a Jhoots Pharmacy and another v Woods* [2012] UKEAT 0454_11_0202). It is irrelevant whether the alleged victimisation was intentional, i.e. it can be for a **conscious or unconscious** reason (*Nagarajan v London Regional Transport* [1999] IRLR 572, HL), although the employer must have **knowledge** of the protected act (*South London Healthcare NHS Trust v Al-Rubeyi* [2010] UKEAT 0269_09_0203). It is arguable the employer must also have knowledge that the act is a protected act, see *Pasab* below: a case which does not sit comfortably with the purpose of the victimisation provisions. In this case, the EAT considered that the claimant's protected act was not, truly, a reason for her dismissal and perhaps its decision in this regard was influenced by the fact her employer did not appear to realise that the claimant's outburst was a protected act.

> EXAMPLE
> 1. In *Pasab Ltd t/a Jhoots Pharmacy and another v Woods*, a Muslim student pharmacist worked at a pharmacy where the pharmacist and the HR director were both Sikh. Some aspects of her working conditions concerned her, for example she was required to give up half of her lunch hour if she wished to pray when, in fact, she prayed for less than 15 minutes a day, and she had raised a grievance about this. The working relationship was not a happy one and matters came to a head when the pharmacist called her into a meeting to discuss her timekeeping. He claimed that she reacted by saying that he and the company were two-faced and "a little Sikh club that only looked after Sikhs". She also allegedly said that the company and pharmacy were "crap". The pharmacist reported her outburst to the HR director, who suspended her over the telephone. At a meeting 2 days later, she denied making the "little Sikh club" remark. The HR director subsequently dismissed her, purportedly for poor timekeeping and breaches of the company's absence reporting procedure. The student brought discrimination, harassment and victimisation claims based upon race and religious belief (the claims were brought under the predecessor legislation now replaced by the Equality Act 2010). Most of her claims were dismissed but the employment tribunal upheld one victimisation complaint. Contrary to her denial, the tribunal found that she had made the "little Sikh club" remark. In evidence, the HR director had accepted that her decision to dismiss the student was influenced by the remark, which she thought was racist. She actually went so far as to tell the tribunal that she would have dismissed her for that alone. However, her evidence that she would have dismissed the student for poor timekeeping and absence recording in any event was rejected by the tribunal. Whilst the student had complained to the pharmacist in a vigorous way, this was because of built-up frustration. Her "little Sikh club" remark was not a generalisation about Sikhs, nor was it racist; it referred to her own experience of working for the company and it was implicit that she was alleging that non-Sikhs were treated less favourably than Sikhs. The tribunal found that this was an allegation of direct religious discrimination and, as it was not made

in bad faith, it was a protected act for victimisation purposes. The tribunal held that the student was dismissed because she had done a protected act and that her dismissal was therefore an act of unlawful victimisation. The EAT upheld the employer's appeal and rejected the student's victimisation complaint. The EAT focused on the reason why the HR director had dismissed the student. The tribunal had accepted that the true reason for dismissal was the HR director's belief that the student had made a racist comment. Having accepted this, it was not open to the tribunal to impute some different reason based on its own assessment of the meaning of the student's "little Sikh club" remark. The EAT held that if the HR director viewed the remark not as a protected act, but as an offensive racist comment, then the reason for dismissal was "some other feature genuinely separable from the implicit complaint of discrimination".

2. In *South London Healthcare NHS Trust v Al-Rubeyi*, a complaint of victimisation was made by a consultant paediatrician, Dr A. The background to the claim was that there had been a history of poor working relationships in the department in which she worked, and Dr A had made a complaint of discrimination against her colleague, Dr I. Dr I then was informed about the complaint but not that it was one of discrimination. Dr I then lodged a complaint against Dr A and threatened to resign rather than resume working with Dr A, who at the time was on sick leave for an unrelated reason. The employer investigated the matter and concluded that while there had been bullying, for which apologies should be made, it did not amount to discrimination. The investigator concluded that the best solution was for Dr A to leave. Dr A claimed that this was victimisation, as it was prompted by the allegation of discrimination against Dr I. It was found as a fact that at the time of Dr I's threat to resign, she had not known the allegation against her was discrimination. The EAT held that in the circumstances there was no connection between the treatment of Dr A and the allegation of discrimination. The reason for the treatment had been the outcome of the investigation which in turn was based on Dr I's threat to resign at a time when Dr I was unaware of any allegation of discrimination. The EAT concluded that there cannot be victimisation where the alleged guilty party is unaware of the allegation of discrimination.

5428 If a comparator is to be used (which is not strictly necessary (see ¶5353)), the **appropriate comparator** in a victimisation claim is a worker who has not brought discrimination proceedings on grounds of race, religion or belief (*Chief Constable of West Yorkshire Police v Khan* [2001] IRLR 830, HL).

There must be a **connection between** the worker's action (for example, in bringing or threatening to make a discrimination claim) and the alleged victimisation (see the example of *Visa International Service Association v Paul* at ¶5353).

4. Harassment

5430 All aspects of race are covered under the relevant provisions of the EqA 2010.

5435 Harassment **occurs** where an employer subjects a worker to unwanted conduct which has the purpose or effect of (s 26 EqA 2010):
– violating that worker's dignity; or
– creating an intimidating, hostile, degrading, humiliating or offensive environment for that worker.

This includes the employer pursuing a discriminatory policy against the religious beliefs held by another employee (*Saini v All Saints Haque Centre and ors* [2009] IRLR 74, EAT).

Also covered is harassment on the grounds of **characteristics associated** (*English v Thomas Sanderson Blinds Ltd* [2009] IRLR 206, CA). While this case concerned harassment on the ground of sexual orientation, the Court remarked that the same interpretation of the legislation would apply to other areas of discrimination such as race and religion.

EXAMPLE In *Queenscourt Ltd v Nyateka* [2006] UKEAT 0182_06_1707, a white manager refused to allow one of his workers who was female and black to attend a meeting, saying to her, "maybe it's because I'm being racist to a black woman". On appeal, the employer argued that racial banter was common in the workplace, with black workers commonly describing one another using racial epithets. In such a context, the employer suggested, it would be unjust for a court to hold that white workers were discriminating and black workers were not. The EAT disagreed, holding that the words said had not been spoken in jest, and had caused real offence. The words amounted to harassment.

MEMO POINTS 1. Harassment is specifically **excluded from the concept of detriment** (s 212(1) EqA 2010) which is a central to the discrimination provisions. Therefore, a claim for harassment covered by s 26 EqA 2010 must be brought under this provision and a complainant cannot argue that his alleged harassment constitutes a detriment under the discrimination provisions.

2. The criminal offence of "**religiously aggravated harassment**" (s 39 Anti-Terrorism, Crime and Security Act 2001) outlaws harassment based on a victim's membership or non-membership of a religious group. A "religious group" is defined as "a group of persons defined by reference to religious belief or lack of religious belief". This is likely to include individuals who are presumed to be members of a religious group (even if they are not), persons who say they are members of a religious group (even if no one else is), and individuals who are not members of any, or any certain, religious group. The outlawed conduct is prohibited generally, including in the workplace. A successful prosecution under the Act (which may be brought by individuals, as well as the Crown Prosecution Service) could pave the way for a worker, subjected to harassment at work, to pursue a claim against the employer under the EqA 2010 as well as the Protection from Harassment Act 1997, for example, for vicarious liability and/or for breach of the duty to protect the worker's health and safety.

5436 It is not essential to demonstrate that the alleged harassment was **intentional** for a claim to succeed. If the complainant cannot establish that the employer's conduct was intentional, the tribunal must consider whether, having regard to all the circumstances, including the perception of the worker concerned, the conduct should reasonably be considered as having that effect (s 26(4) EqA 2010). The **test** is neither entirely objective nor subjective, since some account needs to be taken of the alleged victim's perception. However, it does mean that a complainant who **unreasonably takes offence** at an innocent comment would probably not be considered to have been harassed, although if the conduct was repeated after the complainant made his feelings known, then the repeat conduct could well constitute unlawful harassment.

The EAT has given guidance on the approach to be taken in harassment cases, pointing out that there will often be an overlap between conduct which violates dignity and that which creates an adverse environment (*Richmond Pharmacology Ltd v Dhaliwal* [2009] IRLR 336, EAT). It also pointed out that:
– it was no longer relevant to refer to case law decided before the introduction of harassment as a separate type of discrimination;
– harassment can be established by showing either that the conduct was intended to violate dignity or create an adverse environment;
– liability will only be established if it is reasonable for the claimant to perceive that he has been subjected to a violation of his dignity or an adverse environment; and
– where the reason for the conduct is inherently or overtly discriminatory, it will not be necessary to show what the harasser's reasons were.

EXAMPLE In *Richmond Pharmacology Ltd v Dhaliwal*, the EAT upheld the decision of a tribunal that a remark by an employer suggesting that a female employee of Indian origin might be "married off in India" amounted to harassment on the ground of ethnic origin. The expression used had a stereotypical connotation, its use was on the grounds of her ethnic origin and had the effect of violating the claimant's dignity.

C. Disability

5450 It is unlawful for an employer to discriminate against a **disabled person** in relation to his employment (EqA 2010).

For a discussion as to the **scope** of the relevant legislation (i.e. who is protected in terms of the type of worker, geographical scope and time periods), see ¶¶5215+. Moreover, details as to an employer's liability for his own discriminatory acts, together with those of his workers and agents, as well as individual workers' liability for discrimination, are provided at ¶¶5225+.

It is unlawful for an employer to give **instructions** to a worker **to discriminate** against another worker (s 111(1) EqA 2010). It is also unlawful to (or attempt to) **induce** an unlawful act of disability discrimination by providing or offering to provide another person with a benefit or subjecting, or threatening to subject, him to a detriment. This will be unlawful even if the inducement is not made directly to the person in question, provided it is made in such a way that he is likely to hear of it. For example, the chairman of a holding company, Y Ltd, tries to exert pressure on the managing director of one of Y Ltd's subsidiaries, Z Ltd, to dismiss a disabled worker in contravention of the EqA 2010. Such pressure on the managing director will constitute unlawful conduct. The EHRC can bring proceedings in respect of unlawful instructions to discriminate (s 25 EqA 2006 (as amended)).

Legislation does not protect a **non-disabled worker** who complains that preferential treatment (for example, a reasonable adjustment) is given to a disabled worker.

> MEMO POINTS   Because the EqA 2010 is for the most part a consolidating measure, most of the **case law** based on the **predecessor legislation** will remain relevant under the new legislation. While the majority of provisions dealing with disability remain unchanged, a number of **significant changes** have been made. In particular:
> – the concept of indirect discrimination has been applied to disability discrimination for the first time (¶5509);
> – a new ground of "discrimination arising from disability" has been added to replace discrimination for a disability-related reason (¶5510);
> – the duty to make reasonable adjustments has been changed to add a duty to take reasonable steps to avoid a substantial disadvantage to a disabled person as a result of the lack of an auxiliary aid (¶5530); and
> – the definition of disability has been changed so that it is no longer necessary to consider specific listed capacities.

5451 The question of whether a person **comes within the definition** of disability is the first issue that must be addressed when considering the prospects of cases that come to employment tribunal.

5452 The **definition is** a **legal** and not a medical definition. There are people who are described as disabled by a medical practitioner who are not in fact disabled for the purposes of the EqA 2010. Conversely, there are people who are considered not to be disabled by a doctor, but who are disabled in terms of the definition set out in legislation.

Associative and perceptive discrimination

5453 The EqA 2010 includes protection against **discrimination by association** with regard to all types of discrimination by defining direct discrimination broadly enough to cover discriminating because of association with a person with a protected characteristic (s 13(1) EqA 2010).

Moreover, less favourable treatment based on the **employer's or another worker's perception** of an individual's disability, whether that perception is rightly or wrongly held, is also covered.

1. Definition of disability

5455 A person has a disability if he has a **physical or mental impairment** which has a **substantial and long-term adverse effect** on his ability to carry out **normal day-to-day activities** (s 6(1) EqA 2010).

a. Physical or mental impairment

5457 The term physical or mental impairment should be given its **ordinary meaning**. In many cases, there will be no dispute as to whether an individual suffers from an impairment but not all impairments are readily identifiable, particularly those which are not obviously visible to others. Identifying a physical impairment will often be relatively straightforward compared with identifying a mental impairment.

5458 While there is no exhaustive list of conditions which amount to impairments, some of the different **types of impairment** include:
– sensory impairments, for example, affecting sight or hearing;

– impairments with fluctuating or recurring effects, for example, rheumatoid arthritis, ME/chronic fatigue syndrome, fibromyalgia, depression and epilepsy;
– progressive conditions, for example, motor neurone disease, muscular dystrophy, forms of dementia and lupus;
– organ specific impairments, including respiratory conditions (for example, asthma) and cardiovascular disease (for example, thrombosis, stroke and heart disease);
– developmental impairments, for example, autistic spectrum disorders, dyslexia and dyspraxia;
– learning difficulties;
– mental health conditions and illnesses, for example, depression, schizophrenia, eating disorders, bipolar affective disorders, obsessive compulsive disorders, personality disorders and some self-harming behaviour; and
– impairments caused by injury to the body or brain.

5459 An impairment is some damage, defect, disorder or disease **compared** with a person having a full set of physical and mental equipment in normal condition (*Rugamer v Sony Music Entertainment UK Ltd* [2001] UKEAT 1385_99_2707). This can be either a cause or an effect of an illness (*College of Ripon and York St John v Hobbs* [2002] IRLR 185, EAT, approved by *McNicol v Balfour Beatty Rail Maintenance Ltd* [2002] IRLR 711, CA). An impairment may **result from another illness**, but once an impairment has been established, an individual is not required to further prove that it is caused by an illness. Many physical impairments result from conditions which could not be described as illnesses, for example, genetic deformity or amputation (*Millar v Inland Revenue Commissioners* [2006] IRLR 112, CS).

5460 Effects of a mainly **physical nature** (for example, back pain) **may result from** an underlying **mental impairment**, for example, clinical depression, and vice versa. This has been referred to as **psychological or functional overlay** (*McNicol v Balfour Beatty Rail Maintenance Ltd*, above). The case of *Hobbs*, above, demonstrates that physical symptoms which are caused by psychological disorders may amount to physical impairments.

It may not always be possible, or necessary, to categorise a condition as amounting to either a physical or mental impairment and it may be difficult to establish the underlying cause of such an impairment. However, it is not necessary to establish how an impairment is caused (provided that it does not arise from an excluded condition – ¶5464), but rather to consider the effect(s) of such an impairment (*McNicol v Balfour Beatty Rail Maintenance Ltd*, above).

> **EXAMPLE**
> 1. In *McNicol v Balfour Beatty Rail Maintenance Ltd*, there was no evidence that the cause of M's physical symptoms (progressive muscle wasting and weakness) was an organic disease, but the symptoms themselves were sufficient to fall within the definition of physical impairment, even if it had been proved that the cause was a significant psychological disorder.
> 2. In *Millar v Inland Revenue Commissioners*, the claimant had developed a number of physical symptoms such as photophobia after falling and striking his head at work though no consultant could find any organic cause for his condition. As a result, while the claimant had presented facts to the tribunal which demonstrated that he was suffering an impairment of some kind, the parties disagreed as to whether such an impairment was physical (as the claimant alleged) or mental. If it was physical then the claimant would have satisfied the first part of the definition of a disability. If it was mental, then (under the then law) he would have been required to satisfy the condition that the mental impairment was a clinically well recognised mental illness.

Where the cause of an impairment is **unclear**, it is open to a respondent to seek to disprove the existence of the impairment, including by seeking to prove that the claimed impairment is not genuine (*Hospice of St Mary of Furness v Howard* [2007] IRLR 944, EAT).

5462 By contrast to physical impairments, **mental impairments** can be difficult to identify.

Where a claimant has a mental impairment which is not a mental illness (such as a learning disability), there is no further requirement for it to be clinically well recognised nor is there any further burden of proof. **Expert evidence** of an identified condition and of its nature and degree should be produced (*Dunham v Ashford Windows* [2005] IRLR 608, EAT). Since the decision as to whether a claimant was suffering from a mental impairment is ultimately that of a tribunal, the tribunal must give careful consideration to the expert evidence and consider such evidence in the context of the totality of the evidence before it (*Hill v Clacton Family Trust Ltd* [2005] EWCA Civ 1456).

> EXAMPLE In *Hill v Clacton Family Trust Ltd*, which involved a claimant who alleged she had been suffering from a post-traumatic stress disorder, the tribunal had before it the evidence of two independent and objective psychiatrists, together with a report from a further consultant psychiatrist and a report from a practitioner in traumatology and psychotherapy who was not medically qualified. The Court of Appeal held that the tribunal had been entitled to prefer the evidence of the consultant psychiatrist over that of the traumatology expert. Moreover, although the claimant had been awarded a disability living allowance by the Social Security Appeal Tribunal (SSAT) on the basis that she had suffered a post-traumatic stress disorder, such an award was not conclusive nor binding on the tribunal since the definition of "disability" applied by the SSAT was different to that found in the predecessor legislation. Therefore it was open to the tribunal to reach a different conclusion from that of the SSAT.

Persons who are deemed disabled A person who has been diagnosed with **HIV, multiple sclerosis** or **cancer** is deemed to be disabled from the point of diagnosis (Sch 1 para 6 EqA 2010). Consequently workers do not have to prove that they suffer any substantial and adverse effects from these impairments in order to be regarded as disabled for the purposes of the EqA 2010.

In addition, individuals who are **certified blind, severely sight impaired, sight impaired or partially sighted** by a consultant ophthalmologist will also automatically fulfil the criteria and will be deemed disabled (SI 2010/2128).

5463

Excluded conditions Certain conditions are expressly excluded, **for example** a tendency to set fires, a tendency to steal, a tendency to physical or sexual abuse of others, exhibitionism, voyeurism and hay fever (except where this aggravates another condition). Also excluded are both the tendency to physical abuse as a freestanding tendency and cases where such behaviour is a manifestation of an underlying condition (*Governing Body of X Endowed Primary School v Special Educational Needs and Disability Tribunal and ors* [2009] IRLR 1007, HC). **Addiction** to, or dependency on, alcohol, nicotine or any other substance is also excluded unless the addiction is the result of taking prescribed drugs or because of other medical treatment.

A worker suffering from an impairment which results from an excluded condition such as alcoholism can nonetheless satisfy the definition of disability provided that the impairment satisfies the requirements of the definition of disability (*Power v Panasonic UK Ltd* [2002] UKEAT 0747_01_2401). For example, a person who is addicted to alcohol may also suffer from depression (mental impairment) or liver damage (physical impairment) arising from the addiction. A worker may have both a legitimate impairment and an excluded condition and, where this is the case, the critical question is one of causation (*Edmund Nuttall Ltd v Butterfield* [2005] UKEAT 0028_05_2907). If, for example, the reason for the less favourable treatment is the excluded condition and not the legitimate impairment, the worker's claim will fail. If, however, the legitimate impairment and the excluded condition together form the reason, and the legitimate impairment is an effective cause of the treatment then, on the face of it, discrimination is made out, even where the excluded condition also forms part of the employer's reason for the less favourable treatment.

5464

> EXAMPLE In *Governing Body of X Endowed Primary School v Special Educational Needs and Disability Tribunal and ors*, a disability discrimination claim was brought by the parents of a child with ADHD who was excluded from school after he assaulted a member of staff who was trying to restrain him. The High Court held that both the tendency to physical abuse as a freestanding tendency and cases where such behaviour is a manifestation of an underlying condition fell outside the scope of protected disabilities. However, it considered that the school's failure to provide adequate training on the management of pupils with ADHD, including dealing with non-compliant and disruptive behaviour, was related to the disability ADHD, and not to the tendency to physical abuse. It therefore upheld the decision that the school had failed to make reasonable adjustments.
> Note: While this was not an employment case, the same principle will apply in the employment context.

b. Effect

5469 The mental or physical impairment must have a substantial and long-term adverse effect on an individual's normal day-to-day activities. The limitation suffered must go beyond the normal differences in ability which exist between people.

Substantial and adverse

5470 Substantial **means** more than "minor" or "trivial" (s 212(1) EqA 2010).

The focus is on what the worker cannot do, or can only do with difficulty, rather than on what he can do. Just because a worker can carry out a number of normal day-to-day activities does not mean that the impairment does not adversely and substantially affect his ability to carry out other normal day-to-day activities (for example, *Vicary v British Telecommunications plc* [1999] UKEAT 1297_98_2308).

> EXAMPLE
> 1. In *Goodwin v The Patent Office*, G, a paranoid schizophrenic, was dismissed following complaints from colleagues about his behaviour. The EAT held that the symptoms of his illness, which impaired his ability to concentrate and communicate, did affect his ability to carry out normal day-to-day activities to a substantial degree.
> 2. In *Kapadia v London Borough of Lambeth* [1999] UKEAT 1004_98_2705, K suffered from reactive depression and had difficulty sleeping, suffered from mood swings, appetite loss, lack of motivation, increased difficulty in absorbing and organising information and in communicating. The EAT held that there was sufficient medical evidence to support a finding that K's symptoms had a substantial effect.

5471 Whether an impairment has a substantial effect is a question of fact and a **number of factors** will be taken into account including:
– the effect of any medical treatment (¶5473);
– the time it takes the worker to carry out an activity, compared with the time in which the activity would be expected to be carried out if the worker did not have the impairment;
– the way in which an activity is carried out, compared to the way that the person might be expected to carry out the activity if he did not have the impairment;
– the cumulative effects of the impairment on a person's ability to carry out normal day-to-day activities. A worker may suffer from one impairment that has several consequences, none of which alone amounts to a substantial adverse impact. The cumulative effect of the condition may, however, amount to a substantial adverse effect on the person's ability to carry out normal day-to-day activities;
– the cumulative effects of a number of impairments. This is relevant where a worker suffers from a number of impairments that when viewed separately do not substantially affect his ability to carry out normal day-to-day activities. When taken together the impact may be sufficient (*Vicary v British Telecommunications plc* [1999] UKEAT 1297_98_2308);
– the effects of the worker's behaviour. It is permissible to take into account how far a worker can reasonably be expected to modify his behaviour to reduce the effects of the impairment on normal day-to-day activities. If the worker can behave in a manner which will lead to cessation of the adverse effects of the impairment, he may not meet the definition of disability. Account can also be taken of where a person avoids doing things which cause pain, fatigue or substantial embarrassment because of a loss of energy or motivation. It is not reasonable to conclude that a person who employs an avoidance strategy is not a disabled person. However, where it is possible that the worker's ability to manage the effects of his impairment (i.e. his coping strategy) will break down with the result that the effects recur, this possibility must be taken into account when considering whether the impairment has a substantial adverse effect on the worker (*Virdi v Commissioner of the Police of the Metropolis of London and anor* [2007] IRLR 24, EAT); and
– the effect of environmental factors (for example, temperature, humidity, lighting, the time of day or night, tiredness, stress etc.). Where environmental factors arise from an employer's system of work, the employer may be under a duty to make reasonable adjustments to reduce the effect these have on the worker. For example, a worker's asthma is triggered by exposure to fumes at work, but improves when he is away from work. Before deciding to

dismiss the worker, the employer should seek to make reasonable adjustments. The employer cannot rely on the fact that away from work the worker's condition would improve to such a degree that the impairment would no longer have a substantial adverse affect on their ability to carry out normal day-to-day activities (*Cruickshank v VAW Motorcast Ltd* [2002] IRLR 24, EAT).

5472 Individuals who were **disabled in the past** are also protected, even if they are no longer disabled, provided they met the requirements in the past, i.e. the effects of the past disability must have lasted at least 12 months or recurred within a period not exceeding 12 months following the first occurrence (s 6(4) EqA 2010; Sch 1 para 9(1) and (2) EqA 2010).

> MEMO POINTS   This is the case even for those individuals who were no longer disabled by the time the EqA 2010 was brought into force. For example, a man who, 5 years ago, suffered a mental illness which had a substantial and long-term adverse effect on his ability to carry out normal day-to-day activities is covered by the EqA 2010 as an individual with a past disability, even though there has been no recurrence of his mental illness.

5473 **Treated/corrected impairments** Where an impairment is being treated or corrected, it should be taken to have the effect it would have without the specific treatment (the so-called **deduced effect**); in particular, any medical treatment or use of a prosthesis or any other aid is to be disregarded (Sch 1 para 5(1) and (2) EqA 2010). This applies even if the measures result in the effects being completely under control or not at all apparent. One exception, however, is impaired eyesight correctable by wearing **glasses or contact lenses** (Sch 1 para 5(3) EqA 2010). If the worker's ability to carry out normal day-to-day activities is substantially and adversely affected even where spectacles or contact lenses are used, however, these effects must be considered.

In cases where **medical treatment** has been successful, the worker must provide clear and detailed medical evidence of the symptoms he would have suffered had he not undergone treatment for his condition (*Woodrup v London Borough of Southwark* [2002] EWCA Civ 1716).

> MEMO POINTS   Individuals who are **certified blind, severely sight impaired, sight impaired or partially sighted** by a consultant ophthalmologist will also automatically fulfil the criteria and will be deemed disabled, see ¶5463.

5474 **Continuing treatment** which has the effect of masking or ameliorating a disability so that it does not have a substantial adverse effect should be disregarded if the final outcome of the treatment is not ascertainable or if it is known that a relapse or worsened condition would occur if the treatment was stopped. However, if the effect of continuing medical treatment is to create a **permanent improvement**, then this should be taken into account (*Abadeh v British Telecommunications plc* [2001] ICR 156, EAT).

> EXAMPLE
> 1. In *Kapadia v London Borough of Lambeth* [[1999] UKEAT 1004_98_2705, the EAT ruled that the twenty or so **counselling sessions** which K had undergone over a 2-year period could be regarded as medical treatment and K's condition should have been assessed without reference to that counselling. Consequently, the tribunal had erred in failing to take into account the evidence which showed that, but for the counselling sessions, there was a very strong likelihood that K would suffer a mental breakdown.
> 2. In *Carden v Pickerings Europe Ltd* [2005] IRLR 720, EAT, it was considered that if plates and pins are surgically inserted to successfully correct an impairment and **continue to provide support** and assistance, the impairment is being controlled by an aid and it should be taken to have the effect it would have without the aid. However, if they **lose their functionality**, for example because the bones have successfully knitted together and have recovered their original function, then there is no continuing treatment and the worker's condition is taken as it is (i.e. successfully repaired) and he cannot be said to be suffering from a disability.

5476 **Progressive conditions** A progressive condition is one which is likely to develop and change over a period of time. The category includes conditions which may go through periods of remission, as well as those that show a tendency to worsen. Persons with the progressive conditions of **HIV infection**, **multiple sclerosis** and **cancer** are deemed to be disabled from the point of diagnosis (¶5463).

An impairment(s) suffered by a worker due to a progressive condition will be deemed to have a substantial adverse effect if it has **some adverse effect** on his ability to carry out normal day-to-day activities, and is **likely**, in the future, **to have a substantial effect** (Sch 1 para 8(1) and (2) EqA 2010; *Mowat-Brown v University of Surrey* [2001] UKEAT 462_00_1012). An impairment which has resulted from the **medical treatment** of the progressive condition (*Kirton v Tetrosyl Limited* [2003] IRLR 353, CA) may also be deemed to have a substantial effect. In this case, the worker developed incontinence after medical treatment for prostate cancer and it was held that his incontinence was sufficiently linked to the cancer to result from it, notwithstanding the fact that the worker had undergone surgery in the intervening period.

Some impairments can have long periods of **remission** even though the condition is not extinguished (for example, epilepsy). Consequently, an **impairment** which is "**likely to recur**" will be treated as having a continuing adverse effect on a worker's ability to carry out normal day-to-day activities (Sch 1 para 2(2) EqA 2010). When considering the likelihood of recurrence, a tribunal will consider whether a recurrence "could well happen" rather than whether it is "more probable than not" (*SCA Packaging v Boyle* [2009] IRLR 746, HL overturning *Latchman v Reed Business Information Ltd* [2002] ICR 1453, EAT and *Swift v Chief Constable of Wiltshire Constabulary* [2004] IRLR 540, EAT). Note that it is not necessary for the physical or mental impairment itself to be likely to recur, but rather whether any substantial adverse effect which results from the impairment is likely to recur (*Swift v Chief Constable of Wiltshire Constabulary*, above).

In deciding whether an effect is likely to recur, **subsequent events** are irrelevant in determining whether discrimination occurred. The tribunal is restricted to the knowledge of the employer at the time he took the decision (*McDougall v Richmond Adult Community College* [2008] ICR 431, CA overturning the EAT decision at [2007] IRLR 771, EAT and followed in *Mahon v Accuread Ltd* [2008] UKEAT 0081_08_0107).

All the circumstances of the case should be taken into account, including what the worker could reasonably be expected to do to prevent recurrence, but bearing in mind that controlling methods can break down.

EXAMPLE In *HSBC Bank plc v Clarkson* [2002] UKEAT 205_01_2910, the claimant, who had suffered from two episodes of depression separated by nearly 10 years, was not deemed to be disabled unless it could be shown that each of the episodes of depression had a long-term adverse effect on the claimant's ability to carry out normal day-to-day activities.

5477 In some cases, the worker may be able to **prove the likelihood of future substantial effect** by producing medical evidence of his likely prognosis, but in others, he may be able to rely on statistical evidence (*Mowat-Brown v University of Surrey*, above).

5479 **Severe disfigurements** Most impairments which consist of a severe disfigurement are **deemed** to have a substantial adverse effect on the ability of the person affected to carry out normal day-to-day activities (Sch 1 para 3(1) EqA 2010). It appears to be a matter of degree as to whether a disfigurement will be considered sufficiently severe, but it may also be important to consider whether the feature in question is visible, for example, if there is facial disfigurement. Examples of disfigurements include scars, birthmarks, limb or postural deformities and skin diseases.

Certain disfigurements are expressly **excluded**, for example, tattoos and decorative body piercing (The EqA 2010 (Disability) Regulations SI 2010/2128).

Long-term

5481 An impairment has a long-term effect **if, at the date of the alleged discriminatory act**, it (*Cruickshank v VAW Motorcast Ltd* [2002] IRLR 24, EAT; Sch 1 para 2 EqA 2010):
1. has lasted at least 12 months;
2. is likely (i.e. it is more probable than not) to last:
– at least 12 months; or
– for the rest of the worker's life (including if this is less than 12 months); or
3. is likely to recur if it is in remission (¶5476).

5482 Provided that one of the above conditions is satisfied, it is irrelevant that the adverse effects of the **impairment may change or fluctuate** over the period (for example, certain activities may become more easy or difficult to perform or one adverse effect may be replaced by another).

In **assessing** whether an impairment has a long-term effect, consideration will be given to the typical length of the particular effect on an individual and any relevant factors specific to this individual (for example, their age and state of health). The total period of impairment both before and after the alleged discriminatory act may also be relevant (*Greenwood v British Airways plc* [1999] ICR 969, EAT). Further, two **separate conditions** can be **looked at together** in assessing whether there is a long-term effect **if** the second had developed or was likely to develop from the first (*Patel v Oldham Metropolitan Borough Council and anor* [2010] IRLR 280, EAT).

> EXAMPLE In *Patel v Oldham Metropolitan Borough Council and anor*, a teacher developed inflammation of her spinal cord, which caused pain in her groin and leg. She took a number of periods off work during the course of 2005. In January 2006, she developed a second condition which affected the same areas; she returned to work full time later that year but suffered an injury after which her condition worsened and she was dismissed for incapability. The EAT held that the two separate conditions could be looked at together in assessing whether there was a long-term effect if the second had developed or was likely to develop from the first. It returned the case to an employment judge to assess whether the second condition had developed from the first and whether, taking the two together, there was a long-term effect.

c. Normal day-to-day activities

5485 Normal day-to-day activities refer generally to **domestic activities** which are normal to, and which are carried out fairly regularly by, most people. Examples include shopping, reading, writing, having a conversation or using the telephone, watching television, getting washed and dressed, preparing and eating food, carrying out household tasks, walking and travelling by various forms of transport, and taking part in social activities. A person will not be treated as disabled because he is substantially impaired in an ability to carry out an unusual activity, even if the activity is one that is usual to him, such as playing a particular game, taking part in a particular hobby, playing a musical instrument or playing sport, or performing a highly skilled task. The EAT has held, however, that putting rollers in hair and applying make-up could amount to normal day-to-day activities even though they are types of activities which are carried out almost exclusively by women (*Ekpe v Commissioner of Police of the Metropolis* [2001] UKEAT 1044_00_2505).

5486 Although a worker's particular **work duties** should not be equated with normal day-to-day activities, the EAT has held that the definition of day-to-day activities may comprise activities necessary for participation in professional life (*Paterson v Commissioner of Police for the Metropolis* [2007] IRLR 752, EAT), although this may not always be so (*Chief Constable of Lothian and Borders Police v Cumming* [2010] IRLR 109, EAT). The EAT has also held that night shift working is sufficiently common to be considered to be a normal day-to-day activity (*Chief Constable of Dumfries and Galloway Constabulary v Adams* [2009] IRLR 612, EAT).

> EXAMPLE
> **Activities necessary for participation in professional life day-to-day activities**
> 1. In *Paterson v Commissioner of Police for the Metropolis*, a senior police officer was diagnosed with dyslexia. Following a medical report, it was recommended that he should be given extra time when taking professional examinations. He brought a claim of disability discrimination, alleging that his employers had failed to make reasonable adjustments, particularly in the processes for deciding whether he should be promoted. His employer denied that the officer was disabled, holding that while he might have difficulty in work-related activities such as a professional examination, the officer's impairment had no adverse effect on his ability to carry out normal day-to-day activities. The EAT held that the effect of the officer's dyslexia was to make reading and comprehension more difficult. These were normal day-to-day activities. Further, the EAT held that an inability to take part in professional activities was indeed an inability to carry out normal day-to-day activities. Any other result would invalidate the purposes of the legislation.

2. In *Chief Constable of Dumfries and Galloway Constabulary v Adams*, a police officer who suffered from ME experienced mobility problems when he worked night shifts. His employer allowed him to finish his night shifts early, but he continued to experience difficulties towards the end of shifts. The employer later dismissed him. He made a disability discrimination claim. The EAT considered whether working night shifts was a normal day-to-day activity or whether it related to his particular work and was thus not a "normal" day-to-day activity. It concluded that night-shift working was sufficiently common to fall within the statutory definition even though a minority of workers work at night.

Activities necessary for participation in professional life not day-to-day activities
In *Chief Constable of Lothian and Borders Police v Cumming*, a civilian police employee who was also a special constable applied to be a police officer but failed the medical because the eyesight in her left eye was impaired. While the impairment affected some normal day-to-day activities to a minor extent, the EAT held that exclusion from a profession did not amount to a substantial adverse effect in this case and did not amount to unlawful disability discrimination.

5487 Moreover, if a worker's ability to carry out normal day-to-day activities fluctuates and worsens at work due to the **particular circumstances of his workplace** (for example, if a worker's asthma is exacerbated by environmental conditions at work), then both his activities at work and outside work will be considered in determining whether his impairment has a substantial and long-term adverse effect on his ability to carry out normal day-to-day activities (*Cruickshank v VAW Motorcast Ltd* [2002] IRLR 24, EAT).

5488 In **assessing** whether a worker's activities are affected the focus is on what the worker cannot do or can only do with difficulty, as opposed to what he can do (*Goodwin v The Patent Office* [1999] IRLR 4, EAT).

Even if an impairment does not directly prevent a person from carrying out his normal day-to-day activities, it may still have an **indirect** substantial adverse long-term effect on how he carries out those activities, for example, where the impairment causes pain or fatigue which makes the activity more than usually tiring or where a person has been medically advised to change, limit or refrain from a normal day-to-day activity on account of an impairment.

2. Unlawful

5495 An employer **will be liable** for unlawful disability discrimination **if** (ss 13(1), 15(1), 19(1), 20 EqA 2010; *Clark v TDG Ltd t/a Novacold* [1999] IRLR 318, CA):

a. because of a person's disability, the employer treats that disabled person less favourably than he treats or would treat a person not having that particular disability ("direct discrimination"). It should be noted that it is not possible for an employer to justify such less favourable treatment;

b. the employer applies a provision, criterion or practice to the disabled person which puts people with that disability at a disadvantage, does or would put the disabled worker at a disadvantage, and is not a proportionate means of achieving a legitimate aim ("indirect discrimination");

c. because of something arising in consequence of a person's disability, the employer treats that person less favourably than he treats the person to whom the reason does not apply, in circumstances where the employer knows, or could reasonably be expected to know that the person has a disability, and he cannot justify the less favourable treatment. Less favourable treatment can include dismissal, and the term dismissal includes a reference to constructive dismissal and the non-renewal of a fixed term contract (*Nottinghamshire County Council v Meikle* [2004] IRLR 703, CA; see also ¶8230);

d. the employer fails to comply with the duty to make reasonable adjustments in relation to the disabled person;

e. he victimises a person (whether the person is disabled or not) for a prohibited reason; or

f. he subjects a worker to unwanted conduct which amounts to harassment.

5496 It should be noted that where **other statutory obligations** of the employer conflict with the disability provisions, those other obligations will take precedence provided there are no reasonable adjustments which the employer can make (s 191 EqA 2010; Sch 22 para 1 EqA 2010). For example, health and safety legislative obligations impose an absolute duty on the employer and, if it is clearly impossible for a worker to comply with a particular requirement (for example, to wear protective boots because of a skin condition) and there would be a risk to a worker's health and safety as a result, which could not be adequately controlled (for example, because suitable alternatives could not be found), then the employer's only viable option is not to employ the worker in that particular area. In such circumstances, the anti-discrimination legislation is subordinate to health and safety legislation and the worker is unlikely to succeed with a claim for discrimination if he is dismissed (*Lane Group Plc and anor v Farmiloe* [2004] UKEAT 0352_03_2201; see also ¶5520).

a. Direct discrimination

Direct disability discrimination occurs where an employer, **because of** the disabled person's **disability**, treats the disabled person less favourably than he treats or would treat a person not having that particular disability (s 19 EqA 2010).

5500

The issue is whether a disabled person would have received the less favourable treatment from his employer **but for** his disability (para 3.28 Equality Code). Consequently, if an employer who has generalised, **stereotypical views or assumptions** about a particular disability or its effects treats a disabled person less favourably on these grounds, this is likely to be unlawful direct discrimination since the employer would not make such assumptions about a non-disabled person but instead would consider his individual capabilities (paras 16.43 and 16.61 Equality Code).

5502

EXAMPLE
1. An employer who has advertised for a shop assistant rejects an applicant with a severe facial disfigurement solely on the ground that other workers would be uncomfortable working alongside her. The employer's conduct constitutes unlawful direct discrimination.
2. An employer assumes (wrongly) that blind people cannot use computers and consequently rejects an application for a job involving computers from a blind person. Since the employer has not attempted to consider the individual job applicant's particular circumstances, and he has treated her less favourably because of his wrongly-held assumptions, by not shortlisting her for the position, he is likely to have directly discriminated against her.
3. An employer advertises an internal vacancy for a position within his workforce. The job description indicates that the job would not be suitable for persons with a history of mental illness. Such a "blanket ban" on any workers who have suffered from mental illness will be unlawful since the employer has suggested that he would disregard anyone falling into this category without any consideration of their individual circumstances.

It is essential to **look behind the reason** provided for less favourable treatment by an employer since, although it may appear that an employer has acted for an apparently disability-neutral reason, upon further investigation, it may be discovered that this was merely a pretext for direct discrimination.

5503

Direct discrimination may **sometimes be unconscious** as an employer may act on deeply-held prejudices without realising that he is doing so. Moreover, an employer may directly discriminate against a person even though he is **unaware** of that person's disability (para 3.14 Equality Code).

EXAMPLE
1. In *High Quality Lifestyles v Watts* [2006] IRLR 850, EAT, HQL dismissed an HIV-positive worker on the grounds that he worked with people with learning difficulties, who were prone to acts that included biting. A person who has been diagnosed with HIV is deemed to be disabled (¶5476). Accordingly, the worker claimed that HQL had directly discriminated against him on grounds of disability. The EAT found that there had been no direct discrimination as the dismissal had been on the grounds of the real, if modest, risk of HIV transmission. The EAT did however find that HQL's dismissal had not been objectively justified. It therefore constituted disability-related discrimination.

> 2. In *Cosgrove v Northern Ireland Ambulance Service* [2007] IRLR 397, NICA, a post was advertised for an emergency ambulance worker. The applicant was found to be suffering from psoriasis, a skin condition, to such an extent that he could not be exposed to latex medical equipment, and there would be a risk of infection to patients. Psoriasis is also a disfiguring condition and the applicant argued that he had suffered discrimination on account of his disfigurement. The Northern Ireland Court of Appeal held that this had not been the reason for the differential treatment: it was the risk to patients, rather than his disability, which had caused his application to fail.

5505 **Comparison** The **appropriate comparator** is a person (whether real or hypothetical) without the particular disability whose circumstances (including his abilities) are the same as, or not materially different from, those of the disabled person concerned. In the first example at ¶5502, the appropriate comparator would have been someone without the severe facial disfigurement but who has the same ability as the disabled person to do the job of a shop assistant. In the second example at ¶5502, the appropriate comparator would have been a person who is not blind but who has the same abilities as the blind woman to do the job (s 23 EqA 2010).

> MEMO POINTS Where a **hypothetical comparator** is used, evidence which goes to demonstrate how such a comparator would have been treated is likely to include details of how other people (who do not satisfy the statutory comparison test) were treated in broadly similar circumstances.

5506 It should be noted that it is not essential to find a comparator whose circumstances are the same in every respect provided the comparator's **relevant circumstances** (i.e. including his abilities) are the same as, or not materially different from, those of the disabled person (para 3.29 Equality Code). It is therefore important to focus on those circumstances which are relevant to the matter to which the less favourable treatment relates (para 3.30 Equality Code).

> EXAMPLE A disabled man who has arthritis and is able to type at 30 wpm is rejected from an administrative position which involves typing on the grounds that his typing is too slow. Here the appropriate comparator would be a person who does not have arthritis who also has a typing speed of 30 wpm (and equivalent accuracy rate). It would not be necessary for him to identify a comparator who cannot, for example, lift heavy weights, because this is not a requirement of the job.

5507 For cases being brought under the predecessor legislation, the comparison must be made in the context of the disabled person's abilities as they in fact are as opposed to what they would or might have been had any **reasonable adjustments** which the employer was obliged (but failed) to carry out in respect of that worker been made. However, if the employer has carried out his duty to make reasonable adjustments which have resulted in the disabled person's abilities being improved, then those improved abilities must be considered. There is no equivalent provision in the Equality Code, but the same principle is likely to apply under the EqA 2010.

> EXAMPLE A disabled person with arthritis who applies for an administrative job which includes typing is allowed to use an adapted keyboard for a typing test and produces a test document at 50 wpm. A non-disabled candidate types his test at 30 wpm with the same accuracy rate as that of the disabled applicant. The employer rejects the disabled applicant due to prejudice and the other candidate is successful. The comparator is a person not having arthritis who could type at 50 wpm and the employer is likely to be liable for direct discrimination.

5508 **No justification** It is not open for an employer to justify direct discrimination on the grounds of a person's disability (s 13(1) EqA 2010).

b. Indirect discrimination

5509 The EqA 2010 has extended the scope of indirect discrimination (¶5245) to cases of disability discrimination (s 19 EqA 2010).

In a disability case, indirect discrimination occurs when an employer applies a **provision, criterion or practice** to a disabled person which:
- puts, or would put, disabled persons at a particular disadvantage when compared with persons who do not have that disability;
- puts, or would put, the disabled person at that disadvantage; and
- is not a proportionate means of achieving a legitimate aim.

The appropriate **comparator** in an indirect discrimination case will be the same as in direct discrimination, that is a person (whether real or hypothetical) without the particular disability whose circumstances (including his abilities) are the same as, or not materially different from, those of the disabled person concerned (s 23 EqA 2010).

An employer may **justify** indirect disability discrimination by showing that the treatment is a proportionate means of achieving a legitimate aim; it is unlikely that an employer would be able to do so if there were reasonable adjustments which the employer could have made but has failed to do so.

However, there is **no requirement** that the employer should have **knowledge** that the worker is disabled for there to be liability for indirect discrimination. It is therefore possible that the employer may in some cases be able to establish that indirect discrimination is justified, even where it might have been avoided had adjustments been made, provided the employer could not reasonably have known of the disability, and in that case no duty to make reasonable adjustments would arise (¶5530). Cases decided under the predecessor legislation on disability-related discrimination may be referred to for guidance. If the employer is found to have indirectly discriminated without any intention to do so, a tribunal must consider a declaration or a recommendation as a remedy before considering an award of compensation (s 124(4), (5) EqA 2010).

c. Discrimination arising from disability

5510

An employer must not treat a person less favourably because of something **arising in consequence of his disability** than he treats, or would treat, another person without that disability, unless he can justify the unfavourable treatment by showing that it is a proportionate means of achieving a legitimate aim (s 15 EqA 2010). There must be a connection between the disability and whatever led to the unfavourable treatment (para 5.8 Equality Code).

> EXAMPLE An employer dismisses a visually-impaired employee because he is not able to be as productive as a non-disabled employee. This will be unlawful discrimination related to a disability, unless the employer can show the dismissal is a proportionate means of achieving a legitimate aim.
> A job applicant has a disability which requires the use of a wheelchair. She has the skills and qualifications to perform the job, but the employer is concerned that the wheelchair will get in the way in the office. Consequently, the employer gives the job to a person who is no more suitable for the job but who does not use a wheelchair. The job applicant has been treated less favourably than the successful candidate (by not being offered the job); the reason is connected with a disability (the fact that she uses a wheelchair).

For liability to be incurred under this provision, the employer must **know, or reasonably be expected to know**, that the worker has a disability. Employers should take reasonable steps to find out if a worker has a disability (para 5.15 Equality Code) whilst at the same time respecting the worker's privacy. Particular care is needed where a third party, such as an occupational health adviser, knows of the disability, as the employer is likely to be treated as having knowledge of the disability.

> EXAMPLE An employer dismisses a temporary data entry operator, who has depression, because she does not meet performance targets. Her performance level is a consequence of her disability, which affects her ability to concentrate, and which she has not disclosed to the employer. If the employer is able to show that it is reasonable for him not to have known of the disability, he has not subjected her to discrimination arising from her disability.

5515 **Comparison** There is no requirement for a comparator in the case of discrimination arising from a disability (para 5.6 Equality Code).

5520 **Justification** Discrimination arising from disability treatment will be justified if the treatment is a proportionate means of achieving a legitimate aim (s 15(1)(b) EqA 2010). Where a reasonable adjustment could have been made which would have avoided the unfavourable treatment altogether, or reduced its impact, and the employer has failed to make it, the employer will find it difficult to show that the unfavourable treatment was proportionate (para 5.21 Equality Code). Because an employer will not have discriminated for a reason arising from disability if he does not know (and could not reasonably have known) of the disability, case law decided under the predecessor legislation on the impact of knowledge on the defence of justification will not be relevant in cases of discrimination arising from a disability.

5523 An employer's concerns regarding his **health and safety obligations** is a common reason for less favourable treatment of a disabled worker. Employers should take care to avoid making **stereotypical assumptions** regarding the health and safety implications in relation to particular types of disability, since less favourable treatment based upon such assumptions may itself amount to direct discrimination. However, genuine concerns regarding the health and safety of any worker (including a disabled worker) may be relevant when seeking to rely on the defence of justification for any less favourable treatment of a disabled person. Consequently, if an employer has reason to believe that the effects of a person's disability give rise to a health and safety concern, the employer should arrange for a risk assessment to be carried out, if the existing standard risk assessment procedures do not address the particular concern. However, an employer should not subject a disabled worker or job applicant to a risk assessment where the circumstances of the case do not merit it since such treatment could in itself amount to direct discrimination.

5524 **Long-term sickness absence** which arises from a disability is frequently cited for the less favourable treatment of a disabled worker. An employer should consider **medical information** (for example, doctors' reports, or medical questionnaires) as part of an assessment of the health and safety risks but although such information may justify an adverse decision (for example, to dismiss a worker), there will be no justification where the medical evidence shows that the disability has no effect on the person's ability to do his job. Less favourable treatment in these circumstances may amount to direct discrimination. A tribunal will consider (in relation to establishing an employer's credibility and rationality), any expert medical evidence obtained after an alleged discriminatory act, even if such evidence was not available to the employer at the time. However, a case decided under the predecessor legislation suggests that it must not be used to judge whether or not an employer's decision was justified (*Surrey Police v Marshall* [2002] UKEAT 774_01_0509).

It is also very important to consider whether there are any **reasonable adjustments** which could be made to overcome any issues which may have been identified as a result of the medical information, for example, moving the worker to another job or placing him on reduced hours.

Employers should consider medical information provided in the context of the position concerned and the person's capabilities. However, an employer should not solely **rely** on medical evidence as an influencing factor in reaching his decision. Employers are also advised to **consult** fully with the disabled person concerned, to seek his views about his own capabilities and any reasonable adjustments which could be carried out to enable him to perform his job.

EXAMPLE

1. In *Nottinghamshire County Council v Meikle* [2004] IRLR 703, CA, the employer could not justify paying M half-pay after a prolonged period of absence (100 days) due to her disability (in accordance with its contractual sick pay scheme) since she would have been back at work and entitled to full-pay had the employer complied with his duty to make reasonable adjustments to M's working conditions.

2. In *Rothwell v Pelikan Hardcopy Scotland* (¶5533), a disabled claimant, R, suffering from Parkinson's disease, was on long-term sick leave. The employer requested two medical reports, one of which was pessimistic regarding the worker's chances of returning to work, the other was more optimistic. Prior to the decision to dismiss R, the employer failed to discuss the more optimistic report with him. The EAT held that such consultation with R would have constituted a reasonable adjustment. There had been no urgency on the part of the employer to dismiss R so any delay that such consultation would have caused would have not been unreasonable for the employer to tolerate.

5525 Despite cases decided under the predecessor legislation in which the employer has been found to have discriminated against disabled workers in the implementation of their **sickness policy** (*Nottinghamshire County Council v Meikle* [2004] IRLR 703, CA), the employer is under no absolute obligation not to dismiss a worker for disability-related absence. Much will depend on the facts of each particular case. For example, the EAT has held that an employer will only rarely be required to set aside disability-related absences for the purposes of any sickness policy (*Royal Liverpool NHS Trust v Dunsby* [2005] UKEAT 0426_05_0112).

5526 In another case, the Court of Appeal held that although an employer's **contractual sick pay scheme** (which failed to provide for full pay for disability-related absence) might be said to have indirectly discriminated against disabled workers, it could be justified (*O'Hanlon v Commissioners for HM Revenue and Customs* [2007] IRLR 404, CA). The employer was **not** under a **general obligation** to keep a worker on **full pay** for periods of sickness absence that were related to her disability. In this case, and in contrast to *Nottinghamshire County Council v Meikle* (¶5524), the employer had not failed to make any reasonable adjustments that might have been necessary to enable the disabled worker to return to work.

d. Failure to make reasonable adjustments

5530 The **duty to make** reasonable adjustments **applies where** (s 20(3), (4) and (5) EqA 2010):
– a provision, criterion or practice applied by or on behalf of an employer places a disabled person at a substantial disadvantage compared with a non-disabled person;
– any physical feature(s) of premises occupied by the employer places a disabled person at a substantial disadvantage compared with a non-disabled person; or
– the provision of an auxiliary aid will prevent a disabled person being put at a substantial disadvantage, in comparison with someone who is not disabled.

In such circumstances, the employer, where it is reasonable to do so, will be under a duty to make adjustments or modifications to such provision, criterion, practice, or physical feature, or to provide an auxiliary aid in order to remove that particular disadvantage. Where the adjustment to address the effect of a provision, criterion, practice, or relating to the provision of an auxiliary aid, involves providing information, the employer should ensure that information is in an accessible format (s 20(6) EqA 2010).

MEMO POINTS The provision, criterion or practice need not apply directly to the disabled person. It is possible for there to be a substantial disadvantage despite the provision, criterion or practice only being applied to other employees (*Roberts v North West Ambulance Service* [2011] UKEAT 0085_11_2401).

5531 It is first necessary to **identify** the provision, criterion, practice, physical feature(s) or lack of an auxiliary aid which places the disabled worker or job applicant at a substantial disadvantage when compared to other non-disabled workers/applicants. See ¶¶5540, 5545 for further details.

Once such a provision, criterion, practice, physical feature or need for an auxiliary aid has been identified, the employer is under a duty **to take such steps** as are reasonable in all the circumstances of the case to ensure that the provision, criterion, practice or physical feature ceases to place the disabled person at a substantial disadvantage when compared to other non-disabled persons, including, if appropriate, providing the auxiliary aid. This may result in the employer having to treat the disabled person more favourably than he would treat a non-disabled person (*Archibald v Fife Council* [2004] IRLR 651, HL; ¶5541).

5532 In determining whether there has been a **failure** by the employer to make reasonable adjustments, the tribunal will, in the following order (*Environment Agency v Rowan* [2008] ICR 218, EAT):
1. identify the provision, criterion or practice applied by or on behalf of the employer or the physical feature(s) occupied by the employer;
2. identify the non-disabled comparator(s) (where appropriate); and
3. identify the nature and extent of the alleged substantial disadvantage suffered.

Where the employer has failed to make reasonable adjustments and this has resulted in the employer dismissing the employee, the dismissal is itself an unlawful act of disability discrimination (s 21 EqA 2010; *Fareham College Corporation v Walters* [2009] IRLR 991, EAT).

5533 An employer **cannot justify** a failure to comply with the duty to make reasonable adjustments. The duty is therefore a strict one and an employer's only defence where it is alleged that he has breached the duty is that it was not reasonable for the employer to comply with the duty. For a further discussion of reasonableness, see ¶5552.

Whether it is reasonable for an employer to make adjustments will be **assessed objectively** and, consequently, if the employer has failed to make an adjustment which the tribunal has held to be reasonable, he will have discriminated against the disabled person in question.

A consideration of whether an employer can justify the less favourable treatment of a worker can only take place once it has been established whether there exists a duty on the employer to carry out certain reasonable adjustments and, if so, whether those reasonable adjustments have been made (*Rothwell v Pelikan Hardcopy Scotland* [2006] IRLR 24, EAT(S)).

5534 An employer should consider what reasonable adjustments he can make (*Cosgrove v Caesar & Howie* [2001] IRLR 653, EAT). **Consultation** will enable an employer to make a proper assessment of what might be required to eliminate a disabled person's disadvantage in order to comply with the duty to make reasonable adjustments.

Under the predecessor legislation, there were differing opinions as to **whether** there was an absolute **duty** to **consult**. In two older cases, it was argued that the employer must consult with the worker, and that if the employer has not consulted, he cannot have made a reasonable adjustment (*Mid-Staffordshire General Hospitals NHS Trust v Cambridge* [2003] IRLR 566, EAT; *Southampton City College v Randall* [2005] UKEAT 0372_05_0711). This line of argument is now believed to be wrong. While a failure to consult may be good prima facie **evidence** of whether the duty to make reasonable adjustments has been met or not (*Project Management Institute v Latif* [2007] IRLR 579, EAT), the real test is whether the employer has made reasonable adjustments. If the employer makes the reasonable adjustments, without having consulted, then the employer has fulfilled their duty. If the employer has not made the right reasonable adjustment, then no amount of consultation will remedy that breach (*Tarbuck v Sainsbury's Supermarkets* [2006] IRLR 664, EAT approved in *HM Prison Service v Johnson* [2007] IRLR 951, EAT).

Employers are advised to **agree** any proposed adjustments with the disabled person before carrying them out in a **timely** manner (para 6.32 Equality Code).

EXAMPLE
1. In *Project Management Institute v Latif*, a qualifications body failed to provide reading software for a disabled person with a visual impairment. The EAT found that this failure was unreasonable and was the consequence of the qualification body's failure to focus on the individual needs of the disabled person. Consultation should have taken place.
2. In *Spence v Intype Libra* [2007] UKEAT 0617_06_2704, an IT manager suffered an attack, which left him with two collapsed lungs. His employer offered various routes to enable the worker to return to work, but no adjustments could be agreed. Ultimately, the worker was dismissed. The worker argued that the employer should have obtained a medical report, so as to be in a position to properly evaluate whether, or how, he could return. The EAT disagreed, holding that if the dismissal was a fair dismissal, then it was not made unfair by a failure to consult or obtain a suitable report.

5535 The duty to make adjustments only arises if an employer **knows or could reasonably be expected to know** that a person (including a job applicant or other person who has notified the employer that he may be an applicant for that employment) is disabled and that the employer knows or could reasonably be expected to know that the effect of this is that the person is likely to be placed at a substantial disadvantage by the employer's provisions, criteria, practices, premises and the lack of an auxiliary aid (Sch 8 para 20 EqA 2010; *Secretary of State for the Department for Work and Pensions v Alam* [2010] IRLR 283, EAT). However, an employer must do all he reasonably can be expected to do to find out whether this is the case (para 6.19 Equality Code). Following the introduction of the EqA 2010, the scope for employers to ask applicants health and disability related questions is limited (see ¶5541), but it remains permitted to establish whether reasonable adjustments need to be made to enable the applicant to perform well in an interview or other form of assessment of their suitability for a job (s 60(6)(a) EqA 2010; para 6.18 Equality Code).

EXAMPLE

1. A worker has depression which sometimes causes her to be tearful at work, although this is not known to her employer. The employer makes no effort to find out whether the worker is disabled and, if so, whether a reasonable adjustment could be made to her working arrangements. Instead, the worker is disciplined without being given the opportunity to explain that the problem arises from a disability. The employer may be in breach of the duty to make reasonable adjustments since it has failed to do all it could reasonably be expected to do to establish if the worker is disabled and placed at a substantial disadvantage (para 6.19 Equality Code).

2. In *Eastern and Coastal Kent PCT v Jocelyn Grey* [2009] IRLR 429, EAT, the claimant, who was dyslexic, applied for a promotion. In her application she indicated that she was disabled but did not ask for any adjustments to be made in the recruitment process. She was shortlisted but experienced disability-related problems at interview, in relation to a presentation she was required to make and in understanding questions put to her. The interview panel had not been told of her disability. She received a lower score than other candidates for both her presentation and her answers to questions and so was not selected. The tribunal considered that the respondent knew of the disability, but did not consider whether it did not know, or could not reasonably be expected to have known, whether the claimant was likely to be at a disadvantage at interview, and remitted the claim to another tribunal to reconsider the case.

3. In *Secretary of State for the Department for Work and Pensions v Alam*, an employee, A, suffered from symptoms of depression which affected his concentration and ability to control his feelings and actions. He was disciplined for leaving work without permission, after asking and being refused twice. The EAT held that there was no foundation for the proposition that A was more likely to be disciplined for leaving early than a non-disabled person. In this case, the employer could not reasonably be expected to have known of the disability or that it would have an effect on A, nor did the findings of fact support the conclusion that the disability would make it difficult for A to ask permission to leave early.

4. In *Wilcox v Birmingham Cab Services Limited*[2011] UKEAT 0293_10_2306 an employee, W, with agoraphobia and travel anxiety was not discriminated against or constructively dismissed when she was not relocated permanently to a position nearer to her home. The EAT found that despite the employer receiving a grievance statement referring to the fact that W was disabled, and a report from her cognitive therapist stating that she suffered from "a great deal of anxiety in relation to travel generally", the employer did not know (constructively or otherwise) that W was disabled until it received a psychiatric report during the course of the tribunal proceedings. There were a number of missed opportunities throughout the employment relationship for the employee to make her condition more clear and had she done so, the EAT's decision may well have been different.

Moreover, an employer cannot claim that he did not know about a job applicant's/worker's disability if a **worker or agent of the employer** (for example, a supervisor, personnel officer or occupational health officer) knew that the job applicant/worker was disabled (para 5.18 Equality Code). This rule does not apply where such information is gained by a person who provides services to workers independently of the employer, for example, an independent counselling service (para 5.19 Equality Code).

If the employer is not sure that the impairment actually exists (for example, because it is not visible or noticeable), he can ask the worker to produce **evidence** that the impairment is a disability. For example, where a worker claims to suffer from a mental illness which requires him to take time off work on a frequent but irregular basis, if his employer is not convinced that the worker has a disability, he can ask for evidence of the mental illness claimed.

Where an employer has on an **ongoing** basis failed, over a number of years, to make any reasonable adjustments to eliminate the disadvantage suffered by a worker in serious breach of his duties, a tribunal may find that the employer is also in **breach** of the **implied term of mutual trust and confidence** (*Greenhof v Barnsley Metropolitan Borough Council* [2006] IRLR 98, EAT;

¶1716). It is therefore possible (if unusual) for a worker to treat his employer's ongoing failure to comply with the duty to make reasonable adjustments as a repudiatory breach, entitling him to resign and bring a claim for unfair constructive dismissal (¶8230).

5540 **Provisions, criteria, and practices** The provisions, criteria, and practices that are covered are not defined in the EqA 2010, but according to the Equality Code, they should be construed widely and could include any formal or informal policies, rules, practices, arrangements, criteria, conditions, prerequisites, qualifications or provisions (para 4.5 Equality Code). This would include provisions, criteria, and practices **made by or on behalf of** the employer **in relation to** determining to whom employment should be offered and any term, condition or arrangement on which employment, promotion, a transfer, training or any other benefit is offered or provided. Therefore the **duty** to make reasonable adjustments **applies**, for example, to selection procedures (including premises used for interviews), job offers, and any other contractual arrangements or working conditions. However, only job-related arrangements are covered (6.33 Equality Code; *Kenny v Hampshire Constabulary* [1998] UKEAT 267_98_1410). Consequently, matters such as providing assistance to and from work are **excluded**.

Arrangements for the continuation or termination of employment and redundancy selection criteria are also covered, as are pre-dismissal breaches of duty which result in the worker's dismissal (*Clark v TDG Ltd t/a Novacold* [1999] IRLR 318, CA). Moreover, even if a worker is subject to disciplinary proceedings in which he faces serious allegations of misconduct, an employer will still be liable to comply with the duty to make reasonable adjustments in respect of that worker (*Beart v HM Prison Service* [2003] IRLR 238, CA).

> MEMO POINTS 1. Employers are under a duty to make reasonable adjustments in respect of their **performance-related pay schemes** to improve the performance of their disabled workers who are subject to a substantial disadvantage under them (para 6.33 Equality Code).
> 2. **Contractual sick pay** which is paid by the employer directly to a worker is also included in the ambit of the duty to make reasonable adjustments (*Nottinghamshire County Council v Meikle* [2004] IRLR 703, CA). This might entail making an alteration to a scheme rule if such an adjustment is reasonable.
> 3. See ¶3443 for details of disability discrimination in respect of **occupational pension schemes**.

5541 Where arrangements include **implied conditions** that a worker will be **fit to work** at all times and will be liable to be dismissed if he is unfit to do the work for which he is employed (*Archibald v Fife Council* [2004] IRLR 651, HL), the duty to make reasonable adjustments for a disabled worker is likely to be triggered. In this case, such implied terms place a worker at a substantial disadvantage in comparison to others in the same employment who are not disabled from doing their work (and who are not liable to be dismissed from their position).

Requiring a disabled job applicant to undergo an **occupational health assessment** does not amount to an arrangement, although the occupational health adviser's assessment of whether the job applicant is or is not fit for the job he has applied for and whether the job is stressful or not will amount to an arrangement. Therefore an employer is under a duty to make reasonable adjustments in respect of the adviser's assessment to prevent the job applicant from being placed at a substantial disadvantage in comparison to non-disabled job applicants (*Paul v National Probation Service* [2004] IRLR 190, EAT). Such adjustments could include evaluating the occupational health report in more depth and consulting the job applicant's own medical adviser. See ¶5542 for more information on pre-employment health enquiries.

Further examples of matters which may amount to a provision, criterion or practice are set out in the example below.

> EXAMPLE
> 1. A person suffering from dyslexia, which amounts to a disability, applies for a job where he would be required to write letters within fairly short deadlines. All applicants are required to sit a test on letter-writing abilities. The job applicant can generally write letters very well but finds it difficult to do so in the stressful situation of the test. The employer's requirement that job applicants pass the test within a set period of time could substantially disadvantage the applicant, compared to non-disabled people who would not find such arrangements stressful. The employer would be expected to allow the applicant more time to complete the test, as this would "remedy" the applicant's

position, would not inconvenience the employer very much and would only briefly delay its decision on an appointment.

2. In *Berry v GB Electronics Ltd* [2001] UKEAT 0882_00_1710, an employer informed a deaf worker, together with seven other workers, that he was dismissed for redundancy. Since the employer did not engage a person who could communicate properly with the deaf worker, he only understood that he was dismissed, but not that others had also lost their jobs or that the dismissal was for redundancy. The employer was found to have breached the duty to make reasonable adjustments (for example, the appointment of an interpreter versed in sign language). The discrimination was in the arrangements made for, and the manner of, dismissal.

3. A call centre's normal practice is to employ supervisors only on a full-time basis. A woman with sickle cell anaemia applies for the position of supervisor but because of the pain and fatigue relating to her condition she asks to do the job part-time. The call centre agrees and the offer of work on a part-time basis will amount to a reasonable adjustment to the employer's normal working practice.

5542 It is unlawful for employers to ask applicants questions about any disability or their health (including about previous sickness absence) **during the recruitment process**, up to the point where they have either been offered a job or included in a pool of successful candidates who will be offered a job once there is a vacancy. Health-related questions are, however, permitted in the following limited circumstances (s 60(6) EqA 2010):
– during recruitment to establish whether reasonable adjustments are required to any methods used to assess a person's suitability for a job;
– to establish whether the applicant is able to carry out a function that is intrinsic to the job they have applied for;
– to monitor diversity;
– to take positive action in respect of disabled people, such as implementing a guaranteed interview scheme. In this case, the employer should make it clear that this is the reason for the question;
– where it is a requirement that a job holder has a particular disability, to establish the applicant had that disability; or
– to vet applicants for the purposes of national security.

MEMO POINTS When asking questions to establish whether an applicant can perform an essential part of a job the employer must first take into account any reasonable adjustments which could be made.

Physical features Physical features are **defined as** any permanent or temporary (s 20(1) EqA 2010): **5545**
– feature arising from the design or construction of a building on the premises;
– feature on the premises of any approach to, exit from or access to such a building;
– fixtures, fittings, furnishings, furniture, equipment or materials in or on the premises; or
– other physical element or quality of any land comprised on the premises.

Examples of physical features include (para 6.12 Equality Code):
– steps;
– stairways, lifts and escalators;
– kerbs;
– exterior surfaces and paving;
– parking areas;
– building entrances and exits (including emergency escape routes);
– internal and external doors;
– gates;
– toilet and washing facilities;
– lighting and ventilation;
– floor coverings;
– signs;
– furniture; and
– temporary or movable items.

> EXAMPLE Clear glass doors at the end of a corridor in a particular workplace present a hazard for a visually impaired worker. This is a substantial disadvantage caused by the physical features of the workplace (para 6.12 Equality Code).

There may be occasions where employers **cannot**, **or** are **not required to**, **make changes** to physical features (for example, because the problem lies in premises which the employer does not occupy, such as clients' premises, or because it is not possible to change the premises). In such cases, employers still need to consider whether their work arrangements can be adapted (for example, whether the worker can be allocated other clients or be relocated to another office).

5546 Where an employer **occupies premises under a lease** which does not permit him to make alterations to the premises and he is under a duty to make reasonable adjustments, he must apply to the lessor in writing for consent to make the alteration. The lease will have effect as if it allows the occupier to make alterations with the written consent of the lessor and that the lessor will not withhold consent unreasonably. However, the lessor may attach reasonable conditions to the consent, for example that the occupier repays the lessor's costs in giving the consent and that on expiry of the lease the employer must reinstate the premises to their pre-altered state (Sch 21 EqA 2010). Further details as to the revised procedure for granting consent and the circumstances in which the lessor can reasonably withhold consent can be found in the EqA 2010 (Disability) Regulations (SI 2010/2128).

5547 **Auxiliary aids** The obligation to provide an auxiliary aid as a reasonable adjustment is a new introduction under the EqA 2010. The duty arises when, if the auxiliary aid were not provided, a worker would be put at a substantial disadvantage, in comparison with non-disabled workers (s 20(5) EqA 2010). The term auxiliary aid also includes auxiliary services (s 20(11) EqA 2010). Examples of auxiliary aids include an adapted keyboard or text to speech software, and an auxiliary service would include providing a support worker or sign language interpreter (para 6.13 Equality Code).

5548 **Comparison** There is no need to identify a comparator or group whose circumstances are the same, or nearly the same, as those of the disabled person (para 6.16 Equality Code). This represents a continuation of the position under the predecessor legislation where the Court of Appeal held that the **correct comparator**(s) will be readily identified by reference to the disadvantage caused by the arrangements concerned (*Smith v Churchills Stairlifts plc* [2006] IRLR 41, CA). The comparison should therefore not be made with non-disabled persons generally. In many cases the facts will speak for themselves and the identity of the non-disabled comparators who were not disadvantaged by the arrangements concerned will be clearly discernible from the provision, criterion or practice in question and may not need to be identified (*Fareham College Corporation v Walters* [2009] IRLR 991, EAT).

> EXAMPLE In *Smith v Churchills Stairlifts plc*, the claimant, a disabled person with a condition which precluded him from lifting and carrying heavy objects, had been offered a place on a training course to join the employer's sales force selling radiator cabinets. His place was subsequently withdrawn when the employer decided that all its salesmen would be required to carry a full-sized specimen radiator cabinet and that the claimant would not have been able to do so. The Court of Appeal held that the relevant arrangements in this case were the requirement to carry a full-sized radiator cabinet as well as the fact that the offer of a place on the training course had been subject to the implied condition that the claimant was, or was believed to be, able to carry such a full-sized cabinet and that such an offer was liable to be withdrawn if he was, or was believed to be, unable to carry such a cabinet. Consequently, in respect of the arrangement regarding being able to carry a full-sized cabinet, the correct comparators were those successful applicants who were subject to the same requirement but who were not disadvantaged by it as they had not been rejected. In respect of the arrangement regarding the liability of the offer of a place on the training course being withdrawn, the correct comparators were those persons who had been admitted on to the course.

5549 **Substantial disadvantage** Substantial disadvantages are **those which are** not minor or trivial (s 212(1) EqA 2010). The important question is not whether a provision, criterion, practice, physical feature or lack of auxiliary aid is capable of causing a substantial disadvantage to a disabled person but that it in fact does have this effect on him (or would do if he were doing the job at the time). For example, a worker who is confined to a wheelchair finds it impossible to get through a particular doorway or if there are clear glass doors at the end of a corridor these may present a workplace hazard for a worker with impaired vision. In the example of the worker who is confined to a wheelchair, if there is a reasonably easy alternative route to the same destination, the employer is unlikely to be required to widen the particular doorway to enable passage by the worker.

Redundancy will only be considered a substantial disadvantage where it is on grounds of disability (*NTL v Difolco* [2006] EWCA Civ 1508). In this case, a manager suffered an accident at work and became disabled. While off sick, a replacement was promoted to her post. The Court of Appeal held that the manager had not been made redundant for reason of disability, but because the replacement scored more highly in a selection test. As the manager had suffered no discrimination, there was no substantial disadvantage. The duty to make reasonable adjustments never arose.

Adjustments

The following is a **non-exhaustive list of examples** of the range of adjustments that may need to be considered depending on the particular disadvantages of the disabled worker in question (whilst some of the examples come from sources that are no longer in force in relation to the EqA 2010, they still offer valuable guidance):

– **adjustments to premises**. For example, widening a doorway, providing a ramp or moving furniture for a wheelchair user, relocating light switches, door handles or shelves for someone who has difficulty in reaching, or providing appropriate contrast in décor to help the safe mobility of a visually impaired person;

– **reallocating duties** to another person. For example, an employer might reallocate minor or subsidiary duties to another worker if a disabled person has difficulty doing them. A situation in which this might arise is where a disabled worker suffers from vertigo and his job occasionally involves going on to an open roof of a building;

– **transferring to fill an existing vacancy**. When a worker becomes disabled or his impairment worsens so that he cannot continue in his current job, and there is no reasonable adjustment that would enable him to do so, the worker should be considered for suitable vacancies. Reasonable retraining should also be provided. Furthermore, depending on all the facts of the case and, in particular, what is reasonable, a reasonable adjustment might be to transfer a worker to a job at a slightly higher grade (in addition to a position at the same or lower grade) and this would entail actually appointing the worker to the job as opposed to simply allowing him to apply for such a position (*Archibald v Fife Council* [2004] IRLR 651, HL). In reaching its decision in this case, the House of Lords (now called the Supreme Court) held that such a reasonable adjustment could therefore entail treating a disabled worker more favourably than non-disabled workers. Employers are not, however, required to redeploy workers if there are no vacancies or if a particular transfer will only have limited positive benefit for the worker;

– **altering working hours or training**. Flexibility in hours, the provision of additional breaks or permitting the disabled person to work part-time may be appropriate to accommodate the needs of a disabled person;

– **assigning to a different place of work or training**. It may be reasonable, for example, to transfer a person with a hearing impairment from an open-plan office to a more acoustically suitable environment, or to move a wheelchair user from a third floor office to a ground floor office;

– **allowing time off for rehabilitation, assessment or treatment**. An employer should consider allowing a disabled person extra time off during working or training hours for the purposes of rehabilitation, assessment or treatment;

– **appropriate training or mentoring** (whether for the disabled person or any other person). This may be training on equipment especially designed for the disabled person or training which is provided to all workers but which has to be adapted because of the disability. The Court of Appeal has allowed a decision of disability discrimination to stand even though the tribunal, which had held that the employer had failed to make reasonable adjustments by

failing to retrain the worker, had failed to specify precisely what training the employer should have provided. The failure to retrain the worker at all meant that it was not necessary to be more specific (*Electronic Data Systems Ltd v Travis* [2004] EWCA Civ 1256);
- **acquiring or modifying equipment**. For example, an employer may need to provide special equipment such as an adapted keyboard to a worker affected by RSI or an adapted telephone for a worker with a hearing impairment. An employer is not required to provide or modify equipment for personal purposes unconnected with work;
- **modifying instructions or reference manuals**. An employer may be required to provide instructions and manuals in braille, on audio tape or orally with individual demonstration;
- **modifying procedures for testing or assessment**. An example would be allowing a job applicant with restricted manual dexterity to give oral instead of written responses in a test;
- **providing a reader or interpreter**. An employer may be required to provide a person with a visual impairment with a reader at particular times during the working day, for example to read post; and/or
- **providing supervision or other support**. It could be appropriate for an employer to provide a worker whose disability leads to uncertainty or lack of confidence with help from a colleague.

5551 Sometimes it may be necessary to take a **combination** of steps. The above list is by no means exhaustive (*Chief Constable of South Yorkshire Police v Jelic* [2010] UKEAT 0491_09_2904). **Other steps** an employer might need to take include (para 6.33 Equality Code):
- conducting a **proper assessment** of what reasonable adjustments may be required;
- permitting the disabled person to undertake **flexible working** or allowing him to take a period of **disability leave**;
- participating in **supported employment schemes**. For example, a worker might want to make private phone calls during the working day to a support worker at a scheme;
- **employing a support worker** to assist the worker. For example, where an adviser with a visual impairment is sometimes required to make home visits, the employer might employ a support worker to assist him on these visits;
- **modifying disciplinary or grievance procedures**. For example, this might include allowing a disabled worker to be accompanied by a companion who is a friend (as opposed to a colleague) to act as an advocate at a grievance meeting or, in the case of a deaf worker, allowing a BSL interpreter to attend;
- **adjusting redundancy selection criteria**. For example, an employer might discount any disability-related absence when taking absences into account as a criterion for redundancy selection, so that a worker with an autoimmune disease who has taken several short periods of absence during the year due to his condition is not disadvantaged.

> EXAMPLE In *Chief Constable of South Yorkshire Police v Jelic*, the EAT considered the scope of the employer's duty to make reasonable adjustments where an employee is disabled. A police officer suffering from chronic anxiety syndrome was medically retired from the force after a period working in a job where he did not have face-to-face contact with the public. When advice was received that he was unlikely to recover enough to return to front-line police work, the employer began a performance management procedure and retired him without considering other options. The EAT accepted his argument that it would have been a reasonable adjustment to move him into a role then held by another officer, who would have to be redeployed elsewhere. Although the guidance in the legislation did not mention this as an option, that guidance was not exhaustive and what is a reasonable adjustment will depend on all the circumstances. For example in this case, the police was a disciplined service and even if the other officer had objected he could have been instructed to swap jobs, an instruction with which he would have to comply. Another adjustment involving medically retiring the officer and then re-employing him in another role (a civilian support staff role) would also have been reasonable.

5552 **Whether reasonable to make** Where the duty has arisen, the employer must take such steps as are reasonable in order to avoid the disadvantage, or in the case of an auxiliary aid, to provide the auxiliary aid (s 20(3), (4) and (5) EqA 2010).

Whether a particular adjustment is reasonable will be **determined objectively**, i.e. on the basis of what a reasonable employer should have done. In making this evaluation tribunals may take account of a **number of factors**, in particular (para 6.29 Equality Code):
– the **effectiveness** of the step in preventing a disadvantage. It is unlikely to be reasonable for an employer to have to make an adjustment involving little benefit to the disabled person (*Hay v Surrey County Council* [2007] EWCA Civ 93). The employer should consider consulting the worker on the proposed adjustment as he is most likely to know if it will be effective;
– the **practicability** of the step. It is more likely to be reasonable for an employer to take a step which is easy than one which is difficult, though in some circumstances it may be reasonable to have to take a step even though it is difficult. The amount of warning regarding the disability which the employer receives may be relevant. If, for example, a job applicant does not tell a prospective employer about his disability until the interview, this may cause adjustments that would otherwise be manageable to become impracticable;
– the **financial and other costs** of the adjustment and the **extent of any disruption**. An adjustment is likely to be regarded as reasonable if the cost of it is insignificant and the step entailed is not disruptive. However, even an adjustment that has a significant cost associated with it might still be cost-effective in overall terms and therefore be reasonable to make (para 6.25 Equality Code). Moreover, the greater the **employer's financial or other resources**, the more likely it is that it will be reasonable for the employer to make a more costly adjustment. For larger employers, it is good practice to dedicate a specific budget for reasonable adjustments. Further, if **financial assistance** is available, for example, from a government programme or voluntary body, it may be reasonable for an employer to make an adjustment where that adjustment would have been too costly without that assistance. In any event, as a matter of good practice, employers should first consider the effectiveness and practicability of a particular adjustment before assessing the financial aspect;
– the value of the worker's **experience and expertise** to the employer will also be relevant. Assessing this will involve consideration of the amount invested in the worker, his length of service and his expected future service, his level of skill and knowledge, the quality of the worker's relationships with clients, and the level of the worker's pay; and
– the **nature of the employer's activities** and the **size of undertaking**. The larger the number of staff employed by the employer, the more likely it is that it will be reasonable for the employer to make certain adjustments, for example, reallocating some of a disabled worker's duties or transferring him to an existing vacancy.

EXAMPLE
1. In *Arthur v Northern Ireland Housing Executive* [2007] NICA 25, the Court of Appeal considered the case of a person with mild to moderate dyslexia who applied for a management trainee post with a housing executive. Psychometric tests were set to determine who would be interviewed and the candidate was allowed 20% extra time. The candidate scored poorly and was not invited to interview. He claimed that the result was discriminatory and in breach of the executive's disability code of practice, which provided that "testing will only be applied to disabled candidates where appropriate". The Court held that despite the provisions of the employer's code, the employer's legal duty was only to put the candidate on an equal footing with other non-disabled candidates and this had been done.
2. In *Garrett v Lidl Ltd* [2009] UKEAT 0541_08_1612, a disabled employee made complaints that her employer had failed to make reasonable adjustments to her working conditions. Her disability was caused by fibromyalgia syndrome, which caused pain, fatigue and stiffness. She worked as a manager in the employer's store in Woolwich under a contract which included a mobility clause. Working practices there caused her a number of problems; for example she was unable to take the breaks she needed, and her duties included tasks such as working on the tills which caused her difficulties. These problems did not arise at larger stores with more staff. The employer moved her to a larger store where the adjustments she had requested were made, and her salary was left out of account in calculating productivity. She argued that she should have stayed at the smaller store which was more convenient for her, with the same adjustment made in respect of her salary. The EAT held that relocating the employee to the larger store instead was a reasonable adjustment by the employer, taking into account the facts that she had previously worked at different locations and that there was a mobility clause in her contract.
3. In *Cordell v Foreign and Commonwealth Office* [2011] UKEAT 0016_11_0510, a profoundly deaf employee argued that her employer (the FCO) should have made the reasonable adjustment of paying for lipspeaker support in order that she could take up a post in Kazakhstan. The FCO had refused to

provide this support principally on the ground of cost but also because there was some doubt as to whether continuity of lipspeaker support could be guaranteed in Kazakhstan. The employee brought claims for both direct disability discrimination and a failure to make reasonable adjustments, but was unsuccessful in both claims. For her unsuccessful reasonable adjustments claim, the employee relied heavily on the fact that the FCO would have to pay similar sums to staff with large numbers of children for their school education whilst on assignments abroad, and that this similarity in expenditure made the lipspeaker support a reasonable adjustment. The EAT held that whilst this was a relevant consideration, it was not the only significant factor and could not be used to establish conclusively that the requested adjustment was reasonable, particularly given the difficulty in measuring the value of one type of expenditure over another. There were other relevant factors, such as the fact that there was no general FCO policy to address cases where financial assistance was required in order to take up a post (for example, for individuals who were unable to take a post overseas because their spouse/partner would have to give up a well-paid job in the UK). The EAT held that the original tribunal had not ignored any relevant factors and had been perfectly entitled to consider this case in the context of the FCO's total budget and their budget for reasonable adjustments (of which the lipspeakers would have taken up half across the entire FCO).

4. In *Salford NHS Primary Care Trust v Smith* [2011] UKEAT 0507_10_2608, the EAT held that where a disabled claimant, S, was signed off by her GP (and was later deemed to be "unfit for work of any kind" by an occupational health physician), her employer was not required to either make suggestions as to work that S may be able to undertake (and then ask S's doctor to review the suggestions) or to permit a career break. Such things were not reasonable adjustments that were required to be made by the employer to be able to defend a disability discrimination claim. Matters such as consultations, trials and exploratory investigations do not qualify as reasonable adjustments in themselves and a career break being used in this fashion would be highly irregular and would in no way be a substitute for long-term sick leave. S's inability to comply with the employer's previous suggestions (such as the exploration of re-training or keeping in touch with fellow employees), coupled with the medical reports stating that she was unfit for work of any kind, and the fact that she had failed to attend either of the two meetings put forward by her employer in order to discuss her situation, meant that it was reasonable for her employer to conclude that she was incapable of carrying out any role, regardless of the number of hours required.

5554 **Other factors** include the effect which any adjustment would have on other workers, adjustments already made for other disabled workers and the extent to which the disabled worker co-operates with the employer's proposed adjustment. So, for example, an employer who had already taken steps which satisfied the duty to make reasonable adjustments was not required to pursue the option of another adjustment (in this case a phased return), particularly as the worker did not have an expected return date (*Home Office v Collins* [2005] EWCA Civ 598).

In relation to **private households**, factors to be taken into account in determining the reasonableness of an adjustment include, in particular, the extent to which making the adjustment would disrupt that household or disturb any resident of the household.

5555 Where a worker **proposes certain adjustments**, the employer is required to consider them. Indeed, when assessing whether an employer has met his duty of reasonable adjustments, tribunals will consider the extent to which all the adjustments requested by a worker might have alleviated his symptoms and assisted him at work (*Fu v London Borough of Camden* [2001] IRLR 186, EAT). If a particular adjustment is considered to be unreasonable an employer ought to consider whether he can make other, reasonable, adjustments.

5556 A disabled person may not be **required to contribute** to the cost of an adjustment (s 20(7) EqA 2010). However, a disabled worker may offer to provide certain equipment to assist the performance of his work. If this is the case, it may be reasonable for the employer to accept the offer as well as to take additional steps to allow the disabled person to use the equipment.

EXAMPLE A disabled person applies for a job which involves the use of a company car for business travel. The worker has an adapted car of her own which she is willing to use on business. In these circumstances, it may be reasonable for the employer to allow this and to pay the worker a reasonable car allowance (even though it may not have been reasonable for the employer to provide an adapted company car or to pay an allowance to cover alternative travel arrangements).

5557 In circumstances where a reasonable adjustment requires the **co-operation of other workers** (for example, where some duties are reallocated), the employer must ensure that such co-operation takes place (para 6.35 Equality Code). Lack of co-operation from co-workers is unlikely to be a defence to a claim of failure to make reasonable adjustments unless the employer can show that he took steps to address the unco-operative behaviour. There may also be issues of **confidentiality** as other workers, supervisors, personnel officers etc may have to be informed of the adjustment. In such cases the employer should keep the reason for making the adjustment confidential if he would not have made a similar disclosure about a non-disabled worker for an equally legitimate management purpose.

No justification

5560 It is not possible for an employer to objectively justify a failure to comply with the duty to make reasonable adjustments. Instead, employers are expected to focus on what adjustments are necessary and whether it is reasonable to make such adjustments.

e. Victimisation

5565 It is **not necessary** for a person to have (or to have had) a disability to be able to claim victimisation, but where the person who suffers the less favourable treatment has a disability, that **disability will be disregarded** for the purposes of comparing him/her to others whose circumstances are the same as his/hers. A common situation in which a claim for victimisation under the disability discrimination provisions is brought is when a non-disabled worker has given evidence in support of an employment tribunal claim brought by a disabled colleague.

5566 Victimisation **occurs** when a worker is subjected to less favourable treatment than others whose circumstances are the same as his/hers because he/she has done one or more of the following protected acts under the EqA 2010:
– brought proceedings against his/her employer or any other worker (¶5350);
– given evidence or information in connection with proceedings brought by another person under the EqA 2010;
– taken any other action for the purposes of or in connection with the EqA 2010; or
– made any allegation (whether or not express) against his/her employer or any other worker of a contravention of the EqA 2010.
This extends to a **suspicion** by the employer that the worker intends to do any of these things.

EXAMPLE A disabled worker complains of discrimination, having been refused a promotion at work. His colleague gives evidence at the tribunal hearing in support of his claim. Subsequently, the colleague is made redundant as a result of this. This less favourable treatment will amount to victimisation (para 9.3 Equality Code).

MEMO POINTS As originally enacted, the EqA 2010 only provided protection against victimisation for acts which contravened that legislation. The provision was amended by the EqA 2010 (Commencement No. 4, Savings, Consequential, Transitional, Transitory and Incidental Provisions and Revocation Order 2010 (SI 2010/2317)) to cover victimisation for protected acts under the predecessor legislation.

5567 However, there will be **no protection** for a worker if the allegation made by him, or evidence or information given by him was **false** and not made (or given) in good faith (s 27(3) EqA 2010).

5568 The claimant must show that he has been subjected to a detriment **because** he has done a protected act, or the employer believes that he has done so.

5569 **No comparator** is required.

f. Harassment

5570 Harassment is a distinct form of disability discrimination (s 26(1) EqA 2010).

Harassment **occurs** where an employer, for a reason which relates to a disability, subjects a person to unwanted conduct which has the purpose or effect of (s 26 EqA 2010):
– violating the person's dignity; or
– creating an intimidating, hostile, degrading, humiliating or offensive environment for him.

> EXAMPLE Workers make offensive remarks to a co-worker about his child's severe disfigurement. This is harassment related to disability (para 7.10 Equality Code).

5571 The courts will take into account what the purpose of the alleged behaviour was, i.e. whether it was **intentional**. If the purpose of the behaviour was to cause one of the effects listed above (i.e. to violate a person's dignity or to create an intimidating, hostile, degrading or offensive environment), unlawful harassment will have occurred regardless of whether the complainant did actually experience the intended effect. If there was no intention to cause one of the relevant effects, unlawful harassment will still have occurred if the complainant has suffered from one of the effects (paras 7.16–17 Equality Code). In reaching a decision the tribunal must consider whether, having regard to all the circumstances, including in particular the perception of the disabled person, the conduct should reasonably be considered as having that effect (s 26(4) EqA 2010).

Consequently, the **test** is neither entirely objective nor subjective, since some account needs to be taken of the alleged victim's perception. However, it does mean that a complainant who **unreasonably takes offence** at an innocent comment would probably not be considered to have been harassed, although if the conduct was repeated after the complainant made his feelings known, then the repeat conduct could well constitute unlawful harassment.

D. Age

5600 Age discrimination is unlawful (EqA 2010). This has a considerable impact on many employment policies and practices, including recruitment and other pre-employment issues, occupational pension schemes, retirement ages, redundancy and the law regarding unfair dismissal. Where the age discrimination provisions impact on these other areas of employment law and practice, this is discussed under the relevant subject topics. See ¶¶543, 3444, 8200, 8390, 8411, 8422, 8575, 8991, and 9005 respectively.

> MEMO POINTS Since 1 October 2012, age discrimination has been banned in the **provision of goods and services** to those over the age of 18. Service providers are still able to provide different services to different age groups if they can objectively justify the different treatment (¶¶5614+), establish a need for positive action (¶5623), or establish that one of the general exceptions or one of a number of specific exceptions applies. For more information, the Government Equalities Office has a number of specific guides for small businesses, private clubs and associations as well as a general overview for service providers which can be found at flmemo.co.uk/em5600.

5601 As with most of the protected characteristics, the EqA 2010 **covers** direct and indirect discrimination (¶5605), victimisation (¶5640) and harassment (¶5645) on the grounds of age.

In certain circumstances, an employer will be able to **justify** indirect and even direct age discrimination if he can demonstrate that the discriminatory treatment amounts to a proportionate means of achieving a legitimate aim. This is not the case under most of the other strands of anti-discrimination legislation, under which direct discrimination can usually only be justified on narrow grounds (such as positive action or where there is an occupational requirement (¶¶5280, 5397)).

1. Direct and indirect

Both direct and indirect age discrimination are unlawful though there are certain circumstances in which an employer may be able to **justify** such discrimination. In addition, as noted above in relation to most other strands of anti-discrimination legislation, direct age discrimination may also be lawful where **positive action** or **occupational requirements** apply. Moreover, there are a number of **specific exemptions** where age-based requirements will be justified.

a. Unlawful

Direct age discrimination occurs where an employer (A) treats a person (B) less favourably than he treats or would treat others on the grounds of that person's actual or apparent age (s 13 EqA 2010).

Such treatment will **not** amount to direct age **discrimination if** the employer can demonstrate that it is a proportionate means of achieving a legitimate aim, i.e. if the disadvantage suffered is proportionately balanced against the needs of the employer in the successful running of his business (s 13(2) EqA 2010; ¶¶5615+).

> EXAMPLE
> **Examples relating to recruitment**
> 1. In *Canadian Imperial Bank of Commerce v A Beck* [2010] UKEAT 0141_10_2408, B, an employee in his early 40s, was made redundant from his post as head of marketing by a bank, C. After B was made redundant, C sought to recruit a new marketing team and in the person specification for a post for which B was otherwise qualified required that the person should be "younger". B brought various claims, including age discrimination. The EAT upheld the employment tribunal decision that this amounted to age discrimination and commented that the use of the word "younger" in the person specification was clearly discriminatory and shifted the burden of proof to C to show that its actions had not been discriminatory.
> 2. In *Wilkinson v Springwell Engineering Company Ltd*, ET case 2507420/07, the employer dismissed their 18 year old employee and told her that "she was too young for the job" and they "needed someone older with more experience". The tribunal held that the former administrative assistant had been discriminated against on grounds of age and found that the employer had made a stereotypical assumption about experience and capability based on age.
> 3. During an interview, A, a job applicant, tells her prospective employer that she obtained her professional qualification 30 years ago. Because of her age, the employer decides not to offer her the job, despite the fact that she has all the skills and competencies required for the position. This will amount to direct discrimination.
> 4. B applies for a position as a sales assistant in a shop which markets its clothes at young people under 30. The retailer rejects B because she is over 40 and it feels she does not represent its target market. Again, this will amount to direct discrimination.
>
> **Example relating to dismissal**
> In *London Borough of Tower Hamlets v Wooster* [2009] UKEAT 0441_08_1009, an employee seconded by a council to a social landlord was made redundant when the secondment ended. At the time he was dismissed he was just under the age at which he would be entitled to take his full local authority pension. The EAT found that, while it would have been beyond the council's powers to extend the employee's service in order to ensure he could take early retirement, the evidence was that the reason why the council had not made efforts to redeploy the claimant was to avoid the cost of his early retirement pension, which constituted direct age discrimination.

Indirect age discrimination occurs when an employer applies a policy, provision, criterion or working practice (PCP) which, although on the face of it is neutral and applicable equally to all workers, in fact inadvertently puts a certain group of workers at a disadvantage in comparison to other workers (s 19 EqA 2010). It is irrelevant whether or not the alleged discrimination is intentional.

Such an application of a PCP will **not** amount to indirect age **discrimination if** the employer can demonstrate that it is a proportionate means of achieving a legitimate aim, i.e. if the disadvantage suffered is proportionately balanced against the needs of the employer in the successful running of his business (s 19(2) EqA 2010; ¶¶5615+).

It is irrelevant **whether or not** the alleged discrimination is **intentional**.

EXAMPLE

Examples relating to recruitment
1. An employer advertises a position, stating that a minimum of 7-10 years' experience is required. Such a requirement will indirectly discriminate against younger workers since a considerably larger number of younger workers than older workers will be unable to meet this criterion.
2. A job advert specifies that an employer is looking for university graduates to fill a position, for which a professional qualification is required. Since many more people attend university today than was the case 25 years ago, it is likely that there are considerably fewer older applicants who can meet this criterion than younger applicants, even though they may well hold the requisite professional qualification. Unless the employer can justify this criterion, this may be found to amount to unlawful indirect age discrimination.

Examples relating to dismissal
1. In *Homer v Chief Constable of West Yorkshire Police* [2012] UKSC 15, H, was employed as a legal adviser by a police force. At the time he was appointed, the force required legal advisers to have either a law degree or "exceptional experience/skills in criminal law". H had formerly been a police inspector for 30 years and thus satisfied the second requirement. In 2005, 10 years after his appointment, the force increased pay levels for legal advisers and introduced a career structure based on three thresholds linked to salary increments. The changes were introduced because the force had identified a failure to pay market rates and a lack of career structure as being the main obstacles to recruitment and retention of legal advisers. However, legal advisers needed a degree level qualification to be categorised as level three under the new career structure. Due to the length of the degree course, the earliest H could obtain a degree was over a year after he would reach the force's compulsory retirement age of 65. After his internal appeal to be placed on level three was rejected, he brought an indirect age discrimination claim. Both the EAT and Court of Appeal concluded that there had been no indirect discrimination; the employee's impending retirement, not his age, was the barrier to his promotion. The Supreme Court, however, allowed the appeal and held that "a requirement which works to the comparative disadvantage of a person approaching compulsory retirement age is indirectly discriminatory on grounds of age". It is incorrect to compare someone approaching compulsory retirement with someone choosing to leave the workplace for other reasons because their circumstances are materially different. The requirement to hold a degree is unlawful indirect age discrimination unless it can be justified.
2. In *Martin v SS Photay and Associates*, ET case 1100242/07, a worker was dismissed ostensibly on health grounds from her post as a cleaner at a dental surgery. The dismissal took place just two days after her 70th birthday, which she had invited work colleagues to celebrate. The employer had obtained no medical evidence to substantiate its health fears and there appeared to be no genuine need for the dismissal. The tribunal held that the worker had been treated less favourably on grounds of her age.

MEMO POINTS 1. A person will be able to bring a claim for direct age discrimination based on less favourable treatment on the grounds of his **perceived age**, whether or not this is in fact his actual age. It is not necessary for an individual to disclose his age in order to bring such a claim and there will be no defence for an employer who claims that the claimant is in fact older or younger than he appeared to be.
2. **References to age group** mean a group of persons defined by reference to a particular age or a range of ages. It is not necessary for them to all be of the same age.

5611 For a discussion as to the **scope** of the relevant legislation (i.e. who is protected in terms of the type of worker, geographical scope and time periods), see ¶¶5215+. **Employers' liabilities** for discriminatory acts, together with those of their workers and agents, as well as individual **workers' liability** for discrimination, are covered at ¶¶5225+.

In the context of the legislation, **dismissal includes** the expiry (without renewal) of a fixed-term contract and constructive dismissal (s 39(7) and (8) EqA 2010).

b. Lawful

5614 In certain circumstances, either direct or indirect age discrimination may be lawful, notably where:
– an employer can justify it as a proportionate means of achieving a legitimate aim;
– there is an occupational requirement (OR) that a person must be of a certain age;

– the employer wishes to undertake positive action measures where he can demonstrate that workers of a particular age or age group are at a career disadvantage or are under-represented in the organisation;
– the discrimination is covered by one of the specific exemptions or exceptions outlined in the EqA 2010; or
– a job applicant is already over (or within 6 months of reaching) the employer's normal retirement age (NRA) at the date of the application. However, note that any NRA must be objectively justified as a proportionate means of achieving a legitimate aim (see below).

Justification

5615 Both direct and indirect age discrimination may be justified and lawful **if an employer can demonstrate** that the less favourable treatment, or provision, criterion or practice, amounts to a proportionate means of achieving a legitimate aim (ss 13(2) and 19(2)(d) EqA 2010).

EXAMPLE In *ABN Amro Management Services Ltd and anor v Hogben* [2009] UKEAT 0266_09_0111, a 42 year old manager, H, made an age discrimination claim after he was selected for redundancy, and not offered an alternative post, following a company takeover. H also complained that the employer did not pay a proportion of a discretionary bonus as part of his termination payment. Managers at a more senior level who were made redundant earlier had been given their bonuses but the employer changed its approach when the next layer of management, which included H, was considered for redundancy, and decided to pay bonuses only in exceptional circumstances. H's final claim was that employees with shorter service received disproportionately high contractual redundancy payments under a scheme where employees were entitled to a month's pay for each year of service with a minimum entitlement of 9 months' pay regardless of length of service. The EAT decided that:
– the claims relating to selection for redundancy and non-selection for alternative employment should not be allowed to proceed, because it was clear that H was in a similar age bracket to the employees who were kept on;
– the claim relating to bonus was also too weak to proceed. H argued that there was a disproportionate impact on his age group because the more senior managers who had been made redundant earlier were likely to have been older. This also failed because the decision to dismiss senior managers first was a legitimate approach, and the change in practice relating to bonuses was unrelated to age; and
– the only claim which could be allowed to go forward to a full hearing concerned the contractual redundancy payments, where the employer would be required to show that the weighting in the scheme was justified.

MEMO POINTS With regard to justification, the Directive uses the terms "**proportionate**" and "**appropriate and necessary**" interchangeably, although the EqA 2010 uses the term "proportionate" throughout for the sake of consistency.

5616 A legitimate aim must relate to a genuine need of the employer and cannot be related to age discrimination itself. In its guidance for employers, Acas suggests that a **legitimate aim** might include:
– economic factors such as business needs and efficiency;
– the health, welfare and safety of the individual concerned (including the protection of young people or older workers); or
– the particular training requirements of the job.

While the **avoidance of cost** is not, in itself, a legitimate aim, it can be one factor provided there are other factors; a principle known as the "cost-plus" approach (*Woodcock v Cumbria Primary Care Trust* [2012] EWCA Civ 330; *Cross and ors v British Airways Plc* [2005] UKEAT 0572_04_2305).

EXAMPLE **Examples of legitimate aims**
1. In *MacCulloch v ICI* [2008] IRLR 846, EAT, a contractual redundancy scheme directly discriminated in favour of older workers. The tribunal identified that the scheme had legitimate aims to reward loyalty, protect those more vulnerable in the labour market and to encourage older workers to leave and allow the recruitment of younger workers. However, the tribunal failed to give consideration to the issue of whether the means was proportionate and the case was sent back to the same tribunal to consider that issue.
2. In *Loxley v BAE Systems* [2008] IRLR 853, EAT, a contractual redundancy scheme discriminated against older workers by excluding workers over 60 who were entitled to take their pension under the

employer's contributory scheme. The EAT held that while it might be relevant to take into account the fact that employees were entitled to take a pension, the tribunal had not adequately analysed whether the exclusion of employees of pensionable age from the redundancy scheme was proportionate and the case was sent back to a different tribunal to consider that issue.

3. In *Rolls Royce plc v Unite the Union* [2010] ICR 1, CA, length of service was used as a criterion for redundancy selection in a collective agreement. The Court of Appeal upheld the High Court's decision that use of a matrix giving weight to long service amounted to a benefit to long-serving employees, but that it was a proportionate means of achieving a legitimate aim and was justified. The legitimate aims identified were rewarding loyalty and experience and protecting older members of the workforce at a time when it might be hard to find new employment.

4. In *Pulham and ors v London Borough of Barking and Dagenham* [2010] IRLR 184, EAT, a council operated a pay protection scheme which preserved a system of increments for employees with 25 years' or more service who were over the age of 55. An employee made a complaint of age discrimination because she was excluded from the scheme. She had completed 25 years' service but was not yet 55. The employer had already identified the scheme as discriminatory and negotiated a collective agreement under which existing beneficiaries would continue to receive increments but the scheme would be closed to new entrants, to avoid the expense of having to allow all long-serving employees, irrespective of age, into the scheme. The EAT held that, while it was possible to justify continuing a pay differential for a period, in this particular case the tribunal dealing with the case had placed too much reliance on the fact that it had been continued under a negotiated agreement, and had also mistakenly treated the fact that the employer had no funds to allocate to rectify the discrimination as a justification. The case was therefore returned to a new tribunal to reconsider whether, on the evidence, the discrimination was justified.

5. In *Woodcock v Cumbria Primary Care Trust*, the Court of Appeal considered whether the employer was justified in short cutting a redundancy process, in order to avoid an imminent pension liability. The case involved the chief executive of a Primary Care Trust (PCT), W. It was decided that several PCTs would merge. The chief executives of the various PCTs had to apply for new chief executive roles and redeployment support was given. Their employment was guaranteed until summer 2007 and there was an expectation that notice would be given so that those who were unsuccessful in securing new roles could be made redundant at that time. W's applications for other roles were unsuccessful and he was informed, in September 2006, that he was formally at risk of redundancy and that he would be given 12 months' contractual notice of dismissal. It appeared that alternative employment would be found and so the giving of that notice was delayed. However, by April 2007, when it was clear that no alternative employment could be found, he was invited to a meeting to start the redundancy process. The earliest mutually convenient date they could agree upon was in early June 2007. The PCT believed that he was trying to delay so that his employment would end after his 50th birthday in mid-June 2008, when he would become entitled to an enhanced pension, at an additional cost of £500,000 – £1 million. Therefore, he was given 12 months' notice that, in the absence of alternative employment, he would be made redundant on 22 May 2008. This meant that the formal redundancy consultation meeting took place just under a fortnight after he had been given notice. He brought a direct age discrimination claim and the tribunal held that he had been treated less favourably on the grounds of age. However, the tribunal went on to find that treatment justified; the giving of the notice early was a proportionate means of achieving a legitimate aim. W appealed. The EAT held the tribunal had been correct in identifying justification for the discrimination: W's role had become genuinely redundant in early 2006, the PCT had already been generous in not giving 12 months' notice of dismissal a year earlier and he could have had no legitimate expectation of notice not being given by May 2007 at the latest. The fact he was within "striking distance" of his enhanced pension rights was an unexpected windfall, which the PCT could legitimately seek to prevent. W further appealed to the Court of Appeal, who also dismissed his appeal. On the unusual facts of this case, the PCT's actions could not be characterised as having been solely aimed at saving or avoiding costs and the dismissal had been justified as a proportionate means of achieving the legitimate aim of implementing his redundancy.

5617 In its guidance for employers, Acas suggests that **proportionate means**:
– what the employer is doing must actually contribute to a legitimate aim, for example, if the aim is to encourage loyalty, then the employer must demonstrate that the discriminatory effect does in fact encourage loyalty;
– the discriminatory effect must be significantly outweighed by the importance and benefits of the legitimate aim; and
– the employer has no reasonable alternative to the discriminatory effect. If this is not the case, then the employer must try to achieve the legitimate aim by less or non-discriminatory means instead.

EXAMPLE

Examples of justification
1. In *Bloxham v Freshfield Bruckhaus Deringer*, ET case 2205086/06, a high-profile case concerning a senior lawyer who was reported to be claiming £4.5 million in damages for age discrimination in complaint against a pension scheme that offered significantly improved benefits to those retiring at age 55 or older, the tribunal found for the employer. The tribunal accepted that the provision was potentially discriminatory, but found that the means adopted by the firm in adopting the scheme (including a lengthy and thorough consultation) were proportionate, and that the intention of the firm (to make the scheme more financially sustainable and fairer for younger partners) was legitimate. It followed that any discrimination was justified.
2. In *Wolf v Stadt Frankfurt am Main* [2010] IRLR 244, ECJ, the Court of Justice of the European Union accepted the argument that the German fire service was justified in applying a maximum age limit of 30 for applicants for jobs in grades required to participate actively in fire fighting and rescue, on the grounds that there was evidence that older workers would lack the requisite physical fitness. The age limit was a proportionate measure as it served to maintain a balance of firefighters in the younger age group.
3. In *Petersen v Berufungsausschuss für Zahnärzte für den Bezirk Westfalen-Lippe and ors* [2010] IRLR 254, ECJ, the Court of Justice of the European Union made a preliminary ruling that a maximum age limit of 68 for dentists working in publicly funded practice is potentially justified as a means of providing opportunities for younger dentists to find work in the health service. An argument that it was necessary for the protection of public health failed because there was no age limit for dentists working in private practice. The question of proportionality was referred back to the national courts.
4. In *Kraft Foods UK Ltd v Hastie* [2010] UKEAT 0024_10_0607, the claimant was entitled to a generous contractual redundancy payment scheme. Under its terms redundancy payments were capped at the amount of basic pay the employee would have received had they worked until retirement. The claimant argued that this had a disproportionate impact on those approaching retirement age. The Court of Appeal held that while this was the case, the employer was justified in imposing a cap which prevented employees receiving a windfall which would leave them better off than if they had worked through to retirement.
Note: This case was decided before the abolition of the default retirement age and in workforces with no NRA the windfall argument may no longer apply because it will be impossible to say with any certainly how long a worker would have continued working.

Examples of no justification
1. In *Hampton v Lord Chancellor and anor* [2008] IRLR 258, ET, a Crown employee, H, held the judicial office of recorder, which was a fee paid role, and was retired when he attained the age of 65. However, the statutory retirement age for Crown employees was 70. The reason for his retirement at 65 was because the Lord Chancellor had a policy that more senior judicial salaried appointments (for example High Court judges) would normally be preceded by 2 years' service in a fee paid appointment and it was argued that the reduction of the retirement age for recorders was necessary to ensure there was a pool of candidates for such judicial posts. However, the tribunal found that only 3% of recorders were appointed to these positions per year and while it considered that maintaining a reasonable flow of candidates for posts in the full-time, salaried judiciary was a legitimate aim, the reduction of retirement age was discriminatory and was not a proportionate means of achieving it. Consequently, H had been discriminated against.
2. In *Kücükdeveci v Swedex GmbH and Co KG* [2010] IRLR 346, ECJ, the Court of Justice of the European Union considered a provision of German law whereby service before the age of 25 is excluded for the purposes of calculating minimum notice periods. The claimant in the case had been employed from the age of 18, and had been working for the same employer for 10 years when she was dismissed. Her employer gave her 2 months' notice, on the basis that 3 years of her employment counted. The Court of Justice of the European Union held that this was direct discrimination and was not justified. While it was accepted that there were legitimate reasons for the difference in treatment – workforce flexibility being one – the means used was not "appropriate and necessary", because the rule applied to all employees who start work before they are 25, irrespective of their age at dismissal, and so the defence of justification failed. Where, as in this case, national law conflicts with European law, the Court of Justice of the European Union confirmed that a court or tribunal may disapply national law.
Comment: Although a similar exclusion of service under the age of 18 has been removed from the UK redundancy scheme, there may now be challenges to the weighting of redundancy payments and the basic award in favour of older workers based on this case.

5618 When making internal decisions as to whether he needs to justify an age discriminatory effect, an employer should ensure that all **records** as to how the decision was made are kept on file in case the decision is challenged at a later date.

Occupational requirement

5620 An occupational requirement allows an employer to treat job applicants and workers differently on the grounds of their age in limited circumstances. An occupational requirement may be relied on by an employer where, having regard to the nature of the employment or the context in which it is carried out, possessing an age-related characteristic is an **occupational requirement** and applying that requirement is a proportionate means of achieving a legitimate aim (Sch 9 para 1 EqA 2010). An employer must carefully consider whether the nature of the job and the context in which it is carried out merits the application of an occupational requirement. Acas advises that employers should also **review** whether, over the course of time, an occupational requirement continues to apply in respect of a particular post.

The EqA 2010 does not give examples as to what may constitute an occupational requirement. However, the Government has maintained that the occupational requirement exceptions will consolidate the predecessor law exceptions, so it is worth noting the old exceptions as they are still likely to apply. Under the predecessor legislation, age could constitute an occupational requirement in relation to:
− recruitment: the arrangements an employer makes for the purpose of determining who should be offered employment or in refusing to offer, or deliberately not offering, a person employment;
− promotion, transfer and training: the opportunities which an employer affords a person for promotion, a transfer, training or receiving any other benefit, or in refusing to offer such opportunities; or
− dismissal from a post.

> EXAMPLE An organisation, F, which advises on and promotes rights for older people, may be able to demonstrate that it is essential that its chief executive, the public face of the organisation, is of a particular age group. However, any such assertion by F will need to be supported by evidence that the age of the chief executive is a genuine and determining occupational requirement.

Positive action

5623 Where it reasonably appears to an employer that positive action **is required to** prevent or compensate for disadvantages linked to age suffered by persons of a particular age or age group doing particular work or likely to take up that work, the employer is permitted to take certain steps to reduce the disadvantages (s 158 EqA 2010):

However, it should be noted that these provisions do **not permit positive discrimination** as such. See ¶¶5243 and 5282 for further detail.

> EXAMPLE C Ltd, a transport company, realises from its internal monitoring procedures that the company has a mature age profile with disproportionately few workers under 40. It decides to take positive action to attract more applicants from wider age groups and in its next job advertisement states "We welcome applications from everyone, irrespective of age, but since we are under-represented by people under 40, we would especially welcome applications from these jobseekers. Appointment will be on merit alone."

Specific exceptions

5625 In addition to justification, occupational requirement and positive action, there are a number of specific exemptions where **age-based requirements** will be **justified**.

5626 **Service-related pay and benefits** Employers are not precluded from linking the length of service of a worker as a criterion to award or increase benefits.

The **rationale** behind service-related pay and benefits is that it assists employers with their employment planning in that they can develop ways of attracting, retaining and rewarding experienced workers. Moreover, linking pay and benefits to length of service helps to maintain **workforce stability** by rewarding loyalty (as opposed to performance). Without such provisions, pay and benefits which are linked to length of service are potentially indirectly discriminatory on the grounds of age since older workers are more likely to have a longer length of service than younger workers.

These provisions relate to both pay and non-pay benefits, such as annual leave or company cars.

In order to rely on one of these exemptions, an employer must have **evidence** from which he can conclude that there is a genuine benefit to the organisation in putting such service-related pay and benefits in place. This could, for example, be obtained via staff surveys, monitoring or focus groups.

5627 There is a total exemption in respect of benefits which are linked to **service of 5 years or less** (Sch 9 para 10 EqA 2010). This means that employers will be able to use pay scales which reflect increasing experience or to make certain benefits available to workers who have completed a minimum qualifying period of service.

With regard to any benefit which is only available to workers who have completed **more than 5 years' service**, the use of length of service as a criterion for qualification for the benefit will not discriminate unlawfully on grounds of age if it reasonably appears to the employer that it fulfils a business need, for example, by encouraging the loyalty or motivation, or rewarding the experience, of some or all of its workers (Sch 9 para 10(2) EqA 2010).

MEMO POINTS **Statutory transfer schemes** should be included when calculating length of service (Employment Equality (Age) Regulations 2006 (Amendment) Regulations SI 2008/573).

5630 **Enhanced redundancy payments** Employers can either follow the statutory redundancy payment (SRP) scheme (¶9005) or provide enhanced redundancy pay over and above the statutory minimum set out in the SRP scheme.

It will not be unlawful for an employer who wishes to make an enhanced redundancy payment, which is calculated using criteria used under the SRP scheme, to a worker who (Sch 9 para 13 EqA 2010):
– is entitled to a statutory redundancy payment (¶8990);
– would have been entitled to a statutory redundancy payment but for the qualifying requirement of 2 years' continuous service; or
– with or without 2 years' continuous service, agreed to the termination of his employment in circumstances where, had he been dismissed, the dismissal would have been by reason of redundancy.

An employer who chooses to **raise or amend** the **statutory redundancy payment scheme** can (Sch 9 para 13 EqA 2010):
– raise or remove the maximum amount of a week's pay (¶2923); and/or
– multiply the amounts used for each age band by more than one.

An employer can also then multiply the total amount by a figure of more than one, whether he has followed the statutory redundancy payment scheme rules or amended the statutory redundancy payment scheme as mentioned above.

If he chooses to amend the statutory redundancy payment scheme, he must make the same adjustments to each of the three age bands, for example, by applying any increased maximum week's pay to all three bands or multiplying the appropriate amounts by the same factor for each of the three bands.

5631 If an employer wishes to use his **own method of calculating** an enhanced redundancy payment based on length of service, this would potentially need to meet the test for justification under the regulations insofar as the employer's own scheme is discriminatory on the grounds of age since the exception for service-related pay and benefits does not extend to enhanced redundancy payments.

5636 **Insurance and related financial benefits** Where an employer has arranged for workers to receive insurance or a related financial service, such as life assurance cover, it is **not unlawful to** cease to provide such cover when a worker reaches the age of 65 or the state retirement age, whichever is the greater. This fairly recent change (which came into force in April 2011) expanded the exception which previously applied only to those retiring early as a result of ill health and related only to life assurance (SI 2011/1069; Sch 9 para 14 EqA 2010).

5637 **National minimum wage** The **age bands** contained in the National Minimum Wage Act (NMWA 1998; ¶2865) remain lawful (Sch 9 para 1 EqA 2010).

This means that an employer can continue to pay 16 and 17 year old workers less than those aged over 17, and 18 to 21 year old workers less than those aged over 21, provided he bases his pay structure on the national minimum wage legislation and pays those in the lower age group(s) less than the adult minimum wage. Where workers in the lower age group and workers in the adult age group are paid at different levels, but both at or above the adult rate of the national minimum wage, there is no longer any reason to provide a special exemption based on the national minimum wage and the normal rules on justification (¶5615) will apply.

> MEMO POINTS The Government considered abolishing this exemption under the EqA 2010 but they decided to maintain the national minimum wage bands as they felt them to be objectively justified and a means of making it easier for young people to find work.

5638 **Statutory authority** Where a statutory authority or provision discriminates on the grounds of age, **any act undertaken in order to comply** with a requirement of any other statutory authority or provision will be lawful (Sch 22 para 1 EqA 2010). This provides an employer with an absolute defence if he is forced to discriminate on the grounds of age in order to comply with age-based requirements set out in another piece of legislation, although if that other piece of legislation contains merely a discretion to act in an age-discriminatory manner, then an employer will not be able to rely on the statutory authority exception.

> EXAMPLE A pub is prohibited from employing persons under 18 in a bar when it is open for the sale or consumption of alcohol under the Licensing Act 1964. If the pub refuses employment to a 17 year old, it will be able to rely on the statutory authority exception.

2. Victimisation

5640 Victimisation on the grounds of age occurs when a worker is subjected to **less favourable treatment** than others **because** he has (in respect of the EqA 2010) (s 27 EqA 2010):
– brought proceedings against his employer, another worker or a third party;
– given evidence or information in connection with such proceedings brought by another person against his employer, another worker or a third party;
– taken any other action under or by reference to the EqA 2010; or
– made any allegation against his employer, another worker or a third party which would amount to a contravention of the EqA 2010.

For example, a worker may be victimised by being labelled a troublemaker or being denied promotion or training.

Protection extends to situations where there is a **threat** by the worker to do any of these things or a suspicion by the employer that the worker intends to do any of them. A worker is also protected if he is victimised by his employer for his protected acts against a former employer or third party.

However, a worker will not be protected if his allegation, evidence or information was **false** and not made (or given) in good faith (s 27(3) EqA 2010).

> EXAMPLE A worker at H Ltd brings a claim for discrimination on the grounds of age against his employer and asks J, a work colleague, to give evidence on his behalf at the employment tribunal. J agrees. However, when J subsequently applies for a promotion at H Ltd, the promotion is denied, even though he is able to demonstrate he has all the necessary skills and experience required for the role. J's manager maintains that he is a troublemaker because he gave evidence against his employer at the tribunal and should not be promoted. This will amount to victimisation.

3. Harassment

5645 Harassment on the grounds of age occurs where a worker is subjected to **unwanted conduct** on the grounds of age, which has the **purpose or effect of** (s 26 EqA 2010):
– violating that worker's dignity; or
– creating an intimidating, hostile, degrading, humiliating or offensive environment for that worker.

5646 It is irrelevant whether the harassment is **intentional** or not. It may be unintentional and subtle or may constitute more obvious bullying. Acas suggests that it may involve nicknames, teasing or name calling which, although without malice, will be upsetting for the worker on the receiving end of the conduct. It may involve the particular worker's age or the age of others with whom the worker associates. Moreover, it could involve conduct which is targeted not at an individual worker but may amount to a general organisational culture, for example, one in which the telling of ageist jokes is tolerated and condoned.

Conduct will only be regarded as having the above effect if, having regard to all the circumstances, including the worker's perception, it should be reasonably considered as having that effect (s 26(4) EqA 2010). Therefore an oversensitive complainant who **unreasonably takes offence** at a perfectly innocent comment would probably not be considered to have suffered harassment.

EXAMPLE
1. K, a younger worker, is continually told by older colleagues that he is "wet behind the ears". K finds the constant references to his age humiliating and distressing. It is likely that this conduct would amount to harassment.
2. L, an older worker, is on the receiving end of teasing comments made at his employer's social gathering, during which some of his colleagues describe him as an "old fogey". This could amount to harassment, and the employer could be held liable.

SECTION 2

Equal pay

5650 A worker who has been treated less favourably on the **grounds of sex** may bring an equal pay claim under the provisions of the EqA 2010. The claim is an alternative to a claim of sex discrimination (¶5260). Although a claim will commonly mention both heads as alternatives, a worker will only be able to claim successfully under equal pay or under sex discrimination, not under both (ss 70, 71 EqA 2010).

Equal pay is the **appropriate remedy** where the inequality concerns reimbursement and the source of the inequality is a provision of the employment contract, for example, a term regarding bonuses, share option schemes, pension or salary (¶2830). Where the inequality concerns non-contractual payments, a sex discrimination claim is the appropriate remedy. Sometimes disputes arise as to whether payments are contractual or not, such as where discretionary bonus or share option schemes are in place. In these cases, it is common for claimants to plead under both heads of claim and the court will then determine which claim to consider (see *Hosso v European Credit Management Ltd* [2011] EWCA Civ 1589, where the High Court held that a discretionary share option scheme was not contractual and that the claim was therefore one of sex discrimination rather than of equal pay).

Where a worker claims to have suffered pay discrimination for a reason **other than sex**, the appropriate remedy is a discrimination claim on grounds of age, disability, gender reassignment, marriage and civil partnership, pregnancy and maternity, race, religion or belief, sex or sexual orientation.

In contrast to the other provisions of the EqA 2010, which operate negatively (i.e. by outlawing discrimination), the equal pay provisions work positively by **implying into every contract** a sex equality clause, which overrides any unequal term by which a worker is paid less than a comparator (s 66 EqA 2010).

> MEMO POINTS The **sources** of this separate form of action are the Equal Pay Directive (EC Directive 1975/117), and article 157 of the Treaty on the Functioning of the European Union (previously article 141 of the Treaty of Rome) which stipulates the principle of equal pay for equal work or work of equal value. Where possible, the EqA 2010 will be interpreted in a way which gives effect to European provisions. In addition, claimants who are employed in the public sector can rely directly on article 157.

1. Scope of protection

5653 Both **men and women** are protected by the equal pay provisions.

The equal pay provisions **apply** to job applicants, workers (including part-time and full-time workers and those working under a contract of apprenticeship) and, in certain circumstances, former workers.

As with the other strands of discrimination (¶5215), the EqA 2010 is silent as to the territorial scope of the equal pay provisions. See ¶¶5215+ for consideration of how the territorial scope of the provisions can be determined under the current provisions.

5654 **Pay secrecy clauses** are unenforceable in certain circumstances (s 77 EqA 2010). This means that an employer will not be able to prevent his workers from discussing their terms and conditions in relation to pay with other colleagues, including former colleagues, and also other third parties if the disclosure is made, or sought, in order to find out whether or not there is a connection between pay and a protected characteristic (for example, during discussions with a trade union official). The provisions do not allow the breach of confidentiality clauses, for example by allowing someone to discuss their pay with a competitor if they are not contractually entitled to do so.

> MEMO POINTS Seeking, making (or seeking to make) and receiving a relevant pay disclosure are all protected acts for the purposes of the victimisation provisions.

Sex equality clause

5655 The equal pay provisions have the effect of equalising **any term or condition** of employment that discriminates between men and women. The equal pay provisions in the EqA 2010 are very similar, with regards to the equality clause, to the Equal Pay Act 1970 (the predecessor legislation), which was found to determine a broad range of terms, **including** terms relating to salary, commission, bonuses, company cars, holiday pay, travel allowances, maternity, severance, sick and redundancy pay, guaranteed overtime working, sporting and social facilities, occupational pensions and unfair dismissal compensation.

> MEMO POINTS Although, as yet, there is no case law to help us in determining the extent to which the equal pay provisions under the EqA 2010 will stretch, similar provisions in the Equal Pay Act 1970 and the originating European legislation, article 141 of the Treaty of Rome (now article 157 of the Treaty on the Functioning of the European Union), have been used in cases far beyond what most people would think of as pay. In *Rutherford v Secretary of State for Trade and Industry (No 2)* [2006] IRLR 551, HL, for example, two claimant men sought to disapply provisions of UK law that prevented male workers over the age of 65 from claiming for unfair dismissal or redundancy. These provisions were challenged as a breach of article 141.

As previously mentioned, the EqA 2010 implies into each contract of employment a sex equality clause if it does not already contain one (s 66 EqA 2010). Such a clause will operate to **modify** a person's **employment contract**, if any term of it is less favourable to A than a term of a similar kind in an employment contract of B, a comparator of the opposite sex, where A is employed on work that is equal to the work that B does. **Equal value** means (s 65 EqA 2010):
– like the comparator's work;
– work rated as equivalent to the comparator's work; or
– work of equal value to that done by the comparator.

5656 "**Like work**" means that the work carried out by the complainant must be the same or of a broadly similar nature to that carried out by the worker of the opposite sex, and that there are no important differences in the tasks actually performed. What is actually carried out in practice is significant, not what is simply in the employment contract (*E Coomes (Holdings) Ltd v Shields* [1978] IRLR 263, CA). A tribunal will analyse the duties concerned and the circumstances in which they are carried out, for example, the degree of responsibility in the job (*Eaton Ltd v Nuttall* [1977] ICR 272, EAT). Trivial differences will be disregarded (*Capper Pass v Lawton* [1976] IRLR 366, EAT). A difference in the times of day or night in which work is carried out should also be disregarded (*Dugdale v Kraft Foods Ltd* [1976] UKEAT 277_76_1076). Further, the fact that a promoted woman undertakes more duties than her male predecessor does not mean that she is not undertaking like work for the purposes of bringing an equal pay claim (*Sita UK Ltd v Hope* [2005] UKEAT 0787_04_0803).

5657 "**Work rated as equivalent**" covers situations where a job evaluation has rated a worker's job as equivalent to that of a member of the opposite sex under various headings, such as effort, skill and responsibility. This will also cover circumstances in which the jobs would have been rated as equivalent but for the fact that the evaluation was made using different values for men and women on the same demand under any heading. The evaluation must be carried out objectively and be capable of being applied impartially (*Eaton Ltd v Nuttall* [1977] ICR 272, EAT), and both parties must accept its validity in order for it to be relied on (*Arnold v Beecham Group Ltd* [1982] IRLR 307, EAT).

5658 "**Work of equal value**" applies where a worker is not engaged on like work with, or work rated as equivalent to, a member of the opposite sex, but his/her work is of equal value to the work done by a member of the opposite sex, in terms of the demands made on him/her with regard to effort, skill and decision etc. An evaluation must not take into consideration factors which discriminate on the grounds of sex (*Rummler v Dato-Druck GmbH* [1986] EUECJ R-237/85).

There is a special procedure for dealing with work of equal value claims (¶5721).

2. Unlawful

5660 As with claims under the sex discrimination provisions, **direct** discrimination, for example, when an employer institutes a policy in which men are paid more than women simply because they are men, is rarely found.

5662 In practice, the majority of cases concern **indirect** discrimination and inequality of pay, i.e. situations where, on the face of it, a complainant and his/her comparator enjoy equally favourable contractual terms, but where a beneficial term of the contract is contingent on the fulfilment of a condition or requirement with which, in reality, fewer members of one sex than the other can comply. How a complainant will prove unequal pay will vary from case to case, but the court will usually expect some evidence of a **link** between different pay and one or more **factors related to gender**.

In relation to the predecessor legislation, the EAT has held that tribunals are not required to always adopt a formulaic approach in considering whether there is sex-related pay discrimination and disparate impact, and this is likely to hold true for the equal pay provisions under the EqA 2010. A tribunal instead must be satisfied on the evidence before it that the pay difference was caused by a factor related to the differences in sex between the complainant and his/her comparator. The fundamental question is whether there is a **causative link** between the claimant's sex and the fact that he/she is paid less. Such a link can be established in different ways (*Ministry of Defence v Armstrong and ors* [2004] IRLR 672, EAT).

5663 In cases where indirect pay discrimination is alleged, it is very common for the workers complaining of discrimination to **provide statistics** showing two distinct groups; an advantaged group, predominantly composed of men, and a disadvantaged group, containing a significant number of women (*Bailey and ors v Home Office* [2005] IRLR 369, CA). In this case, the Court held that tribunals are concerned to determine whether what might seem like a gender-neutral practice in reality disguises the fact that female workers are being disadvantaged as compared to male comparators to an extent that indicates that the inequality is due to gender.

5664 In a useful decision, the EAT has distinguished between **two routes** by which a claimant can raise a presumption of indirect discrimination, which in turn will require an employer to justify the difference in pay (*Villalba v Merrill Lynch & Co* [2006] IRLR 437, EAT). The **first route** is to identify some barrier, where a **provision, criterion or practice** operates to the disadvantage of one gender. A common situation occurs when **part-timers** are treated less favourably. This affects women disproportionately, because women's caring role is more likely to prevent them from complying with a provision, criterion or practice that full-time hours must be worked to receive a higher rate of pay.

The **second route** is to show **disparate impact** between two groups, as typically when certain jobs for historical reasons or by reason of gender stereotyping, are dominated by different genders, and are paid at different rates. One example is **occupational segregation** in the health service, where "female" groups such as speech therapists have been paid less than "male" groups such as pharmacists or psychologists (*Enderby v Frenchay Health Authority and Secretary of State for Health* [1993] IRLR 591, ECJ). The statistical evidence required to raise the presumption of indirect discrimination would probably be greater where a claimant adopted the "two groups" approach.

5665 Where the case is **almost wholly based** on **statistics**, there is a consequently greater requirement that the statistics should prove the discrimination claimed.

> EXAMPLE *Tyne and Wear Passenger Transport Executive (trading as Nexus) v Best and ors* [2006] UKEAT 0627_05_2112 concerned two groups of workers, one made up of people who drove underground trains, and the other made up of workers who worked both as drivers and fare collectors. The first group was better paid than the second group. In each group, men were the large majority, forming 92% of the first group, and 85% of the second. The EAT held that such statistical evidence would inevitably be less persuasive than evidence where there was a majority of men in the advantaged group and a majority of women in the disadvantaged group. In the absence of evidence that a particular provision, criterion or practice discriminated indirectly against women, the statistical evidence was not enough to demonstrate unequal pay.

Comparison

5667 The equal pay provisions differ from the other strands of discrimination with regards to comparators. A complainant under the equal pay provisions is required to name a comparator who is an **actual person**, whereas it is possible under other areas of discrimination law, including sex discrimination, to compare one's treatment to that of a **hypothetical** comparator.

In cases of direct discrimination where there is no actual comparator and the claim has not been defeated by a material factor defence (¶5680), a claim can be brought under the sex discrimination provisions, and in such circumstances a hypothetical comparator can be used (s 71(2) EqA 2010). However, it will often be difficult to establish a prima facie case that will be successful without any actual comparison, such as where one party simply claims that they are being paid too little because of their sex and they have solely hypothetical comparisons to make. It is more likely that such cases will arise where the complainant has real comparisons to make, but they do not exactly fit the requirements of the equal pay provisions, for example, where the pay differential between two parties doing work that is not of equal value is disproportionately large, or where a successor comparator (which is unlikely to be accepted under the equal pay provisions (¶5669)) is paid significantly more for doing work of equal value. The Court of Justice of the European Union has also held that a claimant under article 157 of the Treaty on the Functioning of the European Union (previously article 141 of the Treaty of Rome) (¶5676) does not have to rely on an actual comparator and can instead provide **statistical data**, where the source of the discrimination is some rule of a national government (*Allonby v Accrington and Rossendale College and ors* [2004] IRLR 224, ECJ).

> **EXAMPLE** In *Allonby v Accrington and Rossendale College and ors*, following a business reorganisation, a college lecturer, A, and 340 other lecturers were dismissed as part-time workers and re-engaged as agency workers. The policies of the Department of Education had the consequence that the Teachers' Pension Scheme was closed to all those who were not workers. Following A's dismissal, as an independent contractor, she could no longer make payments under the superannuation scheme. Since both male and female lecturers were affected by the prohibition, A could not identify a male comparator. She argued successfully, however, that the Government's policy of closing the superannuation scheme to agency workers discriminated against part-time lecturers in general, a predominantly female group.

5668 **Pregnant workers or recent mothers** have no need to cite a comparator (para 91 Equal Pay Code; *Alabaster v (1) Barclays Bank plc and (2) The Secretary of State for Social Security* [2005] ICR 1246, CA).

A male worker is also prevented from bringing a claim in order to match a woman's entitlement to maternity pay or leave (Sch 7 para 2 EqA 2010).

5669 Any comparator must be in the **same employment** as the claimant.

There is no requirement, however, that the comparator should be at exactly the same **grade** as him/her. A claim was allowed under the Equal Pay Act 1970 when workers were rated more highly but paid less than their comparators (*Redcar and Cleveland Borough Council v Bainbridge and ors* [2007] IRLR 91, EAT).

The comparator need not have worked contemporaneously with the complainant (s 64(2) EqA 2010). Case law decided under the predecessor legislation established that a comparator could be a worker of the opposite sex who was the claimant's **predecessor** (*Kells v Pilkington* [2002] IRLR 693, EAT). Conversely, it was also established that it was not possible to use a **successor** complainant on the basis that this would require excessive speculation and hypothesising (*Walton Centre for Neurology and Neuro Surgery NHS Trust v Brewley* [2008] ICR 1047, EAT). The Explanatory Notes state that this provision was created to preserve the impact of preexisting case law, i.e. "that a comparator need not be someone who is employed at the same time as the person making a claim under these provisions, but could be a predecessor in the job". It is therefore unlikely that a successor comparator would be allowed by the courts, despite the rather broad wording of the new provision.

5670 Moreover, the chosen comparator can be a worker at **another establishment of the employer** in GB, if he/she is employed under common terms and conditions of employment as the complainant (s 79(4) EqA 2010; *Hartlepool Borough Council and anor v Dolphin and ors* [2009] IRLR 168, EAT; *Leverton v Clwyd County Council* [1984] IRLR 28, HL; *British Coal v Smith* [1996] IRLR 406, HL).

Where workers are employed at the **same establishment**, there is no requirement for there to be common terms and conditions of employment. Generally, an establishment will be defined largely by the location, such as a group of buildings or a factory complex, and the existence of a central management function does not mean that workplaces within an overarching organisation will necessarily form part of a single establishment (*City of Edinburgh Council v Wilkinson and ors* [2011] ScotCS CSIH_70).

> **EXAMPLE**
> **Same establishment or common terms and conditions**
> 1. In *Leverton v Clwyd County Council*, a school nursery nurse was able to compare herself with clerical staff employed by the same council, but not working in schools. The House of Lords allowed the use of the clerical staff as comparators for the reason that they were employed on common terms and conditions derived from the same collective agreement.
> 2. The House of Lords allowed a different approach in *British Coal v Smith*, where canteen workers and cleaners working in mines sought to compare themselves to surface mineworkers and clerical workers working in other establishments, who were subject to different collective agreements. The Lords held that a claimant could rely on such comparators, if they could show that the terms and conditions upon which the comparators would be employed, were they to be employed at the same establishment, would be broadly similar.
> 3. In *South Tyneside Metropolitan Borough Council v Anderson and ors* [2007] IRLR 715, CA, a female classroom assistant and a male road sweeper were employed in different establishments by the same council. Although their job descriptions and the content of their work was different, both were employed

on the same grade of the same scale. These facts were enough to constitute common terms and conditions of employment.

4. In *City of Edinburgh Council v Wilkinson and ors*, the Court of Session decided that female council workers in administrative, professional and technical grades making equal pay claims could compare themselves with male manual workers who were employed by the council in a number of different locations. Although the two sets of employees were not employed at the same establishment, largely due to the differing physical locations of their work, they were employed under common terms and conditions (as per a contractually binding collective agreement that all of the workers were likely to have known about).

Not in same establishment or with common terms and conditions

1. In *White v Burton's Foods Ltd* [2010] UKEAT 0514_09_0607, a production planning manager named comparators at other sites run by the same company. They worked in a similar capacity but under different terms and conditions. The sites where they worked had been bought from other companies, and the terms and conditions applying there had never been harmonised with those where the claimant worked, and no common staff handbook had ever been produced. In addition, each site was managed locally with its own HR function, different recognised trade unions and separate disciplinary and grievance procedures. The EAT held that, in the circumstances, the comparators were not in the same employment.

5672 The equality clause applies to each **individual term** of a contract. A court or tribunal is not required to consider the contract as a whole. If any term is inferior, a claimant may succeed.

EXAMPLE In *Hayward v Cammell Laird Shipbuilders Ltd* [1988] ICR 464, HL, the House of Lords considered the case of a female applicant whose total pay was superior to that of her male comparator, but there were individual provisions which were inferior. On that basis, she was entitled to succeed.

When making a comparison of a complainant's terms with those of his/her comparator, however, it has been held that the **basic hourly rate, fixed bonuses** and **attendance allowances** form part of the same contractual term, relating to the entire payment received for the performance of the contract by workers during normal working hours. On this basis, these terms should be aggregated when making the comparison, rather than looked at as separate terms of the contract (*Degnan and ors v Redcar and Cleveland Borough Council* [2005] IRLR 615, CA).

5674 **Claim brought by group of workers** Where an equal pay claim is brought by a group of workers, the group **must find another** comparator group. The comparator should not be artificial or arbitrary. The right size of the group to be used as a comparator will depend on all the facts of the case (*Cheshire and Wirral Partnership NHS Trust v Abbott* [2006] IRLR 546, CA).

It used to be thought that when choosing the appropriate comparator, and assessing whether the disadvantage had a significant impact, it was always better to begin from the advantaged rather than the disadvantaged group. The Court of Appeal has, however, held that this is not the case: the right approach will depend on the facts of the case (*Grundy v British Airways Plc* [2008] IRLR 74, CA).

EXAMPLE In *Grundy v British Airways Plc*, an airline operated a policy that cabin crew could be employed on one of two grades. Those agreeing to work full-time had the benefit of a salary, plus cost of living pay rises and incremental pay rises. Those working part-time received a proportion of the same salary and the cost of living pay rises but not the incremental pay rises. Inevitably, their pay fell behind. In 1994 there were 495 part-time staff out of a total of 9,915: 471 of them were women and 24 were men. In deciding on appropriate pools for comparison, in order to assess the impact of the disadvantage, the Court of Appeal had to consider whether it was right to begin from the advantaged group or the disadvantaged group. If the former approach had been adopted, the evidence of sex discrimination would be slight: women were a majority in both the advantaged and the disadvantaged groups. On the other hand, if the comparison began from the disadvantaged group, then women outnumbered men considerably, by a ratio of 20 to 1.

5676 **Using the EC Treaty to pursue a claim or establish a comparator** Where a worker is **employed by a public authority** (for example, a government department, a local authority, or a health or education authority), he/she can rely directly on article 157 of the Treaty on the Functioning of the European Union (previously article 141 of the Treaty of Rome) (¶5650) if he/she believes that the Directive gives greater rights than the UK implementing regulations.

When pursuing a claim under article 157, a worker **can compare** himself/herself to a comparator employed by another employer, provided he/she can demonstrate that any difference in pay is attributable to a "single source" (i.e. a body which is responsible for the inequality of pay and which can restore equality of pay) (*Lawrence v Regent Office Care* [2002] IRLR 822, ECJ; see also *Allonby v Accrington and Rossendale College and ors* [2004] IRLR 224, ECJ; *Robertson and ors v Department for Environment, Food and Rural Affairs* [2005] IRLR 363, CA; *Armstrong and ors v Newcastle upon Tyne NHS Hospital Trust* [2006] IRLR 124, CA; and *South Tyneside Metropolitan Borough Council v Middleton and ors*, EAT case 0684/05).

EXAMPLE

1. In *Robertson and ors v Department for Environment, Food and Rural Affairs*, a case which involved a pay differential between civil servants working in two different governmental departments, each department had been delegated responsibility for setting its own workers' pay and conditions. The Court held that although the claimants and their comparators were all employed by the Crown, there was no single body which was responsible for the inequality and which could remedy it.
2. In *Armstrong and ors v Newcastle upon Tyne NHS Hospital Trust*, the Court of Appeal held that it is insufficient for an equal pay claimant to establish that he/she has the same employer as his/her comparator(s) for the purposes of comparing pay. Instead, a claimant must demonstrate that his/her employer is also the body responsible for setting the terms and conditions of employment of both the claimant and his/her comparator(s), i.e. a "single source" to which responsibility for setting terms and conditions of both groups of workers is traceable. Without such a single source, an equal pay claim will not succeed.
3. In *South Tyneside Metropolitan Borough Council v Middleton and ors*, the EAT held that female support staff working in state-owned community schools were in the "same employment" as male workers employed by Hartlepool Borough Council, whereas staff employed on identical grades but working for voluntary-aided schools were not in the same employment as the male comparators.

MEMO POINTS In most instances, a worker and his/her comparator whose pay can be equalised by a single source are likely to be in the same employment (see test above at ¶5669), but it is possible that there may be circumstances where this is not so. In such circumstances it is thought that comparison to a comparator employed by another employer, provided he/she can demonstrate that any difference in pay is attributable to a "single source", may be relied on even where the **general basis is the UK equality provisions** (*Defrenne v Sabena* [1976] ICR 547, ECJ).

"Piggyback" claims Claims for equal pay by **men comparing** themselves **to women who are themselves bringing equal pay claims** using other men as comparators can be brought as, if the women are successful in their claims, the women comparators would be paid more than the male claimants for like work (*McAvoy and ors v South Tyneside Borough Council and ors* [2009] UKEAT 0006_08_2406). A man can therefore claim equal pay with a woman who is paid a higher rate for like work as a result of her own equal pay claim. This is often called a "piggyback" claim. Such a claim can extend to any period of arrears awarded to the female comparator, and also cover any bonuses paid to the woman in settlement of her equal pay claim. It is permissible for a man to start proceedings before the equal pay claim made by the female comparator is completed and the claim will be **contingent** on the success of the female comparator's claim.

5677

3. Lawful

Material factor defence

In an equal pay case, the employer is not required to provide equal pay and benefits where he can **prove** that the **difference** is due to a material factor other than sex (s 69 EqA 2010).

5680

To qualify as a material factor accounting for the discrepancy in salary, the reasons for it at the time that the difference in earnings is challenged must be examined, and it is for the employer to show that the factor is material. For example, where the employer has redcircled an employee's pay, the reason for introducing the pay protection and the reason for continuing it should be considered when comparing that pay to another's (*Fearnon and ors v Smurfit Corrugated Cases (Lurgan) Ltd* [2009] IRLR 132, NICA). Under the EqA 2010, there is an additional statutory requirement that any material factor that leads to a disadvantage can be justified as a proportionate means of achieving a legitimate aim (s 69(1)(b) EqA 2010). Although this is a statutory addition, it is unlikely to create a real difference to the way that equal pay claims are decided, because case law decided under the predecessor legislation established that it was necessary to show objective justification for discriminatory pay practices. The examples below are from cases brought under predecessor legislation, hence the reference to "genuine material factors". Despite the differences between the old and new law mentioned above, they are likely to be upheld under the EqA 2010.

EXAMPLE

Genuine material factor defence failed:
In *Francis v London Underground Ltd*, ET case 3201872/04, a manager brought an equal pay claim, citing as her comparator a male colleague who was paid 24% more than her while working on the same grade. Her employer responded that the male colleague's pay was protected, in that his previous post had been displaced in an internal re-organisation. The tribunal accepted that this was potentially a valid genuine material factor defence. On the facts of the case, however, it transpired that when the male colleague had been moved into this position, his pay had been significantly higher than it had been in his previous post. The tribunal concluded that the real difference for the disparity in pay was that the man asked for higher pay and it was given to him. This was part of a general failure in the organisation, where men typically commenced part-way up the pay scales, and women at the bottom of them.

Genuine material factor defence succeeded:
1. In *Blackburn and anor v Chief Constable of West Midlands Police* [2009] IRLR 135, CA, a police force offered a bonus scheme to reward workers who volunteered for night-time working. A worker claimed that the scheme tended to discriminate against women, who for childcare reasons were less likely than men to be able to do night-time work. The CA held that the EAT had been entitled to find that the employer's reason for paying officers who agreed to work night-shifts more was to reward those officers in light of the social, psychological and other stresses that such work creates. Any discrimination was objectively justified in light of that aim.
2. In *Savage v Regent Office Care*, ET case 1701154/05, a female regional manager claimed that she was employed on like work with five male regional managers who were paid more than her. An analysis of the comparators showed that the size of the regions, the mileage required, the number of contracts, and the number of staff for which each was responsible varied considerably. The responsibilities of the other managers was greater, as was the amount of work they were required to do. Accordingly, the material factor defence succeeded.
3. In *Skills Development Scotland Co Ltd v Buchanan and anor* [2011] UKEAT 0042_10_2505, the EAT held that where employees are inherited on different pay rates following a TUPE transfer, these differences are permissible if the reason is solely a result of the TUPE transfer, i.e. it is for a gender neutral reason. In this case, the disparity remained over 6 years after the transfer had taken place. The EAT also commented that an employer is not obliged to freeze salaries as a means of rectifying a disparity. Note: This may not apply if the new employer inherits what he knows to be a pre-existing gender bias.

5681 However, an employer will **not be required to justify** material factors which he has raised in defence to an equal pay claim regarding differences in pay if there is no suggestion that those material factors are either directly or indirectly discriminatory on the grounds of sex (*Glasgow City Council and ors v Marshall and ors* [2000] ICR 196, HL; *Parliamentary Commissioner for Administration and another v Fernandez* [2003] UKEAT 0137_03_0509). This principle has been restated by the Court of Appeal, which held that an employer does not need to provide justification for a disparity of pay unless the reason for the disparity (i.e. the material factor upon which the employer is seeking to rely in order to objectively justify such a disparity) is tainted by sex discrimination (*Armstrong and ors v Newcastle upon Tyne NHS Hospital Trust* [2006] IRLR 124, CA followed in *Gibson v Sheffield City Council* [2010] IRLR 331, CA).

EXAMPLE In *Gibson v Sheffield City Council*, an equal pay claim was made by cleaners whose work was rated as equivalent to that of gardeners and street cleaners who were paid more as a result of productivity bonuses which had been incorporated into their basic pay. The Court of Appeal confirmed the approach taken in *Armstrong and ors v Newcastle upon Tyne NHS Hospital Trust* that, unless the reason for the disparity is tainted by sex discrimination, the employer does not have to justify that material factor. In this particular case, the difference of pay arose from an indirectly discriminatory practice, in giving productivity bonuses for work predominantly done by men and not for work predominantly done by women, so the employer had to show that the difference was justified.

> MEMO POINTS The decision in *Armstrong* has been criticised for seeming to suggest that even where a difference is related to sex, it is still capable of justification; an approach that would run contrary to the statute and to Court of Justice of the European Union authority (*Enderby v Frenchay Health Authority* [1993] IRLR 591, ECJ). The Court of Appeal in *Armstrong* also did not refer to the Court of Justice of the European Union case of *Brunnhofer*, during which the Court of Justice of the European Union spoke of the employer being under an absolute duty to justify any difference in pay (*Brunnhofer v Bank der Osterreichischen Postsparkasse AG* [2001] IRLR 571, ECJ).

Examples of "genuine material factor" defences which have been successful under the predecessor legislation include:
- responsibility (*Edmonds v Computer Services (South West) Ltd* [1977] IRLR 359, EAT);
- experience (*Tyldesley v TML Plastics Ltd* [1996] ICR 356, EAT);
- the application of an objective non-discriminatory grading structure (*National Vulcan Engineering Insurance Co Ltd v Wade* [1978] IRLR 225, CA);
- physical effort where a job is physically unpleasant (*Christie and others v John E Haith Ltd* [2003] IRLR 670, EAT);
- the preservation of favourable terms following a TUPE transfer (*King's College London v Clark* [2003] UKEAT 1049_02_0509);
- performance, attendance and wet weather bonuses (*Redcar and Cleveland Borough Council v Bainbridge and ors (No. 1)* [2007] IRLR 984, CA); and
- length of service. As a general rule, a pay system which rewards workers who have longer service is acceptable and legitimate as length of service goes hand in hand with experience and experience generally enables the worker to perform his duties better. This has been held so even if this means that such pay differences have a disproportionately adverse effect on women (*Handels-og Kontorfunktionaerenes Forbund I Danmark v Dansk Arbejdsgiverforening, Case 109/88* [1990] EUECJ R-179/88; *Cadman v Health and Safety Executive, Case C-17/05* [2006] ICR 1623, ECJ). However, an employer may be required to justify using a length of service criterion for pay and in adopting such a criterion in the first place if an employee can show that there is evidence that, if proved, would establish that the criterion was not justified (*Wilson v Health and Safety Executive* [2010] IRLR 59, CA). Further, length of service benefits may also be subject to challenge on other grounds, including age discrimination (¶5627).

The above is not a closed list. The EAT has held that there is no limitation on the matters which may potentially be relied upon as a genuine material factor (*Davies v McCartneys* [1989] IRLR 439, EAT) (which will equally apply to "material factors" under the EqA 2010).

5682

Work of equal value evaluation

In respect of work of equal value claims, the tribunal can, and usually will, require that an objective and non-discriminatory job evaluation assessment has been undertaken to assess whether or not the worker and his/her comparator do work of equal value (s 131 EqA 2010; ¶5721).

5683

Other factors

Where **pay protection schemes** are introduced to cushion the effect of a job evaluation scheme, their effects are inevitably indirectly discriminatory. The purpose of this type of scheme is to protect, for a period of time, a group of workers whose pay has been higher, but whose work has now been rated as equivalent to that of a lower paid group. If the purpose of the scheme is to defend individuals from the potentially disastrous effects of a sudden drop in pay, the Court of Appeal has held that, in principle, the material factor defence can apply, provided the employer can demonstrate, on the facts, that the scheme is objectively justified (*Redcar & Cleveland Borough Council v Bainbridge and ors (No. 1); Surtees v Middlesbrough Borough Council* [2008] IRLR 776, CA).

5684

5685 Other defences have had more mixed results. Some employers have successfully relied on an argument that pay differentials or bonuses were caused by **market forces**, including scarcity in the local labour market, a shortage of particular skills, and the need to pay the going rate in order to fill a particular vacancy (*Rainey v Greater Glasgow Health Board* [1987] ICR 129, HL; *Cumbria County Council v Dow and ors and conjoined appeal (No. 1)* [2008] IRLR 91, EAT). Where, however, market differentials have been driven by the greater bargaining power of male-dominated careers, the same defence has been unsuccessful, as in the case of *North Yorkshire County Council v Ratcliffe and ors*, where the House of Lords (now called the Supreme Court) accepted that the general tendency for caterers to be paid less than male manual workers arose from a general perception that catering was women's work and that women could be paid less because their role in society was to stay at home and look after children (*North Yorkshire County Council v Ratcliffe and ors* [1995] ICR 833, HL).

Performance-related pay will be easier to justify where it can be shown that managers across an institution have received suitable equality training. Where that has not taken place, there is a danger that managers may evaluate performance on a subjective and even discriminatory basis.

SECTION 3

Enforcement and remedies

5700 Workers have a range of remedies in respect of discrimination claims, the most common being compensation for which there is no limit. In addition, various organisations also have enforcement powers.

I. Tribunal claim

5710 Workers who suffer unlawful discrimination, harassment or unequal pay can make a complaint to a tribunal. To help them assess whether they have a claim or should bring a claim, they can serve their employers with a questionnaire.

Questionnaires

5711 To assist in deciding whether to bring proceedings and in formulating and presenting his/her case, a worker can serve a discrimination or equal pay questionnaire, as appropriate, on his/her employer (s 138 EqA 2010). With regard to discrimination questionnaires, the worker can also serve it on any other person against whom he/she may have a complaint.

The questionnaire and replies to the questionnaire must be in a **prescribed form** (The EqA 2010 (Obtaining Information) Order SI 2010/2194).

> *MEMO POINTS* The Government is **proposing to repeal** statutory questionnaires, though the relevant regulations remain active at the time of publication. The impending change is part of a draft bill called the Enterprise and Regulatory Reform Bill which is proceeding through Parliament and any further developments will be covered by our updating service.

5712 In responding to questionnaires, an employer must ensure that he does not breach his obligations regarding **data protection** towards the named comparator(s) (¶5940). It is advisable, therefore, particularly in relation to equal pay, that before disclosing details of salary, bonus and benefit packages, the employer obtains the consent of the comparator(s). If no consent is given, the employer should consider providing the requested information in terms of groups of relevant workers (for example, the range of bonuses in any given range of workers) as opposed to details of specific workers' packages.

5713 A questionnaire (and any replies) will be **admissible as evidence** in tribunal proceedings **if it is served**:
– before proceedings have been brought, though in the case of discrimination questionnaires this must be within 3 months of the act complained of being done; or
– within 28 days of the date proceedings were lodged (i.e. started), or later at the discretion of the tribunal.

Further, if admissible, the tribunal can also draw **inferences**, including an inference that a discriminatory act (including harassment) has taken place/worker has suffered unequal pay, if it appears that the employer deliberately and without reasonable excuse **failed to reply within** 8 weeks beginning on the day on which the questionnaire was served on him, or if his reply is evasive or equivocal (s 138(3) EqA 2010). However, such inferences are not automatic and will depend on the circumstances (*D'Silva v NATFHE and ors* [2008] IRLR 412, EAT).

Bringing a claim

5720 Workers may present a complaint to a tribunal if their employer has committed an unlawful act of **discrimination or harassment** against them or there is **inequality with regard to their pay** (s 120 EqA 2010).

For these purposes, a discriminatory act is **deemed** to have **occurred** if the complaint:
– concerns a contractual term: the "act" is treated as having been done throughout the contract;
– is about an "act" extending over a period of time: it is treated as having been done at the end of that period, and can include acts which take place after the termination of employment if there is a sufficiently close connection between the employment relationship and the act in question; or
– is about a deliberate omission: it is treated as having been done when the person in question decided on the omission. As it can be difficult to determine when a person decided not to do something, the tribunal will look at inconsistencies and will consider periods of inactivity by the employer in order to determine whether there has been an unlawful "deliberate omission".

> MEMO POINTS The EHRC has a specific duty to consider and, where appropriate, **assist claimants**, for example, by arranging legal advice or representation, by seeking to reach a settlement of any dispute, or by providing other suitable support.

5721 With regard to **equal value claims** in relation to equal pay (¶5658), there is a **special procedure** (s 131 EqA 2010). This procedure was introduced to simplify the rules in equal value cases which had been found to result in litigation that was significantly more lengthy and complex than other equal pay cases.

At the **first stage** of the special procedure, the tribunal will make a number of rulings, including whether:
– the work of the claimant and the comparator have been given equal value in a job evaluation scheme (if so, then unless the job evaluation scheme is found to have been discriminatory, the claim must be struck out); and
– the tribunal will determine the question of equal value itself or ask a member of a panel of independent experts to prepare a report. For example, the EAT has held that the fact that the jobs of the claimant and comparator were similarly rated under a job evaluation study did not mean that they had previously been of equal value and a report was required to give a detailed one-on-one comparison (*Hovell v Ashford and St Peter's Hospital NHS Trust* [2009] IRLR 734, CA).

The tribunal will also make rulings as to directions. Where a report is required, then, in the **second stage** of the procedure, the independent expert will be invited to present his/her report to the tribunal. The independent expert must be granted access to the employer's premises to carry out his/her investigations. Any questions that either party has to the independent expert must be submitted in writing. At the **third stage** of the procedure, the tribunal will determine whether the work is in fact of equal value, and whether any difference in pay is objectively justified (¶5681).

Where there have been **changes in the job content** of either the claimant or comparator during the period covered by the equal pay claim, the tribunal must assess whether the jobs were comparable at each point where there has been a change. However, it is acceptable for the tribunal to deal with the comparison as at the date the claim was made initially. Changes in job content over the entire period could then be dealt with later by additional expert evidence if necessary (*Potter and ors v North Cumbria Acute Hospitals NHS Trust* [2009] IRLR 22, EAT).

5722 **Time limit** The time limit for presentation of **discrimination and harassment complaints** is 3 months from the time that the act (or omission) complained of was done (s 123 EqA 2010). For further details on the relevant start date in relation to discrimination cases, see ¶¶9460+. However, the tribunal may consider a complaint which is made **out of time**, if in all the circumstances, it considers that it would be just and equitable to do so (¶9475).

To be an **omission** for these purposes, it must be deliberate. Where an employer fails to make a reasonable adjustment proposed by the worker and this omission is said to constitute an act continuing for the remaining duration of the claimant's employment, the time limit begins to run from the date on which the employer **declined to make** an adjustment (*Humphries v Chevler Packaging* [2006] UKEAT 0224_06_2407). Where the employer does not actively refuse to make a reasonable adjustment, but **fails to make it through lack of diligence or competence**, and this omission is said to constitute an act continuing for the remaining duration of the claimant's employment, the time limit will begin to run from when the employer might reasonably have been expected to do the omitted act (*Matuszowicz v Kingston upon Hull City Council* [2009] IRLR 288, CA).

5723 The time limit for bringing an **equal pay claim** is ordinarily 6 months from the ending of the contract of employment to which the claim relates, or from the ending of a stable employment relationship formed by a series of short-term contracts (s 129 EqA 2010; *Preston v Wolverhampton Healthcare NHS Trust* [2001] IRLR 237, HL). Likewise, if there are a number of different contracts during the course of that employment, the time limit for bringing the claim does not start to run until that stable relationship ends (*North Cumbria University Hospitals NHS Trust v Fox and ors* [2010] EWCA Civ 729; *Slack and ors v Cumbria County Council* [2009] IRLR 463, CA overturning *Cumbria County Council v Dow and ors (No. 2)* [2008] IRLR 109, EAT).

> EXAMPLE In *North Cumbria University Hospitals NHS Trust v Fox and ors*, nurses' terms and conditions of employment were changed after the introduction of a new single collective agreement in the NHS. Some of these nurses named new comparators in existing proceedings and, as adding a new comparator is treated as making a new claim, a decision was needed about whether the claim had been made within the 6-month time limit. The employer argued that the change in employment terms amounted to the end of a stable employment relationship. The Court of Appeal rejected that approach; even if the change was a fundamental one, the nurses were carrying on doing the same job for the same employer. This could be characterised as a stable employment relationship which had not ended, so that the claims were in time.

A claim can, however, be started at any time during a worker's employment and, in certain circumstances, the 6-month time limit can be **extended** where (s 129(1) EqA 2010):
– an employer has deliberately concealed a fact from the worker which is relevant to his/her equal pay claim and the worker did not or could not reasonably have discovered the concealment until after the employment relationship ended. In such cases, a claim must be brought within 6 months of the date on which the worker discovered the concealment (or could, with reasonable diligence, have discovered it); and
– a worker is either a minor or of unsound mind at any time during the 6 months which follows the end of his/her employment. In such cases, a claim must be brought within 6 months of the worker ceasing to be a minor or of unsound mind.

Where a **worker transfers** to a new employer **under TUPE**, any equal pay claim must be brought within 6 months of the end of the employment to which the claim relates, i.e. with regard to claims relating to the transferor, within 6 months of the date of the transfer (*Gutridge and ors v Sodexo Ltd and anor* [2009] IRLR 721, CA; *Powerhouse Retail Ltd and ors v Burroughs and ors* [2006] IRLR 381, HL; *Unison v Allen and ors* [2008] ICR 114, EAT). Such claims can be made against the transferee as this right transfers under TUPE as long they are brought within this 6-month deadline (¶7972). This does not apply to equal pay claims relating to an occupational pension scheme, which must be brought against the transferor and not the transferee as the transferee does not generally inherit the transferor's occupational pension obligations under TUPE (¶7992).

Equal pay claims can also be brought in the **civil courts after the time limit** to claim in the employment **tribunal has expired**, effectively extending the time limit to bring such claims from 6 months from termination in the employment tribunal to 6 years from the date of the last breach of contract (i.e. the last failure to pay equally) in the civil courts (*Birmingham City Council v Abdulla* [2012] UKSC 47). This is a significant decision which effectively extends the time available to bring a valid claim from 6 months to 6 years. Potentially, it may encourage a new breed of "piggyback" claims (¶5677) with former staff bringing equal pay claims in the civil courts relying upon successful claims which have been brought by their former colleagues. However, it seems likely that the amount of back pay which can be claimed will be reduced by an amount which corresponds to the delay in bringing the claim e.g. if a claim is delayed by 3 years and then brought in the civil court, the maximum compensation which could be awarded would be 3 years (making a total of 6 years) (¶5770).

Multiple claims

One difficulty is raised where an individual brings a claim referring to **multiple types** of discrimination. For example, a Muslim worker may claim that he has suffered discrimination on grounds of both race and religion, or a person who is both black and gay may claim to have suffered particular discrimination, including perhaps racism from white gay fellow workers and homophobia from black colleagues. With regard to such claims, the Court of Appeal held that the **correct approach** was to disaggregate each strand of discrimination, and provide separate evidence for each (*Law Society v Bahl* [2004] IRLR 799, CA). This is particularly important with regard to multiple claims based on similar grounds. For example it is common for workers bringing claims of religious discrimination also to claim racial discrimination in the alternative, and tribunals should take care to distinguish between the two claims. Further, it is inappropriate for a tribunal to assume that because one form of discrimination is proved, the other also automatically is (*Royal Mail Group Plc v Jan*, EAT case 0101/07).

5724

> EXAMPLE In *Law Society v Bahl*, an Asian woman, B, claimed that she had received less favourable treatment on both grounds together: that some women had discriminated against her because she was Asian, some Asian colleagues because she was a woman, and her employer specifically because she was both. Both the EAT and Court of Appeal held that in so far as B sought to prove that she had suffered discrimination as a woman, she should provide a male comparator, and in so far as she claimed discrimination on grounds of her race, she should provide a non-Asian comparator who did not suffer, or would not have suffered, discrimination.

A different problem arises where an individual's protection against discrimination is in **competition with** his own obligations under anti-discrimination law. This problem typically arises where a worker is disciplined for discriminating against a fellow worker, but responds by claiming that he is himself a victim of discrimination: for example, where a Christian worker has distributed homophobic literature in the workplace, and the Christian worker is sanctioned, he may attempt to seek protection from disciplinary sanction under the shelter of the prohibition against discrimination on grounds of religion or belief. However, in the few cases where claimants have attempted to use religion as such a shield, the tribunals have resolutely refused to find in their favour (*Apelogun-Gabriels v London Borough of Lambeth*, ET case 2301976/05).

> MEMO POINTS The EqA 2010 contains provisions permitting **dual discrimination** claims (for example, claims that a person has suffered discrimination on the grounds of being both black and gay). These provisions are **not yet in force**, and the Government has announced its intention to delay the commencement of these provisions. Any future developments will be covered by our updating service.
> Despite the provisions on dual discrimination not yet being in force, tribunals may be willing to find such discrimination under the ordinary direct discrimination provisions – they were certainly prepared to do so under the predecessor legislation. In *Ministry of Defence v Debique* [2009] UKEAT 0048_09_1210, a tribunal combined two provisions, criteria or practices to find both sex and race

discrimination. Upholding the decision, the EAT recognised that discrimination is often a multi-faceted experience which cannot always be compartmentalised.

Evidence

5725 Workers rarely have **direct evidence** of discrimination and employers will very rarely admit to such behaviour. Consequently, findings of discrimination are usually based on **inferences**, drawn by tribunals from any difference in treatment and circumstantial evidence as to the grounds for this. This can include any false or evasive answers by employers including any responses to questionnaires (*King v Great Britain-China Centre* [1991] IRLR 513, CA). See ¶5730 regarding the process by which tribunals should approach discrimination and harassment claims.

5726 When considering whether an adverse inference can be drawn, tribunals are under a duty to consider not only an employer's responses to a statutory discrimination questionnaire, but also **any other explanation for the alleged discrimination** provided by the employer in response to a claimant's question(s) in writing, for example, in his response to a tribunal claim (formerly referred to as a notice of appearance), or in reply to a request for additional information (formerly referred to as further and better particulars) (*Dattani v Chief Constable of West Mercia Police* [2005] UKEAT 0385_04_0702: in this case, the EAT held that an inference could be drawn from the responses provided by the employer in his notice of appearance, further and better particulars and a written explanation sent to the claimant).

5727 The **credibility of a witness** will be considered in the light of all the surrounding circumstances and previous history of the case, particularly where it is possible that he might have been subconsciously swayed by a prejudicial or discriminatory attitude (*Anya v University of Oxford* [2001] IRLR 377, CA; *Williams v YKK (UK) Ltd* [2002] UKEAT 0408_01_2202).

Burden of proof

5730 **Reverse burden of proof** Where, at a hearing, the **claimant proves facts** from which the tribunal could conclude, in the **absence of an adequate explanation**, that the employer has (or is to be treated as having) committed an unlawful act of discrimination, harassment or unequal pay, the tribunal must uphold the complaint unless the employer (and any other respondent) proves that he did not commit (or is not to be treated as having committed) the act complained of (s 136 EqA 2010).

Therefore, there is a **two-stage process**:
1. the claimant must prove facts from which the tribunal could conclude, in the absence of an adequate explanation, that the respondent has committed, or is to be treated as having committed, an unlawful act against the claimant; and
2. to successfully defend a claim, the respondent must prove that he did not commit, or is not to be treated as having committed, the unlawful act.

A claimant can satisfy the first stage where the **evidence is neutral** and equally points to a discriminatory or innocent explanation of the underlying reason for the conduct complained of, and he is not required to prove facts which point towards discrimination more than towards an innocent explanation (*Cunningham v Quedos Ltd and anor* [2003] UKEAT 0298_03_2008).

With regard to the second stage of the process, an employer cannot discharge the burden of proof by simply providing **plausible explanations** for the treatment of the worker which were not discredited by the worker (*EB v BA* [2006] IRLR 471, CA). It is not up to a worker to discredit inherently plausible explanations provided by the employer, but rather for the employer to ensure that he has discharged his burden of proof by providing evidence that his treatment of the worker had not been discriminatory.

Where there are sufficient facts to make a **primary case against a third party** accused of aiding an employer's discrimination, the burden of proof passes on to that third party, to disprove an inference of discrimination (*Cunningham v Quedos Ltd and anor*, above).

5731 The EAT has produced some guidance (referred to as the Barton guidelines) for tribunals regarding the **shift in** the **burden of proof** from worker to employer (*Barton v Investec Henderson Crosthwaite Securities Ltd* [2003] IRLR 332, EAT). These guidelines have been revised and upheld by the Court of Appeal and the Supreme Court and are summarised below (*Igen Ltd (formerly Leeds Careers Guidance) and ors v Wong*; *Chamberlin Solicitors and anor v Emokpae*; *Brunel University v Webster* [2005] IRLR 258, CA; *Hewage v Grampian Health Board* [2012] UKSC 37).

1. A claimant must prove, on the balance of probabilities, facts from which the tribunal could conclude, in the absence of an adequate explanation, that the respondent has, or is to be treated as having, committed an act of unlawful discrimination against the claimant.
2. If the claimant does not prove such facts, his/her claim will fail.
3. In deciding whether the claimant has proved such facts, the tribunal must bear in mind that it is unusual to find direct evidence of discrimination and that, in some cases, the discrimination will not have been intentional but rather based on an assumption that the claimant "would not have fitted in".
4. Moreover, the tribunal must take into account the fact that the outcome of this first stage of the analysis will usually depend on what inferences can be properly drawn from the primary facts found by the tribunal.
5. The word "could" set out at 1. above is important, since at this stage the tribunal is not required to reach a definitive determination that the facts proved by the claimant lead the tribunal to conclude that there was unlawful discrimination. The tribunal must consider the primary facts before it can determine what inferences can be drawn from them.
6. At this stage, in considering what inferences or conclusions can be drawn, the tribunal must assume that there is no adequate explanation for those facts.
7. An inference can include, if appropriate, any inference that it is just and equitable to conclude from an evasive or equivocal reply to a discrimination questionnaire etc.
8. The tribunal must consider whether any Code of Practice is relevant and, if so, take such Code of Practice into account. Consequently, inferences can be drawn from any failure by the respondent to follow a relevant Code of Practice.
9. If a claimant has proved facts from which the tribunal could conclude that the respondent has treated the claimant less favourably on the grounds of sex, race etc., then the burden of proof will shift to the respondent.
10. The respondent must then prove that he did not commit, or is not to be treated as having committed, the unlawful discriminatory act.
11. To discharge the burden of proof, the respondent must prove, on the balance of probabilities, that the treatment was in no sense whatsoever on the grounds of sex, race, disability, etc.
12. The tribunal must assess whether the explanation advanced by the respondent is adequate to discharge the burden.
13. To this end, the tribunal would normally expect cogent evidence from the respondent and must consider carefully any explanations provided regarding a failure to deal with a discrimination/equal pay questionnaire and/or relevant Code of Practice.

These guidelines should be applied **reasonably** and **flexibly** and not schematically. In the first stage, for example, a claimant is required to prove facts from which the tribunal could conclude that the respondent has committed an act of unlawful discrimination. In this first stage, the burden is on the claimant. However, that does not mean that only the claimant's evidence is relevant at this stage: if, for example, the claimant made what turned out to be a false statement of fact, then it would be reasonable to check this statement against the evidence of the employer (*Laing v Manchester City Council* [2006] ICR 1519, EAT). The Court of Appeal has gone further, arguing that the evidence of the employer should usually be considered at both stages of the process (*Madarassy v Nomura International* [2007] IRLR 246, CA).

The question of whether a claimant has proved enough for the burden of proof to shift will depend on the facts of each individual case.

5732

EXAMPLE
Examples of claimant proving sufficient facts for the burden of proof to shift
1. In *James v Gina Shoes Ltd and ors* [2012] UKEAT 0384_11_1801, a production manager at a shoe factory brought constructive unfair dismissal and age discrimination claims. He pointed to derogatory ageist remarks made by the managing director in the context of performance management. The managing director had made his unhappiness at the employee's performance clear. He had asked the sales and marketing director to shadow the employee, after which the employee took stress-

related sick leave. A meeting took place a week later, at which the managing director asked the employee directly whether it was his age that caused him not to be able to meet their expectations. He also said that it may have been possible to train the employee if he was younger. These comments upset the employee and he later resigned. During a subsequent grievance meeting, a further comment to the effect that "you can't teach an old dog new tricks" was made by the managing director. The EAT held that the derogatory ageist remarks plainly shifted the burden of proof to the employer.

2. In *Dresdner Kleinwort Wasserstein Ltd v Adebayo* [2005] UKEAT 0569_04_2203, the EAT held that if there are only two candidates for a vacancy, both are equally well qualified, both are of different races, and one is not appointed, that may be sufficient for the burden to shift.

Examples of claimant not proving sufficient facts for the burden of proof to shift

1. In *Brown v London Borough of Croydon and anor* [2007] EWCA Civ 32, where a white manager brought complaints to a black worker about his working manner, and the black worker responded by commencing a tribunal claim for discrimination, but could not bring any other evidence to show that the manager's acts were discriminatory, the Court of Appeal held that the worker had not done enough for the burden to shift.

2. In *Network Rail Infrastructure Ltd v Griffiths-Henry* [2006] UKEAT 0642_05_2305, where there were nine workers competing for five vacancies, the fact that one was not appointed was not sufficient in itself for the burden to shift.

5733 In **equal pay claims**, once a worker can prove that there is a **lack of transparency** in the **employer's pay structure** and/or he has failed to comply with the equal pay questionnaire, this will be sufficient for the claimant to satisfy the first stage of the two-stage process (*Barton v Investec Henderson Crosthwaite Securities Ltd* [2003] IRLR 332, EAT).

5734 **Exception to reverse burden of proof** The EqA 2010 has harmonised provisions in relation to the burden of proof in discrimination cases, so that the reverse burden of proof applies in relation to all protected characteristics. The only exception to the reverse burden of proof retained under the EqA 2010 is in relation to criminal proceedings brought under the Act (s 136(5) EqA 2010).

A. Remedies – discrimination

5735 Where a tribunal finds that a **complaint is well founded**, it may make one or more of three possible orders (s 124 EqA 2010):
a. declaration: this is an order declaring the rights of the complainant and the respondent in relation to the act complained of;
b. compensation: an order requiring the respondent to pay compensation to the complainant; and/or
c. a recommendation.

> MEMO POINTS The Government is **proposing** to allow tribunals to order employers to **conduct pay audits and publish the results** where they have found that the employer has committed equal pay discrimination. The impending change is part of a draft bill called the Enterprise and Regulatory Reform Bill which is proceeding through Parliament. Any further developments will be covered by our updating service.

1. Declaration

5738 If a tribunal finds that an applicant has been discriminated against or subjected to unlawful harassment, it can make a declaration as to the **rights of the parties** in relation to the matters which are the subject of the complaint. This may assist in ensuring, where there is a continuing relationship between the parties, that they each know what is required in order to avoid further discrimination in the future. It will also be the most appropriate remedy where there is no continuing relationship or financial loss but there has been an act of discrimination.

MEMO POINTS The Government is **proposing to repeal** the tribunals' **power to make wider recommendations** that apply to all of an employer's workers. This decision was made following a consultation on various employment issues, and the other changes that are being progressed as a result of this consultation have been included in a draft bill that is currently going through parliament (see memo points to ¶¶5370, 5711, 5231 and 5735). However, at the time of publication, this change was not to be included in the draft bill and it is unclear how and when it will be brought in. Any further developments will be covered by our updating service.

2. Compensation

5740

The principal differences between compensation for discrimination and compensation for unfair dismissal (¶8570) are that in discrimination cases, compensation may be **awarded for injury to feelings**, and there is **no upper limit** on the amount of compensation which may be awarded.

Compensation for unlawful discrimination falls under **two heads**:
– **financial loss**: loss of earnings and benefits both past and future; and
– **non-financial loss**: an amount awarded for injury to feelings and, in certain circumstances, aggravated damages.

Where a worker has been unlawfully discriminated against and is **subsequently unfairly dismissed** by the employer, the fact of the subsequent dismissal does not operate to end the employer's liability for losses arising from the unlawful discrimination (which would have the effect of bringing all further losses from the date of the dismissal under the rules for unfair dismissal, and would therefore be subject to the statutory cap) since the employer is not permitted to rely on a second unlawful act to terminate his liability for the first (*HM Prison Service v Beart (No. 2)* [2005] EWCA Civ 467).

EXAMPLE In *H M Prison Service v Beart (No. 2)*, B's psychiatric injury arising from her employer's discrimination which impacted on her ability to work continued beyond the date of the unfair dismissal. Since B had been unfairly dismissed, there was no reason for her to not be compensated for losses flowing from the act of discrimination beyond the date of her dismissal.

A tribunal must not make an order for compensation for unintentional indirect discrimination unless it has **first considered whether** a declaration or recommendation is appropriate (s 124(5) EqA 2010).

5742

Where employers are **vicariously liable** for a worker's act of discrimination, it will normally be the employer who is required to make a payment in compensation to the complainant. However, if an individual has been named by the complainant as a personal respondent to a claim, the fact that his employer is vicariously liable for his discriminatory act does not necessarily mean that he will escape the consequences of his liability. In such cases, the tribunal may make an order that the individual respondent should also make a payment of compensation to the complainant. If the employer successfully defends himself against a claim for vicarious liability, by showing that he took such steps as were reasonably practicable to prevent his worker from unlawfully discriminating, the tribunal may order the individual worker alone to compensate the complainant.

5743

EXAMPLE In *Miles v Gilbank* [2006] ICR 12, EAT, affirmed on appeal ([2006] IRLR 538, CA), the tribunal was entitled to hold M jointly and severally liable to pay the award to G since, as a senior manager (and effectively the owner of the employing company, which had been dissolved by the time of the EAT hearing), M had consciously encouraged a discriminatory culture to grow which targeted the claimant.

The **ordinary rules of mitigation apply**, so in discrimination cases a complainant is under a duty to mitigate his loss just as he/she would be in an unfair dismissal case (¶8620).

5744

EXAMPLE In *Debique v MOD* [2011] UKEAT 0075_11_1509, the EAT upheld the employment tribunal's decision that the employee had failed to mitigate her loss when she unreasonably refused an offer of alternative employment made by her employer during her notice period to terminate her service. The employee was a female soldier originally from the Caribbean. She had brought successful sex and race discrimination claims arising from difficulties she had in juggling her childcare needs and her role as a deployable soldier (that is, a soldier who could be deployed on active service with little notice). During her notice period, the MOD offered to post her in a non-deployable role for 5 years. The EAT upheld the tribunal's decision that she had unreasonably refused that offer; the non-deployable nature of the role, combined with the excellent childcare facilities nearby and the stability that the posting would offer her for 5 years, would have adequately addressed her childcare difficulties. The EAT recognised that there may be situations where a discriminatory course of conduct has caused such upset that it may not be fair to expect the employee to make a wholly rational analysis of an offer of re-engagement from the former employer, but this was not one of them. Although the employee had lost some faith in her employer, this had not been a primary factor in her decision to refuse the offer. By unreasonably refusing the posting she had failed to mitigate her loss, and the tribunal's decision to limit her compensation to an injury to feelings award was upheld.

A woman **dismissed for a pregnancy-related reason** may not be able to recover compensation for a period of more than 6 months after the date of childbirth, unless she is actively looking for work after that date (*Ministry of Defence v Cannock* [1994] IRLR 509, EAT). However, a tribunal can take account of the **difficulties** faced by a woman with a young child when seeking work (*Ministry of Defence v Hunt* [1995] UKEAT 85_95_0812).

5745 The burden of having to **prove a failure to mitigate loss** is on the person who asserts it. If the employer wants to raise this point then he will have to produce comprehensive evidence of employment opportunities available to the complainant by such means as expert evidence, copy advertisements and the like. Moreover, it is not sufficient for an employer to show that such opportunities are reasonable – instead, he must prove that the worker acted unreasonably in failing to utilise such opportunities (*Wilding v British Telecommunications plc* [2002] IRLR 524, CA).

It is possible for a worker to fulfil the duty to mitigate his loss by deciding to **retrain in a new profession** for a job which would place his earnings on a par with the position he had lost in circumstances in which the employer is unable to demonstrate that there is any suitable alternative employment for which the worker should and could have applied (*Orthet Ltd v Vince-Cain* [2004] IRLR 857, EAT).

Financial loss

5746 The amount awarded must put the complaining worker, so far as is possible, in the position he would have been had the act of discrimination not occurred (*Ministry of Defence v Wheeler* [1998] IRLR 23, CA). It is the complaining worker's own personal loss which is to be taken into account by the tribunal, not any hypothetical loss which has been calculated on the basis of how a "reasonable employer" might have behaved. There is **no limit** on the amount of compensation which can be awarded under this head.

While **stigma damages** would not usually be awarded specifically to compensate a person for the disadvantage in the job market they will suffer as a consequence of bringing a discrimination claim (i.e. the claimant may be stigmatised as potential employers may be more reluctant to hire a person who has taken legal proceedings against a previous employer), it was a factor to be considered when assessing future loss of earnings (*Chagger v Abbey National Plc and anor* [2010] IRLR 47, CA). **Other considerations** include the fact that it is generally easier to obtain employment from a current job than from the status of being unemployed, and the state of the labour market in question at time of dismissal. In cases where the complainant has shown that an unlawful act of **discrimination resulted in a lost chance**, the tribunal will calculate the award of compensation in accordance with the percentage chance that has been lost.

> EXAMPLE In *Brash-Hall v Getty* [2006] EWCA Civ 531, a worker was constructively dismissed while on maternity leave. The tribunal found that the worker would have returned to work after maternity leave and would then have declined a new job offered to her as part of the employer's subsequent restructuring of its business. This finding meant that the worker was entitled to three months' pay in lieu of notice under her employer's contractual severance package.

5747 In cases of discrimination, tribunals are also entitled to make an award on a **joint and several basis**, as between the respondents (if there is more than one) (*Way and anor v Crouch* [2005] IRLR 603, EAT). This means that each respondent is held to be jointly liable but one respondent can be pursued for 100% of the total award, leaving them to pursue the co-respondents for a contribution. The reasoning for making awards on this basis is that just because more than one respondent may have "caused harm", that does not diminish another "harm doer's" liability. The respective responsibility of the respondents may be relevant in determining the contributions that they should each make between themselves, but it is not relevant to their liability. If **co-respondents** do wish to **pursue** each other for a **contribution**, they may be able to do so in the civil courts using the Civil Liability (Contribution) Act 1978: the EAT has held that tribunals have no jurisdiction to hear claims under this Act and that they must be heard in the civil courts, though there is a question mark as to whether contribution claims arising out of tribunal (rather than civil court) proceedings can be brought under the Act at all because the EAT has given a non-binding opinion that the Act only relates to claims brought in the civil courts (*Brennan and ors v Sunderland City Council and ors* [2011] UKEAT 0286_11_0205). If this non-binding opinion is correct then it leaves co-respondents in a vulnerable position if a successful claimant chooses to enforce against one party only. When deciding to make a joint and several award, tribunals should not use the parties' relative financial resources as a basis.

EXAMPLE
1. In *London Borough of Hackney v Sivanandan and ors* [2011] UKEAT 0075_10_2705, an employee was victimised in the course of her unsuccessful application for two different jobs following her previous successful claim of race discrimination by both employer and individual employee respondents. She was awarded compensation for which the respondents were to be held jointly and severally liable. The EAT reversed the ET's decision and held that there was to be no apportionment of the compensation awarded between the parties. The award made in this case was for over £400,000.
2. In *Bungay and anor v Saini and ors* [2011] UKEAT 0331_10_2709, two employees successfully brought claims of religious discrimination against their employer and two members of the employer's board. The tribunal found that these two members of the employer's board, who were not themselves employees, had been the prime movers in a campaign of discrimination targeting the employees because of their Hindu faith. The EAT upheld the tribunal's decision that the board members were agents of the employer with joint and several liability for the discrimination awards, including awards of aggravated damages, and they endorsed the approach taken in example 1.

Non-financial loss

5748 **Injury to feelings** Although an award for injury to feelings will not automatically be made since a sense of injury must be proved by the complainant, it will often be easy for a complainant to prove, in the sense that tribunals will not take much persuading, that an act of discrimination has injured the complainant's feelings (*Ministry of Defence v Cannock* [1994] IRLR 509, EAT). Consequently, an award for injury to feelings will be made in almost every case.

Compensation can be recovered for any losses which are a **direct consequence** of the discriminatory act, whether or not such losses were reasonably foreseeable (*Essa v Laing Ltd* [2004] IRLR 313, CA). However, compensation should not be awarded for losses which result from the actions of the complainant, for example, in unreasonably refusing medical treatment or failing to follow medical advice.

5749 Where **different types of discrimination** arise from the **same facts**, one award may be appropriate, but where loss flows from different forms of discrimination and does **not** arise out of the **same facts**, the tribunal will consider each award separately before determining whether the total sum of the awards is proportionate and that there is no double counting (*Al Jumard v Clywd Leisure Ltd and ors* [2008] IRLR 345, EAT).

EXAMPLE In *Al Jumard v Clywd Leisure Ltd and ors*, the claimant, who worked as a duty manager at a leisure centre, successfully claimed that he had been subjected to race discrimination, disability discrimination and victimisation. He was awarded £13,000 for injury to feelings arising from race discrimination and disability discrimination, but no separate award was made for injury to feelings arising from the victimisation. The EAT held that the tribunal should have considered whether to make a separate injury to feelings award for victimisation before going on to consider whether the overall sum was proportionate to the injury suffered.

5750 The EAT has set out useful **guidance** for tribunals in **calculating an award** for injury to feelings (*Armitage and ors v Johnson* [1997] IRLR 162, EAT). The principles to be applied are as follows:
a. awards for injury to feelings should be compensatory without being punitive. Feelings of indignation at the discriminatory conduct should not be allowed to inflate the award;
b. the amount awarded should not be so low as to diminish respect for the anti-discrimination legislation;
c. awards should be generally similar to the range of awards in personal injury cases;
d. tribunals should remind themselves of the value in everyday life of the sum they have in mind; and
e. tribunals should bear in mind the need for public respect for the level of awards made.

An award of damages in respect of injury to feelings in a discrimination claim is **not taxable** and, as such, tribunals do not need to take into account income tax when determining the amount to be awarded (*Orthet Ltd v Vince-Cain* [2004] IRLR 857, EAT).

5751 In respect of injury to feelings in cases of **sex and race discrimination**, the Court of Appeal has set out **three bands of compensation** which should be applied in assessing such awards (*Vento v Chief Constable of West Yorkshire Police (No 2)* [2003] IRLR 102, CA increased for inflationary purposes by *Da'Bell v NSPCC* [2010] IRLR 19, EAT):
– Top band: £18,000 – £30,000 for awards in the most serious cases of discrimination, for example, where it has taken place over a long period of time;
– Middle band: £6,000 – £18,000 for cases which, although serious, do not merit an award in the top band; and
– Lowest band: £500 – £6,000 for less serious cases, for example, where the discrimination occurred in a single incident (see also *Essa v Laing Ltd*, ¶5748, in which it was held that an award of £5,000 was held to be in the appropriate band for a one-off incident of racial abuse).

Most cases will fall into the lowest band and it appears that an award of at least £500 is generally regarded as the **minimum** appropriate level, although an award of £750 for racial taunts has been held to be so inadequate by the EAT that it was wrong in law (*Doshoki v Draegar* [2001] UKEAT 0939_01_1601). However, it is within the discretion of a tribunal to make an award of £500 for injury to feelings and, while principles have evolved as to the level of such awards, there are no rules as to minimum amounts (*Greig v Initial Security Ltd* [2005] UKEAT 0036_05_1910). Employers should note, however, that there is **no cap** on the amount that can be awarded and awards reaching tens of thousands of pounds have been made on a number of occasions. Moreover, the EAT has demonstrated that it is willing to overturn tribunal awards which it considers inadequate (*Doshoki v Draegar*, above).

> EXAMPLE In *Miles v Gilbank* [2006] ICR 12, EAT, affirmed on appeal ([2006] IRLR 538, CA), the EAT held that an award at the very top of the highest band in respect of injury to feelings in a sex discrimination claim was not "manifestly excessive". The tribunal had made very clear findings of fact that the claimant, G, had been subjected to a "vicious" catalogue of behaviour, amounting to an "inhumane and sustained campaign of bullying and discrimination" by the respondent (M, who was the manager and major shareholder in the company which employed G). The "campaign" had been "targeted, deliberate, repeated and consciously inflicted", demonstrating both a lack of concern for the welfare of G and also a callous disregard for the life of her unborn child.

> MEMO POINTS 1. It is expected that the *Vento* guidance from the Court of Appeal will be followed in cases involving discrimination on **grounds other than sex and race** (*London Borough of Hackney v Adams* [2003] IRLR 402, EAT, a case involving discrimination on trade union grounds).
> 2. The EAT has applied the *Vento* guidelines regarding compensation in respect of injury to feelings to a case of **sexual harassment** (*Carney v Rouf and anor* [2004] UKEAT 0353_04_0211). In this case, in applying the guidelines, relevant factors included the fact that there was persistent harassment over a matter of months, the employer's denial of any discriminatory behaviour (requiring the

claimant to go through what had happened to her at the hearing), and the fact that the harassment had been conducted by one of the owners of the business and not a junior worker.

Any injury to feelings suffered by the complainant which is not in fact **related to the act of unlawful discrimination** will be disregarded by the tribunal in assessing the level of award for injury to feelings.

5752

> EXAMPLE In *Coleman v Skyrail Oceanic Ltd (t/a Goodmos Tours)* [1981] IRLR 398, CA, a female travel booking clerk married a male worker in a competing agency. After it became evident that information was leaked from one agency to the other, the two employers met and decided that the female worker should be dismissed. Their assumption was that the husband was the main breadwinner. The dismissal was held to be unfair and discriminatory on the grounds of sex. The tribunal's award of £1,000 for injury to feelings was based on the assumption that the dismissal would injure the claimant's reputation (i.e. it would be assumed that she leaked the confidential information). However, the Court of Appeal reduced the award to £100 as such injury did not relate to sex discrimination and, therefore, could not be the subject of an award for injury to feelings.

However, if a claimant is **not aware** that the reason for the treatment causing him injury is victimisation, he may still be entitled to compensation for the distress he has suffered (*Taylor v XLN Telecom Ltd and ors* [2010] IRLR 499, EAT).

> EXAMPLE In *Taylor v XLN Telecom Ltd and ors*, the claimant was dismissed on the grounds of poor performance after he had made allegations that one of his managers had behaved in a racially offensive way. The employment tribunal decided not to award compensation for injury to feelings on the grounds that the claimant had not known that the reason for his dismissal had been unlawful victimisation. On appeal, the EAT held that while the injury to feelings or to health had to be attributable to the victimisation, the fact that the claimant was not aware that the reason for the treatment causing him injury was victimisation did not mean he was not entitled to compensation for the distress he had suffered. The case was returned to the same tribunal to assess the amount of compensation.

When an act of discrimination has resulted in the onset of a **psychiatric illness**, the complainant may recover **compensation for personal injury** in addition to an award for **injury to feelings** (*Sheriff v Klyne Tugs (Lowestoft) Ltd* [1999] IRLR 481, CA). Note that, in practice, it may be difficult to separate injury to feelings and psychiatric injury since it may be almost impossible to say with any precision when the distress inflicted on the complainant by the act of discrimination became a recognised psychiatric illness such as depression (*HM Prison Service v Salmon* [2001] IRLR 425, EAT). In such cases, where there is a risk of double compensation, a tribunal can make a single award for injury to feelings, which includes an element for psychiatric injury.

5753

Because of developments in case law relating to psychiatric injury, it is now extremely common for complainants to bring forward evidence of psychiatric injury, and employers facing claims of discrimination should be aware that the state of health of the individual is likely to be an issue. In addition, tribunals often award damages for actual costs incurred, such as for counselling.

Aggravated damages The tribunal may also make an award of aggravated damages where the employer has behaved in a **high-handed, malicious, insulting or oppressive manner** in committing the act of discrimination or, where the employer's conduct of his defence of discrimination proceedings is designed to be intimidatory and cause maximum unease to the worker (*Alexander v The Home Office* [1988] IRLR 190, CA; *Zaiwalla & Co v Walia* [2002] IRLR 697, EAT). These requirements involve some special element in the conduct of the discriminator, which takes the case beyond the ordinary run of discrimination cases and the fact that there has been discrimination. The fact that the victim has been upset or distressed or even injured in his health as a result of the discrimination is not of itself enough. However, the employer's behaviour need not be deliberate or conscious to be considered to be high-handed, malicious, insulting or oppressive (*Leeds Rhinos Rugby Club and ors v Sterling* [2001] UKEAT 0267_01_1710).

5754

When making an award for aggravated damages, behaviour that has taken place after employment has terminated can be taken into account.

> **EXAMPLE** In *Bungay and anor v Saini and ors* [2011] UKEAT 0331_10_2709, two employees successfully brought claims of religious discrimination against their employer and two members of the employer's board. A campaign of discrimination targeting the employees because of their Hindu faith led to the employees being dismissed, and culminated in the board members making a malicious complaint to the police after the employees' employment had ended and they had issued discrimination complaints. In considering whether the tribunal had erred by taking into account conduct which had occurred post-employment in making an aggravated damages award, the EAT noted that there was authority for post-dismissal behaviour being taken into account, and confirmed that "there is no rule of law which restricts the circumstances in which aggravated damages may be awarded". The tribunal had been entitled to make an aggravated damages award because there was a causal link between the campaign of discrimination during employment and the malicious act of making an unfounded complaint to the police after the employment had ended.

Aggravated damages are compensatory, not punitive (*Singh v University Hospital NHS Trust* [2002] UKEAT 1409_01_1102). They are distinct from compensation for injury to feelings and should not be aggregated with, and treated as part of, any damages for injury to feelings (*Scott v Commissioners of Inland Revenue* [2004] IRLR 713, CA). However, the totality of the awards for non-financial loss will be considered to ensure that there is no double counting (*Ministry of Defence v Fletcher* [2010] IRLR 25, EAT; *Wardle v Credit Agricole Corporate and Investment Bank (known as Calyon UK)* [2010] UKEAT 0535_09_1407).

> **EXAMPLE** In *British Telecommunications plc v Reid* [2004] IRLR 327, CA, the Court of Appeal upheld an award for aggravated damages where the employer took over a year to complete its investigation into the worker's grievance that he had been subjected to racially discriminatory language. This had been further exacerbated by the employer who, during the investigation, promoted the alleged perpetrators of the discrimination whilst relocating the worker.

5755 **Exemplary damages** Exemplary damages may be awarded where a servant of the government has acted arbitrarily or unconstitutionally, or where the respondent's conduct has been calculated to make a personal profit in excess of any sums which can be paid to the claimants by way of compensation (*Kuddus (AP) v Chief Constable of Leicestershire Constabulary* [2001] UKHL 29).

> **EXAMPLE** In *Ministry of Defence v Fletcher* [2010] IRLR 25, EAT, the EAT considered a case where a tribunal awarded both exemplary and aggravated damages to a female soldier who suffered sexual harassment and victimisation. During the hearing of her claim she was cross-examined unnecessarily about her psychiatric history and sexual orientation. The tribunal awarded:
> – £30,000 (at the top of the upper band for compensation (¶5751)) for injury to feelings;
> – aggravated damages of £20,000 to reflect the victimisation by means of disciplinary procedures, the poor procedures used to deal with her grievance, and the manner in which the defence was conducted; and
> – exemplary damages of £50,000 on the ground that the army had failed to provide an adequate means of addressing her grievances.
> The EAT held that:
> – the level of aggravated damages should be reduced to £8,000 to avoid double counting in relation to the totality of the awards for non-pecuniary compensation (¶5754); and
> – it was wrong to award exemplary damages for the way in which the case had been conducted as, although deplorable, the conduct did not meet the high threshold for such an award. The EAT went on to comment that £50,000 would, in any event, have been excessive, as it represented the absolute maximum amount which could be awarded, and that if an award of exemplary damages had been appropriate in this case, it should have been no more than £7,500.

3. Recommendation

5760 The tribunal can make a recommendation that the **respondent take action** for the purpose of "obviating or reducing" the adverse effect on the complainant of any act of discrimination complained of, short of positive discrimination. It must specify a period of time for compliance. Under the predecessor legislation, this was qualified so that the order would be to take action which the tribunal considered practicable (in cases of sex, sexual orientation, racial and religion or belief discrimination) or reasonable in all the circumstances of the case (disability discrimination cases). Case law relating to the predecessor legislation suggests that it is not possible for a tribunal to make a recommendation which simply aims to rectify the effect of some other act(s), including those of a third party (*Leeds Rhinos Rugby Club and ors v Sterling* [2001] UKEAT 0267_01_1710).

A recommendation might **relate to matters such as** the removal of a discriminatory requirement, for example, a minimum height requirement. It should not be used where monetary compensation is more appropriate (i.e. a recommendation should not order an increase in pay) (*Irvine v Prestcold* [1981] IRLR 281, CA). Nor is it appropriate to recommend that an applicant who has been refused a job or promotion because of discrimination should be given the next job which becomes available, as this would be unfair to other people who might be suitable (*Noone v N W Thames RHA (No 2)* [1988] IRLR 530, CA).

5761 The existing power to make a recommendation can be of limited practical effect. Tribunals are not able to recommend that an employer discontinues a discriminatory practice (*Ministry of Defence v Jeremiah* [1978] IRLR 402, EAT) nor are they able to recommend that an employer should promote a successful complainant to the next suitable vacancy since such a promotion without consideration of other applicants (who may have superior qualifications) could in itself amount to direct discrimination (*British Gas plc v Sharma* [1991] IRLR 101, EAT).

However, in *Vento*, a tribunal recommended that the Chief Constable should send to the complainant a written apology in specific terms set out by the tribunal, marked for the attention of prospective employers (*Chief Constable of Yorkshire Police v Vento (No 2)* [2002] IRLR 177, EAT). In addition, the tribunal directed (and the EAT upheld on appeal) that the Deputy Chief Constable should interview officers who were involved in the discrimination, and discuss with them certain aspects of the judgment of the tribunals in the case. It was said that in cases of "institutional discrimination", it was good practice to discuss and address the tribunal's findings with those concerned. However, the EAT ruled that it was not appropriate to recommend that the officers concerned be invited to apologise in writing to the claimant nor that the Chief Constable report to the claimant the result of the interviews and whether or not individual officers agreed to apologise.

MEMO POINTS   *Vento* was overturned on appeal to the Court of Appeal but this point remains unaffected (*Chief Constable of Yorkshire Police v Vento (No 2)* [2003] IRLR 102, CA).

5762 If the employer, without reasonable justification, **fails to comply** with a recommendation, the tribunal can, if it thinks it just and equitable to do so, increase any compensation previously awarded (or may award compensation if it did not previously do so) (s 124(7) EqA 2010).

B. Remedies – equal pay

5770 When an equal pay **claim is successful**, the complainant is entitled to an **order** declaring his/her rights. This is likely to have the practical effect that **future pay** will be increased to the level of the comparator's pay, or the complainant's contractual terms will be improved to match those of his/her comparator. Once the order has been made, the complainant has a contractual right to the increased pay or improved terms.

In addition, a tribunal may award **compensation** in respect of arrears of pay (in effect, damages for breach of the implied clause on equal pay) or in respect of breaches of other contractual terms. The **amount recoverable** by a worker is **up to** 6 years' arrears, starting with the date of the claim (s 132 EqA 2010). Where an equal pay claim comes about because a job evaluation has rated a worker's job as equivalent to a job done by a member of the opposite sex, the appropriate compensation, the EAT has ruled, is arrears for the period since the job evaluation. This cannot be more than 6 years' arrears, and will typically be less (*Bainbridge and ors v Redcar & Cleveland Borough Council (No. 2)* [2007] IRLR 494, EAT).

MEMO POINTS 1. In contrast to other areas of discrimination, which are more restrictive, equal pay **claims may be brought** not just in the employment tribunal but also in the **High Court or county court** (s 127 EqA 2010). In these courts, a number of reliefs are available including declarations and injunctions, which are not available to the tribunal. Where, however, claims are brought in these courts and it appears that a case could more conveniently be brought in the employment tribunal, these courts have discretion to refer the matter to the tribunal.

Equal pay claims can be brought in the civil courts **after the time limit** to claim in the employment **tribunal has expired**, effectively extending the time limit to bring such claims from 6 months from termination in the employment tribunal to 6 years from the date of the last breach of contract (i.e. the last failure to pay equally) in the civil courts (*Birmingham City Council v Abdulla* [2012] UKSC 47). This is a significant decision which effectively extends the time available to bring a valid claim from 6 months (¶5723) to 6 years. Potentially, it may encourage a new breed of "piggyback" claims (¶5677) with former staff bringing equal pay claims in the civil courts relying upon successful claims which have been brought by their former colleagues. However, it seems likely that the amount of back pay which can be claimed will be reduced by an amount which corresponds to the delay in bringing the claim e.g. if a claim is delayed by 3 years and then brought in the civil court, the maximum compensation which could be awarded would be 3 years (making a total of 6 years).

2. The 6-year **limit** on arrears is **extendable** in certain circumstances, namely in respect of a worker from whom an employer deliberately concealed facts relevant to his/her equal pay claim, and a worker who is either a minor or of unsound mind. Proceedings must be commenced within 6 years of the facts becoming known or the claimant ceasing to be disabled (s 129 EqA 2010; s 2ZA EPA 1970).

3. In contrast to the general rule preventing any claimant from bringing the same, or substantially the same case, to the court twice, a worker is not prevented from bringing fresh proceedings for equal pay, where the same worker has previously made a complaint against the same employer covering the same period of time, but in the new complaint the worker cites a **new comparator** (*Bainbridge and ors v Redcar & Cleveland Borough Council (No. 2)* [2007] IRLR 494, EAT).

5772 Damages for **non-financial loss**, such as injury to feelings, together with aggravated or exemplary damages, cannot be recovered in equal pay claims (as confirmed in *Council of the City of Newcastle Upon Tyne v Allan and ors, Degnan and ors v Redcar and Cleveland Borough Council* [2005] IRLR 504, EAT).

5773 In relation to claims regarding differential access rules to employers' **pension schemes**, claims can go back to 1976 but must be brought either during employment or within 6 years of its termination (¶3439).

II. Enforcement

5790 The **Equality and Human Rights Commission** (EHRC) has powers to investigate unlawful discrimination.

The EHRC can conduct an **inquiry** (s 16 EqA 2006), or an **investigation** (s 20 EqA 2006) where it suspects that the person or organisation concerned has committed a discriminatory act or acts contrary to anti-discrimination legislation. In carrying out an inquiry or an investigation, the EHRC has powers to compel a person to give information, produce documents or provide oral evidence.

The result of an inquiry will be a **report**. An employment tribunal is entitled to have regard to the report, but will not be bound by its findings.

The result of an investigation may be a report. In addition, the EHRC has the power to issue an **unlawful act notice** (s 21 EqA 2006). Such a notice may include a requirement for an action to be prepared and recommendations for future action. The person to whom the notice applies may appeal within 6 weeks on the grounds that the unlawful act was not committed or that the requirement is unreasonable.

Moreover, after an investigation, or as a measure to forestall an investigation, the EHRC may also reach a **binding agreement** with a person or organisation (s 23 EqA 2006). Where such an agreement is reached, the EHRC is also able to apply for an **injunction** to restrain an organisation from committing an unlawful act.

Failing to comply with a EHRC request or order or giving false information is a summary offence.

The EHRC can also bring proceedings in relation to unlawful instructions to discriminate (s 25 EqA 2006).

5791

SECTION 4

Best practice

In brief, the term "best practice" encompasses the steps which an employer should take to comply with current UK equal opportunities legislation and future obligations that are on the horizon, recommendations by the Equality and Human Rights Commission, and common practice within each sector.

5800

This section contains **general guidance** on the steps employers can take to ensure best practice within their organisation. However, these guidelines must be used flexibly, since the action an organisation should take will depend on and vary with its type, size, resources and needs.

> MEMO POINTS **Public sector bodies** are subject to a single equality duty which requires them to take equality issues into account in their decision making and to advance equality of opportunity. Specific duties require them to publish certain information in connection with their compliance with the single equality duty on a regular basis (s 149(1) EqA 2010; SI 2011/2260).
> The Government has announced that it also intends to review the scope of this duty. Any further developments will be covered by our updating service.

Equality policy

As a **starting point**, the EHRC recommends that all employers formulate, adopt and implement a written equality policy. A written policy focuses attention on the employer's commitment to develop and to use employment procedures and practices which do not discriminate and which provide genuine equality of opportunity for all workers. That commitment is expressed publicly in a manner that the employer can control and manage.

5802

Work practices and procedures

Before an employer adopts an equal opportunities policy for the first time, and thereafter at regular intervals, it is advisable to review the employment practices, procedures and systems that already exist, to ensure that they support equal opportunities in the workplace. It is not uncommon for employers to find that a practice or procedure which appears neutral in fact disadvantages workers who have a particular protected characteristic, for reasons which are neither job-related nor required for the safe or efficient running of the organisation. Such procedures and practices are unlawful, even if the employer never intended to discriminate nor appreciated that they in fact had a discriminatory effect.

5805

Eight specific areas for employers to consider when reviewing their practices and procedures are discussed briefly below.

5806

1. Recruitment practices and job advertisements Employers need to ensure that job advertisements comply with anti-discrimination legislation. It is unlawful for an employer to publish or cause to be published an advert which indicates or might reasonably be understood as indicating an intention to discriminate on any of the protected grounds.

5807

The Equality Code sets out extensive guidance on recruitment policies, procedures and practices including recommendations to:
– review job descriptions and person specifications each time a post is to be fulfilled to avoid imposing unnecessary requirements;
– ensure that job descriptions accurately describe the job in question;
– ensure that criteria relating to skills or knowledge are not unnecessarily restrictive;
– ensure that criteria in a person specification can be justified for that particular job; or
– avoid unnecessary health criteria for a post, and ensure that any criteria which relate to health, physical fitness or disability can be justified.

It is generally unlawful to ask questions about health or disability before the offer of a job is made or a person is placed in a pool of people to be offered a job (s 60 EqA 2010). There are six exceptions to this rule:
– to establish whether reasonable adjustments need to be made in the recruitment process;
– where the question relates to a person's ability to carry out a function that is intrinsic to that job;
– for the purposes of monitoring the diversity of applicants;
– so applicants can benefit from positive action such as a guaranteed interview scheme;
– where there is an occupational requirement for a person with a particular disability; or
– for national security purposes.

MEMO POINTS When asking questions to establish whether an applicant can perform an essential part of a job the employer must first take into account any reasonable adjustments which could be made.

The Equality Code recommends, in relation to job advertisements, that they should:
– accurately reflect the requirements of the job to avoid deterring applicants;
– not include any wording that suggests the employer may directly discriminate against any applicant by using language such as "youthful" or "fit";
– avoid indicating that indirectly discriminatory criteria will be applied; and
– avoid suggesting that reasonable adjustments will not be made for disabled applicants.

In addition to the specific words used in an advertisement, caution should be exercised with regard to graphics, photographs, illustrations and the overall impression given.

Moreover, an advert indicating that a job is open only to persons who are (or who are not) **union members** will lead to a conclusive presumption that work has been refused on union membership grounds and thus, in general, unlawfully (s 137(3) TULRCA 1992).

EXAMPLE Where an employer **advertises a work placement** with a sign reading "We are sorry but because our offices are on the first floor they are not accessible to disabled people", such a notice is likely to be unlawful. Where, conversely, the sign reads "although our offices are on the first floor, we welcome applications from disabled people and are willing to make reasonable adjustments", such an advertisement will be lawful.

MEMO POINTS Although an individual cannot at present make a **complaint about a discriminatory advertisement** under UK law, they may be able to do so under EU law (*Centrum voor Gelijkheid van Kansen en voor Racismbestridning v Firm Feryn NV, Case C 54/07* [2008] IRLR 732, ECJ, a case involving discrimination on trade union grounds).

5808 As a matter of best practice, employers should:
– avoid placing adverts in publications or areas which are generally restricted to, for example, members of one sex, since this may, effectively, preclude a wider range of applicants;
– word advertisements in a way that would encourage applications from all suitable candidates, regardless of age, sex, sexual orientation, maternity and pregnancy, marriage or civil partnership status, gender reassignment, race, religion or belief, or disability. Employers are allowed to include a statement in advertisements that they welcome applications from disabled persons. Employers who are committed to equal opportunities may state that they are equal opportunities employers;
– review all advertising material and accompanying literature, to ensure that it does not present workers in stereotyped roles. For example, it may not be appropriate to have pictures only of male skiers when recruiting ski instructors; and

– avoid prescribing requirements which are not necessary for the performance of the job. For example, length of residence or experience in the UK is unlikely to be a justified requirement for most jobs. If a job is largely sedentary, there is no reason to specify that job applicants must be "energetic". Where a post requires limited load carrying, it may not be acceptable to say that only "strong, able-bodied" persons should apply.

5809 Employers should **avoid** recruiting through existing workers and word-of-mouth as this risks recreating any tendency there is in the existing staff population for certain groups to prosper and others to be excluded.

Likewise, when **recruiting through** employment agencies, job centres, career offices or schools, employers should not confine their recruitment efforts unjustifiably to agencies, job centres, career offices or schools which, because of their particular source of applicants, provide only or mainly applicants of a particular gender or from a particular racial or religious group.

5810 In a limited number of situations, employers are allowed to fill a post with a worker who has a particular protected characteristic. These cases fall under the **occupational requirement** (OR) exception (¶¶5290, 5340, 5402, 5620). When a vacancy for such a post comes up, employers need to examine whether, in all the circumstances, they can still rely on the occupational requirement exception. If the answer is no, employers must open the vacancy to everyone.

Similarly, just because it might have been justifiable in the past not to offer a post to a person suffering from a disability, employers must not assume that the post should never be filled by a **disabled worker**. Every application must be considered individually in light of the applicant's situation and the relevant surrounding circumstances (including, for example, medical and scientific advances).

2. Selection criteria and methods

5811 **Questions** asked at interview, **tests** given to candidates to complete and other **methods of assessing** a person's suitability for a particular post must not be unlawfully discriminatory. Thus, questions should not be put to job applicants, for example, of one sex or sexual orientation only, or of a particular racial group, religion or belief, age or age group, or to disabled workers (for example, asking female applicants only if they have effective childcare arrangements, asking black or Asian candidates only to provide evidence of the right to work in the UK, or asking only gay applicants to undergo medical tests to prove they are HIV negative).

It is often assumed, incorrectly, that it is enough if an employer asks all candidates the same questions. While this is a good starting point, employers must appreciate that how they use the information may also be discriminatory.

5812 Questions on application forms **should not suggest** that the employer will take into account factors which can result in discrimination. For example, is it necessary to ask whether candidates are married, intend to marry, have children or practise any religion? This type of question can undermine applicants' confidence in the selection process; make it difficult for the employer to recruit the best person for the job; make it harder for selectors/interviewers to do their job in a non-discriminatory way; and make it almost impossible for the employer to defend himself if he later faces a discrimination claim. There should not be **questions on marital or civil partnership status** or **number or age of children**.

On the other hand, some questions can improve selection by highlighting "hidden" skills and assets of workers. For example, questions on unpaid work may help female and disabled applicants to demonstrate that they have the necessary experience and/or skills relevant to the vacancy.

5813 It may be necessary for an employer to accept an application in a different **form** in order to accommodate **disabled job applicants** (for example, a voice-recorded application).

5814 Employers should make sure the **arrangements** they make for holding tests or interviews, or using assessment centres, do not put any candidates at a disadvantage on **racial grounds**; for example, because the dates or times coincide with religious festivals or observance, or because they fail to take account of dietary needs or cultural norms.

Where employers carry out a full monitoring process as part of their equal opportunities policy, details of workers' age, sex, marital status, sexual orientation, race, religion and state of health/disability will be needed. It is recommended that such **monitoring information** should be sought on a separate form or on a tear-off slip which should not be available to those making selection decisions. Ideally, the employer should explain on the form his reasons for requesting the information. Employers should not use the information provided as part of the monitoring exercise to reach a decision about the suitability of a job applicant for a particular post. Employers must be aware of their obligations under the Data Protection Act 1998 in regard to such information (¶¶5845, 5900).

5815 Employers should **examine their job selection criteria** to ensure that they are job-specific and are not (intentionally or otherwise) unlawfully discriminatory. In most cases, therefore, employers are advised to:
– limit their required qualifications to those which are necessary for the proper and safe performance of the job. For example, employers should not ask for a higher level of education or a higher standard of English than is needed for the safe and effective performance of the job;
– allow job applicants to make an application in a different form/manner. For example, an employer should not disqualify a job applicant because he is unable to complete the application form unassisted, unless the ability to do this is a valid test of the standard of English and communication required for the safe and effective performance of the job;
– review requirements for a demonstrable career path. Unless such a career path can be objectively justified as a pre-requisite for the safe and effective performance of the job, there is a risk that the requirement will discriminate against female workers, non-English workers or disabled workers, whose career might not have followed the usual route;
– accept overseas qualifications which are comparable with UK qualifications; and
– review their selection tests and ensure that irrelevant questions or exercises are removed. For example, questions on matters which may be unfamiliar to racial minority applicants should be removed, unless knowledge of these matters is essential for the proper performance of the job.

5816 **3. Shortlisting, interviewing and selection** Much of the guidance applicable to selection criteria and methods also applies in respect of shortlisting, interviewing and selection. In addition, however, **staff responsible** for shortlisting, interviewing and selecting candidates **should be**:
a. informed of the job selection criteria;
b. instructed to apply the job selection criteria objectively and consistently; and
c. given training on equal opportunities. This should deal with, for example:
– the effects that generalised assumptions can have on selection decisions;
– the importance of thinking ahead when interviewing a disabled applicant so that adequate preparations/reasonable adjustments are made. Staff should be aware that they may have to make an adjustment when a disabled applicant arrives for an interview even if they did not know in advance of the disability;
– the need to consider a disabled applicant's ability to do the job effectively, on the assumption that a reasonable adjustment can be made;
– asking only about a disability if it is relevant for the performance of the job, and it will be useful to discuss what could reasonably be done to adjust working arrangements to assist the applicant to perform the job safely and effectively. For example, it may be appropriate to ask whether the worker will require extra leave as a result of the disability, because this can be a factor relevant to the person's suitability for the job; and
– how effectively to interview applicants who are returning to work after a period away (for example, because of childcare responsibilities), disabled applicants, or applicants of a different race. For example, staff should be instructed to ensure that the interviewer's eyes are at the same level as the applicant's when interviewing a wheelchair user.

Wherever possible, shortlisting and interviewing should be done by more than one person or should, at least, be checked by a more senior manager. Staff involved in the selection process should receive training on the employer's equality policy.

5817 In addition, the Equality Code recommends (para 16.46 Equality Code) that employers make arrangements to **keep data**, including application forms and documents relating to each stage of the recruitment process, for 12 months, in case of any complaints about decisions or procedures, or requests for the information under the Data Protection Act 1998, or, where appropriate, the Freedom of Information Act 2000. The documentation should include:
– job advertisement, job description or person specifications used in recruitment;
– records of discussions and decisions by members of the selection panel (for example, on marking standards or interview questions);
– notes taken by each member of the panel during the interviews;
– each panel member's marks at each stage of the process (for example, on the application form, any selection tests and each interview question); and
– all correspondence with the candidates.

5818 **4. Promotion, transfer and training practices** Where an employer considers the promotion of a worker, many of the factors which apply to the selection of an external applicant will apply. In addition, and more specifically, best practice suggests that employers should:
– publicise vacancies, training and transfer opportunities to all eligible workers in a way that will encourage a broad range of applicants;
– review selection, assessment and appraisal systems to ensure that they are not unlawfully discriminatory;
– review promotion and career development patterns to ensure that the required qualifications/career patterns are objectively justified for the job at hand. For example, is length of service a justified criterion? In some cases, it can lead to unlawful sex discrimination as it may adversely affect more women than men;
– objectively consider candidates with differing career patterns when general ability and personal qualities are the main requirements for promotion to a post;
– review rules which restrict or preclude transfer between certain jobs. It may be that workers of one sex, or particular racial group or religion, or who are disabled or are above or below a certain age are concentrated in sections from which transfers are traditionally restricted without real justification. If these rules are found to be unlawfully discriminatory, or potentially so, they should be changed;
– review policies and practices for selection for training and personal development. If considerably more workers of one group attend certain training/undertake certain forms of personal development the reasons for this need to be identified. It may be that the content of the course or the way workers are selected to attend is discriminatory. In such a case, assumptions, policies and practices may have to be changed; and
– remove age limits for access to training and promotion, unless the employer can justify such limits as being a proportionate means of achieving a legitimate aim.

5819 **5. Terms of employment, benefits, facilities and services** To ensure that terms of employment, benefits, facilities and services are not unlawfully discriminatory, employers must, at the outset, **review** these, their potential and actual impact on all workers, and **consider** whether and how these terms, facilities etc. square with UK equal opportunities legislation.

The most appropriate steps for an employer to take will depend on the particular circumstances, for example, the size of the organisation, the structure of the workforce (for example, male/female-dominated, multi-racial, small or large number of disabled workers), the resources of the organisation etc. Below are examples of a number of areas in which employers may need or want to take action.

Flexible work arrangements

5820 Job-sharing, part-time working, homeworking and other atypical work patterns are often regarded as a concession to female workers with childcare responsibilities. However, workers of each sex increasingly seek to balance their work and personal lives. Accordingly, there is increased demand on employers to provide working patterns that allow workers to maintain a fulfilling career while having adequate time for life outside work. Employers should consider introducing or developing a standard flexible working policy which sets out the types of flexible working which they offer and the procedure for requesting such arrangements.

A flexible work arrangement policy should provide a consistent, universally accessible framework. Changes to working hours and patterns should not be made ad hoc on the basis of a "deal" between a worker and the employer (if only because this could lead to a claim of discrimination by a worker whose request is not accommodated). Any restrictions on eligibility under the policy must be based on real operational needs and must be objectively justifiable. Employers should review the restrictions regularly to ensure that they remain justifiable and, if not, they must be removed.

5821 Ideally, a flexible working policy should:
– offer flexible working to all workers irrespective of sex or other potentially discriminatory grounds;
– not impose obligatory restrictions on the type of post(s) open for job sharing/flexible hours etc. Unless there are good operational reasons, flexible working should be offered regardless of grade. Any restriction ought to be based on real operational needs and not on any assumptions that certain jobs carry too much responsibility. Restrictions based on such assumptions may result in a "glass ceiling" preventing certain workers (for example, women or disabled workers) from reaching senior positions and thereby deprive the organisation of a valuable resource of managerial/senior expertise;
– ensure that training is available to all workers, regardless of their working patterns;
– apply to workers regardless of their length of service (such a qualification can indirectly discriminate against women who tend to have shorter careers, or take more breaks in their careers because of domestic responsibilities);
– not set an arbitrary limit on the number of jobs that can be worked flexibly;
– include provision for real attempts to facilitate flexible working, for example, make efforts to find a jobshare partner where jobsharing is requested; and
– set out provisions for leave, pay and other benefits which are equal (but pro-rated) to those available to full-time workers.

> MEMO POINTS   Certain parents have the **right to request flexible work arrangements** and there are specific procedures for employers and workers to follow when dealing with the request (¶¶4690+).

Cultural/religious needs

5822 Workers may have particular cultural/religious needs which conflict with their work requirements (for example, with regard to work patterns and working hours). In such cases, employers should consider whether it is reasonably practicable to vary or adapt the work requirements to accommodate the workers' specific cultural and religious needs. For example, Friday evenings are religious holidays for observant Jews, and it may be reasonable to allow Jewish workers to leave work early on Fridays, especially where they have the opportunity to make up those hours at other times. Fridays are also religious holidays in the Islamic calendar, and many Muslim workers would be grateful for the opportunity to attend mosques on Friday lunchtimes. Where such requests are made, and there is no business reason to refuse them, they should be considered carefully.

In general, an employer should consider allowing workers to observe prayer times and religious holidays if insistence on attendance at work during those times is not justifiable and working time could be made up by the workers at other times.

Social occasions may also provide an environment for indirect discrimination: if an employer has a habit of regularly organising events at which alcohol is likely to be consumed, he should reflect that many Muslim workers do not drink, and take every effort to ensure that such workers are not excluded from attending events, nor excluded in any other fashion if they do attend.

Sometimes a failure to accommodate religious requirements can amount to indirect discrimination, but such discrimination can be justified in certain circumstances. For further discussion on indirect discrimination see ¶¶5410+, and for discussion on justification see ¶¶5418+.

MEMO POINTS Further guidance may be obtained from Acas which has prepared a guide for employers dealing with the requirements of the main religions practised in the UK.

Leave policies

Generally speaking, annual leave, domestic leave and other special leave arrangements should be applied consistently. For example, if a worker requests extended leave to visit relatives in his country of origin and the employer has a policy which allows for the accumulation of annual leave, the policy should be applied consistently.

Bereavement policies should reflect certain religions' requirements for burial within 24-48 hours of death.

Benefits and workers' partners

Where employers offer benefits to workers in respect of their spouses (for example, bereavement benefits or private medical insurance for a worker's spouse or family), they must offer the same benefit to workers who are in a civil partnership (¶5325). In addition, although it is not unlawful to restrict benefits to spouses and civil partners and to exclude workers who have neither, it is best practice to offer them to all workers, irrespective of their marital status.

Communication and language training

Employers are not obliged by law to provide language training, but where staff are employed with limited English (for example, because they are foreign nationals), the employer should consider providing language training as a means of improving efficiency, promotion prospects, health and safety, and understanding between the employer, staff and unions. By way of an example, an employer may consider providing:
– interpretation and translation facilities, for example, in the communication of terms of employment and employment policies and procedures;
– training in English language and communication skills;
– translated safety signs; and
– training for managers and supervisors about the background and culture of racial minority groups.

Dress and appearance

Certain jobs may require workers to wear **uniforms** or **protective clothing** (for reasons of **safety** or **hygiene**) and some employers require workers to maintain a **high standard of dress** and appearance. If the employer has such expectations, his requirements should be made a term of the contract, which should expressly state that a failure to adhere to the dress code may result in disciplinary action.

A **dress code** may be different for men and women, but must not **discriminate** on the grounds of **sex**, **race** or **religion**.

A number of cases have concerned whether it is discriminatory to require male and female workers to wear different uniforms. In 1977, the EAT held that it was lawful to refuse female retail staff permission to attend work in trousers, even though they might have been required to go up and down book-stacks (*Schmidt v Austicks Bookshops Ltd* [1977] IRLR 360, EAT). However, in 1993, an employment tribunal concluded that dismissing a female worker for wearing trousers was unfair (*Stoke-on-Trent Community Transport v Cresswell*, IT case 23968/92), and other tribunals since have taken a similar approach (*Owen v Professional Golf Association*, ET case 1303043/98).

Employers may adopt a dress code requiring **conventional appearance** with differing requirements for men and women, provided that it enforces compliance of those differing requirements in the same way for both genders (*Dansie v The Commissioner of Police for the Metropolis* [2009] UKEAT 0234_09_2010). However, workplaces that operate **dress-down policies** are likely to find it harder to benefit from a "conventional appearance" defence, and dress-down codes should be formulated to be as similar for each sex as possible. However, it has been held that requiring male staff to wear a collar and tie will not necessarily constitute less favourable treatment. The question is whether the level of smartness required by the employer can only be achieved by imposing such a requirement (*Department for Work and Pensions v Thompson* [2004] IRLR 348, EAT).

> **EXAMPLE** In *Dansie v The Commissioner of Police for the Metropolis*, a male trainee police officer asked before he attended basic training whether wearing his long hair in a bun would comply with the employer's dress code, which required recruits to wear hair above the collar or, if long, fastened close to the head. Although he was told that it would, when he started training he was told to get his hair cut. He made a claim of sex discrimination. The EAT upheld the decision of a tribunal that the dress code, looked at as a whole, was balanced in the way it treated the sexes and that there had been no less favourable treatment, because a woman would also have been required to comply with the code in so far as it affected her.

Uniforms have now evolved so that they are nearly always unisex. However, the employer may impose other standards of dress that may be discriminatory. In any event, the employer should have a **convincing reason** for requiring a particular dress code, and should refrain from reasons based purely on subjective taste (*Catharell v Glyn Nuttall Ltd*, IT case 7935/81).

The dress code should also take into account the **racial and religious requirements** of workers. In general, the employer should be aware that certain members of his workforce may not be able to conform to a dress code that goes against their cultural or religious beliefs and should, wherever possible, allow for this. There are instances where the law specifically addresses religious requirements, for example, the requirement of wearing a helmet on a construction site does not extend to a Sikh who is wearing a turban (s 12 Employment Act 1989 as amended by Sch 26 para 5 EqA 2010).

> **EXAMPLE**
>
> **Discrimination on the grounds of religion or belief**
> In *R (on the application of Watkins-Singh) v Governing Body of Aberdare Girls' High School* [2008] EWHC 1865 (Admin), the High Court held that a schoolgirl had been discriminated against when she had not been allowed to wear her Kara (a bangle which was contrary to the school's dress policy) as, despite not being an actual requirement of being a Sikh, she, like many other Sikhs, genuinely believed for reasonable grounds that it was of exceptional importance to her racial identity or her religious belief.
>
> **No discrimination on the grounds of religion or belief**
> In *Eweida v British Airways Plc* [2010] EWCA Civ 80, the Court of Appeal considered the case of a BA employee suspended for wearing a cross which was visible over her uniform, contrary to the company's dress code. The code allowed any jewellery which remained covered by the uniform, and permitted the wearing of visible religious symbols or clothing which were regarded as mandatory, such as the hijab, turban or skull cap. The Court of Appeal upheld the decision of the EAT that there had been no indirect discrimination in this case. It was accepted that the wearing of the cross was the employee's own personal choice rather than something required by scripture, and the employee had been unable to show that there are enough Christians who consider it essential to wear such a visible symbol of their faith to establish that there was a group disadvantaged by the rule. The Court also disagreed with the view of the employment tribunal that the dress code would have been disproportionate. It commented that where different groups in the workforce have conflicting views on a dress code, a blanket ban may in some cases be the only fair solution.
> It should be noted that the Equality and Human Rights Commission (EHRC) has submitted an intervention to the European Court of Human Rights (ECHR) stating that the UK courts had made incorrect decisions in relation to the cases of *Eweida* and *Chaplin* (an unreported tribunal decision following the Court of Appeal decision in *Eweida* which also involved an employee not being permitted to wear a crucifix, as a manifestation of their Christian beliefs, at work). Both of these cases held that indirect discrimination could not be established because the employees could not identify other people sharing their religion who would be put at that particular disadvantage. The EHRC claims that, whilst the European legislation has been properly incorporated into domestic statutes, the domestic legislation is being misinterpreted by the UK courts and, in particular, it is open to the courts to use hypothetical comparators. They also make the general point that group disadvantage may be more difficult to identify in cases of religious discrimination because diverse religious beliefs are legitimately subject to individual interpretation. The EHRC also argues that the fact that not all Christians wear a cross should not "necessarily undermine the rights of those Christians for whom the display of the cross is an essential and reasonable aspect of their autonomous interpretation of their faith". Although there is a proportionality test that allows employers to refuse their employees permission to manifest their religious belief (for example, on the grounds of health and safety), the EHRC submits that the courts did not apply this test with sufficient rigour in these cases. It invites the court to find that "if an individual's desire to manifest a belief is motivated by a

genuinely held belief that attains a certain level of cogency and seriousness", then the rights of article 9 (which guarantee freedom of thought, conscience and religion) should apply.
For further details, see: flmemo.co.uk/em5826, and we will keep you informed of any developments via our updating service.

Although it is still common for dress policies to set out different rules for male and female workers, it is very unusual for dress policies to require workers to wear different clothing according to their different racial or religious backgrounds. In practice, therefore, where individuals have challenged dress codes, arguing that they discriminate on grounds of race or religion or belief, they have done so by claiming that the discrimination was indirect. Indirect discrimination, in contrast to direct discrimination, is subject to a justification defence. In a high-profile case, a school was able to defend its policy that a bi-lingual support worker should not teach pupils with her face covered, by arguing that such a policy was in the interest of the children's education as it impeded effective communication (*Azmi v Kirklees Metropolitan Council* [2007] ICR 1154, EAT).

The Human Rights Act 1998 may also have an impact on the employer's ability to impose dress/appearance requirements, as it enshrines the right to **freedom of expression** and the ability to exercise that right without discrimination. In another high-profile case, however, the House of Lords (now called the Supreme Court) held that a schoolgirl's right to practise her religion did not allow her to manifest her religion at any time or place. In consequence, a school did not discriminate against her where it allowed female Muslim students to wear a shalwar kameez but not a jilbab (*R (on the application of Begum) v Head Teacher and Governors of Denbigh High School* [2006] UKHL 15).

EXAMPLE
1. In *Smith v Safeway* [1996] IRLR 456, CA, the Court of Appeal upheld the employer's rule under which a male delicatessen assistant was dismissed for having such long hair that it would no longer keep under his cap. The argument that the rule that required him to keep his hair short went well beyond his appearance at work, and was discriminatory compared to the rules for female colleagues, was rejected. In that case the Court was prepared to permit the employer considerable leeway in establishing the image that he wanted to project.
2. In *Catharell v Glyn Nuttall Ltd*, C's dismissal for refusing to have his hair cut was unfair since, provided the performance of his job (as an electrician) or the employer's business was not detrimentally affected, the length of his hair was a matter of his own personal taste.
3. In *Harris v NKL Automotive Ltd and First Matrix Consultancy UK Ltd* [2007] UKEAT 0134_07_0310, where a dreadlocked Rastafarian driver was dismissed for his untidy appearance, the EAT held that the reason for the dismissal was not a company prohibition against dreadlocks (a policy which would in all probability have indirectly discriminated on the grounds of religion or belief) but a prohibition against untidy hair. Accordingly, there was no discrimination.

6. Grievance and disciplinary procedures and victimisation

It is unlawful to discriminate in the operation of any dispute resolution procedure, for example, by instigating a disciplinary procedure against a worker because he has complained of discrimination or harassment, or has assisted another to make such a complaint.

It is vital that employers ensure that grievances which are based on or relate to a worker's sex, sexual orientation, pregnancy or maternity, marriage or civil partnership status, gender reassignment, race, religion or belief, disability, or age, are taken seriously, are investigated promptly and thoroughly and, as far as possible, are kept confidential. Employers ought not to treat complaints of such a nature lightly.

Employers should review and, where necessary, adjust their grievance and disciplinary procedures to avoid placing a disabled worker at a substantial disadvantage. For example, where a worker with a learning disability is required to attend a disciplinary hearing, he should be allowed to bring a colleague or a guardian or friend with him, and may have to be given longer than normal to prepare for the hearing.

7. Dismissal, selection for redundancy and other detrimental treatment

There is a risk of unlawful discrimination when an employer dismisses or selects a worker for redundancy. Employers must take appropriate precautions to ensure that their procedures and actions do

not discriminate unlawfully. What **steps** are **needed** will depend on all the circumstances, including the nature and size of the organisation, the employer's resources, the worker(s) in question etc. Generally speaking, employers are advised to ensure that:
– staff responsible for selecting workers for dismissal or redundancy are given equal opportunities training and are instructed not to select workers on discriminatory grounds;
– their redundancy selection criteria are not directly or indirectly discriminatory (for example, selection on the basis of a sickness absence record can be unlawfully discriminatory against female and/or disabled workers, and a last in-first out selection policy for redundancy is likely to be discriminatory on the grounds of age against younger workers who have not worked for their employer as long as older workers);
– workers of one group are not dismissed for performance or behaviour which would be overlooked or condoned in a worker belonging to another group, and any necessary reasonable adjustments are made before a disabled worker is dismissed for poor performance;
– eligibility conditions for voluntary redundancy apply equally to all workers in the same (or not materially different) circumstances, regardless of any protected characteristics that they may have;
– where there is a change in working conditions (for example, the employer has a new shift structure), the new arrangements do not contravene equal opportunities legislation (for example, a new shift system does not make it considerably harder for female workers than male workers to attend work); and
– employers take all reasonably practical steps to ensure that a standard of behaviour is observed which ensures dignity at work. Workers should not be subjected to unwanted conduct which has the purpose or effect of violating their dignity or creating an intimidating, hostile, degrading, humiliating or offensive working environment on discriminatory grounds. The careful formulation, dissemination and implementation of an equal opportunities policy should go a long way towards fulfilling an employer's obligations in this respect.

5831   **8. Preferential treatment**   It is not lawful for an employer to discriminate positively in favour of any group of workers. It is lawful, however, to take **positive action** (¶5623). Such action is most likely to be proportionate and justified where it is taken on the basis of an **impact assessment**, as where, for example, an employer has a race equality policy which requires him to monitor his staff population on a regular basis, and the results of this monitoring show a noticeable demographic contrast between the nature of the organisation's clients, and the profile of its staff. The following are just some of the steps that may be open to an employer:
– providing training to existing workers for work which is traditionally the preserve of workers of the opposite sex (for example, training female staff for technical or managerial jobs and training male staff to do administrative or secretarial work);
– providing training to staff of an under-represented racial group or religion or belief for promotion, for example, language training; and
– setting up recruitment and training schemes for school leavers which are designed to reach members of the under-represented group.

Monitoring equal opportunities

5835   An employer may benefit from monitoring the composition of his workforce. The fact that an employer has monitored the diversity of his workforce is often **taken into account** by the tribunals when dealing with claims based on discrimination.

If the workforce is small, the employer may not need to make a formal assessment of his workforce, as the diversity (or lack of it) will be readily apparent. Appendix 2 of the Equality Code sets out guidance on monitoring.

5836   Monitoring should not be a mere paper exercise. Through monitoring, an employer will be able to identify areas where there may be existing problems, or potential problems, which may or may not indicate that there are equality issues. His findings may assist him in identifying:
– unfairness in opportunities, which may be a result of unlawful discrimination;
– whether his workforce reflects the local community appropriately; and
– the effectiveness of his equal opportunities policy.

Having identified areas of deficiencies, the employer can decide how best to deal with them, if at all. If, for example, the findings show that there are differences in the pay rates of different groups of workers, he should ascertain whether there is a valid reason for this. Similarly, the results of the monitoring may show that workers are not being recruited from the local community. There may be valid reasons for this, but it may be indicative of racial discrimination in his recruitment methods. Unless the employer addresses such issues, he will remain vulnerable and open to action under the anti-discrimination legislation.

5837

The **extent** of the **monitoring** will depend on the employer's objectives. The following types of monitoring are likely to be acceptable:
– the constitution of the workforce based on, for example, ethnicity, sex, religion, sexual orientation, disability, age or age group, part-time workers and their respective jobs (what section, what type of work, what grade);
– differences in pay between different groups, and the reasons for such differences;
– trends in training opportunities, transfers and promotions between the different groups, and if they are different, the reasons why;
– the effectiveness of company procedures on grievance/harassment;
– the disciplinary procedure and whether it has universal application across the workforce;
– accessibility of the workplace for disabled people; and
– whether one group of workers is more likely to resign than others.

5839

Through monitoring, the employer is more likely to have a secure basis to develop equality in the workplace and ensure that he reaches the widest pool of talent when recruiting. The employer will also benefit by retaining workers, thereby reducing recruitment and training costs. If it is evident that an employer is being proactive and ensuring equality of opportunity the public perception of that employer may also be improved. There is also likely to be an improvement in the morale of the workforce if the employer is seen to be taking equality issues seriously.

To ensure the integrity of monitoring systems, the EHRC recommends that employers:
– consult workers, trade unions and other workplace representatives to make sure that they understand the reasons for introducing monitoring before asking workers for information;
– assure all workers that information gathered will be used in the strictest confidence, and keep it in confidence;
– analyse the information regularly; and
– make sure that managers responsible for monitoring, and anyone else involved in the process, are properly trained in data protection.

5840

Data protection issues

Monitoring Monitoring the diversity of a workforce, and processing the related data, is clearly an accepted employment practice provided it is used to promote equality of opportunity (¶5951). However, employers must still ensure that they comply with the **data protection rules** (¶5945) (for example, where the **data is sensitive** (¶5925), explicit consent should be obtained).

5845

As **good practice**, employers should (part 2.5 Employment practice data protection code (DP Code)):
– ensure that all equal opportunities monitoring satisfies a sensitive data condition;
– where possible, ensure that the information is collected in anonymised form. Information that identifies individual workers should only be used where it is necessary to do so to enable a meaningful monitoring; and
– design questions to ensure data is accurate and not excessive. For example, employers should not limit the range of choices of ethnic origin to the extent that individuals are forced to make a choice they consider does not properly describe them.

Employers are also advised to follow the DP Code's general **recommendations** with regard to data management (¶6000).

CHAPTER 17

Data protection and privacy

OUTLINE

		¶¶				¶¶
SECTION 1	**Data protection**	5910	SECTION 2	**Monitoring and surveillance**		6150
A	Scope of protection	5920				
	Personal and sensitive data	5925	A	General standards		6160
B	Employer obligations	5940	B	Monitoring electronic communication		6190
1	Data protection principles	5945	1	Data protection compliance		6200
2	Disclosure of information	5970	2	Interception requirements		6220
	Marketing	5973	C	Other specific forms of surveillance		6230
	Fraud detection	5974		Video and audio		6233
	Publication of personal and sensitive information	5975		In-vehicle monitoring		6237
	Business mergers and acquisitions	5977		Non-employment information		6240
	Official requests for information	5979	D	Covert monitoring		6250
3	Subject access requests	5980				
4	Notification	5990	SECTION 3	**Email, internet and social media issues**		6260
C	Data management	6000				
1	Collecting and handling records	6003				
2	Retention of records	6015	SECTION 4	**Right to privacy**		6285
D	Remedies	6040				

Employers are required by law to meet certain **obligations** when obtaining, handling or using workers' personal information or when monitoring their acts/communications (Data Protection Act 1998 (DPA 1998); Regulation of Investigatory Powers Act 2000; Human Rights Act 1998 and the implied duty of trust and confidence).

5900

Email and internet issues, including those relating to social media, and the right to privacy are also discussed in sections 3 and 4.

SECTION 1

Data protection

When personal information is collected, used or stored by an employer, he has an **obligation to protect** that information from being improperly used or distributed. The individual whose personal details are being held or used also has a **right to know** exactly what information is being held and the reasons why.

5910

Protection is provided under the Data Protection Act 1998 (DPA 1998) through the **data protection principles** which apply when personal information relating to a living individual is

5911

processed. Most of the principles amount to no more than good employment practice and the aim of the DPA 1998, and its related Employment Practice Data Protection Code (DP Code), is intended to ensure that employers develop a culture in which privacy, data protection security and maintaining the confidentiality of personal information are all taken seriously.

The DP Code sets out **good practice recommendations** and key points and possible actions for employers to follow. There are four parts which deal respectively with recruitment and selection, employment records, monitoring at work and medical testing. The recommendations are designed to help employers comply with the requirements of the DPA 1998. In an enforcement action, the non-implementation of these recommendations may be cited by the Information Commissioner to show that the employer has not complied with his obligations under the data protection principles. Likewise, in a tribunal or court claim, failure to comply may be accepted by the tribunal or court as evidence of a breach of the DPA 1998 unless the employer can prove that the particular requirement was met in some equally or more effective way.

MEMO POINTS The **Information Commissioner** enforces and oversees the DPA 1998 and is an independent supervisory authority. The Commissioner's duties include the promotion of good information handling and the encouragement of codes of practice for data controllers. The Commissioner produces the DP Code (see above) and a code of practice on CCTV monitoring. In addition, the Commissioner has also published **legal guidance** notes, which serve as a reference document for employers and their advisers, and **model contract clauses**.

5912 There are **four parts** to the DP Code:
– Part 1: Recruitment and selection, on job applications and pre-employment vetting. In particular it covers: advertising, dealing with applications, verifying applicants' details, short-listing, interviewing, vetting and the retention of recruitment records;
– Part 2: Employment records, on the collection, storage, disclosure and deletion of employment records. In particular it covers: managing data, collecting and keeping employment records, security, sickness and accident records, pension and insurance schemes, equal opportunities monitoring, marketing, fraud detection, workers' access to information about themselves, and dealing with disclosure requests, references, publication and other disclosures, mergers and acquisitions, discipline, grievance and dismissal, outsourcing data processing and the retention of records;
– Part 3: Monitoring at work, on the monitoring of workers. In particular it covers: the monitoring of electronic communications, video and audio monitoring, covert monitoring, in-vehicle monitoring and monitoring through information from third parties. The Information Commissioner has also produced supplementary guidance which is designed to be read alongside the relevant good practice recommendations given in Part 3 and provides additional notes and examples; and
– Part 4: Medical information, on occupational health, medical testing, and drug and genetic screening.

A. Scope of protection

Data subjects

5920 **Workers** and other individuals who are working, or who have worked (for example, casual labour, agency workers or past workers) or might work (for example, job applicants), for the employer are **entitled to protection** by the data protection principles as data subjects.

Data controller

5922 As the **employer** determines the purpose for which personal data is to be kept, and the manner in which it is to be processed, he is a data controller and **must comply** with the data protection principles if he (s 5 DPA 1998):

– is established in the UK. This includes those who maintain an office, branch or agency or have a regular practice in the UK;
– processes personal or sensitive data in the context of his business; and
– determines (either alone or with other persons) the purposes for which and the manner in which the data is or is to be processed.

Employers that are not established in the UK or any other EEA state but **use equipment in the UK** for processing data, otherwise than for transit purposes, will also be subject to the data protection principles.

EXAMPLE
1. A Ltd is a subsidiary company of B Ltd. The records of A Ltd's staff are kept on the computer of B Ltd. A Ltd use the records for general personnel management. B Ltd use them for staff allocation and progression planning within the group. Both A Ltd and B Ltd will be data controllers for the records of A Ltd's staff.
2. Personal data from country C is routed through the UK to country D. Unless some substantive processing operation is carried out on such data in the UK, it is deemed to be in transit and not subject to the data protection principles.

Personal and sensitive data

The data protection principles apply whenever personal or sensitive data is **processed** (see Processing below). Information can be processed either by **automated systems**, such as computers, telephones, audio or video systems that process information automatically, or by the means of a **relevant filing system**, where information is contained within a system that is structured by reference to either individuals or to criteria relating to individuals and which is readily accessible. A relevant filing system can be either electronic (computer programmes) or manual (paper-based) files from which specific information on the worker can be retrieved, for example files with the worker's name or individual reference number from which information such as his start date or last appraisal can be ascertained.

The Information Commissioner has given detailed **guidance** on when **manual files** will be deemed to be a relevant filing system and has indicated that such files will only be covered if they are sufficiently structured, indexed, divided or referenced to allow the retrieval of personal data without leafing through the files. To help identify whether a manual file is covered, the Commissioner has devised the "**temp test**":

"Would a temp be able to extract specific information from the manual files about an individual without any particular knowledge of the employer's type of work or documents?"

It should be noted that the Commissioner has commented that, as a result of this guidance, very few manual files will be covered.

MEMO POINTS   The Freedom of Information Act extends the definition of data with regard to information held by **public sector bodies** and, as a result, such authorities will have to ensure that from 2005 unstructured manual personal data (except for unstructured manual personnel records) is accurate, up to date and accessible (Freedom of Information Act 2000).

Personal data is information that relates to a person who can be identified from that data or from other information that the employer has or is likely to have. It might include:
– salary details;
– sickness and attendance records;
– notification forms naming next of kin/beneficiaries;
– annual assessments; or
– bank account details.

Also included are any opinions about a worker and any indication of the intentions of the employer or other person with respect to that person.

However, it does not necessarily follow that because a person is **mentioned by name** in a document held by a data controller that such a document amounts to personal data. A document will only constitute personal data if it is sufficiently **relevant or proximate** to the person concerned (*Durant v Financial Services Authority* [2003] EWCA Civ 1746). As a result of *Durant*, the Information Commissioner has issued a detailed commentary on what amounts to personal data and has confirmed that data will only be personal if it can be linked to an **identifiable individual** (for example, where his name appears together with his address, telephone number or information regarding hobbies, or where the data contains information about his medical history, salary, tax liabilities, bank statements or spending preferences).

However, **documents** that, when viewed on their own, would not be regarded as "personal" could become construed as such when **viewed** all **together** (*Johnson v Medical Defence Union [2004] EWHC 347 (Ch)*).

5927 **Special protection** is given when personal information, **considered as sensitive**, is processed, such as (s 2 DPA 1998):
– racial or ethnic origin;
– political opinions, religious beliefs or other beliefs of a similar nature;
– trade union membership;
– physical or mental health;
– sexual life; or
– the commission or alleged commission of any offence, or any proceedings for any offence committed or alleged to have been committed, and/or the disposal of any such proceedings or sentence given.

5928 **Information** is **not protected** if it does not identify an individual, such as:
– general reports that do not name or use identifying information such as job titles;
– manual files that are not part of a filing system; or
– reports on individuals that are anonymised.

> MEMO POINTS Information will be anonymised where it is stripped of all factors by which an individual may be identified. However, this does not apply where there is a cross-reference to other information which identifies the individual.

Processing

5930 Personal and sensitive data will be processed if the employer does any of the following with it (s 1 DPA 1998):
a. obtaining, recording or **holding** it; or
b. carrying out **any operation** or set of operations on it including:
– organisation, adaptation or alteration;
– retrieval, consultation or use;
– disclosure by transmission, dissemination or otherwise making available; or
– alignment, combination, blocking, erasure or destruction.

These actions encompass most activities that are performed by an employer on personal information that he keeps on his workers. Even when an employer strips identifying factors from personal data in order to anonymise it he will be considered to be processing that data.

> EXAMPLE
> 1. Short-listing job applicants on the basis of information provided on application forms (being a structured set of information) involves the processing of personal data as it requires consultation and use of the personal information. Interviewing and the obtaining and recording of information from an interview will involve processing where information on the applicant is collated in a structured form.
> 2. The destruction of old personnel records, whether computerised or part of a "relevant filing system", will fall within the definition of processing.
> 3. If the test results are to be kept on computer or recorded in a structured manner, the taking of a blood or urine sample and its subsequent analysis to test for drugs involves the processing of personal data. In any event, the analysis is likely to be processed if it is undertaken by automated equipment.

With regard to **what amounts to a single operation**, by a majority the Court of Appeal has held that the **selection of information** (in this case from various electronic files and manual (i.e. paper) files) **and** the **resultant non-automated** (i.e. human) **analysis** of this information recorded electronically cannot be considered to be one continuous and single processing operation (*Johnson v Medical Defence Union (No 2)* [2007] EWCA Civ 262). To consider otherwise would result in the fairness of a decision being subject to data protection rules rather than employment law.

> **MEMO POINTS** This case is the second case regarding data protection issues the complainant has brought against the Medical Defence Union. The first case in 2004, which was not appealed, is covered in ¶¶5926, 5982.

5931 Specific obligations apply to the data controller where **another entity**, known as a data processor, **processes data on his behalf**. A **data processor** can be any person, other than a worker of the data controller, who merely provides a processing service and operates under the data controller's instructions. Full responsibility remains with the data controller even where a data processor acts on his behalf. See ¶6005 for further details about using data processors.

> **EXAMPLE** Examples of data processors:
> 1. From example 1 at ¶5923, B Ltd, if it makes no use of the information but merely provides the computer facility on which A Ltd maintains its staff records.
> 2. A self-employed consultant reorganising and updating A Ltd's personnel records.
> 3. A payroll company used by A Ltd.
> 4. An organisation that provides a secure facility for storage of archived manual personnel records of A Ltd.

5933 **Right to prevent processing** Data subjects have the **right to prevent** processing if it may cause damage or distress (see Remedies below).

This right **does not exist** if the worker has given his **consent** to the processing or where it is necessary to comply with a legal obligation or to protect a worker's vital interests (s 10 DPA 1998). The worker has the **right to withdraw** his consent at any time.

B. Employer obligations

5940 When collecting, using or storing personal information the employer, as data controller, must observe **three fundamental obligations**:
– abiding by the data protection principles;
– observing the rights of data subjects to disclosure; and
– notification (where required).

1. Data protection principles

5945 The employer, as data controller, must comply with the data protection principles when **personal or sensitive data is processed**. **Specific exceptions** apply in some employment situations, for example where it is necessary to safeguard national security or prevent or detect crime (ss 28-29 DPA 1998).

In summary, these principles state that data must be:
– fairly and lawfully processed;
– processed for limited purposes;
– adequate, relevant and not excessive;
– accurate;
– not kept longer than necessary;
– processed in accordance with the data subject's rights;
– secure; and
– not transferred to countries without adequate protection.

> **MEMO POINTS** 1. The eight data protection principles are contained in Schedule 1 of the DPA 1998. Schedules 2 and 3 set out the conditions required to meet the 1st principle requirements

when processing personal and sensitive data. Schedule 4 applies to cases where the 8th principle (transfer of data outside the EEA) does not apply. The processing of sensitive data is also subject to the provisions of the Data Protection (Processing of Sensitive Personal Data) Order which contains conditions additional to those of Schedule 3 (SI 2000/417).

1st principle

5948 Personal data must be **processed fairly and lawfully** and shall not be processed unless at least one of the conditions contained in Schedule 2 is met. Where the **data is sensitive** at least one of the conditions of Schedule 3 must also be met.

5949 **Processed fairly** Whether data is processed fairly will depend on the **manner** in which it was obtained and whether the worker was **aware** of the purposes for which it was being obtained, such as where the worker consents with full knowledge of the purpose for which the information is to be used, knows who the data controller is, and has all the information required to ensure that the processing is fair (Sch 1 DPA 1998). Consent should be unambiguous and should be allowed to be withdrawn at any time.

5950 In addition, **personal data** may not be processed unless **at least one of the following conditions** is met (Sch 2 DPA 1998):
a. the worker has given his **consent** to the processing; or
b. processing is necessary:
– for the performance of the worker's contract or the taking of steps at the request of a prospective worker with a view to entering into a contract;
– to comply with any legal obligations of the employer (other than obligations imposed by contract);
– to protect the vital interests of a worker (this possibly only applies to life threatening situations, for example, if the worker is badly injured and his employer has medical information that would be vital to his recovery);
– for the administration of justice or for the exercise of any function conferred by an Act of Parliament; or
– for purposes of a legitimate interest pursued by the employer or third party to whom data is disclosed except where this is prejudicial to rights and freedoms or legitimate interests of the worker.

5951 Where **sensitive data** is processed the employer must **also meet one of the following conditions** (Sch 3 DPA 1998):
a. the worker has given **explicit consent** to the processing;
b. processing is necessary:
– and imposed on the employer by law in connection with the employment;
– to protect the vital interests of the worker where his consent cannot be given or the data controller cannot be reasonably expected to obtain it;
– for the administration of justice or in the exercise of any function conferred by an Act of Parliament; or
– in connection with any legal proceedings or prospective proceedings, for obtaining legal advice, or otherwise necessary for the purpose of establishing, exercising or defending legal rights; or
c. the processing is required for the **purpose** of identifying or keeping under review the existence or absence **of equal opportunities**, on the basis of race or ethnicity, with a view to enabling such equality to be promoted or maintained.

> MEMO POINTS 1. The Data Protection (Processing of Sensitive Personal Data) Order sets out more detailed provisions for the processing of sensitive data that is in the substantial public interest and necessary for the prevention or detection of an unlawful act and where the consent of the individual need not be obtained. It also sets out the requirements for processing information in establishing and administering an **occupational pension scheme** and information that is required to determine eligibility for, and benefits payable under, such a scheme (SI 2000/417).

2. Schedule 3 of the DPA 1998 contains other conditions that do not apply to employment situations, including the right of **trade unions**, or other non-profit organisations, to process personal data relating to its members subject to appropriate safeguards being in place, and requiring the data subject's consent prior to transferring personal data to others (Sch 3 DPA 1998).

5952 Where an employer has received the personal data from a third party, for example where he has received information from a former employer, he **must inform the worker** as soon as is practicable that he holds such information as a data controller, the purpose for which that data is to be used and any further information necessary to ensure that the processing of that data will be fair. Failure to do this could amount to the processing of the data being deemed unfair (Sch 1 DPA 1998).

However, the employer **need not inform** the worker if to do so would involve a disproportionate effort, or if the processing is necessary for compliance of a legal (but not contractual) obligation of the employer. The Commissioner recognises that what is disproportionate will depend on the circumstances, taking into account the time and cost to the employer. Where an employer wants to rely on the **grounds of disproportionate effort** he should keep a record as to the circumstances he has taken into account. Neither of these exemptions removes the employer's obligation to process the information fairly and the worker is still entitled to ask to see the information.

5953 **Processed lawfully** Personal data will not be processed lawfully if it has been **obtained through deception**, fraud or where there is a breach of the implied duty of trust and confidence.

2nd principle

5955 Personal data must be **obtained** only for **one or more specified and lawful** purposes and must not be processed further in any manner that is incompatible with those purposes.

3rd principle

5957 Personal data must be **adequate, relevant and not excessive** in relation to the purpose or purposes for which it is processed i.e. the employer should only hold personal data that he actually needs.

4th principle

5959 Personal data must be **accurate** and where necessary kept **up to date**.

5th principle

5961 Personal data processed for any purpose or purposes must be **kept no longer than is necessary** for that purpose.

6th principle

5963 Personal data must be processed **in accordance** with the **rights of data subjects**.

7th principle

5965 Appropriate **technical and organisational measures** should be taken against unauthorised or unlawful processing of personal data and against accidental loss or destruction of or damage to personal data.

The employer should have **adequate security precautions** in place to prevent the loss, destruction or unauthorised disclosure of personal data. Where a data processor processes data on the employer's behalf, a written contract should be in place to ensure that the data processor has adequate security and will only process the data according to the employer's instructions.

8th principle

5967 Personal data **must not be transferred** to a country or territory **outside the EEA** unless there is adequate protection for the rights and freedoms of data subjects in relation to the processing of personal information about them.

> **MEMO POINTS** The EC has decided that the following non-EEA countries and agreements have an adequate level of protection by reason of their domestic law or international commitments. Data transfers to such countries require no additional safeguards. At present, these are: Switzerland, Canada, Argentina, Guernsey, Jersey, the Isle of Man, the US Department of Commerce's Safe Harbor Privacy Principles, and the transfer of Air Passenger Name Record data to the US Department of Homeland Security. An up-to-date list of Community findings is available at flmemo.co.uk/em5967.

5968 Transfers can still take place as long as an adequate level of protection is ensured by **other means** in the particular circumstances of the transfer. For example, the employer should consider using contractual terms to protect that data. The European Commission has devised a set of **model clauses** to be included in contracts and has set out when it is appropriate for these to be used. See flmemo.co.uk/em5968a and flmemo.co.uk/em5968b for further details.

Multinational organisations who wish to transfer personal data outside the EEA but within their group of companies can do so with adequate protection by adopting binding codes of corporate conduct known as binding corporate rules. The use of binding corporate rules to ensure adequacy requires approval from the data protection authorities in the countries in which the group is processing personal data. See flmemo.co.uk/em5968b for further details.

5969 If the employer cannot ensure adequate protection, **specific and informed consent** for the transfer must be obtained from the data subjects.

2. Disclosure of information

5970 When an employer decides to disclose information about workers he should balance the benefits against the reasonable expectations of his workers that their privacy will be respected, and there is an implied duty of trust and confidence that personal information will not be disclosed where there is an expectation that it will remain confidential.

5971 **Specific data protection issues** regarding disclosure are covered as follows:

Business mergers and acquisitions	¶5977
Fraud detection	¶5974
Marketing	¶5973
Occupational sick pay schemes (OSP)	¶4175
Official requests for information	¶5979
Pension/insurance schemes	¶3445 and ¶4206
Publication of personal and sensitive information	¶5975
References	¶8328
Sickness records	¶4223

5973 **Marketing** The employer may wish to market his or third party products or services to workers.

If so, as good practice, the employer should (part 2.6 DP Code):
- inform workers of any intention to use personal information to deliver advertising or marketing messages and should make sure that they can opt-out of any such campaigns; and
- obtain explicit and freely given consent.

Fraud detection The employer should not disclose any information gathered for fraud detection purposes to any third party unless (part 2.7 DP Code):
- he is required to do so by law;
- he believes that failure to do so will prejudice the prevention or detection of a crime; or
- the disclosure is provided for in the worker's contract.

5974

Publication of personal and sensitive information There may be circumstances when the employer makes a discretionary disclosure, for example, where the employer publishes personal information in an annual report or in marketing material. Discretionary disclosure may also be expected, for example, by academic staff where information about their fields of expertise and research interests is to be widely disseminated, including on the internet. However, the majority of workers will not expect personal data to be so disclosed.

As good practice, the employer should only publish information where (part 2.11.1 DP Code):
- there is a **legal obligation** to do so;
- the information is clearly **not intrusive**;
- the worker has **consented** to the disclosure; or
- the information is in a form which does **not identify individual workers**.

Where the worker's consent has been obtained the employer should ensure that the worker is aware of the extent of the information and its use and publication, and the implications of this. The worker should be genuinely **free not to consent** to the publication of the information.

5975

Furthermore, personal/sensitive information should only be **supplied to a trade union** for its recruitment purposes if (part 2.11.3 DP Code):
- the trade union is recognised by the employer;
- the information is limited to that necessary for a recruitment approach; and
- each worker has been advised and has been given a clear opportunity to object.

Aggregated or statistical information about the workforce should be sufficient information for **collective bargaining purposes** and the employer should not assume that information about individual workers must be given to a trade union involved in collective bargaining negotiations.

5976

Business mergers and acquisitions Where the employer is involved in a business merger or acquisition he may be required to disclose personal information relating to his workers.

As good practice, the **employer should** (part 2.12 DP Code):
- wherever practicable, anonymise such data;
- apply conditions to its release, such as securing assurances that it will be only used in the evaluation of assets and liabilities, treated in confidence and destroyed or returned after use;
- advise workers of such disclosure wherever practicable and, if the merger or acquisition takes place, he should ensure that workers are aware of the extent to which their records are to be transferred to their new employer;
- ensure that a sensitive personal data condition (see data protection principles above) is satisfied if such data is to be transferred; and
- if data is to be transferred abroad outside the EEA, ensure that there is a proper basis for making the transfer.

The **new employer** who acquires a workforce as a result of a merger or acquisition will take on the responsibility for the type and extent of personal data retained by him as well as the liability of data controller. He should, therefore, ensure that the records that he retains are accurate and relevant and should not retain excessive information.

5977

Further, the Information Commissioner has issued guidance specifically on compliance with data protection law during the process of **pre- and post-transfer information and consultation** (¶8092). It confirms that disclosure **under TUPE** is permitted because it is required by law, and gives guidelines for the management of providing employee information. It recommends that:

5978

– parties should comply with general data protection principles when disclosing information. In particular they should ensure that disclosed information is accurate, up to date and secure;
– care should be taken to ensure that there is no transfer of excessive or irrelevant data;
– if the information requested is additional to that required by TUPE, it should, if possible, be provided anonymously and should only be disclosed with the consent of employees. Additional precautions should be taken to ensure that it is only used for the purpose of the transfer and not kept after use; and
– after transfer the new employer should delete or destroy any transferred personnel information which is no longer needed.

5979 **Official requests for information** An employer may receive **written** requests for information or access to electronic records from authorised officers (e.g. Jobcentre Plus or a local authority) in connection with claims for social security or housing benefits made by their employee or former employee (s 109B(1) Social Security Administration Act 1992). Authorised officers can also request to visit business premises (usually on notice) if they have reason to believe benefit fraud is taking place and that documents relating to the business are kept there (s 109C Social Security Administration Act 1992).

The **purpose** of the information request must be:
– ascertaining whether a social security benefit is/was payable;
– investigating the circumstances in which an accident, injury or disease arose, which in turn gave rise, or may give rise, to a claim for industrial injuries benefit or any other social security benefit;
– ascertaining whether the provisions of the social security legislation are being, have been or are likely to be contravened; or
– preventing, detecting and securing evidence of the commission of benefit offences.

The authorised officer must have reasonable grounds to believe that the employer has the information (or access to it) and the written notice must specify a particular employee/ex-employee. While the Code of Practice issued by the DWP states that authorised officers should only make a request if they have "reasonable grounds to suspect that benefit fraud is being, or has been, committed" this does not appear to be a statutory requirement in respect of requests to employers. Consequently, given the wide purpose for which information can be requested, it is inadvisable for employers to ignore or refuse such requests properly made, although they can question why they have been asked to provide information. Further, the Code of Practice confirms that an initial refusal to provide information will not be considered an intentional delay or obstruction, where the refusal is given in order to seek legal advice before responding.

The Code of Practice contains a non-exhaustive list of the kind of **information which may be requested**, including an employee's name and address, date of birth, wage details and payroll number, periods of employment, hours of work, employment status, bank details, NI number and details of dates, and pension payments. They may also ask for original or photocopied documents. The Code of Practice confirms that authorised officers "will only request information that they need and will take account of the burden this would place on the business, as well as their own needs."

Employers must **provide the information** requested to the authorised officer within the time and in the format specified in the notice. The Data Protection Act permits disclosure in these circumstances (s 35(1) DPA 1998).

It is a **criminal offence**, punishable upon summary conviction by a fine not exceeding £1,000, to (s 111 Social Security Administration Act 1992):
– intentionally delay or obstruct an authorised officer in the exercise of his powers;
– refuse or neglect to allow access to electronic records; or
– refuse or neglect to answer any question or to furnish any information or produce any document when required to do so.

If an offence (i.e. refusal to provide information) is committed with the consent or connivance of, or is attributable to any neglect on the part of, a director or other similar officer, the individual, as well as the body corporate, shall be guilty of the offence.

3. Subject access requests

5980 Workers have a **right to know** what **information** is kept about them by their employer. This is known as "subject access". The information held by the employer may include records on health and sickness, disciplinary or training, performance reviews, emails and even interview notes. A worker may make a **request in writing** to a prospective, current or past employer for a copy of all his personal information that is processed by that person/organisation. The right to such information is not limited to information kept electronically but also extends to structured paper records (¶5925). The employer may **charge a fee** of up to £10 for responding to each request. The request does not have to state that it is made in connection with the DPA 1998, although to do so will ensure that the employer recognises the request as such.

5981 As good practice, the **employer should** (part 2.8 DP Code):
– **establish a system** so that subject access requests are recognised and all information about a worker located so that the employer can **respond to the request within** 40 days of it being received;
– **check the identity** of anyone making a subject access request to ensure that information is only given to the person who is entitled to receive it. In smaller organisations, identity checks may not be necessary, but in larger organisations employers should not assume that all requests are genuine and appropriate checks will be necessary;
– **provide** the worker with a **hard copy** of information kept, making clear any codes and the sources for the information;
– **make a judgement** as to what information, which concerns the identities of third parties, it is reasonable to withhold;
– **inform** managers and other relevant people in the organisation of the nature of the information that is to be released pursuant to subject access requests from workers;
– ensure that workers are promptly, or in any event within 40 days, provided with a **statement of** how any **automated decision-making process**, to which they are subject, is used and how it works; and
– ensure that any **computer system** that is purchased will enable the employer to retrieve all the information relating to any given individual without difficulty. The employer should ensure that if automated decisions about workers are to be used then the supplier of the system should provide him with information enabling him to respond fully to requests about that system.

> MEMO POINTS The Information Commissioner has also published a **Good Practice Note** in relation to subject access requests and **references**, which clarifies how the DPA 1998 applies to employment references (¶8329).

5982 In addition, the employer:
– should ensure that the information given is intelligible, includes sources, and if possible is in **hard copy** form unless disproportionate effort is involved in copying it. Although disproportionate effort is not defined, factors to be taken into account would include the cost, the length of time involved, the difficulty and the size of the employer. Where there is a disproportionate effort some form of access still has to be given;
– should **remove all information** which identifies a third party (usually another worker), for example, where a complaint has been made about the worker, the release of the document of complaint would identify the complainant. While the employer could, in that case, remove the complainant's name, in other circumstances the third party may still be identifiable. The employer must strike a balance between the worker's right of access and the right of the third party to privacy. If the other person has consented to the information being released, or it is reasonable in all the circumstances to comply with the request without the other's consent, then the employer must make the disclosure. A High Court decision has confirmed that the names of third parties can be removed from data if they do not necessarily form part of the personal data, although in certain circumstances such information is disclosable without requiring the consent of those third parties (*Johnson v Medical Defence Union* [2004] EWHC 347 (Ch)); and
– is under no obligation to disclose documents which had been produced electronically but are **no longer in electronic form** and are only held in paper form. The form in which a

4. Notification

5990 Data controllers should notify the Information Commissioner before they process personal data. However, this will **not apply to most employers** as they will be exempt if they only process personal data **for the purposes of**:
- staff administration (including payroll);
- advertising, marketing and public relations (of the employer's business); or
- accounts and records.

5991 In addition, notification is **not required** in any event where personal data is:
- recorded only in a manual filing system; or
- a health or educational record,

unless the processing is likely to cause substantial damage or distress to the data subject or significantly prejudice their rights or freedoms (s 17 DPA 1998).

Some **not for profit organisations** are also exempt from notification.

> MEMO POINTS   Detailed guidance about the notification exemptions can be found in the Information Commissioner's publication – *Notification Exemptions – A self-assessment guide*. Any data controller who believes it may be exempt must refer to this guidance.

5992 In **all other circumstances**, the employer will be **required** to notify the Commissioner and he must submit his notification prior to processing personal data. The notification details are then put on the register, which is a public document. The details show the employer's name and address and the name and address of his UK representative (if he has one); a description of the personal data being held by him and any recipient who might receive such data; any country outside the EEA where the data may be sent; and any exempt data.

If the personal data maintained by the employer falls partly within and partly outside the above exemptions, for example where personal data is recorded in both a manual filing system and on a computer, the employer should notify the Commissioner as to the non-exempt data and make a statement of fact confirming that he holds exempt data. Alternatively, the employer may choose to voluntarily notify the Commissioner of all the personal data he controls, regardless of whether it is held on computer or not.

5993 As part of the notification process an annual **registration fee** is payable. There is a two-tiered fee structure. The fee for a data controller in tier 1 is £35 and the fee for tier 2 is £500. A data controller will be in tier 2 if it has 250 or more members of staff and either has a turnover of at least £25.9 million or is a public authority. Charities and small occupational pension schemes are exempt from tier 2. Notification is **valid for 1 year**, following which the employer is obliged to renew with any amendments that are necessary. The employer must also provide a general description of the security measures taken to protect the personal data, although this will not appear on the public register. Notification does not equate to compliance with the data protection principles.

Failure to notify is an offence (ss 17, 21 DPA 1998) and it remains open to the Commissioner to investigate and prosecute those who are required to notify but have not done so.

C. Data management

6000 All employers hold personal data and probably some sensitive personal data on their workers. This will have been collected during the recruitment process, through appraisals, sick notes, the administering of certain benefits, for example permanent health insurance, and through any monitoring of communications as discussed in the previous sections. Ideally, data protection compliance should be seen as an **integral part** of the employer's procedures and practices rather than as a standalone requirement. An employer's written procedures relating to the keeping of workers' records should **incorporate** the relevant good practice recommendations of the DP Code, which should extend to all staff and the processing of all **personal and sensitive data**, not just to the more obvious departments such as human resources and payroll. Data protection compliance should be viewed as a multi-disciplinary matter so that all staff are aware that they each have a part to play in securing compliance. The procedures should be regularly reviewed and where necessary updated.

Consequently, employers should allocate responsibility, establish what personal data is processed and ensure that employment practices comply with the data protection principles.

6001

As good practice, **employers should** (part 2 DP Code):
– establish a person within the organisation **who is responsible** for ensuring employment practices and procedures comply with the data protection principles, for example a senior manager in a human resources function or someone in a comparable position, or, where the organisation is small, the employer himself. This is a continuing responsibility and a means of checking that procedures are followed in practice should be established;
– ensure that each departmental line manager and business area which may process workers' personal or sensitive information is **aware of their responsibilities** for data protection compliance and, if necessary, amend working practices to accommodate them;
– **assess** what personal information on workers is kept, and who is responsible for it;
– **eliminate** the collection of personal information that is irrelevant or unnecessary to the employment relationship. If sensitive data is collected then a sensitive data condition should be satisfied (¶5951);
– ensure that **workers are aware** of the extent to which they can be criminally liable if they knowingly or recklessly disclose personal data outside the employer's policies or procedures. Serious breaches of the data protection principles should be made a disciplinary offence;
– allocate responsibility for making a valid **notification** to the Information Commissioner if required (see above), and maintain it in accordance with the notification requirements; and
– **consult** with trade unions or other workers' representatives, if any, or workers themselves over the development and implementation of employment practices and procedures that involve the processing of personal information.

Specific data protection issues are covered as follows:

6002

Equal opportunities monitoring	¶5845
Discipline, grievance and dismissal	¶6504
Information about workers' health	¶4920
Occupational sick pay schemes	¶4175
Pension/insurance schemes	¶3445 and ¶4206
Recruitment and selection	¶676
References	¶¶8328+
Sickness records	¶4223

1. Collecting and handling records

It is not generally necessary to obtain workers' consent to keep general employment records and it will usually be sufficient to ensure that they are aware that records are being kept and for what purpose. However, consent may be necessary with regard to sensitive data.

6003

As good practice, the **employer should** (part 2.1 DP Code):
– ensure that newly appointed **workers** are made **aware** of the nature and source of any information stored about them, how it is used and to whom it may be disclosed;

– ensure that all **workers understand** their rights under the DPA 1998 and their right of access to information held about them;
– make sure that there is a **clear and foreseeable need for the information** and that the information collected meets that need. Any extraneous information should either not be collected or be removed;
– regularly **provide workers** with a copy of the **information about them that may be subject to change**, for example home addresses. Workers should be asked to check such information to ensure that their records are up to date and accurate; and
– **maintain and review** all systems for collecting and retaining information to enable accuracy, consistency, and validity checks to be carried out.

Using data processors

6005 Often employers outsource the processing of information they hold to third parties, referred to here as data processors. When using a data processor the employer should ensure that appropriate **security measures** are adopted and complied with (part 2.14 DP Code). To this end, the employer should have a **written contract** with the data processor which ensures that security is maintained and that personal information is processed only on the employer's instructions. Where the use of a data processor would involve the transfer of information about a worker outside the EEA, the employer should ensure that there is a proper basis for making the transfer. The data processor should comply with the same standards for the collection, processing and retention of personal information as apply to the employer as a data controller.

6006 Further, **contract/agency staff** will be data processors if they process personal data for the employer. The reliability of such staff that have access to workers' records and other personal data should be checked no less thoroughly than in the case of workers who have a similar level of access. Consequently, they should have written contracts that ensure they only process data in accordance with instructions and that they keep the data secure.

Prevention of unauthorised access

6010 The basic principle is that information about workers should **only be available** to those who need it to do their job. The employer should be aware that access rights should be based on genuine need and not seniority. Where workers need to access personal information as part of their job, the employer should check their reliability and they should be made aware of the security regime. Where appropriate, a confidentiality clause should be inserted into their contract of employment.

As good practice, the **employer should** (part 2.2 DP Code):
– apply proper **security standards** that take account of the risks of unauthorised access to or accidental loss or destruction of or damage to employment records;
– **institute a system** of secure cabinets, access controls and passwords that ensure staff access employment records only when they have a legitimate business need to do so;
– use the **audit trail** capabilities of automated systems to track who accesses and amends personal data;
– take steps to ensure the **reliability of staff** that have access to worker records. This will involve training and ensuring that workers understand their responsibilities. Confidentiality clauses should be included in contracts of employment;
– ensure that if **records are taken off-site**, for example on a laptop, that this is controlled and only necessary information is taken. Staff should be made aware of appropriate security rules and procedures, for example the laptop must be secure or in view at all times, to protect such information; and
– take account of the **risks of transmitting confidential information** by fax or email. Such information should only be transmitted between locations if a secure network or comparable arrangement is in place. In the case of email, employers should provide some technical means of ensuring security, such as effective password protection and encryption.

2. Retention of records

6015 As good practice, the **employer should** (part 2.15 DP Code):
– establish and adhere to **standard retention times** for categories of information held on the records of workers and former workers. The retention periods should be based on business needs, taking into account any professional guidelines;
– **anonymise** any data about workers and former workers where practicable;
– if the holding of records containing information on **criminal convictions** of workers is justified, ensure that the information is deleted once the conviction is "spent" (¶613); and
– ensure that records which are to be **disposed of** are securely and effectively destroyed.

6016 No specific retention **period** is given in the DPA 1998, but the DP Code does provide that any period the employer decides on must be based on **business need** and should take into account any **professional guidelines**. Employers should be aware that the DPA 1998 **does not override** any statutory requirement to retain records, for example in relation to certain aspects of health and safety or income tax. Therefore, the employer must strike a balance between ensuring that personnel information is not kept for longer than is necessary but not deleting it where there is a real business need to retain it. The retention of records for health and safety purposes, for example, is likely to be different in the case of those working with hazardous substances to those working in an office environment.

The employer should **not retain** personal information on the basis that it may be useful one day. Instead he should take into account any relevant professional guidelines or statutory requirement and should:
– adopt a risk analysis approach by considering what realistically would be the consequences for the business, the workers, former workers and others, if personal information that is only occasionally accessed is no longer available;
– treat items of information individually or in logical groupings. All of the information in a record should not be retained just because there is a need for some of it to be retained; and
– use the principle of proportionality to help decide which records should be retained, i.e. records about a large number of workers should not be retained for a lengthy period on the off-chance that one of them at some point might question some aspect of his employment.

> **MEMO POINTS** The Information Commissioner's Office (ICO) has published guidance on deleting and archiving personal data. The guidance sets out what the ICO means by deletion, archiving and putting personal data "beyond use", and it was issued to counteract the problem of data controllers informing people that their personal data has been deleted when, in reality, it has been archived in such a way that allows it to be re-instated. The guidance suggests that organisations should put safeguards in place for information that has been deleted but remains in its possession. The guidance can be found at flmemo.co.uk/em6016.

D. Remedies

6040 A worker may **ask his employer** in writing **not to process personal data**, or ask him to stop processing it, where it is causing, or is likely to cause, substantial unwarranted damage or substantial distress to the worker or anyone else. The employer who has received such a request must **respond within** 21 days stating whether he is going to comply with the request or not. If the employer believes that the request is unjustified then he must give the reasons.

A worker can also submit a **subject access request** to find out what personal or sensitive data is held about him (¶5980).

Applications to the Information Commissioner

6043 Workers can write to the Commissioner stating that their employer has failed to comply with his obligations. The Commissioner may:

- **make an assessment** as to whether it is likely or unlikely that the employer has complied with the data protection principles;
- **issue enforcement proceedings** if he is satisfied that the data controller has contravened one of the data protection principles; or
- **recommend** that the worker apply to court, alleging a failure to comply with the subject access provisions.

6044 The Commissioner has a **wide discretion** as to how an assessment is carried out. Should he determine that there has been non-compliance then he may take the matter up directly with the data controller, and is **empowered to enforce** the data protection principles against any data controller where he is satisfied that any of the principles have been, or are being, contravened.

6045 An employer who receives an enforcement notice from the Commissioner may **appeal** to the independent data protection tribunal. However, if the tribunal upholds the Commissioner's decision, failure to comply becomes a criminal offence. The tribunal may substitute its own decision for the Commissioner's if it sees fit.

> MEMO POINTS The Information Commissioner has the power to issue **penalties** to data controllers of up to £500,000 for serious data protection breaches of a kind likely to cause substantial damage or distress (ss 55A and 55B DPA 1998).

Applications to civil courts

6047 The worker may also apply to the civil courts if (ss 7-12 DPA 1998):
- his employer fails to respond to his requests;
- personal data held by his employer is inaccurate; or
- the employer has based an opinion about the worker on inaccurate data.

The courts have the power to order the employer to comply with his obligations or, in the case of inaccurate data or an opinion based on such data, make an order to rectify, block, erase or destroy that data (s 14 DPA 1998).

In addition, the worker may be **entitled to compensation** if he can prove that he has suffered damage as a result of the employer not meeting his obligations (s 13 DPA 1998). The court may order compensation for any **associated distress** as well. A claim for distress alone is unlikely to succeed.

SECTION 2

Monitoring and surveillance

6150 Many employers make some **checks** on the **quantity and quality** of work produced by their workers, for example counting the number of calls made on a daily or weekly basis by telesales workers. Such monitoring of work output is often termed **performance monitoring**. Employers may also check their workers' behaviour and their conformity with company policies, procedures and any legal requirements, for example compliance with health and safety rules or discrimination rules. This is commonly termed **surveillance**.

6151 Traditionally, performance monitoring and surveillance was conducted solely through human observation by way of managers and foremen. However, newer **methods of monitoring and surveillance** by automated and electronic means are now commonplace, such as telephone monitoring, CCTV cameras and email interception, and all have the potential of being extremely intrusive.

6152 Where an employer **intends to monitor** his workers, any monitoring should be carried out subject to a written monitoring policy, should be proportionate and needs to be justified by some benefit that it brings to the employer (see below). Further, covert monitoring, i.e.

monitoring about which the subject of it is unaware, is only justifiable in exceptional circumstances (see ¶¶6250+).

If workers are monitored without their knowledge in the absence of a monitoring policy (unless covert monitoring is justifiable), then this may breach the workers' right to privacy (under art 8, European Convention on Human Rights; *Copland v UK – 62617/00* [2007] ECHR 253, ECJ).

A. General standards

Monitoring will usually be considered to be intrusive and workers have **legitimate expectations** to have a degree of privacy at work as well as to keeping their personal lives private. Any adverse impact on these expectations as a result of any monitoring must be **justified** by the benefits it gives to the employer (DPA 1998). Monitoring that cannot be justified and is excessive **may also be contrary** to the Human Rights Act 1998 and may breach the employer's implied duty of trust and confidence (Human Rights Act 1998).

6160

Policy on monitoring/surveillance It is advisable that employers have or introduce a policy on monitoring if they plan to monitor their workers. The policy should be workable and user friendly.

6163

If the reason for the monitoring is the **enforcement** of the employer's **rules or standards**, they should be clearly **set out** in a policy which refers to the associated monitoring and workers should be made aware of the policy. Where the rules and standards apply to the use of emails and internet access in the workplace, for example, they should be set out in a policy that is made known and is readily accessible to the workers to which it applies. The employer should also specify the safeguards that are in place to protect the worker's personal data and its confidentiality.

The most **widely applicable** monitoring policy is often on internet usage and emails, and it should set out what is acceptable use in the business culture in which employees work, and should emphasise the need for maintaining productivity, the problem of viruses and the legal consequences of sending emails as well as the fact that they are often no substitute for an actual conversation (¶6260).

6164

Impact assessments

Employers, in all but the most straightforward of cases, should carry out a formal or informal impact assessment to help them decide if and how to carry out any monitoring and this will involve:
a. identifying the purpose of the monitoring and its proposed benefit;
b. identifying any adverse impact. This includes the intrusion the monitoring would have on the workers' private lives, whether workers will be able to limit any intrusion, whether confidential or sensitive information will be seen by others (for example IT workers) and whether it will have any impact on the relationship with the employer or other bodies;
c. considering any alternatives to monitoring or different ways in which it could be carried out. For example, the employer should consider whether less intrusive methods would obtain the same desired benefit, such as effective training, supervision and clear communication from managers or limiting the proposed monitoring to a small group of workers which have either been suspected of wrong-doing or are in an area of high risk to the business. Where the monitoring could be automated this may also make the monitoring less intrusive, as will spot-checking or auditing instead of continuous monitoring (although this may not be the case where the spot-checking or auditing requires human intervention);
d. taking into account the obligations that occur when monitoring. In particular, employers must ensure that they comply with the data protection principles which require that all personal information obtained through monitoring be processed legally and fairly and in accordance with the data protection principles (¶5945). They must also comply with the

6165

specific standards that apply to the processing of sensitive data and, when collecting sensitive data about a worker's health, racial origin or sex life, must satisfy one of the sensitive data conditions (¶5951). Workers must also be informed of any monitoring and employers must consider the implications of workers' rights to obtain copies of information about themselves gathered through monitoring; and

e. **deciding whether** the monitoring is **justified**. This must take due consideration of steps a. to d., balancing the benefits against any adverse impact while placing particular emphasis on the need to be fair to individual workers. Where electronic communications are involved, any intrusion must be no more than absolutely necessary. Any **significant intrusion** into the private lives of workers will not normally be justified unless there is a real risk to the employer's business. Account should also be taken of the results of any consultation with trade union or other staff representatives.

Good practice recommendations

6167 As good practice, the **employer should** (part 3.1 DP Code):
– be clear about the **purpose** of the monitoring. This should be identified before the monitoring takes places. Employers should not monitor workers just because a customer for their products or services requires it unless it can be justified;
– be satisfied that the particular **method** chosen is justified by the benefits. This again should be identified before the monitoring is to start and it is best if this is done by an impact assessment (see above);
– make sure that **workers are aware** of the nature, extent and reasons for any monitoring, unless (exceptionally) covert monitoring is justified. This includes informing workers what monitoring is taking place and why and making sure they are regularly reminded that monitoring is occurring;
– keep to a minimum those who have **access to the information**. Wherever possible, access should be confined to those with relevant responsibilities working in a specific function such as the human resources department. Access to personal information obtained through monitoring must be limited and those with such access should be subject to confidentiality and security requirements and should be properly trained as necessary;
– ensure that the information gathered should **not be used for any other purpose** unless it is clearly in an individual worker's interest to do so or it reveals an activity that the employer cannot reasonably be expected to ignore;
– ensure that where the information may have an **adverse impact on an individual worker**, he should be given the opportunity to see the information and make representations, for example to explain or challenge the information, before any action is taken against him; and
– make sure that the workers' **right of access** to information held about them is not compromised and that the monitoring system can meet this requirement.

B. Monitoring electronic communication

6190 Electronic communication **includes** telephone, fax, email, voicemail and internet access. As well as the **requirement** to comply with the general standards in section A, there are also specific good practice recommendations in relation to the monitoring of electronic communication. Further, where employers intercept communications as part of their monitoring they must also ensure that they are acting lawfully (see below).

There are **risks and liabilities** (see ¶6260) associated with workers' use of electronic communications, in particular email and internet access, which may require monitoring. The **introduction of a policy** can serve to minimise the potential for these risks and abuses by setting out clear guidelines and restrictions and by stating what, if any, monitoring takes place.

1. Data protection compliance

As good practice, if he is considering monitoring workers, the **employer should** (part 3.2 DP Code):
– ensure the monitoring is **legal** (see subsection 2 below);
– consider whether the monitoring is **justified**, preferably by using an impact assessment. Alternatives should be considered, for example, if the issue is security, whether encryption and passwords will be sufficient or whether the proposed monitoring can be automated as such systems are likely to be less intrusive. With regard to any monitoring, workers should be informed of its nature and extent and the reason for it. Information regarding private calls or email should not be used, unless it reveals an activity that no employer could reasonably be expected to ignore;
– with regard to **phone calls**: particular care must be taken before phone calls or voicemails are monitored, as such monitoring is more intrusive and therefore harder to justify. Where phone lines are provided at workers' homes or company mobile phones are provided for personal use, expectation of privacy will be even higher. Where it is essential, **alternatives should be considered** such as whether itemised call records will suffice. If voicemails need to be checked for business calls while workers are absent, they should be made aware of this and that in such circumstances it may be unavoidable that some personal messages may be heard. Where calls are monitored, ensure that external callers know that calls may be monitored and the purpose behind it, unless this is obvious; and
– with regard to **emails and the internet**: wherever possible, employers should avoid opening emails, especially those which are clearly shown to be private. To this end, workers should be encouraged to **mark emails** as **personal** where appropriate. Private emails should only be monitored in exceptional circumstances. If possible, email monitoring should be confined to the address/heading of the email, unless it is essential to examine the content.
If it is necessary to check emails while workers are absent, they should be made aware of this. A system of marking up emails to help identify private emails should be encouraged and where possible private emails should not be opened.
Workers should be informed of the extent to which information about their internet access and emails is retained in the system and for how long.

Policies

As good practice, employers should establish a policy if they wish to monitor electronic communication. Workers must be made aware of the policy and its contents. In particular, as good practice, the **policy should** (part 3.2 DP Code):
– clearly state **when** phones (including mobile phones, where relevant), email systems and the internet can be used for **private access and communications**;
– clearly state the **extent of allowable private use**, for example whether overseas phone calls can be made and/or whether certain types of email attachments can be received or sent. This should also include what is allowable for private use with regard to the employer's equipment when it is used from home or off site;
– clearly state what, if any, restrictions apply to **internet access**, for example, whether there are prohibitions regarding downloading or copying information from the internet and/or whether certain material should not be viewed, for example offensive material (in such cases, what is considered to be offensive should also be defined, for example material which is racist or pornographic);
– advise workers of the general **need to exercise care** and what alternatives can be used to ensure confidentiality, for example medical reports should be sent by internal post rather than email;
– explain the **purposes and extent of any monitoring** and how it will be carried out; and
– explain how the policy is **enforced** and what penalties exist for a breach of policy.

2. Interception requirements

Interception of workers' communication by employers is an **offence** (s 1 Regulation of Investigatory Powers Act 2000). The employer may, however, have the **lawful authority** to intercept such communications in certain circumstances, such as where there is specific consent. In addition, specific circumstances which give the employer lawful authority to intercept are contained in the Telecommunications (Lawful Business Practice) (Interception of Communications) Regulations 2000 (SI 2000/2699).

Unlawful interception

6221 It is unlawful for any person who controls a private telecommunications system, or for another person with the controller's consent, to intercept communications made on that system unless they have lawful authority to do so (s 1(3) Regulation of Investigatory Powers Act 2000). Situations where a third party has hacked into an employer's private telecoms system and intercepted communications are not covered by the Regulation of Investigatory Powers Act.

A **private telecommunications system** is defined as one attached to a public telecoms system by equipment located in the UK (s 2(1) Regulation of Investigatory Powers Act 2000).

> EXAMPLE Any company telephone or email system which is attached to a public system is included. Therefore, if an employer has a telephone system by which his workers can make internal telephone calls, it will be within the definition if these workers can also make external telephone calls using the same system. However, an internal system that is not connected in any way to a public system will not be included.

6222 **Communication** is **defined** as including speech, music, sounds, visual images or data of any description, for example, telephone conversations, emails and other written communication (s 81 Regulation of Investigatory Powers Act 2000).

6223 Communication is **intercepted** if the employer (or someone acting on his behalf) (s 2(2) Regulation of Investigatory Powers Act 2000):
a. modifies or interferes with the telecommunications system or its operation; or
b. monitors transmissions made by:
– means of the system; or
– tapping to or from apparatus in the system,
to make some or all of the content available to the employer (or any other person other than the sender or the intended recipient).

Therefore, the monitoring of the **number of emails or telephone calls** is not interception unless the contents are opened or the calls are listened to.

Interception must occur **during transmission** of the communication (s 2(2), (7), (8) Regulation of Investigatory Powers Act 2000). This includes the period when the communication is being stored, for example an answerphone message or an email in an inbox. Interception must be **performed in the UK**. Either the sender or intended recipient of the communication must also be located in the UK.

> MEMO POINTS A telephone call **transmission** is **completed** when the sound exits the telephone receiver and therefore the recording of a conversation using a microphone held near to a telephone receiver was not an interception (R v Hardy [2002] EWCA Crim 3012).

Lawful interception

6225 Communication may be lawfully intercepted if the employer has reasonable grounds for believing that both the **sender and recipient have consented** (s 3(1) Regulation of Investigatory Powers Act 2000). This exception can be used where the communication is between workers of the same organisation and the employer has obtained consent from his workers (usually by incorporating written consent into their contracts of employment).

6226 In addition, an employer's interception of his worker's communications for **specific purposes** is recognised as being lawful. Even in these circumstances, however, the employer should make all reasonable efforts to **inform potential users** that the interception may be made. Examples of **making reasonable efforts** to inform potential non-worker users that interceptions may be made could be putting an automatic message on all out-going emails etc warning that they may be monitored/read or having a recorded message for any customers telephoning which states that calls may be recorded for monitoring or training purposes.

The specific purposes include the **monitoring or keeping a record** of communications in order to (reg 3 SI 2000/2699):
– establish the existence of facts, or to ascertain compliance with procedures applicable to the employer's business;
– ascertain or demonstrate the standards followed by workers using the communications system, such as telephone operators or telesales teams; or
– prevent or detect crime, investigate or detect unauthorised use of telecommunications systems (for example, monitoring to ensure worker compliance with the employer's internet and email policy), or secure the effective operation of the system (for example, monitoring for viruses and other threats).

Other instances of lawful interception are when the employer monitors communications between its workers and any confidential voice counselling or support service so long as it is free of charge and provides anonymity of the caller, or where he monitors incoming communications to determine whether they are business or personal communications.

6227

C. Other specific forms of surveillance

In some circumstances, an employer may want to monitor his workers by other means, for example by CCTV cameras or audio devices. As well as the requirement to comply with the general standards in section A, there are also specific good practice recommendations in relation to video and audio monitoring, vehicle monitoring and monitoring through third party information.

6230

Video and audio

Video monitoring covers the use of CCTV within the workplace. Audio monitoring concerns the recording of face-to-face conversations (as opposed to telephone calls, which is electronic monitoring). Video and audio monitoring must be kept to an absolute minimum and, consequently, it is unlikely that **continuous use** of video or audio monitoring is justifiable save in circumstances where there are particular safety or security risks, for example in a shop where there is a high likelihood of robbery. Covert monitoring (see below) by such equipment is only justifiable in specific circumstances where open monitoring would prejudice the detection of a crime or the apprehension of offenders.

6233

> MEMO POINTS   The separate **code of practice on CCTV monitoring**, which is of more general application than monitoring at work, also provides useful guidance.

As good practice, the **employer should** (part 3.3 DP Code):
– consider, preferably using an impact assessment, whether the benefits will **justify** the adverse impact. Where possible, any monitoring should be targeted to areas of particular risk and confined to areas where the expectations of privacy are low;
– give workers a **clear notification** that the monitoring is taking place and where, and the reasons for it, unless covert monitoring is justified (see below); and
– ensure that **non-workers**, such as visitors or customers, who may be inadvertently monitored by the system, are **aware** that the monitoring is taking place and the reasons for it.

6234

In-vehicle monitoring

Monitoring of vehicle movements of company cars and vans etc, where the vehicle is **allocated to a specific driver**, for example by means of tachograph systems as well as tracking devices, must comply with the data protection standards.

As good practice, the **employer should** (part 3.5 DP Code):
– consider, preferably using an impact assessment, whether the benefits will **justify** the adverse impact. In making an assessment the employer should consider whether the monitoring can be limited to exclude information on the private use of the vehicle. If the private

6237

use of the vehicle is allowed then monitoring of private usage will rarely be justified. Where vehicles are supplied both for business and private use, employers should provide workers with the ability to disable any monitoring device when the vehicle is being used privately. In the case where the employer is obliged by law to monitor the worker's use of the vehicle this will take precedence; and
– **make clear in a policy** the nature and extent of any monitoring and to what extent private use is allowed. Workers affected must be made aware of the policy.

Non-employment information

6240 Some employers may wish to monitor the behaviour of their workers through information **held by third parties** to which they have access, for example public record information such as the electoral roll and the Register of County Court Judgments. Information concerning criminal convictions must be obtained from the Disclosure and Barring Service (¶619).

Employers must not use credit reference agencies which check their customers to monitor or vet workers. Likewise, information which an employer has about a worker because they are also a customer/client/supplier must not be used.

As good practice, the **employer should** (part 3.6 DP Code):
– consider, preferably using an impact assessment, whether the benefits will **justify** the adverse impact. A worker's financial circumstances should not be monitored unless the employer has evidence showing that a worker who is in financial difficulties poses a significant risk to the employer;
– **inform workers** what information sources are to be used to carry out the checks, and why they are to be carried out;
– ensure that those carrying out the monitoring are **properly trained** and that there are rules to prevent the disclosure of information obtained through the monitoring; and
– **avoid retaining** any information obtained by the monitoring. Only a record that the check took place and the result obtained should be kept. Any records should not normally be retained for more than 6 months.

D. Covert monitoring

6250 Covert monitoring, that is monitoring about which the subject of it is unaware, is only justifiable in **exceptional circumstances**, where informing the worker that surveillance is taking place may prejudice national security, the prevention or detection of crime, the apprehension or prosecution of offenders or the assessment of any tax or duty (Part IV DPA 1998). As well as the requirement to comply with the general standards in sections A and B, there are also specific good practice recommendations.

If a private investigator is used, the employer must make sure that the investigator is contractually required to act in accordance with the employer's obligations.

6251 As good practice, the **employer should** (part 3.4 DP Code):
– normally require that **senior management authorise** any covert monitoring. To be **justified** they must be satisfied that there are grounds for suspecting criminal activity or malpractice and that notifying the workers concerned would prejudice its prevention or detection;
– ensure that any covert monitoring is **strictly targeted** and performed within a specified limited timeframe. The number of people involved should be likewise limited;
– ensure that covert monitoring is **not used in** areas in which workers have a reasonable expectation of privacy, for example in private offices or toilets. Where exceptionally it is necessary to monitor such an area there should be an intention to involve the police; and
– ensure that there are clear rules limiting the **disclosure and access** to the information obtained. Any information obtained should **only be used** for the purpose of the covert monitoring and any other information gathered should be destroyed unless it reveals information that no employer could reasonably be expected to ignore.

6252 The **right to privacy** (¶6285) may also have an impact on any covert monitoring the employer undertakes. For example, undercover surveillance cameras which were used to "spy" on an employee, M, whom the employer suspected of falsifying his timesheets in relation to call-outs and periods in which he attended his workplace, did raise a presumption that the right to respect for private life (art 8 European Convention on Human Rights; Human Rights Act 1998) was being breached, but the determining factor was held to be whether the employer's actions in carrying out the surveillance was proportionate to the employee's alleged misconduct (*McGowan v Scottish Water* [2005] IRLR 167, EAT).

EXAMPLE
Surveillance proportionate
1. In *McGowan v Scottish Water*, the EAT held that the employee's alleged misconduct had forced the employer to investigate the matter and, since the objective of the surveillance was to establish how many times the employee left his house to attend the workplace which would then affect the accuracy or otherwise of his timesheet, the covert surveillance went to the **root of the investigation** that the employer was bound to carry out to protect its assets and was therefore proportionate. In effect, the employer (which was a public body) was allowed to investigate what had amounted to a criminal activity and was therefore justified and proportionate. Consequently, M's dismissal had not been unfair.
2. In *McCann v Clydebank College* [2010] UKEAT 0061_09_1706, a part-time employee, M, was dismissed after he was caught working in his own business while signed off and receiving sick pay from his employers, C. There was no express rule against working elsewhere while off sick, and C had known that M had other work before his sickness absence began. M argued that:
– he had not been working during hours when he was contracted to work for C; and
– C's investigation methods, which involved putting him under surveillance, were a breach of his right to privacy.
The EAT found that M had not established, on the facts, that he was only working in his own time, and noted that when challenged the employee had not been open about his actions. Further, in any event, where an employer was paying sick pay, it was entitled to object to the employee doing paid work elsewhere, because the employee was able to earn money, and because the other work may delay his recovery. The dismissal was therefore fair in this case, although if the situation had been ambiguous or there had been an innocent misunderstanding, the position might have been different. The allegation regarding the invasion of privacy failed, in part because the decision to dismiss did not depend on the surveillance, and secondly because surveillance was proportionate in this instance.
Note: For a contrasting case of where an employee on sick leave was unfairly dismissed for misconduct when she carried on with a second part-time job, for which she was still medically fit, without permission from the first employer, see ¶4231.

Surveillance not proportionate
In *Copland v UK – 62617/00* [2007] ECHR 253, ECJ, a secretary, C, worked for a further education college. The college had no monitoring policy. For several months, the secretary was monitored by her employer when using telephone, email and internet. The ostensible purpose of monitoring was to ascertain whether the applicant was making excessive use of her employer's facilities for her own personal benefit. The European Court of Human Rights ruled that the conduct of the employer had breached C's right to privacy under article 8 of the European Convention on Human Rights.

SECTION 3

Email, internet and social media issues

6260 The use of internet and email at work is widespread and, while there are many commercial and organisational advantages, there are also **risks and liabilities** associated with employee use of these media, including viruses, legal claims, unauthorised access, and inadvertent formation of contractual obligations. The introduction of a **policy** on such use can serve to minimise the risk to the employer by setting out clear guidelines and restrictions. Breach of the email and internet policy should be made a disciplinary offence. The employer should monitor use to ensure compliance, although there may be restrictions on his right to do so.

To be able to effectively enforce the policy, employers should also ensure that they enforce the policy consistently.

A separate social media policy may also be useful (¶6282).

6261 Any monitoring of electronic communication requires compliance with the general standards (¶6160), specific good practice recommendations (¶6190) and, where appropriate, good practice recommendations on covert monitoring (¶6250). Further, where employers intercept communications as part of their monitoring they must also ensure that they are acting lawfully (¶6225).

6262 The **key elements** of an email and internet **policy** are:
– notification that email and internet are provided for business-related purposes only, or guidelines as to what level of personal use is acceptable;
– guidelines on access to and use of computer systems and software, and details of computer security procedures;
– notification that emails may be read by the employer and use of computer facilities monitored;
– a ban on sending pornographic, discriminatory and other obscene material, and a warning that doing so may leave the employee open to criminal and civil liability;
– a ban on downloading and sending defamatory messages, informing employees that derogatory remarks, even when intended as a joke, can constitute libel or unlawful discrimination or harassment;
– a reminder that back-up systems and retrieval capabilities mean that deletion of a message or file may not remove it entirely from the system;
– a warning that legally binding contracts can (even inadvertently) be formed by email correspondence; and
– a warning that breach of the email and internet policy and any guidelines on access/use of computer systems and software may result in disciplinary action up to and including summary dismissal.

Some of these areas are expanded below.

Breach of confidentiality

6264 The use of email increases the risk of **accidental disclosure** of the employer's confidential information, especially if the email goes to the wrong recipient. A company policy could protect against this by stating that no highly sensitive company information or confidential material should be sent by email. However, this approach should be weighed against the cost and environmental benefits of having a "paper-free" office.

In order to minimise the effect of accidental disclosure, it is advisable to ensure that all emails carry a confidentiality statement.

Email also makes it easier for disgruntled employees to make **unauthorised disclosures** of sensitive information. Further, a departing employee can take confidential information with him by saving it on a disk or downloading it to his home computer or laptop. After the termination of employment, confidential information is only protected to the extent that it amounts to a trade secret (¶2301), or if there is an express restrictive covenant (¶2550).

Computer viruses

6266 Computer viruses can be transmitted if software and other files are downloaded. The employer's policy should outline procedures to avoid the risk of his systems being corrupted, for example scanning all discs for viruses.

Defamation

6268 An email may constitute a defamatory statement (libel), as may a message posted on the internet. The employee may be liable for any damage caused to the reputation of the subject of the statement. The employer may also be liable by virtue of vicarious liability (¶1205) or as a publisher or disseminator of the offending statement.

A defence may be available to the employer as disseminator of a defamatory statement if he can show that (s 1 Defamation Act 1996):
– he was not the author, editor or publisher of the statement;
– he took reasonable care in relation to its publication; and
– he did not know, and had no reason to believe, that what he did caused or contributed to the publication of a defamatory statement.

The courts will consider the extent to which the employer had responsibility for the statement and the nature or circumstances of its publication. The employer's defence will be strengthened if he has issued clear guidance to employees about acceptable usage of email and internet, and if he has monitored employee use in order to identify and deal with any abuse.

Formation of contracts

6270

Employees may inadvertently enter into contracts on the employer's behalf or vary terms which the employer will be obliged to honour. An email exchange (once printed out) is capable of amounting to an agreement in writing signed by the parties (*Hall v Cognos Ltd*, ET case 1803325/97).

Harassment

6272

The contents of email (for example, jokes or pornographic images or text) can give rise to complaints of harassment (i.e. unwanted, unsolicited and inappropriate words or conduct affecting the dignity of another person), and other claims on the grounds of discrimination. See ¶¶5360, 5380, 5570 and chapter 16 generally.

> EXAMPLE In *Morse v Future Reality Ltd* [1996] ET case 54571/95, an employment tribunal awarded M compensation for sexual harassment based on the fact that her male colleagues often looked at pornography downloaded from the internet, which, together with their bad language and the general atmosphere of obscenity, caused her to feel uncomfortable at work.

6273

Employers are legally obliged to protect employees from harassment and may be liable for any discrimination perpetrated by their employees. In order to defend any claims, the employer must show that he took all reasonably practicable steps to prevent employees from committing acts of discrimination. This will include having and successfully implementing equal opportunities and harassment policies, supervising the use of emails, and dealing with any problems that arise.

The internet and email policy itself should draw employees' attention to the potential liability attached to email abuse, and set guidelines for acceptable usage.

6274

The employer's disciplinary and/or email and internet policy should also make it clear that downloading and/or circulating pornography constitutes gross misconduct (¶6537). If it is not clear, the mere use of the internet for these purposes may not be grounds for summary dismissal, unless the material is extreme enough to be classified as obscene (in which case publication would also be a criminal offence).

If the employee is not permitted to use the internet for personal use at all, downloading or circulating pornography will be a breach of contract in any case, and may result in disciplinary action. Whether summary dismissal is justified in those circumstances will depend on whether the employee's breach is repudiatory (¶1701). It will be easier for an employer to defend an unfair dismissal claim if the employee was made aware of the potential consequences of breach of the policy.

Intellectual property

6276

Copyright may be infringed where employees download articles and other materials from the internet. Software can also be downloaded and software licences may be infringed if unlicensed software is installed.

Personal use of the internet

6278 Employers may suffer a loss of productivity if employees are allowed unregulated access to the internet. The internet policy should establish the scope of permitted use. If the employee's work is suffering, the matter should be dealt with normally as a performance issue.

Unauthorised access/dissemination

6280 While outsiders can generally be kept out of an organisation's computer systems by means of security technology such as "firewalls", employees may be able to gain unauthorised access. It is therefore important for the employer to have rules governing proper use and access. This could be a separate computer and software usage policy, or could be combined with the internet and email policy.

The policy should state that computer misuse may result in disciplinary action, including summary dismissal for serious cases. If it does not, the employer may not be justified in summarily dismissing an employee who has gained unauthorised access, unless the case is sufficiently serious to warrant such action (for example, if the employee's activities constitute a criminal offence (Computer Misuse Act 1990; DPA 1998)).

If an employee deliberately gains **unauthorised access** to a computer containing information to which he is not entitled (for example, by using someone else's password), it is likely that a summary dismissal would be justified, especially where the employer has issued guidelines and warned of the consequences of breach (*Denco Ltd v Joinson* [1991] ICR 172, EAT). Such action is comparable to dishonesty, which would breach the employee's implied duty of fidelity (¶1213).

6281 Particular care should be taken when using email to **transmit confidential information**. Failure to take appropriate security measures could result in a breach of the 7th data protection principle (¶5965). It should be noted that while encryption may protect email in transit the transmission may still be vulnerable at either end. Further, even when a confidential email is "deleted" a copy may nevertheless be retained on the system. There are also risks with the use of fax. A confidential fax message may be received on a machine to which many people have access. It can also easily be misdirected, for example, by mis-keying the fax number of the intended recipient.

To protect his workers from the unauthorised dissemination of personal data, the **employer should**:
– ensure that he has an information systems security policy which properly addresses the risk of transmitting worker information by email;
– only transmit information between locations if a secure network or comparable arrangements are in place or if, in the case of email, encryption is used;
– ensure that all copies of emails and fax messages received by managers which contain sensitive information are held securely and that access to them is restricted;
– provide a means whereby managers can permanently delete such emails from personal workstations, and that they are held responsible for doing so. Checks should be made to ensure that "deleted" information is permanently deleted and not just stored on a server. The employer should be always aware that those providing IT support have access to the server; and
– draw to the attention of all workers the risks of sending confidential or sensitive personal information by email or fax.

Social media issues

6282 Social media allows users to communicate instantly with each other or to share data in a public forum. It includes **social and business networking websites** such as Facebook, MySpace, Twitter and LinkedIn and also covers video and image sharing websites such as YouTube and Flickr, as well as **personal blogs**. Social media has made a massive impact on the workplace over the last decade and employers face an array of challenges in dealing with it. These include monitoring usage, protecting intellectual property and confidential information, preventing defamation, protecting business reputation and preventing online discrimination, harassment and cyber-bullying by or of employees. Whilst employers cannot prohibit employees accessing such sites in their own time using their own equipment, employers can try to ensure employees do not adversely damage their reputation, affect their client relationships or expose them to legal liability. Many businesses **ban access** to social media sites at work. Others **allow limited access** (for example outside normal working hours such as lunch breaks) and some permit more **unrestricted access** (for example, reasonable and appropriate use during normal working hours with guidance as to what is reasonable and appropriate). Probably the most important part of any **social media policy** will be its social media rules section which should be stated to apply regardless of whether employees' access is during working hours using their employer's equipment or in their own time using their own equipment. The rules in a policy should set out a list of employee prohibitions when using social media websites, for example that they must not engage in any online activity which may damage the employer's business or reputation; post material which is offensive, abusive or derogatory; or disclose confidential information. However, the extent to which an employer can enforce such prohibitions will depend upon the facts of the particular situation.

EXAMPLE

1. In *Novak v Phones 4U Ltd* [2012] UKEAT 0279_12_1409, the EAT has held that discriminatory comments made by colleagues via Facebook are capable of forming a continuing act of discrimination.
2. Whereas in *Smith v Trafford Housing Trust* [2012] EWHC 3221 (Ch), the High Court held that a Christian housing manager was entitled to express his views about gay marriage on Facebook and that doing so did not constitute misconduct despite the employer having policies which prohibited bringing the employer into disrepute and causing offence to colleagues, which specifically prohibited such comments being made on social media sites. Despite the fact that many of his colleagues were linked to his site as Facebook friends, it was clear that he was not using the site for work-related purposes. His comments had been made in his own time, using his own equipment, and although his comments had offended a colleague, this was a necessary price to be paid for freedom of speech and for diversity of opinion and beliefs in the workplace. His demotion was therefore in breach of contract.

SECTION 4

Right to privacy

6285 Many employers voluntarily act in a socially responsible manner with respect to personal information relating to their workers and act in accordance with the data protection principles (see above) in keeping that information confidential and not distributing it to others. Outside the data protection principles, in relation to seeking **damages for privacy infringement**, the courts have been struggling with whether they could develop a new tort of privacy or whether claims should only be brought as a breach of confidence, and what the impact was of the European Convention of Human Rights which was brought into force in the UK by the Human Rights Act 1998.

However, the issue of whether there should be a new tort now seems to be settled. While for a period a number of judgments suggested that a new tort of privacy was developing (*Douglas v Hello! Ltd* [2001] QB 967; *Venable & Thompson v News Group Newspapers* [2002] EWCA Civ 1143 and *H (A Healthcare Worker) v Associated Newspapers Ltd v N (A Health Authority)* [2002] EWCA Civ 195), more recent cases have indicated that such a new tort is impractical, not necessary or even impossible (*OBG Ltd and ors v Allan and others, Douglas and another v Hello! Ltd and others, Mainstream Properties Ltd v Young and others* [2007] IRLR 608, HL; *Campbell v MGN Limited* [2004] UKHL 22, HL; *HRH Prince of Wales v Associated Newspapers Ltd* [2006] EWCA Civ 1776; *Wainwright v Home Office* [2003] UKHL 53; *A v B & C* [2002] 3 WLR 542, CA).

6286 Instead, the courts have **adapted the action for breach of confidence** to provide a remedy for the unauthorised disclosure of personal data. This development has been mediated by the analogy of the right to privacy conferred by article 8 of the European Convention on Human Rights and has required a balancing of that right against the right to freedom of expression conferred by article 10 (*OBG Ltd and ors v Allan and others, Douglas and another v Hello! Ltd and others, Mainstream Properties Ltd v Young and others* [2007] IRLR 608, HL). Indeed two earlier Court of Appeal cases also stated that the courts must consider the right to privacy under the European Convention of Human Rights (European Convention on Human Rights which has been directly incorporated by the Human Rights Act 1998) in relation to breach of confidence claims (*McKennitt and others v Ash and anor* [2006] EWCA Civ 1714 applying the decision of the European Court of Human Rights in *Van Hannover v Germany* (2005) 40 EHRR 1 confirmed in *HRH Prince of Wales v Associated Newspapers Ltd* [2006] EWCA Civ 1776).

The UK courts and tribunals are bound to apply domestic legislation in a **manner compatible** with the European Convention on Human Rights unless prevented from doing so by primary legislation, i.e. Acts of Parliament (s 3 Human Rights Act 1998). Therefore, courts and tribunals are bound to interpret legislation to make it compatible unless it is impossible to do so, i.e. unless it is clearly incompatible with the wording of an Act. This goes beyond interpretation and the courts **must take into account** the human rights principles in resolving any legislative ambiguity and in applying common law. Further, as the UK courts and tribunals are public authorities, they should **act in conformity** with the human rights principles (s 6 Human Rights Act 1998).

6287 The right to privacy and family life, home and correspondence under article 8 of the **European Convention on Human Rights** itself can include activities of a professional or business nature (*Niemietz v Germany* [1992] 16 EHRR 97) and there is also an express reference to correspondence, which includes all types of communication, including email and telephonic (Human Rights Act 1998; European Convention on Human Rights).

The **UK courts and tribunals** may be expected, therefore, to recognise the worker's right to a reasonable expectation of privacy in claims for unfair dismissal or breach of the implied term of trust and confidence (*Halford v United Kingdom* [1997] IRLR 471, ECHR). A worker, for example, may possibly claim that his dismissal was unfair if the evidence behind the reason for dismissal was obtained from the secret use of CCTV surveillance which was in breach of privacy and not justifiable under the DP Code. The same principles may also apply to intrusive body searching, drug and alcohol testing and similar activities. It must, however, be emphasised that this is an indication as to how courts and tribunals may act and there is no guarantee that they will do so in relation to private employers.

> EXAMPLE In *Halford v United Kingdom*, which was a case taken to the European Court of Human Rights by a public employee (before the Act came into force, public employees had to take breaches of the Convention to the European Court), H was a senior police officer who alleged that the telephone line, which she had been given by her employer (a police authority) for her to make private calls, had been tapped by them. The Court held that unless H had been given prior warning that her calls were liable to interception, she had a reasonable expectation of privacy. Further, even if this was not so, the police authority would still need to justify the tapping under article 8(2).

> MEMO POINTS 1. The Human Rights Act 1998, which directly incorporates the European Convention on Human Rights, **offers direct protection** in relation to fundamental human rights in the UK against public authorities. This means that an individual who believes his right to privacy has been infringed by a **public authority** may seek direct recourse in the UK courts. Consequently, workers can only directly rely on the Human Rights Act if the employer is a public authority employer. Hybrid (i.e. mixed bodies which are part authority/part public, such as the BBC) and non-public bodies, such as a private limited company or a PLC, are not public authorities.
> 2. It was partly as a result of *Halford* that Parliament introduced the Regulation of Investigatory Powers Act 2000 to regulate interceptions on private telecommunications systems (¶6220).

6288 However, there are **limits to its application** (*Pay v Lancashire Probation Service* [2004] ICR 187, EAT and *X v Y* [2004] ICR 1634, CA). In both these cases, activities out of work were not held to be private because they were done in public places and consequently could be taken into account in deciding whether to dismiss the employee. For example, in the first case, the employer, in deciding whether to dismiss P, could take into account the fact that P, who was a probation officer working with sex offenders, was performing in fetish clubs and merchandising bondage, domination and sado-masochism goods. Further, with regard to this case, the complainant, after failing to get leave to appeal to the Court of Appeal, brought a claim to the European Court of Human Rights on various grounds including under article 8 of the Convention on the grounds that his dismissal constituted a disproportionate interference with his right to respect for his private life (*Pay v UK – 32792/05* [2009] IRLR 139, ECHR). All of his claims failed; in relation to article 8 the Court held that his dismissal had been justified as a proportionate means to achieving a legitimate aim given the nature of his work with sex offenders, the fact that he had not been willing to alter his behaviour and that there was a risk of adverse publicity which could bring the probationary service into disrepute.

CHAPTER 18

Training and performance

OUTLINE

	¶¶
SECTION 1 **Training** 6310	A Making a request 6410
	B Procedure for considering request ... 6415
Requirement to train 6320	Right to be accompanied at a meeting ... 6430
Right of young persons to take time off .. 6330	C Withdrawal of request 6435
Discrimination 6340	D Employee's duties in relation to agreed
A Trainees and apprentices 6349	study or training 6440
B Government-backed training	E Remedies 6445
initiatives 6370	
1 Apprenticeship programmes and national	
traineeships 6375	SECTION 3 **Evaluation, guidelines and benchmarking** 6450
2 Work Programme 6380	
C EU and UK government assignment	
support 6390	
	Job evaluation and banding 6451
	Behavioural guidelines 6455
SECTION 2 **Time to train applications** 6400	Competence statements 6460
	Appraisals and performance management 6465
Qualifying employees 6404	Benchmarking 6470

Training ensures that employees have the **requisite skills** for their job. Further, developing employees' skills and abilities so that they can progress within the company should assist in their retention as well as ensuring a skilled and able workforce. Although there is no implied term requiring an employer to train an employee, failure to adequately train, properly instruct or support an employee may result in a variety of legal consequences (see ¶6320).

As well as training employees, employers may also have **trainees and apprentices**, who are required to undergo specific training and are subject to special rules. There are also a number of Government-backed training **initiatives** that help young people and those who may find it more difficult to return to work.

Finally, **work experience** can be a useful tool for those who would like to find out more about, and gain experience in, a particular job or organisation. Employers also benefit by gaining an opportunity to assess and encourage young graduates. Work experience can take a variety of forms: sandwich or work placements, participation in work-based projects, work shadowing, internships, and voluntary, part-time and vacation work.

MEMO POINTS With regard to work experience, readers are referred to the National Council for Work Experience at flmemo.co.uk/em6300 for more information.

6300

Union learning representatives (ULRs) are another potentially useful resource in the training of the workforce.

6301

6302 The following groups are specifically **entitled to paid time off** to study or train:

Type of employee	Purpose of time off	¶¶
Under notice of redundancy	Make arrangements for training for future employment	¶8885
Young persons	Study or training for a relevant qualification	¶6330
Trade union representatives	Undergo training so that they can carry out their duties	¶7153
Union learning representatives	Carry out training and learning functions	¶7155
Safety representatives and representatives of employee safety	Undergo training so that they can carry out their duties	¶4930
Employee representatives and candidates in election	Undergo training so that they can carry out their duties	¶8931
Trustees of occupational pension scheme	Undergo training so that they can carry out their duties	¶3432

6303 Employees who work for large businesses with 250 or more employees also have a **statutory right to request time off to undertake relevant training**. Such requests need to meet certain conditions in order to qualify for the scheme. See section 2 at ¶6400 for further details.

6304 There are various methods of **monitoring and assessing performance** of employees. On a larger organisational scale, benchmarking is often used to measure standards.

SECTION 1

Training

Types of training

6310 The **induction stage** is usually the first time the employer will formally assess the employee's training requirements and formulate a personal training plan, if necessary. Certain groups of employees may require special attention, such as school and college leavers and those who have been out of the workplace, for example to care for children, to change direction in their careers, or to spend some time working abroad. Health and safety training, for example, is particularly important in the case of young new recruits who may have little or no experience of workplace environments, therefore making them more vulnerable to accidents. Likewise, employees who have been out of the workplace may require additional training and experience to enable them to feel confident in their new jobs.

After the induction stage, training and employee development is usually discussed and planned as a result of the employer's **appraisal/performance management system**.

6311 Training may be **formal or informal** and is usually a combination of the two.

6312 **Formal training** and most qualifications are sought through specialist training providers such as universities, colleges of further and higher education and private training organisations. Some employers have obtained approval to run their own qualifications which, as well as tailoring the training to meet their needs, may also be cost effective where numbers are sufficiently large to justify the effort and the costs involved in becoming a recognised centre.

There are a large number of **qualifications** available. The Office of Qualifications and Examinations Regulator (Ofqual) keeps an up-to-date national database of qualifications and awarding bodies (for example, BTEC, City and Guilds, Edexcel and OCR) for each qualification. These awarding bodies will in turn usually be able to provide details of the centres that are approved to run the qualifications they award.

As well as the main group of awarding bodies, there are sector-oriented awarding bodies and others which focus on a particular group of employees, for example the Hospitality Awarding Body (HAB) and Chartered Institute of Management.

An employer may also use NVQs (National Vocational Qualifications). Technical competence will usually include qualifications and working experience with assessment by work-based assessors with internal and external verification to ensure the requisite standards are met.

> MEMO POINTS The Apprenticeships, Skills, Children And Learning Act 2009 established the Office of Qualifications and Examinations Regulator (Ofqual) as an independent regulator of qualifications and assessments, while the Qualifications and Curriculum Authority (QCA) continues to exercise its non-regulatory role under the new name of the Qualifications and Curriculum Development Agency (QCDA).

Informal techniques include coaching, mentoring, job shadowing, buddy training and experiential learning. These are all work based and there is a measure of overlap between the various approaches. Due to their informality, this may result in a haphazard learning process, and a training programme or checklist of the required learning points is often useful.

Where appropriate, secondment can also be a useful tool in developing the skills and experience of employees.

6313

Requirement to train

There is **no implied term** requiring the employer to train an employee (*White v London Transport Executive* [1981] IRLR 261, EAT).

6320

However, **not providing** adequate training, proper instruction and support may result in:
1. A **breach of contract**, if there is an express term relating to the training of the employee.
2. A **breach of** the common law **duty of care**, if loss or injury is suffered by the employee or others to whom the employer owes a duty of care.
3. **Liability for discrimination because of age, disability, gender reassignment, marriage and civil partnership, pregnancy and maternity, race, religion or belief, sex or sexual orientation**, if the employer has directly or indirectly discriminated against the employee. For example, management training that occurs at weekends or in the evenings may be difficult or impossible for women with family responsibilities to attend and is, therefore, indirectly discriminatory, or only paying part-time workers their normal pay to attend full-time training may indirectly discriminate against women. Where there may be the potential for discrimination, reasonable alternative arrangements should be made available, for example by rescheduling or providing alternatives to residential training. In the same context, employers must give equal access to training to part-time workers as they do to comparable full-time workers and to fixed-term employees as they do to comparable permanent employees.
Liability for unlawful discrimination may also occur if managers and employees have not been trained to implement an equal opportunities policy correctly, as the mere fact of having a policy will not give the employer a defence against any such claim if it has not been implemented.
4. A contributing reason, and in exceptional circumstances the main reason, supporting a **claim for unfair dismissal** if the employee is dismissed for incompetence or poor performance (*J Davison v Kent Meters Ltd* [1975] IRLR 145, IT). This also covers providing inadequate training to a newly promoted employee (*F Burrows v Ace Caravan Co (Hull) Ltd* [1972] IRLR 4, IT) and unfairly dismissing an employee for poor performance where it was due to a lack of trained subordinates (*Woodward v Beeston Boiler Co Ltd* [1973] IRLR 7, IT).
Training is important as the issue of fair procedure is often crucial in determining whether a dismissal for incapability was fair. A tribunal will consider what steps a reasonable employer would have taken, and what steps the employer could have taken, to minimise the risk of poor performance by providing adequate training and supervision.
5. In exceptional cases, a **claim for constructive dismissal**, where the failure to give adequate support is sufficiently serious (*Associated Tyre Specialists (Eastern) Ltd v Waterhouse* [1976] IRLR 386, EAT). In this case, a supervisor was given insufficient support in relation to her role as a supervisor and in relation as to how to improve her supervision skills. As a result, her

resignation following a walk out of her staff was held to be a constructive dismissal resulting in her having been unfairly dismissed.

6. A **breach of** the employer's **health and safety obligations** (for example, under an employer's general statutory duty to ensure the health and safety of his workers). This may also have implications with regard to an employer's insurance cover.

6325 **Refusal by employee to train**   Most **disciplinary procedures** will treat the failure to participate in training as an offence meriting disciplinary action, the severity of which would depend on the importance and type of the training refused. For example, if the employee has unreasonably refused to undertake training which is required by the health and safety rules, an employer may be entitled to dismiss him. Likewise, in the case where an employer is seeking external accreditation to a quality standard, for example ISO 9001: 2008, and the holding of that quality standard has implications on the type of work that the organisation can undertake, he may be able to insist that an employee undergoes relevant training.

Where an employee has refused to train, which may have a future negative impact on his employment conditions, this should be examined carefully to ensure that there are no **issues of discrimination** (see 3. at ¶6320).

6326 Employers may place a **contractual requirement** that employees will participate in appropriate training. In such cases, a refusal may also amount to a breach of contract.

6327 Where substantial costs have been incurred in training the employee, it may be possible for the employer to **recover** some or all of his costs if the employee leaves the company within a set period after completing the course or if he fails to complete it successfully (¶2849). In such cases, there should be a written agreement prior to the training commencing to cover the potential recovery of training costs and a sliding scale regarding recovery is often used to reflect the amount of benefit the employer has received so that, for example, an employee leaving 12 months later would pay less than an employee leaving 2 weeks later.

Right of young persons to take time off

6330 A young employed person has the right to take **paid** time off work for study and training (ss 63A-63C ERA 1996 (inserted by s 32 Teaching and Higher Education Act 1998)). A young person is **defined** as someone who is 16 or 17 years old, who is not in full-time secondary or further education, and has not got any level 2 qualifications (for example, GCSEs in five subjects at grades A*-C, an NVQ level 2, and certain other qualifications such as a BTEC First Diploma).

> MEMO POINTS   The Education and Skills Act 2008 will introduce a new right which replaces the existing right to time off. Basically, once in force, employers will be under a duty not to employ in full-time employment those over compulsory school age but under 18 who do not have a level 3 qualification (for example, A levels in two subjects), unless the employer provides relevant training or education. This will be in line with increasing the age for young people (who have not attained a level 3 qualification) to remain in education or training to 17 in 2013 and to 18 in 2015. Any further developments will be covered by our updating service.

6331 The employer must allow the employee a **reasonable amount** of time off to study or train for a level 2 qualification that will help the employee's future employment prospects, taking into account all the circumstances and in particular:
– the requirements of the study or training; and
– the circumstances of the business of the employer and the effect of the employee's time off on the running of that business.

6332 Time off to train is **paid at** the appropriate hourly rate. See ¶3935.

Discrimination

6340 **By employers**   An employer may not discriminate on the grounds of sex, race, disability, age, religion or belief, marriage and civil partnership, pregnancy and maternity, gender reassignment or sexual orientation in offering employees an **opportunity to undergo training**.

Nor should an employer refuse to afford or deliberately not afford training to employees on such grounds.

Vacation placement schemes are included as training for these purposes (*Treasury Solicitor's Department v Chenge* [2007] IRLR 386, EAT).

> EXAMPLE
> 1. Failure or refusal to offer a female employee a training course because she is pregnant will amount to direct sex discrimination.
> 2. Refusal to consider alternative training arrangements where access to a training room is impossible for an employee who is a wheelchair user is likely to constitute disability discrimination (failure to make reasonable adjustments).
> 3. A policy of paying part-time employees their usual wage to attend full-time training courses, when full-time employees were compensated in full is indirectly discriminatory against women unless objectively justified (*Arbeiterwohlfahrt der Stadt Berlin e V v Bötel* [1992] IRLR 423, ECJ).

6341 In certain limited circumstances, an employer may take **positive action** which would otherwise give rise to a discrimination complaint (see chapter 16).

In addition, in certain circumstances, it is lawful to provide facilities or services to **meet the special needs** of persons of a particular group in relation to their education, training, welfare, or any ancillary benefits (see again chapter 16 for further details).

> EXAMPLE An employer may not be discriminating unlawfully if he provides language training to employees who were born overseas or who had disrupted education in their country of origin, with the result that they are unable to communicate effectively.

6342 The employer is required to make reasonable adjustments for **disabled employees** (¶5530).

6345 **By qualifying and training bodies** It is unlawful for authorities and bodies which can confer an **authorisation or qualification** that is needed for, or will facilitate, engagement in a particular profession or trade to discriminate on the grounds of age, disability, gender reassignment, marriage and civil partnership, pregnancy and maternity, race, religion or belief, sex or sexual orientation (s 53 EqA 2010):
– in the arrangements for deciding upon whom to confer a relevant qualification;
– in the terms on which they are prepared to confer authorisation of qualification;
– by refusing or deliberately omitting to grant an authorisation or qualification;
– by withdrawing or varying the terms on which an applicant holds a qualification or authorisation; or
– by subjecting an applicant to any other detriment.

Moreover, such bodies are under a duty to make reasonable adjustments (¶5530). However, applying a competence standard to a disabled person is not disability discrimination, provided the application of the standard is justified.

Similarly, it is unlawful for such qualifying bodies to subject to harassment or to victimise on the grounds of age, disability, gender reassignment, marriage and civil partnership, pregnancy and maternity, race, religion or belief, sex or sexual orientation any person who holds or applies for such a qualification.

> MEMO POINTS However, where an authority or body provides an **independent complaint and appeal process** (for example, the Specialist Training Authority, by virtue of the Medical Act 1983), a claim for race discrimination may not be brought against that authority or body in an employment tribunal (*Chaudhary v Specialist Training Authority appeal panel and ors (No. 2)* [2005] EWCA Civ 282). In this case, the Specialist Training Authority and its appeal panel provided the claimant with a fair and public hearing by an independent and impartial tribunal established by law and complied with his right to a fair trial under article 6 of the European Convention of Human Rights (Art 6 European Convention of Human Rights). The option of applying for judicial review of the appeal panel's decision remained available to the claimant.

6348 Persons and bodies that provide, or make arrangements for the provision of, **vocational training** must not discriminate on the grounds of age, disability, gender reassignment, marriage and civil partnership, pregnancy and maternity, race, religion or belief, sex or sexual orientation (ss 55, 56 EqA 2010):

– in the arrangements they make for selecting persons to whom to provide, or to whom to offer to provide, the service;
– in the terms on which they are prepared to afford access to training;
– by refusing or deliberately omitting to grant access to training;
– by terminating the training; or
– by subjecting an applicant to any other detriment.

Moreover, such bodies are under a duty to make reasonable adjustments (¶5530).

Similarly, it is unlawful for a provider of vocational training to subject to harassment or victimise on the grounds of age, disability, gender reassignment, marriage and civil partnership, pregnancy and maternity, race, religion or belief, sex or sexual orientation any person seeking or undergoing vocational training.

A. Trainees and apprentices

6349 Traineeships and apprenticeships are useful methods for training the next generation of workers and Government support may be available in certain circumstances (¶¶6370+). The Government has also recently legislated on a new form of apprenticeship (¶6353) which may appeal more to employers than traditional apprenticeships (¶6352). Further, the age for young people (who have not attained a level 3 qualification) to remain in education or training will rise to 17 in 2013 and to 18 in 2015. Once this comes into effect, young people post-16 years will need to:
– be in full-time education, such as school, college or home education;
– participate in work-based learning, such as an apprenticeship; or
– be in part-time education or training if they are employed, self-employed or volunteering for more than 20 hours a week.

Any further developments will be covered by our updating service.

> MEMO POINTS It will be for local authorities to ensure that young people in their area participate and to provide support. The Government has delayed enforcement proposals which included fining those who do not participate.

Trainees

6350 Trainees under a **training contract** will often have an express term that makes the contract terminable if the trainee does not satisfactorily complete his training, or if there is no suitable position available for him within the company at the end of the traineeship.

Trainees who are **not employees** under their contract, for example students on work placements who are gaining experience in their chosen profession, are not entitled to the main body of employment rights. However, employers must ensure compliance with the health and safety regulations (¶¶4800+) and the working time rules (¶¶3600+).

Often trainees are engaged under a **tripartite arrangement** involving an employer, an institution and the trainee themselves. In determining whether a tripartite agreement has resulted in a contract of employment between the trainee and the employer, the tribunal will consider what the dominant purpose of the arrangement was (*M & P Steelcraft Ltd v Ellis* [2008] IRLR 355, EAT). In this case, concerning a prisoner on a work placement under a three-way agreement, the EAT held that the main purpose was the rehabilitation of the offender and that there was no binding contract. In certain circumstances, a tripartite arrangement can result in the creation of a contract of apprenticeship (¶6378).

Apprentices

6351 Apprenticeships are a **hybrid of training and working**: they enable apprentices to obtain on-the-job training by combining learning (which often includes day release to external providers) and work experience. They lead to nationally recognised qualifications and are for a fixed term. The training element of the apprenticeship is often fully or partially government funded. The primary benefit to apprentices is that they can earn a wage (often quite modest) while acquiring skills in a business that may well keep them on after their training has finished. The primary benefits to employers are that they should save on recruitment costs, retain skills that more senior members of the organisation have by passing them down to new apprentices, and as the apprenticeship progresses the apprentice should be productive and represent good value for money.

6352 **Traditionally**, apprenticeships were governed by **common law**, though most apprenticeships that commenced after 6 April 2012 are governed by individual agreements as set out by legislation (see ¶6353 below). Due to the incremental development of the law surrounding traditional apprentices, many aspects of their legal status are unclear. Although they are employees, their status differs to that of regular employees and they are a distinct entity from a legal point of view. They enjoy many of the same rights as regular employees, though they also have greater protection in terms of the sort of training and treatment they can expect and how their apprenticeships can be brought to an end.

The primary purpose of traditional apprenticeships is training and work done is considered secondary. As a consequence, the employer undertakes a much wider responsibility towards an apprentice than he does towards an employee (*Whitely v Marton* [2003] IRLR 197, EAT). In return, the apprentice must serve his "master". There is also a greater degree of control than that normally given to an employer over an employee, due to the training nature of the relationship. The amount of disciplinary power that a master may have over an apprentice will vary depending on the maturity and qualifications of the apprentice, and the extent to which he, like his master, is regulated by any professional code of conduct.

A traditional apprenticeship will be based on an agreement between the apprentice (or his parents or guardian if he is a minor) and the employer, and must be for a fixed period or until specified qualifications are achieved. Consequently, it is not terminable on notice, nor can it be terminated for misconduct in the same way as an ordinary contract of employment could be (the threshold is much higher). Further, apprentices cannot be made redundant unless there has been a fundamental change in the employer's business that has resulted in the redundancy situation (*Whitely v Marton*, *Wallace v C A Roofing Services Ltd* [1996] IRLR 435, QBD). If an apprentice brings a successful claim for wrongful dismissal, the loss claimed could be for the loss of wages until the end of the apprenticeship and also compensation for the loss of training and status, so the consequences of terminating a traditional apprenticeship early can be significant for the employer. Apprenticeship contracts should be made in writing and signed; an oral contract of apprenticeship, although legally valid, is unenforceable unless and until it is acted upon (*Edmonds v Lawson QC* [2000] EWCA Civ 69).

6353 **New apprenticeships**, commencing from 6 April 2012, are normally governed by legislation if they are created under a valid apprenticeship agreement (Apprenticeships, Skills, Children and Learning Act 2009 referred to here as "the Act"). They are available to anyone who is over 16 and who is not in full-time education, provided that there is a contract of service/employment between the apprentice and employer, and the apprentice can be a new or existing employee. The Act was created in order bring apprenticeships in line with normal employees in terms of the rights that they have and the way that their contracts can be brought to an end: the underlying aim was to make apprenticeships more appealing to employers, who were perceived as being reluctant to offer apprenticeships because of how difficult it was to terminate them if the relationship did not go to plan. The Act introduced the **apprenticeship agreement**, which is a contract of service, not one of apprenticeship (Apprenticeships (Form of Apprenticeship Agreement) Regulations SI 2012/844, referred to here as "the Regulations"). As such, it is similar to a regular employment contract (with some additional requirements) and can be ended in the same way. In order for the agreement to be a valid apprenticeship agreement (and to avoid the apprenticeship being viewed as a common law apprenticeship), it must meet the **following conditions**:

1. include an undertaking that the apprentice will work for the employer;
2. be in the prescribed form (as laid down in the Regulations). There is no model agreement, but it must be in the form of a written statement of terms, a written contract of employment or a letter of engagement and it must include the basic terms of employment which are

given to all employees (¶¶1400+), as well as details of the skill, trade or occupation in which the apprentice is being trained;
3. state that it is governed by the laws of England and Wales; and
4. state that it is entered into in connection with a qualifying apprenticeship framework.

Although not specified by the Regulations, it would also be wise to include details of what is expected of the apprentice, both in terms of general discipline and what he will need to do in order to pass the scheme; details of time off that will be allowed for college, if relevant; a probationary period; as well as any clawback of any training fees that the employer had to meet should the agreement be terminated early.

Although apprenticeships governed by the Act are easier to terminate than those governed by the common law, as with any type of employment, employers must follow fair dismissal procedures, even where the employment is coming to an end simply because of the conclusion of the fixed-term apprenticeship agreement (if there was no role for the apprentice to move into at the end of his training, the dismissal would be for "some other substantial reason", see ¶¶8530+).

6354 All apprentices, including those governed by both the common law and the Act are:
– protected by the **anti-discrimination laws**;
– entitled to work in a **healthy and safe workplace**;
– entitled to a **minimum wage** unless on a programme-led apprenticeship scheme (¶¶2868-9);
– protected by the **working time rules**;
– entitled to **statutory sick pay**;
– entitled to **equal treatment** if they work **part-time**; and
– entitled to **parents' and carers' rights**, including maternity, paternity, and adoption pay.

> MEMO POINTS   There is some debate as to whether or not the specific apprentice minimum wage (¶2869) applies to apprentices governed by the Act, simply because the relevant regulations (National Minimum Wage Regulations SI 1999/584 as amended) refer to "contracts of apprenticeship" rather than "apprenticeship agreements" as per the Act. It is unlikely that it was the Government's intention to exclude this class of apprentice, though until this is clarified either by the Government or a test case we will not know for certain. At present there is therefore an argument that apprentices governed by the Act are entitled to the minimum wage as though they were regular employees.

B. Government-backed training initiatives

6370 There are a number of initiatives that help young people and those who may find it more difficult to return to work, and that aid vocational training.

> MEMO POINTS   1. In 2010, the Apprenticeships, Skills, Children and Learning Act 2009 dissolved the Learning and Skills Council for England (LSC) and moved the **responsibility** for the planning and funding of all education for those who are over compulsory school age but under 19 to **local authorities**. In addition, the **Young People's Learning Agency** (YPLA) was established as a non-departmental public body to support and enable local authorities to discharge their new duties.
> 2. Also in 2010, the LSC's responsibility for post-19 education and training transferred to the Chief Executive for Skills Funding who is responsible for the new **Skills Funding Agency** (SFA).

1. Apprenticeship programmes and national traineeships

6375 **Apprenticeship programmes** are schemes aimed at enhancing the vocational skills of the workforce and primarily targeted at those in the **16-24 age bracket** with employers receiving financial assistance towards the cost of training.

A Young Apprenticeship scheme for **14-16 year olds** is a 2-year programme aimed at giving pupils the chance to gain experience before possibly moving onto an apprenticeship at 16.

There are also apprenticeship opportunities for people **aged 25 and over**.

6376 At present there are **three levels** of apprenticeship: apprenticeships, advanced apprenticeships, and a programme-led apprenticeship (PLA). The last of these enables an apprentice to begin their studies at college and gain work experience before moving onto a full apprenticeship with an employer. The requirements of any apprenticeship programme will depend on the sector. There are also some regional variations in the frameworks.

Status

6378 Government-backed apprenticeships, where there is a tripartite apprenticeship agreement in which the employer provides the opportunity for work experience while the training is done by, and/or under the auspices of, a training agent or provider and/or a college or council, can result in common law contracts of apprenticeship (*Flett v Matheson* [2006] ICR 673, CA).

2. Work Programme

6380 The Work Programme (previously called New Deal) scheme is aimed at **assisting** those who would otherwise have difficulty entering paid employment. Employers also get assistance, and in some cases funding, to help and encourage them to recruit such employees.

6381 Its strategy is based on **local partnerships** between employers, local authorities, training providers, Jobcentres, environmental groups, volunteer organisations and others. The partnerships are co-ordinated by Jobcentre Plus or in some cases by the private sector. Work Programme is developing at different rates in different parts of the United Kingdom, so it is worthwhile checking precise details of schemes offered in a particular area. As different bodies have responsibility for promoting and developing the initiatives, the vocabulary and approach may also vary.

C. EU and UK government assignment support

6390 UK employers may be eligible for grants under a **European funding programme (Leonardo programme)** when assigning or seconding an employee to another EU member state for vocational training. The programme is open to a wide range of public and private sector organisations and to companies active in training or concerned by training issues. The vocational training, however, must be part of a structured vocational training programme leading to a recognised qualification in the UK. For more information, see flmemo.co.uk/em6390a

Periods of vocational training acquired in another EU member state can also be registered in a **Europass**. This provides the trainee with a record of his training placements which is recognised outside the member state where the training is based. The document is issued by the European Commission and distributed in each member state through the relevant National Agency. The UK National Europass Centre administers the system in the UK. For more information, see flmemo.co.uk/em6390b

SECTION 2

Time to train applications

6400 The right to request time off to undertake relevant training applies to **businesses with 250 or more employees** (s 40 Apprenticeships, Skills, Children and Learning Act 2009 which inserts ss 63D-63K into the ERA 1996). Moreover, a qualifying condition of 26 weeks' continuous employment applies and certain groups are excluded. However, employers are free to offer enhanced rights so, for example, they may wish to offer the right to all employees so that they use the same procedure to formally consider training requests from all their staff.

While employee requests may involve agreeing time away from their duties, the primary focus of the new right is employers agreeing relevant training with their staff. The entitlement does not give employees the right to time off and, if the employer refuses an application, the tribunals cannot force the employer to give the employee time off. Rather the right is a **procedure** that employees can use to facilitate the discussion for, and mutual agreement of, taking time off to undertake training that is relevant to their work (be it in their current role or in a future one). Consequently, the **initial onus** is on the employee to present a carefully thought-out application well in advance of when he would like the time off to train/study. On receipt of an application, the employer must follow a set procedure, with him only refusing a request where the study or training will not help the employee's productivity or performance, or there is a clear business reason for doing so. It is up to the employer and employee to agree as to how to meet any costs. There is no obligation on the employer for the time off to be paid, or for the employer to pay for the training. In practice, many employers may agree to paid time off and/or paying for or contributing towards training, recognising the value of the investment.

The process is similar to that for requests to work flexibly (¶4690). The extent to which this new time to train right is used will undoubtedly depend on what else the employer already has in place, for example employees may already be raising their training and development needs at annual performance reviews.

MEMO POINTS 1. This right was introduced in April 2010. Following a consultation on extending the right to employees of small and medium-sized organisations (i.e. those with **fewer than 250 employees**) the Government has announced that this will not occur until April 2015 at the earliest. Formal evaluation will be undertaken in due course to determine whether the right should be extended then, remain as now or be repealed. Any further developments will be covered by our updating service.
2. In certain circumstances a **young person** has the **right to take paid time off work** for study and training, see ¶6330.

Type of study or training

6402 The study or training **must** set out to **improve** both the employee's effectiveness and the performance of the employer's business (s 63D(4) ERA 1996).

Study or training is a broad concept and can follow accredited programmes (leading to the award of a recognised qualification) or shorter unaccredited training sessions that help employees develop specific skills relevant to their job, workplace or business. This includes training or study (s 63E ERA 1996):
– undertaken on the employer's premises or elsewhere (including at the employee's home);
– undertaken by the employee while performing his duties of employment or separately;
– provided or supervised by the employer or by a third party (for example, an external provider or college);
– undertaken without supervision;
– undertaken within or outside the United Kingdom; and
– that leads or does not lead to the award of a qualification.

Qualifying employees

6404 The right only applies to employees who have been **continuously employed** for at least 26 weeks (s 63D(6) ERA 1996; SI 2010/800).

6405 **Exclusions** Further, **children and young persons** whose learning needs are already catered for in other ways are excluded (s 63D(7) ERA 1996). This category includes:
– those of compulsory school age;
– those who are 16 or 17 years old who have a duty to participate in education or training (once that duty comes into force); and
– young persons who already have a statutory right to paid time off for study or training (¶6330).

Agency workers are also specifically excluded (s 63D(7)(e) ERA 1996).

A. Making a request

Form and content of application The application must be **dated and in writing** and can be by letter, on a form provided by the employer or by email (reg 4 SI 2010/156).

If an employee has **previously made an application**, he **must wait** a year before making a further application to the same employer (s 63F(1) ERA 1996). However, employers must **ignore an earlier application**, at an employee's request, even where it is within a year of the current application, if (reg 3 SI 2010/155):
a. the employee failed to start the agreed study or training due to:
– an emergency or unforeseen circumstance beyond his control; or
– the cancellation of the study or training (unless this was the employee's responsibility); or
b. where the employee makes a mistake and applied too soon after his last request and has told his employer about his mistake when making his next application and has asked for the earlier application to be withdrawn.

The application must (s 63D(5), s 63E(4) ERA 1996; reg 3 SI 2010/156):
a. state that the **application** is being **made under** the statutory right to request time off to train (i.e. that it is made under "Section 63D of the Employment Rights Act 1996");
b. give details of the **proposed study or training**, including:
– the subject matter;
– where and when it will take place;
– who will provide or supervise it; and
– what qualification (if any) it will lead to;
c. explain **how** the employee thinks the proposed study or training will **improve**:
– the employee's effectiveness in the employer's business; and
– the performance of the employer's business; and
d. give the date and method of submission (i.e. by letter, form or email) of any **previous application**.

As best practice employers should **acknowledge** the application.
Alternatively, if the employee has **failed to provide all of the required information**, it is good practice to inform the employee of what he has omitted and ask him to re-submit the application.

6410

6411

6412

B. Procedure for considering request

Meeting to hear request The employer must hold a **meeting** with the employee to discuss the request **within** 28 days of receipt of the application, unless the employer has already agreed to it in writing (reg 4 SI 2010/155).

Where the **manager** who would ordinarily consider the application is **absent** due to annual leave or sickness, this **period only starts** to run from the earlier of the manager's return or 28 days after the receipt of the application (reg 15 SI 2010/155).

<u>MEMO POINTS</u> The applicant has the **right to be accompanied** at the meeting (¶6430).

The **time and place** of the meeting must be convenient to the employer and the employee (reg 13 SI 2010/155).

If the employee **more than once fails to attend** a meeting to discuss a request without reasonable cause, the employer can treat the request as withdrawn (¶6435). In such circumstances, the employer must inform the employee in writing that he considers the employee's request to be withdrawn.

6415

6416

6418 **Making the decision** Employers must **consider** all applications and establish whether the request will improve the employee's productivity or performance and can be accommodated within the needs of the business (¶6423).

> EXAMPLE There may be many instances where the employer is happy to accept in full the employee's proposals for training as set out in his request. There may also be instances where, while happy to accept the request, the employer considers that the training needs can be met in a different way. For example, the employer may prefer to deliver training in-house rather than use an external training provider, or he may be aware of different courses or qualifications that the employer believes would better meet the training needs of the employee.

6419 If the employer has received a valid request but feels that he **needs additional information** before he can give the request proper consideration, the employer can ask the employee to provide it. If the employee unreasonably refuses to provide this additional information, the employer can treat the request as withdrawn (¶6435). In such circumstances, the employer must inform the employee in writing that he considers the employee's request to be withdrawn.

6420 **Notification of decision** Within 14 days of the meeting, the employer must inform the employee in a **written dated form** that he either (regs 5-6 SI 2010/155):
1. **agrees** to the request:
a. specifying:
– the subject matter;
– where and when it will take place;
– who will provide or supervise the training; and
– what qualification (if any) it will lead to; and
b. clarifying:
– whether any remuneration will be paid for the time spent undertaking the agreed study or training;
– any changes to the employee's working hours in order to accommodate the agreed study or training; and
– how any tuition fees or other direct costs of the agreed study or training will be met;
2. **rejects** the request:
a. setting out clear business grounds why the application cannot be accepted, including sufficient explanation as to why these reasons apply (¶6423); and
b. giving details of the appeal procedure (¶6425); or
3. **agrees in part** to the request:
a. making clear which part of the application is agreed and which part is refused; and
b. giving the information in 1. and 2. above.

6421 Where the employer and employee **agree to a variation**, the written dated form must (reg 7 SI 2010/155):
a. make clear:
– the variation agreed;
– whether any remuneration will be paid for the time spent undertaking the agreed study or training;
– any changes to the employee's working hours in order to accommodate the agreed study or training; and
– how any tuition fees or other direct costs of the agreed study or training will be met; and
b. be supported by written evidence of the employee's agreement to that variation.

BIS recommends drafting the written evidence with the employee during the meeting where this is discussed.

> EXAMPLE The employer agrees to an employee's request, but foresees circumstances where he may later need to withdraw that agreement. In such cases, the employer should agree with the employee the circumstances in which he will withdraw his agreement.

6422 If the agreement requires a change to the employee's terms and conditions, for example, a change in working hours or because the training time will be unpaid, the employer's normal procedures should be followed as for any agreed contractual variation (¶1638).

6423 **Grounds for refusal** The permissible reasons for refusal **must relate** to one or more of **the following** business grounds (s 63F ERA 1996):
a. the proposed study or training would not improve:
– the employee's effectiveness in the employer's business; or
– the performance of the employer's business; or
b. there is:
– a burden of additional costs;
– a detrimental effect on the ability to meet customer demand;
– an inability to reorganise the work among existing staff;
– an inability to recruit additional staff;
– a detrimental impact on quality and performance;
– an insufficiency of work during the periods the employee proposes to work; or
– a planned structural change or changes.

6425 **Appealing a refusal** The employee can appeal against any refusal by giving **written dated notice** within 14 days of the notification of the decision (regs 8-9 SI 2010/155). This must set out the grounds of appeal.

> EXAMPLE While there are no restrictions on the grounds for appeal, common grounds for appeal are likely to be that:
> – the employee challenges a fact given by the employer to explain why a business ground applies;
> – a new fact has come to light (for example another employee is now prepared to cover the time the employee wants off to train); or
> – the employee proposes a varied studying or training pattern that accommodates the business grounds set out in the refusal.

6426 If the employer does not accept the grounds of appeal, he must hold a **meeting to discuss the appeal within** 14 days of receiving the employee's written notification (reg 10 SI 2010/155). BIS recommends that, if it is practical, the appeal should be heard by a different manager to the person who considered the employee's initial request.

The **time and place** of the meeting must be convenient to the employer and the employee (reg 13 SI 2010/155).

If the employee **more than once fails to attend** a meeting to discuss an appeal without reasonable cause, the employer can treat the appeal as withdrawn. In such circumstances, the employer must inform the employee in writing that he considers the appeal to be withdrawn.

> MEMO POINTS The applicant has the **right to be accompanied** at the appeal (¶6430).

6427 Within 14 days of the appeal meeting, the employer must inform the employee in a **written dated form** that he either (regs 11-12 SI 2010/155):
– **upholds** the appeal, specifying the information required as set out in ¶6420; or
– **dismisses** the appeal, stating the grounds for the dismissal, including sufficient explanation as to why these grounds apply.

Extension of procedural time limits

6428 Any of the preceding time limits can be extended if the employer and employee agree (reg 14 SI 2010/155).

In all circumstances, the employer must send a **dated written record** of the agreed extension to the employee stating the process to which the extension relates and the date on which the extension ends.

Right to be accompanied at a meeting

6430 The employee has the right to be accompanied to the meeting to discuss the request or the appeal by a colleague, or a trade union representative as long as he also works for the employer (reg 16 SI 2010/155). The employee can ask whether a companion from outside the employer's organisation can attend, for example a trade union representative who is not employed by the employer, though the employer is under no obligation to accept such a request. The **role of the companion** is to support the employee and to this end he can address the meeting on behalf of the employee and confer with the employee during it, but cannot answer questions on behalf of the employee.

> MEMO POINTS There is no statutory right for the companion to be a trade union representative (i.e. a trade union representative regardless of whether he is also employed by the employer) in contrast to the right to be accompanied to discipline or grievance hearings (¶6782).

6431 The employee should **contact his companion** as soon as he is given the date of the meeting. If the companion is **unable to make** this date, the employer must accept an alternative time as proposed by the employee that is convenient for all parties and which takes place within 7 days of the date of the original meeting. If this cannot be achieved, the employee should consider an alternative companion.

6432 Companions are entitled to **paid time off** to act as a companion (reg 16(8) SI 2010/155) (¶3910).

C. Withdrawal of request

6435 **Employees can withdraw** their application at any time by notifying their employer orally or in writing. In such cases, they cannot make a new application within 12 months of the date on which the application was made (reg 19 SI 2010/155) except in certain circumstances (¶6410).

The **employer can also deem** that the **application has been withdrawn if** the employee (¶¶6416, 6419, 6426):
- misses two meetings to discuss the request/appeal without reasonable cause; or
- unreasonably refuses to provide the employer with information necessary for him to be able to consider the application.

6436 The employer must **confirm the withdrawal** of the application in writing (unless already so provided by the employee).

D. Employee's duties in relation to agreed study or training

6440 Where the employer has agreed an application or part of an application, the employee is under a duty to inform the employer by giving **written dated notice** within 14 days if he (s 63H ERA 1996; reg 20 SI 2010/155):
- **fails to start or complete** the agreed study or training; or
- undertakes, or proposes to undertake, **study or training that is different** to what has been agreed.

E. Remedies

Failure to consider request

6445 An employee has the **right to complain** to a tribunal if the employer has not followed the correct procedure with regard to the request or has rejected the application on a ground that is not a valid permissible reason or based on incorrect facts (s 63I ERA 1996).

Where the tribunal has held that the complaint is well founded, it can **order** the employer to (s 63J ERA 1996; reg 6 SI 2010/156):
– reconsider the request; and/or
– pay the employee such compensation as the tribunal considers just and equitable in all the circumstances, up to a limit of 8 weeks' pay, subject to the statutory cap (¶2923).

6446 Employees can also bring a separate claim if the employer has **not allowed an employee to be accompanied** at a meeting/appeal (reg 17 SI 2010/155). Where the tribunal has held that the complaint is well founded, it can make an **order** for compensation of up to 2 weeks' pay, subject to the statutory cap (¶2923).

Right not to be dismissed or suffer detriment

6447 Employees have the right not to be dismissed for exercising their right to request time off to study or train and any such dismissal will be automatically unfair (¶8390) (s 104E ERA 1996; reg 18 SI 2010/155). An employee also has the right not to be subjected to any detriment (short of dismissal) on the same grounds (s 47F ERA 1996). The same protection against dismissal and detriment applies to those who accompany or seek to accompany an employee to a meeting/appeal.

> MEMO POINTS What amounts to a "**detriment**" is not defined by the ERA 1996, but case law on discrimination has held that it is whether a reasonable worker would feel he has been disadvantaged by reason of his employer's acts (¶5279).

SECTION 3

Evaluation, guidelines and benchmarking

6450 Performance can be judged, monitored, reviewed, assessed and encouraged by the methods outlined below.

Job evaluation and banding

6451 Job evaluation provides a structured and transparent method of **comparing jobs** that are different in terms of duties and responsibilities with the aim of being able to position the jobs in terms of levels of authority and pay. It is not a method for evaluating personal performance. In legal terms, job evaluation is important as a technique when it helps ensure compliance with anti-discrimination legislation by being used as the basis for a fair and equal pay and reward structure. It is also often carried out when organisations are changing, for example expanding or restructuring or to support comparison with external job market rates.

There are a number of job evaluation schemes available, usually through specialist providers. The essentials of the various schemes tend to be broadly similar although the detailed content may vary.

There are fundamentally two approaches, analytical and non-analytical. The analytical approach is more common and breaks the job down into its components, whereas the non-analytical approach compares each job in its entirety (for example, ranking jobs against one another).

Acas provide an advisory booklet on job evaluation at flmemo.co.uk/em6451

6452 In an analytical job evaluation certain factors are defined against which the job is assessed. These factors are then further subdivided into several components. A common approach is a rating of up to ten points for each component, the more significant the component for the business the higher the score. Jobs can then be grouped to reflect their positioning by adding together the scores. The various factors can also be given a weighting, for example one factor may be considered to be twice as important as another and this can be reflected in the rating system.

No single job evaluation system is equally applicable to all organisations. Some adjustments are needed to tailor a job evaluation system to an organisation.

6453 The common **standard factors** are as follows:
– **skill, knowledge and expertise**, for example educational qualifications or the knowledge and understanding which are unique within the organisation;
– **management or supervisory responsibility**, for example the level and type of supervisory or management responsibility activities that the employee is expected to undertake;
– **decision-making responsibility**, for example the degree of autonomy and the impact of the job on the organisation's core aims and objectives;
– **job difficulty**, for example the amount of disruption to plans that the employee has to tolerate, such as sudden changes in the workload that cannot be anticipated; and
– **adding value**, for example impact on the customer.

Behavioural guidelines

6455 There are a number of areas where behavioural guidelines remain key. They are mainly detailed in disciplinary rules and standard operating procedures. These define the two extremes of behavioural guidelines:
– **disciplinary rules** define what is considered unacceptable behaviour and the associated procedures determine how breaches of those rules will be dealt with; and
– **standard operating procedures** define the desired or required "good" behaviour. Standard operating procedures are most often used in the context of quality control and assurance. Where the job, process or procedures add value to the final outcome, then the more clearly and accurately they are defined, the easier it is to ensure quality.

Competence statements

6460 Competence statements are a definition of the **knowledge, skills and capabilities** underlying a job. There can be a degree of overlap between the competences required for a number of jobs. As a result, organisations that define jobs by their competences often do so in terms of groups of related jobs, usually called "job families".

6461 Job competence is commonly based on the working skills, knowledge and attitudes that underlie the ability to do a job effectively. The **key requirements** for assessment of competence are:
– currency: recent demonstration;
– reliability: demonstration over a period of time and in different situations;
– validity: use of procedures that are relevant to the skills or knowledge being assessed;
– authenticity: done in a way that ensures that the work or outcomes can be clearly assigned to the employee being assessed; and
– consistency: demonstration of the same standard or level of performance despite changing circumstances and conditions.

A **key method** of assessing competence is through job cycle checklists.

Appraisals and performance management

6465 Appraisals or performance management reviews are generally accepted as **good human resource practice**. The processes can have an impact on discipline, promotion, redundancy and equal treatment situations and consequently must be performed fairly using best practice procedures. For example, in employment disputes and disciplinary cases, employees and employers may wish to refer to the content of appraisals or performance reviews as evidence of a history of problems or an exemplary working record.

Both appraisals and performance management reviews provide an opportunity for an employee to evaluate his job and performance with his line manager as well as giving an opportunity to plan his development within the organisation and highlight any training needs.

There should be an **internal appeal procedure** in place where an employee does not agree with the assessment of his performance and/or no agreement is possible on an action plan.

Appraisal and performance management processes are, at first sight, very similar in the way they are conducted. The differences between them could be summarised as follows:

6466

Appraisal	Performance management
Regular interview procedure	Continual review of performance
Focus on working methods	Focus on job outcomes
Leading towards an Action Plan to be reviewed at a fixed period	Leading towards an Action Plan to be reviewed continuously
Information from manager to employee	Discussion of information to which both have prior access

There are a number of other reviews possible:
– **group performance reviews** where output and performance are dependent entirely on group rather than individual effort;
– **360 degree feedback** resulting in assessment and feedback on performance from "all angles": essentially from the employee's peers, those that he manages, himself, and his line manager; and
– **self-assessment of performance**.

6467

Discrimination in the appraisal and promotion process An employer must not discriminate, on the grounds of sex, race, disability, religion or belief, marriage and civil partnership, pregnancy and maternity, sexual orientation, or age, against an employee in the appraisal process or in the way he affords an employee access to opportunities for promotion or by refusing or deliberately omitting to afford him access to such opportunities.

6468

An appraisal can have a critical effect on an employee's career development, promotion prospects, pay rise, access to benefits and continuation of employment (for example, a poor appraisal may render an employee more susceptible to selection for redundancy). An employee who believes that his poor appraisal was **unjustified and biased** on the grounds of age, disability, gender reassignment, marriage and civil partnership, pregnancy and maternity, race, religion or belief, sex or sexual orientation could complain of being subjected to a detriment. It is, therefore, vital to ensure that the staff who perform appraisals are **adequately trained** and fully **understand** their **employer's equal opportunities obligations**. It is often advisable to train appraising staff and to carry out appraisal audits. In all cases, appraisals should be carried out objectively and consistently.

Special care and consideration should be taken when **appraising a disabled employee**. The appraisal process may have to be adapted to prevent substantial disadvantage to the employee. For example, if an employee is deaf, a person versed in sign language may have to be present at the appraisal meeting. In addition, appraisal criteria may need to be altered. Moreover, working arrangements may need to be reviewed as a result of the appraisal. For example, if a disabled employee's job performance has been affected by his disability, it will be necessary to consider making reasonable adjustments to facilitate his working arrangements.

Employers must also ensure that **selection procedures for internal promotion** are as carefully and objectively set as for external appointments. This means that selection criteria should be drawn up and a fair and objective process applied, which will generally include an internal advertisement. Any advertisement must not indicate, or be reasonably understood to indicate, an intention on the part of the employer to discriminate unlawfully. In most cases, they should be gender, age and race neutral, and ought not to contain any indication that the employer will not accept applicants with a disability or will be reluctant to make reasonable adjustments. Job advertisements are discussed generally at ¶590.

6469

Benchmarking

6470 Benchmarking enables an organisation to measure their level of effectiveness. The term "benchmarking" in this context refers to comparing those indicators of performance by which an organisation measures its standards and quality against a best practice. This best practice may be, for example, the "industry best" for a particular activity, world class organisations working in the same field or best practice standards

So, for example, if a manufacturing company wants to measure the performance of its distribution department, it may decide to compare itself against a leading distribution company and not a competing manufacturing company.

Benchmark indicators can relate to any area of performance. For example, in most working environments there is an expected relationship between the costs of materials and/or labour and the costs of the product or service.

6471 The **actual measures** that an organisation might benchmark itself against will vary considerably. The following table sets out examples of the activities that companies from different sectors might benchmark themselves against:

Supply chain	Manufacturing	Product development and sales
Time between order and delivery	Changeover times	Time needed to recover investment
Number of late deliveries	Injuries and accidents (including lost time incidents)	Costs of changes to products
Condition of goods on arrival	Machine efficiency, process yield or down time	Costs of marketing/advertising
Percentage of deliveries undertaken by own staff	Output per person per hour worked	Training/skills needed for new market
Percentage of deliveries undertaken by contractors	Management to workforce ratios	Market size needed for profitable return on investment
Number and cost of returns	Adherence to preventative maintenance schedules	
Training/qualifications of staff	Costs of quality measures	
Customer satisfaction	Workforce communications	

6472 Identifying a benchmarking partner can be difficult and it is better if both sides benefit equally. In recent years both employers' organisations and government departments have taken steps to help organisations find suitable benchmarking partners.

There are also specialist firms who sell benchmarking studies for certain areas.

6473 Where benchmarking exercises have applications across all organisations, it is common for them to be formulated into **recognised standards**, for example:

a. the ISO standards, in particular the ISO management system standards (for example the 9000, 14000, and 22000 series). For further details, see the ISO website by following this link: flmemo.co.uk/em6473a;

b. the Business Excellence Model of the European Foundation for Quality Management (EFQM). This is mainly an internally assessed quality standard, but external assessment is also possible and is gaining in popularity. For further details, see the EFQM website by following this link: flmemo.co.uk/em6473b;

c. GoodCorporation Standard, which is a human resource focused quality and social responsibility standard covering the way in which the organisation behaves towards its employees, customers, suppliers, shareholders, the environment and the local community. For further details, see the GoodCorporation website by following this link: flmemo.co.uk/em6473c; and

d. Investors in People (IIP), which is a human resource focused quality standard. It provides a best practice standard for the training and development of the organisation's workforce and an external assessment process. For further details, see the IIP website by following this link: flmemo.co.uk/em6473d

CHAPTER 19

Discipline and grievance

OUTLINE	¶¶

| 1 | Scope | 6505 |
| 2 | Policies and procedures | 6525 |

SECTION 1 Discipline 6530

A	Disciplinary rules	6534
1	Formulation	6535
2	Application	6545
B	Procedures	6555
1	Formulation	6557
2	Operation	6574
	Investigation	6585
	Letter to employee	6605
	Disciplinary hearing	6610
	Decision	6625
3	Sanctions	6630
	Warnings	6631
	Penalties short of dismissal	6633
	Dismissal	6634
4	Records	6645
C	Dealing with particular issues	6650
1	Absence	6650
2	Poor performance	6660
D	Special cases	6670
	Trade union officials	6670
	Criminal charges or convictions outside employment	6671
	Isolated employees	6676

E	Appeal procedure	6680
1	Formulation	6685
2	Operation	6690
	Appeal hearing	6690
	Decision	6695
F	Effect on tribunal claims	6699

SECTION 2 Grievance procedures 6730

1	Formulation	6739
2	Operation	6757
	Raising the grievance	6764
	Grievance meeting	6766
	Appeal	6768
	Records	6771
3	Effect on tribunal claims	6772

SECTION 3 Right to be accompanied 6780

Entitlement	6780
Type of hearing	6781
Choice of companion	6782
Training	6785
Arranging the hearing	6786
Companion's role	6788
Enforcement and remedies	6790

6500 **Disciplinary issues** arise when problems of conduct or, in some cases, performance are identified by the employer, who consequently seeks to address them through his established procedures. **Grievances**, on the other hand, are raised by employees, who may have concerns or complaints about their terms and conditions of employment, their working environment or relationships with other staff.

6501 Employers and employees **should follow** the Code of Practice issued by the Advisory, Conciliation and Arbitration Service (Acas) on discipline and grievance (referred to in this chapter as "the Code") (Employment Act 2008; SI 2008/3232; DG Code). The Code comprises four sections: a foreword which is purely advisory, and the main sections which are an introduction setting out general principles applicable to all disciplinary and grievance matters, and two further sections dealing with disciplinary and grievance matters respectively. Under this system, if the employee subsequently brings a successful tribunal claim, the tribunal has a **discretion to adjust any award** upwards or downwards by up to 25% if either the employer or employee has unreasonably failed to comply with any part of the Code, other than the foreword. The Code is complemented by a non-statutory Acas Guide providing more detailed good practice advice.

Following **best practice principles** should also ensure that the employer has acted reasonably and that dismissals under the general unfair dismissal scheme are procedurally fair (¶¶8435+).

> MEMO POINTS 1. The **Code** does **not apply** with regard to dismissals for **redundancy**, or with regard to the **non-renewal of fixed-term contracts**. However, employers should still follow the guidance within it to ensure that dismissals are fair (¶¶8800+, ¶1996). Further, the Code does not apply to grievances raised on behalf of two or more employees by a representative of a recognised trade union or other appropriate workplace representative. Such grievances should be dealt with by the organisation's **collective grievance** process.
> 2. Following an independent review of employment dispute resolution procedures, the **statutory dispute resolution procedures** were **repealed** in 2009 and replaced by the present system.

6503 At certain disciplinary or grievance hearings, there is a **statutory right to be accompanied** by a work colleague or trade union official (s 10 ERelA 1999). See ¶6780 for further details.

6504 Employers must ensure that they comply with the data protection principles (¶5945) when **processing information** in relation to disciplinary or grievance proceedings. In particular, employers must make sure that those investigating such matters do not gather any information by deception and that unsubstantiated allegations are removed unless there is some exceptional reason not to do so. All records should be of a good enough quality to support any conclusion drawn from them.

Employers should:
– not access or use information kept about a worker, just because it might have some relevance, if such access or use is incompatible with the purpose for which the information was originally gathered or if it is disproportionate to the seriousness of the matter under investigation;
– have clear procedures about how spent disciplinary warnings are dealt with; and
– ensure that if a worker is dismissed, an accurate reason is recorded which ties in with what the worker has been told.

1. Scope

6505 Most employees are subject to disciplinary rules and procedures and grievance procedures. Whether an employer's disciplinary rules and procedures and grievance procedures apply to workers (for discussion as to status, see ¶13) will depend on the contractual arrangements between them. The present system **applies to employees only** and the tribunal's discretion to adjust any award on failure to comply with the Code will only apply to claims brought by employees (*Local Government Yorkshire and Humber v Shah* [2012] UKEAT 0587_11_1906).

However, as these rules and procedures have broader benefits in ensuring harmonious industrial relations in the workplace in general, it is recommended that, as a matter of **good employment practice**, the standards set out in the Code are also applied to grievance and disciplinary proceedings involving workers. Therefore, while the sections on discipline and grievance in this chapter refer to employees, it is recommended that employers consider applying those sections to their workers in general.

However, some provisions will only apply to employees, such as those referring to an employee's right to a statement of written particulars (¶1400), the right to bring a claim of unfair dismissal and the right to request a written statement of reasons for dismissal (¶8310).

The **right to be accompanied** at disciplinary and grievance hearings, on the other hand, specifically applies to all workers regardless of the contractual arrangements as to discipline and grievance between them (¶6780).

6510 Under the present system, while there is **no absolute obligation** to follow a set procedure, in practice, both employers and employees will need to follow the recommendations of the Code wherever an employer needs to address disciplinary or performance issues, or an employee raises a concern, problem or complaint with the employer. If a claim is subsequently made in the employment tribunal and it is found that either party has unreasonably failed to follow the Code, the tribunal has a discretion to **increase or decrease any award** it makes by up to 25%. Further, the Code is **admissible in evidence** in any proceedings before a tribunal, and any provision which appears to the tribunal to be relevant to any question arising in the proceedings (for example, whether a dismissal is unfair) is required to be **taken into account** in determining that question. It will also be taken into account by the arbitrators if the claim is being determined under the Acas arbitration scheme (¶9360). However, it should be noted that a failure on the part of an employer to observe any of the provisions of the Code does not of itself render him liable to any proceedings.

The **size and resources** of the employer should always be taken into account. In small organisations it may sometimes not be practicable to take all of the steps set out in the Code. However, the key elements of good practice that employers and employees should work to should be followed.

6511 Acas has also published **guidance** which expands on the Code's provisions and provides numerous examples and sample letters and notices, together with a practical online questions and answers page on discipline, dismissal and grievances (found on the Acas website at flmemo.co.uk/em6511).

General requirements

6513 Both employers and employees should, where practicable and reasonable to do so, follow the recommendations of the Code in both disciplinary and grievance matters. Where the matter relates to an employee's performance, rather than his conduct, they should be followed even though it may be under a separate procedure. The general principles to be observed in every case under the Code are as follows (rule 4 DG Code):

Both sides should:
– deal with issues promptly and without unreasonable delay; and
– act consistently.

Employers should:
– carry out any necessary investigation before acting;
– tell employees the basis of any problem and give them an opportunity to put their case before any decision is made;
– allow workers to be accompanied at any formal disciplinary or grievance meeting; and
– give employees an opportunity to appeal against any decision.

EXAMPLE In *Sandsfield Gravel Co Ltd v Loving* [2009] UKEAT 0415_08_2804, the EAT considered what an employer must do to comply with the previous statutory disciplinary and dismissal system. In this case, the operator of a holiday park dismissed a park manager for misconduct after she was seen driving a company van in the park with a glass of wine in her hand. Investigations carried out before each of a disciplinary hearing and an appeal indicated other areas of misconduct but the employer provided no details of these other than to refer to "Conduct whilst at work, bad language, sharp and abrasive attitude" in a letter arranging the disciplinary hearing. No specific incidents or examples were given. The EAT took the view that the tribunal were correct to conclude that this did not give the employee sufficient detail to allow her to put her side of the story. The EAT then went on to decide that the tribunal had substituted its own judgment of what was reasonable in the circumstances and directed that a new tribunal consider whether any deduction should be made from the compensation awarded to reflect the employee's conduct or the possibility that the employee might have been dismissed anyway if the correct procedure had been followed.

Note: Although this case was decided in relation to the old system of disciplinary and dismissal procedures (see ¶6501), it is also a reminder of one of the best practice principles to follow when disciplining employees.

Failure to comply

6514 If an employee successfully brings a claim under one of the jurisdictions listed in the memo point below and it appears to a tribunal that either employer or employee has unreasonably failed to follow the provisions of the Code, the tribunal may increase or reduce the award made by up to 25%.

> MEMO POINTS The **statutory jurisdictions** are as follows (Sch A2 TULRCA 1992 as inserted by s 3 Employment Act 2008):
> **a.** inequality in employment (s 120, 127 EqA 2010);
> **b.** detriment in relation to trade union membership and activities and union recognition rights (ss 145A, 145B, 146, Sch A1 para 156 TULRCA 1992);
> **c.** unauthorised deductions and payments (s 23 ERA 1996);
> **d.** detriment in employment (s 48 ERA 1996);
> **e.** unfair dismissal (s 111 ERA 1996);
> **f.** redundancy payments (s 163 ERA 1996);
> **g.** detriment in relation to national minimum wage (s 24 NMWA 1998);
> **h.** breach of employment contract and termination (SI 1994/1623; SI 1994/1624);
> **i.** breach of Working Time Regulations (reg 30 SI 1998/1833; reg 17 SI 2008/1660);
> **j.** detriment relating to European Works Councils (reg 32 SI 1999/3323);
> **k.** detriment relating to domestic information and consultation in the workplace (reg 33 SI 2004/3426);
> **l.** detriment relating to European Public Limited-Liability Companies (reg 45 SI 2004/2326);
> **m.** detriment relating to occupational and personal pension schemes (Sch para 8 SI 2006/349);
> **n.** detriment relating to involvement in a European Cooperative Society (reg 34 SI 2006/2059);
> **o.** breach of Cross-border Railway Services (Working Time) Regulations (reg 17 SI 2008/1660); and
> **p.** detriment in connection with a prohibited blacklist (reg 9 SI 2010/493).

2. Policies and procedures

6525 Subject to a qualifying period of 1 month's continuous service, employers are obliged by statute to provide a **written statement of employment particulars** to all employees, containing specified information, **within** the first 2 months of an employee's employment (ss 1-7, 198 ERA 1996; ¶1405).

The written statement must **specify** not only the disciplinary rules applicable to an employee but also any procedures relating to dismissing or taking disciplinary action in respect of an employee (or should refer the employee to a reasonably accessible document in which such procedures can be found) (s 3(1) ERA 1996, as amended by s 35 EA 2002). In addition, the statement must specify the grievance procedure applicable not only in respect of any disciplinary action taken in respect of an employee but also in respect of any decision to dismiss him.

6526 **Failure to provide a written statement** or providing a statement which is **incomplete** or **inaccurate** may give rise to the employer being additionally liable to pay compensation to an employee who has brought a claim before a tribunal (¶1465).

A tribunal which finds in favour of an employee (whether or not it makes an award to him) in respect of his claim must make an **award** of 2 weeks' pay and can **increase** this award to 4 weeks' pay (if it considers it just and equitable to do so) if, at the time the proceedings began, the employer was in breach of his duty to provide a full and accurate written statement of particulars (s 38(2), (3) EA 2002). The amount of a week's pay is subject to a statutory cap, see ¶¶2920+.

> MEMO POINTS These provisions do not provide employees with a standalone remedy if an employer is only in default of the requirement to provide written particulars.

6527 Further, the Code states that the rules and procedures for handling discipline and grievances should be in writing and be specific and clear (rule 2 DG Code).

SECTION 1

Discipline

6530 Disciplinary arrangements should consist of two elements, namely rules and procedures.

There is **no direct obligation** on an employer to introduce disciplinary rules. However, employers should have disciplinary procedures in place if they are to ensure that any disciplinary dismissal or other action taken in respect of an employee is fair, and the Code states that the rules and procedures for handling discipline and grievances should be in writing and be specific and clear (¶6527). Further, employers are obliged by statute to **provide written information** about their disciplinary rules and procedures (¶6525).

Disciplinary rules

6531 Disciplinary rules set standards to be observed by all staff to whom they apply, and make clear to employees what is expected of them, and the consequences of breaking the rules or failing to reach the required standards.

It is advisable for disciplinary rules to be **contractual terms**, so that a breach by the employee will be a breach of contract.

Disciplinary procedures

6532 Disciplinary procedures are an aid to good management in that they can help the employer to deal fairly and consistently with any disciplinary problems.

It is advisable for the procedures to be **non-contractual**, so the employer can retain as much flexibility as possible when implementing them.

If they are **contractual**, an employee may be able to:
– argue that his contract has been breached if his employer deviates even slightly from the agreed procedures (*Gunton v Richmond-upon-Thames London Borough Council* [1980] IRLR 321, CA);
– obtain an injunction restraining the employer from dismissing in breach (¶1700) or, as in the case below, taking disciplinary proceedings;

> EXAMPLE In *Mezey v South West London and St George's Mental Health NHS Trust* [2010] EWCA Civ 293, a hospital trust started an enquiry into the competence of a consultant psychiatrist, M, after a mentally ill patient absconded and killed a stranger when M allowed him to take unescorted leave in the hospital grounds before a full assessment of his condition had been completed. The enquiry decided that although the decision was a mistake, M was not at serious fault. M's contract incorporated separate procedures dealing with professional conduct and professional competence. Her employer then started disciplinary proceedings under the procedure appropriate for issues relating to capability to practice. The Court of Appeal found, in the light of the findings of the enquiry, that M's decision did not amount to serious professional incompetence and that her capability to practice was not called in question by it, it was not open to the employer to take disciplinary proceedings, and the Court of Appeal therefore upheld an injunction granted in the High Court preventing the employer from taking disciplinary proceedings.

– bring a claim of wrongful dismissal (¶8155) if the employer dismisses him in breach; and
– resign and claim that he has been constructively dismissed if the employer commits a fundamental breach by imposing a disciplinary sanction (such as suspension or demotion) without following the contractual procedures (*Post Office v Strange* [1981] IRLR 515, EAT).

6533 An employee cannot argue that, if the contractual procedure had been followed, he would still have been employed on the date that would give him sufficient qualifying service to bring a claim of unfair dismissal (¶8410).

A. Disciplinary rules

6534 The disciplinary rules should be specific, clear and fair and should reflect the needs of the particular organisation, including the type of work, working conditions, size and location of the employer. One set of rules cannot cover every situation, and should, therefore, state that they are not exhaustive.

1. Formulation

6535 Policy on discipline should ideally be formulated by the employer with the involvement of employees (and trade union or other employee representatives, where applicable).

6536 The disciplinary rules should be **reviewed** from time to time in order to reflect developments in employment legislation, technological or social developments and/or good practice. If amendments or additions are made to the rules, these should only be implemented after reasonable notice has been given to employees and, where appropriate, their representatives consulted. In general, changes to individual contracts will require employee consent (¶1600).

6537 When formulating disciplinary rules, the following **general principles** should be observed:
– the rules should specify clearly and concisely those requirements that are necessary for the efficient and safe performance of work and the maintenance of satisfactory relations within the workforce and between employees and management;
– the rules should be set out clearly and concisely in writing and be readily available to all staff (for example, on a notice board or, in larger organisations, in the staff handbook or on the company intranet), and management is responsible for ensuring that employees know and understand them (for example, by giving each employee a copy, perhaps as part of the induction programme for new employees); and
– employees should be made aware of the likely consequences of breaking the rules, and the type of conduct which may warrant summary dismissal (¶8155).

6538 The disciplinary rules should inform employees of the likely consequences of breaking the disciplinary rules. In particular, it is usual for disciplinary rules to **cover** issues of misconduct and to specify that serious cases will be treated as gross misconduct.

6540 **Misconduct and gross misconduct** Misconduct is conduct which initially requires disciplinary action other than dismissal, such as a minor breach of company rules, policies and procedures, minor damage to company property, unsatisfactory attendance and/or poor timekeeping, unauthorised absence, and failure to meet appropriate and expected standards of work (though in such cases it may be more appropriate to use a capability procedure rather than a disciplinary procedure, depending on the nature of the failure). If further misconduct takes place, dismissal may ultimately be an appropriate sanction.

Gross misconduct is misconduct serious enough to destroy the contract between employer and employee, and irretrievably break down the working relationship and trust between them (*Dunn and anor v AAH Ltd* [2010] IRLR 709, CA). This has been held to be either a deliberate wrongdoing or very considerable negligence (*Sandwell and West Birmingham Hospitals NHS Trust v Westwood* [2009] UKEAT 0032_09_1712). The disciplinary rules should indicate that such conduct may warrant summary dismissal, i.e. dismissal without notice. Examples may include theft or fraud; physical violence or bullying; deliberate and serious damage to property; serious misuse of an organisation's property or name; deliberately accessing internet sites containing pornographic, offensive or obscene material; serious insubordination; unlawful discrimination or harassment; bringing the organisation into serious disrepute; serious incapability at work brought on by alcohol or illegal drugs; causing loss, damage or injury through serious negligence; a serious breach of health and safety rules; and a serious breach of confidence.

6541 It is common for the employer to provide a **non-exhaustive list** of those acts which constitute misconduct and those which amount to gross misconduct, including those determined by the nature of his business. Some types of conduct will obviously amount to misconduct (such as fighting) or gross misconduct (such as dishonestly claiming overtime), and it is, therefore, not always necessary to specify them as such in the rules (*C A Parsons & Co Limited v McLoughlin* [1978] IRLR 65, EAT).

As it is not always obvious whether a particular offence amounts to gross misconduct, it is still useful to give examples of gross misconduct as the employer will more clearly be **justified in dismissing** an employee without notice if it is obvious that the employee should have known that such conduct would result in summary dismissal (*Meyer Dunmore International Ltd v Rogers* [1978] IRLR 167, EAT). Regardless of any stated examples, to avoid a claim of unfair dismissal, the employer must in any case be able to show that dismissal was a reasonable sanction to impose in the circumstances (*Ladbroke Racing Ltd v Arnott* [1983] IRLR 154, CS).

Regardless of whether the employer is justified in dismissing the employee without notice, a **fair disciplinary process**, including a right of appeal, should still be followed before deciding whether gross misconduct has occurred.

2. Application

6545 Employers should ensure that their managers and supervisors are familiar with the disciplinary rules and are **trained** to apply them in a consistent and fair manner.

The employer should ensure that every employee knows and understands the applicable disciplinary rules, including employees whose **first language is not English** or who have **reading difficulties**.

6546 **Consistency** The rules should be applied consistently but not inflexibly, and the employer must take into account any **mitigating or aggravating circumstances** in a particular case. He should deal with each case on its own merits, as employment tribunals hearing unfair dismissal claims will always consider whether the employer acted fairly in all the circumstances of the case (and consistency will merely be one factor).

Inconsistency may arise as a result of:
– different treatment of employees in a sufficiently similar position (both in the past and subsequently) (*Post Office v Fennell* [1981] IRLR 221, CA; *Eagle Star Insurance Co Ltd v Hayward* [1981] ICR 860, EAT); or
– different treatment of a particular employee from one occasion to the next.

An employee may argue that the rules have been applied inconsistently if (*Hadjioannou v Coral Casinos* [1981] IRLR 352, EAT followed in *Paul v East Surrey District Health Authority* [1995] IRLR 305, CA):
– he was led to believe that certain categories of conduct would be ignored or not punished by dismissal;
– decisions made in other cases support an inference that the reason stated by the employer for the dismissal is not the real reason; or
– decisions made by the employer in truly comparable cases support an argument that it was not reasonable to dismiss the employee in the circumstances.

EXAMPLE In Wincanton plc v Atkinson and anor [2011] UKEAT 0040_11_1907, the EAT held that it was fair to dismiss two drivers who had failed to renew their HGV driving licences, despite the fact that 6 years previously a driver who had made the same mistake was not subjected to any disciplinary action. The claimants were dismayed when they found out that their licences had lapsed, accepted that this mistake was misconduct and immediately put in place steps to obtain a new licence. However, they were dismissed and during the ensuing tribunal proceedings the employer was able to point to other instances of dismissal in similar circumstances. The employer also pointed out that, with regard to the case from 6 years earlier, the regulatory regime applicable to HGV driving at that time was much more lenient and the manager who had dealt with the situation did not have the authority to act as he did. The EAT found that the tribunal had placed too much emphasis on the case from 6 years earlier and that dismissal was in the range of reasonable responses given the collectively agreed disciplinary policy and the potential risks to the employer of invalid insurance and the fact that the regulator could take action that could jeopardise the operating licence.

If the employer wants to take a **different attitude towards a particular rule** (for example, where his established and well-known practice has been to ignore an express rule and he now wishes it to be observed), he must give employees sufficient advance warning of this change.

6548 **Discretion** The employer can retain some **flexibility** by stating in the rules that gross misconduct "will normally" or "may" result in summary dismissal. In unfair dismissal cases, a tribunal will take this element of discretion into account in deciding whether the employer acted reasonably in treating a particular case of gross misconduct as a sufficient reason for dismissal. However, an employee cannot rely on such flexible wording to claim that dismissal was not the likely result of gross misconduct (*Proctor v British Gypsum Ltd* [1991] UKEAT 535_89_2407).

> EXAMPLE In *Proctor v British Gypsum Ltd*, the rules stated that gross misconduct (including fighting) "may result in dismissal". P was dismissed for fighting. He argued that dismissal was inconsistent with the penalty imposed in similar circumstances in the past. The EAT held that the dismissal was fair, and that the discretionary wording could not be relied on to indicate that there was a general practice that dismissal would not be the likely result of the misconduct in question.

6550 **Dealing with several suspects** Where one of a number of employees could have committed a particular offence for which the sanction is dismissal, the employer should implement the disciplinary procedure in the usual way for each employee involved. The usual fairness requirement of having "a genuine belief on reasonable grounds after reasonable investigation" (¶8505) that a particular employee committed the offence is modified if, after investigation, no single culprit can be identified. The employer will be justified in **disciplining all members** of the group if:
– he has a reasonable belief that one or more persons committed the act;
– the group of employees who could have committed the act has been reasonably identified;
– each member of the group was individually capable of committing the act; and
– the individual perpetrator cannot reasonably be identified.

The fact that one or more of those employees was **not dismissed** does not make the dismissal of any others unfair as long as the employer can show that he had "solid and sensible grounds", which do not have to be related to the relevant offence, for **differentiating** between the employees (*Frames Snooker Centre v Boyce* 1992] UKEAT 265_90_1805). Such differentiation should not, however, be made on discriminatory grounds.

B. Procedures

6555 If an employee breaches a disciplinary rule, the employer must consider whether to deal with the matter **informally**, or whether to invoke his **formal disciplinary procedures**. The foreword to the Code recommends resolving issues informally where possible, or entering into mediation by an independent third party. If an employer does not, for any reason, seek to resolve a matter informally or by mediation, this will not have any impact on the award in any subsequent tribunal proceedings as these recommendations fall outside the main body of the Code and no adjustment can be made to any award. The employer's decision as to which route to use is likely to depend on the seriousness of the breach, and whether it was a first offence.

The employer may have separate procedures for dealing with issues of **conduct and capability**.

In any case, any hearing which might result in a formal warning or some other disciplinary action will trigger the statutory **right to be accompanied** (¶6780).

1. Formulation

6557 The concept of **natural justice** demands that employees should be:
– informed in advance of any disciplinary hearing of the allegations that are being made against them, together with the supporting evidence;
– subject to an unbiased and impartial tribunal;
– given the opportunity to challenge the allegations and evidence before decisions are reached; and
– given the right of appeal against any decisions taken against them.

A disciplinary procedure should therefore be designed to ensure compliance with these requirements, which should be observed in respect of all employees regardless of the size of the organisation. Breach of natural justice is not an independent ground of complaint if an employee is dismissed, but will be an important factor in **assessing fairness** for the purposes of an unfair dismissal claim (*Slater v Leicestershire Health Authority* [1989] IRLR 16, CA).

MEMO POINTS **Re-visiting previous disciplinary decisions** will generally be against the principle of natural justice. In exceptional circumstances, re-visiting decisions may be justified but this will be very rare and employers should be wary of doing so (see ¶6641).

6558 As a result of the broad concept of natural justice, **good disciplinary procedures** should:
– be in writing, specify to whom they apply, and provide for matters to be addressed without undue delay;
– be non-discriminatory;
– provide for proceedings, witness statements and records to be kept confidential;
– indicate the disciplinary actions which may be taken and specify the levels of management which have the authority to take the various forms of disciplinary action;
– provide for careful investigation before disciplinary action is taken;
– provide for employees to be informed of the complaints against them, together with the supporting evidence, in advance of the disciplinary hearing;
– provide employees with an opportunity to state their case before decisions are reached;
– allow workers to be accompanied at any formal disciplinary hearing (¶6780). There is no breach of natural justice in refusing to allow legal representation at a disciplinary hearing (unless a dismissal could have greater consequences for the employee, such as the loss of his future career in his chosen profession (see ¶6559));
– ensure that, except for gross misconduct, no employee is dismissed for a first breach of discipline;
– ensure that employees are given an explanation for any penalty imposed; and
– provide a right of appeal (normally to a more senior manager) and specify the appeal procedure.

6559 Likewise, the Acas Code sets out the **following basic principles of fairness** that employers should follow if a matter cannot be resolved informally or it is not appropriate to attempt an informal resolution:
1. Ensure that all issues are dealt with promptly and act consistently, treating like cases alike (rule 4 DG Code).
2. Investigate the matter to establish the facts of the case, if necessary holding an investigatory meeting. It may be appropriate to allow the employee to be accompanied at any such meeting, although it is not strictly necessary. Wherever possible, the member of management carrying out the investigation should not be involved in making any disciplinary decisions (rule 5-7 DG Code).
3. If after investigation it appears that there are grounds to take disciplinary action, write to the employee setting out the problem and its possible consequences, and setting a time and place for a disciplinary meeting. That letter should remind the employee of his right to be

accompanied. Normally copies of any written evidence should be provided with the notification (rule 9-10 DG Code).

4. Ensure that the meeting is held without unreasonable delay, while giving the employee reasonable time to prepare his case (rule 11 DG Code). At the meeting, the employer should explain the complaint made and go through the evidence. The employee should be given a reasonable opportunity to ask questions, respond to the allegations and evidence and call relevant witnesses. Either side should give advance notice if they intend to call witnesses (rule 12 DG Code). Where an employee is persistently unable or unwilling to attend a disciplinary meeting without good cause, the employer can make a decision on the evidence available in his absence (rule 24 DG Code).

5. Allow the employee to exercise his right to be accompanied (rule 13-16 DG Code).

6. After the meeting decide whether disciplinary action is required and, if so, what that should be, and then write to the employee with the decision (rule 17 DG Code).

7. Provide an opportunity to appeal if the employee is not satisfied with the decision made. The employee should set out the grounds of their appeal in writing. Appeals should be heard without unreasonable delay and ideally at an agreed time and place. The employer should arrange for the appeal to be dealt with impartially and if possible by a member of management who has not previously been involved in the case. Employees must be allowed to exercise their right to be accompanied. The employer should notify the employee of the outcome of the appeal in writing as soon as possible (rule 25-28 DG Code).

6560 **Human rights considerations** Where a misconduct dismissal is likely to result in the **loss of an individual's future career** in his chosen profession or where it may have **greater consequences** for the employee than **losing his job**, for example if dismissal may also lead to a ban from further employment involving children or is in effect a criminal charge being dealt with by disciplinary proceedings, the employer's investigation, disciplinary process and appeal must be particularly fair and thorough, and the evidence of misconduct must be particularly clear and cogent (*Crawford and anor v Suffolk Mental Health Partnership NHS Trust* [2012] EWCA Civ 138).

Further, in cases where the right to practice a particular profession is in question, civil rights are being determined. This means that human rights issues arise and individuals in these situations are entitled to additional protection due to provisions that safeguard their right to a fair and public hearing (Human Rights Act 1998; art 6 European Convention on Human Rights and Fundamental Freedoms). The main issue flowing from this is the right to have **legal representation** at an internal hearing (*Kulkarni v Milton Keynes Hospital NHS Foundation Trust* [2009] IRLR 829, CA), or at a hearing presided over by a regulatory body (such as the General Medical Council, the Law Society, or the General Dental Council). This right will be relevant to employers of medical professionals, those providing educational or care services to children or vulnerable adults and other regulated professions. However, it does not apply where the disciplinary hearing does not have a greater impact, or where there is a further right of appeal that would involve a complete re-hearing of the case (*R (on the application of G) v Governors of X School* [2011] UKSC 30; *Puri, R (on the application of) v Bradford Teaching Hospitals NHS Foundation Trust* [2011] EWHC 970 (Admin); *R (on the application of Kirk) v Middlesbrough Borough Council and ors* [2010] IRLR 699, HC; *Preiss v General Dental Council* [2001] IRLR 696, PC).

An employee could also be entitled to an **independent decision maker** (*Mattu v University Hospitals of Coventry and Warwickshire NHS Trust* [2012] EWCA Civ 641).

> **EXAMPLE**
> 1. In *R (on the application of G) v Governors of X School*, the Supreme Court held that a teaching assistant, who was accused of sexual misconduct with a minor, was not entitled to legal representation at an internal disciplinary hearing. He could not rely on article 6 and the right to a fair trial because there was not sufficient proximity between the school's decision to dismiss him and the outcome of the statutory barring procedure carried out by the Independent Safeguarding Authority (ISA). In considering the legal test, the judgment stated that the school's decision would not have a "substantial influence or effect" on the ISA's decision (which could prevent the teaching assistant from working with children in the future). The ISA expected to make their own findings and there was no basis upon which to assume that they would not be able to make a decision independently from that of the school governors'.

2. In *Puri, R (on the application of) v Bradford Teaching Hospitals NHS Foundation Trust* [2011] EWHC 970 (Admin), the High Court held that disciplinary proceedings that led to the dismissal of a consultant doctor were, in this case, not career-threatening and that article 6 of the European Convention on Human Rights (right to a fair trial) was therefore not invoked in relation to the internal proceedings. It should be noted that the doctor in this case had been dismissed for reasons relating to his conduct rather than his clinical abilities, he had been able to obtain a position in private practice, and the court held that it would not be impossible for him to return to the NHS in a suitable role – this was an important factor in their decision to assess his dismissal from his NHS post as not being career-threatening.

3. In *R (on the application of Kirk) v Middlesbrough Borough Council and ors*, the employer, a child protection charity, started internal disciplinary proceedings against a social worker, K, when an allegation was made against her after she failed to inform them of a child protection investigation in which she was involved. K applied for an injunction delaying disciplinary proceedings and a declaration that she was entitled to legal representation at the disciplinary hearing when it was held. Both applications failed, because the disciplinary hearing was about her failure to disclose the investigation, and would not, therefore, deal with issues as to whether she had placed a child at risk. It would not have an impact on a decision as to whether she should be allowed to work with children, and so the exception, that legal representation at the disciplinary hearing should be allowed where a dismissal could have greater consequences for an employee than losing his job, did not apply.

4. In *Mattu v University Hospitals of Coventry and Warwickshire NHS Trust*, the Court of Appeal held that a doctor, M, was not entitled to an independent decision maker in the question of his dismissal from an NHS Trust. Article 6 was not invoked because his dismissal had no impact on his medical registration and he was still able to pursue his career within the NHS and privately (it was relevant that M's clinical skills had not been questioned – the issues in his case were disciplinary rather than clinical). The Court pointed out that even if M was unable to find alternative work, it would be because other Trusts were exercising their lawful freedom not to employ him: article 6 is concerned with legal rights and obligations and the gravity of the consequences of such decisions does not alter their nature. In other words, it would be too complex a situation if parties were arguing over the likelihood of an employee obtaining alternative employment in the field as a determining factor as to whether article 6 was invoked.

2. Operation

6574 It is essential that all managers and, where appropriate, employee representatives understand the procedures. **Training** in their use and operation may be required.

6575 The disciplinary procedure should be observed in all cases unless there are exceptional circumstances. Even if the procedure is non-contractual, a failure to follow it may give rise to a complaint of **unfair dismissal** if it indicates that the employer acted unfairly in the circumstances (*Polkey v A E Dayton Services Ltd* [1987] IRLR 503, HL). For example, an employer may be held to be acting unreasonably if he does not follow a collectively agreed procedure, unless it is inherently defective (*East Hertfordshire District Council v K Boyten* [1977] IRLR 347, EAT). However, a breach of agreed procedures will not automatically make the dismissal unfair (it will be a factor in assessing the overall fairness of the employer's actions) (*Westminster City Council v Cabaj* [1996] IRLR 399, CA).

MEMO POINTS A failure to follow an internal disciplinary procedure might lead the tribunal to draw an inference of unlawful discrimination (*Birmingham City Council v Samuels* [2007] UKEAT 0208_07_2410).

6577 There are **possible financial implications** for failure to comply with an appropriate disciplinary procedure (¶6514).

6578 To amount to a **fair dismissal**, the reason for the dismissal (i.e. the breach of the rules) must fall within one of the five statutory fair reasons, "conduct" being the most likely to be relevant in a disciplinary situation (¶8422). The disciplinary procedures are especially important, as at a tribunal hearing an unfair dismissal claim will take account of whether a fair procedure was followed, i.e. that the employer acted fairly in all the circumstances in dismissing the employee (¶8500).

For details of the rules relating to **procedural defects** in disciplinary procedures in unfair dismissal claims, see ¶¶8630+.

6579 When dealing with disciplinary cases, employers must also ensure that they do not **discriminate** against any employee in respect of their disciplinary rules and procedures on the grounds of age, disability, gender reassignment, marriage and civil partnership, pregnancy and maternity, race, religion or belief, sex or sexual orientation. For example, a pregnant woman may be disciplined for a reason that is unconnected with her pregnancy, such as theft, but not on the grounds of her pregnancy.

> EXAMPLE In *Sidhu v Aerospace Composite Technology* [2000] IRLR 602, CA, the Court held that a disciplinary policy that ignored all types of provocation, including racial provocation, was not discriminatory because the application of the policy was not race-specific.

6580 **Grievance about the dismissal and disciplinary procedure** If the employee raises a grievance during the disciplinary procedure, for example if he is **dissatisfied** with the **handling of the disciplinary matter** (for example, the behaviour of the investigating manager), the employer should consider suspending the disciplinary process for a short time in order to deal with the grievance. It may be necessary for a different manager to deal with the remainder of the disciplinary process, although this may not be possible in smaller organisations. If the disciplinary case and the grievance are related, it may be appropriate to deal with the two concurrently.

Investigation

6585 The first step when a disciplinary matter arises is for an appropriate supervisor or manager to **establish the facts** as soon as possible before recollections fade. He should therefore obtain statements from available witnesses where appropriate, and keep written records for later reference. The employer should also check if there are **any special circumstances** to be taken into account, for example any personal or other outside issues affecting performance or conduct, and investigate any **explanations** put forward by the employee. Finally, the employer should check that the **standards of other employees** are acceptable, and that the employee has not been unfairly singled out.

Where an **investigatory meeting** is held solely for the purpose of establishing the relevant facts of the case, the supervisor or manager should inform the employee that it is not a disciplinary meeting.

Where possible, in a misconduct case, different managers should deal with the investigations and any subsequent disciplinary procedure.

> EXAMPLE In *Compass Group UK and Ireland Ltd t/a Eurest v Okoro* [2009] UKEAT 0055_08_1805, an assistant catering manager, O, was dismissed for theft of an iPod which had been sent to her employers as a gift by a supplier. Her manager locked it in a drawer saying that it was so that O could not steal it, which she treated as a joke. O took it home, and when asked by the manager if she knew where it was, she indicated that she did. The manager reported the matter and the company then suspended O and started disciplinary proceedings. O immediately told her manager that she had the iPod. As soon as she realised that the matter was being taken seriously she explained that she had taken it as a joke and returned it unopened and unused. She also explained that she and the manager in question often played pranks of this sort on each other. The EAT upheld the decision that the dismissal was unfair because the employer had not investigated O's explanation properly to consider whether it should be treated as a mitigating factor. The EAT commented that there is no universal rule that if an employee admits misconduct an investigation is unnecessary; it is part of the overall issue of whether it is reasonable to dismiss in the particular case.

> MEMO POINTS An investigation that continues longer than an ordinary investigation would do can amount to a detriment for **discrimination** purposes, even though the employee is unaware that the investigation is continuing (*Garry v London Borough of Ealing* [2001] IRLR 681, CA).

6586 If any **informant** wishes to **remain anonymous**, his evidence should be treated with care. In such cases, the following **guidelines** should be observed (*Linfood Cash and Carry Ltd v Thomson* [1989] IRLR 235, EAT):

1. A written statement should be compiled of the information given by the informant, taken initially without regard to the fact that anonymity is to be preserved. It may subsequently be

necessary to omit or erase certain parts of the statement before it is disclosed to others in order to prevent identification. The statement should include information on:
– the date, time and place of any observation or incident;
– the informant's opportunity and ability to observe clearly and with accuracy;
– the circumstantial evidence, such as knowledge of a system or arrangement or the reason for the presence of the informer and why certain small details are memorable; and
– whether the informant suffered at the hands of the employee or has any other reason to fabricate, whether from a personal grudge or any other reason or principle.
2. Further investigation can then take place either to confirm or undermine the information given. Ideally that information should be corroborated, although in some cases it may not be possible.
3. It may be appropriate to make tactful inquiries into the character and background of the informant or any other information which may tend to add or detract from the value of the information.
4. If the employer is satisfied that the informant's fear of disclosing his identity is genuine, the employer will have to decide whether or not to continue with the disciplinary process. If it is to continue, the informant should be interviewed by the responsible manager at each stage of the process so that the manager can satisfy himself as to the weight to be given to the informant's evidence, and the informant's written statement (with omissions where necessary to prevent identification) should be made available to the employee and his representative.
5. It is particularly important where evidence has been taken from an informant that full and careful notes are taken during disciplinary procedures, and if evidence is to be taken from the investigating officer at the hearing, it should, where possible, be prepared in writing.

However, depending on the circumstances of the case, it may not always be necessary to strictly adhere to these guidelines. Where there are **real fears** that informants in a disciplinary investigation will suffer **retaliation and reprisals** for having co-operated with management, it is not unreasonable for an employer to protect the identities of such informants by restricting knowledge of their identities to only one member of management (*Ramsey and ors v Walkers Snack Foods Ltd* [2004] UKEAT 0601_03_1302). In this case, the anonymity of the informants did not affect the fairness of the employees' dismissals, despite the informants' witness statements lacking in detail and the fact that the informants had not been questioned by the managers involved in the disciplinary investigation or subsequent dismissals. Even though the guidelines were not strictly adhered to in this case, there were two additional problems which had not arisen in *Linfood Cash and Carry Ltd v Thomson*, above: the informants refused to sign a witness statement unless it had been sufficiently edited to remove any chance of identifying them and they were unwilling to be questioned by any other members of management.

A tribunal considering whether the dismissal of an employee in such circumstances was fair must strike a **balance** between the **competing needs** of the employer (who may not want to inform the employee of the allegations against him in order to protect the identity of the informants) and the employee (who will want to know the case against him), as well as establishing whether the employer's procedure fell within the band of reasonable responses (¶8508) (*Surrey County Council v Henderson* [2005] UKEAT 0326_05_2311).

6588

To **defend a claim of unfair dismissal** on grounds of misconduct, the employer must have a genuine belief in the employee's guilt, held on reasonable grounds having carried out such investigation as was reasonable in all the circumstances (¶8505). An investigation is important for the following reasons:
a. to enable the employer to establish the facts on which his decision will be based; and
b. to provide the employee with an opportunity to:
– respond to the allegations against him; and
– reveal any mitigating circumstances (which may affect the disciplinary sanction imposed).

To **establish dishonesty**, for example, the employer must ask himself two questions (*R v Ghosh* [1982] QB 1053, CA):
1. Was what was done dishonest according to the standards of reasonable and honest people?
2. If so, did the employee realise that what he was doing was dishonest by those standards?

In many cases, there will be no doubt about the answer, but the circumstances may require investigation, for example, to ascertain the seriousness of the offence or whether there are any mitigating factors (*John Lewis plc v Coyne* [2000] UKEAT 581_99_0712).

There is no principle of law that dismissal will always be a **fair sanction** for dishonesty, and there may be mitigating factors in certain cases (*Tesco Stores Ltd v Othman-Khalid* [2001] UKEAT 385_00_2111). However, case law indicates that even in trivial cases of dishonesty, dismissal will normally be within the range of reasonable responses open to an employer (*Murphy v Trust Houses Forte Hotels Ltd* [1977] IRLR 186, EAT; see ¶8508 regarding the "range of reasonable responses").

If an employee has **admitted misconduct** (either at the investigation stage or during the disciplinary hearing), the employer can reasonably act on that admission (*RSPB v Croucher* [1984] IRLR 425, EAT). However, where the employee admits the physical elements of the offence but there is some **doubt as to his intention**, some investigation may still be required (*John Lewis plc v Coyne*). In any case, the employer will still be obliged to follow a fair procedure generally (*Whitbread plc (t/a Whitbread Medway Inns) v Hall* [2001] IRLR 275, CA). Similarly, if the employee **pleads guilty** to, or is convicted of, a criminal offence, the employer is entitled to assume the employee's guilt (*P v Nottingham County Council* [1992] IRLR 362, CA).

EXAMPLE

1. In *John Lewis plc v Coyne*, the store had a rule against using work telephones for personal calls (which was considered to amount to dishonesty) and warned that misuse could lead to dismissal. C admitted making personal calls and the store dismissed her without further investigation as it considered her actions to be objectively dishonest. The EAT held that an investigation was required as the test for dishonesty is not simply an objective one but should be considered in the light of individual circumstances, including whether C considered her actions to be dishonest.

2. In *Knight v Treherne Care and Consultancy Ltd* [2009] UKEAT 0384_08_1504, K, the financial director of a care home organisation, was dismissed after allegations had been made that she had misled the board of directors about financial matters. After allegations were raised at a board meeting, she was suspended and a third party, A, was appointed to investigate the matter and held a meeting with K. During the course of investigations carried out after that meeting further allegations were made. Some were discussed at an adjourned meeting but more arose later. A wrote to the board recommending that K be dismissed. The board accepted the recommendation and dismissed her. An appeal was handled by another third party who confirmed that the board had been right to dismiss K on the basis of the same information available to A. An employment tribunal made findings that there had been no proper disciplinary hearing and that the dismissal was unfair. The EAT criticised the tribunal's decision for failing to explain clearly how it had come to that conclusion, but commented that if there had been no proper disciplinary hearing the dismissal would be unfair under the general principles of fairness. In particular, where allegations of dishonest conduct are made they must be put clearly to the employee so that the employee has an opportunity to respond. It sent the matter to a new tribunal to hear the case afresh.

6589 The courts have not laid down rigid criteria of what an adequate investigation will involve (it will be a question of degree in each case) (*Bentley Engineering Co Ltd v Mistry* [1978] IRLR 436, EAT). An investigation may be **inadequate** for the following reasons, which may make a subsequent dismissal unfair:
– failure to allow the employee an opportunity to offer an explanation (*McLaren v National Coal Board* [1988] IRLR 215, CA);
– failure to take statements from available witnesses before recollections fade or delay in carrying out the investigation (*RSPCA v Cruden* [1986] IRLR 83, EAT);
– employees' explanation rejected without proper enquiry (*Francis v Ford Motor Company* [1975] IRLR 25, IT);
– reliance on hearsay evidence alone (*Gordon v F Medhurst Ltd Bromley* [1972] IRLR 47, IT); or
– investigation after the decision to dismiss had been taken was a charade and therefore insufficient (*Robert Whiting Designs Ltd v Lamb* [1978] ICR 89, EAT).

MEMO POINTS If an investigation is not carried out properly in the first instance, a **complete and thorough reappraisal** of the accusations at the hearing stage may remedy this (*Lewis v HSBC Bank* [2006] UKEAT 0364_06_1912; ¶6618).

6595 **Suspension** In most cases, it will not be necessary to suspend the employee **during the investigation stage** and suspension as a knee-jerk reaction to allegations of misconduct may be a breach of the duty of trust and confidence (*Crawford and anor v Suffolk Mental Health Partnership NHS Trust* [2012] EWCA Civ 138). However, a brief period of suspension on full pay may be necessary in the following circumstances (to allow unhindered investigations to be carried out):
– preliminary investigations indicate that there is a potentially serious case, i.e. one involving gross misconduct; and
– the relationships at work have broken down or it is considered that there are risks to the employer's property or he has responsibilities to other parties (e.g. other employees or customers).

After the initial investigation has been completed, suspension will often be an appropriate course of action in cases of **serious misconduct**. If an employer chooses not to suspend an employee between the completion of an initial investigation and the disciplinary process commencing, this may be taken into account when assessing whether there were reasonable grounds for believing that misconduct sufficiently serious to warrant dismissal had been committed, which will consequently have a significant impact on establishing whether or not a dismissal is fair (*Graham v The Secretary of State for Work And Pensions (Jobcentre Plus)* [2012] EWCA Civ 903).

The employee should be informed that suspension on **full pay** is not considered to be a disciplinary action. Suspension **without pay** or with **reduced pay** is only possible where the contract of employment so provides. However, this should be exceptional as it will, in itself, amount to a disciplinary penalty.

6596 Before suspending an employee pending investigation, the employer should **consider** whether there is an **alternative** to suspension, such as a transfer. Where a suspension is imposed, it should be as **brief as possible** and kept **under review**. If a suspension continues for longer than necessary the employer may be in breach of contract. Even if there is a contractual right to suspend (¶6597), a failure to follow **correct procedures** before exercising the right may lead to a breach of contract claim, particularly in the case of skilled workers or those with professional qualifications.

For example, in a case where a paid suspension was not appropriate, the High Court (confirmed by the Court of Appeal) granted an interim (i.e. temporary) **injunction** to restrain an employer from suspending an employee with pay pending the outcome of internal disciplinary proceedings (*Mezey v South West London and St George's Mental Health NHS Trust* [2007] IRLR 237, HC ([2007] IRLR 244, CA)). In this case, the Court of Appeal, in supporting the use of the interim injunction in such circumstances, emphasised that suspension changed the status quo from work to no work and, as it inevitably casts a shadow over the employee's competence, there was no reason of principle why a court could not restrain an employer from suspending an employee in the same way that it may stay a dismissal.

EXAMPLE In *Gogay v Hertfordshire County Council* [2000] IRLR 703, CA, a care worker, G, was suspended pending the outcome of an investigation into allegations of sexual abuse of a child in her care. The Court of Appeal accepted that the Council was in breach of the implied term of trust and confidence because it had no reasonable and proper cause to suspend G, as it had not carried out preliminary investigations to determine the exact nature of the allegations. Consequently, there were no reasonable grounds for believing that the child would suffer harm unless G was suspended and the Council should have considered alternatives to suspension.

6597 The employer should reserve an **express contractual right** to suspend the employee in order to defeat any argument that there is an implied obligation to provide work (¶1233). If there is no express right, the employer may be in breach of contract.

6598 If an employer suspends an employee in circumstances where it **amounts to a detrimental act** (for example under the whistleblowing provisions), the suspension will be regarded as a continuing act. Consequently, time will begin to run from the end of the period of suspension for the purposes of calculating time limits (*Tait v Redcar and Cleveland Borough Council* [2008] UKEAT 0096_08_0204).

6600 **Post-investigation** Following the investigation, the employer may **decide to**:
– drop the matter (if the employee has a satisfactory explanation or the employer feels that there is insufficient evidence);
– deal with the matter on an informal basis (where the circumstances do not warrant implementation of the formal procedures because, for example, the matter is a minor one); or
– arrange for the matter to be dealt with under the formal procedures.

6601 Minor cases of misconduct and most cases of poor performance may warrant **informal advice, coaching and counselling**. If necessary, an **informal oral warning** could be issued, together with a discussion of how the employee needs to improve. This discussion should be held in private, where possible, and should be two-way, allowing the employee to put forward explanations of his conduct or performance.

The employee should be informed how his performance or **conduct** will be **reviewed**, over what period, and any consequences of a failure to improve (for example, implementation of the formal disciplinary procedure). It should be made clear that informal warnings and/or counselling are not part of the formal procedures, although a note should be kept for reference purposes.

Letter to employee

6605 If the employer decides that **formal action** is necessary, the first step in any formal process is to **inform** the employee in writing what it is that he is alleged to have done wrong and the reasons why his conduct or capability is not acceptable. It is important at this stage for employers to take care that the disciplinary charge(s) is framed precisely and accurately, since an employee can only be disciplined for the charge which has been put to him (*Strouthos v London Underground Ltd* [2004] IRLR 636, CA). On the other hand, where the words of the letter are ambiguous, they may suffice, if the employee is aware of the charges against him (*Draper v Mears Ltd* [2006] IRLR 869, EAT).

The notification must also **invite** the employee to attend a meeting at which the conduct or capability issue can be discussed. The meeting should ideally be arranged at a mutually convenient time and location which is reasonable for both parties and the employer should check that everyone who is required to attend the meeting is available. The employee should be given sufficient time to prepare his case, but there should not be an unreasonable delay so as to prevent the parties' memories from fading. Finally, employers must ensure that the notification sets out the employee's statutory right to be accompanied.

6607 In advance of making arrangements for the meeting, the employer should:
– ensure that all the **relevant facts are available**, for example disciplinary records, absence or sickness records and witness statements;
– arrange, where possible, for a second member of management to be present to **take notes**, and to act as a witness;
– consider whether any arrangements need to be made to cater for any **language difficulties** or **disabilities** of any person attending (bearing in mind the duty to make reasonable adjustments under the disability discrimination provisions of the EqA 2010 (¶5530; *Cave v Goodwin* [2004] EWCA Civ 391; *Johnson & Johnson Medical Ltd v Filmer* [2001] UKEAT 1087_00_1203) (for example, it may be necessary to provide an interpreter or wheelchair access));
– plan how the meeting will be **structured**, making notes of points that need to be covered;
– arrange for **witnesses** to attend (unless the employee accepts in advance that their statements are statements of fact). If a witness is someone from outside the organisation who is not prepared or unable to attend, the employer should try and get a written statement from him; and
– establish what disciplinary action was taken in **similar circumstances** in the past.

Disciplinary hearing

6610 The meeting **should be held** as privately as possible, in a suitable room, and the employer should ensure that there are no interruptions.

Attendance Both employers and employees should make every effort to attend meetings which have been arranged. If an employee (or his companion – ¶6786) **cannot attend** a meeting, he must inform the employer, in advance whenever possible, so that the meeting can be rearranged. However, if the employee is persistently unable or unwilling to attend disciplinary meetings without good reason, the employer may decide the outcome of the procedure in his absence.

6612

Conducting a meeting There are no set legal rules to be followed for a disciplinary hearing, and much will depend on the particular circumstances and whether the employer has set out any procedural guidelines. To avoid any allegation of prejudice, the hearing should ideally be **conducted by** an independent person, i.e. someone other than the person who made the complaint against the employee or who carried out, or was involved in, the investigation stage, and further, that person should be impartial (i.e. have no personal interest, financial or otherwise, in the outcome). The person chosen should have the employer's **authority** to impose any relevant penalty, and must act in good faith.

6615

EXAMPLE In *R v Chief Constable of Merseyside Police ex parte Bennion* [2001] IRLR 442, CA, the Chief Constable was held to be impartial when hearing B's disciplinary case, despite the fact that her sex discrimination claim was pending against him in his capacity as head of the force (i.e. not against him personally). He had no disqualifying personal interest arising from his involvement in different capacities in either set of proceedings and it was held that there was no real danger of bias.

MEMO POINTS The above case focuses on the statutory responsibility of a chief constable to hear disciplinary proceedings. It could, in practice, also apply to **chief executives in private organisations** (i.e. they should not regard themselves as disabled by tribunal proceedings from being involved in internal disciplinary matters, unless they have a personal interest in the outcome of the tribunal proceedings).

During the **introductory stage** of the hearing, the person conducting the hearing (who should be a manager with the authority to take a disciplinary decision) should:
– introduce those present and explain the reason for their attendance;
– confirm that the hearing is a disciplinary one to consider whether dismissal or any other disciplinary action should be taken; and
– explain how the hearing will be conducted.

6617

The person conducting the hearing should then explain the nature of the complaint, review the evidence, give any witnesses an opportunity to comment and ensure that the employee (and his representative) is allowed to see any witness statements or is told very clearly of the allegations and evidence raised. As long as the employee is told of the accusations against him and given a full opportunity to respond, there will not necessarily be a breach of natural justice if witness statements are not disclosed. The fairness of the procedure will be a question of fact in each case (*Hussain v Elonex plc* [1999] IRLR 420, CA). The **employee** should have **time to consider** the evidence, so it will normally be appropriate to disclose any statements **in advance** of the hearing. If witnesses are called at the hearing, the employee should be given the opportunity to raise any issues with them, but it is not essential that he is given a chance to cross-examine them (*Santamera v Express Cargo Forwarding t/a IEC Ltd* [2002] UKEAT 780_01_2611).

6618

The **employer** must strike a balance between the desirability of protecting any informants who are genuinely in fear of reprisals, and the need to provide a fair hearing. If the employer is relying on the **statements of an informant** who wishes to remain anonymous, the informant's motives should be examined, and corroborative evidence sought at the investigation stage. If the employee or his representative raise any issues which should be put to the informant, it may be desirable to adjourn the hearing so that the informant can be questioned on those matters.

A **complete and thorough reappraisal** of the accusations at this stage may remedy an improper investigation (*Lewis v HSBC Bank* [2006] UKEAT 0364_06_1912).

EXAMPLE In *Lewis v HSBC Bank*, a colleague accused another employee, L, of performing a lewd act in the work gym. The investigation of the allegation was discriminatory. However, the subsequent

> disciplinary hearing involved a thorough non-discriminatory reappraisal of the case. In these circumstances, the fairness of the disciplinary hearing was found to outweigh the unfairness of the initial investigation and L was unsuccessful in his claim of less favourable treatment with regard to his dismissal.

6619 The **employee** should be invited to **state his case**, ask questions, present evidence, and call witnesses. If witnesses are unable to attend, the hearing should be adjourned unless it is clear that their evidence will not affect the substance of the complaint.

The employer should consider any explanations or other special circumstances put forward by the employee. If he has not offered an explanation, he should be invited to do so. The employer's approach should be formal but polite, using questions (both open-ended and closed, as appropriate) to clarify all the issues.

6620 If it becomes clear that the employee has provided an **adequate explanation** or that there is **no real evidence** to support the allegation, the proceedings should be stopped.

If **new facts** emerge during the hearing, the employer must decide whether further investigation is required, in which case the hearing should be adjourned to be reconvened when the investigation is completed.

6621 If the employee becomes **emotionally distressed** during the hearing, he should be given time to compose himself before continuing. If it is not possible to continue the hearing, it should be adjourned and resumed at a later date.

While the employee (and perhaps some of the witnesses) may be highly charged, **abusive language**, threatened physical violence or other misconduct should not be tolerated. The interview should be adjourned and reconvened at a later date, where that misconduct can also be considered (provided that its inclusion in the issues being addressed has been made clear to the employee).

6622 At the end of the hearing, the employer should **summarise** the main points concerning the offence, the main points raised by the employee, and any matters that need to be checked.

Decision

6625 **Unless** the case is particularly **straightforward**, the hearing should be adjourned before a decision is reached. This allows any further investigation to be completed, and a proper consideration of all the matters raised. The employee should be told about the result of any further investigations, and should be given the opportunity to respond if relevant. If the facts are disputed, the manager conducting the hearing should decide which version is the most probable.

6626 If the employee is found to have committed an offence, before imposing a disciplinary sanction, the **employer should consider**:
– the gravity of the offence, and whether the disciplinary procedure indicates what the likely penalty will be as a result of the offence in question;
– the penalty imposed in similar cases in the past (although each case must be considered on its merits and its own facts);
– any mitigating circumstances (e.g. health, domestic problems, provocation, ignorance of the rule or inconsistent treatment in the past);
– the employee's disciplinary record, employment history and position; and
– whether the proposed penalty is reasonable in all the circumstances.

The employer **should not consider** any further allegations which were not addressed at the investigation/disciplinary hearing stages, as this would be contrary to natural justice (and may be a breach of the employer's own procedures) (*Barros D'Sa v University Hospital Coventry and Warwickshire NHS Trust* [2001] IRLR 691, CA). Since it is not open to a disciplinary panel to find an employee guilty of matters which go beyond the charge originally put to him, it is important that the employer takes care, when formally framing the disciplinary charge, to ensure that it is framed precisely and accurately (*Strouthos v London Underground Ltd* [2004] IRLR 636, CA).

6627 The employer can consider **previous warnings** given for other reasons in deciding whether to dismiss. The significance that can be given to **previous unrelated warnings** will depend on the particular case (*Auguste Noel Ltd v Curtis* [1990] IRLR 326, EAT). For a discussion regards the treatment of spent warnings, see ¶6632.

> EXAMPLE In *Auguste Noel Ltd v Curtis*, C was given a final warning in October 1987 concerning his relationship with other employees, and a final warning in February 1988 for unsatisfactory documentation and absenteeism. In March 1988, the employers dismissed him for mishandling company property. The EAT held that his employer was entitled to take into account the existence of the warnings, how many there had been, the substance of the complaint on each occasion, and the dates and periods between them, as long as to do so was fair and just in the circumstances.

6628 Once a decision has been reached, the employee should be given the **following information**:
– the decision, the reason for it, and the penalty;
– how long any warning given will last and the consequences of further misconduct;
– where improvement is required, what is expected, over what period, and how it will be assessed; and
– the procedure and timescale for lodging an appeal (especially where the decision is to dismiss).

The above information should also be **notified in writing** to the employee with a copy being kept on his personnel file. The letter should ideally be handed to the employee, who should be asked to sign a copy acknowledging receipt. If this cannot be achieved for any reason, a note should be placed on the personnel file, and a copy of the written notification sent to the employee's home address by recorded delivery.

3. Sanctions

6630 The factors the employer should consider when deciding on the appropriate sanction are discussed above. The following formal sanctions are available (rule 17-22 DG Code):
– first written warning;
– final written warning;
– penalties short of dismissal; and
– dismissal (with or without notice).

Warnings

6631 Where misconduct is confirmed or the employee is found to be performing unsatisfactorily, a **first written warning** can be given.

Where the matter is sufficiently serious, or in the case of further misconduct (where the employee has received a previous warning), a **final written warning** may be given, together with a statement setting out what the consequences of recurrence of the offence would be. This should only be given once the employee has had an opportunity to present his case at a meeting with the employer. The final written warning should provide the employee with details of, and the grounds for, the complaint and should warn the employee that if there is no improvement in his conduct, he may be subject to further disciplinary action, including dismissal. The employee should also be informed of the right to appeal against the warning. Employers should consider carefully whether a disciplinary offence justifies the imposition of a final written warning, since the **disproportionate use** of such a warning for a minor offence could constitute a fundamental breach of the employee's contract, entitling him to resign and claim constructive dismissal (*Stanley Cole (Wainfleet) Ltd v Sheridan* [2003] IRLR 52, EAT; see also ¶8230).

6632 **Spent warnings** Unless special agreed circumstances apply, a disciplinary warning should normally be disregarded for disciplinary purposes after a **specified period** of satisfactory conduct, which should be established when the disciplinary procedure is being drawn up. As an approximate guide, warnings for **minor offences** should usually be disregarded after a maximum of 6 months, while final warnings should usually be disregarded after 12 months or more, although what is reasonable will depend on all the circumstances of the case. For example there is no reason why it cannot be longer if the nature of the misconduct justifies it, and in particular if the imposition of a lesser penalty is an act of leniency. An employer might also be justified in extending the period of the warning with respect to a later act of gross misconduct which is the same or substantially the same as that for which the earlier final warning was given.

Where a disciplinary procedure specifies a time period beyond which warnings will be disregarded, while they should not normally be taken into account after they have expired, there is no absolute rule to this effect. If the circumstances warrant it, it may be reasonable to take an expired warning into account, for example if it has only recently expired (*Airbus UK Ltd v Webb* [2008] IRLR 309, CA). However, employers should be cautious in this regard.

In cases of **serious misconduct** (which verges on gross misconduct), it may be justifiable for disciplinary warnings to remain "live". In such circumstances, the employee should be told that the warning will remain active, and that any recurrence will/may lead to dismissal. If an employee's conduct or performance lapses soon after a warning expires, the employer should take this lapse into account when deciding how long any new warning should last.

Although a spent warning will be disregarded for disciplinary purposes, a **record** of it may be kept on file (¶6645).

> EXAMPLE
> 1. In *Diosynth Ltd v Thomson* [2006] IRLR 284, CS, an employer who issued a written warning to an employee, stating that such a warning would cease to have effect after 12 months, acted unreasonably in later trying to rely on the existence of such a warning 4 months after it had expired to justify the dismissal of the employee for a further act of misconduct. In this case, the employer admitted that had the warning not previously been on file, then the employee would not have been dismissed. In treating the warning as if it remained in force beyond the specified 12 months, the employer had not acted within the range of reasonable responses in deciding to dismiss the employee (¶8508). An employee is entitled to reasonably expect that a warning will expire after 12 months if this is what has been expressly indicated in the warning given to him.
> 2. In *Airbus UK Ltd v Webb* [2008] IRLR 309, CA, an employer dismissed an aircraft fitter for watching television in a locker room when he ought to have been working. Four other workers in the same position were not dismissed. In contrast to his colleagues who had clean disciplinary records, the worker had been given a final warning for a similar act of misconduct some 13 months before. While the final warning given with respect to the earlier misconduct had expired after 12 months it was still a relevant circumstance which the employer was entitled to take into account when deciding whether or not to dismiss.

Penalties short of dismissal

6633 Provided these penalties are allowed for in the contract (for example, in disciplinary rules which have been incorporated), instead of, or following, a final written warning, the employer could consider imposing a penalty short of dismissal, such as **disciplinary transfer**, **disciplinary suspension without pay** (but only for such period as the contract permits, which must also be reasonable in the circumstances), **demotion**, **loss of seniority**, or **loss of salary increment**. Note that if there is **no contractual right** to impose such penalties, then any demotion or other such penalties may amount to a fundamental **breach of contract**, allowing the employee to resign and claim that he has been constructively dismissed (*Hilton v Shiner Ltd – Builders Merchants* [2001] UKEAT 9_00_2405) unless the employee has expressly consented to the penalty as an alternative to dismissal (*Saminaden v Barnet Enfield and Haringey NHS Trust* [2008] UKEAT 0018_08_0707).

Dismissal

6634 The **final disciplinary sanction** will be dismissal. The decision to dismiss an employee must only be taken by a manager who has authority to make such decisions. In most cases, dismissal should be the sanction only if, despite warnings, conduct or performance does not improve. However, in some circumstances it may be appropriate to enter the procedure at the written warning or final written warning stage. Dismissals **for a first offence** may be justified in cases of gross misconduct, and also where the employee has made it clear that he is not prepared to alter his attitudes (such that a warning would be futile).

Other than in cases of gross misconduct, the employee should receive the appropriate **period of notice** (statutory or contractual, whichever is greater) or payment in lieu of notice.

In exceptional cases, where the misconduct is not so serious as to destroy the relationship of trust and confidence between employer and employee, the employer should consider whether **suitable alternative employment** is available.

6635 If the employer is considering imposing the disciplinary sanction of dismissal, he should decide whether the breach of the particular rule constitutes a **fair reason** for dismissal, such as misconduct (¶8490). If it does, the employer may have a defence to a claim of unfair dismissal if he has also followed a fair procedure (¶8500).

6636 It should be noted that employees with 2 years' continuous service starting on or after 6 April 2012 have a right to request a **written statement of reasons** for dismissal (¶8310). Employees who started their period of continuous service before this date have a qualifying period of 1 year.

MEMO POINTS   Women who are dismissed while **pregnant or during their maternity leave** must be given written reasons for their dismissal regardless of their length of service and whether or not they have requested reasons (¶4763).

6640 **Gross misconduct**   The employer must give employees a clear indication of the type of misconduct that will warrant summarily dismissing an employee for gross misconduct, which should only take place after the normal investigation process is completed (¶6540) (rule 23 DG Code). The employee must still be told of the allegations against him, and given an opportunity to state his case before any decision to summarily dismiss him is taken.

Re-visiting disciplinary decisions

6641 As a general rule, once the disciplinary process has been exhausted for a particular issue then the internal proceedings in relation to that issue should be at an end. In other words, an employee should not be **disciplined twice** over the same concern unless significant new evidence comes to light. It may be possible in certain circumstances to do so, but this will be extremely rare and employers will find it **very difficult to justify**.

EXAMPLE   In *Christou and anor v London Borough of Haringey* [2012] UKEAT 0298_11_2505, the EAT had to consider an exceptional case involving a council's decision to dismiss two social workers (C and W) for gross misconduct, as a result of their involvement in the "Baby P" scandal, and in particular whether the dismissal was fair in circumstances where they had previously been disciplined and penalised for the same acts of misconduct. The council had two contractual disciplinary procedures: a simplified disciplinary procedure (in which there was no appeal against the maximum sanction of a written warning) and a full disciplinary procedure (in which dismissal could be an outcome). After Baby P's death, both social workers were subjected to the simplified disciplinary procedure and were given written warnings. Around 6 months later there was a public outcry and the then Secretary of State for Children, Schools and Families announced an investigation into child protection and child welfare services in the area. On the same day, C and W were put on leave. A report was published a month later stating that the council's safeguarding services were inadequate and needed urgent and sustained attention and the interim Director of Children's Services re-investigated the issues in Baby P's case, including the involvement of C and W. After this investigation, C and W were re-disciplined under the full disciplinary procedure which resulted in them being summarily dismissed for gross misconduct. C and W brought claims for unfair dismissal. The employment tribunal found that the dismissals were fair. Whilst acknowledging that the death of Baby P and the media and political pressure placed upon the council were possible drivers for the dismissals, the tribunal held that the true reason for C and W being dismissed was their misconduct and not the other external factors. When considering whether the dismissals fell within the "range of reasonable responses", the tribunal took account of the fact that there had been two disciplinary procedures for the same acts of misconduct. The tribunal, by a majority, found that as the new management team considered the previous disciplinary action taken was inadequate, the council was justified in bringing the second disciplinary proceedings against C and W. The EAT upheld this decision and found that the new management team had reasonably taken the view that the misconduct was considerably more serious than was suitable to be dealt with under the simplified disciplinary procedure. The tribunal had been correct to take into account the earlier written warnings and the previous disciplinary procedures when deciding that dismissal was within the range of reasonable responses.

4. Records

6645 In order to ensure consistency in the application of the disciplinary procedure, records of **decisions** should be kept. These should be confidential, and should be retained in accordance with the disciplinary procedure and data protection principles (Data Protection Act 1998; ¶5945). The records should give the following **details**:
– the nature of any offence;
– the employee's defence or mitigation;
– the action taken and the reasons for it;
– whether an appeal was lodged and, if so, the outcome;
– any grievances raised during the disciplinary procedure; and
– any subsequent developments.

Copies of meeting records, including copies of any formal minutes that have been taken at meetings, should be provided to the employee, although in certain circumstances (for example, to protect the anonymity of a witness) an employer will be justified in withholding some information.

C. Dealing with particular issues

1. Absence

6650 The employer should ensure that employees know who (and when) to **notify** when they are absent from work. In cases of sickness, they should know when self-certification is acceptable, and when a doctor's medical certificate will be required.

The employer should **monitor** absence levels by keeping records showing lateness, and the duration of and reasons for any absences. By examining such records, the employer will be able to identify those employees who are regularly absent, and a pattern may be identifiable, allowing problems to be addressed at an early stage.

6651 **Absence on medical grounds** (such as injury, disability and illness) should be treated as a capability issue, whereas other types of absence may give rise to disciplinary issues. Medical absences should be treated sympathetically (¶4280). When considering how to handle such cases, the employer should consider:
– **how soon** the employee's health and attendance will improve;
– whether there is **suitable alternative work** available to give him;
– what **effect** his absence will have on the organisation;
– whether there have been any **other similar cases** and, if so, how they were handled; and
– whether the illness is a result of a **disability**, in which case the employer should bear in mind his statutory obligations not to treat an employee less favourably on the grounds of or for a reason relating to his disability, and his duty to make reasonable adjustments to accommodate disabled employees (¶¶5500, 5510, 5530).

6652 If the employee has a record of **frequent self-certified absences** without any medical advice in support, he should be asked to consult a doctor to establish whether any treatment is necessary, and it may be appropriate for the employer to carry out an assessment as to whether the underlying reason is work-related.

Employees suffering from **alcohol or drug addiction** should be encouraged to seek help and treatment. Alcohol or drug abuse and/or possession, on the other hand, may give rise to disciplinary issues. The employer may have a policy specifically aimed at dealing with such issues (¶5055).

6653 In some cases, an employee may suffer from a medical condition that makes him **unacceptable to fellow employees**, who may threaten or even take industrial action or otherwise bring pressure on the employer to dismiss. Such action/pressure will not be taken into account by an employment tribunal when assessing the fairness of a dismissal, so the employer must consider all other relevant factors, as he will not be able to rely on disruption to production caused by industrial action to justify his decision (s 107 ERA 1996). He should in particular also consider whether the medical condition is a disability.

6654 Where the absence arises from **taking care of dependants**, the employer should respect the employee's right to take reasonable time off (¶4740).

6655 All **unexpected absences** should be investigated promptly, and the employee asked to give an explanation. If there are no acceptable reasons for the absence, the matter should be treated as a conduct issue, and dealt with under the disciplinary procedure, in which case the employee should be told what improvement in attendance is expected, and warned of the likely consequences of failure to improve. If there is no improvement, the employer should take into account the following factors when deciding the appropriate action:
– the employee's age, length of service, and performance;
– the likelihood of an improvement in attendance;
– the availability of suitable alternative work; and
– the effect of past and future absences on the business.

Persistent absence must be dealt with promptly, firmly and consistently to show the employee (and staff in general) that absence is regarded as a serious matter and may result in dismissal.

6656 If an employee takes **holiday without authorisation**, or fails to return from holiday or a period of extended leave on the agreed date, the disciplinary procedure (including a full investigation) should be applied in the usual way.

Before deciding to dismiss an employee in these circumstances, the employer must take into account the employee's age, length of service, past attendance record, and any explanation put forward by him.

> MEMO POINTS In some circumstances employees can absent themselves from work to deal with domestic emergencies concerning their dependants and, provided they have complied with the relevant procedures, they should not be subjected to a detriment or dismissed for doing so (¶¶4740+).

2. Poor performance

6660 Employees are contractually obliged to perform to a satisfactory level (¶1202). Employers should set **realistic and measurable standards** of performance for the job. Careful **recruitment and selection** will minimise the risk of poor performance, as the employer should explain the required standards (and the consequences of failing to meet them) to employees at the outset of the employment (or promotion), and ensure that job descriptions convey the main purpose and scope of the job and the tasks involved.

Proper **training and supervision** are key to the achievement of satisfactory performance, and employers should give employees help and encouragement to reach the required standards. Performance should be discussed on a regular basis, either informally or formally, by means of **appraisal or performance management** systems (¶6465).

Performance should be monitored closely during any **probation period** (¶940).

6661 If an employee **fails to perform** to the required standard, the matter should be investigated to ascertain the reason for the poor performance.

Reason	Action
External factors, e.g. market forces affecting sales figures	Not disciplinary issue
Change in nature of job	Consider whether to treat as redundancy, rather than capability or conduct
Lack of required skills	Where practicable, assistance through training/coaching, monitoring of performance, and reasonable time to reach required standard. If no improvement, consider disciplinary procedure.
Sickness/disability	Treat sympathetically as capability issue
Negligence or lack of application	Disciplinary action through normal procedure or separate capability procedure

6662 If the **matter is a disciplinary one**, employers should consider whether it can be dealt with informally by talking to the employee in private. Where necessary, the employer should normally issue a **warning**, and give the employee an opportunity to improve by setting a reasonable target and timescale together with any appropriate assistance (*Polkey v A E Dayton Services Ltd* [1987] IRLR 503, HL). In all cases, criticism should be constructive, with the emphasis being on finding ways for the employee to improve and for the improvement to be sustained. The employer should clearly set out what needs to be done, how the employee's performance or conduct will be reviewed, and over what period. It is useful to confirm any agreed action in writing.

An employee should only be dismissed for poor performance **without previous warnings** if the actual or potential consequences of his single, negligent error are, or could be, extremely serious (for example, pilot error endangering passengers) (*Taylor v Alidair Ltd* [1978] IRLR 82, CA). The disciplinary procedure should indicate that such cases may result in summary dismissal.

There are no set rules as to the **period for improvement**, and the time will depend on the particular employee, his status, position, service, past performance, and the degree to which he is underperforming.

The **number of warnings** given in a particular case will depend on the levels of improvement required and on the seniority of the employee involved. **More senior employees** may be expected to have the necessary experience for their position, and so the employer may consider that only one warning is appropriate. Only in rare cases will an act of incapability justify immediate dismissal without warning.

6663 The employer may need to put in place special arrangements for employees on **short-term contracts** and **probationary employees**, as the term of their contract or probation period may not accommodate the employer's usual warning procedures.

6664 Performance should be **monitored** and a **review meeting** scheduled.

If the employee **fails to improve** despite warnings and/or additional training, the employer should consider moving him to a suitable alternative job, if available and if provided for by the contract. Otherwise, this variation may require the employee's consent. A failure to consider alternative positions may render a dismissal unfair.

Demotion could be considered where provided for by the contract.

If there is no suitable alternative position, the employer may be justified in **dismissing** the employee.

6665 The employer may be tempted to **penalise poor performance** by making a deduction from the employee's pay. However, employees are protected from **unlawful pay deductions** and compulsory payments (¶3050) and employers should ensure that any variation to an employee's contractual pay (for example, as a result of a demotion) is agreed to by the employee.

Records A note of any discussions with the employee, and the decisions reached, should be kept. **6666**

D. Special cases

Trade union officials

Normal disciplinary standards apply to employees acting as trade union representatives. However, if they are the subject of disciplinary proceedings, the circumstances of the case should be discussed with a senior trade union representative or full-time official at an early stage, after obtaining the employee's agreement (rule 29 DG Code). Otherwise, the action may be seen as an attack on the union, which may lead to a serious dispute. **6670**

Criminal charges or convictions outside employment

If an employee is charged with, or convicted of, an offence, the employer will need to consider the facts of the case and decide whether the employee's conduct is serious enough to be treated as a formal disciplinary matter. The disciplinary procedure should only be implemented if the charge or offence **relates** (directly or indirectly) **to the employee's job** (i.e. it must affect the employee's suitability to do the job and his relationship with his employer, work colleagues and customers), making the employee unsuitable for his type of work (rule 30 DG Code). **6671**

Off-duty conduct that has **no bearing on the employment** will not justify disciplinary action unless it is within the band of responses of a reasonable employer.

An employee charged with a criminal offence is not necessarily guilty of it and he should not be dismissed solely because a **charge is pending**, even where he is employed in a sensitive post (*Securicor Guarding Ltd v R* [1994] IRLR 633, EAT). A **spent conviction** (¶613) will not provide proper grounds for dismissal (*Property Guards Ltd v Taylor and Kershaw* [1982] IRLR 175, EAT). On the other hand, **acquittal** of a criminal charge does not make any subsequent disciplinary action based on the same event unlawful (*Saeed v Greater London Council (Inner London Education Authority)* [1986] IRLR 23, QBD). **6672**

Any disciplinary decision should be made on a reasonable belief that a disciplinary offence has been committed following a reasonable **investigation** into the circumstances of the case. The employer does not have to establish the employee's criminal guilt by means of his own independent investigation. **6673**

The employer should not postpone taking disciplinary action merely because the **outcome of the prosecution** is not known. Further, the disciplinary penalty should not depend on the outcome of any criminal trial.

The employee may be advised by his lawyer that taking part in a disciplinary investigation or hearing may prejudice the outcome of criminal proceedings. If the employee **refuses to co-operate** with the employer's disciplinary procedure, the employer should advise him in writing that, unless he co-operates, a disciplinary decision will be taken on the basis of the information available, and could result in dismissal. The employer will then need to consider whether the evidence available to him is strong enough to justify a disciplinary warning or dismissal.

However, it may be appropriate to **adjourn disciplinary proceedings** until the criminal proceedings are completed. Further, where the employer's disciplinary policy allows for adjournments for matters directly related to the subject of a criminal investigation this has been held to be an implied contractual term (*Lakshmi v Mid Cheshire Hospitals NHS Trust* [2008] EWHC 878 (QB)). Where it is appropriate to await the outcome of criminal proceedings the employer can rely on a **court decision** or the **verdict of a jury** (*P v Nottingham County Council* [1992] IRLR 362, CA; *Post Office v Liddiard* [2001] EWCA Civ 940 (¶6675)), although he should still follow a fair procedure, including giving the employee an opportunity to explain his conduct. The **police** should not be asked to conduct any investigation on behalf of the employer, nor should they be present at any disciplinary hearing or interview (*Read v Phoenix Preservation Society* [1985] IRLR 93, EAT). However, it may be possible to use **witness statements** given as part of a police investigation (*Rhondda Cynon Taf County Borough Council v Close* [2008] IRLR 868, EAT).

6674 If the employee will be absent from work while in **custody or on remand**, the employer must consider whether his job can be kept open during that time (this is not a disciplinary matter). If it is unlikely that the employee will be able to return to the job, it may be argued that the contract of employment has been frustrated, in which case there will be no dismissal (the contract terminates by operation of law). This argument may be accepted where the frustrating event (i.e. the imprisonment) makes performance of the contract clearly impossible (¶8285).

If the employee **loses a licence** (for example, his driving licence) as a result of a conviction such that continued employment in a particular job will be illegal, the employer should consider whether suitable alternative work is available.

> MEMO POINTS If the employee will be absent from work while in custody or on remand, the employee has no recourse under the unlawful deduction of wages legislation if the employer does not pay his wages during this period (¶3007).

6675 The employer should **not automatically dismiss** the employee merely because of the charge or offence, or because of absence from work as a result of being remanded in custody. **Dismissal** will only be **justified** if this sanction is within the band of responses of a reasonable employer (¶8437), which will be the case where the offence is one that makes the employee unsuitable for his type of work (in which case the normal disciplinary rules and procedure should be followed).

> EXAMPLE
> 1. In *Post Office v Liddiard* (¶6673), L was convicted of **football hooliganism**. Due to press coverage, the Post Office claimed that he had brought it into disrepute and therefore dismissed him. The Court held that misconduct unconnected to the workplace could justify dismissal if this sanction was within the band of responses of a reasonable employer.
> 2. In *Norfolk County Council v Bernard* [1979] IRLR 220, EAT, B, a drama teacher, was convicted of **possession of cannabis**. The EAT held that, in the circumstances, the dismissal was unfair.
> 3. In *Nottinghamshire County Council v Bowly* [1978] IRLR 252, EAT, B was convicted of a **sexual offence**. The dismissal was held to be fair.
> 4. In *Moore v C & A Modes* [1981] IRLR 71, EAT, M, a section leader in a retail store, was fairly dismissed after 20 years' service after being caught **shoplifting** in another store.
> 5. In *Leach v The Office of Communications (OFCOM)* [2012] EWCA Civ 959, the Court of Appeal considered a situation where an employer, OFCOM, dismissed an employee, L, after **allegations of child abuse** were made against him. OFCOM have a duty to have regard to the interests of children but do not provide services for children, and L had no contact with children in his job. L was tried in Cambodia on two separate occasions of offences against children (he was acquitted of the first set prior to being dismissed by OFCOM and convicted of the second set after the EAT hearing). L did not inform OFCOM about the first set of proceedings and lied in order to hide the situation from them. After L was acquitted of them, a UK-based specialist police unit brought the proceedings to the attention of OFCOM along with further allegations in the form of limited disclosure, which the officers concerned described as "the tip of the iceberg". Although initially OFCOM supported L, they ultimately dismissed him on the ground that they had lost trust and confidence in him. The Court of Appeal set out the following general points as to how an employer should treat **third party disclosures** of information or allegations about an employee. The employer should:
> – assess for itself, as far a practicable, the reliability of what it has been told;
> – check the integrity of the informant body and the safeguards within its internal processes concerning the accuracy of the information supplied; and
> – consider the likely effect of disclosure and whether there was cogent evidence of a pressing need for disclosure to the employer.
> The Court of Appeal noted the difficulty in balancing the risk of injustice to an employee in losing his job, on the basis of unproven and untested allegations, with the fact that the employer could not be expected to simply ignore the disclosure made to them by the police. Here, the employer sought clarification, confirmation and some further disclosure before holding an internal disciplinary hearing during which L was able to put his case. At the end of the process, it notified L of his

> summary dismissal on the basis that it had to accept the advice from the police that L continued to be a risk to children and that this was a breach of trust and confidence (in the context of the risk of reputational damage to the employer if it did not dismiss him), which justified a dismissal on the ground of some other substantial reason (SOSR). Looking at all the circumstances, this was within the range of reasonable responses. The Court of Appeal also upheld the finding that L had not been wrongly dismissed because his lies and lack of frankness abused the trust and confidence placed in him to a degree that was sufficiently serious to justify his summary dismissal.

Isolated employees

6676 The employer will need to give special consideration to the handling of disciplinary matters in the case of employees to whom the full procedure may not be immediately available, such as **night shift** workers and employees in **isolated workplaces**. For example, the employer could allow the employee paid time off so that he can attend a disciplinary hearing on the main site during normal working hours. Alternatively, if a number of the employee's colleagues need to attend as witnesses, it may be more practical to hold the hearing on the night shift or at the employee's site.

E. Appeal procedure

6680 The employer must allow the employee the **opportunity to appeal** against the decision to dismiss or take disciplinary action. See ¶6514 for the implications if the employer fails to allow his employee the opportunity to appeal and ¶6705 with regard to the implications if the employee fails to appeal.

An employee may wish to appeal a disciplinary decision on the **grounds** that he considers it to be unfair, the penalty too severe, or the disciplinary procedure defective, or he may wish to put forward new evidence.

The appeal hearing may impact on the **date of dismissal** (¶8340).

1. Formulation

6685 An opportunity to appeal against a disciplinary decision is essential to natural justice. It is recommended that the appeal procedure should:
– provide for appeals to be dealt with as promptly as possible (a time limit for hearing the appeal should be set);
– specify any time limit within which the appeal must be lodged (this may vary between organisations but 5 working days is usually appropriate);
– provide for the appeal to be heard by a manager or managers who has/have not previously been involved in the disciplinary procedure (although this may not be possible in small organisations, in which case the person dealing with the appeal should act as impartially as possible); and
– specify the action which may be taken by the person dealing with the appeal.

Employees should let their employers know the **grounds for** their **appeal** in writing.

2. Operation

Appeal hearing

6690 The employee should be informed of the **arrangements** for appeal hearings, including his statutory right to be accompanied (¶6780), and any other rights under the procedure. These arrangements will be similar to those for the disciplinary hearing (¶6610). When preparing

6691 for the hearing, the employer should ensure that the relevant records are available. The person hearing the appeal should review these documents in advance of the hearing.

It must be decided whether the appeal is a re-hearing or review.

A **review** (i.e. starting with the question of whether the disciplinary hearing had been correct) will generally be appropriate only where there is no new evidence and no question of there being any defects in the procedure to date, for example where the employee does not dispute his guilt but feels that the penalty imposed is too harsh.

A **re-hearing** (i.e. approaching the matter as if for the first time) will be appropriate in most other cases, in particular where there is new evidence or to remedy any defect in the earlier procedure. If there is any doubt, the appeal hearing should proceed as a re-hearing, as this may impact on the fairness of the dismissal (¶8500). Where **additional evidence** is being adduced at an internal appeal, it is not essential for an employer to conduct a full re-hearing of the disciplinary hearing (as opposed to a review) if the evidence relates to allegations which were raised at the original disciplinary hearing. However, if the new evidence relates to a matter which was not already considered at the original disciplinary hearing, then the employer must consider such evidence as an entirely separate disciplinary matter (*Arriva North West & Wales v Colebourn* [2005] UKEAT 0439_05_1810).

6692 One line of authority had suggested that where a **disciplinary appeal results in dismissal**, for that appeal to be fair, it should be a "re-hearing" and not a "review". In rejection of that approach, the Court of Appeal found there was no such rule of law. The **reasonableness of the appeal procedure** is subject to no general test. It will depend on the facts of each case (*Taylor v OSC Group Ltd* [2006] ICR 1602, CA).

Further, the EAT has reiterated the principle that a tribunal must give **consideration to all material** which emerges during the course of an internal appeal process in determining whether a dismissal is fair and a tribunal should not therefore limit itself in ascertaining an employer's belief to facts which were known to the employer at the time of the dismissal (*Arriva North West & Wales v Colebourn*, above, and citing *West Midlands Co-operative Society Ltd v Tipton*, ¶8439).

6693 The person/manager **conducting** the appeal should:
– introduce those present to the employee and explain the purpose of the hearing (i.e. whether it is a review or a re-hearing), how it will be conducted and what powers the appeal panel has;
– ask the employee to state the grounds for his appeal; and
– allow the employee, or his representative, the opportunity to comment on any new evidence.

As for the disciplinary hearing, the manager should deal with all the relevant issues, summarising them when concluding the hearing, and adjourn the hearing in order to consider the appropriate decision.

6694 See ¶¶6612+ with regard to attendance.

Decision

6695 When deciding whether to uphold or revoke the disciplinary decision, the appeal panel should take into account the same **considerations** as applied to the earlier decision (¶6625), and also consider the reasons for that decision, if available, and any new evidence put forward by the employee.

It is recommended that the appeal panel should not impose a penalty which is more severe than that being appealed. The appeal panel should not hesitate to **overturn a previous decision** where it is clear that it was incorrect, and impose a lesser penalty. If this action is taken, it will be useful for the matter to be subsequently discussed with the manager who took the disciplinary decision, and to consider whether further training of that manager is required.

6696 The appeal panel cannot find that the dismissal was **justified** for a **different reason** than that previously relied on, as the fairness of any dismissal is judged in the light of the reason relied on at the time of the dismissal (*Monie v Coral Racing Ltd* [1980] IRLR 464, CA). If the appeal panel finds that dismissal is justified but on **different grounds**, the original dismissal should not stand. To ensure that he acts fairly, the employer must look at the matter afresh in order to decide whether a subsequent dismissal on the new information is appropriate.

6697 **New information** which comes to light after the dismissal can be considered at the appeal stage to decide whether the decision to dismiss for the stated reason should stand (*West Midlands Co-operative Society Ltd v Tipton* [1986] IRLR 112, HL; *Board of Governors, The National Heart & Chest Hospitals v Nambiar* [1981] IRLR 196, EAT).

> EXAMPLE In *Board of Governors, The National Heart & Chest Hospitals v Nambiar*, N twice refused to comply with a lawful order from his employer, and walked out of work. During the disciplinary investigation, N claimed that he had refused because of pressure of work. His employer rejected his claim and dismissed him with pay in lieu of notice. N appealed and presented new evidence (medical reports) to the internal appeal panel, which sought further expert medical opinion as to the cause of his conduct. The appeal panel upheld the decision to dismiss, but recommended that, in the light of the new evidence, the employer should seek to employ N in suitable alternative work, if available. N refused offers of other work and claimed unfair dismissal. The EAT held that N was not unfairly dismissed as, on the basis of all the evidence, the internal appeal tribunal had acted reasonably in recommending that he should not be reinstated to his original post.

6698 The employee should be informed of the **outcome** of the appeal and the reasons for the decision as soon as possible. The employee should also be informed if the decision constitutes the final stage in the appeal procedure. This information should be confirmed in writing, and the employee should be asked to acknowledge receipt. Where he refuses to do so, a note should be made on the personnel file, and the **written notification** sent to his home address by recorded delivery.

F. Effect on tribunal claims

6699 The employee may wish to bring a tribunal claim, with or without instigating an internal appeal.

Time limits

6700 When bringing an employment tribunal claim, the employee should usually do so **within** the normal time limits (¶9450). This is usually 3 months from the date of the act or omission complained of. The tribunal has a continuing discretion to extend these time limits in certain circumstances (¶9465).

If an **internal appeal** is **still in progress** as the time limit for bringing an employment claim approaches, it is advisable for the employee to consider preserving his position by presenting a claim with a request that the matter not be set down for hearing until the internal appeal has been completed.

Failure to appeal

6705 A failure to appeal against dismissal does not amount to an acceptance that the dismissal was fair (the employee can still bring a claim of unfair dismissal (*Chrystie v Rolls-Royce (1971) Ltd* [1976] IRLR 336, EAT)) and will merely be of **evidential value** as to the employee's attitude at the time of dismissal. It may, however, lead to the tribunal deciding to reduce **any award** (¶6514). Similarly if the employer fails to allow the employee to appeal, the tribunal may likewise increase any award.

> **EXAMPLE** In *Chrystie v Rolls-Royce (1971) Ltd*, C was asked to attend a disciplinary hearing after he had assaulted a fellow employee. He failed to attend and the employers sent him a letter of dismissal. This letter crossed in the post with a letter from C, explaining that he had been ill and giving his account of the incident. The employers nevertheless allowed the dismissal to stand. The EAT rejected the argument that C had acquiesced in his dismissal by failing to appeal, and accepted that his dismissal had been unfair.

6707 If the **employer prevents the employee** from exercising a **contractual right of appeal**, the dismissal may be held to be unfair (*West Midlands Co-operative Society Ltd v Tipton* [1986] IRLR 112, HL). This will depend on whether the employee was thereby denied the opportunity of showing that the employer's real reason for the dismissal could not reasonably be treated as a sufficient one for the statutory test of fairness (*Westminster City Council v Cabaj* [1996] IRLR 399, CA).

SECTION 2

Grievance procedures

6730 **General principles** Employees may have **concerns, problems or complaints** that they want to raise with their employer. Like with disciplinary matters, employers should have grievance procedures in place so that grievances can be dealt with fairly, consistently and efficiently.

A grievance procedure is a process whereby an employee's concerns, problems or complaints on a particular issue are raised and addressed. If grievances are not dealt with, or are badly handled, the situation may deteriorate, and may lead to poor performance, resignations, complaints to tribunals or courts (including constructive dismissal claims), and possibly a wider dispute with employees in general. It is a matter of good employment practice for employers to have grievance procedures in place so that grievances can be dealt with fairly, consistently and efficiently.

> **MEMO POINTS** The Code does not apply to **collective grievances**, which should be handled under the employer's collective grievance process.

6732 There is an **implied term** that an employee's grievances will be promptly and properly dealt with. It is also important to bear in mind the **general requirements** applicable to the statutory dispute resolution procedures which stipulate that each action and step under the procedure must be taken without unreasonable delay (¶6513).

6733 An employee has a statutory **right to be accompanied** at grievance hearings (¶6780).

6734 **Issues** that may be the subject of employees' grievances include:
– terms and conditions of employment;
– health and safety;
– relationships at work;
– bullying and harassment;
– new working practices;
– organisational change; or
– equal opportunities.

6735 An employee may also have a grievance in relation to the **operation of the disciplinary procedure** (¶6580). Where an employee raises a **grievance during a disciplinary process** it may be appropriate to temporarily suspend the process to deal with the grievance. Where the **grievance and disciplinary cases are related** it may be appropriate to deal with both issues concurrently (rule 44 DG Code).

6736 It is advisable for the grievance procedure to be **non-contractual**. If the procedure is **contractual** and the employer fails to comply with even a minor part of it, the employee may have grounds to resign and claim constructive dismissal (¶8230).

1. Formulation

6739 The **aim** of a good procedure is to deal with the employee's grievance quickly, fairly, and at the lowest appropriate level within the organisation in order that matters do not escalate unnecessarily.

Senior management is **responsible** for developing the organisation's grievance procedure, but this cannot be done effectively without the input of employees and their representatives (including trade unions, where recognised), and of the levels of management responsible for the procedure's operation.

Grievance procedures **should**:
– be simple;
– be in writing;
– enable an employee's line manager to deal informally with a grievance if possible; and
– allow the employee to be accompanied by a companion at meetings.

They should also be quick to implement and confidential.

6740 The employer should ensure that all employees are **aware of and understand** the procedure, with every employee being given his own copy or provided with access to it (for example, by including it in the staff handbook or by putting it on the company intranet). This may be covered as part of an induction programme, with explanations of the procedures being given as required (¶926).

Special allowance should be made for individuals whose **first language is not English** or who have a **visual impairment** or some **other impairment** (see also ¶5530).

6742 The Acas Code sets out the **following basic principles of fairness** that employees and employers should follow if a matter cannot be resolved informally:

1. Employees should ensure that all issues are dealt with promptly and act consistently, treating like cases alike (rule 4 DG Code).
2. The employee should let the employer know the nature of his grievance in writing and without unreasonable delay. Where possible this should be to a manager who is not the subject of the grievance (rule 31 DG Code).
3. Where appropriate, investigations should be made to establish the facts of the case (rule 4 DG Code).
4. The employer should hold a meeting to discuss the grievance without unreasonable delay. Both parties and any companion of the employee should make every effort to attend the meeting (rule 32-33 DG Code).
5. Allow the employee to exercise his right to be accompanied (rule 34-37 DG Code).
6. At the meeting the employee should be allowed to explain his grievance and how he thinks it should be resolved. Consideration should be given to adjourning the meeting for any investigation that might be necessary (rule 33 DG Code).
7. After the meeting the employer should write to the employee without unreasonable delay to let him know what the outcome is and, where appropriate, set out what action the employer intends to take to resolve the grievance. The employer should also inform the employee of his right to appeal if he is not satisfied (rule 38 DG Code).
8. Where the employee does not feel that his grievance has been satisfactorily resolved, he should let the employer know that he wishes to appeal in writing and without unreasonable delay. Appeals should be heard without unreasonable delay and the employer should notify the employee of the time and place of the appeal in advance. Appeals should be dealt with impartially, and if possible by a manager not previously involved in the case. Workers have a statutory right to be accompanied. The outcome of the appeal should be provided in writing without unreasonable delay (rule 39-43 DG Code).

2. Operation

6757 If the employee's grievance is of a routine nature, it may best be resolved **informally** by discussion with his immediate line manager, who should keep a note of any such discussion. Working out an informal solution to the grievance allows issues to be resolved quickly and may be beneficial where there is a close personal relationship between a manager and an employee.

If the grievance **cannot be resolved informally**, the formal grievance procedure should be implemented.

If necessary, supervisors, managers, and employee representatives should be **trained** in the procedure's use.

6759 A failure to take an employee's grievance seriously may itself amount to **discrimination** (¶5829). For example, employers should not ignore or treat lightly grievances from **members of particular racial groups** on the assumption that they are over-sensitive about discrimination.

Further, any action taken against an employee because he has brought a complaint under a grievance procedure may amount to **unlawful victimisation** (¶5240).

6761 **Specific procedures** Some employers may have specific procedures to deal with particularly sensitive issues, such as **discrimination** (on grounds of age, disability, gender reassignment, marriage and civil partnership, pregnancy and maternity, race, religion or belief, sex or sexual orientation). Where the employer has in place separate procedures for dealing with such issues, these should be used instead of the normal grievance procedure, provided they incorporate the statutory minimum requirements. If there is no separate procedure, these issues should, at least, be addressed specifically in the general grievance procedure.

6762 Some employers may have a **whistleblowing** procedure to deal with concerns raised by employees about wrongdoing in their organisation. This will encourage employees to raise such concerns internally, rather than going directly to a regulatory authority or, for example, the press (¶2700).

6763 If the company has safety representatives and a safety committee, there may be no need for a separate **health and safety** procedure. In their absence, the employer may have such a procedure, so that employees can formally raise any grievances they may have.

Raising the grievance

6764 The employee should let the employer know the nature of his grievance **in writing**. This should usually be to the employee's line manager. Where the grievance is against the line manager the employee should approach another manager in the organisation if possible or raise the issue with the organisation's HR department if there is one. If the grievance concerns the person to whom the complaint would normally be addressed, then the employee may approach that person's manager or another manager in the organisation. This may prove more difficult for smaller organisations where it may not be possible for a different person to hear the grievance. If this is the case, the person to whom the grievance is addressed should deal with it as impartially as possible.

If there are any reasons as to why the employee might find setting out his grievance in writing difficult, for example if his **first language is not English** or he has **reading difficulties**, he should be encouraged to seek assistance from colleagues, or a trade union or other employee representative.

Grievance meeting

6766 On receipt of the written grievance, the manager concerned must invite the employee to attend a meeting to discuss the grievance as soon as possible and inform him that he has the right to be accompanied should he wish (¶6780). The manager and employee should agree a **mutually convenient** time and a **private location** for the meeting where they will not, if possible, be interrupted.

In **advance of the meeting**, the employer should:
- arrange, where possible, for a second member of management to be present to **take notes** and to act as a witness; and
- find out whether **similar grievances** have been raised before and, if so, how they have been resolved, including any follow-up action that has been necessary.

The employee must take all reasonable steps to attend the meeting. See ¶6612 for the consequences of either party **failing to attend** a meeting.

At the meeting, the employee should be given the opportunity to explain his complaint and how he would like to see it settled. It may be necessary to make allowances for any reasonable "letting off steam" if the employee is under stress. If it becomes clear to the manager during the course of the meeting that he is not sure how to deal with the grievance or that further investigation is necessary, he should **adjourn** the meeting to seek further advice or make further enquiries. In some cases it may be helpful to use a neutral mediator to help sort out a grievance and maintain working relationships.

Before **responding** to the grievance, the manager must give the employee's explanation careful consideration.

The manager should respond **in writing** to the employee's grievance **within** a reasonable time and inform the employee of his right to appeal against the decision if he is not happy with it. It is usually reasonable for the employer to respond within 5 working days, but if this is not possible, the manager should explain the delay to the employee and inform him of when he can expect a response.

Appeal

If the employee is not satisfied with the decision taken in respect of his grievance, he may wish to exercise his right of appeal. The employee should **inform** his employer that he wishes to exercise his right of appeal, in writing and without unreasonable delay. In response, the employer must invite the employee to attend a further meeting (¶6680). If possible, this **appeal meeting** should be heard by a manager other than the one who heard the original grievance. This may prove difficult in smaller organisations, and if this is not an option, the person to whom the original grievance was raised should deal with the appeal as impartially as possible.

After the appeal meeting, the employer should write to the employee to inform him of the **outcome** of the appeal meeting as soon as possible and should explain that this is the final stage of the grievance procedure.

Records

The employer should keep records giving the following details:
- the nature of the grievance;
- a copy of the written grievance;
- the employer's response;
- any action taken;
- whether there was an appeal and, if so, the outcome; and
- any subsequent developments.

These records should be confidential, and should be retained in accordance with the data protection principles (¶5945). Copies of any meeting records should be given to the employee, although in certain circumstances some information may be withheld (for example, to protect a witness).

3. Effect on tribunal claims

Failure to raise grievance

Failure to raise and discuss the grievance may have an **impact on the amount of any award** (¶6514).

Time limits

6777 When bringing an employment tribunal claim, the employee should usually do so **within** the normal time limits (¶9452). This is usually 3 months from the date of the act or omission complained of. The tribunal has a continuing discretion to extend these time limits in certain circumstances (¶9465).

SECTION 3
Right to be accompanied

Entitlement

6780 Workers have a statutory right to be accompanied by a single fellow worker or trade union official where they are required or invited by the employer to attend disciplinary or grievance hearings, and reasonably request (orally or in writing) to exercise their right (s 10 ERelA 1999).

The employer should ensure that his dismissal, disciplinary and grievance procedures provide for the statutory right to be accompanied, and that it is applied at all disciplinary and grievance hearings.

This right is in addition to any contractual rights, and applies to all **workers** (¶13), regardless of length of service. For these purposes, the definition specifically includes agency and home workers (s 13 ERelA 1999). Casual, temporary, and part-time workers will also be covered if they meet the general definition of worker.

> MEMO POINTS 1. It should be noted that while generally there is no breach of natural justice in refusing to allow legal representation at a disciplinary hearing, where a dismissal could have **greater consequences** for an employee than losing his job, for example if dismissal may also lead to a ban from further employment involving children or is in effect a criminal charge being dealt with by disciplinary proceedings, an employee is entitled to have legal representation at the internal hearing as part of his right to a fair trial under art 6 of the European Convention of Human Rights and under the concept of natural justice (*G, R (on the application of) v X School and ors* [2010] IRLR 222, CA; *Kulkarni v Milton Keynes Hospital NHS Foundation Trust* [2009] IRLR 829, CA). This exception will be relevant to employers of medical professionals, those providing educational or care services to children or vulnerable adults and other regulated professions. However, it does not apply where the disciplinary hearing does not have a greater impact (*R (on the application of Kirk) v Middlesbrough Borough Council and ors* [2010] IRLR 699, HC).
> 2. Dismissal by reason of **redundancy** is not a disciplinary matter and therefore the right to be accompanied has been held not to apply to a hearing to inform the worker that he is being made redundant (*Heathmill Multimedia Asp Ltd v Jones* [2005] UKEAT 0200_03_1006).

Type of hearing

6781 A **disciplinary hearing** includes hearings that could result in:
– the administration of a formal warning to a worker (i.e. a warning, whether about conduct or capability, that will be placed on the worker's record);
– the taking of some other action in respect of a worker by the employer (for example, suspension without pay, demotion or dismissal); or
– the confirmation of a warning issued or some other action taken (i.e. appeal hearings where a sanction might be endorsed or removed) (s 13(4) ERelA 1999).

Most formal disciplinary hearings will fall within the definition, although earlier **investigatory** stages in the process will not necessarily be covered. Although there may be no statutory right to be accompanied at investigatory meetings, employers may consider it appropriate to allow employees to be accompanied, particularly if the worker is disabled, has difficulty speaking English or may become distressed.

> **EXAMPLE**
> 1. In *Skiggs v South West Trains Limited* [2005] UKEAT 0763_03_0703, a meeting held to investigate a grievance about a worker who had previously been disciplined did not constitute a disciplinary hearing and the worker was therefore not entitled to be accompanied. It is a question of fact and degree in each case as to whether a preliminary factual inquiry has transformed into a disciplinary hearing.
> 2. In *OCS Group Limited and Taylor* [2005] UKEAT 0803_04_2305, the EAT upheld the tribunal's decision that an employer had failed to make reasonable adjustments for disability in the disciplinary process for a profoundly deaf employee (the case was appealed further on other grounds, but this principle remains unaffected).

Informal interviews or **counselling sessions** which do not result in a formal warning or other action will not be disciplinary hearings, and the right to be accompanied will not apply.

However, an **oral warning** which is **subsequently confirmed** in writing and becomes part of a worker's disciplinary record will constitute a formal warning and gives rise to the right to be accompanied (*London Underground Ltd v Ferenc-Batchelor* [2002] UKEAT 1039_01_2910). Likewise, if it becomes clear during an investigative or informal interview that formal disciplinary action may be needed, the interview should be terminated and a formal hearing convened at which the worker will have the right to be accompanied.

A **grievance hearing** is a hearing which concerns the performance of a duty by an employer in relation to a worker, which means a legal duty arising from statute or common law, such as contractual obligations. It will be up to the courts to decide this question. However, the following examples may assist:

> **EXAMPLE**
> 1. A worker's request for a pay rise will not amount to a grievance hearing unless it is specifically provided for in the contract, or it raises issues of equal pay.
> 2. A complaint following refusal of a request for new terms and conditions (for example, a request for car parking facilities) will not amount to a grievance where these are not already provided for in the contract. However, if the complaint is made by a disabled worker who needs such facilities in order to attend work, the employer may be under a statutory duty to the worker, in which case the right to be accompanied would apply.
> 3. A complaint about the application of a contractual grading or promotional exercise will amount to a grievance.
> 4. Grievances arising out of day-to-day friction between fellow workers are unlikely to involve breach of a legal duty unless the friction develops into incidents of bullying or harassment, which would give rise to a legal duty of care.

However, it is generally good practice to allow workers to be accompanied at a formal grievance meeting even when the statutory right does not apply.

Choice of companion

The worker's companion can be a **fellow worker** or a **trade union official**, and it is for the worker and not the employer to decide (ss 1, 119 TULRCA 1992; s 10(3) ERelA 1999).

6782

The employment **contract** may extend the category of person who may accompany the worker, for example to include a partner, spouse or legal representative. For example, if a worker is **disabled**, the employer should consider whether it might be reasonable to allow him to be accompanied by his partner or spouse because of his disability.

> **MEMO POINTS** A companion can only attend in a **union capacity** if he is either a full-time official, or certified by his union as having the necessary experience or training to perform such a role. This applies to all workplaces regardless of whether there is a recognised trade union.

The **employer can refuse** the worker's request to be accompanied if it is not reasonable. It would, for example, not be reasonable for a worker to insist on being accompanied by a colleague:
- whose presence would prejudice the hearing;
- who might have a conflict of interest; or
- who is located at a geographically remote site when there is someone suitably qualified on site.

6783

6784 The person who the worker chooses as his companion has the **right to refuse to accompany** him. If he accepts, he has the right to a reasonable amount of **paid time off** during working hours to participate in and prepare for the hearing (¶3910) (s 10(6) ERelA 1999).

Training

6785 Training will be important both for employers and trade unions. Managers will need to know and be able to apply the rules and procedures. Unions should ensure their officials are both experienced in performing this role and provided with periodic refresher training. Organisations may benefit from joint management/trade union training.

Arranging the hearing

6786 The employer is entitled to set the time and date of the hearing. However, it is **good practice** to agree a mutually convenient time and location and, where possible, the companion should have a say in the date and time of a hearing. Where the **chosen companion cannot attend** on the date proposed, the worker can offer an alternative time and date so long as it is reasonable, and is within the following 5 working days (s 10(4)(5) ERelA 1999). A "working day" does not include Saturdays, Sundays, Christmas Day, Good Friday, or statutory bank holidays (s 13(6) ERelA 1999).

It may be unreasonable for the worker to propose a new date where he knows that the relevant manager is going to be unavailable, unless another manager could conduct the hearing.

6787 If the companion is **disabled**, the employer should cater for this by considering whether physical adjustments are necessary, in the same way as he would for a worker's disability.

Companion's role

6788 **Before** the hearing takes place, the worker should inform the employer who his companion will be. In certain circumstances, it may be useful for the companion and employer to make contact before the hearing (for example, where the companion is an official of a non-recognised trade union).

The companion has the **right to address** the hearing in order to (s 10(2A)-(2C) ERelA 1999 as amended by s 37 ERelA 2004):
– confer with the worker;
– put across the worker's case;
– sum up the worker's case; and
– respond on the worker's behalf to any view expressed at the hearing.

However, the companion has **no right** to:
– answer questions on the worker's behalf;
– address the hearing if the worker does not want him to; or
– prevent the employer from explaining his case.

Beyond that, it is for the employer to decide the scope of the companion's involvement. Given the importance of his role, it is **good practice** to allow the worker's companion to ask questions and participate as fully as possible.

Enforcement and remedies

6790 A worker can complain to an employment tribunal if his employer **fails to comply with a reasonable request** to be accompanied, or if the employer **refuses to rearrange** to a reasonably convenient date (s 11(1) ERelA 1999).

The tribunal can award **compensation** of up to 2 weeks' pay (this will be subject to the statutory cap – ¶2923). If the worker can show that his lack of opportunity to be accompanied rendered a dismissal unfair, or was discriminatory, then compensation may also be awarded for those complaints.

6791 A worker can also complain to the tribunal if his employer **subjects him to any detriment** as a result of his exercising, or seeking to exercise, his right to be accompanied or to have a hearing rescheduled (s 12 ERelA 1999), or for acting or seeking to act as a companion (and, in the case of trade union officials, regardless of whether he has the same employer as the worker exercising the right to be accompanied).

If a worker is **dismissed** on the ground that he exercised, or sought to exercise, the right to be accompanied or the right to have a hearing rescheduled, or for acting or seeking to **act as a companion** (and, in the case of trade union officials, regardless of whether he has the same employer as the worker exercising the right to be accompanied), that dismissal will be automatically unfair (¶8390).

6793

Further, **unfair dismissal protection** and compensation, including the right to interim relief (¶8700), is extended to apply to "workers", as well as "employees" (s 12(5), (6) ERelA 1999).

CHAPTER 20

Payroll and NIC

OUTLINE

SECTION 1 **PAYE**	6810
A General principles	6810
Persons liable	6812
Income liable	6814
Taxable period	6817
B PAYE deductions	6820
Setting up a new payroll	6821
1 PAYE codes	6825
2 Calculation	6840
3 New and leaving employees	6850
4 Payment	6860
Electronic payments	6864
Non-electronic payments	6867
Interest	6869
5 Annual summaries	6875
C Other payments and deductions	6890
1 Benefits and expense payments	6895
Dispensations	6900
PAYE settlement agreements	6902

2 State imposed payments and deductions	6905
SSP, SMP, SAP and SPP	6907
Student loan deductions	6911
SECTION 2 **NICs in relation to employment**	6925
A General concepts	6925
Liability for contributions	6928
National Insurance number	6933
B Contributions	6940
1 Class 1 contributions	6940
2 Class 1A contributions	6980
3 Class 1B contributions	6990
C Overseas issues	7000
1 General principles	7005
2 Application of the rules	7020

6800 The Pay As You Earn (PAYE) system is a method of **collecting income tax at source** from employment income, pensions and taxable state benefits. Other topics which are closely related to PAYE earnings are benefits, expenses, and statutory payments, all of which are administered by the employer, and interact closely with PAYE deductions.

Employed earners and their employers must also **pay National Insurance contributions** (NICs). The mechanics of the PAYE system are also used for collecting NICs.

Construction Industry Scheme (CIS)

6802 There are special provisions for certain payments made to subcontractors in the construction industry. The main contractor may have obligations to:
– deduct tax from such payments;
– pay the tax over to HMRC;
– maintain the statutory records; and
– submit returns.

The definition of a contractor is widely drawn, and can include any person whose average annual expenditure on construction operations exceeds £1 million. For further details see *Tax Memo* or HMRC's website at flmemo.co.uk/em6802

SECTION 1
PAYE

A. General principles

6810 The aim of the PAYE system is to ensure that the correct amount of tax is deducted from each individual's income, according to his personal circumstances, and paid to HMRC at regular intervals. The administrative burden is placed on the employer, who has four main obligations:
– to calculate and deduct the correct amounts;
– to pay the correct amounts over to HMRC by the correct day;
– to keep detailed records for each employee, and make appropriate reports to HMRC; and
– to provide each employee with the appropriate information so he can check the deductions made, and complete his self-assessment tax return if relevant.

Persons liable

6812 All **employers** are automatically obliged to operate PAYE for their employees, if they have a presence in the UK. For these purposes, the term "employer" is deemed to include the payers of taxable pension income (such as scheme administrators) and taxable state benefits (the Department for Work and Pensions (DWP)). The term "**employee**" includes full and part-time employees, casual labourers, pensioners, directors and office holders.

There are **special rules** in the following situations:

Situation	Details	Person liable	Reference
Agency workers [1]	If: – client pays worker direct; – agency is overseas; or – client pays someone else overseas (i.e. not the worker or agency)	Client	s 688 ITEPA 2003
	Otherwise	Agency	
Intermediaries	If an employee works for, and is paid by, a person who is not the contractual employer	Intermediary [2]	s 687 ITEPA 2003
	Individual caught by personal service company rules, so that deemed employment income arises		
Employees of a contractor	Employees work for a client while being employed by a contractor	Contractor, but can also be client [3]	s 691 ITEPA 2003
Tips distributed by person who is not employer [4]	Independent person, known as the troncmaster, distributes the tips Employer has no involvement in the distribution	Troncmaster	s 692 ITEPA 2003; reg 100 SI 2003/2682
Employee of overseas employer	Working for an entity which has presence in the UK (e.g. a branch) Irrelevant who pays employee's earnings	UK entity [5]	s 689 ITEPA 2003

Situation	Details	Person liable	Reference
No UK employer or intermediary	Working for an entity which has no UK presence	Employee	regs 141-147 SI 2003/2682

1. This distinction is for PAYE purposes only.
2. Where the intermediary fails to deduct tax under PAYE, the end client becomes ultimately responsible.
3. HMRC can issue a direction to the client to make deductions under PAYE.
4. Employer must notify HMRC where a tronc commences, and the following published guidance applies:
– cash gratuities paid direct to the employee must be declared by him to HMRC and an adjustment will be made to his PAYE code. There is no entry to be made on the payroll;
– gratuities (cash, credit card or cheque) collected by the employer, and paid to the employee, should be subject to PAYE operated by the employer; and
– gratuities collected by the employer which are passed to the troncmaster must be subject to PAYE operated by the troncmaster. Alternatively, the employer can operate PAYE as the troncmaster's agent, so long as separate records are retained by the troncmaster.
For NICs treatment, see ¶6946.
5. Where the employee is in UK for fewer than 60 days, income tax is not due and PAYE is not required to be operated.

Income liable

6814 An immediate deduction under PAYE **applies to** all taxable cash payments (including cash vouchers) received from the employment relationship, including termination payments, pensions and statutory payments for sickness and parenting (s 683 ITEPA 2003). In practice, with the exception of benefits in kind and reimbursed expenses, any items treated as employment income are earnings for this purpose.

In addition, a PAYE deduction must be operated on any round sum allowances. The employee may then make a claim for tax relief in respect of any qualifying expenditure (¶3278).

6815 As a general rule, **payments in kind** are not subject to immediate deductions under the PAYE scheme (although they will be taken into account when the PAYE code for the next tax year is calculated).

> MEMO POINTS However, in a bid to counter perceived avoidance, immediate PAYE deductions must be made in respect of payments in the form of **readily convertible assets**, basically assets where the employer has already arranged a sale for the employee or a market exists. The amount liable to PAYE is the cost to the employer of providing the employee with the asset.
> In addition, **non-cash vouchers** will be liable where they are can be exchanged for cash, or a readily convertible asset.

Taxable period

6817 The **tax year runs** from 6 April to 5 April in the following year, for example the 2012-2013 tax year started on 6 April 2012 and ends on 5 April 2013. Most employees are paid weekly or monthly and therefore the tax year is **divided into** tax weeks and months, starting on 6 April. Tax months therefore end on the 5th day of each calendar month.

A tax year contains 52 weeks. However, as a calendar year has 52 weeks and an extra day (or two in a leap year), it is possible for employees to be paid during tax week 53, for which there are special rules.

B. PAYE deductions

6820 The employer has many obligations concerning the calculation and deduction of PAYE and the administrative requirements for earnings. Every employer must run a payroll, which identifies each employee, the gross amount paid, and the deductions withheld and paid over to HMRC.

For the administrative requirements applicable to benefits in kind, see ¶6895.

Setting up a new payroll

6821 When setting up a payroll system, the employer should **notify** HMRC. The payroll will be given a unique PAYE reference which should be recorded on any correspondence. There is also substantial guidance for employers on the HMRC and GOV.UK websites (flmemo.co.uk/em6821a and flmemo.co.uk/em6821b respectively).

1. PAYE codes

6825 A PAYE code is issued by HMRC to tell the employer how much of an employee's salary can be paid without the deduction of tax (SI 2003/2682).

The code generally consists of up to 3 digits and a suffix letter (although in some circumstances the letter will be a prefix, or there may be no numbers).

6826 A **notice** (**P2**) showing the calculation will be issued to the **employee**, who can object to it, or it can subsequently be amended where his circumstances change. The **employer** will **receive notification** of the code to use (on **P6**), but not details of the calculation. He should continue to use the code until notified by HMRC of any amendments. At the **start of a new tax year**, the employer should follow the guidance on notices **P7X** and **P9X**, and if any other alterations are required due to Budget changes, he will be informed on notice **P6(T)** in respect of each affected employee.

Where an employer has **not received a PAYE code** in respect of an employee, he must notify HMRC where any payment he makes exceeds the PAYE threshold (£156 per week or £675 per month for 2012/13, and £182 or £787 per month for 2013/14).

6827 When an individual first **starts work** for an employer, the PAYE code is usually notified on form P45 (¶6850).

If there is a **change to** the employee's **circumstances** during the tax year, a new P2 notice will be issued, and the employer will be informed via a new P6 notice.

Number

6829 The number usually **indicates** the amount of tax-free salary for a tax year, with the exception of K codes (¶6833). The number is calculated by adding together all the allowances to which an individual is entitled, and then reducing this for anything on which tax needs to be recovered, taking into account the employee's personal circumstances.

Once the total figure is calculated, the last digit is dropped to give the PAYE code number.

Letter

6831 The letter generally **indicates** the type of personal allowance to which the employee is entitled, and is used by HMRC to make re-coding easier.

6832 A **standard code** will include one of the following letters as the suffix, each corresponding to a different type of personal allowance and in some cases the expected highest rate of tax applicable. If allowances are changed, which usually happens in the Budget, HMRC can normally issue the employer with instructions on how to alter all codes with the same suffix, avoiding the need to issue revised codes for every single employee.

Letter	Meaning
L	Personal allowance
P	Maximum age related allowance for individuals under 75
Y	Maximum age related allowance for individuals aged at least 75

MEMO POINTS As an exception, where the suffix is the **letter T**, it means that the code must be reviewed annually by HMRC and the employer cannot automatically amend it. HMRC will issue a new code to take account of any changes.

The following **special codes** operate in a different way.

Letter	Meaning	Situation where normally used
0T	Tax to be deducted in the order of basic rate, higher rate, then additional rate, with no allowances	Allowances already used against other income
NT	No tax to be deducted	Employee overseas
BR	Basic rate tax to be deducted with no relief for allowances	Employee has more than one employment and is using his allowances against the other employment income
D (followed by a number)	Whole of the employee's salary to be taxed at the higher rate where the number is 0, or at the additional rate if the number is 1	For some directors, or individual liable to higher or additional rate tax who have more than one employment
K (followed by a number)	Creates additional taxable pay because code deductions (e.g. benefits in kind) exceed allowances	Employee with sizeable benefits
E	Emergency code which gives personal allowance only	Employee starting work with no previous code

Individuals with **more than one employment** require separate PAYE codes for each employment. The personal allowance will generally be given in full against the earnings from one of those employments.

2. Calculation

Many payroll systems are **computerised and automatically calculate** the PAYE deductions. Otherwise, there are **two manual methods** which can be used:
– HMRC PAYE tax tables; or
– the alternative method, where the employer calculates the PAYE deductions using the actual tax rates and thresholds. Note that the taxable pay to date must still be calculated using the HMRC pay adjustment tables.
For further details, see *Tax Memo* or HMRC Booklet E13.

Recording requirements

Whichever method is used, a separate record must be maintained of the pay and tax deductions on a cumulative basis for each employee. The official form for recording the information is the **deductions working sheet**, **form P11**. There is no requirement to use the P11 (or an approved substitute) but, in all cases, the information required to complete the P11 must be maintained in some format. The P11 has a row for each tax week during the year, and entries should be made on the row for the tax week during which the payment is made.

> MEMO POINTS If the employer has agreed that the **employee is to be paid free of tax**, or a fixed amount after deductions, the actual payment is deemed to be the net salary and must therefore be grossed up. Special tax tables are provided for this purpose, and a special deductions working sheet (**P11 (FOT)**) must be used.

Retention

An employer is **obliged** to retain full details of the pay and benefits provided to his employees. This includes all the payroll records and other supporting documents, for example time sheets and petty cash vouchers. These records must be retained for a minimum of 3 years from the end of the tax year to which they relate.

Incorrect deductions

6846 It is the **responsibility of the employer** to ensure that the correct deductions are made from the employee's salary. The position for incorrect deductions depends on whether the mistake is discovered during the same tax year.

If the mistake is **discovered** after the **end of the tax year**, it is not possible to correct the error. Therefore, HMRC should be informed of the full circumstances of the case. If the mistake is discovered **during the tax year**, and the mistake is that **too much tax** has been deducted, the P11 should be annotated with the correct figures as appropriate (while leaving the original entries legible). A refund should then be made to the employee at the next pay day. If, however, there has been an **underdeduction** of tax, the employer is held responsible and usually the tax is recovered from him. HMRC must be informed of the error as soon as possible, and a determination will be issued.

MEMO POINTS   The employer may **appeal** the determination, otherwise the amount stated becomes final after 30 days have elapsed from the issue of the notice.

6847 An **employee will be obliged** to pay further tax where HMRC accept that:
– a genuine error occurred and that the employer took reasonable care; or
– the employee was complicit in the underdeduction, and had knowledge of it.

This will usually be achieved by amending the PAYE code. Under no circumstances may the employer simply make an increased deduction from the employee's next earnings.

An **employer may request** in writing that an HMRC direction is made to recover underpaid PAYE from an employee.

MEMO POINTS   1. The **procedure** is as follows:
– the employer must request in writing that a direction is made;
– if this request is refused, the employer has 30 days in which to appeal; and
– if the request is authorised, a notice will be sent to the employee who then has 30 days in which to appeal.
2. The grounds of an **appeal** must be one of the following:
– the employer did not take reasonable care;
– the employer did not act in good faith; or
– the amount of the tax in the notice is incorrect.

3. New and leaving employees

New employees

6850 The **employee** is required to **supply form P45** in respect of his previous employment to his new employer, and this automatically gives the employer sufficient information to process the payroll.

The **employer** must complete part 3 of the form and submit it online to HMRC.

6851 If the employee **does not supply** form P45, it is usually **necessary to complete form P46**, unless the employee is going to work for the employer for less than a week. The employee and the employer should each complete the relevant sections of the form, which should then be submitted online to HMRC.

The following codes should be used until another code is notified by HMRC.

Employee's situation	PAYE code
Has not signed form P46	0T on non-cumulative basis
First employment since the preceding 6 April, and the employee has not since received: – jobseeker's allowance or taxable employment and support allowance [1]; or – a retirement pension or an occupational pension	E

Employee's situation	PAYE code
Not receiving a retirement pension or an occupational pension and since the preceding 6 April has: – had another employment, but is no longer receiving any earnings from it; or – received jobseeker's allowance or taxable employment and support allowance [1] but this has now ceased	E week1/month1 basis
Has another employment which is continuing or is in receipt of a retirement pension or occupational pension.	BR
1. The Government plans to phase in a new welfare benefit, Universal Credit (a new single payment for people who are looking for work or who are on a low income), from 2013 to replace income-based jobseeker's allowance, income-related employment and support allowance, income support, child tax credits, working tax credits, and housing benefit.	

MEMO POINTS Details of employees who are **seconded to work in the UK** while remaining employed by an overseas employer should be entered on form P46(Expat).

Leaving employees

When an employee leaves the employment, the **employer must** usually:
– complete **form P45**; and
– annotate the deductions working sheet (**form P11**) with the employee's leaving date.

Where a **payment** is made to the employee **after the issue** of the P45, then the employer must deduct PAYE from the payment on a non-cumulative basis using code 0T.

If the **employee retires** and the employer is paying a future pension, this is not a cessation of the employment and form P45 is not required. Instead, **form P46(Pen)** must be completed and submitted online to HMRC within 14 days of the change of circumstances. A copy of the form should also be given to the employee within the same period.

MEMO POINTS 1. **Agencies** must issue a P45 to an agency worker when the worker stops doing work for the agency, or when the agency has not paid him for 3 months.
2. **On the death** of:
a. an employee, the employer must provide a P45, deduct tax at the basic rate on any taxable payments made after the issue of the form, and submit it online to HMRC; or
b. a pensioner, pension payers should continue to deduct tax, except for payments where the P45 has been issued and the payment is made in the next tax year. In this case, basic rate tax should be deducted.
In either case, no information needs to be provided on the P45 regarding the personal representatives or payments to be made.

Form P45 shows the pay and tax details to the date of leaving, the last tax week/month for which the employee was paid and the last recorded PAYE code.

The form is in 4 parts:

Part	Function
1	Former employer should submit it online to HMRC
1A	For the employee to keep
2	For the new employer to retain
3	New employer completes it and submits it online to HMRC

If **no further employment is taken up**, the form can be used to obtain a refund of tax if appropriate, for example in respect of the personal allowances for which relief has not yet been given. Alternatively a pension payer, or the unemployment office, may require it.

Failure to submit forms online

Penalties apply to employers who fail to submit their joiner and leaver information online, subject to an appeal on the grounds that either:
– the required return has been submitted;

- the amount of penalty is incorrect; or
- a reasonable excuse applies.

4. Payment

6860 The due date for the payment of deductions to HMRC is independent of when the employee receives his pay.

Amount

6862 The amount which must be paid to HMRC is calculated as follows (reg 68 SI 2003/2682):

	£
Income tax	X
Class 1 primary NICs	X
Class 1 secondary NICs	X
Student loan repayments	X
CIS deductions	X
	X
Less: Refunds of tax and NICs to employees [1]	(X)
SMP, SAP, SPP [2]	(X)
Recoverable SSP [2]	(X)
PAYE due	X

Note:
1. Paid out of income tax deducted where possible.
2. Paid out of NICs deducted where possible. Excludes any amounts funded separately by HMRC.

> MEMO POINTS 1. For **foreign employees** who come to work in the UK, some employers agree to meet the UK tax bill and provide a fixed net salary. This is known as tax equalisation. There is a system of modified PAYE which applies in this situation, which allows the employer to make monthly estimated payments of PAYE, based on the grossed-up salary, by the usual due dates. Any shortfall is then payable by 31 January following the affected tax year, although interest will still run from April. The due date for the report of any non-cash benefits (on forms P11D and P11D(b)) is also delayed until 31 January following the affected tax year.
> 2. Employers no longer have any involvement in **working tax credits**.

Electronic payments

6864 If the employer has **250 or more employees**, PAYE must be paid electronically, on time and in full, otherwise interest and penalties may apply (reg 199 SI 2003/2682).

6865 The **due date** for electronic payments is the 22nd of the month.

> MEMO POINTS Where the 22nd falls on a **weekend or bank holiday**, the payment must reach HMRC's bank account no later than the last working day before the 22nd.

Non-electronic payments

6867 If the employer has **fewer than 250 employees**, PAYE can be paid via cheque. The normal **due date** is 14 days after the end of the relevant tax month (reg 69 SI 2003/2682).

By **exception**, employers may make quarterly payments where the **average monthly PAYE is less than** £1,500. Payments must be made within 14 days of the end of each quarter which, for these purposes, end on 5 July, 5 October, 5 January and 5 April.

Deductions made using the **direct collection method** are also made quarterly.

Interest

6869 Interest is automatically **charged** on any amounts outstanding on 19 April (22 April for electronic payments) following the end of the tax year. The amount outstanding is the net due after deducting any amounts recoverable from HMRC. Interest runs from the due date until the date payment is made.

Interest will also be due on any amounts **overpaid**, and will run from the due date (or date of payment if later) until the date a refund is made.

Penalties

Unless a time to pay arrangement has been made, penalties apply to late payments of PAYE. There is a right of appeal against all penalties, and no penalty will be charged if there is a reasonable excuse for the failure.

6870

5. Annual summaries

The tax year end is a busy time for employers, because compliance for the tax year just ended is required, and the new tax year must be started.

6875

In addition to the forms completed on an ongoing basis, the employer must complete a number of **forms at the end of the tax year** as detailed in the table below. Employers providing employees with benefits in kind or paying for expenses must also complete **returns regarding these benefits and expense payments**. These are detailed in ¶6895.

6877

Almost all employers must now submit certain forms electronically, as indicated in the table below.

Form	Function	Due date	Electronic submission required?
P35	Annual summary of deductions employer has made	19 May	✓
P38A	Annual summary of employees receiving pay gross	19 May	✓
P14	Employee specific summary of pay and deductions made	19 May	✓
P60	Employee's copy of P14	31 May	N/A
P11D	Employee specific summary of benefits and expenses (employees earning £8,500 +)	6 July	✓
P9D	Employee's summary of benefits and expenses (lower paid employees)	6 July	✓

MEMO POINTS 1. The following employers are **exempt** from the rule requiring electronic submission:
– those employers whose religious beliefs are incompatible with the use of electronic communications;
– employers who are authorised to operate the simplified deduction scheme for personal employees (i.e. those who provide domestic/personal service for the employer or his family at the employer's home) and who have not received an incentive payment for filing online; and
– care and support employers (i.e. those who employ a person to provide domestic/personal services at or from the employer's home to the employer or his family, and the recipient of those services has a physical or mental disability, or is elderly or infirm), who have not received an online filing incentive payment in respect of any of the last 3 tax years.
2. Where a **termination payment** has been made in the tax year, the employer must report this by the following 6 July.
3. Where any event involving **shares or options** awarded to employees has occurred in the tax year, the employer may need to make a report.

For the employer The employer's annual summary is known as **form P35**. This form shows the total NIC and PAYE deductions for all employees and summarises the information from each deductions working sheet. The employer must sign and **submit** the form to HMRC by 19 May following the end of the tax year. HMRC apply quality standard checks to all P35 returns. These ensure all boxes have been completed and the figures add up.

6878

If **no return is due** (i.e. no deductions worksheet has been completed for any employee in the tax year), HMRC should be informed.

6879 Where **no deductions have been made** during the year for **certain employees**, the employer must also complete and submit **form P38A** by 19 May following the end of the tax year. The employees concerned are those who either:
– worked for the employer for more than a week;
– earned in excess of £100 in the tax year; or
– earned in excess of the PAYE threshold at any time.

6880 **For the employee** The annual summary of pay, tax and NICs for an individual employee is known as **form P14**, which must be completed for each employee on the payroll at any time during the tax year who has earned more than the PAYE threshold. The form is in fact three copies of the same information prepared for the following recipients:
a. HMRC (tax copy);
b. HMRC (National Insurance copy); and
c. the employee, whose copy is actually called form P60.

The first two copies of form P14 must be **submitted by** 19 May following the end of the tax year.

Form P60 must be provided to each employee who is on the payroll on the last day of the tax year by the following 31 May. There is no requirement to provide a form P60 for any employees who left during the tax year, although a leaver is entitled to ask for the details in order that he may complete his tax return. The employer is allowed to provide a **duplicate** P60 on request, as long as the copy is clearly marked as such.

6881 **Penalties** A penalty regime is in place regarding the **late filing** of returns. Penalties also apply to most **incorrect** PAYE forms (excluding P11Ds and P9Ds), but no penalty will be levied unless a taxpayer has been careless, or made a deliberate error by understating or concealing the tax due.

> MEMO POINTS See *Tax Memo* for further information concerning penalties.

C. Other payments and deductions

6890 The employer often remunerates his employees in payments other than cash, namely benefits in kind. In addition, the employer is required to make certain payments in compliance with state imposed obligations.

1. Benefits and expense payments

Reporting obligations

6895 An employer providing an employee with benefits in kind, or paying for expenses, has reporting obligations to HMRC. The returns enable HMRC to adjust the employee's PAYE code to collect the additional tax due on any benefits, and also provide information for the employee to complete his self-assessment return, where relevant.

Subject to any exemption (see memo point to ¶6877), employers must **submit** these forms **online**.

Form	Function	Due date	Electronic submission required?
P11D	Employee specific summary of benefits and expenses (employees earning £8,500+)	6 July	✓
P9D	Employee's summary of benefits and expenses (lower paid employees)	6 July	✓

An employer **must make** a return in respect of benefits provided to employees and expenses incurred, **unless covered** by a dispensation or PAYE settlement agreement. The return required is usually a **form P11D**, with the exception of a non-director employee who earns less than £8,500 per annum (¶3146), when a **form P9D** is used instead. A form must be completed for each employee in receipt of taxable benefits in kind or expenses during the tax year, including employees who have left.

Further, the employer must submit a **declaration** in respect of all forms P11D (**form P11D(b)**) confirming that all required returns have been made and submitted. All forms and the P11D(b) must be **submitted** to HMRC **by** 6 July following the end of the tax year. Where no P11Ds are due, the declaration should still be completed and submitted by the due date.

The employer must also **provide the employee** with a copy of the information (not necessarily a copy of the form) by 6 July. Employees who have left may ask for return information within 3 years from the end of the tax year of leaving.

> MEMO POINTS For lower paid employees, the **P9D** is a much simpler form which only requires details of expense payments, accommodation provided, benefits which are able to be realised in cash, and vouchers. There is no requirement to file a P11D(b), as the submission of a copy of each P9D is sufficient.

6897

In addition, a **form P46(Car)** is required when:
– a car is first provided to a relevant employee (broadly, directors and those employees earning at a rate of more than £8,500 per annum);
– an additional car is provided to the employee;
– the employee ceases to have a company car; or
– a lower paid employee (those earning less than £8,500 per annum) for whom a car is provided starts to earn more than £8,500 per annum.

The P46(Car) must be **submitted within** 28 days of the end of the quarter in which the circumstances change. Quarters end on 5 July, 5 October, 5 January and 5 April.

> MEMO POINTS Since 6 April 2009, a **replacement of a car** provided to an employee (e.g. an upgrade or newer model) is no longer a reportable event.

6898

Penalties A penalty regime is in place regarding the **late filing** of returns, or where an **incorrect return** is submitted.

> MEMO POINTS There are no penalties for failing to file or filing late form P46(Car). However, if the form is delayed, the employee will not be paying the correct amount of tax, and so he will face a tax bill at the end of the tax year.

6899

Dispensations

Where HMRC are satisfied that employees provided with a particular expense payment would be entitled to a tax deduction for that amount, a dispensation may be **granted** to the employer (s 65 ITEPA 2003). An employee will be **excluded** from a dispensation where it would result in his earnings being reduced below £8,500 per annum.

A dispensation authorises the employer not to report the specific expense, and therefore the employee is not required to submit any related claim (¶3278). This is simply a matter of administrative convenience, and does not result in a reduction of tax, merely in a reduction of forms.

Items covered by the dispensation are not subject to income tax or NICs, and commonly include business travel, subsistence and professional subscriptions. However, taxable benefits, such as a company car or medical insurance cannot be included.

6900

The employer should **apply** for a dispensation by completing **form P11DX**, setting out the items which he feels should be covered. HMRC will require evidence of the employer's control procedures to ensure that only appropriate items are included, and where controls are weak, the dispensation will be restricted.

Once a dispensation has been agreed, the employer will be sent a **notice setting out** the exact **terms** of the agreement, which will specify the expenses which are covered. The dispensation **remains valid** for as long as the circumstances do not change. HMRC may

6901

withdraw the dispensation by giving notice to the employer. It is important that the terms of the dispensation are reviewed on a regular basis (at least annually) to ensure that the employer is not vulnerable to an HMRC challenge over the treatment of employee benefits and expenses.

> **MEMO POINTS** 1. **Control procedures** include checks and verification by someone other than the employee incurring the expense, and where possible claims should be vouched.
> 2. In relation to **controlling directors**, a dispensation will only be granted where HMRC are satisfied that no additional tax is at risk. However, this should not deter small businesses from applying, as dispensations are often granted (at least in part). In particular, HMRC have confirmed that where an accountant reviews all expense reimbursements in the course of his usual work (e.g. to prepare the VAT returns), this would be considered to be an independent check.
> 3. The effect of a dispensation can be **backdated** to the beginning of the tax year in which the application was made.
> 4. **Mileage payments** made to employees for use of their own car are not covered by a dispensation. If the payments made are at or below the published HMRC rates (¶3303), no reporting is necessary. Higher rates should be reported on form P11D.
> 5. Employers have the option to use the benchmark rates for **daily subsistence payments**. There is no need to report such payments which are at or below the published HMRC rates (¶3307). The employer may still agree a bespoke system of payments with HMRC under a dispensation.

PAYE settlement agreements

6902 Where it would prove **difficult or impractical** to calculate the value of certain benefits and expenses provided to employees, the employer may decide to enter into a PAYE settlement agreement (PSA) (regs 105-107 SI 2003/683). Under the agreement, the **employer pays** tax and Class 1B NICs on the items covered by the PSA, and these items are excluded from any other PAYE return. As the settlement of an employee's liability is a benefit in itself, the tax due is calculated on a grossed-up basis (i.e. the employer must estimate the amount of the benefit liable to tax, relate this to the employees who have enjoyed the benefit, and gross it up at each employee's marginal rate of tax (basic, higher or additional)). Therefore, although the PSA may reduce the employer's administrative burden, there is a real tax cost which the employer suffers.

The **types of items** which may be included in an agreement are – HMRC SP 5/96:
– minor benefits, e.g. small gifts;
– benefits paid irregularly, such as relocation expenses in excess of £8,000;
– benefits shared between employees, e.g. an expensive staff party; or
– benefits for which it is difficult to compute the tax using the normal rules.

PSAs are **negotiated** annually with HMRC, at any time before 6 July following the tax year. Once a PSA is in force, it is **renewable annually** provided circumstances do not change. The scope of the PSA may be **amended** by negotiation.

6903 The **due date** for tax under a PSA is 19 October (22 October if paying electronically) following the end of the tax year to which it relates. Interest may be charged on any amounts unpaid at that date.

Taxed award schemes

6904 Entities with a UK presence who provide non-cash incentives to either their own or another entity's employees can apply to HMRC's Incentive Award Unit to set up a taxed award scheme. As most employers prefer to use a PSA instead, these schemes are usually entered into by third parties only.

2. State imposed payments and deductions

6905 Payroll systems are being used to administer certain state benefits. In addition to statutory sick pay, and statutory parental payments, employers are also required to make deductions in respect of student loan repayments. HMRC provide all employers with a manual providing guidance on the operation of each scheme and the tables used in calculating payments.

MEMO POINTS The employer may also be bound to make a deduction from his employee's earnings if the courts have made an attachment of earnings order (¶¶3017+).

SSP, SMP, SAP and SPP

Payments of SSP, SMP, SAP and SPP are subject to PAYE and NIC deductions and must be recorded on the deductions working sheet (P11) (¶6842) and on the annual returns (¶¶6877+).

For all other details regarding these payments, see chapter 13, "Sickness, injury and absence", and chapter 14, "Rights of parents and carers".

6907

Student loan deductions

Employers are also responsible for **collecting** student loan payments from employees, which are not deductible for tax or NIC purposes (reg 35 SI 2000/944). The loans are only repayable once the earnings from employment exceed a certain threshold (£15,795 since 6 April 2012). HMRC publish a special table to show the amount of the deduction required.

Student loan deductions should be made where HMRC have sent a start notification, and should not be made after a stop notification. The P11 should be annotated to indicate that deductions are being made.

6911

MEMO POINTS 1. **Earnings** is measured in the same way as for Class 1 NIC purposes.
2. If a **new employee** provides a P45 which indicates that student loan deductions are due (or ticks the relevant box on form P46), the new employer should make the deductions without notification from HMRC.
3. If an **employee leaves** while student loan deductions are being made, the P45 should be annotated accordingly.

SECTION 2

NICs in relation to employment

A. General concepts

The UK maintains a National Insurance fund which aims to provide subsistence level benefits to those in need. All individuals covered by the scheme are given a National Insurance number. The collection of National Insurance is administered by the National Insurance Contributions Office (NICO), which is part of HMRC.

6925

Various contributions may be payable in **respect of the employment** of an employed earner, as follows:

Class 1 contributions are payable in respect of earnings by both the employer and employee.

Class 1A contributions are paid in respect of benefits in kind by the employer.

Class 1B contributions are payable by the employer where he has entered into a PAYE settlement agreement with HMRC (¶6902).

For National Insurance purposes, an individual is an **employed earner** if he is gainfully employed in the UK receiving employment income (s 2 SSCBA 1992). Basically, the same rules apply to decide whether an individual is an employee for NIC purposes as for income tax, including the provisions relating to personal and managed service companies.

6926

MEMO POINTS An employer can deduct employer's Class 1, Class 1A and Class 1B NICs when computing his own taxable profits (for the purpose of corporation tax or income tax).

Liability for contributions

6928 Liability for contributions **starts** once an individual attains the age of 16. The specific rules for the starting date for each class of contribution are included in the appropriate section.

Liability for most contributions **ceases** when an individual reaches pensionable age, except for contributions payable by the employer in respect of employees (Class 1 secondary, Class 1A and Class 1B) which remain payable after pensionable age is attained.

6929 For men, **pensionable age** is currently 65. For women, the pensionable age is currently increasing from 60 to 65, and this affects women who were born on or after 6 April 1950. The retirement age for both sexes will rise to 66 by October 2020 (Pensions Act 2011).

For more details of the proposals, and for a state pension age calculator, see flmemo.co.uk/em6929

Link between contributions and benefits

6931 The entitlement to certain benefits is linked to an individual's contributions to the fund. In addition, some benefits, known as **contributory benefits**, are paid at a higher level based on contributions. **Non-contributory benefits** are generally paid from the general taxation revenues, rather than from the National Insurance fund, and may be means tested.

To be entitled to the maximum rate of **long-term benefits** an individual has historically been required to have a full contributions record for approximately 90% of their adult life. However, for individuals **reaching state pension age on or after 6 April 2010**, 30 years of contributions will be sufficient to obtain a full basic state pension. Entitlement to **short-term benefits** is based on contributions over a short period, and each benefit has specific rules.

Classes 1, 1A and 1B in relation to employment carry the following entitlements to benefits:

Class	Long-term benefits	Short-term benefits
1 (primary)	Earnings-related state pension [1] Bereavement allowance Widowed parent's allowance Bereavement payment	Employment and support allowance [2] Jobseeker's allowance (contribution based) [2] Maternity allowance
1 (secondary)	None	None
1A	None	None
1B	None	None

1. Employees may decide to opt out of the earnings-related element of the state pension scheme, and make independent arrangements. A reduced level of Class 1 primary contribution is payable in these circumstances.
2. The Government plans to phase in a new welfare benefit, Universal Credit (a new single payment for people who are looking for work or who are on a low income), from 2013 to replace income-based jobseeker's allowance, income-related employment and support allowance, income support, child tax credits, working tax credits, and housing benefit.

National Insurance number

6933 All individuals within the National Insurance scheme are given an identifying number. The National Insurance (NI) number comprises a prefix of two letters, followed by six digits and a single letter suffix, for example AB123456C.

As a rule, an individual is **issued** with an NI number shortly before his 16th birthday. If an individual has not been issued with a number, he should apply for one at a Jobcentre Plus office or contact the National Insurance Registrations Helpline on 0845 915 7006.

When an individual starts work for an employer, he will be asked for his NI number. If the number is not available, the employer may use a **temporary number**, which is comprised of the prefix TN followed by the employee's date of birth in six-digit format and then a suffix of either M if male or F if female (for example TN010795M). If the employee does not provide his proper NI number within 8 weeks, the employer should apply to HMRC, either to trace an existing number or issue a new number as appropriate.

B. Contributions

1. Class 1 contributions

6940 Earnings of an employed earner, such as salary, are liable to Class 1 NICs. Contributions are only payable if earnings reach a minimum level, and the rate of contribution depends on who is paying the contribution. For the rules specific to directors, see ¶6967.

Persons liable

6942 Contributions may be payable by the primary contributor and the secondary contributor:
– the **primary contributor** is the employed earner (referred to throughout as the employee); and
– the **secondary contributor** will usually be the employer or, in the case of an office holder, the body responsible for paying the earnings (referred to throughout as the employer).

Contributions are only payable by employed earners aged 16 and over and any earnings paid before an earner's 16th birthday are ignored. Primary contributions cease being payable once the employee reaches pensionable age (¶6929), and any earnings paid after that date are liable only to secondary contributions, for which there is no upper age limit.

Income liable

6944 Contributions are **payable in respect of** the gross earnings of the employment (Sch 3 SI 2001/1004 and HMRC Leaflet CWG2). Dividend income, rent and interest on loan accounts are therefore excluded.

In the main, **taxable employment income** is liable to Class 1 NICs as shown in the following table (s 3 SSCBA 1992):

Remuneration	Detail	Earnings for Class 1 NIC purposes	Taxable
Wages, salary, overtime and bonuses		✓	✓
Inducement payments		✓	✓
Restrictive covenant payments subject to income tax		✓	✓
Certain employment tribunal awards	A reinstatement order or a re-engagement order An order for the continuation of the employment A protective award (NIC should be calculated on the gross amount of the award)	✓	✓
Payments in lieu of notice where contractual		✓	✓
Redundancy and termination payments		x	✓ (above £30,000)
Damages payment under contract when employee injured		✓	✓
Reimbursed expenses	All business related	x	x
	Not all business related	✓	✓

Remuneration	Detail	Earnings for Class 1 NIC purposes	Taxable
Round sum allowance	Covers specific business expenses only	x	x
	Does not cover specific business expenses	✓	✓
Personal incidental expenses paid	Not exceeding £5 per night for UK trips and £10 per night for overseas trips	x	x
	In excess of above limits	✓	✓
Tax paid on behalf of employee		✓	✓
Council tax for living accommodation not job related		✓	✓
Clothing allowance other than for uniform		✓	✓
Meal allowances		✓	✓
Parking fines		✓	✓
Scholarship income		✓	x
Luncheon vouchers	Up to 15p per day (until 5 April 2013)	x	x
	Excess over 15p per day	✓	✓
Non-cash vouchers	Long service awards	x	x
	Social functions which fulfil the relevant income tax conditions	x	x
	One mobile phone	x	x
	Eye tests and special corrective appliances	x	x
	Health screenings and medical check ups	x	x
	Other vouchers	✓	✓
Childcare vouchers	Up to the weekly limit (¶3173)	x	x
	Above the weekly limit (¶3173)	✓	✓
Payments under the up-front childcare fund		x	x
Loans written off		✓	✓
Share remuneration outside an approved scheme		✓	✓
Statutory pay in respect of parenthood, adoption and sickness		✓	✓

MEMO POINTS The following expenses paid by the employer are **treated slightly differently** under the NIC rules:
– removal expenses, where no Class 1 NIC is payable on any amount. However, Class 1A NIC is due on expenses exceeding $8,000; and
– mileage expenses, where the NIC-free rate is 45p per mile up to any level of mileage.

The following items are **not deductible** for NIC purposes, representing a different treatment from income tax purposes:
– expenses incurred wholly, exclusively and necessarily for the duties of employment by the employee which are not reimbursed by the employer;
– charitable donations under the payroll deduction scheme; or
– employee contributions to registered pension schemes (including both personal and employer-provided schemes).

Class 1 NICs are also payable on the following **payments in kind** (Sch 3 SI 2001/1004): **6945**
a. those which can be exchanged for cash (known as readily convertible assets); and
b. any pecuniary liability of the employee met by the employer, where the employee enters into a contract for any goods or services and the employer pays for it by reimbursing the employee's expenditure or settling the bill directly with the provider, e.g. healthcare insurance.

Tips and gratuities Tips and gratuities are outside the scope of NICs unless the **employer has control** over their distribution. Therefore, cash payments given directly to a waiter are not earnings, but tips included on the credit card slip, and therefore distributed by the employer, are earnings. **6946**

In summary, tips and gratuities are **treated as follows** – HMRC Booklet E24:

Scenario		NIC applies?
No involvement of employer or tronc – tip goes direct to employee		No
Employee has contractual right to precise amount of money sourced from tips		Yes
No contractual right to tip	Employer decides who receives it and how much is received	Yes
	Employer has no such control (independent tronc)	No

Time of recognition

Contributions **become payable** at the earlier of when: **6948**
– the earnings payment is actually made (e.g. when the payment is credited to the employee's bank account); or
– the employee is absolutely entitled to be paid, even if the pay is not drawn until a later date.

Payments in respect of restrictive covenants which were received by an employee after his contract had been terminated are still subject to NICs (*RCI Europe Ltd v Woods* [2003] EWHC 3129 (Ch)).

Where earnings are received in **advance** by an employee who is not a director, the NIC treatment of a payment depends on whether: **6949**
– the employee has an absolute entitlement to the income when the payment is received (when it will be liable to NICs); or
– the payment is effectively a loan of money (which is not liable to NICs).

An inducement payment may be liable to NICs if it relates to the employment, even where that employment has not yet commenced.

a. Calculation

Calculation of the NIC liability requires the application of specific rates to bands of income received in a measured period. The NIC must then be paid to HMRC. **6950**

Earnings periods

An earnings period is simply the amount of time between payments of earnings, and is usually at least a week. **6952**

Earnings periods **must begin** on the first day of the tax year (i.e. 6 April) and run consecutively. This means that weekly or monthly earnings periods will correspond with the tax weeks and months used in the operation of the PAYE system (¶6817).

Where an employee is paid at **regular intervals** (for example monthly), the earnings period is simply the interval at which the employee is usually paid. Where employees are paid at **6953** regular intervals but the actual **date of payment changes**, the earnings period is the regular interval.

Where payments are made **irregularly**, and there is **no overriding regular payment** interval, the earnings period for each payment will be the period for which the earnings are paid (or 1 week if longer).

If an employee receives earnings on **two bases** (for example monthly salary with 6-monthly bonuses), the earnings period is the shortest interval between payments.

> MEMO POINTS   A **leaving** employee may receive payments bundled together which would have been received separately if the employment had continued. In this case, the normal earnings periods will still apply to each payment, as follows:
> – regular payments received after ceasing employment are subject to NICs in the usual manner, as if the ex-employee were still employed; and
> – one-off payments after cessation are subject to a weekly earnings period.

Rates

6955   The rates **depend on**:
– who is liable for the contribution (employee or employer); and
– whether special circumstances apply (¶6965).

The standard rate is by far the most usual case and for 2012/13 the rate of **employee's primary contributions** is 12% on earnings which fall between the employee's primary threshold and upper earnings limit, and 2% on any excess earnings. The standard rate of the **employer's secondary contributions** is 13.8% and applies to all earnings in excess of the employer's earnings threshold, which is set at £144 per week (£624 per month) for 2012/13 (£148 per week (£642 per month) for 2013/14).

Earnings period		Employee's NIC rate
2012/13 weekly thresholds	2012/13 monthly thresholds	
£146 to £817	£634 to £3,540	12%
Over £817	Over £3,540	2%
2013/14 weekly thresholds	2013/14 monthly thresholds	
£149 to £797	£646 to £3,454	12%
Over £797	Over £3,454	2%

> MEMO POINTS   There is also a **lower earnings limit** of £107 per week for 2012/13 and £109 per week for 2013/14, but no contributions are actually payable until earnings exceed the employee's earnings threshold. Weekly earnings between the lower limit and primary threshold carry entitlement to benefits, and employees who earn over the lower limit should still be included on the payroll, even where there is no NIC liability.

Calculation methods

6957   To calculate contributions, the **following methods** can be used:
– the tables provided by HMRC; or
– the exact percentage method. This is generally only used by **computerised payroll systems** (or for directors' earnings) and involves multiplying the exact amount of earnings subject to contributions for the earnings period by the appropriate rate. It must be used where the earnings period is not a multiple of a week or a month (e.g. every 10 days) but is at least a week.

b. Payment

6960   The person **liable** for the payment of both primary and secondary contributions is the employer (secondary contributor), although the primary contributions are recoverable from the employee by deduction from salary (Sch 1 para 3 SSCBA 1992).

Class 1 contributions are generally **collected** via the PAYE system, which determines the interest and penalties which apply to contributions paid late.

MEMO POINTS **Exceptionally**, contributions may be collected via a system known as **direct collection**, which means that the primary contributor is liable for paying contributions to HMRC. The same payment requirements and penalty provisions apply as for contributions paid by the secondary contributor.

Where an **underpayment** of primary contributions has been made as a result of a mistake (i.e. an error in good faith), the employer can recover it by making deductions from the employee's subsequent earnings. The extra amount which can be deducted is, however, limited to the usual primary contributions due on his earnings. If recovery is not made by the end of the tax year following that in which the mistake arose, the employer must suffer any remaining shortfall.

6961

MEMO POINTS 1. Where an employee's earnings from more than one employment are **aggregated**, the primary contributions may be recovered from any part of his earnings.
2. Where an underpayment has occurred, the correct amounts actually due should be entered on the annual **payroll returns**.

c. Special cases

For the following types of individuals, the rules outlined above are modified:
– directors; and
– employees with more than one job.

6965

MEMO POINTS 1. Reduced rate contributions are payable by **married women and widows** who, **before 12 May 1977**, elected to pay reduced contributions, and provided that the woman's circumstances have not changed since (e.g. she has not divorced or remarried after becoming widowed). Any such change must be notified to HMRC.
2. Since 6 April 2012, **contracting-out** of the earnings-related element of the state pension scheme (known as **S2P**) is no longer possible through a money-purchase (defined-contribution) occupational pension scheme, a personal pension or a stakeholder pension, although for the time being contracting out through an occupational salary-related (defined-benefit) scheme is still allowed. Contracting out is now rare, but where contracted out rates apply both primary and secondary contributions are payable at a discounted rate up to a certain point.

Directors

Special rules apply when calculating contributions in respect of directors, because otherwise their remuneration packages could be subject to manipulation resulting in the deferral, or even avoidance, of NICs (HMRC Leaflet CA44).

6967

MEMO POINTS For these purposes a director is **defined** as a:
– member of the board of directors (or similar body) which manages the company;
– single director (or similar person) who manages the company;
– member of the company where the company is managed by its members; or
– shadow director, being any person in accordance with whose directions (other than in a professional capacity) the company directors are accustomed to act.

A director's earnings will **include** all the items treated as earnings for employees, as well as any fees paid to him.

6968

If the director is also an employee of the company, both sets of earnings should be aggregated when calculating the contributions payable.

A director's remuneration is usually approved by the members of the company, and so any amounts **received in advance** of such approval cannot strictly be earnings. However, the rule for NICs is that income is recognised at the earlier of when:
– payment is made; and
– earnings are approved.

6969

If any income is voted to a director but subsequently waived or refunded to the company, it is still included as earnings when voted.

6970 Where the director **maintains an account with the company** to which remuneration is usually credited, amounts are included as earnings (and therefore liable to NICs) when credited to the account. Provided the account remains in credit, no further contributions are due.

If the **account becomes overdrawn** (or the overdrawn amount increases), contributions will be due if the withdrawal is in anticipation of further earnings being credited to the account. However, where the withdrawal is in anticipation of the introduction of funds from another source (for example dividends), no contributions are payable.

6971 **Rates** **Usually**, each time a director is paid, contributions are calculated on the total earnings to date and any contributions already paid are deducted. Directors are deemed to have an annual earnings period regardless of the interval at which they are paid, so the rates are applied on an annual basis. Where a director resigns his position during the tax year, he will still have an annual earnings period for that tax year.

MEMO POINTS   The only **exception** is where a director is appointed after the start of the tax year in question, in which case the director has a pro-rata annual earnings period. The pro-rata period runs from the date the director was appointed to the end of the tax year and, for these purposes, the tax year is deemed to have 52 weeks (if the director is appointed in week 53, his earnings period will be 1 week).

6972 **Methods of calculation** Directors' NICs may be calculated **using** either:
a. the alternative method, where:
− the director is paid at regular intervals (which is treated as the earnings period);
− the earnings exceed the lower earnings limit; and
− the director agrees to contributions being calculated in this way; or
b. the normal method, in any other case.
Either tables or the exact percentage calculation can be used in conjunction with either method.

MEMO POINTS   The alternative method allows contributions to be calculated in accordance with the normal rules for employees throughout the tax year, with **an adjustment** when making the final earnings payment for the tax year (or the termination of the directorship if earlier). The adjustment recalculates the NIC liability using the annual thresholds. This should lead to a more even spread of NICs, although a large bonus soon after 6 April will result in a large amount of primary Class 1 NICs being due at the end of the year.

More than one employment

6974 Where an employee has more than one employment, each is normally considered separately when calculating NICs. In such cases it is **usual** to pay primary Class 1 NICs as normal in one employment, and apply for deferment in respect of any other. In certain circumstances, an employee may overpay contributions, and he may be entitled to a refund.

As an **exception**, earnings will be combined in the following situations (unless it is too impractical):
− the employments are with the same employer;
− the two employers are carrying out business in association, sharing profits or sharing resources such as accommodation or personnel; or
− where only one employer, or some other person, is treated as the secondary contributor.

Where such **aggregation** applies, the secondary contributors must decide how to operate the primary Class 1 NIC deduction.

2. Class 1A contributions

6980 Contributions are **payable** by the secondary contributor (usually the employer), in respect of benefits in kind (see ¶3150) provided for relevant employees (broadly, directors and those employees earning at a rate of more than £8,500 per annum) (s 10 SSCBA 1992 and HMRC Leaflet CWG5). No contributions are payable in respect of benefits provided to lower paid employees.

The following benefits are **excluded** from liability (Sch 3 SI 2001/1004):
- earnings subject to Class 1 NICs;
- exempt benefits for employment income purposes;
- those included within a PAYE settlement;
- those covered by a dispensation;
- childcare benefits. If provided in a workplace nursery, the whole cost is exempt. Otherwise, the weekly limit is exempt;
- shares in the employer's company. Only if not readily convertible assets. Exemption does not include deemed loans relating to shares which are taxable;
- tips and gratuities (see ¶6946); and
- redundancy payments (current HMRC practice).

Where benefits are provided to employees for business use and any **private use is insignificant**, no NICs will be due. There is no legal definition of insignificant although HMRC have provided guidelines in respect of each type of benefit. This exemption does not apply to the use of cars, boats or aircraft, or the provision of an improvement or extension to living accommodation.

6981

Where **private use is significant** and the employee does not reimburse the employer, NICs will be due on the taxable benefit relating to the mixed use. Unlike for tax purposes, no deduction is made for any business use. For example, Class 1A NICs will be levied on the full cost of an employer-provided chauffeur, even if he drives 50% for business purposes.

Calculation and payment

The employer's declaration form includes a calculation of Class 1A contributions. The method is simply to total all the relevant benefits on the P11D and multiply the total by the Class 1A contribution **rate**, which is set at the standard rate for secondary contributions (¶6955).

6982

Contributions are **payable** in a single amount on 19 July following the tax year, unless payment is being made electronically, when the due date is 22 July. While payments can be made electronically, there is no obligation to do so. Interest may be charged on any amounts paid late.

Reporting requirements

The employer's reporting requirements are satisfied by completion of form P11D(b), which includes a declaration by the employer that the details are fully and truly stated to the best of his knowledge.

6984

The latest date that the form can be submitted is 6 July following the tax year.

3. Class 1B contributions

Where an employer has entered into a **PAYE settlement agreement** (¶6902), known as a PSA, Class 1B NICs are due on the items covered by the agreement, payable in a single lump sum (s 10A SSCBA 1992).

6990

The following **amounts are liable**:
- total value of the items covered by the PSA which would otherwise give rise to a Class 1 or Class 1A NIC liability; and
- the income tax payable by the employer.

Contributions are at the standard **rate** for Class 1 secondary contributions (¶6955) and are **payable** on the same date as the related income tax, i.e. 19 October following the tax year to which it relates (extended to 22 October where payment is being made electronically).

C. Overseas issues

7000 NICs are generally payable by anyone working in the UK. Individuals working in the UK on a short-term basis, and those leaving the UK who wish to maintain their entitlement to benefits, may be able to take advantage of special rules which exist between the members of the European Economic Area (EEA). The UK has also entered into a limited number of reciprocal agreements with certain other countries (¶7035).

> *MEMO POINTS* The term UK includes Great Britain and Northern Ireland because, even though Northern Ireland has its own system, the same principles apply.

1. General principles

7005 The liability for NICs is **linked to** an individual's residence status and whether he is present in the UK. Special rules apply to ensure that individuals do not pay contributions in more than one country during the period in which they arrive in, or leave, the UK.

On arrival in the UK, anyone planning to work should apply for a National Insurance number (¶6933).

Presence

7007 It is usually clear whether an individual is present in the UK, as presence is simply a matter of fact.

> *MEMO POINTS* **Directors** of UK registered companies, if they are not resident in the EEA or countries with which the UK has a reciprocal agreement, may ignore certain visits to the UK to attend board meetings, where:
> – no more than ten board meetings each requiring a maximum presence of 2 days are attended in a year; or
> – if there is only one board meeting, the meeting does not last more than 14 days.

Residence and ordinary residence

7009 There is no statutory **definition** for either residence or ordinary residence for National Insurance purposes. Residence and ordinary residence are a question of fact, and although these terms are generally given their meaning for income tax purposes, there are some differences as set out below.

7010 **Residence** has a greater permanence than presence, and may continue even while an individual is temporarily absent, if the individual intends to remain resident. Where an individual leaves the UK for an unknown period of time, this will usually bring his residence status to an end.

Claiming contributory benefits is a strong indication that an individual is resident.

7011 An individual will be **ordinarily resident** in a country where he normally lives and has a settled mode of life. It can be generally concluded that it is difficult for an individual to make himself not ordinarily resident for NIC purposes, even when he is not present in the UK.

HMRC have set out practical guidelines, which are summarised below.

Factor	Indication of ordinary residence
Home retained in UK during overseas work	Strong
Home available for person's use when he returns from abroad	
Home let while away	Longer lease would indicate not ordinarily resident

Factor	Indication of ordinary residence
Person returns to the UK during a period of employment abroad	The more frequent or longer the UK visits, the stronger the indication
Person visits family who have remained in UK, including holidays at UK home	
Person returns to UK in connection with his overseas work e.g. to present a report or attend training sessions	Not an indication
Partner and/or children are with the person abroad	Probably not ordinarily resident, especially where family home is no longer retained and only occasional visits are made to the UK
Person has lived in UK for a substantial period of time before working abroad	The longer the period, the stronger is the presumption of ordinary residence
Person will return to UK after employment abroad	The earlier the return, the stronger the presumption of ordinary residence
UK bank account maintained	Not particularly relevant
Still registered with UK doctor	

Liability to UK NICs

7013 An **employee** is liable for Class 1 primary contributions if he is either resident, present (subject to temporary absences), or ordinarily resident in the UK at the time of the employment.

7014 Whenever there is a primary contribution, there is usually is a secondary contribution. The **employer** is liable for Class 1 secondary contributions if the employer either:
– is resident or present in the UK when the secondary contributions become payable; or
– has a place of business in the UK at that time.

> MEMO POINTS 1. HMRC consider the following to be a **place of business**, where:
> – the employer's premises are occupied lawfully; and
> – employees undertake activity at the premises, in the course of the employer's business.
> 2. The following are used as **indicators of premises**:
> – a registered office address;
> – a lease or rental agreement;
> – headed paper or business cards showing the address;
> – an entry in the telephone or trade directory; and
> – a name plate.
> 3. An **overseas company** with a UK branch will have a UK place of business, but a UK subsidiary, while itself having a UK presence, will not constitute a UK place of business for its overseas parent.
> 4. If expatriates are outside the scope of UK NICs, no **Class 1A** NICs are payable by the employer even where P11D forms are still completed.

2. Application of the rules

7020 The operation of the above rules means individuals arriving in, or leaving, the UK may be liable to contributions in more than one country at the same time. Special provisions therefore apply to **limit** the **double charge** in some circumstances, by determining that an individual is subject to contributions in one country only. Unlike income tax, there is no set off of liabilities of one country against another.

7021 There are **three different regimes** which apply, depending on whether the individual is moving between the UK and:
a. an EEA member state;
b. a country with which the UK has a reciprocal agreement, which may be either full, covering both NICs and benefits, or a Double Contributions Convention (DCC), which covers NIC liability only; or
c. the rest of the world.

> MEMO POINTS Further information can be found on the services and benefits area of the DWP's website via flmemo.co.uk/em7021

---

a. Moving within the EEA

7025 The overriding principle is that nationals of any EEA member state should **only be subject** to the social security legislation of one state.

> MEMO POINTS **Switzerland** is treated as part of the EEA for these purposes.

7026 An employee is **liable** to social security contributions **in the state** in which he works, regardless of where he lives, or the location of his employer's place of business. So where an employee takes on work overseas under a contract with a **new employer**, he will be liable to contributions in the overseas state from day one.

Where an employee **remains employed by his home employer**, and he is posted overseas, the NIC treatment will depend on the length of the assignment.

> MEMO POINTS Where an employee **works in multiple member states** at the same time (whether for the same or different employers), he will generally be liable to contributions in the state in which he habitually resides, provided he performs a substantial part of his duties there or where he works for a number of employers resident in other member states. While the occasional business trip to another state will be ignored for these purposes, an employee working a couple of days a month on a regular basis would be working in more than one state. Otherwise he will be liable to contributions in the state in which his employer has its place of business or registered office.

Short temporary assignments

7028 For these purposes, a short assignment is **not expected to last more than** 24 months. Where the employee is not replacing another employee, he will remain liable to home contributions (i.e. contributions in the country in which he has his home), as long as a certificate of coverage (normally a Form A1 but in some cases an E101 or E102) is obtained.

> MEMO POINTS To obtain a **certificate of coverage**, the employer should apply to the social security authority in the home state with the appropriate evidence (such as the employment contract). This document satisfies the authorities in the other member state that contributions are not required.

Longer-term temporary assignments

7029 The **default treatment** is that an employee will pay contributions in the overseas state from day one.

By **exception**, it may be possible to remain liable for home contributions for a period of up to 5 years, where any of the following criteria apply:
– the employee has special skills or knowledge which are not available in the local labour market;
– the employer has specific objectives with which the employee is familiar and for which his services are required; or
– unusually, it is shown to be in the employee's best interest (for example where the employee is nearing retirement).

> MEMO POINTS 1. If one or more of the above exceptions apply, an **application** should be made to the social security authority in the home state setting out the circumstances of the case. If they agree with the application, they will seek the host state's approval to continuing home contributions. Often the host state will examine the employee's history to see that he has a sufficient contributions record in the home state, and has not just spent a minimal amount of time there in order to pay cheaper contributions.
> 2. Eventually, an employee may **develop stronger ties** with the state where he is working, which means that he would need to pay contributions in that state in any event.

b. Reciprocal agreement countries

The UK has entered into reciprocal agreements with a number of countries. Each agreement is unique, although they have many common features and generally include provisions similar to those between EEA member states.

The **general aim** of a reciprocal agreement is to ensure that an individual is only liable to contributions in one of the countries concerned, usually the country in which the individual is working.

> MEMO POINTS The reciprocal agreement countries are: Barbados, Bermuda, Bosnia-Herzegovina, Canada, Croatia, Isle of Man, Israel, Jamaica, Japan, Jersey and Guernsey, Korea, Macedonia, Mauritius, Philippines, Serbia and Montenegro, Turkey and the United States of America.

An individual may continue to pay home contributions (i.e. contributions in the country in which he has his home) if he **works temporarily** in another country. The **definition** of temporary differs according to the country concerned.

If the period of the assignment is extended due to **unforeseen circumstances**, the individual is generally permitted to continue to pay home contributions for a further period. These provisions only apply if the individual was paying contributions in the home country before the assignment.

Applications to pay home contributions should be made in the same way as for employees working in the EEA, using form A1 or E101/E102.

c. Other countries

Where an individual moves between the UK and a country for which no special arrangements exist, **liability for contributions** may arise in more than one country. The rules for determining whether contributions in the UK are required are set out below.

Broadly, an employee:
– arriving in the UK will not be required to pay NICs for the first 52 weeks of their stay; and
– leaving the UK is required to continue paying NICs for the first 52 weeks of their absence.

Coming to the UK

Primary and secondary Class 1 NICs are generally **payable from** the date an individual takes up employment in the UK.

However, an exception will arise where the individual is **posted temporarily** to the UK and all of the following circumstances apply:
– the employee is not ordinarily resident or employed in the UK (apart from the temporary posting);
– the posting arises in the course of an employment carried on mainly outside the UK; and
– the employer has his main place of business outside the UK.

If these criteria are met, no primary or secondary Class 1 contributions are payable from the date of last entry into the UK until the employee has been resident in the UK for a continuous period of 52 contribution weeks.

> MEMO POINTS **Students working in the UK** may be exempt from contributions in the following situations:
> a. where a student pursuing a full-time course of study outside the UK takes up temporary employment during a vacation (not at the end of the course) which is similar to, or related to, the course of study; or
> b. where a student, who occupies a position comparable with that of an apprentice with someone outside the UK, commences employment in the UK before the age of 25 which is similar to, or related to, the apprenticeship.

Leaving the UK

In this case, the employer and employee will often have a **double charge** to NIC, in the UK and the host country. Primary and secondary Class 1 contributions continue to be payable for 52 weeks after the employee leaves the UK if all of the following apply:

- the employee is ordinarily resident in the UK;
- the employee was resident immediately before taking up the employment overseas; and
- the employer has a place of business in the UK.

Otherwise all liability to NICs ceases on the leaving date.

> MEMO POINTS   If an individual employed abroad **changes employer**, the first employer's liability for contributions ceases with the last payment due from him. In this case, further liability for contributions will be dependent upon the three criteria above.

Return to the UK and further employment abroad

7046 If the employee **temporarily returns** to the UK **before the end of the 52-week period**, in any of the following situations, contributions continue to be payable until the period has expired:
- during paid leave (i.e. holiday);
- during sick leave; or
- for a temporary period of employment.

If the temporary employment begins **after the 52-week period** has expired, contributions are not payable for the first 6 weeks of UK duties.

If the temporary assignment lasts for more than 6 weeks, UK contributions may be payable in the normal way unless the duties are merely incidental to the overseas employment (for example training).

7047 Full liability to UK NICs will recommence on an individual's **permanent return** to the UK, and so contributions will be due on the first payment of UK earnings unless both of the following conditions are satisfied:
- the employee is on paid leave from the employer pending termination of that employment; and
- the 52-week contribution period had ended before the return to the UK.

In this situation, contributions are not required for the period of paid leave unless the employee takes up employment with a different employer during that period. The new employer will, of course, be required to deduct contributions in the normal way.

7048 If, **after returning to the UK** following employment abroad, the employee takes up **further employment abroad**, a further 52-week period of contributions will be due if the conditions in ¶7044 are satisfied. So if the employee was not resident in the UK before taking up the new post, no UK NICs will be due during the further employment abroad.

CHAPTER 21
Trade unions, collective bargaining and industrial action

OUTLINE

SECTION 1 **Trade unions**	7115
Independence	7119
Recognition	7121
A Structure	7125
Officials and representatives	7125
Members	7128
B Obligations to members	7138
C Representative and participatory rights	7149
1 Members' rights to be represented by union	7150
2 Members', representatives' and ULRs' rights to time off	7151
D Certification Officer	7160

SECTION 2 **Recognition and derecognition**	7200
A Recognition	7210
1 Voluntary recognition	7214
2 Statutory recognition	7225
Subsequent change to the business	7228
3 Semi-voluntary recognition	7290
B Derecognition	7340
C Access to workers during recognition and derecognition ballots	7350

SECTION 3 **Collective bargaining**	7360
A Where union is voluntarily recognised	7363
1 Scope of bargaining	7363
2 Method of bargaining	7365
3 Enforceability of collective agreements	7367
Between employer and worker	7368
Between union and either employer or worker	7382
B Where a union is recognised by the statutory procedure	7383
1 Scope of bargaining	7383
2 Method of bargaining	7385
Consultation over training	7388
3 Enforceability of collective agreements	7389
C Where union is semi-voluntarily recognised	7391
D Duties during bargaining	7395
E Collective disputes	7397

SECTION 4 **Strikes and other industrial action**	7400
A Industrial action	7410
1 Lawful action	7416
a Lawful purpose	7417
b Supported by a ballot	7443
c Ballot requirements	7455
d Calling an action	7485
e Notice of action	7490
f Duration of ballot result	7492
2 Picketing	7495
B Employer's rights	7510
1 Withhold pay	7515
2 Dismiss workers	7520
3 Specific remedies	7523
Injunction	7528
Damages	7529
C Third party rights	7540
D Criminal penalties	7550
E "No strike" clauses	7556

SECTION 5 **Individual rights**	7560
A Members	7563
Blacklisting	7565
B Non-members	7578
C In relation to recognition and derecognition	7586
D Remedies	7589

7100 Nearly one in three UK workers belongs to a trade union (referred to as a union throughout this chapter) and around four in ten have their employment contract regulated through collective bargaining between unions and employers. Union rights generally apply to **workers** (see general definition of worker at ¶13) although some individual rights (¶7560) are restricted to **employees** only (¶11).

Union rights may be collective or individual. **Collective rights** are those where the union itself and its representatives and members gain protection or immunity in connection with the exercise of their collective functions. An example is the protection of certain forms of industrial action. Unions can call industrial action, even though its impact will be to induce workers to break their contracts, and will be protected from legal challenge, provided that they have complied with certain rules regarding the nature and origins of the dispute and the process by which the action was called. Their legal funds are, at least in part, protected even where industrial action is called in breach of the legal rules.

Individual rights protect the individual worker in his relationship with the employer. Members of independent unions and non-members are legally protected against refusal of employment, dismissal or other detriment by the employer on the grounds of their individual status as union members or not.

Unions **register** annually with the Certification Officer (CO) (¶7160) and the fact that an organisation is included in a list of unions, kept by the CO, is sufficient evidence that it is a union (s 2 TULRCA 1992). The most recent report of the CO lists approximately 170 unions, with around 7.3 million members. Many of these unions are small, single-employer organisations. Most of the larger unions affiliate to the TUC (Trades Union Congress). Over 50 unions are affiliated, with a combined membership of nearly 6.5 million.

Much of the **law** that affects unions is to be found in the Trade Union and Labour Relations (Consolidation) Act 1992 (TULRCA 1992) and the Employment Relations Acts 1999 and 2004 (ERelA 1999; ERelA 2004). The provisions of these Acts are outlined where relevant below.

SECTION 1

Trade unions

7115 A union is **defined** as an organisation, temporary or permanent, consisting "wholly or mainly of workers", whose principal purpose is "the regulation of relations" between workers and employers or employers' organisations (s 1(a) TULRCA 1992). This purpose is normally achieved through collective bargaining (¶7360). The definition includes an organisation consisting of affiliated unions, such as the Trades Union Congress (TUC). It also includes temporary organisations, provided that these have some sort of organisation, which will usually be manifested by a name, rules and evidence of meetings (*Frost v Clarke & Smith Manufacturing Co Ltd* [1973] IRLR 216, CA). On the other hand, the size, capacity and effectiveness of an organisation are irrelevant in deciding whether an organisation is a union or not (*British Association of Advisers and Lecturers in Physical Education v National Union of Teachers* [1986] IRLR 497, HC).

7117 A union cannot register as a company and only has quasi-corporate status (s 10 TULRCA 1992). A union has the right to **make contracts**, sue and be sued and can have criminal proceedings brought against it. Its members cannot sue the union in negligence except where the negligence arises in the course of a legal action which the union has employed solicitors to handle (*Friend v Institution of Professionals, Managers and Specialists* [1999] IRLR 173, QBD).

A union cannot hold **property** in its own name. Instead a union's property is held in the name of its trustees, and there are certain legal restrictions on the way that its funds can be utilised. Most notably it cannot use its property to indemnify unlawful conduct, for example by paying any penalties or compensation imposed for offences or contempt of court committed by one of its representatives or members (s 15(1) TULRCA 1992).

A union cannot sue, or be sued, for **defamation** (*Electrical, Electronic, Telecommunication and Plumbing Union v Times Newspapers* [1980] QB 585).

Independence

The exercise of certain union rights depends on the union establishing that it is an independent body, not under the domination or control of, or subject to interference from, an employer or a group of employers. Only independent unions may be granted recognition under the statutory recognition procedure (¶7225; although there is no requirement that a union should be independent in order to be voluntarily recognised).

Right against employer	Person protected	Whether union must be recognised	¶¶
Reasonable time off for union activities	Members of unions, representatives and Union Learning Representatives (ULRs)	Yes	¶7151
Paid time off to perform duties	Representatives and ULRs	Yes	¶7156
Reasonable time off for training	Representatives and ULRs	Yes	¶¶7153, 7155
Not to suffer a detriment on union grounds	Members of unions	No	¶7566
Not to be dismissed or selected for redundancy on union grounds	Members of unions	No	¶7574

Factors to be considered when assessing the **degree of independence** a union has from an employer include its history, membership, structure, finances, whether it receives facilities from the employer, and its negotiating record (*Blue Circle Staff Association v Certification Officer* [1977] IRLR 20, EAT).

Conclusive **evidence** of a union's independence comes in the form of a certificate of independence issued by the Certification Officer (CO) (¶7160). Unions wishing to establish their independence must apply for this certificate. The CO can withdraw a certificate of independence, if he is of the opinion that a union is no longer independent.

> MEMO POINTS 1. The definition of independence relates only to the relationship between the union and the employer. There is no requirement for a union to be politically independent. A union may have political objects. It may organise a **political fund**, which may make payments to political campaigns or even to political parties. Its members cannot be required, however, to belong to any party or to contribute to a political fund (ss 71-96 TULRCA 1992).
> 2. Under the Compensation Act 2006, persons providing a regulated claims management service need to be authorised. Almost any activity in relation to claims, from simply referring claims through to representing clients, is covered. Independent unions are excluded. In practice, this means that other than in the exceptional circumstances where non-independent unions are authorised, they may not **represent individuals** at an employment tribunal.

Recognition

The **purpose** of recognition is to enable collective bargaining (¶7360). Where a union has been recognised (¶7200), it can **negotiate** pay and other terms and conditions of employment on behalf of a group of workers. Negotiation will result in a collective agreement.

In large sectors of industry, levels of pay and other principal terms and conditions for individual workers are set by terms negotiated between unions and employers and documented in collective agreements.

Recognised unions also acquire the **right to be consulted** for collective bargaining purposes (see ¶7395, and for other certain specific situations ¶7651).

Members of independent unions, representatives and Union Learning Representatives also gain rights to time off where a union is recognised (¶¶7151+).

> MEMO POINTS 1. The definitions of collective agreement and collective bargaining are different for voluntarily recognised unions (¶7214) and for unions recognised under the statutory recognition procedure (¶7225).
> 2. Some collective agreements contain a "no strike" provision, which attempts to prohibit or restrict the right of workers to take industrial action. These clauses are discussed at ¶7556 below.

A. Structure

Officials and representatives

7125 **Elected national officers** At the **head of the union** organisation there will commonly be a general secretary, president and national executive committee. Each of these office holders must be elected by secret postal ballot (s 46 TULRCA 1992).

A member of the executive committee is any person who "under the rules of the union" may attend and speak at all or some of the meetings of the executive, otherwise than for the purpose of providing the committee with factual information or with technical or professional advice.

7126 **Union employees** The union may also employ **officials**, who will not normally be elected to their posts unless required under the union's own rules.

In addition, the union will employ **administrative staff**, who will service the organisation, its officers and its members. The union's trustees, usually elected by the membership as a whole, are responsible for checking that its finances and affairs are in order.

7127 **Lay representatives** Beneath the above structure of national office holders and union employees are workers who have been elected to local union positions but who remain employed by the employer. Such "lay" representatives may go by different names depending on the industry and the workplace.

The union rulebook will prescribe how members of this group are selected.

This layer services the union's members by providing advice and representation at a local or workplace level.

> MEMO POINTS 1. Common names for lay representatives in industry include branch secretaries, branch chairs, members of the union committee, workplace representatives, or (in journalism and printing) mother or father of the chapel. This chapter uses the word "officials" to designate union employees with a representative function and "representatives" to designate union lay representatives.
> 2. An employer is most likely to deal, on a day-to-day basis, with lay representatives. There will be circumstances, however, where an employer may have to deal with union officials. For example, union officials may conduct collective bargaining, depending on the terms of the recognition agreement (¶7216).
> 3. In each individual workplace, it is common for a union to distinguish between different lay representative roles, such as branch secretary and treasurer or chair. In the statute, however, there is no distinction between different lay representatives: each is protected by the same rights against unfair selection, dismissal and other detriment (¶7560).

Members

7128 The members of the union and the union itself are **governed by** its rules, which are its written rules or any other written provision forming part of the contract between a member and the other members (s 20(7) TULRCA 1992). The union rulebook sets out the terms of its contract with its members (¶7144). It also usually includes the union's main principles and objectives. The union's rules may be amended through decisions taken by the union's policy-making bodies, for example the union's annual conference.

B. Obligations to members

A union has a number of specified obligations imposed on it by statute and common law. The most important duties are:
- not to unlawfully exclude or expel a member;
- not to unjustifiably discipline a member;
- to abide by its own rules; and
- not to discriminate.

Further duties are set out in a table below (¶7148).

Duty not to unlawfully exclude or expel a member A union **may** exclude a person from membership **only** on the **grounds** that (s 174(2) TULRCA 1992):
- the person does not satisfy, or no longer satisfies, a membership requirement contained in the union rulebook;
- the person does not qualify, or no longer qualifies, for membership of the union by reason of the union operating only in a particular part of Great Britain;
- in the case of a union whose purpose is the regulation of relations between its members and one particular employer or a number of particular employers who are associated, the person is not, or is no longer, employed by that employer or one of those employers; or
- the exclusion or expulsion is entirely attributable to the person's conduct (although see below regarding conduct relating to membership of a political party).

A union **may not exclude** or expel an individual on the **grounds** of (s 174(4), (4A) TULRCA 1992):
- his current or former membership of a union;
- his current or former employment; or
- his current or former membership of a political party.

However, with regard to an individual's membership this protection does not apply if the **membership of** the **political party** is contrary to a rule or objective of the union (s 174(4C) TULRCA 1992; SI 2009/603). Nor will this protection apply where the union excludes or expels the individual on the grounds of his **conduct**, where the conduct is wholly or mainly attributable to activities undertaken by an individual as a member of a political party, unless the decision to exclude or expel is not taken in accordance with the union's rules or is taken unfairly or where the individual would lose his livelihood or suffer other exceptional hardship as a result of his exclusion or expulsion.

> MEMO POINTS   Following the success of the claimant in *Lee v ASLEF*, amendments to the law were introduced to clarify the distinction between membership of a party and political activities (*Lee v Aslef* [2004] UKEAT 0625_03_2402). The union concerned, ASLEF, then brought a case to the European Court of Human Rights, arguing that UK legislation contradicted the union's right of association (art 11 European Convention of Human Rights). The Court ruled that ASLEF's rights had indeed been restricted and that a union should have greater autonomy to decide whether the political party membership of individuals should debar them from belonging to the union (*Associated Society of Locomotive Engineers & Firemen v United Kingdom* [2007] IRLR 361, ECHR). This has led to further amendments to the law, which have been brought in by the Employment Act 2008.

An individual who **claims** that membership has been denied to him or that the union has unreasonably excluded or expelled him can present a claim to a tribunal.

An individual must make the claim **within** 6 months, which is calculated from the date of the refusal of membership or expulsion. The tribunal can extend this period where it believes that it was not reasonably practicable for the individual to present the claim in time (s 175 TULRCA 1992).

The minimum **compensatory award** is £8,400 and the maximum award is £87,700 (i.e. 30 times the maximum amount of a week's pay for unfair dismissal (¶2920) plus the maximum compensatory award for unfair dismissal (¶8587)).

> MEMO POINTS   The meaning of "not reasonably practicable" should be construed in the same way as the equivalent wording contained in the unfair dismissal legislation (s 111(2) ERA 1996) (*GMB v Hamm* [2000] UKEAT 246_00_1511).

7142 **Duty not to unjustifiably discipline a member** A union may not unjustifiably discipline a member (ss 64-67 TULRCA 1992). Disciplinary action includes expulsion, fines, refusal to accept contributions, depriving members of union benefits, encouraging another union to exclude the member or doing anything else detrimental to the member (*Nalgo v Killorn and Simm* [1990] IRLR 464, EAT). A suspension from membership also amounts to a disciplinary action; however, a mere recommendation for disciplinary action, without it having been carried out, will not give rise to a claim (*TGWU v Webber* [1990] IRLR 462, EAT), neither will a letter before action (*Beaumont v Amicus MSF* [2007] ICR 341, EAT).

Disciplinary action is **automatically unjust** where it is imposed on the **grounds** that the member has (s 65 TULRCA 1992):
– failed to support or participate in industrial action;
– continued to work to his contract despite the industrial action;
– asserted, otherwise than falsely and in bad faith, that the union, its officials or its representatives have breached their legal obligations;
– encouraged others to continue working during industrial action;
– failed to comply with any unjustifiable disciplinary penalty already imposed;
– worked or is proposing to work with non-union members; or
– sought assistance from the CO.

7143 A member or former member can make a **claim** to an employment tribunal, which can declare that the disciplinary action was unjustified (s 66 TULRCA 1992). The claim must be presented **within** 3 months of the action complained of, unless the tribunal believes that it was not reasonably practicable to have done so.

If the claim is successful the tribunal may make a **declaration** that a union has unjustifiably disciplined its member. Where a declaration is made, the union must take all necessary steps to ensure that the effects of the disciplinary action are revoked (*Beaumont v Amicus MSF* [2004] UKEAT 0122_03_1202). This will involve positive and unequivocal action and not simply notifying the member's union branch that the disciplinary action has been reversed.

Moreover, after such a declaration, the member/former member can also pursue a claim for **compensation** and/or reimbursement of any fine/penalty paid (s 67 TULRCA 1992). A claim can only be made after 4 weeks from the date of the declaration but must be made before the end of 6 months from this date. Compensation is awarded in accordance with what is just and equitable. This will not be limited to compensation for failure to revoke the unjustifiable disciplinary action and can include compensation for the manner of the disciplinary action and its effects on the member. Compensation will be calculated on the same basis as compensation in sex or race victimisation cases (*Massey v UNIFI* [2008] ICR 62, CA). The minimum compensatory award is £8,400 and the maximum award is £87,700 (i.e. 30 times the maximum amount of a week's pay for unfair dismissal (¶2920) plus the maximum compensatory award for unfair dismissal (¶8587)).

7144 **Duty to abide by own rules** The union must abide by its own rules and non-compliance will amount to a breach of contract between the union and its members (*Lee v Showman's Guild of Great Britain* [1952] 2 QB 329). For example, if a rule states that the union "will" provide members with professional assistance to pursue legal claims, a refusal to do so will amount to a breach of contract.

A union member may bring a **claim** to the CO that the union has breached or threatened to breach its rules. This can occur where the alleged breach relates to (s 108A TULRCA 1992):
– appointments or elections of officials;
– disciplinary proceedings;
– balloting, other than for industrial action; or
– the constitution or proceedings of any policy-making executive body of the union.

A union member making a complaint has to show that reasonable steps have been taken to resolve the matter internally. The complaint has to be made **within** 6 months.

7145 Members may challenge, in the civil courts, the validity of a union **executive's decision** where that decision is taken in breach of the union's own rulebook. A union member has an individual contractual right to do so (*Wise v Union of Shop Distributors and Allied Workers* [1996] IRLR 609, ChD). However, there are limits to how far the courts will go in investigating the internal affairs of a union. For example, the powers of investigation of the High Court do not extend to a situation where there has already been an internal process where alleged irregularities have been properly investigated (*Hamlet v GMB* [1986] IRLR 293, ChD).

Duty not to discriminate Unions must not discriminate against or victimise members or persons applying for membership of the union on the **grounds** of any **protected characteristics** under the Equality Act 2010, i.e. sex, race, religion or belief, sexual orientation, age, gender reassignment, disability, marriage and civil partnership or pregnancy and maternity, (s 57 Equality Act 2010):
– in the terms on which they are willing to admit members;
– by depriving an existing member of his membership or varying his terms of membership;
– in the arrangements they make for deciding to whom to offer membership of the organisation;
– in the way they afford a member access to opportunities for receiving benefits, facilities or services;
– by subjecting a member to any other detriment; or
– by failing to make reasonable adjustments, including the provision of an auxiliary aid, in respect of any provision, criterion or practice applied by or on behalf of the union or any physical feature of premises occupied by it which places a disabled person at a substantial disadvantage in comparison to persons who are not disabled in order to prevent the disabled person from suffering that disadvantage.

7146

Unions also have a duty not to harass a member or applicant on the basis of any of the protected characteristics.

Unions that discriminate may be subject to tribunal **claims**. The normal principles of anti-discrimination law apply (¶¶5200+), although the reverse burden of proof (¶¶5730+) does not apply in victimisation claims against trade unions (*Croad v University and College Union* [2011] UKEAT 0012_11_1306).

7147

EXAMPLE
Discrimination
In *Allen and ors v GMB* [2008] EWCA Civ 810, a union negotiated an equal pay agreement with a council, but was influenced by the employer's claims of poverty and by its own desire not to rock the boat, and did not explain to its members that the deal on offer was substantially less than they were likely to receive if they were successful before a tribunal. The Court of Appeal held that the union had discriminated against its members by:
a. giving pay security priority over equal pay; and
b. failing to explain properly to members that the deal on offer for back pay was substantially less than they were likely to receive if they were successful before a tribunal.

No discrimination
1. In *British Medical Association v Chaudhary* [2007] IRLR 800, CA, a doctor claimed that the British Medical Association (BMA) had failed to properly investigate his claim of race discrimination against various NHS bodies. The tribunal found that if the BMA had not discriminated against the claimant, by failing to support his case, it would have provided support which would have resulted in the doctor having a 50% chance of putting his career right. On appeal, the Court of Appeal held that the policy of the BMA had been to support cases which had a better than even chance of success. The claimant's case against the NHS bodies had never been strong. Neither the Association's legal policy nor its implementation had been discriminatory. Accordingly, the tribunal's decision was reversed.
2. In *Croad v University and College Union*, the EAT held in favour of a trade union who refused to fund a member's tribunal claims against both her employer and the union itself. The employee, C, was subject to disciplinary proceedings, for which she sought assistance from her union. She was suffering with anxiety, depression and dyslexia and she sought a level of assistance that the union decided it was unable to provide (such as attending meetings that C could not attend herself, and writing certain letters for her). C brought a tribunal claim against her employer, which included a claim for disability discrimination. C was repeatedly told that if she failed to follow the union's advice in respect of her dealings with her employer then support could be withdrawn. C then brought proceedings against the union for disability discrimination and victimisation, and her legal representation was withdrawn. The EAT agreed with the tribunal that the union had not failed in its duty to make reasonable adjustments either in respect of the way it communicated with her or in its failure

to go beyond the general practice as to how it would assist members. In terms of her victimisation claim, the EAT also agreed with the tribunal's finding that the withdrawal of support was not because C had brought proceedings or indicated that reasonable adjustments had not been made (which was the alleged protected act that she claimed led to the victimisation), but because of C's failure to follow the union's advice and because there would be a conflict of interest if the union were to represent her in a claim against her employer if the union faced linked proceedings itself.

7148 **Further duties** The following table sets out a union's main other duties to its members:

Duty	Unions must	Legislation reference (TULRCA 1992)
To use union property lawfully	– not use funds to pay or secure a lawful penalty; and – not allow a union trustee to use the union's property unlawfully. A member of a union may apply to the High Court, to require the return of the property or its value to the union, or to make an order protecting or recovering the property of the union.	ss 15-16
To maintain a register of members' names and addresses	– compile and maintain a register of the names and addresses of their members, to be used for elections and ballots; – ensure that the entries in the register are accurate and up-to-date; and – allow their members to check the register. Where there is a failure to meet this duty, a member may apply to the CO (¶7160) or to the High Court.	s 24
To keep accounts	– keep proper accounting records of their transactions, assets and liabilities. Where there is a failure to meet this duty, the union commits a criminal offence, for which the relevant official or representative of the union may be liable to a fine or imprisonment.	ss 28-29, 45
To permit members to inspect records	– enable their members to see any accounting records going back 6 years. A member may enforce this right by applying to the CO (¶7160) or to the High Court.	ss 30-31
To file and supply annual returns	– file annual returns with the CO, including income and expenditure, a year-end balance sheet and any other accounts that the CO might require. Returns must give details of salaries paid to the president, general secretary and members of the executive. This information must be available to members and anyone else who requests it. Where there is a failure to meet this duty, the union commits a criminal offence, for which the relevant official or representative of the union may be liable to a fine or imprisonment.	ss 32, 45
To appoint an auditor	– appoint a qualified auditor, unless the union is very small. Certain persons are excluded from holding the office. Where there is a failure to meet this duty, the union commits a criminal offence, for which the relevant official or representative of the union may be liable to a fine or imprisonment.	ss 33-37
To hold elections	– hold regular elections for positions of general secretary, president, and for membership of the union's national executive. Members have the right to stand for election and to vote. Where there is a failure to meet this duty, a member or a candidate may apply to the CO (¶7160) or to the High Court.	ss 46, 47, 49-50

Duty	Unions must	Legislation reference (TULRCA 1992)
To ballot before industrial action	– hold a ballot for taking action; – only take action if a majority supports it in the ballot; and – only take action of the type supported by the majority. Members have the right to bring an action to the High Court complaining of a breach (¶7453).	s 62
To ballot on the existence of the union's political fund	– not use funds for political purposes unless there is a fund; – not set up a fund unless there has been a ballot; and – not continue the fund for more than 10 years without holding further ballots. Where there is a failure to meet this duty, a member may apply to the CO (¶7160).	ss 71-76
To allow abstentions from the fund	– allow members to decline to make contributions to the political fund. Where a union deducts funds from a member who objects to payment, the member may complain to the CO (¶7160). Where deductions are made by the employer, the member may complain to the tribunal.	ss 84-88

C. Representative and participatory rights

7149 **Workers** have rights to be represented in the workplace, and where the worker is a member of a union, representation will normally be made by a union representative or official.

Where a union is independent and recognised, the **employer** must give reasonable time off to trade union members, representatives and union learning representatives (ULRs) in order to enable them to participate in union activities. Representatives and ULRs also have an entitlement to be paid for any time taken off to perform their duties or for their training.

1. Members' rights to be represented by union

7150 Recognised unions provide support to members and represent them during individual employment disputes. A member may, for example, approach a union representative and ask him for assistance with bringing a grievance, or with support in preparing for a disciplinary meeting or a tribunal hearing.

Workers have a right to be represented by a union official or representative at a grievance or disciplinary hearing (¶6780).

Depending on the terms of the union's rulebook (¶7144), a **union** may be obliged to represent its members at such meetings or at employment tribunal hearings, although it is more common for the union's responsibilities to be merely discretionary.

At the union's discretion, these services may sometimes be offered to non-members as well as members of a union.

MEMO POINTS It is possible that a worker may seek union representation at a wider class of meetings, for example annual performance review meetings or meetings to discuss an application for flexible working. In such circumstances, an **employer** should respond by considering first whether the worker has an express right to representation (for example, because the right is set out in a contractual document, or in the voluntary recognition agreement, if there is one (¶7216)), and second, whether the worker has an implied right to representation (for example, because it is established custom and practice in the workplace). If neither argument applies, then it will be a matter of discretion for the employer as to whether or not he accepts the request.

2. Members', representatives' and ULRs' rights to time off

7151 Members, representatives and union learning representatives (ULRs) of independent recognised unions have a statutory right to reasonable time off for union activities and duties. Representatives and ULRs also have an entitlement to be paid for any time taken off to perform their duties or for their training.

The extent of time off for members, representatives and ULRs must be **reasonable** in all the circumstances having regard to the Acas Code of Practice on Time off for Trade Union Duties and Activities, referred to as the Code in this section (ss 168(3), 168A(8), 170(3) TULRCA 1992; SI 2009/3223).

Factors such as the needs of the business, and the amount and duration of time off in relation to these needs, are important considerations in deciding if the employer acted reasonably. The number and frequency of similar periods of time off, which have been permitted by the employer, will also be considered to determine if the employer acted reasonably (Borders Regional Council v Maule [1993] IRLR 199, EAT; Thomas Scott & Sons (Bakers) Ltd v Allen [1983] IRLR 329, CA). An employer can act reasonably even if he refuses a valid request for time off if he was not fully aware of the purposes for which time off was requested. There may be a range of reasonable conduct within which the employer may act (Ministry of Defence v Crook and Irving [1982] IRLR 488, EAT). Whether the employer acted reasonably is a question of fact.

> EXAMPLE
> 1. In Thomas Scott & Sons (Bakers) Ltd v Allen, the employer was not unreasonable in refusing to give paid time off to all 11 shop stewards to attend a union meeting on the busiest day of the week.
> 2. In Ministry of Defence v Crook and Irving, C, a shop steward, requested time off for a training course. The employer refused, as he was unaware that the course had been broadened and was now relevant to shop stewards. The EAT held that the employer had acted reasonably.

> MEMO POINTS The Code emphasises co-operation between employers and unions in relation to time off and stresses that arrangements should be agreed for handling time off. The **provisions of the Code** are admissible in evidence and may be taken into account in determining any question arising during employment tribunal proceedings relating to time off for trade union duties and activities. However, failure to observe any provision of the Code does not of itself render a person liable to any proceedings.

7152 **Members** Members may take reasonable time off to (s 170(1) TULRCA 1992):
– take part in union activities; or
– access the services of a ULR.

Reasonable time off will **include** time off for attending union meetings, union conferences and other union bodies like local councils and regional meetings of the union. It does **not include** taking time off for industrial action, whether or not in contemplation or furtherance of a trade dispute. The right to time off for the purpose of accessing the services of a ULR only applies if the ULR himself would be entitled to time off for the purpose of carrying out his duties in relation to the employee.

The union activity must be directly linked to the relationship between the employee, the employer and the union (Luce v London Borough of Bexley [1990] IRLR 422, EAT).

> EXAMPLE In Luce v London Borough of Bexley, a teacher, who was a union member, attended a union-organised lobby of Parliament against the Education Reform Bill. This lobby presented political and ideological objections to the proposed legislation which would affect the teaching profession but did not directly concern the employer. As there was no direct link to the employer, the teacher had no statutory right to time off to attend the lobby.

The Code recommends that members should get unpaid time off for attending workplace meetings to discuss and vote on the outcome of negotiations, meetings with officials to discuss issues relevant to the workplace, voting in properly conducted ballots on industrial action and voting in union elections. It also recommends that where the member is acting as a representative he should be given time off to attend branch, area or regional meetings, meetings of representative policy-making bodies, such as the union's principal executive or its annual conference, and meetings with officials to discuss issues relevant to the workplace.

Representatives A union representative may take reasonable time off to carry out his representative duties or undergo training (that has been approved by the Trades Union Congress or by the independent union of which he is a representative). Reasonable time off will **include** time to enable the representative to take part in (s 168(1), (2) TULRCA 1992):
– negotiations with the employer related to or connected with collective bargaining;
– functions which the employer has agreed may be performed by the union; or
– negotiations concerning redundancies (¶8931) or the transfer of employees (¶8071).

The Code gives the following examples of matters that would be related to or connected with collective bargaining:
– preparing for negotiations;
– informing members of progress;
– explaining outcomes to members; and
– preparing for meetings with the employer about matters for which the trade union has only representational rights.

Reasonable time off does **not include** time off to carry out internal union duties or to be involved with another employer's employee disputes.

The union must expressly or impliedly **require the attendance** of the representative at its meetings in order for such attendance to amount to the carrying out of his duties as a representative (*Ashley v Ministry of Defence* [1984] IRLR 57, EAT). What matters are those representative duties which the union considers as making it necessary for the representative to attend, and not the duties that the representative may subjectively think are desirable.

> EXAMPLE In *Ashley v Ministry of Defence*, an unofficial shop stewards' meeting, which was not authorised by the union and which the union did not request its stewards to attend, was held not to be a meeting that the representative had the right to time off to attend.

A tribunal will consider all the circumstances in ascertaining whether a meeting is **sufficiently close** or proximate **to industrial relations** between the employer and his employees for a representative to be entitled to have time off to carry out representative duties (*British Bakeries (Northern) Ltd v Aldington* [1988] IRLR 177, EAT). This will be a question of fact.

Attending **preparatory, explanatory or advisory** meetings will be considered to be sufficiently proximate if such meetings have some direct relevance to the industrial relations between the employer and its employees (*Beal v Beecham Group Ltd* [1982] IRLR 192, CA). For example, attending a meeting to exchange information may not be directly relevant but determining policies nationally may be (depending what the policies are). A tribunal will consider all the circumstances in deciding whether a particular preparatory or advisory committee is sufficiently close to the carrying out of industrial relations negotiations.

Union Learning Representatives (ULRs) A Union Learning Representative (ULR) is entitled to take reasonable time off to carry out his duties as a ULR, provided that the union concerned has given written notice to the employer and the ULR is sufficiently trained.

Reasonable time off will **include** time off for (s 168A(1), (2) TULRCA 1992):
– analysing learning or training needs;
– providing information and advice about learning or training matters;
– arranging learning or training;
– promoting the value of learning or training;
– consulting with the employer regarding learning and training;
– preparing to carry out any of the above activities; and
– undergoing the relevant training to carry out ULR duties.

Reasonable time off does **not include** time off where a ULR has not been trained by the date on which his union gives written notice to the employer that he is a ULR, or within 6 months of the employer receiving such written notice (s 168A(3), (4) TULRCA 1992).

A ULR can demonstrate to his union that he has received sufficient training to carry out ULR duties by completing a **training course** approved by the TUC or the independent union to which the ULR belongs, or by demonstrating that he has previously gained the necessary skills and experience to operate as a ULR. Such expertise could be gained from experience in other areas of work, including teaching, counselling, careers guidance or human resources etc.

Payment

7156 Members have **no right** to be paid for taking part in union activities, although the Code recommends that consideration should be given to payment if this would ensure that union meetings are more representative.

Representatives and **ULRs** have the **right to be remunerated** for the time taken off in order to do trade union duties (s 169(1) TULRCA 1992).

The Code recommends that the employer pays either the amount that the representatives would have earned had they worked during the time taken off or, where earnings vary with the work done, an amount calculated by reference to the average hourly earnings for the work they are employed to do.

An **employer** only **has to** pay for the hours on the course when the worker would have worked (*Hairsine v Kingston upon Hull City Council* [1991] UKEAT 544_89_0907). There is no statutory requirement to pay for time off where the duty is carried out at a time when the representative would not otherwise have been at work, but staff who work part time will be entitled to be paid if staff who work full time would be entitled to be paid (*Davies v Neath Port Talbot County Borough Council* [1999] IRLR 769, EAT). In all cases the **amount** of time off must be **reasonable**.

> EXAMPLE
> 1. In *Hairsine v Kingston upon Hull City Council*, H worked an evening shift between 3pm and 11pm. He attended a union training course that took place between 9am and 4pm and then worked only part of his shift before going home. The EAT held that he was not entitled to be paid for the time spent on the training course prior to 3pm, or for that part of the shift which he had not worked because he had gone home.
> 2. In *Davies v Neath Port Talbot County Borough Council*, a part-time employee who attended a full-time training course was entitled to be paid for the entirety of the time spent on the training course.

Procedure

7157 The request must be made and brought to the attention of the employer by the member, representative or ULR concerned. Only then does the employee have a right to complain to a tribunal if the employer refuses, ignores it, or fails to respond (*Ryford Ltd v Drinkwater* [1995] UKEAT 723_94_2405).

Employees should give employers as much **notice** as possible and provide details of the:
– purpose of the time off;
– intended location; and
– timing and duration of time off required.

Remedy for failure to allow time off

7159 Union members, representatives and ULRs can complain to an employment tribunal where an employer has failed to allow time off or, in the case of representatives and ULRs, has failed to pay for time taken off, and can seek compensation or an award for payment (ss 168, 168A, 169, 172 TULRCA 1992; *Skiggs v South West Trains Limited* [2005] UKEAT 0763_03_0703).

D. Certification Officer

7160 The Certification Officer (CO) is a government-appointed official who is responsible for the registration and legal regulation of unions. The **main functions** of the CO are to (ss 3, 6, 124, 258 TULRCA 1992):
– maintain a list of unions and of employers' organisations and receive their annual returns;
– certify whether a union is independent;

- produce an annual report; and
- ensure that the statutory requirements relating to accounting records, annual returns, auditors, the election of union executives, financial affairs, political funds, the procedures for amalgamations and transfers of engagements, and changes of union names are complied with.

> MEMO POINTS   In practice, the CO maintains two separate lists of unions: one which contains all unions in Britain, and another of all the independent unions.

The CO must also deal with **complaints** by union members:
- that a union has failed to comply with the legal provisions relating to the holding of secret postal ballots for electing members of its executive committee, president and general secretary;
- about alleged or threatened breaches of the union's own rules;
- about alleged breaches of political fund rules; or
- about the conduct of merger ballots.

Union members making complaints to the CO must do so **within** 6 months of the alleged breach, threatened breach or conclusion of any internal enquiry. Before accepting a complaint, the CO has to be convinced that all reasonable steps were taken to resolve the claim internally. If a complaint is accepted, the CO will call a hearing and give the applicant and the union an opportunity to be heard.

7162

At any stage of the proceedings, the CO may **strike out** an application or complaint on the grounds that (s 256B TULRCA 1992):
- it, or anything in it, is scandalous, vexatious, has no reasonable prospect of success or is otherwise misconceived;
- proceedings have been conducted in a scandalous, vexatious or unreasonable manner; or
- there has been an excessive delay in proceedings.

7163

If, however, the CO is satisfied that the complaint is successful, he can make a **declaration** and a **binding enforcement order** requiring the union to undertake the necessary steps to remedy the breach. He may also pay expenses to the complainant if these are incurred for the purpose of attending hearings.

Appeals from a decision of the CO on points of law go to the Employment Appeal Tribunal (EAT).

7164

SECTION 2

Recognition and derecognition

The statutory purpose of a union is to regulate relations between workers and employers (s 1 TULRCA 1992). In order to be able to do this, the union must be recognised by the employer.

7200

A union is recognised by an employer (or two or more associated employers) if it is entitled to negotiate pay and other terms and conditions of employment on behalf of a group of workers (s 178 TULRCA 1992).

Negotiation is called collective bargaining and its definition differs according to the method by which a union has been recognised, i.e. either by reference to the legislation (**statutory recognition**) or by **voluntary** agreement between the parties (where the employer has decided to recognise a union without reference to the legislation).

Many such voluntary arrangements existed prior to, and have continued to come into existence since, the introduction of the statutory procedures and a clear distinction must be drawn between such non-statutory voluntary arrangements and statutory "voluntary" arrangements, referred to in this chapter as **semi-voluntary** recognition arrangements.

7205 Workers are afforded some protection under the statutory recognition provisions if they are **dismissed** or **subjected to a detriment** for a reason in connection with recognition or derecognition of a union (paras 156-162 Sch A1 TULRCA 1992) (¶7586).

A dismissal on grounds of recognition or derecognition will be for an inadmissible reason (¶7587) and workers will not need to have any particular period of continuous employment in order to bring an unfair dismissal claim.

The employment protection in this respect only applies to unions which are being recognised (or derecognised) under the statutory provisions set out in Schedule A1 and, therefore, will not apply to purely voluntary recognition arrangements (Sch A1 TULRCA 1992).

> MEMO POINTS If a trade union member or representative was dismissed or subjected to a detriment on the grounds that he was acting to obtain **voluntary recognition** of a union, then in all probability the member would also be protected by the general rights prohibiting an employer from subjecting union members and representatives to detriment including dismissal on the grounds of taking part in union activities (¶¶7566, 7574), as the seeking of recognition would almost certainly come within the definition of union activities.

7208 A summary of the different **types** of recognition and the **main characteristics** of each is as follows:

	Statutory	Semi-voluntary	Voluntary
Recognition procedure	Prescribed by statute (¶7225)	Prescribed by statute (¶7225)	By agreement between employer and union(s) (¶7214)
Does the union need to be independent?	Yes		No
Size of employer	Employer must have at least 21 workers		No minimum size requirement
Enforceability	Recognition is legally binding on employer and union; there are prescribed derecognition procedures (¶7340)		Not legally binding (so recognition can be withdrawn at any time) unless parties expressly agree otherwise
Subject of collective bargaining	Pay, hours and holiday, although parties can extend scope of bargaining by agreement		Agreed by parties and not subject to any statutory restrictions
Consequences	Statutory definition limits scope of bargaining (¶7383), duties to agree on method of collective bargaining (or have one imposed by Central Arbitration Committee, ¶7385) and to consult on training (¶7388)	Statutory duties to agree on method of collective bargaining (or have one imposed by Central Arbitration Committee, ¶7391)	Scope and method of collective bargaining to depend on collective agreement plus expanded legal definition of collective bargaining (¶7363)
Right of union members and representatives not to be subject to a detriment	Protected when seeking to obtain or prevent, or supporting or not supporting, recognition		Only if union is independent
Right of union members and representatives to time off for activities?	Yes		Only if union is independent

A. Recognition

7210 There are several ways in which a union may have come to be recognised for the purposes of collective bargaining. Where a union is recognised, typically, the union will have had a presence in a sector for several years. The union will have been recognised for some time as the appropriate union to represent workers employed by a particular employer or at a certain workplace or on a given grade.

7211 Where, however, an employer has only recently been established, or where a union has only recently begun to organise in a particular sector, the union will not be recognised and will seek recognition. Typically, it will begin to do so by making an initial approach. Usually, it will seek **voluntary recognition** (¶7214), based on the employer's consent. There is no obligation on the employer to agree.

When an employer has made it clear that he will not recognise the union, a union may seek to compel recognition, by demonstrating that it has majority support in a workplace. The **statutory recognition** procedures were first introduced in their current form in 2000 (Sch A1 TULRCA 1992). They only apply to employers with 21 or more workers, and to independent unions (¶7119).

7212 Despite the existence of the statutory recognition procedures, relatively few unions have sought to make use of them, and it has been far more common for employers and unions to favour voluntary recognition. For **unions**, one key drawback of the statutory recognition procedure is that when a union has been recognised under it, collective bargaining is likely to take place around a much narrower set of issues (¶7383). For **employers**, the statutory processes are complex and unwieldy. Many employers would prefer to agree with a union the terms of a voluntary recognition arrangement rather than have a heavily regulated statutory recognition arrangement imposed on them.

1. Voluntary recognition

7214 Voluntary recognition can take many **different forms**. In smaller organisations, recognition may be relatively informal, with issues emerging on an ad hoc basis. In large organisations, where there is a history of different unions representing workers at different grades, several unions may be recognised, each having responsibility for representing a particular group (or "bargaining unit") of workers. A union may be recognised to represent workers in a particular grade, or at a given employer, or in a certain group of companies.

> MEMO POINTS There is no requirement that a union should be independent in order to be voluntarily recognised.

7215 Recognition will normally be manifested by a **written agreement**. Where, however, an employer has **impliedly** recognised a union, without concluding a written agreement, by its conduct over a period of time, a court may find that the union has been recognised (*National Union of Teachers v Charles Ingram and Co Ltd* [1977] IRLR 147, EAT).

Recognition agreement

7216 The form that a voluntary recognition agreement should take is not set out by the legislation. Where an employer agrees to recognise a union, it is, however, best practice if the agreement is set down in a written document.

It is appropriate to state the **scope** of collective bargaining (for example, pay, hours, holidays, terms and conditions; for a full list, see ¶7363). The agreement should also set out the intended **method** by which collective bargaining will take place: this may take in issues such the composition of the meeting, the arrangements for regulating the meeting and the degree of formality of the meeting (¶7365).

A voluntary recognition agreement will not be legally **enforceable**, unless the parties record in writing their express intention otherwise (s 179 TULRCA 1992). Unless the parties expressly provide for the voluntary agreement to be enforceable, any deviation from the terms of a collective bargaining method, or indeed a complete withdrawal of voluntary recognition, will not give rise to a legal challenge. The risk of industrial action should, however, be borne in mind.

If the employer intends that the terms of **collective agreements** negotiated under the auspices of a recognition agreement are to be enforceable between himself and the union or his workers (¶7367), this should be in the agreement. If, in addition, the employer intends to be bound by **national** as well as local **agreements**, that intention should be set out in the agreement. If it is not stated, the relationship between agreements conducted at different levels may be unclear (¶7375).

It is also helpful to set out the means for **resolving** any collective **disputes** (¶7397).

It is appropriate for a recognition agreement to set out the **facilities** which will be granted to the union: depending on the size of the employer and its relationship with the union, these may include physical resources (rooms, photocopying machines, computers), agreed paid or unpaid time off for union members, representatives or learning representatives to get involved in union activities or duties (¶7151), and (more rarely) administrative support.

The agreement should also have a set duration and specify the arrangements for its renewal or renegotiation. It should **also be** signed and dated.

Application for recognition

7219 Where a union approaches the employer for the first time to request voluntary recognition, it is likely that any initial approach will be relatively informal. There is no requirement for an initial request to take any particular form or to use any particular words. It is an entirely discretionary matter for the employer to choose whether he accepts or rejects the request for recognition.

> MEMO POINTS   When an employer rejects a union's application for voluntary recognition, it is up to the union to decide whether it will then make an application for statutory recognition.

2. Statutory recognition

7225 The statutory recognition procedure is designed to enable a union to compel recognition in circumstances where the employer opposes it.

The statutory recognition process is divided into several **stages** which are set out in the table at ¶7227, below.

The **Central Arbitration Committee** (CAC), an independent judicial body which also has several other industrial relations functions, oversees the statutory recognition procedure. The CAC website can be found at flmemo.co.uk/em7225

For statutory recognition to be granted, several **requirements** have to be met. The most important are:
– the union must make an initial approach to the employer;
– the union must be independent;
– a period for negotiation must pass;
– the employer must not have reached an existing recognition agreement with any other union;
– the employer must employ 21 or more workers;
– the bargaining unit for which the union seeks recognition must be appropriate;
– within the appropriate bargaining unit, at least 10% of the workers must be members of the union; and
– the union must show that a majority of workers in the bargaining unit would be likely to favour recognition.

If the requirements set out in the above list are met, the CAC has a number of powers, including the power to make a declaration that a union is, or is not, recognised.

If the **CAC** has **declared** that a union is recognised, statutory derecognition may not be invoked until **at least** 3 years have passed. Conversely, where the CAC has declared that a union is not recognised, any further application may not be made by that union in respect of the same bargaining unit within 3 years.

> MEMO POINTS   A **bargaining unit** is the group of workers for which a union seeks recognition. Depending on industrial relations in the sector, the unit may be defined broadly (e.g. "Union A seeks to be the recognised union for all employers of Employer B") or narrowly ("Union C seeks to be the recognised union for all full-time permanent employees of Employer D working in the print room at the site in the town of E, and paid on the Employer's wage bands F, G and H").

Statutory recognition is a relatively complex and often lengthy process. It is also confrontational, with the union providing evidence in favour of recognition and the employer often contesting it. The desire to avoid unnecessary litigation sometimes leads unions and employers to opt out of the process mid-way through. It is possible for an employer and a union, having begun this process, but without concluding it, to **reach agreement** for recognition. Where that takes place, after the employer has received a request under this procedure, agreement will be deemed to be semi-voluntary (para 52(2) Sch A1 TULRCA 1992; ¶7290).

7226

The **essential features** of an application are set out in the following table:

7227

Stage	Requirements	Effect on subsequent bargaining if recognition agreed at this stage	Legislative reference (Sch A1 TULRCA 1992)
Formal request for recognition	– Union application in writing – Application must identify union and state that request is under the statutory procedure – Request must be received	Recognition will be deemed to be semi-voluntary (¶¶7290, 7391)	para 8
Period of negotiation	– 10 working days to negotiate bargaining unit and recognition – Period can be extended by further 20 working days – Either party may request assistance from Acas – Where employer requests Acas' involvement, and union refuses involvement or Acas' proposal, union may not refer to CAC		para 10
Reference to CAC	If no agreement or agreement on bargaining unit only, union may make reference to the CAC		paras 11-12
CAC will assess whether admissibility requirements met	For CAC to accept reference: – employer must have more than 21 workers [1]; – union must be independent [2]; – 10% of the bargaining unit must be union members; – must be no recognition agreement with any other union [3]; and – union must be able to show likely majority support [4]		paras 33-36
Determination of bargaining unit	Bargaining unit to be negotiated between parties or determined by CAC. Must be appropriate. CAC will take into account: – the views of the parties; – existing national and local bargaining arrangements; – location and characteristics of the workers; and – desirability of avoiding small fragmented bargaining units		paras 18-19

Stage	Requirements	Effect on subsequent bargaining if recognition agreed at this stage	Legislative reference (Sch A1 TULRCA 1992)
Assessing support for recognition	If majority of bargaining unit are union members, recognition will be automatic. If a significant number of the union members within the bargaining unit do not want recognition, the CAC may require a recognition ballot. Ballot may take the form of a workplace vote or a postal ballot. A qualified independent person will be appointed to organise it [5]. Each side must refrain from unfair practice. For the CAC to grant recognition, the majority of those voting plus at least 40% of the workers in the relevant bargaining unit must vote for it.	If majority membership or support in recognition ballot, recognition will be deemed to be statutory	paras 22-29

1. An employer has 21 or more workers if he has 21 or more workers on the day he receives the request, or an average of at least 21 workers in the 13 weeks ending with that day (para 7 Sch A1 TULRCA 1992).
2. A union can provide evidence of its independent status by means of a certificate of independence issued by the Certification Officer (¶7160).
3. In general, a union may not seek recognition where another union is already recognised (*R (on the application of the National Union of Journalists) v CAC and MGN Ltd* [2006] IRLR 53, CA). There are, however, limited exceptions to this rule. A union may apply to the CAC if it has a limited voluntary recognition agreement and it wishes to extend the agreement so that the union and the employer can bargain over pay, hours and holiday. A second union may also approach the CAC where a first union is recognised, but the first union is not independent (para 35 Sch A1 TULRCA 1992).
4. Typically, a union will show likely majority support by evidence of membership data and petition evidence from non-members. The CAC will evaluate this information in light of the CAC's own experience, as well as evidence as to custom and practice in the industry concerned.
5. A person may be a qualified independent person if he is a practising solicitor, a qualified accountant, or a member of one of six specified bodies (Recognition and Derecognition Ballots (Qualified Persons) Order SI 2000/1306).

Subsequent change to the business

7228 Where a **union has been recognised** by way of the statutory recognition procedures to represent workers employed by a particular business, and the business undergoes change, there are further processes to enable the bargaining unit to be changed or ended.

If either the union or the employer believes that the original **bargaining unit** (¶7225 memo point) is **no longer appropriate**, or **no longer exists**, that party may make an application to the CAC.

In effect, these are two alternative strategies. Where a union or an employer argues successfully that the bargaining unit is inappropriate, the result is that a new bargaining unit is established. Where an employer argues successfully that the bargaining unit has ceased to exist, the result is that the union is derecognised.

Procedure	Bargaining unit is inappropriate	Legislative reference (Sch A1 TULRCA 1992)	Bargaining unit has ceased to exist	Legislative reference (Sch A1 TULRCA 1992)
Step 1	Union or employer applies to CAC: application must be on specified form and accompanied by documentation.	para 92	Employer notifies union, copy to CAC: notice must identify the unit which has ceased to exist and give date from which bargaining will cease.	para 74(1), (2)
Step 2	CAC determines whether bargaining unit remains appropriate: if unit is appropriate CAC will take no further action.	paras 66-68	CAC has 10 days to decide whether application conforms to requirements.	para 74(7)

Procedure	Bargaining unit is inappropriate	Legislative reference (Sch A1 TULRCA 1992)	Bargaining unit has ceased to exist	Legislative reference (Sch A1 TULRCA 1992)
Step 3	If CAC decides unit is now inappropriate, parties will have 10 days to agree new unit.	para 69	The union has 10 days to challenge the notice; if the union does not challenge, bargaining unit will cease. The challenge must be in a prescribed form.	para 74(6)
Step 4	If parties do not agree, CAC will determine unit, taking into account factors including: the need for the unit to be compatible with effective management; the views of the employer or union; existing national and local bargaining arrangements; the desirability of avoiding small, fragmented units; the characteristics and location of workers falling into the original unit.	para 79(4)	CAC will determine whether unit has ceased to exist. It will ask both parties to give evidence and then must decide the question within 10 days. If the CAC decides the unit has ceased to exist it must make a declaration to this effect. Conversely, where the unit still exists, the CAC will instruct the parties to this effect.	para 77

3. Semi-voluntary recognition

7290 Subject to the statutory recognition procedure (¶7225) having been followed, a union will have a right to request statutory recognition. However, at each stage of the procedure, the legislation promotes agreement between the parties as a preference to persisting with the formal procedure. If the parties are able to reach an agreement on recognition during the formal process, the agreement is commonly referred to as "semi-voluntary". Such an agreement is described in the legislation as an **agreement for recognition** (para 52 Sch A1 TULRCA 1992).

7293 Where a union is recognised under this procedure, the method and scope of collective bargaining will be determined by the recognition agreement negotiated between the employer and the union (¶7391).

B. Derecognition

7340 Derecognition is the process by which an employer ceases to recognise a union as being entitled to bargain on behalf of workers within the bargaining unit. How this can be done will depend on how recognition was obtained.

Where a union has been **voluntarily recognised** by the employer, it can be derecognised at any time, usually without any legal recourse being available to the union. Where an employer derecognises a voluntarily-recognised union, however, he is required to do so formally. A union may not be derecognised by implication (*Union of Shop, Distributive and Allied Workers v Sketchley Ltd* [1981] IRLR 291, EAT).

Where a union has been **recognised** by the employer as a result of the **statutory procedure**, or where a union has been recognised **semi-voluntarily**, it can only be derecognised by way of a statutory derecognition procedure.

Statutory procedure

7341 Applications for statutory derecognition can be made on any one of six grounds:

Grounds of derecognition	Procedure	Legislative reference (Sch A1 TULRCA 1992)
Number of workers	If, at the end of the 3-year period for which statutory recognition must be granted, the employer has less than 21 workers, he can notify the union that the bargaining arrangements will cease to have effect from a given date. If the CAC accepts that fewer than 21 workers are employed by an employer in a relevant 13-week period, the CAC will issue an order terminating recognition.	paras 99-103
Request by employer to end bargaining arrangements	At the end of the 3-year period for which statutory recognition must be granted, an employer may apply to the CAC to hold a derecognition ballot.[1] The CAC must be satisfied that at least 10% of the workers in the bargaining unit favour an end to the bargaining arrangements and that a majority of workers constituting the bargaining unit would be likely to favour the end of recognition. If these conditions are met, the CAC may order a ballot.	paras 104-111
Request by worker to end bargaining arrangements	At the end of the 3-year period for which statutory recognition must be granted, a worker (or group of workers) may apply to the CAC to hold a derecognition ballot.[1] The CAC must be satisfied that at least 10% of the workers in the bargaining unit favour an end to the bargaining arrangements and a majority of workers in the unit would be likely to favour derecognition. If these conditions are met, the CAC may order a ballot.	paras 112-116
Request by employer where recognition had been automatic	Where the CAC has previously declared the union entitled to recognition without holding a ballot on the ground that most of the workers in the bargaining unit were union members, the employer may subsequently apply at any time to the CAC for the holding of a ballot to decide whether the bargaining arrangements should be ended.[1] The CAC must be satisfied that fewer than half of the workers constituting the bargaining unit are members of the union. If this condition is met, the CAC may order a ballot.	paras 122-133
Union never independent	A worker (or group of workers) may apply at any time to the CAC to hold a derecognition ballot on the grounds that the union is not independent.[1] The CAC must be satisfied that the union is not an independent union, that at least 10% of the workers in the bargaining unit favour an end to the bargaining arrangements, and that a majority of workers constituting the bargaining unit are likely to favour the end of recognition.	paras 134-147
Union loses independence	Where a union possessed a certificate of independence at the time that it obtained statutory recognition, but its certificate is later withdrawn at any time by the CAC, the bargaining arrangements will cease to have effect from the moment that the certificate is withdrawn. If the certificate of independence is re-issued, statutory recognition will be reinstated.	paras 148-55

1. Where the CAC orders a derecognition ballot, each side must follow the Code of Practice on Access and Unfair Practices During Recognition and Derecognition Ballots (¶7350).

C. Access to workers during recognition and derecognition ballots

During recognition and derecognition ballots, employers must give the union such access to the workers within the bargaining unit as is **reasonable** to enable the union to inform the workers of the object of the ballot and to seek their support (para 26(3) Sch A1 TULRCA 1992).

The BIS Code of Practice on Access and Unfair Practices During Recognition and Derecognition Ballots (referred to as "the Code" in this section) provides guidance.

> MEMO POINTS The Code is not legally binding but it will be admissible in evidence in any proceedings before any court or the CAC where it considers the Code relevant.

Access arrangements Access will vary according to the type of workplace involved and the characteristics of the workforce. The **aim** is to ensure that the union can reach the workers involved during the balloting process to inform them of its objectives and seek their support. Once the CAC has given the parties notice of the fact that it intends to hold a ballot, the **parties should meet** to discuss access arrangements. The parties should record an **access agreement** in writing. An access agreement should include:
– the union's programme for when, where and how it will access the workers;
– details of whether the union will access the workers on-site or off-site; and
– details of any mechanisms for resolving disagreements about implementing access arrangements.

Where appropriate, the employer's existing methods of communicating with the workforce should be adopted.

Employer's disclosure of information In order for the union to formulate its access proposals, the union may require certain information from the employer. It is reasonable for the employer to be expected to disclose information **relating to the workplace(s)** such as:
– typical methods of communicating with his workforce;
– workplace premises;
– patterns of work; and
– plans to put across his views to the workers about the recognition or derecognition of the union.

The employer should **not disclose** information regarding names or addresses (postal or email) of the workers in the bargaining unit, **unless** the individuals concerned have **authorised** the disclosure.

Role of Acas If an employer and union **fail to agree access arrangements** voluntarily, they may apply to Acas to conciliate differences. The appointed Acas officer will aim to assist the parties in resolving their differences on access arrangements in an impartial manner.

If no agreement can be reached, the CAC may then be asked to intervene. The CAC may consider delaying the ballot in order to provide extra time in which to reach an agreement on access arrangements or it may simply adjudicate and make an order.

Union surgeries Where appropriate, union "surgeries" can be organised at the workplace during working hours in order to give each worker an opportunity to meet with a union representative on an individual basis or in small groups. Workers who attend surgeries (or any other meetings with unions) should be paid in full unless the surgery or meeting takes place outside working hours when the worker would not have received payment from the employer in any event.

Communications with workers The **union should be able to**:
– display written material at the workplace (employers should, where practicable, provide a noticeboard);
– use the employer's website; and
– use internal email.

The **employer** should **take into consideration** the difficulties faced by unions in communicating with workers who might not work or be present full time in the workplace, for example part-time workers, home-workers, those on parental, maternity, paternity or adoption leave or those on sick leave.

The employer should be receptive to a union's suggestions for securing access to such workers.

7357 The Code suggests that **joint activities** between the employer and union should be encouraged. The Code envisages the use of a joint noticeboard informing the workers of the union's and the employer's activities or joint meetings where equal time is allocated to the union and the employer to put arguments either for or against recognition.

7358 While active **campaigning** by the parties is expected during the recognition and derecognition ballots, it must be undertaken responsibly on both sides and acrimonious situations should be avoided. There is, for example, a clear difference in practice between an employer making fair comments about job prospects and intimidatory behaviour designed to scare workers to vote against recognition.

7359 On an application by the union, the CAC may decide whether the employer has failed to allow reasonable access. If the CAC reaches such a decision, the CAC may order an employer to remedy the breach. Where such an order is made, and the breach continues, the CAC may order that the union is recognised, or not derecognised.

An employer may not make an application to the CAC that a union has failed in its duties under the Code. Where, however, the union has made an application to the CAC in complaint of a breach by the employer, the CAC may take into account the conduct of the union.

SECTION 3

Collective bargaining

7360 The purpose of a union is to regulate relations between employers and workers (¶7115). The means by which this is achieved is collective bargaining.

Collective bargaining takes place by way of formal negotiations. Representatives of the employer meet periodically with representatives of the union to negotiate and agree changes to the terms and conditions of work. In practice, the **scope** and the **method** of collective bargaining and the **enforceability** of collective agreements are all likely to depend on whether the union is recognised voluntarily (¶7214), semi-voluntarily (¶7290) or by means of the statutory method (¶7225).

Collective bargaining takes place to secure agreement. Where bargaining takes place, but there is no agreement, a collective dispute may result (¶7397).

A. Where a union is voluntarily recognised

1. Scope of bargaining

7363 A **collective agreement** is an agreement relating to one or more of the following (s 178 TULRCA 1992):
– terms and conditions of work;
– physical conditions;
– engagement or non-engagement of workers;

- termination or suspension of employment;
- allocation of work between workers or groups of workers;
- disciplinary matters;
- union membership;
- facilities for union representatives; and
- machinery for negotiation and consultation, and other procedures relating to these matters, including the recognition of a union by an employer to represent workers in the negotiation of such procedures.

Collective bargaining may relate to any of the matters set out above.

It should be noted that the phrase "terms and conditions of work" is drawn widely. Only rarely will a collective agreement be excluded from this definition.

Depending on the terms of the recognition agreement, a narrower definition may be agreed locally.

2. Method of bargaining

The recognition agreement will determine the method of collective bargaining. **7365**

The agreement should specify the **composition** of any bargaining **meetings**. Most often, a group of managers representing a single employer will meet with a group of union representatives from a single recognised union. As well as meetings of a single employer and a single union, it is also common to find a single employer meeting with two or more recognised unions at once. Normally, there will be some rough parity between the numbers representing each side.

The agreement should set out the **arrangements for regulating** the meeting. The meeting may have a single person appointed as chair, or two agreed chairs, or chairs may be appointed at each meeting. Decisions will normally be taken by consensus.

The agreement should set out any **other formalities** of the meetings. In any company, large or small, all agreed changes to company policies should be recorded in writing. Apart from this requirement, meetings in smaller companies may be relatively informal. At larger employers, or where an issue is likely to be controversial, greater formality will be found. Meetings will take place according to an agreed calendar. An individual will normally have responsibility for taking minutes of the meetings.

3. Enforceability of collective agreements

In general, the question of whether a collective agreement is enforceable will depend on which of the parties (i.e. the employer, the union or the worker) seeks to enforce it. **7367**

As a matter of policy, the courts have tended to hold that the union negotiates only on behalf of workers. Rather than the union having legal rights (or responsibilities), the courts have held that an agreement binds the employer and his workers.

So, for example, if an employer reaches a collective agreement with a union to pay his workers an increased salary, but fails to make the increased payment, then unless certain requirements have been met as to the form of the agreement (¶7382), only a worker, and not the union, will be able to sue to enforce the agreement.

Not all collective agreements will be enforceable, meanwhile, even between an employer and a worker.

Between employer and worker

For a term to be enforceable, the collective agreement must be incorporated into the worker's contract. **7368**

If the terms of the agreement are **incorporated**, it does not matter that the terms are not legally enforceable between the union and the employer, or that the worker does not approve of them (*Tocher v General Motors Scotland Ltd* [1981] IRLR 55, EAT) or is not a member of the union (*Young v Canadian Northern Railway Company* [1931] AC 83, PC), or even that the union representative negotiating the collective agreement has not consulted with the workforce over such terms or is not considered by the union to be a proper signatory (*Harris v Richard Lawson Autologistics Ltd* [2002] ICR 765, CA).

If the terms are **not incorporated**, they will not be enforceable merely because the employer joins the employers' association that negotiated the agreement (*Hamilton v Futura Floors Ltd* [1990] IRLR 478, CS), nor will they be enforceable merely because the worker joins the union that negotiated the agreement.

7369 **Incorporation into an individual worker's contract** The provisions of a collective agreement may be **expressly** incorporated into a worker's contract by agreement with the worker (for example, where the contract of employment provides for incorporation).

Although it is unusual for a contract to state explicitly which collective agreements are or will be incorporated into it, there are definite advantages to clarity, in reducing the opportunities for subsequent dispute.

7370 Situations may arise where it is **not clear** whether a term is to be **incorporated** or not.

This may occur, for example, where a worker's employment **contract** makes no reference to collective bargaining, or does makes reference to collective bargaining, but does so in a vague or general fashion and it is not clear whether the intention is actually that terms should be incorporated or not.

> [EXAMPLE] If the contract states that collective agreements will "usually" be incorporated, but there is no mechanism to establish whether an agreement is ripe for usual incorporation or not, the status of the agreement will be unclear.

This may also happen when a **collective agreement** makes no reference to incorporation or is in other ways vaguely drafted, or covers a topic that is usually considered inappropriate for incorporation.

> [EXAMPLE] Where a redundancy agreement is designed to cover a particular period but does not state clearly the intended duration of the agreement, the status of the agreement will be unclear.

7371 In situations where it is not clear whether a term is in fact to be incorporated or not, the provisions of a collective contract may be **impliedly** incorporated by virtue of the custom and practice within the industry. Clear evidence is required to establish custom and practice (*Henry v London General Transport Services Ltd* [2002] IRLR 472, CA). If such an inference would be inconsistent with an express contractual term, no such inference will be drawn (*Gascol Conversions Ltd v J W Mercer* [1974] IRLR 155, CA).

7372 **Intention of employer and worker** The single most important factor in deciding whether part of a collective agreement is to be incorporated into individual contracts will be the **evidence** as to the contractual intention of the employer and the worker (¶1117).

If the intention was for the terms to be incorporated, the terms will bind, even where there are words in an agreement to the effect that it will not bind (*Marley v Forward Trust Group Ltd* [1986] IRLR 369, CA).

> [EXAMPLE] In *Marley v Forward Trust Group Ltd*, the provisions of a collective agreement relating to enhanced redundancy payments were incorporated into M's contract. The collective agreement itself stated that the provisions were binding in honour only as between the employer and the union. However, the Court held that M could rely on the redundancy provisions as being a legally binding term of his contract.

7373 The courts are likely to **analyse** an agreement **term by term**, rather than as a whole.

If a collective agreement is expressly incorporated but by general words, it will be for the courts to consider, together with the words of incorporation, whether any part of the agreement is suitable to be a term of the individual's contract.

If it is not suitable, the inference will be that the part is not incorporated.

> **EXAMPLE**
> 1. In *Stenson, Torrie and Marshall v West Dunbartonshire Council* [2007] UKEAT 0089_06_0908, the EAT considered the situation of three wardens employed under contracts which provided, among other things, that salary and conditions were "in accordance with" a particular collective agreement. On a close reading of the contracts it became clear that some provisions of the collective agreement had been adopted wholesale, while other provisions had been disregarded entirely. It followed that terms of the collective agreement relating to allowances for night-time working, which were not mentioned in the individual employment contracts, had not been incorporated into them.
> 2. In *Bristol City Council v Deadman* [2007] IRLR 888, CA, the Court of Appeal considered two collective agreements: one was an equality policy and the other a procedure for investigating complaints of harassment. The first was found to be merely indicative of the sorts of standards that the council considered appropriate, and not sufficiently precise to be contractual. The second document, although issued in conjunction with the first, was more precise. It was a formal procedure for complaint handling, which was intended to be binding. Accordingly, the Court held that its terms had become contractually binding terms of employment.
> 3. In *Malone and ors v British Airways Plc* [2010] EWCA Civ 1225, the Court of Appeal considered whether a term within a collective agreement allowing for minimum staffing levels was contractually binding. They held that, despite the collective agreement's inclusion in the employees' written contracts, the term in question could not have been intended to have contractual effect because, if it had, the employees would have been entitled to refuse to work if the staffing levels had not been met, and this would have been disastrous for the employer's business. The term was intended as an undertaking to the employees and was made with the intention both to protect jobs and to protect the cabin crews collectively against excessive demands in terms of work and effort: it was intended to be binding only in honour, although it created a danger that, if breached, industrial action would follow.

To avoid ambiguity, the employer may therefore wish to specify in the contract which terms are incorporated.

7374
If there is no express incorporation, incorporation may only be inferred if the particular provision is suitable by its nature and character to be a term of the contract.

Where the terms of a collective agreement are for some reason **inappropriate** to be treated as incorporated into the contract, the courts have not incorporated them. Such terms include:
– consultation and procedural issues, including redundancy provisions (a "last in first out" selection procedure) (*Alexander v Standard Telephones & Cables Ltd (No 2)* [1991] IRLR 286, QBD; *LTI Ltd v Radford* [2000] UKEAT 164_00_1506; *Kaur v MG Rover Group Ltd* [2005] IRLR 40, CA);

> **EXAMPLE** In *Kaur v MG Rover Group Ltd*, the Court held that the statement "There will be no compulsory redundancy" in a collective agreement which covered other manpower and industrial relations issues was merely aspirational, vague and only related to a commitment at a collective level. It was therefore not a provision which could be incorporated into the worker's individual contract.

– broad policy issues (e.g. long-term plans on business continuity, retraining and redundancy) (*British Leyland (UK) Ltd v McQuilken* [1978] IRLR 245, EAT);
– collective issues (e.g. collective bargaining) (*Tadd v Eastwood and Daily Telegraph Ltd* [1983] IRLR 320, QBD; *National Coal Board v National Union of Mineworkers* [1986] IRLR 439, ChD);
– union recognition; and
– "no strike" clauses. Note that incorporation of a provision of a collective agreement restricting a worker's right to take industrial action is prohibited, unless certain conditions are met (¶7556).

7375
Where **bargaining** takes place at **different levels**, incompatible, competing agreements may result (for example, both national and local agreements suggesting different pay for the same employment).

If there is a conflict between those agreements, the question as to which terms are incorporated into the individual contract will depend on the intention of the employer and worker.

If, for example, a **local agreement** was made **after** a national agreement and commented on or varied the national agreement, then it would be appropriate to conclude that the local agreement was intended to bind (*Barnett v NCB* [1978] ICR 1102, EAT). In another case, the EAT held that since local agreements are usually more immediate, there is a presumption that they are intended to have priority, unless there is a clear inference to be drawn from the evidence as to the contrary intention of the parties (*Gascol Conversions Ltd v J W Mercer* [1974] IRLR 155, CA).

A linked problem arises where a national agreement gives authority to employers and to unions to negotiate agreement at a **local** level, but **agreement is not reached**. For example, when two unions are represented in the local arrangements, and the larger union accepts the proposals while the smaller union rejects them. In a case where this factual situation arose, the EAT looked to the arrangements made for the national bargaining, and found that a very high level of consensus was required before agreements could be reached. It followed that if the local agreement was to have precedence over the national agreement, then a similarly high level of consensus would be required of the local agreement (*South Tyneside MBC v Graham* [2003] UKEAT 0107_03_3110).

7376 **Variation of an incorporated term** Where there is a collective agreement, and it is varied by a subsequent collective agreement, for the terms of the new agreement to be incorporated into the employment contract the employer and the worker must intend incorporation to take place.

If there is an **express agreement** to incorporate provisions of collective agreements as renegotiated from time to time, then any variations will automatically vary the individual contract (*Higgins v Cables Montague Contracts Ltd* [1994] UKEAT 564_93_0202).

> EXAMPLE In *Higgins v Cables Montague Contracts Ltd*, H's statement of particulars stated that his terms of employment were in accordance with, and subject to, collective agreements currently in force between the company and the union. The EAT held that an agreement between the company and the union to reduce wages by 20% as a result of the company's financial difficulties was binding on H.

7377 If there is **no agreement** to incorporate collectively agreed terms as renegotiated from time to time, variations to the collective agreements must be incorporated into the individual contract, either by individual agreement or by virtue of custom and practice.

It may be possible to **infer an agreement** to vary the contract by the parties' conduct, i.e. the application by the employer of the revised terms and the acceptance of those terms by the worker.

There will be a very strong presumption that the parties to the individual contract will have intended that such terms should continue, if the consequence of not doing so would be that there would be no binding contractual terms at all (*Framptons Ltd v Badger* [2006] UKEAT 0138_06_0906).

7378 The **employer** cannot change a term incorporated into an individual contract by a **unilateral variation**, abrogation or withdrawal from the collective agreement but must agree with the recognised union to vary the collective agreement.

If the collective agreement is not varied by agreement, the individual contracts will remain unaffected (*Robertson and Jackson v British Gas Corporation* [1983] IRLR 302, CA; *Lee v GEC Plessey Telecommunications* [1993] IRLR 383, QBD).

Similarly, a **worker** cannot **unilaterally withdraw** his agreement once he has agreed that the provisions of a collective agreement are incorporated into his contract (*Tocher v General Motors Scotland Ltd* [1981] IRLR 55, EAT). If the worker resigns as a union member, he will still be bound.

7379 **Special cases** If the terms of the collective agreement have been incorporated into the individual worker's contract, the **termination of the collective agreement** will not remove those terms from the individual contract and the parties can continue to enforce them (*Robertson and Jackson v British Gas Corporation* [1983] IRLR 302, CA).

7380 Similarly, if the **business transfers to a new employer** under the transfer (TUPE) regulations (¶7900), any collective agreement made between the original employer and a union recognised by him in respect of the transferring workers (and incorporated into their contracts of employment) will have effect after the transfer as if made between the transferee employer

Between union and either employer or worker

7382 A collective agreement will **only** be **enforceable** between a union and an employer where the agreement is in writing and expressly states that the parties intend the agreement to constitute a binding contract between the parties (s 179(1), (2) TULRCA 1992).

In practice, if only because employers are rarely willing to be bound in this fashion, these requirements are rarely met.

A collective agreement will not usually be enforceable between a union and a worker. The union does, however, have a duty to its members to negotiate in good faith (¶7396), which can give rise to legal duties.

B. Where union is recognised by the statutory procedure

1. Scope of bargaining

7383 Under the statutory recognition procedure, a **narrow definition** of collective bargaining applies. The union will have authority to conduct negotiations only on pay, hours and holidays and on training (para 3(3) Sch A1 TULRCA 1992).

The definition of "pay" does not include terms relating to a person's membership of, or rights under, an occupational or personal pension scheme (s 171A(1) TULRCA 1992).

2. Method of bargaining

7385 Where the CAC has issued a declaration of recognition, the parties then should negotiate a collective agreement. Following the declaration of recognition, the parties have 30 working days to agree on a method of collective bargaining (para 30 Sch A1 TULRCA 1992).

If agreement on the bargaining method **is not reached** within this timescale, the CAC will specify the method to be used. In doing so, it will have regard to the "model method" (¶7386). The parties may also apply to the CAC where, following a declaration of recognition, they have agreed on a method but one party has failed to carry out the agreement (para 32 Sch A1 TULRCA 1992).

7386 **Model method** The model method provides for a **joint negotiating body** (JNB), comprised of at least three representatives from the union and three from the employer, which should be established to discuss and negotiate pay, hours and holidays of workers in the bargaining unit. Each union recognised by the employer is entitled to at least one seat on the JNB. The union representatives on the JNB may be workers employed by the employer or individuals employed by the union as union officials (Trade Union Recognition (Method of Collective Bargaining) Order SI 2000/1300).

Under the model method, the parties set aside half a working day for each JNB meeting unless agreed otherwise. Ordinarily JNB meetings should be held during normal working time.

The employer and union are required to have regard to the Acas Code of Practice on Time Off for Trade Union Duties and Activities and ensure that there is no unwarranted or unjustified failure to adhere to the Code (¶3910).

7387 A **specific bargaining procedure**, as follows, is set out in the model method, including a suggested timetable for the parties to deal with proposals of adjustments to pay, hours and holidays on an annual basis. There is no provision for the parties to negotiate outside this timescale.

Stage		Requirements
Step 1	Union submits pay claim	Must be in writing, must normally be submitted at least a month before the date when the employer normally alters pay; where there is no established date, union shall submit claim within 3 months of method being imposed and by this date in subsequent rounds
Step 2	Negotiation	Within 10 days of submission of claim, there should be a JNB meeting (3 present from each side, 50% attendance required for quorum)
Step 3	Employer responds to claim	Response should be provided within 15 days, in writing or at subsequent JNB meeting
Step 4	Negotiation	If no agreement, another JNB meeting should be held within 10 days of receipt of employer's response
Step 5	Further negotiation	If still no agreement, another JNB meeting should be held within 10 days: at this meeting, the union may add up to two union officials to its negotiating team and the employer may add up to two workers or officials of an employer's organisation
Step 6	Approach to Acas	If still no agreement, either or both sides have 5 days to approach Acas to arrange further negotiations

7388 **Consultation over training** Once statutory recognition has been granted, the employer will also be under a duty to consult over training with the union (s 70B TULRCA 1992) (unless the agreement has been otherwise varied by the parties). The employer must invite the union to send representatives to a meeting with the employer for the purposes of consultation about:
– the employer's training policy;
– the employer's training plans during the following 6 months; and
– reporting about training since the previous 6-monthly meeting.

The first meeting must be held within 6 months of the day on which the CAC specifies the bargaining method. At least 2 weeks before a meeting the employer must provide the union with any information without which the union's representatives would be impeded, to a material extent, at the meeting (s 70B(4) TULRCA 1992).

A union may bring a complaint to an employment tribunal if an employer **fails to comply** with its duties in respect of consultation over training (s 70C(1) TULRCA 1992). The complaint has to be brought within 3 months, beginning with the date of the failure to consult, or within such period as the tribunal considers reasonable (s 70C(2) TULRCA 1992). Where a complaint is successful, a tribunal may make a declaration to that effect and, in addition, may make an award of compensation to be paid by the employer to each member of the bargaining unit. The amount shall not, in relation to each person, exceed 2 weeks' pay (¶2920).

3. Enforceability of collective agreements

7389 The method imposed by the CAC, including the model method, **constitutes** a legally binding contract between the parties. However, the parties **may agree** to vary its terms, including the removal of its legally binding status.

Once the CAC has imposed a method of collective bargaining, an employer may **not vary** the contractual terms affecting pay, hours and holidays of any workers within the bargaining unit **unless** he has first negotiated his proposals with the union in accordance with the bargaining method.

The employer's duties refer to collective terms. Individual workers will not be prevented from discussing or negotiating with their employer the terms of their contract of employment which differ from the terms of any collective agreement which has been entered into by the employer and union as a result of collective bargaining conducted by this method.

Either party may apply for an order for specific performance if the other party **breaches** any **provision** of the collective bargaining method (para 31(6) Sch A1 TULRCA 1992). A failure to comply with an order for specific performance would constitute a contempt of court.

C. Where union is semi-voluntarily recognised

The **scope** of collective bargaining can be agreed by the parties or will be imposed on the parties by the CAC. The parties are not restricted to bargaining over pay, hours and holidays (para 54(3) Sch A1 TULRCA 1992). The parties can widen the scope of the matters to be dealt with by collective bargaining in the recognition agreement. The scope of a collective agreement cannot, however, be wider than the scope allowed under the statutory definition of a collective agreement (¶7363). 7391

The **method** of collective bargaining also can be agreed or will be imposed on the parties by the CAC. If the parties reach an agreement for recognition, they must try to negotiate a bargaining method within 30 working days. If no agreement is reached during the initial period, the parties may apply to the CAC for assistance (para 58(3) Sch A1 TULRCA 1992). 7392

Where the parties do not agree as to a collective bargaining method, the CAC will try to promote agreement. If the parties cannot agree a collective bargaining method within 20 working days (starting with the date on which the CAC accepts the application), the CAC will specify the method by which the parties are to conduct collective bargaining (para 63(2) Sch A1 TULRCA 1992). The CAC will take into consideration the model method (¶7386) when specifying the bargaining method to be implemented.

Collective agreements negotiated between employers and semi-voluntarily recognised unions will have the same **enforceability** as agreements negotiated between employers and voluntarily recognised unions (¶¶7367+). 7393

D. Duties during bargaining

Employer duty to disclose information

When bargaining with an employer, the **representatives of a recognised union** have the right to have information disclosed to them where (s 181 TULRCA 1992): 7395
– without it, the union representatives would be materially impeded in carrying on collective bargaining, and
– it would be in accordance with good industrial relations practice for the information to be disclosed.

Where an employer has previously agreed to bargain with a union, with respect to a certain matter, the employer may not use the union's legitimate request for information as an excuse to refuse to bargain with it any further on this matter or at all (*British Petroleum Chemicals Ltd and Transport and General Workers Union* [1986] CAC award 86/1).

EXAMPLE In *British Petroleum Chemicals Ltd and Transport and General Workers Union*, an employer refused to disclose information concerning a pension scheme on the grounds that, even if the information was disclosed, the employer had no intention of negotiating its contents with the union. The Central Arbitration Committee held, however, that the employer had previously agreed to recognise the union for the purposes of negotiating over pensions, and therefore that the union was entitled to the information.

The employer is **not**, however, **obliged to disclose information** where the disclosure would (s 182 TULRCA 1992):
- be against the interests of national security;
- contravene a prohibition imposed by or under an enactment;
- breach a confidence reposed in him by another person;
- relate specifically to an individual;
- cause substantial injury to his undertaking for reasons other than its effect on collective bargaining; or
- reveal material obtained by him for the purpose of bringing, prosecuting or defending any legal proceedings.

> MEMO POINTS   As well as the right to bargain collectively with the employer, representatives of recognised unions **also** have the **right to be informed and consulted on certain, specific topics**, which are listed at ¶7651. In addition, members of trade unions, like other workers, benefit from the rights to information and consultation in the workplace, which are set out in more detail at Chapter 22.

Union duty to negotiate with care

7396 A union also has duties to its members. Where a union **negotiates negligently**, with the result that an agreement causes unjustifiable loss to its members, or where it **misrepresents** an agreement to its members, the members may be able to bring a claim against the union. Where the union has a statutory duty, as under the provisions of the Equality Act 2010 (¶7146), and the appropriate forum for a remedy is an employment tribunal, a member may bring an action there.

> MEMO POINTS   In *GMB v Allen and ors* [2007] IRLR 752, EAT (decision confirmed on appeal at [2008] IRLR 690, CA), a union misrepresented an employer's offer to its members, suggesting that the offer was more favourable than it actually was. The EAT declared that, on the facts, the members might have succeeded in a case of breach of an implied duty of fair representation or loss through misrepresentation, but as these claims had not been pleaded, the case was not decided on this point.

E. Collective disputes

7397 Not all negotiations between an employer and a union will result in agreement. Typically, the **recognition agreement** (¶7216) will contain **procedures** for remedying disputes between the union and the employer. Such procedures may require the union to declare a trade dispute (¶7417).

Under the terms of the recognition agreement, there may be compulsory dispute resolution procedures, including appeals to higher levels of management than those involved in negotiations to date, or to the employer's governing body, or to some other organisation. The recognition agreement may also give some role to Acas (¶9201), which offers its services as a mediator in trade disputes.

Where an employer and a union cannot agree, the union may consider taking industrial action (¶7400).

SECTION 4

Strikes and other industrial action

7400 **Strike action** is action that involves the total withdrawal of labour. It does not have to be indefinite ("continuous") and may include 1-day or even shorter stoppages. Strikes often involve workers leaving the workplace, and there may be picketing to prevent non-strikers from attending at work. Less commonly, strikes may involve workers entering and occupying a workplace.

Action short of a strike includes overtime bans and call-out bans, a work to rule or any other action that falls short of a total withdrawal of labour.

UK legislation on industrial action is very restrictive, when compared to that of other EU member states and the norms of good practice as set out by the International Labour Organisation. There is **no** general **right to strike** or to take any other form of industrial action, including action short of a strike, and under common law industrial action amounts to a breach of contract.

How significant the breach is will depend on all the circumstances. If the breach is sufficiently serious and amounts to a fundamental breach, the employer may be justified in **dismissing** the individual (¶7520).

The law gives **legal immunities** in certain circumstances, protecting the individual striker against unfair dismissal, and the union against civil litigation, by the employer, where the industrial action is conducted strictly in accordance with the statutory provisions. For action to be **protected**, a ballot must have been held. There are also strict requirements regarding the union to give notice to the employer (¶7490). Where these requirements have not been met, the most common remedy available to an employer is an injunction prohibiting the action from going ahead.

Where industrial action takes place and is unprotected, or where improper picketing takes place, strike action may be unlawful. In such circumstances, the union, its officers and strikers may all be liable for legal action in the civil courts.

A. Industrial action

Industrial action **includes** any concerted action by workers to bring about, or prevent, changes to terms and conditions or to any other working arrangements. **7410**

Industrial action is most commonly identified with strike action, but includes any action aimed at persuasion, for example, a work to rule, an overtime ban, "work without enthusiasm", a refusal to cover for others, or a refusal to do specific tasks. The fact that there is no contractual obligation to undertake certain duties (for example, overtime) does not mean that it cannot amount to industrial action, when taken with the aim of achieving changes at work.

1. Lawful action

For any industrial action to be **protected**, the following conditions must be met: **7416**
– the proposed industrial action must have a lawful purpose;
– it must be supported by a ballot;
– the ballot itself is subject to a series of procedural requirements;
– the action must be lawfully called;
– the union must notify the employer of its intention to take action; and
– the action must take place within the duration of the ballot result.

Any worker taking unlawful industrial action will be risking dismissal, and will not have the right to submit an unfair dismissal claim to a tribunal.

a. Lawful purpose

For any industrial action to be protected, it must fall within the statutory **definition** of a **trade dispute**, namely a dispute between workers and their employer, which relates wholly or mainly to one or more of the following (s 244 TULRCA 1992): **7417**

– terms and conditions of employment, or the physical conditions in which any workers are required to work;
– engagement or non-engagement, or termination or suspension of employment or the duties of employment, of one or more workers;
– the allocation of work or the duties of employment between workers or groups of workers;
– matters of discipline;
– a worker's membership or non-membership of a union;
– facilities for representatives of unions; and
– the machinery for negotiation or consultation and other procedures relating to any of the above matters, including the recognition by employers or employers' associations of the right of a union to represent workers in such negotiation or consultation or in the carrying out of such procedures.

The phrase "terms and conditions of employment" is widely drawn and has been held to include, for example:
– action by teachers to prevent a disruptive pupil from returning to schooling (*P v National Association of Schoolmasters and Union of Women Teachers* [2001] IRLR 532, CA); and
– action to prevent the introduction of a voluntary productivity scheme (*BT plc v CWU* [2004] IRLR 58).

It is important to emphasise that any industrial action taken in contemplation or furtherance of a dispute that does not come within this definition will not be protected.

Various possible **disputes** fall **outside** this definition.

7418 **1. To compel union membership** (s 222 TULRCA 1992) Any action aimed at forcing the employer to employ union members is not a trade dispute. Industrial action which occurs due to the belief that an employer is employing, or might employ, a non-union member, or might fail to discriminate against a non-member, is unprotected. Similarly, industrial action which amounts to an inducement or attempted inducement to introduce a requirement of union membership into a contract is unprotected.

Pressure to impose a union recognition requirement into a contract or a proposed contract or a refusal to deal with a person on the grounds of union exclusion is also unprotected.

7419 **2. Where the dispute is political** Any dispute that is in some way connected with government policies is likely to be defined as a political dispute (*London Borough of Wandsworth v National Union of Schoolmasters and Union of Women Teachers* [1993] IRLR 344, CA; *Westminster City Council v Unison* [2001] IRLR 524, CA).

Although the courts have provided some guidance as to what will or will not be included, the dividing line between protected and unprotected action sometimes seems fine.

EXAMPLE
1. In *London Borough of Wandsworth v National Union of Schoolmasters and Union of Women Teachers*, a dispute over the new national curriculum and its impact in schools on the working conditions of teachers was defined as a political dispute.
2. In *Westminster City Council v Unison*, a dispute about a change of employer following a proposal to "externalise" the functions of a local council to a private company, to which employees objected on the basis that they wished to remain employees of the local council, was defined as political.

7420 **3. In response to the dismissal of unofficial strikers** (s 223 TULRCA 1992) Industrial action taken in response to the dismissal of unofficial strikers is not protected, regardless of whether the action is carried out in compliance with all of the legal rules and has been representatively sanctioned by the union.

7421 **4. Where workers are taking secondary action** (s 224 TULRCA 1992) Secondary action, sometimes called "solidarity" or "sympathy" action, involves calling on those employed by another employer to take industrial action in support of the dispute where there is no actual dispute with the secondary employer.

Industrial action taken by workers, employed by a third party employer, in support for those in dispute is outside the protection of the immunities. Secondary picketing, which aims to picket workers in another workplace, is similarly outside the protection.

5. Where reason for dispute differs If the reason that the union gives for calling industrial action is not the main cause of the dispute, the action will not be protected. However, where the union honestly believes that the dispute is over an issue which it has identified, its immunity will not be lost (London Borough of Newham v NALGO [1993] IRLR 83, CA).

6. Where there is no actual dispute Any industrial action will not be protected if there is no actual dispute in existence (London Underground Ltd v NUR [1989] IRLR 341, QBD).

EXAMPLE In *London Underground Ltd v NUR*, the Court ruled that industrial action would not be protected because matters were included in the ballot form which were not yet the subject of a dispute.

7. A dispute between groups of workers or another party A demarcation dispute between one group of workers and another is not covered and would, therefore, never be protected. A dispute with a party other than the employer is also not covered (Connex South Eastern v RMT [1999] IRLR 249, CA).

EXAMPLE In *Connex South Eastern v RMT*, the Court ruled that rail safety, the ostensible cause of the dispute, was not the responsibility of the employer. It followed that the dispute was not protected.

8. Disputes over future terms and conditions A dispute over future terms and conditions of employment cannot be the subject of a legitimate trade dispute (UNISON v United Kingdom [2002] IRLR 497). The restriction on future disputes is contained within TULRCA 1992. In *UNISON v United Kingdom* [2002] IRLR 497, the European Court of Human Rights held that this statutory restriction contravened the right to freedom of association under the European Convention on Human Rights (art 11 European Convention on Human Rights). The Court, however, went on to allow that such a restriction was both justified and proportionate.

EXAMPLE In *UNISON v United Kingdom*, the ownership of a hospital was to be transferred under the TUPE Regulations. The employer refused to seek a guarantee from the transferee that terms and conditions of employment would be protected. The union called a ballot in response to this failure. The employer sought an injunction prohibiting the strike and was successful. The ECHR declined to overturn this ruling.

9. Supply of goods Industrial action is unprotected if it:
– interferes with the supply of goods or services or can reasonably be expected to do so, or there is an allegation that breaches of contracts have been induced or threatened; and
– the reason, or one of the reasons for this is that a supplier does not recognise unions or does not negotiate or consult with them.

A term in a contract for the supply of goods and services is void in so far as it purports to require a party to the contract to recognise a union or to negotiate or consult with it. A refusal to deal with a supplier of goods or services because the supplier does not recognise unions is also prohibited, as is the exclusion, for example from tender applications, of a supplier on similar grounds. Any party adversely affected by such action can bring a claim for a breach of statutory duty.

b. Supported by a ballot

An act done by a union to induce someone to take part in or continue to take part in a trade dispute is not protected unless it has the support of a ballot (s 226 TULRCA 1992). Action is deemed to be supported by a ballot where the workers who are entitled to vote did so in favour of the action and it was reasonable to assume that the union's members would be called upon to take industrial action. It will only be taken to have the support of a ballot in the **following circumstances**:
– all of the rules about the procedure for holding the ballot, notification and declaration of the results are complied with;
– the majority voting in the ballot answered affirmatively to the question on industrial action; and

– the industrial action, authorised by the ballot, is called by the person specified in the ballot to do so.

A ballot would not be unlawful simply because the union had campaigned for its members to vote in a particular way. The fact that a union has called for a "yes" vote and is clearly partisan does not nullify the ballot. A union is "perfectly entitled to be partisan" as long as it complies with the legislation (*London Borough of Newham v NALGO* [1993] IRLR 83, CA).

7445 **Ballots of over 50 members** Where the number of members who would be entitled to vote in an industrial action ballot exceeds 50, the union must appoint an **independent scrutineer** before the ballot takes place (s 226B TULRCA 1992).

The scrutineer has to take appropriate steps to enable **a report** to be made to the union on the conduct of the ballot, by no later than 4 weeks after the ballot. The report must indicate whether the scrutineer is satisfied that the legal requirements were complied with. The report must also show whether the scrutineer was satisfied with the arrangements for producing, storing, distributing, handling and counting the voting papers.

The scrutineer's report should indicate whether he was able to carry out his functions without interference by the union, its representatives, members or workers.

7446 An employer has the **right to see a copy** of this report, provided that a request is made to the union within 6 months of the ballot. Individual members of the union who were entitled to vote in the ballot also have this right. The union can specify a reasonable fee to provide the report.

7447 **Separate employers** Industrial action at one location, where all the relevant workers are covered by the **same terms and conditions**, can be by single ballot, even if the action would affect more than one employer. If the terms and conditions are different, separate ballots must be held.

> EXAMPLE In *University of Central England v National and Local Government Officers' Association* [1993] IRLR 81, QBD, a single ballot which covered college staff employed by several different employers was still valid, since the subject matter of the dispute related to common terms and conditions.

7448 **Separate workplaces** A union may be required to hold separate ballots where members are working in different workplaces (ss 226(3), 228 TULRCA 1992). However, it can organise an aggregated ballot where there is at least one individual who is affected by the dispute in each of the workplaces aggregated into the single ballot. Ballots can also be aggregated where linked by occupation and employer(s).

Where there are separate ballots for different workplaces, industrial action can only be taken to have the support of a ballot if the majority in the specific workplace has voted in favour of the industrial action.

Members to be balloted

7449 The union has to give the **right to vote** in the ballot to all of its members who (it is reasonably believed at the time of the ballot) might be called on by the union to take part in industrial action (s 227 TULRCA 1992). If the union ballots either too widely or too narrowly it could lose its protection in respect of the proposed action. However, where there is a failure to comply which is accidental and unlikely to affect the ballot result, the mere fact that some members were added in or left out will not jeopardise the lawfulness of the ballot.

7450 If a union **fails to send out ballot papers** to a substantial number of members whom the union could reasonably have expected to be called on to take industrial action, the industrial action may be restrained on the basis that at least some of the members who were not balloted would have been induced to strike (*National Union of Rail, Maritime and Transport Workers v Midland Mainline Ltd* [2001] IRLR 813, CA). However, if members have joined the union after the date of the ballot it can still induce them to take industrial action (*London Underground Ltd v National Union of Rail, Maritime and Transport Workers* [1996] ICR 170, CA).

Overseas members In the case of members of the union who are working overseas during the period when votes are being cast, the union has the right to decide whether or not it will entitle them to vote (ss 227-230 TULRCA 1992). If it does decide to do so it does not have to comply with the rules on separate workplace ballots, marking the ballot paper and the conduct of the ballot in relation to the votes of these members. However, it must, when providing information on the outcome of the ballot, be able to distinguish between the results of those members who are overseas and those who are not.

Breach of members' right to ballot

A member of a union who claims that members (including himself) are likely to be induced to take industrial action without the support of a ballot can apply for a **court order** (s 62 TULRCA 1992). If granted, it will require the union to take steps to ensure that there is no further or continued inducement of members to take industrial action. It is irrelevant that the union's inducement may have been ineffective.

c. Ballot requirements

To comply with **procedural** requirements, ballots must be:
– commenced within a specified timescale;
– notified in advance to the employer;
– in secret;
– by post;
– fairly and accurately counted;
– independently scrutinised (if the ballot is of over 50 members); and
– prepared so as to inform the worker of the extent of the legal protection against dismissal.

The BIS Code of Practice on Industrial Action Ballots and Notice to Employers gives **guidance** to employers and unions to promote the improvement of industrial relations and good practice in the conduct of industrial action ballots. It gives guidance on situations where a ballot would be appropriate and on the steps that unions must take to comply with the law on ballots.

The Court of Appeal has also provided a thorough analysis of the requirements for a properly conducted ballot and has considered both the statutory provisions and the relevant case law in some detail (*National Union of Rail, Maritime and Transport Workers v Serco Ltd (t/a Serco Docklands)* [2011] EWCA Civ 226). In this case, the Court emphasised that a **certain limited degree of flexibility** should be allowed within balloting requirements, though of course this flexibility must be exercised within the numerous statutory rules that must still be observed.

EXAMPLE
1. In *National Union of Rail, Maritime and Transport Workers v Serco Ltd (t/a Serco Docklands)*, the Court of Appeal allowed two linked appeals by unions against interim injunctions that had prevented them from striking. The High Court had granted the injunctions on the basis that the member ballots had not been properly conducted on numerous grounds. The most significant issues considered were whether the fact that inaccurate members lists had led to two more individuals voting was sufficiently accidental under the terms of the statute, the exact requirements on information to be given in the ballot notice and the strike notice, whether the "de minimis"' principle could apply to breaching the duty to give accurate figures, and the parameters of the requirement to give information including lists of figures for workplace and job categories, along with information as to how these figures were calculated.
2. In *London Underground Ltd v Associated Society of Locomotive Engineers and Firemen* [2011] EWHC 3506 (QB), there was a dispute between the trade union ASLEF and London Underground Ltd (LU) over payments to train drivers for working on Boxing Day. In November 2011, ASLEF posted a notice on its website that members would shortly be asked to vote in favour of industrial action on Boxing Day. The same notice was carried in the December 2011 issue of the ASLEF journal sent to all its members. Two days after the notice was posted on its website, ASLEF notified LU that its members were to be balloted on the Boxing Day working dispute and that those to be balloted were "All Train Operator and Instructor Operator members of ASLEF employed by you and paying their membership subscriptions by check off at [listed depots]" plus 789 specified union members. In mid-December 2011, ASLEF sent LU the ballot result – 920 people, of the 998 who had voted,

had voted in favour of strike action. ASLEF also issued a notice stating that the executive committee had resolved to call for strike action on 3 additional days in 2012 (16 January and 3 and 13 February). LU applied for an interim injunction to prevent the Boxing Day strike going ahead, arguing that ASLEF had failed to tell its members of the full extent of the proposed action (having balloted its members for a mandate to strike on Boxing Day, ASLEF had called for strike action on three further days). In addition, LU argued that around 75% of those balloted would not be expecting to work on Boxing Day and as such ASLEF could not have reasonably believed those members would be called upon to take part in the industrial action.

The High Court refused to grant an interim injunction to prevent the industrial action. The Court held that the union's publicity material was not intended to limit the industrial action to Boxing Day alone (in particular, similar industrial action in 2010 had been balloted in similar terms and had taken place over several days). Further, entitlement to vote was not restricted to those who would actually take the industrial action by striking; it extended to those who might associate themselves with it, e.g. by joining picket lines.

MEMO POINTS The Code of Practice is not legally binding but may be taken into account by a tribunal or court in deciding whether an industrial action is lawful.

Advance notice requirements

7463 There are **four key stages** when the union must communicate in writing with the employer and failure to comply with any of these stages will remove the union's immunity from the industrial action (s 226A TULRCA 1992). At each of these stages, the notice requirements are as follows.

7464 **1. Notice to employer** At least 7 days **before the opening day** of the ballot (i.e. the first day when a voting paper is sent to any member entitled to vote), the union must take reasonable steps to ensure that it gives the employer notice of its intention to hold a ballot (s 226A(1)(a) TULRCA 1992). It must specify the date that it reasonably expects the ballot will begin and provide specific information (see below).

Where the **validity** of a ballot notice is at **issue**, it is important to consider the notice objectively and in context, rather than the subjective intentions of the union or the subjective view of the company (*English, Welsh and Scottish Railway Ltd and anor v National Union of Rail, Maritime and Transport Workers* [2004] EWCA Civ 1539).

The union must provide certain information to the employer who is believed to be the employer of those entitled to vote in the ballot. The union must provide a **list** of the categories of worker to which the workers concerned belong and a list of the workplaces at which they work. The union must also provide **figures** of the total number of workers concerned, in relation to each category and each workplace, together with an **explanation** of how those figures were calculated.

EXAMPLE In *EDF Energy Powerlink Ltd v National Union of Rail, Maritime and Transport Workers* [2010] IRLR 114, HC, the only category specified was "engineer/technician", which was taken from the union's database. The employers argued that this was not sufficient to allow it to identify which employees were being balloted. It had no records itself of which of its 270 employees were union members as subscriptions were not deducted at source, and three of its sites were involved in the dispute. The High Court held that the union had not adequately identified the types of employees to be balloted and that it would have been practicable for the union to obtain fuller details from its shop stewards at each of the workplaces. It commented that although the Code of Practice on Industrial Action Ballots and Notice to Employers refers to the union's records as one source of information on the categories of employees, other sources should also be taken into account where the union's own database will not enable the employer to identify which workers may be called out on strike as a result of a ballot. It therefore granted an injunction preventing the union calling a strike notice on the basis of the ballot.

7465 **2. Sample ballot paper** At least 3 days **before the ballot commences**, the employer must receive a sample copy of the voting paper to be sent to those workers who the union reasonably believes will be entitled to vote (s 226A(1)(b) TULRCA 1992).

3. Notice of result The union must notify the employer of the result as soon as is reasonably practicable **after** the result of the ballot has been declared (s 231A TULRCA 1992). The union must take the necessary steps to ensure that the employer is informed of the number of votes cast. He must also be told the number answering "yes" and the number answering "no" to the question or questions, and the number of spoiled votes.

4. Notice of date of commencement Not later than 7 days **before the industrial action** is due to start, the employer must be given written notice of the date of commencement of industrial action (s 234A(1)(a) TULRCA 1992). The employer must also be told whether the intended action is to be continuous (i.e. an "all out" strike) or discontinuous (¶7490).

During the ballot, the union will need to write to its members with a letter containing the voting form and the members will need to write back with their votes. Depending on the method of postage, normally 7 or 14 days are allowed (¶7475).

Voting paper

In order to comply with the rules as to its **content**, the voting paper must (s 229 TULRCA 1992):
– state the name of the independent scrutineer where there is a ballot of over 50 members;
– clearly specify the address to which, and date by which, it must be returned;
– be uniquely numbered;
– contain a question (however framed) which requires the person answering it to say, by "yes" or "no", whether they are prepared to take part (or continue to take part) in a strike (where the action proposed is action short of a full strike, the question has to specify that form of action);
– specify who is authorised to call on members to take industrial action; and
– contain the following statement:

"If you take part in a strike or other industrial action, you may be in breach of your contract of employment. However, if you are dismissed for taking part in a strike or other industrial action, which is called officially and is otherwise lawful, the dismissal will be unfair if it takes place fewer than 12 weeks after you started taking part in the action, and depending on the circumstances may be unfair if it takes place later."

This reference to industrial action being potentially in breach of contract must appear, even where it is the case that the action proposed would not amount to a breach of contract.

A union seeking a mandate both for a **strike and for action short of a strike** has to ask two separate questions (s 229(2) TULRCA 1992). The policy underlying the statute is to allow workers who wish to take industrial action short of strike action, but not strike action, the opportunity to vote accordingly. Where a ballot asked workers whether they wanted to take part in industrial action "up to and including a strike", the subsequent action was not protected (*Post Office v Union of Communication Workers* [1990] IRLR 143, CA).

The union does not, however, have to aggregate the results of the answers to each question. If it obtains a simple majority for one question, it has the right to call industrial action which accords with that question. An employer cannot challenge the legitimacy of the industrial action because a higher proportion of workers had voted on the other question (*West Midlands Travel v TGWU* [1994] IRLR 578, CA).

The fact that the union has not defined or prescribed every single issue in dispute in the ballot paper will not make the ballot void (*Associated British Ports v TGWU* [1989] IRLR 291, HL).

Voting procedure

All members who are entitled to vote must be allowed to do so **without interference** from the union or its members, representatives or workers (s 230 TULRCA 1992). There is, however, no prohibition on interference by the employer or any third party.

The voting must be "as far as is reasonably practicable" **without cost to the individual**. This might mean that the union could be required to provide pre-paid envelopes for posting completed voting papers.

7475 Voting must be **in secret** and every voter has to have a voting paper sent **by post** to his home address or any other address he has chosen. The member must be given a convenient opportunity to vote by post. Failing to send out a few forms due to a minor error would not automatically invalidate the ballot.

At least 7 days have to be allowed for the first-class return of the voting papers. If the ballot is being returned by second-class post then at least 14 days should be allowed for return of the voting papers.

The votes must be **fairly and accurately** counted.

Right to challenge legality of ballot

7480 **Employers and union members** can challenge the legality of a ballot. An employer may apply to the High Court where it is alleged that a union intending to authorise industrial action has not complied with all of the legal requirements concerning the ballot, including:
– whether notice was properly served on the employer before the ballot was held and before the industrial action began;
– whether the correct workers were balloted;
– whether the requirements regarding the conduct of the ballot were adhered to; and
– any other matters related to the ballot.

However, **minor unintentional errors** in conducting a strike ballot will not generally invalidate its results (s 232B TULRCA 1992; *Re P, a minor* [2003] ICR 386, HL).

d. Calling an action

7485 Only the individual specified by the union as having the **authority to call** industrial action can do so (s 233 TULRCA 1992). In some unions, this power lies solely in the hands of the general secretary. In others, it may be the executive committee or a regional official who can call on members to take industrial action.

The **name** of the person empowered to call industrial action **must be included** in any ballot form. Legality is preserved as long as this name is included.

> EXAMPLE In *Tanks & Drums v TGWU* [1991] IRLR 373, CA, the Court rejected an employer's challenge to the legality of the strike on the grounds that, although the ballot paper specified that the union's general secretary was the person with the power to call the industrial action, the call was dependent on the judgement of local representatives, as they were charged with concluding a satisfactory settlement.

7486 Additionally, there must have been no call for industrial action before the date of the ballot. The call for industrial action must be made while the ballot is still effective.

e. Notice of action

7490 Once the ballot results are known, they must be brought to the attention of the employer. Employers must be given **written notice** of the action at least 7 days **before the industrial action** is due to begin (s 234A TULRCA 1992). The notice must include:
– specific information about the group of **workers to be called upon** to take industrial action, which mirrors the requirements for the written notice of the ballot (¶7464);
– the type of industrial action intended, including whether it is **continuous** (for example an all out strike) or **discontinuous** (where it is intended to take place only on some days, but not others); and
– the **date** or dates when it will **begin**.

If a union fails to take such steps as are reasonable to give proper notice, the industrial action will lose its immunity and will be open to challenge by the employer if it goes ahead. If the union ceases to authorise or endorse industrial action and then, at a later date, decides to re-authorise or endorse, the original notice to the employer no longer applies and the union will have to give new notice.

f. Duration of ballot result

A ballot normally **ceases to have effect** at the end of 4 weeks from the last day on which voting could have taken place, **except** in the following circumstances (s 234 TULRCA 1992):
– where industrial action commences within this 4-week period;
– where the employer and union have agreed to extend the 4 weeks by up to another 4 weeks (8 weeks in total) to allow for further negotiation; or
– where the action was due to begin within 4 weeks, and has been delayed due to legal proceedings, and has been called within an overall 12-week period.

The **weeks are calculated** by counting the last day for voting as day one.

7492

If industrial action commences and is suspended for negotiations, a union may re-impose the action without having to re-ballot (*Monsanto plc v TGWU* [1986] IRLR 406, CA). The gap between the **suspension of action** and its re-imposition should not be too long, however, or the ballot will no longer provide immunity. It will be a question of fact and degree whether industrial action is sufficiently continuous for it to be capable of being supported by a single ballot (*Post Office v Union of Communication Workers* [1990] IRLR 143, CA).

7493

> EXAMPLE
> **Industrial action covered by ballot**
> Where a ballot was followed by strike action, but strikes were suspended for 14 days to enable negotiations to take place, the ballot result covered the resumption of strikes (*Monsanto plc v TGWU*).
>
> **Industrial action not covered by ballot**
> Where a ballot was followed by a series of 1-day strikes which lasted for 3 months, and then by a break of 9 months, during which the union adopted different strategies to influence the employer and public opinion, before then resuming strike action over a period of another 5 months, the Court of Appeal held that the duration of the original ballot result was complete and the ballot ceased to protect the action. During the time when the strikes had been halted, significant changes in the composition of the workforce occurred (*Post Office v Union of Communication Workers*). Workers who had not been balloted were called upon to take strike action and conversely workers who had been balloted were no longer in the workplace and therefore not called upon to take action.

Where action is discontinuous and where time has passed between the first day of strikes and subsequent days, an employer can apply to have the ballot result set aside where (s 234(4) TULRCA 1992):
– the result of the ballot no longer represents the views of the union members concerned; or
– an event is likely to occur as a result of which members would vote against action if another ballot were to be held.

7494

2. Picketing

Workers have the **right to picket** when they are involved in a trade dispute. However, their legal right is **limited** to where the picket is:
– at their own workplace (*Rayware Ltd v TGWU* [1989] IRLR 134, CA);
– peaceful; and
– for the purpose of peacefully persuading others not to cross their picket line.

7495

> EXAMPLE In *Rayware Ltd v TGWU*, the Court held that picketing at the entrance to a trading estate, rather than the actual entrance of the company with which the pickets were in dispute, was lawful. The entrance to the trading estate was the nearest point the pickets could reach without trespassing on private property.

A picket will be **unlawful** if it goes **further than peaceful persuasion**. A member "in contemplation or furtherance of a trade dispute" can attend "at or near his own place of work" but only if the purpose is peacefully to obtain or communicate information, or persuade a person to work or abstain from working.

In particular, picketing may result in the committing of common law torts, including:
– trespass to the highway (where a person uses the highway for a purpose outside that prescribed by law);
– private nuisance (where a person causes an unreasonable interference with another's enjoyment of property); and
– public nuisance (where an act causes harm or potential harm to a class of the Crown's subjects).

Remedies for the above torts include injunction and damages.

Unlawful picketing may also result in criminal offences (¶7550).

7496 **Union officials** (including lay union representatives) have the right to attend at or near the place of work of their members who are in dispute and whom they represent.

7497 Difficulties are likely to arise where the workers have **no specified work location**, perhaps because they work from more than one location or travel in the course of their work.

For such workers, the **appropriate location** for any picketing depends on where they normally work. If someone normally works at more than one place or somewhere where it would be impracticable to picket, then their place of work, for the purpose of the right to picket peacefully, will be any premises of their employer or from which work is administered (*Union Traffic Ltd v TGWU* [1989] IRLR 127, CA).

> EXAMPLE In *Union Traffic Ltd v TGWU*, the Court held that drivers who normally worked from one depot, but occasionally from others, could not lawfully picket the other depots since these were not their normal place of work.

7498 If the **pickets are no longer employed** by the employer (i.e. because they have been dismissed), the appropriate location for the purpose of a lawful picketing is the location that would have been appropriate had the individual remained in employment.

7499 While the legislation itself is silent as to the **numbers who may picket** at any one time, the BIS Code of Practice on Picketing recommends that pickets and their organisers should ensure that in general the number of pickets does not exceed six at any entrance to a workplace. Where issues relating to the number of pickets have come to the courts they have generally viewed large-scale pickets as being in breach of the law (*Thomas v National Union of Mineworkers (South Wales Area)* [1985] IRLR 136, ChD).

> EXAMPLE In *Thomas v National Union of Mineworkers (South Wales Area)*, the Court held that a picket was in breach of the common law tort of nuisance, even though there were just six pickets that stood at the gate, because around 60 demonstrated across the road. Consequently, an injunction could be applied to restrain it.

B. Employer's rights

7510 Where there is an industrial action, employers may respond by **withholding pay or** by moving to **dismiss** those taking industrial action, provided that the dismissal is in compliance with the law (¶8101).

Further, an employer whose workers take (or threaten to take) unprotected industrial action has the right to commence legal proceedings. Proceedings can be brought against the union and/or the individuals taking the industrial action. The most commonly used remedy is the injunction, a court order which carries with it potential further penalties, including action for contempt of court, if not complied with.

1. Withhold pay

7515 An employer whose workers are taking any industrial action, regardless of whether it is protected of not, has the right to withhold pay. Where workers are taking partial industrial action, for example, by working to rule or refusing to handle specified pieces of work, the employer may withhold **part pay** in return for part performance of the contract (*Miles v Wakefield Metropolitan District Council* [1987] IRLR 193, HL). Indeed, an employer may even withhold **entire wages**, where workers refuse to undertake part of their contractual duties, no matter how small these duties are, provided that the employer makes it clear that part performance of the contract is not acceptable (*Wiluszynski v London Borough of Tower Hamlets* [1989] IRLR 259, CA). For a worker to sue for wages due under a contract, he must prove a readiness and willingness to discharge all contractual obligations, including implied obligations so that, provided the employer indicates that partial performance is not enough, he will defend any such claim.

MEMO POINTS Pay during industrial action short of strike action is further discussed at ¶3007.

7516 The employer's rights to withhold pay extend to **workers** who, though they are carrying out, or are willing to carry out, their full duties, are nevertheless still **supporting an industrial dispute** (*British Telecommunications plc v Ticehurst and Thompson* [1992] IRLR 219, CA).

EXAMPLE In *British Telecommunications plc v Ticehurst and Thompson*, an employee, on her return to work after a 2-day strike, was asked to sign a loyalty pledge specifying that she would not take part in any further industrial action for the duration of the dispute. She refused to sign and was excluded from work, on a daily basis, until the dispute was formally settled. She claimed that an unlawful deduction had been made to her wages, since she was at all times ready and willing to perform the full range of her duties. However, the Court held that, by withdrawing her "goodwill", she had breached an implied term in her employment contract to "serve her employer faithfully", even if the work she would have carried out would not have been disrupted.

7517 **Pay deductions** which are due to industrial action do not come under the general protection which workers have against unlawful deductions (¶3050; *Sunderland Polytechnic v Evans* [1993] IRLR 196, EAT). In such cases, the worker can only challenge the contractual validity of the deduction.

2. Dismiss workers

7520 Where workers are taking industrial action an employer may **lawfully dismiss** them, **unless**:
1. The **industrial action is protected** and the date of dismissal is (ss 237, 238, 238A TULRCA 1992):
a. within the protected period; or
b. after the end of the protected period but:
– the employee had ceased to take part in the industrial action before the end of that period; or
– the employer has failed to take any steps that might have been reasonable to resolve the dispute; or
2. At the date of dismissal (¶8340), during an **unprotected industrial action or a lock-out**, other relevant employees involved in the action or lock-out were not dismissed.

MEMO POINTS 1. The **protected period** is normally the first 12 weeks of industrial action. This period can, however, be extended where an employee is locked out by the employer during a period of protected industrial action.
2. **Relevant employees** are, in relation to a (s 238 TULRCA 1992):
– lock-out, employees who were directly interested in the dispute in contemplation or furtherance of which the lock-out occurred; or
– strike or other industrial action, those employees at the establishment of the employer at or from which the complainant works, and who, at the date of his dismissal were taking part in the action.

3. Workers may not be lawfully dismissed where they merely support, but do **not actually participate** in, the industrial action (*Naylor v Orton and Smith* [1983] IRLR 233, EAT).

7521 To determine whether the **employer** has **taken any procedural steps** that might have been reasonable to attempt to resolve the dispute, the courts will look at whether the union and the employer agreed to use a **conciliation or mediation services provider** and, if so, whether they co-operated in arranging meetings with that provider, fulfilled any commitments given during the process or answered any reasonable question put to them during the conciliation or mediation (s 238B TULRCA 1992).

7522 Where an employee has not been lawfully dismissed, any dismissal will be treated as being **automatically unfair** (¶8390), regardless of the employee's length of continuous employment.

3. Specific remedies

7523 Where **industrial action** is **unprotected and** the union is guilty of a civil **tort**, the employer may be able to bring a civil action against the union or against a worker or a group of workers.

The action will typically take the form of an injunction to prevent the unlawful action. It may take the form of a claim for damages.

7528 **Injunction** An employer can apply to the High Court to obtain an injunction (or interdict, in Scotland) (ss 20(6), 221 TULRCA 1992; see ¶1771). The **effect** of the injunction is that the union will be required to take any steps that the court considers appropriate to ensure that there is no further inducement of persons to take part in industrial action. If a union **fails to comply** with the injunction, proceedings can be taken for contempt of court. Such proceedings can result in the imposition of a fine, sequestration or imprisonment (*Richard Read (Transport) Ltd and anor v National Union of Mineworkers (South Wales Area)* [1985] IRLR 67, QBD).

Any application for an injunction should be brought to the attention of the party named in it (most commonly, the union), where that party is likely to claim that the action complained of was in contemplation or furtherance of a trade dispute and may wish to defend the application.

> MEMO POINTS Injunctions are unlikely to be granted for merely technical "breaches": the set provisions that are needed to be satisfied for industrial action to be lawful should not be given restrictive meanings and they are not designed to trip up a union or unduly restrict a worker's right to strike (¶7456).

7529 **Damages** Employers may also bring claims for damages against unions and individuals where unprotected industrial action has caused financial loss.

In general, claims for damages are relatively rarely sought for the following reasons:
– in claims against the union itself the amount of damages is limited, making it unlikely that the employer will successfully recover any financial loss; and
– claims against workers, although not subject to a statutory maximum, are rarely pursued because in most cases the employer's wish will be for the industrial action to end so that normal working can resume.

7530 If claims are pursued **against individuals**, the employer has to be able to allocate to that individual the amount of the loss directly attributable to that individual's actions. For example, the court can order a claim for damages against individual pickets.

It is usually difficult to do this and often, where it has been attempted, the action has failed.

If claims are pursued **against the union**, and the losses are reasonably foreseeable as a result of the union's actions, the courts can make an award of damages against the union.

The **amount of damages** is subject to a maximum that is linked to the size of the union. Smaller unions are subject to a lower level of liability than large unions, as follows:

Size of union by membership	Maximum award
Fewer than 5,000	£10,000
Between 5,000 – 24,999	£50,000
Between 25,000 – 99,999	£125,000
100,000 or more	£250,000

MEMO POINTS These **limits** on damages **do not apply** where the proceedings in tort are:
– for personal injury (including any disease or impairment of a person's physical or mental condition) as a result of negligence, nuisance or breach of duty;
– for breach of a duty that is imposed by any rule of law or by or under any enactment, where this is in connection with the ownership, occupation, possession, control or use of property, whether real or personal; or
– by virtue of a claim under the Consumer Protection Act 1987.

An employer seeking to sue a union for damages as a result of unprotected industrial action needs to be aware of the size of the union as this, and not the loss sustained, could determine the amount awarded.

7531 The maximum amount that can be awarded is subject to the discretion of the court (s 35A Supreme Court Act 1981). It does not include any **award of interest** on the sum outstanding in respect of the loss sustained by the employer (*Boxfoldia LTD v NGA (1982)* [1988] IRLR 383, QBD).

EXAMPLE In *Boxfoldia LTD v NGA (1982)*, the court exercised this discretion to award an additional amount of £50,000 in respect of interest, in addition to the maximum amount of £250,000 which it could award based on the size of the union.

7532 An award against a union, its trustees, or against members or officials of a union can be made against any property of the union unless it is **protected property** (s 23 TULRCA 1992). Protected property **includes**:
– the property of individual members of the union, officials and trustees;
– the political fund (¶7120 memo point); and
– any separate provident benefit funds.

Where there are such rules, they must already have been in operation at the time when the legal proceedings were begun. A union has no power to create protected property retrospectively.

MEMO POINTS The **provident benefit funds** that remain protected are those from which payment is expressly made to members during sickness, injury, unemployment and retirement, in cases of accident, as funeral benefits, or to compensate for the loss of a member's tools.

Union's protection against litigation

7534 Unions have specific protection from certain tort (i.e. civil wrong) liabilities which arise "in contemplation or furtherance" of a trade dispute. This protection is **limited to** the torts of:
– inducing another person to break a contract;
– interfering or inducing another person to interfere with its performance;
– threatening to break or interfere with a contract, either by the union or by another person; and
– lawful means conspiracy (this occurs when two or more people combine to do or procure an act which would not be actionable in tort if the act was done without combination. For an example of this tort, see *Lonrho v Fayed (no. 5)* [1993] 1 WLR 1489).

These exemptions give unions protection where they **call on their members to take industrial action**, provided that it is in furtherance of a trade dispute and that the above balloting and procedural conditions are met (¶¶7416+).

7535 **Repudiation of action** A union can avoid legal liability for unlawful industrial action if it repudiates the action "as soon as is reasonably practicable" after it comes to the knowledge of any member of its executive, its president or general secretary (s 21 TULRCA 1992). Repudiation **must amount to** "an open disavowal and disowning of the acts of the representatives concerned" to be effective (*Express & Star Ltd v NGA (1982)* [1985] IRLR 455, QBD).

To repudiate the action, the union has to give **written notice** of repudiation, without delay, to the committee or representative who endorsed or authorised the action. The union also has to do its best to give individual written notice, of the fact and date of the repudiation, to every member who is taking, or who might take part in, the action.

The notice to members must contain the following prescribed words (s 21(3) TULRCA 1992):

"Your union has repudiated the call (or calls) for industrial action to which this notice relates and will give no support to unofficial industrial action taken in response to it (or them). If you are dismissed while taking unofficial industrial action, you will have no right to complain of unfair dismissal."

The union must also give the **employer** of every such member written notice of the repudiation.

Finally, any person who is a **party to a commercial contract** whose performance has been or may be interfered with as a result of the industrial action can also demand from the union a written notice of repudiation within 3 months after the unlawful industrial action has been repudiated (s 21(6) TULRCA 1992). A commercial contract for this purpose is any contract other than one of employment or a contract to personally perform work or services.

Failure to give notice as required or on request will invalidate the repudiation, leaving the union responsible for unprotected industrial action.

7536 A union's formal repudiation of unlawful industrial action will not be valid if it continues to **act** in a manner that is **inconsistent with** its **repudiation**. Therefore, if a union issues a written notice of repudiation but its executive, president or general secretary continues to support industrial action (for example by providing financial or other assistance), the repudiation is invalid.

7537 Where industrial **action** is **repudiated** and a **worker continues to take part** in it, the employer may dismiss the striking worker, who will have no right to complain of unfair dismissal (s 237(1) TULRCA 1992).

C. Third party rights

7540 Any person or organisation can apply to the High Court for an **injunction** or to the county court or High Court for **damages** where:
– a union or any other person has done, or is likely to do, an unlawful act to induce industrial action; and
– the effect of the action will be to prevent, delay or reduce the quality of goods or services to him.

Individuals and organisations who are not a party to the dispute but who claim that it has affected or could affect their rights to goods and services can take steps to have the action prevented (s 235 TULRCA 1992).

7541 In effect, a **potential customer** can complain where a service which he might have required is affected in any way due to industrial action (*Falconer v Aslef and NUR* [1986] IRLR 331, CC).

EXAMPLE In *Falconer v Aslef and NUR*, a commuter, F, who was unable to travel due to an industrial dispute successfully brought an action in the county court, but not against British Rail from whom he had bought a ticket and with whom he, therefore, had a contract. Instead, he brought a claim against the unions which had authorised unprotected industrial action and interfered with F's contract with BR.

D. Criminal penalties

7550 Picketing may also involve criminal offences (s 241 TULRCA 1992), the most common of which are:
– obstruction of the highway;
– criminal damage; and
– common assault.

7551 Individual pickets may also be criminally liable under the old offence of **watching and besetting**. This is committed where, with a view to compelling another person to do or not to do something, which he has a legal right to do, a person "wrongfully and without legal authority":
– uses violence or intimidates;
– persistently follows that person;
– hides tools, clothes or property or otherwise deprives or hinders that person from using them;
– "watches or besets" that person's home or place of business; or
– together with two or more persons follows that person in a "disorderly" manner.

7552 The High Court has held that where industrial action takes the form of a "**work in**" or "**sit in**", this will usually constitute "besetting" (*Galt v Philip and ors* [1984] IRLR 156, HCJ).

EXAMPLE In *Galt v Philip and ors*, the Court ruled that a "work in" by laboratory staff was illegal. Denying access to the laboratory, with a view to compelling others not to do what they had a legal right to do, was held to amount to "besetting."

7553 A police constable can **arrest, without warrant**, anyone who is reasonably suspected of committing any of these offences. The **penalty** on conviction can be a fine and up to 6 months' imprisonment.

Payment of members' penalties

7554 A union may not use its funds to pay any member's penalty for contempt (s 15 TULRCA 1992).

E. "No strike" clauses

7556 Some collective agreements may contain a provision attempting to prohibit or restrict the right of workers to strike or engage in other industrial action. Any such so-called "no strike" clauses will be **precluded** from being incorporated into the contract of employment of an individual worker **unless** the collective agreement (s 180 TULRCA 1992):
– is in writing;
– expressly states that the no strike provision will be incorporated into an individual contract of employment;
– has been entered into by one or more unions, all of which are independent;
– is reasonably accessible at the place of work of a worker to whom the strike clauses apply and is available to be consulted upon during working hours; and
– is one where each trade union which is a party to the agreement is an independent trade union,

and the terms relating to industrial action are expressly or impliedly incorporated into the individual worker's contract of employment.

It is not possible for a collective agreement or individual contract of employment to **contract out** of the above conditions (s 180(3) TULRCA 1992).

SECTION 5
Individual rights

7560 Members of unions have a number of rights at work. At the heart of these individual rights is the notion of choice: employees have the right to choose to join or not to join a union and where an employer infringes these rights, they can bring a claim against the employer. The rights in this section are also designed to protect employees and workers against any form of discrimination on the grounds of their union status, with most protection offered to members of independent unions.

A. Members

1. Refusal of employment

7563 A potential employee has the right not to be refused employment on the **grounds** that he (s 137(1) TULRCA 1992):
– is a member of a union; or
– refuses an unlawful requirement from the employer.

The prohibition on unlawful requirements prevents the employer from making it a condition of employment that the applicant ceases to be a union member or ceases to pay union subscriptions.

> EXAMPLE
> 1. In *Beaver Management Services v Archeson* [2012] UKEAT 0268_11_1406, an employee who was a leading trade union activist was held to have had a job offer withdrawn on the grounds of his union membership, even though this was not the reason given (he was told that he had been chosen because he was the last person to have been offered the job whereas he had in fact been one of the first people who had been contacted about the role).
> 2. In *Harrison v Kent County Council* [1995] UKEAT 824_94_0802, a known union activist successfully brought a claim against his employer when he failed to obtain a new job even though he was told it was not because he was a union member but because he was unco-operative and "anti-management".

7564 A refusal of employment **occurs** if the employer does any of the following (s 137(5) TULRCA 1992):
– refuses to process or deliberately omits to consider an application or enquiry;
– causes the applicant to withdraw his application or enquiry;
– refuses or deliberately omits to offer the employment;
– makes an offer of employment on terms that no reasonable employer, wanting to fill the post, would offer; or
– makes an offer but then withdraws the offer or causes the applicant not to accept it.

> EXAMPLE
> 1. A person could be held to be refused employment if he was not selected for a vacancy after being asked at his interview whether there could be a conflict of interest between being a union member and being a worker with a managerial role.
> 2. An individual applies for a job and is sent details of the main terms and conditions. In the course of his job interview, it is established that he is the best candidate but is also an active union member. The employer offers the job but on significantly worse pay and conditions than would be appropriate for the particular position on offer. As a result, the applicant is unable to accept the offer.

Blacklisting

7565 The compilation, dissemination and use of blacklists, which contain details of trade union members and activists and whose purpose is to discriminate against these workers on grounds of their trade union membership or trade union activities, is **prohibited** (Employment Relations Act 1999 (Blacklists) Regulations SI 2010/493).

Claims can be made to the employment tribunal where a person has been **refused employment or employment agency services** (reg 6 SI 2010/493) or has been subjected to a **detriment** (reg 9 SI 2010/493) for a reason relating to a blacklist. Any **dismissal** of an employee in such circumstances will also be automatically unfair (s 104F ERA 1996). As a result, no qualifying period of continuous employment is necessary (s 108(3)(gk) ERA 1996). An employee will also be unfairly dismissed if the reason or principal reason for selecting him for redundancy is due to a blacklist (s 105(7M) ERA 1996). For the minimum basic award applicable in such cases, see ¶8577.

Alternatively, where a person has suffered or will suffer a loss due to the use or apprehended use of a blacklist, he can apply to the **civil courts for damages** for breach of statutory duty, including damages for injury to feelings (reg 13 SI 2010/493). A person cannot claim compensation from the employment tribunal and damages from the court in respect of the same conduct (reg 13(5) SI 2010/493).

Those affected can also **apply** to the civil courts **for orders** restraining or preventing the compilation, use, sale or supply of the blacklist in question, and for these purposes it does not matter if the person is also bringing a claim before the employment tribunal (reg 13(4) SI 2010/493).

2. Right not to suffer a detriment

A worker has the right not to be subject to any detriment by any act or omission of his employer where the employer's purpose is to prevent or deter him from being, or seeking to become, a member, or taking part in the activities, or accessing the services, of an independent union (s 146(1)(a)-(b) TULRCA 1992).

7566

"Detriment" includes denying a worker promotion, taking disciplinary action based on union activities, and altering a worker's shift patterns, if the reason for doing this is to thwart his union activities or victimise him. Specific **examples** of detriments have included withholding pay rises (*Ridgway v Coal Board* [1987] IRLR 80), denying car parking space (*Carlson v Post Office* [1981] IRLR 158, EAT), and failing to short-list a candidate for promotion (*Cleveland Ambulance NHS Trust v Blane* [1997] IRLR 332, EAT).

7567

If a worker makes a derogatory remark about another worker at a union meeting, which results in the employer taking disciplinary action, the employer's action may amount to detriment.

Refusing to recognise or deal with a union representative will also amount to detriment.

Sanctions The employer may not subject the worker to detriment where the employer's purpose is to prevent or deter him from **taking part in union activities**, or **making use of union services**, at an appropriate time. An **appropriate time** is defined as a time outside the member's working hours (i.e. any time when, in accordance with his contract of employment, he is required to be at work) or within these hours in accordance with arrangements agreed with his employer.

7569

The employer's agreement that a union may arrange its activities for a particular time **can be established** by custom and practice. For example, the EAT held that it was possible for an employer to impliedly consent to conversations taking place in relation to union activities during working hours when he allowed workers to talk about anything they wished to while they worked, provided that it did not interfere with the proper completion of the work or was otherwise disruptive (*Zucker v Astrid Jewels Ltd* [1978] IRLR 385, EAT).

The employer's agreement **cannot be inferred**, however, merely from an employer's silence (*Marley Tile Co Ltd v Shaw* [1980] IRLR 25, CA).

In considering a complaint, a tribunal will look to **evidence** of the employer's **intention** (*London Borough of Southwark v Whillier* [2001] EWCA Civ 808; *Yewdall v Secretary of State for Work and Pensions* [2005] UKEAT 0071_05_1907; *Gallacher v Department of Transport* [2001] ICR 142; *Smyth-Britt v Chubb Security Personnel* [2003] UKEAT 0620_03_2111).

7571

> **EXAMPLE**
> **Intention to deter union membership**
> In *London Borough of Southwark v Whillier*, an employer offered an employee a promotion but then informed the employee that his pay rise would be withheld until such time as he had given up his union

duties. The Court of Appeal held that the employer's intention had been to deter the employee from carrying out any further union duties.

No intention to deter union membership
1. In *Yewdall v Secretary of State for Work and Pensions*, the claimant, while a union member and engaged in activities with the union, was acting in his capacity as a health and safety officer for the employer and was therefore held not to have been engaged in union activities.
2. In *Gallacher v Department of Transport*, a union group assistant secretary with full remission from his work duties applied for a promotion, but was unsuccessful. The Court of Appeal held that there was no detrimental purpose as the employer's purpose had been to ensure that only those with the appropriate experience were promoted.
3. In *Smyth-Britt v Chubb Security Personnel*, an employer removed a worker, who was a union representative, from a client's site because of pressure from that client to remove him due to his union activities. The EAT held that the employer's purpose was not to deter union membership but to protect his business relationship with a third party. Although it was the client's purpose to deter or prevent the worker from taking part in union activities, there was no statutory provision to make such third party pressure unlawful.

7573 **Inducement** The prohibition on subjecting a worker to a detriment also includes situations where an employer offers an economic inducement to a worker. An **employer may not** make an offer to a worker for the sole or main **purpose** of inducing the worker (s 145A TULRCA 1992):
– not to be or not to seek to become a member of an independent union;
– not to take part, at an appropriate time, in the activities of that independent union; or
– not to make use, at an appropriate time, of the union's services.

Such inducements are also unlawful if the result of the worker's acceptance of the employer's offer would be that the worker's terms and conditions would not be determined by a collective agreement negotiated on behalf of a union which is recognised or seeking to be recognised by the employer (s 145B TULRCA 1992).

3. Dismissal or selection for redundancy

7574 An employee has a right not to be dismissed on grounds of union membership. A dismissal or selection for redundancy is **automatically** unfair if the **reason** or **principal reason** is that the employee (ss 152, 153 TULRCA 1992):
– is, or proposes to become, a member of an independent union;
– has taken part or was proposing to take part in union activities at an appropriate time;
– has made use of the services of his union at an appropriate time; or
– refuses to accept an unlawful inducement (¶7573).

As well as membership of an independent union, union activities are protected (*Bass Taverns v Burgess* [1995] IRLR 596, CA; *Fitzpatrick v British Railways Board* [1991] IRLR 376, CA). In order to be protected, however, there is no need for a union member to have engaged in activities: it is enough for the union member to make a request for information or to be a recipient of services (*Discount Tobacco v Armitage* [1990] IRLR 15, EAT).

EXAMPLE
1. In *Fitzpatrick v British Railways Board*, an employer dismissed an employee because he had become aware of the employee's **past union activities** in a previous job and the only basis for the dismissal was the fear that the employee would repeat those activities in his present employment. The employee was successful in his unfair dismissal claim.
2. In *Bass Taverns v Burgess*, an employer dismissed an employee who, in the course of his union activities, **criticised the employer**. The employer was successful when he relied on a defence that the employee was a manager and therefore under an obligation to advance harmonious relationships between the employer and staff.

The protection against redundancy or dismissal is also extended to employees making use of a union representative's services in negotiating terms and conditions (*Speciality Care plc v Pachela* [1996] UKEAT 937_94_0803).

MEMO POINTS 1. See ¶7569 for the definitions of "appropriate time" and "working hours".
2. In contrast to a standard unfair dismissal claim, this right accrues on the first day of employment and is not subject to any qualifying period (¶¶8393-4).

Ostensible and real reasons When looking at the reason given for dismissal of a union representative, it is likely that the employer and the union will claim that the dismissal was for different reasons. Where an employer alleges that union membership or activities were irrelevant to their decision, the **tribunal** may **substitute** the correct reason for the ostensible reason given by the employer, provided the facts have been established (*Dundon v GPT* [1995] UKEAT 118_93_0702; *Afzal v Europackaging* [2006] UKEAT 0411_06_2510; *O'Dea v ISC Chemicals Ltd* [1995] IRLR 599, CA).

7576

EXAMPLE

Unfair selection
1. In *Dundon v GPT*, D, a senior shop steward agreed with his employer that although he was employed and paid as a technical services operator, he could work as a packing operator, so that he could devote half of his time to his union activities. Following a reorganisation, the packing department closed down and D was made redundant after scoring badly on a work assessment. His selection was held to be unfair, even though the employer had not been malicious in selecting him for redundancy or deliberately dismissed him because of his union activities.
2. In *Afzal v Europackaging*, an employee was ostensibly dismissed for taking unauthorised leave, but on investigation by the tribunal it became clear that because the employee was an active trade unionist and father of the union chapel, the employer had failed to give him a fair hearing under the statutory dismissal procedure. In effect, the dismissal was for trade union activities, and was unfair.

Fair selection
In *O'Dea v ISC Chemicals Ltd*, an employee's work had been arranged to fit in with his union activities and he was chosen for redundancy because the job was identified as redundant. His selection for redundancy was not unfair.

B. Non-members

1. Refusal of employment

A potential employee has the right not to be refused employment on the **grounds** that he (s 137(1) TULRCA 1992):
– is not a member of a union; or
– refuses an unlawful requirement from the employer.

This protection prohibits the employer from requiring the potential employee to become a union member, or to pay union subscriptions.

The phrase "refusal of employment" has the same meaning as when an employer refuses employment to a union member (¶7564).

7578

MEMO POINTS An employer must not have a "closed shop" arrangement under which employment is offered only to persons **approved by a union** (s 137(4) TULRCA 1992).

2. Right not to suffer a detriment

A worker has the right not to be subject to any detriment by any act, or deliberate failure to act, by his employer, where the **employer's purpose** is to (s 146 TULRCA 1992):
– compel him to be or become a member of any union or of a particular union; or
– enforce a requirement that, in the event of the worker not being a member of any union or of a particular union, he must make one or more payments (or suffer deductions from his salary) for union subscriptions.

The term "detriment" has the same meaning as when an employer refuses employment to a union member (¶7567).

7581

7582 **Inducement** An employer may not make an inducement to a worker for the sole or main purpose of inducing the worker to be or become a member of any union or of a particular union (s 145A TULRCA 1992).

3. Dismissal or selection for redundancy

7583 An employee will be **automatically** unfairly dismissed if the **reason** or **principal reason** for his dismissal or selection for redundancy is that he (ss 152(1)(c), (3), 153 TULRCA 1992):
– was not a member of any union or of a particular union;
– refused, or proposed to refuse, to become or remain a member of any union or of a particular union; or
– refused, or proposed to refuse, to pay the equivalent of union subscriptions or objected, or proposed to object, to make such payments (or suffer such deductions from his salary).

> MEMO POINTS In contrast to a standard unfair dismissal claim, this right is not subject to any qualifying period (¶¶8393-4).

C. In relation to recognition and derecognition

7586 A worker has the right not to be subject to any detriment by any act or omission of his employer in connection with the statutory recognition and derecognition procedures (paras 156-160 Sch A1 TULRCA 1992). In particular, a worker must **not suffer detriment** for the **reason** that he:
– acted with a view to obtaining or preventing recognition of a union;
– supported or did not support recognition of a union;
– acted with a view to securing or preventing the ending of bargaining arrangements;
– supported or did not support the ending of bargaining arrangements;
– influenced or sought to influence the way in which votes were to be cast by other workers in a ballot;
– influenced or sought to influence other workers to vote or to abstain from voting in a ballot; or
– voted in such a ballot.

These provisions apply regardless of the length of the worker's continuous service.

This protection against detrimental treatment **only applies** in respect of statutory recognition and derecognition provisions, and does not extend to purely voluntary recognition arrangements (for a discussion of detriment in the context of voluntary recognition, see memo points to ¶7205).

7587 An employee who is dismissed (or selected for redundancy) for a reason connected with one of the specified reasons under the statutory recognition and derecognition procedures will be deemed to have been **automatically unfairly dismissed** for any of the reasons above (paras 161, 162 Sch A1 TULRCA 1992; ¶¶8393-4).

D. Remedies

1. Refusal of employment

7589 A job applicant who is refused employment on the grounds of union membership or non-membership has the right to complain to an employment tribunal (ss 139, 140 TULRCA 1992).

The complaint has to be brought **within** 3 months, beginning with the date when the conduct complained of occurred (¶9455). A tribunal may **extend** this period where it was not reasonably practicable to present the claim before it ended (¶9466).

If either the employer or the claimant claims that the refusal of employment was induced by a **third party**, such as a union, then the employer or claimant can ask for the third party to be joined in the action.

If the claim is successful, the tribunal will make a declaration to that effect and order that the individual is paid **compensation** up to a maximum of £74,200.

7590

The tribunal can also recommend the employer takes, within a specified period, any **other action** it thinks practicable to reduce the adverse effect suffered by the complaint. Potential remedies include an order that the complainant is appointed to the original vacancy.

2. Right not to suffer a detriment

A worker who is subject to a detriment has the right to complain to an employment tribunal (ss 149-150 TULRCA 1992).

7592

The **timescale** for making a complaint and the mechanism for involving third parties are the same as where an employee complains of being refused employment on union grounds (¶7589).

If the claim is successful, the tribunal will make a declaration to that effect and order that the individual is paid **compensation**. The amount of compensation will be the sum the tribunal regards as just and equitable in all the circumstances.

7593

Non-financial loss, i.e. injury to health or feelings, sustained because of the infringement can be claimed (*Brassington v Cauldon Wholesale Ltd* [1977] IRLR 479, EAT; *Cleveland Ambulance NHS Trust v Blane* [1997] IRLR 332, EAT). The amount of any compensation for injury to feelings in such cases will not necessarily be lower than that awarded in claims involving any other types of discrimination, and in each case it is necessary to focus on the level of injury suffered (*London Borough of Hackney v Adams* [2003] IRLR 402, EAT; see also ¶5748).

For a successful complaint of **unlawful inducement**, there is a fixed award of £3,600 (s 145E TULRCA 1992).

EXAMPLE
1. In *Cleveland Ambulance NHS Trust v Blane*, a worker who was not short-listed for a promotional post because of his union activities won damages for injury to feelings.
2. In *London Borough of Hackney v Adams*, LBH withdrew an offer of promotion to A when it became aware of her union activities. A tribunal awarded her £5,000 compensation for the humiliation and distress suffered.

A tribunal can reduce the compensation where it considers that the worker to any extent caused or contributed to the situation (s 149(6) TULRCA 1992). However, the tribunal must not consider the worker's conduct where the conduct relates to an employer's requirements regarding union membership (s 155 TULRCA 1992).

3. Dismissal or selection for redundancy

In contrast to other unfair dismissal cases, an employee who has been dismissed or selected for redundancy on union grounds has the right to apply to a tribunal to have a **dismissal** (including a dismissal for redundancy) **suspended** pending a full hearing of his unfair dismissal claim (ss 160-166 TULRCA 1992).

7595

The application has to be made to the tribunal **within** 7 days of the dismissal.

If the dismissal is of a union member, an application must be supported by a **certificate** in writing signed by an authorised official of the independent union of which the employee was (or had proposed to become) a member, stating that there are reasonable grounds for supposing that the reason for the dismissal or the principal reason was the one set out in the complaint.

The claim will be heard at an **interim hearing**.

Once an application has been made, the tribunal has to give the employer a copy of the application and the union certificate, together with notice of the date, time and place of the hearing.

7596 **Interim hearing** At the interim hearing, the tribunal will state if it is **likely** to **uphold** the unfair dismissal claim.

If so, it will ask the employer, if present, whether, pending the full hearing or settlement, he will **reinstate** the employee or re-engage him on no less favourable terms and conditions. If the employer agrees, the tribunal will make an order to that effect (s 163 TULRCA 1992).

If the employer states that he is willing to **re-engage** the employee in **another job**, and specifies the terms and conditions on which he is willing to do so, the tribunal will ask the employee whether he is willing to accept the job on those terms and conditions.

If the employee accepts the job, the tribunal will make an order to that effect. If not, the tribunal will make an **order for continuation** of the contract of employment if it considers the refusal is reasonable.

An order for continuation has the effect that the contract of employment continues in force for the purposes of pay and all employment benefits purposes (s 164 TULRCA 1992). The order will be in force from the date of the dismissal until the tribunal gives its decision on the substantive dismissal claim. The tribunal will state how much should be paid to the employee in each normal pay period and this is based on what the employee would reasonably have been expected to earn.

If an employer fails to attend or states that he is unwilling to reinstate or re-engage, the tribunal will make an order for continuation (s 163 TULRCA 1992). If the employer fails to comply with a **continuation order**, he will be ordered to pay compensation to take account of the fact that the employee's rights have been infringed, together with any loss of earnings as a result of this failure (s 166 TULRCA 1992).

If there is a **change in circumstances**, the employer or employee can, at any time after the continuation order has been made, apply to the tribunal to have the order revoked or varied (s 165 TULRCA 1992).

7597 At the main hearing, if either the employer or the employee claims that a dismissal was induced by a **third party**, usually the union, by calling or threatening industrial action, they can ask for that party to be joined in the action (s 160 TULRCA 1992). The tribunal will allow a third party to be joined prior to the beginning of the hearing although it may refuse to do so once the hearing has begun. No request can be made after an award of compensation or an order for reinstatement or re-engagement.

7598 The tribunal may award compensation, reinstatement or re-engagement. The **compensatory award** is assessed under the standard rules for compensation (¶8585), save that where an employee is dismissed or made redundant on union grounds, this is an automatically unfair dismissal and subject to a minimum award (s 34 ERA 1999), which is currently £5,500.

Further, if the tribunal orders reinstatement or re-engagement, but the employer refuses to comply, it will give an **additional award** of between 26 and 52 weeks' pay subject to the statutory cap (¶2923).

Where the tribunal has ordered at an **interim hearing** that an employer reinstates or engages an employee, the employee will be engaged in effect on full pay until the case is resolved. Where the employee then goes on to lose the substantive complaint of unfair dismissal, these payments will not be recoverable (*Initial Textile Services v Rendell* [1991] UKEAT 383_91_2307).

4. Detriment or dismissal in relation to statutory recognition and derecognition

A worker who is subject to any **detriment**, including dismissal, in connection with any of the specified grounds under the statutory recognition and derecognition procedures can complain to an employment tribunal **within** 3 months of the date of the act or failure of the employer.

Should a tribunal find that a complaint is well founded, it may award **compensation** according to what it considers just and equitable in all the circumstances. If a worker's complaint is upheld and the detriment complained of is the termination of his contract (not a contract of employment), then compensation may be awarded, subject to the statutory limits for basic and compensatory awards under the unfair dismissal legislation (¶8570).

An employee who has been dismissed should bring an **unfair dismissal** claim. There is no minimum qualifying period for the right to claim unfair dismissal (para 164 Sch A1 TULRCA 1992; ¶¶8393-4).

7599

CHAPTER 22

Information and consultation in the workplace

OUTLINE

SECTION 1 Domestic information and consultation 7655

I Scope 7658
  Applicability 7659
  Employee thresholds 7660
II Negotiated agreement 7665
  Three-year moratorium 7667
  1 Employee request 7670
    a Pre-existing agreement 7675
    b Endorsement ballot 7685
  2 Employer notification 7695
  3 Negotiations to reach an agreement ... 7700
    a Negotiating representatives 7702
    b Conduct of negotiations 7710
  4 Requirements for negotiated agreement . 7718
    Form and content 7718
    Information and consultation representatives 7722
    Employee approval 7723
III Standard agreement 7730
  1 Information and consultation representatives 7733
  2 Standard information and consultation provisions 7745

  a Information to be provided 7750
  Developments regarding activities and economic situation 7752
  Situation, structure and development of employment 7754
  Changes in work organisation or contractual relations 7756
  b Conduct of consultation 7760
IV Enforcement and remedies 7765
  a Breach of negotiated or standard agreement 7770
  b Representatives' and candidates' remedies 7780
  c General employees' remedies 7783

SECTION 2 European works councils 7785

1 Scope 7787
2 Establishment of a European works council 7797
  a Agreed negotiations 7801
  b Statutory default model 7825
3 Enforcement and remedies 7842
  a General remedies 7845
  b Individual remedies 7851

Employers with 50 or more employees are required to inform and consult **UK-based employees** on an **ongoing basis** about potential measures and decisions that will **affect** their **employment prospects** and which are likely to lead to **substantial changes** in the workplace.

In addition, certain larger employers (¶7787) with **employees in more than one EU member state** have to negotiate the establishment of a European Works Council (EWC) or an information and consultation procedure as a means of exchanging views and establishing dialogue between management and employees. EWCs are discussed in section 2.

7650

As well as the possibility of elected representatives under an information and consultation agreement and/or EWC as discussed in this chapter, workplace or other representatives may need to be **consulted in a variety of situations**. These are dealt with more fully in other chapters:

7651

Regarding occupational and personal pension schemes	¶3448
Health and safety (health and safety representatives)	¶¶4910+
Dealing with trade unions	¶¶7149+
Transfer of an undertaking (elected or appointed representatives)	¶¶8062+
Collective redundancies (elected or appointed representatives)	¶¶8925+

SECTION 1

Domestic information and consultation

7655 Certain large employers are required to establish information and consultation arrangements in their workplace (Information and Consultation of Employees Regulations SI 2004/3426, referred to in this chapter as "the regulations").

> MEMO POINTS 1. These regulations were introduced in April 2005 to give effect to the European **Directive** on Information and Consultation (EC Directive 2002/14).
> 2. Employers cannot **exclude or limit** the **application of the regulations**, and any agreement (for example, an employment contract) which attempts to contract out of the regulations will be void (reg 39 SI 2004/3426).
> 3. BIS has published **guidance notes** to the regulations.
> Acas has also produced an **advisory booklet** on Employee Communications and Consultation, which aims to assist employers, employees and their representatives in developing effective arrangements for communications and consultation (the booklet can be found at flmemo.co.uk/em7655).

I. Scope

7658 These obligations apply to all employers with **50 or more employees**.

Employers with **fewer than 50 employees** are not subject to the regulations.

> MEMO POINTS The Government has indicated that, as a matter of **good practice**, all businesses, regardless of their size or the nature of their activities, are encouraged to inform and consult with their employees on an ongoing basis about matters which affect them in a way which is appropriate for their particular circumstances.

Applicability

7659 The regulations apply to **undertakings** whose registered or head office, or principal place of business, is situated in GB (reg 3(1) SI 2004/3426). An undertaking is **defined** as a public or private undertaking carrying out an economic activity, whether or not operating for gain (reg 2 SI 2004/3426). Ultimately, whether an organisation falls within the definition of an undertaking carrying out an economic activity for the purposes of the regulations will be determined by the Central Arbitration Committee (CAC) and, on appeal, the EAT and higher courts.

> MEMO POINTS 1. **Further guidance** as to what may constitute an "**undertaking**" and an "**economic activity**" may be found in Court of Justice of the European Union and UK case law interpreting the application of the Acquired Rights Directive and the TUPE regulations (¶¶7912, 7932). BIS guidance suggests that the regulations principally cover companies (as opposed to organisational entities such as establishments or business divisions within a company), partnerships, co-operatives, mutual building and friendly societies, associations, trade unions, charities and individuals who are employers. It is possible that the regulations also cover educational establishments, NHS trusts and Government bodies.

2. Where an undertaking's registered office is situated in GB but its **head office or principal place of business** is located **in Northern Ireland** or vice versa, the regulations will only apply if the majority of its employees are employed in GB (reg 3(2) SI 2004/3426). Separate legislation implements the European Directive on Information and Consultation in Northern Ireland. Once it is determined whether the regulations or the Northern Irish legislation applies, this legislation will apply to employees throughout the undertaking, whether they are employed in GB or Northern Ireland.

Employee thresholds

In order to determine whether the 50-employee threshold is met, it is necessary to **calculate the number of employees** working for that employer in the UK. This is done by taking the average number of employees employed (whether for whole or part of the month) in the previous **12 calendar months** (reg 4(1) SI 2004/3426). This calculation refers to 12 completed calendar months prior to the event that triggers an obligation on the employer to negotiate an Information and Consultation (IC) agreement (¶7665). If an organisation has **existed for less than 12 months**, the number of actual months that it has existed must be used (reg 4(4) SI 2004/3426).

MEMO POINTS 1. Only employees are counted and **workers** who are not employees are excluded.
2. **Part-time employees** are normally to be counted as if they worked full-time. However, for the purpose of the number thresholds only, an employer can choose to treat any part-time employee who works **75 hours or less** in any whole month within the relevant 12-month period as representing half a full-time employee (reg 4(3) SI 2004/3426). Any absence from work or overtime worked by the employee is disregarded when determining whether he is contracted to work 75 hours or less per month. An employer can only choose to count a part-time employee as representing half a full-time employee for those months in which he was employed part-time throughout the whole month. If an employee is employed on a full-time basis during any whole or part month, he must be counted as a full-time employee for that month. Moreover, if an employee works under a contract for **more than 75 hours** per month, he is deemed to be a full-time employee even though his employer may regard him as "part-time" in comparison to other employees in the business.

Access to employee data Should employees wish to make an employee request to trigger the obligation to negotiate a negotiated agreement, they will need access to employee figures. An employee (or employee representative) is entitled to make a **data request** to his employer for information on the number of people employed by the undertaking in the UK to enable him to determine whether the employee threshold is met and to determine what number of employees constitutes 10% of employees employed by the undertaking for the purposes of the negotiations (¶7670) (reg 5 SI 2004/3426). The request must be **dated** and **in writing**.

If the employer **fails to provide** the necessary employee data **within** 1 month of a valid request or the data provided is considered false or incomplete in any material respect, the employee (or employee representative) can complain to the CAC, which, if it considers the complaint to be well-founded, will order the employer to disclose the data within a given period not less than 1 week from the date of the order (reg 6 SI 2004/3426). Employees who believe their employer has failed to provide the required data are advised to consider trying to resolve the matter informally with their employer before making a formal complaint to the CAC.

EXAMPLE A trade union, which had made an employee data request to an employer for the purposes of determining the number of people employed by the employer's undertaking in the UK and to ascertain which sites, establishments or plants were considered to form part of the undertaking, was entitled to more information than just the bare facts that the employer employed a total of [x] number of employees (*Amicus v Macmillan Publishers Ltd*, CAC Case 1C/4/2005). In this case before the CAC, the employer was under an obligation to provide more than this, by way of a breakdown of the number of sites and how many employees were employed at each site. The CAC rejected the employer's argument that some of this information was already in the public domain (on its website). The CAC went on to hold that the regulations envisage that the data disclosed should be able to be verified by the recipient, who would then be able to take a view as to whether it had been supplied with false or incomplete data in any material respect.

MEMO POINTS The term "**employee representative**" is not defined in the regulations and can be a trade union official or some other third party.

II. Negotiated agreement

7665 The process of reaching a negotiated agreement will be **triggered by** either (regs 7, 11 SI 2004/3426):
– a valid employee request to initiate negotiations (¶7670); or
– a valid employer notification of his decision to initiate negotiations (¶7695).

Whichever way the process of reaching a negotiated agreement is triggered, the rules governing the actual **process** of negotiations and the **requirements** for the negotiated agreement are the same (¶7700, 7718).

Three-year moratorium

7667 There are **restrictions** as to when employee requests and employer notifications can be made. A 3-year moratorium (i.e. suspension) on employee requests or employer notifications applies where the request or notification is made **within 3 years of** (reg 12 SI 2004/3426):
– where a negotiated agreement (¶7665) is in place, the date the agreement was drawn up, unless it has been terminated during that period;
– where a standard agreement (¶7730) is in place, the date it started to apply; or
– where a pre-existing agreement (¶7675) is in place and an employee request to negotiate a new negotiated agreement has not been endorsed by ballot, the date of that request.

Once an agreement covering information and consultation is in place (whether it is under a negotiated, standard or pre-existing agreement), either party is prevented from unilaterally starting the process of putting new information and consultation arrangements in place, although they can mutually agree to terminate the current information and consultation arrangements.

The moratorium will not apply where there have been **material changes in the undertaking** during the 3-year period which mean that either (reg 12(2) SI 2004/3426):
– there is no longer a valid pre-existing agreement(s) which covers all the employees in the undertaking(s) or can no longer be treated as being approved by employees; or
– where there has been a negotiated agreement, it no longer covers all the employees in the undertaking.

Such material changes could, for example, arise from a significant group restructuring.

1. Employee request

7670 The process of reaching a negotiated agreement will usually be triggered by an employee request to initiate negotiations. The request must be **in writing** and **specify** the names of the employees making it and the date on which it is sent. Employees are advised to sign and date the request to avoid disputes as to whether they do in fact support the request.

To be **valid**, a request must consist either of (reg 7(2) SI 2004/3426):
– a single request made by at least 10% of the employees in the undertaking; or
– a number of separate requests made on the same or different days by employees which, when taken in aggregate, amount to at least 10% of the employees in the undertaking, provided the requests fall within a rolling 6-month period.

The figure of 10% of employees is **subject to a minimum** of 15 and a **maximum** of 2,500, so that if a company has fewer than 150 employees, a request will only be valid if at least 15 employees make the request. Similarly, in large companies with more than 25,000 employees, a request will be valid so long as 2,500 employees have made the request. Any part-time employee is to be counted as representing a full-time employee for the purposes of the request, even if the employer chooses to count him as representing half a full-time employee for the purposes of the number thresholds (¶7660).

> EXAMPLE An undertaking employs a workforce of 30,000. A total of 2,900 employees make a request to initiate negotiations to reach a negotiated agreement. Although the normal 10% threshold has not been met, the request will nevertheless be valid since it is only necessary for 2,500 employees to make the request.

> MEMO POINTS Employers are advised to **retain** records of **employee requests** for 6 months which, on their own, do not meet the 10% threshold, in case any further requests are made which would, in aggregate, amount to a valid request as set out above.

A request must be **sent to** the employer at its registered office, head office or principal place of business (reg 7(4) SI 2004/3426). **7671**

Should the employee(s) making the request **wish to remain anonymous**, he can send the request to the employer via the CAC (reg 7(4) SI 2004/3426). The CAC does not forward the names of the employees to the employer but will notify the employer that a request has been made and seek such information from the employer that is necessary to ascertain the number and names of the employees who have made the request (reg 7(5) SI 2004/3426). The employer must provide this information to the CAC as soon as reasonably practicable.

> MEMO POINTS If an employer has already received other **employee requests during the previous 6 months** which, when taken alone, did not meet the 10% threshold, he is advised to provide the CAC with the names of the employees making the previous request(s) to avoid the problem of double-counting.

Each request must be **dated**. In the case of a single request, or a number of single requests made on the same day, this will normally be the date it is sent to the employer, but in the case of anonymous requests, it is the date the CAC informs the employer and employees of how many employees have made the request (reg 7(7) SI 2004/3426). With regard to aggregated requests made on different days, the relevant date is the day on which the 10% threshold (¶7670) is met, or the date the CAC informs the parties that the threshold has been met. **7672**

Where an **employer believes** that an employee **request** is **not valid** on the grounds that (reg 13 SI 2004/3426): **7673**
– it does not meet one or more of the validity requirements (¶7670);
– a 3-year moratorium on further employee requests is in place (¶7667); and/or
– the regulations did not apply to the undertaking concerned on the date the request was made,
he may apply to the CAC, within 1 month of the date on which the request was made, for a **declaration** as to whether the request is valid.

If the CAC **upholds the complaint** that the employee request is not valid, the parties will be prevented from proceeding any further with the process of negotiating to reach an agreement covering information and consultation (reg 7(9) SI 2004/3426). If the CAC **rejects the complaint**, the employer must then initiate discussions for a negotiated agreement.

> MEMO POINTS As a matter of **good practice**, employers are advised to acknowledge receipt of the request, inform the workforce as a whole of the request and explain how they intend to respond to it, though these steps are not required by the regulations. This will assist in avoiding confusion as to whether or not an employer believes the request is valid.

a. Pre-existing agreement

If a valid **employee request** has been **made by fewer than 40% of employees** in the undertaking, an employer who already has in place one or more valid pre-existing agreements on the date the request is made will not necessarily be obliged to commence negotiations for a negotiated agreement. In these circumstances, an employer can choose either to ballot **7675** the workforce to establish whether it endorses the employee request (¶7685) or not to ballot the workforce but commence negotiations to reach a new agreement on information and consultation (reg 8(2) SI 2004/3426).

If the employee request has been made by **40% or more of employees** in the undertaking, the employer has no choice but to initiate negotiations for a negotiated agreement (¶7700).

Criteria for pre-existing agreement(s)

7676 For a pre-existing agreement to be **valid**, it must, on the date on which the employee request is made (reg 8(1) SI 2004/3426):
– be in writing;
– cover all the employees of the undertaking, though it could include employees in other undertakings (for example, in group companies – ¶7678);
– set out how the employer is to inform and consult with employees or their representatives; and
– have been approved by the employees.

> MEMO POINTS 1. The regulations do not stipulate what constitutes **employee approval** of a pre-existing agreement, but BIS suggests that approval might be demonstrated by ballot endorsement, support through signatures, or agreement with employee representatives (including recognised union officials) who represent a majority of the workforce.
> The CAC has held that existing agreements which provided for negotiation and consultation with union representatives for employees without differentiating between union members and non-members did in fact cover those employees who were not members of one of the recognised unions (*Stewart v Moray Council* [2006] IRLR 168, EAT). Indeed in this case, the union representatives represented all groups of employees and, moreover, a majority of the workforce belonged to one of the recognised unions. The criterion of "employee approval" was therefore satisfied. In the first appeal to the EAT under these regulations, the EAT has confirmed the CAC's decision (*Stewart v Moray Council* [2006] IRLR 592, EAT): "employee approval" **means** approval of the majority.
> 2. Employers who wish to put in place a valid pre-existing agreement **prior to the regulations being applicable** to them should review their existing information and consultation agreements to ensure that they meet the criteria specified. This might include, for example, extending existing arrangements to cover all employees, putting in place new consultation arrangements covering the whole workforce, and/or seeking approval for existing agreements.

7677 A **collective agreement** (¶7363) might be a valid pre-existing agreement even if it does not cover all the employees in the undertaking, provided one or more other valid pre-existing agreements cover the remainder of the employees who fall outside the scope of the collective agreement.

However, a **European Works Council (EWC) agreement** (¶7785) is not a valid pre-existing agreement since it focuses on transnational, rather than domestic, issues.

7678 **Pre-existing agreement covering more than one undertaking** Where a pre-existing agreement which meets all the validity criteria covers employees in more than one undertaking, the employers can choose to hold a **combined endorsement ballot** of the employee request rather than holding separate ballots in respect of each of the undertakings (reg 9 SI 2004/3426).

A combined endorsement ballot can only be held if **fewer than 40% of employees** in all the undertakings covered by the agreement made one or more requests for the negotiated agreement. Requests from employees in different undertakings covered by one pre-existing agreement will be aggregated if they are made within a rolling period of 6 months. Note that, rather than holding a combined endorsement ballot, it is still open to the employer to simply hold an endorsement ballot in respect of the employees in the undertaking from which the request was made (reg 9(3) SI 2004/3426).

If **40% or more employees** in all the undertakings covered by the agreement made the request, then the obligation on the employer to negotiate a new IC agreement is triggered (¶7700).

> **EXAMPLE** A valid employee request to negotiate an information and consultation agreement is made in respect of an undertaking, X. The organisation already has in place a valid pre-existing agreement which covers employees in its two subsidiary companies, Y and Z. The employee request in relation to X, when aggregated with employee requests made by employees of Y and Z during the preceding 6 months, is made by 30% of the total number of employees employed by X, Y and Z. It is therefore possible for X, Y and Z to hold a combined endorsement ballot to endorse the request in respect of all the employees employed by X, Y and Z. However, X can alternatively choose simply to hold an endorsement ballot in respect of its own workforce.

Similarly, it is possible for one pre-existing agreement to provide for different information and consultation arrangements to apply to different parts of one undertaking or for there to be several pre-existing agreements, each of which covers only part of an undertaking.

Complaints regarding pre-existing agreement(s)

Where an employee (or employee representative) believes that there is no valid pre-existing agreement in place which entitles the employer(s) to hold an endorsement ballot (or, if applicable, a combined endorsement ballot), he can complain to the CAC, provided he does so **within** 21 days of the employer's notification of his intention to hold an endorsement ballot (or combined endorsement ballot) (reg 10(1) SI 2004/3426). Where a complaint has been made, an employer is advised to wait for the CAC's decision before going ahead with the ballot.

If the employee's complaint is **upheld by the CAC**, it must order the employer to start negotiations for a new negotiated agreement or, where an employer proposes to hold a combined endorsement ballot, it will either order the employer to initiate negotiations for a new agreement (if the employer has expressed a preference for this) or to conduct a single endorsement ballot in respect of the undertaking from which a valid employee request was made (provided there is a valid pre-existing agreement covering that undertaking).

If the complaint is **not upheld**, the employer is free to hold the endorsement ballot.

b. Endorsement ballot

If a valid employee request has been made by **fewer than 40% of employees** in the undertaking, the employer can choose to hold an endorsement ballot rather than start negotiations for a negotiated agreement (reg 8(2) SI 2004/3426).

If he decides to hold a ballot, he must, **within** 1 month of the employee request, **inform in writing** all the employees in the undertaking (or, in the case of a combined endorsement ballot, all the employees in that group of undertakings) that he intends to do so (reg 8(3) SI 2004/3426).

An employee (or employee representative) who believes that his employer has **failed to inform employees** that he intends to hold an endorsement ballot within the time limit can apply for a declaration from the CAC which, if upheld, will oblige the employer to start discussions for a negotiated agreement (reg 8(7) SI 2004/3426).

The employer must make arrangements for the ballot to be held as soon as is reasonably practicable but in any event **no earlier than** 21 days of having informed employees of the ballot. During this period, employees have an opportunity to complain about the validity of the pre-existing agreement(s) (¶7680).

If, having informed employees of his intention to hold an endorsement ballot, an employer **fails to hold a ballot**, an employee (or employee representative) can complain to the CAC which, if the complaint is well-founded, must make an order requiring the employer to hold a ballot by a given date (reg 8(8), (9) SI 2004/3426).

Conduct of the ballot

The employer must ensure as far as is reasonably practicable that the arrangements for the ballot are fair and that every individual who is employed by the undertaking on the day of the ballot is entitled to vote in it (reg 8(4) SI 2004/3426). The ballot must be conducted so that voting takes place in secret and the votes are counted accurately.

One way of ensuring the fairness of the endorsement ballot would be to appoint an **independent scrutineer** to supervise its conduct, although this is not required by the regulations.

7688 If an employee (or employee representative) believes that his employer has **failed to meet** any of the **ballot requirements**, he can complain to the CAC within 21 days of the ballot. If his complaint is upheld, the CAC will make an order that either the employer initiates negotiations for a new negotiated agreement (if the employer has already indicated that he would prefer to do this) or that the ballot should be held again (reg 10(2), (3) SI 2004/3426).

Result of the ballot

7689 The **employer must inform** the employees of the result of the ballot as soon as is reasonably practicable.

7690 An **employee request** is **endorsed** if 40% or more of the employees in the undertaking, plus the majority of the employees who voted in the ballot, vote in favour of it (reg 8(6) SI 2004/3426). The employer will then be under an obligation to start the negotiation process to reach a negotiated agreement. Where a pre-existing agreement covers more than one undertaking, the employer's obligation to start negotiations applies to all of the undertakings in respect of which a ballot was held and not just in respect of the undertaking from which the employee request was made. Where there is more than one undertaking, an employer is free to negotiate a new negotiated agreement applying to all of the undertakings covered by the pre-existing agreement or a separate agreement in respect of each of the undertakings.

This does not mean that pre-existing agreements already put in place by the employer no longer continue to have any force (for example, a collective agreement with a trade union which provides for collective bargaining over pay, hours and holiday). However, it means that the pre-existing agreement is not sufficient to fulfil the employer's obligations under the regulations and that a new negotiated agreement (or, if the parties fail to reach an agreement, the standard IC provisions) must be put in place.

7691 However, if the **employee request** is **not endorsed**, the employer is not obliged to initiate negotiations for a negotiated agreement (reg 7(8) SI 2004/3426). Furthermore, a **3-year moratorium** on any further employee requests from employees in any of the undertakings in which an endorsement ballot was held comes into effect from the date of the employee request (reg 12(1) SI 2004/3426) (¶7667).

2. Employer notification

7695 As an alternative to an employee request, the process of negotiations for a negotiated agreement can be initiated by an employer notification.

A **valid** notification must (reg 11 SI 2004/3426):
– state that the employer intends to start negotiations for an IC agreement and that notification is given for the purpose of the regulations;
– state the date on which the notification is issued; and
– be published in order to bring it to the attention of, so far as is reasonably practicable, all the employees in the undertaking (or if the employer wishes to negotiate a single IC agreement covering more than one undertaking, the employees in each undertaking covered).

Once a valid notification has been given, the process of negotiating a negotiated IC agreement will begin (¶7700).

7696 Where an employee (or employee representative) considers that an employer notification is **not valid** on the grounds that it does not meet one of the requirements above or that the employer is restricted from issuing a notification by a 3-year moratorium which is in place (¶7667), he may apply to the CAC, within 1 month of the date on which the notification was made, for a **declaration** as to whether the notification is valid (reg 13 SI 2004/3426).

Where appropriate, employees are advised to first inform the employer on an **informal basis** that they believe a notification is not valid, or that the regulations do not apply to the undertaking, before bringing a complaint to the CAC, in case there has been a misunderstanding between the parties regarding the application of the regulations to the undertaking concerned.

If the CAC **upholds the complaint** that the employer notification is not valid, the employer will be prevented from continuing any further with the process of negotiating to reach an agreement (reg 7(9) SI 2004/3426). If the CAC **rejects the complaint** and declares the notification is valid, the employer will be required to initiate negotiations.

3. Negotiations to reach an agreement

Before any negotiations can take place, the employer must first arrange for the election or appointment of negotiating representatives. The regulations lay down how such election or appointment must take place, as well as certain provisions regarding the conduct of the negotiations.

7700

a. Negotiating representatives

Election or appointment

Following a valid employee request (which, if necessary, has been endorsed by a workforce ballot – ¶7685) or employer notification, the employer must, as soon as is reasonably practicable, make arrangements for the election or appointment of negotiating representatives who will represent employees in the negotiations for an agreement with the employer (reg 14(1) SI 2004/3426). Whether negotiating representatives are elected or appointed is left to the discretion of the employer, although it is possible to use both methods, for example, with regard to different parts in an undertaking. The employer is not entitled, however, to take any part in the decision as to who is elected or appointed.

7702

There are no requirements regarding the **number of representatives**, and the employer must simply ensure that a sufficient number are elected or appointed. If the undertaking is split into different parts, then it may be appropriate for employees to elect or appoint representatives from each part of the undertaking. Similarly, if it is proposed that a negotiated agreement will cover employees in more than one undertaking, for example, in a group of companies, then it may be appropriate to have one (or more) negotiating representative(s) from each undertaking to be represented.

The employer must ensure that all employees are entitled to take part in the election or appointment of the representatives and that, following their election or appointment, all employees will be represented by one or more representatives (reg 14(2) SI 2004/3426). If it is proposed that a negotiated agreement will cover more than one undertaking, employees in all the undertakings covered must be entitled to take part in the election or appointment.

Once such representatives have been elected or appointed by employees, the employer must inform employees of the identity of the representatives and invite the representatives to enter into negotiations to reach an agreement (reg 14(1) SI 2004/3426).

<u>MEMO POINTS</u> It will not always be the case that the individuals who are elected or appointed as negotiating representatives will be the same people as the **IC representatives** (¶7733), who will be informed and consulted by the employer under the arrangements set out in the negotiated agreement. In addition, it should not be assumed that **trade union representatives** should become negotiating representatives, although they are likely to be well placed to take on such a role.

Complaints regarding election or appointment If an employee (or employee representative) believes that one or both of the requirements for the election or appointment of negotiating representatives has not been met, he can, **within** 21 days of the election or

7704

appointment, bring a complaint to the CAC (reg 15(1) SI 2004/3426). Where the CAC upholds a complaint, it will order the employer to arrange for the process of election or appointment to take place again within a prescribed period.

Role

7705 The role of the negotiating representatives is significant in representing employees' interests when negotiating the information and consultation arrangements with the employer. Negotiating representatives will therefore need to ensure that they represent **employees' views** regarding what arrangements they wish to put in place, including, for example:
- the method, subject matter, timing and frequency of information and consultation;
- how IC representatives will be chosen and replaced;
- who will represent the employer at information and consultation meetings;
- the method by which the employer will respond to the views put across at such meetings; and
- the circumstances in which the arrangements under the negotiated agreement can be amended or terminated.

Right to paid time off

7706 A negotiating representative has the right to take **reasonable** paid time off during his working hours to perform his functions (regs 27, 28 SI 2004/3426) and is entitled to be paid at the **appropriate hourly rate**, the amount of which will depend on whether his contractual hours vary or not (¶¶3935+). Any contractual remuneration paid to him in respect of a period of time off will go towards discharging the statutory liability for paid time off for that period (reg 28(7) SI 2004/3426).

7707 An employee who is **unreasonably refused** time off to perform his functions as a negotiating representative or is not paid (wholly or in part) in respect of such time off can bring a complaint to an employment tribunal (reg 29(1) SI 2004/3426). Complaints must be made within 3 months beginning with the day on which the time off was taken or on which it is alleged the time off should have been permitted (reg 29(2) SI 2004/3426). However, a tribunal can extend this period if it is satisfied that it was not reasonably practicable for the employee to make the complaint in time.

If the claim is successful, the **tribunal must** make a declaration to that effect and/or order the employer to pay (reg 29 SI 2004/3426):
- the employee the amount equal to the remuneration he would have been entitled to had the employer not refused to permit him to take time off; or
- the amount due to the employee if he has taken time off but the employer has refused to pay him in whole or in part.

b. Conduct of negotiations

Time limit for starting negotiations

7710 The **employer must initiate** negotiations to reach a negotiated agreement with employee representatives as soon as reasonably practicable (reg 14(3) SI 2004/3426; *Darnton v Bournemouth University* [2010] IRLR 294, EAT).

This requirement is effectively **suspended** in respect of any period during which:
- an endorsement ballot (including a combined endorsement ballot) is held (¶7685);
- any complaint regarding an endorsement or combined endorsement ballot is determined (¶7688);
- any dispute regarding the validity of the employee request or employer notification is determined (¶¶7673, 7696); or
- any complaint regarding the election or appointment of employee negotiating representatives is determined (¶7704).

If the employer **fails to initiate negotiations** within a reasonable time, the standard information and consultation provisions (¶7745) will apply from the earlier date of (reg 18(1) SI 2004/3426):
– 6 months from the date of the valid employee request or employer notification; or
– the election of information and consultation representatives under the standard information and consultation provisions.

During the negotiations, the parties are under a duty to work in a **spirit of co-operation** and with due regard for their reciprocal rights and obligations, taking into account the interests of both the undertaking(s) and the employees (reg 21 SI 2004/3426).

7711

Duration of negotiations

Negotiations between the employer and employee representatives can **continue for up to** 6 months from the date beginning 3 months after the employee request or employer notification was made (reg 14(3) SI 2004/3426).

7712

The negotiating period is effectively **suspended** in respect of any period during which any complaint regarding the employee approval ballot (¶7725) of a negotiated agreement is determined, including any further period during which the ballot is re-held if required by the CAC (reg 14(4) SI 2004/3426).

If, before the end of the negotiating period, the parties have not yet reached agreement, the employer and a majority of the negotiating representatives can mutually agree to **extend without limit** the negotiating period (reg 14(5) SI 2004/3426). It is not possible for one party to unilaterally impose an extension.

7713

Failure to reach agreement

If the parties fail to reach an agreement within the 6-month period or any extended period which has been agreed between the parties, the **standard information and consultation provisions** (¶7745) will **apply from** the earlier date of (reg 18(1) SI 2004/3426):
– 6 months from the date on which the time limit expires; or
– the election of the information and consultation representatives under the standard information and consultation provisions.

7715

This provides the parties with an **additional limited period** in which the parties may be able to reach agreement before the standard information and consultation provisions begin to apply. Employers should note that if, at the end of this additional 6-month period, they have failed to arrange for the election of information and consultation representatives (¶7733), they will be liable to a fine (¶7777).

EXAMPLE In a second round of litigation before the CAC concerning the parties from ¶7664 (*Amicus v Macmillan Publishers Ltd* [2007] IRLR 378, CAC), the employer, MP Ltd, received a request to negotiate an information and consultation agreement on 15 March 2006 from around 14% of its employees. MP Ltd had a pre-existing agreement in place, but this only affected one of its sites. MP Ltd neither negotiated with its employees, nor reached an agreement with them, nor allowed information and consultation representatives to be elected. The employer was asked on 15 March to hold a vote to elect information and consultation representatives but by 15 October 2006 had not done so. The CAC therefore gave an order requiring an election to be held.

4. Requirements for negotiated agreement

Form and content

Considerable flexibility is provided to the parties in agreeing the scope and provisions of the negotiated agreement so they can tailor the agreement towards the particular circumstances of the organisation.

7718

However, the regulations require that a negotiated agreement, which can be either a **single agreement** or consist of **separate parts** (e.g. sections, divisions, units or establishments) **covering different employees** which, when taken together, cover all the employees in the undertaking (or, if more than one, each of the undertakings), **must** (reg 16(1) SI 2004/3426):

a. set out the circumstances in which the employer must inform and consult the employees;

b. be:
– in writing;
– dated;
– approved by employees (¶7723); and
– signed by, or on behalf of, the employer (or, in the case of an agreement which covers more than one undertaking, each of the employers); and

c. either provide for the appointment or election of information and consultation representatives whom the employer must inform and consult or provide that the employer informs and consults directly with employees (or both) (¶7722).

Where a negotiated agreement consists of different parts, each part can make different provisions in respect of the requirements set out above (reg 16(2) SI 2004/3426).

> MEMO POINTS   The **date** of the negotiated agreement will determine the start of the 3-year moratorium on further employee requests or employer notifications.

7720 **Specific matters** such as the method, subject matter, timing and frequency of information and consultation are not prescribed by the regulations, but must be determined by the negotiations between the employer and negotiating representatives. The "default" standard information and consultation provisions (¶7745) can be used as a guide as to content of the information and consultation arrangements should the parties wish.

BIS guidance suggests the following framework of provisions could be used as a basis for deciding what arrangements need to be covered in any such negotiated agreement, including:

– **coverage**, for example a definition of "undertaking", which employees will be covered, whether separate arrangements will cover different parts of the undertaking and the scope of any agreements with trade unions;

– **methods** of informing and consulting, for example the type of arrangements to be set up, including whether there should be representatives or direct consultation with employees (or both), how any representatives will be chosen, how long they will serve and how they will be replaced, any facilities and time off for employee representatives, and any obligations on the representatives to report back to employees and/or seek the views of the workforce;

– **frequency** and **timing** of information and consultation, for example how often information and consultation will take place and when;

– **subject matter**, for example the types of topics which will be covered by the obligations to inform and consult and how those topics will be chosen, including how the agendas of meetings will be decided;

– **information and consultation**, for example the type and nature of the information to be provided, how the views/opinions of the employees could be expressed, what the employer will do in response and who will represent management in any meeting with information and consultation representatives;

– **statutory consultation requirements**, for example how other legal requirements on the employer to consult employees (for example, regarding collective redundancies, TUPE transfers, European Works Councils etc) will be handled and whether there will be any overlap with the information and consultation arrangements set up under the negotiated agreement;

– **confidential information**, for example how confidential or price-sensitive information will be dealt with, the obligations on any recipients of confidential information and any disciplinary measures for breaches of confidentiality;

– **disputes**, for example how disputes are resolved and the enforceability of any pre-existing agreement(s);

– **restructuring**, for example what the implications of any company restructuring would be for the information and consultation arrangements agreed; and

– **duration**, for example the parties might want to include provisions regarding the duration of the agreement and the circumstances in which it can be reviewed, revised or terminated.

MEMO POINTS Special provisions apply to **confidential information and documents** (¶7746).

Information and consultation representatives

A negotiated agreement must provide for either the **election or appointment** of information and consultation representatives (referred to as IC representatives) or for the employer to inform and **consult directly** with the workforce. It is possible for an agreement to provide for both forms of arrangement and this is a matter for the parties to agree.

The employer and negotiating representatives must, if they agree that information and consultation should take place through IC representatives, also decide on how many IC representatives there will be, who they will represent, when and how they will be replaced, and whether anyone other than an employee can hold the position.

7722

Employee approval

A negotiated agreement will be approved by the employees if it has been **signed by** (reg 16(3) SI 2004/3426):
a. all the negotiating representatives; or
b. a majority of the negotiating representatives and either approved:
– in writing by at least 50% of employees in the undertaking (or, where the agreement covers more than one undertaking, group of undertakings); or
– by at least 50% of employees voting in a ballot.

7723

MEMO POINTS Where a negotiated agreement consists of **different parts**, each part must be approved in accordance with identical provisions (reg 16(4) SI 2004/3426).

Ballot An employer is **not obliged** to hold a ballot to seek employee approval of a negotiated agreement. However, **if** he **chooses** to do so, he must ensure, as far as is reasonably practicable, that the arrangements he makes for the ballot are fair and that all employees (who are employed on the date of the ballot) in the undertaking (or in the part of the undertaking to which the agreement relates, if appropriate) are entitled to vote in it (reg 16(5) SI 2004/3426).

7725

The ballot must be **conducted** so that, as far as is reasonably practicable, the voting takes place in secret and that the votes are accurately counted. As soon as is reasonably practicable after the date of the ballot, the employer must inform the employees who were entitled to vote in it of the result (reg 16(6) SI 2004/3426).

MEMO POINTS One way of ensuring the fairness of the endorsement ballot would be to appoint an independent scrutineer to supervise its conduct, although this is not required by the regulations.

A negotiating representative who believes that the arrangements for the ballot do not satisfy all the requirements set out above can bring a **complaint regarding** the **conduct** of the ballot to the CAC **within** 21 days of the date of the ballot (reg 17 SI 2004/3426). Where the CAC upholds a complaint, it will order the employer to re-hold the ballot within a specified period.

7726

III. Standard agreement

If, following a valid employee request or employer notification, the employer **fails to initiate negotiations** for a negotiated agreement or the parties enter into negotiations but **fail to reach an agreement** within the 6-month period (or any extended period which had been mutually agreed between the parties), the standard information and consultation provisions (referred to as the standard IC provisions) will apply (reg 18 SI 2004/3426). It should be noted that the standard IC provisions will apply to each individual undertaking separately and any

7730

information and consultation arrangements made under the standard IC provisions cannot cover more than one undertaking.

When implementing the standard IC provisions, the parties are under a duty to work in a **spirit of co-operation** and with due regard for their reciprocal rights and obligations, taking into account the interests of both the undertaking and the employees (reg 21 SI 2004/3426).

7731 **Negotiated agreement** It is important to note that, where the standard IC provisions apply, the employer and the IC representatives who have been elected under the standard IC provisions can, at any time, reach a negotiated agreement under which provisions **other than the standard IC provisions** will apply (reg 18(2), (3) SI 2004/3426). Such an agreement can only take effect if it complies with the requirements for a negotiated agreement (¶7718) and is signed by the majority of IC representatives.

Where such an agreement has been reached, the **3-year moratorium** will apply to any further employee requests or employer notification from the date of the agreement (¶7667).

1. Information and consultation representatives

7733 Before the standard IC provisions start to apply, the employer must arrange a **ballot to elect** the relevant number of IC representatives (reg 19, Sch 2 SI 2004/3426). For each 50 employees (or part thereof), one representative must be elected, subject to a **minimum** of two and **maximum** of 25. Therefore, a company with 100 employees will need two IC representatives and a company with 180 employees will need four.

> MEMO POINTS It is not necessary for the same people who are elected **negotiating representatives** to also be elected as IC representatives.

Arrangements for ballot

7734 The requirements for the arrangements and conduct of the ballot are set out at Schedule 2 (Sch 2 SI 2004/3426).

The employer can choose whether to hold a **single ballot** or **separate ballots** in respect of different constituencies, if the employer considers that the IC representatives elected would better reflect the interests of the employees as a whole (para 1 Sch 2 SI 2004/3426). Once he has formulated his proposed arrangements for the ballot, the employer must, as far as is reasonably practicable, **consult** with employee representatives (for example, trade union or negotiating representatives) or employees regarding the arrangements and make any necessary modifications following consultation. He must then **publish** the final arrangements for the ballot in such a way that they are, as far as is reasonably practicable, brought to the attention of his employees (and employee representatives).

Any employee can stand as a candidate, provided he is employed at the latest time at which a person is allowed to stand. However, if, at any point, the **number of candidates** equals or is less than the relevant number of IC representatives (¶7733), those candidates will become the IC representatives and the employer will not have to conduct a ballot.

Every employee in the undertaking must be **entitled to vote**.

Conduct of ballot

7735 The employer must **appoint** an **independent ballot supervisor** to supervise the conduct of the ballot (para 2 Sch 2 SI 2004/3426). A person will be an independent ballot supervisor if the employer reasonably believes that he will carry out his functions competently and the employer has no reasonable grounds to believe that his independence might reasonably be called into question. The ballot supervisor must be able to carry out his functions without interference and the employer must comply with all reasonable requests made by the ballot supervisor in connection with the conduct of the ballot (para 8 Sch 2 SI 2004/3426).

The **role** of the ballot supervisor is to supervise the conduct of the ballot in accordance with the arrangements set out above (para 9 Sch 2 SI 2004/3426). The ballot cannot be held before the employer has published the final ballot arrangements and, where no complaint of defective ballot arrangements has been made, before the expiry of 21 days beginning with the date on which the arrangements were published. Alternatively, where a complaint regarding defective ballot arrangements has been made (¶7738), the ballot cannot be held before the complaint has been determined and the arrangements have been modified as required by the CAC.

The ballot must be conducted so as to secure that, as far as is reasonably practicable, all those entitled to vote can do so in secret, all those entitled to stand as candidates can do so, and all the votes are fairly and accurately counted.

The ballot supervisor must publish the **results of the ballot** to the employer, candidates and voters as soon as reasonably practicable (para 10 Sch 2 SI 2004/3426).

7736 Within 1 month of the ballot results being published, the ballot supervisor can publish an **ineffective ballot report** if he considers (whether or not on the basis of representations made to him) that:
– any of the requirements regarding the conduct of the ballot were not met and the result of the ballot would have been different;
– there was interference with the carrying out of his functions; or
– the employer failed to comply with his reasonable requests so that he was unable to form a proper judgement as to whether each of the requirements for the ballot had been met.

This report should be published to the employer, candidates and voters.

Where such a report is published, the outcome of the ballot (or separate ballots, if appropriate) will be void and the employer(s) must **re-hold the ballot(s)**.

7737 All **costs** relating to the conduct of the ballot, including payment of the ballot supervisor, must be paid by the employer, whether or not the supervisor has declared the ballot ineffective (para 15 Sch 2 SI 2004/3426).

Complaints regarding arrangements and conduct

7738 Any employee (or employee representative) who considers that the **ballot arrangements** are **defective** can **complain** to the CAC **within** 21 days of the final arrangements having been published (para 3 Sch 2 SI 2004/3426). The CAC will **uphold a complaint** if the arrangements for the ballot set out above are not met and may make an order specifying what modifications the employer must make to the arrangements or which requirements set out above should be satisfied.

If an employer has actually **failed to make arrangements** for such a ballot, an employee (or employee representative) can bring a complaint to the CAC (reg 19(4) SI 2004/3426). If the CAC **upholds the complaint**, it will order the employer to arrange, or re-arrange, and hold the ballot. Moreover, the employee (or employee representative) can, within 3 months of the CAC declaration, apply to the EAT for the employer to be issued with a fine (regs 19(6), 22(6) SI 2004/3426) (¶7777).

Right to paid time off

7740 An IC representative has the right to take **reasonable** paid time off during his working hours to perform his functions (regs 27, 28 SI 2004/3426) and is entitled to be paid at the **appropriate hourly rate**, the amount of which will depend on whether his contractual hours vary or not (¶¶3935+). Any contractual remuneration paid to him in respect of a period of time off will go towards discharging the statutory liability for paid time off for that period (reg 28(7) SI 2004/3426).

7741 An employee who is **unreasonably refused** time off to perform his functions as an IC representative or is not paid (wholly or in part) in respect of such time off can bring a complaint to an employment tribunal (reg 29(1) SI 2004/3426). Complaints must be made within 3 months beginning with the day on which the time off was taken or on which it is alleged the time off should have been permitted (reg 29(2) SI 2004/3426). However, a tribunal can extend this period if it is satisfied that it was not reasonably practicable for the employee to make the complaint in time.

If the claim is successful, the **tribunal must** make a declaration to that effect and/or order the employer to pay (reg 29 SI 2004/3426):
– the employee the amount equal to the remuneration he would have been entitled to had the employer not refused to permit him to take time off; or
– the amount due to the employee if he has taken time off but the employer has refused to pay him in whole or in part.

2. Standard information and consultation provisions

7745 If the standard information and consultation provisions (referred to as the standard IC provisions) apply, the regulations require employers to comply with the standard IC provisions set out below in respect of the information to be provided and the way the consultation is to be conducted.

Confidential information

7746 Under either a standard or negotiated agreement, an employer is permitted to **withhold or restrict** what information or documentation is released to IC representatives (and any persons to whom the IC representatives may wish to further disclose the information or documentation) where, when viewed objectively, such disclosure would seriously harm the functioning of, or would be prejudicial to, the undertaking (regs 25, 26 SI 2004/3426). This provision will apply when information is so confidential that, if leaked, it would cause serious harm or prejudice to the functioning of the undertaking.

> MEMO POINTS Employers should bear in mind **their own confidentiality obligations** (if applicable) when deciding what information or documents can be provided to IC representatives, for example, under the UK Listing Rules or the City Code on Takeovers and Mergers.

7747 Where there is a **dispute** between the employer and the IC representatives or, where no IC representatives have been elected or appointed, an employee or employee representative, **as to the confidentiality** of a piece of information or document which the employer has withheld, either party can apply to the CAC for a declaration as to whether or not the information or document is of such a confidential nature that, when viewed objectively, its disclosure would seriously harm the functioning of, or be prejudicial to, the undertaking (reg 26(2) SI 2004/3426). If the CAC makes a **declaration against the employer**, it will order the disclosure of the information or document, specifying the person(s) to whom the information or document should be disclosed, any terms on which it is to be disclosed and the date before which disclosure must take place (reg 26(3), (4) SI 2004/3426). Before applying to the CAC, however, the parties are advised to seek to resolve the dispute informally.

7748 Where an **employer releases** information or documentation to IC representatives on **terms that require them to keep it confidential** or restrict the categories of persons to whom the information or documentation can be further disclosed, the IC representatives must not disclose such information or documentation except where the employer has expressly permitted them to do so (reg 25(1) SI 2005/3426). It is for an employer to ensure that he makes it clear what information and documentation is to be kept confidential and if any restrictions are to be placed on further disclosure by the recipients to other persons. For example, an employer might allow IC representatives to disclose information to their professional advisers. Employers are advised, however, to make clear that any further recipients of the information are to be bound by an obligation of confidentiality as well.

If a recipient of information or documentation **breaches his duty of confidentiality**, the employer can bring an action against him for breach of a statutory duty (reg 25(3) SI 2004/3426). However, if the recipient reasonably believed that the disclosure was protected under the whistleblowing regulations (¶2700), there will be no breach of duty (reg 25(5) SI 2004/3426).

A recipient of information or documentation from the employer can apply to the CAC for a **declaration** as to **whether** it was **reasonable** for the employer **to impose a duty of confidentiality** in respect of the information or documentation (reg 25(6) SI 2004/3426). If the CAC considers that the disclosure of the information or document by the recipient would not or would not be likely to harm the legitimate interests of the undertaking, it will declare that it was not reasonable for the employer to require the recipient to hold the information or document in confidence (reg 25(7) SI 2004/3426). The recipient(s) of any such information or documentation will therefore no longer be under any duty of confidentiality.

a. Information to be provided

The **specific matters** about which an employer must inform and consult with IC representatives are (reg 20(1) SI 2004/3426):
a. the recent and probable developments in respect of the undertaking's activities and economic situation;
b. the situation, structure and probable development of employment within the undertaking and any anticipatory measures envisaged, in particular, where there is a threat to employment within the undertaking; and
c. decisions likely to lead to substantial changes in work organisation or in contractual relations.

BIS guidance (below) suggests what type of information might be included within these categories, although it will depend largely on the particular circumstances of the undertaking concerned.

An employer is obliged to ensure that consultation on matters referred to in **b**. and **c**. above takes place. He must therefore ensure that the information is **provided at such time and in such a way with such content** as appropriate to enable the IC representatives to adequately study and, if necessary, prepare for consultation regarding such matters (reg 20(2) SI 2004/3426).

7750

Category a: developments regarding activities and economic situation

The standard IC provisions imply that the purpose of this category of information is to provide IC representatives with information which will enable them to **understand** the **background** against which subsequent decisions affecting employment, work organisation or contractual relations are made. Information will include past and future probable developments, which implies that only matters which are more than just a mere possibility need to be disclosed. It should be noted that an employer is not obliged to consult in respect of such information, but simply to provide it to IC representatives.

BIS guidance suggests that the following types of information might be included in respect of the undertaking's **activities**:
– the launch of new products or services or the discontinuation of others;
– changes in senior management;
– takeovers, mergers, acquisitions, sales and other restructuring involving the undertaking;
– reorganisation of the workforce within the undertaking;
– developments in new methods of working; and
– changes to the aims, objectives, strategy or business plan of the undertaking.

BIS guidance regarding the undertaking's **economic situation** suggests that the following information might be included:
– trading conditions, the competitive market in which the undertaking operates, future forecasts for the sector and the level of demand; and
– the undertaking's financial situation based on its accounts.

7752

Category b: situation, structure and development of employment

Unlike information to be provided in category **a**. above, the employer must consult with IC representatives regarding information provided under this category.

7754

BIS guidance suggests that the emphasis regarding this category of information is on the overall **number of employees** within the undertaking and that it therefore might include information regarding:
- the recruitment of new staff and redundancies (both voluntary and compulsory);
- employee turnover;
- the possibility of moving to reduced hours working or the need for overtime;
- changes in retirement policy and early retirement schemes;
- the distribution of employees in the undertaking, both geographically and organisationally; and
- the reorganisation, redeployment or transfer of posts within an undertaking.

BIS guidance suggests that the term "threat to employment" refers to employee training and skill development so as to increase the "employability and adaptability" of affected employees.

Category c: changes in work organisation or contractual relations

7756 This category of information includes information regarding **collective redundancies** (¶8730) and **business transfers** (¶7900). Again, employers are obliged to consult with IC representatives regarding any information provided under this category.

BIS guidance suggests that information regarding changes in **work organisation** might include:
- changes to the level or distribution of employment within the undertaking;
- changes to flexible working, part-time and overtime policies;
- the introduction of different work patterns, including shift work, reduced hours or overtime; or
- the introduction of new technology or equipment and any subsequent need for training.

BIS guidance also suggests that **contractual relations** refer to the contractual relationship between employer and employee and that such information would include:
- a change of employer resulting from a business transfer;
- variations to employees' terms and conditions, except for pay or benefits with a monetary value since these are specifically excluded;
- the introduction of, or a change to, compulsory retirement age;
- changes to an occupational pension scheme where there is a contractual right to become a member; and
- changes in disciplinary and grievance procedures.

b. Conduct of consultation

7760 The employer must consult with IC representatives regarding **information provided under** categories **b.** and **c.** above (¶¶7750+). The employer must ensure that consultation is conducted in such a way so as to ensure that the timing, method and content of the consultation is appropriate (reg 20(4) SI 2004/3426), although there is no guidance as to the required **frequency** or **timing** of consultation, save that the regulations imply that consultation should be ongoing and regular. The frequency and timing of consultation is likely to fluctuate, depending on whether there is much change under way within an undertaking.

Consultation is designed to be a **two-way process based on** the information the employer provides as well as any opinion expressed by the IC representatives. Moreover, the IC representatives must be able to meet the appropriate level of management at the employer, depending on the subject matter, and to obtain a reasoned response from the employer to any opinion the representatives have given. These provisions are aimed at ensuring that there is a genuine consideration by the employer of any views expressed by the IC representatives during the course of the consultation process. IC representatives may therefore disagree with decisions which have been made or may express suggestions for modifying employer's proposals. However, whilst an employer is not obliged to necessarily follow the opinions expressed by the IC representatives, the regulations do imply that meaningful consultation requires the employer to seek and consider views expressed prior to making such decisions.

It is **good practice**, though not a requirement of the regulations, for the IC representatives to report back to the employees they represent and/or to obtain their views following consultation with the employer to ensure that the views of the workforce are reflected.

7762 In addition, with regard to information in category **c**. regarding **collective redundancies**, **business transfers**, and changes to **occupational and personal pension schemes**, the consultation must take place with a view to reaching an agreement on decisions within the employer's power (reg 20(4) SI 2004/3426). This overlaps with the employer's separate consultation duties under TULRCA 1992 (¶8915), the TUPE regulations (¶8060) and the Occupational and Personal Pension Schemes (Consultation by Employers and Miscellaneous Amendment) Regulations (SI 2006/349).

However, once an employer is under a statutory duty to consult representatives under the relevant legislative provisions, the **duty to inform and consult** under these regulations **will cease**, provided he has notified the IC representatives in writing that he will be complying with his duty under either TULRCA, TUPE or the Occupational and Personal Pension Schemes (Consultation by Employers and Miscellaneous Amendment) Regulations (as appropriate) (reg 20(5) SI 2004/3426). This notification needs to be made each time a collective redundancy situation or business transfer arises. However, an employer can choose to consult under both sets of legislation should he wish.

IV. Enforcement and remedies

7765 Where either a **negotiated agreement** or the **standard IC provisions** have come into effect, the following statutory enforcement provisions will apply. Employers who fail to implement their information and consultation obligations, under either type of agreement, risk being liable to a fine (¶7777).

Where, however, a valid **pre-existing agreement** is in place, the statutory enforcement provisions do not apply and such an agreement will only be enforceable if the methods of enforcement have been expressly agreed by the parties in the agreement itself or if the agreement has contractual force (¶1117).

7766 The regulations provide for a formal means of addressing an **employer's failure to comply** with his obligations under a negotiated agreement or, if applicable, the standard IC provisions, but employees (or their representatives) are advised to consider trying to resolve the matter informally before bringing a formal complaint to the CAC. There is no provision allowing for an employer to bring a **complaint against IC representatives or individual employees** save in respect of a breach of confidentiality (¶7748).

7767 **Employee, IC and negotiating representatives** have a **statutory right to paid time off** to carry out their duties as representatives (¶¶7740, 7706). Moreover, both representatives and candidates have the **right not to be unfairly dismissed** or **suffer a detriment** in respect of their functions as a representative or candidate.

Furthermore, **general employees** within an undertaking are afforded the **right not to be unfairly dismissed** or **suffer a detriment** in respect of various matters connected to the negotiation of information and consultation arrangements within the undertaking.

a. Breach of negotiated or standard agreement

7770 With regard to a **negotiated agreement**, a complaint might be brought if the employer fails to comply with one of the terms of the agreement. This could include, for example, that the employer has failed to:

- establish the information and consultation arrangements provided for by the agreement;
- arrange for the election or appointment of IC representatives;
- provide adequate or timely information; or
- consult in the way established by the agreement.

With regard to a **standard agreement**, a complaint can be brought regarding an employer's failure to arrange for the election of IC representatives (¶7738) or in respect of any failure by the employer to comply with one or more of the standard IC provisions (¶7745). This could include, for example, if the employer has failed to:
- arrange for the election of IC representatives;
- adequately provide the information in categories **a**., **b**. or **c**. (¶¶7750+) or to consult in a genuine and meaningful way;
- provide such information in a timely manner;
- meet the IC representatives or send the appropriate level of management to such a meeting; or
- listen to representatives' opinions being expressed and give a reasoned response to such opinions.

Complaint to CAC

7772 Where an employer fails to comply with the terms of a negotiated agreement or, if applicable, the standard IC provisions, a complaint can be made to the CAC in respect of such failure **within** 3 months of the alleged failure (reg 22(1), (2) SI 2004/3426). Where IC representatives have been elected or appointed, they can bring a complaint. If there are no IC representatives, an employee or employee representative can bring the complaint (reg 22(3) SI 2004/3426).

Any complaint or application to the CAC must be made **in writing** and in the **form** required by the CAC (reg 35(1) SI 2004/3426). The CAC will make any **appropriate enquiries** of the parties that it sees fit and, so far as is reasonably practicable, any party with a proper interest in the complaint or application will have an opportunity to be heard by the CAC (reg 35(2) SI 2004/3426). If, as part of its enquiries, the CAC makes a **reasonable request** for **information or documents** from one or both of the parties, it can draw adverse inferences from any failure to comply with such a request (reg 35(3) SI 2004/3426).

Where an employer fails to inform and consult as required by a standard agreement, he cannot rely on a **failure by** a **person who controls the employer** (either directly or indirectly) to provide information to the employer as a valid reason for the employer failing to inform and consult (reg 20(6) SI 2004/3426).

7774 If it considers that the matter is reasonably likely to be settled by conciliation, the CAC can **refer** the complaint or application **to Acas** and will notify the parties accordingly (reg 38 SI 2004/3426). Acas is not under a duty to assist the parties to conciliate and if it decides that the matter is not appropriate for conciliation, or if it has unsuccessfully tried to resolve the dispute, Acas will notify the CAC which must then hear and determine the complaint or application (reg 35(3)-(5) SI 2004/3426). See ¶9218 for a discussion as to Acas' involvement in the conciliation process.

7775 Where the CAC **upholds a complaint**, it will make a declaration to that effect and may order the employer to take such steps as are necessary to comply with the terms of the negotiated agreement or, as the case may be, the standard IC provisions, specifying what steps the employer is required to take and the timeframe in which he must take them (reg 22(4), (5) SI 2004/3426). However, any order made by the CAC cannot have the effect of suspending, or altering the effect of, any act done or agreement made by the employer, or preventing or delaying any such act or agreement he proposes to do or make (reg 22(9) SI 2004/3426).

The CAC must make any declaration or order under these regulations **in writing** and state its **reasons** for making it (reg 35(5) SI 2004/3426). If necessary, a CAC declaration or order can be **enforced** in the civil courts (¶9850).

Appeals

7776 Appeals from a CAC declaration or order on a point of law can be made to the EAT and will be subject to the usual rules regarding timing and form as appeals from the employment tribunal (¶9740). If there is an appeal, any penalty notice (see below) will be suspended while the appeal is ongoing.

Fines

7777 If the CAC makes a declaration and upholds a complaint regarding an employer's failure to (regs 19(6), 22(6) SI 2004/3426):
- inform and consult as required by a negotiated or (if applicable) standard agreement; or
- make arrangements for a ballot to elect IC representatives under the standard agreement, the complainant can **apply to the EAT within** 3 months of the declaration for a penalty notice containing a fine to be imposed on the employer, which is payable to the Secretary of State for BIS (reg 22(6) SI 2004/3426).

Fines cannot be ordered in respect of any other complaints or applications to the CAC, for example, where an employer withholds information on employee numbers (¶7664).

The EAT can hear representations from the employer regarding his failure to comply with the terms of the negotiated agreement or, if applicable, the standard IC provisions. However, unless the EAT is satisfied that, on having heard the employer's representations, his failure resulted from a **reason beyond the employer's control** or that he has some other **reasonable excuse** for his failure, the EAT must impose a fine.

7778 The penalty notice will **specify** the (reg 23(1) SI 2004/3426):
- **amount** of the fine, which **cannot exceed** £75,000;
- **date** by which it must be paid, which cannot be earlier than the end of the period within which an appeal against a declaration or order by the CAC can be made (see ¶9756 regarding the timing of appeals to the EAT); and
- **nature** of the employer's failure and the period to which the fine relates.

In **determining the amount** of the fine, the EAT must take into account the (reg 23(3) SI 2004/3426):
- gravity of the failure;
- period of time over which the failure occurred;
- reason for the failure;
- number of employees affected by the failure; and
- number of employees in the undertaking(s).

> EXAMPLE In a third round of litigation concerning the parties from ¶7664 and ¶7715 (*Amicus v Macmillan Publishers Ltd* [2007] IRLR 885, EAT), an employer, MP Ltd, unreasonably failed to hold a ballot to elect information and consultation representatives. The union then applied to the EAT for a penalty notice. This was the first such case to appear before the EAT. The EAT considered that the failure in this case was a significant one: it was not the company's first breach of the regulations. At the time of the EAT hearing, the company had still not acted on the order of the CAC, indeed its only suggestion to the union had been the offer of a further meeting to discuss the administration of a possible future election. This meeting would take place 6 months after the CAC order. Such conduct the EAT described as "unacceptable dragging of feet" and "an aggravation of the breach". The EAT imposed a fine of £55,000.

7779 If an employer **fails to pay** the fine before the time limit specified in the penalty notice and the period during which an appeal may be made has expired without the employer having made an appeal, or such an appeal has been made and determined (against the employer), the fine can be recovered by the government from the employer as a civil debt.

b. Representatives' and candidates' remedies

7780 Note the specific provisions relating to a representative's or candidate's **statutory right to reasonable paid time off** and any remedies for breaches of this right (¶¶7741, 7707).

Right not to be unfairly dismissed or suffer a detriment

7782 An employee representative, negotiating representative or IC representative (whether elected or appointed under a negotiated or standard agreement), or any candidate for such a position, will be **automatically** unfairly dismissed if the **reason** or **principal reason** is that he (reg 30 SI 2004/3426):
– has performed or proposed to perform any of the functions or activities of a representative or candidate;
– exercised or proposed to exercise his right to paid time off to carry out the functions of a representative or candidate; or
– requested paid time off to carry out the functions of a representative or candidate.

A representative will not be unfairly dismissed if the reason or principal reason for his dismissal is that, in his performance of his functions or activities, he **breached** his **confidentiality obligations** to the employer (¶7748), unless he reasonably believed that he had acted in accordance with the whistleblowing rules (¶2700). For the purposes of automatically unfair dismissal, no **qualifying period of service** is required and there is **no upper age limit** on the right to bring a claim of unfair dismissal (¶8390).

Further, such representatives have the **right not to suffer a detriment** (which does not amount to a dismissal) on the same reason(s) or ground(s) as above (reg 32 SI 2004/3426).

Representatives and candidates who are **also employees** of the employer are further protected from the right not to be unfairly dismissed or suffer a detriment for the reasons and grounds listed below (¶7783).

c. General employees' remedies

Right not to be unfairly dismissed or suffer a detriment

7783 An employee, whether or not he falls within one of the categories of representative mentioned above, is protected from being unfairly dismissed or suffering a detriment (which does not amount to a dismissal) if the **reason** or **principal reason** for his dismissal is that he (reg 30(6), (7) SI 2004/3426):
a. brought, or proposed to bring, tribunal proceedings to enforce a right or secure an entitlement conferred on him by these regulations, whether or not the employee has the right or entitlement or whether or not it has been infringed, provided that the claim to the right and (if applicable) the claim that it has been infringed has been made in good faith;
b. exercised, or proposed to exercise, any entitlement to apply or complain to the CAC or EAT, or to exercise the right to appeal, in connection with any rights conferred by these regulations;
c. requested, or proposed to request, data (¶7664);
d. acted with a view to securing that an agreement was or was not negotiated or that the standard IC provisions did or did not become applicable;
e. indicated that he supported or did not support the coming into existence of a negotiated agreement or the application of the standard IC provisions;
f. stood as a candidate in an election to become either a negotiating or IC representative;
g. influenced or sought to influence by lawful means the way in which votes were to be cast by other employees in a ballot arranged under these regulations;
h. voted in any ballot under these regulations;
i. expressed doubts, whether to a ballot supervisor or otherwise, as to whether the ballot had been properly conducted; or
j. proposed to do, failed to do, or proposed to decline to do, any of the things mentioned in **d.** to **i.** above.

SECTION 2

European works councils

7785 Certain **larger employers** with **employees in more than one EEA member state** are subject to regulations under which they may be required to inform and consult with their employees at European level through the establishment of a European works council (EWC) or information and consultation procedure set up for this purpose (Transnational Information and Consultation of Employees Regulations, referred to in this section as "the regulations" (SI 1999/3323 as amended by SI 2010/1088, the provisions of which came into force on 5 June 2011, save for a few which came into force on 1 October 2011)).

Employers cannot **exclude or limit** the **application of the regulations**, and any agreement (for example, an employment contract) which attempts to contract out of the regulations will be void (reg 40 SI 1999/3323).

> MEMO POINTS   The regulations came into force in January 2000 to implement the European Works Council Directive (EC Directive 1994/45) in the UK. The **principal objective** of the Directive and its implementing regulations is to provide a means of establishing a dialogue between employers and employees through which an exchange of views can take place.
> A revised set of requirements came into force on 5 June 2011 to reflect the changes introduced by a new Directive (EC Directive 2009/38).

7786 For EWCs created **on or after 5 June 2011** (and those which were established by agreement after 15 December 1999 under agreements which were not revised in the 2 years before 5 June 2011) there:
– are requirements on central management to supply information in a set way and form;
– is a different, and more prescriptive, requirement about how and when consultation must take place between central management and EWCs;
– are provisions detailing how consultation between the EWC and central management should be conducted (this requirement was already in place in the default model);
– are provisions which limit consultation to transnational issues;
– are provisions which link consultation to consultation at a national level;
– is a requirement for EWC and SNB members to be trained or given time off with pay to attend training;
– is a requirement on central management to provide the means required for EWCs to operate (this requirement previously existed in the default model); and
– is a different formula to determine membership of the SNB.

1. Scope

7787 The regulations **apply to** Community-scale undertakings or groups of undertakings. A **Community-scale undertaking** is an undertaking with at least 1,000 employees within the EEA member states and at least 150 employees who are employed in each of at least two EEA member states (reg 2 SI 1999/3323). A Community-scale **group of undertakings** means a group of undertakings with at least 1,000 employees between them within the EEA member states, at least two of which must each employ 150 or more employees.

> MEMO POINTS   The regulations do not apply, however, to certain undertakings which already had in place a **voluntary agreement** providing for the transnational information and consultation of employees which covers the entire workforce in the member states, provided the agreement had been concluded **by 15 December 1999** (if the undertaking was subject to the original directive solely as a result of the Extension Directive (so-called article 3 agreements)) or by 22 September 1996 (if the undertaking was subject to the original European Works Council Directive (so-called article 13 agreements)) (regs 44, 45 SI 1999/3323).

7794 Should employees wish to make an employee request to trigger the obligation to negotiate an agreement for an EWC or information and consultation procedure, they may need access to employee numbers in order to determine whether an establishment or undertaking is part of a Community-scale undertaking or group of undertakings. An employee (or employee representative) is **entitled to request information** from the management of an establishment or undertaking in the UK for this purpose (reg 7 SI 1999/3323). If the management **fails to provide** the information, the employee (or employee representative) can complain to the Central Arbitration Committee (CAC) which, if it considers the complaint well-founded, will order the management to disclose the required information to the employee (or employee representative) (reg 8 SI 1999/3323).

2. Establishment of a European works council

7797 Negotiations to establish an EWC or information and consultation procedure can be **initiated** in two ways: either an undertaking can initiate negotiations on its own initiative (reg 9(5) SI 1999/3323) or, more likely, the obligation to begin negotiations arises following a request made by employees (or employee representatives). If no such employee request is made, central management is under no obligation to initiate negotiations.

Employee request

7798 Central management must initiate negotiations to establish an EWC or information and consultation procedure where employees (or employee representatives) have made a valid request and on the relevant date the undertaking is a Community-scale undertaking or the group of undertakings is a Community-scale group of undertakings (reg 9 SI 1999/3323).

7799 To be **valid**, a request must consist of:
– a single request made by at least 100 employees (or employee representatives who represent at least that number) in at least two undertakings/establishments in at least two different member states; or
– a number of separate requests made on the same or different days by employees (or employee representatives) which, when taken in aggregate, mean that at least 100 employees (or employee representatives who represent at least that number), in at least two undertakings/establishments in at least two different member states, have made requests.

Each single or separate request must be **in writing** and **sent to** either the central or local management of the undertaking/establishment, **specifying** the date on which it was sent.

> *MEMO POINTS* Where there have been **previous failed negotiations** to establish an EWC or information and consultation procedure, the request can be made no earlier than 2 years from the conclusion of the previous negotiations unless agreed to otherwise by the special negotiating body (¶7802) and central management.

7800 Where central management considers that a **request** (or separate request) is **not valid**, it can apply to the CAC for a **declaration** as to whether the request is valid (reg 10 SI 1999/3323).

a. Agreed negotiations

7801 The process of negotiating an EWC or information and consultation procedure takes place between central management and a special negotiating body (SNB) which represents the employees in the negotiations.

Special negotiating body (SNB)

7802 Following either a valid request or central management having indicated a wish to initiate the negotiation process, steps must be taken to set up an SNB which will conduct negotiations for the establishment of an EWC on behalf of all employees in each of the member states in which the undertaking or group of undertakings has operations.

The **role** of the SNB, together with central management, is to conclude a written agreement detailing the scope, composition, functions and term of office of an EWC or the arrangements for implementing an information and consultation procedure (reg 11 SI 1999/3323).

The **composition** of the SNB is determined by the formula specified in the regulations of the member state in which the central management is located (or, where the central management is outside the member states, the country in which its representative agent is located). The SNB must **inform** central management and local managements of the composition of the SNB (reg 12 SI 1999/3323). For example, in the UK for those covered by the 5 June 2011 changes (¶7786), the SNB must have at least one member from each EEA member state where the company has employees and at least one member for each 10% or part of 10% of the total number of employees employed in each member state. For those not covered by the 5 June 2011 changes, the SNB should have at least one member from each EEA member state where the company has employees and one additional member where between 25% and 49% of employees are employed in that member state, two additional members where between 50% and 74% of employees are employed in that member state and three additional members where 75% or more employees are employed in that member state.

7803

Management in the UK must arrange for the holding of a ballot of all UK employees within the undertaking/establishment to **elect the UK members** of the SNB **unless**, for example, there is already an existing consultative committee in place (regs 13, 15 SI 1999/3323).

7804

Conduct of negotiations

Once the SNB has been established, the central management and the SNB must negotiate in a **spirit of co-operation** with a view to reaching a written agreement outlining the detailed arrangements for the information and consultation of employees in the Community-scale undertaking or group of undertakings (reg 17 SI 1999/3323). For the purposes of the negotiations, the SNB can bring along **additional experts** if it so wishes. Central management must pay for any **reasonable expenses** relating to the negotiations that are necessary for the SNB to carry out its functions. For those covered by the 5 June 2011 changes (¶7786), UK members of the SNB are also entitled to receive **paid time off** from their employer to attend any necessary **training**.

7820

It is for the SNB to decide not to open negotiations with central management or to terminate them (reg 16 SI 1999/3323). Any such decision must be taken by at least two-thirds of the votes cast by the SNB members. If the SNB takes such a decision, the negotiations process will cease and any subsequent request to invoke negotiations for the establishment of an EWC or information and consultation procedure cannot take place for another 2 years from the date of the SNB decision, unless central management and the SNB agree otherwise.

The parties are free to establish an information and consultation procedure instead of an EWC.

Scope and content of agreement

If the parties decide that they wish to establish an EWC, the arrangements for establishing an EWC are largely left to them to agree. This means that arrangements can vary widely between one EWC and another. However, the agreement must cover the following:
a. which undertakings of the Community-scale group of undertakings or establishments of the Community-scale undertaking will be covered;
b. the composition of the EWC, the number of members and their term of office;
c. the functions and procedure for informing and consulting the EWC;
d. the venue, duration and frequency of EWC meetings;
e. the financial and material resources to be allocated to the EWC;
f. how long the agreement will last and the procedure for renegotiating a new agreement; and
g. for those covered by the 5 June 2011 changes (¶7786):
– how the consultative dialogue with the EWC should be linked to other consultative dialogues at national level;
– whether a select committee should be set up and, if so, how it will operate; and
– transnational issues only.

7821

With regard to any further provisions in the agreement, parties may find it useful to adopt some or all of the provisions of the statutory "default" model EWC agreement (Sch 1 SI 1999/3323).

7823 Once an EWC or information and consultation procedure has been established, both central management and the EWC or information and consultation representatives have a legal duty to work in a **spirit of co-operation** with regard to their reciprocal rights and obligations (reg 19 SI 1999/3323). There is also a statutory duty of confidentiality and the central management may, in certain circumstances, withhold information if its disclosure is likely to prejudice or cause serious harm to the undertaking concerned. Further, for those covered by the 5 June 2011 changes (¶7786), the central management has specific duties in relation to providing information to the EWC representatives or information and consultation representatives.

b. Statutory default model

7825 A statutory default model EWC will **apply** if, in respect of the date on which a valid request to negotiate an EWC or information and consultation procedure is made (¶7799) (reg 18 SI 1999/3323):
– **within 6 months**, central management refuses to commence negotiations; or
– **after 3 years**, the parties have failed to reach an agreement to establish an EWC or information and consultation procedure (and the SNB has not made a decision about entering into or withdrawing from such negotiations).

The **rules** relating to the statutory default model are much less flexible on the composition of the EWC, what it can discuss during EWC meetings and how the EWC should work.

7826 A statutory model EWC **will operate for** at least 4 years, at the end of which the members of the EWC can decide whether it wishes to negotiate a new EWC, the terms of which the parties will mutually agree, or to continue with the statutory arrangements (para 10 Sch 1 SI 1999/3323). Should the EWC wish to negotiate a new agreement, it must notify the central management in writing. The central management must then enter into negotiation with the EWC as if it were an SNB (¶7801).

3. Enforcement and remedies

7842 Enforcement of the regulations is through the Central Arbitration Committee (CAC) and Employment Appeal Tribunal (EAT) in GB. The CAC generally determines matters such as whether an undertaking is covered by the regulations and matters regarding the procedure for establishing an EWC, and its involvement is discussed where relevant throughout the section. The EAT, on the other hand, generally hears disputes regarding the operation of an EWC or a failure to establish one, together with appeals on points of law from the CAC. Both the CAC and EAT can refer cases to Acas, where they consider conciliation would be useful.

a. General remedies

Failure to establish EWC or information and consultation procedure

7845 Where an SNB (or, if no SNB exists, an employee, employee representative or former member of an SNB (if one previously existed)) considers that the parties have reached an agreement to establish an EWC or information and consultation procedure, or that the statutory default model EWC applies (¶7825), and that, due to a failure of central management, the EWC or information and consultation procedure has not been established at all or has not been established fully in accordance with the terms of the agreement, it can **bring a complaint** to the EAT (reg 20 SI 1999/3323).

Where the EAT finds a complaint **well-founded**, it must make a decision to that effect and can order the central management to take such steps as are necessary to establish the EWC or information and consultation procedure (whether in accordance with the procedure for establishing a mutually-agreed EWC or the statutory model).

In addition, the EAT must issue a **written penalty notice**, requiring central management to pay a fine of **up to** £100,000 to the Exchequer in respect of the failure, unless the EAT is satisfied that the failure resulted from a reason beyond the control of central management or that it has some other reasonable excuse for its failure (regs 20, 22 SI 1999/3323).

When **determining the amount** of the fine, the EAT will take into account the following factors:
– gravity of the failure;
– period of time over which the failure has occurred;
– reason for the failure;
– number of employees affected by the failure; and
– number of employees of the Community-scale undertaking or group of undertakings in the member states.

Disputes regarding operation of EWC or information and consultation procedure

Either central management or an EWC (or, in a case concerning an information and consultation procedure, the information and consultation representatives) which considers that the terms of an EWC agreement or information and consultation procedure (whether established by mutual agreement or based on the statutory model) have not been complied with by the other party to the agreement can **bring a complaint** to the EAT (reg 21 SI 1999/3323).

Where the EAT finds a complaint is **well-founded**, it must make a decision to that effect and can order the defaulting party to take such steps as are necessary to comply with the terms of the EWC agreement (or, if relevant, the statutory model) or information and consultation procedure.

If the **defaulting party** is **central management**, the EAT must in addition issue a written penalty notice, requiring central management to pay a **fine of up to** £100,000 to the Exchequer in respect of the non-compliance unless the EAT is satisfied that the non-compliance resulted from a reason beyond the central management's control or that it has some other reasonable excuse for the failure to comply (regs 21, 22 SI 1999/3323).

See ¶7848 for a discussion of the provisions relating to the imposition of a **fine**.

b. Individual remedies

Individual employees are afforded protection under the regulations if they are dismissed (or selected for redundancy) unfairly or subjected to a detriment for a reason in connection with their membership, candidature, or activities in relation to an SNB or EWC, or in relation to their involvement as an information and consultation representative. There is also protection for employees generally if they are dismissed or subjected to a detriment for other reasons related to EWCs. In addition, certain employees have the right to take reasonable paid time off to train or carry out their functions in respect of an SNB or EWC or in relation to their involvement as an information and consultation representative and can enforce such a right through the employment tribunal.

Right not to be unfairly dismissed or subjected to a detriment

An employee who is a **member of an SNB or EWC** or an **information and consultation representative member** (or a **candidate** in an election to become such a member or representative) can bring a claim for unfair dismissal (including unfair redundancy dismissal) or in respect of a detriment (other than dismissal) to which he has been subjected if the **reason**

for the dismissal (including selection for redundancy) **or detriment** is that the employee has (regs 28, 29, 31, 32 SI 1999/3323):
a. performed, or proposed to perform, any functions or activities as such a member, representative or candidate; or
b. made, or proposes to make, a request (including via a person acting on his behalf) to take time off to perform such functions (¶7855).

If such an employee has, in the course of performing his functions or activities, disclosed any confidential information in breach of his statutory duty of confidentiality, then he will lose the protection afforded under **a.** above unless he reasonably believed that his disclosure amounted to a "protected disclosure" under the whistleblowing legislation (¶2715).

7853 **Any employee**, whether or not he falls into the category of employee listed above (¶7852), can bring a claim for unfair dismissal (including unfair redundancy dismissal) or in respect of a detriment (other than dismissal) to which he has been subjected if the **reason for the dismissal** (including selection for redundancy) **or detriment** is that the employee (regs 28, 29, 31 SI 1999/3323):
– took, or proposed to take, any proceedings before an employment tribunal to enforce a right or secure an entitlement conferred on him by these regulations. It is irrelevant if it later transpires that the employee does not have the right concerned or whether or not it was infringed provided that his claim to the right (and, if applicable, his claim that it has been infringed) was made in good faith;
– exercised, or proposed to exercise, any entitlement to apply or complain to the EAT or CAC, conferred by these regulations;
– requested, or proposed to request, information regarding employee numbers (¶7794);

or that he (or proposed to, failed to, or proposed to decline to):
– acted with a view to securing that an SNB, EWC or information and consultation procedure did or did not come into existence;
– indicated that he did or did not support the coming into existence of an SNB, EWC or an information and consultation procedure;
– stood as a candidate in an election to become a member of an SNB, EWC or an information and consultation representative;
– influenced or sought to influence the way in which votes were to be cast by other employees in a ballot arranged under these regulations;
– voted in such a ballot; or
– expressed doubts, whether to a ballot supervisor or otherwise, as to whether such a ballot had been properly conducted.

7854 The reasons set out above are inadmissible reasons and, consequently, any such dismissal (or selection for redundancy) will be **automatically unfair** which means that an employee does not have to have any particular period of continuous employment (¶8393).

Right to time off

7855 An employee who is a **member of an SNB or EWC** or an **information and consultation representative member** (or a **candidate** in an election to become such a member or representative) is entitled to take reasonable time off during his working hours to perform his functions as such a member, representative or candidate (reg 25 SI 1999/3323).

For those covered by the 5 June 2011 changes (¶7786), such an employee is also entitled to take reasonable time off to train.

Time off is to be **paid** at the appropriate hourly rate (reg 26 SI 1999/3323) (¶¶3935+).

7856 An employee who has been **unreasonably refused time off** or has **not been paid** in respect of any time off, whether in whole or in part, can bring a claim to an employment tribunal (reg 27 SI 1999/3323). He must **bring his claim within** 3 months beginning with the date on which the time off was taken or on which he alleges time off should have been permitted by his employer.

If the tribunal finds an employee's claim is **well-founded**, it will make a declaration to that effect and, in respect of a failure to permit an employee to take reasonable time off, will order the employer to pay an amount to the employee equal to the remuneration to which he would have been entitled had he been permitted to take time off. In respect of a failure to pay for any reasonable time off, the tribunal will order the employer to pay to the employee an amount which it finds is due to him.

CHAPTER 23

Lay-off and short-time working

OUTLINE

SECTION 1 **Guarantee payments** 7860	SECTION 2 **Redundancy payments** 7875
Amount payable 7865	Scope 7877
Remedies 7870	Eligibility 7880
	Contested claims 7887
	Uncontested claims 7890
	Calculation 7891
	Death of employer or employee 7892

7858 Where an employer cannot provide work, an employee may be entitled to a statutory guarantee payment.

If the employee has been laid off or put on short-time working, he may be entitled to a statutory redundancy payment if his employer terminates his employment. This provides the employee with a remedy where the employer has laid off the employee or put him on short-time working instead of making him redundant in the hope that this will result in the employee leaving of his own accord.

SECTION 1

Guarantee payments

7860 An employee has a statutory right to a minimum guarantee payment for every workless day where the employer cannot provide him with work.

Employers should pay full contractual pay in such circumstances unless there is an express term to reduce pay. Otherwise, the employer may be liable under his employee's implied right to be paid (¶2806).

7861 To be entitled to a guarantee payment, **employees** must be **continuously employed** for 1 month ending with the day before the workless day (s 29 ERA 1996).

7862 The right arises when **work** of the kind which the employee is employed to do **is not provided** to him during any part of his normal working hours in a workday **due to** (s 28 ERA 1996):
– a decrease in the employer's business requirements for that work; or
– any other event affecting the normal working of the employer's business in relation to that work.

When this occurs, the day will be treated as a workless day. On the other hand, if there is an agreement to vary hours which results in certain days not being worked then any such days will not be categorised as workless days (*Abercrombie and ors v Aga Rangemaster Ltd* [2012] UKEAT 0099_12_1010).

> **EXAMPLE** In *Abercrombie and ors v Aga Rangemaster Ltd*, the EAT considered whether an agreed temporary variation to employees's normal working hours meant that the employees could not claim a guarantee payment. The case involved hourly-paid factory workers, all of whom were GMB union members. In December 2008, the GMB members voted in favour of a temporary reduction in working hours and pay from 39 to 34 hours per week, so as to avoid a redundancy exercise. This involved compressing their hours into a 4-day week, with Fridays off. GMB asked the employer, A Ltd, to confirm that it would be paying guarantee payments during the period of the revised working pattern. A Ltd refused to make those payments, pointing out that the reduction in working hours was the result of an agreed variation to the contracts. The employees issued claims for failure to make guarantee payments. At the hearing of those claims, an employment judge (sitting alone) held that there had been a clear temporary variation of the employees' contracts, with the result that the employees were not normally required to work on Fridays during the period of the revised working pattern. As such, they were not entitled to guarantee payments for those Fridays. The EAT dismissed the employees' appeal and held that the temporary agreed variation of working hours meant that the normal working hours for guarantee payment purposes had also changed. As such, the employees had no entitlement to guarantee payments; there were no days (or parts of days) on which the employees were not provided with work which they would, in accordance with their varied contract, be required to work. The EAT suggested that tribunals must look at the particular day when it is said that the employee was not provided with work and consider whether that was a day upon which the employee was normally required to work. Here, the agreed variation to the contracts meant that the employees were no longer normally required to work on the Fridays in question.

7863 Where a **shift or night worker**'s shift starts before midnight and ends the following day, the workless day will be taken to be the day he started the shift if it is, or would normally be, longer in duration before midnight. If not, it will be treated as falling wholly on the second day (s 28(4), (5) ERA 1996).

7864 An employee is not **entitled** to a guarantee payment if (s 29(3)-(5) ERA 1996):
– his employer fails to provide work as a result of a **strike**, lock-out or other industrial action involving any employee of his employer or of an associated employer;
– his employer has offered **suitable alternative work** and he has unreasonably refused. Suitable alternative work need not be within his normal contractual duties but have to take into account his skill, geographic location, pay and hours; or
– he does not comply with his employer's **reasonable requirements** which are made with a view to ensuring that his services are available, for example a requirement to telephone to find out about availability of other alternative work.

Amount payable

7865 The amount payable for a workless day is **calculated** by multiplying the number of normal working hours in that day by the guaranteed hourly rate (s 30 ERA 1996).

7866 The **guaranteed hourly rate** is 1 week's pay (¶2920) divided by the number of **normal working hours** for that week. If the employee works **variable hours** from week to week, the number of working hours for 1 week's pay is calculated by taking the average number of working hours over the 12 weeks ending with the last complete week before the workless day. If the employee has not been employed for 12 weeks, the working hours are calculated by the number which will fairly represent the number of normal working hours in a week taking into account the employee's reasonable expectations in accordance with his contractual terms and the experience of comparable employees (s 30(3) ERA 1996).

If the employee works on **short-time**, the calculation is based on the original contract (s 30(5) ERA 1996).

7867 This is subject to a **maximum amount payable** for a workless day of £24.20 from 1 February 2013 and is only payable **for a maximum of** 5 workless days in any 3-month period (SI 2012/3007).

Any **contractual amounts** paid by the employer with regard to a workless day will go towards discharging this amount (s 32 ERA 1996). Therefore, if an employee is paid on a weekly or monthly basis, these payments will go towards discharging any statutory liability in that period. Offsetting the statutory entitlement does not discount the workless days in question and therefore will count towards the maximum of 5 workless days in any 3-month period (*Cartwright v G Claney Ltd* [1983] IRLR 355, EAT).

Remedies

The employee can bring a claim to an employment tribunal if his employer has failed to pay the whole or part of a guarantee payment entitlement (s 34 ERA 1996).

The **time limit** for bringing a claim is 3 months beginning with the workless day. The tribunal can **extend** this period if it is satisfied that it was not reasonably practicable to have presented the claim in time. In such cases the tribunal will indicate what extension is reasonable.

Where the tribunal finds that the complaint is well-founded it will **order** the employer to pay the worker as appropriate.

SECTION 2

Redundancy payments

If an employee has been laid off or put on short-time working, he may be entitled to a statutory redundancy payment under a specific statutory scheme if his employer terminates his contract by giving notice and satisfies the eligibility requirements (see below).

Contractual redundancy schemes which give enhanced redundancy payments do not normally apply to lay-off or short-time working.

The **collective consultation obligation** does not apply as it arises only when the employer proposes to dismiss, and in the case of lay-off and short-time working, it is the employee who gives notice of termination.

Scope

The **lay-off** provisions apply when an employee is not provided with the work he is employed to do and on which his contractual remuneration depends, such that he will not be entitled to any remuneration for the period of the lay-off (for example, pieceworkers) (s 147(1) ERA 1996). Receipt of a statutory guarantee payment (see above) will not prevent the lay-off provisions applying.

The **short-time working** provisions apply when an employee is provided with less work by the employer, such that his remuneration for any week is less than half a week's pay (for example, pieceworkers and timeworkers) (s 147(2) ERA 1996) (¶2920). Again, guarantee payments do not affect the application of these provisions.

An employer needs a **contractual right** (express or implied) to lay off an employee or put him on short-time working. An implied right will only exist where there is a custom for that particular employment that is reasonable, certain and notorious, such that the employee would have expected the term to be included as part of the agreement.

If there is **no contractual right**, the employer will be in fundamental breach of contract if he imposes lay-off or short-time working, entitling the employee to accept the breach, resign, and claim constructive dismissal (including, possibly, a claim for a redundancy payment under the general rules). Alternatively, the employee can choose not to treat himself as dismissed, waive the breach, and claim redundancy under the specific lay-off/short-time working provisions by resigning with notice.

If the employee has **actually been dismissed** in connection with a period of lay-off or short-time working, he must bring a claim for a redundancy payment under the general rules (s 151 ERA 1996).

7879 It has been held that there is an implied contractual term that any lay-off will only be **for a reasonable period**, and that breach of this term will entitle the employee to claim constructive dismissal for redundancy (*A Dakri & Co Ltd v Tiffen* [1981] IRLR 57, EAT), although it has also been held that the employee's remedy for a lengthy period of lay-off is to claim a redundancy payment under the specific statutory scheme (*Kenneth MacRae & Co Ltd v Dawson* [1984] IRLR 5, EAT).

Eligibility

7880 Firstly, the employee **must satisfy** the eligibility requirements under the general statutory redundancy payment scheme (including the completion of 2 years' continuous service) (¶8990).

7881 Secondly, the employee must:
– work under a contract according to which his pay is dependent on the provision of work by the employer (for example, workers paid per piece of work done);
– have been laid off or put on short-time working for the requisite period (¶7882);
– have been available for work (i.e. an employee on sick leave will not be eligible);
– comply with the statutory notification procedure (¶7884);
– in contested cases, apply to the tribunal for a decision (¶7888); and
– resign his employment by giving notice (¶7886).
An employee may be entitled to a redundancy payment in these circumstances even if he also receives a statutory guarantee payment from the employer (see section 1).

7882 **Requisite period** The employee must have been laid off or put on short-time working (or a combination of the two) for either (s 148(2) ERA 1996):
– 4 or more consecutive weeks; or
– a total of 6 weeks (of which no more than 3 are consecutive) in any period of 13 weeks.
For these purposes, a week ends with a Saturday, unless the employee's pay is calculated by reference to a week ending with a different day, in which case it ends with that day (s 235(1) ERA 1996).

7883 A week of lay-off or short-time working caused wholly or mainly by a **strike or lock-out** will not count towards the requisite period (s 154(b) ERA 1996), whether or not:
– the employee participates in the strike or lock-out;
– the strike or lock-out is in the employee's trade or industry; or
– the strike or lock-out takes place in Great Britain.

> MEMO POINTS For these purposes, a **strike** is defined as (s 235(5) ERA 1996):
> – the cessation of work by a group of workers; or
> – the refusal of workers to continue to work as a consequence of a dispute,
> to compel the employer (or to aid other workers in compelling their employer) to accept/not to accept terms or conditions of or affecting employment.
> A **lock-out** is defined as (s 235(4) ERA 1996):
> – the closing of a place of employment;
> – the suspension of work; or
> – the refusal by an employer to continue to employ workers in consequence of a dispute,
> with a view to compelling workers, or to aid another employer in compelling his workers, to accept terms or conditions of or affecting employment.

7884 **Notice of intention to claim** The employee must give the employer written notice of his intention to claim a redundancy payment on, or **within** 4 weeks of, the last day of the lay-off or short-time working on which the claim is based (s 148 ERA 1996). This time limit cannot be extended.

The notice must be **served by** (s 179(2) ERA 1996):
– delivery to the employer or a person designated by him;

– post to the employer at the employee's workplace (or to the designated person at a designated address); or
– leaving it for the designated person at a designated place.

If the notice is **served before** the employee has completed the requisite period of lay-off or short-time working (¶7882), it will be invalid and the claim for a redundancy payment will fail (*Allinson v Drew Simmons Engineering Ltd* [1985] ICR 488, EAT), although the employee could cure the defect by sending another notice within the time limit.

If the employee is dismissed for misconduct or taking part in a strike **after service** of the notice, he cannot claim a redundancy payment based on lay-off or short-time working, but will have to rely on the express dismissal and the general redundancy payment rules. However, in this case, the employer will not be able to rely on the fact that the dismissal was not for redundancy to thwart the employee's claim for a payment (¶¶8992+), although the tribunal will have a discretion to reduce the amount of the payment (¶9006).

7885

Notice of termination The employee will not be entitled to a redundancy payment if his employment subsists, so he must terminate his employment by giving 1 week's (i.e. 7 days') notice (or contractual notice, if longer) either (s 150(1), (3) ERA 1996):
– within 3 weeks of the employer's failure to give, or his withdrawal of, a counter-notice (or his service of a late or invalid notice) (see below for service of counter-notice); or
– in contested cases, within 3 weeks of notification to the employee of the tribunal's decision (ignoring any appeal).
This notice does not have to be in writing.

7886

Contested claims

If the employer opposes the claim, he must serve a **written counter-notice** within 7 days of service of the employee's notice (s 149 ERA 1996). It must clearly state that the employer intends to contest the employee's claim for a redundancy payment.

7887

The counter-notice must be **served by** (s 179(1) ERA 1996):
– delivery to the employee;
– leaving it for the employee at his usual or last-known place of residence; or
– post to the employee at that address.

The employer can **withdraw** his counter-notice at any time by giving a written notice of withdrawal.

If the employer has served (and not withdrawn) a counter-notice, the **employee must apply** to a tribunal for a decision (s 149 ERA 1996).

7888

If the employee does not satisfy the eligibility criteria (¶7880), the employer can **defend the claim** on that basis (whether or not he has served a counter-notice).

7889

Otherwise, the employer can only defend a claim if, when the employee served his notice, it was reasonably to be expected that a period of at least 13 weeks of normal working (i.e. no lay-off or short-time) (under the same contract of employment) would be resumed within the next 4 weeks (s 152 ERA 1996). To rely on this defence, the employer must have served a valid counter-notice. If the employee continues to be laid-off or on short-time working throughout the 4 weeks, the employer's defence will fail.

> MEMO POINTS An employee who unreasonably refuses an offer of **suitable alternative employment** may lose his entitlement to a statutory redundancy payment (¶8996). It is not clear whether this applies to the specific statutory provisions relating to lay-off and short-time working, or whether it is confined to situations where there has been a dismissal for redundancy, although it is thought that the latter approach is more likely to be taken by the courts and tribunals.

Uncontested claims

If the employer does not serve a counter-notice (or withdraws his counter-notice), the employee who satisfies the eligibility criteria (¶7880) will be entitled to a redundancy payment as if he had been dismissed for redundancy.

7890

Calculation

7891 The redundancy payment is calculated in the same way as in the general scheme (¶8990).

The **relevant date** for calculation purposes is the last day of the last week of lay-off or short-time working on which the employee is relying (s 153 ERA 1996).

Death of employer or employee

7892 If an **individual employer** dies after the employee has been laid off or put on short-time working for 1 or more weeks but **before** he has served a **notice of intention to claim**, the week in which the employer dies and the week in which the employee is taken on by the employer's personal representatives are treated as consecutive weeks for the purposes of the requisite period (¶7882) if the personal representatives lay the employee off or put him on short-time working for 1 or more weeks (s 175(2) ERA 1996).

If the employer dies within 4 weeks of receiving the employee's notice of intention to claim but before he has given **notice to terminate** (or before that notice expires), the position will depend on whether the employee is re-engaged by the personal representatives within 4 weeks of the date of service of the notice of intention to claim. If he is **not re-engaged**, the position is as if the employer had not died and the employee had terminated his employment by giving the required notice. However, the employer's defence is not available to the personal representatives, nor can they serve a counter-notice opposing his claim (s 175(3), (4) ERA 1996). If he is **re-engaged** and is laid off or kept on short-time working for at least 1 week, all the weeks of lay-off or short-time working are deemed to be consecutive and in the same employment (s 175(5) ERA 1996). The time limit for service of his notice of termination is extended by the number of weeks between the employer's death and the date of re-engagement.

7893 If an **employee dies after serving** his notice of intention to claim (but **before giving notice to terminate** the employment), and the time limit for serving a notice to terminate has not expired (see above), the requirement to serve such a notice disappears (s 176(6)(a) ERA 1996). The employee's estate can claim a redundancy payment although the employer is free to raise a defence.

If an employee dies **within 7 days of serving** his notice of intention to claim, the employer is treated as having served a counter-notice (even if he has not actually done so) and may contest proceedings brought by the employee's estate (s 176(6)(b) ERA 1996).

CHAPTER 24

Transfer of the business

OUTLINE

		¶¶
SECTION 1 **Which transfers are covered?**		7910
A Types of transfer		7910
B Identifying a transfer		7930
Business transfer		7931
Service provision change		7936
Special situations		7940
SECTION 2 **Effect**		7950
A Employees protected by TUPE		7952
Timing of transfer		7966
B Rights and liabilities		7970
1 Rights and liabilities which transfer		7970
Contractual obligations		7971
Non-contractual rights and liabilities		7980
Collective agreements		7985
Trade union recognition		7987
2 Rights and liabilities which do not transfer		7990
Share options and other incentives		7990
Occupational pension schemes		7992
Debts owed by insolvent transferor		7998
Criminal liabilities		8002
C Varying terms and conditions		8010
Permitted variations		8015
Business subject to insolvency proceedings		8023
D Dismissal		8030
Liability for dismissals		8037
Defence		8041
SECTION 3 **Information and consultation obligations**		8060
A Duty on transferor and transferee to inform and consult		8062
Informing employees about the transfer		8067
Timing		8075
Failure to comply		8080
Infringement of rights		8089
B Duty on transferor to provide transferee with employee information		8090
Informing transferee about transferring employees		8091
Timing		8093
Failure to comply		8094

7900 Many types of transfers, such as the sale of a business or the contracting out of a service, may be covered by **UK transfer regulations**.

The general **purpose** of such regulations is to safeguard employees' rights when the business in which they work changes hands. Where the regulations apply, their **effect is** that most rights and liabilities transfer automatically from the transferor to the transferee. Transfer-related changes to terms and conditions of employment may be void and dismissals in connection with the transfer may be automatically unfair. Both transferor and transferee are also subject to specific information and consultation obligations.

Parties cannot **contract out** of these regulations when they apply. Being able to identify what constitutes a transfer is central to understanding the scope of TUPE.

7901 **The regulations** governing business transfers in the UK are the Transfer of Undertakings (Protection of Employment) Regulations 2006 (SI 2006/246) (referred to in this chapter as "TUPE" and the "current TUPE regulations"), which were introduced to give effect to European Directive 2001/23, known as the Acquired Rights Directive ("ARD"). The current TUPE regulations revise and supersede the previous TUPE regulations (the Transfer of Undertakings (Protection of Employment) Regulations 1981 (SI 1981/1974) (referred to in this chapter as the "previous TUPE regulations")). This chapter refers to case law made under the current TUPE regulations and, where relevant, reference is also made to the extensive case law and principles developed under the previous TUPE regulations.

MEMO POINTS 1. The current TUPE regulations came into force on 6 April 2006. Transfers which took place **before 6 April 2006** are governed by the previous TUPE regulations.
2. Where an employer is a **public authority** (for example, government departments, local authorities, health or education authorities), its employees can rely directly on the ARD if they believe that the UK has failed to implement it correctly, or that it gives them greater rights than domestic legislation.
3. **BIS guidance** on the current TUPE regulations is referred to throughout this chapter.
4. The Government intends to **review** the current TUPE regulations and any further developments will be covered by our updating service.

SECTION 1

Which transfers are covered?

A. Types of transfer

7910 There are **two definitions** of a TUPE transfer, covering:
1. transfers of undertakings or businesses (referred to in this chapter as "business transfers"); and
2. service provision changes (reg 3(1) SI 2006/246).

These two definitions govern whether TUPE applies. Once TUPE applies, the effect is the same, irrespective of the type of transfer.

It is important to note that the two types of transfer are not mutually exclusive. Some transfers will qualify both as a business transfer and a service provision change.

7912 **Business transfer** TUPE will **apply to** the transfer of an undertaking or business which is situated in the UK immediately before the transfer. There **must be** a transfer of an economic entity which retains its identity (¶7931). TUPE can also apply to the transfer of part of a business (¶7947).

7914 **Service provision change** The definition of a TUPE transfer extends specifically to cover the relationship between clients and the **contractors** who provide services for them. Examples of such services include office cleaning, catering, refuse collection and machinery maintenance. The **purpose** of this extended definition is to provide certainty, create a level playing field for contractors and reduce transaction costs.

TUPE therefore expressly provides for **three scenarios**, covering contracts which are (reg 3(1)(b) SI 2006/246):
– awarded to a contractor (i.e. the service is "contracted out" or "outsourced");
– re-let to a new contractor (i.e. the service is "reassigned"); or
– brought back "in-house" (i.e. the service is "contracted in" or "insourced").

A change in service provision will only effect a TUPE transfer if **three conditions** are satisfied (see ¶7936).

7915 A service provision change may still **qualify as a business transfer** on the basis of case law developed under the previous TUPE regulations (whether or not the three conditions are satisfied) (¶7938).

Where a service provision change does take place, the party responsible for carrying out the activities prior to the change is treated as the **transferor** and the party who carries them out as a result of the change is treated as the **transferee**.

> MEMO POINTS **Sub-contractors** are treated in the same way as contractors under TUPE (reg 2(1) SI 2006/246).

Examples

7919

TUPE **may apply** to:
– the **sale** of a business, or part of a business, as a going concern. This includes transfers of **day-to-day activities**, even where on the face of it there has merely been a share sale (¶7926);
– the **contracting** of an activity; and
– transfers **whether or not** there has been a transfer of **ownership of assets**.

> MEMO POINTS TUPE may also apply to:
> – the transfer of a **lease** on a business such as a pub or a tenanted farm (*Foreningen af Arbejdsledere i Danmark v Daddy's Dance Hall A/S* [1988] IRLR 315, ECJ; *Landsorganisationen i Danmark v Ny Molle Kro* [1987] EUECJ R-287/86);
> – the termination and grant of **franchises and licences**;
> – transfers by **operation of law** (for example, the automatic transfer of a sole trader's estate on his death);
> – transfers between undertakings engaged in economic activities, **whether or not** they are **operating for gain**; and
> – where **directors and sole shareholders** continue to carry on a business with the same employees after the company was struck off the register of companies (*Charlton and Charlton v (1) Charlton Thermosystems (Romsey) Ltd and (2) Ellis* [1995] IRLR 79, EAT).

TUPE does **not apply** to:
– a mere transfer of an asset or **assets**;
– the transfer of **shares** in a company which carries on the undertaking (see also ¶7926); and
– an administrative reorganisation of **public administrative authorities** or the transfer of administrative functions between public administrative authorities (but see also ¶7928).

7923

More complex transfer situations TUPE will apply to company restructures where there has been a transfer of business. Further, there are some exceptions to the general rule that TUPE does not apply to the reorganisation of public administrative authorities, or transfer of functions between public administrative authorities.

7925

TUPE will apply to **company restructures** where this has led to a transfer of business, for example the transfer of business **between** two **subsidiaries** in the same group (*Allen v Amalgamated Construction Co Ltd* [1999] EUECJ C-234/98).

7926

However, **pure share sales** remain outside TUPE, even where the transaction is structured in this way specifically to avoid TUPE (*Brookes v Borough Care Services* [1998] UKEAT 210_98_0408). The mere fact of a **transfer of control**, i.e. ownership of the shares of the company, will not be sufficient to establish the transfer of the business from subsidiary to parent (*Print Factory (London) 1991 Ltd v Millam* [2007] ICR 1331, CA). What is needed for a TUPE transfer is for the overall arrangement to have changed so that the subsidiary's **day-to-day** activities can be shown to have transferred to the parent company. This is simply a question of fact and it is not necessary to look behind the corporate structure to ascertain whether the transaction was in fact more than a share sale alone.

Pure public sector transfers remain outside TUPE, and are covered instead by the Cabinet Office's Statement of Practice (Staff Transfers in the Public Sector).

7928

However, the following transactions involving a public authority fall **within TUPE**:
– the grant of **concessions**, for example, by a public body (*Collino and Chiappero v Telecom Italia SpA* [2000] EUECJ C-343/98);
– the transfer of a **state subsidy from** one **charity** to another (*Dr Sophie Redmond Stichting v Bartol* [1992] EUECJ C-29/91);
– the transfer of an undertaking from a **private body back to a public authority** (*Mayeur v Association Promotion de l'Information Messine (APIM)* [2000] EUECJ C-175/99); and

– the outsourcing of public sector services to the **private sector** or to companies set up and owned by local authorities to manage their services at **arm's length** (referred to as ALMOs in England and ALEOs in Scotland).

B. Identifying a transfer

7930 Identifying a TUPE transfer will **depend on** whether the transaction is a business transfer or a service provision change. In many cases it will be obvious if a transfer falls within TUPE. Where it is not clear or where the matter is in dispute, the parties (or the tribunal determining the question) must examine the issue with great care and in some detail.

Business transfer

7931 The **starting point** for identifying a business transfer is to establish whether there has been a transfer of an economic entity which retains its identity (reg 3(1) SI 2006/246).

The **two issues** (the economic entity and the retention of its identity) should be considered separately (*Cheesman v R Brewer Contracts Ltd* [2001] IRLR 144, EAT).

7932 **Is there an economic entity?** TUPE contains an **express definition** of an economic entity: an organised grouping of resources which has the objective of pursuing an economic activity, whether or not that activity is central or ancillary (reg 3(2) SI 2006/246).

This definition is drawn from case law decided before the current TUPE regulations came into force, which continues to provide guidance. These cases clarify the definition:
– an **activity** does not, of **itself**, constitute an economic entity (*Süzen v Zehnacker Gebäudereinigung GmbH Krankenhausservice und Lefarth GmbH* [1997] EUECJ C-13/95);
– the economic entity should be **structured and autonomous** (*Sánchez Hidalgo v Asociación de Servicios Aser* [1999] IRLR 136, ECJ) but need not necessarily have significant assets; and
– the economic entity should be **stable** and it is unlikely that TUPE will apply to an entity whose activity is limited to performing one specific works contract (*Rygaard v Stro Molle Akustik* [1995] EUECJ C-48/94). An entity may be stable as a matter of practical and industrial reality, even if its long-term future is not assured (*Balfour Beatty Power Networks Ltd and anor v Wilcox and ors* [2007] IRLR 63, CA). What is important is whether the entity can be said to be stable **at the time of transfer** and it is irrelevant as to whether the business can succeed long term.

> EXAMPLE In *Wain v Guernsey Ship Management Ltd* [2007] ICR 1350, CA, the claimants had been working on short-term contracts for a company, Wightlink (Guernsey) Limited (WGL), which supplied personnel to do a variety of jobs on different ferries. WGL decided to change its practices and only employ permanent employees with the result that the claimants were offered the same work by another company, Guernsey Ship Management (with which WGL had entered into an arrangement), for lower pay. The claimants brought an action that this was a TUPE transfer, in order to seek TUPE protection with regard to their terms, but this failed on the grounds that they did not form an economic entity. On appeal, the Court of Appeal held that although, on the one hand, the claimants could be said to belong to a group which could be identified because all members had short-term contracts and fulfilled a specific role in WGL's business, on the other hand they all did **different work, on different vessels**. To the Court's mind, neither factor was conclusive and the tribunal was entitled to hold that, taking both factors into account, this group was not an economic entity.

7934 **Has it retained its identity?** The decisive criterion is that the economic entity retains its identity following the transfer. While maintaining a unit as a distinct entity after transfer is a factor indicating that the identity of the business had been preserved, it is only one of a number of factors to be considered, and the Court of Justice of the European Union has held that a change in organisational structure does not prevent the Directive applying (*Klarenberg v Ferrotron Technologies GmbH* [2009] IRLR 301, ECJ). To establish if an economic entity has retained its identity, consider all the **factors** characterising the transaction, such as (*Spijkers v Gebroeders Benedik Abbattoir CV* [1986] ECR 1119, ECJ):

- the type of undertaking or business;
- whether tangible assets (such as buildings and moveable property) are transferred;
- the value of intangible assets (such as goodwill) at the date of the transfer;
- whether the majority of employees are taken over by the new employer;
- whether customers are transferred;
- the degree of similarity between the activities carried on before and after the alleged transfer; and
- whether there is a cessation of the activities and, if so, for how long.

However, all the above circumstances are merely single factors in the overall assessment to be made and should therefore not be considered in isolation (*Cheesman v R Brewer Contracts Ltd* [2001] IRLR 144, EAT; *RCO Support Services Ltd and anor v Unison* [2002] IRLR 401, CA).

EXAMPLE In *Wood v Caledon Social Club Ltd (Debarred) and anor* [2010] UKEAT 0528_09_1203, a parish council who owned a community centre granted a lease of the centre, which had a premises licence to sell alcohol, to a community association, who employed a bar steward to run the bar. The premises licence was withdrawn, the community association gave up its tenancy and dismissed the bar steward. After a break of several weeks a new community association was formed and obtained a personal liquor licence, operating the bar using volunteers. An employment tribunal held that there was no continuing economic entity because there was no premises licence in place at the time of the transfer. The EAT overturned this finding; there had been a temporary cessation of the bar operation which did not prevent the economic entity retaining its identity.

Service provision change

In order for a change in service provision to fall within the extended definition of a TUPE transfer, the following **three conditions** must be satisfied immediately before the change (reg 3(3) SI 2006/246):

1. there must be an organised grouping of employees situated in Great Britain whose principal purpose is to carry out the activities concerned on behalf of the client. An organised grouping is not simply a group which, without any deliberate planning or intent, mostly works on tasks that benefit a particular client: the employees must be organised "in some sense by reference to the requirements of the client in question" (*Eddie Stobart Ltd v Moreman and ors* [2012] UKEAT 0223_11_1702);
2. the client must intend that the activities will, after the change, be carried out by the transferee other than in connection with a single specific event or task of short-term duration; and
3. the activities must not consist wholly or mainly of the supply of goods for the client's use.

Under these service provision change rules, switching professional services providers, for example law firms and accountants, is unlikely to be a TUPE transfer as long as any existing work is completed by the original firm, i.e. there is a "run off" of services. This is because only work received is likely to be deemed to be part of the services provided: the expectation of and availability to do further work is unlikely to count as an "activity" for the purposes of the TUPE regulations (*Ward Hadaway Solicitors v Love and ors* [2010] UKEAT 0471_09_2503).

Whether workers are providing a service or merely supplying goods is ultimately a factual question (*Pannu v Geo W King Ltd* [2011] UKEAT 0021_11_2112).

EXAMPLE The following examples are from the BIS guidance and case law:

1. **Organised grouping of employees with principal purpose**
a. This will be an **identifiable team** of employees **essentially dedicated to carrying out the activities** that are to transfer (however, they do not need to work exclusively on those activities). Where, for example, a courier service is provided by a contractor but the deliveries and collections are undertaken by different couriers on an ad hoc basis, rather than by an identifiable team of employees, there will be no service provision change under TUPE if a different contractor is subsequently engaged.
b. If just some of the activities in the original service contract are re-tendered and awarded to a new contractor, or the original service contract is split up and **each component is assigned to a different contractor**, this may also constitute a service provision change under TUPE if there is an organised grouping with the principal purpose of carrying out the activities that are transferred.

7936

c. A **single employee** can constitute an organised grouping, e.g. when the cleaning of small business premises is undertaken by a single person employed by a contractor. However, this will not always be the case simply because an individual works solely for one client. In *Seawell Ltd v Ceva Freight (UK) Ltd and anor* [2012] UKEAT 0034_11_1904, an employee, M, was one of a group of employees working in the outbound section of a freight forwarding business. He worked on one client's account for 100% of his time, and other members of the team worked on the client's account for between 0% and 30% of their time. M was held not be an organised grouping for the purposes of TUPE because he was not deliberately organised for the purposes of the client's contract and he did not carry out the activities on his own: he worked as part of a team whose principal purpose was not the client's contract.

d. Even in **single service organisations**, only the employees who **work directly on the services** will transfer, and employees who play wider strategic roles within the organisation providing the services will not transfer. In *Edinburgh Home-Link Partnership and ors v The City of Edinburgh Council and ors* [2012] UKEAT 0061_11_1007, the EAT found that the directors of a charity, EHLP, providing services to a Council, did not fall into the organised grouping of staff who transferred to the Council when they decided to bring the service back "in-house". The directors were concerned with the running and maintenance of the charity for EHLP's benefit, rather than with the direct provision of the transferring services. The correct test is whether the employee was assigned to the group which had, as its principal purpose, the carrying out of the activities for which the client contracted, and in this case the directors did not satisfy that test.

2. Single specific ("one off") event or task

TUPE will not apply where a contractor is engaged to organise a single conference for a client, even if the contractor has established an organised grouping of staff, for example a project team, to carry out the activities involved in fulfilling that task. Therefore, if the client subsequently holds a second conference using a different contractor, the members of the first project team would not be required to transfer.

3. Short-term duration

a. If one contract relating to the security of a major sporting event concerns the provision of security advice over a period of years leading up to the event and another contract concerns the hiring of security staff during the event itself, only the first contract would be potentially covered by TUPE (even though both have a "one-off" character as they relate to a specific event), as it runs for a significantly longer period than the second.

b. In *Liddell's Coaches v Cook and ors* [2012] UKEAT 0025_12_0910, there had been no service provision change where a local authority awarded a coach company a 12-month contract to transport schoolchildren while their school was being rebuilt (the standard contract term usually being 3 to 5 years). The rebuilding of the school was also a "one off" event.

4. Supply of goods

a. If a contractor is engaged to supply sandwiches and drinks to a client's canteen, for the client to sell on to its own staff, TUPE will not apply. If, however, the contract is for the contractor to run the client's staff canteen, this may fall outside the exclusion for the supply of goods and may therefore be covered by TUPE.

b. In *Pannu v Geo W King Ltd* [2011] UKEAT 0021_11_2112, the EAT had to consider whether workers on a manufacturing assembly line, who were dedicated to producing car parts for a specific client, were providing a service or merely supplying goods. The EAT upheld the tribunal's finding that the employees were engaged in the supply of goods not services and that, as such, no service provision change had taken place when the client had switched to a new supplier for the car parts. The fact that the client also paid directly for the components, which were then delivered to the manufacturer by the suppliers, before being checked for safety and assembled into the finished car parts, to the client's specification, did not prevent the contract being one wholly or mainly for the supply of goods. The employer's business activities consisted wholly of the supply of finished goods to its client.

MEMO POINTS 1. It is acknowledged that there could be misuse of the exemption for **one-off services** if longer term contracts are broken up into a series of smaller contracts of a short-term duration. However, it will be a question of intention on the client's part, to ensure that each contract is distinct and not part of a deliberate design to award linked contracts to the same contractor in the future. Such intention can be assessed by an employment tribunal.

2. There is no exclusion of "**procurement**" of goods in the exemption for the supply of goods under TUPE. This ensures that, for example, the outsourcing of a client's procurement department (which clearly provides a service function) would be covered by TUPE.

3. The Court of Justice of the European Union has held that, in respect of the Acquired Rights Directive (**ARD**), a mere service provision change, without the transfer of assets or employees, is not a transfer of an undertaking. This maintains the distinction between the current TUPE regula-

tions in relation to service provision change (which accepts such a change as being a transfer of an undertaking more readily) and many other European jurisdictions (*CLECE (Social policy) French Text* [2010] EUECJ C-463/09). This decision was based upon an undertaking that was always based abroad and had no GB element, and it therefore does not affect the principle established in *Holis Metal Industries Ltd v GMB and Newell Ltd* that outsourcing services from Great Britain to foreign jurisdictions could be deemed a transfer of an undertaking under TUPE even if it would not be deemed as such under the ARD (¶7945).

7937

While in a business transfer the economic entity must retain its identity, in a service provision change it is sufficient that one group or person **ceases** an activity and another group or person **continues** it. There is no implied requirement for those activities to be carried out by the transferee in an identical manner. Further, a **failure** by the new contractor **to take on employees or assets** will not necessarily prevent TUPE applying.

EXAMPLE

Activity continued
In *Metropolitan Resources Ltd v Churchill Dulwich Ltd (in liquidation) and ors* [2009] IRLR 700, EAT, a charity contracted out the provision of accommodation and associated services to provider A. Toward the end of that contract, the charity decided not to renew the contract with A and agreed a contract with B to provide accommodation at a different location, with a slight change in terms because accommodation was to be provided on a shorter term basis. There was an overlap period before the expiry of A's contract, during which some staff stayed on, although no services were actually provided. After expiry, the remaining staff presented themselves for work with B, on the basis that they had been transferred under TUPE, but were sent home. The EAT upheld the decision of the tribunal that the change of contractor amounted to a service provision change. While there were some differences in how the service was to be provided, overall, the same service was to be provided following re-tendering. It was a question of fact, to be decided at tribunal level, whether an activity had ceased to be provided by one contractor and had been taken on by a new contractor.

Activity did not continue
In *OCS Group UK Ltd v Jones and anor* [2009] UKEAT 0038_09_0408, there was a change of catering contractor at BMW's Cowley car plant. A contract for provision of a catering service providing hot food, which was unprofitable, was replaced by a new contract providing cold food only. The EAT upheld the decision of an employment tribunal that the substantially reduced service meant that the activities were not essentially the same as under the original contract, so the transfer did not fall within the definition of a service provision change.

There will be no service provision change if there is not only a change of contractor but also a **change of client** (*McCarrick v Hunter* [2012] EWCA Civ 1399, confirmed by *Taurus Group Ltd v Crofts and anor* [2012] UKEAT 0024_12_2205). For example, if facilities services contracts (such as those for cleaners or security guards) are changed at the same time as the ownership or management of a commercial property, staff assigned to those facilities contracts will not transfer to the new provider, and liability for the termination of the contracts of the existing staff will remain with the original contractor.

EXAMPLE In *McCarrick v Hunter*, an employee of a property management business looked after a portfolio of properties. Two purported TUPE transfers involved changes to the contractors who managed the property portfolio. In February 2009, his original employer, WGL, ceased to carry out property management services in respect of its property portfolio and those services were carried out instead by another company, WCP, on its behalf. Six months later, the mortgagee of the property portfolio appointed receivers to take control of the properties and appointed new property consultants, KS, to manage the properties. The combined effect of the transactions was that the property management services ceased to be carried out by WCP on WGL's behalf and were instead carried out by KS on behalf of the mortgagee/receiver. The tribunal held that both transactions were service provision changes under TUPE. The EAT overturned the tribunal's decision and held that, for this kind of service provision change, the activities carried out by the different contractors before and after the transfer must be carried out for the same client. The Court of Appeal upheld the EAT's decision and confirmed that there will be no service provision change if there is not only a change of contractor but also a change of client.

7938

If a change in contractor **does not qualify** as a service provision change it may still qualify as a business transfer (¶7931). The key elements to be considered to establish whether a change in contractor amounts to a business transfer are:

– whether there had been a transfer of an economic entity (as outlined above); and then
– whether a major part of the workforce, or substantial tangible or intangible assets, were transferred (*Süzen v Zehnacker Gebäudereinigung GmbH Krankenhausservice und Lefarth GmbH* [1997] EUECJ C-13/95; *Oy Liikenne Ab v Liskojarvi* [2001] IRLR 171, ECJ).

Special situations

7940 In some cases it is more difficult to identify a transfer. The most significant are discussed below.

7941 **Transfer by a series of transactions** Transfers are usually effected by **one transaction**. Transfers may also be effected by a **series of two or more transactions** (reg 3(6) SI 2006/246). The series must, as a matter of causation, implement the transfer for TUPE to apply. This is the case, even if there is an **interval of time** between the different transactions, provided the second (and any further) transaction was within the parties' contemplation as being part of a series of transactions at the time the first transaction took place (*Key Communications Ltd v Rose* [2001] UKEAT 1292_00_2303). Where a series of transactions is effected over time, there will be a single point at which employees will transfer in law. The point at which the transfer takes place will be a question of fact in each case. The transfer may therefore take place at the date of the first transaction, even if that is earlier than anyone involved in the transactions anticipated (¶7966; *Celtec v Astley (C-478/03)* [2005] EUECJ C-478/03).

> EXAMPLE
> 1. In *Key Communications Ltd v Rose*, there was a **gap of several months** between the sale of a business to a transferee which had bought it on behalf of a third party, and the subsequent sale of that business by the transferee to that third party. The delay did not prevent TUPE applying.
> 2. In *Foreningen af Arbejdsledere i Danmark v Daddy's Dance Hall A/S* [1988] IRLR 315, ECJ, the transfer of a lease took place in **two phases**. The lessee of restaurant premises dismissed his employees when the lease came to an end. The lessor then granted a new lease to a third party who continued to run the business without any interruption, immediately re-employing the staff of the former lessee. TUPE was deemed to apply.

7943 **Transfers with an international element** While TUPE generally applies to businesses situated within the UK (for business transfers) or Great Britain (for service provision changes), it also extends to a number of situations where employees are located abroad, a business is transferred abroad, or foreign law applies to an employee's contract.

> MEMO POINTS It is anomalous that the territorial scope of the provisions relating to business transfers and service changes differs. This means, for example, that the rules relating to service provision changes do not extend to Northern Ireland, whereas the rules on business transfers do.

7944 Where employees are employed in a **business** situated **in the UK** before transfer but **ordinarily work abroad**, provided they are assigned to a business within the UK they will also transfer to the transferee (reg 3(4)(b), (c) SI 2006/246). The same applies to employees whose contracts are governed by foreign law, i.e. the law of a country outside the UK (for business transfers) and outside Great Britain (for service provision changes) (reg 3(4)(b)(i) SI 2006/246). This could arise where an employee is employed in part of a business situated in the UK but who has a contract with a parent company situated overseas, or where an employee of a UK-based business lives abroad.

> EXAMPLE BIS guidance provides the following examples:
> 1. If there is a transfer of a UK exporting business, the fact that the sales force spends the majority of its working week outside the UK will not prevent TUPE applying to the transfer, as long as the undertaking itself (comprising premises, assets, fixtures and fittings, goodwill, employees etc) is situated in the UK.
> 2. Where a contract to provide website maintenance comes to an end and the client wants to engage a new contractor, if, in the organised grouping of employees that has performed the contract, one of the IT technicians works from home, which is outside the UK, this should not prevent TUPE from applying to the transfer. However, if the whole team of IT technicians works

from home which is outside the UK, then a transfer of the business for which they work would not fall within TUPE as there would be no organised grouping of employees situated in the UK.

7945 In a significant development it has been held that the transfer of a business or service provision change to a location **overseas**, including **outside the EU**, may fall within TUPE (*Holis Metal Industries Ltd v GMB and Newell Ltd* [2007] UKEAT 0171_07_1212).

> MEMO POINTS   The decision in *Holis Metal Industries Ltd v GMB and Newell Ltd* is potentially very far-reaching, particularly with regard to the **outsourcing of services abroad**, and gives rise to many practical and commercial problems. In the case of business transfers not involving a service provision change, TUPE may be excluded by the fact that the business entity does not retain its identity after the transfer when a business is transferred outside the UK, but this restriction does not apply to service provision changes.

7947 **Transfers of part businesses**   If an economic entity is **fragmented** into two or more separate entities, the fragmented entity is capable of retaining its identity on transfer (although each case will turn on its own facts). A matter of importance in this case was that future transferors might try to circumvent the application of TUPE by dividing up an undertaking into smaller fragmented parts (*Fairhurst Ward Abbots Ltd v (1) Botes Building Ltd (2) Vaughan* [2004] IRLR 304, CA).

7948 Where just **part of a business** is transferred, BIS guidance suggests that the resources do not need to be used exclusively in the transferring part of the business. However, where resources are applied in a variable pattern over several parts of a business, there is less likelihood that a transfer of any individual part of a business would qualify as a business transfer.

SECTION 2

Effect

7950 To reflect the broad definition of a transfer, all general **references to a "transfer"** in this chapter relate to both business transfers and service provision changes, unless stated otherwise.

When TUPE applies to a transfer, it has a number of wide-ranging implications. There is an **automatic transfer** of employees, as well as a number of rights and liabilities, from the transferor to the transferee. Transfer-related **changes to terms and conditions** may be void and **dismissals** may be automatically unfair.

Transferors and transferees must therefore be fully aware of the various effects of a TUPE transfer on their workforce and obligations, particularly if they intend to limit their exposure to claims from employees.

A. Employees protected by TUPE

7952 When a TUPE transfer takes place, the transferor's employees transfer automatically to the transferee. It is as if their contracts of employment had originally been made with the transferee (reg 4(1) SI 2006/246). Although transfer is automatic, employees can object to the transfer (¶7962).

If TUPE applies, such employees will be transferred **whether or not** they have been **informed** of the transfer (*Secretary of State for Trade and Industry v Cook* [1997] IRLR 150, EAT) and regardless of any contrary intention of or agreement between the transferor and transferee (*Rotsart de Hertaing v J Benoidt SA* [1996] EUECJ C-305/94).

7953 The **definition of employee** for TUPE purposes is any individual who works for another person under a contract of employment or apprenticeship or otherwise, but not someone who provides services under a contract for services (reg 2(1) SI 2006/246).

> MEMO POINTS The definition of employee under TUPE is wider than the definition of employee under the ERA 1996, in that it includes those who work for someone other than under a contract of employment or apprenticeship. However, it will not necessarily cover all those who fall within the definition of a "worker" (¶13).

7954 The **following matters** may affect whether employees transfer:

7955 **Assignment** Those employees employed by the transferor and assigned to the organised grouping of resources or employees which is subject to the transfer will transfer automatically (reg 4(1) SI 2006/246). Assignment is a question of fact in each case. Case law decided under the previous TUPE regulations continues to provide guidance on establishing who transfers.

The current TUPE regulations expressly exclude employees who are assigned to a business or part of a business on a temporary basis (reg 2(1) SI 2006/246).

BIS guidance suggests that whether an assignment is temporary depends on a number of factors, such as the length of time the employee has been there and whether a date has been set by the transferor for his return or reassignment to another part of the business.

> EXAMPLE In *Gale v Northern General Hospital* [1994] IRLR 292, CA, a student nurse temporarily assigned to a hospital for training purposes was not assigned to the hospital for the purposes of TUPE.

7956 If an employee's contract allows the employer to require him to **work in a part** of an organised grouping that is **not** being **transferred**, the employee could be transferred to that part prior to the transfer, and will therefore not be covered by TUPE. However, a mobility clause in the contracts of employees will only mean that they are not assigned to the business transferred for the purposes of a TUPE transfer if the clause is actually used to transfer the employee (*Securicor Guarding Ltd v Fraser Security Services Ltd* [1996] UKEAT 350_95_1602).

> EXAMPLE In *CPL Distribution Ltd v Todd* [2003] IRLR 28, CA, a personal assistant, T, worked for a manager who was assigned to the part of an undertaking which did not transfer when CPL lost a contract after it was put out to tender. The Court held that T had been effectively assigned to her manager and, accordingly, did not transfer to the transferee, even though most of her work related to the lost contract.

7957 An employee may, alternatively, **work at two or more parts** of an undertaking and only **one is transferred**. In such circumstances, the Court of Justice of the European Union has applied a test of looking at where the employee predominantly worked (*Botzen v Rotterdamsche Droogdok Maatschappij BV*, C-186/83 [1985] EUECJ R-186/83; applied in *Michael Peters Ltd v Farnfield* [1994] UKEAT 533_92_0809). UK tribunals often consider the percentage of time spent in the undertaking as indicating assignment but this test is not applied by the Court of Justice of the European Union, and the matter should be determined by assessing the facts of each case (*Duncan Webb Offset (Maidstone) Limited v Cooper* [1995] UKEAT 47_95_1506). Relevant factors will include:
– the amount of time spent on one part of the business or the other;
– the amount of value given to each part by the employee;
– the terms of the employment contract; and
– how the cost to the employer of the employee's services is allocated between the different parts of the business.

> EXAMPLE
> 1. In *CPL Distribution Ltd v Todd* [2003] IRLR 28, CA, the Court of Appeal confirmed that an employee was not assigned despite the fact that most of her work related to the contract which transferred. She worked as a PA to a manager who had little or no connection with the part transferred, and so neither he nor his PA were assigned to the part transferred.
> 2. In *Skillbase Services Ltd v King* [2005] All ER (D) 106, the Court of Session (Inner House) held that time spent working on a particular project was only one factor to consider in determining whether an employee was assigned to that project when it transferred. Therefore, although two employees spent 80% of their time on the project, only one of them was assigned.

In the case of **service provision change**, where a service is split into two or more parts and transferred to two or more entities, the employees will be allocated between the new service providers using the test in *Botzen*, according to which aspects of the service they predominantly worked on (*Kimberley Group Housing Ltd v Hambley; Angel Services (UK) v Hambley* [2008] UKEAT 0488_07_2504). If the services are too fragmented on transfer, TUPE will not apply (*Clearsprings Management Ltd v Ankers and ors* [2009] UKEAT 0054_08_2402).

> EXAMPLE In *Kimberley Group Housing Ltd v Hambley; Angel Services (UK) v Hambley*, the EAT considered the impact of fragmenting a service when new contractors were appointed by the National Asylum Seekers Service to provide accommodation and pastoral care for asylum seekers. Three new contractors were appointed under the new contracts, whereas previously the service had been provided by four contractors. The new contractors acquired new premises and over a period of time asylum seekers were allocated to new accommodation with one of the three new contractors, individually and at random, rather than moving all those accommodated by one of the old contractors to one of the new contractors in a group. The EAT held that a tribunal had been entitled to find that, on the particular facts of the case, the activities carried on by the old contractors had been so fragmented by the way in which asylum seekers were allocated to new contractors that there was no service provision change, and so TUPE did not apply.

7958 **Termination of contract** Only those employees employed and assigned whose contracts of employment would, if it were not for the effect of TUPE, **be terminated** by the transfer will transfer to the transferee (reg 4(1) SI 2006/246).

7960 **Pre-transfer employment** Employees must be employed and assigned immediately before the transfer in order to be protected by TUPE (reg 4(3) SI 2006/246). This includes any employees on sick leave or maternity leave (*Fairhurst Ward Abbots Ltd v Botes Building Ltd and ors* [2004] EWCA Civ 83) and those working out their notice with the existing employer (the transferor) at the time of transfer (*Marcroft v Heartland (Midlands) Ltd* [2011] EWCA Civ 438).

> EXAMPLE In *Marcroft v Heartland (Midlands) Ltd*, the transferor, PMI, was a firm of brokers of various kinds of insurance and M was employed predominantly in the commercial insurance department of its business. His contract contained a restrictive covenant which he is alleged to have breached by approaching clients with a view to their transferring business to a rival company. There were negotiations for the disposal of the commercial insurance undertaking between PMI and H (the transferee). On 15 September 2009, M, who had become disillusioned with the business, gave notice of his resignation. It was agreed that the notice would expire on 26 October 2009. He was paid for the notice period and he retained the use of the company car and mobile phone until his employment terminated. M was officially informed on 25 September 2009 that it was proposed to sell the commercial insurance business to H. It was agreed that he did not need to attend the office, as there was very little work to be done in the commercial side of the business, but that he would be "on call" at home, if it became necessary. There was no consultation with him about any actual or prospective transfer to H or to anyone else, nor did he receive any documentation about the transfer. Between 25 September and 2 October 2009, when PMI entered into a formal written agreement for the transfer, M did no substantial work although he fielded a few calls and finalised some account details. The written agreement made no reference to M or to the transfer of his contract of employment. At the end of his agreed notice period M went to work for a rival company. H claimed that M's employment was transferred to it by virtue of TUPE and that it was entitled to sue him for breach of the restrictive covenant. The Court of Appeal agreed: M was an employee at the time of transfer and therefore his contract of employment transferred. Further, the Court held that the fact that M was not provided with information and documents or afforded a right to object to the transfer does not avoid the transfer as it is not a condition precedent to an effective transfer of a contract of employment.

TUPE will also apply to employees **dismissed by reason of a transfer** if they would have been employed immediately before the transfer, were it not for their dismissal (¶8030) (*Litster v Forth Dry Dock and Engineering Co Ltd* [1989] IRLR 161, HL).

If an employee is **dismissed for misconduct** prior to a transfer but is **reinstated** by the transferor after the transfer as a result of an appeal process, the dismissal effectively "vanishes". The employee will be deemed to have been employed immediately before the transfer and will transfer to the transferee (*G4S Justice Services (UK) Ltd v (1) Anstey (2) Simpson (3) GSL UK Ltd* [2006] UKEAT 0698_05_3003).

> *MEMO POINTS* There is no obligation on the transferee to provide a job to **former employees** of the transferor. However, the transferee will be responsible for all outstanding liabilities relating to such employees in relation to their former employment (e.g. the transferee would be responsible in an unfair dismissal claim (¶¶7980, 8037)).

7962 Employees who object to a transfer Employees have the right to object to the automatic transfer of their contracts of employment (reg 4(7) SI 2006/246). The **consequence** is that the employees' employment will be deemed to have terminated by operation of law, with no entitlement to compensation for unfair or wrongful dismissal (reg 4(8) SI 2006/246). If, however, an employee can show that his objection was made on the basis of a **substantial change in working conditions** to his material detriment, this may be treated as a dismissal (¶8035). The fact that an employee is not provided with information and documents about a TUPE transfer or afforded a right to object to the transfer does not prevent his contract of employment transferring (*Marcroft v Heartland (Midlands) Ltd* [2011] EWCA Civ 438 and see the example at ¶7960).

7964 As the consequences of objection potentially mean that the employee will lose protection under TUPE, there must be clear **evidence** of the objection. It may be evidenced by a refusal to give consent to the transfer, which is communicated to the transferor or the transferee prior to the transfer (*Hay v George Hanson (Building Contractors) Ltd* [1996] IRLR 427, EAT). A resignation once details of the transfer were known by the employee 2 days after the transfer has been held to be sufficient (*New ISG Ltd v Vernon* [2008] ICR 319, Judge Behrens). However, a **mere expression of unhappiness or concern** will not amount to an objection. "Opting out" of the transfer and accepting a severance payment from the transferor may not amount to an objection where the employee later accepts employment with the transferee (*Senior Heat Treatment Ltd v Bell* [1997] UKEAT 1285_96_2006). Equally, if the employee agrees to work for the transferee after the transfer, even for a short period, this will prevent any objection he makes from amounting to an effective opt-out from the transfer (*Capita Health Solutions v (1) BBC (2) McLean* [2008] UKEAT 0034_07_0105).

If an employee objects to the transfer, the transferor may re-engage the employee on new terms (although continuity of employment will be broken). In such circumstances, it may be possible to argue that a **subsequent dismissal** by the transferor is automatically unfair for being connected to the transfer (*Dunkinson v Meridian Technologies Ltd* [2001] UKEAT 0266_01_3007) (¶8030).

> *MEMO POINTS* There is no requirement that the employer inform an employee of the consequences of any objection.

Timing of transfer

7966 As a **general rule** employees will transfer on the transfer date, e.g. the completion of the contract for the sale of the business.

In relation to a **transfer effected in stages**, by means of a series of two or more transactions, TUPE will apply to anyone employed and assigned immediately before any of those transactions. Where the transfer is effected by a **series of transactions**, the date of a transfer must be a particular point in time (which cannot be postponed to another date at the will of the transferor or transferee), i.e. when the responsibility as employer for carrying on the business of the unit transferred moves from the transferor to the transferee (*Celtec v Astley (C-478/03)* [2005] EUECJ C-478/03).

In a situation where a transfer is effected by a **complex series of events**, the House of Lords has held that the first date at which employees begin to be transferred constitutes the date of transfer to the new employer (*North West Training and Enterprise Council Ltd (t/a Celtec Ltd) v Astley and ors* [2006] ICR 992, HL).

> *MEMO POINTS* The decision of the House of Lords in *Celtec* gives rise to a number of potential problems in cases where responsibilities for an activity are transferred over a period of time, as in the *Celtec* case. In particular, where employees are **seconded** to the transferee **prior to a complete transfer** of the economic entity, the date of the transfer will be brought forward to the date when they are first seconded, which may conflict with the intentions of the parties. Possible results are that the transferor and transferee inadvertently fail to comply with their information and consultation obligations, or that the employees so transferred lose their right to object to the transfer.

B. Rights and liabilities

1. Rights and liabilities which transfer

The effect of TUPE is that (reg 4(2)(a), (b) SI 2006/246):
– all the transferor's **rights, powers, duties and liabilities** under or in connection with employees' contracts of employment transfer to the transferee; and
– any **act or omission** of the transferor before the transfer is deemed to have been an act or omission of or in relation to the transferee.

7970

> MEMO POINTS   The **risk of compensation for claims** may be able to be **reallocated** using warranties and indemnities, see Company Law Memo for more details.

Contractual obligations

Most contractual rights, powers, duties and liabilities, including terms such as pay, benefits and holiday entitlement, transfer to the **transferee**, i.e. the employees' existing terms and conditions will be preserved (reg 4(2)(a) SI 2006/246). Terms relating to occupational pension schemes generally do not transfer (¶7992).

7971

Consequently, the transferor will no longer be liable to the employees after the transfer (*Stirling District Council v Allan* [1995] IRLR 301, CS). For example, if the transferor owed the transferring employees wages prior to the transfer, they must claim any outstanding sums from the transferee after the transfer. Similarly, the transferee can sue an employee for a breach of contract that was committed against the transferor before the transfer. Transferred employees may also make claims against the transferee in respect of the transferor's failure to pay equal pay (*Gutridge and ors v Sodexo Ltd and anor* [2009] IRLR 721, CA). However, this right is limited in time and claims must be made within 6 months of the termination of their employment with the transferor, i.e. within 6 months of the date of transfer (¶5723).

Terms that exist between the transferor and the employee will transfer in their existing form and **cannot be amended** in favour of the transferee, for example by extending the geographical area of a mobility clause to the area served by the transferee (*Tapere v South London and Maudsley NHS Trust* [2009] IRLR 972, EAT).

7972

> EXAMPLE   In *Tapere v South London and Maudsley NHS Trust*, an employee whose contract included a mobility clause was transferred under TUPE from one NHS health trust to another. The clause provided that the employee could be moved within the trust area. After the transfer the transferee sought to enforce the clause by requiring her to move from one location in London to one in another part of the city, which was within the area served by the transferee but had not been within the area served by the transferor. She objected, because it would increase her journey time and interfere with her childcare arrangements. A letter informing her of the date of the move did not reach her before she returned from holiday to find that her colleagues had moved. She resigned and made a constructive dismissal claim. The EAT held that the transferee was only able to use the mobility clause to move her within the area covered by the transferor trust, and so was in breach of contract. It also found that the change had been a material detriment and that the employee was deemed to have been dismissed. The case was sent to a new employment tribunal to consider whether the dismissal was unfair.

While the aim of TUPE and the Acquired Rights Directive (ARD) is to prevent an employee in an undertaking from being prejudiced as a result of a transfer of the undertaking, it is **not** their objective to **confer additional rights** on the employee or to improve his situation (*Jackson v Computershare Investor Services Plc* [2008] ICR 341, CA).

7973

> EXAMPLE   In *Jackson v Computershare Investor Services Plc*, J, a transferred employee, claimed damages from her new employer, CIS, for non-payment of enhanced contractual severance pay. J had joined her original employer in 1999 and was transferred to CIS in 2004. CIS made her redundant in 2005. Her employment contract with her original employer contained no provision for enhanced

> severance pay. However, CIS operated an enhanced severance pay scheme based on a dual system of redundancy terms which distinguished between employees whose date of entry was pre-1 March 2002 (who were entitled to enhanced severance pay) and "New Entrants after 1 March 2002" (who were not so entitled). While these terms were incorporated in, and became part of, J's contract under TUPE when she transferred in 2004, J was not entitled to be treated as a pre-1 March 2002 joiner of CIS by virtue of her deemed continuity of employment with CIS. The pre-1 March 2002 right was an enhanced right which did not transfer to J in 2004.
>
> In a case like this, the rights and duties with regard to the employees will effectively be frozen at the point of transfer. They will be entitled to benefits as if they had always been employed by the transferor employer, which means that they may be entitled to different terms and conditions to those who have always been employed by the transferee employer. In these circumstances, the transferee must take care that the differences in terms and conditions do not inadvertently discriminate indirectly against any group of employees.

7974 Statutory **continuity of employment** will also be preserved, i.e. the transferee must recognise the employee's period of service with the transferor (*Nicholas v Grant (t/a Sandancers Café)* [2006] UKEAT 0198_06_0109). Service with the transferee will be taken into account when calculating rights based on length of service, such as the amount of any future redundancy payment or notice of termination due.

The transferee employer does not need to provide a new statement of employment particulars (¶1400), but must **notify** the transferring employees **in writing** of the change in the employer's identity, and give the date their period of continuous employment began.

7975 **Restrictive covenants** transfer under TUPE but are construed so as to protect the transferor's business, and not the transferee's business. As the subject matter of the restriction will remain unchanged, a covenant against dealings with customers of the employer, for example, will be read as referring to customers of the transferor employer who fell within the definition of the covenant (*Morris Angel & Son Ltd v Hollande* [1993] IRLR 169, CA). This will clearly be problematic if the transferee wishes to enforce the covenant some time after the transfer, when the pool of customers may have changed. However, agreeing a **new covenant** with the transferring employees is also not without difficulty, as an agreed variation connected with the transfer will only be effective in certain limited circumstances (see ¶¶8010+).

7976 Although they may technically transfer under TUPE, some contractual terms specific to the transferor may be meaningless or difficult to implement after the transfer, such as **bonuses or profit-sharing schemes** calculated by reference to the profits of the transferor employer's group of companies. A solution may be for the transferee to establish benefits of "substantial equivalence" to the transferor's scheme (*Mitie Managed Services Ltd v French* [2002] UKEAT 408_00_1204).

True discretionary bonuses will not transfer as there is no contractual obligation to transfer. However, even if the term "**discretionary**" has been used, the whole context of the scheme must be considered to ascertain whether the term "discretionary" does refer to the whole scheme or merely to a particular aspect of it, such as the amount to be paid (*Small and ors v Boots Co PLC and anor* [2009] IRLR 328, EAT).

7977 Where a transferor is contractually obliged to make **contributions** to an **employee's personal pension scheme**, this obligation will transfer in the normal way. A personal pension scheme is not excluded from TUPE in the same way as occupational pension schemes are (¶7992).

Non-contractual rights and liabilities

7980 **Liability for statutory claims** (or circumstances giving rise to them) existing prior to the transfer will transfer to the transferee. For example, a transferee will become liable for a transferor's act of discrimination which took place prior to the transfer in relation to a transferring employee. This will be the case even if the liability related to a contract which preceded the one in place at the time of the transfer, as the Acquired Rights Directive (ARD) refers to rights and obligations arising from the "employment relationship", and TUPE is interpreted in line with this broad concept (*DJM International Ltd v Nicholas* [1995] UKEAT 1218_94_1210). This broad interpretation means that **liabilities** owed to transferring employees **for tortious acts of negligence** (whether the employer's own acts or those of his employees) and **for breaches of statutory duty** will pass to the transferee as arising from the employment relationship (*Taylor v Serviceteam Limited & Waltham Forest Borough Council* [1998] 2CL 57, CC).

Liability for personal injury claims will transfer, as they are connected with the contract of employment.

When a transfer takes place between **private sector** employers, the right of a transferor to an indemnity from his insurers for such claims (under the obligatory employer's liability insurance) will transfer to the transferee, along with liability for any such claims, as it is a right arising from/in connection with the employment contract (*Bernadone v Pall Mall Services Group* [2000] IRLR 487, CA).

Where the transferor is a **public sector** employer, there is generally no equivalent insurance cover to transfer (usually because the public sector employer is not subject to, or is exempt from, the requirement to provide it). TUPE expressly provides for this situation so that, where the transferor is a public sector employer, the transferor and transferee will be jointly and severally liable in respect of personal injury liability arising from an employee's employment with the transferor (reg 17 SI 2006/246). This means that either transferor or transferee can be ordered to bear the whole of the liability, so that if one does not have the resources to pay damages, the employee can recover the whole of his damages from the other.

MEMO POINTS Given that compulsory employers' liability insurance cover can transfer under TUPE, there is a question as to whether **other types of insurance cover** that are contractually provided for (such as permanent health insurance) could also transfer, as arising from or in connection with the employment contract. It is essential for transferees to obtain details of any insurance claims by transferring employees, together with details of the relevant policies. Liability will then be a matter for negotiation between the parties (and possibly their insurers), as the transferee may seek an indemnity.

Exceptions 1. **Liabilities owed to third parties** as a result of the employee's tortious acts will not transfer.
2. Liability for **post-employment victimisation** will not transfer if it occurs **after** the **transfer** takes effect. For example, liability for victimising an employee by refusing to give a reference will not pass to the transferee if the reference is requested after the transfer has taken place, because only existing liabilities can pass under TUPE (*Coutinho v Vision Information Systems (UK) Ltd & Rank Nemo (DMS) Ltd* [2007] UKEAT 0466_06_2008).
3. **Financial obligations** under a **continuation order** where the transferor has refused to reinstate or re-engage the employee pending the hearing of the employee's unfair dismissal claim (¶8703) will not transfer. In such cases, the employee's contract will continue in force in relation to pay and any other employment benefits. However, as it is not a continuing contract of employment, but is instead a purely statutory relationship between the transferor and the former employee which provides for the financial protection of the employee pending the full hearing of his claim, the financial obligations under it will not transfer (*Dowling v (1) M E Ilic Haulage (2) Berkeley Logistics Ltd* [2004] UKEAT 0836_03_0203).

Collective agreements

Collective agreements made between the transferor and a trade union recognised by the transferor to any extent for the purposes of collective bargaining in respect of the transferring employees will transfer as if made by the transferee and that trade union (reg 5 SI 2006/246).

Where **terms** are **incorporated** into individual employment contracts, they will automatically transfer to the transferee under TUPE (reg 4 SI 2006/246). However, a transferee will not be bound by variations to a collective agreement or in relation to new agreements which are **negotiated after** the transfer date (*Werhof v Freeway Traffic Systems GmbH & Co KG* [2006] IRLR 400, ECJ; *Parkwood Leisure Ltd v Alemo-Herron and ors* [2010] IRLR 298, CA).

MEMO POINTS *Parkwood Leisure Ltd v Alemo-Herron and ors* relates to collective agreements and whether changes negotiated after a TUPE transfer or new agreements will bind the transferee. The facts of the case are that at the date of TUPE transfer there were in place collectively agreed terms setting out the pay rates. However, negotiations on a 3-year settlement on pay rates were concluded after the date of transfer and the transferee, being a private sector employer, was not party to the negotiations. The transferee refused to award some of the pay increases for later years. The Court of Appeal followed a Court of Justice of the European Union decision, *Werhof v Freeway Traffic Systems GmbH & Co KG*, and held that a transferee will not be bound by variations to a collective agreement or in relation to new agreements which are negotiated after the transfer date. The Supreme Court on hearing the appeal has decided to seek guidance from the Court of Justice of the European Union as to whether it can give a "dynamic" interpretation to the TUPE regulations than provided for by the Acquired Rights Directive or whether this is not possible following *Werhof v Freeway Traffic Systems GmbH & Co KG* (*Parkwood Leisure Ltd v Alemo-Herron and ors* [2011] UKSC 26). A more dynamic interpretation would allow the Supreme Court to rule that a transferee can be bound by changes to a collective agreement or new agreements negotiated after the transfer date.

7986 In most cases, however, collective agreements are **not automatically incorporated** into individual employment contracts and are binding in honour only. Consequently, for example, where the transferor is not legally bound to offer terms contained in a collective agreement each time a fixed-term contract comes up for renewal, the transferee will similarly not be obliged to offer such collectively agreed terms (*Ralton v Havering College of Further and Higher Education* [2001] IRLR 738, EAT).

> EXAMPLE Where, at the date of the transfer from the public to the private sector, transferring employees' contracts provided for their terms and conditions to be in accordance with a national collective agreement which made no provision for any successor agreement to be incorporated into the employees' contracts, no subsequent collective agreement could be deemed to apply to the employees' terms and conditions without any further reference or incorporation (*Ackinclose and ors v Gateshead Metropolitan Borough Council* [2005] IRLR 79, EAT).

Trade union recognition

7987 If, after the transfer, the transferred employees maintain an **identity distinct** from the remainder of the transferee's undertaking, any independent trade union recognised by the transferor is deemed to be recognised by the transferee (reg 6 SI 2006/246). If there is no separate identity, for example if both the transferred employees and existing employees of the transferee are integrated into a single organisation, the previous trade union recognition lapses and it is up to the union and the employer to renegotiate a new recognition agreement.

Unlike the transfer of collective agreements, recognition is **not restricted** to employees who were employed at the date of the transfer, and so will apply to new joiners who are within the scope of the recognition agreement. However, it is open to the transferee to derecognise the union in the same way that the transferor was able to do so (reg 6(2) SI 2006/246).

2. Rights and liabilities which do not transfer

Share options and other incentives

7990 A transferring employee may hold share options in the transferor company/group. If the business is transferred to the transferee, the employee will be leaving the company or group. Case law indicates that TUPE will not affect any rights under share option schemes where these are separate contracts from the employment contract. Liability in respect of the options will therefore not transfer to the transferee (*Chapman & Elkin v CPS Computer Group plc* [1987] IRLR 463, CA).

Occupational pension schemes

7992 Rights and liabilities relating to the provision of occupational pension schemes which relate to benefits for old age, invalidity or survivors generally do not transfer under TUPE (reg 10 SI 2006/246). Further, a transferring employee cannot claim against the transferor for breach of contract or constructive unfair dismissal arising out of a loss or reduction in his rights under an occupational scheme in consequence of the transfer (reg 10(3) SI 2006/246).

However, since 6 April 2005, transferees must offer, as a condition of employment, a **minimum level of pension protection** under TUPE to qualifying employees (ss 257, 258 Pensions Act 2004; *Transfer of Employment (Pension Protection) Regulations* SI 2005/649).

Qualifying employees include any transferring employee who had an actual or contingent right (i.e. was an active member, eligible to be a member or was in a waiting period before becoming eligible to be a member) in relation to an occupational pension scheme with employer contributions immediately prior to the TUPE transfer. Transferees must offer such qualifying employees either:

a. membership of a **defined benefit** (i.e. final salary) occupational pension scheme, in relation to which the transferee is the employer, which provides for either:
– the value of the benefits to be provided to the member to equal at least 6% of his pensionable pay per year of employment, in addition to any member contributions, and where the member is required to make contributions, for him to contribute at a rate not exceeding 6% of his pensionable pay; or
– the transferee to match member contributions to the scheme up to a maximum of 6% of basic pay;

b. membership of a **money purchase** occupational pension scheme, in relation to which the transferee is the employer, to which the employer must match member contributions up to a maximum of 6% of basic pay (with either party being able to contribute more at their own discretion); or

c. to match member contributions up to 6% of basic pay to a **stakeholder** pension scheme of which the employee is, or is eligible to become, a member (with either party being able to contribute more at their own discretion).

Exception Some pension schemes provide for **age-related benefits** (for example, enhanced redundancy entitlement or early retirement benefits, and the right to be considered for early retirement). Such benefits transfer because they fall outside the scope of the pension rights exclusion from TUPE and are commonly referred to as "Beckmann rights" after the leading case which sets out this exception (*Beckmann v Dynamco Whicheloe Macfarlane Ltd* [2002] EUECJ C-164/00, confirmed by *Martin and ors v South Bank University* [2003] EUECJ C-4/01).

7994

EXAMPLE In *The Procter and Gamble Company v (1)Svenska Cellulosa Aktiebolaget SCA (2) SCA Hygiene Products Manchester Limited (formerly known as SCA Hygiene Investments Ltd)* [2012] EWHC 1257 (Ch), P&G sold part of its business to SCA. The transferring employees of P&G were members of a defined benefit pension scheme that provided for a normal retirement age of 65. Early retirement was subject to the consent of the employer and applied to both active and deferred members on or after becoming 55. Retirement benefits taken before the age of 65 were reduced and the level of this reduction was dependant on whether or not the member had accrued 15 years of service before retiring. Transferring employees became deferred members of the P&G scheme. SCA refused to accept an indemnity from P&G for any transferring Beckmann rights in the sale agreement and instead insisted upon an adjustment to the purchase price to reflect the risk. Following the transfer of the business to SCA, a dispute arose as to the level of the adjustment and during the litigation various questions were raised as to the rights and liabilities that had in fact transferred in order to assess the value that should be attached to them. The court held as follows:
1. a transferring employee's right to be considered for early retirement benefits does transfer under the TUPE Regulations because it does not fall under the "old age, invalidity or survivors" exception. In this case, P&G's discretionary power to grant early retirement benefits and their duty to consider any requests in good faith transferred to SCA;
2. liability to pay the pensions of transferring employees only transfers for the time between the employee taking early retirement and when they reach a normal retirement age, because at this point the benefit becomes one that relates to "old age" and therefore excluded. This means that even where a pension has fallen into payment prior to the normal retirement age, the liability for this benefit ceases to be the responsibility of the transferee when the employee in question reaches the normal retirement age; and
3. employees are not entitled to claim duplicate benefits from both the transferee and the transferor. In this case, SCA's responsibility was limited to the enhanced benefits which were held to be:
– the possibility of taking early retirement, with consent, after the age of 55;
– qualifying for a bridging pension until state retirement age; and

> – for those with less than 15 years' service, offsetting the lost possibility to qualify for enhanced early retirement benefits after obtaining 15 years of service.
> There was no obligation for SCA to provide a duplicate pension.

<u>MEMO POINTS</u> In relation to the **public sector**, the more generous policy set out in the HM Treasury Guidance Note (A Fair Deal for Staff Pensions), annexed to the Cabinet Office Statement of Practice (Staff Transfers in the Public Sector), continues to apply, guaranteeing public sector employees a broadly comparable occupational pension entitlement on transfer to a private sector employer, or subsequently between private sector employers.

The Government has been **consulting** on a range of possibilities **to reform** this policy, though its response has not yet been published. Any further developments will be covered by our updating service.

Normal retirement age

7996 A normal retirement age (i.e. an age that is either a well-known and observed contractual retirement age or, if there is no contractual retirement age or at least not one that is well-known and observed, the age at which individuals in a particular position can reasonably expect to work until, see ¶8206), is not the same as a contractual retirement age and therefore does not fall within the rights, powers, duties and liabilities which transfer under TUPE (*Cross and anor v British Airways plc* [2006] ICR 1239, CA).

<u>MEMO POINTS</u> Given that the default retirement age has been abolished, and considering the consequential difficulties employers have with using normal or contractual retirement ages, this is unlikely to remain a common issue going forward. See ¶¶8200+ for further details relating to retirement under the equality legislation.

Debts owed by insolvent transferor

7998 To aid the sale of insolvent businesses as going concerns, the TUPE regulations include **special provisions** to make it easier for insolvent businesses to be transferred to new employers. This can include "pre-pack" transfers, i.e. where the negotiation of the sale of all or part of the company's assets is prior to the appointment of the administrator, with the administrator effecting that sale immediately on, or shortly after, his appointment (*OTG Ltd v Barke and Luke* [2011] UKEAT 0320_09_1602).

Where a transferor is subject to relevant insolvency proceedings, certain pre-existing debts owed by the transferor to relevant employees will not pass to the transferee. Instead, those employees will be entitled to **claim payments** of these debts from the Secretary of State through the **National Insurance Fund**. The debts covered by the provisions include statutory redundancy pay, arrears of pay, payment in lieu of notice, holiday pay and the basic award compensation for unfair dismissal. Debts created after the transfer, for example a basic award for compensation and notice pay following the unfair dismissal post-transfer by the new employer (the transferee), are not covered (*Pressure Coolers Ltd v Molloy and ors* [2011] UKEAT 0272_10_0906). **Debts** falling **outside these provisions**, or which exceed the relevant statutory upper limit, will still pass to the transferee.

<u>MEMO POINTS</u> 1. "**Relevant insolvency proceedings**" are proceedings which have been instituted in relation to the transferor but not with a view to liquidating his assets and which are under the supervision of an insolvency practitioner (reg 8(6) SI 2006/246; *Secretary of State for Trade and Industry v Slater and ors* [2008] ICR 54, EAT). The current TUPE regulations do not list all the different types of insolvency procedures. BIS guidance states that "relevant insolvency proceedings" means any collective insolvency proceedings in which the whole or part of the business or undertaking is transferred to another entity as a going concern (i.e. covering insolvency proceedings in which all creditors of the debtor may participate, and in relation to which the insolvency office holder owes a duty to all creditors). BIS states that this does not cover winding-up by either creditors or members where there is no such transfer. In *Key2Law (Surrey) LLP v De'Antiquis* [2011] EWCA Civ 1567, the Court of Appeal confirmed that administrations can never be "insolvency proceedings which have been instituted with a view to the liquidation of the assets of the transferor" (see memo point 4). The primary objective of an administration is to rescue the company as a going concern.

2. "**Relevant employees**" are those employees whose contracts of employment automatically transfer under TUPE or those who are unfairly dismissed because of the transfer (¶¶7952, 8030).

3. **Variations to terms** and conditions are also permitted where the transferor is subject to relevant insolvency proceedings (¶8023).

4. Where the transferor is subject to insolvency proceedings that have been instituted with a **view to liquidating his assets** (i.e. there is no rescue package and the insolvent business cannot be sold as a going concern) then the employees' contracts of employments will not transfer (reg 8(7) SI 2006/246). Employees dismissed in such circumstances will be able to apply to BIS for certain state guaranteed payments including statutory redundancy payments (¶9045).

Criminal liabilities

Criminal liabilities do not transfer under TUPE (reg 4(6) SI 2006/246).

8002

C. Varying terms and conditions

Since one of the key aims of TUPE is to protect employees when a business changes hands, the **general position** has always been that employees who transfer under TUPE do so on their existing terms (¶¶7952, 7971) and that changes in contract terms where the reason for the change is solely or principally related to a transfer are void.

8010

The normal rules on variation of terms and conditions will apply to any changes of terms and conditions which are **unconnected** to a transfer (see ¶¶1600+). A reason unconnected with the transfer could include the sudden loss of an expected order by a manufacturing company or a general upturn in demand for a particular service.

In terms of establishing the **connection between a variation and the transfer**, where an employer changes terms and conditions simply because of the transfer, and there are no extenuating circumstances linked to the reason for that decision, then such a change is prompted by reason of the transfer itself. Likewise, where the reason for the change is prompted by a knock-on effect of the transfer (e.g. the need to re-train staff to use different machinery used by the transferee), then the reason will be connected to the transfer.

8011

There is no clearly defined point at which the connection between a variation of terms and the transfer will be broken (*Taylor v Connex South Eastern Limited* [2000] UKEAT 1243_99_0507). It may be that on the particular facts a variation is connected with the transfer even after a year or more has passed. Further, there is no "rule of thumb" used by the courts under TUPE to define a period of time after which it is safe to assume that the transfer did not impact directly or indirectly on the employer's actions. Once the link is broken, a variation can be effected (subject to the normal rules on variation) (*Wilson v St Helens Borough Council* [1998] IRLR 706, HL).

EXAMPLE
Variations connected to transfer
In *Campbell v Martin McColl Ltd* [2011] Hull ET 1804664/2011, the transferee sought to harmonise terms and conditions a year after employees TUPE transferred into its employment. The tribunal held that the harmonisation exercise was connected with the transfer.

Variations not connected to transfer
1. In *Smith and ors v Trustees of Brooklands College* [2011] UKEAT 0128_11_0509, four teaching assistants brought unlawful deductions from wages claims relying upon their assertion that consensual variations in their pay were void because they were made for a reason connected to a TUPE transfer. At the time their contracts were entered into, their pay had been reduced pro-rata to take account of the fact that they worked 43 out of 52 weeks of the year, but took no account of the fact they did not work normal full-time hours (usually 36) in those weeks. Conventional part-time contracts in the education sector make a pro-rata reduction to take into account both the number of weeks worked and the hours worked in a week, but theirs did not do so. Their employment transferred under TUPE and it was not until some 2 years later, having noted the anomaly in the teaching assistants' contracts and reached the conclusion they had been overpaid in error, the respondent's HR Director took steps to reach agreement for a phased reduction in pay to the correct rates. They reluctantly agreed to this phased reduction in January 2010.

The EAT confirmed that the test for deciding whether changes are connected to the transfer is not a "but for" test; the correct approach is to ask: What caused the employer to do it? What was in the HR Director's mind and why did she decide to do it? In this case, the tribunal had been entitled to find as a fact that the reason for the HR Director seeking changes to the contract was her belief that the claimants had been overpaid in error. Her actions could have been taken at any time, irrespective of TUPE. As such, the contractual variations were not void.

2. In *Enterprise Managed Services Ltd v Dance and ors* [2011] UKEAT 0200_11_2190, post-transfer changes to transferring employees' terms, which were driven by the success of pre-transfer changes to the transferee's employees' terms in order to improve productivity, were not transfer-related.

8012 If transferred employees find that a transfer involves or would involve a **substantial change** in their working conditions to their material detriment, they have the right to treat the contract as being terminated by the transferee and claim constructive unfair dismissal (see ¶8035).

Permitted variations

8015 In recognition of the difficulties involved in varying terms and conditions, TUPE permits transferors and transferees **to agree** contractual variations with employees connected with the transfer in the following circumstances:

8016 **Economic, technical or organisational reasons (ETO)** A transfer-related change will be **valid**, subject to the normal rules on contractual variation (¶¶1600+), if it is for an "economic, technical or organisational" ("ETO") reason entailing changes in the workforce.

There is no statutory definition of an ETO reason. BIS guidance and case law regarding identical wording in the previous TUPE regulations suggest that the term is likely to **include reasons** relating to:

a. the profitability or market performance of the transferee's business (i.e. an economic reason);

b. the nature of the equipment or production processes which the transferee operates (i.e. a technical reason); or

c. the management or organisational structure of the transferee's business (i.e. an organisational reason).

8017 Equally, there is no statutory definition of "**entailing changes in the workforce**". However, it is understood to mean that the structure of the workforce must be changed, either by a reduction in the number of employees, or by a change in job functions (*Berriman v Delabole Slate Ltd* [1985] ICR 546, CA as applied and clarified in *Crawford v Swinton Insurance Brokers Ltd* [1990] IRLR 42, EAT; *London Metropolitan University v Sackur and ors* [2006] UKEAT 0286_06_1708). BIS guidance suggests a functional change could involve a new requirement for an employee who held a managerial position to enter into a non-managerial role, or to move from a secretarial to a sales position. The changes can apply to part of the workforce (*Nationwide Building Society v Benn and ors* [2010] UKEAT 0273_09_2707). A change in functions that does not involve a change in the affected employee's function is not an ETO reason (*Miles v Insitu Cleaning Co Ltd* [2012] UKEAT 0157_12_120).

EXAMPLE In *Meter U Ltd v Hardy and ors* [2012] UKEAT 0207_11_2802, the EAT had to consider whether a transferee service provider (i.e. the new contractor), who had dismissed the transferring employees and replaced them with limited company franchisees, had established an ETO reason, meaning that the dismissals were potentially fair. A number of meter readers were employed by two different meter-reading companies. In December 2009, the contracts between those meter-reading companies and an energy company, SP, came to an end. A new contract for meter reading was granted to MU. The business model operated by MU is one of franchises with independent limited companies, typically owned by individual meter readers; they did not employ meter readers directly. It was accepted that there had been a service provision change transfer and that the employees has transferred. MU consulted with the meter readers and offered them the opportunity of forming franchise companies but the employees refused and were ultimately dismissed in April 2010. The employment tribunal had held that the dismissals were for a transfer-related reason and were automatically unfair. They took the view that it must have been the intention of the Acquired Rights Directive, which TUPE implements, to include in the term "workforce" everyone working in the business, whether as employees, franchisees or otherwise. The tribunal held that, as the number of meter readers did not change after the transfer of the contracts, there were no changes to the workforce and, consequently, there was no ETO reason for the dismissals. On appeal, the EAT held that MU had established an economic, technical or organisational reason entailing changes in the workforce and that the dismissals were potentially fair. The EAT held that the term "workforce" excluded limited companies and that the use of corporate franchisees, rather than the transferring employees, to carry out the services entailed changes in the workforce. The case was sent back to the employment tribunal to determine whether the dismissals were handled fairly.

8018 The ability to change contractual terms is a key development, particularly in light of the commercial difficulties often faced by employers in the context of a TUPE transfer. However, varying contractual terms will continue to present **practical difficulties** under the current TUPE regulations. For example, while changes for ETO reasons are permitted, very few variations will entail a change in the structure or composition of the workforce. BIS guidance also confirms that the **desire to achieve harmonisation** is deemed to be by reason of the transfer itself and not an ETO reason (and any change is therefore void).

If the changes are not, overall, disadvantageous to the employees, it is likely that employers will continue to take the **pragmatic approach** often taken under the previous TUPE regulations and consider implementing the changes with **employee consent**, in the expectation that few, if any, employees will complain.

It also remains open to employers, in order to ensure that the new terms are legally binding, to **dismiss and re-engage** the employees on new terms (*British Fuels Ltd v Baxendale and Meade* [1998] IRLR 706, HL). The disadvantage of this course of action is that the dismissals may be automatically unfair if they are for a transfer-connected reason (¶¶8030+). To minimise liability, the employer could ask employees to waive any contractual claims and compromise their right to bring an unfair dismissal claim, in return for a payment calculated by reference to the unfair dismissal basic award (¶8575). If employees are dismissed and reluctantly accept re-engagement on less attractive terms, the consequence of a successful unfair dismissal claim could be an order for either reinstatement on the terms of the old contract, or the tribunal may even re-write the old contract slightly.

EXAMPLE In *Manchester College v Hazel and anor* [2012] UKEAT 0642_11_0907, the EAT considered the position of two employees dismissed as part of a post-transfer harmonisation of terms and found that the employment tribunal had been correct to order their re-engagement. Post-transfer, the new employer began a redundancy exercise and sought to introduce new terms and conditions for the remaining staff including substantial pay cuts, in an attempt to harmonise terms and protect the staff from further redundancies. Both of the teachers were offered new contracts which, amongst other changes, involved pay cuts of 13.2% and 18.5%. They refused the new contracts and were dismissed, but were later re-engaged under the new terms. The employment tribunal found that they had been unfairly dismissed for a reason connected with the transfer: namely their refusal to agree to new terms as part of the College's harmonisation exercise. A majority of the tribunal held that this was not a valid ETO reason, because it did not involve changes in the numbers or functions of employees. Although other employees had been dismissed for redundancy (an ETO reason) the dismissals here were connected with harmonisation (which was not an ETO reason). The dismissals were therefore automatically unfair. The EAT upheld the tribunal's decision that reinstatement was not practicable and that the appropriate order was one for re-engagement based on the new terms and conditions, with their salaries restored to their previous level but "frozen... without cost of living increases or incremental increases until the new pay scale catches up with their salaries".

8020 **Variations favourable to the employee** The second case in which it will be possible to vary terms and conditions where there is a connection between the variation and the transfer is where the **variation is in the employee's favour**. The EAT has held that this does not prevent an employee from **taking advantage of a variation** which he considers more favourable (*Power v Regent Security Services Ltd* [2007] UKEAT 0499_06_2901, confirmed on appeal ([2008] IRLR 66, CA)). The EAT emphasised that this ability to choose which terms to rely on applies to employees only and no similar right is to be conferred on the transferee. On the other hand, the EAT remarked that if the employee wants to, he can object to any variation which he considers to be to his detriment (even if the change has compensating advantages) and can treat it as void. In such situations, the EAT commented that the employee may well have to give up any related compensating benefits obtained under the varied contract as a condition of doing so.

As a result of this case, BIS amended its guidance to make it clear that **changes to contracts agreed by the parties** which are **entirely beneficial to the employee** are not prevented by the current TUPE regulations.

> EXAMPLE In *Power v Regent Security Services Ltd*, the employee's contractual retirement age was agreed as a result of the transfer to be 65 (the employee's contractual retirement age with the transferor had been 60). However, after the transfer the transferee notified the employee that they would be retiring him on his 60th birthday. The EAT held that the employee could rely on his contractual retirement age being 65 so that he was eligible to claim unfair dismissal.

Business subject to insolvency proceedings

8023 The current TUPE regulations make **provision** for insolvent transferors by enabling the parties to vary contracts of employment in order to preserve jobs.

Where a transferor is subject to relevant insolvency proceedings (¶7998), **permitted variations** to transferring employees' terms and conditions can be agreed between the transferor or transferee (or insolvency practitioner) and appropriate representatives of the employees. A permitted variation is one that would normally be void and which is designed to safeguard employment opportunities by ensuring the survival of the undertaking or business or part of the undertaking or business. It may involve reducing pay or establishing other inferior terms and conditions after the transfer and will take effect as a term or condition of the employees' contracts of employment, in place of any term or condition which it varies (reg 9(6) SI 2006/246).

Appropriate representatives can be **trade union** representatives, representatives selected for other purposes (who have authority from the employees to agree permitted variations on their behalf), or representatives elected for the particular purpose of negotiating permitted variations (reg 9(2) SI 2006/246).

> MEMO POINTS Where appropriate representatives are **non-trade union** representatives, additional requirements apply. The agreement recording the permitted variation must be in writing and signed by each of the non-union representatives (or, where that is not reasonably practicable, by an authorised person on the representative's behalf). Before any agreement is made available for signature, the employer must provide all affected employees with copies of the text of the agreement and any guidance which employees might reasonably require to enable them to understand it fully (reg 9(5) SI 2006/246).

D. Dismissal

8030 The current TUPE regulations **set out the circumstances** under which it is unfair for employers to dismiss employees for transfer-connected reasons. The normal rules regarding dismissals will apply to dismissals which are **unconnected** to a transfer (see ¶¶8435+).

Whether a TUPE-related dismissal is either automatically unfair or potentially fair depends on the transferor's or transferee's **sole or principal reason** for the dismissal. The reason to be considered will be that in the mind of the person selling the business, so that in a case where an administrator, just before the company in administration was transferred, dismissed employees because there was not enough money to pay them, it was that reason which was considered (*Dynamex Friction Ltd and Ferotec Ltd v Amicus and ors* [2008] EWCA Civ 381).If the reason is **connected** with the transfer and is **not an ETO reason** (¶8016), then the dismissal will be automatically unfair. However, if the reason is connected with the transfer and **is an ETO reason** then it may be potentially fair subject to the normal rules regarding dismissal (see ¶¶8435+).

8033 To **establish a connection** between a dismissal and the transfer, it is not necessary for the transferor to have had in mind a specific transferee at the time of the dismissal, and it is enough that a possible transfer was the reason for the dismissal (*Morris v John Grose Group Ltd*

[1998] IRLR 499, EAT), although it must be more than "a mere twinkle in the eye" (*Ibex Trading Co Ltd v Walton* [1994] UKEAT 911_93_2106; confirmed by the Court of Appeal in *Spaceright Europe Limited v Baillavoine* [2011] EWCA Civ 1565).

> EXAMPLE In *Spaceright Europe Limited v Baillavoine*, the Chief Executive of a company was dismissed on the day that it was put into administration. The administrators had no particular buyer lined up at the time of dismissal, but selling the company as a going concern, which would involve a transfer of all employees under the TUPE Regulations, was the most likely outcome, and this in fact happened 1 month later. The Chief Executive claimed that he had been unfairly dismissed for a reason connected with the transfer. Despite the fact that no particular transfer was in mind at the time of his dismissal, he claimed that, on the facts of this case, there was a sufficient link between his dismissal and the subsequent TUPE transfer because he claimed that his dismissal took place in order to make the company more attractive for potential buyers. The administrators argued that the Chief Executive had in fact been dismissed due to redundancy: they were running the company in the short term and there was no need for such a senior and expensive employee to work alongside them. The Court of Appeal preferred the arguments of the Chief Executive and found in his favour: his employment was terminated because a company without a chief executive would be easier to sell as any purchaser would either be an existing company with its own leader in place, or a new venture that would recruit from the ranks of the existing directors. The fact that the administrators were not working towards a transfer of the business to a particular buyer at the time of dismissal was not important.

8034 There is no hard and fast rule as to **when the connection** between a dismissal and the transfer **will be broken**. A dismissal which took place nearly 2 years after the transfer has been held to be connected with it, partly because there had been ongoing negotiations throughout that period in relation to changes to the employee's terms and conditions (which he had resisted and which eventually led to his dismissal) (*Taylor v Connex South Eastern Limited* [2000] UKEAT 1243_99_0507). Conversely, dismissals which took place 2 years after a TUPE transfer have been held to be unconnected with the transfer on the basis that they were caused by serious cash-flow problems facing the transferee in the intervening 2-year period (*Norris and ors v Brown and Root Ealing Technical Services Ltd* [2002] UKEAT 386_00_1004).

8035 **Substantial change in working conditions** Where a transfer involves or would involve a substantial change in working conditions to the material detriment of a transferring employee, the employee has the right to treat himself as having been dismissed by the employer (unless the insolvency provisions apply – see ¶8023). This entitles the employee to claim **unfair dismissal** (subject to the normal rules of reasonableness – see ¶¶8435+). The employee will be treated as having been dismissed with notice: no damages will be payable by the employer for a failure to pay wages in relation to the notice period if the employee has failed to work it. Significantly, there is no need to show a breach of contract or a fundamental breach (reg 4(9), (10) SI 2006/246).

This statutory right is separate from the employee's common law right to claim **constructive dismissal** by terminating his contract without notice in acceptance of a repudiatory breach of contract by the employer (reg 4(11) SI 2006/246). This is discussed further at ¶¶8230+.

8036 It is for the tribunals and courts to **determine** what constitutes a substantial change in working conditions (an objective test) and to ascertain whether the employee was entitled to form the view that the change was to his material detriment (a subjective test) (*Abellio London Ltd v Musse and ors* [2012] UKEAT 0283_11_1201). BIS guidance suggests that this may include a major relocation of the workplace, which makes it difficult or much more expensive for an employee to transfer, or the withdrawal of a right to a tenured post.

> EXAMPLE
> 1. In *Abellio London Ltd v Musse and ors*, five bus drivers were employed on a set route, operated by CW, from a depot in West London. Under their contract CW reserved the right to require them to work at other defined work locations and could, subject to consultation, vary the terms of the contract save where the change would diminish a statutory entitlement. The drivers were given a month's notice that CW's contract to operate this route would be transferring to A and the route would relocate 6 miles to a depot in south west London. It was accepted that this was a service provision change transfer and the five drivers were assigned to the transferring bus route. The

drivers resigned due to concerns that the relocation of the route would extend their working day from between 1 to 2 hours. One driver resigned pre-transfer; the other four resigned on the day of transfer. The tribunal upheld their unfair dismissal claims and held that the drivers were constructively dismissed. The change of depot was not permitted by the terms of their contract as the new depot was not one of the locations listed in the claimants' contracts of employment and CW's letter notifying the drivers of the depot change was not a valid variation of the contract because it was not a depot they owned and could operate from. The requirement to relocate was a repudiatory, i.e. fundamental, breach of contract entitling the drivers to resign. It was also a substantial change to the claimants' working conditions to their material detriment; the relocation of 6 miles was substantial bearing in mind the additional travel time it would involve and it was reasonable for the drivers to consider this a material detriment. As such, the drivers had been automatically unfairly dismissed for a transfer-related reason as there was no ETO reason for the dismissals. CW was liable for the pre-transfer dismissal, whereas A was liable for the four dismissals on the day of transfer. Both bus companies appealed. The EAT held that the tribunal was entitled to conclude that the depot relocation was a substantial change. Although the move was only 6 miles, it was a substantial change given the travel difficulties it would cause. The contractual mobility clause was irrelevant; "working conditions" means an employee's actual circumstances, not what he may be required to do under his contract. Each driver had regarded the change as detrimental; they had either raised grievances or concerns with their managers. The fact their working day would be extended by 1 to 2 hours justified the tribunal's decision that the detriment was material. The EAT dismissed A's appeal, but allowed CW's appeal against the decision relating to the driver who had resigned pre-transfer; his case was remitted to the tribunal to determine whether he had objected to the transfer (a factual question unclear from the tribunal decision) (¶¶7962+).

2. In *F & G Cleaners v Saddington and ors* [2012] UKEAT 0140_11_1608, two window cleaners were employed to work on a contract to provide window cleaning services to a local authority. The window cleaning contract transferred to F & G and 2 weeks later they offered the two window cleaners a self-employed arrangement where they would receive a daily rate of pay. They refused and brought unfair dismissal claims against F & G. The employment tribunal and then the EAT upheld their claims. They held that there had been a TUPE transfer and that transferring to F & G under the terms offered would have involved a substantial change in their working conditions to their material detriment. As a result, they were entitled to resign and consider themselves automatically unfairly dismissed by reason of the transfer.

MEMO POINTS   The wording of regulation 4(9) means that the **change in working conditions** does not need to be so significant that it would amount to a fundamental breach of contract, and it will be easier for an employee to establish a dismissal than under the normal rules relating to constructive dismissal (¶¶8230+).

Liability for dismissals

8037 The liability for dismissal of transferring employees **transfers** to the transferee so that the transferee becomes liable for both pre- and post-transfer dismissals (unless there is an ETO reason – ¶8045), as TUPE applies to employees employed by the transferor and assigned to the organised grouping immediately before the transfer and those employees who would have been employed immediately before had they not been unfairly dismissed for a reason connected with the transfer (¶7960). The transferee may therefore wish to seek indemnities from the transferor for pre-transfer dismissals.

8038 If the employee claims **constructive dismissal without first objecting** to the transfer, he will be treated as having been constructively dismissed for a reason connected with the transfer, and liability will pass to the transferee (reg 7(1) SI 2006/246; *Euro-Die (UK) Ltd v (1) Skidmore (2) Genesis Diesinking Ltd* [1999] UKEAT 1158_98_1502).

However, if the employee **objects to the transfer and is constructively dismissed** as a result of substantial changes proposed by the transferee, the transferor will be liable for the dismissal and may wish to obtain an indemnity from the transferee (*University of Oxford v (1) Humphreys (2) Associated Examining Board* [2000] IRLR 183, CA).

MEMO POINTS   This applies despite the principle established in *Litster* that TUPE covers dismissed employees if they would have been employed immediately before the transfer were it not for their dismissal by reason of the transfer (*Litster v Forth Dry Dock and Engineering Co Ltd* [1989] IRLR 161, HL, see ¶7960). However, this case did not deal with objection to the transfer.

A **compromise agreement** between the employee and the transferor reached after the transfer date (perhaps because the parties had assumed that TUPE did not apply) cannot be relied on by the transferee to block an unfair dismissal claim against him (*Thompson v Walon Car Delivery* [1997] UKEAT 256_96_0502).

Defence

An employer may have a defence to an unfair dismissal claim if he can show an **ETO reason** (¶8016).

If an ETO reason is established, the dismissal will be potentially fair and subject to the normal test of reasonableness. It will be treated as having been for either **redundancy**, if the appropriate test of redundancy is met (entitling the employee to claim a redundancy payment) (¶¶8730+), or for **some other substantial reason** (¶8530) (reg 7(3)(b) SI 2006/246). The employer will have to show that he acted reasonably in all the circumstances in treating the reason as a fair reason for dismissal to avoid liability (¶¶8435+). This will normally require the employer to consider alternatives to dismissal and to consult with the employee.

Dismissal by transferor If the transferor dismisses the employee and **can show an ETO reason**, the employee will not be deemed to have been employed immediately before the transfer, and liability for his dismissal (for example, in relation to unfair dismissal procedure) will not transfer to the transferee (*Kerry Foods Ltd v Creber* [1999] UKEAT 1379_97_1110). If, however, the transferor **cannot show an ETO reason**, the dismissal will be automatically unfair and liability will transfer to the transferee.

If the transferor dismisses at the **transferee's request** and can show an ETO reason, he must still act reasonably in all the circumstances, which is likely to require him to consult and consider alternative employment, and possibly to satisfy himself that the transferee's reason for the dismissal is genuine. Given that the liability will rest with the transferor, he may be reluctant to implement dismissals at the transferee's request without obtaining appropriate indemnities.

Further, a transferor employer **cannot rely on** the **transferee's ETO reason** to justify the redundancy of an employee prior to the transfer of the business (*Hynd v (1) Armstrong and ors, (2) Bishops Solicitors and ors* [2007] IRLR 338, CS). The right of a transferee to dismiss for an ETO reason relates only to a reason of its own, i.e. its own future conduct of the business which entails a change in its own workforce. This is so even if the employee could have been fairly dismissed after the transfer, on grounds of redundancy. In *Hynd*, the employee was held to be automatically unfairly dismissed because the transferee had used the transferor's ETO reason (i.e. that the new firm was not going to practice in the area of the employee's expertise) in making the employee redundant before the transfer.

If the transferor can dismiss showing an ETO reason, the transferee benefits from the fact that there are **separate pools for redundancy selection** purposes. If the transferee were to effect the dismissals, he may have to include his existing staff in the selection pool.

However, where the transferor dismisses employees at the transferee's request **to achieve a sale** or in order to make the business more attractive, it is unlikely that the transferor will have an ETO reason as it must relate to the conduct of the business (with which the transferor will no longer be involved) (*Wheeler v (1) Patel (2) J Golding Group of Companies* [1987] IRLR 211, EAT; followed in *Ibex Trading Co Ltd v Walton* [1994] UKEAT 911_93_2106). As long as there is no **collusion** between transferor and transferee, the reason to be considered in establishing whether there is a valid ETO will be that in the mind of the transferor (*Dynamex Friction Ltd and Ferotec Ltd v Amicus and ors* [2008] EWCA Civ 381).

> MEMO POINTS **Receivers of an insolvent transferor** may have an ETO reason if they dismiss at the request of the transferee in circumstances where all employees would have been dismissed had the transferee not agreed to take over the business (*Thompson v SCS Consulting Ltd* [2001] UKEAT 34_00_0309).

8047 If the transferor gives **notice of termination** before the transfer which expires after the transfer, a tribunal would consider the transferor's reasons when determining the fairness of the dismissal (although liability for the dismissal will transfer to the transferee) (*BSG Property Services v Tuck* [1995] UKEAT 245_95_1603).

8048 **Dismissal by transferee** If the transferee dismisses the employee, he will be liable for the dismissal, but may have an ETO reason. It is likely to be easier for the transferee to rely on this, as he will be involved in the future conduct of the business. This may be the case even where he dismisses as a condition of a contract for the provision of services being awarded to him by the transferor in order to reduce ongoing staffing costs (*Whitehouse v Chas A Blatchford & Sons Ltd* [1999] EWCA Civ 1255).

SECTION 3
Information and consultation obligations

8060 TUPE imposes a duty on the **transferor and transferee** to provide information about the transfer and its implications to representatives of their respective workforces before a transfer takes place. If measures are contemplated in connection with the transfer, there is an additional obligation to consult the representatives. There is a **further duty** on the **transferor** to provide information about transferring employees (referred to in the regulations as "employee liability information") to the transferee before the transfer occurs. Each of these duties is discussed below.

8061 There is no **definition of "measures"** but they are widely construed to include any action, step or arrangement amounting to a definite plan or proposal that the employer intends to implement, for example redundancies, relocation, changes to working practices, and effects on pensions and other benefits. Mere possibilities or hopes are excluded (*Institution of Professional Civil Servants v Secretary of State for Defence* [1987] IRLR 373, HC).

> *MEMO POINTS* Certain large employers are also required to inform and consult employees before taking important business decisions by virtue of the European **Information and Consultation Directive** (see Chapter 22).

A. Duty on transferor and transferee to inform and consult

8062 The duty on transferor and transferee is to inform and consult with the appropriate representatives of affected employees (reg 13 SI 2006/246). These are separate duties and the duty to inform (¶8067) is independent of the duty to consult (¶8071) and still applies where no measures were contemplated.

If the transferor or transferee fails to inform or consult, damages can be sought (¶8080). The fact that an employee is not provided with information and documents about a TUPE transfer or afforded a right to object to the transfer does not prevent his contract of employment transferring (*Marcroft v Heartland (Midlands) Ltd* [2011] EWCA Civ 438 and see the example at ¶7960).

> *MEMO POINTS* Many of the requirements in relation to appropriate representatives, elections, protections and failure to comply are as for **collective redundancy consultation** (see ¶8915). If the transferee is likely to make any employees redundant after the transfer, any consultation may also need to comply with these requirements.

8063 **Appropriate representatives** are defined in broadly the same way as they are defined for the purposes of agreeing a permitted variation in relevant insolvency proceedings (¶8023) (reg 13(3) SI 2006/246).

Where a transferor has no recognised union and there are no elected employee representatives (for example, as the result of a failure to elect them), the transferor is nevertheless obliged to invite "affected employees" to elect employee representatives for the purposes of TUPE and, should they fail to do so, the transferor is obliged to inform and consult all affected employees on an individual basis about the matters relating to the transfer prescribed by the regulations (*Howard v Millrise Ltd (t/a Colourflow) (in liquidation) and anor* [2005] IRLR 84, EAT).

Affected employees are broadly defined as any employees of the transferor or the transferee who may be affected by the transfer or by measures taken in connection with it (reg 13(1) SI 2006/246). They may therefore include employees who are to be transferred, their colleagues who will not transfer but whose jobs may be affected by the transfer, or the transferees' existing employees whose jobs may also be affected.

8065

> EXAMPLE   In *Unison v Somerset County Council* [2010] IRLR 207, EAT, two councils outsourced administrative functions from their resources departments to a joint venture company, S. Most employees involved opted to remain council employees and be seconded to S. Unison, the union representing the council employees, made a complaint that not all affected employees had been consulted before the transfer. The argument was based on the fact that council employees who worked outside the two resources departments were affected by the terms of the transfer agreement in that they would not be given advance notice of any vacancies arising within S after the date of transfer. The EAT rejected this argument and held that "affected employees" meant employees who:
> – would be transferred by operation of TUPE;
> – might lose their jobs as a result of the transfer; or
> – were in the process of applying for a job in the transferred part of an organisation at the time of the transfer.
> The term "affected employees" does not extend to all employees of the transferor organisation, simply because they may wish, in the future, to apply for a job in the transferee organisation.

Informing employees about the transfer

Both transferor and transferee must inform the appropriate representatives of their own staff of the following (reg 13(2) SI 2006/246):
– the **fact** that a transfer is to take place, the **date** or proposed date, and the **reason** for it (but they are not obliged to justify the transfer or discuss its merits); and
– the legal, economic and social **implications** of the transfer for any affected employees. This may include an explanation of the legal effect in relation to employment contracts, collective agreements and statutory rights, the impact on pay and benefits, and any relocation plans.

8067

Where the employer is the **transferor**, and he envisages taking **measures** in connection with the transfer in relation to any affected employees, he must inform the appropriate representatives. If the transferor does not envisage any measures, he should confirm that fact.

8068

Where the employer is the **transferee**, and he envisages taking such **measures**, he must also inform the appropriate representatives or, if he does not envisage any measures, confirm that fact. Further, the transferor must also provide information about the transferee's measures or, if no measures are envisaged, confirm that fact. The transferee is obliged to provide the transferor with such information as will allow him to comply with this obligation (for consequences of the transferee's failure to do so, see ¶8084).

Giving **incorrect information** in itself will not breach this obligation, if the transferor/transferee genuinely thinks that the information given is correct (*Royal Mail Group Ltd v Communication Workers Union* [2009] IRLR 1046, CA). However, both transferor and transferee must take reasonable care in providing information in a transfer situation, or they may face claims for **breach of contract** (¶1700). They may also be liable for **negligent misstatement** (*Hagen and ors v ICI Chemicals & Polymers Ltd* [2002] IRLR 31, QBD).

8069

However, liability for negligent misstatement will only arise where:
– a duty of care owed by the employer to the employees is breached (i.e. because the representations are false and could not have been made by someone exercising reasonable care);

– the employees reasonably relied on the representations and suffered loss as a result; and
– the loss is of a kind falling within the scope of the duty.

In most cases, it will be difficult to establish **consequential loss**, as most employees are not in a position to prevent a transfer going ahead or to secure more favourable terms.

8070 **Procedure** The information to be provided must be **given to** the appropriate representatives directly, or **sent** to them **by post** to an address notified by them to the employer or, in the case of trade union representatives, to the union's head or main office (reg 13(5) SI 2006/246). This requirement indicates that the information should be provided **in writing**. It is then up to the representatives to convey the information to the affected employees, which they may do by holding meetings in the workplace or by way of written information.

Consulting about measures

8071 Where the employer is the **transferor**, and he envisages taking **measures** in connection with the transfer in relation to any affected employees, he must not only inform but also consult the appropriate representatives (reg 13(6) SI 2006/246).

Where the **transferee** envisages taking measures, he is not obliged to consult with transferring employees prior to the transfer as he is not yet their employer. Equally, the transferor is not obliged to consult as he will not be taking those measures. There is also no obligation on a transferee to provide information to, or consult with, employees after a TUPE transfer has taken place where the transferee envisages measures after the transfer has been completed (*UCATT v Amicus and ors* [2008] UKEAT 0007_08_1811).

> MEMO POINTS The new employer may have **other obligations** to consult post-transfer (see Chapter 22 on information and consultation in the workplace and Chapter 21 with regard to collective bargaining).

8073 **Procedure** Consultation with appropriate representatives should take place "**with a view to** seeking their agreement to the intended measures", and employers are expressly required to consider any representations made by the appropriate representatives, and to reply to those representations, giving reasons for any rejection of them (reg 13(6), (7) SI 2006/246). The employer must therefore give proper and genuine consideration to the views of the appropriate representatives, and allow them to canvass the opinions and suggestions of the affected employees.

Timing

8075 Where an employer is under a **duty to inform** appropriate representatives about the transfer and its implications, the required information must be provided "**long enough**" before the transfer **to enable consultation** with the appropriate representatives to take place (reg 13(2) SI 2006/246). The duty is triggered where there is a proposed or planned transfer, even if it does not eventually take place (*Banking Insurance and Finance Union v Barclays Bank plc* [1987] IRLR 495, EAT). The timing will therefore depend on the number of employees, their location, and the complexity of the transaction. If appropriate representatives already exist, a period of 2 to 4 weeks may be appropriate. If representatives need to be elected, a longer period will be needed. Periods, such as annual shutdowns, which will affect the time it takes to consult must be taken into consideration (*Cable Realisations Ltd v GMB Northern* [2010] IRLR 42, EAT). Even where **consultation** is **not compulsory**, information should be given in good time so that voluntary consultation can take place (*Institution of Professional Civil Servants v Secretary of State for Defence* [1987] IRLR 373, HC; *Cable Realisations Ltd v GMB Northern*).

Where an employer also has a **duty to consult**, this process should ideally begin before the transfer agreement is signed, so that he can respond in a meaningful way to any representations raised. If it is not, the employer may have failed to comply with his consultation obligations. However, where the transfer is commercially sensitive, reasons of secrecy may outweigh potential liability for failure to fully inform and consult (although note that such reasons are unlikely to offer a defence).

> **EXAMPLE** In *Cable Realisations Ltd v GMB Northern*, a recognised union made a complaint that an employer had failed to provide information sufficiently in advance of a TUPE transfer. The required information was provided on 15 August, just before the employer's annual shutdown when nearly all the employees were on holiday, in respect of a transfer which took place on 3 September. The EAT held that where consultation is not a compulsory requirement because no measures have been proposed, it is still necessary to allow enough time for voluntary consultation to take place after the information is given. It was right to take into account the impact of the shutdown in assessing whether enough time had been allowed. The EAT also upheld an award of 3 weeks' pay as appropriate to the seriousness of the default, applying the same approach as for collective redundancy purposes (see ¶8952).

Failure to comply

Complaints may be brought to an employment tribunal for failure to inform and consult as for collective redundancy consultation (reg 15(1) SI 2006/246) (¶8946). **8080**

> *MEMO POINTS* If a question arises as to whether or not a particular employee representative was an appropriate representative, it is for the employer to show that the representative had the necessary authority to represent the affected employees. If necessary, he must also show that the requirements regarding elections have been satisfied (reg 15(3), (4) SI 2006/246).

Defence There may be **special circumstances** which render it not reasonably practicable for an employer to comply with his duty to inform and consult. If this is the case, the employer must show that he took all such steps towards performing his duty as were reasonably practicable in the circumstances (regs 13(9), 15(2) SI 2006/246). **8082**

> *MEMO POINTS* Where an employer is controlled by another company (e.g. in a group company structure), a **failure by the controller** to provide information to the employer does not constitute special circumstances (reg 15(6) SI 2006/246). Concerns about **confidentiality** or the **mere appointment** of an insolvency practitioner will not provide a defence.

If the complaint is that the transferor failed to provide information on the **measures envisaged by the transferee**, the transferor may have a defence if the transferee failed to give him the requisite information. However, in order to rely on this defence, the transferor must give the transferee notice of that intention, in which case the transferee becomes a party to the proceedings (reg 15(5) SI 2006/246). **8084**

Remedies If the tribunal finds that there has been a **failure by the transferor or transferee** to inform or consult, it can make a declaration to that effect and order the relevant party to pay appropriate compensation to the affected employees (reg 15(7), (8) SI 2006/246). **8085**

Where the complaint is that the transferor failed to provide information on the **measures envisaged by the transferee**, and the transferor can show that the transferee failed to give him the requisite information, the tribunal can make a declaration to that effect and order the transferee to pay appropriate compensation to affected employees.

The **amount of compensation** will be such sum as the tribunal considers just and equitable, having regard to the seriousness of the employer's failure to comply, subject to a **maximum of 13 weeks' pay (uncapped)** (reg 16(3) SI 2006/246). The EAT has confirmed that the approach to assessing compensation for a failure to consult under TUPE is the same as for collective redundancy purposes and that the focus should be on the punitive and deterrent nature of any such award. The maximum should therefore be awarded unless there are mitigating circumstances justifying an appropriate reduction (*Sweetin v Coral Racing* [2006] IRLR 252, EAT).

> **EXAMPLE**
> 1. In *Cable Realisations Ltd v GMB Northern* [2010] IRLR 42, EAT, the EAT held that an award of 3 weeks' pay for failure to inform with regard to voluntary consultation was appropriate by applying the same approach as for collective redundancy purposes.
> 2. In *Todd v Strain and ors* [2010] UKEAT 0057_10_1606, the EAT reduced an award of 13 weeks' pay to 7 weeks' pay, as the employees had been given some, if limited, information and no significant measures had been contemplated.

8087 Where the transferor has failed to inform or consult, the transferor and transferee can be made **jointly and severally liable** for an award of compensation made by a tribunal (reg 15(9) SI 2006/246). Employees may therefore **bring proceedings against** either the transferor or the transferee or, as is more likely, both. Where an order of joint and several liability is made it is not the tribunal's role to apportion liability between the transferor and transferee (*Todd v Strain and ors* [2010] UKEAT 0057_10_1606).

> MEMO POINTS   In cases involving both **collective redundancies and a TUPE transfer**, a separate award for failure to consult may be made in relation to each, with no provision for one to be offset against the other.

Infringement of rights

8089 Any **dismissal** will be automatically unfair if it is on the grounds of an employee's participation in an election either as a candidate or voter or because of his status or activities as a union representative or elected representative (¶8390).

It is also unlawful for an employer to victimise any employee by subjecting him to a **detriment short of dismissal** by any act, or any deliberate failure to act, on those grounds.

B. Duty on transferor to provide transferee with employee information

8090 Transferors are under a statutory duty to provide transferees with specific information to help them understand their rights, duties and obligations in relation to transferring employees. The purpose of this obligation is to enable the transferee to prepare for the arrival of the transferring employees. Employees should also benefit as their new employer will be aware of the obligations he has inherited.

> MEMO POINTS   The transferor and transferee cannot **contract out** of this duty.

Informing transferee about transferring employees

8091 The transferor is obliged to provide the transferee with the following **details** in relation to the transferring employees (reg 11(2) SI 2006/246 as amended by SI 2009/592):
– the **identity** and **age** of the employees;
– information contained in the statutory **written particulars** (¶1400);
– information relating to any **disciplinary action** taken against an employee within the previous 2 years, where a Code of Practice issued under the Trade Union and Labour Relations Act 1992 which relates exclusively or primarily to the resolution of disputes applies (i.e. the Acas Code of Practice on Disciplinary and Grievance Procedures);
– information relating to any **grievances** raised by an employee within the previous 2 years, where a Code of Practice issued under the Trade Union and Labour Relations Act 1992 which relates exclusively or primarily to the resolution of disputes applies (i.e. the Acas Code of Practice on Disciplinary and Grievance Procedures);
– information about any **legal action** brought by an employee against the transferor within the previous 2 years and any potential legal action which the transferor has reasonable grounds to believe may be brought by an employee; and
– information relating to any **collective agreement** which will have effect after the transfer.

The information should **also include** information about anyone who would have been employed by the transferor and assigned to the organised grouping immediately before the transfer if he had not been unfairly dismissed (¶7960). This includes, where a transfer is effected by a series of two or more transactions, anyone so employed immediately before any of those transactions (reg 11(4) SI 2006/246).

Procedure The transferor has a degree of flexibility as to **how to provide the information**, as it can be provided in writing or in other forms which are readily accessible to the transferee (reg 11(1) SI 2006/246). For example, the transferor may send the information as computer data files, as long as the transferee can access that information, or provide access to the transferor's data storage. Where a small number of employees are transferring and small amounts of information are involved, it may be acceptable to provide the information by telephone. The party disclosing information should take care that the method of disclosure complies with the data protection principles (¶5945) when carrying out information and consultation obligations. The main points to bear in mind are that:
– any data disclosed should be accurate, up to date and secure;
– excessive or irrelevant data should not be disclosed;
– if going beyond the disclosure strictly required by TUPE, the employees' consent should first be obtained and additional precautions taken to ensure that it is not retained or used for any purpose other than the transfer; and
– the new employer should delete or destroy any disclosed personnel information which is no longer needed after transfer.

8092

> MEMO POINTS 1. It will be **good practice** for the transferor to consult the transferee first to discuss the appropriate methods.
> 2. **Notification** may be given in more than one instalment. It can also be given indirectly, through a third party (such as the client, in a change of contractor situation) (reg 11(7) SI 2006/246). Once the information is provided, the transferor must also notify the transferee in writing of any change to it (reg 11(5) SI 2006/246).
> 3. The ICO has provided **guidance** on compliance with data protection law during TUPE consultation.

Timing

The information must be correct at a specified date **not more than** 14 days before the date it is notified to the transferee (reg 11(3) SI 2006/246).

8093

Notification must be given **not less than** 14 days before the transfer, or, if special circumstances make this not reasonably practicable, as soon as reasonably practicable thereafter (reg 11(6) SI 2006/246). BIS guidance indicates that it would not be reasonably practicable to provide the information in time if the transferor did not know the identity of the transferee until very late in the process. This may occur, for example, when service contracts are reassigned from one contractor to another by a client or when the transfer takes place at very short notice.

Failure to comply

The transferee may bring a **complaint** to an employment tribunal if the transferor fails to comply with the requirement to inform and consult.

8094

The complaint should be brought **before** the end of 3 months beginning with the date of the transfer, or within such further period as the tribunal considers reasonable where it was not reasonably practicable to present the claim within the 3-month period.

Remedies If the tribunal finds the complaint well-founded, it shall make a declaration to that effect and may award unlimited compensation to be paid by the transferor to the transferee (reg 12(3) SI 2006/246).

8095

The **amount of compensation** shall be just and equitable in all the circumstances, having regard to the:
– loss sustained by the transferee; and
– terms of any contract between the transferor and transferee under which the transferor may be liable to pay sums to the transferee in respect of such failure.

The transferee has a **duty to mitigate** any loss he may sustain (reg 12(6) SI 2006/246). However, the compensation shall be **no less than** £500 for each employee for whom information was not provided or was defective. The tribunal may award a lesser sum if it considers it just and equitable (e.g. if there were only trivial or unwitting breaches of the transferor's duty).

CHAPTER 25

Ending employment

OUTLINE ¶¶

SECTION 1 Termination of employment 8105

I Forms of termination	8115
A Dismissal with notice	8120
1 Notice periods	8123
Contractual notice	8126
Statutory minimum notice	8131
2 Pay in lieu of notice	8145
3 Garden leave	8150
B Dismissal without notice	8155
1 Calculation of damages	8160
Period of loss	8160
Types of loss	8161
Adjustments to net loss	8169
2 Sample calculation	8175
3 Overlap with unfair dismissal awards ..	8177
C Resignation	8180
D Retirement	8199
1 Retiring age	8200
Contractual retiring age	8203
Normal retiring age	8206
2 Fair retirement procedure	8209
3 Early retirement	8228
Impact on pension entitlement	8228
Retirement due to ill health	8229
E Constructive dismissal	8230
Resignation	8238
Affirmation of the contract	8242
Remedies	8248
F Mutual agreement	8260
G Automatic termination	8270
1 Supervening events	8275
Death	8276
Insolvency	8277
2 Frustration	8285
II Termination issues	8300
A Statement of reasons for dismissal ..	8310
B References	8320

C Date of termination	8340
Dismissal with notice	8343
Dismissal without notice	8349
Fixed-term contracts	8356
Trial period in alternative employment ..	8357
Appeals against dismissal	8358

SECTION 2 Unfair dismissal 8380

I Automatic unfair dismissal	8390
Qualifying employees	8393
Inadmissible reasons	8394
II General scheme	8410
A Qualifying employees	8410
Excluded employees	8412
B Reason for dismissal	8420
C Procedure	8435
D Application to specific cases	8450
1 Incapability	8450
a Fair reason	8450
Capability	8451
Incompetence	8452
Ill health	8458
Qualifications	8461
b Fair procedure	8470
2 Misconduct	8490
a Fair reason	8490
b Fair procedure	8500
3 Redundancy	8510
4 Contravention of a duty or restriction ..	8520
a Fair reason	8520
b Fair procedure	8525
5 Some other substantial reason	8530
a Fair reason	8530
Business reorganisations	8532
Confidentiality and competition issues	8537
Temporary contracts	8539
Breakdown of mutual trust and confidence	8541
Breakdown of working relationship	8542

Dismissal at request of third parties	8543
Imprisonment	8544
Genuine belief that dismissal fair	8545
Takeover of the business	8546
b Fair procedure	8550

III Enforcement and remedies 8560
A Compensation 8570
1 Basic award 8575
   Minimum basic award 8577
   Reductions 8578
2 Compensatory award 8585
   a Losses for which compensation can be awarded 8590
   Causation 8591
   Earnings and other benefits 8593
   Pension rights 8601
   Expenses 8608
   Statutory rights 8609
   Manner of dismissal 8610
   b Adjustments to compensation 8615
   Sums paid by the employer 8616
   Mitigation of loss 8620
   Employment would have terminated in any event 8628
   Polkey reduction 8630
   Effect of unreasonable failure to follow code on discipline and grievance 8634
   Contributory fault 8635
   Social security benefits 8643
   c Order for calculating compensatory award 8665
B Reinstatement and re-engagement 8680
   Effect of reinstatement 8681
   Effect of re-engagement 8682
   Relevant factors 8684
   Failure to comply 8688
C Interim relief 8700
D Table of specific remedies 8710

SECTION 3 Redundancy 8730

I Identifying a redundancy dismissal 8740
1 Redundancy situations 8745
   Closure of business 8747
   Closure of employee's workplace 8749
   Diminishing need for employees 8752

2 Dismissal 8765
3 Reason for dismissal 8767
   a "Causation" issues 8767
   b Unfair dismissal 8790

II Managing redundancy 8800
A Redundancy policies 8810
B Contractual terms 8820
C Selection 8830
D Alternative employment 8850
   Offer 8858
   Refusal 8865
   Suitability and reasonableness 8867
   Statutory trial period 8872
   Common law trial period 8876
E Time off 8885

III Consultation and notification requirements 8900
A Individual consultation 8910
B Collective consultation 8915
   Scope 8916
1 Consultation requirements 8925
   Information to be provided 8935
   Timing 8939
   Failure to comply/infringement of rights 8946
2 Notification to the Department for Business, Innovation and Skills (BIS) 8970

IV Statutory redundancy payments 8990
   Entitlement 8990
   Excluded/disqualified employees 8992
   Calculation 9005
   Claims for payment 9010
   Statement of entitlement 9017

SECTION 4 Employee rights on insolvency 9040

1 State guaranteed payments 9045
   a Types of payment 9045
   Statutory redundancy payments 9049
   Debts 9053
   Pension contributions 9056
   b Application procedure 9065
   Remedies 9071
2 Preferential creditor 9080
3 Administrators 9085

8100 The **three main ways** an employment relationship can come to an end (termination by the employer, termination by the employee and termination by mutual agreement) are set out below. Termination may be with or without notice.

In addition, the contract may automatically terminate in certain circumstances, such as where it is "frustrated" by the employee's long-term absence.

8101 When **terminating** the employment of an employee, the employer must do so in accordance with the terms of the **contract** (for example, in relation to notice periods) or he will be liable for breach of contract (¶¶1700+). Breach of contract due to the employer's failure to give the required period of notice is known as wrongful dismissal (¶8155).

In addition, all employees (and, to a certain extent, some workers) enjoy **statutory protection** on dismissal. If the dismissal is discriminatory, the employee may bring a claim of discrimination on the grounds of age, disability, gender reassignment, marriage and civil partnership, pregnancy and maternity, race, religion or belief, sex or sexual orientation (¶¶5200+). Further, if an employee is dismissed for an inadmissible reason, he can bring an unfair dismissal claim (with, generally, no requirement for qualifying service) (¶¶8390+). In such cases, the dismissal will be automatically unfair. Dismissals to which the transfer of business (TUPE) regulations apply are also automatically unfair and special rules apply (¶¶8030+).

Employees with sufficient qualifying service can bring an unfair dismissal claim under the general scheme (¶¶8410+).

8102 Under the general scheme there are five potentially fair reasons to terminate employment: incapability, misconduct, contravention of a duty or restriction, redundancy and some other substantial reason.

Redundancy is a fair reason for dismissal unless (¶¶8730+):
– there is no genuine redundancy situation;
– it is automatically unfair (for example, if the reason for dismissal is the employee's pregnancy); or
– the employer failed to act fairly in all the circumstances. This includes a requirement for individual consultation. In cases of collective redundancies, an employer is also required to consult with trade union or employee representatives and to notify the Department for Business, Innovation and Skills (BIS).

An employee under notice of dismissal for redundancy has a statutory right to **time off work** to seek new employment or to make arrangements for retraining (¶¶8885+), and on dismissal may be entitled to a **statutory redundancy payment** (¶¶8990+). Employees may also benefit from contractual provisions relating to redundancy pay and procedures.

8103 Employees have specific rights and protections if their **employer is insolvent**, including (¶¶9040+):
– a right to apply to the Department for Business, Innovation and Skills (BIS) for certain state guaranteed payments;
– a right to be preferential creditors in respect of certain debts; and
– rights against an administrator in respect of amounts arising during the period of administration (or, in rare cases, administrative receivership).

SECTION 1

Termination of employment

8105 There are three main ways an employment relationship can come to an end: termination by the employer (known as **dismissal**), termination by the employee (known as **resignation**), and termination by **mutual agreement**. Termination may be with or without notice. The contract may **automatically terminate** in certain circumstances, such as where it is "frustrated" by the employee's death.

8106 **Extended meaning of dismissal** To **bring a claim** of unfair dismissal or for a redundancy payment, the employee must show that he has been dismissed. The meaning of dismissal is extended by statute for these purposes to include:
– the **expiry of a fixed-term contract** without its renewal (¶1996), or the termination of a contract for a **specific purpose**/terminable on the occurrence of a specified event;
– **constructive dismissal** (where the employee resigns in response to the employer's fundamental breach of contract) (ss 95(1)(c), 136(1)(c) ERA 1996) (except in redundancy cases, when the fundamental breach is a **lock-out** and the employee resigns without notice (s 136(2) ERA 1996)); and
– the resignation of the employee during the employer notice period under a special statutory procedure whereby he gives a **counter-notice** (for redundancy purposes only, this must be given during the "obligatory period") (ss 95(2), 142 ERA 1996) (¶9000).

For redundancy purposes, dismissal also includes the following:
– **voluntary redundancy** (in contrast to consensual termination/early retirement) (*Burton, Allton & Johnson Ltd v R R V Peck* [1975] IRLR 87, QBD; *Cole v London Borough of Hackney* [1999] UKEAT 973_99_2311);
– termination by **operation of law** (¶8271) as a result of an act of the employer or an event affecting him (for example, death of an individual employer, frustration of the contract at common law, the dissolution of a partnership, the appointment of some receivers and some forms of winding up) (s 136(5) ERA 1996; *British Airport Authority v Fenerty* [1976] ICR 361, EAT; *Pickwell v Lincolnshire County Council* [1992] UKEAT 123_92_1109); and
– special cases where the employment is terminated **by statute** (for example, transfers from one statutory body to another) (s 172 ERA 1996).

A deemed dismissal may also occur in some cases of **variation**, where the changes are so significant that a court finds that the old employment has in fact been terminated and replaced by a new contract (¶1652).

8107 **No dismissal** There is no dismissal in the following cases:
– termination by **mutual agreement**. An employee who agrees to take **early retirement** will not, therefore, be dismissed (*Birch and Humber v The University of Liverpool* [1985] IRLR 165, CA; *Scott v Coalite Fuels and Chemicals Ltd* [1988] IRLR 131, EAT). If, however, an employee is given notice of redundancy and subsequently agrees to take early retirement, he will still be considered to have been dismissed for redundancy unless the employee agrees to the notice of redundancy being withdrawn (*Gateshead Metropolitan Borough Council v Mills* [1995] UKEAT 610_92_2305);
– **resignation** (unless the circumstances give rise to a constructive dismissal or the employee has been forced to resign); and
– termination by **frustration** or **supervening events** (but note the extended meaning of dismissal for redundancy purposes in certain cases of termination by operation of law above).

In certain circumstances, an employee will be deemed not to have been dismissed where he is **subsequently re-engaged** (¶8850).

There is no dismissal when employees transfer automatically from one employer to another under the **transfer of business (TUPE)** regulations (¶7952).

8108 How the employment ends affects whether an employee can bring a claim and the type of claim he may bring. To help employees decide whether they may have a claim against their employer, certain employees are entitled to a **statement of the reasons** for dismissal.

To avoid **liability for breach of contract**, the employer must comply with the terms of the contract (in relation to notice and any applicable termination procedures). To avoid statutory liability for **unfair dismissal**, he must have a fair reason for dismissal and follow a fair procedure. The employee may, depending on the circumstances, be entitled to a contractual and/or statutory **redundancy payment**. The dismissal may also be **discriminatory**, giving rise to a separate claim of age, disability, gender reassignment, marriage and civil partnership, pregnancy and maternity, race, religion or belief, sex or sexual orientation discrimination.

8109 In some cases, the employer and employee may **negotiate the termination** of employment, which commonly involves the payment of a lump sum in return for a waiver of the employee's rights against the employer. This is discussed at ¶9259. The employee's **contract of employment** can deal with a number of issues arising on termination, such as notice requirements, post-termination restraints, return of company property and, in the case of directors, resignation of directorships.

One particularly important issue on termination is the provision of **references**. For the employee, this may be crucial to his securing new employment. From the employer's point of view, he may incur liability, both to the employee and the recipient of any reference provided by him.

It is important to identify the **date of termination** for various reasons, including assessing continuous employment (in order to assess qualifying service periods and the amount of redundancy payments and unfair dismissal awards) and complying with time limits for tribunal claims. This date will depend on the form of termination and, for some purposes, it is postponed. These issues are discussed at ¶8340.

8110

Discrimination

It is unlawful for an employer to discriminate against a person on the grounds of age, disability, gender reassignment, marriage and civil partnership, pregnancy and maternity, race, religion or belief, sex or sexual orientation by dismissing them. See chapter 16 for a detailed discussion of discrimination.

8111

Generally speaking, a dismissal which is unlawfully discriminatory is also likely to be unfair (¶8380). See ¶¶8586+ regarding compensation in such cases. However, the statutory provisions are not the same and do not necessarily lead to the same result. It should be noted that there is **no qualifying service requirement** for bringing a claim in respect of a discriminatory dismissal and there is **no statutory cap** on the amount of **compensation** that can be awarded. Further, injury to feelings and aggravated damages may also be awarded.

It should be noted that discrimination may also amount to constructive dismissal under anti-discrimination laws (¶8249).

I. Forms of termination

The various forms of termination are discussed below. In some cases, it may not be clear whether the employment has in fact ended (for example, because of ambiguity as to words used or as to a party's true intentions, or where a party attempts to withdraw his words).

8115

Identifying a termination

There may be a dispute as to whether the employer (or employee) has in fact terminated the employment where the **actions or words used are ambiguous**. The tribunal or court will take an objective view and consider how those words or actions would have been understood by a reasonable employee (or employer) in the circumstances (including preceding and subsequent events and the nature of the workplace) (*B G Gale Ltd v Gilbert* [1978] IRLR 453, EAT). Further, the general principle of construction applies so that any ambiguity is construed against the party seeking to rely on it (*Graham Group plc v Garratt* [1997] UKEAT 161_97_2002).

8116

If the **words are clear**, the employer (or employee) cannot later state that he did not intend them to have that meaning, unless special circumstances apply (such as words spoken in the heat of the moment, where the other party ought to know they are not meant to be taken seriously or where the employee is mentally impaired) (*Sothern v Franks Charlesly & Co* [1981] IRLR 278, CA; *Sovereign House Security Services Ltd v Savage* [1989] IRLR 115, CA; *Kwik-Fit (GB) Ltd v Lineham* [1991] UKEAT 250_91_2410). Where such circumstances apply, the employer (or employee) would be advised to investigate the other party's **true intentions**.

In general, words of dismissal or resignation cannot **unilaterally** be **withdrawn** once they have been communicated to the other party, although arguably an employer must accept a resignation before it can take effect. Only in special circumstances can a notice to terminate employment be withdrawn unilaterally and "almost invariably in cases in which the

8117

purported notice has been given orally in the heat of the moment by words that may quickly be regretted" (*C F Capital PLC v Willoughby* [2011] EWCA Civ 1115, and see also *Martin v Yeoman Aggregates Ltd* [1983] IRLR 49, EAT). Notice of termination by either party can, of course, be withdrawn **by mutual consent**.

> EXAMPLE In *C F Capital PLC v Willoughby*, an employee was dismissed on the basis that she would be re-engaged immediately on a self-employed contract containing different terms and conditions. A meeting had taken place prior to the dismissal in which both parties discussed this possibility as a way to avoid redundancies, and the meeting ended with the employee expressing interest and requesting further details. After various attempts to find out further information, she received a letter terminating her employment and re-engaging her on a self-employed basis. She took legal advice and, despite the employer claiming that there had been a mistake and immediately offering to retain her on her existing contract and making various attempts to resolve the situation, she refused to accept the retraction of the notice of termination and brought a claim for unfair dismissal. The Court of Appeal disagreed with the original tribunal and found that there had not been a misunderstanding at the original meeting as to what had been agreed (as the employer argued was the case): both parties left the meeting thinking that the employee wanted to consider the self-employment option further but understood that a final agreement had not been reached. The dismissal letter gave unequivocal notice of termination of employment and, despite the employer's prompt protests, the letter was valid as notice of termination and the employee was entitled to take it as such.

8118 Once notice of termination has been given, it is still open to the employer (or employee as the case may be) to terminate immediately during the notice period if the employee (or employer) is in **fundamental breach** (*Ford v Milthorn Toleman Ltd* [1980] IRLR 30, CA).

A. Dismissal with notice

8120 **Statute** implies a minimum notice period into every contract terminable on notice. However, there may also be an **express or implied contractual term**. It is advisable that the notice of termination is in writing. Even if the employer gives the requisite notice, the dismissal may still be **unfair**.

The employee is entitled to the longer of the contractual notice and the statutory minimum notice.

> EXAMPLE
> 1. Employee A has been employed for 2 years and his contractual notice is 1 month. He is entitled to the contractual notice as it is longer than the statutory minimum (which is 2 weeks – see ¶8131 below).
> 2. Employee B has been employed for 8 years and his contractual notice is 1 month. He is entitled to the statutory minimum notice of 8 weeks (see ¶8131 below), as it is longer than the contractual period.

1. Notice periods

8123 To be valid, notice of termination must include the **date of termination** (or information from which it can be ascertained) (*Morton Sundour Fabrics Ltd v Shaw* [1967] ITR 84, DivCt) and be unequivocal. It is not sufficient for an employer to notify the employee that his employment will terminate if he does or does not perform a specified act since such notice could, in theory, be unilaterally withdrawn (*Rai v Somerfield Stores Ltd* [2003] UKEAT 0557_02_1205). Similarly, a warning that the employment will end on or after a certain date does not constitute a valid notice of dismissal (*Doble v Firestone Tyre and Rubber Co Ltd* [1981] IRLR 300, EAT).

> EXAMPLE In *Doble v Firestone Tyre and Rubber Co Ltd*, the employer's announcement that the plant at which D worked would close by a certain date did not amount to a notice of dismissal as the date of termination could not be ascertained with precision from that announcement (which further stated that notice of dismissal would be sent out to individual employees as appropriate).

8124 The date of termination may be **brought forward or postponed** by mutual agreement (*Mowlem Northern Ltd v Watson* [1990] IRLR 500, EAT). If the employee wants to leave before expiry of the employer's notice period, he may still be treated as having been dismissed if the employer so agrees or if the employee serves a statutory **counter-notice** (¶9000). See ¶¶8342, 8346 as to how this may affect the effective date of termination.

8125 Unless the contract states otherwise, notice can be given on any day and, where given **orally**, runs from the start of the next day if given on a day where work has been performed (*West v Kneels Ltd* [1986] IRLR 430, EAT) and, where given **in writing**, will likewise run from the first day after notice has been given and received (*Wang v University of Keele* [2010] UKEAT 0223_10_0804).

Any ambiguity with regard to the date that notice is given should be construed in favour of the recipient (¶8344).

Contractual notice

8126 There is often an **express term** in the contract stating the period of notice required of the employer and the employee to terminate the employment.

8127 This term must be **notified** to the employee in writing as part of the obligation to give written particulars (¶1405). It is also advisable for the contract to require **written notice** of termination. If it does, oral notice may be ineffective.

8128 The contract may specify a different period of notice in respect of any **probationary period**.

8129 If there is no express term, there is an **implied term** that the employment may be terminated on **reasonable notice**. Determining what is reasonable is a mixed question of law and fact, and will depend on all the circumstances of the case, including the grade and remuneration of the employee, his age, length of service, and the usual practice in that trade or industry. Broad guidelines are given in the following table:

Employee	Reasonable notice
Manual workers	Between 2 and 4 weeks
Skilled/managerial staff	3 months
Senior management/director level	Between 3 and 12 months

EXAMPLE In *Clark v Fahrenheit 451 (Communications) Ltd* [1999] UKEAT 591_99_1910, C, an equity director in a new company, was given 1 month's notice of dismissal after 3 months' service. The EAT held that, taking into account the modest nature of the business, and C's length of service, status and seniority, 3 months' notice would have been reasonable in the circumstances.

Statutory minimum notice

8131 Unless he falls within one of the exceptions detailed below, after he has been continuously employed for 1 month, an **employee is entitled to receive** 1 week's notice (s 86(1) ERA 1996). Once he has been employed for 2 years or more, he is entitled to 1 week's notice for each complete year of continuous employment up to a maximum of 12 weeks' notice as set out in the following table.

Length of continuous employment	Employee's notice entitlement
1 month up to 2 years	1 week
2 years	2 weeks
3 years	3 weeks
4 years	4 weeks
5 years	5 weeks
6 years	6 weeks
7 years	7 weeks
8 years	8 weeks

Length of continuous employment	Employee's notice entitlement
9 years	9 weeks
10 years	10 weeks
11 years	11 weeks
12 years and above	12 weeks

8132 An **employee** is also **obliged to give** statutory minimum notice (or the contractual notice, where greater). The statutory minimum period to be given by an employee who has been continuously employed for 1 month or more is 1 week. Unlike the notice that the employer has to give, this does not increase with length of service (s 86(2) ERA 1996; ¶8181).

8134 **Waiver of rights** An employee **cannot contract out** of his right to statutory minimum notice in advance (s 203 ERA 1996). He can, however, waive his right to notice on a particular occasion (including the right to payment in respect of that notice), or accept pay in lieu of notice (see below) (s 86(3) ERA 1996; *Trotter v Forth Ports Authority* [1991] IRLR 419, CS).

8135 **Specific right to payment** Employees who work out their notice under normal working conditions will be paid according to their contract.

However, in certain circumstances an employee who **does not work** for all or part of the statutory minimum notice period is entitled to be paid a minimum wage where the employment is **terminated by notice** (given by the employer or employee) (s 88(1) ERA 1996), unless the contractual notice to be given by the employer exceeds the statutory minimum by 1 week or more (s 87(4) ERA 1996). This right does not arise if the employment is terminated without notice.

The right **applies** where the employee is:
– ready and willing to work but no work is provided for him;
– incapable of work because of sickness or injury (even where sick pay rights have been exhausted by date of dismissal);
– absent from work wholly or partly because of pregnancy, childbirth, or adoption, or on paternity or parental leave; or
– taking holiday in accordance with his contract.

> EXAMPLE Employees C and D are contractually entitled to 4 weeks' notice. C's statutory minimum notice entitlement is 2 weeks and D's is 6 weeks. During the notice period C and D are both on unpaid parental leave. C's contractual notice is greater than his statutory notice by at least 1 week so he is not entitled to any payment while on parental leave. D, on the other hand, is entitled to be paid a minimum wage for the parental leave period which coincides with the statutory notice period.

8136 There is **no right** to be paid where the employee has given notice and subsequently goes on strike (s 91(2) ERA 1996) or where the employee is on leave at his own request (other than taking contractual holiday entitlement) (s 91(3) ERA 1996), although there may be a separate statutory right to be paid for this time off, for example to look for work in a redundancy situation. Further, if the employee otherwise breaches the contract during the notice period, allowing the employer to terminate immediately, there is no right to payment for the rest of the notice period (s 91(4) ERA 1996).

8137 The **amount payable** is determined by multiplying the number of hours covered by the above circumstances by the employee's hourly rate of pay (i.e. a week's pay (¶2920) divided by the number of normal working hours) (s 88 ERA 1996). Where there are no normal working hours, the amount payable is a week's pay for every week of the notice period in which the employee was ready and willing to do work of a reasonable nature and to earn a week's pay (s 89 ERA 1996).

Any payment actually made (sick pay, maternity pay, adoption pay, paternity pay, holiday pay, etc) can be deducted from the amount payable.

If the employer terminates immediately in breach of contract during the notice period, any payment made is taken into account when assessing damages payable to the employee (s 91(3) ERA 1996).

The employee cannot enforce his right to a minimum wage during what would have been the statutory minimum notice period, but this loss will be taken into account when **calculating damages** for wrongful dismissal (¶8160) (s 91(5) ERA 1996).

State guaranteed payments The employee may be able to recover his statutory notice monies from the National Insurance Fund in certain circumstances, for example where the **employer is insolvent** (¶9045).

8138

Resignation during notice period An employee who is under notice of dismissal may wish to leave before the employer's notice expires. To preserve his right to a redundancy payment, he must either agree with the employer to vary the notice period or serve a **counter-notice** on the employer, following specific statutory provisions (¶9000).

8139

2. Pay in lieu of notice

In the employment contract, the employer can reserve the **right to terminate** the employment **immediately** by a payment in lieu of notice (PILON). This is useful when the employer wants the employee to leave work immediately rather than work out the notice period (an alternative would be to have a contractual right to put the employee on garden leave – see below). The employer may also wish to reserve the right to make a payment in lieu of **notice given by the employee**.

8145

Express PILON

If the employer exercises an express PILON and terminates immediately, there will be **no breach of contract** (the employee remains bound by his post-termination contractual obligations). Express PILONs are usually stated to be based on basic salary alone (i.e. not taking into account the value of any benefits that would have been provided to the employee during the notice period, had it been served), and are normally payable even if the employee finds another job immediately.

8146

If the express PILON is stated to be **discretionary** (i.e. "the employer may make a payment in lieu of notice to the employee..."), the employer has a choice whether to exercise the right to pay in lieu or whether to give actual notice (for example, in order to preserve restrictive covenants). Employers could also terminate in breach of contract (¶8148) and choose whether to pay a sum representing damages for wrongful dismissal (although whether HMRC consider this to be a payment for damages rather than a PILON will depend on all the circumstances (¶3135)).

If **dismissing in reliance** upon a **PILON** clause, the letter of dismissal must **clearly state** that the employment is being terminated immediately and, crucially, that a PILON is being relied upon (i.e. that no actual notice is being given). If this is not done, even if the contract has a PILON clause, the employee is entitled to view the dismissal as a repudiatory breach and can affirm his contract until his notice period would expire. Depending on the terms of the contract, it may also be necessary for the payment to be made before the termination date can be effective (*Société Générale v Geys* [2012] UKSC 63).

EXAMPLE In *Geys v Societe Generale*, a bank told its managing director, G, on 29 November that it had decided to terminate his employment with immediate effect, and required him to leave work at once. A letter was given to this effect. His contract provided for 3 months' notice, but included a power to terminate immediately by making a payment in lieu of notice. The parties started negotiating a settlement. During the course of the negotiations, the bank paid a sum of money into G's bank account on 18 December without any explanation. G responded on 2 January by reserving his position about whether the payment was accepted and affirming his contract. The employer then wrote to him on 4 January confirming his dismissal and asserting that he had been paid in lieu of notice on 18 December. The Supreme Court held that the effective date of termination was 6 January: G was not informed that he was being paid in lieu of notice (and therefore being dismissed according to the terms of his contract) until he received the employer's letter dated 4 January (and due to provisions in the employer's handbook this meant that the date G officially received the letter was 6 January).

8147 Where PILON clauses are in the contracts of employees who commit acts of **gross misconduct**, or where other conduct arises that allows an employer to summarily dismiss without notice, then certain complications can arise. For example, confusion can be caused where an employer purports to be summarily dismissing for gross misconduct but also makes a payment in lieu of notice. The EAT has confirmed that in such circumstances an employer does not waive the right to summarily dismiss (or the right to avoid paying benefits such as pension contributions that would have fallen due during the notice period) by choosing to also make a payment in lieu of notice, but care should be taken where employers mix summary dismissal with PILON payments in order that the reason for and manner of dismissal are clear (*Benveniste v Kingston University* [2009] UKEAT 0176_08_1805).

Another area where employers should be particularly careful is where **repudiatory conduct is discovered after notice** has been given and a PILON payment has been promised. In such circumstances, employers are not able to rely on the repudiatory conduct to avoid making the PILON payment, because the employee's claim would be a debt claim, which cannot be won on the basis of knowledge acquired after the fact (in contrast to claims for damages, such as where wrongful dismissal is at issue) (*Cavenagh v William Evans Ltd* [2012] EWCA Civ 697). To avoid this problem, PILON clauses should be drafted either to include an allowance for the PILON monies to be repaid if gross misconduct is discovered at a later date, or to make it a condition of payment that the employee has not committed a repudiatory breach.

No express PILON

8148 If there is no express PILON, the employer could terminate immediately (in **breach of contract**) and pay a sum representing damages for wrongful dismissal (see below), in which case the employee would have to mitigate his loss (for example, by finding another job), and damages could reflect the employee's net loss (i.e. salary after deduction of tax or national insurance). The employee would, in theory, have a right to bring an employment tribunal claim for damages, but the employer's payment may (depending on its calculation) in fact extinguish his loss. If the employer terminates in breach in this way, the employee will not be bound by any post-termination contractual obligations (such as express confidentiality undertakings and restrictive covenants). Employers should be aware, however, that in such a case the payment of a PILON will not release them from any express settlement agreement obligations they have towards the employee (*CRS Computers Ltd v Mackenzie* [2002] UKEAT 1259_01_2504).

Where an employment contract contains an express notice provision, but no express payment in lieu provision (PILON), a **PILON cannot be implied** and an employer will be in breach of contract if he terminates the contract without notice and gives a payment in lieu of notice (*Morrish v NTL Group Ltd* [2007] CSIH 56).

Difference in tax treatment

8149 If the contract contains a PILON (even where this is discretionary), the payment will be subject to the usual income tax and National Insurance deductions. In contrast, damages for wrongful dismissal can be paid tax free up to £30,000 and are not subject to National Insurance deductions. See ¶¶3123+, 3134+ for detail on the taxation of termination payments.

3. Garden leave

8150 Garden leave describes the employer's ability to require the employee to stay at home during the notice period while continuing to pay him as if he were at work. In certain cases, an employer may be able to obtain a garden leave injunction to restrain the employee from competing during the notice period. Garden leave is discussed in detail at ¶2529.

B. Dismissal without notice

8155 An employer is entitled to dismiss the employee without notice (known as **summary dismissal**) if he is in fundamental breach (the contract can specify circumstances in which he may do so, such as for **gross misconduct** (¶6540)). The service agreements of directors and senior employees should also expressly set out the circumstances in which the employment may be terminated without notice.

If the employer is **not entitled** to dismiss summarily, he will be in breach of contract if he does not give the required period of notice (known as **wrongful dismissal**), entitling the employee to a remedy (¶8160).

Even if notice is given (where required), the dismissal may be **unfair**. Conversely, a wrongful dismissal is not necessarily always an unfair dismissal (*BSC Sports and Social Club v Morgan* [1987] IRLR 391, EAT). In determining a wrongful dismissal claim, the tribunal must decide what, as a matter of fact, actually happened and whether what the employee actually did was so fundamental a breach as to justify instant dismissal. In contrast to the test in unfair dismissal cases, the employer's "reasonable belief" of what happened is irrelevant (*London Central Bus Company Ltd v Nana-Addai* [2011] UKEAT 0204_11_2909).

If the employer exercises a PILON (¶8145) and makes a **payment in lieu of notice**, a dismissal without notice will not be a wrongful dismissal. In those circumstances, the employee would have to sue for a sum due under the contract, rather than damages for breach (*Abrahams v Performing Rights Society* [1995] IRLR 486, CA).

The termination of a **fixed-term contract** not determinable on notice prior to its expiry, and the termination of a **contract for a specific purpose** prior to completion of that purpose, will also amount to wrongful dismissal.

8156 The most common remedy for wrongful dismissal is damages, although in rare circumstances an injunction may be granted (¶1732). This section will focus on the **calculation of damages**. As for all breach of contract claims, the **basic aim** when calculating damages is to put the employee, so far as an award of money can do so, in the same situation as if the contract had been properly performed by the employer. If a claim for wrongful dismissal is made in a tribunal, any award is subject to a **statutory maximum** of £25,000. The civil courts are not subject to any such limit.

1. Calculation of damages

Period of loss

8160 In making the calculation, the law assumes that if the employer had not wrongfully terminated the contract, he would have terminated lawfully at the first point when he could have done so (*Lavarack v Woods of Colchester Ltd* [1967] 1 QB 278, CA). The employee's losses are, therefore, limited by reference to that period. This approach contrasts with that taken in unfair dismissal cases where an employee may be awarded compensation for several years' loss of earnings, even where the contract could be terminated by, for example, 3 months' notice.

> EXAMPLE
> 1. Employee E is contractually entitled to 3 months' **notice**. The employer dismisses him without any notice (in circumstances where he was not entitled to do so). E's losses will be limited to the 3-month period of notice which he should have been given. If E had been dismissed with only 1 month's notice, his losses would be calculated on the basis of the balance of the notice period, i.e. 2 months.
> 2. Employee F has a **fixed-term contract** for 2 years (not terminable by notice prior to expiry of the fixed term). The employer dismisses him (in breach of contract) after 6 months. F's losses will be calculated on the basis of the remaining 18 months of the contract.

3. The employer dismisses Employee G without notice (in circumstances where he was not entitled to do so). G's contract entitles him to 3 months' notice, but also incorporates a **contractual disciplinary procedure**, which would have taken 2 weeks to follow properly. The earliest the employment could lawfully have been terminated is therefore 3 months and 2 weeks after the date on which it was actually terminated and losses will be calculated accordingly (*Focsa Services (UK) Ltd v Birkett* [1996] IRLR 325, EAT).

Types of loss

8161 General principles are discussed at ¶1700. The particular types of loss which may be included in the calculation of damages for wrongful dismissal are set out below.

8162 **Loss of earnings and benefits** Damages are calculated by reference to the employee's contractual pay and benefits, which may include pay, commission, bonus, tips, pensions, and share options. If an employee has a contractual right to a **bonus or a pay rise** during the notice period (or fixed term), this will be taken into account in calculating loss of earnings. Many employment contracts refer to discretionary bonuses or pay rises, where the employer may decide to make such payments but is not obliged to. The court or tribunal is entitled to form a view as to what the employer would have done, and is to assume that such discretion would have been exercised reasonably (*Clark v BET plc* [1997] IRLR 348, QBD). Even a bonus clause which appears to give the employer completely unrestricted discretion must be exercised in good faith and not irrationally or perversely (¶2833).

Damages extend to **accrued pension rights** to which the employee would have become entitled had he been given the correct period of notice (*Silvey v Pendragon plc* [2001] IRLR 685, CA).

8163 As the purpose of compensation is to put the employee in the position he would have been in had the employer not breached the contract, the calculation needs to **take account of the tax** he would have paid on his earnings and other benefits. The loss is, therefore, the **net salary and the net value** of any other benefits (such as a company car) after deducting the tax and national insurance contributions which would have been payable.

8164 **Expenses** Expenses that have been incurred as a result of the breach will be included if they would not have been incurred had there been a lawful termination of the contract.

8165 **Loss of statutory rights** An employee who has been summarily dismissed in breach of the employer's contractual **disciplinary procedures** cannot recover damages through a wrongful dismissal claim for the loss of the chance to claim unfair dismissal (*Wise Group (The) v Mitchell* [2005] UKEAT 0693_04_1102 applying *Virgin Net Ltd v Harper* [2003] UKEAT 0111_02_0907 confirmed on appeal *Harper v Virgin Net Ltd* [2004] IRLR 390, CA, and *Johnson v Unisys Ltd* [2001] IRLR 279, HL).

> MEMO POINTS   In coming to its decision in this case, the EAT considered that its earlier decision in *Raspin v United News Shops Ltd* [1999] IRLR 9, EAT was wrongly decided in light of *Virgin Net Ltd v Harper* and *Johnson v Unisys Ltd*.

8166 **Loss due to injury to feelings, etc** Compensation is not recoverable for damages for ongoing financial loss due to **injury to feelings**, **psychiatric injury**, **loss of reputation** and **inability to find new employment** arising from an employee's **dismissal or the manner of his dismissal** (*Johnson v Unisys Ltd* [2001] IRLR 279, HL; *Dunnachie v Kingston upon Hull City Council* [2004] IRLR 727, HL). Unfairness in the circumstances of dismissal does not give rise to a common law action, whether in contract or tort, but must be subject to employment tribunal proceedings.

However, a claim in respect of injury arising from events which are **independent** of, and **prior to**, a dismissal can be brought, provided that the events do not immediately surround the dismissal itself (*McCabe v Cornwall County Council and anor* heard jointly with *Eastwood and Williams v Magnox Electric plc* [2004] IRLR 733, HL). In these cases, the employees had a cause of action relating to the financial loss they had suffered as a result of psychiatric injury caused by their employers' treatment of them in the events leading up to dismissal, which was independent of the action they brought relating to the unfairness of the dismissal.

However, the situation is different where the employee has a claim for breach of an express contractual term (¶¶1726, 6532).

MEMO POINTS However, the implied term of trust and confidence in accordance with a provision in the contract of employment entitling the employer to terminate the **contract with notice for "good cause shown"** only ceases once a decision to dismiss has been made and consequently it subsists during the employer's investigation and evaluation of disciplinary charges (*King v University Court of the University of St Andrews* [2002] IRLR 252, CS).

In rare cases, financial loss associated with **loss of reputation** resulting from a breach of the implied term of trust and confidence during the employment relationship ("**stigma damages**") may be awarded (*Malik v Bank of Credit and Commerce International SA* [1997] IRLR 462, HL), although actual (and not merely hypothetical) loss must be shown, and the stigma must be shown to be the cause of the former employee's failure to find work (*Bank of Credit and Commerce International SA v Ali (No 3)* [2002] IRLR 460, CA).

8167

> **EXAMPLE** In *Malik v Bank of Credit and Commerce International SA*, the bank went into liquidation after having operated for some time in a corrupt and dishonest manner in breach of the implied term of mutual trust and confidence. The employee was entitled to compensation for the financial loss associated with his damaged employment prospects, which had been tainted by the employer's reputation.

Adjustments to net loss

Once the employee's net loss has been assessed, adjustments are made to increase or reduce the award as set out below. Note that an employee who becomes entitled to a **pension** on dismissal is not required to set off the amount which he receives from his pension against any damages for wrongful dismissal (*Hopkins v Norcross plc* [1992] IRLR 304, QBD).

8169

Discount for accelerated receipt If the award contains an element of future loss, which is most likely where there is a long notice period or a fixed-term contract with a long period to run when the award is made, the award will be adjusted to reflect the fact that the employee is receiving an accelerated payment (see ¶8600 for provision for decelerated receipt in relation to unfair dismissal). Instead of receiving his salary in monthly or weekly instalments over a period of time, he will receive his **damages in a lump sum** in advance of the due dates for payment. He will be able to invest this and so a lump sum of, for example, £24,000 paid on 1 January is in practice worth more than 12 monthly payments of £2,000 made over the course of the year. The lump sum is therefore discounted to reflect the amount of compensation awarded and the potential return on investment.

8170

Mitigation The employee has a duty to mitigate his loss, and one way for him to do so is to **seek alternative employment**. If the employer has offered new employment on reasonable terms, the employee may have failed to mitigate his loss if he refuses the offer (¶8620).

The employer will be given credit for **sums earned** by the employee **from another employer** during the period for which compensation is being awarded (or which the employee could have earned had he taken reasonable steps to mitigate his loss). There is no obligation to mitigate if the employer exercises a contractual right to make a **payment in lieu of notice** (¶8145). Mitigation is discussed in more detail in the section on compensation for unfair dismissal (¶8620).

8171

State benefits **Unemployment benefit** is set off (*Parsons v BNM Laboratories Ltd* [1964] 1 QB 95, CA). However, the court has to take into account any loss which is suffered by the employee as a result of the fact that, by not giving him notice, the employer has caused him to claim benefit earlier than would have been the case, so that he will also exhaust his entitlement earlier than he would have done (*Westwood v Secretary of State for Employment* [1984] IRLR 209, HL).

8172

Taxation Damages for wrongful dismissal in excess of £30,000 will be taxable (tax being levied on the excess only) (¶3125; s 406 ITEPA 2003). Where the **damages exceed £30,000**, this tax liability also needs to be brought into the calculation to avoid the employee suffering double taxation. The approach taken is to calculate the total net damages and then gross that figure up to **take account of the tax** which will have to be paid on any excess over £30,000 (*Shove v Downs Surgical plc* [1984] IRLR 17, QBD).

8173

2. Sample calculation

8175 The following calculation illustrates the general principles described above.

> **EXAMPLE** A is employed under a contract which entitled him to 12 months' notice of termination. He is summarily dismissed in breach of that contract. His salary under the contract was £80,000 per annum and in addition he had other benefits with a taxable value of £10,000 per annum.
> He has been able to find a lower paid job which, over the course of the 12-month period for which damages are being calculated, will enable him to earn £15,000 after tax.
> Calculation based on tax rates and allowances for 2012/13.
>
> a. *Calculation of award before grossing up for tax*
>
> | | £ |
> |---|---:|
> | Gross salary for 12 months: | 80,000 |
> | Gross benefits for 12 months: | 10,000 |
> | **Total gross loss**: | 90,000 |
> | Tax on gross salary and benefits: | |
> | Deduct personal allowance: | (8,105) |
> | Taxable income: | 81,895 |
> | Income tax @ 20% on £0 – £34,370 | (6,874) |
> | Income tax @ 40% on taxable income on £34,371 – £150,000 | (19,010) |
> | **Total tax payable** | (25,884) |
> | **Total net loss after tax**: | 64,116 |
> | Less: | |
> | Mitigation | (15,000) |
> | | 49,116 |
> | Deduction for accelerated receipt (e.g. 5%): | (2,456) |
> | Total: | __46,660__ |
>
> b. *Grossing up for tax*
>
> | | £ |
> |---|---:|
> | Award to be grossed up: | 46,660 |
> | Less: tax-free element | (30,000) |
> | Amount to be grossed up: | 16,660 |
>
> To gross up for tax, the sum of £16,660 would be added to any other taxable income which A had (or could be expected to have) for the period in question to determine how much income tax would be payable on that sum. Assuming this results in a finding that it would be taxed at the basic rate of 20%, this would mean tax of £3,332.
> The gross award made to A would therefore be:
>
> | | £ |
> |---|---:|
> | Pre-grossing up award: | 46,660 |
> | Plus: grossing up sum: | 3,332 |
> | Total: | __49,992__ |

3. Overlap with unfair dismissal awards

8177 An employee might claim both unfair dismissal and wrongful dismissal. To some extent, the awards made may overlap. However, the employee is not entitled to be compensated for the same loss twice (*Babcock FATA Ltd v Addison* [1987] IRLR 173, CA).

Neither the **basic award** nor any **additional award** is set off against damages for wrongful dismissal as they are not based on any loss suffered by the employee and so there is no question of double compensation.

The **compensatory award** may well overlap with wrongful dismissal damages, in which case some **set-off** will be required. It will be necessary to identify those elements of the compensatory award (assuming that award has already been made) which cover losses which would otherwise be included in the damages for wrongful dismissal. Obviously, if the wrongful dismissal case has been heard first then the reverse process will need to be carried out by the employment tribunal in calculating the compensatory award. If the cases are heard together, the tribunal will adopt a method of calculating damages to ensure that the employee is not compensated twice.

C. Resignation

8180 Termination by the employee is known as resignation and may be **with or without notice**. The employer can reserve the right to make a payment in lieu of notice given by the employee (¶8145). If the employee resigns, there will be no dismissal (i.e. the employee will not be entitled to bring a claim for redundancy, unfair or wrongful dismissal), unless he has resigned in response to the employer's fundamental breach (i.e. the employee has been constructively dismissed – ¶8230), has resigned during the employer's notice period by serving a statutory counter-notice (¶9000), or has been forced to resign.

8181 **Notice periods** As for employer termination with notice (see above), the employee must give the longer of the **contractual** (express or implied) or statutory notice period. The **statutory minimum** period to be given by an employee who has been continuously employed for 1 month or more is 1 week (this does not increase with length of service) (s 86(2) ERA 1996). See ¶8135 for employee rights to payment during the statutory notice period.

The employee may ask to be **released before the expiry** of his notice period. If this is acceptable to the employer, he should ask the employee to confirm in writing the agreed termination date, and the fact that the employer is released from any further obligations under the contract. Without such confirmation, the employee could argue that the employer merely agreed to release him from his obligation to work out his notice.

8182 **Communication of resignation** There are **no formal requirements** for a resignation but it must be communicated to the employer either orally, in writing or by conduct. It is not, therefore, strictly necessary for the employee clearly to state his intention to resign as this may be inferred from his conduct and the surrounding circumstances (*Johnson v Monty Smith Garages Ltd*, EAT case 657/79). It may be sufficient for the employee to walk out and fail to return to work. There is no need for the employer to **accept** the resignation.

Notice of an **intention to resign** (but without specifying a date) is unlikely to be a valid and effective termination of the employment (*Ely v YKK Fasteners (UK) Ltd* [1993] IRLR 500, CA).

> EXAMPLE In *Ely v YKK Fasteners (UK) Ltd*, E told the employer that he planned to emigrate in order to take up a job offer. The employer recruited a replacement but E subsequently changed his mind. The employer claimed that E had resigned but this was not the case as no formal notice had been given and no termination date could be ascertained from the information he had provided.

8183 **Pressure to resign** If the employer forces the employee to resign, there will be an express dismissal (*Martin v MBS Fastenings (Glynwed) Distribution Ltd* [1983] IRLR 198, CA; *Bickerton v Inver House Distillers Ltd*, EAT case 656/91). If the parties agree that the employee should resign as an alternative to completing disciplinary proceedings (the end result of which could be dismissal), the agreed resignation will not amount to a dismissal (*Staffordshire County Council v Donovan* [1981] IRLR 108, EAT). If the employee is offered an inducement (for example, a financial incentive) to resign, there may be an agreed resignation or alternatively a termination by mutual agreement (¶8260).

The Court of Appeal has given **guidance** as to when a resignation is **by mutual consent or** when it is **forced** resulting in constructive dismissal (*Sandhu v Jan de Rijik Transport Ltd* [2007]

ICR 1137, CA). Resignation, the Court has stated, implies some form of **negotiation and discussion**; it predicates a result which is a genuine choice on the part of the employee. If the employee has had an opportunity to take independent advice and then offers to resign, that fact is powerful evidence pointing towards resignation rather than dismissal. In analysing the case law surrounding the matter, the Court found that there were no cases in which the employee was held to have resigned where the resignation had occurred during the same interview/discussion in which the question of dismissal was raised. Further, in no case was an employee held to have resigned in which the termination of the employee's employment had occurred in a single interview.

> EXAMPLE In *Sandhu v Jan de Rijik Transport Ltd*, S was told to attend a meeting, but was not told in advance what the meeting was to be about. At the meeting, S was informed that his contract was going to end and as a result S negotiated a settlement with regard to his employment ending. S brought a claim for unfair dismissal. The employer argued that as S had negotiated a settlement at that meeting it showed that S had resigned by mutual consent. The Court of Appeal rejected this argument. It could not be said that S had negotiated freely as he had had no warning as to the purpose of the meeting, no advice nor time to reflect. In the Court's judgment, all S had done in negotiating a settlement at that meeting was to do his best on his own to salvage what he could from the inevitable fact that he was going to be dismissed. This was the very antithesis of free, unpressurised negotiation and consequently S had not resigned but had been dismissed.

8184 **Resignation without notice** If the employee does not give the required period of notice, he will be in **breach of contract** unless he has resigned in response to a fundamental breach by the employer (¶8230). There is an argument that the employer can choose whether or not to accept this breach but in practice the employment terminates regardless of the employer's wishes and the question of acceptance is in practice relevant only to establishing the date of termination. For example, the employer may insist on notice if there is a garden leave clause so that he can seek a **garden leave** injunction to ensure that the employee does not compete during the notice period (¶2645). The employee cannot be compelled to work out his notice and although the employer could sue for damages, such actions are rare (¶1750). If the employer withholds the employee's wages, he may be liable for making an unlawful deduction (¶3050).

D. Retirement

8199 Prior to the abolition of the default retirement age, a retirement was a potentially fair dismissal by the employer. As a direct consequence of the abolition of the default retirement procedure, retirement is no longer a potentially fair reason for dismissal in itself; any retirement dismissal must fall within one of the other potentially fair grounds for dismissal, most commonly some other substantial reason (SOSR). If an employee chooses to take **early retirement**, this will usually be a **resignation** rather than a dismissal (in some cases it will be a termination by **mutual agreement** – ¶8260).

On retirement, the employee may be entitled to certain **benefits** (in particular, a **pension**).

> MEMO POINTS The default retirement age was abolished with effect from 6 April 2011, subject to transitional provisions (under the transitional provisions with the maximum extension, 5 October 2012 was the last possible retirement date for those who attained age 65 on or before 30 September 2011 provided 6 to 12 months' notice to retire was given on or before 5 April 2011). Unless it falls within the transitional provisions, any dismissal because of age taking place on or after 6 April 2011 constitutes direct age discrimination.

1. Retiring age

8200 As a direct consequence of the abolition of the default retirement age, 65 can no longer be regarded as the "safe" age at which employees can be retired. To avoid claims for unfair dismissal and age discrimination, it is now necessary to show objective justification for dismissing at this or any set age for retirement. Employers can choose whether to keep a fixed retirement age (or perhaps different ages for different roles) or decide on a case-by-case basis when to retire an employee. In either event, the dismissal will be for "some other substantial reason" and they will have to objectively justify the decision to retire. This may often be difficult to do unless there is a really strong justification (see ¶8209).

Contractual retiring age

8203 The employer may have a **retirement policy** giving a contractual retiring age for the employment (referred to here as the CRA), or one may have arisen by virtue of an established **custom or practice** (¶1180). Note that mere comments made at a job interview regarding the retirement age of the position's predecessor cannot be interpreted as implying a commitment by the employer that the job applicant can retire at the same age as his predecessor (*Tarbert (Loch Fyne) Harbour Authority v Currie*, EAT(S) case 0033/05).

If the employer wishes to **change the CRA**, the normal principles of variation of contract (as discussed at ¶1600) apply.

8204 In order to **avoid liability for sex discrimination**, the CRA must be the same for men and women (*Marshall v Southampton and South-West Hampshire Area Health Authority (Teaching)* [1986] IRLR 140, ECJ). The **state pension age** cannot be a CRA as it is differs according to sex and year of birth. The CRA may, however, differ for **different occupations**.

In order to avoid liability for age discrimination, the CRA must be objectively justified, i.e. the employer can demonstrate that it is a proportionate means of achieving a legitimate aim (see ¶8209 and outlined at ¶5615).

> MEMO POINTS The **state pension age** is to be equalised at age 65 between April 2016 and November 2018. The retirement age for both sexes will rise to 66 by October 2020 (Pensions Act 2011).
> **Pensionable age under occupational pension schemes** (which must also be the same for men and women as pension is "pay" for the purposes of EU equal pay provisions (*Barber v Guardian Royal Exchange Assurance Group* [1990] IRLR 240, ECJ)) is distinct from both the state pension age and any CRA, although it can be the same.

8205 The Department of Work and Pensions (DWP) **code of practice** gives standards of good practice in employment, although it has no formal statutory authority. The code **recommends** that employers:
– base any retirement policy on business needs while also giving individuals as much choice as possible;
– carefully evaluate the loss to their business in terms of skills and abilities in cases of early retirement and consider alternatives to early retirement;
– avoid using age as the sole criterion for early retirement schemes (subject to pension rules);
– use flexible retirement schemes, where possible;
– use phased retirement, where possible, to allow employees to alter the balance of their working and personal lives and prepare for full retirement (also preparing the business for the loss of the employee's skills); and
– make pre-retirement support available for employees.

Normal retiring age

8206 Despite the abolition of the default retirement age, some employers may decide to keep a normal retirement age (referred to here as the NRA) (or perhaps different ages for different roles) which they believe they can objectively justify for the purposes of defending any age discrimination claim. Note though that the existence of an NRA does not automatically render any dismissal at that age automatically fair: the NRA must be objectively justified if the employer is to avoid liability for age discrimination and a fair procedure must be followed if the dismissal is to be deemed fair for "some other substantial reason" (SOSR).

If there is a contractual retiring age (**CRA**) (¶8203), which is well known and observed, this is the normal retiring age (referred to here as the NRA). Where there is **no CRA**, the NRA in respect of an employee is the normal retiring age for employees in the employer's undertaking who hold, or have held, the same kind of position as the employee concerned.

Where there is no CRA, or there is a CRA but it is not well known and observed, in order to determine the NRA, one must examine the reasonable expectations of the group of employees holding the employee's position at the date of dismissal. The relevant group is identified by reference to their status, nature of work and terms of employment, including any terms dealing in particular with retirement (*Barber v Thames Television plc* [1992] IRLR 410, CA). The expectations of the group are determined by reference to the group in general and not merely those employees approaching retirement (*Brooks v British Telecommunications plc* [1992] IRLR 66, CA). Normal is not to be equated with usual, which suggests a narrow, statistical approach.

If the employee occupies a **unique position**, in that there is no other employee employed by the undertaking with the same job, it does not mean that such an employee does not have an NRA (*Wall v British Compressed Air Society* [2004] ICR 408, EAT; confirmed on appeal [2004] IRLR 147, CA). In such cases, the NRA will ordinarily be the CRA.

> MEMO POINTS   Note that an employee's NRA **does not transfer** under TUPE (*Cross and anor v British Airways plc* [2006] ICR 1239, CA). See chapter 24 for further details.

8207 If the **CRA is expressly abandoned** or **regularly departed from** in practice, it will be displaced as the NRA as the group's reasonable expectations will have changed (*Waite v Government Communications Headquarters* [1983] IRLR 341, HL; *Whittle v Manpower Services Commission* [1987] IRLR 441, EAT). However, **limited exceptions** to the CRA will not displace it as the NRA (*Barclays Bank plc v O'Brien* [1994] IRLR 580, CA).

If the employer lawfully **changes the CRA** and the relevant employees are made aware of this change, their expectations will also change and the NRA will be altered (*Barclays Bank plc v O'Brien*).

If, however, the employer attempts to **lower the CRA in breach of contract**, it seems that the NRA will not be affected (*Bratko v Beloit Walmsley Ltd* [1995] UKEAT 798_94_1109). If the employee refuses to agree to a lower CRA, the employer could terminate the current contract by notice and offer new employment on revised terms (¶1655).

8208 On the basis that an employee with a CRA has a reasonable expectation that he will not be retired before this age, the **NRA cannot be lower than the CRA** (*Royal and Sun Alliance Insurance Group plc v Payne* [2005] UKEAT 0122_05_0108). An employer who unilaterally makes the NRA lower than the CRA will therefore be acting in breach of contract.

2. Fair retirement procedure

8209 As a direct result of the abolition of the default retirement age, retirement is no longer a fair reason for dismissal in its own right, and fair retirement dismissals will be classed as being for "some other substantial reason" (SOSR) (¶¶8530+). To avoid claims for unfair dismissal and age discrimination, employers who wish to retire an employee without his consent will only be able to do so using their **own compulsory retirement age** (CRA or NRA) if it can be objectively justified, and this will not always be easy to establish (for an explanation of what constitutes a CRA or NRA see ¶¶8203-8208). Any forced retirement using the CRA or NRA will have to follow a **fair procedure**, though the Government has declined to give further statutory guidelines as to what will constitute a fair procedure. Such dismissals will therefore have to comply with the normal unfair dismissal procedures (¶¶8435+).

To assist, Acas have issued their own guidance for employers entitled "Working without the default retirement age", which provides useful information on what might constitute a fair procedure in these circumstances including giving reasonable notice, consistency of treatment (unless there are exceptional circumstances) and considering any employees' requests to work past the CRA or NRA. The guidance also includes extensive information on how best to communicate with employees to discuss their plans for the future including suggestions such as:

- asking open questions;
- asking employees about their plans for the short, medium and long term; and
- having these discussions with all levels of employees and not just those nearing retirement.

If an employer thinks that he can objectively **justify** a CRA or NRA, he will need to be sure that it is a proportionate means of achieving a legitimate aim (outlined at ¶5615), for example possibly workforce planning, health and safety (which would apply in jobs that require an exceptional level of physical or mental agility, such as air traffic controllers or those in some sectors of the emergency services, although a better approach may be to rely on any extensive fitness testing to identify those unable to perform the role whatever their age and dismiss on the grounds of incapacity if necessary), or encouraging the recruitment of younger workers (*Hörnfeldt v Posten Meddelande AB, Case C-141/11* [2012] EUECJ C-141/11). If they can satisfy this test and follow a fair procedure (which will be governed by the unfair dismissal rules; ¶¶8435+) then the dismissal will be fair. It should be noted that the Court of Justice of the European Union has handed down a judgment that addresses various issues in reference to the objective justification of a compulsory retirement age (*Fuchs and Köhler v Land Hessen, Cases C-159/10 and C-160/10* [2011] EUECJ C-160/10). The judgment appears to give a green flag to justifying compulsory retirement on grounds of cost (considered alongside other factors, which is not dissimilar to our current position in relation to discrimination generally, see ¶5310), to help promote a younger workforce, and to prevent disputes as to older employees' fitness to work. The court also suggested that a test of "reasonableness" was appropriate, rather than one of proportionality. The difference between a test of "reasonableness" and one of proportionality is minimal, though it is interesting that the court decided to use a different test to that previously established without offering an explanation. Indeed, as a whole, the judgment is far from clear, which is evidenced by the numerous different interpretations by commentators. What is clear is that although employers may look to this judgment for general guidance, reliance on any of the specific means of justification is risky, not least because this case related to German public sector workers and their state compulsory retirement age. Whilst the objective justification issues are still relevant to UK retirements where employers want to use their own contractual retirement age, some issues considered in this judgment, such as acting consistently with national social policies, are no longer relevant to cases within the UK.

In respect of a partnership, a compulsory retirement age of 65 may be justified by such aims as (*Seldon v Clarkson Wright and Jakes (a partnership)* [2012] UKSC 16):
- providing promotion opportunities for younger employees;
- facilitating succession planning; and
- promoting a good working environment by reducing the potential for performance management procedures to arise involving older workers.

The Supreme Court in *Seldon* noted that the partner being subjected to compulsory retirement will, at some earlier point of his career, have benefited from the legitimate aims identified. They also hinted clearly in the decision that, in considering objective justification, the tribunal in this case should take into account the fact that, at the time this compulsory retirement took place, there was a default retirement age for employees of 65 (this, of course, no longer applies). The case was sent back to the employment tribunal to consider whether the choice of 65, the firm's chosen retirement age, was a proportionate means of achieving these aims. Employers should also note though that this case concerned partners and so there was more equal bargaining power between the parties than in relation to the classic employer/employee relationship. It may be, therefore, that such arguments are less likely to succeed in an employment case on justifying a retirement age.

In summary employers generally should **be cautious** in imposing a compulsory retirement age and should consider the matter very carefully. They must be able to provide concrete evidence to justify their reasoning as they will need to show that the chosen age was based on a legitimate aim, such as workforce planning or on health and safety grounds, and is a proportionate means of achieving that aim. This is unlikely to be easy.

> MEMO POINTS   If an employer feels that an employee nearing the age that he would expect that employee to retire is **not performing adequately**, normal capability or performance management procedures should be followed (¶¶8451+).

3. Early retirement

Impact on pension entitlement

8228 Pension schemes are discussed at ¶3400. The relevant scheme rules may allow the employee to draw a pension before the employee reaches pensionable age, typically with the employer's consent. Early retirement may be offered as an alternative to redundancy and the scheme may provide for one or more of the following:
- immediate payment of the employee's full pension (with no reduction for early payment);
- payment of part of the pension as a lump sum;
- adding additional years' service for the purpose of calculating pension entitlement; and
- allowing the employee to pay all or part of any termination payment into the scheme in order to increase entitlement.

> MEMO POINTS   HMRC-approved occupational schemes cannot pay pensions before age 50, except in cases of ill health.

Retirement due to ill health

8229 If an employee is dismissed on the grounds of ill health, the employer may potentially be liable for unfair dismissal and disability discrimination. When dealing with an employee who is on long-term sick leave, the employer may therefore wish to consider whether early retirement could be an option. Ill health retirement may entitle the employee to pension benefits.

The rules of an **occupational scheme** normally provide for early retirement due to ill health, commonly granting immediate payment of full pension, perhaps with additional pensionable service added on in order to calculate an enhanced ill health pension. Some schemes apply a tiered system, such that full prospective pensionable service is used for complete incapacity and actual pensionable service is used when the employee can do some work (but not his normal duties).

Some schemes will also allow for commutation on the grounds of **serious ill health**. If so, and the employee's life expectancy is severely shortened, the scheme will commute the whole of his retirement benefit into a lump sum.

Medical evidence is normally required to prove that the employee's ill health prevents him from carrying out his normal employment. Often, the incapacity must be expected or likely to be permanent, with provisions for suspension of pension payments if the employee is able to resume work before reaching pensionable age.

The employer is bound by his duty to act in **good faith** when deciding whether the employee meets any definition of incapacity (*Mihlenstedt v Barclays Bank International Ltd and Barclays Bank plc* [1989] IRLR 522, CA) and the scheme **rules must be construed** in a purposive and practical way (*Derby Daily Telegraph Ltd v The Pensions Ombudsman and Thompson* [1999] IRLR 476, ChD).

> MEMO POINTS   **Personal pensions** can also come into payment early, at a reduced rate, and the employee should check his policy, if necessary.

E. Constructive dismissal

8230 If the employer commits a **fundamental breach** of contract (¶1715), the employee is entitled to treat himself as discharged (i.e. he can immediately terminate the employment without notice) (*Western Excavating (ECC) Ltd v Sharp* [1978] IRLR 27, CA). The contract will not automatically terminate; the **employee must resign** (he normally does so without notice but may give notice if he wishes) before bringing a claim based on the fact that he has been constructively dismissed.

It is important to note that it is only the **employer's actions** that must be considered in determining whether there has been a fundamental breach justifying constructive dismissal (*Tolson v Governing Body of Mixenden Community School* [2003] UKEAT 0124_03_1609). Consequently, it is irrelevant whether or not the employee failed to utilise the employer's grievance procedure as a response to his employer's actions. However, an **employee** is not entitled to treat himself as discharged if he is **already in breach** of the duty of trust and confidence before the acts he complains of take place (*Aberdeen City Council v McNeill* [2010] IRLR 374, EAT).

> EXAMPLE In *Aberdeen City Council v McNeill*, an employee resigned and claimed constructive dismissal while he was under investigation for a number of disciplinary offences, including sexual harassment, drunkenness at work and breaches of confidentiality. He was successful in his claim for unfair dismissal in the employment tribunal. The EAT overturned the decision, finding that the tribunal had failed to take proper account of the claimant's own breaches of contract. It held that he was not entitled to terminate his contract on the ground of the employer's conduct toward him, as he was himself in breach of the duty of trust and confidence before the acts he complained of took place.

8231 An **employer** who has committed a fundamental breach of contract cannot cure it by his **subsequent actions**. However, if the employer takes steps to put matters right after a fundamental breach this does invite the employee to affirm the contract, but the employee is under no obligation to do so and he does not lose the right to accept the breach and claim constructive dismissal (*Buckland v Bournemouth University Higher Education Corp* [2010] IRLR 445, CA). This is not the case with regard to threatened or anticipatory breaches (see ¶8233).

8232 Fundamental breach often occurs in the context of a variation. If the employee **agrees to a variation**, there will be no breach of contract (and so no question of constructive dismissal). If the employer **unilaterally imposes radically different terms**, there may be a deemed express dismissal (¶1652).

An employer may also commit a fundamental breach if he unjustifiably imposes a **disproportionate disciplinary sanction** on an employee (¶6633).

A breach by the employer of the **implied term of trust and confidence** will always be a repudiatory breach for the purposes of a claim of constructive dismissal. For further details as to what amounts to a breach and the duration of the obligation, see ¶¶1245+.

> MEMO POINTS Constructive dismissal in the context of a **business transfer** is discussed at ¶8035.

8233 **Threatened or anticipatory breach** The employee may be justified in resigning if the employer indicates that he **intends to commit** a fundamental breach (an "anticipatory breach"). There must be a clear and unequivocal statement of intention, and vague or conditional proposals of a variation to terms or working practices will not amount to an anticipatory breach. For example, in the absence of a unilateral variation of contract, the **lawful termination** of a contract, coupled with an offer of employment on new terms, will not of itself give rise to a breach of the implied term of trust and confidence nor will it constitute an anticipatory breach (*Kerry Foods v Lynch* [2005] UKEAT 0032_05_2005). A **warning of redundancy** will not normally entitle the employee to claim he has been constructively dismissed (*Secretary of State for Employment v Greenfield*, EAT case 147/89), nor will a rumour that a particular employee is to be made redundant (*Quinn v Weir Systems Ltd* [2001] UKEAT 1317_00_2704), although it has been suggested that a **threat to dismiss** with notice in the context of an anticipated unilateral variation of contract by the employer can be a fundamental anticipatory breach (*Greenaway Harrison Ltd v Wiles* [1993] UKEAT 304_92_1506).

The employee's choice to accept an anticipatory breach and resign must be unequivocal as the employer can **withdraw or remedy** his anticipatory **breach** prior to the employee's acceptance of his repudiation (*Harrison v Norwest Holst Group Administration Ltd* [1985] IRLR 240, CA; *Assamoi v Spirit Pub Company (Services) Ltd* [2011] UKEAT 0050_20_3007).

> EXAMPLE
> 1. In *Harrison v Norwest Holst Group Administration Ltd*, the employer threatened to transfer H's workplace and remove H as a director. H indicated that he would resign if the matter could not be resolved amicably. The employer withdrew the threat before H resigned so he was unable to claim he had been constructively dismissed.
> 2. In *Assamoi v Spirit Pub Company (Services) Ltd*, a rather turbulent employment relationship ended with the employee, A, resigning and bringing a claim for constructive dismissal. The alleged fundamental breach in trust and confidence occurred when A's manager, C, suspended A on full pay and started disciplinary proceedings against him for not attending a meeting to discuss attendance

while A was on holiday, which had in fact been authorised by C. At the resultant investigating meeting, the senior managers investigating the charge vindicated A's position. A chose not to return to work and resigned. The tribunal found that the decision of the senior management at the investigatory meeting prevented the acts of the immediate manager from constituting a breach of trust and confidence.

8234 **Cumulative breaches** A fundamental breach may be based on the cumulative effect of a **series of acts** (*Lewis v Motorworld Garages Ltd* [1985] IRLR 465, CA), such that the last act is the "**last straw**", justifying the employee's resignation. It is not necessary for each act in the series, or even for the last act, to be a fundamental breach in its own right. However, the last straw act must contribute in some way, when taken in conjunction with the cumulative breaches, to a breach of the implied term of trust and confidence, even though that contribution may be relatively insignificant (*London Borough of Waltham Forest v Folu Omilaju* [2005] IRLR 35, CA; *Wishaw and District Housing Association v Moncrieff* [2009] UKEAT 0066_08_2204).

There is no requirement for the employee to demonstrate any particular degree of proximity between the acts relied upon (*Logan v Commissioners of Customs and Excise* [2004] IRLR 63, CA). Further, the series may comprise different incidents if they are united by a common thread (for example, the employer's failure to give the employee the necessary support (*J V Strong and Co Ltd v Hamill* [2000] UKEAT 1179_99_1603)).

On the other hand, an innocuous act of the employer does not become a last straw because the employee misinterprets it (*London Borough of Waltham Forest v Folu Omilaju*; *Wishaw and District Housing Association v Moncrieff*).

> EXAMPLE
> **Last straw**
> In *Abbey National plc v Robinson* (¶8245), R was on sick leave following a complaint that her manager had bullied her (which was upheld). The employer unreasonably failed to remove the manager from R's department so that she could return, thereby committing a fundamental breach. R remained on leave over the course of the next year while continuing to seek a way to return to work. During this time she suffered further insensitive, unsatisfactory and unreasonable treatment. Finally, she attended a meeting in which nothing was resolved. This was the "last straw" and R was entitled to resign and claim she had been constructively dismissed, 10 months after the initial fundamental breach.
>
> **No last straw**
> In *Wishaw and District Housing Association v Moncrieff*, W attended an initial counselling meeting regarding his work performance and shortly afterwards was signed off sick. After he had been absent from work for some months with depression there was an exchange of letters about his absence in which the employer at first indicated that they were considering dismissal for incapability, if he was not fit to work within a further month. In response to a protest from W's advisers, the employer withdrew the proposal and instead suggested a meeting to try and resolve outstanding issues when he was fit for work again. W responded by resigning. He gave as his reasons earlier unfairness in dealing with performance issues and the employer's conduct in relation to his sickness absence. The EAT overturned a finding of unfair dismissal by the employment tribunal. The employer's letters, objectively considered, were innocuous and could not amount to the "last straw".

8235 **Employer's intention** There is no need for the employer to intend to terminate the employment. A constructive dismissal may be identified even if the employer is keen for the employment to continue. There may be a constructive dismissal even where the **employer is unaware** that he is in breach (for example, he may be in fundamental breach of an implied term (*Bliss v South East Thames Regional Health Authority* [1985] IRLR 308, CA)). In cases of anticipatory breach, if the employer **genuinely but mistakenly believes** in a particular interpretation of the contract, there may be no repudiation if he puts forward his interpretation (but there probably will be if he insists on it) (*Financial Techniques (Planning Services) Ltd v Hughes* [1981] IRLR 32, CA). However, the employer's mistaken but genuine belief will not normally of itself prevent his conduct from amounting to a fundamental breach.

> EXAMPLE In *Roberts v Whitecross School* [2012] UKEAT 0070_12_1906, an employer reduced an employee's sick pay after a certain amount of time as a result of a genuine misunderstanding as to the construction of a collective agreement, but was still held to have constructively dismissed the employee.

8236 An employer may be liable for constructive dismissal by virtue of his **vicarious liability** for acts done by employees in the course of their employment (*Hilton International Hotels (UK) Ltd v Protopapa* [1990] IRLR 316, EAT).

> EXAMPLE In *Hilton International Hotels (UK) Ltd v Protopapa*, P was severely reprimanded by her immediate supervisor for making a dental appointment without first asking for permission to be absent from work. She resigned and claimed constructive dismissal. The EAT upheld her claim on the basis that the employer was liable for the acts of the supervisor as the latter was acting within the scope of her employment (the fact that she did not have authority to dismiss P was irrelevant).

Resignation

8238 The employee's resignation must be **communicated** to the employer by words or conduct (*Edwards v Surrey Police* [1999] UKEAT 698_98_0103). This will be a question for the tribunal or court on the facts and evidence in each case.

8239 The tribunal or court must consider whether the fundamental breach **caused** the resignation (*TSB Bank plc v Harris* [1999] UKEAT 1145_97_0112). It does not have to be the sole or principal cause and there can be a **combination of causes** (*Bass v Travis Perkins Trading Company Ltd* [2005] UKEAT 0598_05_1512; *Abbycars (West Horndon) Ltd v Ford* [2008] UKEAT 0472_07_2305; *Logan v Celyn House Ltd* [2012] UKEAT 0069_12_1907). Consequently, an employer cannot avoid liability because the employee has also relied on other, perhaps unjustified or unsubstantiated, reasons.

> EXAMPLE In *Logan v Celyn House Ltd*, the EAT had to consider an employment tribunal's rejection of a constructive dismissal case on the grounds that, despite there having been a repudiatory breach by the employer, the principal reason for the resignation did not amount to a repudiatory breach. The case involved a veterinary nurse who was contractually entitled to 4 weeks' full sick pay. Having been signed off sick, the employer had failed to pay her full pay, but had instead paid her SSP only. She raised grievances about alleged bullying and the employer's failure to pay the contractual sick pay to which she was entitled. Her grievance was rejected, as was her subsequent internal appeal. She resigned as a result, citing both the alleged bullying and the handling of her grievance in respect of the sick pay issue. In considering her constructive unfair dismissal claim, the employment tribunal found that the bullying had been imagined, but the failure to pay her the sick pay to which she was contractually entitled was a repudiatory breach of contract. However, the tribunal rejected her constructive dismissal claim, holding that the principal reason she had resigned was the alleged bullying, not the failure to pay sick pay. On appeal, the EAT overturned the tribunal's decision on this point and substituted a finding of constructive unfair dismissal. The EAT held that the tribunal had been wrong to focus on the principal reason for dismissal; it was sufficient that the failure to pay sick pay had been one of the employee's reasons for resigning.

8240 It is not always necessary for the employee to make the **reason** for his resignation clear to the employer at the time in order to prove that he resigned as a result of the employer's breach (*Weathersfield Ltd (t/a Van & Truck Rentals) v Sargent* [1999] IRLR 94, CA). Whether he did so or not will be one of the factors to be considered by the tribunal when determining this question.

> EXAMPLE In *Weathersfield Ltd (t/a Van & Truck Rentals) v Sargent*, S commenced work as a receptionist at a car hire firm. She resigned after a few days in response to the employer's special policy for black and Asian customers (i.e. she was to tell them that no cars were available). She did not communicate the reason for her resignation until some days later. The Court held that she had been constructively dismissed.

8241 The employee must choose **within a reasonable time** to treat the contract as at an end or he will normally be taken to have affirmed it (see below) (*Western Excavating (ECC) Ltd v Sharp* [1978] IRLR 27, CA).

Affirmation of the contract

8242 The employee can reject the employer's breach but choose not to treat himself as discharged, in which case the employment will continue and there can be no claim of constructive dismissal (the contract is "affirmed"). His remedies in this case are discussed at ¶1710.

8243 The contract may be affirmed by the **employee's behaviour** (i.e. if he acts in a way that is inconsistent with an intention to treat himself as discharged). The employee may avoid this if he tells the employer that he does not accept the breach but **continues to work** for a period **under protest**, perhaps to allow the employer time to remedy the breach (*W E Cox Toner (International) Ltd v Crook* [1981] IRLR 443, EAT). However, this period cannot continue indefinitely and at some stage the contract will be deemed to have been affirmed.

Working out the **notice period** does not affirm the contract.

8244 **Factors** to be taken into account when deciding whether the contract has been affirmed include:
a. the length of any **delay** in resigning (mere delay by itself will be evidence of implied affirmation but will not be conclusive (*Allen v Robles* [1969] 3 All ER 154, CA; *W E Cox Toner (International) Ltd v Crook*)). Delay which is not accompanied by any express or implied affirmation of the contract will not in itself amount to affirmation of the contract, although prolonged delay might be evidence of implied affirmation (*Bass v Travis Perkins Trading Company Ltd* [2005] UKEAT 0598_05_1512). There may be **special circumstances** to excuse a delay, such as:
– mental illness;
– stress-related illness during which the employee is not in a position to make a rational judgement (*Governing Body of St Edmund of Canterbury Catholic High School v Hines* [2003] UKEAT 1138_02_2609);
– time needed to investigate the true position (*Post Office v Roberts* [1980] IRLR 347, EAT);
– the willingness of the employer to give the employee time to decide (*Bliss v South East Thames Regional Health Authority*);
– where new terms are imposed at short or no notice (a reasonable trial period is allowed (¶8876)); or
– absence from work for example, due to sickness (*Burton v Northern Business Systems Ltd* [1994] UKEAT 608_92_1605; see also *El-Hoshi v Pizza Express Restaurants Ltd* [2004] UKEAT 0857_03_2303);
b. continued acceptance of **wages or other benefits**, including sick pay (*Wood & Mott Ltd v Carr* [1996] UKEAT 1025_95_0611), although acceptance of sick pay will not necessarily indicate that the employee has affirmed the contract (*Forbes v Salamis (Marine & Industrial) Ltd* [2004] UKEAT 0085_03_2403; *Bass v Travis Perkins Trading Company Ltd* [2005] UKEAT 0598_05_1512) and, moreover, it is reasonable for the employee to accept wages for a limited time while looking for another job (*Waltons & Morse v Dorrington* [1997] UKEAT 69_97_1905);
c. the **nature of the breach**; and
d. the employee's **length of service** (*Miceli v Signal House Ltd* [1996] UKEAT 180_95_1602).

8245 In cases of **cumulative breach**, it does not matter if the employee has waived earlier acts in the series (even if they amount to a fundamental breach), as it is the end of the series that is relevant in order to identify if the contract has been affirmed (*Abbey National plc v Robinson* [1999] UKEAT 74_3_2411). When deciding whether the final act is a sufficient "trigger" to revive the earlier ones, the tribunal will take into account (*J V Strong and Co Ltd v Hamill* [2000] UKEAT 1179_99_1603):
a. the nature of the incidents;
b. the overall time span;
c. the length of time between the incidents;
d. any factors which may have amounted to a waiver of any earlier breaches; and
e. the nature of any waiver, namely:
– whether it was express or implied; and
– whether it was final or conditional on there being no further breach.

Further, if the individual acts are not fundamental breaches in themselves, there can be no affirmation until the "last straw" trigger.

8246 If the situation involves a **continuing breach** (for example, the failure to provide or operate a proper grievance procedure (*WA Goold (Pearmak) Ltd v McConnell* [1995] IRLR 516, EAT)), the contract is not affirmed by the employee delaying his resignation while the breach continues.

Remedies

8248 If an employee has been constructively dismissed, he may seek compensation for **wrongful dismissal** (¶8160) if he resigned without notice.

As constructive dismissal is a dismissal for the purposes of **unfair dismissal** and **redundancy payments**, the employee may also bring such claims, where appropriate (ss 95(1)(c), 136(1)(c) ERA 1996).

8249

A constructive dismissal will also be a dismissal for the purposes of age, disability, gender reassignment, marriage and civil partnership, pregnancy and maternity, race, religion or belief, sex or sexual orientation **discrimination** claims (the employer's conduct may also amount to "other detriment" for the purposes of such claims) (*Catherall v Michelin Tyre plc* [2002] UKEAT 915_01_2110).

A claim of discrimination (based on dismissal or some other detriment) must be **brought within** 3 months of the employer's fundamental breach (*Commissioner of Police of Metropolis v Harley* [2001] UKEAT 518_00_1902; *Cast v Croydon College* [1998] IRLR 318, CA). Note that this contrasts with the time limit for an unfair constructive dismissal claim, which runs from the effective date of termination (¶8340) (although this may be the same where the employee resigns without notice on the day the breach occurs). See ¶9460 for further details on time limits for discrimination claims.

Unfair constructive dismissal A constructive dismissal may be fair or unfair. If an employee brings a claim of unfair constructive dismissal, he must comply with the general **qualifying conditions** and procedural rules applicable to all unfair dismissal claims (¶8410 and ¶8560). The tribunal will consider the **general questions**, namely whether the employee has been dismissed, whether the employer had a fair reason for dismissal, and whether he followed a fair procedure.

8251

In certain cases, a dismissal is **automatically unfair** (¶8390). For example, an employee can leave his workplace and claim automatic unfair constructive dismissal when he believes that his health and safety is in imminent and serious danger.

The **reason for the dismissal** is the employer's reason for committing the fundamental breach (*Berriman v Delabole Slate Ltd* [1985] ICR 546, CA), and the tribunal will consider whether that reason was sufficient in the circumstances to justify the breach (the criteria applied are generally the same as those in cases of express dismissal – ¶8420). In defending a claim, the employer normally contests that a dismissal has in fact taken place at all, but he should also plead a reason for the dismissal in the alternative, as the tribunal will not investigate the reason of their own volition (*Derby City Council v Marshall* [1979] IRLR 261, EAT).

8252

In many cases the fundamental breach will make the dismissal unfair. However, the following situations may provide a **fair reason** for dismissal:
– conduct or capability dismissals (¶8450);
– redundancy (¶8510); and
– business reorganisations (capable of being a fair reason under the "some other substantial reason" limb – ¶8532).

EXAMPLE
1. In *Ross v What Every Woman Wants*, EAT case 474/87, R's **conduct** entitled his employer to dismiss him summarily but the employer chose to demote him (with a consequent pay cut). Although this was a fundamental breach, R's conduct constituted a fair reason for dismissal.
2. Employee K worked in London. The employer ceased to operate there and required K to move to his offices in Manchester (having no contractual right to do so). K resigned and claimed unfair constructive dismissal. **Redundancy**, however, could provide the employer with a fair reason for dismissal.
3. In *Genower v Ealing Hammersmith and Hounslow Area Health Authority* [1980] IRLR 297, EAT, the employer **reorganised his business** and the resulting **changes to G's job duties** amounted to a fundamental breach entitling him to claim constructive dismissal. However, the reorganisation amounted to a fair reason for dismissal.

Even if the employer establishes a fair reason, the dismissal may still be unfair if he failed to **act reasonably** in all the circumstances in treating that reason as a sufficient reason for dismissal (for example, he failed to consult when seeking to vary terms of employment). See ¶8420 for further detail on the criteria generally applied.

8253

F. Mutual agreement

8260 Although relatively unusual, the employer and employee can agree (orally or in writing) to terminate the employment with effect at any time. This usually arises in cases of voluntary **early retirement**. There will be **no dismissal** (i.e. the employee will not be entitled to bring a claim for redundancy, unfair or wrongful dismissal) (*Birch and Humber v The University of Liverpool* [1985] IRLR 165, CA).

In contrast, there will be a **dismissal** for redundancy purposes if the employee persuades the employer to dismiss him in a redundancy situation, or if he accepts **voluntary redundancy** or agrees to the employer's redundancy proposals (*Burton, Allton & Johnson Ltd v R R V Peck* [1975] IRLR 87, QBD).

If, however, the employee is under any **pressure to agree** (for example, a threat of dismissal in any case), the courts may find that he has actually been dismissed. However, if other factors also influenced the employee's decision (for example, he is offered a financial incentive), the courts may find that he has terminated by mutual agreement (*Sheffield v Oxford Controls Company Ltd* [1979] IRLR 133, EAT; *Hellyer Brothers Ltd v Atkinson and Dickinson* [1992] UKEAT 630_90_3103).

8261 There will be no termination by mutual agreement until **all the terms** of the agreement are agreed (*Asamoah-Boakye v Walter Rodney Housing Association Ltd* [2001] EWCA Civ 851).

> EXAMPLE In *Asamoah-Boakye v Walter Rodney Housing Association Ltd*, A-B and his employer were negotiating terms in relation to the termination of his employment by mutual agreement. The employer required him to enter into a compromise agreement waiving his right to bring an unfair dismissal claim. A-B required the employer to provide an agreed form reference. A-B left his job before the agreement was signed. The Court held that there was no termination by mutual agreement as the agreement had not been signed and the form of reference had yet to be agreed.

8262 In contrast to a termination by mutual agreement, the employer and employee may negotiate the termination and agree that the employee resigns, or the employer dismisses the employee, on a certain date. **Negotiated terminations** are discussed at ¶9315.

8263 The employer and employee may have agreed that the employment should **automatically terminate** on the occurrence of a specified event (¶8270).

G. Automatic termination

8270 An agreement for automatic termination on the **occurrence of a specified event** may be ineffective to exclude statutory employment rights, unless it falls within one of the exceptions to the general prohibition on contracting out (¶9203). Therefore, an agreement that **overstaying holiday leave** would result in automatic termination was void as it purported to limit the employee's right not to be unfairly dismissed and to bring an unfair dismissal claim (*Igbo v Johnson Matthey Chemicals Ltd* [1986] IRLR 215, CA).

8271 The employment may also terminate automatically as a result of a **supervening event** or because it has been **frustrated**. In such cases, the employment terminates by operation of law and there is no actual dismissal or resignation. However, to preserve statutory rights, certain cases will be deemed to be a dismissal.

1. Supervening events

8275 Supervening events include death, certain cases of insolvency (¶8277), permanent closure of the employee's workplace, and automatic termination by statute (i.e. a change in the law makes performance impossible).

MEMO POINTS   In common law, the transfer of an employer's business automatically terminates all existing contracts of employment. The employee's position is, however, normally protected by the **transfer of business (TUPE)** regulations, which transfer the employment to the new employer (¶7952).

Death

The death of the employer or the employee automatically terminates the employment unless there is a term (express or implied) to the contrary (*Farrow v Wilson* [1869] LR 4 CP 744, Court of Common Pleas). However, an employee whose contract is not renewed, or who is not re-engaged, by the person to whom the deceased employer's business passes is treated as dismissed for **redundancy** if the failure to renew or re-engage is wholly or mainly attributable to redundancy (¶9010). If the employee is **re-employed**, his statutory continuity of employment is preserved (s 218(4) ERA 1996).

8276

Claims outstanding at the time of death (including claims of unfair dismissal and for a redundancy payment) can be brought against the deceased employer's personal representatives (s 206(1) ERA 1996) or by the deceased employee's personal representatives, as appropriate (ss 206(3), 207(1) ERA 1996; *Lewisham and Guys Mental Health NHS Trust v Andrews (deceased)* [2000] ICR 707, CA).

Insolvency

A detailed discussion of the law of insolvency is beyond the scope of this book and the following will deal only with its impact on the employment relationship.

8277

The **bankruptcy** of an individual employer does not automatically terminate the employment. The **dissolution of a partnership** (as opposed to the addition or departure of individual partners) (*Briggs v Oates* [1990] IRLR 472, ChD), on the other hand, normally does. **Intervention by a regulatory body** may do so where it results in the regulated firm (for example, a partnership of solicitors) closing down (but does not where the partners are allowed to dispose of their practice as a going concern without dismissing the employees) (*Barnes and anor (t/a Barnes Thomas and Co) v Leavesley and ors* [1999] UKEAT 642_99_0510).

If a company goes into **liquidation or winding up**, its assets are used to pay off its liabilities and the company is dissolved (i.e. it ceases to exist). There are three types of liquidation: compulsory, creditors' voluntary and members' voluntary. A company enters into **compulsory** liquidation by way of a court order, which automatically terminates the employment of all the company's employees. However, the liquidator can waive their dismissal if he needs to carry on the company's business during the winding up. A **voluntary** liquidation (creditors' or members') commences when the shareholders pass a resolution to wind the company up, and the employees' position depends on the circumstances. Their contracts of employment may provide that the company commits a fundamental breach if the business ceases or a resolution to wind the company up is passed. If not, the contracts will usually be terminated when the liquidator is appointed, unless the liquidator needs to carry on the company's business during the winding up.

8278

Certain steps may be taken short of the company's liquidation. A company can be put into **administration** by the company, its directors, a qualifying floating charge holder or by court order (on application by the company, its directors or creditors) under which an administrator is appointed to manage the company's affairs. The appointment of an administrator does not of itself automatically terminate the employment of the company's employees as the administrator is said to be acting as agent of the company (para 69, Sch B1 Insolvency Act 1986). Employment contracts can either be adopted by the administrator or terminated by him within the law. If the administrator causes an employment relationship to continue for more than 14 days after his appointment, he is taken to have adopted the contract (*Powdrill v Watson* [1995] 2 AC 394).

8279

The company will go into **receivership** if the holder of a floating charge created before 15 September 2003 appoints an administrative receiver. The administrative receiver is also an agent of the company (s 44 Insolvency Act 1986) and so his appointment will not usually

terminate the contracts of employment. If the administrative receiver causes an employment relationship to continue for more than 14 days after his appointment, he is taken to have adopted the contract (*Powdrill v Watson*, above). On the other hand, it will be terminated automatically where (*Griffiths v Secretary of State for Social Services* [1974] QB 468):
– the employee's employment is inconsistent with the receiver's activities;
– the receiver and employee enter into a new contract of employment contemporaneously or soon after the receiver's appointment, which is inconsistent with the old one; or
– the receiver's appointment is accompanied by a sale of the company's business.

> MEMO POINTS   The company also goes into receivership where a receiver (or receiver and manager) is appointed as a way of enforcing certain other security over the company's assets. The receiver can adopt a contract of employment, and will be taken to have done so if he allows an employment relationship to continue for more than 14 days after his appointment (*Powdrill v Watson*, above).

8280 Where the **employment is not automatically terminated** by the insolvency, the employees may have to be dismissed. In such cases, the employer (or liquidator/receiver/administrator) should, before sending out dismissal notices, comply with the general rules on **collective redundancy consultation** (¶8915).

8282 Employees of insolvent employers enjoy certain **specific rights and protections**, which are discussed at ¶9040.

2. Frustration

8285 A contract may be frustrated where an unforeseen event makes performance impossible or radically different from what the parties had originally contemplated (*Davis Contractors v Fareham UDC* [1956] AC 696, HL).

Although relatively rare in an employment context, frustration can occur in the following circumstances:
– prolonged or sudden serious illness or disability (discussed at ¶8458);
– imprisonment (see below);
– death (see above);
– total destruction of the workplace;
– conscription into the armed forces; and
– internment as an alien during wartime.

The party asserting that the contract has been frustrated has the **burden of proof**, and he cannot rely on a frustrating event if it has been caused by his **fault or default** (*FC Shepherd & Co Ltd v Jerrom* [1986] IRLR 358, CA). In ascertaining whether an employer has discharged the burden of proof in establishing that a contract of employment has been frustrated on the grounds that the employee has become incapable of performing his duties under that contract, a court must take into consideration the **nature and duration** of the employee's employment (*Gryf-Lowczowski v Hinchingbrooke Healthcare NHS Trust* [2006] IRLR 100, QBD). Where an employee's work was of a **highly-skilled nature** and the termination of his employment contract by frustration would effectively make it highly **unlikely** that he would **find such work elsewhere** in the future, then it is reasonable for the employer to wait longer before considering the contract frustrated than it might otherwise do in different circumstances.

> EXAMPLE **No frustration**
> 1. In *Gryf-Lowczowski v Hinchingbrooke Healthcare NHS Trust*, a specialised NHS surgeon had been absent on special leave for 2 years (due to concerns regarding his work) and the National Clinical Assessment Authority held he could not return to work until he had undergone a re-skilling placement at a different NHS trust. The High Court found, on the evidence before it, that as there was a realistic possibility the surgeon would be able to obtain this necessary re-skilling placement, he was not yet incapable of performing his duties under the contract and the employer could not rely on its assertion that the contract was frustrated.
> 2. In *Jones v Friction Dynamics Ltd (in administration) and ors* [2007] UKEAT 0428_06_2803, an employee had been signed off sick for 6 months in 2001. After that certificate expired he did not return to work, although

he was fit to do so, and there was no further contact between employee and employer until the employer company went into administration in 2003. He remained notionally employed, but did not receive any pay. When the administrator was appointed he wrote to the employee dismissing him. The employee then made a claim for unfair dismissal to the employment tribunal who found that his contract had been frustrated, which meant he was not entitled to any redundancy payment. This decision was overturned by the EAT who held that his contract could not have been frustrated as he had been capable of work since late 2001. His employment had been terminated by the administrator's letter of dismissal, and not by operation of law.

8286 In cases of frustration, the employment ends automatically by operation of law so that there is **no dismissal or resignation**, with the result that there can be no claim for wrongful or unfair dismissal, notice/payment in lieu of notice (*G F Sharp & Co Ltd v McMillan* [1998] IRLR 632, EAT), or for redundancy (unless the frustrating event affects the employer, in which case there is a **deemed dismissal** for statutory redundancy payment purposes (¶8106)), although the employee is entitled to payment for work done before the frustrating event.

The parties cannot choose to keep a frustrated contract alive (*G F Sharp & Co Ltd v McMillan*; *Collins v Secretary of State for Trade and Industry* [2000] EAT 1460_99_2203), although continuity of employment may be preserved if the parties have a voluntary (as opposed to contractual) **continuing relationship** (¶1000).

Imprisonment

8290 If an employee is sentenced to imprisonment, the contract may, depending on the circumstances of the case, be **frustrated** (*F C Shepherd & Co Ltd v Jerrom* [1986] IRLR 358, CA). Relevant factors include the following:
– the length of sentence/likely duration of the employee's absence;
– whether and at what stage it is necessary to replace the employee; and
– whether any replacement employee needs to be permanent rather than temporary.

An employer should not act too hastily, but should consider the likely duration of the employee's absence when making the decision whether to replace him (and not necessarily at the moment the sentence is passed) (*Chakki v United Yeast Co Ltd* [1982] ICR 140, EAT).

The contract may also be frustrated due to **restrictive bail conditions** (for example, that the employee lives in a certain place) or a **remand in custody** while awaiting trial (the factors discussed above will apply).

EXAMPLE In *Four Seasons Healthcare Limited (formerly Cotswold Spa Retirement Hotels Ltd) v Maughan* [2005] IRLR 324, EAT, the employee's employment contract was held not to be frustrated when the police launched an investigation into allegations of patient abuse at the care home at which the employee worked. Neither the act of abusing the patient nor the imposition of bail conditions which prevented the employee from entering the care home amounted to frustration of the contract. The contract was only frustrated when the decision was taken as to the employee's fitness to work (which, in this case, took place when the Crown Court convicted the employee and he was consequently rendered unfit to continue to work under the governing care home regulations).

MEMO POINTS The employee will not be able to argue that by being imprisoned he has committed a fundamental breach of contract permitting the employer to treat himself as discharged in order to create a dismissal for the purposes of an unfair dismissal claim (*F C Shepherd & Co Ltd v Jerrom*, above).

8291 If the contract is **not frustrated**, the employer may be able to dismiss fairly for some other substantial reason (¶8544).

II. Termination issues

8300 In addition to **notice** provisions (including payment in lieu of notice and garden leave options) discussed above, the contract could include terms relating to **confidentiality** and **post-termination restraints**. These are discussed in chapter 9.

8301 For directors, the agreement should also deal with resignation of **directorships** (¶2125).

8302 It is advisable for the contract to oblige the employee to **return company property** when the employment terminates.

A. Statement of reasons for dismissal

8310 If an employee is dismissed (with or without notice) or his fixed-term contract expires without being renewed, he is entitled to **request** (orally or in writing) a written statement of reasons for his dismissal, which must be provided within 14 days of the request (s 92(1) ERA 1996). Generally, to be entitled to make a request, employees who started their employment on or after 6 April 2012 must have 2 years' **continuous employment** ending with the effective date of termination (¶¶8340+) (SI 2012/989). Those who started their period of continuous employment before this date require only 1 year's continuous employment.

No period of employment is required and **no request** for the statement need be made if the employee has been dismissed while **pregnant or on maternity leave** or **adoption leave** (s 92(4), (4A) ERA 1996).

8311 The employer may refer the employee to full reasons given in an **earlier written communication** (a copy must be sent with the employer's reply) (*Kent County Council v Gilham* [1985] IRLR 18, CA).

The reasons given can be used as evidence in any **court or tribunal proceedings**.

8312 The employee can apply to an employment tribunal if the employer unreasonably **fails to provide** the statement of reasons or the employee believes that the reasons given are **inadequate or untrue** (s 93(1) ERA 1996).

It may be unreasonable for an employer to fail to comply even where the employee is fully aware of the reason for dismissal, as the provision enables him to show the reason for dismissal to third parties. The reason given must be sufficiently specific or it will be inadequate. It may be reasonable for the employer not to give a statement where he reasonably believes that there was in fact no dismissal (*Broomsgrove v Eagle Alexander Ltd* [1981] IRLR 127, EAT).

8313 The complaint must be **made within** 3 months from the effective date of termination (see below) (or within such further period as the tribunal considers reasonable where it was not reasonably practicable to comply with that limit) (s 93(3) ERA 1996).

If it upholds the employee's complaint, the **tribunal must order** the employer to pay the employee 2 weeks' pay (uncapped) (see ¶¶2920+ for calculation of a week's pay) and may make a declaration in respect of the employer's reasons for dismissal (s 93(2) ERA 1996).

> EXAMPLE In *Marenghi v Western Baths Club*, [2001] UKEAT 1508_00_1505, M worked as a barmaid. The employer restructured the club so that the bar and kitchen were in the same place and asked M to serve food as well as drinks. She refused and her employment ended. The statement of reasons stated that she had been dismissed and had been made redundant. The EAT held that this statement was inadequate and untrue as the tribunal had found that the dismissal was for "some other substantial reason" (her refusal of a reasonable alternative to her duties). The employer had therefore given the wrong reason in the statement and the tribunal should have awarded M the mandatory 2 weeks' pay.

B. References

8320 There is **no implied term** entitling an employee to a reference. In some cases, the employer may be obliged to give a reference (for example, by a regulatory body or by the terms of a settlement agreement with the employee), or he may be willing to accede to the employee's request for one. As the employee may need a reference to obtain new employment (see ¶704 in relation to references as a pre-condition of employment), it is relatively unusual for the employer to refuse to supply one and a refusal may be discriminatory (see below). Some employers adopt a policy of providing only factual information (such as dates of employment, position held, and salary) when asked for references. This is acceptable providing it is applied in all cases (¶8325).

A reference may be provided **orally** or, more commonly, **in writing**. All written references should be marked "private and confidential" to avoid their disclosure to third parties. References are often **requested by** prospective employers. Character references may also be sought from other organisations, for example in connection with legal proceedings. Financial references may also be requested by lenders or banks, for example in connection with a worker's application for a mortgage. Consequently, a reference may be **general**, or may be a response to a request for **specific details**. Regardless of the type of reference, the employer must take care not to breach the legal duties that he owes both to the recipient of the reference (the new employer) and to the subject (the employee or ex-employee).

8321 The **information provided** may depend on the status of the employee, with a fuller reference being provided for more senior employees. A reference for general staff will commonly include the following:
– length of service;
– positions held;
– competence;
– honesty/integrity;
– absence record;
– time-keeping; and
– reason for leaving.

8322 When deciding whether to provide a reference (or the content of that reference), the employer must **avoid discriminating** against, or victimising, a particular employee (*Coote v Granada Hospitality (No 2)* [1999] UKEAT 1332_95_1905). If the **reason for the refusal** to provide a reference is based on discriminatory grounds, the refusal in itself could amount to a discriminatory act (¶5222). The employer's reason is therefore a crucial factor in determining his liability.

> EXAMPLE
> **Victimisation**
> In *Coote v Granada Hospitality (No 2)*[1999] UKEAT 1332_95_1905, the employer victimised C by failing to provide her with a reference following her sex discrimination claim.
>
> **No victimisation**
> In *Chief Constable of West Yorkshire Police v Khan* [2001] IRLR 830, HL, K brought race discrimination proceedings against his employer. The employer refused to provide him with a reference for new employment while those proceedings were continuing. The Court held that K was not victimised because the reason for the refusal was not the fact that he had brought proceedings, but rather that providing a reference would have amounted to a reassertion of the alleged discriminatory views and would have compromised the employer's position in those proceedings.

8323 The employee cannot bring a **libel** action based on the reference, unless the employer is motivated by malice and knows the information is incorrect.

8324 **Duty of care** If a **reference is provided**, the employer owes the employee (or ex-employee) a duty of care to ensure that it is **accurate**. In such circumstances, there is an implied term that the reference will be compiled (and the information on which it is based will be verified) with reasonable care. If it is not, the employee may have a remedy for **negligent misstatement** (*Spring v Guardian Assurance plc* [1994] IRLR 460, HL). For such a remedy to be available, the employer must **actually have provided** a reference (i.e. the employee cannot argue that any reference given would inevitably include a detrimental statement) (*Legal & General Assurance Ltd v Kirk* [2002] IRLR 124, CA). The **new employer** may also have a claim against the old employer if he suffers any loss as a result of inaccuracies in the reference (for example, if it gives a false picture of the employee's abilities). The employer must, therefore, ensure that a reference can be substantiated.

A recent case has held that this duty of care applied even 6 years after the employee had left his employment, although the facts were unusual in the total lack of care taken in establishing the truth behind the accusations made, and a more measured communication between the old employer and the new employer would have been likely to have been acceptable (*McKie v Swindon College* [2011] EWHC 469 (QB)).

> EXAMPLE In *McKie v Swindon College*, the High Court held in favour of an ex-employee, M, whose former employer, S (a college), 6 years after the end of their employment relationship, sent an email to M's new employer (another college) informing them that they would not allow M on their premises. This was an essential requirement for M's new role. This was explained as being a result of "safeguarding concerns" for their students and serious staff relations problems that came to light following the end of the M's employment. Following this email M was summarily dismissed by his new employer, and the High Court held that this would have been an unfair dismissal had M had 12 months' service. The High Court held that the claims made by S were unsubstantiated and untrue. As this was not part of a formal reference process, the Court had no specific library of case law to rely upon and looked at the general law on negligent misstatement and negligent misrepresentation. It was held that the damage caused to M was foreseeable, there was a sufficiently proximate relationship between the parties (despite the 6-year gap), and it was fair, reasonable and just to impose a duty of care on S to its ex-employee.

> MEMO POINTS **While employed**, it has been held to be part of the implied contractual term of trust and confidence that the employer should exercise reasonable care and skill when providing a reference for existing employees (¶1245).

8325 There is **no duty to provide a full and comprehensive reference** so employers may wish merely to provide an objective **standard form** reference, limited to basic facts and avoiding comments on more subjective issues.

However, the reference must be in substance true, accurate and fair (*Bartholomew v London Borough of Hackney* [1999] IRLR 246, CA) and its fairness will be determined by looking at "the overall balance of the reference and any opinion contained within it" (*Jackson v Liverpool City Council* [2011] EWCA Civ 1068). It must **not be misleading** or create a false impression, or the employer will be negligent.

If the employee leaves while **disciplinary proceedings are pending**, the employer is not obliged to complete that investigation, but he should limit any **unfavourable statements** to matters that have been properly investigated and which he has reasonable grounds to believe are true (*Cox v Sun Alliance Life* [2001] IRLR 448, CA).

> EXAMPLE
> **No breach of duty**
> 1. In *Bartholomew v London Borough of Hackney*, the reference referred to the fact that, at the time he left, B had been suspended pending disciplinary action. B alleged that the reference was negligent as it failed to state that he strongly disputed the charges. Despite this omission, the reference was accurate and fair.
> 2. In *Jackson v Liverpool City Council*, a social worker had a job offer withdrawn when his former employer provided a reference that mentioned allegations had been made about him after his employment was terminated, which had not been investigated or substantiated. The reference made it clear that these issues had not been investigated but would have led to a formal improvement plan (i.e. not directly to disciplinary action) and also pointed out his strengths. A telephone conversation also took place between his former and prospective employers in which his former employer made it clear that because the claimant had left their employment before matters could be investigated, there were some questions that could not be answered in a positive or negative way. It was accepted that the reference was true and accurate, but the issue at hand was whether or not it was fair. Whilst expressing sympathy for the claimant, the Court of Appeal held that the alternatives (such as not providing a reference at all) were not satisfactory and that it was difficult to see how the questions within the reference could have been answered honestly without identifying the concerns and allegations that were raised. The judgment stated that the facts given in the reference will establish its accuracy and truth, but its fairness is determined by looking at "the overall balance of the reference and any opinion contained within it". The Court ruled in favour of the employer and held that the reference had been fair.

> **Breach of duty**
> In *Cox v Sun Alliance Life*, the employer led C's new employer to understand that C had left while disciplinary proceedings involving allegations of financial impropriety were pending. This was held to be an unfair reference because the unfavourable comments were not confined to matters which had been investigated and were, therefore, made without reasonable grounds.

8326 Where a settlement is agreed on termination, the wording of the **reference may be agreed** between the employer and the employee. The employer must, however, still be aware of his duty to new employers when supplying an agreed form reference.

8327 An employee also has the right **not to suffer a detrimental act** or omission (s 47B ERA 1996) and an employer must ensure that any reference he provides is satisfactory. In a case concerning a whistleblower, this right has been held to continue to apply post-employment (*Woodward v Abbey National plc* [2006] IRLR 677, CA not following *Fadipe v Reed Nursing Personnel* [2001] EWCA Civ 1885).

8328 **Data protection** If the employer is asked to provide a reference, he should consider discussing the request with the employee. If **sensitive information** is requested, the employee's explicit consent to disclosure must be obtained to avoid a breach of data protection rules (¶5951).

As **good practice**, the employer should (part 2.9 DP Code):
– have a **clear company policy** which sets out who can give corporate references and in what circumstances. All referees should be made aware of the policy; and
– not give confidential references unless the referee is sure that this is the **worker's wish**. It may also be useful to include on file a record of whether the worker wants references to be provided after he has left.

Employers are also advised to follow the DP Code's general **recommendations** with regard to data management (¶6000).

8329 The Information Commissioner has published a **Good Practice Note** in relation to **subject access requests** and references, which clarifies how the Data Protection Act applies to employment references.

With regard to giving a copy of a **reference** an **employer has written** itself to an employee or ex-employee, if requested, the employer is under no obligation to do so, though it is reasonable to provide a copy if a reference is wholly or largely factual in nature, or if the employee or ex-employee is aware of the appraisal of his work or ability.

However, the position of giving a copy, if requested, of a **reference** an employer has **received from a third party** is different. In such cases, the request must be considered under the normal rules of access (¶¶5980+), i.e. that an individual can have access to information which is about them, but may not necessarily have access to information about other people, including their opinions, provided in confidence. However, even if the reference received is **marked "in confidence"**, this does not automatically mean that all, if any, of the contents are actually confidential and the employer must make an assessment as to what is confidential and can be withheld. An employer cannot sensibly withhold information that is already known to the individual (for example factual information as to employment start and end dates, and absence records). Similarly, information relating to performance, which may well have been discussed with the individual as part of an appraisal system. However, where it is not clear whether the information, including the referee's opinions, is known to the individual, the employer should contact the referee to ask whether they object to the information being provided and, if so, why. Even if the referee objects, the employer must still provide the reference if it is reasonable in all the circumstances to do so, weighing the referee's interest in having their comments treated confidentially against the individual's interest in seeing what has been said about him.

In summary, the Information Commissioner gives a list of the factors that should be taken into account in deciding what is **reasonable to disclose**:
– any express assurance of confidentiality given to the referee;
– any relevant reasons the referee gives for withholding consent;
– the potential or actual effect of the reference on the individual;

– the fact that a reference must be truthful and accurate and that without access to it the individual is not in a position to challenge its accuracy;
– that good employment practice suggests that an individual should have already been advised of any weaknesses; and
– any risk to the referee and whether it is possible to keep the identity of the referee secret.

Finally, as **recommended good practice**:
– in most cases, the information, or a substantial part of it, in a reference should be provided if requested;
– the referee refusing consent does not necessarily justify the employer withholding the information, particularly if it has a significant impact on the individual (for example, it prevents him from taking up a provisional job offer). However, there may be circumstances where it would not be appropriate to release a reference (for example, where there is a realistic threat of violence or intimidation by the individual to the referee);
– the employer should consider whether it is possible to conceal the identity of the referee although often the individual will have a good idea as to who has written the reference; and
– if is not reasonable in all of the circumstances to provide the information without the referee's consent, the employer should consider whether he can summarise the contents in some way so that it protects the identity of the referee, while providing the individual with an overview of what the reference said about him.

C. Date of termination

8340 For the reasons set out below, it is necessary to ascertain the "**effective date of termination**" (EDT), known as the "**relevant date**" for redundancy payment purposes but referred to here as the EDT unless the two need to be distinguished.

The reasons are:
– to comply with **time limits** for tribunal or court claims (for example, unfair dismissal claims must be brought within 3 months from the EDT);
– to identify whether the employee has sufficient continuity of employment to **qualify for a particular statutory right**;
– to calculate the amount of any **statutory redundancy payment** or **unfair dismissal basic award** (which are based on length of continuous employment);
– to identify the calculation date in order to ascertain a "**week's pay**" (for the purposes of various compensation awards, including the unfair dismissal basic award, the failure to consult under collective redundancy obligations and the failure to provide written reasons for dismissal); and
– to determine whether a worker is a **protected shop or betting worker** throughout his period of continuous employment for the purposes of Sunday working.

8341 The EDT **depends on** the **form of termination**, i.e. whether the termination is with or without notice or the expiry of a fixed-term contract. This is discussed in detail below.

In summary, **it is the date** (unfair dismissal: s 97(1) ERA 1996; redundancy: s 145(2) ERA 1996):
– on which notice of termination expires;
– on which termination takes effect (where no notice is served); or
– of expiry of a fixed-term contract.

8342 While the parties may agree to waive a notice period, or to bring forward or put back the end of the notice, and so change the EDT, they cannot agree an EDT different to that imposed by the statutory rules discussed below (*Fitzgerald v University of Kent at Canterbury* [2004] IRLR 300, CA). However, although the EDT is a statutory construct, it can change in certain circumstances, for example where an earlier termination has been held to "disappear" because a resignation without notice has been withdrawn by consent and is subsequently followed by another resignation (*Chelmsford College Corporation v Teal* [2011] UKEAT 0277_11_0701). Likewise, where an employee has been summarily dismissed, an appeal is capable of varying the date of termination to a later date and the employment contract will be treated as having been temporarily revived for this period (*Hawes and Curtis Ltd v Arfan and anor* [2012] UKEAT 0229_12_0106).

EXAMPLE
1. In *Chelmsford College Corporation v Teal*, a lecturer, T, got into a dispute with the college who employed her over their rejection of her claims for overtime payments. The college's refusal of T's overtime claim caused her to write to the college offering her resignation with immediate effect. The college construed this "resignation" as a grievance and invited her to a grievance hearing. The college subsequently confirmed that the overtime claim would be honoured and that they would allow her to rescind her resignation. T then wrote to the college confirming that she was grateful to them for agreeing to allow her to rescind her resignation. However, when a further dispute on another matter arose some weeks later and T's grievance in relation to this was rejected, she resigned again stating that the refusal of her second grievance had been "the final straw". T later brought a claim for constructive dismissal. The question arose as to what T's EDT was. The tribunal and EAT dismissed the college's argument that T's claim had been brought out of time because her first resignation had been effective. T's first resignation had been withdrawn with the college's consent and consequently she had been in continuous employment until her second resignation.
2. In *Hawes and Curtis Ltd v Arfan and anor*, two managers employed in a shop who were dismissed for gross misconduct for their suspected involvement in stock losses amounting to £140,000. They were both given dismissal letters on 5 October 2010 terminating their employment "as of the date of this letter". The employees unsuccessfully appealed against their dismissals and the employer wrote to them on 4 November 2010 confirming that their summary dismissals were being upheld. However, the letters indicated that their effective date of termination was being changed to 4 November 2010. The employees subsequently brought unfair dismissal claims relying upon 4 November as their EDT; if 5 October was their EDT those claims were out of time. The employer did not initially raise an issue with the claims having been brought out of time but, after almost a year, the employer asserted that the EDT was in fact 5 October and that, as such, the claims had been brought out of time. A hearing took place to determine the correct EDT as a preliminary issue. The tribunal held, by a majority, that the EDT was 4 November. The EAT dismissed the appeal against this decision and rejected the suggestion that in cases of summary dismissal the EDT always crystallises on the date of summary dismissal. The EAT held that, in a case of summary dismissal, an appeal is capable of varying the effective date of termination.

Dismissal with notice

When an employee is dismissed with notice, the EDT is the **date the notice expires** (regardless of whether the employee actually attends work during the notice period, and insisting an employee should, or allowing an employee to, stay away from work will not bring forward the EDT) (ss 97(1)(a), 145(2)(a) ERA 1996; *Wedgewood v Minstergate Hull Ltd* [2010] UKEAT 0137_10_1307). The same applies to discrimination claims based on dismissal (*Lupetti v Wrens Old House Ltd* [1984] ICR 348, EAT). See ¶8120 in relation to notice periods.

8343

EXAMPLE In *Wedgewood v Minstergate Hull Ltd*, an employee, W, was given notice of termination of his employment to expire on 1 December. During his notice period it was agreed that W would be released from his duties early on 26 November, but that he would be paid up to 1 December. The question arose of whether the effective date of termination of contract was the date W's notice expired or the date he was released from his duties. When W made an unfair dismissal claim on 28 February, it was rejected as being out of time, on the basis that the termination date had been brought forward to when he was released from his duties. The EAT overturned this; while the parties could have agreed to vary the date of termination in advance, merely allowing the employee to stay away from work did not amount to an agreement to bring forward the date of termination.

If the employer's **notice is ambiguous** as to the intended date for its expiry, it is interpreted to reflect what a reasonable employee would understand it to mean in the light of facts known to him at the time, and any ambiguity will be resolved in the employee's favour (*Chapman v Letheby & Christopher Ltd* [1981] IRLR 440, EAT). A written notice of dismissal will be interpreted without reference to any prior or subsequent oral or written communication, unless it is merely confirming an earlier oral notice of dismissal, in which case the letter can be used to clarify any ambiguity in the earlier notice (*Leech v Preston Borough Council* [1985] IRLR 337, EAT).

8344

8345 If a **payment in lieu of notice** is made, the EDT is as for dismissal without notice (¶8351) unless the intention was actually to dismiss the employee with notice but release him from his obligation to work out the notice (i.e. paid or garden leave situations), in which case the EDT is as stated above.

8346 As noted above (¶8342), the parties can agree to **bring forward or postpone** the date of termination. If the employee gives a **counter-notice** to terminate which expires prior to the employer's notice (¶9000), he may still be treated as having been dismissed by the employer if he leaves before expiry of the employer's notice period, but the EDT will be the date the employee's notice expires (*Thompson v GEC Avionics Ltd* [1991] UKEAT 330_91_0409).

8347 In **constructive dismissal** cases, where the employee resigns with notice, the date of termination is the date the notice expires (*Peterborough Regional College v Gidney* [1998] UKEAT 1270_97_1311).

8348 Where the **employee or employer dies** during the employer's notice period, the contract is treated as having expired by notice terminating on the date of death (ss 133(1), 176(1) ERA 1996).

Dismissal without notice

8349 If the employee is dismissed without notice, the EDT is the date on which the termination takes effect (normally immediately, i.e. when the employer tells the employee that he is dismissed "with immediate effect" or when the employee ceases to work) (ss 97(1)(b), 145(2)(b) ERA 1996).

There is an argument that termination without notice, as a fundamental breach of contract, must be accepted by the innocent party in order to bring the contract to an end, rather than automatically terminating the contract. For statutory purposes, case law indicates that there is **no need for acceptance** (i.e. the employment is terminated automatically by the fundamental breach) (*Kirklees Metropolitan Council v Radecki* [2009] IRLR 555, CA, *Robert Cort & Son Ltd v Charman* [1981] ICR 816, EAT, *Dedman v British Building and Engineering Appliances Ltd* [1974] ICR 53, CA). Therefore, where the employer summarily dismisses the employee, the EDT is the date of dismissal.

> **EXAMPLE** In *Kirklees Metropolitan Council v Radecki*, an employee, R, was suspended, pending disciplinary investigations, and without prejudice negotiations for a compromise agreement were entered into. As a result of these negotiations, a termination date of 31 October 2006 was proposed. However, negotiations broke down and the parties never reached a binding agreement. The employer stopped paying R on 31 October 2006, notifying R in writing that it had done so. In February the following year, R phoned his employer to say that he was no longer represented by his union, that he was rejecting the proposals and requested payment for his outstanding salary. The employer wrote back to R stating that his employment had ended when it had stopped paying him. The Court of Appeal held that the EDT was when the employer ceased to pay R, and notified him that it had done so, as this amounted to a fundamental breach of the contract of employment, bringing it to an end. The EDT was therefore the date on which payment was stopped, and not a later date of when the employer wrote stating that R had been dismissed with effect from the date pay was stopped.

If the **summary dismissal is oral**, it will take effect at the moment it is communicated to the employee (and not at the end of that day or shift (*Octavius Atkinson & Sons Ltd v Morris* [1989] ICR 431, CA)). If the communication is **in writing**, the EDT is the day on which the employee reads it. Tribunals will take into account when letters arrive in the ordinary course of post and the fact that people normally open their post promptly after it arrives. However, if there is a delay, the EDT will be when the employee has actual knowledge of the termination (unless he has deliberately avoided reading the letter) (*Gisda Cyf v Barratt* [2010] UKSC 41; *McMaster v Manchester Airport Plc* [1998] IRLR 112, EAT). If an **employee sends a letter** resigning with immediate effect, the EDT is the date on which the resignation is effectively communicated to the employer (*Horwood v Lincolnshire County Council* [2012] UKEAT 0462_11_0304).

The date on which the employee is sent his **P45** is not relevant for the purposes of ascertaining the EDT (*London Borough of Newham v Ward* [1985] IRLR 509, CA).

> **EXAMPLE**
> 1. In *McMaster v Manchester Airport Plc*, M's letter of dismissal (terminating the employment immediately) was posted to his home. He did not see it until the day after it arrived as he had been away in France on that day. The EDT was the date he read the letter.
> 2. In *Gisda Cyf v Barratt*, the employee was dismissed without notice for gross misconduct. The decision was communicated to her by a recorded delivery letter which was signed for by her partner's son while she was away. Although she was expecting the letter, she did not ask about it until the morning after she returned, 4 days after delivery, when it was found and handed to her. The Supreme Court confirmed the Court of Appeal decision and held that where an employee is dismissed by letter, the dismissal will only take effect when the employee has actual knowledge of the termination which in this case was the date on which she read the letter, not the date on which it arrived.

8350 As for dismissal with notice, any **ambiguity** as to the effect of the dismissal is construed in favour of the employee.

8351 Where a **payment in lieu of notice** is made, the EDT is the date of dismissal (*Dedman v British Building and Engineering Appliances Ltd* [1974] ICR 53, CA).

8352 In cases of **constructive dismissal** where the employee resigns without notice, the EDT is normally the date the employee accepts the breach as terminating the employment (as opposed to the date of the employer's breach). This acceptance must be communicated (by words or conduct) to the employer, so a letter of resignation which purports to terminate the employment immediately cannot do so until it is received by the employer (*Edwards v Surrey Police* [1999] IRLR 456, EAT; *Weathersfield Ltd (t/a Van & Truck Rentals) v Sargent* [1999] IRLR 94, CA). Nevertheless, a fax which sets out an employee's resignation without notice is deemed to have been received by the employer (and therefore communicated to him) at the time it is sent (*Potter and others v R J Temple plc (in liquidation)* [2003] UKEAT 0478_03_1812). It is irrelevant if the fax is sent out of office hours and that the employer will not actually see it until the next working day.

> **MEMO POINTS** Only where the **breach itself inevitably terminates** the employer-employee relationship (for example, where the employee loses a directorship on which his employment depends) will the EDT be the date of the breach rather than the employee's resignation, where different (*BMK Ltd and BMK Holdings Ltd v Logue* [1993] UKEAT 781_92_0502).

8353 **Date of dismissal postponed** Where the employer has given no notice or inadequate notice, the employee's **statutory notice** entitlement is **added on** (i.e. the EDT/relevant date is postponed) for the **following purposes** (ss 97(2), (3), 145(5), (6) ERA 1996):
a. assessing continuous employment for claiming:
– a written statement of reasons for dismissal (s 92(7) ERA 1996);
– unfair dismissal (s 108(1) ERA 1996); and
– a statutory redundancy payment (s 155 ERA 1996); and
b. calculating the amount of an employee's continuous service in respect of:
– redundancy pay entitlement (s 162(1) ERA 1996); and
– unfair dismissal basic award (s 119(1) ERA 1996).
In relation to the EDT, this extension applies to both **express and constructive dismissal** cases (s 97(4) ERA 1996). The relevant date is not deemed postponed in cases of constructive dismissal.

Statutory notice is added on even where the employee has **waived** his right to notice or accepted a **payment in lieu** (*Secretary of State for Employment v Staffordshire County Council* [1989] IRLR 117, CA).

If the **employee dies** after the contract has been terminated but before the date on which proper notice (had it been given) would have expired, the relevant date will be the date of death (not the date on which statutory minimum notice would have expired) (ss 133(2), 176(2) ERA 1996).

8354 **No postponement** Statutory notice is not added on where the employer is entitled to dismiss the employee summarily (for example, because of the employee's **gross misconduct**), or for the purpose of determining the **time limit** for tribunal claims.

8355 If the contract is terminated without notice just before the employee becomes entitled to a certain **contractual benefit** (for example, enhanced pension rights), no notice is added on but the loss will be recoverable as part of a wrongful dismissal claim (¶8161). If the employee would have acquired a particular **statutory right** had the proper notice been given (for example, the right to claim unfair dismissal), the date of termination is not affected and it seems that the loss of chance will not be reflected in any award for wrongful dismissal (*Wise Group (The) v Mitchell* [2005] UKEAT 0693_04_1102 applying *Virgin Net Ltd v Harper* [2003] UKEAT 0111_02_0907 confirmed on appeal *Harper v Virgin Net Ltd* [2004] IRLR 390, CA).

Fixed-term contracts

8356 Where a fixed-term contract expires without being renewed, the EDT is the date of expiry (ss 97(1)(c), 145(2)(c) ERA 1996).

Trial period in alternative employment

8357 In redundancy cases, where the employee works for a trial period in alternative employment (¶8850) and leaves during that period, the relevant date for **qualifying service and payment calculation** purposes is the date of termination of the original contract (s 145(4)(b) ERA 1996). For **time limit** purposes, however, the relevant date is the date of termination of the trial period (or the last trial period, where more than one) (s 145(4)(a) ERA 1996).

Appeals against dismissal

8358 The employee may appeal the decision to dismiss him. If he is **reinstated** on appeal, there will be no dismissal (*Savage v J Sainsbury Ltd* [1980] IRLR 109, CA). If, however, the **decision to dismiss is confirmed**, the EDT will depend on the facts of the case and, in particular, the terms of the disciplinary procedure. Normally the employee is suspended pending the appeal decision and the contract does not subsist, such that the original date of dismissal stands (*Savage v J Sainsbury Ltd*). However, the contract may state that the employment subsists pending the appeal decision, with the dismissal not being implemented until that decision (*Drage v Governors of Greenford High School* [2000] IRLR 314, CA). Frequently, there is no express mention of the status of the employee pending the decision and the tribunal must ascertain the position from all the facts. Whether the employee continues to be paid while on suspension will be an important factor. If an employee's dismissal takes effect prior to the outcome of an appeal and the appeal varies the date of termination to a later date for some reason, the employment contract will be treated as having been temporarily revived for this period (*Hawes and Curtis Ltd v Arfan and anor* [2012] UKEAT 0229_12_0106).

> EXAMPLE In *Savage v J Sainsbury Ltd*, S's contract stated that, pending the appeal decision, S would be suspended without pay but if reinstated would receive full back pay. The Court held that the EDT was the original date of dismissal because the contract indicated that if the appeal failed, the employee would be deprived both of his pay and his right to work from the original dismissal date.

SECTION 2

Unfair dismissal

8380 All employees (and to a certain extent, some workers) also enjoy **statutory protection** on dismissal. If the dismissal is **discriminatory**, the employee may bring a discrimination claim on the grounds of age, disability, gender reassignment, marriage and civil partnership, pregnancy and maternity, race, religion or belief, sex or sexual orientation discrimination. If he is dismissed for an inadmissible reason, he can bring an unfair dismissal claim (with no requirement for qualifying service). In such cases, the dismissal will be **automatically unfair** (¶8390).

Dismissals to which the **transfer of business (TUPE)** regulations apply may also be automatically unfair and special rules apply (¶8030).

Employees with sufficient qualifying service can bring an unfair dismissal claim under the **general scheme** (s 94(1) ERA 1996; see ¶8410).

In order to avoid a claim of unfair dismissal under the general scheme, an employer must be able to show a **statutory fair reason** for dismissal. If he cannot, the dismissal will be unfair.

If he does have a fair reason, the employer must also act fairly in all the circumstances in treating that reason as a fair reason for dismissal. This essentially means that he must follow a **fair procedure**.

If an employee is unfairly dismissed, he can apply to an employment tribunal for a **remedy**.

8381

8382

I. Automatic unfair dismissal

It is automatically unfair to dismiss an employee for **certain inadmissible reasons**.

If there are **several reasons** for dismissal, the dismissal will be automatically unfair if the inadmissible reason is the principal reason for dismissal.

A dismissal will also be automatically unfair if the employee was **selected for redundancy** for an inadmissible reason, where the circumstances constituting the redundancy applied equally to one or more other employees in the same undertaking who held positions similar to that held by the dismissed employee and who have not been dismissed (s 105 ERA 1996).

In certain cases of automatically unfair dismissal, special provisions apply in relation to **remedies** (there may be no statutory cap on compensation, a minimum basic award may apply, and/or interim relief may be available). See the table at ¶8394 for further details.

8390

8391

8392

Qualifying employees

Employees dismissed for the following inadmissible reasons **do not need** to have any particular period of **continuous employment** in order to bring an unfair dismissal claim. If the employee would not otherwise have sufficient continuity of employment to bring a claim under the general scheme (see below), he must prove that the reason for dismissal was an inadmissible one (such that no qualifying service is required) (*Smith v Hayle Town Council* [1978] IRLR 413, CA).

For exclusions to the right to claim, see ¶8412 below.

Some workers (for definition, see ¶13), who are not employees, whose contracts are terminated for one (or more) of the inadmissible reasons shown in the table below, can complain that they have suffered a detriment by the termination of their contracts. The position for workers contrasts with that of employees, who have to bring a claim under the unfair dismissal rules in such circumstances.

8393

Inadmissible reasons

The following table lists the inadmissible reasons and shows who is protected against dismissal or detriment in those circumstances. Both employees and workers who are not employees are protected from being subjected to a **detriment** by any act or deliberate failure to act by their employer relating to one of the inadmissible reasons set out below. However, if the detriment in question amounts to a **dismissal**, then the only remedy available to an

8394

employee is a claim for unfair dismissal, whereas a worker, who is not an employee, whose contract is terminated can complain that he has suffered a detriment. In such cases, compensation is awarded on the same basis as for unfair dismissal.

Reason	Employee	Worker	¶¶
Seeking to enforce rights under part-time workers legislation	✓	✓	¶1920
Seeking to enforce rights under fixed-term employees regulations	✓		¶2013
Making a protected disclosure for the purposes of the whistleblowing legislation [1]	✓	✓	¶¶2763, 2769
Seeking to enforce rights under the national minimum wage regulations	✓	✓	¶2915
Trusteeship of occupational pension scheme	✓		¶3433
Protected shop/betting workers under Sunday trading legislation	✓		¶¶3861-2
Being summoned to attend for jury service or obeying a jury service summons [2]	✓		¶3965
Seeking to enforce rights under the working time regulations	✓	✓	¶4040
Pregnancy and maternity, paternity, adoption, parental, and dependant care leave reasons	✓		¶¶4765, 4771
Seeking to enforce rights under the right to request flexible working regulations	✓		¶4771
Exercising, or seeking to exercise, the right to be accompanied at a meeting to discuss request or appeal regarding flexible working	✓		¶4771
Exercising, or seeking to exercise, the right to accompany an employee at a meeting to discuss request or appeal regarding flexible working	✓	✓	¶¶4767, 4771
Health and safety reasons	✓		¶¶5145-6
Spent convictions [3]	✓		¶6672
Exercising, or seeking to exercise, the right to be accompanied at a disciplinary or grievance hearing, or for accompanying a fellow worker to such a hearing	✓	✓	¶¶6791, 6793
Seeking to enforce rights under the right to request time off to undertake relevant training regulations	✓		¶6447
Exercising, or seeking to exercise, the right to be accompanied at a meeting to discuss request or appeal regarding time off to undertake relevant training regulations	✓		¶6447
Exercising, or seeking to exercise, the right to accompany an employee at a meeting to discuss request or appeal regarding time off to undertake relevant training regulations	✓	✓	¶6447
Trade union reasons: – being, or proposing to be, a member of an independent trade union (or not being, or refusing to become or remain, a member), or taking part, or proposing to take part, in trade union activities, or making use of union services at an appropriate time – taking protected industrial action – trade union recognition or derecognition – unlawful inducement	✓	✓	¶¶7560, 7520, 7569, 7586, 7587
Due to a blacklist whose purpose is to discriminate against workers on grounds of their trade union membership or trade union activities	✓	✓	¶7565
Assertion of a statutory right	✓		¶8395

Reason	Employee	Worker	¶¶
Employee representation: – being an employee representative (or candidate) for collective redundancy consultation or business transfer consultation purposes, or taking part in an election of employee representatives for those purposes – membership of a special negotiating body or European Works Council, or being an information and consultation representative – being a candidate for any of the above under transnational information and consultation legislation	✓		¶¶8957, 8089, 7782, 7785

1. The right not to suffer a detriment on the grounds that a whistleblower has made a protected disclosure can apply after the employment has ended (*Woodward v Abbey National plc (No 1)* [2006] IRLR 677, CA).
2. There is a defence to a claim of automatic unfair dismissal on the ground of jury service if the employer can show that (s 98B ERA 1996):
– the employee's absence would have caused substantial injury to the employer's business; and
– once the employee had been made aware of this, he unreasonably refused or failed to apply to be excused from service or to have service deferred.
3. Although it is not expressly stated in case law, it is generally accepted that a dismissal on the grounds of a spent conviction is automatically unfair without the need to have a particular period of continuous service.

Assertion of statutory rights In relation to the assertion of statutory rights, the employee is protected if he brings proceedings to enforce the right or alleges that the employer has infringed the right (the allegation must be made prior to the dismissal) (s 104 ERA 1996). He need not have specified the right he sought to assert, as long as he made it reasonably clear to the employer what that right was (*Armstrong v Walter Scott Motors (London) Ltd* [2003] UKEAT 766_02_1903). Further, provided the employee acts in good faith, he is protected regardless of whether he is actually entitled to the particular right and regardless of whether that right has in fact been infringed (*Mennell v Newell & Wright (Transport Contractors) Ltd* [1997] IRLR 519, CA). However, it appears that an employee will not be protected if he alleges that the employer has merely proposed or threatened to infringe such a right.

8395

The **relevant statutory rights** include those relating to:
– employment documentation, including written statements of employment particulars, itemised pay statements, and written statement of reasons for dismissal;
– employee payments, including guarantee pay, medical/maternity suspension payments;
– protection against unlawful deductions from pay/unlawful receipt of payments by the employer, deductions of unauthorised or excessive union subscriptions, and requiring the employer to stop payment of a contribution to a union's political fund;
– time off for public duties, jury service, antenatal care, trade union duties and activities, trade union learning representatives' duties or training, employee representatives and candidates' study or training, employee pension scheme trustee duties or training, or to look for work/arrange training prior to redundancy;
– maternity, paternity, parental, adoption and dependant care leave;
– working time, rest periods, breaks and annual leave;
– making a public interest disclosure;
– protection against detriment in health and safety cases, cases relating to Sunday shop or betting work, or on trade union grounds; and
– rights on dismissal, including statutory minimum notice, not to be unfairly dismissed, and to a statutory redundancy payment.

EXAMPLE In *Albion Hotel (Freshwater) Ltd v Maia e Silva* [2002] IRLR 200, EAT, Mr and Mrs S were hotel managers, entitled to an annual bonus dependent on occupancy levels. The hotel did not perform well under their management and at two review meetings when the couple **asserted their right to a bonus**, the employer indicated that no bonus was likely to be payable. They were subsequently dismissed. The EAT agreed that they had been dismissed for asserting a statutory right, namely the right not to suffer an unlawful deduction from wages (the refusal to pay the bonus).

II. General scheme

A. Qualifying employees

8410 **Employees** who satisfy the requirements of continuous employment can bring an unfair dismissal claim, unless they are excluded (s 108(1) ERA 1996; SI 2012/989).

8411 Generally, employees who started their employment on or after 6 April 2012 must have 2 years' **continuous employment** ending on the effective date of termination (¶¶8340+). Those who started their period of continuous employment before this date require only 1 year's continuous employment.

For details on **calculating** statutory continuity, see ¶1040.

> MEMO POINTS 1. Employees **dismissed on medical grounds** in consequence of **certain health and safety requirements or recommendations** only need 1 month's continuous employment (s 108(2) ERA 1996) (¶4985).
> 2. There is no qualifying period with regard to **dismissals for certain inadmissible reasons** (¶¶8393+).

Excluded employees

8412 The following employees cannot bring an unfair dismissal claim:
– those working under **illegal contracts** (¶¶1305+);
– those who have waived the right to claim in a valid **compromise agreement** (¶¶9259+); and
– those taking part in **unprotected industrial actions** in certain circumstances (¶¶7520+).

B. Reason for dismissal

Dismissal

8420 If the dismissal is disputed, the first step in any unfair dismissal claim is for the **employee to show** that he has been dismissed. The definition of dismissal for these purposes is discussed at ¶8106.

8421 Certain employees can ask their employer to provide a written **statement of reasons** for dismissal (¶8310), which can be used as evidence in tribunal proceedings.

8422 Once the employee has shown that he was dismissed, the **employer must show** that the dismissal was for one of the statutory fair reasons (s 98(1) ERA 1996). If he cannot, the dismissal will be substantively unfair (*Timex Corporation v Thomson* [1981] IRLR 522, EAT).

The five **potentially fair reasons** are:
– incapability;
– misconduct;
– redundancy;
– contravention of a duty or restriction; and
– some other substantial reason.

Prior to the abolition of the default retirement age, **retirement** was also a potentially fair dismissal by the employer. As a direct consequence of the abolition of the default retirement procedure, retirement is no longer a potentially fair reason for dismissal in itself; any retirement dismissal must fall within one of the other potentially fair grounds for dismissal, most commonly some other substantial reason. Employers can still operate a compulsory retirement age as a normal retirement age as long as they can objectively justify it, i.e. the employer can demonstrate that it is a proportionate means of achieving a legitimate aim (outlined at ¶5615). If justifiable, such retirements will not amount to unlawful age discrimination (¶5611) or unfair dismissal (¶8380). If an employer wishes to rely on retirement as a reason for a dismissal, he should follow a fair retirement procedure as set out at ¶8209 and ¶8530.

> MEMO POINTS   The default retirement age was abolished with effect from 6 April 2011, subject to transitional provisions (under the transitional provisions with the maximum extension, 5 October 2012 was the last possible retirement date for those who attained age 65 on or before 30 September 2011 provided 6 to 12 months' notice to retire was given on or before 5 April 2011). Unless it falls within the transitional provisions, any dismissal because of age taking place on or after 6 April 2011 constitutes direct age discrimination (EqA 2010).

8423 The tribunal will investigate the **real reason** for the employee's dismissal and may find that the employer has incorrectly labelled the dismissal, in which case it may substitute the correct reason provided the necessary facts have been established (*Abernethy v Mott, Hay and Anderson* [1974] IRLR 213, CA; *Marenghi v Western Baths Club*, [2001] UKEAT 1508_00_1505). It will not do so, however, if the employee would be prejudiced where the difference in grounds goes to facts and substance such that he might have conducted his case in a substantially different way (*Hannan v TNT-IPEC (UK) Ltd* [1986] IRLR 165, EAT). The employer should, therefore, take care when deciding which reason for dismissal to plead when defending a claim (he may plead a different reason in the alternative). This is particularly important as different factors may need to be taken into account when judging the reasonableness of the dismissal for a given reason (*Wilson v Post Office* [2000] IRLR 834, CA). If the tribunal **wrongly categorises** the reason for dismissal, this amounts to an error of law (which can, therefore, be appealed) (*Amor v Galliard Homes Ltd* [2001] UKEAT 47_01_2509; *Wilson v Post Office*, above).

In **establishing the real reason** for a dismissal, the tribunal can look behind the reason given by the employer, even where it may be a potentially fair reason, if the employer may have made this reason a pretext for dismissing the employee on other grounds. For example where an employer, because of his antipathy towards the employee, makes misconduct an excuse to dismiss an employee in circumstances where the employer would not have treated others in a similar way. However, the fact that the employer welcomes the opportunity to dismiss when a reason affords does not render the dismissal unfair as there is a difference between a reason for the dismissal and the enthusiasm with which the employer adopts that reason (*Aslef v Brady* [2006] IRLR 576, EAT). The fact that there is **evidence of circumstances** which could justify the dismissal does not require the tribunal to adopt a presumption that that is the true reason. If the **employee disputes the reason** given for dismissal, it is for the employer to prove which reason was the principal reason for dismissal (*Maund v Penwith District Council* [1984] IRLR 24, CA applied in *Aslef v Brady* [2006] IRLR 576, EAT; *Kuzel v Roche Products Ltd* [2008] IRLR 530, CA).

> EXAMPLE **Categorisation of reason for dismissal**
> In *Wilson v Post Office*, the employer's tribunal defence stated that W was dismissed for "incapability by reason of unsatisfactory attendance record". The Court held that the tribunal incorrectly treated the case as one of incapability by reason of health rather than a case involving dismissal for another substantial reason (namely W's failure to meet the requirements of an agreed attendance procedure). The case was remitted for consideration on the correct basis.

8424 The reason for dismissal in **constructive dismissal** cases is the employer's reason for committing the fundamental breach. Unfair constructive dismissal is discussed in detail at ¶8251.

8425 If the employer **dismisses by giving notice**, the reason for dismissal is determined by reference to the reason when the employment terminates and also by reference to the reason for giving the notice (*Parkinson v March Consulting Ltd* [1997] IRLR 308, CA). The employer may only rely on **facts known to him at the time** of the dismissal when putting forward a potentially fair reason for dismissal. If the facts change between the date of giving notice and the date of termination, the tribunal can have regard to the latter date and the changed facts (*Parkinson v March Consulting Ltd*).

However, the employer cannot rely on **facts** which **emerge after the dismissal** to justify his decision to dismiss, although such facts may affect the amount of compensation awarded (*Devis & Sons Ltd v Atkins* [1977] IRLR 314, HL). Evidence of post-termination events is not, therefore, admissible in tribunal proceedings to establish the fairness or otherwise of a dismissal. It may be admissible in exceptional circumstances if it is relevant to the credibility of a witness or otherwise shows that other evidence given in relation to pre-termination events is inaccurate (*Overton v Healthcall Services Ltd* [2001] UKEAT 282_01_0407). If there is an **internal appeal**, the employer can rely on new information which comes to light to confirm the dismissal for the original reason (but not for a different reason) (*West Midlands Co-operative Society Ltd v Tipton* [1986] IRLR 112, HL).

8426 If the employer is **pressured to dismiss** by reason of the calling, organising, procuring or financing a strike or other industrial action (or the threat of such), that pressure is ignored when determining whether the employer had a fair reason for dismissal (and also whether it was fair in the circumstances to dismiss) (s 107 ERA 1996). However, the trade union/individual who induced the employer to dismiss may be joined in the proceedings and ordered to pay all or part of any compensation awarded (s 160 TULRCA 1992).

C. Procedure

8435 Where the employer has established one of the potentially fair reasons for dismissal, the **tribunal will then consider** whether he acted reasonably in all the circumstances (taking into consideration the size and administrative resources of his undertaking) in treating that reason as a sufficient reason for dismissal (s 98(4) ERA 1996).

8436 Employers who are contemplating dismissing an employee should **follow the Acas Code on discipline and grievance** to avoid any increase to tribunal awards if the employee subsequently brings a successful unfair dismissal claim (¶8634).

Requirement to act reasonably

8437 The dismissal must be within the band or **range of reasonable responses** which a reasonable employer might make, and the tribunal must not substitute its own view for that of the employer (*Iceland Frozen Foods Limited v Jones* [1982] IRLR 439, EAT; *Post Office v Foley and HSBC Bank (formerly Midland Bank) v Madden* [2000] IRLR 827, CA; *Aitkin v Weatherford UK Limited (Court of Session)* [2005] CSIH 26; *Anglia Home Improvements v Kelly* [2005] ICR 242, CA). This is essentially a **question of fact** and so the tribunal's decision cannot normally be appealed (the EAT hears appeals on points of law only and will only otherwise interfere if the tribunal has misdirected itself as to the law, reached a decision contrary to the facts, or if the decision is perverse).

Whether or not the employer's decision to dismiss falls within that range depends on the employer's **state of knowledge** at the time the decision was taken (*Asda Stores Ltd v Malyn* [2001] UKEAT 0066_00_0603). The question is determined in accordance with equity and the substantial merits of the case (i.e. the tribunal should adopt a broad approach of common sense and fairness, avoiding legal and other technicalities (*Earl v Slater & Wheeler (Airlyne) Ltd* [1972] IRLR 115, NIRC)). The tribunal should, therefore, not only consider the **way** in which the **dismissal was carried out**, but also whether the employer acted reasonably in relation to the situation **leading up to the decision to dismiss**. The employer's actions **during** any **notice period** after the decision to dismiss before termination may also be taken into account (*South Tyneside Council v Ward* [2011] UKEAT 0358_10_1207). As noted above, pressure on the employer to dismiss by reason of industrial action is ignored when determining the question of reasonableness.

EXAMPLE In *South Tyneside Council v Ward*, an employee brought a claim for unfair dismissal when she was dismissed after a long period of negotiation in relation to numerous complex grievances (these related both to the individuals managing her and changes that had been made to her workload). Her grievances proved difficult to resolve and, coupled with an occupational health report that she should not return to her post, her employer ultimately gave her notice of dismissal, but informed her that they would continue to try to resolve her grievances and search for suitable alternative employment during her notice period. The employee was uncooperative in relation to her grievances and unreasonably refused a number of offers of suitable alternative employment that were made during her notice period. The EAT held that the tribunal's finding that her dismissal had been unfair was based on a reasoning that effectively stopped the clock at the time that notice was given. They should have considered the possibility that even if the dismissal was unfair at the time of giving notice, it may not have remained so throughout the notice period. On this basis, the case was sent back to the original tribunal to consider the reasonableness of the dismissal as a whole.

To act reasonably, an employer must take into account the **best practice** principles set out in the relevant **codes of practice** (in particular the Acas code on discipline and grievance), and a tribunal will consider whether best practice guidance has been followed, even where the parties themselves do not refer to it (*Lock v Cardiff Railway Co Ltd* [1998] IRLR 358, EAT).

Examples of defects might include:
– inconsistency in treatment;
– a failure to warn an employee of substandard performance;
– a failure to give an employee sufficient detail of the allegations he must face at a disciplinary hearing;
– a failure to warn an employee that the disciplinary sanction of dismissal could be imposed; and
– an appeal being heard by someone with previous involvement in the disciplinary matter.

EXAMPLE
Within range of reasonable responses
In *Weston Recovery Services v Fisher* [2010] UKEAT 0062_10_0710, the employer ran a vehicle recovery business and dismissed one of its drivers without notice for returning a minibus he had borrowed in an unsafe state. The driver brought an unfair dismissal claim, in which the tribunal dealing with the case held that the decision to dismiss was within the range of reasonable responses, but that the offence was not one of gross misconduct. It went on to make a finding of unfair dismissal based on the failure of the employer to give notice. The EAT overturned the decision; if the decision to dismiss was within the range of reasonable responses for a single offence, the employer's failure to give notice of termination did not make the dismissal unfair. However, because there had been no gross misconduct, summary dismissal was a breach of contract and the EAT substituted a finding of wrongful dismissal, awarding loss of earnings for the period of notice.

Not within range of reasonable responses
In *Sarkar v West London Mental Health NHS Trust* [2010] IRLR 508, CA, a consultant psychiatrist was unfairly dismissed when his employer initially handled a disciplinary matter using a lesser dispute resolution procedure (in this case a "fair blame" procedure intended to help resolve workplace disputes and for use in cases of fairly low level breaches of conduct or performance standards), but later invoked its full disciplinary procedure and dismissed him. The Court considered that the tribunal was entitled to conclude that the inconsistency in treatment took the employer's actions outside the range of reasonable responses.

Size and administrative resources Tribunals will also take into account the size and administrative resources of the employer's undertaking. For example, it may not be possible for a small employer to offer alternative employment (see below) (*Bevan Harris Ltd v Gair* [1981] IRLR 520, EAT), or to have an elaborate disciplinary or appeals procedure (*MacKellar v Bolton* [1979] IRLR 59, EAT). However, the size of the undertaking will not justify a failure to properly investigate complaints made against the employee (and which lead to his dismissal) (*Henderson v Granville Tours Ltd* [1982] IRLR 494, EAT), nor will it excuse a complete failure to consult with a potentially redundant employee (although it may affect the nature or formality of the consultation process) (*De Grasse v Stockwell Tools Ltd* [1991] UKEAT 529_89_1111).

8438

Investigation The employer must make his decision having **ascertained all the relevant facts**, and the fairness of that decision is determined by reference to the circumstances

8439

known to him **at the time of the dismissal** (or confirmation of the dismissal following an internal appeal (*West Midlands Co-operative Society Ltd v Tipton* [1986] IRLR 112, HL)). Any investigation conducted by an employer into an employee's alleged misconduct should fall within the same **range of reasonable responses** as in relation to the dismissal itself (*Sainsbury's Supermarkets Ltd v Hitt* [2003] IRLR 23, CA, see ¶8508).

8440 **Consultation and alternative to dismissal** As a matter of best practice, a fair procedure will commonly oblige the employer to consult with the employee and consider alternatives to dismissal.

8441 **Internal appeal against dismissal** As a requirement of best practice there should be a **right of appeal** against the decision to dismiss. **Procedural defects** in the conduct of the appeal could also make an otherwise fair dismissal unfair. An appeal hearing that amounts to a complete rehearing can **cure any defects** (for example, in the consultation process), making a potentially unfair dismissal fair.

A tribunal must give consideration to all **new material** which emerges during the course of an internal appeal process in determining whether a dismissal is fair and should not limit itself in ascertaining an employer's belief to facts which were known to the employer at the time of the dismissal. Where additional evidence is being adduced at an internal appeal, it is not essential for an employer to conduct a full **re-hearing** of the disciplinary hearing (as opposed to a **review**) if the evidence relates to allegations which were raised at the original disciplinary hearing. If the new evidence relates to a matter which was not already considered at the original disciplinary hearing, then the employer must consider such evidence as an entirely separate disciplinary matter (*Arriva North West & Wales v Colebourn* [2005] UKEAT 0439_05_1810). See also ¶8439.

8442 **Other factors** Other factors commonly taken into account by tribunals include:
– **length of service**; and
– **consistency** (in the treatment of employees in a sufficiently similar position and in the treatment of a particular employee from one occasion to the next) (¶6546).

Polkey reduction

8445 Where there is an unfair dismissal (i.e. the tribunal has decided the employer has acted unreasonably), with regard to calculating an unfair dismissal compensatory award, the tribunal must take into account whether the employment may well have terminated anyway had a fair procedure been followed (see ¶¶8630+). This is commonly known as the "Polkey reduction" and applies equally to procedurally unfair dismissals (i.e. the employee would have been dismissed in any event had a proper procedure been followed) and substantively unfair dismissals (i.e. the dismissal would have occurred in any event at a later date for a different fair reason).

D. Application to specific cases

1. Incapability

a. Fair reason

8450 The employer will have a fair reason if the reason (or principal reason) for dismissal relates to "the **capability or qualifications** of the employee for performing work of the kind which he was employed by the employer to do".

The incapability must relate to the kind of **work the employee was employed to do**, which is determined by reference to his current contractual obligations. For the dismissal to be fair, it is not necessary that the employee is unable to perform all of his contractual duties (*Shook v London Borough of Ealing* [1986] IRLR 46, EAT).

Capability

Capability is assessed "by reference to skill, aptitude, health or any other physical or mental quality" (s 98(3)(a) ERA 1990). Incapability, therefore, covers the employee's **incompetence** and also his inability to do the job as a result of **illness**. The approach taken by the employer should vary depending on the type of incapability.

8451

Incompetence Incapability will **include** employees who fail to meet the employer's standards, who work too slowly, or who are physically incapable of doing their job. It also includes those whose mental qualities prevent them from fulfilling their duties.

8452

> EXAMPLE
> 1. In *A J Dunning & Sons (Shopfitters) Ltd v S Jacomb* [1973] IRLR 206, NIRC, J was fairly dismissed for incapability because he **lacked the necessary aptitude and mental qualities** to be co-operative with, and helpful to, important clients.
> 2. In *Abernethy v Mott, Hay and Anderson* [1974] IRLR 213, CA, A was dismissed for unreasonably refusing to work at a site other than the head office. The Court held that his **inflexibility and lack of adaptability** supported a fair dismissal for incapability.

The **test** for a fair capability dismissal is whether the employer **honestly believes** that the employee is incompetent, and that he has **reasonable grounds** for his belief (*Taylor v Alidair Ltd* [1978] IRLR 82, CA). The tribunal cannot substitute its own view of the employee's competence. The employer does not need to prove that his belief was correct. He must show that there was **evidence** available to him that satisfied him of the employee's incompetence and that, relying on that evidence, it was reasonable to dismiss. His belief may, for example, be founded on performance figures or exam results which directly relate to the employee's abilities, customer complaints, complaints from other employees, or evidence from the employee's supervisor or manager (*Cook v Thomas Linnell & Sons Ltd* [1977] IRLR 132, EAT).

8453

The employer's position will be weakened if he has made **other statements** that are **inconsistent** with his assertion of the employee's incapability (for example, in a reference to a prospective employer).

One act of incompetence is not normally sufficient to support a fair dismissal, unless the consequences are so serious that it would be too risky and dangerous to continue the employment (*Taylor v Alidair Ltd*). On the other hand, a **number of minor incidents** over a relatively short period of time resulting in a loss of confidence in the employee's abilities could be a sufficient reason for dismissal, even though individually the incidents would not justify such action (*Miller v Executors of John C Graham* [1978] IRLR 309, EAT).

8454

> EXAMPLE In *Taylor v Alidair Ltd*, T, a **pilot**, was dismissed after landing a plane carrying fare-paying passengers so hard that there was serious damage to the plane. The Court held that this **one-off error of judgement** justified a dismissal for incapability.

Incapability can be difficult to establish in the case of **managers** and other **senior employees**, as the quality of management may be difficult to assess precisely. Case law indicates that it is sufficient for a fair dismissal if the employer comes to the view over a period of time that the employee is incompetent, as long as he has supporting evidence for his view (for example, a fall-off in trade or feedback from colleagues or clients) (*Cook v Thomas Linnell & Sons Ltd*, above).

8456

In some cases, the employee's incompetence may really be **misconduct** (for example, where the employee fails to meet the required standard through his own carelessness, negligence or idleness (*Sutton & Gates (Luton) Ltd v Boxall* [1978] IRLR 486, EAT)). This will affect the way in which the employer should deal with the matter (¶8490).

8457

8458 **Ill health** Incapability due to ill health may relate to **persistent short-term illness** or to **long-term illness**. The employee's ill health may reduce his performance levels or prevent him from carrying out his duties at all if he is absent. In exceptional circumstances, the employee's ill health may **frustrate the contract**, in which case there will be no dismissal (and therefore no possibility of an unfair dismissal claim (¶8285)).

More commonly, the employee's ill health may be a fair **reason for dismissal** and the question will depend on all the facts of the particular case. The following **factors** will be relevant:
– the nature of the illness;
– the length and frequency of absences;
– the likely length of continuing or future absences;
– the employer's need to have work done by that employee; and
– the effect of the absence on his colleagues.

8459 If the ill health has been **caused by the employer's treatment** of the employee, the employee may be able to bring a personal injury claim against him. The fact that the employer caused the illness will not of itself make a dismissal unfair, although the tribunal can take this into consideration (*McAdie v Royal Bank of Scotland* [2007] EWCA Civ 806 confirming *London Fire and Civil Defence Authority v Betty* [1994] UKEAT 483_92_2104) (although where the employer's actions are wilful or malicious, it could make the dismissal unfair (*Edwards v Governors of Hanson School* [2001] UKEAT 314_99_1101)). The employer may be expected to show greater sympathy towards the employee where he has caused the illness, and his actions are likely to be relevant to an assessment of compensation (*Edwards v Governors of Hanson School*).

8460 It may be fair for the employer to dismiss where the employee's ill health makes it **unsafe for him to continue** in his position because of the danger presented to himself or to other employees (*Harper v National Coal Board* [1980] IRLR 260, EAT).

> EXAMPLE
> **Fair dismissal**
> In *Harper v National Coal Board*, H, an epileptic, had on three occasions had a fit during which he (unknowingly) **attacked other employees**. His dismissal was fair despite the fact that his epilepsy did not interfere with his actual job performance.
>
> **Unfair dismissal**
> In *Converform (Darwen) Ltd v Bell* [1981] IRLR 195, EAT, B was a works director at the employer's factory. His dismissal after a heart attack was unfair because the **risk of another heart attack** did not make it unsafe for him to continue in his position, given the nature of his work.

Qualifications

8461 "Qualifications" means "any degree, diploma or other academic, technical or professional qualification relevant to the position" (s 98(3)(b) ERA 1996). It is not always necessary for the employment contract **expressly** to refer to, or require, specific qualifications, as these may be **inferred** from a job advertisement (*Tayside Regional Council v McIntosh* [1982] IRLR 272, EAT), or **implied** from the nature of the position.

8462 In some cases, an employee is engaged on the understanding that he **will obtain a certain qualification**. If he subsequently fails to do so, the dismissal is likely to be fair, even if his performance has otherwise been satisfactory (*Blackman v The Post Office* [1974] IRLR 46, NIRC).

8463 The employer's **requirements** for particular qualifications **may change** over time. A dismissal may be fair where an employee does not meet the new requirements, but the employer must take special care to follow a fair procedure (see below).

8464 A dismissal is likely to be fair where the employee **loses his qualifications** (or if they lapse), although the employer should offer any available suitable alternative employment. Note that this might also be a fair dismissal on the grounds of contravention of a duty or restriction (¶8520).

> **EXAMPLE** In *Tayside Regional Council v McIntosh* (¶8461), M, a car mechanic, was fairly dismissed when he **lost his driving licence** as the job advertisement for the position had specified this as an essential requirement.

b. Fair procedure

8470 In cases of incompetence and ill health alike, the issue of fair procedure is often crucial in determining whether a dismissal for incapability was fair. A **tribunal will consider** what steps a reasonable employer would have taken, and what steps the employer could have taken at the outset to minimise the risk of poor performance and to enable the employee to carry out his duties to a satisfactory standard. These may include the provision of adequate training and supervision, and a satisfactory physical working environment.

Incompetence

8471 Where the employee's incapability is not due to his own negligence or idleness, the matter should be dealt with more sympathetically than cases of misconduct, with plenty of opportunity offered for improvement. It may still be appropriate, however, to treat incompetence as a disciplinary matter, in which case the employer should follow his **disciplinary procedure**. Handling poor performance is discussed at ¶6660.

This will normally require him to take the **following steps**:
– carry out an appraisal of the employee to identify the areas of concern;
– give guidance, supervision and, where necessary, additional training (particularly where an employee is promoted to a new job);
– give the employee a specific period of time for improvement;
– warn the employee of the consequences of failure to improve; and
– review the employee's performance after the specified period.

It may not always be necessary to follow each step, for example in cases of **gross incompetence** ("irredeemable incapability"), a failure to give a warning/opportunity to improve may not make a dismissal unfair (*James v Waltham Holy Cross U.D.C.* [1973] IRLR 202, NIRC; *Taylor v Alidair Ltd* [1978] IRLR 82). Similarly, in the case of **senior employees** (who, it is argued, should be aware of the standards to be met and whether they are meeting them), a warning may not always be necessary (*James v Waltham Holy Cross U.D.C.* [1973] IRLR 202, NIRC).

8472 An employee who has been **promoted** to a job that requires new skills that he proves incapable of acquiring is not automatically entitled to return to his old job (unless the contract provides such a right).

8473 Where, after the above steps have been taken, the employee still fails to meet the required standard (and in particular, where a promoted employee fails to meet the new requirements), the employer should normally consider the availability of **suitable alternative employment**, although this is not always required in cases of incompetence (*Bevan Harris Ltd v Gair* [1981] IRLR 520, EAT).

8474 There should be a **right of appeal** against the decision to dismiss.

Ill health

8475 The management of ill health differs according to whether the illness is short term or long term. These issues are discussed in detail at ¶4245. Handling absence generally is discussed at ¶6650. Persistent short-term absence is commonly treated as a disciplinary matter, while in **long-term** cases the employer will normally take the **following steps**:
– consult with the employee;

- obtain medical evidence (to ascertain whether the employee's health will improve and, if so, whether it will do so within a timescale that the employer's business requirements can accommodate);
- give a warning if there are a large number of short absences and where dismissal is being considered; and
- consider alternatives to dismissal (for example, changing work hours or offering suitable alternative employment).

> EXAMPLE
> 1. In *Elmbridge Housing Trust v O'Donoghue* [2004] EWCA Civ 939, an employee who refused to provide unequivocal consent to her occupational health report being passed to her employer was fairly dismissed on the grounds of capability after 3.5 months on sickness absence. Without access to the occupational health report, the employer was entitled to conclude that she was incapable on the basis of the limited material available to it.
> 2. In *Chaplin v Howard Kennedys Solicitors* [2009] UKEAT 0469_08_2001, an employee refused to consent to the disclosure of her medical records so that her employer could obtain a report on her fitness for work. She was dismissed for misconduct and claimed unfair dismissal. Her dismissal was held to be fair, despite the fact that she was not given another opportunity to agree to disclosure at the disciplinary hearing at which she was dismissed, as she had been given another chance to sign a consent form at an appeal hearing. This had cured the procedural defect and rendered the dismissal fair.
> 3. In *Governing Body of Hastingbury School v Clarke* [2007] UKEAT 0373_07_1712, the EAT found a dismissal unfair where a teacher, C, was dismissed for inappropriate sexual conduct towards school students. When the conduct came to the employer's attention, it had concerns about C's mental health and considered obtaining a medical report to see if this explained his behaviour. However, it instead instigated a disciplinary process and dismissed C for misconduct without waiting for a report. The EAT confirmed the tribunal's decision that no reasonable employer would have ignored the issue of the employee's health during the disciplinary process. After considering psychiatric evidence given at the tribunal hearing, the EAT further held that if a report had been obtained, C would have been fairly dismissed for incapability. The EAT commented that the safety of the children could have been protected by suspending the employee until a report was received. Applying the Polkey principle (¶8630) it held that compensation should be restricted to cover loss of income for the time it would have taken to obtain a report and carry out a fair dismissal on the grounds of incapability, in this case 10 weeks' pay.

8476 Again, there should be a **right of appeal** against the decision to dismiss.

8477 Where an employer has a contractually binding **scheme for early retirement** on the grounds of ill health, it should not dismiss an employee for incapability without first considering whether the employee will be entitled to benefit under the scheme and, if appropriate, implementing it (*First West Yorkshire Ltd t/a First Leeds v Haigh* [2008] IRLR 182, EAT). This is in addition to any right the employee might have to make a claim for breach of contract arising where the employer dismisses the employee in such a way as to deprive him of the right to benefit from such a contract term (¶¶1174, 4203).

The employer should also consider the impact of **disability discrimination** legislation (¶5450). A dismissal could be unfair but not amount to disability discrimination (for example, because the employee's illness does not amount to a disability, as defined). However, it is likely that a discriminatory dismissal will almost always also be unfair.

> EXAMPLE In *First West Yorkshire Ltd t/a First Leeds v Haigh*, the employer offered H, an employee who had been absent for some months, the option of being dismissed or accepting an alternative arrangement which would deprive him of any right to participate in its **early retirement scheme**, before evidence was obtained as to whether H would be fit to return to work before his normal retirement date. The EAT held that while long-term absence is a potentially fair reason for dismissal, fairness required the employer to take reasonable steps to consider whether H would qualify under its ill health retirement scheme before dismissing for sickness.

2. Misconduct

a. Fair reason

8490 The employer will have a fair reason if the reason (or principal reason) for dismissal relates to the conduct of the employee.

To constitute a fair reason, the misconduct must in some way reflect on the employer-employee relationship (*Thomson v Alloa Motor Co Ltd* [1983] IRLR 403, EAT). Misconduct **includes**:
– a breach of the employer's workplace or disciplinary rules (or of the standards of behaviour commonly required by employers) (*McPhie and McDermott v Wimpey Waste Management Ltd* [1981] IRLR 316, EAT);
– a refusal to obey a lawful order (*R Farnborough v The Governors of Edinburgh College of Art* [1974] IRLR 245, NIRC); and
– in limited circumstances (principally relating to criminal charges or convictions), misconduct committed outside the employment (¶6671), although there may be possible human rights implications in such cases.

It is the employee's own conduct which is relevant and not the conduct of those around him (*Wadley v Eager Electrical Ltd* [1986] IRLR 93, EAT).

> EXAMPLE In *Wadley v Eager Electrical Ltd*, W's summary dismissal following his **wife's dismissal for theft** was unfair.

8491 Dismissal for misconduct may be appropriate after a **series of incidents** (provided the employer follows a fair procedure – see below) or, in serious cases of misconduct (known as **gross misconduct** (¶6640)), after a **single incident**. As with all reasons for a fair dismissal, the decision to dismiss must be within the "range of reasonable responses" which a reasonable employer might make.

> EXAMPLE In *Nejjary v Aramark Ltd* [2012] UKEAT 0054_12_3105, N, a hospitality manager responsible for organising the location of and catering for business meetings, brought a claim for unfair dismissal after he was dismissed for gross misconduct. He was initially suspended as a result of two complaints for failures to check that event arrangements were in order. However, shortly after his suspension, the client complained to his employer about N's lack of enthusiasm and asked that he not be assigned to an event they were hosting. The employer concluded, at a disciplinary hearing, that each of the three complaints amounted to gross misconduct and he was therefore dismissed. Although N had a live warning on his disciplinary record and another live warning under appeal, both in respect of previous matters of conduct, the employer did not take those warnings into account because it considered the new set of complaints to be standalone acts of gross misconduct, which did not require the "totting up" of previous warnings in order to dismiss. During N's internal appeal, the appeal officer discounted two of the complaints, but upheld his dismissal in respect of the third complaint. N brought an unfair dismissal claim in which the tribunal held that, had he had a clean disciplinary record, dismissal for that single complaint would have been outside the band of reasonable responses. However, taking into account the previous live warnings for similar issues, it was reasonable for N's employer to treat his misconduct as a sufficient reason to dismiss. In the alternative, if his dismissal was unfair, the tribunal held that N had contributed 100% to his dismissal so that it was not just and equitable to award compensation. On appeal, the EAT overturned the tribunal's decision on both points. The EAT held that the tribunal had wrongly considered parts of the employee's disciplinary record which the employer had not taken into account when deciding to dismiss. The tribunal should have restrained themselves to consideration of the single incident of misconduct relied upon by the employer. As the tribunal had felt that this incident, on its own, was not sufficient for the dismissal to be within the band of reasonable responses, the EAT substituted a finding of unfair dismissal. The EAT went on to overturn the decision of contributory fault because N, having been dismissed by reason of a single instance of misconduct, could not have been said to have contributed to his dismissal by reason of previous matters of conduct which were not in play in the employer's decision to dismiss.

8492 Misconduct may still be a fair reason for dismissal where an employee is dismissed where there is **more than one suspect** (¶6550).

8493 **Breach of disciplinary rules or acceptable standards of behaviour** Disciplinary rules are discussed in detail at ¶6534. In summary, to support a fair dismissal:
a. the rules must be:
– relevant to the employment;
– clear and unambiguous; and
– consistently applied;
b. the matter must be dealt with promptly;
c. other factors, such as length of service, should be taken into account; and
d. the sanction of dismissal must be appropriate in the circumstances.

8494 **Refusal to obey** The dismissal may be fair if the employee has refused to obey a **lawful order**, which is one which the employer is entitled to give according to the employee's contract (for example, refusing to relocate where the contract contains a wide mobility clause). However, not all cases of refusing to obey a lawful order will justify dismissal.

8495 If the employee refuses to obey an order which is outside the scope of the contract (an **unlawful order**), a dismissal may be unfair, but this will depend on the circumstances (*Farrant v The Woodroffe School* [1997] UKEAT 1117_96_0810). The tribunal may find that the employee has caused or contributed to the dismissal (which will affect the amount of compensation awarded).

> EXAMPLE **Unlawful orders**
> 1. In *C W Graham v Anthony Todd (Haulage) Limited* [1975] IRLR 45, IT, G, an apprentice mechanic, was dismissed when he refused to **work overtime**. As the employer could not lawfully require him to work overtime, the dismissal for refusal to obey the unlawful order was unfair.
> 2. In *Brandon and Goold v Murphy Bros* [1983] IRLR 54, EAT, B and G were dismissed for refusing to **work over New Year** so that their employer could meet the demands of its main customer. Despite the fact that they were contractually entitled not to work, the dismissal was fair in all the circumstances.
> 3. In *Ferrie v Western No 3 District Council* [1973] IRLR 162, IT, F was an assistant gardener. He was unfairly dismissed for **refusing** to clear out a pond unaccompanied, as his refusal was reasonable given the **danger** presented by the task.
> 4. In *R F Deegan v T T Norman & Sons Ltd* [1976] IRLR 139, IT, D was the only tacker in the employer's footwear business. He refused the employer's unlawful instruction to **work overtime** so as to process an important order in time. The dismissal was unfair but D's refusal to co-operate had contributed to his dismissal and his compensation was reduced by 50%.

b. Fair procedure

8500 Employers must ensure that they follow a fair procedure. For this reason, it is essential for employers to ensure that they are aware of, and implement, the **best practice principles** which are laid down in the Acas Code on discipline and grievance and other regulatory guidelines. This and other issues relating to fair procedure in misconduct cases are discussed in chapter 19. Details on procedure in relation to **specific topics** are found as follows:

Absence	¶6650
Poor performance	¶6660
Trade union officials	¶6670
Employees facing criminal charges/conviction	¶6671
Isolated employees	¶6676

8501 In summary, **best practice** requires that a fair procedure will normally **include**:
– having clear rules as to required standards of conduct (and sanctions for breach) and making employees aware what actions amount to gross misconduct (¶6540);
– applying the disciplinary rules consistently but not inflexibly (¶6546);
– carrying out an investigation to establish the facts (¶6585);
– giving the employee the opportunity to put his side of the case (¶6619), although it is not always essential that an employee accused of alleged misconduct be allowed to cross-

examine his accusers (¶6618; see also *Santamera v Express Cargo Forwarding t/a IEC Ltd* [2002] UKEAT 780_01_2611);
- having more than one manager involved in the dismissal and disciplinary process (though this may not be possible for smaller organisations) (*Masterfoods (a division of Mars UK Ltd) v Wilson* [2007] ICR 370, EAT). Further, those involved in the process must have an open mind with regard to the outcome of an employee's disciplinary proceedings;
- taking account of the employee's representations before making any disciplinary decision (including any mitigating circumstances);
- deciding on the appropriate sanction (¶6630);
- if the employer decides to dismiss, clearly explaining the reason for the dismissal; and
- giving the employee the opportunity to appeal (¶6680).

Where a misconduct dismissal is likely to result in the **loss of an individual's future career** in their chosen profession, the employer's investigation, disciplinary process and appeal must be particularly fair and thorough, and the evidence of misconduct must be particularly clear and cogent (*Crawford and anor v Suffolk Mental Health Partnership NHS Trust* [2012] EWCA Civ 138).

Note that there is a statutory **right to be accompanied** at certain disciplinary and grievance hearings (¶6780).

8505

The tribunal needs to be satisfied that the employer, at the time of dismissal (*British Home Stores v Burchell* [1978] IRLR 379, EAT, approved in *Post Office v Foley and HSBC Bank (formerly Midland Bank) v Madden* [2000] IRLR 827, CA):
- had a **genuine belief** in the employee's guilt of that misconduct;
- had **reasonable grounds** to hold this belief; and
- carried out such **investigation** as was reasonable in all the circumstances.

This does not apply where there is **more than one suspect** (¶6550).

The first limb relates to fair reason, while the second and third are concerned with the reasonableness of the decision to dismiss (*Post Office v Foley and HSBC Bank (formerly Midland Bank) v Madden*). Each of the three limbs must be satisfied for a fair dismissal. For example, if the employer had a genuine belief in the employee's guilt, having carried out a reasonable investigation, but based his decision on inadequate and unreliable evidence (such that his belief was not held on reasonable grounds), the dismissal will be unfair (*Granges Building Systems Ltd t/a Glostal Monarch v Hill* [1999] UKEAT 666_99_0810). In large organisations, an employer may not be expected to know exculpatory facts known by management (but withheld from him) when taking a decision to dismiss an employee for gross misconduct (*Orr v Milton Keynes Council* [2011] EWCA Civ 62). In *Orr*, by a majority of 2: 1, the Court of Appeal held that the employer could not be deemed to know all information known to its employees, even those at management level, and that a dismissal would be fair provided the appropriate legal test was met (i.e. a reasonable investigation was carried out and there was an honest belief in the employee's guilt based upon reasonable grounds). As a point of principle, Parliament must have meant for large organisations, whilst remaining employers, to dismiss employees on the basis of decisions taken by individuals on its behalf who are not at the most senior level. Although this is a practical decision based on the reality of how large organisations work, employers must still be careful to gather all the information that might be relevant before dismissing an employee. As the judgment highlights, a reasonable investigation must be carried out and failure to do so may render any dismissal unfair and may breach the employer's duty of care towards the employee.

EXAMPLE In *McGowan v Scottish Water* [2005] IRLR 167, EAT, undercover surveillance cameras used to "spy" on an employee who was suspected of falsifying timesheets were deemed to be proportionate to his alleged misconduct. Covert surveillance went to the root of the investigation, enabling the employer to protect its assets, and the dismissal of the employee was therefore deemed to be fair.

In determining whether the test has been satisfied where an employee has been dismissed **before** he attended a **disciplinary hearing**, the tribunal will consider not only what would have happened at that disciplinary hearing had it taken place, but also whether the dismissal would have been fair or unfair, i.e. had the dismissal been made after a disciplinary hearing (*Panama v London Borough of Hackney* [2003] IRLR 278, CA).

To satisfy the fair procedure test, the **employer should have concluded** that it was more likely than not that the employee committed the alleged misconduct. He **cannot take into account** matters which were not known to him at the time of the dismissal in order to defend an unfair dismissal claim (*Devis & Sons Ltd v Atkins* [1977] IRLR 314, HL) (¶8425).

8506 Where the employee is facing **very serious allegations** of misconduct, including criminal conduct, then the seriousness of the criminal charges and their potential implications are relevant circumstances to consider and, as such, a very thorough and careful investigation must be carried out by the employer (*A v B* [2003] IRLR 405, EAT). Likewise, **the more severe the consequences** of dismissal for the employee the greater care an employer will be expected to take in carrying out its disciplinary procedure (*Salford Royal NHS Foundation Trust v Roldan* [2010] IRLR 721, CA).

> EXAMPLE
> 1. In *Salford Royal NHS Foundation Trust v Roldan*, a Filipino nurse was dismissed for allegedly mistreating a patient. When she lost her job she also lost her work permit and the right to remain in the UK. She successfully claimed unfair dismissal on the basis that conflicts of evidence had not been properly investigated and she had not been given clear enough details of a previous incident which was taken into account. The Court of Appeal held that the tribunal was entitled to reach this conclusion, particularly bearing in mind the consequences for dismissal for the claimant. It commented that the more severe the consequences of dismissal for the employee the greater care an employer will be expected to take in carrying out its disciplinary procedure.
> 2. In *Turner v East Midlands Trains* [2012] EWCA Civ 1470, the Court of Appeal held that a former employee, T, who had been dismissed on the grounds of gross misconduct, was not entitled to a more stringent investigation than that provided for under domestic law in order to satisfy her rights under human rights legislation. T was a train conductor and was found to have been purposely producing faulty tickets and selling them to the public, keeping the proceeds for herself. She claimed that although the investigation was adequate for the purposes of domestic law, it did not satisfy the requirements under Article 8 of the European Convention on Human Rights, nor did the "range of reasonable responses" test, which was not sufficiently robust where human rights issues were at play. The Court accepted that Article 8 rights were engaged in this case (because matters relating to a professional or business nature could be included within the realm of private life), but held that T's rights were sufficiently protected by the domestic law, particularly given the heightened requirement for a more stringent investigation where more serious consequences are.

> MEMO POINTS In determining a wrongful dismissal claim, the tribunal must decide what, as a matter of fact, actually happened and whether what the employee actually did was so fundamental a breach as to justify instant dismissal. In contrast to the test in unfair dismissal cases, the employer's "reasonable belief" of what happened is irrelevant (*London Central Bus Company Ltd v Nana-Addai* [2011] UKEAT 0204_11_2909).

8508 **Dismissal** must be within the **range of reasonable responses** which a reasonable employer might make. The range of reasonable responses test is equally applicable to **procedural**, as well as **substantive, fairness** relating to an employer's decision to dismiss an employee (*Centre West London Buses Ltd v Balogun and anor* [2005] UKEAT 0067_05_1910). Consequently, provided that an employer can demonstrate that his actions in deciding to dismiss an employee fell within the range of reasonable responses which a reasonable employer may have, then a tribunal should not substitute its own view as to what was procedurally or substantively fair or not for that of the employer (i.e. it should not ask itself whether a lesser penalty would have been reasonable but rather whether or not dismissal (and the procedure undertaken in respect of that dismissal) was reasonable). In addition, any **investigation** conducted by the employer into an employee's alleged misconduct should fall within the same range of reasonable responses as in relation to the dismissal itself (*Sainsbury's Supermarkets Ltd v Hitt* [2003] IRLR 23, CA). In cases where the **employee admits to the offence** but fails to offer any explanation for his actions at every opportunity he is given to do so, the employer is not under a duty to enquire further into the employee's reason for committing the offence (*Weatherford UK Ltd v Aitken* [2003] UKEAT 0049_03_1812).

> EXAMPLE
> 1. In *Centre West London Buses Ltd v Balogun and anor*, the employees had absented themselves from a disciplinary hearing on the (unreasonable) advice of their union representative. In such circum-

stances, the EAT held that the tribunal had erred in finding that a reasonable employer would have rearranged the hearing to allow the employees to attend. The employer had been entitled to continue the disciplinary hearing in the absence of the two employees.

2. In *Fuller v London Borough of Brent* [2011] EWCA Civ 267, an administrator at a school for children with social and emotional difficulties was involved in two incidents where she intervened when children were being restrained by trained teaching staff. After the first, she was told that the head teacher would speak to her about her interference, but no formal warning was ever given. Disciplinary action was taken after the second incident. The Court of Appeal reinstated the tribunal's decision that it considered the employer was acting unreasonably to dismiss in the circumstances.

3. Redundancy

8510 The employer will have a **fair reason** if the reason (or principal reason) for dismissal is redundancy (as defined – see ¶8740). A **business reorganisation** may not always fall within the statutory definition of redundancy. In such cases, the dismissal may still be fair for some other substantial reason (¶8530).

8511 Although redundancy is a fair reason for dismissal, it is **automatically unfair** to select an employee for redundancy for certain reasons, including pregnancy and health and safety (¶8390).

8512 In order to show that he has acted reasonably, the employer must follow a **fair procedure**. This is discussed at ¶8800.

4. Contravention of a duty or restriction

a. Fair reason

8520 The employer will have a fair reason for dismissal if he can show that he would be acting in breach of legislation by continuing to employ the employee, for example where an employee employed as a driver loses his driving licence (*Fearn v Tayford Motor Co Ltd* [1975] IRLR 336, IT), or where an employee is refused a work permit and so cannot legally work in the UK. The continued employment must **actually contravene** legislation (a genuine but mistaken belief does not suffice, although it may amount to some other substantial reason – ¶8545).

> EXAMPLE In *Kelly v University of Southampton* [2008] ICR 357, EAT, a university employee, K, obtained a 60-month permission to work from the Department for Education and Employment, and a 48-month leave to remain from the Immigration and Nationality Directorate. One month before the leave to remain was due to expire, K informed her university of the deadline. K contacted the personnel department, and with the department's support made an emergency application for her leave to remain to be extended. Before hearing back from the Immigration and Nationality Directorate, the university dismissed K on the basis that had it continued to employ K it would have been in breach of the Immigration Rules. However, the EAT concluded, on a reading of the Immigration Rules, that Parliament had not intended to impose criminal liability on an employer in the (admittedly rare) circumstances that an employee's leave to remain has ceased, while his permission to work remains valid. Further, even where there was a contravention, a decision to dismiss may still be unfair. Whether a dismissal is fair will depend on the circumstances of the case and in this case it was not reasonable for this employer to have dismissed K in breach of its agreement to support her application for extended leave to remain.

b. Fair procedure

8525 The employer's obligation to act reasonably may require him to consult with the employee, informing him of the situation and inviting his views. He should consider whether he could make any reasonable adjustments to the employee's duties to allow him to continue in

5. Some other substantial reason

a. Fair reason

8530 This is the "**catch-all**" category which covers fair reasons not covered by the preceding four categories. To fall within it, the employer must show that the reason (or principal reason) for dismissal is a "substantial reason of a kind such as to justify the dismissal of an employee holding the position which the employee held" (s 98(1)(b) ERA 1996). This is known as the "SOSR" defence. Tribunals must not substitute their own views in such cases but, instead, consider whether the reason advanced by the employer could constitute a SOSR and, if so, whether the employer's decision to dismiss was a reasonable response (*Scott & Co v Richardson* [2005] UKEAT 0074_04_2604). SOSR applies to many varied situations which cannot be fully listed here. In all cases, the general principles set out below should be taken as guidance, and careful attention paid to following a fair procedure.

SOSR **most commonly applies** to action taken by the employer to protect his business, including:
– business reorganisations/changes requiring variations to employment terms to which the employee refuses to agree; and
– dismissal of employees who refuse to enter restrictive covenants necessary for the protection of the employer's legitimate business interests.

As a result of the abolition of the default retirement age and accompanying retirement process, any fair **retirement dismissals** are likely to be classed as SOSR situations. For further details, see ¶¶8199+. For guidance as to appropriate fair procedures, see ¶8209.

Other SOSR situations are described further below.

8531 The SOSR defence is available in the case of an employee who is dismissed for an economic, technical or organisational reason entailing changes in the workforce in the context of a **transfer of an undertaking** (¶8041).

Business reorganisations

8532 A dismissal of an employee who refuses to accept a change in terms and conditions as part of a business reorganisation may be fair if the employer has a "**sound, good business reason**" for the reorganisation (*Hollister v National Farmers' Union* [1979] IRLR 238, CA). There may be an overlap with dismissal for redundancy and it is open to the employer to plead both redundancy and SOSR in the alternative.

The employer must have evidence of the advantages of the changes (*Banerjee v City and East London Area Health Authority* [1979] IRLR 147, EAT), but he need not show that the variation was essential. However, making the business more profitable is unlikely to be seen as a good business reason in itself – the employer should be under some kind of pressure to make the reorganisation.

> EXAMPLE In *Genower v Ealing Hammersmith and Hounslow Area Health Authority* [1980] IRLR 297, EAT, a prosecution in the supplies department in which G worked had led to a reorganisation of the department and a decision that control of the department should not rest with one person for too long. As a result, G's duties and place of work were changed, and he resigned. The EAT held that the dismissal was fair. Referring to *Hollister v National Farmers' Union*, it found that a reorganisation may be a fair reason for dismissal even if the alternative is not that the business would come to a standstill but merely that there would be a **serious effect on the business**.

8533 **Changing working hours** The changes to terms and conditions often involve a requirement to **work overtime** or to agree to **flexible working patterns**.

EXAMPLE
1. In *L Moreton v Selby Protective Clothing Co Ltd* [1974] IRLR 269, IT, the employer sought to vary M's contract to require her to work during the school holidays. This was essential to maintain production and M was given 12 months' notice of the change. M's dismissal for refusing to agree was fair.
2. In *B E Robinson v Flitwick Frames Ltd* [1975] IRLR 261, IT, R was the only employee who refused to work overtime to meet peaks in demand. As the employer's request was reasonable (and also because R would have remained in the bonus pool, making calculation of his entitlement compared to those who worked overtime difficult), he was fairly dismissed.
3. In *Korry Foods v Lynch* [2005] UKEAT 0032_05_2005, the employer sought to persuade L to work a 6-day week to avoid a two-tier system of working, increase the perception that Saturday was a working day and improve the quality of supervisory cover. The employer was able to show an improvement in Saturday trading performance and this was deemed to be sufficient to pass the "low hurdle" of establishing the SOSR defence. There was no need for the employer to demonstrate the quantum of improvement which would be achieved if the changes were made.
4. In *Copsey v WWB Devon Clays Ltd* [2005] IRLR 811, CA, it was held to be fair to dismiss a Christian employee who refused to work on Sundays. The employee argued that the dismissal infringed his freedom to manifest his religion under art 9 of the European Convention on Human Rights. While there were diverging views as to whether art 9 was relevant in this context, it was agreed that any infringement (under the law of unfair dismissal with or without reference to art 9) had been justified as the employer had compelling economic reasons requiring the introduction of a 7-day shift. This case was brought prior to employees having the right not to be discriminated against due to their religion or belief (¶5375). However, the outcome is unlikely to have been different as the change of practice could be justified as a proportionate means of achieving a legitimate aim (in this case, a business necessity which required a change to a 7-day shift pattern).

Relocation A refusal to relocate in order to be within a reasonable distance of the place of work may be a fair reason for dismissal (*Farr v Hoveringham Gravels Ltd* [1972] IRLR 104, IT). **8534**

Opposing interests The tribunal will also take into account the **interests of the employees** when determining whether the employer had a good business reason for dismissal. The reasonableness (or otherwise) of the employee's refusal will also be relevant (*Evans v Elemeta Holdings Ltd* [1982] IRLR 143, EAT). **8535**

EXAMPLE In *Evans v Elemeta Holdings Ltd*, the employer sought to introduce a new contract which included an obligation to work mandatory and unlimited overtime. The EAT found that there was no evidence of an immediate need to introduce that requirement and that it was **reasonable for E to refuse** to agree (his dismissal was, therefore, unfair).

In some cases, however, the **interests** of the employees and those of the employer may be **irreconcilable** and the fairness of the dismissal will be determined by considering whether the employer's decision to dismiss was within the band of responses of a reasonable employer (see below). **8536**

Confidentiality and competition issues

The employer may wish to **introduce a new term** to protect his business interests, i.e. to prevent the disclosure of confidential information to a competitor, or to restrict the ability of employees to resign and set up a competing business. A dismissal for refusal to agree to the new term may be fair. The EAT has confirmed this (refusing to follow its previous approach in *Forshaw v Archcraft* [2004] UKEAT 0677_04_1312) and held that a **dismissal for a failure to agree** to restrictive covenants is capable of constituting a SOSR situation, unless the contract that the employer was seeking to make was so manifestly unreasonable that the purported reason was in fact a cover or a ruse to get rid of the employee (*Willow Oak Developments Ltd t/a Windsor Recruitment v Silverwood and ors* [2006] ICR 1552, CA). Consequently, the consideration of the reasonableness of the new contract, including the **reasonableness of the covenants** sought to be imposed, arises at the stage of deciding fairness (¶¶8435+, 8550) and the EAT outlined the approach that should be taken: **8537**

a. if the proposed covenant appears plainly unreasonable and not severable, it may be easier for a tribunal to conclude that there was unfairness;

b. if the proposed covenant is arguably unenforceable (and/or severable), greater consideration should be given to the approach of the employer (in particular, the amount of time given to consider proposals and the opportunity given for legal advice); and
c. if the covenant is plainly reasonable, then there will still need to be consideration of the fairness of the procedure but the tribunal may well be satisfied that the dismissal was fair.

> EXAMPLE In *R S Components Ltd v Irwin* [1973] IRLR 239, NIRC, the employers' business was being damaged by departing sales employees, who were setting up in competition. In reaction to this, the employers sought to **introduce a new restrictive covenant** in the contracts of the remaining employees, which aimed to prevent competition for 12 months after the termination of their employment. I refused to accept the new covenant and he was dismissed. The NIRC held that the dismissal was fair on the grounds of SOSR, as the employers were entitled to protect their business interests.

8538 It may be fair to dismiss an employee where there is a real **risk of a leak of trade secrets** which could substantially damage the employer's interests, for example, where an employee has close **connections with a competing business**.

> EXAMPLE
> 1. In *D C Foot v Eastern Counties Timber Co Ltd East Harling* [1972] IRLR 83, IT, F was a wages and accounts clerk. She was dismissed when her husband set up a competing business and her dismissal was fair.
> 2. In *Coleman v Skyrail Oceanic Ltd (t/a Goodmos Tours)* [1981] IRLR 398, CA, C was a booking clerk with the employer's travel agency. She was dismissed on her marriage to an employee of a rival firm. Her dismissal was unfair (partly because, despite the fact there had been leaks, C was never accused of being the source, and partly because she was given no warning).
> 3. In *Chandlers (Farm Equipment) Ltd v Rainthorpe* [2005] UKEAT 0753_04_0802, C was dismissed on the grounds that her husband had left the company to work for a competitor. However, there was nothing in C's past conduct to lead her employer to reasonably think that any disclosure to her husband, even unintentionally, would occur. Both she and her husband were long-standing employees with good records and reputations. C's employer had therefore acted unreasonably and her dismissal was unfair.

Temporary contracts

8539 The SOSR defence may apply to the dismissal of an employee who was taken on as a temporary worker, provided it was explained at the outset that the job was only temporary (*Terry v East Sussex County Council* [1976] IRLR 332, EAT; approved in *North Yorkshire County Council v Fay* [1985] IRLR 247, CA).

This applies specifically to employees who are engaged as **replacements** for permanent workers who are absent due to pregnancy or childbirth, or on medical or maternity suspension, provided the return of such workers is the actual reason for dismissal and as long as the employee was informed in writing of the temporary nature of the post (s 106 ERA 1996).

8540 A fair procedure must still be followed; in particular, the employer should offer any available suitable alternative employment (see below).

Breakdown of mutual trust and confidence

8541 Where, as a result of an act of the employee (for example, a conviction for dishonesty), the employer (or his customers) has lost trust and confidence in him, the SOSR defence may apply (*Wadley v Eager Electrical Ltd* [1986] IRLR 93, EAT). However, employers must be mindful not use this as a reason for dismissal when other reasons that may be more difficult to pursue are really at play, such as misconduct. The tribunals have demonstrated a growing awareness of employers using SOSR as a ruse for disguising misconduct dismissals, so where misconduct is at issue the first step should always be rigorously applying the Acas code, rather than looking for a way to mould the situation into a loss of trust and confidence, because unless there is a clear case for this (such as in situations involving dishonesty) it may be difficult to prove.

Breakdown of working relationship

The SOSR defence may apply where the working relationship has broken down (for example, because of a clash of personalities between employees (*Treganowan v Robert Knee & Co Ltd* [1975] IRLR 247, QBD; *Perkin v St George's Healthcare NHS Trust* [2006] ICR 617, CA). However, the breakdown must be irreparable, and the employer should seek to improve relationships and investigate alternatives to dismissal (*Turner v Vestric Ltd* [1981] IRLR 23, EAT). **8542**

Dismissal at request of third parties

The SOSR defence may apply in exceptional circumstances where the employer is requested to dismiss an employee by a third party, for example a major customer (*Scott Packing & Warehousing Co Ltd v Paterson* [1978] IRLR 166, EAT). The employer must be able to show that he had tried to reason with the third party (if he disagreed with them) and that he gave due consideration to the potential injustice suffered by the employee. Consequently, even though there may be injustice if the third party is acting unreasonably, that will not render the dismissal unfair if the employer can show that he did everything he reasonably could have done to avoid dismissing the employee (*Henderson v Connect (South Tyneside) Ltd* [2010] IRLR 466, EAT). **8543**

Imprisonment

Imprisonment may bring the employment to an end by **frustration**, in which case there will be no dismissal (¶8290). **8544**

If, on the facts, the contract cannot be said to be frustrated, the SOSR defence may apply, depending on the nature of the offence, the position held by the employee, and the length of the sentence (*Kingston v British Railways Board* [1984] IRLR 146, CA). Misconduct may also apply (¶8490).

Genuine belief that dismissal fair

The SOSR defence may be available where the employer had a genuine belief that the **reason for dismissal** was fair, even where modern sophisticated opinion can show that his belief has no scientific foundation (*Harper v National Coal Board* [1980] IRLR 260, EAT). **8545**

Similarly, SOSR may apply to a genuine but mistaken belief that continued employment would be unlawful (for example, a breach of the immigration rules) (*London Borough of Hounslow v Klusova* [2008] ICR 396, CA; *Kurumuth v NHS Trust North Middlesex University Hospital* [2011] UKEAT 0524_10_2203; *Bouchaala v Trust House Forte Hotels Ltd* [1980] IRLR 382, EAT).

> **EXAMPLE**
> 1. In *Kurumuth v NHS Trust North Middlesex University Hospital*, an employee, K, had uncertain immigration status as she was going through an appeals process for leave to remain, though she did have a letter from the Home Office stating that she was allowed to be in the UK while her appeal was being determined. Following the introduction of the points-based immigration system, the employer was no longer satisfied that this letter was sufficient proof of her right to work and, after raising enquiries with the UK Border Agency, who failed to provide a clear response, dismissed her. The EAT held that it was not for the tribunal to consider the true factual status in terms of the employee's right to work, but merely to establish if the employer had conducted a reasonable investigation and had a genuine belief upon which the dismissal was based. In this case, the dismissal was reasonable when the UK Border Agency had not satisfied the employer that K had the right to work in the UK.
> 2. In *London Borough of Hounslow v Klusova*, K, a Russian national, was granted, in 1999, limited leave to remain for a period of 5 years until May 2004. In November 2000 she entered the Council's employment. The Council summarily dismissed her in August 2005 on the grounds that K had lost the right to work after her original limited leave to remain had expired. In fact K had made an in-time application to the immigration authorities at the Home Office and as her application had not been properly determined at the date of her dismissal she could have lawfully continued in employment pending its proper determination. The Court of Appeal held that the Council did have a fair reason for dismissing K, as its genuine but mistaken belief was that to continue employing K would be unlawful. However, as the Council had failed to follow the prescribed dismissal procedures K's dismissal was procedurally unfair.

A mistaken belief that the **employee had resigned** (and an insistence on the employment ending when the employee belatedly changed his mind) has been held to be a fair dismissal for SOSR (*Ely v YKK Fasteners (UK) Ltd* [1993] IRLR 500, CA).

Takeover of the business

8546 An employer may be able to argue the SOSR defence in respect of the dismissal of an employee following a successful takeover of the company in which the employee is employed, provided that due regard is given to the position held by the dismissed employee and the dismissal fell within the range of reasonable responses which could be taken by the employer (*Cobley v Forward Technology Industries Ltd* [2003] IRLR 706, CA).

> MEMO POINTS Where the dismissal is related to a TUPE transfer, see ¶8030.

b. Fair procedure

8550 To ensure that any such dismissal is fair, as a matter of **best practice** the employer must normally:
– consult with employees (even if there is an urgent financial need to introduce changes);
– discuss proposed changes with them in advance;
– explain the impact of proposed changes;
– consider and respond to representations and objections raised; and
– consider alternatives to dismissal, such as finding alternative jobs or moving staff to other locations.

The employer's decision to dismiss must be within the **range of responses of a reasonable employer** and the **following factors** will be relevant:
– the terms of the offer, and the number of employees who accepted it (*St John of God (Care Services) Ltd v Brooks* [1992] IRLR 546, EAT);
– the employer's motives (for example, if less favourable terms are offered because the employer was suffering financial difficulties and was trying to increase profits or avoid bankruptcy) (*Catamaran Cruisers Ltd v Williams* [1994] UKEAT 786_93_1301);
– the trade union's recommendation of the changes (*Catamaran Cruisers Ltd v Williams*);
– whether the employees are adversely affected financially (if so, it will be more difficult to persuade a tribunal of the employer's reasonableness); and
– whether the employer is acting reasonably in deciding that the advantage to him of implementing the changes outweighs any disadvantage which the employee might suffer (*Richmond Precision Engineering Ltd v Pearce* [1985] IRLR 179, EAT; *Chubb Fire Security Ltd v Harper* [1983] IRLR 311, EAT).

III. Enforcement and remedies

8560 An employee who wishes to bring an unfair dismissal claim must **apply to** an employment tribunal **within** 3 months of the effective date of termination (¶8340). Where the dismissal is connected with industrial action, the time limit is 6 months. The tribunal has a discretion to **extend the time limit** where it was not reasonably practicable for the claim to be presented on time (it must then be submitted within a reasonable time). For further information on time limits, see ¶9450.

It should be noted that where there is a **dismissal with notice**, it is possible to bring a claim after the notice of dismissal has been given (¶8343) but before the EDT (s 111(3) ERA 1996).

8561 If the **employee dies**, his personal representative can apply to the tribunal or continue existing unfair dismissal proceedings.

8562 If the employee becomes **bankrupt**, he can still pursue a claim of unfair dismissal since the complaint constitutes a claim for **personal relief** (for example, such as a declaration and/or compensation for injured feelings) and does not therefore vest in his trustee in bankruptcy (*Khan v Trident Safeguards Ltd* [2004] IRLR 961, CA).

8563 **Three remedies** are available for unfair dismissal: reinstatement or re-engagement and/or compensation (ss 113, 118 ERA 1996). The employee can indicate which of these remedies he is seeking when submitting his unfair dismissal claim (he is not bound by this indication), and again, if his claim is upheld, when the tribunal explains the remedies available to him. The tribunal can only order reinstatement or re-engagement if the employee so requests (s 112(3) ERA 1996). If he does not, the tribunal can only consider compensation.

In certain circumstances, the employee can apply for **interim relief** (including reinstatement, re-engagement, and continuation of the employment contract) pending the final determination of his claim.

The **table** at the end of this section shows the circumstances in which particular remedies may be available (¶8710).

A. Compensation

8570 Compensation is by far the most commonly made order. An award is in two parts: the basic award and the compensatory award. In some cases, an additional award (¶8689) may also be ordered.

Unlike wrongful dismissal awards, a tribunal award for unfair dismissal is not itself taxable as earnings, but instead will be treated in the same way as payments which are taxed under sections 401 and 403 ITEPA 2003 (¶3125).

8571 Where the employee is **paid less than the national minimum wage**, neither the calculation of a week's pay (¶2920) for a basic award nor the assessment of any compensatory award should be based on what the employee was being paid but should be based on the national minimum wage he should have received (*Paggetti v Cobb* [2002] UKEAT 136_01_2203).

1. Basic award

8575 If the tribunal finds that an employee has been unfairly dismissed and makes a compensation order, it must make a basic award (s 119(1) ERA 1996). This is calculated by reference to age, length of service to the effective date of termination (¶8340), and salary as follows (s 119(2) ERA 1996):
– for each complete year of employment in which the employee was aged 41 or over: 1.5 week's pay;
– for each complete year in which he was aged 22 to 40: 1 week's pay; and
– for each complete year in which he was aged 21 or under: 0.5 week's pay.

The table at ¶9007 for redundancy payments can also be used to calculate the employee's entitlement to a basic award.

A **week's pay** is subject to a statutory cap. For details on this cap and on calculating a week's pay, see ¶2920. **Length of service** is subject to a maximum of 20 years, and is calculated according to statutory continuity of service (contractual agreements relating to continuity are ignored) (¶1040).

The **current maximum** basic award is, therefore, £13,500 (£450 × 20 × 1.5).

8576 In the situations discussed below, the amount of the basic award may be subject to a minimum level, a specific reduction or limit, or a general reduction.

Minimum basic award

8577 If the employee is dismissed (or selected for redundancy) for **certain inadmissible reasons**, there is a specified minimum basic award (before any general reductions (¶8578) are made), currently £5,500 (s 120(1) ERA 1996, s 156 TULRCA 1992).

The inadmissible reasons are:
– trade union membership or activities;
– being an employee representative, candidate, or voter in relation to collective redundancy or business transfer consultation;
– being a workers' representative for health and safety purposes or a member of a safety committee;
– carrying out (or proposing to carry out) health and safety activities (having been designated by the employer to do so);
– being a workforce representative for working time purposes (or a candidate to become one); and
– being a trustee of an occupational pension scheme.

Where an employee is regarded as unfairly dismissed because of a blacklist (¶7565), the amount of the basic award of compensation is £5,500 (s 120(1C) ERA 1996).

> MEMO POINTS If an employer has dismissed an employee and has in doing so unreasonably failed to follow the Acas Code on discipline and grievance, the tribunal has a discretion to **increase any award** it makes by up to 25% (¶8634).

Reductions

8578 In the following circumstances, the basic award is subject to a reduction or limit.

8580 **Certain redundancy dismissals** The basic award payable to an employee who has been dismissed because of redundancy is limited to 2 weeks' pay if (s 121 ERA 1996):
– he has unreasonably refused (or left) suitable alternative employment;
– his contract has been renewed; or
– he has been re-engaged.

8581 **Unreasonable refusal of offer** If the employee has unreasonably refused an offer from the employer which would have effectively **reinstated** him as though he had not been dismissed, the tribunal can reduce the basic award to the extent it considers just and equitable (s 122(1) ERA 1996). The tribunal will consider whether the employee acted unreasonably in refusing the offer, but it is not sufficient for the employer to show that such an offer was reasonable (*Wilding v British Telecommunications plc* [2002] IRLR 524, CA).

However, if the **employment** offered **differs** in any way **from his previous terms**, this reduction will not apply even if the employee's refusal could be considered unreasonable.

8582 **Employee conduct** The tribunal may also reduce the basic award if it feels that it would be just and equitable to do so as a result of the employee's conduct **before the dismissal** (or if the dismissal was with notice, before notice of dismissal was given) (s 122(2) ERA 1996).

The tribunal can take into account **any conduct** on the part of the employee, and not just conduct which caused or contributed to the dismissal. This applies even if the conduct is **discovered after the dismissal** (or giving of notice).

The basic award will not be reduced for employee conduct where the reason (or principal reason) for the dismissal was **redundancy**, unless the reason for selection was an inadmissible one attracting a specified minimum basic award (see above), in which case the reduction only applies to that part (s 122(3) ERA 1996). In most redundancy cases, the basic award and the statutory redundancy payment will be the same amount. This provision enables the tribunal to reduce the part of the basic award over and above the normal basic award which the employee is only entitled to because he was selected for an inadmissible reason.

> EXAMPLE An employee is dismissed for capability (because the employer does not feel he is doing his job well enough) but, for procedural reasons, the dismissal is unfair. The employer subsequently

discovers that the employee has been defrauding him. The tribunal is likely to decide that it would not be just and equitable to order the employer to pay a basic award.

Receipt of other employer payments If the employee has received a **redundancy payment**, this will be set off against the basic award provided that the dismissal was genuinely because of redundancy (s 122(4) ERA 1996; *Boorman v Allmakes Ltd* [1995] IRLR 553, CA). In most redundancy cases, the basic award and the statutory redundancy payment will be the same amount, so effectively this means that the employee's statutory redundancy payment if made will be offset against the basic award.

8583

If the employee has received an award under a designated **dismissal procedures agreement**, the tribunal can reduce the basic award to the extent it considers just and equitable (s 122(3A) ERA 1996).

An **ex gratia payment** made by the employer will only reduce or extinguish the basic award if it can be shown that it was intended to cover this liability. If the ex gratia payment is made in settlement of liability for unfair dismissal in general, there appears to be a presumption that this is intended to cover both the compensatory award and the basic award (*Chelsea Football Club and Athletic Co Ltd v Heath* [1981] IRLR 73, CA). The tribunal must determine as a question of fact whether any part of the payment which was made was intended to cover the basic award.

Blacklist dismissal also dismissal for trade union membership or activities The basic award for a dismissal due to a blacklist shall be reduced or further reduced by the amount of any basic award in respect of the same dismissal on grounds related to trade union membership or activities (s 122(5) ERA 1996).

8584

2. Compensatory award

The **purpose** of compensation is to put the employee, as far as possible, in the position which he would otherwise have been in had he not been unfairly dismissed. It is **not intended to punish** the employer (i.e. the compensation awarded does not increase according to the degree of unfairness). There is, therefore, **no** award of **punitive** or **exemplary damages**.

8585

The compensatory award will be such amount as the tribunal considers just and equitable in all the circumstances having regard to the loss suffered by the employee as a result of the dismissal, subject to the statutory cap (see below) (s 123(1) ERA 1996). Essentially, the tribunal should ask itself two questions: first, is the claimant's dismissal one of the causes of his loss of earnings (this will be a question of fact) and secondly, what compensatory award is just and equitable in all the circumstances (this is a matter of discretion) (*Dignity Funerals Limited v Bruce* [2005] IRLR 189, CS). A tribunal should only consider the second question if there is factual proof that the claimant's loss of earnings was caused to a material extent by his dismissal.

The starting point is, therefore, the employee's losses, but the tribunal has a **wide discretion** and it can refuse to award any compensation at all, even if the employee's loss is significant. It may do so, for example, if the **employee committed serious misconduct** during his employment which did not come to light until after the dismissal, as it may consider that had the employer been aware of the misconduct at the time of the dismissal, he would have been justified in dismissing and could have done so fairly. If an employee is dismissed for incapability, the tribunal may take into account allegations that the **employer caused his illness** when deciding whether it is just and equitable to make a compensatory award (*Edwards v Governors of Hanson School* [2001] UKEAT 314_99_1101). It should also be noted that tribunals must consider the specific facts of each case and should not be constrained by compensation given in earlier tribunal decisions (*Elkouil v Coney Island Ltd* [2002] IRLR 174, EAT).

The amount of the compensatory award may be **reduced or adjusted** to reflect:
– sums paid by the employer;
– the employee's failure to mitigate his loss;
– the possibility that the employee could have been fairly dismissed;

8586

– any contributory fault; and
– whether either party has unreasonably failed to follow the Acas Code on discipline and grievance.

If the employee has received **social security benefits**, part of the award may be recouped by the Government. These are discussed further below. The order in which any such reductions are made is set out at ¶8665 below.

Moreover, where a successful complaint is brought under both the unfair dismissal and **anti-discrimination legislation** (¶8111), compensation will not be awarded twice for the same loss (s 126 ERA 1996).

8587 The compensatory award is subject to a **statutory cap** of £74,200 which is applied once all other deductions and reductions have been made.

There is **no cap** for certain types of automatically unfair dismissal, namely dismissals for "whistleblowing" or health and safety reasons (or selection for redundancy for those reasons). Further, if an award of compensation is made with a reinstatement or re-engagement order (see below), the tribunal can disregard the cap and award compensation equal to the employee's actual loss between termination of employment and the date of reinstatement/re-engagement (s 124(3), (4) ERA 1996).

> MEMO POINTS The Department for Business, Industry and Skills (BIS) launched a consultation "Ending the Employment Relationship" on **proposals** to vary the statutory limit on the compensatory award under powers contained in the Enterprise and Regulatory Reform Bill. The consultation sought views on the current level of the statutory cap and in particular whether it should be reduced. The discretion to reduce the cap would be a wide one; the Government could set the cap at an amount of between one and three times the median annual earnings (currently £25,882 – £77,646). Views were also sought on the introduction of a secondary cap of 12 months' pay, meaning that the statutory cap could vary from employee to employee depending upon their earnings. There were no proposals to change the basic award. Responses were accepted until November 2012. Any further developments will be covered by our updating service.

a. Losses for which compensation can be awarded

8590 The loss for which the tribunal can award compensation **includes** (s 123(2), (3) ERA 1996):
– expenses reasonably incurred by the employee as a result of the dismissal; and
– loss of any benefits which he might reasonably be expected to have had but for the dismissal (though any loss of the right to a redundancy payment (statutory or otherwise) will only be taken into account to the extent that it exceeds the basic award).

Employees can only recover **losses which flow from the dismissal** itself and not for earlier breaches of contract (*GAB Robins (UK) Limited v Triggs* [2008] EWCA Civ 17). However, there is no bar to separate proceedings to recover loss of earnings in respect of contractual breaches prior to dismissal (¶1725).

In making an award of compensation, the tribunal should **set out** the types of loss which it has included and explain how it has carried out the calculation (*Blackwell v GEC Elliott Process Automation Ltd* [1976] IRLR 144, EAT).

> EXAMPLE In *GAB Robins (UK) Limited v Triggs*, a breach of trust and confidence by the employer had led to the employee, T, being absent from work as a result of stress, and prior to dismissal she had been receiving only sick pay. T claimed loss of earnings based on her full rate of pay. The Court held that T's loss in a claim for constructive unfair dismissal must be calculated on the basis of her actual earnings – i.e. sick pay, not the earnings she would have received if the employer had not been in breach of contract.
> Note: It should be noted that the dismissal in this case was constructive with the employee resigning as a result of the employer's breach of trust and confidence. The Court held that while the employer's repudiatory conduct was an essential condition of a constructive dismissal, it was not that conduct that effected the dismissal. It was the employee's acceptance of it. Consequently, damage caused by the conduct prior to the dismissal has to be claimed as a separate cause of action and not as part of an unfair dismissal claim.

Causation

The tribunal can only award compensation in respect of losses which flow from the **employer's actions** (*Leonard v Strathclyde Buses Ltd* [1998] IRLR 693, CS). Therefore, if something happens after the dismissal which breaks the chain of events, the tribunal will not award any further compensation. For example, if an employee suffers a stroke between being dismissed and the tribunal hearing such that he is permanently unable to work, any loss of earnings after that date is attributable to his medical condition and not to the actions of the employer.

8591

> EXAMPLE In *Henderson and ors v Mite Olscot Ltd* [2008] UKEAT 0030_07_0802, the employer, who was running his business at a loss, wished to introduce new terms and conditions. The claimants refused to agree the new terms and were dismissed when the employer closed the business down. The tribunal found that they had been unfairly dismissed, but reduced their compensation for loss of earnings to zero, applying the Polkey reduction (¶8630), on the grounds that employment would not have continued past the date of dismissal in any event. On appeal, the EAT agreed that there would be no compensatory award, but said that the correct way of reaching this conclusion was on the grounds that the losses had not been caused by the dismissal but the claimants' own decision not to accept the deal that was on offer, and so were not recoverable.

Complications can arise if the employee, after being dismissed, **obtains another job which he subsequently loses**.

8592

If the employee takes a **short-term temporary job** which comes to an end, or a job on a short **trial basis** in which he is not kept on, the tribunal may be persuaded that he was only in the position of having to take such a job because the first employer's actions had left him out of work. The earnings from the second employment will be taken into account in calculating compensation, but he should be able to claim further compensation from the original employer for the period after the second job ends.

Where the employee finds a **new job** but **loses it soon afterwards**, his first employer may remain liable for loss of earnings suffered after loss of the new job (*Cowen v Rentokil Initial Services Ltd t/a Initial Transport Services* [2008] UKEAT 0473_07_0603). If, however, the employee takes a new job which **lasts for a reasonable period** of time and then is, for example, made redundant or dismissed for misconduct, it will be more difficult to persuade the tribunal that the first employer should be held responsible for subsequent losses as this will be an intervening event which breaks the chain of causation.

If the employee **enrols on a course** after being unfairly dismissed, he may be entitled to compensation for future losses beyond the date of enrolment (*Khanum v IBC Vehicles Ltd* [1999] UKEAT 685_98_1509).

> EXAMPLE In *Khanum v IBC Vehicles Ltd*, K enrolled on a degree course after being unfairly dismissed. She was entitled to compensation for future losses beyond the date of enrolment as she decided to follow the course because she was unable to obtain a suitable job in her chosen career and needed to retrain. As such, losses incurred while studying were a direct result of her dismissal.

Earnings and other benefits

When calculating compensation for loss of earnings and other benefits, it is the **net equivalent** of such payments which is taken into account (as the employee would have had to pay tax and national insurance on his earnings and other benefits and, therefore, using the gross figures would result in over-compensation).

8593

Loss of earnings is separated into **two parts**:
– loss from dismissal to the date of the hearing; and
– future loss;
and the tribunal must distinguish between the two (*Seafield Holdings Ltd (trading as Seafield Logistics) v Drewett* [2006] UKEAT 0199_06_2706). **Past loss** should be calculated on a "but for" basis: if the acts of the employer were a cause of the dismissal, then the employer will be liable for the employee's loss, even if other causes were also at work. **Future loss**, by contrast, should be calculated by taking into account the percentage chance that some external factor might

have contributed to the employee's inability to work. The employer will only be liable for that proportion of the harm for which he is responsible.

8594 **Loss prior to hearing** The tribunal calculates the **earnings** which the employee would have earned from the employer between the date of the dismissal and the date of the hearing, taking into account any **pay increases or bonuses** which the employee might have been expected to receive during that period. It is not necessary to show a definite contractual entitlement to such bonuses or increases as long as the tribunal is satisfied on the evidence that in practice they would have been received (*York Trailer Co Ltd v Sparkes* [1973] IRLR 348, NIRC).

8595 The tribunal also takes into account **other benefits** such as company car, private health insurance, mobile telephone, and share schemes. The tribunal places a **value** on each benefit, usually on the basis of what it would cost the employee to obtain similar benefits privately. Often the taxable value of the benefit shown on a P11D or the value ascribed by the AA (for company cars) is used as a guide. For items such as company cars and mobile telephones, the tribunal only awards compensation if (and to the extent that) the employee was also allowed to use them for **private use**.

8596 **Future loss** This is more difficult to assess. The tribunal takes into account not only **salary** but also the value of **other benefits** (¶8593).

> MEMO POINTS Where the tribunal is quantifying loss, such as the loss of share options, which is dependent on a number of **uncertain future events** (for example, the likely flotation of a company and resulting share values), it must assess the chance of that event materialising in percentage terms and not on the balance of probabilities (*Selective Beauty UK Ltd v Hayes* [2005] UKEAT 0582_04_0503).

8598 If the **employee is still suffering a loss** at the date of the hearing, either because he remains out of work or he has only been able to obtain work at a lower rate of pay, the tribunal will **consider how long** such loss might be **expected to continue**, which naturally requires a degree of speculation. The Court of Appeal has confirmed this approach and has emphasised that deciding what compensation for future loss is just and equitable "will almost inevitably involve a consideration of uncertainties" (*Thornett v Scope* [2007] ICR 236, CA; *Wardle v Credit Agricole Corporate and Investment Bank* [2011] EWCA Civ 545). The tribunal may **also take into account** the fact that the old employment would have ended fairly in any case, or that the employer had a good reason for dismissal but failed to follow a fair procedure. It can make a reduction to reflect its findings which is discussed further below (see ¶¶8628, 8630+ respectively).

Where an employee has **not found a new job** at the date of the tribunal hearing, the tribunal has to decide when or if he is likely to find a job and, if so, the likely salary. In most cases it is foreseeable that claimants will at some point obtain an equivalent job: this is inevitably a speculative exercise (as already mentioned) and it encompasses the possibilities that the claimant will find a job both sooner and later than predicted. Compensation should stop at the point that a tribunal finds that an equivalent role will be found unless there are exceptional circumstances, such as where a claimant changes career to a less well-paid profession and the mitigation evidence shows this career change to be reasonable. It will be a rare case where **career-long loss** will be appropriate and this would primarily be the case where there was no real prospect of the employee obtaining an equivalent job (*Wardle v Credit Agricole Corporate and Investment Bank*). The tribunal will take into account its own knowledge of the local employment situation and the employee's age, range of skills and previous experience. It is essentially a matter of judgement for the tribunal and since it has a wide discretion, it is rarely possible to challenge its decision on appeal.

Being in **receipt of incapacity benefit** (now called employment and support allowance) does not mean that the employee was incapable of any work and is not a bar to his recovering loss of earnings (*Sheffield Forgemasters International Ltd v Fox, Telindus Ltd v Brading* [2009] ICR 333, EAT).

> MEMO POINTS It should be noted that "Ogden tables" (which provide for an actuarial adjustment of future loss of earnings and benefits) may only be used when the future loss to be assessed is expected to last for the rest of the employee's working life (*Dunnachie v Kingston upon Hull City Council* [2003] UKEAT 0726_02_2205; *HSBC Bank plc v Drage* [2003] UKEAT 0369_02_0807).

8599 If the employee has **obtained a new job** which is likely to continue indefinitely, the loss is the difference between the old pay and the new pay. The tribunal will decide for how long the employee should be compensated in this way. Its task in making this determination is similar to the task it faces in assessing how long an unemployed applicant will remain out of work (see below).

If the employee's new job **pays more** than the old job (taking into account the value of any benefits), and is likely to continue, then he has no continuing loss.

If, at the date of the hearing, the employee is working but it appears likely that his new job **will come to an end** for some reason, then in deciding if any further loss after the end of that employment should be attributed to the original employer, the tribunal will apply the same principles as are described at ¶8591.

8600 As compensation for future loss will be **awarded in a lump sum**, rather than earned over a period of months or years, the tribunal may (particularly if the period in question is a long one) make a reduction to reflect **accelerated receipt**. This is normally around 5%, although the Court of Appeal has expressed the opinion that this figure is out of line with, and somewhat higher than, the percentage applied in other civil cases (for example, the discount for accelerated receipt applied in personal injury cases is 2.5%) (*Bentwood Brothers (Manchester) Ltd v Shepherd* [2003] IRLR 364, CA). A tribunal is also entitled to make allowances for delayed payment when considering compensation and apply a premium to **delayed or decelerated** payments in the same way as deductions are made for accelerated receipt (*Melia v Magna Kansei Ltd* [2006] IRLR 117, CA).

> EXAMPLE An employee, aged 60, was earning £25,000 per year and now earns £20,000 per year in his new employment. The tribunal believes that had he not been dismissed, he would have remained in his previous employment until retiring at 65. It also believes that having found this new job, it is likely that he will remain in it until the same age. The loss is, therefore, £5,000 per year for 5 years: £25,000 (which will probably be subject to a deduction for accelerated receipt).

Pension rights

8601 Loss of pension rights can continue beyond loss of earnings.

Occupational pension schemes fall into **two main categories**:
– final salary (also known as defined benefit); and
– money purchase (also known as defined contribution).

In **final salary** schemes, the pension is based on a fraction (often around 1/60) of the employee's final salary for each complete year of service. An employee's loss on dismissal in relation to a final salary scheme is clearly based on him losing the right to a pension based on his final salary. The employee may, however, be entitled to a deferred pension (see further below) and his loss is therefore broadly based on the difference between the deferred pension and the pension and other benefits he would have received had he not been unfairly dismissed.

In **money purchase** schemes, the pension is based on the level of contributions made by employer and employee. An employee's loss on dismissal is therefore equal to the value of the further contributions the employer would have made. This is normally a fixed percentage of salary and can be worked out fairly easily. The tribunal must then decide how many years' worth of contribution ought to be awarded, which it does by considering what is likely to happen in the future, including the likelihood of the employee finding another job, when, and whether that job will have a pension attached to it. The tribunal also has to consider the other factors considered above in relation to future loss generally. There is no loss in respect of the employee's own future contributions as the compensation awarded for loss of earnings or any earnings from a new job can be paid into a new pension scheme. However, a dismissed employee may be required to pay a penalty for leaving a money purchase scheme early, which will be a loss directly associated with the dismissal.

Pension **loss should be treated** in the same way as any other financial loss in that only losses caused by the dismissal are recoverable (*Aegon UK Corp Services v Roberts* [2009] IRLR 1042, CA). The tribunal must translate pension values into money terms to assess the loss (see ¶¶8602+), although it has been recognised that this is often a difficult and highly speculative exercise.

If the claimant finds another job, this will usually break the chain of causation, in which case no compensation will be appropriate in respect of any aspect of his remuneration, including his pension, from the start of the new job if the overall package is equivalent. If the facts warrant it, it is open to a tribunal to find that the chain of causation is not broken if the new job is lost soon afterwards (see ¶8592), in which case both pay and pension loss will be recoverable after the second dismissal.

8602 One of the most difficult aspects of calculating a compensatory award can be the **assessment of pension loss**, as the calculations required are often complex and based on actuarial values. The summary below provides an overview of the approach taken by tribunals but is no more than a general outline of the principles involved as a more detailed discussion is outside the scope of this book.

Tribunals have been given **guidance** on the assessment of pension loss by a booklet prepared by a committee of Chairmen of Employment Tribunals, the Government Actuary and a member of his department entitled "Compensation for Loss of Pension Rights – Employment Tribunals". While the guidance outlines the position regarding potential loss in relation to state pension provision (for example, the basic state pension, the State Earnings-Related Pension Scheme ("SERPS") and the State Second Pension ("S2P")), the difficulties surrounding the calculation of pension loss arise more frequently in relation to occupational pension schemes.

The guidelines suggest that tribunals should select one of **two different approaches to calculate** future pension loss:
– the simplified approach; or
– the substantial loss approach.

The tribunal's choice of approach will be significant and may make a substantial difference to the amount of compensation awarded for pension loss. While the simplified approach entails a three-stage assessment of loss, the substantial loss approach relies on actuarial tables to calculate the value of the pension rights which would have accrued up to retirement. The difference in the approaches is outlined below.

> MEMO POINTS 1. In *Evans v Barclays Bank plc* [2009] UKEAT 0137_09_1505, an employee lost a job with a final salary pension, and found a new job which carried a money purchase pension. An employment tribunal made use of the "**Ogden tables**" which are normally used for calculating loss in personal injury cases, instead of the guidance provided for the use of tribunals to calculate the difference between the value of the two pension schemes. The employer challenged the method of calculation, but the EAT declined to interfere, because in its view the tribunal had made no error of law in using the tables. Tribunals have a wide discretion to award such compensation as they consider just and equitable, provided that the approach is reasoned, not based on incorrect principles and is not excessive in amount.
> 2. Calculating loss, particularly in relation to final salary schemes, can be complex and **expert actuarial advice** may be required to produce an accurate assessment.

8603 **Simplified approach** The simplified approach is likely to be appropriate in most cases of assessing pension loss. It **involves calculating three stages** of loss:
1. in the case of a final salary scheme, the loss of enhancement of the pension rights which had already accrued at the date of dismissal (because the pension is calculated on the basis of the salary at dismissal, rather than the higher salary which the employee would have had if he had remained in employment until retirement);
2. in all cases, the loss of rights from the date of dismissal to the date of the hearing; and
3. the loss of future pension rights.

8604 In relation to **stage 1**, an employee who leaves a final salary pension scheme early (either because he is dismissed or for any other reason), is entitled to a pension payable at what would have been his retirement date as an annuity for the rest of his life. This is a **deferred** pension. The early leaver therefore receives a deferred pension representing, usually, 1/60th of his salary at the time he leaves, for each year of service with the employer. However, even though this deferred pension will be recalculated to incorporate increases in the cost of living, the deferred pension is likely to be much less as it is based on the salary at the time of dismissal, rather than the final salary the employee would have had if he had remained with the company until retirement.

The guidance recommends that there should be **no compensation** for loss of enhancement of pension rights where the employee is **near to his anticipated retirement date** i.e. within 5 years of retirement.

Similarly, the guidance suggests that it is not appropriate to award compensation for the loss of accrued pension rights where the tribunal makes a finding of fact that the **employment would have terminated in any event** within 1 year.

However, **compensation may be awarded** where the employee had **5 years or more to retirement** and the calculation can be undertaken using an actuarial method, based on a number of assumptions, provided in the guidance.

> MEMO POINTS   Different methods are provided for the private and public sectors based on their different approaches to final salary schemes, for example, the former will usually provide a pension of 1/60th final salary, whereas the latter usually provides 1/80th final salary.

Stage 2 of the simplified approach covers the loss of pension rights from the date of dismissal to the date of the hearing. In relation to a **money purchase** scheme, the calculation will be based on the money value of the additional benefits the employee would have received during this period in relation to the employer's contributions. In relation to a **final salary** scheme, the calculation is not as easy. It is suggested that the employee's loss of earnings during this period should incorporate a sum representing what the employer would have contributed to the pension fund during this period, had the employee still been in employment. If the percentage contributed to the pension fund by the employer is unclear, a figure of 15% (or 20% for non-contributory schemes) of pensionable pay is suggested.

Stage 3 of the simplified approach addresses the loss of future pensions rights from the date of the hearing, and should be used where the period of future earnings is not likely to be more than 2 years. Where the pension is a **money purchase** scheme, the value of the loss during the relevant period is the amount of the contributions which the employer would have made to the scheme. In relation to a **final salary** scheme, the value of the loss is generally the amount of contributions which the employer would have made to the pension fund. Allowances for accelerated payment must be made in both cases.

Substantial loss approach   The guidance suggests that the substantial loss approach may be most **appropriate** where the employee dismissed has been in employment for a lengthy period, the employment is stable and unlikely to be affected by the economic cycle and the employee dismissed has reached an age where he is less likely to be looking for a new position, in other words, the employee has suffered a "career loss" of a particular employment.

This approach may also be appropriate where the employee has:
– found permanent new employment by the time of the hearing and is not likely to move on to a new position in due course;
– not found new employment and the tribunal is satisfied that, on the balance of probabilities, he will not find new employment before state pension age (this may be the case if an employee is significantly disabled and will find it difficult to obtain new employment); or
– not found new employment but the tribunal is satisfied that he will find new employment requiring the tribunal to value all losses to retirement and beyond before reducing the total loss by the percentage chance that the employee would not have continued to retirement in the lost employment.

The simplified approach is **not appropriate** in these circumstances as there is a quantifiable loss which can be assessed using pensions data and the actuarial tables set out in the guidance.

Note that the application of either approach will involve the use of the appendices to the guidance, which are useful for parties and tribunals alike. For example, appendix 1 sets out a checklist for assessing pension loss and appendices 4 to 7 contain the tables of multipliers and factors necessary to calculate pension loss under both the simplified and substantial headings.

Expenses

8608 The tribunal can include a sum for expenses incurred by the employee as a result of the dismissal, including **travelling expenses** incurred looking for a new job, and, in some cases, **removal costs** if the employee can show that the only way he could find a new job was to move house and that it was reasonable for him to do so (*Co-operative Wholesale Society Ltd v Squirrell* (1974) 9 ITR 191, NIRC). If the employee, instead of taking up new employment, **sets up his own business** he may be able to recover the costs of doing so (*Gardiner-Hill v Roland Berger Technics Ltd* [1982] IRLR 498, EAT). The employee **cannot recover** the cost of bringing any legal proceedings under this heading.

Expenses incurred in attending tribunal hearings are dealt with separately and do not form part of the compensatory award (¶9712).

Statutory rights

8609 As many statutory rights are only available to those with certain periods of qualifying service, the dismissed employee is disadvantaged, as he will lose the **built-up period of qualifying service** with the old employer, and will have to start again with a new employer. This will mean that he will have a period of time during which he does not have, for example, the protection of the right not to be unfairly dismissed or the right to a redundancy payment, and will also have to build up his rights to minimum statutory notice again. The tribunal will award a sum, usually around £300, to compensate for this.

Manner of dismissal

8610 The manner of the dismissal will not of itself attract compensation (i.e. there is **no award for injury to feelings** for unfair dismissal) (*Vaughan v Weighpack Ltd* [1974] IRLR 105, NIRC). This has been confirmed by the House of Lords (*Dunnachie v Kingston upon Hull City Council* [2004] IRLR 727, HL).

On rare occasions, the manner of dismissal will be relevant to the issue of compensation where it has **financial implications**, chiefly in relation to mitigation, i.e. if the manner of the dismissal makes it more difficult for the employee to find a new job (for example, because it causes him to become ill), such that the period for which compensation may be ordered is extended.

b. Adjustments to compensation

8615 As discussed above, the compensatory award will be such amount as the tribunal considers just and equitable in all the circumstances, thus giving it **broad discretion** to reduce or adjust compensation as it sees fit. In addition, the compensatory award may be reduced or adjusted in the circumstances set out below, and in the order given at ¶8665.

Sums paid by the employer

8616 Once the tribunal has calculated the total amount of the loss, the employer is entitled to credit for any sums which he has paid to the employee, such as pay in lieu of notice (*MBS v Calo* [1983] IRLR 189, EAT). This will also include any sums paid to the employee from the **transferee** of the employer's business (*Steele v Boston Borough Council* [2002] UKEAT 1083_01_2603).

The order in which this reduction is made in the calculation of compensation is discussed below.

> EXAMPLE In *MBS v Calo*, MBS made an ex gratia payment of 3 months' gross salary to C on dismissal. It was assessed that C would be unemployed for 7 months. The EAT held that the correct approach was to work out 7 months' net pay and then deduct the 3 months' gross salary already paid.

8617 In cases where the tribunal decides that the employee would have been dismissed in any event, perhaps at some later date, the tribunal will have to consider whether any **payment made by the employer would have been made anyway** (*Babcock FATA Ltd v Addison* [1987] IRLR 173, CA). If the payment would have been made anyway, it is not deductible from the compensatory award. If the payment would not have been made anyway, it is deductible.

> EXAMPLE
>
> **No set-off**
> An employee is dismissed and is given an ex gratia payment of £500. The tribunal decides that if a proper procedure had been followed, he would still have been dismissed but that dismissal would have taken place 6 weeks later. However, as the employer had a practice of making an ex gratia payment of £500 to any employee who was dismissed, whatever the circumstances, the employee would have received the payment whenever he was dismissed. In those circumstances, the tribunal would not set off the £500 payment against the loss which it finds the employee to be entitled to for the 6-week period when he should have remained in employment.
>
> **Set off**
> In *DCM Optical Clinic plc v Stark* [2004] UKEAT 0124_04_2105, a payment made to an employee (who was subsequently found to be unfairly dismissed), pursuant to an agreement by the employee to continue to work his contractual notice period, was deemed to be deductible from the compensatory award.

8618 If the employer makes a payment by way of **redundancy compensation**, any surplus after an amount equivalent to the statutory redundancy payment has been set off against the basic award (¶8575) is set off against the compensatory award. In most redundancy cases, the basic award and the statutory redundancy payment will be the same amount, so effectively this means that any contractual redundancy payment over the statutory redundancy entitlement will be offset against compensatory award. The order in which these reductions are made in the calculation of compensation is discussed below at ¶8665.

8619 Any **sums for breach of contract** (including wrongful dismissal) which an employee has been awarded (or received by way of settlement) in other proceedings are also set off to the extent that they cover the same losses, as the employee is not entitled to be compensated for the same loss twice over (¶8177).

Mitigation of loss

8620 Employees have a **duty to mitigate** their loss and consequently where the employee has been **able to find alternative employment** by the date of the tribunal hearing, the tribunal will **offset** the amount of any earnings from such employment from the amount which it awards for loss to date and also may project this forward in order to set it off against future loss. If an employee obtains permanent alternative employment **paying the same or more** during the period between dismissal and the tribunal hearing, he is entitled to his full loss up to the date on which he obtains that higher paid employment and is not required to give credit for the excess of his earnings thereafter (*Whelan v Richardson* [1998] IRLR 114, EAT). In such cases, the employee will not usually be able to claim for future losses beyond this date. However, this will depend on the circumstances and the date the claimant achieves earnings equal to or greater than their pre-dismissal salary may not necessarily be determined to be the cut-off point for calculating future loss (*Islam Channel Ltd v Ridley* [2009] UKEAT 0083_09_0805).

There is an **exception** to this principle in that employees who have been dismissed without notice are usually entitled to full earnings in respect of the notice period they should have been allowed to serve without mitigation (*Norton Tool Co Ltd v Tewson* [1972] ICR 501, NIRC; *Burlo v Langley and anor* [2007] ICR 390, CA). This exception does not apply to constructive dismissals (*Stuart Peters Ltd v Bell* [2009] IRLR 941, CA).

> EXAMPLE
>
> 1. In *Whelan v Richardson*, W was dismissed in August 1995 from a job in which she earned £72 per week. She was unemployed for 2 weeks and then obtained a new job which paid £51.60 per week. She remained in that job for 18 weeks before starting a new job in December 1995 which paid £95.82 per week. The tribunal hearing took place in November 1996, by which time she had

been in the higher paid job for nearly a year. The total earnings since dismissal were actually higher than those she would have earned had she remained in the job from which she was dismissed. However, the EAT upheld the tribunal's decision to award loss of earnings up to the point at which she obtained the higher paid employment in December 1995 (i.e. 2 weeks at £72 and 18 weeks at £20.40 (£72 – £51.60)).

2. In *Islam Channel Ltd v Ridley*, the EAT considered a situation where a dismissed employee mitigated her loss by taking freelance work. Initially, her income was higher than she had been earning before dismissal, but after about 6 months it fell to less than her original earnings. The question arose whether the initial higher earnings should be set off against the later losses. Upholding the decision of the tribunal that she did not have to give credit for the period of higher earnings, the EAT commented that there was no obligation on an employment tribunal to treat the date on which the claimant achieves earnings equal to or greater than their pre-dismissal salary as a cut-off point for calculating losses. Here, the tribunal was entitled to take an overall approach and not take the increased earnings into consideration on the basis that her future earnings as a freelancer were uncertain.

8621 **Failure to mitigate** The compensatory award may be reduced if the employee has not taken reasonable steps to reduce his loss (for example by seeking alternative employment), i.e. if he has failed to mitigate his loss (s 123 ERA 1996).

In such cases, if the employee has **not found alternative employment** by the date of the hearing, or has taken up **employment at a lower rate of pay**, the employer may allege that he has failed to mitigate his loss, in which case the tribunal can reduce his compensation accordingly. Strictly speaking, it is for the **employer to prove** such a failure, and he should give evidence of jobs which have been advertised locally during the relevant period for which he believes the employee would have been suitable. He does not have to prove that the employee would have obtained a particular job, only that it is likely that some employment would have been obtained if reasonable efforts had been made. It is sensible for an **employee** to have **evidence** of the steps which he has taken to find work, including copies of any applications which he has sent off (and any replies), details of his contacts with the employment service or recruitment agencies, and evidence of any other efforts which he has made.

EXAMPLE In *Kelly v University of Southampton* [2010] UKEAT 0139_10_0607, a university lecturer, K, was dismissed unfairly and in breach of contract on the grounds that she did not have the right to work in the UK, her work permit having expired. After she was dismissed, two posts for which she was qualified were advertised by the employer. She expressed an interest in them but did not apply for either (by this stage, K had regularised her position and obtained indefinite leave to remain). When compensation was assessed the employer argued that she had failed to mitigate her loss. She replied that there was no evidence that she would have been appointed, if she had applied for either of them, given the competition for the posts. The EAT upheld the finding of the tribunal that she should only recover loss of earnings up to the date when she might have been appointed to one of the jobs, had she applied. It was entitled to make this finding, based on the facts that she had worked for the university in a similar post for 4 years and that although there had been some criticisms of her work, these were not why she had been dismissed. It was reasonable to conclude that she was likely to be appointed if she had applied.

8622 The tribunal must look at the individual employee and decide whether, on the basis of his particular skills, age and background, he has taken **reasonable steps** to find alternative employment. The employee is expected to do what is reasonable, which means that he is expected to do what a reasonable person would have done if they had no prospect of recovering compensation (*Archbold Freightage Limited v Wilson* [1974] IRLR 10, NIRC). He is not necessarily expected to take the first job that comes along but he will be expected to be able to show that he has been looking for work.

8623 Rather than seek alternative employment, a dismissed employee may decide to **set himself up in business**. Depending on the circumstances of the employee, the tribunal may well find he has acted reasonably by doing so. This is particularly the case where the employee is older, has been with the same employer for a long period of time, and is in a relatively specialist area where alternative employment might be difficult to find (*Gardiner-Hill v Roland Berger Technics Ltd* [1982] IRLR 498, EAT). The tribunal will need to be satisfied that the business has a reasonable prospect of producing an income for the employee. Where it is so satisfied, the tribunal will deduct the reasonable costs of setting up the business from any earnings achieved during the mitigation period.

An employee is likely to have failed to mitigate his loss if he **turns down a job** on a rate of pay which, while lower than that which he received from the employer, would have gone some considerable way to reducing his loss. What it is reasonable for an employee to do will depend on the particular employee and the evidence of the alternative jobs which were available. On the other hand, if an employee is dismissed from a £40,000 per year job and accepts a £10,000 per year job and then makes no further effort to find employment at a higher rate of pay in order to replace the remainder of the lost earnings, he is also likely to be found to have acted unreasonably.

A **refusal to accept employment with the same employer** who has dismissed the employee is less likely to be unreasonable. Further, at the tribunal stage, the employee may indicate that he does not want an order for reinstatement or re-engagement (see below), and this will not be considered as a failure to mitigate his loss.

EXAMPLE In *F & G Cleaners v Saddington and ors* [2012] UKEAT 0140_11_1608, the EAT found that, following a TUPE transfer, two window cleaners did not fail to mitigate their losses when they were dismissed and did not accept offers of self-employment from the transferee employer. The tribunal and the EAT found that they would have given up valuable statutory rights and been financially disadvantaged if they had accepted the offer: it was not reasonable to expect an employee to give up valuable statutory rights to mitigate his loss. The fact that the alternative work offered was on less favourable terms and the fact that the employees were in litigation with the employer when the offer was rejected was relevant. In any event, no duty to mitigate arises until the employee is actually dismissed, which here only occurred at the point when the claimants rejected the offers.

When the **tribunal has found a failure to mitigate**, it has to reduce the compensatory award accordingly. In doing so, it considers when it believes the employee ought to have found alternative employment, and what rate of pay the employee would have received. This is not done on a percentage basis, but is approached by treating the employee as though he has earned the amount the tribunal believes he could have earned from the date when the tribunal believes he could have started earning it.

EXAMPLE
1. Employee A is dismissed on 31 March. The tribunal finds that, had he made a reasonable effort, A would have found alternative employment on the same rate of pay not later than 30 June. The tribunal will award compensation for the period between 1 April and 30 June and no compensation thereafter.
2. Employee B is dismissed on 30 April. Prior to his dismissal, he was earning £100 per week. The tribunal sitting on 1 November decides that he could have obtained a job on £80 per week not later than 30 September. It will award him £100 per week for the period up to 30 September, £20 per week for the period from then until the tribunal hearing, and will calculate future loss on the basis of £20 per week.

Employment would have terminated in any event

In assessing compensation, the tribunal aims to put the employee in the position that he would have been in had he not been dismissed. If, therefore, the tribunal believes that his old employment would have come to an end anyway in circumstances where the termination of his employment would have been fair, it will take this into account (considering also when the dismissal would have taken place) (*James W Cook & Co (Wivenhoe) Ltd v Tipper* [1990] IRLR 386, CA). In assessing whether the old employment would have ended at some point in the future in any event, there may well be cases where there is no evidence that the employment would not have continued definitely, but where there is evidence that it may not have been so, that evidence must be taken into account (*Thornett v Scope* [2007] ICR 236, CA). Just because this may involve making predictions which may be difficult to do does not mean that a tribunal can opt out of their duty to make an assessment on the evidence in front of them.

> **EXAMPLE** In *James W Cook & Co (Wivenhoe) Ltd v Tipper*, T claimed he had been unfairly dismissed from the employer's shipyard in May 1986. The Court held that he could not claim loss beyond September 1986 when the whole shipyard closed and all staff were made redundant. Even if he had not been dismissed in May, his employment would have ended anyway in September and so he did not suffer any loss beyond that point.

Procedural defects

8630 **Polkey reduction** There are some cases where the employer had a **good reason for dismissing** the employee but the dismissal is unfair because of a procedural defect. In such cases, the tribunal considers what would have happened had a fair procedure been followed. If the employer would have dismissed in any event, the tribunal may reduce any compensatory award to reflect the likelihood that the employee would have been dismissed (*Polkey v A E Dayton Services Ltd* [1987] IRLR 503, HL; see also ¶8445 for details of the rules regarding procedural fairness) (known as a "**Polkey reduction**"). It is not necessary for the tribunal to establish whether the unfairness is procedural or substantive: a tribunal is entitled to make a Polkey reduction provided it can undertake a sensible reconstruction of what would have happened had there been no failure by the employer and conclude that the employee would have been dismissed in any event (*Gover and ors v Propertycare Ltd* [2006] ICR 1073, CA). For example, an employee dismissed for misconduct without first being given the opportunity to give his version of events is likely to have been procedurally unfairly dismissed. The evidence, however, might show that even if the employee had been given that opportunity, there would still be sufficient evidence of misconduct to have justified the dismissal.

A Polkey reduction of up to 100% can be made to an employee's compensatory award. If the tribunal is unable to say with certainty what the outcome of a fair procedure would have been, it has to assess the chances that the **employee would have stayed in employment**. If it believes that there is a 25% chance that a fair procedure would have resulted in the employee remaining in employment, it should award 25% of the compensation which it would otherwise have given to the employee. It will be up to the **employer to show** that the employee would (or might) have been dismissed in any event (*Britool Ltd v Roberts* [1993] UKEAT 394_92_0104). It may not be appropriate to assess chance in percentage terms where the tribunal is considering the likelihood of the employee being **fairly dismissed at some point in the future** (as a sliding scale would have to be used). Instead, the tribunal may identify a date by which it concludes the employment would have terminated in any event, and calculate compensation by reference to that period (*O'Donaghue v Redcar and Cleveland Borough Council* [2001] IRLR 615, CA). The correct approach will depend on the facts and circumstances of each particular case. It is clear, however, that if the tribunal is considering making a Polkey reduction to an employee's compensation, then both parties must have an **opportunity to make submissions** on any such reduction (*Market Force (UK) Ltd v Hunt* [2002] IRLR 863, EAT).

8631 A similar principle applies in a case of **unfair selection for redundancy**. The tribunal may be able to say that a fair selection procedure would have meant that the employee was not the one selected for redundancy and so would have stayed in employment. Alternatively, it may only be able to say that had a fair procedure been carried out there was, for example, a 30% chance that the employee would have remained in employment or would have been offered alternative employment. In such a case, it will reduce the compensation accordingly.

Compensation for **failure to consult** prior to a redundancy dismissal is conventionally calculated by reference to the length of time that a proper consultation process would have taken (for example, if it is decided that consultation would have taken 2 weeks, compensation may be calculated on the basis that the employee would have been employed for those further 2 weeks) (*Mining Supplies (Longwall) Ltd v Baker* [1988] IRLR 417, EAT). However, tribunals should not be constrained by this convention but should assess compensation by reference to what would have happened if the employer had acted properly in all the circumstances (*Elkouil v Coney Island Ltd* [2002] IRLR 174, EAT).

> **EXAMPLE** In *Elkouil v Coney Island Ltd*, E was notified on 27 July 1999 that he was being made redundant with immediate effect. The tribunal found that, had the employer followed established procedure

and consulted with him, E would have been employed for a further 2 weeks. However, as it had been clear to the employer by May 1999 that E would be made redundant, the EAT held that he should have been warned earlier and his compensation should, therefore, be calculated by reference to a 10-week period.

Procedural defects may be **so fundamental** that it is not possible for the tribunal to come to any sensible conclusion about what would have happened if a fair procedure had been followed. In such cases, it is appropriate for the tribunal to award full compensation without making any Polkey reduction, and the tribunal should not indulge in an exercise of pure speculation (*King v Eaton Ltd (No 2)* [1998] IRLR 686, CS; *Valueunion Ltd v White* [1999] UKEAT 875_99_1111).

8632

EXAMPLE In *Valueunion Ltd v White*, W only found out that he had been dismissed when he read the employer's notice of appearance in respect of his application for unlawful deductions from wages. In the circumstances, the tribunal was not able to form any view as to what might have happened if a fair procedure had been followed and the EAT upheld its decision to make no reduction.

Effect of unreasonable failure to follow code on discipline and grievance If either party has unreasonably not followed the Acas Code on discipline and grievance, the tribunal may, if it considers it just and equitable in all the circumstances to do so, increase or reduce any award it makes by up to 25% (s 207A (2), (3) TULRCA 1992 as amended by s 3 Employment Act 2008).

8634

MEMO POINTS An employer may be able to avoid the risk of the application of an uplift with regard to any undisputed part of compensation by paying it in advance of any tribunal hearing (*Tim Arrow and Sons (A Firm) v Onley* [2009] UKEAT 0527_08_0406). Although this case was decided in relation to the old statutory disciplinary procedures which have been repealed, this is likely to be applied to the present system.

EXAMPLE In *Tim Arrow and Sons (A Firm) v Onley*, a partnership employed a single employee. When a redundancy situation arose, he was dismissed without any prior warning or consultation and was not paid any notice or redundancy pay. He made an unfair dismissal claim and shortly before the hearing the employer paid him money in lieu of notice and the correct redundancy payment. The dismissal was found to be procedurally unfair. The EAT held that the uplift on compensation for failure to follow the statutory procedures could not be applied to the redundancy payment and notice pay which had been paid before the hearing because these did not represent part of any award made by the tribunal. The modest awards which were made by the tribunal in respect of a period when, had the employee been treated fairly, he would have remained employed (which was held to be one week), and in respect of holiday pay for holidays which had been accrued but not taken at the date of termination, were awarded the maximum uplift.

Contributory fault

If the tribunal finds that the employee has, by his actions, caused or contributed to his dismissal, it **must reduce** compensation by such amount as it considers just and equitable (s 123 ERA 1996; *Optikinetics Ltd v Whooley* [1998] UKEAT 1257_97_1006). It is open to a tribunal to make a reduction of 100% on the basis of contributory conduct (*Devis & Sons Ltd v Atkins* [1977] IRLR 314, HL; *Perkin v St George's Healthcare NHS Trust* [2006] ICR 617, CA).

8635

This reduction can only be made on the basis of the **employee's own conduct**, not the conduct of any other person (unless that person is acting as the employee's agent or under his instructions).

The employee must be allowed to give **evidence** in respect of any question of contributory fault. If the tribunal does make a reduction, it must specify the conduct which has caused it to do so (*Parkers Bakeries Ltd v Palmer* [1977] IRLR 215, EAT).

Unlike reductions to the basic award which apply to any conduct, reductions to the compensatory award are limited to conduct which **caused or contributed** to the dismissal. This means that it is open to the tribunal to reduce the basic and compensatory awards by different proportions, although it is common to apply the same percentage deduction to both (*Charles Robertson (Developments) Ltd v White* [1994] UKEAT 450_93_1711).

8636

The conduct must have contributed to the dismissal, but **not necessarily to the unfairness** of the dismissal. Further, where the employee's conduct gave rise to a situation in which he was dismissed, the tribunal can find that he contributed to his dismissal even where the contributory conduct did not relate to the real reason for dismissal, provided it played a part in the process which led to dismissal (*Robert Whiting Designs Ltd v Lamb* [1978] ICR 89, EAT).

> **EXAMPLE**
> 1. Employee C commits an act of gross misconduct. For procedural reasons, the employer's disciplinary process is found to be inadequate and the dismissal is held to be unfair. C's conduct has not contributed to the **procedural unfairness**, but has, however, contributed to the dismissal (it is because of his conduct that he was dismissed). The conduct can, therefore, be taken into account to make a finding of contributory fault.
> 2. According to the employer, Employee D is dismissed for persistent (unjustified) absenteeism. After examining all the matters discussed during the disciplinary process, the tribunal finds that the real reason for dismissal was, in fact, a general lack of competence. The tribunal can still regard the absenteeism as having **contributed to the dismissal**, as it was because the employee was persistently absent that the disciplinary process was initiated and it was one of the matters which ultimately led to his dismissal.
> 3. In *Lindsay v General Contracting Ltd t/a Pik a Pak Home Electrical* [2000] UKEAT 1096_00_2911, L's letter of dismissal stated that she was dismissed for bad work ethics, bad attitude and disruptive behaviour. The tribunal found that the real reason for dismissal was her joining a trade union. There should have been no reduction for contributory fault as her behaviour **did not contribute** to the dismissal.

8637 The tribunal has a broad discretion in relation to the **types of conduct** which it can take into account. The conduct has to be "**blameworthy**", i.e. action which is "perverse, foolish… or bloody-minded… [or] unreasonable in all the circumstances" (*Nelson v BBC (No 2)* [1979] IRLR 346, CA). The conduct need not amount to a breach of contract or a tort such as negligence. Conduct is not blameworthy if, for example, it consists of refusing to obey an order which would have involved breaking the law. Participating in industrial action (even where this is in breach of contract) is not, in itself, blameworthy (*Courtaulds Northern Spinning Ltd v Moosa* [1984] IRLR 43, EAT). Further, circumstances which are beyond the control of the employee, such as ill health or incompetence (where the employee has made appropriate effort to do his job properly), will not normally be regarded as blameworthy.

8638 Unlike reductions to the basic award, conduct by an employee can **only** be taken into account if it occurred, and was discovered by the employer, **before the dismissal**. This is because conduct that the employer did not know about when he dismissed cannot be said to have contributed to the dismissal. However, in such cases it is still open to the tribunal to find, on the basis of **conduct discovered after the dismissal**, that it would not be just and equitable to award compensation at all (*Devis & Sons Ltd v Atkins* [1977] IRLR 314, HL).

Social security benefits

8643 The treatment of social security benefits is discussed below.

8644 **Income support and job seeker's allowance** Where the employee has received one of these benefits, the Government can recoup payments made from any award (Employment Protection (Recoupment of Jobseeker's Allowance and Income Support) Regulations SI 1996/2349). The tribunal will ask the employee when it is assessing compensation whether or not either of these benefits has been received and, if so, it will structure its order so as to comply with the requirements set out below.

The regulations do not apply where the parties **settle the case privately** (whether or not a conciliation officer has been involved). This can act as an incentive to settling rather than having the award made by the tribunal.

8645 These benefits are treated differently from other types of income when assessing compensation. The tribunal calculates the employee's loss without making any deduction to reflect receipt of these benefits. However, when it makes its award, it must specify how much relates to **loss of earnings** for the period **between dismissal and the date of the award**. This is called the "**prescribed element**", and is arrived at after all appropriate deductions and reductions have been made, and the statutory maximum has been applied. In working out how the prescribed element is affected by the application of the statutory maximum, it is deemed to have been reduced in the same proportion as the compensatory award as a whole.

8646 The Government is entitled to recoup from the employer an amount in respect of benefits paid to the employee by serving a **recoupment notice** on the employer. The notice must be served within 21 days of the conclusion of the hearing or within 9 days after the decision is sent to the parties (21 days if judgment has been reserved), whichever is later. Recoupment is limited to the amount of the prescribed element. This means that the employer may only pay to the employee the balance of the total award over and above the prescribed element until the period for service of a recoupment notice has expired. The tribunal will inform the employer of this and will tell him that he should not pay the employee any part of the prescribed element until either he has received a recoupment notice or has been informed that no notice is to be issued. If a notice is issued, the employer pays the Government the amount which it wishes to recoup from the prescribed element, and any surplus is then paid to the employee.

8647 **Employment and support allowance (previously incapacity benefit)** In assessing the compensatory award of an employee who has been unfairly dismissed, a tribunal is permitted to **deduct in full** an amount equivalent to the amount of any allowance or benefit which the employee has received between the date of his dismissal and the date of the tribunal remedies hearing (*Morgans v Alpha Plus Security Ltd* [2005] IRLR 234, EAT). It was concluded by the EAT in this case that there is no authority to allow a tribunal to disregard any monies received by the employee and that to not take such receipts into account would be to reward an unfairly dismissed employee a "bonus" which would place him in a better position than he would have been in had he not been dismissed.

> MEMO POINTS Compare this to an earlier EAT decision which held that no deduction should be made (*Hilton International Hotels (UK) Ltd v Faraji* [1993] UKEAT 136_93_1511).

8648 However, in relation to any benefits or allowances which are contributory in nature, the EAT has also given guidance which suggests that only **50% of the amount** should be deducted. This is on the basis that it is not just and equitable for either party to benefit fully from the amount of benefits which have been received by the employee but which he has contributed to through the National Insurance system (*Rubenstein v McGloughlin* [1996] IRLR 557, EAT).

8649 **Housing benefit** **No deduction** should be made in respect of housing benefit received by the employee (*Savage v Saxena* [1998] ICR 357, EAT). This is on the basis that housing benefit relates to the needs of the family/household as a whole and not directly to the position of the employee as an individual. It also reflects the fact that the local authority may be able to recover the amount of any housing benefit which it has paid out from any award of compensation which the employee receives, and so a deduction by the tribunal might leave the employee in a position of having effectively to pay it back twice.

c. Order for calculating compensatory award

8665 The order for calculating the compensatory award is as follows (*Digital Equipment Co Ltd v Clements (No. 2)* [1998] IRLR 134, CA; *Heggie v Uniroyal Englebert Tyres* [1999] IRLR 802, CS; *Patel v Clemence Hoar Cummings* [2008] UKEAT 0605_07_2602):
a. calculate the total loss attributable to the employer's actions (this includes any deduction in respect of employee's failure to mitigate his loss) (¶¶8590+);
b. give full credit for sums paid by the employer (¶8616) (other than contractual severance payments to the extent that they exceed the statutory redundancy entitlement (usually equivalent to the basic award) (¶8618)) and money earned by the employee in mitigation (i.e. earnings since dismissal) (¶8620). This includes any sums for breach of contract (including wrongful dismissal) which an employee has been awarded (or received by way of settlement) in other proceedings to the extent that they cover the same losses (¶8619);
c. reduce this amount, if appropriate, to reflect that the employment may well have terminated anyway had a fair procedure been followed (the "Polkey reduction") (¶8630);

d. if appropriate, adjust the amount if either party has unreasonably failed to follow the Acas Code on discipline and grievance (¶8634);

e. increase the amount in respect of any failure by the employer to provide a full or accurate statement of written particulars (¶6525);

f. reduce this amount further, if appropriate, to reflect any contributory fault on the part of the employee (¶8635);

g. deduct the excess of any contractual severance payment over statutory redundancy entitlement (usually equivalent to the basic award) (¶8618);

h. apply the statutory maximum if the amount arrived at exceeds this amount (¶8587); and finally

i. indicate, if appropriate, what part, if any, is a prescribed element for recoupment purposes due to benefits received (¶8645).

The following example shows the difference which can occur by using a different order of calculation.

> EXAMPLE An employee is out of work for 6 months after dismissal with total loss of earnings of £115,000. The employer has made an ex gratia payment of £20,000. The tribunal finds that compensation should be reduced by 20% to reflect contributory fault.
> Using the correct order set out above, £20,000 would first be deducted from £115,000 to give a net loss of £95,000. This would then be reduced by 20% to give £76,000. As this exceeds £74,200 (the statutory maximum), the cap would then be applied so that the compensatory award would be £74,200.
> If instead, the total loss of £115,000 was reduced by 20% to give £92,000, before deducting the ex gratia payment of £20,000, the compensatory award would be only £72,000.
> Another alternative, with even more drastic implications for the employee, would be to apply the statutory cap before making the reduction for ex gratia payment and contributory fault. This would mean that the total loss of £115,000 would be capped at £74,200. £20,000 would then be deducted to leave £54,200, which would then be reduced by 20% to give a compensatory award of only £43,260.

B. Reinstatement and re-engagement

8680 Reinstatement and re-engagement orders require the employer to take the employee back in either the same or a similar role and to pay compensation for earnings lost in the meantime (¶8593).

In deciding whether or not to make one of these orders, the tribunal considers reinstatement first (s 116(1) ERA 1996). If it decides not to order reinstatement, it then goes on to consider re-engagement and, if so, on what terms (s 116(2), (3) ERA 1996).

Effect of reinstatement

8681 If an employee is reinstated, he is treated as if he had not been dismissed (his employment is treated as having continued uninterrupted and **statutory continuity** of employment is preserved) (s 114(1) ERA 1996).

The employee will be entitled to an amount in respect of **loss of benefits** (including **arrears of pay**) between the date of dismissal and the date of reinstatement (s 114(2) ERA 1996). In calculating the sum payable, the tribunal will take into account pay in lieu of notice, ex gratia payments by the employer, and any pay received from any other employer during the relevant period (s 114(4) ERA 1996). If the employee would have benefited from any **improvement** in his terms and conditions (for example, a pay rise or promotion) had he not been dismissed, the employer will be required to give him the benefit of such an improvement with effect from the date on which it would have taken effect had the dismissal not occurred (s 114(3) ERA 1996).

The order will also specify any **other rights and privileges**, such as seniority or pension rights, that must be restored to the employee and will set a time limit for compliance by the employer.

Effect of re-engagement

An order for re-engagement requires the employee to be re-employed (and his **statutory continuity** of employment is preserved), but not necessarily in the same job or on the same terms. It need not even be by the same employer, but can require the employee to be engaged by a **successor** to that employer (i.e. someone who has taken over the business) or an **associated** employer (s 115(1) ERA 1996).

8682

> MEMO POINTS   Employers are treated as being "associated" if one is a company of which the other (directly or indirectly) has control, or both are companies of which a third party (directly or indirectly) has control (s 231 ERA 1996).

In such cases the employee must be engaged in employment **comparable** to that from which he was dismissed, or other suitable employment. The tribunal must specify the **terms** on which re-engagement is to take place. These must, as far as is reasonably practicable, be as favourable as an order for reinstatement, unless the employee has partly contributed to his own dismissal (s 116(4) ERA 1996). The tribunal cannot order re-engagement on substantially more favourable terms (*Rank Xerox (UK) Ltd v Stryczek* [1995] IRLR 568, EAT). The terms of the order will include (s 115(2) ERA 1996):
– the identity of the employer;
– the nature of the employment;
– the remuneration for the employment (i.e. pay and other benefits);
– any amount payable for loss of benefits (including arrears of pay) between the date of dismissal and the date of re-engagement;
– any rights and privileges such as seniority and pension rights which must be restored; and
– the date for compliance.

8683

As in the case of reinstatement orders, any pay in lieu, ex gratia payments or pay from other employers during the relevant period is taken into account in calculating how much the employer must pay for **loss of benefits** (s 115(3) ERA 1996).

Relevant factors

In addition to the **applicant's wishes**, the following factors are taken into account by the tribunal when deciding whether to make an order for reinstatement or re-engagement.

8684

Practicability   The tribunal has to consider whether it is practicable for the employer to comply with such an order. In this context, practicable means more than possible (*Central and North West London NHS Foundation Trust v Abimbola* [2009] UKEAT 0542_08_0304). However, practicability is a relevant but not conclusive factor, so a tribunal may still make an order where it considers that compliance may not be reasonably practicable if it believes that there is still a chance it may succeed (*Timex Corporation v Thomson* [1981] IRLR 522, EAT). In such cases, doubts about the practicability of the order are relevant if the tribunal is subsequently asked to award compensation for non-compliance by the employer (¶8688).

8685

In **assessing** practicability, the tribunal will look at all the circumstances, including the likely atmosphere in the workplace if the employee returns, the degree of trust and confidence which remains, whether there will be any (or enough) work for the employee to do, and the likely attitude of customers or the public (if the job involves contact with these groups). Each case has to be looked at individually. When deciding whether or not to make an order for reinstatement, the tribunal will investigate practicability as a separate factual matter, taking evidence as necessary, and providing reasons in its judgment (*Great Ormond Street Hospital for Children NHS Trust v Patel* [2007] UKEAT 0085_07_2206). The tribunal will be reluctant to make an order which seems likely to lead only to further trouble.

> **EXAMPLE**
>
> **Reinstatement or re-engagement inappropriate**
> 1. In *Wood Group Heavy Industrial Turbines Ltd v Crossan* [1998] IRLR 680, EAT, C was dismissed following allegations of drug dealing in the workplace. The dismissal was held to be unfair (there had not been an adequate investigation). However, as the employer genuinely believed the allegations to be true, the EAT agreed that the relationship of trust and confidence between employer and employee had broken down such that an order for re-engagement was inappropriate.
> 2. In *Coleman and Stephenson v Magnet Joinery Ltd* [1974] IRLR 343, CA, C and S were dismissed after the rest of the workforce threatened to go on strike if the employer continued to employ them after they ceased to be union members. The dismissal was unfair (because the main reason for it was their exercising the right not to be trade union members), but re-engagement was inappropriate as such an order would lead to industrial unrest in the workplace.
> 3. In *Central and North West London NHS Foundation Trust v Abimbola*, a psychiatric nurse successfully made an unfair dismissal claim after he was dismissed for misconduct. The EAT overturned the tribunal's order for reinstatement as it accepted that the relationship of trust and confidence had broken down such that an order for reinstatement was inappropriate. Relevant factors that the tribunal had failed to take into account included the employee having been evasive and dishonest when giving evidence at the remedy hearing, and a final warning and other unproven allegations which had not contributed to the employee's dismissal.
>
> **Reinstatement or re-engagement appropriate**
> In *Manchester College v Hazel and anor* [2012] UKEAT 0642_11_0907, two academic teaching staff transferred employment to a college under a TUPE transfer. Around 5 months later, the college began a redundancy exercise and sought to introduce new terms and conditions for the remaining staff including substantial pay cuts, in an attempt to harmonise terms and protect the staff from further redundancies. Both of the teachers refused new contracts which, amongst other changes, involved pay cuts of 13.2% and 18.5%. They were dismissed and re-engaged on the new terms, which meant that, at the time their claims for unfair dismissal were heard, they remained in the college's employment. The employment tribunal found that they had been unfairly dismissed and held that although reinstatement was not practicable, an order for re-engagement based on the new terms and conditions, with their salaries restored to their previous level but "frozen... without cost of living increases or incremental increases until the new pay scale catches up with their salaries" was appropriate. The EAT rejected the college's argument that it was perverse for the tribunal to hold that reinstatement was not practical, whereas re-engagement was. The college was capable of dealing with any resulting staff discontent and the pay protection ordered would limit the impact of having two staff on different terms.

8686 The tribunal will not take into account the fact that an employer has taken on a **permanent replacement** for the employee (s 116(5) ERA 1996). The tribunal can make an order for reinstatement or re-engagement even if a permanent replacement has been taken on, unless the employer can show that:
– it was not practicable for him to arrange for the employee's work to be done without engaging a permanent replacement (i.e. it could not be done by a temporary replacement or absorbed by other members of staff); or
– the employer waited for a reasonable period after the dismissal (and did not during that time hear from the employee that he wanted to be reinstated or re-engaged) before engaging the permanent replacement, and by that time it was no longer reasonably practicable for him to arrange for the employee's work to be done without engaging a permanent replacement.

8687 **Contributory fault** Where the applicant caused or contributed to his dismissal, the tribunal must consider whether it would be just to order his reinstatement. If, for example, a tribunal has found that an employee was guilty of serious misconduct but his dismissal was unfair for purely procedural reasons, it might be reluctant to order the employer to take him back.

A tribunal may consider that it would not be appropriate to order an employee to be taken back into the same workplace if there is **ill feeling** between him and other employees or management. However, it is not bound to do so and it is for the employer to argue that the ill feeling has caused a breakdown of relationships or a poisoning of the workplace (*Johnson Matthey plc v Watters* [2006] UKEAT 0236_0237_0910). It might be appropriate in such cases for him to be taken back in a different job elsewhere in the employer's business.

Failure to comply

8688 If an order for reinstatement or re-engagement is made, further remedies are available to the employee if the employer fails to comply. Non-compliance may consist of a total failure or refusal to reinstate or re-engage the employee. Alternatively, it may be that the employee is reinstated or re-engaged but the terms of the order are not fully complied with (perhaps because the employer fails to pay all that it is ordered to pay, or because the employee is taken back on different terms from those ordered). In either case, the tribunal can award **compensation** (o 117 ERA 1006).

If there is **partial compliance** (i.e. reinstatement or re-engagement but failure to comply fully with the terms of the order), the compensation is calculated on the basis of the loss sustained by the employee as a result (which may exceed the statutory cap to the extent necessary to compensate for any amount which should have been paid under the original order) (ss 117(2), 124(3) ERA 1996).

If the non-compliance means that the employee has **not been reinstated or re-engaged at all** (or supposed reinstatement but on much inferior terms (*Artisan Press v Srawley and Parker* [1986] IRLR 126, EAT)), the compensation is calculated in the same way as for unfair dismissal.

8689 The tribunal will (unless an exception applies) also make an **additional award** (s 117(3) ERA 1996). A tribunal is entitled to reconsider the amount of loss incurred by an employee between dismissal and the date originally set for reinstatement, even though this exercise will have already been carried out when making the original reinstatement order (¶8681) (*Awotona v South Tyneside Healthcare NHS Trust* [2005] EWCA Civ 217). The statutory cap can be exceeded to the extent necessary to enable the aggregate of the compensatory and additional awards fully to reflect the amount which should have been paid under the original order (s 124(4) ERA 1996; *Selfridges Ltd v Malik* [1997] UKEAT 1352_96_2404). The tribunal has a wide discretion in setting the amount of an additional award, which will be between 26 and 52 weeks' pay (subject to the statutory cap on a week's pay – ¶2923) (s 117(3) ERA 1996). The employer's conduct will be an important factor in deciding the amount payable.

An additional award is **not payable** if the employer can satisfy the tribunal that it was not reasonably practicable for him to comply (s 117(4) ERA 1996). This means that the tribunal has to consider practicability again at this stage. The same considerations will apply as when considering practicability before making the order in the first place (see above). If the employer shows that it was not practicable to comply, the tribunal will award compensation in the normal way.

8690 If the **employee** changes his mind and does not return, he can still ask for compensation but the tribunal must take his **failure to take up reinstatement or re-engagement** into account when considering whether or not he has mitigated his loss unless he had good reasons for not returning (s 117(8) ERA 1996).

Where an **employer fails to comply** with a reinstatement or re-engagement order, an award for loss of benefits (including arrears of pay) forms part of the compensation award and is therefore subject to the statutory cap. The employer is not obliged to pay the compensatory award plus a further sum relating to lost pay and benefits (*Parry v National Westminster Bank plc* [2005] IRLR 193, CA).

C. Interim relief

8700 The **purpose** of an interim relief order is to maintain the status quo pending the final determination of the case. It is only **available** where the applicant claims to have been **unfairly dismissed** for one of the reasons for which a minimum basic award is payable (¶8577) and also in respect of the following reasons (s 161 TULRCA 1992; para 161(2), Sch A1 TULRCA 1992; s 128 ERA 1996):

– the right to accompany or be accompanied at a disciplinary/grievance hearing;

– certain activities relating to trade union recognition/derecognition; and
– making a protected disclosure (i.e. whistleblowing).

8701 **Procedure** An **application** for interim relief must be made within 7 days of the EDT (¶8340), and can only be made if an originating application claiming unfair dismissal on one of the grounds set out above has also been presented (the two applications will normally be presented together).

If made on grounds of **trade union membership or activity**, the application must be accompanied by a certificate signed by an authorised trade union official. The certificate must state that the applicant was (or proposed to become) a member of the trade union at the date of dismissal and that there are reasonable grounds for believing that the dismissal was on trade union grounds.

8702 The tribunal will hear the application as soon as possible after it is submitted. The tribunal will give the employer a copy of the application and (where applicable) the certificate at least 7 days before the **hearing**, along with details of the time, date and place of the hearing.

At the hearing (which may only be **postponed** if the tribunal is satisfied that special circumstances exist), the **applicant must satisfy** the tribunal that it is likely that at the full hearing of his originating application it will be found that he was unfairly dismissed for one of the specified reasons.

If the **tribunal is satisfied** that such a finding is likely, it will explain to the parties the powers available to it. It will then ask the employer (if present) whether or not he is willing to reinstate or re-engage the applicant (on terms not less favourable than would have been applicable had he not been dismissed), pending the final determination of the case.

8703 **Possible orders** If the employer is **willing to reinstate**, the tribunal will make an order accordingly. If the employer is **willing to re-engage on specific terms**, the tribunal will ask the employee if he is willing to accept those terms. If he is, the tribunal will order re-engagement accordingly. If he is not willing, the tribunal will only make an order for the **continuation of the employee's contract** of employment if it considers that the employee's refusal of those terms is reasonable (otherwise it will make no order).

If the employer is **not present** or states that he is **not willing to reinstate or re-engage**, the tribunal will (if satisfied that the unfair dismissal claim is likely to succeed) make an order for the continuation of the employee's contract of employment.

8704 The **effect of a continuation order** is that from the EDT or settlement of the case, the contract remains in force:
– for the purposes of pay or any other benefit derived from the employment, seniority, pension rights and other similar matters; and
– to determine for any purpose (for example, the amount of a basic award or statutory redundancy payment) the employee's period of continuous employment (¶1040).

In the order, the tribunal will specify how much the employer is to pay the employee in respect of each pay period between the date of dismissal and the final determination of the case (based on the amount which the employee could reasonably have been expected to earn during that period). If the employer has made any payment in respect of a particular pay period (either under the contract, e.g. by way of notice pay, or as compensation for breach of contract), that payment will be set off. The recoupment provisions (see above) will be applicable to any sum which the tribunal orders the employer to pay in respect of arrears of pay between dismissal and final determination of the proceedings.

8705 If there is a **change of circumstances** after the making of the order, either party may make a further application to have it revoked or varied.

8706 **Failure to comply** If the tribunal orders reinstatement or re-engagement and the employer fails to comply, the employee can return to the tribunal to ask for:
– an order for continuation of the contract of employment; and/or
– damages.

D. Table of specific remedies

The following table shows the circumstances in which particular remedies may be available.

8710

Reason	Minimum basic award (general) (¶8577)	No cap on compensation (¶8587)	Interim relief (¶8700)	Additional award (¶8689)	Increase to compensatory award (¶8634)
Trade union membership/non-membership or activities	✓		✓		
Certain activities relating to trade union recognition/derecognition			✓		
Being an employee representative, candidate, or voter in relation to collective redundancy or business transfer consultation	✓		✓		
Being a workers' representative for health and safety purposes, or a member of a safety committee, or carrying out (or proposing to carry out) health and safety activities (having been designated by the employer to do so)	✓	✓	✓		
Other health and safety reasons		✓			
Being a workforce representative for working time purposes (or a candidate to become one)	✓				
Making a protected disclosure (i.e. whistleblowing)		✓	✓		
Right to accompany/be accompanied at disciplinary/grievance hearing			✓		
Trusteeship of occupational pension scheme	✓		✓		
Refusal to comply with order for reinstatement/re-engagement		✓		✓	
Employer fails to reasonably follow Acas Code on discipline and grievance					✓
Employer fails to comply with duty to consider procedure regarding retirement	✓		✓		

SECTION 3

Redundancy

In broad terms, an employee is redundant if he becomes surplus to his employer's requirements. Redundancy can be a distressing experience for employees, and employers are advised to develop strategies for managing human resources in order to avoid or reduce job losses, minimise disruption to company performance and ease the process of change (Acas: Redundancy handling).

8730

8731 An employee under notice of dismissal for redundancy has a statutory right to time off work to seek new employment or to make arrangements for retraining. If he is dismissed by reason of redundancy, or laid off or put on short-time working (see chapter 23), an employee may also be entitled to a statutory redundancy payment, although he may lose this entitlement if he unreasonably refuses an offer of suitable alternative employment. Employees may also benefit from contractual provisions relating to redundancy pay and procedures.

8732 Although redundancy is a fair reason for dismissal, an employer may incur liability for unfair dismissal if there is no genuine redundancy situation or the dismissal is automatically unfair (for example, if the reason for dismissal is the employee's pregnancy), or if he fails to act fairly in all the circumstances. This last requirement obliges the employer to implement fair selection, to consult, and to consider alternatives to dismissal.

8733 In addition to individual consultation in order to ensure a fair dismissal process, in cases of collective redundancies, an employer is also required to consult with trade union or employee representatives and to notify BIS.

I. Identifying a redundancy dismissal

8740 **Definition**   An employee is dismissed by reason of redundancy if the dismissal is wholly or mainly attributable to (s 139(1) ERA 1996):
– the fact that his employer has ceased or intends to cease to carry on the business (i) for which the employee was employed by him, or (ii) in the place where the employee was so employed; or
– the fact that the requirements of that business for employees to carry out work (i) of a particular kind, or (ii) of a particular kind in the place where the employee was so employed, have ceased or diminished or are expected to cease or diminish.

8741 The **business** of the employer is treated as one business with the business of any **associated employer** (s 139(2) ERA 1996). Employers are "associated" if one is a company controlled by the other (who may be a company or an individual), or if both are companies controlled by another employer (either a company or an individual) (s 231 ERA 1996). "Company" means a limited company, and "control" means control of more than 50% of the votes attaching to shares. For example, Company A has a 75% stake in both Company B and Company C. The businesses of all three companies are treated as one and the redundancy selection procedure can be applied across the whole group such that, when faced with a redundancy situation, Company C could select employees for redundancy from Company A and B as well as from itself, even if there is no redundancy situation in Company A or B. See "Bumping" at ¶8784 below for further details.

1. Redundancy situations

8745 According to the statutory definition, **three redundancy situations** can be identified:
– closure of the entire business;
– closure of the employee's workplace; and
– a diminishing need for employees to carry out work of a particular kind.

For the purposes of the definition, **cease** and **diminish** mean either a temporary or permanent cessation or diminution respectively, and it is a question of fact for the tribunal whether a temporary closure amounts to a cessation. For example, a 13-week closure of the business for repairs was held to be a temporary cessation for redundancy purposes (*Gemmell v Darngavil Brickworks Ltd* [1967] ITR 20, ET), while a 4-week closure for refurbishment was not (*Whitbread plc (t/a Whitbread Berni Inns) v Flattery* [1994] UKEAT 287_94_1511).

In cases of temporary cessation, employees may be laid off or put on short-time working (¶7858).

> **EXAMPLE** In *Martland & ors v Co-operative Insurance Society Ltd* [2008] UKEAT 0220_07_1004, sales representatives, dismissed for refusing to accept new terms and conditions, claimed redundancy payments. The employer, CIS, had restructured its insurance sales operation in order to address financial difficulties. This involved imposing changes in terms and conditions of employment, including changes in its systems of payment and performance management, and in the day-to-day activities to be undertaken by employees. In particular, sales representatives would visit fewer existing customers, and carry out more "cold calling" of prospective customers. The EAT held that there had been no change in the particular kind of work carried out by the sales force; under the new system they remained salespeople. Consequently, their dismissal could not be said to be due to a reduction in the requirement of the employer for employees to do work of a particular kind, and they were not entitled to any redundancy payment.

8746 If the employer transfers the business (or the part in which the employee is working) to a new owner, the **transfer of business (TUPE) regulations** may apply automatically to continue the employee's employment with the new owner (¶7900). Specific considerations apply to dismissals in transfer situations (¶8030).

Closure of business

8747 The closure of the business may be **permanent or temporary**. A tribunal will not question the justification for the closure (*James W Cook & Co (Wivenhoe) Ltd v Tipper* [1990] IRLR 386, CA).

8748 A **change in the type of business** may amount to a closure of the old business if the new business is sufficiently different in nature and not merely a new way of operating the old business (*Whitbread plc (t/a Whitbread Berni Inns) v Flattery*, [1994] UKEAT 287_94_1511).

Closure of employee's workplace

8749 This redundancy situation will arise if the employer ceases to carry on business at his workplace, even if the **business is transferred** to another site.

8750 The tribunals currently apply a "geographical" or factual (as opposed to "contractual") test in order to determine **where the employee was employed** for redundancy purposes (*Bass Leisure Ltd v Thomas* [1993] UKEAT 47_92_2101; approved in *High Table Ltd v Horst* [1997] IRLR 513, CA). This means that they will take into account where the employee has actually worked under his contract. In most cases, there is one identifiable place of work or, in the case of "travelling jobs" (such as a travelling salesperson), one identifiable area. A temporary change in location is ignored.

8751 **Mobility clause** The mere existence of a contractual **right to transfer the employee** (a mobility clause) will not, therefore, deprive the employee of a redundancy payment. Likewise, mobility obligations may not be invoked once a redundancy procedure has been implemented and where employees have participated in it. However, where the employee is bound by a mobility clause and where the employer has consistently applied a mobility procedure, the employer may rely on the clause and, if the employee refuses, a dismissal will be by reason of misconduct (rather than redundancy), in which case the employee will not be entitled to a redundancy payment.

If there is **no such right**, the employee may be entitled to resign and claim constructive dismissal (¶8230) (and a redundancy payment) if the employer requires him to transfer. However, if the transfer to another workplace amounts to an offer of **suitable alternative employment**, the employee will not be entitled to a redundancy payment if he unreasonably refuses (¶8865).

> **EXAMPLE** In *Home Office v Evans and anor* [2008] ICR 302, CA, the office of the employees, two immigration officers, was relocated elsewhere in the south east. Before the decision was taken to close the office, various assurances were made by the employer that agreed procedures would be followed. These assurances were taken by the employees to be a guarantee that the employer's redundancy procedure would be followed. Once the decision had been taken, however, the employer required the workers to move under mobility clauses in their contract. They refused and resigned, bringing claims for unfair constructive dismissal. In these circumstances the right question to ask, the Court

> held, is not what the intention of the employer was but whether it was legally entitled to invoke the mobility clause. The Court found that in this case the Home Office consistently applied the mobility clause. The redundancy procedure had not been invoked. Accordingly, the immigration officers had not been constructively dismissed, unlawfully or at all.

Diminishing need for employees

8752 This redundancy situation may arise in the following circumstances:
– where work of a particular kind has diminished (i.e. there is **less work**) resulting in a diminished need for employees to carry it out; and
– where work has not diminished, but **fewer employees are needed** to do it, either because they have been replaced (e.g. by outside contractors or new technology), or because of a reorganisation resulting in a more efficient use of labour).

A redundancy situation may be triggered by the **employer's expectation** that there will be a diminishing need for employees (for example, in a merger situation where job losses commonly occur as a result of the streamlining of the merged companies, or where the employer plans to introduce new technology), even where temporary staff are brought in the interim period.

8753 The **test applied** to determine whether an employee is redundant in this situation is as follows (*Safeway Stores plc v Burrell* [1997] IRLR 200, EAT; approved in *Murray v Foyle Meats Ltd* [1999] IRLR 562, HL):
1. Was the employee dismissed (¶8765)?
2. If so, had the requirements of the employer's business for employees to carry out work of a particular kind ceased or diminished, or were they expected to cease or diminish?
3. If so, was the dismissal of the employee caused wholly or mainly by (i.e. "attributable to") the cessation or diminution (¶8767)?

8754 **Less work of a particular kind** If there is **less work** resulting in **fewer employees** being needed in the business, there will be a redundancy situation.

However, there may not necessarily need to be a reduction in headcount in order for a redundancy situation to exist. A **reduction in the hours** required from the **same number of employees** could still amount to a redundancy situation if there is a reduction in the work of a particular kind (*Packman t/a Packman Lucas Associates v Fauchon* [2012] UKEAT 0017_12_1605).

> MEMO POINTS This approach has been questioned in the case of *Welch v The Taxi Owners Association (Grangemouth) Ltd* [2012] UKEAT 0001_12_1506, which was decided a month after *Packman*, though it is likely that *Packman* is the better authority to rely on because the point was more central to this case.

8755 There may also be a redundancy situation where the requirements of the business for a particular kind of employee to carry out work of a particular kind change (*Murphy v Epsom College* [1984] IRLR 271, CA), causing the employer to **redistribute** the same amount of **work** among the **same number of employees** (i.e. replacing one employee with another). For example, where a financial advisory and accountancy firm loses an auditing job because a big client has gone bankrupt, but then wins an equally lucrative contract for tax advice, they would have the same amount of work but may need to replace some of the audit accountants with tax specialists. The skills and attributes of the employees will be relevant in determining whether a redundancy situation exists, i.e. is there really a need to replace one employee with another? (*British Broadcasting Corporation v Farnworth* [1998] UKEAT 1000_97_1307). Whether a reorganisation amounts to redundancy is a question of fact to be decided by the tribunal, and the mere fact of reorganisation (in particular, that an employee is replaced by someone doing a slightly different job) is not conclusive of redundancy (*Shawkat v Nottingham City Hospital NHS Trust* [2001] IRLR 555, CA).

In contrast, there will be no redundancy situation where the work and number of employees required remains the same, but an employee of the same kind but of lower grade or status is required to do it, as **status or qualifications** will not make the work "of a particular kind" (unless they imply special skills, attributes or knowledge) (*Pillinger v Manchester Area Health Authority* [1979] IRLR 430, EAT). Further, the employee's **personal attributes** are not relevant unless they affect his ability to perform the work.

> **EXAMPLE**
> **Redundancy situation**
> 1. In *Murphy v Epsom College*, M was one of two plumbers but he also did some engineering work. When he refused to continue with the engineering work, he was dismissed and replaced by an engineer who also did some plumbing. The Court agreed that the requirements for work of a particular kind had changed, in that the business first required a plumber who could do some engineering, and subsequently required an engineer who could do some plumbing. M was therefore redundant despite the fact that overall requirements for work and employees remained the same (i.e. there was no diminution in the work to be done).
> 2. In *British Broadcasting Corporation v Farnworth*, F was a radio producer graded "Mark 1". The BBC decided it needed a more senior producer and replaced her with a "Mark 2" producer. The EAT held that F was redundant because the BBC required an employee with a different specialism (in terms of experience and ability), even though the overall requirements of the business for employees had not diminished.
>
> **No redundancy situation**
> 1. In *Shawkat v Nottingham City Hospital NHS Trust*, S was appointed as a thoracic surgeon. Following a merger, S was required to do cardiac work as well, thereby cutting down on his thoracic work. S refused, was dismissed and claimed redundancy. The Court held there was no redundancy because, despite the change in work, the employer's requirements for employees to carry out thoracic surgery had not ceased or diminished.
> 2. In *Pillinger v Manchester Area Health Authority*, P was a grade II research officer working on a particular project. When he was promoted to grade IIS, he was dismissed because it was felt that the project warranted only a grade II researcher. The EAT held that there was no redundancy as the work involved was exactly the same, regardless of the grade of researcher who undertook it.

8756 If a redistribution of duties results in the **work done** being **fundamentally different**, such that the new job is "in a different league", there may be a redundancy situation (*D N Robinson v British Island Airways Ltd* [1977] IRLR 477, EAT). If the work changes such that it is of a **different particular kind**, there will be a redundancy situation (*R Denton v Neepsend Ltd* [1976] IRLR 164, ET). Work of a particular kind means work which is distinguished from other work of the same general kind by requiring special aptitudes, skills or knowledge (*J C Amos v Max-Arc Ltd* [1973] IRLR 285, NIRC). If the work changes but nevertheless is of the same kind as the old work, there will be no redundancy.

> **EXAMPLE** **Work of a different particular kind**
> In *R Denton v Neepsend Ltd*, D was employed as a cold saw operator. The cold saw was replaced by an abrasive cutting machine, which D refused to operate. Although the purpose of the work was the same, the operational technique now needed was more sophisticated and onerous as the machine worked at higher speed. The working environment was also different as the machine gave out vapours, fumes and dust not present with the cold saw.

8757 Generally, a **change in employment terms** (for example, the introduction of new working hours or arrangements) will not give rise to redundancy unless the kind of work (in terms of the tasks to be performed) changes, the employee numbers are reduced (*N Johnson v Nottinghamshire Combined Police Authority* [1974] IRLR 20, CA; *Aylward v Glamorgan Holiday Home Limited* [2003] UKEAT 0167_02_0502), or the number of working hours has been reduced (¶8754).

> **EXAMPLE**
> **Night-shift to day-shift**
> 1. In *Macfisheries Ltd v Findlay* [1985] ICR 160, EAT, a change from the night-shift to the day-shift gave rise to **redundancy** as the night-shift was "work of a particular kind", as identified from the nature of the work done on the two shifts, the impact of the shifts on the employee's personal life, and a contractual term protecting F's right not to transfer to the day-shift.
> 2. In *Maher v Photo Trade Processing Ltd*, EAT case 451/83, there was **no redundancy** situation following a change from the night-shift to the day-shift as the work on each shift was substantially the same, and was merely carried out at different hours.
>
> **Part-time to full-time**
> 1. In *Ellis v GA Property Services Ltd*, ET case 13453/89, E, a part-time audio typist, was replaced by a full-time secretary who had other duties in addition to audio typing. The tribunal held that the work was of a different kind and gave rise to **redundancy**.

> **2.** In *Barnes v Gilmartin Associates*, EAT case 825/99, B, a part-time secretary, was replaced by a full-time secretary. There was **no redundancy** as the requirement for employees to carry out secretarial work had not diminished.

8758 **Fewer employees needed**   There will be a redundancy situation where fewer employees are needed as a result of **technological change**, for example the introduction of new machinery or computers (*Scarth v Economic Forestry Ltd* [1973] ICR 322, NIRC). There will, however, be no redundancy situation where the new technology is simply a **new way of performing the same job** (i.e. the work remains of the same particular kind, albeit that the method of doing that work has changed) with no resulting decrease in the need for employees (*Cresswell v Board of Inland Revenue* [1984] IRLR 190, ChD).

8759 A redundancy situation may also arise where the employer replaces employees with **independent contractors**, because he will require fewer "employees" to do the work (although the number of "workers" may be the same as before) (*Baxter v Limb Group of Companies* [1994] IRLR 572, CA). However, if the business need for employees does not diminish and contractors are used as a fallback measure, there will be no redundancy situation (*Bromby & Hoare Ltd v Evans* [1972] ICR 113, NIRC).

> MEMO POINTS   If the employer contracts out the operation of a service, the transfer of business (TUPE) regulations may apply (¶¶7915, 7936).

8760 A redundancy situation may arise where there has been a **reorganisation** (for example, because of over-staffing) resulting in a reallocation of duties even though the amount of available work is the same or even greater (*Carry All Motors Ltd v Pennington* [1980] IRLR 455, EAT). The focus of this situation is on the requirements of the business for employees to carry out the work. However, not every reorganisation dismissal will be a dismissal for redundancy, and the reason for the dismissal must be examined in each case (*Frame It v Brown* [1993] UKEAT 177_93_1611).

8761 If the employee is dismissed simply because the employer cannot afford to keep him on, the dismissal will not be for redundancy unless the employer has decided to reorganise in order to reduce staff numbers. If the employee is **not cost-effective** (for example, because he works too slowly) the dismissal may be by reason of capability (¶8451).

8762 **Flexibility clause**   If an employee appears to be redundant, the employer may seek to avoid a redundancy situation by **redeploying** him to other duties within the scope of his contract (under a "flexibility clause" (¶1618)). The courts used to accept this "contract" test when deciding whether an employee was redundant, but the correct test to be applied is currently as set out above. The employee's contractual terms will only be relevant to the question of whether the dismissal is wholly or mainly attributable to the redundancy situation (¶8767).

2. Dismissal

8765 To satisfy the definition of redundancy, an employee must prove that he has been dismissed. The concept of dismissal includes termination by the employer (with or without notice) and is further extended in certain circumstances, while certain forms of termination will not amount to a dismissal. These issues are discussed in detail at ¶8116.

3. Reason for dismissal

a. "Causation" issues

General principles

8767 There will only be a redundancy dismissal if the dismissal is **attributable wholly or mainly to redundancy** (s 139(1) ERA 1996). If there appears to be **more than one reason** for the dismissal, the tribunal will decide on the balance of probabilities which was the real, or main, reason for the dismissal.

Although tribunals will not concern themselves with the **economic or commercial reason** for the redundancy itself (*James W Cook & Co (Wivenhoe) Ltd v Tipper* [1990] IRLR 386, CA), they will review evidence to determine the **real reason** for dismissal (*Maund v Penwith District Council* [1982] IRLR 399, EAT; *West Kent College v Richardson* [1998] UKEAT 905_97_0212). The test is an objective one, namely (*Baxter v Limb Group of Companies* [1994] IRLR 572, CA):
– was there a redundancy situation at the time of the dismissal?
– if so, was that the reason for the dismissal?

In claims for a redundancy payment (but not in unfair dismissal cases) there is a **presumption** that a dismissal was for redundancy (s 163(2) ERA 1996), so to avoid payment the employer must prove that there was no redundancy situation, or that the redundancy situation was not the sole or main reason for the dismissal.

The **timing** of the dismissal may be an important factor. If the dismissal occurs at the same time as the closure of the business or workplace, the presumption of redundancy will be strengthened (*R A Marshall v Harland & Wolff Ltd* [1972] IRLR 90, NIRC). **8768**

The employee's **contractual terms** may also be relevant. If the employer exercises a flexibility clause (i.e. a contractual right to transfer the employee to other work), the dismissal may be for misconduct rather than redundancy if the employee refuses to obey. If the dismissal is attributable to the redundancy situation, it will be irrelevant that the employer could have transferred the employee to other work. It may, however, be more difficult to identify a redundancy situation in the case of an employee who could have been moved to other work, or who was not carrying out the work in respect of which there was a diminished requirement. **8769**

Once a redundancy situation has arisen, the employer will select employees for redundancy by applying **selection criteria**. These criteria (for example, experience, attendance, disciplinary record) will normally be subsidiary reasons for dismissal, but in rare cases the tribunal may conclude that the criterion itself (for example, incapability) was the real reason for dismissal (*Timex Corporation v Thomson* [1981] IRLR 522, EAT). **8770**

It is possible for the **reason** for dismissal **to change**. For example, an employee who has been given notice of dismissal for redundancy may actually be dismissed for misconduct if, during the notice period, he commits a serious disciplinary breach. **8771**

Once an employer has decided to dismiss an employee for redundancy, he is prevented from dismissing the employee for some other reason in order to **avoid** a **contractual obligation** to make a contractual redundancy payment to the employee, unless the dismissal is for good cause. A summary dismissal for gross misconduct would, for example, constitute good cause (*Jenvey v Australian Broadcasting Corporation* [2002] IRLR 520, QBD) (¶8820). **8772**

Specific cases

Causation issues in relation to specific cases where there may be some doubt are discussed below. **8775**

Voluntary redundancy If there is a genuine redundancy situation, an employee who agrees to, or volunteers for, redundancy will still be considered to have been dismissed for redundancy (as will an employee who agrees to **early retirement** following a notice of redundancy which has not been withdrawn – see ¶8106). **8776**

Fixed-term contracts An employee whose fixed-term contract expires and is not renewed because of a redundancy situation is considered to be dismissed by reason of redundancy. This may occur in the case of lecturers who are employed for single academic terms on a series of fixed-term contracts. The employee may be dismissed for redundancy when each contract expires (*Pfaffinger v City of Liverpool Community College; Muller v Amersham and Wycombe College* **8778**

[1996] UKEAT 423_95_0403). They will only be entitled to a redundancy payment if they have sufficient continuity of service (¶8990).

If, however, an employee has been working under a **temporary fixed-term contract** in order to cover for an absent employee, the non-renewal of the contract on the latter's return will not be by reason of redundancy.

Non-renewal of certain fixed-term contracts which cannot be renewed, such as **contracts of apprenticeship or training**, will not give rise to a redundancy dismissal (*North East Coast Ship Repairers Ltd v Secretary of State for Employment* [1978] IRLR 149, EAT).

8780 **Misconduct** If an employee is dismissed for misconduct at a time when a redundancy situation exists, the misconduct rather than the redundancy may be considered to be the main reason for the dismissal, in which case he will not have been dismissed for redundancy. An employee dismissed for misconduct may lose his entitlement to a redundancy payment (¶9001).

8782 **Industrial action** The threat of closure of the business and/or job losses often provokes industrial action. In such cases, it may be difficult to identify whether employees who take part in the action are dismissed for doing so, or for redundancy, and the tribunal will have to decide the matter on the evidence of each case (*K R Sanders v Ernest A Neale Ltd* [1974] IRLR 236, NIRC). If the industrial action itself forced the employer to cut back his workforce or close down the business, the employees will, depending on the evidence, still be dismissed by reason of redundancy (*K R Sanders v Ernest A Neale Ltd*, above). If there may be more than one reason for the dismissal, the tribunal must decide on the facts of the case which was the main reason (*Baxter v Limb Group of Companies* [1994] IRLR 572, CA).

> EXAMPLE In *Baxter v Limb Group of Companies*, B refused to give up an overtime ban in which he was participating in connection with a dispute over bonuses, and was dismissed. He was subsequently replaced by an independent contractor. The Court reversed the tribunal's ruling that the decision to contract out work meant that there was a redundancy situation when B was dismissed, and found that industrial action was the real reason for the dismissal.

8784 **Bumping** An employee may be dismissed for redundancy where he is **replaced** by another employee who is surplus to requirements within the employer's business, even though there is **no diminution** in the **particular kind of work** carried out by the dismissed employee (known as "bumping" or "transferred redundancy") (*W Gimber & Sons Ltd v Spurrett* [1967] EWHC QB 2; applied in *Elliott Turbomachinery Ltd v Bates* [1981] ICR 218, EAT).

> EXAMPLE In *W Gimber & Sons Ltd v Spurrett*, S, a warehouse manager, was dismissed and replaced by a sales representative whose job had become redundant. The Court held that the dismissal of S was by reason of redundancy.

Indeed, the EAT has held that it may be unfair for an employer, when proposing to dismiss an employee on the grounds of redundancy, not to give consideration to alternative, including subordinate, positions for that employee, even where this may entail bumping another employee. Whether or not a **failure to consider bumping** another employee amounts to unfairness depends on the particular circumstances of each case, including factors such as (*Lionel Leventhal Ltd v North* [2004] UKEAT 0265_04_2710):
– whether or not there is a vacancy;
– how different the two positions are;
– the difference in pay between the two positions;
– the relative length of service of the two employees;
– the qualifications of the employee in danger of redundancy; and
– any other factors which may be relevant to the particular case.

> MEMO POINTS The EAT in *Lionel Leventhal Ltd v North* did not consider the decision in *Byrne v Arvin Meritor LVS (UK) Ltd* [2003] UKEAT 239_02_2201, which held that there is **no duty** on an employer **to consider** bumping one employee in order to avoid making another employee redundant.

8785 A bumping redundancy may occur where an employee is displaced because of a redundancy situation elsewhere within his employer's group of **associated companies** (¶8741).

However, bumping can only occur within the **same business** (*Babar Indian Restaurant v Rawat* [1985] IRLR 57, EAT). The test to be applied is whether the two businesses could be viewed as a "single enterprise".

> EXAMPLE In *Babar Indian Restaurant v Rawat*, R was employed at a restaurant operated by two partners who also operated a frozen food concern, which they closed down. R was sacked to make way for employees from the frozen food concern. The EAT held that he was not redundant because the businesses were separate businesses, and there was no redundancy situation at the restaurant.

b. Unfair dismissal

8790 Redundancy is one of the statutory potentially **fair reasons** for dismissal (¶8422). Note that where the employee claims that his dismissal was not, in fact, by reason of redundancy, there is no statutory presumption of redundancy. However, the employer may dismiss for redundancy and still be **liable** for unfair dismissal if:
– the dismissal, or selection for dismissal, is for an **inadmissible reason** which makes the dismissal **automatically unfair** (¶8390); or
– the employer has **not acted reasonably** in treating redundancy as a sufficient reason for dismissal (for example, because the employer failed to follow a fair procedure – ¶8800).

II. Managing redundancy

8800 If the employer faces a redundancy situation, he must identify the employees at risk of redundancy (i.e. the appropriate selection pool – see ¶8831 below) and then address a number of **issues**, which are summarised in the following table:

Number of employees in redundancy pool	Fair selection (¶8830)	Individual consultation (¶8910)	Alternatives to dismissal (¶8850)	Collective consultation (¶8915)	Notice of dismissal (¶8802)	Time off (¶8885)
1	n/a	✓	✓	n/a	✓	✓
Between 2 and 19	✓	✓	✓	n/a	✓	✓
20 or more	✓	✓	✓	✓	✓	✓

8801 If he is proposing to dismiss 20 or more employees within 90 days, the employer may have to put in place arrangements for **collective consultation** (including the election of representatives). Where 100 or more employees are to be dismissed, consultation must begin at least 90 days before the expiry of the first notice of dismissal, so the employer should make the necessary arrangements as early as possible. The detailed requirements of collective consultation are discussed at ¶8915.

Individual consultation will be relevant in all cases and should also begin as early as possible. As part of this process, the employer should consider alternatives to dismissal, including any suitable alternative employment. These issues are discussed at ¶8910 and ¶8850.

8802 To avoid liability for breach of contract, the employer must give **notice of dismissal** to terminate the employment of an employee who has been selected for redundancy.

8803 Certain employees under notice of dismissal for redundancy have a **right to time off** during working hours to look for new employment or to make arrangements for training for future employment (¶8885).

8804 Although redundancy is a fair reason for dismissal (see above), to avoid **liability for unfair dismissal** the employer must also **act reasonably** in treating redundancy as a sufficient

reason for dismissal, so the careful management of a redundancy situation will be crucial. The general obligation on an employer to act reasonably when dismissing for a fair reason is discussed at ¶¶8435+. In a redundancy context, in order to show that he has acted reasonably, the employer should (*Williams v Compair Maxam Ltd* [1982] IRLR 83, EAT; *Polkey v A E Dayton Services Ltd* [1987] IRLR 503, HL):
– adopt and apply an objective and fair selection procedure (i.e. follow a fair procedure);
– warn and consult the relevant employees, and consult any recognised trade union or, in some cases, elected employee representatives (i.e. have a meaningful consultation); and
– take reasonable steps to investigate the possibility of alternative employment (i.e. consider any alternatives to dismissal).

If the redundancy is unfair, the **employee's remedies** may include, in addition to a statutory redundancy payment, compensation for unfair dismissal (¶8560). The redundancy payment will extinguish the entitlement to the basic award, but a compensatory award may be made.

If there is a failure to provide adequate information, the fact that it is later provided at an **appeal** will not in itself prevent the dismissal from being automatically unfair. However, where an appeal hearing that amounts to a complete rehearing (as opposed to a mere review of the original decision to dismiss) can cure any **defects** (for example, in the consultation process), making a potentially unfair dismissal fair (*Lloyd v Taylor Woodrow Construction* [1999] UKEAT 1116_98_0107).

A. Redundancy policies

8810 If a redundancy situation arises, the employer may deal with it according to the circumstances of the particular case on each occasion, or he may have a **formal redundancy policy** setting out the general approach to be adopted. This policy may be contractual or may serve as mere guidelines, and could be included in the staff handbook. In some cases, the procedure is agreed with union or employee representatives, resulting in a **formal redundancy agreement**. If an employer wishes to establish a formal policy, it is good practice to involve his employees and/or their representatives. Further, adoption and implementation of a reasonable procedure may help the employer avoid liability for unfair dismissal.

8811 The **contents** of a formal procedure will vary according to the size and nature of the employer's organisation, but will normally include:
a. a commitment to maintaining job security, wherever practicable;
b. details of consultation arrangements with trade union or employee representatives (¶8915);
c. measures for minimising or avoiding compulsory redundancies;
d. guidance on selection criteria (¶8830); and
e. details of:
– severance terms;
– relocation expenses;
– appeals/hardship procedures; and
– training and assistance in finding other work.

8812 If the employer wishes to **depart from an agreed procedure**, he should seek the agreement of the trade union or employee representatives, as appropriate. It is useful for the procedure to specify the circumstances in which departures may be necessary. The procedure itself could allow for a degree of **flexibility** so that it can be applied to different redundancy situations and take account of changing economic circumstances. If the procedure is contractual, a failure to follow it will entitle the employee to a remedy for breach of contract (¶1710). In any case, failure to follow agreed procedures may result in industrial action, and may render a dismissal unfair.

8813 Any procedure should be reviewed periodically to ensure that it operates fairly.

B. Contractual terms

8820 In a redundancy situation, in order to avoid liability for breach of contract, the employer must terminate the employment in accordance with the terms of the employee's contract, including any contractual redundancy procedure (see above).

8821 **Notice** The employer must give the employee the **specified period** of notice of termination (or payment in lieu, if applicable). The contractual notice period is subject to statutory minimum requirements (¶8131).

8823 **Redundancy payments** The employer may be obliged by an **express or implied term** to enhance the employee's statutory entitlement. An express right may be set out in the contract of employment or an ancillary document, such as a redundancy policy document or a collective agreement, while an implied term may arise by virtue of custom and practice (¶1180). It should be made clear **whether** the contractual payment is **in addition to or inclusive of** the employee's **statutory redundancy entitlement**.

A contractual redundancy payment may be **based on** a wider variety of factors than the statutory scheme, and different employers may attach different weight to different factors (taking care not to unlawfully discriminate) (*Barry v Midland Bank plc* [1999] IRLR 581, HL).

If an employee can establish a contractual right to an enhanced redundancy payment, the employer will not be able to deny the employee this entitlement by **dismissing** the employee for **another reason without good cause**. A summary dismissal for gross misconduct, for example, would constitute good cause (*Jenvey v Australian Broadcasting Corporation* [2002] IRLR 520, QBD).

MEMO POINTS An employee might be able to argue that a redundancy policy offering enhanced severance terms has become an implied contractual term of his contract by virtue of custom and practice. If an employer wishes to avoid this, he should ensure that he makes clear that the enhanced terms are discretionary and for the purposes of the current redundancy exercise only. If further exercises are envisaged for the future, the employer should consider varying the terms and structure of the enhanced packaged on offer, in order to avoid elevating the terms into implied contractual provisions by virtue of custom and practice.

8825 **Redundancy procedure** The employment contract (or an ancillary document) may set out an agreed redundancy procedure (¶8810).

C. Selection

8830 The employer may have an **agreed selection procedure**, in which case this should be followed (unless the employer considers that, in all the circumstances, a departure from it can be justified) (¶8810).

8831 **Selection pool** Unless all employees are to be dismissed, employers must take care to ensure that the pool of employees from which employees may be selected for redundancy is fairly defined, as the application of otherwise fair selection criteria (see below) to the wrong group will probably amount to unfair dismissal. An agreed or customary procedure may specify a particular selection pool, otherwise the employer must consider the matter and act from genuine motives. In the light of the broad test of redundancy (¶8740), employers may be justified in using a wide pool for selection. When considering whether the **employer acted reasonably**, a tribunal may consider the **following factors**:
– the extent to which other groups of employees are doing the same or similar work;
– the extent to which employees' jobs are interchangeable;

– the employees' contractual job descriptions;
– any agreement with unions as to the selection pool; and
– any background facts which may show that a pool was defined solely for the purposes of weeding out a particular employee.

This does not mean that a **pool of one** will never be fair (see *Halpin v Sandpiper Books Ltd* [2012] UKEAT 0171_11_0602), but an employer seeking to rely upon such a narrow pool must show that he genuinely applied his mind to the issue. Doing so makes it more difficult for the tribunal to find the choice of pool unfair, but not impossible; the tribunal must still apply the band of reasonable responses test to decide if the employer acted reasonably (see *Capita Hartshead Ltd v Byard* [2012] UKEAT 0445_11_2002, where a pool of one was held to be unfair). The underlying message here is that, if a wider pool is probably more appropriate, applying a narrow pool without exceptionally good reasons may render that decision outside the band of reasonable responses.

> EXAMPLE
>
> **Fair selection pool**
> In *Halpin v Sandpiper Books Ltd*, a book distributor sought to expand its market into China. The employee, who did administrative and analysis work, was promoted to the role and posted to China. Whilst he initially continued to do some of his administrative and analysis work, this was over time mostly redistributed amongst other staff in the UK. Eventually, the distribution company decided to outsource their work in China to local book agents. As a result, the employee's role was at risk of redundancy. Extensive consultation took place but, having rejected an offer of alternative part-time administrative work in the UK, the employee was eventually made redundant. The employment tribunal dismissed his unfair dismissal claim stating that in their view the employer had done all that it could to avoid the redundancy and had handled the redundancy process fairly. The employee appealed, arguing that other employees, who had interchangeable skills, should have been included in the pool. He argued that no reasonable employer would have limited the pool in the way his employer had. The EAT dismissed the appeal; the tribunal had not erred in reaching its decision. It is for the employer to decide the pool and it is difficult (although not impossible) to overturn an employer's decision. The pool chosen by the employer was logical; he was the only employee working in China on the work being outsourced. The fact that he had previously undertaken administrative and analysis duties currently being undertaken by other staff did not render the employer's decision to place him in a pool of one unreasonable.
>
> **Unfair selection pool**
> 1. In *Capita Hartshead Ltd v Byard*, the employee, B, was an actuary who managed a number of pension funds. Her employer lost a number of her key clients and, having failed to obtain new work for her, decided to consider a redundancy. Although there were four actuaries managing pension funds on behalf of various clients, her employer concluded that she should be placed in a pool of one. It commenced individual consultation with her, ultimately making her redundant. B claimed unfair dismissal. In the employment tribunal, the employer argued that placing her into a pool of one employee was reasonable because: (a) her workload had reduced (whereas the workload of the other actuaries had not); (b) pension funds must appoint a named scheme actuary and there was a risk of losing clients if they were transferred between actuaries; and (c) if the other actuaries were told that they were at risk of redundancy, when they had not lost clients, team morale would suffer. The tribunal rejected this and held that B's dismissal for redundancy was unfair. The EAT upheld the tribunal's decision; the tribunal had not erred in holding that limiting the size of the pool to one was unreasonable in the circumstances and that other actuaries should have been included in a selection pool. The employer had not genuinely applied its mind to the issue of who should be in the pool: the other actuaries did very similar work, the employee's work had been praised and the risk of losing clients due to a change in scheme actuary was "slight" (indeed previous actuary changes had not caused problems with clients).
> 2. In *Flintshire County Council and ors v Moore (deceased) and anor* [2011] UKEAT 0379_11_1509, a small Welsh primary school, which was forced to undertake a redundancy process because of falling pupil numbers, decided that all the teachers would be in the selection pool save for the head, the deputy head and one teacher who taught in the special needs unit. The EAT upheld the tribunal's decision that the school had wrongly failed to include the teacher who taught in the special needs unit in the selection pool (his post being one for which another teacher in the pool was properly qualified and experienced to do).

8833 **Selection criteria** An agreed procedure may specify the selection criteria to be applied to the pool. If there is no agreed procedure, the employer must adopt fair and objective selection criteria that are most suitable for his business. He must ensure that the balance of skills and experience within the remaining workforce is appropriate to his future operating requirements. The employer should be able to substantiate the criteria adopted (for example, by verifying them by reference to data such as attendance records). Where there is a recognised union, it should be consulted.

Tribunals will rarely set aside an employer's selection criteria unless the criteria fall outside the band of responses open to a reasonable employer (*Drake International Systems Ltd v O'Hare* [2003] UKEAT 0384_03_0209).

> **EXAMPLE**
>
> **Fair selection criteria**
> In *Drake International Systems Ltd v O'Hare*, the tribunal's refusal to interfere with the employer's decision not to exclude industrial injuries from the absence records which were taken into consideration in applying the redundancy selection criteria.
>
> **Unfair selection criteria**
> In *Flintshire County Council and ors v Moore (deceased) and anor* [2011] UKEAT 0379_11_1509, the selection criteria was unfair as it had the practical result of penalising teachers for their own competence. Points were awarded to teachers whose names appeared in the school development plan (SDP) – that is, those who taught in areas the school needed to improve. The two teachers selected did not score any points for that criterion, because the areas in which they taught did not appear on the SDP, precisely because they had done an effective job and those areas of the school were performing well.

8834 An acceptable method of selection is **voluntary redundancy**, whereby employees volunteer to be considered for redundancy dismissal. This may be an expensive method as longer serving employees tend to apply, thus attracting higher statutory redundancy payments. Further, it is common for employers to offer enhanced payments as an incentive to attract staff to volunteer. A further disadvantage is that voluntary redundancy may create an imbalance in the skills and experience of the remaining workforce. To avoid this, the employer could retain the right to confine applications to selected categories of employees, and/or to decide whether a particular employee is actually dismissed. On the positive side, voluntary redundancy is an effective way of reducing staff numbers where necessary without damaging staff morale. If offering voluntary redundancy terms it is important to reserve the right to refuse applications.

8835 **Early retirement** may be considered as an alternative to redundancies. This usually involves the payment of a pension, and thus has its own financial implications. Where specialised staff are involved, early retirement may also result in deficiencies in skills and experience in the remaining workforce.

8836 Where the situation is not resolved by voluntary redundancy or early retirement, **compulsory selection criteria** must be considered. Such criteria are likely to include:

Criterion	Comment
Attendance record	Reasons for poor attendance may be a relevant factor, and period of assessment should be reasonable, not arbitrary. Extent of absences will also be relevant. To avoid disability discrimination, absences due to disability must not be taken into account. Absence due to pregnancy/maternity/paternity/adoption/parental leave/leave to care for dependants should also be ignored. Employer should verify employee's state of health and offer suitable alternative work, where available
Disciplinary record	Records must be compared over reasonable period of time to ensure that they are representative
Skills/qualifications	Assists retention of workforce balanced in terms of skills
Performance/capability	Fair criteria, provided that assessment of performance itself was objective, and performance criteria clearly defined from outset
Length of service	Length of service/Last In First Out (LIFO) may be acceptable to promote loyalty and a stable workforce provided that, as part of a matrix, it is only one of a number of criteria

It will not be fair to select an employee for redundancy because of his **attitude to his work** as this criterion is too subjective. Generally speaking, selection criteria should be as objective as possible but the tribunals recognise that not all aspects of employee capability can be objectively verifiable, such as administration or flexibility. Provided that, overall, the criteria are reasonable, then the fact that some criteria are not capable of objective verification will not be fatal to the scheme (*Nicholls v Rockwell Automation Ltd* [2012] UKEAT 0540_11_2506).

8837 In order to avoid unfair dismissal liability, the selection criteria adopted must also be fairly **applied** (*Boulton & Paul Ltd v Arnold* [1994] UKEAT 341_93_2305; *Carclo Technical Plastics Ltd v Jeyanthikumar* [2010] UKEAT 0129_10_0308). However, tribunals will allow some leeway with regard to the scoring given to employees: they are more concerned with the overall procedural and substantive fairness of the dismissal as opposed to whether each score given is fair, and they are not able to substitute their own views for the employer's in terms of what individual scores should be (*Nicholls v Rockwell Automation Ltd* [2012] UKEAT 0540_11_2506). Bad faith is not required for a decision to be outside the range of reasonable responses (*Northgate HR Ltd v Mercy* [2008] IRLR 222, CA).

> EXAMPLE
> **Selection criteria unfairly applied**
> 1. In *Boulton & Paul Ltd v Arnold*, the selection criteria were performance, length of service, discipline and attendance. The employers took into account every day of absence, which in A's case included an authorised doctor's appointment lasting half an hour. She had no unapproved absence or lateness on her record. She was made redundant on the basis of her low attendance rating, which was held to be unfair.
> 2. In *Carclo Technical Plastics Ltd v Jeyanthikumar*, an employee was selected for redundancy on the basis of her scores on a number of selection criteria. She had a current disciplinary warning on her record regarding inspection standards. The warning was counted twice, once under disciplinary record and once for quality of work. The EAT upheld the finding of a tribunal that the method of selection was unfair and that double counting the warning was an obvious and fundamental procedural error.
>
> **Selection criteria fairly applied**
> In *First Scottish Searching Services Ltd v McDine and anor* [2011] UKEAT 0051_10_1702, the EAT held that the tribunal was wrong to find that the claimants had been unfairly dismissed primarily because there was no moderation system in place between two separate redundancy scoring processes following a TUPE transfer. Following the transfer, all relevant employees went through a redundancy scoring process with employees of the transferee company being scored by their former managers, and employees of the transferor being scored by their own managers under two separate scoring processes, though the same criteria were used for both groups. All employees identified as being at risk were from the transferee group. The EAT held that, in considering the fairness of the dismissals, the tribunal had sought perfection in the redundancy system and had not explored whether the potential risk of unfairness had actually translated into unfairness taking place. The tribunal substituted its view for that of a reasonable employer. Interestingly, the EAT did not find fault with the scoring matrix which, of eight criteria, included five that were subjective.

8838 The employer should also take care to ensure that the selection criteria adopted are consistently applied and **do not discriminate** on the grounds of age, disability, gender reassignment, marriage and civil partnership, pregnancy and maternity, race, religion or belief, sex or sexual orientation, or he may face both an unfair dismissal and a discrimination claim. Selection on the basis of working part-time or on a fixed-term contract may be discriminatory since these could have a greater detrimental effect on women, and need to be objectively justified in order to be lawful (*Whiffen v Milham Ford Girls' School* [2001] IRLR 468, CA; see also *Hendrickson Europe Ltd v Pipe* [2003] UKEAT 0272_02_1504). While employers should ensure that selection criteria are free of age discrimination, **length of service** can be justified as promoting loyalty and a stable workforce, and that, as part of a matrix where it is only one of a number of criteria, it can be proportionate (*Rolls Royce plc v Unite the Union* [2010] ICR 1, CA).

Fixed-term employees who have been discriminated against in their selection for redundancy do not have to argue that their selection constitutes indirect sex discrimination and may have a remedy under the fixed-term employee regulations (¶1951). Likewise with **part-time** workers who may have a remedy under the part-time workers regulations (¶1870).

EXAMPLE In *Eversheds Legal Services Ltd v De Belin* [2011] UKEAT 0352_10_0604, the EAT held that a male employee was discriminated against when his female colleague was give a maximum score in one element of a redundancy exercise. The maximum score was given to her on the basis that she was on maternity leave, had no performance records for the relevant period in that element of the scoring matrix, and had a statutory entitlement to "special treatment" on the basis of her maternity absence. This score was crucial in determining who would be selected for redundancy as the scoring gap between the two employees in question was narrow. The EAT held that awarding a maximum score went beyond what was reasonable and proportionate in the circumstances, and for this aspect of the scoring process the employer should simply have looked at the female employee's performance pre-maternity leave. The male employee had been discriminated against on the grounds of his sex.

MEMO POINTS 1. Note that once an **employee on maternity, adoption or additional paternity leave** is selected for redundancy, special rules apply with regard to offering suitable alternatives (¶4453).
2. Whilst employees who are **armed forces reservists** can be included in the selection pool if this is appropriate, it is a criminal offence for an employer to make a member of the reserve forces redundant on the grounds of his duties as a reservist or his liability to be mobilised. However, before selecting a reservist for redundancy, an employer should consider whether the Reserve Forces (Safeguard of Employment) Act 1985 applies, especially if the reservist has an entitlement to reinstatement following a period of mobilised service or has been reinstated within the past 52 weeks.

8839 Employees in the pool for selection are commonly **assessed** by being marked against selection criteria adopted by the employer. In some cases the different criteria may be given a particular weighting. The fact that the manager selecting employees for redundancy relied on assessments of employees made by others who had direct knowledge of their work does not render the dismissal unfair (*Eaton Ltd v King* [1995] IRLR 75, EAT).

8840 Employees should be given information about the selection criteria their employer is using. However, employees are not entitled to the **disclosure of the assessment** of all staff considered for redundancy, although naturally they should be given their own assessment (*Alexander and anor v Bridgen Enterprises Ltd* [2006] ICR 1277, EAT and note that an employee has the right to make a subject access request to his employer for information kept about him, although the employer has the right to withhold information to protect the identity of others (¶5980)). The employer need only show that the method of selection was fair in general terms, and that it was reasonably applied to the employee concerned (*Buchanan v Tilcon Ltd* [1983] IRLR 417, CS; approved in *British Aerospace plc v Green* [1995] IRLR 433, CA). However, the employer may be found to have failed in his duty to consult with the employee (¶8900) if he fails to disclose details of the **employee's own assessment** and allow the employee the opportunity to contest his selection (*John Brown Engineering Ltd v Brown* [1997] IRLR 90, EAT; see also *Alstom Traction Ltd v Birkenhead* [2002] UKEAT 1131_00_1010).

8842 The employer should consider establishing an **appeals procedure** to deal with complaints that an employee has been unfairly selected (¶8810). Employers must have an appeals procedure for individual redundancies not covered by the collective redundancy legislation.

D. Alternative employment

8850 The employer should offer any available suitable alternative employment to redundant employees. There are two **implications**, the first relates to unfair dismissal, and the second to entitlement to a redundancy payment. Further, there is a specific obligation to offer alternative employment to employees who become redundant while on **maternity or adoption leave** (¶4453).

MEMO POINTS Offers of suitable alternative employment from a **deceased employer**'s personal representatives are discussed below (¶9015).

8851 The employer will be obliged to give the employee a statement of change of his **written particulars** (¶1400) if he accepts and starts a new job.

8853 **Unfair dismissal** As part of a fair redundancy procedure, employers should take **reasonable steps to find** suitable alternative employment **within the company** and, where appropriate, within any **associated employer** (¶8682) (s 146(1) ERA 1996) (this will not be required where the associated employer carries out work completely independent of and distinct from the employing company). The suitability of alternative employment is relevant to a consideration of unfair dismissal. In particular, if the **terms** of the alternative employment are unreasonable, the dismissal of an employee who refuses the offer may be unfair. The employer should not, however, discount alternative employment which involves a decrease in **salary or status**, but should raise any such possibilities as part of the consultation process, although it would normally be appropriate for a senior employee who is prepared to accept an inferior position to make this clear to the employer at an early stage (*Barratt Construction Ltd v Dalrymple* [1984] IRLR 385, EAT).

Where there is more than one possibility of suitable alternative employment available, the employer should normally inform the employee of the **financial prospects** of those positions (*Fisher v Hoopoe Finance Ltd* [2005] UKEAT 0043_05_0206).

> MEMO POINTS   The EAT also noted in this case that if an employee fails to indicate an interest in a particular position and/or fails to request further information (including financial information), the tribunal can take this into account by reducing the basic and compensatory awards on the grounds of **contributory fault** (¶¶8578, 8635).

8854 The reasonableness of the dismissal depends on the circumstances of which the employer was **aware at the time of the dismissal**. If an alternative job comes up **after the dismissal**, a failure to offer it to the employee will not make the dismissal unfair (unless the employer already knew that work would become available within a short time) (*Octavius Atkinson & Sons Ltd v Morris* [1989] ICR 431, CA). Similarly, if, after the dismissal, the employer discovers that the employee would not have accepted any alternative employment, this will not rule out a finding of unfair dismissal (although it may affect compensation).

8855 Whilst selection criteria should mainly be objective and measurable (¶¶8833+), when considering an employee for suitable alternative employment, the **employer can appoint** who it subjectively considers is best for the job.

> EXAMPLE   In *Samsung Electronics (UK) Ltd v Monte-D'Cruz* [2012] UKEAT 0039_11_0103, the employee was one of four senior managers in an electronics firm. The employer decided to combine the four roles into a single head of department position. The claimant was warned he was at risk of redundancy and was invited to apply for the new role and other roles that would be created in a restructure. He was interviewed for the head of department role and was scored using ten competencies that his employer regularly used in the annual assessment process: creativity, challenge, speed, strategic focus, simplicity, self-control/empowerment, customer focus, crisis awareness, continuous innovation and teamwork/leadership. His application was unsuccessful and another internal candidate was appointed. The new head of department was subsequently heavily involved in the reorganisation and creation of several new roles. One of those new jobs was that of Business Region Team Leader (BRTL). The role strongly resembled the employee's old job so he felt he was ideally suited for it. The same criteria were used to score the candidates and an external candidate was appointed. The employee did not apply for any of the other available roles and he was subsequently made redundant. His challenge to his employer's decision not to appoint him to the BRTL role was rejected. He brought an unfair dismissal claim, alleging that his non-appointment to the BRTL role was "engineered" so that an external candidate known to management could be appointed. The employment tribunal found that this was a genuine redundancy but held that the dismissal was unfair because the consultation had been inadequate and the employer's approach to alternative employment was flawed. The tribunal were critical of the fact that the claimant was informed that a reorganisation would take place and found that this constituted "informing rather than consulting". The tribunal criticised the employer for failing to tell the employee at the outset what the selection criteria were for the interview or what would happen if he did not get the job. They were also concerned about the lack of objectivity in the criteria used in assessing the suitability of candidates and the fact that the core competencies were not defined. The tribunal suggested it would not have allowed other members of the team to apply for the BRTL job because it was so close to the

claimant's previous role. The EAT allowed the employer's appeal and dismissed the unfair dismissal claim. There was no basis in this case to characterise the consultation as inadequate; there was no unfairness in the failure to inform the employee what the selection criteria would be in advance and the EAT did not consider it necessary for the employee to be warned what would happen if he failed to get the job. The tribunal had also erred in its approach to suitable alternative employment. Selecting an employee for redundancy and deciding whether a redundant employee should be offered an alternative position are two different situations. The EAT noted that subjectivity is often used as a "dirty word" in the context of redundancy, but not all aspects of an employee's performance are easily objectively measured. There is no obligation on an employer to use objective criteria in the context of an interview for alternative employment and small failings in good interview practice will not, of themselves, render the interview process unfair. The criticisms made by the tribunal tended to suggest that it had fallen into the substitution mindset; the tribunal had gone beyond merely expressing its view about how the employer proceeded and had "crossed the line" and looked at what it considered would have been reasonable for the employer to do, instead of whether what the employer did was unreasonable.

Effect on entitlement to SRP If a redundant employee accepts an offer of suitable alternative employment (subject to his right to a 4-week statutory trial period) or if he unreasonably refuses such an offer he may lose his entitlement to a statutory redundancy payment.

8856

Offer

If the situation has improved since the employer served notice of dismissal, he may be able to offer to re-employ the employee in his old job (i.e. to **renew** his contract). More commonly, the employer (or an associated employer) makes an offer of alternative employment on different terms (i.e. to **re-engage** him). Where terms of employment are different, the employee has a right to a statutory trial period (see below).

8858

There are no statutory requirements as to the form of the offer of re-engagement (it can be **oral or in writing**) (ss 138(1), 141(1) ERA 1996), although it must be sufficiently clear for the employee to understand what is being offered. A written offer is obviously better evidence that an offer has been made. The employer can offer the employee **several different jobs** at once as long as what is offered is specific enough to be capable of acceptance (*Curling v Securicor Ltd* [1992] UKEAT 40_90_2807).

8859

The offer does not need to be detailed (for example, it does not need to contain all the statutory written particulars (*McKindley v William Hill (Scotland) Ltd* [1985] IRLR 492, EAT)), but it is advisable that it specifies any **difference in terms** between the new and old employment (*Havenhand v Thomas Black Ltd* [1968] 2 All ER 1037, DivCt). It is also advisable that the offer states the **date** on which the new employment is to begin (unless it is obvious that it is to continue straight on from the old employment). If the employer cannot give a definite date, the employee may be justified in looking for work elsewhere, and his refusal of the employer's offer may, therefore, be reasonable.

The offer may be **made collectively** (for example by placing it on a staff notice board), as long as it is brought to the employee's notice, is capable of being understood by him, and is in fact read by him (*McCreadie v Thomson and MacIntyre (Patternmakers) Limited* [1971] 2 All ER 1135, HL). If an employee is on sick leave and therefore does not read an offer posted on a staff notice board, no offer will have been made to him (*F Maxwell v Walter Howard Designs Ltd* [1975] IRLR 77, IT).

8860

An offer of renewal or re-engagement should be made even if the **employee indicates that he will refuse** any such offers, as the employer cannot rely on the employee's unreasonable refusal to justify not making a redundancy payment unless an offer is actually made (*Simpson v Dickinson* [1972] ICR 474, NIRC).

8861

If an offer of alternative employment is accepted **before notice of dismissal** is served, this will be an agreed variation to the existing employment contract and there will be no redundancy dismissal. It is also possible for an employee to agree to the variation subject to a trial period, which does not need to be the same as the statutory trial period (see below).

8862

8863 If the offer is made **after notice of dismissal** has been served, the statutory rules apply, in which case the offer should be communicated to the employee by the employer (or the associated employer) before the existing contract terminates (ss 138(1)(a), 141(1) ERA 1996).

In either case, the **new employment must commence** immediately after the termination of the old employment or after an interval of not more than 4 weeks give or take a weekend (ss 138(1)(b), 141(1), 146(2) ERA 1996), in which case the employee is treated as not having been dismissed (for the purposes of redundancy payments but not for unfair dismissal purposes) and statutory continuity will be preserved (s 213(2) ERA 1996).

Refusal

8865 The employee will lose his right to a redundancy payment if he **unreasonably refuses** (either immediately or during a trial period) an offer to **renew** his contract or an offer of **suitable alternative employment** (s 141(2)-(4) ERA 1996). If the employer offers to renew (i.e. on the same terms), the only issue is whether the employee's refusal is reasonable. If he offers to re-engage, the employer must show that the job was suitable and, if so, that the employee's refusal was unreasonable. The employer should, therefore, seek an explanation for any refusal (*Jones v Aston Cabinet Co Ltd* [1973] ICR 292, NIRC).

If the alternative employment is **not suitable**, or if the employee's refusal of renewal or suitable alternative employment is **reasonable**, he will still be entitled to a redundancy payment.

Suitability and reasonableness

8867 The suitability of alternative employment is judged objectively, while the reasonableness of an employee's refusal of such employment is considered subjectively from his point of view at the time of the refusal (*Bird v Stoke-on-Trent Primary Care Trust* [2011] UKEAT 0074_11_2107; *Cambridge & District Co-operative Society Ltd v Ruse* [1993] IRLR 156, EAT). When considering these separate questions, there may be factors common to both (*Spencer and Griffin v Gloucestershire County Council* [1985] IRLR 393, CA). For example, the employee may refuse to accept a job of a lower standard than he considers reasonable. While the alternative employment may be objectively suitable, it may be reasonable for the employee to refuse it on the ground of his personal perception of it.

> EXAMPLE In *Cambridge & District Co-operative Society Ltd v Ruse*, R was the manager of a butcher's shop. He was offered alternative employment as manager of a supermarket butchery department. The EAT held that although the job was suitable alternative employment, R's perceived loss of status made it reasonable for him to refuse it.

8868 **Suitability** covers **factors** relating to the nature of the new employment as they affect the particular employee, such as job content, responsibility, status, terms and conditions (including pay and other benefits, location, working hours), and job prospects. If the job is suitable, a tribunal will go on to consider the question of **reasonableness**, which will involve a consideration of **factors** relating to the employee's personal circumstances, such as domestic arrangements (including childcare responsibilities), housing, schooling, medical grounds, and more general factors, such as the timing of the offer, whether the employee has found other employment, and the employer's financial stability.

8869 If the employer makes a **collective offer** of alternative employment, suitability must be assessed in relation to each individual employee. If the employer states that his offer must be accepted by all or none, the offer will only be considered suitable if it is suitable for all of the employees concerned (*E & J Davis Transport Ltd v Chattaway* [1972] ICR 267, NIRC). Similarly, the reasonableness of refusal must be judged in relation to each employee (*John Fowler (Don Foundry) Ltd v H Parkin* [1975] IRLR 89, QBD).

Statutory trial period

8872 Where there is a **difference in the terms** of the new employment, the employee benefits from a mandatory trial period in order to decide whether the new employment is suitable for him (s 138(2)(a) ERA 1996). There is no right to a trial period where an employee is re-employed on the **same terms**.

The period **begins** when the employee starts work under the new contract (which must start not more than 4 (calendar) weeks after the old contract ends), and **lasts for** 4 (calendar) weeks (s 138(3) ERA 1996; *Benton v Sanderson Kayser Ltd* [1989] IRLR 19, CA).

The employer and employee can agree to **extend** the trial period in order to retrain the employee for the new job (s 138(3)(b)(ii) ERA 1996). The agreement must be (s 138(6) ERA 1996):
a. made before the new job starts; and
b. in writing, and specify the:
– date on which the period of retraining will end; and
– terms and conditions of employment that will apply after the period of retraining.

The employer should warn the employee that he will lose his redundancy entitlement if he **works beyond** the end of the trial period (without agreeing an extension), or the end of the agreed extended period (*Optical Express Ltd v Williams* [2008] ICR 1, EAT).

8873 If the employee is **dismissed during the trial period** for a reason connected with or arising out of the new employment (such as the employee's incapability or unsuitability), the employee will be treated as having been dismissed for redundancy when the old job came to an end (s 138(2)(b)(ii), (4) ERA 1996), and will be entitled to a redundancy payment. If the employee is dismissed for a reason unconnected with the new employment (for example, for misconduct), he will lose his entitlement to a redundancy payment.

If the employee **leaves during the trial period**, he will be treated as having been dismissed for redundancy when the old job came to an end (s 138(2)(b)(i), (4) ERA 1996). He will be treated as having refused the offer of alternative employment and will therefore not be entitled to a redundancy payment if the new job was suitable and he acted unreasonably in leaving it (s 141(4) ERA 1996).

If the employee leaves or is dismissed within the trial period, he will be treated, for **qualifying service and redundancy payment calculation purposes** (¶8990), as having been dismissed when the old job came to an end. For the purposes of an application to the tribunal, however, the **time limit** runs from the date of termination of the trial period (¶8876).

8874 There can be **more than one trial period** if the employee is offered different alternative positions. If none of the alternatives works out and the employee is ultimately dismissed, he is deemed to have been dismissed for redundancy when the original contract ended.

Common law trial period

8876 Where the employer, faced with a redundancy situation, **imposes new terms and conditions** in fundamental breach of contract, the employee can resign and claim constructive dismissal, accept the new terms (resulting in an agreed variation), or continue working for a reasonable trial period in order to decide whether to accept the changes or to resign (*Air Canada v Lee* [1978] IRLR 392, EAT). This period may be longer than the statutory trial period, but should not be much longer or the employee may be deemed to have accepted the new terms.

However, if the **employer expressly terminates** the old employment and offers alternative employment under a new contract, the employee will be entitled to the statutory trial period only, as no question of constructive dismissal will arise.

E. Time off

8885 Certain employees under notice of dismissal for redundancy (see ¶8120 for further details on notice of dismissal) have a **statutory right** to reasonable time off with pay during working hours to look for new employment or to make arrangements for training for future employment (s 52 ERA 1996). The employee's **contract** may enhance the statutory right, for example by providing for further time off with pay.

8886 The **right applies to** employees (workers are excluded) who have been continuously employed for 2 or more years on the later of the following dates:
– the date on which the notice is due to expire; and
– the date on which notice would have expired, had the statutory minimum notice been given.

The right to time off does not depend on **entitlement to a redundancy payment** (which may have been lost, for example due to an unreasonable refusal of suitable alternative employment (*Dutton v Hawker Siddeley Aviation Ltd* [1978] IRLR 390, EAT)).

8887 **Reasonable time off** The employee is entitled to take time off **during working hours**, which is defined as any time when his contract requires him to be at work (s 52(3) ERA 1996). The **amount** of time off is whatever is reasonable in the circumstances, which will depend on the following factors:
– the employee's length of service and attendance record;
– when the dismissal will take effect;
– how easy/difficult it will be for the employee to find another job;
– the timing of the request for time off and the proposed arrangements (i.e. how much time and when); and
– how the time off will affect the employer's work schedules.

It may, therefore, be reasonable for an employer to refuse time off in certain circumstances, such as where the employee refuses to provide details of any appointments or interviews for which he seeks time off (*Dutton v Hawker Siddeley Aviation Ltd*, above).

8888 **Remuneration** The employee is entitled to be paid for the time allowed at the appropriate hourly rate, see ¶3930 for how this is calculated. The entitlement to paid time off is limited to 40% of a total week's pay for the whole notice period (s 53(5) ERA 1996).

> MEMO POINTS A week's pay for these purposes is not subject to the statutory cap (¶8885).

8889 **Remedies** If the employer **unreasonably refuses time off** or **fails to pay** the amount due, the employee can apply to an employment tribunal for a remedy (¶3960).

III. Consultation and notification requirements

8900 **Unfair dismissal** A redundancy dismissal will normally be unfair where the **employee** has not been given prior warning or been consulted (*Polkey v A E Dayton Services Ltd* [1987] IRLR 503, HL). Warning and consultation do not need to be separate steps, rather warning (i.e. giving notice of the risk of redundancy) is an essential prerequisite of the consultation process (*Elkouil v Coney Island Ltd* [2002] IRLR 174, EAT). Only in exceptional circumstances, such as where the employer, at the time of the dismissal, may reasonably take the view that warnings or consultation would be utterly useless or futile, will such dismissals be fair. The test of fairness in such cases is whether an employer acting reasonably could have failed to consult in the given circumstances, and does not require the employer to make a deliberate decision not to consult the employee (*Duffy v Yeomans & Partners Ltd* [1993] UKEAT 530_91_0704).

8901 To ensure a fair procedure, it is advisable also to consult with **any recognised union** as to the selection criteria and their application. In cases of **collective redundancies**, there is a statutory duty to consult with union or employee representatives (see below), and compliance with this duty is a further factor to be taken into account when assessing the reasonableness of a dismissal (*Williams v Compair Maxam Ltd* [1982] IRLR 83, EAT). However, compliance with collective consultation obligations does not make individual consultation unnecessary and the collective consultation obligation is independent of, and in addition to, the individual consultation obligation.

It will be a question of fact and degree in each case whether the consultation that has taken place is so inadequate as to render a dismissal unfair (*Mugford v Midland Bank plc* [1997] IRLR 208, EAT). **Fair consultation** (both collective and individual) will require consultation when proposals are still being formulated, providing adequate information, giving adequate time for a response, and giving proper consideration to any points raised (*R v British Coal Corporation and Secretary of State for Trade and Industry, ex parte Price* [1994] IRLR 72, DivCt; applied in *King v Eaton Ltd* [1996] IRLR 199, CS). Merely informing staff of potential redundancies will not constitute fair consultation (*Mofunanya v Richmond Fellowship* [2003] UKEAT 0449_03_1512). The extent and length of consultation necessary will depend on the facts of each individual case.

8902

A. Individual consultation

Consultation with individual employees selected for redundancy (including those redundant due to expiry and non-renewal of a fixed-term contract (*University of Glasgow v Donaldson and McNally*, EAT(S) case 951/94)) should **begin** as far in advance as possible (and before notice of dismissal is given).

8910

The **employer should**:
– explain the reason for the redundancies;
– explain the selection process, seek the employee's views on the selection criteria and give him an opportunity to explain any factors which may have resulted in his selection for redundancy, such as domestic problems temporarily affecting his performance;
– explain any requirements during the notice period, including the right to time off to look for alternative work (¶8885), and any assistance (such as outplacement counselling) to be provided by the employer;
– explore with the employee ways of avoiding redundancy, such as retraining for other work, making it clear that the employer will look for suitable alternative employment within the organisation (¶8850); and
– ask for volunteers for redundancy.

> EXAMPLE In *Flintshire County Council and ors v Moore (deceased) and anor* [2011] UKEAT 0379_11_1509, a small Welsh primary school was forced to undertake a redundancy process because of a predicted 16.5% shortfall in school funds due to falling pupil numbers. Although the predicted shortfall was first identified in October 2008 and the prospect of redundancies became an increased possibility in January 2009, it was not until March 2009 that the teachers were warned of the need to make redundancies. Importantly, the teachers and their unions were only given 6 days to respond to the proposed selection criteria. The EAT upheld the tribunal's decision that the school had left inadequate time for meaningful and effective consultation.

B. Collective consultation

If the redundancies arise in the context of a **business transfer**, separate TUPE consultation obligations may apply (¶8060).

8915

> MEMO POINTS Consultation requirements are also imposed by the European Information and Consultation Directive, which requires employers with 50 or more employees to consult with their employees before taking important business decisions, particularly where these affect employee rights. See ¶7655 for further details.

Scope

8916 For the consultation obligations to arise, the dismissals must be on the grounds of redundancy, which is presumed to be the case (s 195(2) TULRCA 1992). The duty arises in the **redundancy situations** identified above (¶¶8745+) and may also apply where the employer seeks to impose a **variation to employment terms** by dismissal and re-engagement (¶1677).

Where **20 or more redundancies** are proposed at one establishment **within 90 days**, the employer must **consult** with "appropriate representatives" of the employees who may be affected by the proposed dismissals or by measures taken in connection with them ("affected employees") (s 188 TULRCA 1992, as amended). The employer is also required to **notify** BIS (¶8970). If there is any dispute about which employees are affected, it is for an employment tribunal to decide.

> EXAMPLE The employer is proposing 30 redundancies from among the sales force team. The effect of the redundancies will be to increase the workload of the remaining members of the team and to transfer some of the team's clerical responsibilities to the clerical staff. The employer must consult with elected representatives of both the sales force team and the clerical workers whose working conditions may change as a result of the dismissals.

MEMO POINTS 1. The **relevant legislation** was amended by the Trade Union Reform and Employment Rights Act 1993 and the Collective Redundancies and Transfer of Undertakings (Protection of Employment) (Amendment) Regulations and SI 1999/1925, implementing a European Directive now consolidated in the European Collective Redundancies Directive (Trade Union Reform and Employment Rights Act 1993; SI 1995/2587; SI 1999/1925; EC Directive 1998/59).

2. The **definition** for consultation purposes is broader than that used for redundancy payment purposes, in that it applies to employees dismissed for a reason or reasons which is/are not related to the individual concerned (s 195(1) TULRCA 1992). An employee will not be included where the reason for the proposed redundancy relates to him, i.e. if it has "something to do with him such as something he is, or something he has done" (University of Stirling v University and College Union [2011] UKEAT 0001_11_0811). For example, a fixed-term employee who has a contract of over 3 months should be included within collective consultation criteria if the non-renewal related to a business decision of the employer which did not focus on the individual employee. However, he should not be included within collective consultation criteria if the reason for non-renewal for his fixed-term contract is simply the expiry of the term. This decision is important especially in relation to sectors that habitually use a large number fixed-term contracts such as the educational sector, as was the case here. It should be noted that the law on what amounts to a redundancy dismissal for collective consultation purposes is not completely certain: in an earlier case, also brought by the university and college trade union, in which the employer concerned conceded the point, the EAT was nevertheless content to proceed on the basis that the non-renewal of fixed-term contracts could and did trigger the duty to collectively consult (University of Lancaster v University and College Union [2010] UKEAT 0278_10_2710).

3. Collective agreements dealing with redundancy procedures or the provision of alternative employment covered by an **exemption order** issued by BIS following application by all the parties to the agreement can disapply the statutory obligation to consult (s 157 ERA 1996). While collective redundancy provisions are common between trade unions and employers, exemption orders are rarely used.

4. The Government has published its response to a consultation on **proposals** to change the rules surrounding collective redundancies. In summary, the Government has decided:
– to reduce the 90-day minimum consultation period to a 45-day minimum period for redundancies of 100 or more employees. The aim is "to improve employers' ability to react to changing market conditions and to reduce uncertainty and low morale amongst employees, while ensuring that there could still be full consultation and effective engagement from government agencies." The response emphasises that this is a genuine minimum period and it will still be possible to extend it by agreement;
– that Acas should produce a new non-statutory code of practice;
– not to legislate on the definition of "establishment" for the purposes of deciding whether or not collective consultation is necessary. Instead, it will issue guidance including reference to the following factors: geographical location, management structure, management or financial autonomy, cohesion of the workforce, nature of work undertaken or type of service provided, contractual relationship between employer and employee, and level within the company at which the decision to dismiss is taken;
– to legislate to exclude fixed-term contracts, which have reached their agreed termination point, from collective redundancy consultation obligations (see memo point 2, above). The fixed-term

contract would need to have a clear termination date in order for this exemption to apply, and the employer would also not be able to rely on the exemption if it is considering early termination by reason of redundancy.

The Government intends that the amended legislation and Acas guidance will be in place by 6 April 2013. Further developments will be covered by our updating service.

Calculating number of redundancies When calculating the number of employees an employer proposes to dismiss as redundant for the purposes of collective redundancy obligations, an employer must include any employees he is proposing to **redeploy**, if his proposals objectively amount to withdrawing an employee's existing contract or the proposed changes to the existing contract are so substantial so as to constitute a withdrawal of the entire contract (*Hardy v Tourism South East* [2005] IRLR 242, EAT). **8917**

Employees who accept **voluntary redundancy** count as being dismissed for the purposes of the collective consultation provisions, and are entitled to protective awards in the event of a failure to consult (see below) (*Scotch Premier Meat Ltd v Burns* [2000] UKEAT 1151_99_2804). Consequently, all voluntary redundancies must be included in determining the number of proposed redundancies for the purposes of collective redundancy obligations (*Optare Group Ltd v Transport and General Workers' Union* [2007] IRLR 931, EAT).

Where an employer has started consultation in relation to proposed redundancies, the number of those redundancies is ignored when considering his obligation to consult should **further redundancies** be proposed, unless bad faith can be identified (i.e. the employer intended from the outset to dismiss the combined group as redundant) (s 188(3) TULRCA 1992; *Transport and General Workers Union v Nationwide Haulage Ltd* [1978] IRLR 143, IT). However, as **good practice**, it is advisable in cases of staggered redundancies to start collective consultation as soon as it becomes clear there will be 20 + redundancies (assuming the earlier individual redundancies have not already taken place). **8918**

The consultation provisions **do not apply** to workers who are not employees (for example, independent contractors), nor to short-term employees (i.e. those employed for a fixed term of 3 months or less, or for a specific purpose not expected to last for more than 3 months, who have actually worked for less than 3 months) (s 282 TULRCA 1992). **8919**

MEMO POINTS 1. In contrast, **fixed-term employees** who have a contract of over 3 months should be included within collective consultation criteria if the non-renewal relates to a business decision of the employer which did not focus on the individual employees (see memo point 2 to ¶8916 and memo point 4 to ¶8916 with regard to proposals to exclude such employees).
2. **Overseas employment** is not excluded from the duty to consult (although it is excluded from the duty to notify BIS – ¶8970).

Meaning of establishment The total number of redundancies proposed by the employer may be unimportant – the obligation to consult depends on the number of redundancies at one establishment. There is no statutory definition of establishment and so tribunals have taken a practical approach when deciding whether to add together the number of employees to be made redundant in a business which has **several sites**. The Court of Justice of the European Union has held that "establishment" means the unit to which the redundant employees were assigned to carry out their duties, regardless of whether the power to effect redundancies lies with that unit, and it is a matter of judgment, depending on the circumstances of the particular case, as to whether a business operation constitutes an independent unit or merely forms part of a larger unit (*Rockfon A/S v Specialarbejderforbundet i Danmark, acting for Nielsen* [1996] IRLR 168, ECJ). The Court of Justice has confirmed that its definition of establishment is very broad and that as long as the unit is a distinct entity with a certain degree of permanence and stability, which is assigned to perform one or more given tasks and which has a workforce, technical means and a certain organisational structure to facilitate these tasks, it need not have any legal autonomy, nor need it have economic, financial, administrative or technological autonomy or geographical separation from other units and facilities of the undertaking (*Athinaiki Chartopoiia AE v Panagiuotidis and ors* [2007] IRLR 284, ECJ). It was in this spirit that the Court of Justice held in *Rockfon* that it was not essential for the power to effect redundancies to lie with that unit. Taking into account the Court of Justice's definition of **8921**

establishment, it will be a matter of judgment, depending on the circumstances of the particular case, as to whether a business operation constitutes an independent unit or merely forms part of a larger unit. **Relevant factors** may include (*Lord Advocate v Babcock and Wilcox Ltd* [1972] 1 All ER 1130, HL):
- the exclusive occupation of the premises;
- a degree of permanence;
- some organisation of employees working there;
- administrative functions; and
- the site being a contractual workplace.

> EXAMPLE
> **One establishment**
> 1. In *Barratt Developments (Bradford) Ltd v UCATT* [1977] IRLR 403, EAT, the EAT held that 14 building sites linked to headquarters by telephone was one establishment.
> 2. In *Mills and Allen Ltd v Bulwich* [1999] UKEAT 154_99_2704, the EAT held that a nationwide direct sales team was one establishment, as the team was capable of being a unit of the employer's organisation to which employees at different offices had been assigned.
>
> **Distinct establishments**
> 1. In *National Union of Footwear, Leather & Allied Trades v K Shoemakers Ltd*, COIT 1300/65, unreported, it was held that five factories were distinct establishments as each had a degree of managerial independence, was geographically separate from the others, and was a permanent not a temporary site.
> 2. In *Renfrewshire Council v Educational Institute of Scotland* [2012] UKEAT 0018_12_0410, the EAT overturned the tribunal's decision and held that a Local Education Authority (LEA) was not one establishment for the purposes of collective consultation, and that individual schools were establishments in their own right. The original tribunal judge had focused too much on the fact that the teachers could be instructed to work at other schools under the mobility clauses in their contracts and on the LEA's control over the recruitment, movement and dismissal of teachers. The EAT confirmed that the meaning of "establishment" relates to a physical presence; it largely corresponds to the physical place of work of the employees.

MEMO POINTS   The Government has published its response to a consultation on **proposals** to change the rules surrounding collective redundancies, and this includes a commitment to issue guidance on the meaning of "establishment" in this context. See memo point 4 to ¶8916 for further details.

8922   The number of redundancies is calculated by reference to one employer only, and redundancies made in **associated companies** (¶8682) at the same establishment are treated separately.

8923   **Proposal to dismiss**   The collective obligation applies to **actual and constructive dismissals**, and expiry of fixed-term contracts. There is no duty to consult where there is no dismissal, for example, where the redundancy situation arises as a result of a frustrating event, such as the death of an individual employer.

The obligation may arise in the case of **involuntary redundancies**, such as the making of a **winding-up order**, given that the underlying EU law requires consultation where an establishment's activities are terminated as a result of a judicial decision (it was previously argued that the order, rather than the employer, caused the dismissal, such that there was no proposal to dismiss (*Re Hartlebury Printers Ltd (in liquidation) and ors* [1992] IRLR 516, ChD; *GMB v Rankin and Harrison* [1992] IRLR 514, EAT)). Where a **liquidator, receiver or insolvency administrator** dismisses, he does so as the company's agent such that the duty to consult should apply (although the insolvency may give rise to a defence to claims of failure to consult – ¶8950). It could be argued that an employer in financial difficulties could anticipate his business collapsing and therefore "contemplates" redundancies, which may be sufficient to trigger the duty to consult (see below).

8924   The **duty to consult is triggered** when the employer proposes to dismiss. A proposal to dismiss may arise where an employer has decided on a plan of action which has two alternative scenarios, only one of which necessarily includes redundancies (even if the other is still being considered) (*Scotch Premier Meat Ltd v Burns* [2000] UKEAT 1151_99_2804). The word "propose" in this context connotes an intention on the part of the employer (*Scotch Premier*

Meat Ltd v Burns). It does not matter that the proposal is yet to be approved by the company's shareholders (*Dewhirst Group v GMB Trade Union* [2003] UKEAT 0486_03_1908) or that the proposal is made by a Council officer but not yet ratified by a formal political Council decision (*Leicestershire County Council v Unison* [2005] UKEAT 0066_05_0209). The EAT's construction of "proposing to dismiss" followed the judgment in *Junk v Wolfgang Kuhnel* ([2005] IRLR 310, ECJ) (which requires consultation to begin before notice of dismissal for redundancy is given (see ¶8939 below)) and therefore indicated that this phrase could be read as "proposing to give notice of dismissal".

A proposal to dismiss has been held to arise where:
– there is a proposal to redeploy employees, particularly when the proposal amounts to, or constitutes, a withdrawal of an employee's contract (¶8917; *Hardy v Tourism South East*);
– an employer sought to harmonise his employees' terms and conditions by giving them notice to terminate so that he could re-engage them on new terms (*GMB v Man Truck and Bus UK Ltd* [2000] UKEAT 1151_99_2804);
– the closure of a workplace is proposed and it is recognised that dismissals will inevitably, or almost inevitably, result from the closure (*UK Coal Mining Ltd v National Union of Mineworkers (Northumberland Area) and anor* [2008] ICR 163, EAT); and
– a group of companies has made a business decision which will mean there will be redundancies (*Akavan Erityisalojen Keskusliitto AEK and ors (Social policy)* [2009] EUECJ C-44/08). This is so, even where the decision has been imposed by the parent company and the subsidiary affected does not yet have all the information needed to comply with the obligation. In such a case, missing information can be supplied as the consultation process continues. However, there must be enough information to identify the subsidiary in question for the duty to be triggered.

For consultation to be seen to be meaningful, it is essential for an employer to consult before making any definite redundancy plans and it is not open to an employer to argue that consultation would be futile or utterly useless as a defence for failing to do so (*Middlesbrough Borough Council v TGWU* [2002] IRLR 332, EAT). In any case, the employer must comply with the requirement to consult "in good time" (¶8939).

1. Consultation requirements

8925 The employer must consult the affected employees' **appropriate representatives**. These are either (ss 188(1B), 196(1) TULRCA 1992):
a. representatives of the union if the employees are of a description in respect of which an independent trade union is recognised for collective bargaining purposes (¶7360); or
b. in any other case, employee representatives, employed by the employer at the time of their election or appointment, and who may be either:
– **existing representatives** elected or appointed by the affected employees for purposes other than redundancy consultation but who, having regard to those other purposes and the method of election/appointment, have authority from those employees to receive information and to be consulted about the proposed dismissals on their behalf (for example, members of an existing works council, but not, in the case of redundancies amongst sales staff for example, a committee specifically established to consider the operation of a staff canteen (BIS guidance: Redundancy Consultation and Notification)); or
– employee representatives who have been **specially elected** for the purposes of redundancy consultation (see below).

If there are **trade union representatives**, they must be consulted and, further, the employer can consult with them in respect of affected employees who fit the description of employees within the scope of the recognition agreement, whether or not they are actually union members. If any affected employees do not fit that description, they will be entitled to information and consultation via employee representatives.

8926 The employer is **required to consult** in good faith "with a view to reaching agreement" with the appropriate representatives on the proposed redundancies, in particular in **relation to** ways of (s 188(2) TULRCA 1992):

– avoiding the dismissals;
– reducing the number of dismissals; and
– mitigating the consequences of the dismissals (which may include assistance in redeployment or retraining).

This can include the **reasons for redundancies**, for example the employer is required to consult about the reasons for whether or not a plant should close (*UK Coal Mining Ltd v National Union of Mineworkers (Northumberland Area) and anor* [2008] ICR 163, EAT overruling *R v British Coal Corporation, ex parte Vardy* [1993] IRLR 104, QBD). In a closure context, where it is recognised that dismissals will inevitably, or almost inevitably, result from the closure, dismissals are proposed at the point when the closure is proposed. Consequently, consultation as to the reasons for the closure is required from when the closure is fixed as a clear, albeit provisional, intention i.e. when it is a possibility though not when it is merely mooted as a possibility.

> EXAMPLE In *UK Coal Mining Ltd v National Union of Mineworkers (Northumberland Area) and anor*, the EAT upheld maximum protective awards for failure to consult properly over mass redundancies due to a colliery closure. CM started formal consultation for the proposed redundancies on the grounds that they had to cease production at the colliery for safety reasons. This was not true; the real reason for the closure was the economic difficulties facing the employers. The EAT held that CM had failed to comply with the duty to consult when it gave a deliberately misleading reason for the closure. Firstly, this affected the nature of the subsequent consultation. Secondly, despite CM's argument that it was not obliged to consult over the reason for the colliery closure and consequently it did not matter that it gave misleading information as to it, the EAT held that, given the increased requirements regarding domestic consultations, the collective redundancy consultation requirements must be interpreted to require consultation over the decision to close a workplace which meant that CM had failed to properly consult with the unions.

8927 Employers are therefore under an absolute obligation to consult and to do so meaningfully (*Susie Radin Ltd v GMB* [2004] IRLR 400, CA).

Further, employers are **obliged to negotiate** with employee representatives to find ways to avoid and/or reduce the number of redundancies which may need to be made (*Junk v Wolfgang Kuhnel* [2005] IRLR 310, ECJ). Employee representatives should therefore be given the opportunity to understand the proposals, and should give proper consideration to any counter-proposals before reaching a final decision on the redundancies, although the employer will not be in breach of his duty if agreement is not actually reached.

8928 **Election requirements** The election of employee representatives must satisfy the requirements set out in the table below (under "First election") (s 188A TULRCA 1992). If, following an election, an elected representative ceases to act, leaving any of the affected employees unrepresented, the employees must elect a replacement representative, satisfying the requirements as indicated in the table (s 188A(2) TULRCA 1992).

Requirement	First election	Replacement representative
Employer must: – make such arrangements as reasonably practicable to ensure election is **fair**	✓	✓
– determine **number of representatives** to be elected so all affected employees' interests are sufficiently represented (in terms of their number and classes)	✓	n/a
– determine whether affected employees should be represented by representatives **of all the affected employees** or by representatives **of particular classes** of those employees	✓	n/a
– decide their **term of office** (must be long enough to enable relevant information to be given and consultations to be completed)	✓	n/a
Candidates for election must be affected employees as at election date	✓	✓
No affected employee should be **unreasonably excluded** from standing	✓	✓

Requirement	First election	Replacement representative
All affected employees on election date are **entitled to vote** (they may vote for as many candidates as there are representatives to be elected to represent them or their particular class of employee, as the case may be)	✓	n/a
Election must be conducted to ensure, as far as is reasonably practicable, that voting is **in secret** and votes are **accurately counted**	✓	✓

8929 If the **affected employees delay in electing representatives** where the employer invited them to do so long enough before the time when consultation was required to begin (or information was required to be given), the employer will be taken to have complied with his obligations if he consults or informs as soon as is reasonably practicable after the election (s 188(7A) TULRCA 1992).

8930 If affected employees **fail** to respond to the employer's invitation **to elect representatives** within a "reasonable" time, the employer has to give (in writing) to each affected employee the information which otherwise he would have been required to give to the elected employee representatives (see below) (s 188(7B) TULRCA 1992). "Reasonable" time is not defined, but it is likely to be no later than when the consultation with employee representatives would have begun had any been elected. In these circumstances, the employer may be excused his duty to consult, as the "special circumstances" defence may be available to him (¶8950).

8931 **Rights of employee representatives and candidates** Employee representatives (including union representatives) and, where relevant, candidates have the following rights:
a. reasonable time off with pay to carry out their functions or undergo appropriate training (ss 168, 169 TULRCA 1992; s 61 ERA 1996); and
b. access to (s 188(5A) TULRCA 1992):
– affected employees; and
– appropriate accommodation and facilities.

8932 There is no definition as to how much **time off** is "reasonable" (it may, therefore, be useful for employers to indicate in advance what would be considered reasonable as this is likely to avoid disputes later on). **Candidates** may require time off to lobby affected employees on an individual basis, and to prepare for and hold a general meeting to allow them to present their candidature. **Representatives** should be allowed paid time off to prepare for and attend consultation meetings with the employer, and to report back to affected employees. Time off should also be permitted for appropriate **training** to enable them to perform their functions, although there is no obligation on the employer to investigate or provide such training.

Details on the **payment** for time off and **remedies** for refusal of time off (or failure to make the appropriate payment) are discussed at ¶3960.

8933 Legislation does not prescribe the range of **facilities** that should be provided, but employers may find it useful to establish early, before the election is called, what facilities will be provided. This could include the use of a telephone and facilities relevant to the production of the candidates' election material and its distribution to affected employees. To avoid claims of discrimination, facilities should be provided equally to all candidates (for example, it would be inappropriate to distribute the election material of one candidate and not of another).

Information to be provided

8935 Employers must provide the representatives with relevant information that gives them "enough information about the employer's proposals to be able to take a useful and constructive part in the process of consultation" (BIS guidance).

Each representative should be given, in writing, information which complies with the above description. It **should include** (s 188(4) TULRCA 1992):
- the reasons for the proposed redundancies;
- the numbers and descriptions of employees the employer proposes to dismiss as redundant;
- the total number of employees of any such description employed by the employer at the establishment;
- the proposed method of selecting for redundancy;
- the proposed method and time-scale for carrying out the dismissals (with due regard for any agreed procedures); and
- the proposed method of calculating the amount of any non-statutory redundancy payments.

However, it is not essential that the employer provides information regarding the **economic background** or **context** in which the proposal to make redundancies has arisen (*Securicor Omega Express Ltd v GMB* [2004] IRLR 9, EAT).

The information should be disclosed before the consultation begins, and although the employer is not required to give every last detail of his proposals at the initial stage, he must give **provisional details** in respect of the required information as a basis for discussion with the representatives (*E Green & Son (Castings) Ltd v ASTMS* [1984] IRLR 135, EAT).

8936 The employer must also give the representatives a **copy of the notification** made to BIS (¶8970).

8937 The information should be **given** to each of the appropriate representatives **or sent** to an address notified by them to the employer or, in the case of union representatives, posted to the union's main or head office (s 188(5) TULRCA 1992).

8938 Employee representatives may be asked to accept **confidentiality constraints** for a specified period, so long as this does not inhibit their rights to be sufficiently informed so as to be able to take part in meaningful consultation. Further, Stock Exchange rules do not preclude employee representatives being informed and consulted in advance where collective redundancies are planned in connection with a take-over.

Timing

8939 Following a significant Court of Justice of the European Union ruling, consultation must **be completed before the notice of dismissal** is given (*Junk v Wolfgang Kuhnel* [2005] IRLR 310, ECJ).

Readers should note, however, that the UK legislation rules on when consultation **must commence** still apply and employers must also ensure that where the number of redundancies proposed at one establishment:
- are between 20 and 99, consultation must commence at least 30 days before the first of the dismissals takes effect, i.e. before the expiry of the first notice of dismissal; or
- are 100 or more, consultation must commence at least 90 days before the first of the dismissals takes effect, i.e. before the expiry of the first notice of dismissal.

As consultation must be completed before the notice of dismissal is given the UK rules will usually be complied with in any event. This is because it is expected that this additional requirement will mean employers will have to ensure that they start their consultation period earlier than before. However, where the consultation period is concluded quickly and the notice period is relatively short, it is possible that employers may find that they have to allow for the 30/90-day requirement.

Employers must ensure, as emphasised by BIS in its revised guidance note (Redundancy Consultation and Notification), that the process of consultation begins in **good time**. Indeed, there should be a period of **meaningful consultation** before the notices of termination are sent out (*TGWU v Ledbury Preserves (1928) Ltd* [1986] IRLR 492, EAT), especially given the requirement to consult "with a view to reaching agreement" (¶8926). A tribunal must ask itself whether a consultation process has begun in good time to achieve its aims (i.e. see the factors set out at ¶8926) but a mechanistic or calendar approach cannot be adopted to working out

what is or is not "in good time" (*Amicus v Nissan Motoring Manufacturing (UK) Ltd* [2005] UKEAT 0184_05_2607). In this case, the EAT held that determining the answer to such a question will involve a consideration of a number of factors:
– the numbers of staff and union(s) involved in the process;
– what is a reasonable time for the union to be able to respond to proposals and make counter-suggestions regarding redundancies while the proposals are still at a formative stage;
– the eventual outcome being envisaged, i.e. how many are to be relocated or redeployed; and
– the ancillary issues involved in any redeployment such as re-housing costs and new schooling for children of relocating employees.

The 30/90-day period fixes the start of consultation, but not when it finishes. The **actual period** of consultation can be much longer than the minimum requirement, for example, where there was an ongoing dialogue concerning the same employees and the same prospective redundancies, a 22-month period was considered to constitute one consultation process (even though the issue of redundancies had been deferred for over a year during this period) (*Vauxhall Motors v Transport and General Workers Union* [2006] IRLR 674, EAT). However, the consultation period does not have an unlimited shelf-life and where necessary the employer must start another consultation period to ensure that he complies with the consultation requirements.

Consultation should also **precede any public announcement** of the redundancy programme.

> EXAMPLE In *Amicus v Nissan Motoring Manufacturing (UK) Ltd*, the employer had initially informed and consulted with a company council through which staff issues such as salary rises and terms and conditions of employment were discussed and negotiated. By the time the union had become involved, the proposals were still at a formative stage and, consequently, the union had been able to respond to adequate information and, as a result of their involvement in the consultation process, a significant number of improvements in the proposals had been achieved. Consequently, although the process involving the union had started late, the union officials had in fact played an important and effective role in the consultation process and therefore consultation was deemed to have occurred "in good time".

> MEMO POINTS Following the Court of Justice of the European Union ruling in *Junk*, it may appear artificial that BIS has maintained the 30/90-day rule in its guidance, especially given the Court of Justice's comments that the effectiveness of the information and consultation provisions in the Directive on Collective Redundancies would be jeopardised if employers were allowed to inform and consult subsequent to their decision to terminate employees' contracts of employment. This very clearly imposes an obligation on employers to undertake meaningful consultation to achieve the Directive's objectives of finding ways to avoid and/or reduce the number of redundancies which need to be made.

8940 If they are to comply with these requirements, employers need to have the **structure for consultation** already in place before the relevant period of consultation is due to commence. This may make it more convenient to have a standing representative body with which to consult. Otherwise, if elections need to be held, there is a risk that plans over redundancies will be indirectly revealed at too early a stage.

8941 In order to calculate the applicable consultation period, where the employer subsequently proposes **further redundancies**, each batch in respect of which the employer has already started consultation is, in the absence of bad faith, considered separately (s 188(3) TULRCA 1992).

8942 The employer will not be in breach of the consultation period if he consults or informs as soon as is reasonably practicable after the election of employee representatives where this has been **delayed by the affected employees** (¶8929).

8943 If the employer dismisses before the consultation period has expired, he will be in breach of his statutory obligations and could face a compensation claim. To avoid claims, the employer should **delay the date** of the dismissals.

Failure to comply/infringement of rights

8946 If an employer fails to **consult** as required, or fails to comply with **election requirements**, a complaint may be brought to an employment tribunal as follows (s 189 TULRCA 1992):

Failure:	Complaint by:
Election of employee representative(s)	Any affected employees/employees dismissed as redundant
Any other failure relating to employee representative(s)	Any employee representative(s) to whom failure related [1]
Relating to trade union representative(s)	The trade union
Any other case	Any affected employees/employees dismissed as redundant

1. Where employee representatives have been elected but information or consultation has been inadequate only employee representatives are entitled to make a complaint and affected employees have no direct right to complain of a failure to inform and consult (*Northgate HR Ltd v Mercy* [2008] IRLR 222, CA).

> **MEMO POINTS** Liability for a protective award in respect of failure to carry out collective consultation before making redundancies is a provable debt in the liquidation of a company (*Haine v Day* [2008] IRLR 642, CA).

8947 Affected employees have no remedy if their **representative does not perform** his duties properly, as the right to complain is confined to complaints against the employer.

8948 If a question arises as to whether or not a particular employee representative was an appropriate representative, it is for the employer to show that the **representative had the necessary authority** to represent the affected employees (s 189(1A) TULRCA 1992). If necessary, he must also show that the **requirements regarding elections** have been satisfied (s 189(1)(a), (1B) TULRCA 1992).

8949 Complaints must be brought either before the date on which the last of the dismissals takes effect or within 3 months beginning with that date unless, in the view of the tribunal, it was not reasonably practicable for the complaint to be made in time, in which case it must be brought within such further period as the tribunal considers reasonable (s 189(5) TULRCA 1992) (¶9466).

8950 **Defence** There is a defence for an employer who finds it not reasonably practicable to perform his information and consultation obligations due to **special circumstances**. In such cases, the employer must take all such steps towards performing his duties as are reasonably practicable in those circumstances (s 188(7) TULRCA 1992). It is for the employer to establish the defence (s 189(6) TULRCA 1992). "Special circumstances" is not defined, but case law indicates that the circumstances must be special to the particular case, and "out of the ordinary" or "uncommon" (*Clarks of Hove Ltd v Baker's Union* [1978] IRLR 366, CA). If the circumstances are not sufficient to support the defence, they may nevertheless be taken into account by the tribunal when awarding compensation for failure to comply (see below).

The employer cannot rely on the defence where he **has not received necessary information** from the person controlling him (directly or indirectly) (for example, a head office or parent company), where the latter has made the decision leading to the proposed dismissals.

Moreover, any **delay** between taking a decision which leads to the proposed dismissals and the date on which the employer is informed of it should be disregarded when considering whether the employer can rely on the special circumstances defence (*GMB v AMICUS (AEEU & MSF) and ors* [2003] UKEAT 1094_02_1404).

It is clear that concerns about **confidentiality** will not provide a defence, and the Stock Exchange rules do not preclude consultation in advance of a transaction involving a listed company. It may be possible to consult with appropriate representatives on a confidential basis, although this will obviously be more difficult if employee representatives need to be elected.

There are no special circumstances attaching to the **appointment of a receiver or administrator** (*Re Hartlebury Printers Ltd (in liquidation) and ors* [1992] IRLR 516, ChD), unless the financial deterioration into insolvency or receivership is sufficiently sudden, such as the collapse of take-over negotiations and the immediate denial of further credit by the bank (*USDAW v Leancut Bacon Ltd* [1981] IRLR 295, EAT), or the insolvency is combined with, for example, the destruction of the employer's plant, a general trading boycott or a sudden withdrawal of supplies from the main supplier (*Re Hartlebury Printers Ltd (in liquidation) and ors*).

> EXAMPLE In *Shanahan Engineering Ltd v UNITE* [2010] UKEAT 0411_09_2202, a contractor working on a power station was instructed to reschedule its work, with effect from the next day, which meant that the contractor would need 50 fewer employees to work on site. The next day the contractor selected the employees to be made redundant and the following day issued redundancy notices with one week's pay in lieu of notice. Unite, the union recognised by the contractor, brought proceedings in respect of the failure to consult. While the EAT accepted that the sudden need to reorganise the work schedule did amount to special circumstances, and that it was not reasonably practicable to conduct a consultation process in good time, it held that it would have still been possible to conduct a partial and brief consultation process, so that it upheld the decision of the employment tribunal that the contractor would be liable to pay a protective award. However, the EAT overturned the maximum 90-day protective award made by the tribunal, and said that the lack of time available to consult should be taken into account when assessing the protective award (¶8952). The case was sent back to the tribunal to reconsider the level of protective award.

Remedies for failure to consult/comply with election requirements If a tribunal upholds a complaint, it must make a **declaration** to that effect and may make a **protective award** of up to 90 days' pay for each affected employee, which the employer will be obliged to pay (s 189(2) TULRCA 1992). It appears that only those employees who have been dismissed as redundant, or whom it is proposed to dismiss as redundant, will be covered by the award (s 189(3) TULRCA 1992). Those employees who are otherwise affected by the redundancy situation (¶8916) do not appear to have a right to receive a protective award.

8951

Where a complaint has been **brought by** a recognised trade union (for example for failure to consult with appropriate representatives) on behalf of its members that have been affected, the award can only be made **in relation to** those it represents (*Transport and General Workers Union v Brauer Coley Ltd (in administration)* [2007] ICR 226, EAT). Any employees who are not members and have been affected by a non-union breach (for example, due to a failure to consult) must bring their own claims. Practically speaking, such claims can be brought simultaneously.

The award is **calculated** by reference to a week's pay (¶2920) (uncapped) for each week of the "**protected period**" (s 189(2), (3) TULRCA 1992), which begins with the date on which the first of the dismissals to which the complaint relates takes effect, or the date of the award if earlier, and is as long as the tribunal decides is just and equitable bearing in mind the seriousness of the employer's failure to comply, subject to a **maximum** of 90 days (s 189(4) TULRCA 1992). Tribunals, in deciding the appropriate period, should make the maximum award of 90 days and should only make reductions to it if there are mitigating circumstances which the tribunal, in its discretion, considers just and equitable (*Susie Radin Ltd v GMB* [2004] IRLR 400, CA; *Transport and General Workers Union v Morgan Platts Ltd (in administration)* [2003] UKEAT 0646_02_1003; *Amicus v GBS Tooling Ltd (in administration)* [2005] UKEAT 0100_05_1804). The purpose of the protective award is punitive but should not serve to compensate the employee and, consequently, it is the **seriousness of the default** that should be the primary consideration in calculating the amount to be awarded. **Mitigating factors** should be examined alongside the seriousness of the employer's default and the tribunal is likely to **take into account**:

8952

a. the number of consultation days actually lost;
b. the employee's loss of notice/remuneration;
c. whether the breach was merely technical or minor (for example, providing the information orally rather than in writing) and whether the employer complied in part;
d. the employer's attitude to the consultation process;
e. whether the employer made a genuine mistake in relation to, or was ignorant of, his legal obligations;

f. whether the breach was deliberate;
g. the employer's efforts to find alternative employment;
h. any previous practice of non-consultation; and
i. the extent to which employee representatives were also responsible for the failure.

The tribunal will **not take into account** the employer's ability to pay the protective award and it will be irrelevant that a payment may have to be made by the Government instead of the employer if the latter is insolvent (*Smith and anor v Cherry Lewis Limited* [2004] UKEAT 0455_04_0511).

Therefore, if there is no consultation, or the consultation is meaningless (for example, where there is no exploration of alternatives to redundancy), the maximum award is likely to be made. On the other hand, if, despite the employer's failure to fully comply with his consultation obligation, the employee has not suffered any adverse effects, the tribunal may reduce the award, or make no award at all, although in most cases, an award will be made.

> EXAMPLE **Examples of mitigating factors**
> 1. In *Amicus v GBS Tooling Ltd (in administration)*, the employer failed to carry out any consultation with the union after formulating a proposal to dismiss all employees as redundant because of the company's insolvency. However, the employer had, in prior consultation, kept the union informed of the situation and that redundancies were likely. Although this consultation had taken place prior to formulating the proposal to dismiss, it was deemed to constitute a mitigating factor going to the seriousness of the employer's breach, justifying a reduction in the award.
> 2. In *Lancaster University v The University and College Union* [2010] UKEAT 0278_10_2710, a university followed a practice, over a number of years, of informing a recognised union in advance where fixed-term lecturers might not have their contracts renewed. It did not arrange any form of meeting with the union to discuss the termination of the contracts, although individual meetings were held. A new union representative took over and pointed out that the procedures did not comply with the statutory requirements. The employer did not disagree, but made no significant effort to agree new, compliant procedures, so the union made an application for a protective award. An employment tribunal awarded 60 days' pay, rather than the maximum 90 days, on the basis that the union had condoned the practice for some years. The EAT upheld the award. The tribunal had taken the correct "top down" approach, and it was reasonable for the tribunal to take the fact that the employer had been lulled into a false sense of security into account as a mitigating factor.

8953 If the employee is paid a **Jobseeker's Allowance or income support** during the protected period, the employer must deduct the amount paid from the award and repay it to the Department of Work and Pensions. Note that a **contractual payment** or a payment by way of **damages for breach of contract** in respect of any part of the protected period will not go towards discharging the employer's liability to pay a protective award (and similarly, the protective award will not go towards discharging the employer's liability to make those payments) (*Commission of the European Communities v UK, Case C-382/92* [1994] IRLR 392, ECJ).

8954 The **protective award will be lost** to the extent that an employee would otherwise have remained employed where he is employed during the protected period but is fairly dismissed for a non-redundancy reason (see ¶8916 for definition of redundancy), or unreasonably terminates his employment (s 191(1) TULRCA 1992).

Further, if an employee **unreasonably refuses** an offer of **suitable alternative employment**, he loses the protective award for the period during which he would have been employed, had he not refused (s 191(2), (3) TULRCA 1992). If the employee accepts the alternative employment but reasonably leaves during the trial period (see above), he will still be entitled to the protective award.

If an **employee dies** during the protected period, that period will, for the purposes of calculating his award, end on his death (s 190(5) TULRCA 1992).

8955 If the employer **fails to comply with the award**, the employee can bring a complaint to the tribunal within 3 months of the last day on which the employer failed to make the payment, unless it was not reasonably practicable to bring it within that period (s 192(2) TULRCA 1992).

8956 If the **employer is insolvent**, the employee can apply to BIS for payment of the protective award (¶9053).

Protection for voters, candidates and employee representatives It is **automatically unfair** (¶8390) for an employer to dismiss any worker wholly or mainly because (s 152 TULRCA 1992; s 103 ERA 1996):
– they have participated in the election either as a candidate or voters; or
– of their status or activities as union representatives or elected representatives.

8957

It is also unlawful for an employer to victimise any such worker by subjecting him to a **detriment short of dismissal** by any act, or any deliberate failure to act, on those grounds (s 146 TULRCA 1992; ss 47, 47(1A) ERA 1996).

8958

> EXAMPLE The employer transfers Employee A, removing him from the group of affected employees. The reason, or one of the reasons for this, is to do with the fact that A is a representative. This amounts to detrimental action and gives A the right to a remedy.

2. Notification to the Department for Business, Innovation and Skills (BIS)

Where **20 or more redundancies** are proposed at one establishment **within 90 days** (¶8916), an employer must notify the Department for Business, Innovation and Skills (BIS) of his proposal to dismiss employees as redundant. The timing for this notification is as for the commencement of consultation (¶8939) (s 193(1), (2) TULRCA 1992).

8970

> MEMO POINTS In light of the effect of the Court of Justice of the European Union's decision in *Junk* (*Junk v Wolfgang Kuhnel* [2005] IRLR 310, ECJ; see ¶8939), a small legislative change was made to clarify that an employer must notify BIS before any redundancy notices are sent to affected employees (Collective Redundancies (Amendment) Regulations SI 2006/2387).

The notification provisions **are excluded** in the same circumstances as the consultation provisions (see above). In addition, however, overseas employment is excluded from the duty to notify BIS (s 285 TULRCA 1992).

8971

It is irrelevant whether the redundancies are compulsory or voluntary. Where the employer has already notified BIS of one batch of redundancies, any **further redundancies** are counted separately (s 193(3) TULRCA 1992).

8972

Employers may notify by letter or use Form HR1. The **information required** is similar to that to be provided to employee representatives (¶8935), and must, if consultation is required, identify the trade union or employee representatives concerned and give the date when consultation began. BIS should also be informed if the employer's **proposals change significantly** after the notification has been given – for example, if the dismissal dates change or the numbers to be dismissed increase by twenty or more.

A **copy of the notification** must be provided to the employee representatives, although there does not appear to be any sanction for failure to comply with this requirement (s 193(6) TULRCA 1992).

Failure to notify may lead to criminal proceedings, which could result in a fine, although the special circumstances defence (see above) may apply. Ignorance of the obligation to notify does not amount to special circumstances for the purposes of the defence (*Secretary of State for Employment v Helitron Ltd* [1980] ICR 523, EAT).

8973

IV. Statutory redundancy payments

Entitlement

An employee who has been dismissed by reason of redundancy (¶8740) will be entitled to a statutory redundancy payment if he has completed at least 2 years' continuous employment, unless he is an excluded/disqualified employee.

8990

If the **employer is insolvent or refuses to pay**, the state will guarantee the statutory redundancy payment from the National Insurance Fund (see ¶9049).

Taxation of redundancy payments is discussed at ¶3132.

8991 **Continuous employment** is calculated as at the "relevant date", which is discussed at ¶8340. Periods before the employee's 18th birthday count towards continuous service. However, periods of overseas employment and receipt of a genuine statutory redundancy payment will break continuity (see ¶1025).

Excluded/disqualified employees

8992 The following employees are not entitled to statutory redundancy payments:
- employees who have contracted out of their entitlement (¶¶8993, 8995); and
- employees who have lost their entitlement in certain circumstances (¶¶8996, 9001).

Domestic servants who are close relatives of their employers are also excluded (s 161 ERA 1996).

8993 **Contracting out in advance** Collective agreements dealing with redundancy procedures or the provision of alternative employment covered by an **exemption order** issued by BIS following application by all the parties to the agreement can disapply the statutory redundancy scheme in respect of employees within the scope of the agreement, and set out agreed severance payments and procedures (s 157 ERA 1996). The agreement must indicate that, in the event of disagreement, certain issues (the right to a payment and/or its amount) may be referred to an employment tribunal for decision. While collective redundancy provisions are common between trade unions and employers, exemption orders are rarely used.

8994 Employees on **fixed-term contracts** can **no longer contract out in advance** on an individual basis (¶2003).

8995 **Contracting out once right has arisen** It is only possible to contract out of the employee's right to redundancy pay (or to a statutory trial period in alternative employment – ¶8872) if the agreement between employer and employee meets the statutory requirements of a valid compromise agreement (¶9333) or is reached through an Acas-appointed conciliation officer (¶9305).

8996 **Re-employment or refusal of suitable alternative employment** An employee will lose his entitlement if he is re-employed (such that continuity is preserved) or he unreasonably refuses an offer of reinstatement or suitable alternative employment (or unreasonably leaves during the statutory trial period) (s 141(2)-(4) ERA 1996) (¶8873).

9000 **Resignation during notice period** An employee who is under notice of dismissal may wish to leave before the employer's notice expires. To preserve his right to a redundancy payment, he must serve a **counter-notice** on the employer (s 136(3) ERA 1996). Although it appears that he can give short, even minimal notice (*Ready Case Ltd v Jackson* [1981] IRLR 312, EAT), he must give written notice within the obligatory period of the employer's notice (i.e. the minimum notice required by statute or contract, or the actual notice period if less), which is counted backwards from the date of dismissal specified in the employer's notice. For example, if the employee is entitled to 2 weeks' notice, but the employer actually gives 3 weeks' notice, the employee must serve his counter-notice within the last 2 weeks of the 3-week notice period (and not before).

The **employer may contest** the employee's counter-notice by serving a further written notice on the employee, requiring him to withdraw his counter-notice and serve out the original notice period, and warning him that the employer will contest his right to a redundancy payment if he fails to comply (s 142 ERA 1996). If the **employee refuses**, he is not entitled to any redundancy payment unless he applies to the tribunal, and the tribunal can award all, part or none of the redundancy payment, as it considers just and equitable. If the **employee dies** during the period of his counter-notice, the employer is deemed to have contested that notice (if he has not actually done so), and the employee's estate must apply to an employment tribunal for a redundancy payment (s 176(5) ERA 1996).

Gross misconduct If an employee is **potentially redundant**, he will lose his entitlement if it is subsequently discovered that summary dismissal for gross misconduct is justified (¶6640), and the employer either dismisses without notice, with shorter notice than required by the contract or the statutory minimum, or with full notice but accompanied by a written statement that he would have been entitled to dismiss without notice (s 140(1) ERA 1996).

If the employer has **already given notice of redundancy** when the employee commits the act of gross misconduct, the employer may be able to avoid making a redundancy payment by giving **further notice** that he would have been entitled to summarily dismiss the employee. However, a tribunal may award the whole or part of any redundancy payment in such circumstances (s 140(3), (4) ERA 1996).

If an employee is **on strike** during the redundancy notice period, the employer cannot exclude the right to a redundancy payment by dismissing for gross misconduct (s 140(2) ERA 1996). However, the employer may make **payment conditional** on the employee working an extended notice period (to make up for days lost during the strike) by serving a written **notice of extension**, warning that he will dispute the employee's right to a redundancy payment if the employee does not comply (s 143 ERA 1996). If, on each day of the extension, the employee turns up for work, is unable to comply or reasonably refuses to comply, a tribunal can award all or part of the redundancy payment. If not, the tribunal may not make any award.

Calculation

The statutory redundancy payment is calculated by reference to age, length of service (subject to a cap – see below) to the relevant date (¶8340), and salary (subject to a cap – see below) as follows (s 162(2) ERA 1996):
– for each complete year of employment in which the employee was aged 41 or over: 1.5 week's pay;
– for each complete year in which he was aged 22 to 40: 1 week's pay; and
– for each complete year in which he was aged 21 or under: 0.5 week's pay.
The table on the next page can be used to calculate the employee's entitlement.

A **week's pay** is subject to a statutory cap (see ¶2923). **Length of service** is subject to a maximum of 20 years (s 162(3) ERA 1996), and is calculated according to statutory continuity of service (contractual agreements relating to continuity are ignored) (¶1020).

The **current maximum** statutory redundancy payment is, therefore, £13,500 (£450 × 20 × 1.5).

A tribunal has a **discretion to reduce** the amount of a redundancy payment in the following circumstances where the employee:
– served a counter-notice on the employer, seeking to bring forward the date of dismissal given in the employer's notice, but the employer serves further notice requiring him to work out the notice period in full (¶9000);
– is dismissed for misconduct after notice of dismissal for redundancy was served (¶9001) or after he served a notice of intention to claim a redundancy payment in a lay-off or short-time working case (¶7884); or
– failed to comply with a notice of extension after being on strike (¶9001).

Read off the employee's age and number of complete years' service. The table will then show how many weeks' pay the employee is entitled to.
(See next page)

Age	Service (Years)																		
	2	3	4	5	6	7	8	9	10	11	12	13	14	15	16	17	18	19	20
18 [1]	1																		
19	1	1½																	
20	1	1½	2																
21	1	1½	2	2½															
22	1	1½	2	2½	3														
23	1½	2	2½	3	3½	4													
24	2	2½	3	3½	4	4½	5												
25	2	3	3½	4	4½	5	5½	6											
26	2	3	4	4½	5	5½	6	6½	7										
27	2	3	4	5	5½	6	6½	7	7½	8									
28	2	3	4	5	6	6½	7	7½	8	8½	9								
29	2	3	4	5	6	7	7½	8	8½	9	9½	10							
30	2	3	4	5	6	7	8	8½	9	9½	10	10½	11						
31	2	3	4	5	6	7	8	9	9½	10	10½	11	11½	12					
32	2	3	4	5	6	7	8	9	10	10½	11	11½	12	12½	13				
33	2	3	4	5	6	7	8	9	10	11	11½	12	12½	13	13½	14			
34	2	3	4	5	6	7	8	9	10	11	12	12½	13	13½	14	14½	15		
35	2	3	4	5	6	7	8	9	10	11	12	13	13½	14	14½	15	15½	16	
36	2	3	4	5	6	7	8	9	10	11	12	13	14	14½	15	15½	16	16½	17
37	2	3	4	5	6	7	8	9	10	11	12	13	14	15	15½	16	16½	17	17½
38	2	3	4	5	6	7	8	9	10	11	12	13	14	15	16	16½	17	17½	18
39	2	3	4	5	6	7	8	9	10	11	12	13	14	15	16	17	17½	18	18½
40	2	3	4	5	6	7	8	9	10	11	12	13	14	15	16	17	18	18½	19
41	2	3	4	5	6	7	8	9	10	11	12	13	14	15	16	17	18	19	19½

Service (Years)	2	3	4	5	6	7	8	9	10	11	12	13	14	15	16	17	18	19	20
Age																			
42	2 1/2	3 1/2	4 1/2	5 1/2	6 1/2	7 1/2	8 1/2	9 1/2	10 1/2	11 1/2	12 1/2	13 1/2	14 1/2	15 1/2	16 1/2	17 1/2	13 1/2	19 1/2	20 1/2
43	3	4	5	6	7	8	9	10	11	12	13	14	15	16	17	18	19	20	21
44	3	4 1/2	5 1/2	6 1/2	7 1/2	8 1/2	9 1/2	10 1/2	11 1/2	12 1/2	13 1/2	14 1/2	15 1/2	16 1/2	17 1/2	18 1/2	19 1/2	20 1/2	21 1/2
45	3	4 1/2	6	7	8	9	10	11	12	13	14	15	16	17	18	19	20	21	22
46	3	4 1/2	6	7 1/2	8 1/2	9 1/2	10 1/2	11 1/2	12 1/2	13 1/2	14 1/2	15 1/2	16 1/2	17 1/2	18 1/2	19 1/2	20 1/2	21 1/2	22 1/2
47	3	4 1/2	6	7 1/2	9	10	11	12	13	14	15	16	17	18	19	20	21	22	23
48	3	4 1/2	6	7 1/2	9	10 1/2	11 1/2	12 1/2	13 1/2	14 1/2	15 1/2	16 1/2	17 1/2	18 1/2	19 1/2	20 1/2	21 1/2	22 1/2	23 1/2
49	3	4 1/2	6	7 1/2	9	10 1/2	12	13	14	15	16	17	18	19	20	21	22	23	24
50	3	4 1/2	6	7 1/2	9	10 1/2	12	13 1/2	14 1/2	15 1/2	16 1/2	17 1/2	18 1/2	19 1/2	20 1/2	21 1/2	22 1/2	23 1/2	24 1/2
51	3	4 1/2	6	7 1/2	9	10 1/2	12	13 1/2	15	16	17	18	19	20	21	22	23	24	25
52	3	4 1/2	6	7 1/2	9	10 1/2	12	13 1/2	15	16 1/2	17 1/2	18 1/2	19 1/2	20 1/2	21 1/2	22 1/2	23 1/2	24 1/2	25 1/2
53	3	4 1/2	6	7 1/2	9	10 1/2	12	13 1/2	15	16 1/2	18	19	20	21	22	23	24	25	26
54	3	4 1/2	6	7 1/2	9	10 1/2	12	13 1/2	15	16 1/2	18	19 1/2	20 1/2	21 1/2	22 1/2	23 1/2	24 1/2	25 1/2	26 1/2
55	3	4 1/2	6	7 1/2	9	10 1/2	12	13 1/2	15	16 1/2	18	19 1/2	21	22	23	24	25	26	27
56	3	4 1/2	6	7 1/2	9	10 1/2	12	13 1/2	15	16 1/2	18	19 1/2	21	22 1/2	23 1/2	24 1/2	25 1/2	26 1/2	27 1/2
57	3	4 1/2	6	7 1/2	9	10 1/2	12	13 1/2	15	16 1/2	18	19 1/2	21	22 1/2	24	25	26	27	28
58	3	4 1/2	6	7 1/2	9	10 1/2	12	13 1/2	15	16 1/2	18	19 1/2	21	22 1/2	24	25 1/2	26 1/2	27 1/2	28 1/2
59	3	4 1/2	6	7 1/2	9	10 1/2	12	13 1/2	15	16 1/2	18	19 1/2	21	22 1/2	24	25 1/2	27	28	29
60	3	4 1/2	6	7 1/2	9	10 1/2	12	13 1/2	15	16 1/2	18	19 1/2	21	22 1/2	24	25 1/2	27	28 1/2	29 1/2
61 [2]	3	4 1/2	6	7 1/2	9	10 1/2	12	13 1/2	15	16 1/2	18	19 1/2	21	22 1/2	24	25 1/2	27	28 1/2	30

1. It is possible that an individual could start to build up continuous service before age 16, but this is likely to be rare, and therefore the table has been started from age 18.
2. The same figures should be used when calculating the redundancy payment for a person aged 61 and above.
(Crown Copyright reproduced by permission of the Controller of Her Majesty's Stationery Office from "Ready Reckoner for Redundancy Payments")

Claims for payment

9010 In order to **secure his entitlement** to a statutory redundancy payment, the employee must, **before** the end of 6 months beginning with the relevant date (¶8340) (s 164 ERA 1996):
- agree and receive the payment from the employer;
- make a written claim for payment from the employer;
- bring a claim for payment in an employment tribunal; or
- bring a complaint of unfair dismissal in an employment tribunal.

9011 If the employee secures his entitlement (for example, by making a written claim from the employer), there is no time limit for a **subsequent application** to a tribunal if his entitlement is not paid in full.

> EXAMPLE In *Bentley Engineering Co Ltd v Miller* [1976] IRLR 146, QBD, M was paid a redundancy payment based on 8 years' service within 6 months of the relevant date, thus satisfying the initial time limit. Two years later, an employment tribunal accepted his claim for a redundancy payment based on 23 years' service.

9012 The time limit for tribunal claims can be **extended** up to within 12 months of the relevant date (but no further) if the tribunal considers it just and equitable to do so, having regard to all the circumstances of the case (¶9475), including whether the employee should receive a redundancy payment (s 164(2) ERA 1996).

The statutory time limit only applies to claims under the statutory redundancy scheme. The time limits for **contractual schemes** (for example, exempt schemes set out in a collective agreement – ¶8993) may set out their own time limits. If they do not, the general limitation period for contractual claims will apply (¶9450).

9013 **Compensation for financial loss** With regard to any tribunal claim for payment, tribunals have the power to order employers to compensate workers for any financial loss sustained as a result of the non-payment of redundancy awards (s 7 Employment Act 2008).

9014 **Death of employer or employee** If the **employee dies**, his entitlement to a redundancy payment passes to his estate, and his personal representatives can pursue his claim. If the employee dies within 6 months of the relevant date, the basic **time limit** is 1 year beginning with the relevant date (s 176(7) ERA 1996). If the employee dies during the 6 months following expiry of the normal 6-month time limit, the tribunal may extend this second 6-month time limit to 12 months.

The deceased employee's estate will not be entitled to a redundancy payment if he had been offered **suitable alternative employment**, which would have been unreasonable for him to refuse, and he died (s 176(3), (4)(a), (b) ERA 1996):
- after the offer was made but before deciding whether to accept or reject it;
- during the trial period; or
- having given notice to terminate the trial period.

9015 The **death** of an **individual employer** amounts to a dismissal of the employee for statutory redundancy purposes, and the employee may be entitled to a redundancy payment from the employer's estate (ss 136(5), 139(4) ERA 1996). If, however, the employee accepts an offer of **suitable alternative employment** (¶8867) from the employer's personal representatives, continuity will be preserved and there will be no liability to pay statutory redundancy. The statutory trial period will apply (¶8872), although in this case the new employment must begin within 8 weeks of the termination of the old job, and the offer of new employment does not have to be made before the old job came to an end (s 174 ERA 1996).

9016 It is possible that the transfer of the business from the deceased employer to his personal representatives may amount to the transfer of an undertaking for the purposes of the **business transfer regulations** (¶7910) (although arguably the employees' contracts would not otherwise have been terminated by the transfer, as required by the regulations, but by the employer's death). See chapter 24 for further discussion about the transfer regulations.

Statement of entitlement

9017 When making a redundancy payment, the employer must provide the employee with a statement showing how it was calculated (see above), unless that amount is determined by an employment tribunal following a claim for payment (s 165(1) ERA 1996). It is advisable for the statement to make it clear that the calculation represents the employee's statutory redundancy payment.

Failure to provide the statement is a criminal offence. Further, the employee can give written notice to the employer **demanding a statement** by a specified date (allowing the employer at least 1 week), and failure to comply without reasonable excuse is a further offence (s 165(4) ERA 1996).

SECTION 4

Employee rights on insolvency

9040 A detailed discussion of the law of insolvency is beyond the scope of this book. The **impact** of employer insolvency **on the employment relationship** is discussed at ¶8277. This section will focus on specific employee rights and protections, including the employee's right to apply to the Department for Business, Innovation and Skills (BIS) for certain state guaranteed payments, his treatment as a preferential creditor in respect of certain debts, and his rights against an administrator (or, in rare cases, an administrative receiver) in respect of amounts arising during the period of administration (or receivership).

1. State guaranteed payments

a. Types of payment

9045 Employees of an insolvent employer can apply to BIS for the following state guaranteed payments (payable from the National Insurance Fund):
– **statutory redundancy payments**;
– certain **debts**; and
– unpaid **pension contributions** to an occupational pension scheme or a personal pension scheme.

An employee of an insolvent employer can recover her **statutory maternity pay** from the Commissioners of HM Revenue and Customs (reg 7 Statutory Maternity Pay (General) Regulations 1986, as amended; s 1(2) Social Security Contributions (Transfer of Functions, etc) Act 1999). Likewise, **statutory paternity pay** and **statutory adoption pay** may be recovered (reg 43 SI 2002/2822).

> MEMO POINTS   Where an employer has his registered office in one EU state but also employs workers in **another EU state**, the guarantee institution of the state in which the employee is employed is responsible for making the guaranteed payment (*Everson and Barrass v Secretary of State for Trade and Industry and Bell Lines Ltd* [1999] EUECJ C-198/98).

9046 The **definition of insolvency** depends on whether the employer is an individual or a company (s 166 ERA 1996 (redundancy payments); s 183(2) ERA 1996 (debts)).

An **individual employer** is insolvent if he has:
– been declared bankrupt or has entered a composition or arrangement with his creditors; or
– died and the court has ordered that his estate be administered as an insolvent estate (s 421 Insolvency Act 1986).

> MEMO POINTS   In **Scotland**, an individual employer is insolvent under the first limb if sequestration of his estate has been awarded, or he has executed a trust deed for his creditors or has entered into a composition contract (for detail on an insolvent estate, see s 11A Judicial Factors (Scotland) Act 1889).

9047 A **corporate employer** is insolvent if:
- a winding-up order or administration order has been made, or a resolution for voluntary winding-up has been passed;
- an administrator, a receiver or a manager of the company's undertaking is appointed, or possession has been taken of any company property by or on behalf of debenture holders; or
- a voluntary arrangement under certain insolvency provisions has been approved (Part I Insolvency Act 1986).

> MEMO POINTS 1. If the employee is employed by a **partnership**, each and every partner must meet the definition of individual insolvency (*Secretary of State for Trade and Industry v Forde* [1996] UKEAT 213_96_0310).
> 2. Appointment of a manager/possession by or on behalf of debenture holders does not apply in **Scotland**.

9048 An employer is not insolvent merely because he is unable to pay debts as they fall due or simply stops trading. When making a claim, the **employee must prove**, by direct evidence, that the employer is insolvent (*Secretary of State for Trade and Industry v Walden* [1999] UKEAT 905_98_0107).

Statutory redundancy payments

9049 The employee can recover a so-called employer's payment from BIS if he can show that the employer was liable to make such a payment, he has not been paid (or has been paid only in part) and either:
- he has taken all reasonable steps short of legal proceedings to obtain payment from the employer; or
- the employer is insolvent, as defined (see above).

For these purposes, **legal proceedings** does not include tribunal proceedings, but does include enforcement proceedings, so an employee is normally expected to bring a tribunal claim for a redundancy payment before applying to BIS, but is not required to take enforcement proceedings in respect of a tribunal decision before doing so.

The Secretary of State will make the payment if he is satisfied that the above conditions are met, and in making his decision he must make reasonable enquiries to ascertain the facts and to apply them to the law current at that time (*Secretary of State for Trade and Industry v Lassman* [2000] IRLR 411, CA).

The employee must have completed the necessary period of **qualifying service** to claim a redundancy payment (¶8990).

> MEMO POINTS An employee claiming under a contractual scheme covered by an exemption order (see below) must also have completed the statutory period of qualifying service to claim from the National Insurance Fund, regardless of the scheme rules, although the period of continuous employment is computed in accordance with these rules rather than the statutory provisions (s 167(2) ERA 1996).

9050 The **type of payment** recoverable includes a statutory redundancy payment and also (s 166 ERA 1996):
- an amount payable under an Acas-conciliated settlement or a compromise agreement (including an agreement to submit a dispute to arbitration under the Acas scheme) in respect of a statutory redundancy payment; or
- a termination payment payable in accordance with a collective agreement covered by an exemption order (¶8993).

9051 The **amount of payment** recoverable is as follows:

Claim	Amount
Statutory redundancy payment	Calculated in normal way, with credit given for any amount actually paid by the employer (s 168(1)(a) ERA 1996)
Sum owing under Acas-conciliated settlement or compromise agreement	Lesser of amount owing under agreement or amount of redundancy payment employer would otherwise have been liable to pay (s 168(1)(aa) ERA 1996)

Claim	Amount
Sum payable under exempt scheme	Lesser of amount due under scheme and "relevant redundancy payment" (see memo points) (s 168(2) ERA 1996)

MEMO POINTS Relevant redundancy payment is the statutory redundancy payment to which the employee would otherwise have been entitled, calculated according to the exempted scheme's computation of continuous employment and determination of the relevant date, where different from the statutory provisions.

Where a tribunal has specified the amount of a redundancy payment owing to an employee (or made appropriate findings permitting the amount to be calculated), the employer may be liable to pay **interest** on that amount from 42 days after the tribunal's decision. The interest owing can also be claimed from BIS (*Secretary of State for Employment v Reeves* [1993] UKEAT 104_91_2601).

9052

Debts

The debts listed below may be recovered from BIS if the employer is insolvent (see above), the employment has been terminated, and the employee was entitled to all or part of the debt on the appropriate date (s 182 ERA 1996).

9053

Relevant debt (s 184(1), (2) ERA 1996)	Limit	Appropriate date
Arrears of pay [1]	8 weeks [2]	Date employer becomes insolvent (except protective awards – see below)
Accrued holiday pay [3]	6 weeks	
Protective award	8 weeks [2]	The latest of: – date employer becomes insolvent; – date employment terminates; and – date on which award made
Unfair dismissal basic award		
Statutory minimum notice	[4]	The later of: – date employer becomes insolvent; and – date employment terminates
Reimbursement of whole or part of any fee/premium paid by apprentice		

1. Pay includes commission, overtime, guarantee and time-off payments, protective awards (for failure to consult in collective redundancy situations), and medical and maternity suspension pay. These are assessed on the basis of salary net of tax and National Insurance contributions (NICs) (which are deducted after the statutory cap (see below) is applied) (*Morris v Secretary of State for Employment* [1985] IRLR 297, EAT; confirmed in *Titchener v Secretary of State for Trade and Industry* [2002] ICR 225, EAT).
2. The employee can choose the 8 weeks for which he is owed most, where relevant (*Mann v Secretary of State for Employment* [1999] IRLR 566, HL).
3. This relates to the employee's entitlement in the 12 months ending with the appropriate date and is assessed by reference to net pay.
4. If the employee was wrongfully dismissed, the amount recoverable in respect of statutory notice will reflect his duty to mitigate his loss (*Westwood v Secretary of State for Employment* [1984] IRLR 209, HL) and any state benefits received (which would not have been paid had he not been dismissed) (¶8160).

EXAMPLE **Appropriate date**
Employee A's employer becomes insolvent on 14 October when a receiver is appointed out of court as agent for the company. The receiver dismisses A with immediate effect on 18 October. A can apply to BIS for **arrears of pay** and **accrued holiday pay** up to 14 October (not up to 18 October).

The total amount recoverable for any debt (except for fees/premiums paid by apprentices) is subject to a **statutory cap** (¶2923) or such amount as the Secretary of State may order (or pro-rata for a period less than 1 week) (s 186 ERA 1996). If the **employee is owed more** than the statutory maximum, the rest of the debt will be considered as part of the employer's insolvency proceedings.

9054

9055 The Secretary of State can deduct any amount which the employer would have been able to **offset** (for example, a debt owed by the employee to the employer) (*Secretary of State for Employment v Wilson and BCCI* [1996] IRLR 330, EAT). If the statutory cap is applicable, the Secretary of State is entitled to apply this to the sum and then deduct NICs and other appropriate amounts which the employer would have been able to offset (*Titchener v Secretary of State for Trade and Industry* [2002] ICR 225, EAT). However, if the employee has a claim for arrears of pay in respect of periods before the reference period (in addition to arrears in the reference period), payments made by the employer during the reference period are set against the earlier claims rather than the arrears during the reference period (*Regeling v Bestuur van de Bedrijfsvereniging voor de Metaalnijverheid* [1998] EUECJ C-125/97).

Pension contributions

9056 **Contributions recoverable** are those to be paid by the employer on his own behalf or on behalf of an employee from whose pay a deduction has been made for that purpose, where these remain due from the employer at the date of his insolvency (s 124(2) Pension Schemes Act 1993).

9057 The **maximum amount payable** depends on whether the contribution is an employer or employee contribution as follows:

Type of contribution	Amount payable
Employer	The least of: – arrears of employer contributions accrued within the 12 months immediately preceding date of insolvency; – an amount equal to 10% of the total amount of remuneration [1] paid or payable to employees covered by the scheme in respect of the 12 months immediately preceding date of insolvency; and – (in relation to defined benefit schemes) the amount certified by an actuary as required to pay employees' benefits on dissolution of the scheme
Employee	The amount deducted from the employee's pay in respect of his contributions during the 12 months immediately preceding the date of insolvency [2]

1. Remuneration includes statutory sick and maternity pay, guarantee and time off payments, medical or maternity suspension payments, protective awards, and holiday pay.
2. If an employee recovers a payment in respect of arrears of pay from which his employee contribution would normally have been deducted, he should consider paying his contribution into the scheme in order to preserve his benefits.

MEMO POINTS   The Court of Justice of the European Union has held that the UK has not correctly implemented the EC Directive on Insolvency Protection with regard to pension benefits (art 8 EC Directive 1980/97; *Robins and ors v Secretary of State for Work and Pensions* [2007] IRLR 270, ECJ). The Court held that while there was no obligation to guarantee entitlement to benefits in full, the Directive provides employees/ex-employees with a minimum level of insolvency protection with regard to their acquired and prospective rights to benefits under an occupational pension scheme. UK domestic legislation, the Court concluded, did not meet this minimum standard of protection as unchallenged statements before the Court showed that two of the claimants in the main proceedings would only receive 20% and 49% respectively of the benefits to which they were entitled.

9058 Some schemes are **eligible for pension protection**. These are certain defined benefit pension occupational pension schemes and defined benefit elements of other schemes.

Where, in the case of an occupational pension scheme, an insolvency event has occurred (which includes, in relation to a company, the appointment of an administrative receiver or entering into administration (Pensions Act 2004; see ¶¶8277+)), the **insolvency practitioner** is obliged to **give notice** of this, and the status of the scheme, to the Board of the Pension Protection Fund, the Pensions Regulator and the trustees or managers of the scheme. If the **Board of the Pension Protection Fund assumes responsibility** for eligible schemes, which it may do under a number of complex provisions in the Pensions Act 2004, compensation may then be payable to affected members of the scheme. The compensation may be payable on a periodic or lump sum basis and the amount will vary depending on the age of the member.

b. Application procedure

9065 The **employee** applies for payment by filling in an **application form** (RP1) (available from the administrator, receiver, liquidator or trustee) (RP2 for payments in respect of statutory minimum notice) and returning it to the Redundancy Payments Office of BIS. An application for payment of pension contributions is made by the **administrator** of the pension scheme (in respect of the total amount due to the scheme).

9066 There are no express **time limits**. However, as the state guaranteed redundancy payment depends on the employer's liability to pay, the time limits for claiming a redundancy payment must normally be observed (¶9010). The employee may then apply to BIS if the employer refuses to pay or is **insolvent**. The employee may make an **application to a tribunal** for a redundancy payment from the employer before applying to BIS (if the employer is **not insolvent**, he may be required to do so as part of the obligation to take all reasonable steps to recover payment).

9067 In order to determine the claim for payment, BIS can require the employer or other persons to provide the necessary **information and documents** (s 169 ERA 1996 (redundancy payments); s 190 ERA 1996 (debts); s 157 Pension Schemes Act 1993), and failure to comply without reasonable excuse is a summary offence punishable by a fine. A more serious offence is committed if the employer deliberately or recklessly provides false information.

9068 The Secretary of State can apply to a tribunal **contesting the employee's redundancy entitlement** or the amount claimed (or both) (s 170(1) ERA 1996), even if an earlier tribunal application resulted in an award being made to the employee (*Secretary of State for Employment v Banks* [1983] ICR 48, EAT). There is no time limit.

9069 If an administrator, receiver, liquidator or trustee in bankruptcy is required by law to be appointed, the Secretary of State must delay making any payment in respect of relevant **debts** until he has obtained a **statement** from such person as to the **amount owing** to the employee (unless he is satisfied that he can determine the amount without a statement) (s 187 ERA 1996). Similar provisions apply in relation to **pension contributions** but note that the Secretary of State cannot dispense with the requirement of an actuary's certificate, where applicable (s 125 Pension Schemes Act 1993).

9070 **Transfer of rights** If the Secretary of State makes a payment to the employee, the employee's rights and remedies against his employer are transferred to the Secretary of State, who is therefore entitled to any **money subsequently recovered** from the employer (ss 167(3), (4), 189 ERA 1996). This also applies in relation to the rights of the administrator of the pension scheme in the insolvency proceedings (s 127(1) Pension Schemes Act 1993).

Remedies

9071 Complaints are made to an employment tribunal and the procedure will depend on the type of payment claimed.

9072 **Redundancy payments** The employee can apply to a tribunal if the Secretary of State **refuses his application** for a redundancy payment or **pays less** than the correct amount (the application can be made against the Secretary of State alone, or the employee can join the employer as a party (*Jones v Secretary of State for Employment* [1982] ICR 389, EAT)). There is no time limit.

> MEMO POINTS   The EAT had found that employment tribunals, when hearing cases against BIS, were **not independent and impartial** as required by the European Convention on Human Rights (incorporated by the Human Rights Act), as they are paid for, largely appointed by, and administered by the Secretary of State (*Scanfuture UK Ltd (2) Link v Secretary of State for Trade and Industry* [2001] IRLR 416,

EAT; European Convention on Human Rights; Human Rights Act 1998). **Subsequent amendments** to procedures for appointment, payment and termination of lay members' contracts mean that the right to a fair trial is no longer breached.

9073 **Debts and pension contributions** The applicant for payment can complain to an employment tribunal that the Secretary of State has **failed to make the payment** or has **paid less** than the correct amount (s 188 ERA 1996; s 126 Pension Schemes Act 1993).

He must bring the claim **within** 3 months beginning with the date on which the Secretary of State's decision was communicated to him (or where not reasonably practicable, within such further period as the tribunal considers is reasonable).

If the **tribunal upholds the complaint**, it will make a declaration to that effect and state the amount due (it does not actually order payment).

2. Preferential creditor

9080 An **employee**'s claim to remuneration is treated as a preferential debt and given precedence over other creditors' claims (s 386, Sch 6 Insolvency Act 1986). Also as preferential debts are any sums owing to occupational pension schemes and state scheme premiums and these will take precedence over any sums owing to employees.

Remuneration is **limited to** the 4-month period immediately preceding the employer's insolvency and **includes** wages or salary (including commission), guarantee and time-off payments (to look for work or arrange training on redundancy, for antenatal care, for trade union duties etc), protective awards for failure to consult on collective redundancy, medical and maternity suspension pay, sick pay and accrued holiday pay (Sch 6 paras 9-15 Insolvency Act 1986).

The employee's claim is subject to a **statutory cap** of £900, although this does not apply to accrued holiday pay (Sch 6 Insolvency Act 1986; Insolvency Proceedings (Monetary Limits) Order SI 1986/1966). Claims over the cap and claims other than for remuneration (contractual or statutory) will not rank as a preferential debt.

9081 If the employer's **assets cannot meet all claims** for remuneration, each claim ranks equally and is paid in equal proportions to the other claims.

3. Administrators

9085 An administrator can be **appointed by** the company, its directors, a qualifying floating charge holder or by court order (on application by the company, its directors or creditors) (paras 10, 14, 22 Sch B1 Insolvency Act 1986). The administrator does not incur personal liability to pay sums due to employees. Instead, if the employment contract was adopted by the administrator, certain sums due to employees may have to be paid out as an expense of the administration at the cessation of an administrator's appointment. In such cases, liability for the payments falls on the company's property in the custody or control of the administrator and has priority to most other charges and securities, including the administrator's own remuneration and expenses (para 99 Sch B1 Insolvency Act 1986).

The **sums due to employees** under the above provisions are:
– wages and salary (including holiday pay and sick pay); and
– contributions to an occupational pension scheme.

> MEMO POINTS The Court of Appeal has confirmed that the expenses of an administration rank ahead of paying protective awards (¶¶8951+) and payments in lieu of notice (¶¶8145+) and that therefore protective awards and payments in lieu of notice (subject to a minor exception in relation to the latter) do not attract "super-priority" (*Krasner v McMath* [2005] IRLR 995, CA).
> Holders of a floating charge pre-dating 15 September 2003 may be able to appoint an **administrative receiver**. A receiver (or, a receiver and manager) may also be appointed by the court as a way of enforcing certain other security over the company's assets. The provisions relating to payments by administrative receivers and receivers are similar to those of administrators, except

that administrative receivers are personally liable for certain payments under the contracts (broadly, wages, salary and occupational pension contributions for the period after adoption of the contract during his appointment) and receivers are personally liable for payments during their appointment without any statutory limitation (ss 44, 37 Insolvency Act 1986 respectively). The exact details are outside the scope of this book.

CHAPTER 26

Handling disputes and alternative resolution

OUTLINE	¶¶
SECTION 1 **Handling potential litigious disputes** 9110	Consideration 9250
	Tax issues 9265
	Benefits 9268
A Identifying potential disputes 9115	References 9270
B Taking advice 9130	Return of company property 9272
Availability 9130	Resignations 9274
Timing 9133	Confidentiality and restrictive covenants 9276
First appointment 9136	Reporting requirements 9280
C Gathering information and evidence 9140	Employee's legal fees 9282
1 Documents 9143	Governing law and jurisdiction 9284
2 Physical evidence 9165	D Settlement documentation 9300
3 Witness evidence 9170	1 Agreements reached through conciliation officers 9305
4 Disclosure and privilege 9185	2 Compromise and settlement agreements 9315
SECTION 2 **Resolving employment disputes** 9200	a Types of claim 9318
	Contractual claims 9320
	Statutory rights 9322
I Settlement through negotiation/conciliation 9210	b Types of agreement 9330
	c Conditions for a valid compromise agreement 9333
A Assessing the merits of settlement 9210	3 Signing 9350
B The negotiation/conciliation process 9215	4 Enforcement 9353
1 Involvement of Acas conciliation officers 9218	II **Arbitration** 9360
	Scope 9360
2 Admissions of liability 9227	Access to the scheme 9365
3 Without prejudice negotiations 9230	Withdrawal and settlement 9367
C Settlement proposals and terms 9240	Pre-hearing procedure 9370
Scope 9240	Hearing 9373
Agreed termination 9247	Decision 9376
	Appeals 9380

9100 Where an employment dispute arises, it is usually in the interests of both employer and employee, in terms of saving time, costs, reputation and often, for the employee, emotional distress, to resolve it without resorting to litigation. However, in some cases this will not be possible and the parties will therefore need to rely on the tribunals and courts to resolve the dispute. Section 1 examines the identification of disputes, sources of advice, and the gathering of information and evidence. Section 2 discusses alternative methods of resolving disputes, including negotiation/conciliation and arbitration, and examines the documenting of agreed settlements. Litigation is discussed in chapter 27.

Although reference will be made throughout this section to litigation in employment tribunals, the same principles generally apply to litigation in the courts.

SECTION 1
Handling potential litigious disputes

9110 If litigation cannot be avoided, the parties should prepare themselves as thoroughly as possible in order to bring or defend the case effectively.

In any event, the following steps should be considered:
- identifying possible disputes at an early stage;
- taking appropriate advice;
- identifying the strengths and weaknesses of each side;
- gathering and preserving all relevant evidence (which will include physical evidence, documentary evidence and the evidence of witnesses);
- identifying and using opportunities to resolve the dispute by means other than litigation; and
- knowing the potential costs and other consequences involved in pursuing (and possibly losing) litigation.

A. Identifying potential disputes

9115 Complaints can more easily be resolved if they are identified before a tribunal claim is actually brought. The employer should, therefore, be alert to the possibility of a dispute situation arising and be aware of, and have a means of addressing, employee grievances.

Dispute situations

9116 A dispute may arise in all sorts of different situations, such as where the employer's actions will or may **change the employment relationship**, for example, where he is contemplating a dismissal, the introduction of a new shift system, alterations to commission schemes, adjustments to lunch hours, or the introduction of a dress code.

Changes to the law may give employees new rights which make current practices unlawful. For example, the introduction of the national minimum wage created potential disputes where employees continued to be paid below the minimum rate.

Disputes may also arise between the employer and non-employees, such as a discrimination claim from an unsuccessful candidate in relation to the **recruitment process**.

An employer may be liable for the actions of his employees (or even third parties) (¶¶4825+), for example in connection with racial or sexual harassment (¶¶5227-31), and should therefore be alert to **disputes or friction in the workplace**.

> MEMO POINTS The Government is **proposing to repeal** provisions relating to employers' liability for third party harassment from the EqA 2010. The regulations remain active at the time of publication, though the impending change is part of a draft bill called the Enterprise and Regulatory Reform Bill which is proceeding through Parliament. Any further developments will be covered by our updating service.

Recognising and avoiding potential disputes

9118 The factors set out below will be relevant.

Knowledge of the law An **employer** needs to have at least a basic understanding of employment law, and the rights and obligations imposed by it, in order to identify potential disputes and to avoid or deal with them satisfactorily. Ignorance of the law is no defence to a claim.

Although the ability to avoid a dispute is normally in the hands of the employer, an **employee** needs to know whether there is any legal basis for his complaint.

Policies and procedures The following written procedures will assist the proper handling of a potential dispute (both employer and any aggrieved employee should consult the relevant procedure):
– a dismissal and disciplinary procedure;
– a grievance procedure;
– an equal opportunities procedure;
– a redundancy procedure; and
– staff rules of conduct.

> MEMO POINTS   The employer **must provide** written details of his dismissal, disciplinary and grievance procedures (¶¶1405, 1408).

The employer must ensure that any written procedures are effectively **implemented**. To achieve this, **those who make decisions** affecting employees (e.g. line managers) must be made aware of the applicable procedures, and know and understand their responsibilities.

Following a fair procedure is crucial to defending a claim of **unfair dismissal**, as the employer must have a fair reason for dismissal and follow a fair procedure. Proper implementation of any written procedures will make it easier to satisfy a tribunal that a fair procedure has been followed, and a **departure from the normal procedure** may result in an unfair dismissal, or inference of unlawful discrimination, unless it can be justified and was carefully considered. These issues are discussed further at ¶¶8435+.

B. Taking advice

Availability

Both employers and employees should consider taking legal advice in order to understand their rights and obligations. Advice becomes particularly important if the matter proceeds to litigation, and is available from a number of sources, including:
– solicitors, citizens advice bureaux and law centres;
– employers' associations;
– GOV.UK;
– trade unions;
– Acas;
– official helplines, for example the Equality Advisory Support Service; and
– employment consultants.

Some solicitors offer a **free initial interview** at which they will discuss the case, give an outline of what needs to be done and estimate the likely costs.

Tribunal staff will give assistance in respect of the procedural aspects of claims but cannot give legal advice in relation to the merits of the case.

Acas advisers give objective and impartial advice to employers, employees, employers' associations, workers and trade unions (s213 TULRCA 1992), and such advice may be given at the parties' request or at its own instigation.

Public funding (previously known as legal aid) is not available for pursuing employment tribunal claims in England and Wales (although publicly-funded representation may be available for representation at the EAT). It is, however, available in limited circumstances for claims to employment tribunals in Scotland.

Employees in England and Wales may be entitled to a limited form of aid known as **Legal Help**, which is subject to a means test and enables a solicitor to give advice and assistance (e.g. advising on the merits of a claim, writing letters and preparing the tribunal application). It may also cover the cost of mediation. These costs will be paid by the Legal Services Commission but if the employee subsequently recovers any damages, the costs payable under the Legal Help scheme will be deducted from the amount recovered.

> MEMO POINTS Despite arguments that this may conflict with the right to a fair trial under the Human Rights Act 1998 (which succeeded in Scotland), there are currently no plans to extend public funding to employment claims in England and Wales. Public funding is available in Scotland where the case is both arguable and too complex for the applicant to present the case himself to a minimum level of effectiveness, and the award of public funding is reasonable in the circumstances of the case (Human Rights Act 1998; Advice and Assistance (Advice By Way of Representation) (Scotland) Regulations SI 1997/3070).

Timing

9133 Once a potential dispute has been identified, appropriate advice should be taken at the earliest possible opportunity. If a **dismissal for misconduct**, for example, is being considered, advice should be taken before the disciplinary process begins or as soon as possible thereafter. If **redundancies** are thought necessary, advice should be taken immediately so that a proper consultation procedure can be devised and implemented. Further, it is likely to be more cost-effective to take advice before taking action rather than seek legal advice once a dispute has arisen.

9134 Most employment claims must be presented within relatively short **time limits** (¶9452), as must the employer's response to the claim. If, therefore, an employee is seeking advice about a potential claim after the dismissal (or other act complained of) has taken place, or if an employer is seeking advice after a claim has been started by an employee, swift action is needed.

First appointment

9136 The adviser will need to see all **relevant documents** (it will usually be helpful to send them in advance). He will require all the relevant information in order to give a proper assessment of the case and the likely consequences. If a weakness is identified at the outset, an appropriate strategy can be adopted to minimise its impact. If the weakness only comes to light during the tribunal hearing it will be more difficult to deal with, and the tribunal may question the veracity of a party's evidence if it suspects that the party has withheld information from his own adviser.

C. Gathering information and evidence

9140 Relevant information should be gathered and retained, including:
– documentary evidence (e.g. correspondence including emails, notes of meetings (including any informal notes, diary entries etc), contractual documents);
– physical evidence (e.g. property which has allegedly been damaged); and
– witness evidence.

All relevant documents (or at least copies of them) and other items should be **preserved** so that they can, if necessary, be produced to the tribunal. If the company automatically disposes of or shreds documents, or automatically deletes electronic data, this should be stopped until all relevant information has been retrieved.

Employees will also need to gather any relevant evidence in the same way. They may be able to use their rights under the Data Protection Act 1998 to gain **access to records** held by the employer in their personnel file (Data Protection Act 1998).

The ability to produce relevant documents which support a party's case is also often crucial in conducting successful **negotiations**, as the outcome is inevitably influenced by the parties' views of the relative strengths and weaknesses of each side's case.

Any **letters written in relation to a dispute** should not be unduly emotional, abusive or aggressive, but should be clear, precise and businesslike. If some response or action is required, this should be clearly stated and, if appropriate, should include the time scale for compliance. Correspondence (including any informal notes, diary entries etc) within the employer's organisation (for example, between line managers and the human resources department) may have to be disclosed at the tribunal stage, unless they are covered by "privilege" (discussed below).

9141

It may be appropriate to mark letters "without prejudice" where they relate to a genuine attempt at settlement of a dispute (¶9230).

1. Documents

A **separate file** should be opened to keep all documents relevant to the dispute in chronological order so that they can be easily produced either to an adviser or as part of the disclosure process during litigation (¶9545). **Indexing** these documents will make it less likely that a document is subsequently overlooked, and will save time and expense if it later becomes necessary to compile a full list of documents for disclosure.

9143

If the **original** document cannot be retained (for example, where a letter is sent out), then a **photocopy** (or a second print of a document produced by computer) should be retained.

9144

All documents (or copies) must be complete and legible. It may be necessary for a **typed transcript** of any **handwritten notes** to be prepared (retaining the original in case it is important to show the content of contemporaneous notes if, for example, there is a dispute about what was said at the time).

Where it is important to show that a particular document has been seen or received, an **acknowledgement of receipt** or other proof (for example recorded delivery post) should, where possible, be obtained and retained with the document.

9145

The **date of receipt** of a document may be important. If the document arrived by post, the envelope showing the postmark should be retained. Alternatively, a date stamp or handwritten note on the document itself may be helpful.

Types of document

The documents set out below are normally **relevant** in employment disputes.

9148

Contract of employment This may be contained in a single document or encompass a number of documents, such as an offer letter, a written statement of particulars and a staff handbook.

9149

There may be a number of different contractual documents over a long period of employment with the same employer. The contract governing the employment at the time of the matter in dispute will be most relevant, but **previous contracts** may be helpful for comparison purposes. Where there has been a transfer of the business, the contract may be a document produced by a previous employer.

Any **amendments** to the contract (whether by way of individual letters to the employee or general notices to staff) should also be made available.

Evidence of receipt and/or acceptance of these documents will often also be important.

Personnel file This will contain most, if not all, of the relevant employment documentation. **Background information**, although not directly relevant to the particular dispute, may be useful. For example, information about the employee's **past conduct** could form the basis of an argument that it is not just and equitable to award him any compensation, even though it played no part in the decision to dismiss him.

9150

9151 **Dismissal and/or disciplinary procedure** This may be contained in the employment contract, the staff handbook, or a separate document, and will be most relevant in unfair dismissal cases. Any evidence that the employee is aware of the disciplinary procedure will be important (for example, an acknowledgement of receipt of the staff handbook containing the procedure).

> MEMO POINTS For details as to what information regarding disciplinary rules and procedures should be included in an employee's **written statement of particulars**, see ¶6525.

9152 **Documents arising from disciplinary action** Any previous **written warnings** should be made available, together with evidence of receipt.

Written notes of any **oral warning** should also be retained in accordance with the disciplinary procedure, as well as copies of all **other documents** used in the disciplinary process, including any letter to the employee setting out the complaints against him, requiring him to attend a disciplinary meeting and advising him of his right to be accompanied, any statements or other documents considered at the disciplinary hearing, notes of the meeting, and a copy of the written confirmation of the outcome (including written notice of any rights of appeal).

9153 **Notes of meetings** It may be crucial to prove what was, or was not, said in particular meetings, so comprehensive and accurate notes of any relevant meeting should be kept. Ideally, meeting notes should:
a. be **made**:
– **contemporaneously**, preferably by someone whose sole purpose in attending is to take notes, otherwise by the person conducting the meeting (even if these are only rough notes to form the basis of a more detailed minute to be prepared afterwards). If the employee is accompanied at a disciplinary or grievance hearing, he may wish his companion to take notes on his behalf; or
– **immediately after** the meeting, recalling what was said in as much detail as possible;
b. identify who is present at the meeting, the date and the location. The start and finish times (and the timing of any breaks) should also be recorded, as the length of the meeting can give a better impression of the nature of that meeting. For example, a meeting appearing to have lasted only 5 minutes is unlikely to have included detailed discussion of an allegation of misconduct followed by serious consideration of the appropriate sanction;
c. contain:
– as far as possible, a **verbatim account** of what is said, identifying who said what; or
– a **detailed summary** of what was said by each party; and
d. refer to any documents or other items which were considered in the course of the meeting.

All participants in the meeting should be **provided with a copy** of the note and asked to acknowledge that they agree that it accurately reflects what was said in the meeting or to specify any points which they believe are inaccurate. A party who has been given this opportunity and not raised an objection will find it harder later to convince a tribunal that the note is inaccurate. Evidence that copies of the notes have been sent to the participants (for example, a copy of a covering letter) should be retained. Where there is to be an appeal from the decision of that meeting, the relevant meeting note should be made available prior to the appeal hearing.

If a **typed transcript** is prepared of any handwritten notes, each participant should be provided with a copy of the original notes and the transcript and should be asked to agree both.

9154 **Correspondence** The file relating to the dispute should contain:
– copies of all letters sent out;
– copies or originals of all letters received; and
– evidence of the date of despatch or receipt.

9155 **Evidence relating to remuneration** This may be important with regard to:
– liability (for example, where it is alleged that an employee has been **underpaid** in a breach of contract or unlawful deductions claim); or
– compensation in any type of claim.

The file should, therefore, contain copies of payslips, P45, P60 and P11D (particularly important if the employee's pay is variable because of, for example, overtime or shift allowances), and any documents relating to bonus schemes or commission arrangements (if not included in the contract itself).

Medical evidence In a case involving ill health or incapacity, copies of sick/fit notes, correspondence with the employee's GP and any medical reports should be included in the file of documents. The employer may also have attendance records or self-certification forms, which may also be necessary to prove absence. 9156

The employee would also be advised to keep copies of any such documents and may also wish to obtain a letter from his GP or any specialist treating him, confirming his condition.

Evidence relating to mitigation If an **employer** wishes to claim that an employee has not fully mitigated his loss (i.e. taken steps to minimise it) in order to reduce any compensation payable (¶8620), he should compile a dossier containing copies of any job advertisements which the employee might reasonably be expected to pursue. There is no need to prove that the employee could have obtained any particular job. 9158

Conversely, an **employee** should retain copies of all applications, letters of rejection, and a note of any interviews or other efforts made to find alternative employment (for example, a diary noting his contacts with the local job centre or recruitment agencies). He should also be able to produce evidence of pay and other remuneration received from any employment which he has obtained since his dismissal.

Diaries/other notes Those involved in a potential dispute should make a note in a diary as and when any incident or discussion occurs. This will be helpful in later demonstrating to a tribunal that a party's version of events is correct. Other notes, for example records of calls between the HR department and the disciplinary officer, will also be both relevant and, in most cases, discloseable. 9159

Handling documents

The tribunal or court normally prefers to see the document in its original form. If, therefore, the parties wish to make **annotations** on a document, this should be done on a copy. Similarly, if certain sections of a document need to be **blacked out** for reasons of confidentiality, a clean copy should be retained. 9162

2. Physical evidence

Physical evidence will be important where, for example, an employee is accused of damaging employer property. Items of physical evidence may include damaged equipment, computer records, tachograph records, CCTV footage and surveillance videos, clocking in or till records, stolen property, alcohol or drugs found in the employee's possession or clinical analysis reports following drug or alcohol testing on the employee, or examples of deficient workmanship. Care should be taken to ensure that any such items (assuming they belong to the employer) are taken out of the employee's custody and that the employer is himself not committing a criminal offence by retaining them, e.g. possession of illegal drugs. 9165

If the damaged item can be **retained**, it should be placed somewhere secure. Steps should be taken to ensure that it is not interfered with prior to any tribunal hearing. 9166

If the item is too large, or if it needs to be repaired or cleaned, **photographs** should be taken as soon as possible after the incident is discovered. The date and time at which the photographs are taken should be recorded. Where possible, the actual damage should be **inspected** by the person who is conducting the disciplinary process before any repairs or cleaning take place. A note should be made identifying who was present at the inspection, what was seen and the date and time it took place. If an employee is suspected of having caused the damage, a **joint inspection** may be appropriate.

If the dispute relates to **computer records** then a screen print, paper print-out or back-up copy of the relevant records should be made in order to record the problem. Alternatively, a **forensic report** from IT specialists may be necessary, particularly in cases of breaches of confidentiality or where employees are suspected of establishing competing businesses: forensic specialists can often recover deleted or encrypted files and track precisely when certain actions were taken by employees.

3. Witness evidence

9170 As part of a proper disciplinary procedure, the employer should **obtain written statements** from all relevant witnesses. He should certainly do so once a potential litigious dispute is identified. There are three types of statement:
– statements taken for use as **evidence** in the disciplinary process;
– statements taken after the relevant event(s) in order to **provide information** in relation to it; and
– **formal** statements prepared for use at a tribunal hearing.

The statements prepared during a disciplinary process or as part of an information-gathering exercise may not necessarily be those which are used as formal statements at the tribunal (though they will be disclosable as evidence). The latter are likely to be prepared by the parties' legal advisers in a more formal format, taking into account any additional matters which come to light in the course of preparing for the hearing.

Informal statements taken for the purposes of a disciplinary procedure or in the early stages of preparing for litigation (discussed below) may form the basis of any formal statements subsequently prepared. They will also be important as they will have been prepared during or shortly after the events in question before memories fade. They may also serve as a basis for challenging any different version of events put forward by any witness at a later stage.

Preparation

9172 Statements are **generally** prepared in **one of two ways**:
– the witness is asked to write down in as much detail as possible his recollection of the relevant events; or
– the party seeking the statement interviews the witness and writes out a statement on the basis of that interview.

Whichever method is adopted, the statement must, as far as possible, be in the witness' own words. An attempt to influence what is said or put a more helpful gloss on the evidence may result in harmful discrepancies if the witness is subsequently (during tribunal proceedings) cross-examined on his statement.

If the statement is not prepared by the witness himself, he should be encouraged to make any **corrections, additions, or deletions** so that the statement accurately reflects his own recollection.

To obtain a balanced assessment of the case, statements should ideally be taken from **everyone who has been involved** in, or who has witnessed, the relevant events (and not only from those who are thought likely to be most helpful to that party's case).

Each witness should **prepare** his own statement **independently** where possible, rather than after having read the statements of other witnesses. Once all the statements have been gathered, **supplementary statements** can be sought from witnesses if points made in one statement cast doubt or cause confusion in relation to points made in another.

Evidence of a party's spouse or other closely connected person who is **not independent** is not worthless and should still be obtained. A tribunal will take into account the lack of independence when assessing their credibility.

If a professional adviser is engaged, the task of interviewing witnesses and preparing statements is likely to be taken on by him.

Content

9174 Witnesses should give a full and frank account of their recollection of events, including anything which is detrimental to a party's case, as it is better to identify any weaknesses at the outset (rather than in the course of the hearing). Statements should be confined to **relevant facts** so far as possible, and should not contain legal argument.

Witnesses should make clear in their statements what they actually saw or are aware of from their own **direct knowledge**, and what they are recounting on the basis of having been told by someone else, and whether something they say is merely their **opinion or speculation**, as opposed to a statement of fact.

If a witness' evidence relies on a document, it is sufficient to **refer to the document** and, if necessary, to a particular paragraph or section (rather than recite its entire contents). Now that witness statements are generally taken as read by the judge, rather than read out during the course of the hearing by the witnesses, it is particularly important to refer to specific paragraphs of supporting documents in order that it is straightforward for the tribunal to find the relevant points easily.

Nicknames and abbreviations should not normally be used. Where a person is referred to, that person's position in the business should be identified where appropriate. If a term is used which is **technical** or has a **specific meaning** within a particular business, an explanation should be given. If **locations** are being described, a photograph or a plan showing the layout could be attached.

If a witness cannot recall exact dates or times, an **approximation** should be given (but it should be made clear that it is an approximation). Similarly, if there is anything that the witness cannot remember with certainty, he should make this clear.

Format

9176 It is desirable for witness statements to:
- be **typed** (where relevant, the original handwritten version should be retained);
- be divided into **numbered paragraphs**;
- start with a brief **introduction** explaining who the witness is and what his involvement is;
- deal with events in **chronological** order; and
- be **signed and dated** by the witness (after having read through it) to show that he agrees with its contents.

Use at tribunal

9178 The witness should be advised that his statement may later form the **basis of his evidence** at a tribunal hearing under oath. If this is likely, each witness should be asked to confirm in writing whether he is prepared to attend a tribunal hearing to give evidence if required. This will indicate whether or not **witness orders** will be needed (¶9553).

---

4. Disclosure and privilege

9185 The parties may be ordered by the tribunal to disclose **relevant documents** (irrelevant documents do not need to be disclosed) (¶9545). Those involved in a potential dispute should be made aware that documents they create may have to be disclosed in this way, unless they are protected from disclosure by a legal rule called "privilege". This applies to correspondence between a party and his legal advisers and other documents (e.g. early drafts of witness statements) prepared for the purpose of litigation. Privilege is discussed further at ¶9551.

When a party is preparing his file of documents in readiness for litigation, it is important to distinguish between evidential documents (including final drafts of witness statements) and any earlier **draft statements** or other **documents** which are **not intended for disclosure** (including statements of any witnesses whom the party does not intend to call). Preferably these should be kept in a separate file or otherwise marked in order to prevent inadvertent disclosure.

> **MEMO POINTS** Any statements taken as **part of a disciplinary investigation** will need to be disclosed irrespective of whether the witness will be called to give evidence. Additionally, relevant documents which are not otherwise privileged must be disclosed regardless of whether the party holding the document wishes to rely upon it.

SECTION 2
Resolving employment disputes

9200 If the parties have not already attempted to resolve their dispute, they should consider the prospect of settlement once proceedings are commenced or threatened and before the matter comes to a hearing. The likelihood of settlement will depend on the relative strengths and weaknesses of the opposing cases, the reasonableness of the parties involved, the demands and expectations of the claimant and the ability (and willingness) of the other party to meet those demands.

> **MEMO POINTS** The Government is looking into introducing a system of "protected conversations": that is, discussions with an employee about a proposed termination package with no need for there to be an existing dispute (thus including situations where the without prejudice rule would not apply), and not to have those conversations used in evidence for a future ordinary unfair dismissal claim. The aim is to enable employers and employees to have frank discussions at either's request to aid dispute resolution. A consultation took place on this (and other matters relating to ending employment relationships, such as renaming compromise agreements as "settlement agreements" and encouraging their use) in November 2012, and any further developments will be covered by our updating service when available.

9201 The Advisory Conciliation and Arbitration Service (**Acas**) often plays a significant role in the resolution of employment disputes. It is a statutory body set up to provide advisory, conciliation and arbitration services, with a general duty to promote the improvement of industrial relations. It intervenes both in individual employment disputes (discussed below) and in wider trade disputes.

9202 Whether or not the services of Acas are available, the parties should consider conducting their own negotiations, either directly or through professional advisers such as solicitors, with a view to arriving at an **agreed settlement**, which should be **documented** in a compromise or settlement agreement as appropriate.

9203 In order to avoid pressure being put on employees to sign away their rights, there is a **general prohibition on contracting out of statutory rights** such that any provision in an agreement is void in so far as it purports to exclude or limit the operation of those rights or prevents an employee from bringing or continuing a claim under them (s 203(3) ERA 1996). For example, any attempt to exclude the right to bring a claim of unfair dismissal will be, on the face of it, void.

There are three main **exceptions**:
– where an agreement is made with the involvement of an Acas conciliation officer under the statutory conciliation procedures (¶9305);
– where a valid compromise agreement has been reached (¶9333); and
– where Acas has referred the dispute to arbitration (¶9360).

9204 If the parties cannot agree a settlement, the matter may be referred to **arbitration** (in cases of unfair dismissal claims), or may come before an **employment tribunal** or court. Litigation is discussed in chapter 27.

> **MEMO POINTS** The Government is also looking into setting up a "Rapid Resolution" scheme as an alternative to an employment tribunal hearing for simple or low value cases such as holiday pay. This is now part of a draft bill called the Enterprise and Regulatory Reform Bill which is proceeding through Parliament. Further developments will be covered by our updating service when available.

I. Settlement through negotiation/conciliation

A. Assessing the merits of settlement

Before entering into negotiations, each party should **assess**:
- his chances of winning the case if it were to go before a tribunal or court;
- the level of compensation (or other remedies) available to the successful party;
- the amount of time and effort that will need to be devoted to bringing or defending the case (particularly for the employer);
- the legal and other costs involved, including the likelihood of the successful party recovering his costs from the unsuccessful party;
- what sort of adverse publicity the case may generate; and
- what the other party actually wants from the proceedings.

9210

Initially, each party will only be able to form a provisional view on the above matters, with each factor being **reassessed** in the light of further information obtained during a negotiation process. For example, the employee may have evidence of which the employer was unaware, legal arguments which he had not considered, or may be more interested in obtaining an apology or a reference than compensation. If relevant, the employer should also find out whether the employee has found another job, which will affect any estimate of compensation.

> MEMO POINTS There are **plans to introduce tribunal fees** from summer 2013 (see memo point to ¶9510), and from this time on such fees will be an additional consideration for both employees and employers (who are very likely to be ordered to reimburse the fees paid by the employee if they are unsuccessful in their defence of the claim).

Even if the **employer** believes, or is advised, that he has a **strong case**, it may still be commercially sensible for him to make a **token offer** in order to avoid incurring significant **legal costs** (which are not usually recoverable from the employee (¶9705)), and wasting **management time and resources** in preparing for and possibly attending a tribunal hearing. Dealing with tribunal claims can also be **stressful** for those involved and result in **adverse publicity**, even if the case is ultimately won.

9211

Where the **employer** has a **weak case** (or it is not clear who is likely to succeed), a more **substantial offer** may be required to settle the matter without the need for a hearing.

9212

Similar factors are relevant when an **employee** is deciding whether or not to accept an offer of settlement, although he may, as a **matter of principle**, have a greater interest in proceeding to a tribunal hearing to have his day in court. The employer may also, however, be unwilling to settle where the case against him has no merit, and may prefer to continue to defend it regardless of the cost.

9213

B. The negotiation/conciliation process

The settlement process should be **started** at the earliest possible opportunity in order to maximise the potential costs savings. The process **may continue** until all matters (i.e. both liability and remedy) are decided by the tribunal. If properly handled, the negotiation process should not prejudice either party's case in the event that it is not possible to reach a settlement.

9215

The parties are often unwilling to make the **first move** in commencing negotiations because they fear that it will prejudice their case and/or that it will be seen as a sign of weakness. Where **Acas** is involved, this fear is often reduced as Acas takes the initiative by contacting each party.

The **format** for the conciliation procedure will depend largely on the particular conciliation officer involved and the attitudes of the parties. In most cases, the conciliation officer consults with both parties by telephone and passes their respective views back and forth in the hope of achieving some common ground. This often assists in identifying those facts which are agreed and those which are in dispute, highlighting the perceived strengths and weaknesses of each case and identifying each party's estimate of any possible compensation. In some cases, meetings may be arranged with the parties either jointly or separately.

When discussing a case with the conciliation officer, a party may give certain information to him so that he has a complete picture of the case but may prefer not to have that information communicated to the other party. Parties should take care to ensure that the conciliation officer is aware of which information he can pass on and which he cannot.

Scheme for Acas involvement in EAT cases

9216 The EAT has issued a Conciliation Protocol (EAT/Acas Protocol 2007), which enables Acas to be involved in certain EAT cases. Those that may be suitable for conciliation include cases:
– relating to monetary awards only;
– where the overwhelmingly likely result of a successful appeal would be a remission back to the tribunal;
– that concern remedies; or
– where the parties' employment relationship is continuing.

For further details, see ¶9760.

1. Involvement of Acas conciliation officers

9218 Acas appoints officers to intervene in the conciliation of disputes, with the **aim** of assisting their resolution without the need for a tribunal hearing (s 211 TULRCA 1992). A conciliation officer may be an Acas employee or an independent external appointee (the latter might be more appropriate if, for example, specialist knowledge of a particular industry is required) (s 210(2) TULRCA 1992).

The conciliation officer's **role** is to impartially and objectively promote a settlement of the dispute without the need for a tribunal hearing. He will not put forward a particular settlement or attempt to decide the merits of a case. He has **no duty** to **advise either party** on the effect of relevant legislation. Further, where a financial settlement is reached, he is not obliged to ensure that such an agreement is fair to both parties (*Moore v Duport Furniture Products Limited* [1982] IRLR 31, HL confirmed in *Clarke and ors v Redcar and Cleveland Borough Council, Wilson and ors v Stockton-on-Tees Borough Council* [2006] ICR 897, EAT). Likewise, a conciliation officer must never advise parties as to the merits of their case.

The conciliation officer is required, where appropriate, to **encourage the use of** other procedures available for the settlement of grievances (for example, the employer's internal grievance or appeal procedures, if these have not already been used (s 18(6) Employment Tribunals Act 1996)).

In **unfair dismissal** cases, the conciliation officer's **priority** is to try to promote the reinstatement or re-engagement of the complainant. If this is not possible, he will seek to promote settlement by way of compensation (s 18(4), (5) Employment Tribunals Act 1996).

> MEMO POINTS It is not for the tribunals to consider whether the officer correctly interpreted his duties and it will be sufficient that the conciliation officer intended and purported to act according to his duties. However, if a conciliation officer **acts in bad faith** or adopts unfair methods when promoting a settlement, this may be a situation where the agreement might be set aside and might not operate as a bar to proceedings (*Slack v Greenham* [1983] IRLR 271, EAT; *Clarke and ors v Redcar and Cleveland Borough Council, Wilson and ors v Stockton-on-Tees Borough Council,* above).

9219 Acas' **duty to** offer free conciliation services with regard to employment tribunal claims continues **throughout** the **proceedings** until the tribunal delivers a judgment (s 6 Employment Act 2008, which repeals ss 18(2A) and 19(2) Employment Tribunals Act 1996).

Further, Acas officers have a discretionary power to offer conciliation in a **pre-tribunal dispute** although they can refuse to do so, even if both parties request it, without having to give a reason (s 5 Employment Act 2008, which amends s 18(3) Employment Tribunals Act 1996). This enables Acas to prioritise cases and relieves it from an obligation to offer conciliation in pre-tribunal disputes where there is no prospect of success.

> MEMO POINTS The Government has published **proposals** to require claims to be submitted to Acas before they can be lodged with the employment tribunal. It is proposed that Acas would then have a specified period (up to 1 month) to offer pre-claim conciliation in all cases. This is now part of a draft bill called the Enterprise and Regulatory Reform Bill which is proceeding through Parliament. Further developments will be covered by our updating service when available.

2. Admissions of liability

9227 In some cases, where the employer's liability is obvious, he may **admit liability** so that the parties can move on to **discuss compensation**. In most cases, however, liability is **contested**, but the negotiations may, nonetheless, be successfully concluded without any admission by the employer. This may be acceptable to the employee if he is satisfied with the terms of the settlement, although sometimes it is important to him to prove that the employer was in the wrong (or to get the employer to acknowledge that).

3. Without prejudice negotiations

9230 "Without prejudice" means that if discussions take place with a view to **trying to agree a settlement** but this is not achieved, the contents of those **discussions** (and even the fact that they have taken place) **cannot be disclosed to the tribunal** and a party will not be prejudiced by any offer made in the process. Although the tribunal is aware that, in most cases, some discussion takes place, it will not be influenced by that fact when deciding whether or not a party is liable.

> EXAMPLE In the course of negotiations, an employer offers £10,000 in settlement. The employee seeks £14,000 and it is not possible to reach agreement. A tribunal finds the employer liable and awards the employee £8,000. The employee cannot argue that the employer should be ordered to pay at least £10,000 because he had previously offered that sum. The offer cannot be disclosed to the tribunal and if for any reason it is disclosed, the tribunal must disregard it.

9231 If a tribunal is satisfied that the **purpose of the discussions** was to explore settlement, it will generally be prepared to regard them as without prejudice even if they have **not** been **expressly described** as such. However, it is sensible to specify that discussions or offers are "without prejudice" to avoid unnecessary arguments. On the other hand, the **mere use of the words** will not automatically result in protection from disclosure if the discussions do not relate to a genuine attempt to settle a dispute and if the parties are not on an equal footing (*BNP Paribas v Mezzotero* [2004] IRLR 508, EAT). As an **exception** to the "without prejudice" rule, statements may be admissible if there is **perjury, blackmail or other unambiguous impropriety** during the discussions (*Woodward v Santander UK Plc* [2010] UKEAT 0250_09_2505). Further, where a **dispute** arises as to the interpretation of a **settlement agreement**, prior negotiations that would otherwise be deemed as being without prejudice will also become disclosable: this is known as the "interpretation exception" (*Oceanbulk Shipping and Trading SA v TMT Asia Ltd and ors* [2010] UKSC 44). Consequently, an alleged **discriminatory act** will only be admissible if it amounts to unambiguous impropriety. This runs slightly contrary to previous EAT decisions which indicated that evidence of discrimination and evidence of victimisation on grounds of whistleblowing will never be protected (*BNP Paribas v Mezzotero*; *Hudson v University of Oxford*, EAT case 0488/05).

It is recommended that **employers ensure that they**:
– are attempting to resolve an existing dispute before embarking on any "without prejudice" discussions;
– give advance notice that the meeting is proposed to be "without prejudice" where possible and before starting any such discussion that they explain what it means and find out if the employee wishes to accept or decline the chance to have such a discussion;
– clearly state what dispute the discussions are aimed at settling and that the discussions are an alternative to dealing with this issue in the usual way, again emphasising that the employee is not forced to take part. In particular, it should be highlighted that whatever is proposed is an option to be considered rather than a stark choice between acceptance or dismissal;
– adjourn the meeting after any proposal has been made to allow the employee to consider the contents of the proposal before making a decision;
– put the proposal in writing where appropriate; and
– take extra care that nothing is said which will either undermine the duty of trust and confidence (¶1245) or is discriminatory or which may be considered to be an act of victimisation.

EXAMPLE
Disclosure inadmissible – without prejudice rule
1. In *Woodward v Santander UK Plc*, an employee making a complaint of victimisation sought to rely on refusal to provide a reference during "without prejudice" negotiations which led to the settlement of a previous claim. The EAT declined to allow her to do so as it held that the refusal did not amount to unambiguous impropriety.
2. In *Barnetson v Framlington Group Ltd* [2007] ICR 1439, CA, a senior manager, B, was employed on a payment package including share options and bonuses. His employer proposed to terminate his employment and commenced negotiations with B to that end. The negotiations were unsuccessful, and B was dismissed under terms of his contract which purported to allow payment of reduced wages in the event of early termination. B then brought a claim for wrongful dismissal. As part of his attempt to provide evidence for his claim, B proposed to put the evidence of the discussions before the High Court. The employer argued that the negotiations had been conducted on a without prejudice basis and the information should be subject to privilege. The High Court found that the evidence could not be privileged, as the purpose of the negotiations had been to avert rather than conclude a dispute and it declined to exclude the evidence. This the Court of Appeal held was wrong. The purpose of the without prejudice rule is to prevent parties from having to resort to litigation. It followed that there was no need for either party to have commenced litigation, before the rule applied. On the facts of the case, the negotiations had commenced after the employer had decided to terminate B's employment and, at this time, his contractual entitlement was already in doubt. The Court therefore held that the evidence of the discussions was privileged and could not be disclosed before a tribunal.

Disclosure admissible – exception to without prejudice rule
1. In *BNP Paribas v Mezzotero*, M, after raising a grievance with her employer about her treatment on return from maternity leave, was called to a meeting at which she was told after it had begun that it was on a "without prejudice" basis and that her job was no longer viable and a "redundancy" package was proposed. M was told that this was independent of her grievance which was still being investigated. The EAT held that M could use the contents of this meeting as evidence of further discrimination in her claim of sex discrimination because it was not a genuine attempt to settle M's complaint (although M had wanted changes to her job, she had wanted her employment to continue). It further held that M had been in a vulnerable and unequal position, having only been informed that the meeting was "without prejudice" once it had started.
2. In *Hudson v University of Oxford*, a university employee, H, was subject to a disciplinary hearing, at which he was informed that he would be dismissed. Shortly before the hearing, H made a series of disclosures, alleging that his employer was engaged in a series of criminal frauds. These allegations were withheld from the disciplinary hearing. In subsequent correspondence with H, the university insisted that he would be dismissed, relying for its argument not on the findings of the disciplinary hearing, but on its contempt for the employee's allegations of fraud. The letter was marked "without prejudice". The EAT held that, at least potentially, the contents of the letter could be read as an admission that one reason for the employee's dismissal was his attempt to highlight a perceived wrongdoing and, treating the victimisation of the employee on grounds of whistleblowing as an example of discrimination, the letter could not be privileged and should be admissible before a tribunal.
3. In *Brunel University and anor v Vaseghi and anor* [2007] ICR 592, CA, two lecturers brought complaints of racial discrimination against their employer. The university attempted to settle their claims. The vice

> chancellor sent a communication to all staff criticising the employees and accusing them of making unfounded allegations accompanied by unwarranted demands for money. The employees then brought grievances against the employer under the university's grievance procedure, as a preliminary to a victimisation claim. The Court of Appeal held that the university had waived privilege during the grievance meetings and the settlement negotiations could be discussed as evidence. The meetings were not an attempt to resolve an existing dispute, but in fact a "mini-trial" (independent adjudicators had been invited in and evidence was called and findings of fact made). Further, although the university had sought to exclude the evidence of the meetings as being subject to the without privilege rule, the university had also made reference to the same hearings in its ET3 response to the claim and in its witness statements. This too, the Court argued, was evidence that the university had waived privilege.

9232 An offer should clearly indicate whether it includes an **admission of liability**, as if a party appears to admit liability without any qualification, he may be held to that admission and only the remainder of the discussion (relating to remedies) will be regarded as without prejudice. If a party does not intend to be held to an admission of liability, he should state that such admission is made only for the purposes of negotiation and that he reserves the right to **dispute liability** if negotiations fail and the matter proceeds to a hearing.

9233 The protection afforded to "without prejudice" negotiations is largely removed **once agreement is reached**. If one party, having accepted a settlement offer without qualification, then tries to get out of that agreement (whether Acas has been involved or not), evidence can be put before the court or tribunal to prove the **existence of a settlement agreement** settling the proceedings.

9234 All **negotiations conducted through Acas** are without prejudice and confidential. Therefore, any information communicated to a conciliation officer by a party to a case is not admissible in evidence before a tribunal except with the consent of that party, even if it is the only evidence in relation to a certain matter (s 18(7) Employment Tribunals Act 1996). Evidence which exists separately from any communication to a conciliation officer can be put before the tribunal if it would otherwise be admissible (for example, a document provided to a conciliation officer which was already available to both parties).

C. Settlement proposals and terms

Scope

9240 It is recommended that settlement proposals are set out in writing to avoid confusion and misunderstanding as to the scope of any proposed settlement. For example, when discussing compensation for unfair dismissal, the parties should **clarify** whether **any figures** mentioned include the basic award or are in addition to it. If **more than one claim** is being made, it should be made clear whether any offer is intended to settle all claims or just one of them.

9241 A **dismissal in connection with the transfer of an undertaking** to which the business transfer regulations apply (¶8030) gives rise to a potential litigious dispute. It is, therefore, advisable for the employer to obtain a waiver of the employee's right to bring a claim for unfair dismissal, in the form of a validly signed compromise agreement. In these cases it is not always clear **who should be a party** to the agreement. If the dismissal takes effect prior to the transfer date, the **transferor employer** should be a party to the agreement. In this case, the benefit of the waiver would transfer from the transferor to the **transferee employer**. However, to ensure that he can rely on it, a transferee employer would also be advised to be a party to the agreement. In any event, it is essential that the agreement makes it clear against whom the claims are being settled in order to avoid subsequent litigation over this point, particularly with regard to joint and several liabilities such as the duty to inform and consult (*Tamang and anor v ACT Security Ltd and anor* [2012] UKEAT 0046_12_3108). A compromise agreement between the employee and the transferor reached after the transfer date (perhaps because the parties had assumed that TUPE did not apply) cannot be relied on by the transferee to block an unfair dismissal claim against him (*Thompson v Walon Car Delivery* [1997] UKEAT 256_96_0502).

> **EXAMPLE** In *Thompson v Walon Car Delivery*, a company, BRS, was to transfer its business to Walon under the transfer regulations. Walon did not want to take on T and other BRS staff, and so BRS intended to dismiss them, asking them to enter into compromise agreements. The agreements were not signed prior to the transfer date, and liability for the employees' dismissals transferred to Walon. The agreements were signed after the transfer date but as Walon was not a party, T could bring an unfair dismissal claim against it.

MEMO POINTS With regard to business transfers, the **risk of claims** may be able to be **reallocated** using warranties and indemnities, see *Company Law Memo* for more details.

9242 A party should ensure that all the **terms** which he requires are **agreed in principle** before final negotiations on the written agreement start in order that the settlement does not fall through at a later stage. This particularly applies to fundamental terms that are essential requirements of the respective parties, where failure to have them incorporated into the written agreement would prevent the deal from being finalised. For example, often an employer's requirement for the terms of the settlement and the circumstances leading to the dismissal to be kept **confidential** will be crucial, as will an employee's requirement for an agreed **reference**. Additionally, parties may want to include conditional terms, such as **warranties** that must be followed in order that payment will be made: if such terms are to be condition precedents for making a payment under the agreement, then they could be controversial and should ideally be agreed in advance.

9243 While the terms of the settlement are still subject to negotiation, it is advisable to head any draft agreements "**subject to contract**" to indicate that final agreement has not yet been reached. Once it has (and prior to the execution of the agreement), the heading (and any "without prejudice" label (¶9233)) should be removed.

9244 Unless a party has been deliberately misled by the other party, he will not usually be able to **withdraw from an agreement** simply because he has become aware of some matter which would have caused him not to make the agreement had he known about it at the time.

9245 In addition to meeting the statutorily prescribed conditions for compromise agreements (¶9333), a settlement agreement may contain the terms discussed below, depending on the circumstances.

Agreed termination

9247 A settlement commonly involves an agreed termination of the employment. It is advisable for this not to be described as a **resignation**, as the employer may not be able to make a bona fide damages payment for breach of contract in these circumstances, which could particularly be a problem with regard to the dismissal of a director.

This may also have **adverse tax implications**, in that the payment may not fall within the favourable treatment applied to genuine compensation payments for loss of office/position (¶3125). Note that case law indicates that any payment made in connection with a consensual termination will not benefit from favourable tax treatment but will be taxed in full as earnings from employment (*Richardson (HM Inspector of Taxes) v Delaney* [2001] IRLR 663). To fall within the favourable tax treatment, the employer would have to terminate before terms are agreed or offer settlement on a non-negotiable basis. If the parties attempt to agree terms informally prior to termination and subsequently document those terms in an agreement, HMRC may nevertheless argue that the termination was in fact by mutual agreement.

9248 If the settlement is agreed before the termination actually takes effect, HMRC may attempt to argue that the settlement is a variation of the employment contract, with the result that payments made under the varied contract are fully taxable as earnings (¶3125).

Consideration

As for any legally binding agreement, a settlement or compromise agreement must be supported by consideration. This is usually the payment of money to the employee in return for his waiver of rights.

9250

Settlement payment The starting point for any settlement proposal is normally a **calculation of the likely award** which would be made to the employee if he succeeded at the tribunal. This notional figure could be reduced if it is thought likely that the tribunal would make **reductions** for factors such as mitigation, contributory fault or the likelihood of dismissal having occurred in any event. The employer would then argue that this figure should be further reduced to reflect what is known as "**litigation risk**". In other words, if, for example, the likely award to an employee if he is successful is £10,000 (after appropriate reductions), but the employer's view is that the employee has only a 60% chance of winning the case, then he may consider an offer of £6,000 to be appropriate. If the employee does not want to accept a figure on this basis and the employer still wants to reach a settlement, he may want to consider offering a premium in order to avoid losing management time and to take account of any concerns as to the impact that a claim may have on his reputation.

9251

When considering an offer, an **employee** should take into account:
- his chances of success and the likely award;
- the possibility of reductions (for example, for contributory fault);
- his chances of finding alternative employment; and
- the costs which he will save by accepting an offer.

9252

An employee who is confident of obtaining £9,000 at the tribunal may think it prudent to accept an offer of £8,000 if it is likely to cost him £1,500 to get to the tribunal.

The employer could propose that the **payments are staggered**, for example, to take account of the fact that the employee may quickly find new employment (thus reducing his potential loss). In such cases, the agreement could provide that payments will cease if the employee starts a new job. The employee could be asked to give an undertaking, when entering the settlement agreement, that he has not yet started or obtained new employment.

9253

If there is **no formal compromise of statutory claims**, an employer may consider staggering payment of the settlement monies, with the final payment being made, for example, 4 months after the termination date, on condition that no tribunal claim has been brought. The period reflects the time within which the majority of tribunal claims must be brought (although the tribunal does have discretion to extend these time limits). This wording may provide the employee with a financial incentive, but without a valid compromise agreement, it would not prevent him from bringing statutory claims against the employer. It is therefore a risky approach and not advisable.

If the employee participates in an **approved retirement benefit scheme**, it may be possible for all or part of the termination payment to be made into the scheme, with advantageous tax treatment (¶3127). A further option would be for the employer to purchase an approved annuity for the employee.

9254

The **timing** of the termination payment (i.e. whether it is made before or after the termination of employment and delivery of the P45) will be relevant to its tax treatment (see ¶¶3122+ for information on the tax treatment of termination payments).

9255

Other forms of employer consideration Other forms of employer consideration may include allowing the employee to **keep his company car**. In this case, the employer should check the terms of the leasing and insurance arrangements to ensure that this would be permitted. The employer could offer to continue the employee's **health insurance** cover, again checking that the policy allows this.

9257

An employee may be prepared to accept a lower sum in compensation in return for the employer agreeing to a settlement which also includes items which the tribunal could not include in any order, such as a **reference**, which is discussed below.

9258

Some employees attach great importance simply to obtaining an **acknowledgement from the employer** that his actions were wrong. Equally, many employers wish to make settlement only on terms that liability is not admitted.

9259 Employee's waiver of rights It is important to ensure that the agreement specifies **all possible claims** which the parties **wish to settle**. Although it is common to use words such as "in full and final settlement of all claims arising from the employee's employment or its termination", such words will be construed as being limited to matters within the presumed contemplation of the parties at the time, and will not extend to any possible claims outside of this (*Livingstone v Hepworth Refractories plc* [1991] UKEAT 643_90_0512; *Bank of Credit and Commerce International SA v Ali* [2001] IRLR 292, HL). The waiver should, therefore, be **carefully drafted** to specify all actual claims to be waived, together with any potential claims (however remote), so that it is clear that such claims are contemplated at the time of the agreement.

> EXAMPLE In *Bank of Credit and Commerce International SA v Ali*, the employee had signed a compromise agreement which was stated to be "in full and final settlement of all or any claims whether under statute, common law or in equity of whatsoever nature that exist or may exist". Some time later, the employees sought to claim "stigma" damages arising out of the fact that the way in which BCCI had been conducting its business had made it more difficult for them to find employment because of their previous association with it. Such a claim was not recognised at the time the compromise agreement was signed (it only became subsequently recognised as a claim by the House of Lords some 8 years later). Consequently, despite the very wide wording of the compromise agreement, the House of Lords in this case held that it could not be construed as covering claims which neither the employer nor employee could have had in mind when signing the agreement. The House of Lords did suggest, however, that it would be possible, by using suitably specific wording, to exclude such claims if that was what was intended.

9260 Waivers of any **future rights** may be unenforceable as a matter of public policy and/or because the parties were unaware of such rights at the time of the agreement, although a compromise agreement can waive future claims if it does so in a plain and unequivocal manner (for a fuller discussion, see ¶9336). If a waiver of future rights is included, it is advisable for further wording to state that the waiver does not extend to any claim or other right of action which would render it void or unenforceable.

> EXAMPLE Employee A enters into a settlement agreement with his employer, a car manufacturer, waiving his future rights against the employer. Some years later, A buys a car made by the former employer which, due to defect, causes A to have an accident in which he suffers severe injuries. A court deciding A's claim against his former employer is likely to refuse to uphold the waiver on grounds of public policy.

9261 It is common specifically to exclude any claims for **personal injury** (save for known personal injuries) or **accrued pension rights** from any general words of settlement.

9262 If the employer is part of a **group of companies**, it may be appropriate to extend the employee's waiver (and other undertakings) to cover other group companies.

Tax issues

9265 These are often important in the context of agreed settlements. The tax treatment of termination payments is discussed at ¶¶3122+. It is possible to **allocate separate consideration** to the various elements of the settlement. This would show that there has been valid consideration for the employee's waiver of potentially numerous different statutory or contractual claims (rather than one payment being said to cover everything together), and it may also have an impact on the tax treatment.

9266 If there is any doubt as to whether tax should be deducted from the settlement payment, advance clearance could be sought from HMRC. If there is insufficient time to seek clearance, the employer could consider seeking a tax indemnity from the employee so that he can recover from the employee any tax (and employee's NIC) found to be payable if all or part of the payment is paid gross. However, the indemnity is only of benefit to the employer if the employee has the financial means to meet it.

Benefits

The termination may have an impact on benefits provided to the employee and his contract or relevant scheme rules, such as those relating to pensions, shares and bonuses, should be checked for this. The settlement agreement should cover what will happen to any such benefits on termination. Share scheme rules, for example, may provide for the employee's **share options** to be exercisable within a certain period of the termination date, or to lapse on termination, subject to the directors' discretion. In the latter case, the employer is in a strong negotiating position. As part of the settlement, the employee may agree not to exercise his options, and to waive any rights which he may have in respect of the scheme. This **waiver** may not be covered by the employee's general waiver and should be dealt with **separately**.

9268

References

The provision of a reference is likely to be of some value to the employee as he may encounter great difficulty in securing alternative employment without one. The settlement terms may, therefore, include an **agreed form of reference**, which will either be given to the employee to submit to future prospective employers or which the former employer agrees will be supplied in response to any requests for a reference. The wording should be consistent with any reason for the termination given in the settlement agreement and any reports to regulatory bodies. For further information on the provision of references generally, see ¶8320.

9270

Return of company property

As part of the settlement, the employer may have agreed that the employee can retain certain property until the termination date, or may have given such property to him as part of the settlement package. If the employment has not yet terminated, the employee may acquire further company property after the date of the agreement. The wording of the agreement should reflect the arrangements made.

9272

Resignations

The employer should ensure that the employee resigns all directorships and other offices (for example, company secretary, pension scheme trustee) as part of the settlement.

9274

Confidentiality and restrictive covenants

Confidentiality is almost always accounted for in a compromise agreement to some extent, and this can be to the benefit of both employees and employers. There may already be provisions in the employee's existing service agreement/contract of employment which are stated to apply after the termination, such as confidentiality undertakings and restrictive covenants. The employee should be **reminded of** these **existing obligations** in the settlement documentation. If the employer has terminated the employment in breach of contract, he will not be able to enforce these existing post-termination obligations and, if agreed within the settlement, the employer must **repeat the obligations** (as opposed to merely referring to them) in the settlement agreement (they could be annexed as a schedule).

9276

If there are no existing provisions, or if existing obligations are insufficient, the employer could seek to include completely **new obligations** in the settlement agreement. For further detail on drafting confidentiality clauses and on restrictive covenants, see ¶2450 and ¶2520 respectively.

> MEMO POINTS 1. If the settlement agreement repeats or imposes restrictive covenants, the consideration for those covenants is subject to special **tax treatment**, normally resulting in it being fully taxable as earnings (¶3140). To mitigate the amount that may be taxable as a result, a separate amount (reflecting the value of the covenants to the employer) should be allocated to the covenants to avoid the risk that the whole settlement payment may become taxable under this special tax regime. As confidentiality undertakings are arguably also restrictions on the employee's activities, there is a risk that they would also be subject to this special tax treatment.

2. Even in high profile public sector dismissals, **employee privacy** is likely to be valued more than the public's right to hold institutions accountable for the way that public money is spent, though this will not always be the case, particularly where the employee has behaved in such a way that a settlement pay-out is unnecessary (see both *Trago Mills (South Devon) Ltd v Information Commissioner* [2012] UKFTT 2012_0028 (GRC) and *T W Gibson v Information Commissioner* [2011] UKFTT EA_2010_0095 (GRC) for contrasting examples of applications under the Freedom of Information Act (¶5925) for disclosure of compromise agreements between public authorities and their employees that were unsuccessful (in relation to the first case) and successful (in relation to the second)).

Reporting requirements

9280 The employer may be legally obliged to report the **employee's dismissal** to the stock exchange and/or regulatory bodies. In some cases, reasons for the dismissal must be given. Care should be taken to ensure that the reasons given for the dismissal are consistent in the settlement documentation and the report (and any reference – see above).

Any **confidentiality undertaking** in relation to the termination and the terms of the agreement must allow for any required disclosures (see above).

Employee's legal fees

9282 It is not uncommon for the employer to pay a **contribution** towards an employee's legal costs in entering into a compromise or settlement agreement. There is a **tax concession** (i.e. no tax will be payable) if the payment is made direct to the employee's adviser in full or partial discharge of fees incurred by the employee obtaining independent advice upon the compromise agreement, and the payment is provided for in the settlement documentation.

Governing law and jurisdiction

9284 If the employment has an international element, the employer should consider including an express jurisdiction and governing law provision (¶2255).

D. Settlement documentation

9300 All agreements should be recorded **in writing**. If the agreement is reached through Acas, the conciliation officer will prepare the written agreement. Otherwise, the agreement may be in the form of:
– a formal compromise agreement which satisfies the various statutory requirements (¶9333);
– a less formal settlement agreement (which may be satisfactory if the time limit for any further statutory claims by the employee has passed);
– a combination compromise and settlement agreement; or
– an order made by the court or tribunal recording the terms of the parties' settlement.

> MEMO POINTS If the terms of the settlement agreement are **not** recorded **in writing**, there is a danger that they will be difficult to prove and enforce later, and it is also possible that there could be a dispute as to whether the terms were agreed in full and final settlement (*Whiley v Christopher Clark Workshops Ltd* [2002] UKEAT 1403_01_1009).

1. Agreements reached through conciliation officers

9305 In order for the exception to the prohibition on contracting out of statutory rights to apply (¶9203), the conciliation officer must be involved in the process which leads to the agreement. He must have "taken action", which means that Acas will not simply approve agreements which have already been reached without its involvement (s203(2)(e) ERA 1996). In such cases, the parties will have to draw up a compromise agreement instead.

Form

9306 Acas will normally draw up the agreement using a standard form known as a "**COT3**", though any form of agreement will be sufficient. Although it is advisable (and standard practice) for the agreement to be in writing, an **oral agreement** may be sufficient (*Gilbert v Kembridge Fibres Limited* [1984] IRLR 52, EAT). Therefore, if a party reaches an agreement through the conciliation officer but subsequently refuses to sign the written record of that agreement, the other party can put forward evidence to demonstrate that agreement was reached. If this is accepted, the agreement will be valid. The normal contractual principles of offer and acceptance are applied, and a binding agreement will only exist where both parties intend it (*Duru v Granada Retail Catering Ltd* [2000] UKEAT 281_00_2106).

Content

9308 Settlement terms are discussed above at ¶¶9240+.

2. Compromise and settlement agreements

9315 If a conciliation officer is not involved, the parties should document their agreement in a compromise or settlement agreement (or a combined compromise and settlement agreement).

> MEMO POINTS The Government has consulted on various changes to settling employment claims including:
> – renaming compromise agreements as "settlement agreements" (this is currently part of a draft bill called the Enterprise and Regulatory Reform Bill which is proceeding through Parliament);
> – a statutory Acas Code of Practice on settlement agreements, to include an optional model settlement agreement, guidance notes and model letters that employers can use to propose settlement;
> – setting a guideline tariff to help parties set the level of the severance payment; and
> – the proposed "protected conversations" regime.
> Further developments will be covered by our updating service when available.

9316 Where a claim is compromised for an agreed amount and the employee remains in employment, that compromise does not affect his **continuity of employment** and he can rely on the period of service dating back to the commencement of his employment to satisfy any necessary qualifying period with regard to any subsequent claim.

a. Types of claim

9318 The method of settlement will depend on whether the matter deals only with contractual entitlements or involves statutory rights.

Contractual claims

9320 An agreement between the parties to settle a contract claim will prevent the parties from bringing or continuing a claim before a court or tribunal (which has jurisdiction to hear certain contractual claims (¶9425)) (Employment Tribunals Extension of Jurisdiction (England and Wales) Order SI 1994/1623 and s 3(2) Employment Tribunals Act 1996). There is **no prohibition against contracting out** of the right to bring such claims, and there is no requirement for a settlement agreement to be drawn up by a conciliation officer, or to be in a prescribed form.

Statutory rights

9322 There is an **exception to the general prohibition** on contracting out of statutory rights if the agreement meets the statutorily prescribed conditions for compromise agreements (see below). If the conditions are not met, the relevant provision will be void, and the employee will be free to bring a claim even if he has already received a payment in respect of that agreement (*Council of Engineering Institutions v R E Maddison* [1976] IRLR 389, EAT). However, if such a payment is made, the tribunal may take it into account in making any award of compensation.

> **EXAMPLE** In *Council of Engineering Institutions v R E Maddison*, the employer made M redundant and gave him a letter enclosing a cheque for £1,600 for severance (including his redundancy entitlement), acceptance of which was stated to be in final settlement of all claims. The letter did not meet the requirements for a compromise agreement, and the EAT confirmed that M could pursue his unfair dismissal claim.

9323 The same statutory requirements apply to any **agreement as to the level of compensation** made between the parties after the tribunal has determined liability, but before it has awarded compensation. If such a payment is made but the agreement does not meet the statutory requirements, the tribunal may decide that it would not be "just and equitable" to award any further compensation if the agreement was reached without undue persuasion or pressure (*Courage Take Home Trade Ltd v Keys* [1986] IRLR 427, EAT), or may take any such payment into account in making any compensation award.

9324 The **complaints** that may be compromised are:

Complaint	Reference
Discrimination claims	EqA 2010
Infringement of certain trade union rights, including: • not to be unjustifiably disciplined • not to suffer deduction of unauthorised/excessive subscriptions • exemption/objection to contributing to political fund • not to be refused employment or service of employment agency on grounds related to union membership • not to suffer action short of dismissal on grounds related to union membership or activities • to paid time off for carrying out trade union duties and time off for union activities and training • to paid time off for carrying out trade union learning representative activities and training • not to be excluded/expelled from union • to protective award for failure to consult	TULRCA 1992, as specified in Employment Tribunals Act 1996
Infringement of general employment rights, including: • to an itemised pay statement • not to suffer unauthorised deductions from wages or to have to make payments to employer • to a guarantee payment • to a written statement of reasons for dismissal • to a redundancy payment • not to suffer detriment on grounds of: – health and safety issues – Sunday working for shop and betting workers – being a trustee of an occupational pension scheme – being an employee representative – making a request for time off for study or training • to time off: – for public duties – to look for work/make arrangements for training in redundancy situations – for antenatal care – for pension scheme trustee duties – for employee representative duties – for young persons for study or training – to care for dependants • to remuneration on suspension on medical grounds • not to be unfairly dismissed	ERA 1996, as specified in Employment Tribunals Act 1996

Complaint	Reference
Infringement of rights under Working Time Regulations, including: • to minimum rest periods • to weekly rest periods • to rest breaks • to annual leave/holiday pay • to compensatory rest	SI 1998/1833
Infringement of rights under national minimum wage legislation, including: • to access records • to minimum wage • not to suffer detriment for enforcing minimum wage rights	NMWA 1998, as specified in Employment Tribunals Act 1996
Infringement of rights of part-time workers not to be treated less favourably	SI 2000/1551
Infringement of rights of fixed-term employees not to be treated less favourably	SI 2002/2034
Infringement of right not to be subjected to a detriment or unfairly dismissed on grounds connected with pregnancy, childbirth, or taking maternity, adoption or paternity or parental leave	ERA 1996; SI 1999/3312; SI 2002/2788
Infringement of right to request flexible working	ERA 1996
Infringement of rights under the transnational information and consultation regulations	SI 1999/3323
Infringement of rights under the information and consultation of employees regulations	SI 2004/3426
Infringement of right to be accompanied at disciplinary and grievance hearings or detriment connected with that right	ERelA 1999
Right not to be unfairly dismissed in connection with a TUPE transfer	ERA 1996; SI 2006/246
Claims for detriment relating to occupational and personal pension schemes	SI 2006/349

9325

It is **not possible** for an employee to **contract out** of his right to:
1. **statutory minimum notice** (i.e. he will be entitled to the statutory minimum despite any term in his contract providing for less notice), although he can waive his right to notice on a particular occasion or accept a payment in lieu of notice, which, depending on the amount, may extinguish his right to damages, as he may effectively have already been compensated for his loss (s 203(1)(a) ERA 1996; s 86(3) ERA 1996);
2. be collectively informed and consulted with in relation to **collective redundancies** (s 288(2) TULRCA 1992);
3. be collectively informed and consulted with in relation a **TUPE transfer** or for payment of the equivalent of a "protective award" (reg 18 SI 2006/246);
4. equal treatment as an **agency worker**, access to employment or facilities as an agency worker or detriment or dismissal for asserting those rights (reg 15 SI 2010/93);
5. not be refused employment or the services of an employment agency or to be subjected to a detriment for a reason related to an unlawful **blacklist of trade union members** (reg 16 SI 2010/493);
6. statutory **paternity, maternity** and **adoption pay** (ss 164 & 171ZF Social Security and Contributions Act 1992);
7. accrued **pension** rights (s 91 Pensions Act 1995); and
8. **personal injury** claims that have not yet arisen (s 16 UCTA 1977; s 1 Law Reform (Personal Injuries) Act 1948).

MEMO POINTS **Acas** has the **power to conciliate** in relation to claims 2, 3, 4 and 5 above.

b. Types of agreement

9330 A **compromise agreement** is used to compromise statutory claims. It is an agreement between employer and employee to settle a dispute and to refrain from commencing or continuing with certain tribunal proceedings. A compromise agreement is not, therefore, limited to complaints that have already been presented to an employment tribunal (*Lunt v Merseyside Tec Ltd* [1999] IRLR 458, EAT).

A **settlement agreement** is used to settle contractual claims.

It is possible for a **single combined agreement** to be used to settle both statutory and contractual claims, although this document must comply with the strict requirements applicable to statutory claims.

If both contractual and statutory claims are waived in the same agreement, it is possible for the waiver (i.e. the term stating that the parties will refrain from commencing or continuing with certain proceedings) to be upheld in respect of the contractual claims, even if the agreement is void in respect of statutory claims (for failure to meet the statutorily prescribed requirements) (*Sutherland v Network Appliance Ltd* [2001] IRLR 12, EAT).

> EXAMPLE In *Sutherland v Network Appliance Ltd*, S's employer agreed in a letter to pay him a sum of money in respect of the termination of his employment with a waiver "in full and final settlement of any claims". The letter did not comply with the conditions for valid compromise agreements. The EAT held that the agreement was void only in so far as it purported to exclude statutory rights, and that S's contractual claims had been validly compromised. S could, therefore, only pursue his statutory claims.

c. Conditions for a valid compromise agreement

9333 In order to be valid, the compromise agreement must meet a number of conditions, which are set out below.

Form

9334 The agreement must be **in writing**.

Particular complaint or proceedings

9335 Compromise agreements must be **tailored to the individual circumstances** of each particular case otherwise they will not be effective. A "blanket" agreement (e.g. "in full and final settlement of all claims which the applicant has or may have against the respondent arising from his employment or the termination thereof") is not permitted in respect of statutory claims (*Lunt v Merseyside Tec Ltd* [1999] IRLR 458, EAT). This has been reinforced by the Court of Appeal in *University of East London v Hinton* where it held that a general clause in a compromise agreement purporting to be in full and final settlement of all claims was not sufficient to prevent a subsequent claim (*University of East London v Hinton* [2005] ICR 1260, CA). The Court emphasised that compromise agreements must "**relate to the particular proceedings**" to be compromised and set out **good practice standards** as follows:
– if **actual proceedings** are to be compromised: the particulars of the proceedings and of the particular allegations made in them should be inserted in the compromise agreement in the form of a brief factual and legal description; and
– if the compromise is of a particular claim raised which is **not yet the subject of proceedings**: the particulars of the nature of the allegations and of the statute under which they are made or the common law basis of the alleged claim should be inserted in the compromise agreement in the form of a brief factual and legal description.

However, although a particular complaint must be adequately specified it is not necessary for there to have been a "history of communication or dialogue about the matter" (*McWilliam and ors v Glasgow City Council* [2011] UKEAT 0036_10_1003).

9336 A compromise agreement can cover **future claims** of which an employee does not and could not have had knowledge, provided the terms of the agreement are absolutely plain and unequivocal and each actual or potential claim must at least be identified by a generic description or reference to the section giving rise to the claim (*Hilton UK Hotels Ltd v McNaughton* [2002] UKEAT 1437_01_0603).

If there are **several claims** to be compromised, they should be listed separately. A single compromise agreement can cover claims under more than one statute (*Lunt v Merseyside Tec Ltd*, see above).

9337 Although there is no requirement to do so, it may be convenient to include any **contractual claim** in the compromise agreement where the facts relied on support both a statutory and a contractual claim (thus making a single combined agreement). If it is included, the particular breach of contract should also be clearly described.

Relevant independent adviser

9339 The employee must receive advice from a "relevant independent adviser" as to the terms and effect of the agreement and, in particular, its effect on his ability to pursue his rights before a tribunal. However, it is not necessary for the adviser to address whether or not the employee is receiving a good deal in order for him to properly advise as to the "terms and effect of the proposed contract" (*McWilliam and ors v Glasgow City Council* [2011] UKEAT 0036_10_1003). The agreement must **identify** the adviser.

A relevant independent adviser **can be**:
– a qualified lawyer (i.e. a barrister who is practising or employed to give legal advice, a solicitor who holds a practising certificate, or a person other than a barrister or solicitor who is an authorised advocate or authorised litigator, for example, certain legal executives (Courts and Legal Services Act 1990));
– an officer, official, employee or member of an independent trade union who has been certified in writing by the trade union as competent to give advice and as authorised to do so on its behalf;
– a person who works at an advice centre (whether as an employee or a volunteer) who has been certified in writing by the centre as competent to give advice and authorised to do so on its behalf; and
– a qualified legal executive who is employed by a solicitors' practice and who is supervised by a solicitor who holds a practising certificate in providing such advice in relation to compromise agreements.

The adviser is **not independent** if:
– he is employed by or acting for the employer or an associated employer;
– in relation to trade union or advice centre advisers, the trade union or advice centre is the employer or an associated employer; or
– in relation to advice centre advisers, the employee pays for the advice.

An adviser can still be sufficiently independent even if he is paid by the employer.

> EXAMPLE In *McWilliam and ors v Glasgow City Council*, the EAT considered the validity of the compromise agreements that a group of claimants entered into in relation to equal pay claims against Glasgow City Council, and held that it was not necessary for an adviser to address whether or not a client was receiving a good deal in order for them to properly advise as to the "terms and effect of the proposed contract" (in this case the clients had been offered a group presentation followed by individual meetings in which they were told by their solicitor that they could not advise them on whether or not they had a good equal pay claim and what it would be worth). The EAT also held that the advisers were sufficiently independent and could not be said to have been "acting in the matter" for the employer as well as the claimants, on the basis that the advisers were paid by the employer to advise on multiple compromise agreements, and the fact that the approach that would be taken in giving the advice (i.e. a group presentation followed by individual meetings) and the changes that were made to the generic form of the agreements had been negotiated prior to meeting with the clients. Indeed, the EAT held that the advisers had considered themselves subject to the normal duty of care owed to clients.

> **MEMO POINTS** There is a potential problem with the drafting of the Equality Act 2010 which may, upon one interpretation, render it impossible to obtain independent legal advice upon the terms of a compromise agreement settling **discrimination claims**. Until this uncertainty is resolved, it is sensible to settle such claims via a COT3 or via Acas pre-claim conciliation.

9340 The adviser must be covered by a contract of **insurance or an indemnity** provided for members of a profession or professional body covering the risk of a claim by the employee in respect of any loss arising as a result of his advice.

9341 It is advisable for the employer to get **written confirmation** from the employee's adviser (either in the compromise agreement or in a separate letter) that he qualifies as a relevant independent adviser, has the necessary insurance cover, and has advised the employee as to the terms and effect of the agreement. There is no statutory requirement for the adviser to sign the compromise agreement, but this is often done in practice, and avoids the need for separate confirmation. However, some advisers prefer to sign a schedule to the agreement, rather than the agreement itself.

Reference to statutory conditions

9344 The agreement must state that the statutory conditions are satisfied. Statutory claims that can be legally compromised can only be excluded if the compromise agreement or contract refers to the relevant provisions of each statute.

> **EXAMPLE** In *Lunt v Merseyside Tec Ltd*, see above, although L's letter to her employers did contemplate a sex discrimination claim, the compromise agreement did not state that the conditions regulating compromise contracts in the then SDA 1975 had been satisfied. L was therefore allowed to proceed with her sex discrimination claim.

3. Signing

9350 The agreements are often signed by the **parties' representatives** rather than the parties themselves, and each side should take care to check that the representative with whom they are negotiating has **authority** to do so (for example, by being named in the appropriate box on the claim or response form).

Where a representative signs the agreement, the party will be bound by the agreement provided his representative has actual or apparent (or "ostensible") authority to act on his behalf. **Ostensible authority** is taken to exist in the case of legal advisers and has also been held to exist in relation to an adviser from a Citizens Advice Bureau who was named as representative by a party and held himself out as having authority to negotiate and reach settlement on behalf of that party (*Freeman v Sovereign Chickens Limited* [1991] UKEAT 514_89_2707). Ostensible authority arises not from what the apparent agent says to the third party but from what the person for whom he claims to act says or does (*Gloystarne & Co Ltd v Martin* [2001] IRLR 15, EAT).

> **EXAMPLE** In *Gloystarne & Co Ltd v Martin*, the trade union official who had conducted negotiations with the employers was not named as a representative on M's originating application, and M had not indicated to the employers in any way that the official had authority to act on his behalf. The EAT accepted that the official had no ostensible authority, so M was able to proceed with his claim for unfair dismissal even though his "representative" had concluded an agreement with the employers.

9351 If the adviser has **no actual authority to act**, the party for whom he signs may have a case against him, but the other party to the dispute will be able to rely on the agreement if the adviser had ostensible authority.

4. Enforcement

9353 Compromise and settlement agreements (including COT3 agreements) made **before termination** can be enforced as a contract claim in a tribunal, or by way of an action in the civil courts.

However, a tribunal does not have jurisdiction to enforce agreements entered into **after termination** and any claims would have to be brought in the civil courts.

> EXAMPLE In *Gibb v Maidstone and Tunbridge Wells NHS Trust* [2010] IRLR 786, CA, the Court of Appeal overturned a decision of the High Court not to enforce a compromise agreement for more than the maximum statutory compensation because it was irrationally generous and so exceeded the power of the NHS Trust employer to agree it. There were many factors a public body could take into account in negotiating a settlement figure, including the employee's long service and difficulty in finding alternative employment, and in the circumstances the payment was not beyond the scope of the Trust's powers. The compromise agreement was therefore enforceable. The Court also remarked that even if the terms of the agreement had been outside the Trust's powers, the employee would have been permitted to enforce it on the equitable basis that the Trust would have been unjustly enriched if it had not met its obligations under the agreement.

> MEMO POINTS The recovery of sums payable under **Acas-supervised compromises** (i.e. an Acas-brokered settlement, or compromise, to avoid proceedings or bring proceedings to an end) are **directly enforceable in the county courts** (s 142 Tribunals, Courts and Enforcement Act 2007 which adds a new s 19A Employment Tribunals Act 1996; Tribunals, Courts and Enforcement Act 2007 (Commencement No. 6 and Transitional Provisions) Order SI 2008/2696).

II. Arbitration

Scope

As an alternative to bringing tribunal claims for unfair dismissal (¶8380) or in relation to the statutory right to request flexible working (¶4690), such claims can be referred to the Acas Arbitration Scheme. Arbitration is different from conciliation (where a conciliation officer attempts to promote agreement between the parties), as the arbitrator (after hearing from both parties) decides how the dispute should be resolved. The scheme is intended to be confidential, relatively fast, cost-efficient, non-legalistic and informal. **9360**

Once the parties have agreed to refer the unfair dismissal or request for flexible working claim to arbitration, they cannot then return to the tribunal in respect of that claim. If the applicant also has **other claims** (even where these are linked to the unfair dismissal or request for flexible working claim), those claims will still have to be pursued in the tribunal (and the relevant time limits must still be observed).

> MEMO POINTS The scheme has been extended to **Scotland** and the revised scheme is contained in the Schedule to the Acas Arbitration Scheme (England and Wales) Order (SI 2004/753).
> Further guidance is available from Acas, which has published a guide to the scheme (The Acas arbitration scheme for resolution of unfair dismissal disputes: a guide to the scheme) (referred to in this section as the "**Acas Guide**") and an introductory leaflet (How Acas can help: choosing our arbitration scheme).

Once the parties consent to arbitration, this will be an **exception to the general prohibition on contracting out** of statutory rights (¶9203). **9361**

The scheme is not designed to deal with complex legal issues (for example, **jurisdictional issues** such as qualifying service and compliance with time limits are not considered). The Acas Guide indicates that arbitration is not suitable for cases which raise questions of **EU law** (for example, where the reason for the dismissal is sex discrimination or relates to the transfer of an undertaking or the exercise of rights under the Working Time Regulations). However, the arbitrator must apply EU law and the Human Rights Act 1998 and can appoint a legal adviser to provide guidance if any such issues arise (Human Rights Act 1998). Alternatively or additionally, a party to the arbitration can (with the permission of the arbitrator or the agreement of the other party) apply to the High Court or the Central London County Court for it to determine any such point of law. **9362**

9363 The **arbitrator's role** is twofold: he decides whether the dismissal was **fair or unfair**, and he determines remedies. He will take account of general principles of fairness and good practice rather than applying strict law or legal precedent (i.e. he need not follow the statutory concept of reasonableness or the test for a fair dismissal laid down by case law). Although he should not substitute what he would have done for the actions taken by the employer, the arbitrator can make use of his own experience of accepted standards in the workplace.

In respect of unfair dismissal claims, the scheme operates on the assumption that there has been an actual dismissal and will, therefore, not be suitable in cases of **constructive dismissal** (unless the employer concedes that there has been a dismissal or a tribunal has made such a finding). Further, there is no explicit requirement for arbitrators to consider whether the reason for dismissal is one of the statutory fair reasons, which suggests that the potentially fair reasons for dismissal will not be confined to those reasons. Arbitrators only need to "have regard to" statutory provisions on **automatically unfair dismissal**, which means that the particular reason for dismissal will merely be a factor to be taken into account when deciding the fairness of a dismissal (rather than being determinative), so these claims will not normally be suitable for arbitration.

Access to the scheme

9365 The employee must have either an **existing tribunal application** pending or grounds to bring such a claim. To use the scheme, both parties to the dispute must enter an **arbitration agreement** (reached with the assistance of an Acas conciliator or in the format of a compromise agreement drawn up by their advisers), and must also sign a **waiver form** (one for each party), confirming they understand and accept the arbitration process and waiving certain rights (including, for example, the right to a public hearing and the cross-examination of witnesses). The agreement cannot seek to vary the provisions of the scheme.

The agreement (and waivers) must be received by Acas **within** 6 weeks of its conclusion by the parties (although an arbitrator can extend this time if it was not reasonably practicable to comply with it). Where such consent is given, Acas will refer the dispute to the arbitration of an arbitrator (who is a person (other than an Acas officer or employee) appointed by Acas for the purpose). The arbitrator is obliged to disclose any circumstances which may affect his impartiality in the matter.

Withdrawal and settlement

9367 The employee may withdraw from the arbitration by giving written notice, and the claim will be dismissed. There is no right to re-open the original claim to the tribunal. Once an arbitration agreement has been concluded and accepted by Acas, the employer cannot withdraw from the scheme.

9368 The parties are free to reach a settlement of their dispute at any stage, in which case the arbitrator can terminate the arbitration on receipt of a joint written request of the parties, and (if so requested by the parties) can record the settlement (in so far as it is relates to the unfair dismissal claim and the remedies he can award) as an "agreed award".

Pre-hearing procedure

9370 Where a tribunal application had been made, the parties are invited to submit details of their claim or defence (as the case may be). In any case, they should submit a **written statement of their case** at least 14 days before the arbitration hearing, together with any supporting documentation (for example, the contract of employment, warning and dismissal letters) or evidence (for example, witness statements), and (where appropriate) a list (including title/role) of the people who will attend the hearing or be called as witnesses.

9371 The arbitrator may issue **directions**, for example, in relation to the production of relevant documents and the attendance of witnesses, although he has no power to compel a party to comply (but may draw an adverse inference from such a failure). He can also call the parties to a **preliminary hearing**, for example to address differences between the parties over the availability or exchange of documents.

Hearing

An arbitration hearing must be held which, unlike a tribunal hearing, will be in private, and held at a location convenient and accessible to the parties. The arbitrator can set the date and location of the hearing if the parties do not agree.

The hearing will normally last for not more than half a day. If a **party does not attend** the hearing without good cause, the arbitrator can hear the matter in his absence or adjourn it. Where the absent party is the employee, the arbitrator can dismiss the claim if the employee does not subsequently give a satisfactory explanation for non-attendance.

The hearing will be **inquisitorial** rather than adversarial (i.e. the arbitrator will ask the parties questions in order to find out the facts, as opposed to each party giving evidence and being cross-examined by the other, as in tribunal cases). The arbitrator will not apply strict rules as to the admissibility, relevance or weight of evidence.

The parties may be **represented**, although no special status is given to representatives (the parties will be liable for any fees or expenses incurred as a result). **Public funding** may be available under the Legal Help scheme for limited initial advice and preparation for the hearing (¶9131).

9373

The Acas Guide suggests a hearing procedure, although it emphasises that the procedures are flexible and can be adapted by the arbitrator to suit the circumstances. According to the suggested procedure, the hearing will be in **four sections** as follows:
– introduction (of those present and points of procedure);
– oral presentations (opening statements (the employer usually goes first) summarising the parties' main arguments and commenting on the other party's written submissions);
– discussion of the issues (the arbitrator questions the parties, seeks views on remedies, and requests information relevant to the calculation of compensation); and
– closing statements.

9374

Decision

The arbitrator will not announce his decision at the hearing but will send the parties (through Acas) a written decision, called an **award**, within 3 weeks of it being signed and dated by him. In it, the arbitrator will summarise each party's case, set out his main considerations, his decision and any remedy. The award is confidential.

9376

The **remedies** that an arbitrator can grant include compensation and orders of reinstatement or re-engagement. Awards are enforceable in the High Court or county courts. Where the employer fails to comply with an order of reinstatement or re-engagement, the employee can apply to a tribunal for appropriate compensation.

9377

Costs are not recoverable from the other party, although the arbitrator may include an element for costs incurred by the employee personally attending the hearing in any award of compensation.

9378

Appeals

The award of an arbitrator sitting in England and Wales is final (except on certain narrow grounds relating to EU law and the Human Rights Act 1998), although a right of appeal to the Court of Session is given in respect of arbitrations held in Scotland. In England and Wales, the arbitrator's award can be **challenged** (as opposed to appealed) on the following grounds:
– **substantive jurisdiction**, i.e. that the dispute was not in fact one which should have been referred to arbitration or that the award dealt with matters outside the scope of the arbitration agreement; or
– **serious irregularity**, i.e. on the basis of the way in which the arbitration was conducted.
Such challenges must be made in the High Court or Central London County Court within 28 days of the date of the award.

9380

CHAPTER 27

Employment claims

OUTLINE

	¶¶

SECTION 1 Jurisdiction and time limits 9410

I Where to bring a claim 9415
- **A Employment tribunals** 9420
  - Statutory claims 9424
  - Breach of contract 9425
  - European Union Law 9432
  - Human Rights Act 1998 9435
- **B Civil courts** 9440
  - The High Court 9440
  - The county courts 9443

II Time limits 9450
- Courts 9451
- Tribunals 9452
1. Calculating the relevant period 9455
   - Identifying the relevant start date 9457
2. Extension of time limits 9465
   - Not reasonably practicable test 9466
   - Just and equitable test 9475
3. Time limits for main tribunal claims ... 9490

SECTION 2 Tribunal claims 9500

Decisions without a hearing 9502

I Commencement of proceedings 9510
- Commencement of a claim 9510
- Submission of a defence 9519
- Default judgments 9526

II Pre-hearing 9530
1. Amendments to the claim or response 9530
   - Claim 9534
   - Response 9537
2. Additional information 9539
3. Disclosure and inspection of documents 9545
   - Confidentiality issues 9549
   - Legal professional privilege 9551
4. Witness orders 9553

5. Directions 9560
6. Expert evidence 9563
7. Hopeless or vexatious cases 9566
   - Pre-hearing reviews 9567
   - Deposit to continue proceedings 9570
   - Striking out 9573
   - Restriction of proceedings orders 9576
8. Entitlement to bring or contest proceedings 9580
9. Restricted reporting orders 9583
10. Freezing injunctions 9590

III Main hearing 9600
1. Composition of tribunal 9605
2. Fairness and natural justice 9610
   - Opportunity to be heard 9611
   - Bias 9612
3. Public hearings 9619
4. Listing the case for hearing 9623
5. Preparation for the hearing 9633
6. Representation 9640
7. The hearing itself 9645
   - Form 9645
   - Failure to attend 9648
   - Initial matters 9655
   - Who goes first? 9656
   - Evidence 9660
   - Submissions of no case to answer ... 9675
   - Final submissions 9680

IV Decision 9690
1. Points of procedure 9690
2. Remedies 9700
3. Recovering costs or preparation time 9702
   - Costs or preparation time 9702
   - Wasted costs 9711
   - Expenses 9712
4. Enforcement of awards 9715
   - Interest 9716
5. Review 9718

V	Appeals	9740	Review and appeals	9805
A	Employment Appeal Tribunal	9745	B Court of Appeal	9820
1	Grounds	9748	C UK Supreme Court	9830
	Final orders	9748	D Referral to the Court of Justice	
	Interim orders and decisions	9754	of the European Union	9840
2	Commencement	9755		
3	Case listing	9760	SECTION 3 **Claims in the civil**	
	Rule 3(7) cases	9761	**courts**	9850
	Preliminary hearing and directions	9762		
	Full hearing and fast track cases	9765	Commencing proceedings	9851
4	Procedure	9770	Directions	9853
	Contesting the appeal and cross-appeals	9770	Hearing	9854
	Interim applications	9775	Decision	9855
	Preparation for the hearing	9779	Remedies	9856
	Appeal hearing	9788	Costs	9857
	Decision	9794	Appeals	9858

9400 If a **dispute cannot be resolved** between the parties, the aggrieved party (normally the employee) will have to bring legal proceedings in order to seek a remedy. However, some statutory employment rights are only available after a qualifying period of continuous employment (¶1080). Before commencing any litigation, an employee will, therefore, have to find out whether such a period is required, and, if so, whether he fulfils that requirement. No such qualifying period is required in relation to breach of contract claims.

As the majority of employment claims are heard by employment tribunals, this chapter will focus on tribunal procedure, with a summary only of civil court procedure at ¶9850.

MEMO POINTS   It is an offence to provide **claims management services** without authorisation or exemption (Compensation Act 2006). Consequently, claims management firms must be registered before they can advise and handle employment compensatory claims.
Those exempted include:
– legal practitioners acting in the normal course of practice;
– charities and not-for-profit advice agencies;
– trades unions certified as independent; and
– individuals acting otherwise than in the course of business. This includes networks of individuals, operating through a website for example, provided it is not done for reward.

SECTION 1

Jurisdiction and time limits

9410 The aggrieved party must identify in **which forum** his claim should be commenced. In most employment disputes, claims must be brought in the employment tribunals. Some claims (for example, personal injury claims) must be brought in the ordinary civil courts (i.e. the High Court or the county court). In some cases the aggrieved party may be able to choose his forum, and the choice will be influenced by factors such as cost, time limits, speed, convenience and funding. A claimant will often be estopped (i.e. prevented) from bringing a claim in one court when he has already issued proceedings in another forum (¶9631).

MEMO POINTS   The Government is also looking into setting up a "Rapid Resolution" scheme as an alternative to an employment tribunal hearing in simple cases such as holiday pay. Any further developments will be covered in our updating service when available.

9411 A claim must be presented within the **time limit** specified for that type of claim. Most employment disputes are heard by employment tribunals, a forum which is intended to provide a quick and informal means of resolving disputes, and the time limit within which the action must be brought is generally short.

I. Where to bring a claim

9415

Forum	Claim	Para.
Tribunal	Statutory claims	¶9424
Civil courts	Personal injury claims Breach of contract: – during employment – over tribunal cap – where tribunal time limit expired – particular types of breach	¶9442 ¶9425 ¶9425 ¶9428 ¶9442 ¶9442
Choice	Breach of contract: – arising or outstanding on termination – within tribunal cap – within tribunal time limit Equal pay claims	¶9425 ¶9425 ¶9428 ¶9452 ¶¶5723, 5770

A. Employment tribunals

9420 Employment tribunals (referred to in this chapter as "a/the tribunal") can hear statutory claims and certain claims for breach of contract.

> *MEMO POINTS* 1. The constitution and **rules of procedure** (referred to in this section as "the Rules" and "ETR") of the tribunals are set out in legislation (Employment Tribunals (Constitution and Rules of Procedure) Regulations SI 2004/1861 as amended ("the Regulations")).
> 2. The Government has been consulting on a **new set of rules and procedure** for employment tribunals. The consultation, based on a review of the rules which was published early in 2012, contains a number of recommendations including:
> – new rules on case management, such as simplified and streamlined procedures for preliminary hearings and withdrawing cases;
> – new Presidential guidance on what to expect and what will be expected at tribunal; and
> – a standalone rule for employment tribunals and judges to encourage and facilitate the use of alternative forms of dispute resolution at all appropriate stages of the tribunal process.
> The Government also sought evidence and views on wider issues relating to the employment tribunal system, such as encouraging better compliance with employment tribunal orders for awards. Responses were taken until November 2012. It is expected that the new rules will come into force in **April 2013** and further developments will be covered by our updating service.
> 3. Tribunals are subject to the **overriding objective** to deal with cases justly, which includes ensuring the parties are on an equal footing, saving expense, dealing with the cases in ways which are proportionate to the complexity or importance of the issues, and ensuring that they are dealt with fairly and expeditiously (reg 3(1) SI 2004/1861).

Geographical jurisdiction The Rules and Regulations cover England, Wales and Scotland. **9423**
Tribunals in **England and Wales** can deal with cases where (reg 19(1) SI 2004/1861):
– the respondent (i.e. the party defending the claim) (or one of the respondents) resides or carries on business in England or Wales;
– if the matter had given rise to a county court action, the cause of action would have arisen (wholly or partly) in England or Wales (for example, if the breach of contract occurred in England or Wales); or

– the proceedings are to determine a question which has been referred to the tribunal by a court in England or Wales.

Similar, but different, provisions apply to tribunals in **Scotland**, which can only deal with proceedings where (reg 19(2) SI 2004/1861):
– the respondent (or one of the respondents) resides or carries on business in Scotland;
– the proceedings relate to a contract of employment which is or was executed or performed in Scotland; or
– the proceedings are to determine a question which has been referred to the tribunal by a sheriff in Scotland.

Cases can be **transferred** between Scotland and England and Wales where appropriate (for example, if a number of claims against a company with employees around the UK are brought in both Scotland and England, it may be convenient for them all to be heard by the same tribunal if they all involve the same issue) (rule 57 ETR).

Statutory claims

9424 Tribunals do not have any common law jurisdiction. Nevertheless they have a wide and growing statutory jurisdiction – the **main complaints** which may be brought by **employees** (and, in appropriate cases, by **workers**) are set out below:

Complaint	Statute
Written statement of employment particulars Deductions from wages Detriment for exercising various statutory rights Time off for various circumstances, such as for antenatal care, performance of public duties, and to care for dependants Maternity, adoption, paternity and parental leave Right to request flexible working Written reasons for dismissal Unfair dismissal Redundancy payments	ERA 1996
Discrimination claims	EqA 2010
Working time	SI 1998/1833
Minimum wage	NMWA 1998
Equality for fixed-term employees	SI 2002/2034
Equality for part-time workers	SI 2000/1551
Continuity of employment on transfer of undertaking	SI 2006/246
Trade union rights	TULRCA 1992
Health and safety rights	HSWA 1974

Breach of contract

9425 Tribunals can hear **claims** brought by **employees** for damages for breach of, or any sum due under:
– a contract of employment; or
– any other contract connected with employment, including compromise agreements concluded before termination of employment (*Rock-It Cargo Ltd v Green* [1997] UKEAT 255_97_1006).

The tribunal's **jurisdiction is limited**, however, to claims which either arise on **termination** of the contract of employment or are outstanding on its termination.

Consequently, tribunals have **no jurisdiction** to hear a breach of contract claim in respect of compromise agreements not finalised until **after termination**, even if the claim arose because of the termination (*Miller Bros and F P Bulter Ltd v Johnston* [2002] UKEAT 407_01_1403 followed in *Byrnell v British Telecommunications plc* [2004] UKEAT 0383_04_0411). Likewise, tribunals have no jurisdiction to hear a breach of contract claim that was commenced **before the termination**

(*Capek v Lincolnshire County Council* [2000] EWCA Civ 181). Any such claims must be brought in the High Court or county court as appropriate.

> EXAMPLE
> 1. An employer fails to pay his employee holiday pay due to him under his contract. The **employment continues**, so his breach of contract claim cannot be brought in the tribunal and must be brought in the civil courts. Note, however, that he may be able to make a tribunal claim based on a statutory breach under the working time regulations.
> 2. If, however, the **employment ends** for whatever reason, the employee may bring his breach of contract claim in the tribunal.
> 3. If both parties agree in a valid **compromise agreement** on a lump sum to be paid on termination, and the employer fails to pay the employee, he could bring a claim to enforce the agreement in the tribunal. If, however, the compromise agreement is agreed after termination, it will not be enforceable in the tribunal and a claim would have to be brought in the civil courts.

> MEMO POINTS The tribunal's jurisdiction comes from an extension order (Art 3 Employment Tribunals Extension of Jurisdiction (England & Wales) Order SI 1994/1623).

An **employer** cannot bring a breach of contract claim against an employee in the tribunal unless he is first claimed against by the employee, in which case the employer can **counterclaim** against the employee for any damages or other sum which the employer claims to be owed under the contract (Art 3 SI 1994/1623). If the employer does counterclaim, he will be allowed to proceed with that claim even if the employee's own claim is dismissed, withdrawn or settled. If the employee has not made a claim, the employer would have to bring his claim in the civil courts.

9426

> EXAMPLE In *Wright v Weed Control Ltd* [2008] UKEAT 0492_07_2901, the employee was a managing director of a company who committed a number of serious breaches of the implied term of trust and confidence, causing the employer to suffer significant financial losses. He was dismissed and unsuccessfully claimed unfair dismissal. The employer successfully counterclaimed for breach of contract in the tribunal and was awarded damages of £18,159.79.

Tribunals have **no jurisdiction** to hear breach of contract claims based on any of the following (Art 5 SI 1994/1623):
– confidentiality obligations;
– covenants in restraint of trade (e.g. non-competition or non-solicitation clauses);
– terms relating to the provision of living accommodation for the employee; and
– terms relating to intellectual property.

9427

Compensation The amount of compensation which a tribunal can award in a breach of contract claim is **limited** to £25,000 (Art 10 SI 1994/1623). The full range of remedies available in breach of contract cases is considered at ¶1700.

9428

European Union law

Tribunals cannot hear claims brought directly under the law of the European Union if the complaint is a free-standing one and not linked to a complaint under domestic UK legislation (*Barber v Staffordshire County Council* [1996] IRLR 209, CA).

9432

> EXAMPLE In *Barber v Staffordshire County Council*, it was held that article 119 of the Treaty of Rome (now article 143 of the Treaty on the Functioning of the European Union), which deals with equal pay, did not create any separate right to claim unfair dismissal or a redundancy payment. The claimant could only claim those rights on the basis of the UK statutes.

However, tribunals must, of course, have regard to and apply EU law when hearing any case under domestic legislation (*Biggs v Somerset County Council* [1996] IRLR 203, CA).

9433

> EXAMPLE In *Biggs v Somerset County Council*, it was pointed out that the tribunal could have used article 119 of the Treaty of Rome (now article 143 of the Treaty on the Functioning of the European Union) to override the requirement which then existed for employees to work a minimum number of hours per week before they could claim unfair dismissal (as this made it more difficult for women to claim).

Human Rights Act 1998

9435 As tribunals are public authorities, they must not act in a way which is incompatible with any of the rights set out in the Human Rights Act (such as the right to a fair trial, the right to respect for private and family life and freedom of expression).

In practice, the **right to a fair trial** (Art 6(1) European Convention on Human Rights) has the most immediate impact on tribunals, although many of the principles inherent in this right are already imposed by the tribunal's rules of procedure and the rules of natural justice. Tribunals will have to ensure that their decisions do not infringe this right. This may affect the following decisions:
- whether evidence should be excluded (for example, if evidence has been obtained by means of covert surveillance or monitoring of communications in breach of the right to privacy);
- whether parties should be allowed to call witnesses of whom the other party has not been given notice;
- whether parties presented with a large amount of documentation just before the hearing should be allowed an adjournment to consider it;
- whether hearings should be postponed if a witness is not available; and
- whether the tribunal or court is independent and impartial (¶9612). In deciding this, the test has been held to be whether a fair-minded and informed observer would conclude that there was a real possibility of bias (Re Medicaments and Related Classes of Goods [2001] ICR 564, CA).

The right to a fair trial will also involve an effort by tribunals to avoid unnecessary delay in resolving a claimant's claim (Somjee v UK [2002] IRLR 886, ECHR).

An argument has been put forward, so far without success, that the non-availability of **legal aid** for tribunal proceedings in England and Wales breaches the right to a fair trial (this argument succeeded in Scotland). The availability of legal advice is discussed at ¶9131.

9436 Tribunals also have to **interpret domestic legislation** in a way which is compatible with the rights in the Human Rights Act 1998 (¶6286).

> EXAMPLE In *MacDonald v Ministry of Defence* [2000] IRLR 748, EAT, the Scottish EAT interpreted the word "sex" in the Sex Discrimination Act 1975 to include sexual orientation as this was the definition used in the European Convention on Human Rights. Although the decision was subsequently overruled, and relied on the Convention rather than the 1998 Act (which was not in force at the relevant time), it demonstrates the type of argument which can be put forward. Note that sexual orientation discrimination provisions are now in force.

B. Civil courts

The High Court

9440 The High Court of Justice is the principal court of civil jurisdiction for England and Wales. It is **divided into** three Divisions – the Family Division (FD), the Chancery Division (ChD) and the Queen's Bench Division (QBD). Employment cases are heard in either the Queen's Bench Division or the Chancery Division.

> MEMO POINTS The **rules of procedure** of the High Court are set out in the Civil Procedure Rules (SI 1998/3121, as amended).

9441 The High Court has **no jurisdiction** to hear claims regarding the various statutory claims which are reserved for the tribunal (see above).

> EXAMPLE In *Barber v RJB Mining (UK) Limited* [1999] IRLR 308, QBD, the Court decided that it did not have jurisdiction to deal with any complaint that the limit on a worker's average weekly working time had been exceeded as this was specifically reserved for enforcement by the Health and Safety Executive, nor could it hear any complaint of detriment, which was a matter for the tribunal.

The High Court has **jurisdiction** to hear any dispute not specifically reserved to another tribunal, including:
– breach of contract claims (of any amount and especially where the tribunal time limit has expired (¶9452)), including claims to enforce restrictive covenants by way of injunctions or damages;
– breach of the equality clause, i.e. equal pay (especially where the tribunal time limit has expired (¶5723));
– disputes as to the interpretation of employment contracts, where a declaration is sought; and
– personal injury claims arising out of employment.

The county courts

The county courts deal largely with the same type of claims as the High Court (the more complex a claim is or the higher its value is, the more likely it is that it will be heard by the High Court rather than the county court), are governed by the same rules of procedure (see above), and may award the same remedies.

II. Time limits

In deciding whether or not the time limit has been complied with, it is important to be able to ascertain (a) when the period of time commenced and ended, and (b) when the application was presented. These are discussed below.

Courts

In the High Court or county court, breach of contract claims must be **brought within** 6 years of the breach, while personal injury claims must be made within 3 years.

> MEMO POINTS 1. If a contract is executed as a **deed**, the limitation period is 12 years rather than 6 years.
> 2. Special rules apply for children or patients being treated under the Mental Health Act 1983 bringing personal injury claims. In the case of a child, the 3 year time limit begins from the date of their 18th birthday and in the case of a patient treated under the Mental Health Act 1983, the 3 year deadline begins from the date they are discharged as a patient.

Tribunals

In the tribunals, most applications must be **made within** 3 months of the matter complained of occurring, and some time limits are even shorter.

A **table** showing the time limits for the main types of tribunal claim is at ¶9490.

Time limits are strictly enforced, which means that a party who fails to present his claim within the specified time is likely to lose any chance of doing so. The parties **cannot agree to extend or waive** the time limit (*Radakovits v Abbey National plc* [2010] IRLR 307, CA), although a tribunal has power to do so in certain circumstances, set out below. Unless the time limit has been extended, a tribunal cannot hear a case which is presented out of time (*Rogers v Bodfari (Transport) Ltd* [1973] IRLR 172, NIRC), and if it does, its decision will be a nullity (even if the employer did not raise the issue) and can be set aside.

1. Calculating the relevant period

The periods for presenting claims are expressed in different ways in respect of different types of claim. If an application has to be presented within a specified period "**beginning with**" a certain date, then in calculating the period, that date should be included (*Trow v Ind Coope (West Midlands) Ltd* [1967] 2 All ER 900, CA). This is the most commonly used formula. If, however, the application must be presented within a specified period "**after**" or "**from**" a particular date, that date is not included.

In either formulation, time runs from the beginning of the relevant day, and runs until midnight on the last day of the period.

Where reference is made to a "**month**", this is interpreted as meaning a calendar month.

> EXAMPLE
> 1. A complaint of race discrimination must be presented before the end of the period of 3 months **beginning when** the act complained of was done, as follows:
>
> | Date of act complained of | Last day for presentation |
> |---|---|
> | 31 March | 30 June |
> | 1 April | 30 June |
> | 26 June | 25 September |
> | 1 December | 28 February (or 29 February if a leap year) |
>
> 2. If, however, something is to be done within 14 days **after** 1 January, then it would have to be done by midnight on 15 January.

9456 The time limit may expire on a Saturday, Sunday or public holiday when the **tribunal office is closed**. In general, this does not affect the time limit, as presentation of an application does not involve any action on the part of the tribunal and it is sufficient for it to be posted through the office's letterbox (for example, by hand delivery on that day) (*Swainston v Hetton Victory Club Ltd* [1983] IRLR 164, CA). If the tribunal has no letterbox or other means to allow applications to be delivered when it is closed, presentation on the next day on which it is open may be regarded as having taken place on time (*Ford v Stakis Hotels & Inns Ltd* [1988] IRLR 46, EAT). However, as this is not entirely certain, the safest course is to ensure that applications are presented well within the appropriate time limit.

Identifying the relevant start date

9457 The relevant start date for calculating the relevant period depends on the type of claim, as set out below.

9458 **Unfair dismissal/redundancy** With regard to unfair dismissal claims, the relevant start date is the effective date of termination ("EDT"). The relevant start date for redundancy payment claims is referred to as the "relevant date". Both are discussed at ¶8340. For time limit purposes, where an employee has been dismissed without notice, the EDT or relevant date is extended by the addition of statutory minimum notice (s 97(2) ERA 1996).

An employee who has been given **notice of dismissal** can present his unfair dismissal claim before the EDT, even though the limit does not start to run until then (s 111(3) ERA 1996). This will also apply in cases of **constructive dismissal** where an employee has given notice to terminate his employment (*Presley v Llanelli Borough Council* [1979] IRLR 381, EAT).

> EXAMPLE In *Governing Body of Wishmorecross School v Balado* [2011] UKEAT 0199_11_1207, an employee was allowed to present a complaint of unfair dismissal after notice was given but before her EDT.

9459 However, if an employee presents an application before he has been given notice of dismissal or if no question of notice arises (for example, where he is told that his fixed-term contract will not be renewed and he issues an application before the date of expiry of that contract), the **application is premature** and will be rejected.

9460 **Discrimination** The relevant date is normally the date on which the act (or omission) complained of was done. It is, therefore, necessary to identify that act (or omission) and then determine when the time limit expires. If the act of discrimination is a **dismissal**, time will normally run from the date on which the dismissal takes effect (¶8341) and will not be affected by any internal appeal procedure (unless the employment contract states that employment continues pending the outcome of the appeal) (¶8358).

However, if it can be shown that the **rejection of an appeal against dismissal** was itself tainted by discrimination, this can constitute a separate act of discrimination so that the time limit can be calculated from the date of rejection.

A discriminatory act that **extends over the period** of an individual's employment is treated as having been done at the end of the employment (*Cast v Croydon College* [1998] IRLR 318, CA). A tribunal will consider whether there was an act of discrimination extending over a period of time as opposed to a series of unconnected acts (*Hendricks v Commissioner of Police of the Metropolis* [2003] IRLR 96, CA, overturning the EAT ruling) and in doing so will look at the substance of the complaint (*Lyfar v Brighton and Sussex University Hospitals Trust* [2006] EWCA Civ 1548) and whether the same individuals were involved (*Aziz v First Division Association (FDA)* [2010] EWCA Civ 304). Where there is a **continuing act or a series of linked acts**, time is calculated from the last date of either the continuing act or the series of acts. Note that a continuing act of discrimination can include acts which take place after the termination of employment if there is a sufficiently close connection between the employment relationship and the acts in question (*BHS Ltd and anor v Walker and anor* [2005] UKEAT 0001_05_1105). However, discrimination which takes place after a tribunal claim has been lodged cannot be taken into account in determining whether or not there has been a continuing act of discrimination (*Robertson v Bexley Community Centre t/a Leisure Link* [2003] IRLR 434, CA).

> EXAMPLE In *Novak v Phones 4U Ltd* [2012] UKEAT 0279_12_1409, the EAT held that postings on Facebook about an employee, made by his colleagues, were capable of forming part of a continuing act for the purposes of his discrimination claim. The claim involved a manager of a phone store, N, who was of American national origin, who became disabled after a fall at work. A number of his colleagues made fun of his accident on Facebook. He brought claims for disability and race discrimination, harassment and victimisation. At a pre-hearing review an employment judge had to decide whether his claims had been brought in time, by determining whether there had been a continuing act. The Facebook postings had been made over a period spanning 17 weeks, but there had been a 7-week gap within the period, when no postings were made. One aspect of the claims made against the employer was that it had failed to take steps to stop the continuing Facebook postings. N had submitted his claims within time for the second set of postings, but his claim was out of time for the earlier set of postings, unless the two sets of postings were sufficiently linked to create a single continuing act. The judge at first instance concluded that the two sets of postings were not linked, in part because some of the employees involved were different and in part because of the 7-week gap between the two groups of postings. On appeal, the EAT held that the judge had erred in deciding that the two sets of Facebook postings were not linked as one continuous act; it was reasonably arguable that they were. Overall, there was clearly a connection between the postings in terms of the colleagues involved, their subject matter and their timing. The claim was therefore brought in time in relation to both the earlier and later set of postings and the case was sent back to the tribunal for a full hearing. The EAT acknowledged that the tribunal hearing this claim will need to consider whether or not the fact that the postings remained on Facebook walls of those participating in the exchanges, long after the exchanges themselves ended, meant that the acts continued throughout the period when they could be accessed and viewed by the perpetrator's Facebook friends. In short, does a discriminatory comment made via Facebook occur at the point the exchange begins, when it ends or only when the posting is permanently deleted? We will keep you informed with our updating service if and when the tribunal decision in this matter is reported.

A **job applicant** cannot complain of a policy of continuing discrimination based on a general discriminatory recruitment policy. Time runs in relation to the specific post for which the claimant applied (*Tyagi v BBC World Service* [2001] IRLR 465, CA).

> EXAMPLE In *Cast v Croydon College*, the employer refused to allow C to work part-time. This was a continuing act because there was evidence that the employer had a policy which required the holder of C's post to work full-time. C was allowed to proceed with her claim even though it was submitted more than 3 months after the initial rejection of her request to work part-time.

There is a distinction between a continuing act and the **continuing consequences** of an act (*Barclays Bank plc v Kapur* [1991] IRLR 136, HL). A rule or policy which remains in place and continues to have a discriminatory effect for as long as it remains in place is treated as continuing (*Cast v Croydon College*). On the other hand, a decision not to promote an employee which means that he remains on a lower level of pay is treated as a one-off act and is not regarded as a continuing act simply because he continues to suffer from the consequences of that lower rate of pay from this date.

9462 **Unlawful deductions from wages** Where there is a **series of deductions**, time runs from the last of such deductions. Therefore, if an employee should be paid £30 per week but by reason of an unlawful deduction is only paid £25 per week for 6 months, he can present his claim within 3 months from the last date on which a deduction was made.

9463 **Breach of contract** Claims made to the tribunal cannot be presented before the termination of employment and must be submitted within 3 months after the employment ends (*Capek v Lincolnshire County Council* [2000] EWCA Civ 181).

2. Extension of time limits

9465 Although time limits are strictly enforced, the tribunal can extend them on **two principal grounds**:
– where it was not reasonably practicable for the complaint to be presented in time and the delay is reasonable (the "not reasonably practicable" test, applicable to the vast majority of claims, including unfair dismissal); and
– where the tribunal considers it just and equitable to extend time in all the circumstances (the "just and equitable" test, applicable principally to discrimination cases).

The **table** of time limits given at ¶9490 identifies which test is applied in considering requests for extensions.

Not reasonably practicable test

9466 This is the stricter test of the two, and the tribunal must be satisfied that:
– the claimant has shown that it was not reasonably practicable to present his application in time; and
– the application has been presented within a reasonable time.

The tribunal will consider the above steps in order and will only go on to consider the second limb if it is satisfied in relation to the first.

9467 **What constitutes "not reasonably practicable"?** To satisfy the first limb of the test, the employee does not have to prove that it was not physically possible, although he must go further than showing that he had a good excuse for failure and that it was not reasonable to have expected him to comply. The test lies somewhere between the two and has been described as a requirement to show that it was not "reasonably feasible" (*Palmer & Saunders v Southend-on-Sea Borough Council* [1984] IRLR 119, CA).

Each case has to be decided on its own facts and the tribunal has to decide if the excuse given by the employee effectively prevented him from submitting his application in time. In considering this, the tribunal will weigh up all relevant factors, including the prejudice to each party of allowing or not allowing an extension of time (*Elizabeth Duff Travel Ltd v Bray* [2001] UKEAT 517_01_1209).

9468 A **serious illness** which prevents a claimant taking professional advice during the period where an application could be presented might be sufficient. In such circumstances, the tribunal will consider when and for how much of the period the claimant was afflicted by this condition. A claimant who hopes to resolve the case through the use of internal appeal procedures during the first few weeks of the time limit and then is struck down by illness for the remainder of the period may be able successfully to argue that it was not reasonably practicable for him to submit the application in time (*Schultz v Esso Petroleum Ltd* [1999] IRLR 488, CA). However, a claimant who is ill during the first few weeks of the time limit but in good health for the remainder of the period is likely to be unsuccessful.

A **serious drug addiction** may also prevent a claimant from presenting his claim within the required time limit. In the case of *Imperial Tobacco Ltd v Wright* [2005] UKEAT 0919_04_2207, the employee (who was an existing heroin addict) had been summarily dismissed by his employer and returned to heroin abuse following his dismissal. In holding that it was not reasonably practicable for him to present his claim for unfair dismissal within the time limit, the EAT emphasised that tribunals must make a finding on the facts of each case as to whether it was reasonably practicable for an employee to present his claim in time. It was unreal, in the circumstances of this case, to regard the impracticability of presenting the claim in time as being the result of the claimant's voluntary choice.

9469 A claimant who is aware of his right to bring a claim but chooses not to for **commercial or other reasons** is unlikely to persuade a tribunal that it was not reasonably practicable to act earlier (*Birmingham Optical Group plc v Johnson* [1995] ICR 459, EAT).

9470 It used to be the case that a claimant's failure to present his claim in time arising from his own **ignorance of his rights** (or even from **incorrect advice** given to him by his legal advisers) would not generally justify an extension of time (*Walls Meat Co Ltd v Khan* [1978] IRLR 499, CA) (unlike the approach taken under the "just and equitable" test (see below)).

However, the EAT now takes a **less stringent view** (*Marks and Spencer plc v Williams Ryan* [2005] ICR 1293, CA). This does not mean that this will automatically happen and it will depend on the circumstances (*Royal Bank of Scotland Plc v Theobald* [2007] UKEAT 0444_06_1001) and the test is whether the claimant is reasonably ignorant of a time limit (*John Lewis Partnership v Charman* [2011] UKEAT 0079_11_2403).

> EXAMPLE
>
> **Claim allowed to proceed**
> 1. In *Marks and Spencer plc v Williams Ryan*, the employee was unaware that, in order to protect her position, she needed to present her unfair dismissal complaint to the tribunal within the normal time limit as she had received **advice from** the **Citizens Advice Bureau** that she needed to exhaust her employer's internal dispute resolution procedures before submitting a claim. The Court held the employee could proceed with her claim even though it was out of time because of the incorrect advice she had been given.
> 2. In *Jean Sorelle Limited v Rybak* [1991] IRLR 153, EAT, erroneous advice by a member of the **tribunal's own staff** was held to give grounds for an extension of the time limit to present the claim which was out of time.
> 3. In *John Lewis Partnership v Charman*, the claimant had been in the midst of an internal appeal process against his dismissal when the time limit to bring an unfair dismissal complaint expired. He was "young and inexperienced" and did not think about bringing legal proceedings while his appeal process was ongoing. He had taken no legal advice and his sole source of guidance was his father. Here, the claimant's ignorance was reasonable and the claim was presented within a further period which was reasonable (more than 5 weeks after the time limit expired, though the EAT did comment that this was "on the generous side").
>
> **Claim not allowed to proceed**
> In *Royal Bank of Scotland Plc v Theobald*, like in *Marks and Spencer plc v Williams Ryan*, the employee was unaware that, in order to protect his position, he needed to present his unfair dismissal complaint to the tribunal within the normal time limit as he had received incorrect advice from the Citizens Advice Bureau that he needed to exhaust his employer's internal dispute resolution procedures before submitting a claim. However, this case was different in that the internal dispute resolution procedure concluded before the end of the time limit (by 1-2 days) and as there were no grounds given on which to conclude that it was not reasonably practicable for the claim to be presented in the part of the 3 months that remained after the appeal process was completed and as no reasons were given to show that it was presented in a reasonable time after the end of the 3-month period, the EAT held that no extension of the time limit was justifiable and the applicant was not allowed to proceed.

9471 A claimant who becomes **aware of new facts** which change his understanding of his situation may be able to persuade a tribunal to extend time. For example, an employee may be made redundant and subsequently become aware of facts (such as the engagement of other employees) which suggest that there was not a genuine redundancy situation after all (*Machine Tool Industry Research Association v Simpson* [1988] IRLR 212, CA).

9472 An extension will not be granted on the grounds that the employee delays in order to await the **outcome of other civil or criminal proceedings**. In such a case, an appropriate course of action is to present the tribunal application but ask for it to be **adjourned** pending the outcome of those other proceedings.

9473 If a **posted** application **fails to arrive in time**, the tribunal will consider whether it was reasonable for the claimant to have expected that it would arrive in time. For these purposes, a claimant can rely on the **ordinary course of the post** and, if an application would, in the normal course of post, have been presented before the expiry of the time limit (although not immediately after), then the claimant should not be penalised for posting the application at the last possible moment (*Consignia v Sealy* [2002] IRLR 624, CA). Further guidance on the presentation of claims was laid down by the Court of Appeal in *Consignia v Sealy*, which, among other things, states that a first class letter will, in the ordinary course of the post, be **delivered on** the second day after it was posted, excluding Sundays and public/bank holidays (followed in *Metcalfe v Cygnet Health Care Ltd* [2005] UKEAT 0421_05_1212). A tribunal might be prepared to grant an extension where the failure is due to a **postal strike or other postal delay**.

Where a claim is submitted **electronically**, a strict view will be taken about whether the claim has been submitted in time (*Miller v Community Links Trust Ltd* [2007] UKEAT 0486_07_2910; *Beasley v National Grid Electricity Transmission* [2007] UKEAT 0626_06_0608). In *Miller*, the claimant electronically submitted his claim at 23.59.59 on the last day he had to make his claim. It was received at 00.00.08 and was held to be 9 seconds out of time.

Where applications are submitted towards the end of the time limit period, the tribunal is also likely to consider what **efforts** have been made to **check receipt** (for example, by telephoning the tribunal to confirm that it has been received). However, in the case of a claimant who is **not legally represented**, the EAT has indicated that there is no duty to check whether his application has been received (*Grossman v Barnet Healthcare* [2002] UKEAT 0134_01_2202; see also *Peters v Sat Katar Co Ltd* [2003] IRLR 574, CA, in relation to appeals to the EAT).

9474 Reasonable time Once the reason for not being able to present an application is removed, the second limb of the test is that a claimant should present his application as quickly as possible. How long will be allowed for this will depend on all the circumstances of the particular case and not just the length of the delay (*Marley (UK) Limited v Anderson* [1993] UKEAT 603_93_1711).

Just and equitable test

9475 In cases to which this test applies, the tribunal has a wide discretion to extend the time limit if it believes that it is just and equitable in the circumstances of the case (*Chief Constable of Lincolnshire Police v Caston* [2010] IRLR 327, CA). The tribunal is entitled to take into consideration any factors which it considers to be relevant, including whether the claimant can show a good reason for not presenting the claim in time and whether he acted reasonably promptly once it became apparent to him that a claim was appropriate.

In relation to the **delay**, the tribunal will also take into account:
– the length;
– whether it will affect the ability of witnesses to give their evidence;
– whether it has been contributed to in any way by the other party (for example, by refusing to provide relevant information); and
– what steps have been taken by the claimant to obtain appropriate professional advice.

A **good reason** for the delay may be:
– defective professional advice, including incorrect legal advice as to the time limit in which the claimant needed to submit his claim (*Chohan v Derby Law Centre* [2004] IRLR 685, EAT; *Benjamin-Cole v Great Ormond Street Hospital for Sick Children NHS Trust* [2010] UKEAT 0356_09_0501);
– where a claimant becomes aware of old documentation which changes his understanding of his position (*Southwark London Borough Council v Afolabi* [2003] IRLR 220, CA);

– pursuing an internal appeal or grievance procedure (although this will merely be one of the factors to be taken into account (*Robinson v Post Office* [2000] IRLR 804, EAT; confirmed in *Apelogun-Gabriels v London Borough of Lambeth* [2002] IRLR 116, CA)); and
– (with regard to a claim for disability discrimination) where the reason for failing to submit the claim in time was based on the claimant's reluctance to admit that he was so ill with depression as to be disabled (*Department for Constitutional Affairs v Jones* [2007] EWCA Civ 894).

EXAMPLE
Good reason for delay
1. In *Benjamin-Cole v Great Ormond Street Hospital for Sick Children NHS Trust*, the EAT ordered a new hearing of whether it was just and equitable to extend time for making a claim. The employment tribunal who dealt with the case took the view that the employee, who had been advised incorrectly by a voluntary advice worker about the time limit for bringing her claim, bore responsibility for the failure to lodge the claim in time, and should have taken action herself to try to meet the time limit. The EAT found that this was not supported by the facts and stated that although sometimes the conduct of the employee is a relevant factor in delay, as a matter of general principle where a claimant puts matters in the hands of a skilled adviser it would not be reasonable to expect the claimant to issue proceedings himself.
2. In *Southwark London Borough Council v Afolabi*, there was a delay of 9 years before the claimant discovered old documents which changed his understanding of his position. In this case, the Court of Appeal emphasised that such a delay was exceptional and that its decision was also based on the fact that the respondent had failed to provide any evidence supporting its submission that such a delay would not allow there to be a fair trial.

No good reason for delay
In *Robinson v Post Office*, it was held that it would not be just and equitable to allow R to proceed with a late application under the Disability Discrimination Act (he had waited until after his internal appeal) as he was aware of the time limit, was able to conduct his own affairs, and chose not to submit his application in time.

9476 The tribunal will consider the **prejudice to the parties**, i.e. that which the claimant would suffer as a result of not being allowed to proceed, compared to that which will be suffered by the respondent if the case is allowed to go ahead.

9477 An extension is more likely to be granted if the **claim is connected** to another claim which has already been submitted within the appropriate time but not yet heard (for example, where an attempt is being made to add a sex discrimination claim to an unfair dismissal claim which has already been submitted).

9478 It may be that a higher authority, such as the EAT or the Court of Appeal, makes a decision which **changes the interpretation of the law**. This could provide grounds for granting an extension if it was reasonable for the claimant to have concluded, on the previous interpretation of the law, that he had no case and only to realise after the expiry of the time limit and the change in the law that he did have a potential claim.

3. Time limits for main tribunal claims

9490 The following table sets out the main time limits and the test which will be applied in deciding whether or not extensions should be granted. "J & E" refers to the "just and equitable" test (see above), while "NRP" refers to the "not reasonably practicable" test (see above). See ¶8340 for detail on the EDT (effective date of termination) and relevant date.

Complaint	Time Limit	Test for extension	Reference
Discrimination claims	3 months beginning with date of act complained of	J & E	EqA 2010
Equal pay/value	6 months beginning with termination of employment	None	

Complaint	Time Limit	Test for extension	Reference
Unfair dismissal (*)	3 months beginning with EDT	NRP	ERA 1996
Unfair dismissal for taking part in official industrial action	6 months from date of dismissal (which is date notice given (if employer gave notice) or else EDT)	NRP	
Interim relief pending determination of certain complaints of unfair dismissal (¶8700)	7 days immediately following the EDT	None	
Written statement of reasons for dismissal (*)	3 months beginning with EDT	NRP	
Redundancy payment (*)	6 months beginning with relevant date	J & E (and see ¶9010)	
Written statement of employment particulars (*)	3 months beginning with date on which employment ceased	NRP	
Itemised pay statement	3 months beginning with date on which employment ceased	NRP	
Guarantee pay (*)	3 months beginning with day for which payment claimed	NRP	
Time off for: – public duties – dependants – pension scheme trustees – redundant employee to look for work (*) – employee representatives – study or training – health and safety representatives and candidates – trade union duties and activities	3 months from date of failure to allow time off/day taken off or date when time off should have been allowed	NRP	ERA 1996; Health and Safety (Consultation with Employees) Regulations SI 1996/1513; Safety Representatives and Safety Committees Regulations SI 1977/500; TULRCA 1992
Refusal to permit exercise of rights or failure to make payments in respect of annual leave	3 months beginning with date when exercise of right should have been permitted or date when payment was payable	NRP	Working Time Regulations SI 1998/1833
Time off for antenatal care	3 months beginning with date of appointment	NRP	ERA 1996
Parental leave (*)	3 months beginning with date of matters complained of	NRP	
Maternity, paternity and adoption leave and pay (*)	3 months beginning with date of matters complained of	NRP	
Infringement of right to request flexible working (*)	3 months beginning with date of last act or failure	NRP	
Suspension from work on medical, or maternity, grounds (*)	3 months beginning with first day of suspension	NRP	
Less favourable treatment and detriment relating to part-time workers	3 months beginning with date (or last date) of less favourable treatment or detriment	J & E	Part-time Workers (Prevention of Less Favourable Treatment) Regulations SI 2000/1551

Complaint	Time Limit	Test for extension	Reference
Less favourable treatment and detriment relating to fixed-term employees	3 months beginning with date (or last date) of less favourable treatment or detriment	J & E	Fixed-term Employees (Prevention of Less Favourable Treatment) Regulations SI 2002/2034
Right to be accompanied at a disciplinary or grievance hearing: – failure (or threat to fail) to comply – detriment relating to right	3 months beginning with date of failure or threat	NRP	ERelA 1999
Detriment relating to: – health and safety – Sunday working – working time – protected disclosure – duties of occupational pension trustee – functions of employee representative – leave for study/training, family or domestic reasons – enforcement of rights to national minimum wage	3 months beginning with date of last act or failure	NRP	ERA 1996; NMWA 1998
Transfer of undertaking: – failure to inform or consult – failure to comply with compensation order for failure to inform or consult	3 months beginning with date of completion of transfer 3 months beginning with date of tribunal's order	NRP	TUPE Regulations SI 1981/1784
Redundancy consultation: – failure to consult – failure to pay protective award	Before dismissal or 3 months beginning with date on which dismissal takes effect 3 months beginning with last day in respect of which complaint made	NRP	TULRCA 1992
Unauthorised deduction of union subscriptions	3 months beginning with date of deduction	NRP	
Trade union membership: refusal of employment	3 months beginning with date of conduct complained of	NRP	
Trade union membership or activities or making use of union services: dismissal and victimisation	3 months beginning with date of last act or failure	NRP	
Unlawful inducement relating to trade union membership, activities or collective bargaining: dismissal and victimisation	3 months beginning with date of last act or failure	NRP	
Breach of contract claim by employee	3 months beginning with EDT or (if no EDT) last working day (6 years from breach in civil courts)	NRP	SI 1994/1623
Breach of contract counterclaim by employer	6 weeks beginning with date of receipt of employee's claim (6 years from breach in civil courts)	NRP	

* A qualifying period of service applies (¶1080).

SECTION 2

Tribunal claims

9500 The **litigation process is commenced** by lodging a claim. If the other party wishes to defend the proceedings, he will need to file a response.

9501 In order to bring cases to a hearing as quickly and efficiently as possible, and to ensure that the issues to be determined at the main hearing are clear both to the parties and the tribunal, the tribunal may deal with the following matters **before the main hearing** (and these can be the subject of an **interim order** granted by the tribunal):
- the contents of the claim and the response;
- disclosure and exchange of documents;
- witness statements and witness orders;
- the issue of a default judgment in an uncontested case; and
- striking out of hopeless cases.

Pre-hearing procedure is covered at ¶9530.

9502 Tribunal procedure **at the main hearing** (discussed at ¶9600) aims to ensure the fair and efficient handling of the case, with rules governing the composition of the tribunal, representation, publicity and evidence.

Tribunals can **decide** cases **without any hearing** if all the parties have consented in writing (s 7(3A), (3AA) Employment Tribunals Act 1996 as amended by the Employment Act 2008).

Consent of parties is not required with regard to **default judgments** issued without a hearing (¶9526).

9503 Tribunal decisions may be **appealed** on points of law to the Employment Appeal Tribunal (EAT), and from there, to higher courts. Appeals are discussed further at ¶9740, together with details on relevant European issues.

Publicity

9504 Following a ruling by the Information Commissioner under the Freedom of Information Act 2000, the **names and addresses of respondents** in employment tribunal proceedings can be **disclosed**. The ruling will not apply to claimants' details, which will continue to be confidential. The Secretary of the Employment Tribunal Office is also responsible for maintaining a **public register** of applications, appeals and decisions (¶¶9517, 9698).

9505 Further, since 1 April 2009, **employers who fail to pay awards** made by employment tribunals or the EAT, and who have had enforcement proceedings brought against them, will be entered onto the **Register of Judgments, Orders and Fines**. This register is available to the public and is used by banks, building societies and credit companies when considering applications for credit.

I. Commencement of proceedings

Commencement of a claim

9510 A claim is commenced by presenting details of the claim in writing to an Employment Tribunal Office (rule 1(1) ETR). Presentation may be carried out by post or fax, or online via the Employment Tribunals' website.

The claim should be **addressed to** the Secretary of the Employment Tribunal Office (the "Secretary"). The Secretary will submit it to the appropriate regional Employment Tribunal

Office. These offices are set up to cover specific geographic areas and each has a Regional Secretary who deals with the administration of the employment tribunal within his region. Any function of the Secretary may be performed by the Regional Secretary or by a person acting with the authority of the Secretary (rule 60(3) ETR). The term Secretary will be used throughout this section even though a Regional Secretary may be acting with his authority. The **appropriate Regional Office** might be the one that covers the postcode area specified in the ET1 Form, i.e. where the claimant worked or where the subject matter of the complaint occurred, although it could also be presented either at the Central Office or at any other regional Employment Tribunal Office (rule 61 ETR).

MEMO POINTS The Ministry of Justice has published its response to its consultation to **introduce fees** in the employment tribunal and the Employment Appeal Tribunal. The Government plans to introduce a two-stage fee structure in **summer 2013** which will depend on the type of the claim and the stage in the proceedings. For example, an unfair dismissal or discrimination claim would incur a commencement fee of £250 and a hearing fee of £950, whereas a less complicated claim such as unlawful deduction of wages would incur a commencement fee of £160 and a hearing fee of £250. Where there are multiple claimants, the fees will be greater and will depend on the number of claimants. Additional fees will also be payable for other stages/proceedings by the requesting party, for example for an application to set aside a default judgment. There will also be a fee of £400 to appeal to the EAT with a further £1200 to be paid before the hearing. An individual may be eligible for a full remission (where no fee is payable) or a part remission (where a contribution towards the fee is required). No fee will be payable if the applicant is on certain state benefits or if their annual gross income is less than a certain amount which will depend on whether they are single or in a couple and how many children they have. Full or part remission will also occur if their and, if applicable, their partner's monthly disposable income is below certain amounts. This is the same remission system which already exists for civil court users. Wider consultation on remissions was set to take place in autumn 2012 due to the proposals to introduce a new welfare benefit, Universal Credit (a new single payment for people who are looking for work or who are on a low income), which the Government plans to launch in 2013 to replace income-based Jobseeker's Allowance, income-related Employment and Support Allowance, Income Support, Child Tax Credits Working, Tax Credits, and Housing Benefit. However, the consultation did not take place. Further developments will be covered by our updating service.

Form A standard form (**Form ET1**) is mandatory (SI 2005/435). This form, which can be obtained from tribunals and from Jobcentres, requires the **following information** to be given: **9511**
– the name and address of the employee ("the claimant");
– a UK address for correspondence, if different;
– the name and address of those against whom the case is brought ("the respondent(s)");
– the grounds on which relief is sought (i.e. sufficient information to show what sort of complaint is being made); and
– if whether since leaving the employment of the respondent, the claimant has obtained new employment and, if so, the details of his new salary.

Where a claimant is required to provide minimum information in his claim form, his failure to do so should not immediately render it inadmissible (*Richardson v U Mole Limited* [2005] UKEAT 0179_05_0906).

In other cases on the admissibility of claim forms, the EAT has repeatedly criticised the Rules and emphasised that they must **not be interpreted** so as to **deny a claimant access** to the tribunal system (*Grimmer v KLM Cityhopper UK* [2005] IRLR 596, EAT) and that they are "simply a procedural vehicle to enable important statutory claims to be advanced before the tribunal service" (*Hamling v Coxlease School Ltd* [2007] IRLR 8, EAT).

Consequently, a claimant will have given sufficient details of a **complaint** if it **can be discerned** from the details provided on the claim form that the claimant is complaining of an alleged breach of an employment right which falls within the jurisdiction of the tribunal. This threshold for access should, in the interests of justice, be kept low. If it becomes necessary, as a case proceeds, for additional information to be obtained (for example, to clarify the issues) this can be requested, either by application from either party or by the judge on his own initiative (¶9539).

Likewise, **whether** any **omission is relevant** and, if so, whether it is also **material** has to be answered in the affirmative before a claim form can be rejected for being incomplete. In

Hamling v Coxlease School Ltd, the fact that the claimant's solicitors' address was given instead of her own was not relevant or material as the form had been submitted and signed by the solicitors on the claimant's behalf, full particulars for the representatives had been given and the form indicated that if representative details were given all further communication would be with the representative.

Similarly, tribunals should not be overly prescriptive if they receive **long and very detailed** claim forms. The proper way to deal with long and complicated forms is to identify the issues at a case management discussion rather than instructing a claimant to significantly reduce the length of his or her claim form (*Fairbank v Care Management Group* [2012] UKEAT 0139_12_2003). However, if a claim form is excessively long to the point that it constitutes unreasonable conduct, then a costs order could be made at the end of proceedings.

> MEMO POINTS If a claimant fails to use the form, his claim will be returned to him together with an explanation of why the claim has been rejected and a copy of the prescribed form (rule 3(1) ETR).

9512 **Presentation** The claim may be **presented by** hand, post or electronic communication (rule 61(1) ETR). Claims can also be submitted online on the Employment Tribunals' website, see flmemo.co.uk/em9512

It is presented upon **receipt** in the tribunal office (*Hammond v Haigh Castle & Co Ltd* [1973] 2 All ER 289, NIRC). A claim is **deemed** to have been **received** (unless proved otherwise) either when delivered in the ordinary course of the **post** or (in the case of **personal delivery**) on the date of delivery (rule 61(2) ETR). **Online applications** will usually be received very shortly after being sent. When submitting a claim online it is important to ensure that the claimant's place of work is stated where it is different from the employer's address. Otherwise the central server may relay the form to the wrong jurisdiction, for example where the claimant worked in Scotland, but the employer's address was in England (as happened in *McFadyen and ors v PB Recovery Ltd and ors* [2009] UKEAT 0072_08_3107).

It is advisable that **confirmation of receipt** should always be obtained.

For discussion of the **timing** of presentation see ¶9450.

9513 **Pre-acceptance procedure** When the claim is received, the Secretary will **review** it to establish whether or not the claim (or part of it) can be accepted by the tribunal (rule 2(1) ETR).

A claim will **not** be **accepted** if one or more of the following circumstances applies (rule 3(1), (2) ETR):
– the mandatory claim form has not been used;
– the claim form does not include all the relevant information required; or
– the tribunal does not have power to consider the claim (for example, if it seeks a relief which the tribunal does not have power to give).

The Secretary will refer the claim, together with his statement of reasons for not accepting it, to the judge who will decide whether the claim (or part of it) should be allowed to proceed. The Secretary will inform the claimant in writing of the judge's decision as soon as reasonably practicable, together with information on how that decision may be reviewed or appealed (rule 3 ETR).

> MEMO POINTS The claimant can apply to the tribunal to **review its decision** not to accept his claim on the grounds that the decision was wrongly made as a result of an administrative error or that it is in the interests of justice to do so (see ¶9720 for further details).

9514 **Tribunal action on acceptance of claim** If the claim (or part of it) is accepted, the **Secretary sends a copy** of it to each respondent and records in writing the date on which it was sent (rule 2(2)(a) ETR). He will give **notice to every party** (in writing) of the case number which has been assigned to it and the address to which notices and other communications to the Secretary must be sent (rule 2(2)(b) ETR). The Secretary sends a **further notice to the respondent** which includes information about the means and time limit for entering a response to the claim, the consequences of the failure to do so and the right to receive a copy of the decision.

MEMO POINTS   If only **part of a claim** is **accepted**, the Secretary will inform the parties which part(s) of the claim have not been accepted and that the tribunal will not deal with those part(s) unless they are accepted at a later date.

9515 The Secretary must notify the parties (in every case where legislation provides for conciliation) that the **services of a conciliation officer** may be available to them (rule 2(2)(d) ETR) (¶9218).

9516 **Copies of all documents** and notices in the case are sent by the Secretary to:
– an appropriate conciliation officer, if relevant;
– the Secretary of State for BIS if the proceedings may involve payment out of the National Insurance Fund (for example where a redundancy payment or notice pay is being claimed from an insolvent employer); and
– the Equality and Human Rights Commission in equal pay, sex, race and disability discrimination cases.

9517 The Secretary is responsible for maintaining a **public register** of applications, appeals and decisions. The Secretary must enter a copy of the following documents in the register:
a. any judgment (including any costs, expenses, preparation time or wasted costs order); and
b. any written reasons provided in relation to any judgment (unless the evidence has been heard in private and the tribunal or judge orders otherwise).

MEMO POINTS   In cases which involve allegations of the commission of a **sexual offence**, the Secretary can omit or delete from the register or any judgment, document or record of proceedings any identifying matter which is likely to lead members of the public to identify any person affected by or making such an allegation (¶9583).

9518 **Multiple claimants**   Often, a number of claimants will have identical or very similar cases, for example, where a large number of claimants have been made redundant by the same employer. In such cases the tribunal can order one claimant to represent the interests of all the claimants, order all the applications to be heard and dealt with together, or permit two or more applications to be submitted in a single document by claimants claiming the same relief in respect of the same set of facts (rules 10(2)(j), 1(7) ETR).

Submission of a defence

9519 If he wishes to contest the proceedings, the respondent must enter a defence to the proceedings called a **response** (rule 4(1) ETR).

9520 **Form**   A standard form (**Form ET3**) is sent out to the respondent by the Secretary along with the copy of the ET1, and this form must be used (SI 2005/435). The following **information** will be required:
– the respondent's full name and address;
– a correspondence address in the UK if different;
– a statement of whether or not he intends to defend the claim (in whole or in part); and
– if he does intend to defend it, on what grounds.

MEMO POINTS   If a respondent fails to use the prescribed form, his response will be returned to him together with an explanation of why the response has been rejected and a copy of the prescribed form (rule 6(1) ETR).

9521 **Entering a defence**   The response must be **addressed to** the Secretary and be **presented** by the respondent (using the same **methods** of presentation as are allowed for the claim (¶9512)) **within** 28 days of the date on which a copy of the claim was sent to him (not including the date of receipt).

This applies even if the claim form is **never received** by the respondent (*Bone v Fabon Projects Ltd* [2006] IRLR 908, EAT). In such circumstances where the respondent has failed to enter a response as a result, he can either make an application for an extension so that he can enter a late response (see below) or, if he is too late to make such an application and is time barred, he can seek a review of the decision not to accept his response (¶¶9718+). On review, the tribunal can extend the time limit in which a response can be presented if it considers it is just and equitable to do so.

Where a **respondent is legally represented**, the respondent or his representative must, at the same time as the application is sent to the Employment Tribunal Office, **provide all other parties** with the following information in writing (rule 4(4A) ETR as inserted by SI 2008/3240):
– details of the application and the reasons why it is made;
– notification that any objection to the application must be sent to the Employment Tribunal Office within 7 days of receiving the application or, if a hearing of any type is due to take place before then, before the date of that hearing; and
– that any objection to the application must be copied to both the Employment Tribunal Office and all other parties.

Further, the respondent or his representative must confirm in writing to the Employment Tribunal Office that this rule has been complied with. The above time limit of 7 days may be extended where the judge or tribunal considers it in the interests of justice to do so.

Where a **respondent is not legally represented**, the Secretary shall send a copy of the application to all other parties and inform them of the matters listed above.

9522 Where a respondent wishes to present a **late response**, an application for an **extension of time** must be made (rule 4(4) ETR). The application must be presented to the tribunal **within 28 days** of the date on which the respondent was sent a copy of the claim (excluding the date on which the claim was received) and must explain why the respondent cannot comply with the time limit. A respondent may apply for **more than one extension** of time to enter his response (*Skinners Hastings Ltd v Wilkin* [2001] UKEAT 1023_00_2102).

In considering the application, the tribunal (which may consist of a judge sitting alone) will have regard to the following **factors**:
– the reasons given for the failure or anticipated failure to present the response in time;
– the relative prejudice to the parties of granting or not granting the extension; and
– the merits of the respondent's proposed defence.

This will often be done without the tribunal requiring the parties to attend a hearing, but it is open to the tribunal to invite the views of the claimant in writing, and/or convene a hearing before making its decision.

The tribunal will only extend the time limit in which a response can be presented if it considers that it is just and equitable to do so.

9523 **Pre-acceptance procedure** On receipt of the response, the Secretary will consider whether the response should be accepted (rule 5(1) ETR).

The response will **not** be **accepted** if one or more of the following circumstances applies (rule 6(1), (2) ETR):
– the mandatory response form has not been used;
– the response does not include all the required relevant information; or
– the response has not been presented within the relevant time limit.

If the Secretary considers that the response should not be accepted for either of the two latter reasons, the Secretary must refer the response, together with an explanation as to why he does not accept it, to the judge who will decide whether or not the response should be accepted in respect of these grounds.

If the judge decides that the response **should be accepted**, he will inform the Secretary in writing and the Secretary will accept the response and deal with it accordingly (¶9524).

If the judge decides that the response **should not be accepted**, the judge will record his decision, together with the reasons for it, in writing in a document signed by him, and the parties will be informed of this decision by the Secretary. The Secretary will also notify the respondent of the consequences of that decision and that the respondent may apply for the decision to be reviewed or appeal against it. The response will be returned to the respondent and the claim will be dealt with as if no response had been presented (rule 6(5), (6) ETR).

MEMO POINTS The respondent can apply to the tribunal to **review its decision** not to accept his response on the grounds that the decision was wrongly made as a result of an administrative error or that it is in the interests of justice to do so (see ¶9718 for further details).

Tribunal action on acceptance of response If the response is accepted, on receipt, the **Secretary sends a copy** of it to each other party and records in writing the date on which this is done (rule 5(2) ETR). **9524**

Multiple claimants Where there are multiple claimants (¶9518), the response form can include the response to more than one claim where the relief sought arises out of the same set of facts provided that the respondent (rule 4(5) ETR): **9525**
– intends to resist all the claims and the grounds for doing so are the same in relation to each claim; or
– does not intend to resist any of the claims.

Moreover, a single response form can be used by more than one respondent to a single claim provided that (rule 4(6) ETR):
– each respondent intends to resist the claim and the grounds for doing so are the same for each respondent; or
– none of the respondents intends to resist the claim.

Failure to enter defence or defence not accepted

Default judgments **Automatic** default judgments will be ordered by the judge in circumstances in which the claimant's claim is effectively uncontested. If, at any time after the relevant time limit for presenting a response has passed (and the respondent has not been granted an extension of time in which to submit a response), the judge will issue a default judgment to determine the claim without a hearing **if** (s 7(3A), (3AA) and (3AB) Employment Tribunals Act 1996 as amended by s 4 Employment Act 2008; rules 8(1), (2) ETR as amended by SI 2008/3240): **9526**
– the respondent has **failed to enter a response**;
– the **response** has **not been accepted**; or
– the respondent has indicated in his response that he **does not contest** the claim.

If the judge does **not have enough information** to issue a default judgment, he may require the respondent to provide additional information (rule 8(1A) ETR). The judge will then decide whether to make a default judgment based on that information or, if the respondent fails to provide the information requested, make a default judgment (rule 8(1B) ETR).

No default judgment will be entered **if** (rule 8(2A), (6) ETR):
– the tribunal does not have jurisdiction to consider the claim;
– there is sufficient evidence to conclude that the respondent did not receive the claim form; or
– the claim has already been settled via a compromise agreement or Acas conciliation.

The default judgment must be in writing and signed by the judge. The Secretary will then send a copy of it to the parties, Acas, and, if the proceedings were referred to the tribunal by a court, to the relevant court. **9527**

A respondent may, however, apply to have the default judgment reviewed in certain circumstances (¶9726; rules 8(5), 33(1) ETR).

Taking no further part in proceedings If a respondent **fails to enter a response**, or his response is **not accepted**, he is not entitled to take any further part in the proceedings except to (rule 9 ETR): **9528**
– apply for written reasons for the tribunal's decision (¶9691);
– apply for a review of a default judgment (¶9726);
– apply for a review of the tribunal's decision not to accept his response under its pre-acceptance procedure (¶9718);
– take part as a witness if called by another person; or
– receive a copy of a decision.

A party who has been precluded from taking any further part in employment tribunal proceedings for having failed to enter a response will **nevertheless be able to** appeal a decision of the employment tribunal since appeals to the EAT are governed by different rules of procedure (*Atos Origin IT Services UK Ltd v Haddock* [2005] IRLR 20, EAT) (¶9745).

II. Pre-hearing

1. Amendments to the claim or response

9530 It is obviously advisable when submitting a claim or response to ensure that it accurately states the case which the party wishes to put forward. It is often the case, however, that a party will subsequently wish to amend his claim or response because of a **mistake** in the original document or as a result of **new facts** which have since come to light. The tribunal has a general discretion to allow amendments (rule 10 ETR).

9531 **Timing** An application to amend may be made at any time – before, at, or even after the hearing of the case (*Selkent Bus Co. Ltd v Moore* [1996] UKEAT 151_96_0205), although any application made less than 10 days before the hearing will only be considered if it was not reasonably practicable to make the application sooner or if the judge considers that it is in the interests of justice to consider it late (rule 11(2) ETR). The application should ideally be made as soon as it becomes apparent that it is necessary, as a tribunal will not look favourably on a party changing the basis of his case at a late stage due to the additional time and costs incurred as a result.

9532 **Procedure** Most applications for amendment are made in advance of the hearing. Amendment applications are one of the interlocutory matters which can be dealt with by a judge sitting alone (¶9607).

The application can be made either in the form of a letter setting out the amendment required or by submitting a copy of the ET1/ET3 marked up with the proposed amendments. Even if the application is made during the course of the main hearing (in which case it is less likely to be successful, particularly if it relates to a totally new point, partly because the other party will not have sufficient time to prepare a response), the applying party should give the other party notice of the wording of the amendment and there should be an opportunity for a response to be given before the tribunal makes its decision (*Ladbrokes Racing Ltd v Traynor* [2007] UKEAT 0067_06_0310).

The tribunal may be able to determine the application to amend without the need for a hearing if the application relates to a **simple minor or clerical error** or is **not particularly controversial**. A legally represented party must send the other party a copy of the application, explain his reasons for making it and give the other party 7 days to raise **any objections** to the tribunal; he must also notify the tribunal that he has complied with these requirements (rule 11 ETR). If the party proposing the amendment is unrepresented, the tribunal will contact the other party to deal with this point. If the other party has no objection, the tribunal can go ahead and make the order approving the amendment and the other party is then usually permitted to amend his claim or response to account for the amendment(s) if necessary. If the **other party does object**, a hearing is normally held so that both parties can put forward their arguments. Where the other party has not been consulted, he will have the opportunity to object after being notified of the amendment and his objections should then be considered and, if necessary, a further order made.

9533 **Decision** In making its decision, the tribunal will attempt to strike a balance between the interests of the parties, and will take account of all the circumstances, including the **following considerations** (*Selkent Bus Co. Ltd v Moore* [1996] UKEAT 151_96_0205):

– the nature of the amendment (i.e. whether it is minor or substantial);
– if it would effectively introduce a new claim, whether the relevant time limit for such a claim has expired and, if so, whether time should be extended under the appropriate statutory provision; and
– whether there has been a delay in making the application and, if so, the reason for the delay.

Given the possibility that time limits for new claims may have expired, amendments to the claim often raise more difficult questions than amendments to the response. Further, the Court of Appeal has held that a **new claim** can **only be introduced** as an amendment to the original claim form if the facts on which this new claim is to be based were particularised in the original claim form (*Ali v Office of National Statistics* [2005] IRLR 201, CA).

A decision to allow an amendment is a judgment rather than an order, therefore tribunals must give reasons for their decisions (*Ladbrokes Racing Ltd v Traynor* [2007] UKEAT 0067_06_0310).

EXAMPLE In *Ali v Office of National Statistics*, the Court of Appeal held that as there was nothing in the applicant's original claim of race discrimination which supported his later request for an amendment to include a claim of indirect race discrimination his amendment could not be granted.

Claim

In addition to considering the general factors mentioned above, the tribunal will consider whether the effect of the application would, in fact, be to introduce a **new claim**, or merely to apply a **new label** to facts already presented. Tribunals are more willing to allow amendments which fall into the second category.

9534

Late claims may be added where it is simply a question of re-labelling facts which have already been set out in the claim form without the necessity of extending time. Where there is no causal link and a new claim is needed, the tribunal will consider whether time should be extended.

EXAMPLE
New claim
In *Foxtons Ltd v Ruwiel* [2008] UKEAT 0056_08_1803, the EAT held that the claimant should not have been allowed to add a sex discrimination claim to an existing unfair dismissal claim as, although the employee had made complaints about being bullied and unfairly criticised for her manner of dress at work, she had not said that the reason for this unfair treatment was due to her sex. By the time the application to amend was made, the time limit had expired for discrimination claims. The **lack of** that **causal link** in the original claim meant that the case was not one of mere re-labelling and so the case was sent back to the tribunal to consider whether time should be extended.

New label
1. If the claimant has set out various facts which he claims amount to unfair dismissal, and then later seeks to amend his claim form to say that the **same facts** also amount to race discrimination, the tribunal is likely to consider the amendment and whether the relevant time limit should be extended if he is out of time.
2. In *Enterprise Liverpool Ltd v Jonas and ors* [2009] UKEAT 0112_09_2407, the EAT upheld the decision of an employment tribunal to allow an amendment to a complaint regarding failure to consult prior to a TUPE transfer. Several employees made complaints in their own names about lack of consultation. They submitted the claims within the correct time limit. They were then advised that it was only permissible for their trade unions to bring such claims because the trade unions were recognised by their employer. By that time it was too late to submit new claims, so they applied to amend the **claim to substitute** their respective unions as **claimants**. The EAT upheld the tribunal decision that the amendment did not introduce a new claim but changed the basis of an existing claim.

MEMO POINTS Where the effect of the application would be to introduce a **new claim**, the tribunal should consider whether to **amend the existing application** and allow the new claim or whether **fresh proceedings** need to be brought. The EAT has held that the tests for allowing new claims brought by late amendment and for bringing fresh claims will in practice have the same outcome, although it acknowledged that there may be a small difference in perception as to how difficult it is to discharge the burden of satisfying the tests, deriving from the differently worded tests (*Mouteng v Select Services Partner Ltd* [2008] UKEAT 0059_08_1803).

9535 **New respondents** The application may be to add a new respondent who was not previously involved in the proceedings, for example, if there is confusion as to which member of a group of companies is the correct employer, or if it transpires that there has been a transfer of an undertaking covered by the business transfer regulations.

The only person who may be joined to the proceedings is a person against whom the claimant is seeking relief (not a person whom the respondent considers ought to share or take liability) (*Eemtrans v McMahon* [2000] UKEAT 797_00_1107).

The tribunal can order the addition or substitution of respondents, either of its own motion or on the application of any person (which could be someone other than a party to the proceedings, such as the Secretary of State, who could apply to be joined in proceedings in which he has an interest, for example where BIS could be liable to meet redundancy payments) (rule 10 ETR). It can also (of its own motion or upon application) dismiss from the proceedings any party which appears to it not to have had, or to have ceased to have, any direct interest in the claim.

A tribunal can order the addition or substitution of the respondent regardless of the **time limits**, provided the original claim was itself submitted within the appropriate time limit. The tribunal **approaches** the question in the following way (*Cocking v Sandhurst (Stationers) Limited* [1974] ICR 650, NIRC):
1. It will consider whether the original unamended **claim** is **valid** (¶9511). If it is not, then it cannot be amended and a new claim will be required.
2. If it is valid, the tribunal will consider whether it was presented within the relevant **time limit** for the amended claim. If it was not, the tribunal will not allow the proposed amendment.
3. If it was, the tribunal has a **discretion** whether or not to allow the addition or substitution. In deciding whether or not to exercise this discretion the tribunal should:
– be satisfied that the mistake as to the correct respondent was genuine, and was not misleading or such as to cause reasonable doubt as to the identity of the person intending to claim (or, as the case may be, to be claimed against); and
– have regard to all the circumstances of the case, in particular any injustice or hardship which may be caused to any of the parties, including those proposed to be added, if the proposed amendment was allowed or refused.

9536 It is even possible for the correct respondent to be substituted for another **after the final decision** has been made by the tribunal, although the new respondent may be able to apply for a review of the original decision if he was not aware of the proceedings (*Watts v Seven Kings Motor Company* [1983] ICR 135, EAT).

> EXAMPLE In *Watts v Seven Kings Motor Company*, the tribunal had made an order awarding compensation against a particular respondent (Seven Kings Motor Company Limited), but it was subsequently discovered that the true employer was in fact an individual trading as Seven Kings Motor Company (i.e. not a limited company). The EAT made an order substituting the true employer for the named respondent as it was satisfied that the true proprietor had been aware of the proceedings.

Response

9537 The tribunal is only entitled to find for the respondent on the grounds that have been specifically pleaded. If, therefore, the respondent has put forward a defence on the basis of one ground when, in fact, the evidence suggests that another would be more appropriate, his defence will fail. It may be essential, therefore, for a respondent to seek an amendment to his response.

If applications are made **during the hearing**, the tribunal will **consider** whether or not the amendment would substantially alter the basis on which the case has been proceeding and, in particular, whether it would require the presentation of substantial additional evidence or the recalling of witnesses.

If the respondent is simply seeking to apply a **new label** to the same set of facts, an application will generally be allowed, even at a late stage.

If the proposed amendment introduces a whole **new line of defence**, a tribunal will be less willing to grant a late amendment.

> EXAMPLE
> **New label**
> 1. In an unfair dismissal claim, the employer's defence referred to the employee's failure to meet the required standards of work. This could amount to either a capability reason for dismissal or a reason related to conduct. As it is often difficult to determine whether someone is unwilling (misconduct) or unable (capability) to do their job properly, the tribunal will look favourably on a request to amend.
>
> **New defence**
> 2. The claimant has claimed that he has been constructively dismissed. The respondent's defence has been that there was no dismissal but, at a late stage, he attempts to introduce a new line of argument suggesting that, if there was a dismissal, then there was a good reason for it. Such an amendment is likely to be rejected.

2. Additional information

9539 A copy of the claim is sent to the respondent, and a copy of the response is sent to the claimant. These documents give the parties formal notice of either the claim which they face or the defence which will be put up against it. It may be that either the claimant or the respondent feels that the document sent to him does **not** contain **enough information** to enable him properly to understand the other party's case, in which case, he can apply to the tribunal for an order for additional information. The tribunal can order a party to provide in writing additional information as to the grounds on which that party relies and of any facts and contentions relevant to those grounds (rule 10(1), (2)(b) ETR).

The **purpose** of seeking additional information is not to produce evidence but to clarify the main points of the case put forward by a party. If, for example, a respondent simply stated that the reason for dismissal was that the claimant was not capable of doing his job, it is likely that the respondent would be ordered to provide additional information which establishes the reason for the incapability. If a claimant states that he has been victimised, it would be reasonable to require him to state by whom and in what way.

9541 **Written answers** The tribunal may require a party to provide written answers to any question where it considers that the answer may help to **clarify any issue** likely to arise for determination in the proceedings, and that it would be likely to assist the progress of the proceedings for that answer to be available to the tribunal (rule 10(1), (2)(f) ETR). Its **purpose** is to narrow the issues before the hearing begins.

9542 **Timing and procedure** The tribunal may make an order for additional information or written answers of its own motion or on the application of either party (who is normally expected to have first requested the other party to provide them **voluntarily**). No particular form of request is required. A letter is the usual way to request information.

An order can be made at any time and can be issued by the judge in considering the papers before him in the absence of the parties or at a hearing. The tribunal may lay down a **time limit** for provision of the additional information or written answers (rule 10(3) ETR), and will send copies of both the questions and the answers to all the relevant parties.

9543 **Failure to comply** If a party fails to comply with an order for additional information or written answers, the sanctions are the same as for failure to comply with other orders and practice directions, namely striking out and/or costs or preparation time (¶9562).

3. Disclosure and inspection of documents

9545 Unlike the High Court, in the tribunal there is no automatic process of disclosure (also known as "discovery") or inspection (including the taking of copies) of documents. A party **does not need voluntarily to disclose** any documents to the other party (but if he does disclose some documents, he must not be selective in order to give an unfair or misleading impression of the case) (*Birds Eye Walls Ltd v Harrison* [1985] IRLR 47, EAT). Documents will, of course, form a very important part of many cases. The tribunal, therefore, can order disclosure of **relevant** documents and it is common practice for the tribunal to order disclosure as a matter of routine.

9546 The **purpose** of disclosure and inspection is to bring to light the documents which are relevant, and to ensure that the whole picture is presented. A party must, however, have a case to begin with, and must be able to show that the document of which he is seeking disclosure is relevant to it. He cannot simply go on a "fishing expedition" and demand the production of all types of documents in order to try and deduce whether or not there is a case to be made. The claimant will also have to show that disclosure is necessary for the fair disposal of the claim or to save expense (rule 10(5) ETR). For example, in cases arising out of selection for redundancy, the tribunal will only order disclosure of documents relating to the selection process if the claimant can show some basis for saying that the process was unfair. It will not simply order production of the documents to enable the claimant to find out if the process was fair or not (*British Aerospace plc v Green* [1995] IRLR 433, CA). However, claimants may use their right to make a subject access request under the Date Protection Act 1998 (¶¶5980+) to bypass the need to persuade a tribunal that particular documents should be disclosed or if they do not know what documents are held by the respondent.

The fact that some documents are **confidential** will not provide immunity from disclosure if they are relevant to the fair disposal of proceedings (*Beck v Canadian Imperial Bank of Commerce* [2009] IRLR 740, CA).

EXAMPLE In *Beck v Canadian Imperial Bank of Commerce*, the Court of Appeal confirmed the EAT's decision to overturn the employment tribunal's refusal of a request for disclosure of documents relating to a grievance raised by another employee about his **selection for redundancy**. The claimant alleged that the employer had a policy of favouring Canadian nationals and had obtained information which had emerged in the course of a grievance raised by a colleague which appeared to support this contention, and sought additional disclosure of documents regarding the earlier grievance and redundancy process. The employer resisted the request on the ground that the material was not relevant to the claimant's case, but the Court held that the allegation of a discriminatory policy was supported by some evidence and it was therefore impossible for the case to be decided fairly without disclosure.

9547 **Timing and procedure** Either of its own motion, or on the application of either party, the tribunal can order such disclosure and/or inspection of documents and information as might be granted by a county court (or, in Scotland, a sheriff) (rule 10(2)(d) ETR). It is normal, before applying to the tribunal for an order, to request the other party to give disclosure or inspection **voluntarily**.

Such requests or applications for orders should always be made as early as possible. The application may be made at any time and no particular form is required. The tribunal can set a **time limit** for complying with any order it makes and can specify the place at which disclosure or inspection of material should take place. The order can be made by a judge sitting alone.

9548 **Failure to comply** If a party fails to comply with such an order without reasonable excuse, he will be liable to be punished on summary conviction (i.e. conviction by the Magistrates' Court) by a **fine** (currently up to £1,000) (s 7(4) Employment Tribunals Act 1996). The order must contain a statement warning of the consequences of failure to comply and the amount of the current maximum fine (rule 10(6) ETR).

In addition, the tribunal can impose the same sanctions as for failure to comply with other orders and directions, namely striking out and/or costs or preparation time.

Confidentiality issues

9549 Such issues often arise in relation to documents which a party wishes to have disclosed to him. This happens particularly in discrimination cases where the claimant is seeking disclosure of documents which he hopes will show that another employee had been treated more favourably. A party might have in his possession:
– documents which are relevant to the case but which contain additional information which either is not relevant or is confidential; or
– documents which are relevant but disclosure of which might breach a duty of confidentiality to other people not involved in the case.

9550 **Procedure** Where a party seeks disclosure of a document which may include confidential information, there are a number of ways in which this can be dealt with. Tribunals may review the documents in order to consider whether there is any way in which the confidential elements of the documents could be deleted or concealed so that the general substance of the document can be disclosed. For example, an objection to disclosing names of certain people referred to in the documents could be overcome by replacing the names with letters of the alphabet. This review may be carried out either by the tribunal hearing the case or, in advance, by another tribunal, depending on the circumstances (such as the availability of tribunal members). Another option is for a fresh document to be prepared which recites the relevant parts of the original documents while omitting the confidential details. The fresh document would then be checked against the originals by, for example, the judge. In this way, the relevant parts could be disclosed to the parties without disclosing those parts which it was felt should not be disclosed.

> EXAMPLE In *Asda Stores Ltd v Thompson* [2001] UKEAT 1096_01_1110, in which T and others were dismissed for allegedly supplying and using drugs at an office party, witness statements were given by other employees who wished to remain anonymous. The EAT held that it had not been necessary for the tribunal to order full disclosure of the statements in order for the proceedings to have been conducted fairly, but instead the tribunal should have considered ordering the statements to be disclosed subject to the identities of the witnesses not being revealed.

Legal professional privilege

9551 A party cannot require another party to disclose documents and other communications which are **privileged from disclosure** on the grounds of legal professional privilege. This **covers** communications between:
– a party and his legal advisers, provided the communications were confidential and made for the purpose of obtaining or giving legal advice; and
– a party or his legal advisers and a third party, if those communications have been made for the purpose of existing or contemplated litigation.

Legal professional privilege does not apply to any professional other than a qualified lawyer (*R (on the application of Prudential PLC and anor) v Special Commissioner of Income Tax and anor* [2010] EWCA Civ 1094). It does not therefore extend to non-legally qualified advisers such as employment consultants (*New Victoria Hospital v Ryan* [1993] IRLR 202, EAT; confirmed in *Knight v King Edward Grammar School* [1998] UKEAT 963_98_0112).

4. Witness orders

9553 Most witnesses **attend** tribunal hearings **voluntarily** at the request of a party, and they should be invited to do so before any application is made for a witness order (*Dada v Metal Box Company Limited* [1974] IRLR 251, NIRC). However, tribunals can order the attendance of any witness and can also order him to produce any document or information which relates to the claim (rule 10(2)(c) ETR).

Where a witness attends voluntarily, it will usually be possible for the party calling that witness (or his representative) to prepare a **written statement** of the witness' evidence in advance of the hearing (¶9635). This enables the party to approach the hearing with some confidence as to what the witness is going to say. This is unlikely to be possible where a witness has to be compelled to attend and so the risks involved in calling such a witness are much greater.

9554 **Timing and procedure** If a witness order is required, it may be made by a tribunal of its own motion or on the application of a party at any time. No particular form is required. The order may be made by a judge sitting alone (rule 12 ETR). A tribunal will be unlikely to grant a witness order at the main hearing unless there is good reason as to why the order has not been applied for earlier (for example, that the witness' relevance to the proceedings only became known in the course of the hearing, or that prior to the hearing it was reasonable to believe that the witness would attend voluntarily). Where a witness order is made at the hearing, the hearing may have to be **adjourned** until the witness attends, unless there are other witnesses who can be conveniently dealt with in the meantime (which is only likely to be possible if the hearing is listed for more than 1 day).

9555 The tribunal has **discretion** as to whether or not to grant a witness order. In exercising its discretion, the tribunal will **consider**:
– whether the witness is able to give **evidence which is relevant** to the issues in dispute; and
– whether the party applying for the order can satisfy it that it is **necessary** to issue a witness order.

The party applying for the order will need to give the tribunal some indication of the substance of the evidence which the witness would be able to give (it is not necessary to produce a full proof (i.e. statement) of that evidence), and demonstrate the extent to which it is relevant. The tribunal does not have to be satisfied in every case that the proposed witness would be **unwilling to attend voluntarily**. An order may also be appropriate if the proposed witness is **equivocal** in his response to a request to attend, if he **fails to respond** to such a request, or where it would be easier for a willing witness to attend if a witness order were to be obtained (perhaps because his **employer** is **unwilling** to release him).

If a witness is ordered to attend, he can apply to the tribunal to have the order varied (for example, as to the date or time) or set aside (rule 11 ETR).

9556 **Failure to comply** Failure to comply with a witness order is an offence punishable on summary conviction (i.e. conviction by the Magistrates' Court) by a **fine** (currently up to £1,000) (s 7(4) Employment Tribunals Act 1996). The order must contain a statement warning of the consequences of failure to comply and the amount of the current maximum fine (rule 10(6) ETR).

The tribunal can also make an award in respect of costs or preparation time or strike out the claim or response where there is non-compliance with a witness order (presumably only where one of the parties is in default in failing to comply with the witness order).

5. Directions

9560 Although tribunal procedure is intended to be relatively informal, tribunals can give directions at any time on any matter arising in connection with the proceedings to ensure that cases proceed as swiftly and efficiently as possible (rule 10(1) ETR). Effective case management can narrow the issues, define them more clearly and reduce the time which has to be devoted to the final hearing.

Tribunals can conduct **case management discussions** (i.e. interim hearings) at any time during the tribunal process in order to address matters of procedure and case management. These discussions shall be held in private and, consequently, matters such as a person's civil rights or obligations cannot be dealt with at such a discussion (rule 17 ETR as amended by

SI 2005/1865). Directions as to how the claim should proceed can be decided at such case management discussions, which are frequently conducted by telephone.

> MEMO POINTS   The Government has been consulting on **proposals** for more flexible case management powers and the use of legal officers to deal with certain case management functions. Further developments will be covered by our updating service when available.

Timing and procedure   Directions may be given by the tribunal of its own motion or on the application of a party made by notice in writing to the Secretary (no particular form is required).

The **nature and extent** of the directions given depend on the complexity of the case. In **most cases**, tribunals will, as a matter of course, issue standard directions dealing with:
– exchange of witness statements;
– exchange of relevant documents; and
– preparation of an agreed bundle of documents for use at the hearing.

In **more complicated cases**, directions may be required to cover matters such as:
– agreed chronology of events;
– submission of skeleton arguments;
– exchange of medical evidence;
– matters to be dealt with as preliminary issues;
– statements of agreed facts; and
– time estimate for the hearing (as in most cases the standard directions or listing order issued by the tribunal will allow for 1 day only).

Directions will be given by a judge sitting alone and may be made with or without a hearing (*Sterling Developments (London) Ltd v Pagano* [2007] IRLR 471, EAT; *Halford v Sharples* [1992] ICR 146, EAT). The need for a hearing will generally be determined by the complexity of the case. Parties will often try to **agree directions** to avoid the need for a hearing. The agreed directions are then submitted to the tribunal for approval.

An order can also be made striking out the claim/response unless certain steps are taken by a specified time. Such orders are often called "**unless orders**".

9561

Failure to comply   If a party fails to comply with a direction, the tribunal can strike out the whole or part of his claim/response and, where appropriate, may make an award of costs or preparation time against him (rule 13(1) ETR). Such orders are not made, however, until the party who has not complied has been given an opportunity to put forward reasons as to why the tribunal should not do so. However, with regard to unless orders, the strike out will happen automatically if the order is breached, without the need for a separate striking out order (rule 13(2) ETR) and the tribunal has no discretion not to strike out (*Scottish Ambulance Service v Laing* [2012] UKEAT 0038_12_1710).

9562

6. Expert evidence

Obtaining expert evidence   There are **guidelines** as to how expert evidence should be obtained (*De Keyser Ltd v Wilson* [2001] IRLR 324, EAT):
– before instructing an expert, a party should seek guidance from the tribunal (by correspondence or at a directions hearing) as to whether such evidence will be acceptable;
– joint instruction of experts is preferred (in which case the parties should agree how the expert's fees and expenses will be shared). Although joint instruction is preferred and the normal convention, there may be circumstances where it is useful to appoint two expert witnesses, for example in cases involving very substantial claims or where key evidence is disputed (*Hospice of St Mary of Furness v Howard* [2007] IRLR 944, EAT; *Mid-Devon District Council v Stevenson* [2007] UKEAT 0196_07_1810);
– the tribunal may set a time limit for the parties to agree the identity of the expert and the terms of a joint letter of instruction (if the parties do not agree within that time, the tribunal

9563

can intervene to assist them to reach agreement), and set a date for his report to be made available;
- if one party instructs his own expert, the weight of his evidence may be increased if the terms of his instruction were submitted to the other party for agreement (or at least for comment) before being finalised;
- any letter of instruction should specify in detail any particular questions that the expert is to answer and any general subjects he is to address (in all cases, the tribunal can give formal directions as to these issues);
- instructions are to avoid partisanship and the letter should emphasise the expert's over-riding duty to the tribunal;
- where each party instructs his own expert, the tribunal should, in the absence of agreement between the parties, give a timetable for disclosure/exchange of their reports and for meetings between them (see below), and possibly for the raising of supplementary questions and disclosure/exchange of answers; and
- where separate experts are instructed, they should meet on a "without prejudice" basis to try to resolve points of dispute. Where possible, a schedule of agreed issues/points of dispute should then be produced and disclosed.

The guidelines suggest that tribunals should consider awarding costs against a party who **fails to follow** the above steps.

EXAMPLE
1. In *Hospice of St Mary of Furness v Howard*, the employee suffered from an undiagnosed back condition. The total size of the claim was £500,000. The parties originally agreed to instruct a joint expert, but while the expert's evidence covered one key issue for the tribunal (the question of whether pains were caused by a particular condition), the employer maintained that it did not satisfactorily address another key issue in the litigation, which was whether the claimant suffered from any genuine impairment at all. Faced with substantial claims, the EAT held that a tribunal should adopt the procedure of a civil court, which in similar circumstances would allow each party to ask questions of the expert witness and, if questions did not resolve a matter in dispute, would allow a second expert to be called.
2. In *Mid-Devon District Council v Stevenson*, regarding a disability discrimination claim worth nearly £100,000, an expert had initially been instructed by one party, the claimant, at a time when the facts of the claimant's disability had been largely unknown. There was no risk that the instruction of another expert would delay the substantive hearing and the request for another expert to be called was granted.
3. In *Government Communications Headquarters v Bacchus* [2012] UKEAT 0373_12_0608, an employee brought various claims against his employer, including disability discrimination. Having been unable to agree a joint expert, the employee had refused to attend appointments with any of the employer's chosen medical experts and he breached a tribunal order requiring him to do so. This left the employer unable to obtain its own medical evidence. So that the employer could properly prepare its defence the EAT granted an unless order, i.e. an order requiring the employee to attend a medical appointment and if he failed to do so his claims would be struck out for non-compliance.

9564 **Challenging an expert** A party wishing to challenge the evidence of an expert witness should give advance warning that this is the case so that arrangements can be made for the expert to attend the tribunal and be cross-examined about his report (*Mahon v Accuread Ltd* [2008] UKEAT 0081_08_0107).

EXAMPLE In *Mahon v Accuread Ltd*, the tribunal rejected an expert report to the effect that the claimant was disabled, on the basis of its own observation of the claimant in cross-examination, and without cross-examining the expert. The EAT overturned the judgment of the tribunal for several reasons. The question of whether a claimant was disabled should be judged on the basis of the evidence available at the time of the alleged discriminatory act, not as at the time of the hearing. It was also unfair to judge the matter on the basis of the tribunal's own observations, and without there being an opportunity for the expert to be cross-examined on his evidence.

9565 **Liability of an expert** Expert witnesses can be sued in negligence in relation to the evidence that they give although negligence will not be easy to prove (*Jones v Kaney* [2011] UKSC 13).

7. Hopeless or vexatious cases

In order to try to eliminate hopeless or vexatious cases at an early stage (and thus alleviate the burden on tribunal resources and save the parties' time and expense), the tribunal has the power to order a pre-hearing review at which the tribunal may make various orders, including the payment of a **deposit** in order to continue the proceedings or the **striking out** of a claim and/or response in whole or in part.

9566

A party who has acted vexatiously, abusively, disruptively or otherwise unreasonably, or whose bringing or conducting of the proceedings has been misconceived, may have a **costs or preparation time order** awarded against him (¶9702). "Misconceived" includes having no reasonable prospect of success. Tribunals can issue a "**costs warning**" to try to deter misconceived applications, but before doing so must consider the effect of such a warning on the claimant's decision to proceed with his claim, taking into account whether such a warning is proportionate to the actual risk of substantial costs being awarded against the claimant (*Gee v Shell UK Ltd* [2003] IRLR 82, CA).

A party who repeatedly brings vexatious claims may have his **right to submit new claims** restricted (¶9576).

> **MEMO POINTS** The Government has been consulting on **proposals** to make the power to order deposits and to strike out claims more flexible. Further developments will be covered by our updating service when available.

Pre-hearing reviews

The **purpose** of a pre-hearing review is to carry out a preliminary consideration of the proceedings at which the tribunal may (rule 18(2) ETR):
- determine any interim or preliminary matter relating to the proceedings;
- issue any order within its powers;
- order that a deposit be paid without hearing evidence (¶9570); and
- consider any oral or written representations or evidence.

9567

In addition, despite the preliminary nature of a pre-hearing review, it is possible for the tribunal to make a judgment or order at the pre-hearing review which results in the proceedings being **struck out** (¶9573) or **dismissed** or otherwise determined with the result that a full hearing is no longer necessary (rule 18(5) ETR).

Timing and procedure The pre-hearing review may be ordered either by the tribunal of its own motion or on the application of either party, at any time **prior to the main hearing**, by notice in writing to the Secretary (no particular form is required) (rule 11(1) ETR). If one of the parties has requested that such a judgment or order be made, then the judgment or order must be made at the pre-hearing review (or the full hearing), but if no request has been made, then the tribunal can make such judgment or order in the absence of the parties. The party against whom an order or judgment is proposed to be made must be given **advance notice** of the pre-hearing review so that he has an opportunity to submit written representations or put forward oral arguments as to why the judgment or order should not be made (rule 19(1) ETR).

9568

A pre-hearing review can be **conducted by** a judge sitting alone, although it can be conducted by a tribunal if a party so requests in writing at least 10 days before the date on which the pre-hearing review is due to take place and the judge considers that one or more substantive issues of fact are likely to be determined and that this would be desirable (rule 18(3) ETR). The members of the tribunal which sit to determine the pre-hearing review (or the judge if sitting alone) are not allowed to play any part in the tribunal which ultimately sits to hear the case if, at the pre-hearing review, a requirement to pay a deposit has been considered (rule 18(9) ETR).

The tribunal **will consider** the contents of the claim and response, any representations made in writing and any oral argument advanced by or on behalf of a party. It is not a hearing of the evidence of the case.

9569

Deposit to continue proceedings

9570 If, at the pre-hearing review, the tribunal believes that the contentions put forward by a party in relation to any matter to be determined by it have **little reasonable prospect of success**, that party may be **ordered to pay** a deposit of up to £1,000 as a condition of being allowed to continue to take part in the proceedings relating to that matter (rule 20(4) ETR; SI 2012/468). A tribunal can only make this order if it has taken reasonable steps to ascertain that party's **ability to pay** and has taken such information into account in determining the amount (rule 20(2) ETR).

The tribunal can reconsider its decision if there is a **material change** in the factual circumstances or a relevant change in the law (it will therefore need to consider the basis of its previous decision in order to assess whether such a change has occurred) (*Maurice v Betterware (UK) Ltd* [1999] UKEAT 1030_99_0712).

The tribunal's decision and its reasons must be **recorded** in writing, and a copy must be sent to the parties, accompanied by a **note explaining** that if the party against whom the order is made persists in participating in the proceedings, he may have an award of costs or preparation time made against him and could lose his deposit (rule 20(3) ETR).

9571 An order to pay a deposit as a condition of being allowed to take part in proceedings does not constitute a judgment and **cannot be reviewed** (*Sodexho Ltd v Gibbons* [2005] ICR 1647, EAT). However, a **strike out** for failure to comply with a deposit order does constitute a judgment and can be reviewed (¶9720).

9572 **Payment of the deposit** The deposit must be paid within 21 days from the day on which the written order is sent to the party who is required to pay it. That party can ask the tribunal to extend the 21-day period by up to 14 days, but to do so he must make his application in writing within the 21-day period (rule 20(4) ETR). If the deposit is **not paid** within the required period (including any extension), the claim/response (or the relevant parts of such documents) is automatically struck out and the tribunal has no discretion to overlook the failure.

If the party pays the deposit and proceeds with the case but ultimately has a costs or preparation time order made against him, the deposit is **used** in satisfaction or part satisfaction of the award of costs, with any balance of the deposit which exceeds the costs award being returned to him (rule 47(2) ETR). If a deposit is paid and the party continues and wins (or loses but does not have an award of costs made against him) his deposit will be **refunded** to him. It will also be refunded if he withdraws from the proceedings before they reach the final hearing.

Striking out

9573 At the pre-hearing review, the tribunal can strike out or amend all or part of any claim or response on the grounds that it is **scandalous, vexatious, or has no reasonable prospect of success** or if the claimant or respondent (or their representatives) has **conducted the proceedings** in a scandalous, unreasonable or vexatious manner (rule 18(7) (b), (c) ETR).

The misconduct does not have to **take place** in the tribunal hearing room as long as it can be said to take place in the conduct of the proceedings (*Harmony Healthcare plc v Drewery* [2000] UKEAT 866_00_2107; *Bolch v Chipman* [2004] IRLR 140, EAT).

A tribunal can also exercise its discretion to strike out a claim on the basis that the claimant has acted unreasonably in his **preparation for an appeal** (*Neckles v Yorkshire Rider Ltd* [2001] UKEAT 517_00_0102). In this case, the claimant had produced a transcript made from an unauthorised tape recording of the tribunal hearing but had refused to explain to even the employment tribunal how he had obtained the transcript. The unauthorised recording had been a deliberate breach of rules and constituted scandalous conduct.

A striking-out order must be **proportionate** to the offensive conduct (*De Keyser Ltd v Wilson* [2001] IRLR 324, EAT) and the Court of Appeal has emphasised the importance of proportionality as an important check in deciding whether to strike out a claim (*Ezsias v North Glamorgan National Health Trust* [2007] IRLR 603, CA; *Blockbuster Entertainment Ltd v James* [2006] IRLR 630, CA). Where an application for a strike-out has been made on the grounds that a case has **no reasonable**

prospects of success, the application would only be granted in exceptional circumstances, such as where it can be demonstrated that the central facts of the case are patently untrue. Where there is a **core of disputed facts**, it is not for the tribunal to conduct a mini-trial without all of the evidence available, and it would be an "error of law for the tribunal to pre-empt the determination of a full hearing by striking out" (*Tayside Public Transport Company Limited (t/a Travel Dundee) v James Reilly* [2012] ScotCS CSIH_46; *Ezsias v North Glamorgan National Health Trust*). It would also take something very unusual to justify the striking out, on procedural grounds, of a claim which has arrived at the point of trial (*Blockbuster Entertainment Ltd v James*). For example, although the last-minute production of documents or a late demand for them may result in a high risk of such requests being refused if they cannot be accommodated, only in extreme cases would it justify or even contribute to the justification of striking out. **Serious intimidation** will mean that it is not possible for there to be a fair trial, and, in most cases, it will be proportionate to strike out a claim or response (*Force One Utilities v Hatfield* [2009] IRLR 45, EAT).

In **discrimination cases**, there is also a higher threshold and therefore only in the most exceptional cases should a claimant's claim be struck out (*Jiad v Byford* [2003] IRLR 232, CA). As **whistleblowing** cases concern similar issues this higher threshold applies to such cases as well (*Ezsias v North Glamorgan National Health Trust*).

> **EXAMPLE**
> **Strike out**
> 1. In *Harmony Healthcare plc v Drewery*, the employer's representative assaulted D's representative in the **tribunal waiting room** when demanding the return of witness statements. The tribunal was entitled to strike out the response.
> 2. In *Edmondson v BMI Healthcare* [2002] UKEAT 0654_01_0103, the claimant's lay representative repeatedly interrupted proceedings **during the hearing**, interfered with evidence being given by E and acted in an agitated manner. The EAT upheld the tribunal's decision to strike out E's claim on the basis that not only was her representative's conduct unreasonable, but also on the ground that it was impossible for a fair trial to continue.
> 3. In *Force One Utilities v Hatfield*, a senior manager had made **intimidating remarks** to the claimant in the tribunal car park during the hearing. The EAT upheld the tribunal's decision to strike out the response.
>
> **No strike out**
> In *De Keyser Ltd v Wilson*, the employer was granted an order to appoint a medical expert to examine W's allegation that her illness was attributable entirely to her work. The employer's representatives attempted to prejudice the doctor to her disadvantage. The EAT held that striking out was **disproportionate** and that the correct response would have been to ensure the correct instruction of another doctor.

> **MEMO POINTS** Where it is alleged that the claimant is **delusional**, there is a presumption that the party has capacity to continue to act in proceedings (*Johnson v Edwardian International Hotels Ltd* [2008] UKEAT 0588_07_0205). Cases where there is evidence justifying a finding of incapacity are likely to be exceptional. However, where there is a risk that the conduct, including alleged mental incapacity, of one of the parties is such as to cause serious unfairness to the other party or to make the case truly unmanageable, the claim may have to be struck out.

9574 The tribunal can also strike out a claim for **want of prosecution** by the claimant (i.e. where the claimant does not take appropriate steps to bring the proceedings to a hearing or does not do so quickly enough) (rule 18(7)(d) ETR). An "unless" order, that the claim will be struck out if the claimant fails to take the steps ordered by the tribunal (¶9561), may be appropriate before striking out the claim, for example if a claimant has already obtained judgment on liability, but his obstructive attitude has resulted in very lengthy delays in relation to the remedies hearing (*Abegaze v Shrewsbury College of Arts and Technology* [2010] IRLR 238, CA).

Moreover, the tribunal can strike out a claim where it considers that it is **no longer possible to have a fair hearing** in those proceedings (rule 18(7)(f) ETR).

> **EXAMPLE** In *Riley v The Crown Prosecution Service* [2012] UKEAT 0043_12_1306, the EAT struck out a claim on the basis that it was no longer possible to have a fair hearing. This was held to be the case because the claimant was suffering from severe depression and psychotic symptoms which were held to be a direct result of her ongoing legal battle, and her condition would not change in the foreseeable

future. Her illness meant that she could not cope with dealing with the dispute and had applied for various postponements, both in respect of the internal and tribunal proceedings. In this case the fact that a fair trial was no longer possible for all concerned took precedence over the claimant's right to a fair trial, though in many cases involving ill health a postponement will be an alternative solution.

9575 **Timing and procedure** An order to strike out may be made at any stage of the proceedings either by the tribunal of its own motion or on the application of either party. An order to strike out for want of prosecution may be made either of the tribunal's own motion or on the application of the respondent. In all cases, the order must not be made until the party to be struck out has been given an **opportunity to show cause** why (i.e. persuade the tribunal that) the order should not be made (*En'Wezoh v London Forum Hotel Ltd* [1999] UKEAT 1153_98_2603). The tribunal normally writes to the relevant party inviting him to respond.

Restriction of proceedings orders

9576 A party who **repeatedly issues** "vexatious" (i.e. **hopeless or malicious**) applications can have a restriction of proceedings order made against them by the EAT (s 33 Employment Tribunals Act 1996). Such an order is not a denial of the right to a fair hearing protected by the Human Rights Act 1998 (Human Rights Act 1998; *Attorney General v Wheen* [2001] IRLR 91). The order has the **effect** of requiring the party in the future to obtain permission from the EAT before they can commence or continue any proceedings.

9577 **Timing and procedure** The order can only be made on the application of the Attorney General, and can be for a specified period or indefinite. The procedure is rarely used. It is no defence for the allegedly vexatious claimant to say that he has always withdrawn his applications once a tribunal has ordered him to pay a deposit.

EXAMPLE
1. In *Attorney General v Bentley* [2012] UKEAT 0556_11_0305, the Court of Appeal upheld an EAT restriction of proceedings order against B, who had embarked upon 31 separate sets of tribunal proceedings. In many of those cases multiple respondents were listed, resulting in at least 44 separate respondents being involved. The background to the claims was that B would apply for roles or inform potential employers that he was available for work, and when he did not receive an offer of work he would issue proceedings for age discrimination, sometimes alongside disability discrimination and victimisation. B did not attend any scheduled hearings in any of the claims, and none of his claims were ever met with any success whatsoever. This behaviour was found to be an abuse of the tribunal system and sufficiently vexatious to warrant an order being put in place. As B's pattern of behaviour was not linked to a particular dispute and was not likely to come to a natural end, the restriction of proceedings order was designated as being for an indefinite period.
2. In *Attorney General v Wheen* [2000] EAT 1301_99_1804 (approved by Court of Appeal [2001] IRLR 91, CA), W had over a period of time launched 13 sets of tribunal proceedings, all of which had failed. The EAT held that he had issued vexatious proceedings "habitually, persistently and without any reasonable ground", thus justifying the order.

8. Entitlement to bring or contest proceedings

9580 There may be a question as to the entitlement of a party to bring or contest the proceedings, which may be dealt with at the **pre-hearing review** (rule 18(7)(a) ETR). Situations where this could occur include:
– where it appears that the claimant may not have sufficient **qualifying service** to bring the claim which he has presented (¶1080);
– where the claim may have been presented **out of time** (¶9450); or
– where there may be a question as to the **true status of the claimant** (i.e. whether he is employed or self-employed).

EXAMPLE An employee commences employment on 25 April 2011 and presents an unfair dismissal claim after he is dismissed on 20 April 2012. As it appears that he has not completed the requisite

1 year of continuous employment (because his employment commenced before 6 April 2012 (¶8411)), it will be appropriate to decide the question of continuous employment first as a separate issue. If the tribunal then finds that he does not have sufficient continuous employment, the claim will be dismissed and the parties will not be put to the effort and expense of preparing and presenting evidence in relation to the fairness of the dismissal. If, on the other hand, the tribunal finds that there was sufficient continuous employment (for example, because it appears he was dismissed for a reason which does not require any qualifying period (¶1080) or because his effective date of termination is extended by the addition of his statutory minimum period of notice (¶8131)), the case can proceed to a full hearing.

Timing and procedure For a discussion as to the timing and procedure for an application by a party for a judgment or order to be made at a pre-hearing review in respect of the entitlement of the other party to bring or contest proceedings, see ¶9568.

9581

The hearing of such an issue will generally also involve the hearing of **evidence**. It is possible to deal with such an application at the beginning of the main hearing. However, if the evidence required to determine the issue of entitlement to bring or contest proceedings and the evidence required to determine the claim **overlap** to a large extent, the tribunal may prefer to consider the whole picture and deal with all the issues at once at the main hearing.

EXAMPLE An employee, who started work before 6 April 2012, is dismissed without notice a few days short of completing 1 year's service (¶8411). If he is not guilty of gross misconduct, he is entitled to 1 week's statutory notice which he can add on to take him over 1 year's continuous service. If he is guilty of gross misconduct, he is not entitled to such notice. Since the question of whether or not there was gross misconduct is also likely to be highly relevant to the fairness of the dismissal, the tribunal will probably want to deal with all the issues at the main hearing after having heard all the evidence.

9. Restricted reporting orders

The tribunal can make a restricted reporting order (either temporary or full) in any case which involves allegations of sexual misconduct or in a disability discrimination claim in which evidence of a personal nature is likely to be heard by the tribunal (rule 50(1) ETR), as can the EAT (rule 23 EATR).

9583

Sexual misconduct is defined as the commission of a sexual offence, sexual harassment or other adverse conduct of whatever nature related to sex (whether such conduct is of a sexual character itself or is sexual by reference to the sex or sexual orientation of the person at whom the conduct is directed). **Evidence of a personal nature** means any evidence of a medical or intimate nature which might reasonably be assumed to be likely to cause significant embarrassment if reported.

MEMO POINTS 1. There is no power under the Rules to make such an order in cases of sexual discrimination not involving allegations of sexual misconduct (for example, to protect the **anonymity of a transsexual** (*Chief Constable of the West Yorkshire Police v A* [2000] IRLR 465)), although European law may provide such a power where the claimant would be deprived of an effective remedy if the order were not made.
2. Once a **case has been withdrawn**, a tribunal has no power to lift a restricted reporting order made earlier, as the case is no longer in existence (*Davidson v McMillan* [2010] IRLR 439, CS).

Timing and procedure The order may be made at any time **before** the **tribunal's decision** in respect of the claim, and may be made either on the application of a party by notice in writing to the Secretary (no particular form is required) or of its own motion (rule 50(2) ETR). If a party thinks that a restricted reporting order is appropriate, it is obviously sensible to make the application in advance of the main hearing and certainly not later than the start of the main hearing (otherwise the damage may have been done before the order is made). If the application is made in advance of the hearing, the order can be made by a judge sitting alone.

9584

Before making such an order, the tribunal must give each party the opportunity to advance oral arguments at a **hearing** (either the main hearing or at a pre-hearing review) if they wish to do so.

9585 **Decision** In deciding whether or not to make a restricted reporting order, the tribunal will balance the interests of all concerned, including the interest of the public and the press. Such orders are not granted automatically and are a matter for the tribunal's discretion.

The **order must specify** the persons who are not to be identified. It will remain in force (unless revoked earlier, which might happen if it was no longer intended to call the evidence which had led to the order being made) until the final decision of the claim (which means the decision at a remedies hearing if the matter is adjourned following a "liability only" decision (*Chief Constable of the West Yorkshire Police v A* – see memo point at ¶9583 above)).

The Secretary must ensure that a notice of the fact that a restricted reporting order has been made is **displayed** on the tribunal notice board along with any list of the proceedings taking place before the tribunal and on the door of the room in which the proceedings are taking place.

9586 It is an **offence** to publish identifying matter in contravention of a restricted reporting order, and on summary conviction (i.e. conviction by a magistrates' court) a fine (not exceeding £5,000 (£10,000 in Scotland)) can be imposed. Those who may be convicted of the offence include editors and publishers of newspapers, corporate bodies responsible for the publication and directors or managers of such corporate bodies (s 11(2)(3) Employment Tribunals Act 1996).

10. Freezing injunctions

9590 In a significant ruling which may strengthen the tactics of applicants with potentially large claims, the High Court has confirmed that it has jurisdiction to grant a freezing injunction in respect of a pre-existing action which is in the employment tribunal. To succeed **there must be** a pre-existing cause of action at the time of the application which presents a very strong case for compensation. Further, it must be shown that there is a **real risk** that the respondent's assets will be dissipated unless he is prevented from doing so (*Amicus v Dynamex Friction Ltd and another* [2005] IRLR 724).

> MEMO POINTS A freezing injunction **freezes the assets** of a party pending an action to ensure that those assets will still be available to satisfy any award which may be made in the future.
> Freezing injunctions can be made at any time after a cause of action has been brought although such injunctions are **usually brought** as soon as the claim is made as, where there is a real risk of dissipation of assets, time is very often of the essence.

III. Main hearing

9600 After all the preliminary issues have been dealt with, the case will be heard by the tribunal to determine the outstanding procedural or substantive issues or to dispose of the proceedings.

1. Composition of tribunal

9605 **Full composition** When an employment tribunal sits to hear a complex case, it will usually be made up of an Employment Judge (drawn from a legally qualified panel (e.g. solicitors or barristers)), and **two lay members**: one drawn from a panel of lay members from the **employee side** of industry (e.g. with a trade union background) and one from a panel of lay members from the **employer side** of industry (reg 8 SI 2004/1861). When hearing cases, lay members are impartial and independent, and must not show bias based on their own particular background (see below). Some judges are appointed on a full-time basis, while others sit only part-time. The lay members are all part-time.

By convention, in **sex or race discrimination cases** at least one member of the tribunal will be a woman or, as the case may be, have special experience of race relations. There is, however, no statutory requirement that this should be the case and the hearing will still be valid if this convention is not followed.

9606 If the parties consent, the hearing can be conducted by a **judge and one lay member**, in which case the judge has a casting vote if necessary (reg 9 (3) SI 2004/1861; s 4(1) (b) Employment Tribunals Act 1996). If, for example, a member of the tribunal is taken ill on the day of the hearing and no replacement is available, the parties may prefer to proceed rather than have the hearing postponed to another day.

Such **consent must be informed** (*Rabahallah v BT Group plc* [2005] IRLR 184, EAT). In this case, where a lay member of the panel became unavailable during the proceedings, the unrepresented applicant should have been told the identity of the remaining lay member (i.e. whether they represented the employer's or the employee's side of the industry) before her consent to continue the case was requested.

MEMO POINTS   This applies the Court of Appeal's ruling in *De Haney v Brent Mind* (that informed consent must be given before the EAT can hear an appeal by just the judge and one lay member) (*De Haney v Brent Mind* [2004] ICR 348, CA; ¶9789) to proceedings at tribunal level.

9607 **Employment Judge sitting on his own**   The judge can hear a matter on his own where the parties have **consented** (perhaps in order to obtain an earlier hearing date), in which case the judge may do so even if consent is subsequently withdrawn, and where the **respondent is not contesting** the case.

Additionally, the **following complaints** will be heard by a judge sitting on his own without the need for the consent of the parties, unless the judge considers a full tribunal is more appropriate (¶¶9608+) (s 4(3) Employment Tribunals Act 1996 as amended):
– unfair dismissal (recently added by SI 2012/988);
– certain deductions of trade union subscriptions from wages;
– failure to supply a written statement of particulars of employment;
– unlawful deductions from wages;
– failure to consult under the regulations relating to business transfers;
– failure to keep records under the national minimum wage legislation;
– breach of contract;
– redundancy payments;
– guarantee payments and certain claims relating to insolvent employers;
– complaints relating to medical and maternity suspensions; and
– stage 1 equal value claims (¶5721).

A judge can also sit alone to determine the **entitlement** of a party **to bring or contest** proceedings (¶9580). However, this power should not be used as a matter of course as many of these issues (particularly where the facts are in dispute) would benefit from the **input of the lay members**, with their experience of industrial practice (*Sutcliffe v Big C's Marine* [1998] UKEAT 1326_96_2205).

9608 However, a case must be heard by a **full tribunal** if the judge decides that this is appropriate (s 4(5) Employment Tribunals Act 1996). When reaching his decision, the judge will have regard to the **following factors**:
– any views of any of the parties as to whether or not the proceedings ought to be heard in either of those ways;
– whether there is a likelihood of a dispute arising on the facts which makes it desirable for the proceedings to be heard by a full tribunal;
– whether there is a likelihood of an issue of law arising which would make it desirable for the proceedings to be heard by a judge sitting alone; and
– whether there are other proceedings which might be heard concurrently but which are not proceedings specified as being capable of being heard by a judge sitting alone.

The judge **must consider** these factors before proceeding to sit on his own. If the judge fails to do so, his decision can be **challenged**. It does not, however, affect his jurisdiction and so the decision is not a nullity. If, for example, the parties had expressly agreed to the judge sitting alone, then his decision is likely to be upheld even if the judge had not explicitly considered the various factors (*Post Office v Howell* [2000] IRLR 224, EAT).

9609 The EAT has given **guidance** as to when a judge should hear a matter on his own and in doing so emphasised that this question is a judicial, not administrative, decision (*Sterling Developments (London) Ltd v Pagano* [2007] IRLR 471, EAT):

– where **interim case management discussions** (i.e. interim hearings) are held prior to the substantive hearing, the judge conducting the interim hearings should inform the parties as to whether, in his opinion, the substantive hearing is to be before a full panel or a judge alone, applying the rules that certain complaints will be heard by a judge sitting on his own unless it is inappropriate to do so. To this end, the judge will invite any submissions as to whether he should exercise his discretion for the hearing to take place before a full panel (see ¶9608 above). A simple explanation of the respective merits of trial mode should be given to the parties, particularly unrepresented parties. If representations are made the judge should rule on the point, giving brief reasons for his ruling. The mode of trial, judge alone or full tribunal, will then be recorded in the judge's written order; or

– where **no interim hearing** has been held, a judge (if appropriate the Regional Employment Judge, by direction to the Secretary) must ensure that the notice of hearing (see ¶9623) states whether the hearing is to be before a full panel or judge alone; if the latter, parties should be expressly invited to make representations if they wish as to why the hearing should take place before a full panel, giving reasons, including those factors which the judge will have regard to in exercising his discretion (see again ¶9608 above). Any such representations will then be considered, after obtaining the views of all parties, and a judicial decision, with reasons, made by a judge.

Following this, **unless there are any representations or appeal**, the mode of hearing will be settled, subject to any change of circumstances which requires the hearing judge to revisit the question of composition. In the absence of any such point being raised, the EAT emphasised that it could see no reason why the final hearing should be susceptible to challenge on a point of law, the relevant judicial decision having been taken earlier, either at an interim hearing or in the form of standard directions.

2. Fairness and natural justice

9610 The tribunal, like any court, has a duty to follow the principles of natural justice at all stages in the proceedings but particularly at the final hearing. The two most important principles involved are that each side should be given a proper **opportunity to be heard** and present his case, and that the tribunal should be **impartial** and not be biased or give the appearance of bias.

Opportunity to be heard

9611 Each party (or his representative) must be allowed to **put his case** or **make submissions** on any issue upon which the tribunal is asked to decide (*Chapman v Simon* [1993] EWCA Civ 37). The tribunal should, therefore, not prevent a party from commenting on points raised by the other side. Further, the tribunal should not decide on an issue which it has identified as being of importance to the decision which it has to make without hearing from both parties. For example, if the parties have not addressed the question of contributory fault during a hearing, the tribunal cannot make a decision in relation to contribution without first asking the parties to express their views (or call evidence) in relation to the matter, nor can it rely on previous legal decisions without giving the parties the opportunity to make submissions on those decisions (*Albion Hotel (Freshwater) Ltd v Maia e Silva* [2002] IRLR 200, EAT). However, once the tribunal has raised a particular issue, the parties must ensure that all relevant evidence is brought to support their contentions (¶9660).

Bias

9612 The right to a fair trial by an **independent and impartial tribunal** is a statutory right (Human Rights Act 1998) and a basic principle of natural justice. The principle is so important that the appearance of bias ("apparent bias") is as unacceptable as "actual bias" (*Locabail (UK) Ltd v Bayfield Properties Ltd* [2000] IRLR 96, CA).

9613 **Actual bias** This arises where a judge (or tribunal member) is actually affected in his decision by **partiality or prejudice** towards or against one party. Such cases are rare and, for obvious reasons, difficult to prove.

9614 **Apparent bias** The **test** to determine whether there has been apparent bias is whether a fair-minded and informed observer would conclude that there was a real possibility or danger that the tribunal was biased (*In Re Medicaments and Related Classes of Goods* [2001] ICR 564, CA; *Porter v Magill* [2002] 2 AC 357, HL).

Apparent bias usually arises where a **judge** (**or tribunal member**) has an **interest in the outcome**. If such an interest exists (even if he has put it entirely from his mind), it is not acceptable for him to be involved in the case. The issue is not whether the judge is linked to one of the parties, but whether the outcome of the case could realistically affect the judge's own interests and, therefore, his decision (for example, where the judge has a substantial shareholding in a company which is involved in a case, or the judge plays an active part in a charity which promotes a cause which is also supported by one of the parties (*R v Bow Street Metropolitan Magistrate, ex parte Pinochet Ugarte (No2)* [1999] 2 WLR 272, HL)). There is no apparent bias if the **personal interest is so small** that it would be incapable of affecting his decision. If there is any doubt, the judge or tribunal member will be disqualified. **Indirect interests**, such as those of a spouse or other relative of the judge, are considered in the same light.

9615 Instances of apparent bias can **also arise**:
– in the context of a **tribunal's preliminary views** regarding the outcome of a case before it. It is acceptable for a tribunal to indicate to the parties its current thinking before the case has been concluded, provided only if it stresses that such views are provisional (*Jiminez v London Borough of Southwark* [2003] IRLR 477, CA). In this case, no apparent bias arose when a tribunal expressed a preliminary view on the treatment of the employee by the employer, having heard almost all the evidence save for evidence to be given by an insignificant witness, but before the parties had made their closing submissions;
– if the tribunal (or any member of it) appears, even unconsciously, to be **discriminating against the claimant**. For example, by prolonged questioning by the judge as to how the claimant viewed her own skin colour and by making comparisons with his own skin colour resulting in a fair-minded observer concluding that the remarks made were likely to cause the claimant to feel unsettled, humiliated and embarrassed and that there was a real possibility that the judge was biased, albeit unconsciously (*Diem v Crystal Services plc* [2005] UKEAT 0398_05_1612);
– if the tribunal (or any member of it) "oversteps the line" and crosses the boundary between rigorous questioning and offensive cross-examination in relation to their **questioning and intervention of one party's case** such that a fair-minded observer would be left with a clear impression that party did not have a fair hearing (*Calor Gas Ltd v Bray* [2005] UKEAT 0633_04_1209);
– if the judge acts in an **undignified and intemperate fashion** (*Howell and ors v Millais and ors* [2007] EWCA Civ 720). In this case, a judge had applied for a post with a firm of solicitors. When his application was unsuccessful, he described the firm as "insulting" and "condescending". Shortly afterwards, a case came before the same judge in which one of the parties was a partner of the same firm. Counsel for the applicants invited the judge to stand down. Rather than doing so, he ordered a preliminary hearing. At that hearing, he interviewed a witness vigorously, as if cross-examining him. He threatened counsel with "professional consequences", and acted throughout in an undignified and intemperate fashion. An appeal against the judge's decision not to stand down was allowed;

– if the tribunal (or any member of it) is seen to have behaved as if it had **closed its mind** against one of the parties. For example, before any witness evidence had been heard the judge commenting that the respondent would face "an upward struggle", which could lead a fair-minded and informed observer to conclude that there was a real possibility or danger that the tribunal was biased (*Project v Hutt* [2006] UKEAT 0065_05_0604);

– if a **tribunal member cannot give his full attention** to the proceedings, for example, if he has consumed alcohol or fallen asleep (*Stansbury v Datapulse plc and anor* [2004] IRLR 466, CA);

– where a tribunal member was a full-time **trade union official** hearing a **case concerning alleged victimisation by another union** closely connected to that union (*Hamilton v GMB (Northern Region)* [2007] IRLR 391, EAT). In this case, the complainant had been disciplined for flouting a policy which was shared by both UNISON and GMB. As one of the tribunal panel had been a senior official of UNISON, she could be expected to support her own union's policy which the complainant was questioning as to its lawfulness and reasonableness, Further, she was closely connected with individuals who were involved in the case. In these circumstances, a reasonable person would take the view that there was a real possibility of bias; and

– where **counsel who has previously sat as a part-time judge** at the EAT appears as an advocate before one or more of the EAT lay members. With regard to this, the House of Lords (now the Supreme Court) has stated that this practice should cease since confidence in the judicial system would be reduced (*Lawal v Northern Spirit Ltd* [2003] IRLR 538, HL). On the other hand, the EAT has held that there was no bias where the **judge** of the tribunal hearing the case had made, in an **earlier unconnected case**, a costs order (because of the way the proceedings had been conducted) against a party the claimant had represented in his capacity as a union representative (*Lodwick v London Borough of Southwark* [2005] UKEAT 0116_05_1306). This decision was given after the Court of Appeal had ruled that the EAT did have jurisdiction to hear the issue and the EAT in coming to its decision drew upon the Court of Appeal's ruling that in these circumstances "something more" is required to establish bias. The EAT also confirmed that, had it been in any doubt as to the issue of bias, the matter would have been put firmly beyond doubt due to the way in which the claimant was assisted by the tribunal during the hearing and in the formulation of his case. Another EAT has likewise held that parties cannot generally assume or expect that **findings adverse to a party in one case** entitle that party to a different judge or tribunal in a later case (*Ansar v Lloyds TSB Bank plc and ors* [2007] IRLR 211, CA). The mere fact that a complaint is made does not mean that the judge or member should automatically decide to withdraw. Again "something more" is required.

9616 **Impact of bias** The judge (or tribunal member) himself must be alert to the possibilities of bias, and should **stand down** from the case at the **earliest possible moment** (preferably before any objection is raised). If a party is aware of a judge's interest, he should draw it to the attention of the tribunal before the start of the hearing. If he fails to raise the matter at the hearing, a party may waive his right to complain of bias (*Anthony v Governing Body of Hillcrest School* [2001] UKEAT 1193_00_1403).

The Court of Appeal has provided **guidance** as to the procedure tribunals should adopt in cases in which there is a real possibility that the test for apparent bias would be met (*Jones v DAS Legal Expenses Insurance Co Ltd* [2004] IRLR 218, CA). In such cases, the Court of Appeal stated that if another judge or tribunal member is available to hear the case they should do so, otherwise:

– the judge should take time to fully explain to the parties what the facts are, why the issue of bias has arisen at such a late stage in the proceedings, and why (if appropriate) there is no other judge or tribunal who is available to hear the case on that day;
– the judge's explanation should be mechanically recorded, if possible;
– the judge should explain the parties' options to them, including asking the judge or tribunal to stand down. They should be told that if they do not object at this stage of the proceedings, they will lose the right to object on this issue later on;
– if the parties decide not to proceed with the case that day, they should be informed of the likely re-listing dates; and

– the parties should be informed that they have time to reflect on the issue before deciding whether to object to the judge or tribunal continuing to hear the case. If a person is not legally represented, he might be referred to the Citizens' Advice Bureau, chief clerk or listing officer.

Bias will normally mean the judge's disqualification from further involvement in the case. If the **case has already been determined**, such bias will normally give a party **grounds for** having the decision set aside (¶9753).

3. Public hearings

Unless an exception applies (see below), tribunal hearings must be held in public and **failure to have a public hearing** will make any decision which the tribunal has made unlawful and liable to be set aside (rule 26(3) ETR). The test for deciding whether a hearing is in public is whether the public has unimpeded access to it (and not whether a member of the public is actually prevented from attending it) (*Storer v British Gas plc* [2000] IRLR 495).

> EXAMPLE In *Storer v British Gas plc*, there was no tribunal room available to deal with S's case. Instead, it was heard in the Employment Judge's office which was in an area of the building marked "private no admittance to public beyond this point" and secured by a door with a push button coded lock. The Court decided that this did not constitute a hearing in public and so set aside the tribunal's decision, and remitted the case to be re-heard by another tribunal.

> MEMO POINTS In *Storer v British Gas plc*, the Court of Appeal appeared, in passing, to suggest that **all hearings** (including pre-hearing reviews) should be held in public.

While it will generally be easier to justify a lesser step, such as **anonymisation of witnesses**, than holding a hearing in private (*AB v Ministry of Defence (Rev 1)* [2009] UKEAT 0101_09_2407), the tribunal will exercise its discretion to **hear evidence in private** in the following circumstances:
– if disclosure of information contained in the evidence would **contravene any statute** (for example, the Official Secrets Act) (rule 16(1)(a) ETR);
– if the evidence consists of information which has been communicated to a witness in confidence or which he has obtained under a **duty of confidence** (rule 16(1)(b) ETR); or
– if the evidence consists of information which if disclosed would cause substantial **injury to any undertaking** of the witness (or any undertaking in which he works) for reasons other than its effect on negotiations in respect of a trade dispute (for example, the disclosure of trade secrets) (rule 16(1)(c) ETR).

> MEMO POINTS A hearing may be held in private if a Minister of the Crown has directed a tribunal to sit in private on grounds of **national security** (rule 54(1)(a) ETR) or if the evidence relates to matters which would be against the interest of national security to be heard in public (where no order has been made by a Minister) (rule 54(2)(a) ETR). This will not be contrary to European and human rights law where a special advocate represents the interests of the claimant (*Home Office v Tariq* [2011] UKSC 35). However, there is no absolute rule that requires the gist of the allegations (i.e. sufficient information about the allegations to enable an effective challenge) to be given. Art 6 of the European Convention of Human Rights only requires such disclosure in cases involving the liberty of the subject (i.e. in criminal proceedings and not in cases involving employment claims).

An **application** for a hearing to be held in private will normally be made at the commencement of the hearing or during the hearing if the need arises in respect of a particular witness.

If a tribunal does sit in private, it has to decide **who should be allowed to attend** the hearing. Obviously, the members of the tribunal, the tribunal staff, the parties and their representatives, and the witness giving evidence at the time will have to be present, but more difficult questions arise in relation to, for example, a party's spouse whom that party wishes to be in attendance. The tribunal will decide whether there is any need for that person to be there (for example, if their assistance is required in presenting a case) and whether any prejudice would be caused by their presence.

Where the specific rules discussed above do not apply, a tribunal cannot use its **general power to regulate its own procedure** (rule 10(1) ETR) to sit in private (*R v Southampton Industrial Tribunal, ex parte INS Newsgroup Ltd and Express Newspapers plc* [1995] IRLR 247, EAT), and the parties' and witnesses' only recourse is an application for a restricted reporting order, where such orders are available (¶9583).

> EXAMPLE In *R v Southampton Industrial Tribunal, ex parte INS Newsgroup Ltd and Express Newspapers plc*, allegations of indecent assault were raised. The tribunal had made a restricted reporting order which had allegedly been breached by a newspaper. The tribunal then made an order excluding the public and the press at certain stages in the proceedings when "salacious or sensitive" evidence was to be read. It did so under its general power to regulate its own procedure. The EAT held that this was not a legitimate use of that power.

4. Listing the case for hearing

9623 The President of the Employment Tribunals, Vice-President, or a regional Employment Judge will decide when and where the hearing of the claim should take place (rule 27(1) ETR). Unless they consent to shorter notice, the parties must normally be given at least 14 days' notice of the hearing date (rule 14(4) ETR). The **notice of hearing** will also set out information about:
a. attending the hearing;
b. where the case will be heard, the date and the time of the hearing;
c. the calling of witnesses and the bringing of documents; and
d. the opportunity to be represented by another person or to make written representations.

The tribunal normally lists more cases on each day than could actually be heard in the expectation that many will settle prior to the hearing. If too few settle, some cases may have to be removed from the list shortly before the hearing date, start later than the allocated time, or even be postponed on the day itself.

Time estimate

9624 Cases are **normally listed** for hearing for a single day. If a party believes that the case will take **more than 1 day** because of the number of witnesses or the amount of legal argument involved, they must notify the tribunal beforehand, preferably having agreed a time estimate with the other party. Often this is dealt with at the pre-hearing review, if there is one.

If no estimate is given (or if the case takes longer than expected) and the case is **not completed** in the time allotted, it is not normally possible to continue the case on the following day, as the lay members (and sometimes the judge) are part-time. The case will be **adjourned** to a later date that is convenient to all those involved, resulting in a potential **delay** of several weeks or months, which may make it more difficult to deal with the evidence in a coherent way.

Postponement

9625 In many cases, the tribunal initially sends out a notice of hearing without consulting the parties as to convenient dates, although many tribunals now send out a pre-listing questionnaire in which they ask the parties to provide time estimates for the hearing. In cases where finding a date convenient to all concerned is likely to be difficult, the tribunal often gives an indication of the period during which it intends to hold the hearing and asks the parties to submit a list of dates within that period which would not be suitable.

If a party **requests** a postponement of the hearing date **due to illness**, the onus is on him to prove that his inability to attend is genuine and that a postponement is necessary (*Teinaz v London Borough of Wandsworth* [2002] IRLR 721, CA; *Andreou v Lord Chancellor's Department* [2002] IRLR 728, CA). If a claimant receives **medical advice** informing him **not to attend a tribunal hearing**, then he cannot be expected to attend to prove he is unable to attend (*Teinaz v London Borough of Wandsworth*, above). However, if a claimant simply receives **medical advice** informing him **not to attend work**, then it does not automatically follow that he is unable to attend a tribunal hearing (*Andreou v Lord Chancellor's Department*, above).

9626 Unless there are exceptional circumstances, requests for postponements **must be made** in writing within 14 days of the date of the notice of hearing. It is important, therefore, as soon as the notice of hearing is received, that the party or his representative confirms the availability of all potential witnesses on the date allocated.

A judge has a wide **discretion** to postpone the day or time fixed for a hearing (rule 10(2)(m) ETR), especially where this will allow the parties to pursue efforts towards conciliation. In any event, if the parties are subject to a statutory fixed period of conciliation, the hearing must be postponed until after the conciliation period has ended (¶9219). The judge's duty is to do as he thinks best in the interest of justice in each individual case (*Carter v Credit Change Ltd* [1979] IRLR 361, CA). He also has to take into account the Human Rights Act (in particular, the right to a fair trial) (Human Rights Act 1998).

Before deciding on a request for a postponement, the tribunal normally gives each party the opportunity to make **representations** (orally or in writing) as to why the hearing should or should not be postponed.

If the tribunal grants a postponement on the application of a party, it can make an order in respect of **costs or preparation time** in favour of or against (depending on the circumstances) the party requesting the postponement (rules 40(1), 44(1) ETR).

EXAMPLE In *London Fire and Civil Defence Authority v Samuels* [2000] UKEAT 450_00_2206, a directions hearing was held at which the main hearing was listed for 14-18 August. The employer's barrister was unaware that a key witness was unavailable on those dates (he therefore raised no objection). The employer's subsequent request for a postponement was refused as the barrister should have had available dates at the directions hearing and the key witness would not be greatly inconvenienced by having to attend. The interests of justice/administrative efficiency in bringing the matter to a hearing were also taken into account.

Pending decisions by other courts Employment disputes can give rise to cases not only in the tribunal but also in the High Court and county court, and there will often be a significant degree of **overlap** between such cases. For example, a dismissal could give rise to an unfair dismissal case in the tribunal but also to a wrongful dismissal (breach of contract) case in the High Court or county court (where, for example, the employee's loss exceeds the £25,000 limit on contractual claims in the tribunals). Although the legal remedies sought are different, many of the facts to be considered will be the same. Tribunals will, therefore, often be asked to postpone the main tribunal hearing (also referred to as "to stay proceedings") until after the High Court (or county court) has made its decision in any related case.

9628

When faced with such an application, the tribunal will consider **factors** such as:
– the delay which will inevitably result;
– the degree of overlap between the issues in the two sets of proceedings;
– the complexity of the issues;
– the nature of the evidence;
– the sums being claimed in each case; and
– the legal principle of "res judicata" (¶9631).

It may be **undesirable** for the tribunal **to deal** with the case before the High Court (or county court) for the following reasons:
– the rules of evidence in the High Court are much stricter and the procedures are more formal (a High Court judge could, therefore, be forced to accept a finding of fact by a tribunal which it would not have been appropriate for him to have made applying the stricter rules of evidence);
– the High Court claim will often involve much larger sums than could be awarded by the employment tribunal;
– the High Court claim may also involve counterclaims by the employer which could not be made in the employment tribunal; and
– the successful party in the High Court would be able to recover his costs from his opponent, which is less likely to be the case in the tribunal.

9629

The tribunal may, therefore, postpone the main hearing (or any preliminary hearing dealing with overlapping factual issues) until after concurrent High Court or county court proceedings, particularly if the claimant indicates that he has only issued his tribunal proceedings in order to comply with the applicable time limit for tribunal claims. Postponement of tribunal proceedings can only be ordered where **concurrent proceedings have been issued**. Postponement will not be ordered where the claimant has **only stated an intention to pursue a claim(s)** in the High Court, for example by sending the respondent a letter before action together with draft particulars of claim (*Halstead v Paymentshield Group Holdings Ltd* [2012] EWCA Civ 524).

Similar consideration will apply where there are concurrent proceedings in **foreign jurisdictions** or **criminal proceedings**.

> EXAMPLE In *Mindimaxnox LLP v Gover and anor* [2010] UKEAT 0225_10_0712, the EAT overturned the tribunal's decision not to stay tribunal proceedings after considering the following factors in what was essentially a bonus claim:
> – the complexity of the factual and legal issues as the High Court is the more appropriate forum for more complex issues;
> – the undesirability of tribunal decisions made in advance of High Court decisions as the High Court Judge will find it difficult not to be bound by the findings;
> – the extent of overlap as where there is considerable overlap it is appropriate to cede to the High Court; and
> – the sums being claimed in each case as where the claim is much very smaller in the tribunal it is appropriate to determine the High Court claim first.
> The EAT concluded that it would give satisfaction for the central issues here, in terms at least of money, and some of the issues relating to share ownership, to be determined once in the High Court.

9630 **With regard to dismissal claims in connection with industrial action** Where a claimant alleges that he has been dismissed for participation in official industrial action and court proceedings are taking place to determine whether or not that industrial action is covered by the protections given by trade union legislation, the tribunal may adjourn the application until those court proceedings have been concluded (rule 10(2) ETR).

Res judicata

9631 In simple terms, res judicata (sometimes referred to as "issue estoppel") **means** that once an issue has been decided in one court it should not be reopened in another court.

Res judicata may **be applied** where:
– tribunal or court **makes a decision** on the facts of a case after hearing the evidence and such a finding could bind another court who had to **determine similar issues** in an overlapping case. This does not apply where the court or tribunal in the earlier proceedings has **exceeded its jurisdiction** in what they have been asked to determine and expressed views on other matters and such matters can be the subject of future claims (*Foster v Bon Groundwork Ltd* [2012] EWCA Civ 252). This has also not prevented an employee from bringing fresh proceedings for equal pay, where the same employee has previously made a complaint against the same employer covering the same period of time, but in the new complaint the employee cites a **new comparator** (*Bainbridge and ors v Redcar & Cleveland Borough Council (No. 2)* [2007] IRLR 494, EAT, by a 2-1 majority);
– a claimant **withdraws** his claim before it is decided **such that it is dismissed**. In such circumstances he may be prevented from bringing a fresh claim based on the same facts ("cause of action estoppel"), depending on the reason for the withdrawal, which the tribunal should ascertain (*Ako v Rothschild Asset Management Ltd* [2002] IRLR 348, CA). The reasons for the withdrawal must be made clear (*London Borough of Enfield v Sivanandan* [2005] EWCA Civ 10). As a result, where a party seeks to withdraw all or part of a claim, the other party will generally be entitled to have the proceedings dismissed (which will prevent any fresh claims based on the same facts), unless there is a good reason for the withdrawal (rule 25(4) ETR as amended by SI 2008/3240; *Verdin v Harrods Ltd* [2006] IRLR 437, EAT). In this case it was held that there was a good reason and the claimant was allowed to withdraw part of her claim without it being dismissed so that she could issue proceedings for breach of contract in the High Court, which would enable her to recover damages in excess of £25,000 (as tribunals can only award up to £25,000 for breach of contract) if the tribunal rejected her claim that her employer's failure to pay her in lieu of notice was due to victimisation; and

– further to the parties agreeing in writing to an Acas-conciliated settlement with regard to a claim, the tribunal has **automatically dismissed** the claim. This will occur within 28 days of receiving written notification of the settlement terms and of the withdrawal (rule 25A ETR as inserted by SI 2008/3240).

Once a claim is dismissed, a claimant may not commence a further claim based on the same or substantially the same cause of action, unless the decision to dismiss is later reversed on review or appeal (rule 25(4) ETR as amended by SI 2008/3240). Whether this will be allowed will depend on whether there is a good reason to do so.

> EXAMPLE
> 1. In *London Borough of Enfield v Sivanandan*, the Court of Appeal was satisfied that the claimant's breach of contract claim in the tribunal had been struck out with her other claims (of race and sex discrimination, victimisation, and unfair dismissal) on the grounds that they were scandalous, vexatious and with no reasonable prospect of success. As a result, her attempt to re-litigate it in the High Court on the basis that her breach of contract claim had been withdrawn from the tribunal to allow her to pursue the civil proceedings (where the amount that could be awarded was not limited to £25,000) failed.
> 2. In *Fraser v HLMAD Ltd* [2006] IRLR 687, CA, the Court of Appeal held that the claimant, who had successfully pursued a wrongful dismissal claim in the employment tribunal, could not bring proceedings in the High Court to recover any excess damages over the tribunal limit of £25,000 for wrongful dismissal awards. His claim in the High Court was not held to be a separate action so that once the tribunal gave its final judgment on the wrongful dismissal claim before it, the cause of action for wrongful dismissal "merged" into the tribunal's judgment and was extinguished. This is so even though the claimant had issued proceedings in the High Court for the recovery of any such excess and had specified in his claim form to the tribunal that he reserved the right to pursue an action in the High Court for this purpose.

9632 **Reserving right to bring proceedings elsewhere** If the claimant has reserved the right to bring proceedings in a different court, he may be allowed to do so (*Sajid v Sussex Muslim Society* [2002] IRLR 113, CA).

5. Preparation for the hearing

9633 The tribunal will usually give directions on matters such as the exchange of witness statements and preparation of bundles of documents (¶9560). Even if it has not done so, it is clearly in the interests of both the parties and the tribunal that such matters should be addressed.

9634 **Bundle of documents** At the hearing, documents should be presented in a way which makes them easy to find and identify, particularly if they are numerous. The parties should agree a bundle of documents **containing** all correspondence and other documents on which they intend to rely at the hearing. The bundle should be in chronological order and have numbered pages.

If there is any dispute as to the **admissibility or authenticity** of any document, then (unless it can be dealt with at a case management discussion or pre-hearing review) such documents should still be included in the bundle but the issue should be raised at the beginning of the hearing.

Where a full tribunal is hearing the claim, **at least six copies** of the bundle should be prepared – three for the tribunal, one for each party and one for use by witnesses as they give evidence. The party preparing the bundle (which will usually be the claimant or his representative) should ensure that all the photocopies in the bundle are legible, in a logical order (usually chronological) and numbered. It is helpful to include an **index** at the beginning of the bundle identifying the page numbers of each document.

9635 **Witness statements** Witness statements may be based on statements produced at an earlier stage in the dispute, or as part of a disciplinary process (see ¶9170 for information as to their preparation, content and format). Usually tribunals will order that there should be simultaneous exchange of witness statements a certain number of days prior to the hearing and that no further witnesses statements may be relied upon at the hearing without the tribunal's permission. As with bundles of documents, at least six copies of witness statements should be prepared.

Unless the employment judge or tribunal otherwise directs, witness statements are **taken as read** at the hearing instead of requiring witnesses to attend to give evidence (SI 2012/468).

9636 Tribunals should exercise their discretion in relation to **confidential witness statements** and order disclosure in an anonymised and redacted form if necessary (*Asda Stores Ltd v Thompson* [2001] UKEAT 1096_01_1110). In exercising its discretion, a tribunal will consider the risk of reprisals, any promise of confidentiality and whether the disclosure of the statements and their origin are necessary for the fair disposal of the case.

9637 **Written representations** Parties can submit written representations to be considered at the hearing. If they wish to do so they should send them to the Secretary at least 7 days before the hearing and copy them to the other parties at the same time (rule 14(5) ETR). This will generally happen if a party does **not intend to appear** at the hearing. The tribunal will have to decide **how much weight** to attach to such representations. They will not normally be given as much weight as evidence which has been given orally and tested by cross-examination.

Occasionally, a tribunal will direct that the parties supply written submissions before the hearing. However, if it does so, the tribunal must wait to receive written submissions from both parties before making its decision, particularly if there was no delay in the lodging of the submissions by either party (*Mayor and Burgesses of London Borough of Haringey v Akpan* [2001] UKEAT 974_00_1601).

6. Representation

9640 A party can present his case in person or be represented by a barrister or solicitor, a trade union representative or employers' association representative, or by any other person of his choice (s 6(1) Employment Tribunals Act 1996). Most parties are represented at hearings (statistics suggest that respondents are more likely to be legally represented than claimants). See ¶9130 for details on the availability of legal advice.

9641 A tribunal has no power to interfere with a party's **choice of representative** and **cannot exclude** a representative, although it does have power to control the way in which a representative conducts a case before it (*Bache v Essex County Council* [2000] EWCA Civ 3, confirmed in *Dispatch Management Services (UK) Ltd v Douglas* [2001] UKEAT 902_01_0412; rules 10(1), 27(1) ETR).

> MEMO POINTS It should be noted that a tribunal can make a **wasted costs order** against a party's representative in certain circumstances (¶9711).

9642 If a party is **unrepresented** (and particularly if his opponent is represented), the tribunal will attempt to ensure that he is not prejudiced as a result. The judge cannot present a party's case for him or tell him what evidence to call, but the judge will try to explain the procedure and the relevant law, and assist him in presenting his case properly. For example, if an unrepresented party is giving evidence, a judge may adopt a more interventionist approach by asking questions to elicit the evidence which the party wishes to put before the tribunal.

7. The hearing itself

Form

9645 Tribunal procedure is designed to be relatively **informal**. A tribunal has a **wide discretion** as to how the proceedings should be conducted, and can conduct the hearing in such a way as it considers most appropriate for the clarification of the issues before it and for the just handling of the proceedings, making such enquiries of the people appearing before it and the witnesses as it considers appropriate (rule 10(1) ETR; *Hart v English Heritage (Historic Buildings and Monuments Commission for England)* [2006] UKEAT 0055_06_2302). Tribunals are specifically required to avoid formality as far as is appropriate, and are not bound by the strict rules of evidence which are applied in court (so that for example, a more relaxed approach is taken to hearsay evidence (¶9667)). Parties, their representatives and witnesses remain seated while addressing the tribunal or giving evidence.

Some degree of **structure** is, of course, necessary to ensure that the proceedings are dealt with efficiently and to this extent the procedure is similar to that in court. The more complicated a case, the more likely it is that a greater degree of formality will be introduced to ensure that all the issues are properly explored and that the case is properly understood.

Each party may give evidence, call and question witnesses, and address the tribunal (rule 27(2) ETR). The judge is obliged to make notes of the evidence and representations put forward during the hearing. There is no right to make any **opening statement**, but the party going first will often, particularly in more complicated cases, give the tribunal a brief outline of his case before calling the first witness. Whether or not this is allowed is within the discretion of the judge.

9646

In England and Wales (though not in Scotland), **witnesses** are allowed to be present in the tribunal room before they give their evidence. A party may, however, ask the tribunal to exclude any witness prior to giving his evidence.

9647

The tribunal may require witnesses to give evidence on oath or by affirming (rule 27(3) ETR). When witnesses are giving their evidence, they should address the tribunal even though the questions are being put by a party or his representative. The tribunal judge should be addressed as Sir or Madam.

Failure to attend

Where a party fails to attend the hearing and is not represented, the tribunal has to decide whether to dismiss the application, dispose of it in the absence of either the claimant or the respondent or adjourn the hearing to a later date (rule 27(5) ETR). Before making its decision, however, the **tribunal must consider**:
– the claim/response submitted by the absent party, and any written representations or answers (rule 27(6) ETR); and
– any information available to it as to the reason for non-attendance and whether the absent party had intended to appear.

9648

In doing so, the tribunal must be **pro-active in making enquiries** to try to ascertain why the absent party has not attended and if they had intended to appear (*Cooke v Glenrose Fish Co.* [2004] IRLR 866, EAT). In most cases this means that the tribunal should telephone the absent party or at the very least consider whether it is appropriate to do so. Further, enquiries should be made of the other party as to any news they may have and whether they knew if the absent party had intended to come and, consequently, whether it was possible that the absence was due to the absent party being delayed or having forgotten the matter.

In making its decision, the **tribunal must explain its reasons** as to why it has taken the decision to dismiss, dispose of, or adjourn the application (*Robinson v Home Office* [2001] UKEAT 533_01_1909). Failure to do so will result in a breach of the right to a fair trial under the Human Rights Act. However, the tribunal is not under a duty to be satisfied that the respondent has established a good defence to the claim being brought by a non-attending claimant before dismissing such a claim (*Roberts v Skelmersdale College* [2004] IRLR 69, CA).

A party who is unable to attend for whatever reason, or who is going to be late, should, therefore, make every effort to contact the tribunal before the time appointed for the hearing in order to explain his absence.

Normally, the tribunal clerk will try and contact the absent party to find out whether or not he **intends to appear**. If the party does intend to appear and is able to get to the tribunal within a reasonable time, the tribunal may be prepared to **give him time** to get there (particularly if it has other cases which it may deal with in the meantime). Alternatively, if he does

9649

intend to appear but is unable to get there on that day and has a **good reason**, the appropriate decision for the tribunal is to **adjourn** to a later date.

In either case, if the delay results in the case not being finished on that day, it is likely that the tribunal will make an order for **costs or preparation time** against the absent or late party, unless he can put forward a good reason (rules 40(4), 44(4) ETR).

9650 If the clerk finds that the absent party **does not intend to appear**, the tribunal will normally dismiss the case (if the party in question is the claimant) or deal with the case in the absence of that party (either the claimant or the respondent). In either case, it is likely that a **costs or preparation time order** will be awarded against the absent party, although in the case of an absent respondent, a costs or preparation time award is only likely if the claimant is successful in the case.

9651 If **no contact** can be made or if the tribunal nonetheless continues with the hearing and dismisses the case or proceeds with it in the absence of a party, the absent party is entitled to apply to the tribunal for a **review** of the tribunal's decision, which may be successful if he had a good reason for not attending the hearing (¶¶9718+).

Initial matters

9655 There are often a number of "**housekeeping**" points to be dealt with at the start of a hearing, including any of the following applications:
– for a restricted reporting order;
– for the hearing to be held in private;
– to amend the claim/response;
– with regard to disputed documents; or
– for permission to call witnesses whose evidence has not been exchanged in accordance with directions.

The judge may also give, or be requested to give, **guidance** as to how he intends to deal with different issues. For example, it is common practice in **unfair dismissal** cases for liability to be dealt with first and for the tribunal then to hear evidence in relation to compensation and other remedies only if the claimant is found to have been unfairly dismissed. There may also be questions as to whether any allegation that a claimant has contributed to his dismissal should be dealt with as part of the main evidence on the dismissal or as part of the subsequent determination of remedy. It is useful for all concerned to know exactly how the tribunal wishes to deal with these matters at the outset so that evidence can be led and representations made at the appropriate time.

Who goes first?

9656 The **general rule** is that the party who has the burden of proving his case should present his case first (*Gill v Harold Andrews Sheepbridge Ltd* [1974] IRLR 109, NIRC). This is, however, subject to the tribunal's discretion, and it may decide that it is more convenient to take the evidence in a different order.

In **unfair dismissal cases**, this will depend on whether or not the dismissal is admitted. If the respondent does **not admit dismissing** the employee (which most often arises in constructive dismissal cases), the claimant will have to present his case first as he must prove the dismissal. If the respondent **does admit** that the claimant was dismissed then, since the respondent must prove the reason for the dismissal, the respondent will go first. In most unfair dismissal cases, therefore, the employer's case is presented first.

In **discrimination cases**, once the claimant has established a prima facie case (i.e. a case to be answered), the burden of proving that the actions taken were not discriminatory shifts to the respondent. The question of who goes first is, therefore, likely to depend on whether the tribunal decides after reviewing the claim and the response that a prima facie case exists before any evidence is heard.

Evidence

The presentation of evidence at the main hearing and the rules relating to admissibility of evidence are discussed below.

9660

> MEMO POINTS Judicial proceedings **immunity** (i.e. where an individual cannot face proceedings in relation to witness evidence that they have given, save in relation to prosecution for perjury, civil proceedings for malicious prosecution, or an order for costs) applies to witnesses in respect of all types of **discrimination** claims, including **victimisation** claims (*Parmar v East Leicester Medical Practice* [2010] UKEAT 0022_10_0511). In this case, the claimant, P, had brought a claim against his employer for race discrimination. His claim was unsuccessful but in the course of proceedings witness evidence was produced that, according to P, contained untruths created solely because of his protected act of bringing a race discrimination claim. P claimed that this amounted to victimisation. The primary issue was whether or not the witnesses (most of whom were partners in a medical practice, which was the named respondent) were protected by judicial proceedings immunity. The EAT held that they were: this was a matter of public interest and although it may sometimes cause injustice, there were other ways of holding witnesses to account (such as costs awards and criminal prosecutions for perjury).

Presentation Each party will call the witnesses that he believes can produce the evidence to support his case. Although a contrary view has been expressed in some cases, the general view is that it is for a party or his representative to decide the **order** in which he puts forward his witnesses (*Barnes v BPC (Business Forms) Ltd* [1975] IRLR 313, QBD).

9661

It is up to the parties to ensure that **all relevant evidence** is put before the tribunal. The tribunal does not have any obligation to point out any gaps in the evidence or make any further investigation to try and fill them (*Mensah v East Herts NHS Trust* [1998] IRLR 531, CA), although it may try to be helpful, particularly where a party is unrepresented.

Each witness (including the parties themselves if giving evidence) will give their evidence. The tribunal usually simply asks the witness to confirm that it is his **written statement** and that he has signed it and accepted it as his evidence, in which case the tribunal members will read the statements themselves.

9662

Where a written statement is read, the tribunal normally allows the party presenting the case (or his representative) to ask **further questions** of the witness either as he proceeds with the statement or after it has been read, for example to deal with matters raised by the other parties' statements. It is sensible, however, to check with the tribunal at the beginning of the hearing as to how it wishes to handle this. The tribunal members will often ask questions of their own during or after the reading.

A party (or his representative) must not ask leading questions of his own witnesses. A **leading question** is one which suggests its own answer (and usually can be answered simply yes or no). For example, "When you went into the room, did you see Fred taking money from the till?" is a leading question, whereas "When you went into the room, did you see anyone there and, if so, what were they doing?" is not. Leading questions asked in relation to non-controversial matters, such as "Are you Fred Smith?", "Did you work for the respondent?" will not normally be objected to.

Once a witness has completed his evidence (and been asked any additional questions by the party who has called him or his representative), that witness is **cross-examined** by the other party or his representative. Cross-examination involves questioning the witness about any parts of his evidence which are disputed. It will also involve putting to the witness the contrary version of events which the other party wishes to prove. It is important in cross-examination that any aspect of a witness' evidence which is disputed is put to him and tested. If it is not, the tribunal may find that the evidence is not disputed. **Leading questions** are allowed in cross-examination.

9663

Once the first party's witnesses have given evidence and been cross-examined, the same process is repeated with all the witnesses for the other party.

If a party chooses not to call a witness, the other party cannot insist that he is called so that they can cross-examine the witness (*Power v Greater Manchester Police Authority* [2010] UKEAT

0087_10_2904). In this case, a claimant in a discrimination claim complained that the respondent's failure to call a witness at a hearing was a breach of his right to a fair trial under the Human Rights Act, because he was not able to cross-examine her. The EAT held that the right to cross-examine witnesses applies in criminal cases and not to employment tribunal claims. However, the EAT pointed out that if a respondent chooses not to call a witness who may be able to give evidence about, for example, the reason for dismissal, then that will have implications for the credibility of the respondent's case, and may make it more difficult for a respondent to establish, for example, a non-discriminatory reason for its actions.

MEMO POINTS It is, of course, open to a party to seek a witness order to require a witness to give evidence (¶¶9553+).

9664 Sometimes, as a matter of convenience, it may be necessary to depart from this sequence. For example, if a witness is, for good reason, only able to attend the hearing at a certain time then it may be necessary for that witness' evidence to be heard **out of sequence**.

9665 Parties should take care to ensure that they bring out from each witness all the relevant information which that witness has while they are giving evidence as the tribunal will be reluctant to allow a party to **recall a witness** later without good reason.

9666 **Rules** Tribunals are **not bound** by the strict rules of evidence applied in the civil courts, although those rules are not to be completely disregarded. These rules have developed in order to ensure fairness and consistency in the way in which evidence is dealt with and so tribunals do follow the basic principles.

It is open to a tribunal in exercising its case management powers to keep the **evidence and cross-examination within reasonable bounds**, for example, it can use its discretion to exclude evidence which, although strictly relevant, is of peripheral relevance or is, for instance, repetitive (*Digby v East Cambridgeshire District Council* [2007] IRLR 585, EAT). However, it must exercise its discretion judiciously and it must not exclude evidence which is material to the claim and any decision to do so will be perverse.

EXAMPLE In *Digby v East Cambridgeshire District Council*, the tribunal excluded evidence relating to the circumstances surrounding the issue of a final warning in an unfair dismissal claim. As the final warning had been highly material to the claimant's subsequent dismissal, the claimant had been effectively prevented from advancing his case for unfair dismissal and the tribunal's exercise of its discretion in excluding the evidence was perverse. A substantive hearing before a fresh tribunal was ordered.

9667 A tribunal may admit "hearsay evidence" (which would not normally be admitted in civil courts), unless it considers that doing so could adversely affect its ability to reach a proper decision in the case (*Coral Squash Club Ltd v Matthews* [1979] IRLR 390, EAT). **Hearsay evidence** is evidence given by someone who does not have direct knowledge of the facts which he is putting forward but was told of them by someone else. For example, "I saw Fred hit Jim" is not hearsay evidence but "Jim told me that Fred hit him" is.

9668 Tribunals are also able to take a less restrictive approach to what is known as "**similar fact evidence**". In a criminal court, it will not normally be admissible to try and prove that someone did something on a particular occasion by leading evidence to show that he has done the same thing on a previous occasion. A tribunal is entitled to admit such evidence, although it will consider what weight should be attached to it (*Docherty v Reddy* [1977] ICR 365, EAT).

9669 The tribunal is also entitled to consider **confessions or admissions** made in circumstances which would make them inadmissible in criminal proceedings (*Dhaliwal v British Airways Board* [1985] ICR 513, EAT), but will, of course, have to have regard to the right to a fair trial under the Human Rights Act.

9670 Communications which are "**without prejudice**" (¶9230) are privileged from disclosure and so inadmissible in tribunal proceedings in the same way as in any other court.

A covert recording of disciplinary and internal appeal hearings by an employee may be admissible in tribunal hearings (*Dogherty v Chairman and Governors of Amwell View School* [2007] ICR 135, EAT). However, this cannot extend to any discussions and deliberations the disciplinary panel have with regard to the merits of the case in private and any such secret recording cannot be used.

Submissions of no case to answer

As the party bearing the formal burden of proving his case normally presents his evidence first, it sometimes becomes clear **at the end of the first party's case** that it has no prospect of success. The other party may make a submission that there is no case to answer, i.e. that the first party has not put forward any evidence which would enable the tribunal to find in his favour. If the tribunal agrees, it will dismiss the case without the need for the other party to present his case. Alternatively, where a case is clearly misconceived (i.e. has no reasonable prospects of success), the tribunal may exercise its power to **strike out** (¶9573).

However, the use of submissions of no case to answer is not encouraged and tribunals will approach such an application with caution. The **preferred approach** is to hear from both sides before making a decision and even where the onus of proof lies on the applicant, as in discrimination cases, it will only be in "exceptional or frivolous" cases that it will be right for a tribunal to stop a case at "half-time" (*Ridley v GEC Machines Ltd* [1977] 13 ITR 195, EAT; *Clark v Watford Borough Council* [1999] UKEAT 43_99_1404, confirmed by *Logan v Commissioners of Customs and Excise* [2004] IRLR 63, CA; *Boulding v Land Securities Trillium (Media Service) Ltd* [2006] UKEAT 0023_06_0305).

In **unfair dismissal** cases where the **dismissal is admitted** and the respondent goes first, the preferred view is that it is not appropriate for the case to be determined at the end of the respondent's case without hearing from the claimant (*Hackney London Borough Council v Usher* [1996] UKEAT 1143_95_1912). This is partly because there is not strictly any burden of proof on any party in unfair dismissal cases, and also because there may be questions of contributory fault which have to be determined (which can only be done after hearing evidence from the claimant).

However, where the dismissal is **not admitted**, the claimant goes first, and if at the end of his case it is clear that there is no evidence to support the contention that he was dismissed, a submission of no case to answer may be appropriate and successful.

Final submissions

After both parties have presented their evidence, each party (or his representative) may put forward submissions to the tribunal, **summarising** the evidence in support of his case, **highlighting** the perceived weaknesses in the other side's case, referring the tribunal to the appropriate law and explaining how (in his view) it should be applied to the facts of the case.

Such submissions are usually put forward **orally at the hearing**. The tribunal may ask the parties to put forward **written submissions** for consideration subsequently if they consent (*London Borough of Barking & Dagenham v Oguoko* [1999] UKEAT 819_98_2709). Written submissions are submitted to the tribunal, which must serve a copy on the other party. If the receiving party has any comments to make on the other party's submissions, he should send those comments to the tribunal within a stated period. **Comments in reply** (to oral or written submissions) are limited to correcting factual errors in the submissions or replying to new points of law raised in the other side's submissions. It is not an opportunity to make good any deficiencies in that party's own original submissions. If a party **fails to comment**, the tribunal will assume that he has no further comment to make and will make its decision on the basis of the submissions which it has received. A party who had **no opportunity to comment** is entitled to apply for a review of the decision and to state what further comments he would have made had he been given that opportunity.

IV. Decision

1. Points of procedure

9690 Decisions are **taken by** majority with each of the three tribunal members having one vote (rule 28(4) ETR). It is, therefore, quite legitimate for the lay members to outvote the legally qualified judge. Although this does sometimes happen, **most decisions are unanimous**. If only a judge and one lay member are sitting, the judge has a **casting vote**.

The Court of Appeal has given **guidance** on tribunals **giving majority judgments** (*Anglia Home Improvements v Kelly* [2005] ICR 242, CA). The Court commented that it is undesirable, on the whole, for tribunals to reach split decisions although it accepted that in some cases it is inevitable. Tribunals should, if it is possible to do so, make all efforts to reach an unanimous decision and to this end should allow themselves more time to make the decision by reserving the decision rather than giving it extempore (i.e. at the time). Extempore decisions of majority judgments were also criticised in that they may not provide an adequate set of extended reasons (as happened in this case). Further, practically speaking, where a tribunal cannot agree, it was preferable, in general, for the judge to reserve the decision so that it could be written up and circulated to the lay members, giving them not just the opportunity to see that their views were correctly expressed but also the opportunity to reflect on the grounds of disagreement, especially where they are in disagreement with the judge as to the outcome of the case.

9691 **Form** The decision must be recorded in writing and signed by the judge (rule 29(1) ETR). As well as giving its decision (for example, whether or not the claimant has been unfairly dismissed), the tribunal will also give **written reasons** for its decision provided (rule 30(3) ETR):
– a party makes a written request for extended reasons within 14 days of the date on which the judgment is sent to the parties (although this time limit can be extended where the tribunal considers it just and equitable to do so); or
– they have been requested by the EAT.

Written reasons must be signed by the judge, and the Secretary will send a copy of them to all the parties in the proceedings (rule 30(2), (4) ETR). In practice, the decision and the reasons will generally be given in the same document but this need not be the case.

Written reasons provided must also include a **statement of any compensation** or payment awarded, and a breakdown or description of its **calculation**. Where a decision on compensation has been deferred to a later hearing, the written reasons for the decision on the merits and the statement setting out the tribunal's reasoning in relation to compensation may be in different documents. As well as the statement of compensation, written reasons will go into detail regarding the evidence, the tribunal's analysis of it and the application of the law. It is essential that written reasons should be requested in any case where an **appeal** is being considered. A notice of appeal can only be lodged after written reasons have been given.

9692 **Timing** In many cases, the judge announces the tribunal's decision **at the end of the hearing**, together with the tribunal's reasons. The practice is for these to be tape recorded as the judge is delivering them. They are later typed up and sent out to the parties if a request is made for written reasons.

Alternatively, perhaps because of a shortage of time, the judge only announces the tribunal's decision (i.e. which side has won) at the end of the hearing. The reasons are then prepared separately and sent out to the parties **at a later date**.

In some cases, the tribunal may **reserve its decision**. This means that the parties will not be notified of the outcome of the case on the day of the hearing. The decision and the reasons will be prepared, perhaps after further deliberation by the tribunal at a later date, and sent out **in due course** to the parties. This is likely to happen in more complicated cases or where there is insufficient time at the end of the hearing for the tribunal to complete its deliberations and deliver its decision.

9693 The right to appeal a decision of an employment tribunal as set out by statute is confined to questions of law and consequently the **unsafeness of a decision due to the delay** cannot be an independent ground of appeal and it is not possible to equate unsafeness of the decision with the loss of the right to a fair trial as a matter of fact (*Bangs v Connex South Eastern Ltd* [2005] IRLR 389, CA, followed in *Wandsworth Borough Council v Warner* [2005] UKEAT 0671_04_0607). The ground of appeal must be whether the delay made the decision unsafe **on the grounds of perversity** (i.e. as a result of the delay the decision was one which no reasonable tribunal properly directing itself under law would have reached). This is often extremely difficult to establish (¶9749).

However, in exceptional cases, unreasonable delay may be treated as a serious procedural error or material irregularity giving rise to a **question of law "in the proceedings before the tribunal"**, for example if this resulted in the appellant being deprived of the substance of his right to a fair trial (under Art 6 of the European Convention on Human Rights (incorporated into domestic law by the Human Rights Act 1998)) and as a result it would be unfair or unjust to allow the delayed decision to stand. The Court commented that this test was, on the one hand, less stringent than the perversity ground of appeal, but it was, on the other hand, more stringent than the previous "unsafe" decision test formulated and applied by the EAT (*Kwamin v Abbey National plc; Birmingham City Council v Mtize; Martin v London Borough of Southwark; Connex South Eastern Ltd v Bangs* [2004] IRLR 516, EAT (overturned by CA decision)) as it required the existence of a question of law.

9695 **Content** A tribunal decision consists principally of two parts. It first sets out the tribunal's **findings of fact**, followed by the tribunal's **application of the law** to those facts. It may also summarise the arguments put by each side.

9696 **Written reasons** must set out the issues identified as being relevant to the claim, which issues (if any) were not determined and why, findings of fact relevant to the issues which have been determined, a concise statement of the applicable law, and how the relevant findings of fact and applicable law have been analysed by the tribunal in order to determine the issues (rule 30(6) ETR). Failure to comply could amount to an error of law (*Greenwood v NWF Retail* [2011] UKEAT 0409_09_0218). In particular, the tribunal must provide **sufficient information** to enable the parties to understand why they have won or lost (*Meek v City of Birmingham District Council* [1987] IRLR 250, CA), and to enable the EAT or the Court of Appeal in any subsequent appeal to understand the basis on which the tribunal has reached its decision in order to determine if any question of law arises. This will involve **identifying the evidential documents** upon which it has made its finding and explaining how it reached its decision (*Tran v Greenwich Vietnam Community* [2002] IRLR 735, CA). At the same time, however, tribunals are discouraged from being overly formal or legalistic. In **unfair dismissal cases**, the tribunal must specify what it has found to be the principal reason for the dismissal (and the facts which have led to that conclusion), and show that it has applied the correct test in deciding whether or not the employer has acted reasonably in all the circumstances. If it reduces compensation because of the employee's contributory fault, it must also specify the behaviour which it is relying on in order to make this reduction.

Where the decision has been **reached by majority**, the views of the majority and minority should be set out separately and distinctly in separate paragraphs (*Parkers Bakeries Ltd v Palmer* [1977] IRLR 215, EAT).

9698 **Registration** Once a tribunal decision and the reasons for it have been recorded in writing, they are entered by the Secretary in the register (rule 32(1) ETR). This means that the decision and reasons are open to **public inspection**. If the hearing has been held in private, only the decision (and not the reasons) is registered (rule 32(2) ETR).

> MEMO POINTS Where the case involves the alleged commission of a **sexual offence**, the identity of the alleged victim or offender is deleted from the reasons before it is registered (rule 49 ETR).

2. Remedies

9700 The remedies which the tribunal can order differ according to the type of claim, and are, therefore, discussed in the relevant chapters. A summary for the main claims is given in the table below.

Claim	Remedy	Para.
Unfair dismissal	Reinstatement	¶8680
	Re-engagement	¶8680
	Compensation	¶8570
	Interim relief	¶8700
Discrimination	Declarations	¶5738
	Recommendations	¶5760
	Compensation	¶5740
	Non-discrimination notices	¶5790
Breach of contract	Declaration	¶1740
	Compensation (subject to financial limit ¶9428)	¶1725

MEMO POINTS The Government has announced **plans to introduce** a provision for employment tribunals to levy a **financial penalty** on employers found to have breached employment rights with a discretion not to penalise inadvertent errors. This is now part of a draft bill called the Enterprise and Regulatory Reform Bill which is proceeding through Parliament. Further developments will be covered by our updating service when available.

9701 The most common remedy is **compensation**, which is an option for the tribunal in most types of case. The purpose of a compensation award is not to punish the employer but to attempt as far as possible to put the employee in the position he would have been in but for the employer's default. In the vast majority of cases, the principal element of any compensation award will be **loss of earnings**. This is likely to include (a) loss of earnings between the date of the act complained of and the tribunal hearing and (b) a sum to represent the tribunal's estimate of future loss of earnings.

An employee seeking compensation has a duty to **mitigate** his loss, i.e. he must take reasonable steps to minimise the loss which he suffers. The most obvious example is that an employee who is claiming compensation as a result of being dismissed must make reasonable efforts to find another job.

3. Recovering costs or preparation time

Costs or preparation time

9702 Tribunals are permitted to **make orders** in respect of either a party's costs in relation to a set of proceedings or the time a party (the receiving party) who is not legally represented at the main hearing has spent in preparing for the proceedings (rules 38-47 ETR).

Costs are defined as fees, charges, disbursements or expenses incurred by or on behalf of a party in relation to the proceedings. Expenses incurred by a witness in attending a tribunal to give evidence are also recoverable (rule 3(1)c ETR as inserted by SI 2012/468).

Preparation time covers time spent up to, but not including any time spent at, a main hearing by (rule 42(3) ETR):
– the receiving party or his employees in carrying out preparatory work directly relating to the proceedings; and
– the receiving party's legal or other advisers relating to the conduct of the proceedings.

Unlike the civil courts where the loser normally pays the winner's costs, the tribunal can only award orders for costs or preparation time in certain circumstances. Whether an order is made for costs or for preparation time will depend on whether the receiving party is legally represented or not. If the receiving party is **legally represented**, only a costs order can be made. If the receiving party is **not legally represented**, only a preparation time order can be made. A tribunal cannot, therefore, make both a preparation time order and a costs order in favour of the same party in the same proceedings. However, where a preparation time order has been made in favour of one party, the tribunal can make a costs order in favour of another party in the same proceedings (rule 46(1) ETR).

MEMO POINTS 1. **A person is legally represented** if they are represented by a barrister or solicitor (England and Wales), an advocate or solicitor (Scotland), or a member of the Bar of Northern Ireland or a solicitor of the Supreme Court of Northern Ireland (rule 38(5) ETR; s 71 Courts and Legal Services Act 1990).
2. In **Scotland**, the terms "costs" and "costs orders" are references to "expenses" and "orders for expenses" respectively.
3. A party who is **represented by in-house lawyers** is entitled to recover his costs in the same way as a party represented by independent solicitors (*Wiggin Alloys Ltd v Jenkins* [1981] IRLR 275, EAT).
4. The tribunal must **not pre-judge** the issue of costs: whilst a tribunal is entitled to make findings about a party's credibility or conduct in dealing with the question of liability, it should not express concluded views which seemingly anticipate arguments which may arise on the question of costs (*Oni v NHS Leicester City (formerly Leicester City Primary Care Trust)* [2012] UKEAT 0144_12_1209).

Circumstances in which order can be made A costs or preparation time order (as appropriate) can be made **against** either a claimant or a respondent where (rules 40, 44 ETR):
– costs have been incurred, allowances paid or preparation time spent as a result of a **postponement or adjournment** of a hearing or pre-hearing review on the application of a party; and/or
– a party has **not complied with** an order or practice direction made by the tribunal.

Moreover, if a party, in bringing the claim, or he or his representative in conducting the claim, has **acted vexatiously, abusively, disruptively or otherwise unreasonably**, or the bringing of or conducting of the claim has been **misconceived**, the tribunal must consider making a costs or preparation time order against him (rules 40(2), 44(2) ETR).

A claim is **misconceived** (i.e. it has no reasonable prospect of success) when it is so poor that the other side does not even have to respond to the points raised for the claim to fail. If this is the case, however late the claimant comes to this conclusion, the claimant must abandon his case and should not regard the tribunal hearing as "a free opportunity to come to court simply because the case is listed" (*Thorpe v Eaton Electrical Limited* [2004] UKEAT 0497_04_0612). In other words, a claimant cannot have his day in court if he knows he has no chance of success without the danger of a costs order being made against him of wasted time and expense. A claimant acts **vexatiously** if he brings a hopeless claim out of spite to harass his employers or for some other improper motive, rather than in order to recover compensation. This is an abuse of the procedure. **Demonstrating** that a claimant has acted vexatiously or that his claim was misconceived is not an easy task. It is not enough that the case has been lost, or that by the end of the case it becomes clear that the case was hopeless. The tribunal has to consider whether the parties should have realised prior to the hearing that the case was hopeless.

Unreasonable conduct covers a wider range of circumstances, such as bringing a case based on a lie, and behaviour by a party or his representative which unnecessarily extends the length of the hearing or the cost to the other party. Such conduct may occur either before or during the hearing. It may also take place in the context of settlement negotiations (*Kopel v Safeway Stores plc* [2003] UKEAT 0281_02_1104; *Raggett v John Lewis Plc* [2012] UKEAT 0082_12_1708).

EXAMPLE
1. In *Khan v Kirklees Metropolitan Borough Council* [2007] EWCA Civ 1342, the Court of Appeal approved the decision of a tribunal that a claimant should be liable for costs of £83,000, following vexatious conduct at a tribunal hearing that lasted for 49 days. The claimant was a supply teacher in a school and brought an action in 2001, which was heard by a Chairman who was a school governor, albeit in a different area. In 2005 the same claimant began a further action against the Chairman and his school, the action having as one of its aims to embarrass the Chairman in relation to the 2001

claim. The conduct of the claimant gave adequate grounds for the tribunal to conclude that he had behaved unreasonably.

2. In *Kopel v Safeway Stores plc*, EAT held that a tribunal did not err in making a costs order against a claimant on the grounds that part of her complaint was seriously misconceived and that her failure to accept a substantial settlement sum offered by her employer during proceedings was unreasonable. Unreasonable refusal of a settlement offer was also held to be relevant to establishing unreasonable conduct in *Raggett v John Lewis Plc*.

3. In *Daleside Nursing Home v Mathew* [2009] UKEAT 0519_08_1802 and *Dunedin Canmore Housing Association v Donaldson* [2009] UKEAT 0014_09_0807, the EAT held that a tribunal must consider, and should make, an order for costs where a claim is brought which is based on a lie by the claimant. In the first case, the claimant made an allegation of racial abuse which the tribunal found was a lie. In the second case, the claimant lied about whether she had breached a confidentiality clause in a compromise agreement she was seeking to enforce. She had in fact disclosed its terms to two people. In both cases, the EAT held that it was perverse for a tribunal to fail to conclude that a claimant was acting unreasonably in bringing a claim based on a lie.

9704 The same rules apply to a **respondent**. Pursuing a defence which has no merit carries the same risks as pursuing a hopeless application. A respondent has the same responsibility not to conduct his case unreasonably before and during the hearing. Note, however, that it is the respondent's conduct in relation to the proceedings which is considered, not his conduct in relation to the actual dismissal or other cause for complaint.

9705 Furthermore, where a party has been ordered to pay a **deposit** as a condition of being permitted to continue to take part in the proceedings (¶9570) and the tribunal has found against that party but no award of costs or preparation time has been made against him, the tribunal must consider whether or not to make a costs or preparation order against that party on the ground that he conducted the proceedings unreasonably in persisting in having the matter determined (rule 47(1) ETR). However, the tribunal must have considered the document recording the order to pay a deposit and believe that the grounds for judgment against the party are the same grounds as those for considering that his contentions had little reasonable prospect of success.

9707 **Circumstances in which order must be made** A costs or preparation time order (as appropriate) must be made against a respondent where, in an **unfair dismissal claim**, the main hearing has been **postponed or adjourned** and (rules 39, 43 ETR):
– the claimant has expressed a wish for reinstatement or re-engagement which has been communicated to the respondent not less than 7 days before the hearing; and
– the postponement or adjournment of the hearing has been caused by the respondent's failure, without special reason, to provide reasonable evidence as to the availability of the job from which the claimant was dismissed or of comparable or suitable employment.

Such an order will relate to any costs incurred or preparation time spent as a result of the postponement or adjournment of the hearing.

9708 **Timing and procedure** A costs or preparation time order may be made by the tribunal acting on its own motion or at any time during the proceedings on the **application of a party** (rules 38(7), 42(5) ETR). An application by a party can be made at the end of a hearing or in writing to the Employment Tribunal Office **within** 28 days from the date of the judgment (this will be the date of the hearing if the judgment was issued orally or the date on which the written judgment was sent to the parties). An application made after this date will not be accepted or considered by the tribunal unless it considers it in the interests of justice to do so.

No order can be made unless the party against whom the order may be made has been given the opportunity to give **reasons why the order should not be made** (this will include the opportunity to give reasons orally to the tribunal at the hearing) (rules 38(9), 42(7) ETR).

The **tribunal's written reasons** as to why the order has been made will be provided if a request has been made for reasons within 14 days of the date of the order. Any such written reasons will be sent to all parties to the proceedings (rules 38(10), 42(8) ETR).

9709 **Amount of the order** The tribunal can order **costs** in three ways (rule 41(1) ETR; SI 2012/468):
– an order for a specified sum not exceeding £20,000;
– an order for a specified sum agreed by the parties (whether more or less than £20,000); or
– an order for the whole or part of the costs to be assessed if not otherwise agreed (this can exceed £20,000).

This means that the tribunal's own power to decide a figure for costs is **capped** at £20,000. If it believes that the costs payable should exceed this, then it will make an **order for assessment** of those costs and the party who is to have his costs paid must submit a detailed bill to the county court where it will be assessed, usually by a district judge. The process of assessment involves the judge determining whether or not it was reasonable for the party to incur costs in respect of each aspect of the case, and whether the amounts claimed are themselves reasonable. The parties are entitled to make submissions to the judge as to why they believe the costs claimed are or are not reasonable and the judge can strike out or reduce particular elements of the costs in order to arrive at a final figure, which can be more or less than £20,000.

In **assessing** the **amount of preparation time** spent, the tribunal must assess the number of preparatory hours on the basis of (rule 45(1) ETR):
– information provided by the receiving party; and
– the tribunal's own assessment of what it considers to be a reasonable and proportionate amount of time to spend on such preparatory work. In doing so, the tribunal can consider matters such as the complexity of the proceedings, the number of witnesses and documentation required.

Having assessed the amount of preparation time, the tribunal must apply an **hourly rate** of £32 to that figure in order to calculate the amount payable to the receiving party (rule 45(4) ETR). The preparation time order is, however, subject to a **maximum** amount of £20,000 (rule 45(2) ETR).

VAT should not be included in the costs award calculations if the recipient of the award is able to reclaim the VAT elsewhere (*Raggett v John Lewis Plc* [2012] UKEAT 0082_12_1708).

MEMO POINTS From **6 April 2013**, the hourly rate will be £33.

9710 In deciding on the level of costs or preparation time, the tribunal may take into account the paying party's **ability to pay** (rules 41(2), 45(3) ETR). The EAT has suggested that tribunals should encourage parties to use the county court Form EX140 where they would like their means to be taken into account in a costs hearing (*Oni v NHS Leicester City (formerly Leicester City Primary Care Trust)* [2012] UKEAT 0144_12_1209).

MEMO POINTS The tribunal can also take into account the **means of a trade union** which is supporting the claimants in deciding whether or not to make an award of costs. This is only likely to happen, however, if some fault on the part of the union has led to the costs order (*Beynon and ors v Scadden and ors* [1999] IRLR 700, EAT).

Wasted costs

9711 Tribunals (and the EAT) have the power to make "wasted costs" orders directly against a party's representative who is then personally liable to make the payment under the order (rule 48 ETR). Wasted costs are **defined as** any costs incurred by a party as a result of any improper, unreasonable, or negligent act or omission by a party's representative, or as any costs incurred after the representative's act or omission which, in the light of such act or omission, the tribunal considers it unreasonable to expect the party who incurred the costs to pay them (rule 48(3) ETR). In a wasted costs order, a tribunal or judge **may order a representative** to meet the whole or part of any wasted costs of any party, including his own client, and/or to reimburse the Secretary of State the amount paid in any allowances in connection with a person's attendance at the hearing (rule 48(2) ETR). There is no limit as to the amount of a wasted costs order. However, before making a wasted costs order, the tribunal can take into account the representative's **ability to pay**.

Before the order is made, the representative will be given the opportunity to make oral or written representations as to why an order should not be made (*Ridehalgh v Horsefield and anor* [1994] EWCA Civ 40 approved in *Medcalf v Weatherill and anor* [2002] UKHL 27). If the tribunal considers that the case was hopeless, it should consider whether the legal representative committed an abuse of the court in continuing with such a case and should also consider his state of mind as to whether he made any continuing assessment of the merits of the case and whether, if correctly advised, his party would have withdrawn (*Mitchells Solicitors v Funkwerk Information Technologies Ltd* [2008] UKEAT 0541_07_0804). Tribunals should, in considering whether to make a wasted costs order (*Godfrey Morgan Solicitors Ltd v Cobalt Systems Ltd* [2011] UKEAT 0608_10_3108):

1. refer to the relevant authorities and not confuse the principles applying to applications for "ordinary" costs (¶9702) with those for wasted costs;
2. apply a three-stage test:
– has the legal representative of whom complaint is made acted improperly, unreasonably or negligently?
– if so, did such conduct cause the applicant to incur unnecessary costs? and
– if so, is it in all the circumstances just to order the legal representative to compensate the applicant for the whole or any part of the relevant costs?
3. ensure the right procedure in the circumstances is applied;
4. be aware of the issues surrounding assessing available evidence if legal privilege has not been waived; and
5. give clear reasons for any order as such orders are disproportionately likely to generate appeals.

With regard to the procedure, this should be as summary as is consistent with fairness, bearing in mind that wasted costs orders will often involve not only quite large sums but also what may be very serious criticisms of the representative's competence or conduct which may have serious repercussions for the representative. The only essential element, as mentioned above, is that the representative against whom the application is made has a reasonable opportunity to make representations as to whether an order should be made. It may be open to one or more of the parties to submit to the tribunal that it can rely on written statements. On the other hand, an oral hearing, with live evidence, may be necessary and in such circumstances evidence may be needed to be tested in cross-examination (as was the case in *Godfrey Morgan Solicitors Ltd v Cobalt Systems Ltd* [2011] UKEAT 0608_10_3108).

> EXAMPLE In *Godfrey Morgan Solicitors Ltd v Cobalt Systems Ltd*, an employment claim was brought under a contingency fee arrangement. The employer, the respondent to the claim, refused to contemplate settlement and as the case progressed to tribunal the claimant was told by his solicitors that he needed to fund a barrister for the hearing. The claimant was unable and unwilling to do this, holding that it had not been made sufficiently clear to him that he would need to pay any costs up front (despite the wording of the conditional fee agreement which had set this out). The claimant also gave evidence that he had not been properly advised at this stage and had he been so he would have instructed his solicitors to withdraw his claim. Instead, the claim limped on until it was withdrawn at a much later date. As a result, a wasted costs order was made against the claimant's solicitors for the unnecessary costs incurred by the employer in preparing for trial from the date at which the claimant would have withdrawn his claim if he had been properly advised. The EAT upheld this order: the failure to ensure that the claim was withdrawn sooner was in breach of the representative's duty to the tribunal and put the employer to very substantial expense.
> **Note**: In this case, the claimant's solicitors had evidence which demonstrated that the claimant had in fact been properly advised. However, they only sought to introduce their file which contained this evidence for the first time at the costs hearing and the EAT held that the tribunal was within its rights to disallow this evidence for not having been put before it in good time given that an order for disclosure of documents had been made, albeit in rather unsatisfactory terms, 3 months earlier.

On request within 14 days of the date of the wasted costs order, the tribunal will provide **written reasons** as to why such an order was made.

> MEMO POINTS 1. A **representative** who is **not acting in pursuit of profit** with regard to the tribunal proceedings cannot have a wasted costs order made against him. Nor can a representative who is an **employee of a party** have a wasted costs order made against him.

2. The **party in whose favour** the wasted costs order is made does not have to be legally represented.

Expenses

In April 2012, the automatic state-funded expenses for witnesses were withdrawn and only the expenses of witnesses called to give **medical evidence** will be covered where these have been approved before the hearing. Any other witnesses called by either party should be paid by that party, unless the employment judge or tribunal orders the other party to pay the expenses incurred by a witness in attending a tribunal to give evidence (¶9702).

4. Enforcement of awards

The tribunals do not have their own enforcement procedure. However, the recovery of tribunal awards is **directly enforceable** in the county courts and the High Court (s 27 Tribunals, Courts and Enforcement Act 2007; SI 2008/2696) and the outstanding balance can be recovered using the same enforcement **procedures** as are available where there is non-compliance with a county court or High Court order, including:
– attachment of earnings (an order whereby the employer of the defaulting party is ordered to make a deduction from that party's wages and pay it direct to the court);
– execution against goods (where the bailiffs are sent to seize property owned by the defaulting party which can then be sold to raise money to satisfy the debt);
– garnishee proceedings (where the contents of bank accounts can be seized);
– bankruptcy proceedings; and
– charging orders against land (where the debt is secured against land owned by the defaulting party so that the debt can be satisfied out of the proceeds of sale).

Employers who **fail to pay awards** made by employment tribunals or the EAT, and who have had enforcement proceedings brought against them, will be **entered onto the Register of Judgments, Orders and Fines** (SI 2009/474). This register is available to the public and is used by banks, building societies and credit companies when considering applications for credit.

MEMO POINTS Failure to pay compensation for discrimination may amount to **post-employment victimisation** and be a ground for new proceedings (*Coutinho v Rank Nemo (DMS) Ltd* [2009] IRLR 672, CA).

Interest

Where a tribunal orders a sum of money to be paid (other than costs and expenses), interest will eventually accrue if it remains unpaid (Employment Tribunals (Interest) Order SI 1990/479). If the full sum is paid within 42 days of the date on which the tribunal's written decision containing the order to pay is sent to the parties (the "**relevant decision day**"), no interest will be payable. If, however, it remains unpaid at that time, interest will be calculated from the end of that period (the "**calculation day**") until payment at a **rate** specified by statute (currently 8% per annum (s 17 Judgments Act 1838 as amended by SI 1993/564)). Effectively, therefore, interest only starts to accrue after the period for lodging an appeal ends (¶9756). Special provisions apply to interest on awards and orders of compensation in discrimination cases (SI 1996/2803).

The Secretary of the Employment Tribunal is obliged to send with the decision containing the award a **notice** specifying the relevant decision day, the calculation day and the rate of interest. If he omits to do so, this does not affect the liability to pay interest.

The relevant decision day remains the same even if the **amount** is subsequently **varied on appeal** (although interest will be calculated on the basis of the revised amount). If the amount awarded on appeal is subsequently varied again in a further appeal, then again this does not affect the relevant decision day. If the original tribunal decision did not award any money but a subsequent appeal decision does, then the relevant decision day is the date on which that appeal decision is sent to the parties.

> **EXAMPLE**
> 1. The tribunal's written decision is sent to the parties on 3 January, containing an order to pay £1,000. The relevant decision day is 3 January. The calculation day is 15 February. If payment is made before 15 February, no interest will be payable. If payment is made after 15 February, interest will be calculated at 8% (from 15 February until the date of payment) on £1,000.
> 2. An appeal is lodged against the above decision and no payment is made while the appeal is pending. The EAT decides in December that the award should be £750 instead of £1,000. The relevant decision day remains 3 January, which means that the calculation day remains 15 February. Interest will be calculated from 15 February until the date of payment, but on £750 rather than £1000.
> A further appeal goes to the Court of Appeal, which decides that the correct award is in fact £2,000. Interest will still be calculated from 15 February but on £2,000.
> 3. The tribunal finds that the employee has been unfairly dismissed but orders no compensation because it finds that he contributed to his dismissal to the extent of 100%. The decision is sent out in December. On appeal to the EAT, the tribunal's finding on contribution is overturned and the EAT orders the employer to pay him the sum of £1,000. The EAT's decision is sent to the parties on 4 June. The relevant decision day will be 4 June and the calculation date will be 42 days after that.

9717 Interest is not payable on any part of the award which is **recouped** by the government in respect of benefit payments (¶8586).

> **EXAMPLE** The tribunal awards £1000 for loss of earnings, of which £250 is subject to recoupment. Interest will only be payable on £750.

5. Review

9718 In a review, the tribunal reviews its own judgment or decision. In contrast, in the case of an appeal, a superior court or tribunal is asked to decide whether or not the tribunal's judgment or decision was correct. The following **judgments or decisions** can be reviewed (rules 33(1), 34(1) ETR):
– a default judgment;
– a decision not to accept a claim, response or counterclaim; and
– a judgment other than a default judgment, but including an order for costs, preparation time or wasted costs.

> **MEMO POINTS** 1. **Default judgments** are dealt with separately and are discussed at ¶9726.
> 2. The EAT has reiterated that a tribunal has the power to review a decision by a judge **not to accept a claim form** (*Richardson v U Mole Limited* [2005] UKEAT 0179_05_0906, the judge referring in particular to his earlier judgment in *Moroak t/a Blake Envelopes v Cromie*).

9719 **Grounds for review** A judgment or decision can only be reviewed on the **following grounds** (rule 34(3) ETR):
– the decision was wrongly made as a result of an administrative error by the tribunal staff;
– a party did not receive notice of the proceedings leading to the decision;
– the decision was made in the absence of a party; or
– new evidence has become available since the conclusion of the hearing (but only if its existence could not have been reasonably known of or foreseen at the time of the hearing).

> **MEMO POINTS** 1. An application for review will be properly constituted if the grounds for review **can be discerned** from the application (*Sodexho Ltd v Gibbons* [2005] ICR 1647, EAT). In the event of any doubt, the judge, either on his own initiative or on an application of the opposing party, may seek additional information.
> 2. **Administrative error** covers errors by the parties as well as tribunal staff (*Sodexho Ltd v Gibbons*).
> 3. In most cases, where claimants wish to challenge a tribunal decision because they have **new evidence**, the usual course should be to apply for a review of the decision rather than appeal to the EAT (¶9752) (*Adegbuji v Meteor Parking Ltd* [2010] UKEAT 1570_09_2104).

9720 A decision may also be reviewed if the **interests of justice** require it and this should not be construed restrictively (*Sodexho Ltd v Gibbons*). Where a tribunal reviews a decision not to accept a claim, response or counterclaim on these grounds, the EAT has held that the power to review applies not just to the **content** of the claim/response/counterclaim in question, but also to its **timing** (despite the strict time limits which normally apply) (*Moroak t/a Blake Envelopes v Cromie* [2005] UKEAT 0093_05_1904). In this case, the response was 44 minutes late and the EAT held that, in the interests of justice, the decision to reject the response on this ground could be reviewed.

Further, where a **mistake or procedural shortcoming** has been made by both parties and the judge, there may also be grounds to review the decision in the interests of justice (*Williams v Ferrosan Ltd* [2004] IRLR 607, EAT). For example, a tribunal may review a decision in the interests of justice where there has been a procedural shortcoming which was a consequence of the parties having been denied a fair opportunity to present their case (*Trimble v Supertravel Ltd* [1982] IRLR 451, EAT). If this happens, even significant errors of law which have resulted from the procedural shortcoming can be reviewed. However, where both parties had a fair opportunity to present their case and where the tribunal decision was reached in the light of all relevant arguments, errors of law should be dealt with by way of appeal.

Procedure A review can take place either following an application by a party or if the tribunal itself decides that it is appropriate. **9722**

A **party can apply** for a review either orally at the hearing or in writing to the Secretary (setting out the reasons for requesting a review), not later than 14 days after the written decision has been sent to the parties (rule 35(1) ETR), although this can be extended by the tribunal.

If the **tribunal itself decides** that a review should be carried out, it must send a notice to each of the parties explaining why it proposes to do so and giving them the opportunity to make representations as to why there should be no review. A tribunal may decide to hold a review if, for example, it had decided the case on the basis of the law as it understood it but subsequently discovered that the EAT or a higher court had made a decision altering the law. The **tribunal's notice** must be sent out not later than 14 days after the date on which the decision was sent to the parties (rule 36(2) ETR).

Given the relatively short period in which an **appeal** may be lodged (¶9756), a party wishing to appeal may often have to lodge his appeal while a review is still pending. In such cases, the tribunal will decide whether to **adjourn the review** pending the outcome of the appeal or proceed as normal. The decision is likely to depend on whether the appeal is on the same or different grounds as the request for a review. **9723**

Conduct Applications for review are **heard by** the original tribunal which decided the case unless this is not practicable (for example, because one of the members has died or is not available within a reasonable period of time for other reasons), in which case a freshly constituted tribunal will deal with the review. If the review is taking place at the instigation of the tribunal itself rather than on the application of a party, then only the original tribunal (or judge) can conduct such a review. If that is not practicable, a different tribunal or judge will be appointed. **9724**

In **considering an application** for review, the tribunal must take account of all relevant factors, and should balance the possible prejudice to the parties of allowing or refusing the application (*British School of Motoring v Fowler* [2006] UKEAT 0059_06_2402). In this case, a Chairwoman, who had treated a letter explaining why a response had not been filed in time as an application for a review, had erred in refusing it after having sought the views of the applicant without recourse to the respondent.

Outcome After hearing the review, the tribunal can confirm its decision, vary it, or revoke it (rule 36(3) ETR). **9725**

If the decision is **revoked**, the tribunal has to order the decision to be taken again which may be either before the same tribunal or a differently constituted tribunal. The power to **vary** a decision is, however, a wide one and may enable the tribunal to substitute an entirely different decision without having to revoke the original decision and then hold a re-hearing. If it is clear after the review not only that the original decision cannot stand but also what the decision ought to have been, then variation is the most appropriate course. If, however, it is only clear that the original decision cannot stand but further consideration of the evidence or further argument is required, revocation and re-hearing will be the most likely outcome.

Default judgments

9726 A party can apply to have a default judgment against or in favour of him reviewed (rule 33(1) ETR). His application must be made in writing to the Employment Tribunal Office **within** 14 days of the date on which the default judgment was sent to the parties. This time limit can be **extended** by a judge if he considers it just and equitable to do so. In his application, the party must state why the default judgment should be varied or revoked. If the **respondent** is the party **applying** for the review, he must also include his proposed response to the claim, an application for an extension of the time limit for presenting the response and an explanation as to why he did not comply with the rules for submitting a response (rule 33(2) ETR).

Judges have the power to review default judgments **without** the **need for an application** by one of the parties if there has been an administrative error, a party did not receive notice of the proceedings or one or more of the parties was absent when the decision to enter default judgment was made (rule 33(8) ETR as inserted by SI 2008/3240).

A review of a default judgment must be **conducted by** a judge in public and notice of the hearing and a copy of the application must be sent to all other parties to the proceedings. A review of a default judgment need not be in public if all the parties to the proceedings consent in writing to a review without a hearing (rule 33(3) ETR as amended by SI 2008/3240).

9727 The jurisdiction to review a default judgment is a just and equitable one and the judge must have regard to whether there is a "**good reason**" for the response not having been presented in time, although this is not determinative, and does not rule out the consideration of other discretionary factors (*Pendragon plc t/a CD Bramall Bradford v Copus* [2005] UKEAT 0317_05_1107).

If the respondent has a **reasonable prospect of successfully responding** to the claim or part of it, the judge may **revoke or vary** all or part of the default judgment. If the judge decides that the default judgment should be varied or revoked and that the respondent should be allowed to respond to the claim, the Secretary will accept the response and the tribunal will take the usual steps that apply on acceptance of a valid response (¶9514).

The judge may **refuse** the application for a review, or vary, revoke or confirm the default judgment. The judgment must be revoked if the whole of the claim has been **settled** by Acas conciliation or a valid compromise agreement (¶9333).

V. Appeals

9740 Appeals from decisions of tribunals on points of law are heard by the Employment Appeal Tribunal (EAT), and from there, by the higher courts.

A. Employment Appeal Tribunal

9745 Appeals from employment tribunals on questions of law are dealt with by the Employment Appeal Tribunal (EAT), which (although it may sit at any time and in any place throughout GB) in practice sits permanently in Glasgow and London, and only occasionally sits elsewhere.

> *MEMO POINTS* 1. The EAT is a statutory body whose constitution is set out in Part II of the Employment Tribunals Act 1996, and whose **rules of procedure** are set out in the Employment Appeal

Tribunal Rules (SI 1993/2854), as amended (SI 2001/1128; SI 2001/1476; SI 2004/2526) (referred to in this section as the "EAT Rules" and "EATR").

The EAT issued a revised **Practice Direction (PD)** in 2008 (superseding all previous PDs), which applies to all appeals from tribunals unless specifically excluded by the EAT Rules. The full text of the EAT PD is set out at [2008] IRLR 621. The EAT have also issued **Practice Statements** in 2005 and 2012 which are referred to where relevant below.

The EAT is also subject to the **EAT/Acas Protocol 2007** which sets out the procedure to be followed where the EAT considers a case may be suitable for conciliation (¶9760).

2. The EAT is subject to the **overriding objective** of dealing with cases justly (rule 2A EATR; as inserted by reg 3 SI 2004/2526). As with employment tribunals, this includes ensuring that the parties are on an equal footing, saving expense, dealing with the case in ways which are proportionate to the importance and complexity of the issues and ensuring that it is dealt with expeditiously and fairly. The parties must assist the EAT in furthering this objective.

The EAT has also emphasised that it has a **broad and generous discretion** in applying the EAT Rules and PD so as to achieve the overriding objective of dealing with cases justly (¶9759).

3. A refusal by the EAT to **sit in Wales** where the appeal is against a decision of an employment tribunal sitting in Wales, and a refusal to conduct a hearing in Welsh, does not contravene the Welsh Language Act 1993 or the European Convention on Human Rights (*Williams v Cowell* [2000] ICR 85).

4. The rules of procedure are slightly different in **Scotland**, in particular, the rules relating to skeleton arguments (¶9786) (these do not apply to appeals in Scotland) and the rules regarding the handing down of judgments and appeals from the EAT (in Scotland, appeals are made to the Court of Session).

The EAT also hears appeals on a question of law arising in any proceedings of the **Central Arbitration Committee** in connection with European Works Councils, domestic information or consultation requirements or from any declaration or order made by it. It also has jurisdiction to hear appeals from decisions of the **Certification Officer** for Trade Unions and Employers' Associations.

9746

Any documents sent to the EAT should be addressed to the **Registrar** (rule 35 EATR), who has both administrative and quasi-judicial functions.

9747

1. Grounds

Final orders

A tribunal decision can only be appealed on a **question of law**: it is not for the EAT to take over the tribunal's role as an "industrial jury" and re-hear a case in the absence of an error of law (*case* [2010] UKEAT 0453_09_2104). To succeed in an appeal, therefore, a **party must show** that (*British Telecommunications plc v Sheridan* [1990] IRLR 27, CA):
– there is no evidence to support a particular conclusion or finding of fact. However, the fact that there is no evidence to support a particular conclusion or finding of fact will not automatically invalidate the tribunal's decision and the EAT will consider the error in light of all the facts of the case (*Munu v Great Ormond Street Hospital NHS Trust and ors* [2007] UKEAT 0287_07_0511);
– the decision was either perverse (i.e. one which no reasonable tribunal properly directing itself under law would have reached) or obviously wrong; or
– the tribunal misdirected itself in law, or misunderstood or misapplied the law.

Unless one of these categories applies, the EAT cannot interfere with the tribunal's **finding of fact**.

9748

> EXAMPLE
> 1. Witness A says in his evidence to the tribunal that he personally handed a letter to witness B. Witness B in his evidence denies ever having received such a letter. The tribunal, having heard both witnesses and assessed their credibility, decides that it believes witness A rather than witness B. This is a **question of fact** for the tribunal to decide and the EAT will not interfere with this decision.
> 2. The facts are as in the previous example, but there is also a question as to the effect of the letter. The letter, which is dated 14 March, states that B's employment is "terminated forthwith". The tribunal finds that the letter was handed to B by A on 17 March. The tribunal has to decide

whether the effect of the letter is to terminate B's employment on 14 March (the date of the letter) or 17 March (the date on which it was received). This is a **question of law**, which could be the subject of an appeal.

9749 The Court of Appeal has set out guidance as to when an **appeal** on the **grounds of perversity** can be brought (*Yeboah v Crofton* [2002] IRLR 634, CA).

9751 **New points of law**   As a general rule, the EAT will not allow an appeal on a new point of law that should have been raised at the tribunal (*Kumchyk v Derby City Council* [1978] UKEAT 122_78_2407, confirmed in *Glennie v Independent Magazines (UK) Ltd* [1999] IRLR 719, [1999] EWCA Civ 1611), nor will it, generally speaking, allow a point of law that was conceded at the tribunal to be re-opened (*Jones v Governing Body of Burdett Coutts School* [1999] ICR 38, [1998] EWCA Civ 602, [1998] IRLR 521). However, the EAT will allow such appeals in exceptional circumstances. It **may do so** if, for example, the legal point is so fundamental and well established that the tribunal should have considered it, even if it was not argued by the parties (such as the test for a fair dismissal for misconduct, i.e. whether the employer had a reasonable belief in the employee's guilt, held on reasonable grounds, following a reasonable investigation). The EAT has given detailed guidance as to when it will exceptionally allow a point of law to be raised on appeal where it has not been raised in the tribunal, emphasising that this is solely within the discretion of the EAT (*Secretary of State for Health and anor v Rance and ors and conjoined appeals* [2007] IRLR 665, EAT). The guidance is as follows:
1. there is a **discretion** to allow a new point of law to be argued in the EAT which covers new points and the re-opening of conceded points;
2. this discretion will be exercised only in **exceptional circumstances**. It is **even more exceptional** to exercise this discretion where fresh issues of fact will have to be investigated;
3. where the new point **relates to jurisdiction**, this is not a trump card requiring the point to be taken: it remains discretionary;
4. the **discretion may be exercised** in any of the following circumstances which are given as examples:
– it would be unjust to allow the other party to get away with some deception or unfair conduct which meant that the point was not taken before;
– the point can be taken if the EAT is in possession of all the material necessary to dispose of the matter fairly without recourse to a further hearing;
– the new point enables the EAT plainly to say from existing material that the tribunal judgment was a nullity;
– the EAT can see a glaring injustice in refusing to allow an unrepresented party to rely on evidence which could have been adduced at the tribunal;
– the EAT can see an obvious knock-out point;
– the issue is a discrete one of pure law requiring no further factual enquiry; or
– it is of particular public importance for a legal point to be decided provided no further factual investigation and no further evaluation by a tribunal is required; and
5. the **discretion is not to be exercised** where, by way of example:
– what is relied upon is a chance of establishing lack of jurisdiction by calling fresh evidence;
– the issue arises as a result of lack of skill by a represented party;
– the point was not taken before as a result of a tactical decision by a representative or a party;
– all the material is before the EAT but what is required is an evaluation and an assessment of this material and application of the law to it by a tribunal;
– a represented party has fought and lost a jurisdictional issue and now seeks a new hearing. This applies whether the jurisdictional issue is the same as that originally canvassed or is a different way of establishing jurisdiction from that originally canvassed; and
– what is relied upon is the high value of the case.

EXAMPLE   In *Secretary of State for Health and anor v Rance and ors and conjoined appeals*, the EAT exercised its discretion in allowing a point conceded at the tribunal to be reopened on appeal. The exceptional circumstances included the fact that the issue went to jurisdiction, these were four test cases representing 120 similar concessions in a mass litigation affecting 11,000 employees. Further, the error had been administrative not tactical, the respondents applied in each case for a tribunal review as well as appealing and no further investigation into the facts was required in order to do justice.

The respondent has an **opportunity to object** to a new point of law being raised by stating his objection in writing **within** 14 days of receiving the notice of appeal (if a preliminary hearing has been ordered) or, if the appeal is listed for a full hearing without a preliminary hearing, in a respondent's answer.

New evidence The EAT will exercise its discretion as to whether to admit evidence not put before the tribunal, having regard to its overriding objective (¶9745). An EAT Practice Statement was issued in April 2012 (set out at [2012] IRLR 523) stating that where a party wishes the EAT to consider evidence that had not been seen at the tribunal, it is likely that an order will be made staying any further action on the appeal (or dismissing it as having no reasonable prospects of success) until an application has been put to the tribunal to review its judgment (¶9719). This is because an appeal relating to fresh evidence will, generally, not be based on an error in law on the tribunal's part (which is the basis of the EAT's jurisdiction), and it is also more logical for the tribunal to deal with such applications as its experience of the case in question will enable it to best assess matters. It also relieves a certain caseload burden on the EAT. Although the time limits for applying for a review in the tribunal are shorter than those for lodging an appeal, there is scope to extend the time limit in appropriate cases. After this application has been made to the tribunal, it will still be open to the party to argue that the tribunal made an error of law with regard to any refusal of the tribunal to review the decision.

9752

Even where the EAT does hear fresh evidence appeals, it will only permit them in limited circumstances. A party seeking to put new evidence forward must be able to show the EAT that it (*Ladd v Marshall* [1954] 1 WLR 1489; *Wileman v Minilec Engineering Limited* [1988] IRLR 144, EAT):
– could not have been obtained with reasonable diligence for use at the tribunal;
– is relevant and would probably have an important influence on the result of the case (though it need not necessarily be decisive); and
– is apparently credible (though it need not be incontrovertible).
A party who decides to withhold evidence at the tribunal hearing stage will not, therefore, be able to introduce it at the EAT.

Bias and improper conduct Bias by the judge or a tribunal member in reaching their decision will normally give a party grounds for appealing to have the decision set aside (¶9612). **Full particulars** of any complaint about the conduct of the tribunal (including bias, apparent bias or improper conduct by the judge or tribunal members, or any procedural irregularity) must be included in the appellant's notice of appeal (para 11.1 EAT PD). If the respondent wishes to complain of bias or improper conduct, the full particulars of his complaint must be set out (if there is a Preliminary Hearing (PH) (¶9762)) in his cross-appeal or written submissions or (if there is no PH) in his written answer (para 11.4 EAT PD). Before or at the case listing stage (¶9760), the judge or Registrar may postpone a decision to list the case in a particular track and direct the party complaining of bias (or his representative) to provide a sworn statement setting out the full particulars of all allegations of bias or misconduct (para 11.2 EAT PD). At the case listing stage, the Registrar may ask the party complaining of bias if he intends to proceed with the allegation(s) and may warn him that the **unsuccessful pursuit** of such allegation(s) could put him at risk of a costs order. If the appeal is allocated to a PH or FH track (¶9765), the EAT can (para 11.3 EAT PD):
– require the party complaining of bias (or his representative) to provide a sworn statement (if not already provided);
– require a sworn statement or obtain a witness statement from the parties, any representative of the parties or any other person present at the tribunal hearing or a relevant part of it (save for the tribunal judge or any lay members who heard the case, who it can merely invite to provide a sworn statement) (*Facey v Midas Retail Security* [2000] UKEAT 966_98_0905); and
– seek comments on all sworn statements or witness statements from the judge or tribunal members.

9753

The Court of Appeal has also provided **guidance** on how appellate tribunals and courts should handle such complaints and has stated that the appellate tribunal may have to make judgments of fact to be able to resolve any factual disputes relating to such a complaint (*Stansbury v Data pulse plc and anor* [2004] IRLR 466, CA).

Interim orders and decisions

9754 A party can also appeal to the EAT against an interim order or decision made by the tribunal (for example, an order for disclosure of certain documents or a striking out order). As with final orders, the EAT can only intervene if the tribunal has made an **error of law**, i.e. if (*Adams and Raynor v West Sussex County Council* [1990] IRLR 215, EAT):
- the order is not one which the tribunal has power to make;
- the tribunal has not followed the relevant "guiding legal principles" (which will depend on the order made) in relation to the exercise of its discretion; or
- the tribunal has exercised its discretion in an unreasonable or irrational manner (i.e. can be challenged on what are known as "Wednesbury principles").

2. Commencement

9755 **Form** The **notice of appeal** must be, or be substantially, in accordance with **Form 1** (in the amended form annexed to the Practice Direction (substituted by Employment Appeal Tribunal (Amendment) Rules SI 2005/1871)) or **Forms 1A or 2** of the Schedule to the Rules and must **identify** the date of the judgment, decision or order being appealed (para 2.1 EAT PD). It must also clearly identify the grounds of appeal and state the order the appellant seeks (para 2.4 EAT PD). With regard to **perversity appeals**, it will not be sufficient to merely state words to the effect that "the judgment or order was contrary to the evidence" or that "there was no evidence to support the judgment or order" or that "the judgment or order was one which no reasonable tribunal could have reached and was perverse" unless the notice of appeal also sets out full particulars of the matters relied on in support of these general grounds (para 2.6 EAT PD).

Copies of the judgment, decision or order appealed against and of the employment tribunal's written reasons, together with a copy of the claim (ET1) and the response (ET3) must be attached, or if not, a written explanation must be given. A notice of appeal without such documentation will not be validly lodged (para 2.1 EAT PD).

Notices of appeal can be **sent** to the EAT **by** post, hand delivery, fax or other electronic communication.

> MEMO POINTS The Government plans to **introduce a fee** of £400 to appeal to the EAT with a further £1,200 to be paid before the hearing in **summer 2013**. Further developments will be covered by our updating service.

9756 **Timing** The notice of appeal must be **submitted within** 42 days (rule 3(3) EATR; as amended by reg 4 SI 2004/2526):
1. in the case of an appeal against a **judgment of the employment tribunal**:
- from the date on which written reasons were sent to the parties, where those written reasons were requested orally at the hearing or within 14 days of the date on which the written record of the judgment was sent to the parties, or were reserved and given in writing by the employment tribunal;
- from the date on which a document containing edited reasons for the tribunal judgment given in relation to national security proceedings was sent to the parties; or
- from the date on which a written record of the tribunal judgment was sent to the parties where the written reasons for the judgment were not requested orally at the hearing before the employment tribunal or in writing within 14 days of the date on which the written record of the judgment was sent to the parties and were not reserved and given in writing by the employment tribunal; or

2. in the case of an appeal against an **order of the employment tribunal**, from the date of that order.

> MEMO POINTS   The Practice Direction gives **additional guidance** as follows (para 1.8 EAT PD):
> – the day that the employment tribunal decision is sent to parties does not count and the notice of appeal must arrive at the EAT by 4pm on or before that day 6 weeks (i.e. 42 days) later;
> – when a date is given for serving a document or for doing some other act, the complete document must be received by the EAT or the relevant party by 4pm on that date. Any document received after 4pm will be deemed to be lodged on the next working day; and
> – all days count, but if a time limit expires on a day when the central office of the EAT, or the EAT office in Edinburgh (as appropriate), is closed, it is extended to the next working day except where the time limit is 5 days (e.g. an appeal against a Registrar's order or direction) in which case Saturdays, Sundays, Christmas Day, Good Friday and bank holidays do not count.

9757

If it appears that compliance with the **time limit** may be **difficult**, it was previously recommended that the party serves a notice of appeal containing as much information as possible, accompanied by a covering letter indicating the difficulty in which he finds himself, and that it may be necessary to apply to amend the notice at a later date (¶9759). However, where the appellant is not able to provide a copy of the tribunal's written reasons with his notice of appeal, the EAT has indicated that it will take a strict approach in such cases (*Kanapathiar v London Borough of Harrow* [2003] IRLR 571, EAT).

9758

If the **time limit is missed**, an extension of time can be applied for, but it must be accompanied by a notice of appeal in proper form, together with a written application for an extension of time, explaining clearly and concisely the reasons for the delay in lodging the notice of appeal (para 3 EAT PD). The EAT in a **Practice Statement** issued on 3 February 2005 (set out at [2005] IRLR 189) emphasised the importance of strict compliance with the time limit, and that it will not accept ignorance of the limit as an excuse.

Further, the EAT has looked at the existing case law on this area and the Practice Statement in detail and given **guidance** as to when it will allow an extension of time if the time limit to submit a notice of appeal has been missed, emphasising that such extensions will only be granted in exceptional circumstances and that the judge should focus on the following three questions: 1. What is the explanation for the delay? 2. Does it provide a good excuse for the default? and 3. Are there circumstances which justify the tribunal taking the exceptional step of allowing an extension of time? (*Muschett v London Borough of Hounslow* [2007] UKEAT 0281_07_0608 applying *Kanapathiar v London Borough of Harrow* [2003] IRLR 571, EAT; *United Arab Emirates v Abdelghafar* [1995] IRLR 243, EAT; *Aziz v Bethnal Green City Challenge Company Ltd* [2000] IRLR 111, CA; *Woodward v Abbey National Plc* [2005] IRLR 782, EAT; *Steeds v Peverel Management Services Ltd* [2001] EWCA Civ 419 as applied to an employment tribunal case in *Chohan v Derby Law Centre* [2004] IRLR 685, EAT; and *Jurkowska v Hlmad Ltd* [2008] IRLR 430, CA).

The guidance is summarised **as follows**:
a. the EAT will be more strict about time limits on appeal than at first instance and the 42-day time limit will only be relaxed in rare and exceptional cases;
b. there is no excuse even in the case of an unrepresented party for ignorance of the time limits or procedure; however, the fault of a legal adviser with regard to the time limit may be a factor which, when combined with others, might contribute to the exercise of discretion;
c. the EAT must be satisfied that there is a full honest and acceptable explanation of the reasons for the delay and it will be astute to any evidence of procedural abuse or intentional default;
d. in an ordinary case, a good explanation and excuse will need to be shown, but even if the explanation does not amount to a good excuse, there may still be exceptional circumstances which justify an extension of time anyway; and
e. the EAT will have regard to the length of delay and why a notice of appeal was not submitted through the entirety of the time limit. With regard to the latter point, this means that an analytic approach should be taken to different parts of the period. For example, if a claimant receives the judgment and resolves to appeal in week 1 but suffers a stroke and is physically unable to lodge an appeal in time, a sympathetic approach would be forthcoming for the second segment and also for the first as it would not be just to debar someone for not acting immediately on receipt of a judgment. However, a less sympathetic approach to

the first segment might be taken if the stroke occurred in week 6. All would depend on the facts adduced in explanation for not acting during that time.

If the reason for the missed time limit is due to a **postal delay**, the EAT has indicated that represented appellants will be expected to have enquired in good time to ensure that their appeal has been received by the EAT. However in respect of unrepresented appellants, there is no duty to check with the EAT as to whether the appeal has been received (*Peters v Sat Katar Co Ltd* [2003] IRLR 574, CA; see also ¶9473 in respect of employment tribunal claims). It is not usually a good reason to miss the time limit on the grounds that an application for litigation support from public **funds** has been made, but not yet determined; or that support is being sought from, but has not yet been provided by, some other body, such as a trade union, employers' association or the Equality and Human Rights Commission (para 3.8 EAT PD).

The **Registrar will** usually **determine** whether or not such a request should be granted, but it is possible to **appeal from the Registrar's decision** to a judge. The judge can either hear the appeal on his own or refer it to a full decision of the EAT. Any appeal against the Registrar's decision must be made within 5 days of the date when the Registrar's decision was sent to the parties.

> EXAMPLE   In *O'Cathail v Transport for London* [2012] EWCA Civ 1004, the Court of Appeal upheld the EAT's decision to refuse an extension of time to an applicant, O, who was disabled (he suffered from depression). O lodged his notice of appeal 1 day ahead of the 42-day time limit but without a copy of the original tribunal decision along with its reasons, which is a requirement to bring an appeal. Due to stress, O did not lodge his completed notice of appeal until the day after the time limit had expired. His appeal was rejected as being out of time. He appealed this decision, relying on unopposed medical evidence that he suffered from anxiety, depression and panic attacks exacerbated by court hearings. The EAT judge held that there was no evidence to explain why he had not lodged his notice of appeal before the very last moment. Although O's disability contributed to him not being able to lodge the additional documents in time, the true reason that his appeal was not lodged in time was that he had left it to the last minute and he ran the risk that, if something went wrong, he may not have time to remedy it. The Court of Appeal agreed with this judgment and stated that, although there are critics of the tough approach that the EAT takes to time limits, the approach is necessary in order to treat people equally, to consider the conflicting positions of both parties, and to protect the public interest in providing good judicial administration.

> MEMO POINTS   In any case of doubt or difficulty, a notice of appeal should be lodged in time and an application made to the Registrar for directions (para 3.9 EAT PD).

9759 **Amendment of the notice of appeal**   The notice of appeal may only be amended by an order of the EAT on a separate **interim application** and that application should be made as soon as need for the amendment is known (rule 19 EATR; para 2.7 EAT PD). The application must be accompanied by a draft of the amended notice of appeal which makes clear the precise amendments sought. Parties are encouraged to make such applications at the preliminary hearing (PH) (see below) or (if one is ordered) at the directions hearing (para 4.1 EAT PD).

Permission may be granted if the proposed amendment is produced at the hearing. However, if the other party has not been notified of the proposed amendment and the appeal cannot proceed but for the amendment, then the opposing party can apply on notice to vary or discharge the permission to proceed.

If the proposed amendment is **not produced at the PH**, then the appellant can apply in writing for permission to amend the notice of appeal within 14 days of the PH, provided he gives notice to the other party. If the proposed amendment is critical to the appeal being allowed to proceed, then the EAT can at the PH order for the appeal to be dismissed if the appellant does not apply for permission to amend.

If the appellant is **permitted** to amend his appeal, then he must make any amendments within a period of time specified by the EAT. The respondent will be sent a copy and will have 14 days in which to object. **Objections** are only likely to be sustained if the amendment would cause prejudice to the other party. If permission to amend the notice of appeal is given, and the respondent has already filed an answer, he is allowed to make consequential amendments to his answer without permission within the same 14-day period. If the amendment is **not permitted**, then either party can apply to the EAT as to the hearing or disposal of the appeal.

The EAT has given **guidance** as to the principles which should be applied when considering applications to amend notices of appeal (*Khudados v Leggate* [2005] ICR 1013, CA, applied in *Readman v Devon Primary Care Trust* [2011] UKEAT 0116_11_0109). It emphasised that it has a **broad and generous discretion** in applying the EAT Rules and Practice Direction so as to achieve the overriding objective of **dealing with cases justly**. In doing so, the following are among the **matters to be taken into account** in determining whether an amendment should be allowed:
– whether the applicant has complied with the requirement that an application for permission to amend a notice of appeal should be made as soon as the need for the amendment is known (as set out above). This is of considerable importance and it is not simply aspirational or an expression of hope;
– whether the applicant has given a full, honest and acceptable explanation for any delay or failure to comply;
– if allowed, the extent to which the proposed amendment would cause any delay. For example, proposed amendments that raise a point of law closely related to existing grounds of appeal, or offer limited particulars that flesh out existing grounds, are much more likely to be allowed than wholly new grounds of perversity raising issues of complex fact and requiring consideration of a volume of documents, including witness statements and notes of evidence, which would, if allowed, cause delay and extra expense;
– whether the amendment would cause prejudice to the other party, and whether refusing the amendment would cause prejudice to the applicant by depriving him of fairly arguable grounds of appeal. It should be noted though that any prejudice caused by refusing permission to amend to an applicant who seeks permission to amend by adding fairly arguable grounds, but who has failed in a significant way to comply with the EAT Rules and Practice Direction, or who has delayed excessively, is likely to carry less weight than where an applicant has not delayed and has acted in accordance with the EAT Rules and Practice Direction;
– in some cases it may be necessary to consider the merits of the proposed amendments since, as a general rule, they must raise a point of law which gives the appeal a reasonable prospect of success at a full hearing; and
– regard must be had to the public interest in ensuring that business in the EAT is conducted expeditiously and that its resources are used efficiently.

3. Case listing

On receiving a notice of appeal, a case manager will check the notice of appeal to ensure compliance with rules on lodging of appropriate papers and time limits. Thereafter, a judge will decide which one of **four case tracks** the appeal should occupy and will give directions to the parties (para 9 EAT PD):
1. where it appears to a judge that a notice of appeal discloses no reasonable grounds for bringing an appeal or is an abuse of the EAT's process or is otherwise likely to obstruct the just disposal of the proceedings, the appeal will be dealt with in accordance with rule 3(7) (¶9761). Where the judge considers more material is needed, either to form an opinion under rule 3(7) or to send the case to a hearing track (see points 2, 3 and 4 below), the judge may direct that more information is given of the ground; and in cases alleging bias or procedural irregularity may order a stay while the appellant or a representative is ordered to provide an affidavit;
2. the appeal will be listed for a preliminary hearing (PH) to determine whether the appeal has merit and a reasonable prospect of success (if so, it will go to a full hearing);
3. the appeal will be listed for a full hearing (FH), without the need for a PH; or
4. the appeal will be listed for a fast track full hearing (FTFH) due to its importance or if it deals with an interim order of the tribunal requiring compliance within a specified time limit.

However, in cases where the EAT considers there is potential for some or all of the matters in dispute between the parties to be resolved by way of **Acas conciliation**, it may exercise its power and give directions as to any steps it sees fit in relation to conciliation or other

9760

settlement (rule 36 EATR; EAT/Acas Protocol 2007). Consequently, the **sifting procedure** described above **may be modified**, particularly with regard to appeals:
- relating to monetary awards only;
- where the overwhelmingly likely result of a successful appeal would be a remission back to the tribunal;
- that concern remedies; or
- where the parties' employment relationship is continuing.

The modified procedure **is as follows**:
1. a judge, after deciding whether to sift the appeal to a hearing track, and whether or not to continue any stay, may give a direction to:
- require the parties to consider conciliation by Acas, and, if asked, to attend a meeting called by, or respond to other communications from, the nominated Acas officer;
- send the papers to the nominated Acas officer, inviting the officer to conciliate a settlement of the appeal or of the ground; and
- require the appellant to report back to the EAT on the outcome;

To assist the parties and the Acas officer, the judge may indicate brief reasons for considering why conciliation might be sought. In every appropriate case, the following paragraph will be included in an order made on the papers or at a hearing: "Pursuant to Rule 36 and the EAT/Acas Protocol 2007, it is considered that there is potential for some or all of the matters at issue between parties being resolved by means of conciliation. The papers will be sent to an Acas Officer. The parties are each directed to give consideration to any offer of conciliation and respond promptly to any invitation made by the Acas Officer. The Appellant is directed within 28 days of the seal date of this Order to inform the EAT what has occurred, when any necessary further directions can be given."; and

2. after the appellant has reported back to the EAT, the judge will decide what further steps should be directed in the appeal. If a settlement has been achieved, the appeal, or any particular ground, will be dismissed by the Registrar on withdrawal by the appellant. If requested by the parties, the terms of the settlement may be annexed as a Schedule to the Registrar's Order. Where the parties seek to have the appeal allowed by consent, adequate reasons must be given.

At any stage, the Registrar or a judge can require the parties to **report to the EAT** on steps taken between the parties towards conciliation with the assistance of the Acas officer, but not with regard to the substance of any such conciliated settlement (para 22 EAT PD).

Rule 3(7) cases

9761 If, having received a notice of appeal, the judge or Registrar decides that the notice of appeal discloses no reasonable grounds for bringing the appeal or is an abuse of the EAT's process or is otherwise likely to obstruct the just disposal of the proceedings, the judge or Registrar will notify the appellant of his reasons and no further action will be taken on the notice of appeal (rule 3(7) EATR; as amended by reg 4 SI 2004/2526).

If the claimant **accepts** this, no further action will be taken on that appeal but he can lodge a fresh appeal either within the original time limit (if still applicable) or within 28 days from the date the notification was given to him. On the other hand, if the appellant **contests** this, the appellant must activate the prescribed procedure (rule 3(8)-(10) EATR, as amended) within 28 days of the date the notification was given to him. The claimant can request an oral hearing before a judge to challenge the decision and if it appears to the judge or Registrar that the notice of appeal gave insufficient grounds of, or lacked clarity in identifying, a point of law, he can postpone any decision under rule 3(7), pending further explanation or clarification (para 2.5 EAT PD).

Preliminary hearing (PH) and directions

9762 Where the EAT's jurisdiction is not at issue, the judge or Registrar may nevertheless decide to list the appeal for a PH, the **purpose** of which is to determine whether the notice of appeal raises a valid point of law which gives rise to a reasonable prospect of success (paras 9.7 – .18

EAT PD). Alternatively, the EAT may consider that there is some other compelling reason that the appeal should go to an FH.

The aim of the PH is to eliminate at an early stage those appeals which have **no prospect of success**.

> MEMO POINTS   If a party intends to cite any authority at a PH, he must lodge three copies (one copy if the judge is sitting alone) no less than 10 days before the hearing, and additional copies for any other parties notified (para 14.6 EATPD). However, the EAT produces a list of familiar authorities of which copies do not need to be provided (¶9780). Authorities should be bundled, indexed and incorporated into one agreed bundle.

Hearing and decision   Only the appellant (or his representative) need **attend**, unless the respondent has indicated that he intends to cross-appeal. The appellant will be invited to make submissions on whether the notice of appeal raises a reasonably arguable point of law. The respondent will not be allowed to present any arguments relating to the merits of the appeal, although he may make submissions in relation to directions, and will be allowed to make submissions in relation to any cross-appeal (see below).

The hearing will be short (usually not more than an hour), and if a reasonably arguable point of law is established, the EAT will allow the **appeal to go forward** to a full hearing on all or only some of the grounds of appeal. If the appeal is **allowed to proceed**, it will be assigned to a listing category (¶9765) and the EAT may also give **directions** covering matters such as exchange of documents, time estimates, applications for fresh evidence, production of the judge's notes of evidence (¶9782) and amendments to the notice of appeal.

If a reasonably arguable point of law has not been established, the EAT will give a judgment explaining why the **appeal** is to be **dismissed**, whether in whole or in part.

9763

Further directions   In order to ensure that appeals are dealt with as swiftly and efficiently as possible, parties are encouraged to ensure that all necessary directions are obtained at the PH. Later applications for directions are only considered if the EAT is satisfied that there was a **good reason** for failing to apply for them at the PH (rule 19 EATR). Such applications are also likely to result in the party applying being ordered to pay the costs (even if he is successful in obtaining the directions).

The EAT also has power to give directions of its own motion at any stage in the proceedings (rule 25 EATR). At this stage, it will give further directions relating to, for example, a time estimate, any application for fresh evidence, the exchange of skeleton arguments and the appellant's chronology, and bundles of documents and authorities for use at the FH.

9764

Full hearing (FH) and fast track cases (FTFH)

If a judge or the Registrar decides to list the case for an FH without the need for a PH, then he will consider what directions should be given to the parties (see below). Each appeal will be assigned a listing category (which can be altered at the President's discretion) (para 9.18 EAT PD):
– P: recommended to be heard in the President's list;
– A: complex, and raising point(s) of public importance; and
– B: any other case.

Although FH cases are generally heard in the order in which they are received by the EAT, in certain circumstances an appeal may be listed for the fast track, in which case it will be heard as soon as it can be fitted into the list.

9765

Fast track appeals are normally one of the following appeals where (para 9.20 EAT PD):
– the parties have applied, and there are merits, for an expedited hearing;
– the parties are appealing against an interim order, directions, or decisions of the tribunal which require action within a specified period;
– other applications to the tribunal or EAT depend on the outcome of the appeal;
– one or both parties have sought a reference to the Court of Justice of the European Union or a declaration of incompatibility under the Human Rights Act 1998; or

9766

– one of the parties has sought an order for reinstatement, re-engagement, interim relief or (in discrimination cases) recommendation for action.

4. Procedure

Contesting the appeal and cross-appeals

9770 After the appeal has been allocated to a particular track listing, or after a PH at which an appeal has been permitted to proceed to FH, the **EAT will send** to the respondent the **notice of appeal**, together with any permitted amendments, written submissions and/or skeleton argument lodged by the appellant.

9771 If the respondent wishes to contest the appeal, he must deliver a **written answer** within 14 days of the date of the notice of appeal (para 10.1 EAT PD). If he fails to meet this time limit, the respondent may be prevented from taking part in the appeal unless he obtains permission to serve his answer out of time.

At the same time as lodging and serving the written answer, the respondent may also wish to **appeal against the tribunal decision** (or a certain aspect of it) (known as a **cross-appeal**). If his answer contains a cross-appeal, the appellant must lodge and serve his reply within 14 days of service. In his written submissions he must state whether his cross-appeal is **conditional**, i.e. he intends to cross-appeal only if the other party's appeal is allowed to proceed to an FH, or whether it is **unconditional**, i.e. he wishes to cross-appeal regardless of whether or not the other party's appeal is allowed to proceed.

In such cases, the cross-appeal is also **considered at the PH**. The party putting forward the cross-appeal is entitled to appear and must satisfy the EAT that there is a reasonably arguable point of law in the cross-appeal. The EAT treats the cross-appeal in the same way as it does the original appeal and will decide whether or not it should be allowed to go forward to an FH.

> EXAMPLE A tribunal finds that an employee has been unfairly dismissed but reduces compensation by 80% to reflect contributory fault. The employee may wish to appeal against the finding of contributory fault, while the employer may wish to cross-appeal against the finding of unfair dismissal itself.

9772 **Directions** After the respondent has lodged and served his written answer (and any cross-appeal), the Registrar may invite the parties to apply for directions. At this stage, he may give any appropriate directions that he sees fit of his own motion or, alternatively, may fix a date for the parties to attend a directions hearing (para 10.2 EAT PD).

9773 **Failure to deliver answer** A respondent who fails to lodge his written answer may be prevented from taking any further part in the proceedings, but the EAT has discretion to make such order as it thinks just in the circumstances. As for notices of appeal, it is possible to apply for an **extension of time** (see above).

9774 **Amendment of answer** The procedure for amending a respondent's answer is as for the notice of appeal (see above).

Interim applications

9775 While parties are encouraged to ensure that all directions are given at the PH, it is possible to make interim applications (for example, amendments to notice of appeal or answer, joinder of additional parties, consolidation with other appeals, directions dealing with evidence and arrangements for the hearing).

9776 **Form and procedure** Such applications should be made in writing and must specify the direction or order sought. An interim application will in the first instance be dealt with by the Registrar who will serve a copy of the application on the other party and notify both parties of how he intends to deal with it. In general, applications will be dealt with at an **oral hearing** unless the application is not opposed (in which case an order may be made without the parties having to attend) or where the Registrar decides that it can be dealt with by way of **written submissions** from the parties. If the application is to strike out pleadings or to prevent a party in default from taking any further part in the proceedings, the application will usually be heard before the start of the main appeal hearing.

Conduct and appeal The Registrar will normally deal with interim applications, having regard to the EAT's overriding objective. However, the Registrar may refer the matter either to the President or a judge (who may themselves refer it on to a full division of the EAT if they think it appropriate or refer it back to the Registrar with such directions as they think fit). Interim applications for a **restricted reporting order** or for permission to **start or continue** to make **a claim** in any proceedings before an employment tribunal must be disposed of by the President or a judge (rule 20 EATR; as amended by reg 13 SI 2004/2526).

9777

Decisions made by the Registrar can be appealed to a judge, who again can refer it to a full division of the EAT or determine the appeal himself. Notice of any such appeal should be given to the EAT within 5 days of the Registrar's decision.

Preparation for the hearing

Preparation will include the collation of relevant documents, (possibly) the production of the judge's notes, and the service of a skeleton argument.

9779

Documents Any documents **relevant** to the point of law on which the appeal is based (i.e. not necessarily all documents produced at the tribunal stage) should be sent to the EAT as soon as possible, and subject to the time limits set out below.

9780

Responsibility for the preparation of the **core bundle** of papers for use at the hearing lies with both parties and their advisers, although ultimately, the appellant is responsible, following consultation with the other parties (para 6.1 EAT PD). It is also the responsibility of the parties to **retain copies** of all documents and correspondence, including hearing bundles, sent to the EAT since the EAT will not retain a bundle used at one hearing for any subsequent hearing (para 6.1 EAT PD). **Guidance** as to which documents should appear in the core bundle is found in the Practice Direction (para 6 EAT PD).

If the **parties disagree** over the content of the bundles, they can apply to the Registrar for directions, or the Registrar may give such directions of his own motion.

> MEMO POINTS   The EAT issued a Practice Statement in April 2012 (set out at [2012] IRLR 523) outlining **best practice** in relation to the use of **authorities**. It gives the following guidance:
> 1. use photo or online copies of formal reports, such as the ICRs or IRLRs, rather than those available from other online resources;
> 2. cases should be presented in chronological order;
> 3. relevant passages on which a party intends to rely should be sidelined and/or highlighted clearly;
> 4. if ring binders are used, they should be properly tabulated;
> 5. there is no need to include copies of the EAT's familiar authorities (a list of which is kept on the EAT's website). If parties wish to rely on these authorities then it is sufficient to simply identify the relevant principle by reference to the paragraph number(s);
> 6. generally speaking no more than ten authorities should be used unless the scale of the appeal requires it and parties should be prepared to justify more extensive citation (the Practice Statement highlights a civil appeal Practice Direction which establishes this rule in respect of the EAT in England, and states that the same general principle applies to the EATs of Scotland and Wales as per the EAT's current Practice Direction); and
> 7. cases should set out a legal principle rather than be merely illustrative.

The **time limits** for lodging a core bundle vary depending on where the appeal has been allocated (i.e. which track). For **PH cases**, lodge four copies (two copies if the judge is sitting alone) of the bundle as soon as possible after service of the notice of appeal and no later than 28 days from the date of the relevant order (para 6.5 EAT PD). In **FH cases**, the parties

9781

must agree on a core bundle and the appellant is responsible for lodging four copies (two if the judge is sitting alone) of the bundle with the EAT no later than 28 days from the date of the relevant order (para 6.6 EAT PD). In respect of **warned list** (¶9792) and **fast track** cases, the bundles should be lodged as soon as possible and (unless the hearing date is earlier than 7 days later) not later than 7 days after the parties have been notified that the case is expedited or in the warned list (para 6.7 EAT PD).

9782 **Evidence before employment tribunal and Employment Judge's notes** Parties who consider that it is necessary to **refer to evidence** heard before the employment tribunal which does not sufficiently appear from the tribunal's decision or reasons can apply for such evidence to be produced before the EAT (para 7 EAT PD).

Ordinarily, an **appellant should make his application** when he submits his notice of appeal. However, in exceptional circumstances, he can apply later (para 7.1 EAT PD). A **respondent** must make such an application with his answer, or before if possible.

The party seeking production **must state** the issues in the appeal in respect of which the evidence is required, the names of those witnesses in respect of whose evidence the notes are required, and the parts of the witness' evidence alleged to be necessary.

9783 The application will be **considered on** the papers, **or by** the Registrar or a judge at PH stage. The Registrar or judge may:
– determine the application; or
– give directions for written representations (if they have not already been lodged).

However, the Registrar or judge will **ordinarily make** an order requiring the party to give notice to the other party(ies) to the appeal/cross-appeal. The notice will require the other party(ies) to co-operate in agreeing, within 21 days (unless a shorter period is ordered), a statement or note of the relevant evidence. All parties are required to use their best endeavours to agree such a statement or note (para 7.3 EAT PD).

If the parties **fail to agree**, either party may apply for directions from the EAT within 7 days. The directions may include (para 7.4 EAT PD):
– resolution of the disagreement on the written submissions or at a hearing;
– the administration by one party to the other(s) of, or a request to the judge to respond to, a questionnaire; or
– if the EAT is satisfied that it is necessary, a request that the judge produce his notes of evidence either in whole or in part.

9784 The **EAT must be satisfied** that production of the notes is necessary to enable the appeal to be dealt with fairly, for example if it is alleged that there is no evidence to support a particular finding of fact, or that the tribunal failed to make a relevant finding of fact which it ought to have made on the basis of the evidence as put forward, or that a finding of fact is perverse in the sense that no tribunal properly directed could have reached that conclusion. If the EAT considers that the notes should be produced, the judge is then obliged to provide them.

If a party believes that the judge's **notes of evidence are inaccurate**, the EAT has suggested that the proper procedure should be as follows (*Dexine Rubber Company Limited v Alker* [1977] ICR 434, EAT):
– the party should submit his criticism to the advocate for the opposite party;
– the criticism should then be submitted to the judge; and
– if the judge, having considered the criticisms, confirms that in his view this note is accurate, then unless there is a joint confirmation from both opposing advocates that they believe otherwise, the EAT will accept the judge's notes as being accurate.

A note of evidence is not to be produced and supplied to the parties to enable the parties to embark on a "**fishing expedition**" to establish grounds or additional grounds of appeal or because they have not kept their own notes of the evidence. If an application for such a note is found by the EAT to have been unreasonably made or if there is unreasonable lack of co-operation in agreeing a relevant note or statement, the party behaving unreasonably is at risk of being ordered to **pay costs** (para 7.7 EAT PD).

New evidence Any application to include new evidence should be **lodged at** the EAT with the notice of appeal or the respondent's answer, as appropriate (para 8 EAT PD). The application and copy should be served on the other parties. Details of the nature and substance of such evidence together with the date when the party first became aware of its existence should be included and copies of any relevant documents should be lodged and served. The evidence and representations in support of the application must address the principles set out at ¶9752.

The application will be **considered by** the Registrar or a judge on the papers (or, if appropriate, at a PH) who may determine the issue or give directions for a hearing or may seek comments from the judge (para 8.4 EAT PD).

A party wishing to **resist the application** must, within 14 days of it being sent, submit any representations in response to the EAT and other parties.

9785

Skeleton arguments Parties in all appeals are required to serve a skeleton argument on the EAT **in advance of** the hearing date for the appeal.

The skeleton argument should briefly **identify and summarise** the points in the legal argument to be put forward by that party, specifying statutory provisions and authorities to be relied on. The skeleton argument should also set out the **form of order** which the party seeks from the EAT. As well as the skeleton argument, the appellant should also submit a **written chronology** of relevant events. Where possible, the chronology should be agreed by both parties.

9786

> MEMO POINTS The parties must co-operate in agreeing a list of case authorities and jointly or severally lodge a list and three bundles of copies (one copy if the judge is sitting alone) of the authorities to be cited at the EAT no later than 7 days before the FH (para 14.7 EAT PD).

The **time limits** for submitting skeleton arguments vary depending on where (i.e. which track) the appeal has been allocated (para 13.9 EAT PD).

In respect of **FH appeals**, parties must lodge with the EAT and exchange their skeleton arguments no later than 14 days before the hearing. For **PH appeals**, the skeleton arguments must be lodged with the EAT no later than 10 days before the date fixed for the PH or, if the PH is listed for less than 7 days' notice, the skeleton arguments should be lodged as soon as possible after notification of the hearing date. If both parties are to be present at the PH, then they must also exchange them within these time limits. In respect of **warned list** (¶9792) and **fast track** cases, the skeleton arguments must be lodged as soon as possible and, unless the hearing date is at less than 7 days' notice, in any event within 7 days of notification of the hearing date.

9787

Appeal hearing

The appeal will be heard by an appeal panel, as described below.

9788

Composition of appeal panel When an appeal is heard, the EAT panel will in **most cases consist of** a judge and either two or four (usually two) lay members (s 28 Employment Tribunals Act 1996). The parties can consent to an appeal being heard by a judge and either one or three lay members. Where there is an even number of lay members, there must be an equal number representing employers and employees.

9789

If the parties are asked to consent to an appeal being heard by just the judge and one appointed lay member, then the consent must be informed (*De Haney v Brent Mind* [2004] ICR 348, CA). In this case, the unrepresented appellant had given her consent for the appeal to be heard by the judge and one lay member, but she had not realised until the hearing itself that the lay member had represented the employer's side of industry (see memo point below).

> MEMO POINTS EAT **judges** are selected from judges of the High Court and Court of Appeal (and at least one judge of the Court of Session in Scotland) (s 22(1) Employment Tribunals Act 1996). Additional judges can be appointed either to fill vacancies temporarily or to assist in the disposal of business. The **lay members** are appointed on the basis of their experience of industrial relations, some of whom represent the employee's side of industry and others the employer's side (s 22 Employment Tribunals Act 1996).

9790 If the tribunal decision appealed against was taken by a judge sitting alone, then the appeal would be heard by a **judge sitting alone** unless the judge directs otherwise (s 28 Employment Tribunals Act 1996).

> MEMO POINTS   There are special provisions regarding cases involving **national security**. If a Minister of the Crown so directs, then such an appeal is heard by the President of the EAT sitting alone.

9791 **Representation and legal aid** As in the tribunal, a party may appear in person or be **represented** by a barrister or a solicitor, a trade union representative, an employer's association representative, or by any other person whom he desires to represent him (s 9(1) Employment Tribunals Act 1996).

Legal aid is available for bringing or defending cases in the EAT.

> MEMO POINTS   The Legal Aid Board which used to administer legal aid has been replaced by the **Legal Services Commission** (LSC). Eligibility assessment for funding is made to the LSC through a solicitor or advice agency.

9792 **Date of hearing** The EAT will normally try to agree a date for the main appeal hearing with the parties. Cases will either be given a **fixed date** or placed in a **warned list**, which is prepared at the beginning of each month. The parties (or their representatives) are informed if their case is included in this list. If fixed date cases settle or are withdrawn, cases from the warned list will be called on in their place and the parties will be notified as soon as possible of the hearing date.

9793 **Procedure** EAT hearings are **held in public** but the same exceptions apply as in the case of employment tribunals (¶¶9619+).

As appeals are on a point of law, most appeals will only involve **legal argument**. However, if **witness evidence** is required, the EAT can hear evidence on oath and can order witnesses to attend.

The appellant will normally **go first**.

Decision

9794 Decisions can be **made by** majority (most are unanimous).

If **judgment is reserved**, the parties are notified of the date on which it will be handed down in writing and a copy of the judgment will be provided to all parties (para 18 EAT PD). Where a **judgment is delivered** at the FH, no transcript of it will be provided unless either party applies for it within 14 days or if the EAT so directs that the judgment should be transcribed (para 18.5 EAT PD). It should be noted that all FH judgments which are transcribed or handed down will be posted onto the EAT website and are accessible by the public.

9795 **EAT orders** After hearing an appeal, the EAT can make an order:
a. **dismissing** the appeal; or
b. **allowing** the appeal; and:
– substituting its own decision for that of the tribunal; or
– remitting the case (i.e. sending it back) to either the same or a different tribunal for a complete re-hearing or further consideration of a particular point.

The EAT's order is **sealed** by the Registrar before being sent to the parties.

9796 Where an **appeal is allowed**, the nature of the error of law identified will determine whether the EAT **substitutes its own decision or remits** the case. If the tribunal has misdirected itself as to the law, its decision can only stand if the EAT considers that the conclusion is plainly and unarguably right notwithstanding the misdirection (Moore v University of Greenwich [2002] UKEAT 0942_01_0507). However, if the EAT believes that **further consideration of the facts** is required, then it will remit the case. If, however, no further consideration of the facts is necessary but the **decision is plainly wrong** because of the way in which the tribunal has applied the law, the EAT will be more willing to substitute its own decision. It can only do so if a proper application of the law would inevitably have led the tribunal to a certain conclusion. If, however, in applying the law properly, the tribunal could have come to one of a number of different conclusions, the case will be remitted. The EAT can also remit the case for **fuller reasons** from the tribunal prior to a further hearing on appeal (*English v Emery Reimbold and Strick Ltd* [2003] IRLR 710, CA; *Burns v Consignia plc (No. 2)* [2004] IRLR 425, EAT followed and confirmed in *Barke v Seetec Business Technology Centre Ltd* [2005] IRLR 633, EAT). This process is generally known as the **Burns/Barke** procedure.

If a case is to be remitted, the EAT will also decide whether it should be remitted **back to the same tribunal** that heard the case originally or when it should be remitted **to a fresh tribunal** (which would require a full re-hearing of the case). The **relevant factors** which will be considered are as follows (*Sinclair Roche and Temperley and ors v Heard and anor* [2004] IRLR 763, EAT):

– **proportionality**. Where there is sufficient money at stake the question of costs does not offend on the grounds of proportionality although this may not be a decisive, or even an important, factor. Likewise, the distress and inconvenience of the parties in reliving a hearing must be weighed up although this will not be greatly less by virtue of the extra time taken by a fully, rather than partially remitted, hearing;

– **passage of time**. A matter should not be sent back to the same tribunal if there is a real risk that it will have forgotten about the case. However, tribunals should normally be able to refresh their minds from notes of evidence and submissions if the case occurred relatively recently. Further, the longer the case the more likely a tribunal is to remember it. In this case, the hearing which was over a year ago was held to be in the minds of the original tribunal as the hearing was relatively lengthy and the tribunal had come back to the case over that year in giving its reserved decision followed later by its promulgated decision, as well as having a remedies hearing and various chambers' meetings;

– **bias or partiality**. A matter will not be sent back to the same tribunal where there is a question of bias or the risk of pre-judgment or partiality;

– **totally flawed decision**. It is not ordinarily appropriate to send a matter back to a tribunal where the first hearing was wholly flawed or there was a complete mishandling of it. The appellate tribunal must have confidence that, with guidance, the tribunal can get it right second time;

– **second bite at the cherry**. A matter must not be sent back to the same tribunal if, on the face of it, the tribunal has already made up its mind in relation to all the matters before it; and

– **tribunal professionalism**. On the balance of all the above facts, an appellate tribunal should ordinarily consider that, in the absence of clear indications to the contrary, it should be assumed that the tribunal below is capable of a professional approach to dealing with a matter on remission. It follows that where a tribunal is corrected on an honest misunderstanding or misapplication of the legally required approach (not amounting to a "totally flawed" decision), then, unless it appears that the tribunal has so thoroughly committed itself that a rethink appears impracticable, there is the presumption that it will go about the tasks set out on remission in a professional way, paying careful attention to the guidance given to it by the appellate tribunal.

Consent orders The EAT should be informed immediately if:
– an appellant decides to **abandon or withdraw an appeal**;
– the parties agree a **compromise**; or
– the parties agree that the **appeal should be allowed** and that the tribunal order should be reversed or varied or the matter remitted on the ground that the decision contains an error of law.

The EAT's permission is required in order to **withdraw an appeal**. If the parties have agreed an order for withdrawal, it should be submitted to the EAT for approval. If the parties are agreed that the appeal should be withdrawn but do not agree to the terms of a proposed order (which might arise if the respondent wishes to apply for costs against the appellant), the EAT will arrange a hearing to determine the outstanding matters. If the application to withdraw is made close to the main appeal hearing, the EAT may require the attendance of the appellant (or his representative) to explain the reasons for the delay in making a decision not to pursue the appeal, and in such circumstances may be minded to award costs and/or wasted costs (¶9800).

If the agreement is that the **appeal should be allowed**, the EAT normally has a hearing to decide whether or not the order should be made (although it can decide on the papers alone). To save costs it may only require one party to attend to put forward the reasons why the order should be made.

9798 **Previous decisions and precedent** The EAT is bound by decisions of the **Court of Appeal** and **Supreme Court** on English Law, and decisions of the Court of Session (Inner House) and Supreme Court on Scottish Law (i.e. it must follow these decisions in later cases).

Decisions of the **High Court** in England and Wales, and of the Outer House of the Court of Session in Scotland, are regarded as being highly persuasive (i.e. the EAT will normally follow them unless it is persuaded that there is a good reason why it should not do so).

The EAT is not bound by its **own previous decisions**. It will, however, depart from them only in exceptional circumstances or where there are previous inconsistencies. When faced with **inconsistent decisions** the EAT attempts to resolve any conflicts and, if necessary, will direct employment tribunals as to which decision should be followed and which should be disregarded.

9799 **Decisions of the EAT** (whether sitting in England and Wales or Scotland) are binding on all employment tribunals in England, Wales or Scotland.

9800 **Costs** The position on costs is similar to that in the tribunal (¶9702). An order for costs may be made where the EAT considers that **proceedings were unnecessary, improper or vexatious**, or that there has been **unreasonable delay** or **other unreasonable conduct** in bringing or conducting the proceedings (rule 34A EATR; as inserted by reg 21 SI 2004/2526). This might include a party who pursued an obviously hopeless appeal, or if a party abandoned an appeal at the last minute or failed to attend the appeal hearing without good excuse. For discussion of vexatious proceedings, unreasonable conduct etc, see ¶9566.

The fact that an appeal has gone through the sifting stage (¶9760) does not prevent it from having a costs order made against the appeal (*Iron and Steel Trades Confederation v ASW Ltd (in liquidation)* [2004] IRLR 926, EAT). However, it will be a factor in deciding whether such an order should be made.

9801 A party may be ordered to pay all or part of the costs or expenses **occurred by another party**. The EAT may either **assess the costs** itself or refer the matter to the taxing officer authorised by the President of the EAT to assess costs or expenses. Where the taxing officer assesses costs, his decision may be appealed to a judge. Alternatively, the parties may agree on a sum to be paid between themselves.

There is **no cap** on the costs which may be awarded by the EAT. However, the EAT will take into account the paying party's **ability to pay** when considering the amount of a costs order (rule 34B EATR; as inserted by reg 21 SI 2004/2526).

Where the EAT makes a costs order **in favour of** a **party who is not legally represented**, the costs (excluding disbursements) cannot exceed two-thirds of the amount which would have been allowed if the party had been legally represented (rule 34D EATR; as inserted by reg 21 SI 2004/2526). The **costs allowed** include costs for work and disbursements which would have been allowed if the work had been done or the disbursements made by a legal representative on the party's behalf, payments reasonably made by him for legal services relating to the conduct of the proceedings, costs in obtaining expert assistance in assessing the costs claim and other expenses incurred by him in relation to the proceedings (including expenditure on his employees, but not including any allowance paid to a witness to attend the appeal hearing). If the unrepresented party can prove his financial loss for the time reasonably spent on doing the work in relation to the proceedings, the costs will cover this amount. Where he cannot prove his financial loss, his costs will be calculated by the EAT for an amount of time which the EAT considers reasonably spent on doing the work at the rate of £32 per hour.

MEMO POINTS   From **6 April 2013**, the hourly rate will be increased to £33.

Wasted costs   The EAT is also able to make a wasted costs order against a party's representative if it considers that the representative has acted improperly, unreasonably, or negligently in relation to the proceedings (rule 34C EATR; as inserted by reg 21 SI 2004/2526). The rules relating to wasted costs are the same as in respect of the employment tribunal (¶9711).

Review and appeals

The EAT has a similar power to **review** its own orders (and, if appropriate, to revoke or vary them) as the tribunal (¶9718). It **can do so if** (rule 33 EATR):
– the order was wrongly made as a result of an error on the part of the EAT or its staff;
– a party did not receive proper notice of the proceedings leading to the order; or
– the interests of justice require a review.

The EAT can decide of its own motion to have a review (though it rarely does so), or a party can apply for a review within 14 days of the date of the order. A clerical mistake in any order may be corrected at any time by order of a judge or a member of the appeal panel.

Where an application for review is made, it may be considered on paper by the judge who heard the original appeal or made the original order (para 20 EAT PD). In such circumstances, where the judge in question had sat alone without lay members, he will deal with the application as he thinks fit. If, on the other hand, the judge had sat with lay members and, on consideration of the application on paper, thinks that an order may need to be varied or revoked, he will give notice to the other party and consult with the original lay members either on paper or in open court.

Decisions of the EAT can be **appealed** to the Court of Appeal on a point of law. The appeal procedure is discussed below.

B. Court of Appeal

Appeals from the EAT and the High Court are dealt with by the Court of Appeal (Civil Division), which has appellate jurisdiction only (i.e. it only hears appeals against the decisions of lower courts in England and Wales; cases do not start there). The Court of Appeal sits in London at the Royal Courts of Justice. In Scotland, the appeal is to the Inner House of the Court of Session, which sits in Edinburgh.

Like the EAT, the Court of Appeal can only consider appeals on a **point of law** and cannot interfere with findings of fact.

The appeal must be **lodged** with the Court of Appeal not later than 4 weeks after the date on which the EAT's order is sealed by the Registrar of the EAT.

Before lodging an appeal, an application for **permission to appeal** must be made at the EAT hearing or when a reserved judgment is handed down, or in writing within 7 days of the hearing or handing down of the judgment (para 21 EAT PD). If not made at this stage, or if the EAT refuses permission, then permission must be sought from the Court of Appeal within 21 days of the sealed order. If a transcript is requested after the hearing with a view to making an application for permission to appeal, then the potential appellant must apply for an extension of time for permission to appeal if necessary. The application **must state** the point of law and the grounds on which the appeal is based.

Appeals are **heard by** a panel of three senior judges (known as Lord or Lady Justice X), who decide whether or not to allow the appeal by majority if they are unable to reach a unanimous decision.

9823 Further, where the Court of Appeal disagrees with the decision of the court or tribunal below, it will normally substitute its own **decision** (unlike the EAT which often remits cases to be heard again by the same or another tribunal).

9824 Decisions of the Court of Appeal may be **appealed** to the Supreme Court (see below).

C. UK Supreme Court

9830 The Supreme Court is the highest appellate court in the United Kingdom and consists of Justices (previously called Lords of Appeal in Ordinary ("Law Lords")). It hears appeals on a **point of law** from the Court of Appeal (and from the Inner House of the Court of Session in Scotland). **Permission to appeal** is required either from the Court of Appeal (or Court of Session) or the Supreme Court. Permission is normally only granted in cases where the point at issue is of general public importance.

> MEMO POINTS 1. The **rules of procedure** of the Supreme Court are set out in legislation (Supreme Court Rules SI 2009/1603). The Supreme Court also has its own **Practice Directions** (which replace the Civil, Criminal and Taxation Practice Directions and standing orders of the Appellate Committee of the House of Lords).
> 2. The UK Supreme Court came into being on 1 October 2009 and **replaced** the **House of Lords** in its judicial capacity and jurisdiction (Constitutional Reform Act 2005).

9831 A **notice of appeal** must be filed within 42 days of the date of the order or decision of the court below. Where the permission to appeal has been granted by the Supreme Court, the application for permission to appeal will stand as the notice of appeal and the appellant must, within 14 days of the grant by the Court of permission to appeal, file notice that he wishes to proceed with his appeal.

9832 Appeals are normally **heard by** five judges. In cases of particular importance, seven judges may sit. Appeals are decided by majority if a unanimous decision cannot be reached.

9833 **Judgments** are given on a day notified in advance. One week's notice will normally be given.
The Supreme Court is not bound by its own **previous decisions**.

9834 The decision of the Supreme Court is final, i.e. there is **no further right of appeal**.

D. Referral to the Court of Justice of the European Union

9840 The courts of member states (including the EAT and employment tribunals) can refer questions relating to the **interpretation of EU law** to the Court of Justice of the European Union (CJEU) (previously called the European Court of Justice (ECJ)) for a **preliminary ruling**. EU law does not usually have direct effect – it needs to be implemented by the introduction of domestic laws in each member state (for example, the Working Time Regulations 1998 implement the EU Working Time Directive). Questions may, therefore, arise as to whether a member state has fully complied with its obligation or as to the interpretation which should be given to domestic legislation in order to give effect to the EU law. Such questions may be referred to the CJEU so that it can give guidance and ensure uniform application across the member states.

The CJEU comprises 15 judges and eight advocates general, appointed by the member states. The judges select one of their number to serve as President. An **advocate general** delivers an impartial opinion on a case (in open court) before the **judges** make their decision. The judges do not have to follow the advocate general's opinion, but his opinion can usually be taken as a guide to the way in which the CJEU will ultimately decide the case.

Procedure The national court **submits the questions** which it wishes to have determined (usually in the form of a judgment). This is then translated into all the official EU languages and distributed to all member states, the Commission and the Council of Ministers. A **notice** is published in the Official Journal of the European Communities.

9841

The parties and those to whom the request is distributed have 2 months in which to **submit written observations** to the CJEU. Unlike domestic claims, **legal aid** may be applied for, the decision whether to grant it being made by a chamber of the CJEU.

The case is summarised in a **report** which is made public. A **public hearing** is then held at which the parties argue the case and are questioned by the judges and the advocate general. The CJEU sits either in **plenary session** (all 15 judges) or in **chambers** of three or five judges. A plenary session is held if a member state or EU institution which is a party to the case requests it to do so, or if the case is particularly complex or important.

A few weeks later the advocate general delivers his **opinion** in open court. The judges will subsequently deliberate on the basis of a draft judgment which one of them has prepared.

When they have all agreed on the final text of the **judgment**, it will be delivered in open court. Decisions of the CJEU are by majority. No dissenting opinions are given.

MEMO POINTS The EU Commission or another member state may bring proceedings against a **member state** alleging that it has **not fulfilled its obligations** under EU law. For example, the CJEU ruled that the UK Government was obliged to implement the Working Time Directive, rejecting the UK Government's argument that the UK was not bound by the Directive.

Normally an appeal court **makes the referral** (i.e. the EAT, Court of Appeal or Supreme Court). While it is unusual for cases to be referred directly to the CJEU by an employment tribunal, a tribunal does also have the power to do so.

9842

EXAMPLE In *Attridge Law and anor v Coleman* [2007] IRLR 88, EAT, a tribunal referred the questions of whether the European Equal Treatment Framework Directive covered carers and whether the then domestic legislation should be read in light of the Directive. An appeal to the EAT against the referral was unsuccessful.

SECTION 3

Claims in the civil courts

The county courts are governed by the same rules of procedure as the High Court, and may award the same remedies.

9850

Commencing proceedings

Claims are commenced by service of a **claim form** setting out the basis for the claim and the remedies sought. This form may include the particulars of the claim, or these may be sent separately. The person making the claim is called the claimant, and the other party, the defendant.

9851

The defendant must serve an **acknowledgement of service** within 14 days' service of the claim form stating whether or not he intends to defend the claim. Within 28 days from service of the particulars of claim, he must serve a **defence** in which he sets out his grounds for defending the claim.

9852

Directions

The Court plays an active part in the management of the case and will give directions to bring it to trial as efficiently as possible. The procedural rules require the parties to proceedings to disclose the existence of relevant documents to each other and/or to allow inspection of such documents. The directions set out a timetable for discovery and inspection, and also

9853

deal with matters such as exchange of witness statements, exchange of expert evidence, and preparation of trial bundles.

Hearing

9854 The trial will be held in public before a judge, sitting without a jury. The procedure at the trial is similar to, but more formal than, that at a tribunal hearing. Each party (normally represented by a barrister) will make an **opening statement**. They will then call their **witnesses** who will each give their evidence and be cross-examined by the other party's representative. The judge may also ask questions. Each party will then make his **closing submissions**. As in the tribunal, the party with the burden of proof will generally go first.

Decision

9855 The judge may either give his decision at the end of the trial or reserve it to be handed down later. When the judge gives his decision, he normally also gives a **judgment** setting out his reasoning. If the judgment is not handed down in writing, a transcript may be obtained later through the Court Service.

Remedies

9856 The High Court may award damages, and also has the power to grant injunctions and declarations.

Costs

9857 In the High Court, the party who loses the case normally has to pay the costs of the party who wins. If the parties cannot agree the figure for costs, costs are assessed as described above for tribunal claims. Costs are also awarded at interlocutory stages so that if, for example, a party has to make an application to the Court in relation to inspection of documents, the party who "wins" that application is normally entitled to have his costs (in respect of that application) paid by the other party regardless of the final outcome of the case.

Appeals

9858 A decision of the High Court may be appealed initially to the Court of Appeal on a point of law (¶9820).

Appendix

OUTLINE	¶¶
Model statement of particulars	9900
Model contract of employment for general staff	9910
Model discipline and grievance policy	9915
Main social benefits	9920

Model statement of particulars

9900

Name and address of Company:

Name of Employee:

Date:

This statement sets out the particulars of your employment with [*Company*] which are required to be given to you under the Employment Rights Act 1996. The particulars are correct as at [*date*].

1. Start date and period of continuous employment

Your employment commenced on [*date*]. [Your period of continuous employment began on [*date*].] OR [No employment with a previous employer counts as continuous employment with [*Company*].]

2. Job title and duties

Your job title is [*job title*]. [The main duties of your position are [set out in the attached job description] OR [*describe main characteristics of job duties*].] [From time to time and at its absolute discretion, [*Company*] may require you to perform other duties to meet its business needs.]

3. Warranty

You warrant that you have the unconditional right to work in the UK. You agree to notify [*Company*] immediately should there be a change in your circumstances which may affect your right to work in the UK. [1]

4. Duration of employment [2]

[If you wish to terminate your employment, you must give [*Company*] [*period – minimum 1 week's*] prior written notice. Subject to [*Company*]'s right to terminate without notice [or payment in lieu of notice] in cases of gross misconduct or other serious breach (including your ceasing to be entitled to work in the UK), if [*Company*] wishes to terminate your employment, you will be given [1 week's notice during your first 2 years of employment and then an additional week's notice for each additional complete year of service up to a maximum of 12 weeks' notice].]

OR

[Your employment is for a fixed-term and will terminate on [date].] [It may be terminated at any time before the expiry of the fixed-term by either party giving to the other [applicable notice period]' prior written notice.]

OR

[Your employment is not intended to be permanent and is expected to continue until [date]. Either party may terminate your employment by giving to the other [applicable notice period]' prior written notice.]

5. Place of work

Your usual place of work is [address] [although from time to time and at the absolute discretion of [Company] you may be required to work at [other locations] on a temporary or permanent basis].

[[Company] may require you to [live and] work in [location outside UK] [on a temporary basis] for more than 1 month. Further details are provided [in clause [6] below].]

6. [Work outside the UK]

[It is anticipated that your posting to [location] will be for [period] [, subject to the absolute discretion of [Company] to change the period of your posting]. During that time your salary will be paid in [currency] and you will additionally be entitled to [additional remuneration or benefits, if any]. At the end of your posting, [terms and conditions relating to return to UK].]

7. Hours of work

Your normal hours of work are from [time] to [time] [Monday to Friday inclusive], with a [1 hour] [paid/unpaid] lunch break per day.

[You will not be required to work overtime.] OR [You may from time to time be required to work overtime. You are not entitled to any payment for overtime [unless agreed in advance with [job title]].] OR [Any overtime worked will be paid at the rate of £[amount] per hour.]

If overtime is worked, you must complete overtime sheets and return them to [the HR Department] to enable [Company] to comply with its obligations under the Working Time Regulations 1998 as amended ("the Regulations").

8. Remuneration

Your remuneration is £[amount] per [time period] subject to deductions for tax and NICs, payable by [method of payment] [interval of payment] on or about [time of payment].

You authorise [Company] both at any time during your employment and on the termination of your employment, to deduct from your salary payment and any sums [Company] is liable to repay to you any amount which you owe to [Company] from time to time including (but not limited to) any outstanding loans, advances, payments for excess holiday and overpayment of wages and you expressly consent to any such deductions pursuant to Part II of the Employment Rights Act 1996.

9. Pension

[[Company]'s pension arrangements are explained in [reasonably accessible document, such as the staff handbook].]

OR

[[Company] operates a [non-]contributory pension scheme, which you will be eligible to join [on commencement of employment/after completing [number] [weeks/months]' employment], subject to the rules of the scheme from time to time in force. Further details of the scheme are set out in a separate pensions booklet available from [details].]

OR

[[Company] has set up a Stakeholder Pension Scheme which you are eligible to join [on commencement of employment/after completing [number] [weeks/months]' employment], subject to the rules of the scheme from time to time in force. [[Company] does not contrib-

ute to the scheme.] Further details of the scheme are set out in a separate pensions booklet available from [*details*].]
OR

[[*Company*] does not operate a pension scheme in relation to your employment.] ³

[A contracting-out certificate under the Pension Schemes Act 1993 is [not] in force in respect of your employment.] ⁴

10. Annual leave

The leave year runs from [*date*] to [*date*]. You are entitled[, in addition to [English and Welsh] bank and public holidays,] to [*number*] days' paid holiday in each holiday year, accruing on a [*daily*] basis. ⁵ You will be paid [your normal basic remuneration] during such holidays. Your entitlement will be pro-rated in the year of joining and leaving [*Company*].

[You are required to use part of your annual entitlement during [*Company*]'s shutdown period in [*time/dates*]. [*Company*] will notify you by [*method and timing of notification*] of the exact number of days' holiday affected by this provision and the dates on which they must be taken.]

You must take your holiday at times convenient to [*Company*] and you must obtain the prior written approval of [*job title*] before taking a holiday. You are required to give at least [2 weeks'] notice of a proposed holiday. [No more than [*number*] days' holiday can be taken together unless [*job title*] gives permission.] [You must take at least [*number*] consecutive days' holiday in each holiday year.] [[*Company*] has the right to require you to use any outstanding holiday entitlement by the end of the holiday leave year, where possible. Any holiday entitlement not used in a holiday year will be forfeited save where a period of statutory maternity, paternity or adoption leave or a period of sickness has prevented you from taking your statutory entitlement to holiday in the preceding leave year [and any such leave carried over must be used within [18] months of your return to work, unless you become absent again for any of these reasons, in which case the [18] month period will be frozen until your return to work].] ⁶

You will be entitled to a payment in lieu of any holiday which has accrued but not been taken on the termination of your employment. [You will not accrue any contractual holiday entitlement during any period of notice (whether given by [*Company*] or you), save that your entitlement to annual leave pursuant to the Regulations shall continue to accrue during such period.] If, on the termination of your employment, you have taken holidays in excess of your entitlement, [*Company*] may deduct from your final salary an amount equal to the gross salary paid to you in respect of such holidays and you expressly consent to any such deductions pursuant to Part II of the Employment Rights Act 1996.

11. Sickness absence

[[*Company*]'s sick pay arrangements are explained in [*reasonably accessible document, such as the staff handbook*].]
OR

[If you are absent from work due to sickness or injury, you (or someone on your behalf) must inform [*job title*] of the reason for and likely duration of your absence no later than [*time*] on the first day of absence ⁷. If your sickness absence lasts 7 calendar days or less, you must complete a self-certification form on your return to work ⁸. For absences lasting more than 7 calendar days, you must produce a medical certificate from your doctor stating the reason for your absence. You must keep [*job title*] regularly informed of your absence and the likely duration of your absence. Further medical certificates are required for each further [week] of sickness absence. [Failure to notify [*Company*] of your absence may render you subject to disciplinary action and may also bar you from receiving sick pay.]

[[*Company*] may require you to undergo a medical examination at its expense and the results of any such examination may be disclosed to [*Company* [and its advisers]].] ⁹

[[*Company*] does not operate a sick pay scheme. Your entitlement is to Statutory Sick Pay (SSP) only.] OR [Subject to any right [*Company*] may have to terminate your employment and subject to your complying with all statutory and contractual notification requirements, you will be paid your normal basic remuneration (inclusive of any Statutory Sick Pay (SSP)) [and provided with all contractual benefits] for [*number*] working days of absence due to sickness or injury in any calendar year. Thereafter, you will be paid half your normal basic remuneration (inclusive of any SSP) [and provided all contractual benefits] for a further [*number*] working days of absence due to sickness or injury in that calendar year. Any payments to which you are entitled under any social security scheme (whether or not claimed by you) may be deducted from any sick pay paid to you by [*Company*]. Entitlement to payment is subject to your compliance with this clause [11].]

12. Discipline and grievances

The disciplinary rules and procedure and grievance procedure applicable to you are [attached to this statement] OR [set out in [*reasonably accessible document, such as the staff handbook*] [10]. These rules form part of the terms and conditions of your employment but any procedure is given by way of guideline only and does not have contractual effect.

13. Suspension

[*Company*] has the right to suspend you on normal pay for a period of up to [*number*] days in order to investigate any disciplinary allegations against you.

14. Collective agreements

[There are no collective agreements which affect the terms and conditions of your employment.]

OR

[The collective agreement(s) between [*parties*] directly affect(s) your terms and conditions of employment [*details of terms and conditions affected*].]

I acknowledge receipt of this statement.

Signed... (employee)

Dated...

---

1. The inclusion of the warranty regarding the right to work is not part of the information that has to be provided as evidence in writing of the employee's terms (¶1420), but it is a useful addition to include.
2. See clause 16 of ¶¶9910 for suggested wording for a payment in lieu of notice clause and provisions relating to gross misconduct.
3. Use only if employer falls outside scope of the automatic enrolment requirements (see ¶3402).
4. Since 6 April 2012, contracting out will no longer be possible through a money-purchase (defined-contribution) occupational pension scheme, a personal pension or a stakeholder pension, and those who are contracted out will be brought back into the S2P. For the time being, contracting out through an occupational salary-related (defined benefit) scheme will still be allowed. Contracting out is now rare, however, at present, statutory statements/contracts should still state whether there is a contracting out certificate in force.
5. Paid leave on bank or public holidays will count towards annual statutory entitlement (see ¶4009). For the minimum entitlement to annual statutory leave, see ¶4005.
6. For more information on the carrying over of statutory holiday not taken due to statutory maternity, paternity or adoption leave, see ¶4442 and in relation to sick leave, see ¶¶4102, 4103.
7. For SSP purposes, an employer cannot specify notification before a specific time on the first qualifying day.
8. For SSP purposes, an employer cannot insist on evidence of incapacity for the first 7 days of sickness.
9. If this clause is used, the employee should also be asked for their express consent to a medical examination and the disclosure of the report to the employer (see ¶4213).
10. It is important to have a comprehensive set of discipline and grievance rules and procedures in order to ensure a smooth resolution to workplace disputes where possible. This will help to ensure legal compliance, particularly with the Acas Code.

Model contract of employment for general staff

*This is an example of a short form contract of employment for general staff. More **senior staff** may need more complex and **additional clauses**, for example on intellectual property, garden leave and post-termination restrictive covenants.*

* *Clauses marked with an asterisk indicate that the information is required to be provided as part of the employer's obligation to give written particulars (¶1400).*

This Contract of Employment is made on [*date*] between:

(1) * [*Company*] of [*address*] ("[*Company*]") and

(2) * [*Employee*] of [*address*] ("you").

This Contract sets out the terms of your employment with [*Company*].

1. * Start date and period of continuous employment

[Your employment commenced on [*date*].] OR [Subject to the conditions set out [in your offer letter/below] being fulfilled, your employment will commence on [*date*].]

[*List any conditions, e.g. satisfactory medical, references, work permit etc*]

[Your period of continuous employment began on [*date*].] OR [No employment with a previous employer counts as continuous employment with [*Company*].]

2. * Job title and duties

Your job title is [*job title*]. [The main duties of your position are [set out in the attached job description] OR [*describe main characteristics of job duties*].] [From time to time and at its absolute discretion, [*Company*] may require you to perform any other reasonable duties within your capabilities and/or to move you to [another department] in order to meet its business needs.] [You will report to [*job title*] or such person(s) as may be notified to you from time to time.]

[[*Company*] reserves the right to transfer your employment to [another group company] and/or to second you to [such a company, OR *other company/organisation*].]

3. Warranty

You warrant that you have the unconditional right to work in the UK. Should this right be withdrawn or should your status materially change, you agree to notify [*Company*] immediately. [*Company*] reserves the right to terminate your employment, with or without notice (as appropriate) should your right to work in the UK be withdrawn. Any misrepresentation of your employment status is a serious disciplinary offence which may result in your summary dismissal.

4. [Probation]

[Your employment is subject to an initial probationary period of up to [*number*] months, during which your performance and conduct will be appraised and monitored. [*Company*] reserves the right to extend your probationary period should this be considered necessary by [*job title*].

During the probationary period, your employment may be terminated by [*Company*] or by you giving [*notice period during probation, if different from general position*]. On successful completion of the probationary period, the provisions of clause [16] will apply in respect of the termination of your employment. Clause [16.3] will apply during your probationary period.]

5. * Place of work

Your usual place of work is [*address*][, although from time to time and at the absolute discretion of [*Company*] you may be required on reasonable prior notice to work at [*other locations*] on a temporary or permanent basis]. [*Company*] reserves the right to extend the list of required locations provided that these are within [*number*] miles of any location listed above on giving you reasonable notice.

[You may be required at the absolute discretion of [*Company*] to undertake travel within the United Kingdom and internationally from time to time for the proper performance of your duties.]

[[*Company*] may require you to [live and] work in [*location outside UK*] [on a temporary basis] for more than 1 month. Further details are provided [in clause [6]].]

6. * [Work outside the UK]

[It is anticipated that your posting to [*location*] will be for [*period*][, subject to the absolute discretion of [*Company*] to change the period of your posting]. During that time your salary will be paid in [*currency*] and you will additionally be entitled to [*additional remuneration or benefits, if any*]. At the end of your posting, [*terms and conditions relating to return to UK*].]

7. * Hours of work

Your normal hours of work are from [*time*] to [*time*] [Monday to Friday inclusive], with a [1 hour] lunch break per day. [From time to time you may be required to work reasonable additional hours without pay for the proper and effective performance of your duties.]

[You will not be required to work overtime.] OR [You may from time to time be required to work overtime. You are not entitled to any payment for overtime [unless agreed in advance with [*job title*]].] OR [Any overtime worked will be paid at the rate of £[*amount*] per hour.]

[Compliance with regulations on working time]

[If overtime is worked, you must complete overtime sheets and return them to [the HR Department] to enable [*Company*] to comply with its obligations under the Working Time Regulations 1998, as amended ("the Regulations").]

The Regulations prohibit employees from exceeding the average weekly limit on working time (48 hours per week) unless they have agreed that the limit will not apply to them.

[You agree that the 48-hour limit on average weekly working time specified in the Regulations will not apply to your working time (including any overtime worked). This agreement will apply indefinitely, subject to your giving [*Company*] [*period of notice – up to 3 months*]' written notice if you wish to withdraw your agreement.] [1]

[You will record your working hours [*describe applicable recording method*] or as notified by [*Company*] from time to time. Failure to do so will be a disciplinary offence and [*Company*]'s disciplinary procedures may be invoked.]

[You may, with [*Company*]'s prior written permission, take up employment with another employer. If you do so, you must notify [*Company*] of any hours worked for the other employer. If your total working time (including those additional hours) may result in your exceeding the limit on average weekly working time, you agree to opt-out of that limit.] [2]

In this contract, "working time" means any time during which you are working at [*Company*]'s disposal and carrying out your duties, and will include [*examples*]. "Working time" does not include [*examples*].

8. * Remuneration

Your remuneration is £[*amount*] per [*time period*] subject to deductions for tax and NICs, payable by [*method of payment*] [*interval of payment*] on or about [*time of payment*].

Salary will be reviewed annually on or around [*date*] in each year. [There is no obligation on [*Company*] to increase the level of your basic salary at a review. [*Company*] reserves the right to decrease salary at a review if deemed appropriate.] Any increase awarded in one year will not create any right or entitlement or set any precedent in relation to subsequent years. Any revision to your salary will take effect from [*date/period after review*]. Your salary will not be reviewed after notice of termination has been given by either party.

[You may be eligible to participate in [*Company*]'s [discretionary] bonus scheme, subject to the rules of that scheme from time to time in force. [*Company*] reserves the right to change the rules of the scheme from time to time at its absolute discretion. [The decision to award a bonus in any given year and the amount of any such bonus is at [*Company*]'s absolute discretion. Payment of a bonus in a particular bonus year will not create any right or entitlement to a bonus in any subsequent bonus years.]]

You authorise [*Company*] both at any time during your employment and on the termination of your employment to deduct from your salary payment, and any sums [*Company*] is liable to pay to you, any amount from time to time which you owe to [*Company*] including but not limited to any outstanding loans, advances, payments for excess holiday and overpayment of wages and you expressly consent to any such deductions pursuant to Part II of the Employment Rights Act 1996.

9. **Other benefits**
   9.1. * **Pension**

   [[*Company*]'s pension arrangements are explained in [*reasonably accessible document, such as the staff handbook*].]

   OR

   [[*Company*] operates a [non-]contributory pension [and life insurance] scheme, which you will be eligible to join [on commencement of employment/after completing [*number*] [weeks/months]' employment], subject to the rules of the scheme from time to time in force. Further details of the scheme are set out in a separate pensions booklet available from [*insert details*].]

   OR

   [[*Company*] operates a Stakeholder Pension Scheme which you are eligible to join [on commencement of employment/after completing [*number*] [weeks/months]' employment], subject to the rules of the scheme from time to time in force. [[*Company*] does not contribute to the scheme.] Further details of the scheme are set out in a separate pensions booklet available from [*insert details*].]

   OR

   [[*Company*] does not operate a pension scheme in relation to your employment.] [3]

   [* A contracting-out certificate under the Pension Schemes Act 1993 is [not] in force in respect of your employment.] [4]

   9.2. **[Private medical cover]**

   [You will, subject to meeting any conditions or eligibility criteria imposed by the insurance provider and subject to the rules of any such scheme from time to time in force, be eligible for such free private medical insurance as [*Company*] may from time to time arrange. Further details [are set out in [*the Staff Handbook*]/will be provided to you separately].

   [*Company*] reserves the right to cease to offer private medical insurance or to substitute another provider, or to alter the benefits available to you under, or the terms and conditions of, any scheme or schemes at any time and no compensation will be paid to you. [*Company*] will not be liable in the event of any failure by or refusal from any provider or providers to provide cover or any application of any conditions or limitations to the benefit or benefits by any provider or providers.]

   9.3. **[Permanent health insurance]**

   [Subject to [*Company*]'s right to terminate your employment, if you comply with any eligibility or other conditions imposed by [*Company*] or by the relevant insurance provider, you may be eligible to receive payments under [*Company*]'s permanent health insurance arrangements. The terms and level of such cover will be in accordance with the [*Company*]'s policy and the rules of the scheme from time to time in force. Further details [are set out in [the Staff Handbook]] OR [will be provided to you separately]. Any entitlement to payments under the permanent health insurance scheme will be inclusive of any entitlement you may have to statutory holiday pay accrued during a period of sick leave.

   [*Company*] reserves the right to cease to offer permanent health insurance or to substitute another provider, or to alter the benefits available to you under, or the terms and conditions of, any scheme or schemes at any time and no compensation will be paid to you. [Company] will not be liable in the event of any failure by or refusal from any provider or providers to provide cover or any application of any conditions or limitations to the benefit or benefits by any provider or providers.]

9.4. **[Company car]**

[You will be eligible to participate in [Company]'s company car scheme, subject to the rules of the scheme from time to time in force. Participation is conditional on you having and retaining a valid full UK driving licence. Further details [are set out in [the Staff Handbook]/will be provided to you separately].]

9.5. **Other (share schemes, professional subscriptions, lunch vouchers)**

[insert details]

10. **[Expenses]**

[[Company] will reimburse (against production of satisfactory receipts) all reasonable expenses wholly, exclusively and necessarily incurred by you in the performance of your duties.

[Any credit or charge card provided to you by [Company] must only be used for expenses properly incurred by you in the performance of the duties of your employment.] Abuse or misuse of any company credit or charge cards may result in disciplinary action being taken against you, including dismissal.]

11. * **Annual leave**

The leave year runs from [date] to [date]. You are entitled[, in addition to English and Welsh bank and public holidays,] to [number] days' paid holiday in each holiday year, accruing on a [daily] basis. [5] You will be paid [your normal basic remuneration] during such holidays. Your entitlement will be pro-rated in the year of joining and leaving [Company].

[You are required to use part of your annual entitlement during [Company]'s shutdown period in [time/dates]. [Company] will notify you by [method and timing of notification] of the exact number of days' holiday affected by this provision and the dates on which they must be taken.]

You must take your holiday at times convenient to [Company] and you must obtain the prior written approval of [job title] before taking a holiday. You are required to give at least [2 weeks]' notice of a proposed holiday. [No more than [number] days' holiday can be taken together unless [job title] gives permission.] [You must take at least [number] consecutive days' holiday in each holiday year.] [[Company] has the right to require you to use any outstanding holiday entitlement by the end of the holiday leave year, where possible. Any holiday entitlement not used in a holiday year will be forfeited save where a period of statutory maternity, paternity or adoption leave or a period of sickness has prevented you from taking your statutory entitlement to holiday in the preceding leave year [and any such leave carried over must be used within [18] months of your return to work, unless you become absent again for any of these reasons, in which case the [18] month period will be frozen until your return to work].] [6]

You will be entitled to a payment in lieu of holiday which has accrued but not been taken on the termination of your employment. [You will not accrue any contractual holiday entitlement during any period of notice (whether given by [Company] or you), save that your entitlement to annual leave pursuant to the Regulations shall continue to accrue during such period.] If, on the termination of your employment, you have taken holidays in excess of your entitlement, [Company] may deduct from your final salary an amount equal to the gross salary paid to you in respect of such holidays and you expressly consent to any such deductions pursuant to Part II of the Employment Rights Act 1996.

12. * **Sickness absence**

12.1. [[Company]'s sick pay arrangements are explained in [reasonably accessible document, such as the staff handbook].]

OR

[If you are absent from work due to sickness or injury, you (or someone on your behalf) must inform [job title] of the reason for and likely duration of your absence no later than [*time*] on the first day of absence [7]. If your sickness absence lasts 7 calendar days or less, you must complete a self-certification form on your return to work [8]. For absences lasting more than 7 calendar days, you must produce a medical certificate from your doctor stating the reason for your absence. You must keep [*job title*] regularly informed of your absence and the likely duration of your absence. Further medical certificates are required for each further [*week*] of sickness absence.] [Failure to notify [*Company*] of your absence may render you subject to disciplinary action and may also bar you from receiving sick pay.]

12.2. [*Company*] may require you to undergo a medical examination at its expense by a medical practitioner appointed or approved by [*Company*] and you agree to a medical examination and authorise that medical practitioner to disclose to [*Company* [and its advisors]] the result of the examination and discuss with it [or them] any matters arising from the examination which might impair the proper performance of your duties.

12.3 [[*Company*] does not operate a sick pay scheme. Your entitlement is to Statutory Sick Pay (SSP) only.] OR [Subject to any right [*Company*] may have to terminate your employment, you will be paid your normal basic remuneration (inclusive of any Statutory Sick Pay (SSP)) [and provided all contractual benefits] for [*number*] working days of absence due to sickness or injury in any calendar year. Thereafter, you will be paid half your normal basic remuneration (inclusive of any SSP) [and provided all contractual benefits] for a further [*number*] working days of absence due to sickness or injury in that calendar year. Any payments to which you are entitled under any social security scheme (whether or not claimed by you) may be deducted from any sick pay paid to you by [*Company*]. Entitlement to payment is subject to your compliance with this clause [12].]

[12.4. [*Company*] at all times reserves the right to withhold, discontinue or request repayment of any contractual sick pay if:

    12.4.1. you fail to follow [*Company*]'s absence procedure;

    12.4.2. [*Company*] is satisfied that there has been an abuse of the sick pay arrangements or misrepresentation of your health; or

    12.4.3. you behave in a way likely to delay, hinder or impede your recovery.]

13. Outside interests

For the duration of this contract (including without limitation any period of garden leave), you will not undertake any other employment [without the prior written permission of [*job title*]], or undertake any external posts or positions or engage in any outside activity, paid or unpaid, which might interfere with the effective discharge of your duties or adversely affect [*Company*] in any way. [If such permission is given, you must advise [*Company*] of your additional working hours and [*Company*] reserves the right to withdraw its consent at its absolute discretion.]

14. Confidentiality and return of company property

You will not, except as authorised by [*Company*] or as required by law or your duties, use, divulge or disclose to any person, firm or organisation, any client or trade secrets or other confidential or commercial information relating to the organisation, business, finances, clients, customers, dealings and affairs of [*Company*] which may come to your knowledge during your employment.

For the purposes of this contract, trade secrets and confidential information include [*insert examples, such as information relating to the Company's trading position (e.g. client/customer lists, details of suppliers), product and sales information, and documents marked as confidential*]. This list is by way of illustration only and is not exhaustive.

A breach of this clause may render you subject to disciplinary action.

This restriction will continue to apply after the termination of your employment but will not apply to information which becomes public (other than through unauthorised disclosure by you).

This clause is not intended to exclude or restrict your right to make a protected disclosure under Part IVA Employment Rights Act 1996 if you reasonably believe a harmful or illegal activity is being undertaken. In such a case, you [are encouraged to discuss your concerns with [*job title*]/should refer to [*Company*]'s whistleblowing policy].

On the termination of your employment or at [*Company*]'s request, you will immediately return to [*Company*] all property belonging or relating to [*Company*] that is in your possession or under your control. [For the avoidance of doubt, this includes (but is not limited to) [your company car, keys, security cards, [*list other property*]], and all documents, records, correspondence, papers and other materials (and any copies thereof), whether in hard copy or in electronic or machine readable form, made or kept by, or provided to, you during your employment.] You will not retain any copies or extracts of such material.

15. * **Discipline and grievances**

The disciplinary rules and procedure and grievance procedure applicable to you are set out in [Appendix below/*reasonably accessible document, such as the staff handbook*] [9]. These rules form part of the terms and conditions of your employment but any procedure is given by way of guideline only and does not have contractual effect.

16. * **Termination of employment**

16.1. [If you wish to terminate your employment, you must give [*Company*] [*period – minimum 1 week*'s] prior written notice. Subject to [*Company*]'s right to terminate without notice [or payment in lieu of notice] in cases of gross misconduct, if [*Company*] wishes to terminate your employment, you will be given [1 week's notice during your first 2 years of employment and then an additional week's notice for each additional complete year of service up, to a maximum of 12 weeks' notice].] [*cross-refer to notice period during probation, if different*]

OR

[Your employment is for a fixed-term and will terminate on [*date*].] [It may be terminated at any time before expiry of the fixed-term by either party giving to the other [*applicable notice period*]' prior written notice.]

OR

[Your employment is not intended to be permanent and is expected to continue until [*date*]. Either party may terminate your employment by giving to the other [*applicable notice period*]' prior written notice.]

16.2. [[*Company*] reserves the right, at its sole and absolute discretion, to pay salary (based on the basic salary set out above) in lieu of any required period of notice (whether given by you or [*Company*]), less any deductions [*Company*] is required to make by law.]

16.3. Notwithstanding the other provisions of this clause [16], your employment may be terminated immediately by [*Company*] without notice [or payment in lieu of notice] if you are guilty of gross misconduct, gross negligence or in any way fundamentally breach your employment contract with [*Company*]. The following are examples of conduct which would entitle [*Company*] to terminate your employment without notice or pay in lieu of notice: [10]

– theft, fraud or any act of dishonesty;

– any act or attempted act of violence or abusive behaviour towards people or property; or

– any serious act of insubordination or refusal to carry out reasonable requests.

This list is intended as a guide and is not exhaustive.

16.4. If you are absent for a total period of [*period*] (including Saturdays, Sundays and public holidays) in any period of 12 months due to sickness or injury, [*Company*] may terminate your employment [immediately by written notice/by giving you [*shorter period of notice than clause [16]*]]. [[*Company*] may terminate your employment notwithstanding any entitlement you may have to claim benefits under any permanent health insurance scheme and shall not be liable to compensate you for the loss of any such benefits.]

16.5. [*Company*] reserves the right at any time to suspend you on full pay [and contractual benefits] from the performance of some or all of your duties under this contract in connection with any investigation or matter with which you are involved for such period as [*Company*] in its absolute discretion shall decide.

16.6. During any such period referred to in clause [16.5]:

16.6.1. you shall, if requested by [*Company*], refrain from contacting or communicating with [employees, customers, clients and professional contacts] of [*Company*];

16.6.2. [*Company*] shall be entitled to make such announcements or statements to its [employees, customers, clients and professional contacts] or any other third parties concerning you as [*Company*] in its absolute discretion shall decide; and

16.6.3. [*Company*] shall be under no obligation to provide any work for you and you shall continue to be bound by the express and implied duties of your employment.

16.7. [Your normal retirement age is [*age*].] You will be given notice of termination of employment which will not be less than 6 months and not less than the notice you are entitled to under this agreement to expire on the date you reach [*normal retirement age*]. [11]

17. Data protection

In relation to Personal Data and Sensitive Personal Data (as defined by the Data Protection Act 1998) provided by you to [*Company*], you give your consent to the Company and any Group Company holding and processing sensitive personal data about or relating to you for the purposes of performing your contract of employment, including but not limited to:
- 17.1. monitoring sickness absence;
- 17.2. administering personnel records and any disciplinary issues;
- 17.3. performance reviews;
- 17.4. administering remuneration;
- 17.5. references; and
- 17.6. providing information to third parties such as potential purchasers of the business.

By signing this agreement you also expressly consent to personal data about you being transferred to a country or territory outside the EEA. You further agree that [*Company*] may make sensitive personal data available to any Group Company, regulatory bodies, courts or tribunals, potential or future employers and potential purchasers of the business in which you are employed.

18. Monitoring

You accept that you have no expectation of privacy while using [*Company*]'s computer equipment for internet access. Information passing through or stored on [*Company*]'s equipment may be monitored, accessed, reviewed, copied, modified or deleted as [*Company*] considers necessary.

You agree that [*Company*] may monitor and record any or all communications made by you using the Company's electronic communications system [and telephone] to ensure the proper compliance with Company rules and regulations. You have read [*Company*]'s non-contractual email policy and agree with its contents. You agree to comply at all times with [*Company*]'s non-contractual email policy set out in [the Staff Handbook].

19. Statutory particulars

This contract [and the attached Appendix] contain the written particulars of employment which [*Company*] is obliged to provide you under the Employment Rights Act 1996.

20. * Collective agreements

[There are no collective agreements which affect the terms and conditions of your employment.] OR [The collective agreement(s) between [*parties*] directly affect your terms and conditions of employment [*details of terms and conditions affected*].]

21. Policies and procedures

You agree to comply with the rules, policies and procedures of [*Company*] from time to time in force, although these do not form part of your contract of employment (unless stated otherwise).

22. Whole agreement

This contract supersedes any previous oral or written agreement between [Company] and you in relation to the matters dealt within it. It contains the whole agreement between [Company] and you relating to your employment as at the date of the contract, except for any terms implied by law that cannot be excluded by the agreement of the parties. [12]

23. Third party rights

The Contracts (Rights of Third Parties) Act 1999 shall not apply to this agreement and no third party shall be entitled to enforce any term of this agreement against [Company].

24. Governing law and jurisdiction

This contract will be governed by and interpreted in accordance with English law. [Company] and you submit to the exclusive jurisdiction of the English Courts and Tribunals in relation to any claim or matter arising in connection with this contract.

Please sign and return the duplicate copy of this Contract of Employment to indicate your acceptance of its terms.

Signed...

Date...

For and on behalf of [Company]

I agree to the above terms and conditions.

Signed...

Date...

[Employee]

APPENDIX Unless expressly stated otherwise, the following particulars are given by way of guideline only and do not form part of your Contract of Employment.

[Disciplinary procedure]

[insert full disciplinary procedure here]

[Grievance procedure]

[insert full grievance procedure here]

---

1. The Court of Justice of the European Union has emphasised that a worker's consent to opt out of the average weekly time limit should be given expressly and freely (see ¶3688).
2. Add if the option for undertaking other employment with permission is used in clause 13.
3. Use only if employer falls outside scope of the automatic enrolment requirements (see ¶3402).
4. Since 6 April 2012, contracting out will no longer be possible through a money-purchase (defined-contribution) occupational pension scheme, a personal pension or a stakeholder pension, and those who are contracted out will be brought back into the S2P. For the time being, contracting out through an occupational salary-related (defined benefit) scheme will still be allowed. Contracting out is now rare, however, at present, statutory statements/contracts should still state whether there is a contracting out certificate in force.
5. Paid leave on bank or public holidays will count towards annual statutory entitlement (see ¶4009). For the minimum entitlement to annual statutory leave, see ¶4005.
6. For more information on the carrying over of statutory holiday not taken due to statutory maternity, paternity or adoption leave, see ¶4442 and in relation to sick leave, see ¶¶4102, 4103.
7. For SSP purposes, an employer cannot specify notification before a specific time on the first qualifying day.
8. For SSP purposes, an employer cannot insist on evidence of incapacity for the first 7 days of sickness.
9. It is important to have a comprehensive set of discipline and grievance rules and procedures in order to ensure a smooth resolution to workplace disputes where possible. This will help to ensure legal compliance, particularly with the Acas Code.
10. This list should be consistent with policies on disciplinary matters.
11. The default retirement age and the accompanying procedures have not been included in this clause as, following the abolition of the default retirement age of 65, it is no longer possible to rely on it or its accompanying retirement procedure (which relates both to the default and normal retirement ages). Employers who wish to retire an employee without his consent will only be able to do so where they have an objectively justifiable normal retirement age, and this will not always be easy to establish (see ¶8209).
12. This clause will need to be amended if contractual terms are also contained within company policies or procedures or a staff handbook.

Model discipline and grievance policy

See chapter 19 for a full discussion of discipline and grievance issues in the workplace. If the employee subsequently brings a successful tribunal claim, the tribunal has a discretion to adjust any award upwards or downwards by up to 25% if either the employer or employee has unreasonably failed to comply with any part of the Acas Code on disciplinary and grievance procedures, other than the foreword.

This policy is designed to meet the requirements of both the statutory dispute resolution procedures and the Code. For the law on unfair dismissal, see chapter 25. While the procedures outlined in this policy reflect the Code, compliance with them does not guarantee that the action will be considered "fair" should the employee bring an unfair dismissal complaint or another complaint based on detrimental treatment.

Employers may need to depart from some of the procedural stages, depending on the size of the organisation and administrative resources.

Overview

The Company is committed to maintaining high standards of conduct, competence and performance in the workplace and will address all disciplinary matters fairly and appropriately.

The Company also aims to ensure that employees have every opportunity to raise issues arising out of their employment and that all grievances are properly heard and resolved.

All employees will be treated fairly and consistently although it may be necessary to treat similar cases differently according to the circumstances, and the Company will endeavour to complete disciplinary and grievance procedures without unreasonable delay.

This procedure reflects your and our legal rights and obligations but does not form part of your contractual terms of employment. It can be departed from, amended or replaced at any time at the Company's discretion. This includes the Company's right to jump stages of the procedure. The procedure does not apply in redundancy or retirement cases or on the non-renewal of a fixed-term contract. It applies to all employees irrespective of length of service or working arrangements but not to self-employed, casual or other categories of worker. [However, we reserve the right not to apply the procedure where an employee has service of less than 2 years' service.] [1]

This procedure has been agreed with staff and/or employee representatives. [2] We will involve staff and/or employee representatives in consultation over any proposed review of this procedure. [3]

We understand and respect the need for confidentiality and we expect all members of staff involved in any investigation or disciplinary proceedings to maintain strict confidentiality and to comply with Data Protection Act 1998 principles when handling sensitive personal data. [4] Any breach of confidentiality may result in disciplinary proceedings being taken against the person committing the breach.

General principles

The following principles apply to every stage of the Company's disciplinary and grievance procedures:

1. The Company will investigate any complaints and allegations promptly and will not take any action until the matter has been fully investigated.
2. So far as reasonably practicable, any disciplinary hearing will be dealt with by a member of management who has not previously been involved in investigating the matter.
3. Following investigation, the Company will notify you in writing of any allegations or complaints against you and of the time and date of a disciplinary hearing at which they will be considered.
4. You will normally be given the opportunity to see the evidence relied upon by the Company (including any witness statements save where a witness' identity is to be kept

confidential), and will be able to present your own evidence at a disciplinary or grievance hearing before any decision is made. The Company will, where practicable, give you reasonable advance notice of any witnesses it has asked to be present at a hearing and if you wish to call witnesses you should give the Company reasonable advance notice that you wish to do so. You will not usually be allowed to ask questions of witnesses.

5. You must take all reasonable steps to attend meetings and must cooperate fully with us in any investigation or when responding to any questions.

6. You are entitled to be accompanied to any disciplinary or grievance meeting by a work colleague or trade union representative (except for any investigatory meeting). You can confer with your companion and he/she can ask questions but he/she cannot answer questions on your behalf. You should notify us well in advance of the meeting who your companion is. If you (or your chosen companion) are not available to attend a meeting on the appointed date, you may propose an alternative time which is reasonable and falls within [5] working days of the appointed date. However, if you twice fail to attend a meeting without good reason, you may forfeit your right to attend and we may have to make a decision based on the evidence available to us.

7. Any decision and reasons will be communicated to you in writing, if possible within [1 week] of the hearing or as soon as reasonably practicable thereafter. You will be given the opportunity to appeal against any decision. In appeal meetings which are not the first meeting, as far as reasonably practicable, the Company will be represented by a more senior manager than attended the first meeting.

8. Where appropriate, the Company may suspend you during any investigation. Any such suspension will be kept as brief as possible and will be kept under review. If you are suspended pending investigation, this will not represent a disciplinary sanction and your contract of employment will continue in force. [5]

9. If you raise a grievance during a disciplinary process the Company may, if it is appropriate to do so, temporarily suspend the disciplinary process while it deals with your grievance. If the grievance you raise is connected to the disciplinary process, the Company may decide to deal with both procedures at the same time.

10. If you are disabled and require adjustments to be made to any part of the procedure to overcome any difficulty that you may have, you should raise this immediately with [the HR department].

Investigation [6]

At any stage and before any formal action has been taken we will, where appropriate, carry out an investigation. Where possible the investigation will be carried out by someone other than the person who will hear any disciplinary hearing which may result. You will be notified in writing about the alleged misconduct and what the sanctions may be if found proven.

How much investigation is necessary will depend on the facts and complexity of each case. It may be necessary to speak to witnesses and to take statements.

You are not entitled to be accompanied by a companion at any investigatory interview although if you feel disadvantaged by this, for example if you are hard of hearing and would like an interpreter, you should discuss your requirements with [the HR department] and, if appropriate, we will agree.

It may be necessary to suspend you on full pay from work for no longer than necessary when carrying out an investigation. Whilst on suspension you remain under strict duties of confidentiality and good faith and must not discuss the matter under investigation nor should you contact any employees, clients or customers of the Company other than as agreed with us.

Discipline

The Company may follow this disciplinary procedure if your conduct, competence or performance is inappropriate or unacceptable. The procedure may be implemented at any stage if your conduct warrants such action and if the Company considers it appropriate in the circumstances.

You will not usually be dismissed for a first breach of the Company's rules, policies and procedures, except in the case of gross misconduct. You should always abide by the express terms in your contract of employment and by your implied terms of good faith and loyalty.

Misconduct The following are examples of misconduct:
– minor breach of Company rules, policies and procedures;
– minor damage to Company property;
– unsatisfactory attendance and/or poor timekeeping;
– unauthorised absence; and
– failure to meet the appropriate and expected standards of work.

This list is intended as a guide and is not exhaustive.

If the offence being investigated concerns a criminal matter which is being investigated by the police or you are subject to criminal charges we will not normally await the outcome of any court proceedings but will carry out our own investigation and follow our own procedure when considering what action to take.

You are reminded that the outcome of any police investigation may not affect any internal disciplinary proceedings.

Gross misconduct The following are examples of gross misconduct (entitling the Company to terminate your employment without notice or payment in lieu of notice):
– theft, fraud or any act of dishonesty;
– any act or attempted act of violence or abusive behaviour towards people or property;
– any serious act of insubordination or refusal to carry out reasonable requests;
– major breach of Company rules, policies and procedures;
– deliberate and/or major damage to Company property;
– unauthorised or unreasonable absence or consistently poor timekeeping;
– serious neglect of duties or incompetence;
– serious breach of health and safety obligations;
– deliberately accessing internet sites containing pornographic, violent, racist, obscene or otherwise offensive or unlawful material;
– serious incapability at work brought on by alcohol or illegal drugs;
– serious breach of confidence;
– any form of discrimination, victimisation, harassment or bullying on the grounds of sex, pregnancy or maternity, marital or civil partnership status, gender reassignment, sexual orientation, race, colour, ethnic or national origin, religion or belief, disability or age;
– any other breach of the Company's policy on bullying or harassment;
– any act likely to bring the Company into disrepute.

This list is intended as a guide and is not exhaustive.

Disciplinary action: types of action

If your conduct, competence or performance is inappropriate or unacceptable, the Company may attempt to resolve the matter on an informal basis, depending on the seriousness of the offence. All formal warnings will be issued after a hearing and you have the right to appeal against any such warning issued to you. If, however, the matter cannot be resolved on this basis, the Company will consider the following action:

[Oral warning If your conduct, competence or performance is unacceptable, you may receive an oral warning. You will be informed of the reasons for the warning and, where relevant, the improvement required from you. A note of the oral warning will normally be entered on your personnel file but will not be taken into account when considering future offences.]

First written warning If your conduct, competence or performance does not improve, or any further unacceptable conduct, competence or performance occurs, you will receive a written warning. You will be informed of the reasons for the warning and, where relevant, the improvement required from you. A copy of this written warning will be kept on your personnel file.

Final written warning If your conduct, competence or performance does not improve, or any further unacceptable conduct, competence or performance occurs, you will receive a final written warning. You will be informed that if your conduct, competence or performance does not reach an acceptable standard, your employment may be terminated. A copy of this final written warning will be kept on your personnel file. All warnings will indicate the type of misconduct which has occurred and what is required of you. It will also indicate the length of time the warning will remain live and what will happen if you reoffend.

Dismissal If your conduct, competence or performance does not improve, or any further unacceptable conduct, competence or performance occurs, you may be dismissed. If it appears that there may be grounds on which your employment may be terminated summarily, the Company may begin with this stage of the procedure.

Length of warning In the case of [oral and] first written warnings, a warning will usually apply for 6 months, after which it will lapse. A final written warning will usually apply for 12 months before lapsing. The Company reserves the right to extend a warning in appropriate circumstances.

Other sanctions We may consider sanctions alternative to dismissal, including suspension without pay, demotion, loss of seniority, transfer to another department or reduced pay.

Disciplinary procedure: contemplating dismissal or certain disciplinary action

If the Company is contemplating dismissal or other disciplinary action provided for in your contract (e.g. demotion or reallocation of duties), it will apply the following procedure:

Notification [The HR Department] will set out in writing your alleged conduct, characteristics or other circumstances which have led the Company to contemplate dismissing or taking disciplinary action against you and the reasons why this conduct is not acceptable. [The HR Department] will send a copy of the statement to you and invite you to attend a meeting, as soon as reasonably practicable, to discuss the matter.

Disciplinary hearing A meeting will take place to discuss the allegations before any action is taken. You have the right to call witnesses and we will go through the evidence with you during the meeting. At the hearing the charges against you will be reviewed.

You will be given adequate time to prepare your case before a hearing is held and you will be given an opportunity to put forward your views before any decision is made. It may be necessary to adjourn any hearing if we need to carry out further investigations or time to consider our decision.

A decision will be given, if reasonably practicable, within [5] working days of the meeting, and confirmed to you in writing. You will be notified of your right to appeal the decision.

Appeal If you wish to appeal, you must inform [the HR Department] in writing within [5] working days of receipt of the decision, setting out the grounds of your appeal. If you raise new matters we may need to carry out a fresh investigation.

You will be invited to attend a meeting to discuss your grounds of appeal. Where possible, your appeal will be heard by the next most senior manager who was not involved in the decision from which the appeal is made. The appeal hearing may be a review or a complete rehearing, at our discretion and depending on the facts of the case.

A decision will be given, if reasonably practicable, within [5] working days of the meeting, and confirmed to you in writing. This decision will be final and you will have no further right of appeal.

Grievance procedure

This procedure is designed to encourage good working relations and the quick and fair resolution of grievances concerning work-related matters. A grievance may be about a wide range of matters including dissatisfaction about your terms of employment or difficulties with working relationships. It may be more appropriate in some cases to use a different policy (see below). [This procedure does not apply where a grievance is brought on behalf of two or more employees by a trade union or other appropriate workplace representatives.]

If you have a grievance which requires resolution, you should in the first instance discuss the matter on an informal basis with [your line manager]. The Company hopes that most grievances can be fully resolved at this stage. As with the disciplinary procedure, this procedure does not form part of your contractual terms of employment and may be replaced, departed from or amended at any time at the Company's discretion.

Notification If the grievance cannot be resolved on an informal basis (or if your manager is the subject, or part of the subject, of your grievance), you should set out your grievance in writing and send a copy of it to [the HR Department]. Your grievance should clearly set out what you are complaining about, making the details as specific as possible. A general complaint will be difficult for us to address and we may ask further clarifying questions. A copy of your grievance will be kept on your file and processed in accordance with Data Protection Act principles. [7] [The HR Department] will invite you to attend a meeting, as soon as reasonably practicable, to discuss your grievance.

Prior to the meeting, you must ensure that you have informed [the HR Department] in full what the basis is for your grievance.

Meeting A meeting will take place as promptly as reasonably practicable to discuss your grievance. You can be accompanied (see above).

A decision will be given, if reasonably practicable, within [5] working days of the meeting, and confirmed to you in writing. You will be notified of your right to appeal the decision.

Appeal If you wish to appeal, you must inform [the HR Department] in writing within [5] working days of receipt of the decision, setting out the grounds of your appeal. You will be invited to attend a meeting to discuss your grounds of appeal. [Where possible, your appeal will be heard by another appropriate senior manager who was not involved in the decision from which the appeal is made.]

A decision will be given, if reasonably practicable, within [5] working days of the meeting, and confirmed to you in writing. This decision will be final and you will have no further right of appeal.

Other procedures If your grievance relates to any disciplinary action or a dismissal, you should appeal the decision under the Company's disciplinary procedure.

If you have a grievance which relates to discrimination, victimisation, harassment or bullying, you should refer in the first instance to [the Company's equal opportunities policy].

If you wish to raise any concerns about a wrongdoing or suspected wrongdoing within the Company, you should refer in the first instance to [the Company's whistleblowing policy. This includes any concerns about possible bribery or corrupt practices].

---

1. As employees with less than 2 years' service do not qualify for protection against unfair dismissal (1 year if they started their employment before 6 April 2012: ¶8411), in some circumstances employers may not wish to follow the full disciplinary procedure before dismissing employees with short service. However, note that no qualifying period applies in the case of dismissal for certain reasons for example pregnancy and maternity-related dismissals. See ¶8394 for a list of inadmissible reasons for dismissal where no qualifying period applies.
2. Insert these words if the procedure is an agreed one. It is good practice to consult with employees when introducing a policy of this nature, and if a trade union is recognised, it may form part of a collective agreement. See ¶7363 for an outline of the contents of voluntary collective agreements.
3. Employers of more than 50 employees are obliged to provide employee representatives with information about this type of change see ¶7756.
4. See ¶5940 for an outline of an employer's obligations regarding to handling personal data relating to employees.
5. Suspension may be appropriate, for example, where there is a risk of further misconduct or interference in the investigation. See ¶6595 for more information on suspending employees pending investigation.
6. It should be made clear to the employee that any investigatory meeting is not a disciplinary hearing. See ¶6585 for an outline of the legal issues involved in investigating disciplinary offences. Employees are not entitled to be accompanied at meetings which are purely investigatory, but it may be helpful to allow this in some cases.
7. See ¶5945 for an outline of the data protection principles, and ¶¶6000+ for general guidance on data management.

Main social benefits

9920 Below are details of the main social benefits (other than statutory sick pay which is discussed in chapter 13 and statutory maternity/adoption/paternity pay which are discussed in chapter 14). Claims should always been made straight away or as soon as possible otherwise the benefit may be lost.

Contact details for a person's:

- **local social security office** and **local jobcentre** can be found at: flmemo.co.uk/em9920a
- **nearest Revenue and Customs enquiry centre** can be found at: flmemo.co.uk/em9920b

The Government is **proposing to introduce a new welfare benefit, Universal Credit** (a new single payment for people who are looking for work or who are on a low income), which it plans to launch in 2013 to replace income-based Jobseeker's Allowance, income-related Employment and Support Allowance, Income Support, Child Tax Credits Working, Tax Credits, and Housing Benefit. Further developments will be covered by our updating service.

Main social benefit	What is it?	How to claim
Income Support	Income support for those on a low income and generally with savings of £16,000 or under. If have to sign on at the Jobcentre, cannot get Income Support.	Claim forms available from local social security office.
Jobseeker's Allowance	Paid if capable of working and available and actively seeking work.	Contact local jobcentre.
Council Tax Benefit	Help towards council tax. Do not have to get any other benefits to be eligible. Does not matter if already get discount on council tax, for example if living alone.	Claim forms available from local social security office. If Income Support or Jobseeker's Allowance is being claimed, a person will get relevant forms with claim pack. In such cases, he should return them as appropriate with his Income Support or Jobseeker's Allowance claim form.
Housing Benefit	Help towards rent. Do not have to get any other benefits to be eligible. If claiming Income Support or Jobseeker's Allowance, may be able to get help with other housing costs as part of benefit.	Claim forms available from local social security office. If Income Support or Jobseeker's Allowance is being claimed, a person will get relevant forms with claim pack. In such cases, he should return them as appropriate with his Income Support or Jobseeker's Allowance claim form.
Employment and Support Allowance (previously Incapacity Benefit)	Paid if SSP has ended or person cannot get SSP.	Claim forms available from local social security office.
Disability Living Allowance	Paid if need help looking after, have severe difficulty walking or need help getting around. Different rates depending on how disability affects person.	Claim forms available from local social security office.

Main social benefit	What is it?	How to claim
Child Benefit	A benefit for those bringing up children.	Claim packs available from local social security office or by ringing Child Benefit Centre. If child has just been born, claim pack may be included in Bounty Pack from hospital.
State Pension	Retirement pension when obtained state pension age. Made up of Basic Pension and Additional State Pension.	Contact pension centre or local social security office.
Work Programme (previously New Deal)	For those who are claiming Jobseeker's Allowance (JSA). The referral point will depend on the type of claimant, but is generally 9 months for 18 to 24 year olds and 12 months for those aged 25 or over. Some travel concessions may be available.	Contact local jobcentre.
Work Trial and Employment on Trial	Possibility of trying out a job without risking losing benefits.	Contact local jobcentre.
Job Grant; Return-to-work Credit; In-work Credit; In-work Emergency Discretion Fund	Various payments or credits on returning to work.	Contact local jobcentre.
Maternity Allowance	For pregnant women who cannot get Statutory Maternity Pay.	Contact local social security office.
Working Tax Credit	Tax credit for working households on low incomes.	Application packs are available from local Revenue and Customs enquiry centre, social security office and jobcentre.
Child Tax Credit	Tax credit for those (whether or not they work) who are responsible for child/children or qualifying young person(s).	Application packs are available from local Revenue and Customs enquiry centre, social security office and jobcentre.

Index

The numbers refer to paragraphs and the plus sign (+) indicates that the entry covers a number of paragraphs.

A

A week's pay: See Week's pay

Abroad, work: See Overseas work

Absence from work: 4100+
As disciplinary offence: 6650+
Due to custody or on remand: 6674
Whether automatically commences maternity leave: 4430+
Whether fair redundancy selection criterion: 8836

Acas:
Conciliation:
   Tribunal claim: 9218
   EAT appeal: 9216
Arbitration: 9360+
Assistance:
   Access arrangements during recognition/derecognition: 7353

Access:
To employee information: 5970

Access agreement:
During recognition and derecognition: 7351

Accidents at work: See Health and safety

Accommodation:
Tax of benefit: 3200+, 3215+
Communal:
   Lawful discriminatory action: 5280

Accompanied, right to be:
Main entry: 6780+

Accompanied, right to be *(continued)*
At disciplinary and grievance proceedings:
   Relevance in determining fairness of dismissal: 8501
At meeting/appeal regarding flexible working: 4720+
At meeting/appeal regarding time to train application: 6430+
National minimum wage:
   To view records: 2901
Notification:
   Disciplinary hearing: 6612
   Grievance procedure: 6766
   Internal appeal hearing: 6690

Account for profits:
Employee duty: 1217
Director duty: 2139
Due to breach of duties: 2665, 1775

Accountability: See Account for profits

Accounting requirements:
Director duty: 2155
Union duty: 7148

Acquired Rights Directive: See TUPE

Additional adoption leave (AAL): See Leave

Additional award: See Award

Additional information (regarding tribunal claims): 9539+

Additional maternity leave (AML): See Leave

Additional paternity leave (APAL):
See Leave

Adjournment:
Disciplinary hearing: 6621, 6625
Tribunal hearing:
 Due to failure to attend: 9648+

Adjustments: See Reasonable adjustments

Administration order: See Insolvency

Administrative receiver: See Insolvency

Adoption leave: See Leave

Advisory, Conciliation and Arbitration Service: See Acas

Advocate general: See Court of Justice of the European Union

Age:
Discrimination: See Age discrimination
Whether fair redundancy selection criterion: 8838
Effect on calculating basic award: 8575
Effect on calculating statutory redundancy pay: 9005

Age discrimination:
Main entry: 5600+
During recruitment: 543
Retiring age: 8200+
Fair retirement procedure: 8209+
Occupational pension scheme: 3444

Age retirement: See Retirement

Agencies:
Relationship with agency worker: 2045+
Duties and obligations: 2052+, 2066
Use of in recruitment: 585
 Data protection issues regarding advertising: 678

Agency worker: 2040+

Agreement:
With third party to assign employee: 2222+
Regarding continuity of employment:
 Where gap between contracts with the same employer (greater than one week): 1019

See also under specific types (e.g. Contract (of employment), Service agreement, Apprentice, COT3 agreement)

Alcohol:
See Drug/alcohol misuse

Alternative employment: (option of)
Redundancy situation: 8850+
As disciplinary sanction: 6634
Consideration of by employer:
 With regard to poor performance: 6664
 Relevance in determining fairness of dismissal: 8473
Effect on calculation of damages for wrongful dismissal: 8171
For removal of risk:
 New/expectant mother: 4953
Refusal:
 Effect on protective award: 8954
 Effect on SRP: 8996
 Effect on guarantee payment: 7864
See also Trial period

Amendment:
To ET pleadings: 9532
To EAT pleadings:
 Notice of appeal: 9759
 Written answer: 9774

AML: See Leave

Annual leave: See Leave

Annual returns:
Filing duties:
 Employer: 6875+
Filing duties:
 Union: 7148

Antenatal care:
Paid time off:
 Main entry: 4411+
 Remedies (specific): 4780+

Anti-poaching covenants: See Restrictive covenants

Appeal:
Internal:
 Against disciplinary sanction: 6680+
 Against selection for redundancy: 8842
 As rehearing: 8441
 Effect on date of termination: 8358
 Effect of new evidence: 8425
 Effect on fairness of dismissal: 8441
 Natural justice requirement: 6685
 Requirement to advise: 6628
 Requirement for fair procedure: 8474, 8476, 8501
External:
 Extended statement of reasons for tribunal decision: 9691
 EAT: 9740+
 Court of Appeal: 9820+
 Supreme Court: 9830+
 High Court: 9858

Appeal *(continued)*
Against decision of certification officer: 7164
Against arbitration award: 9380

Applicable law: 2255+

Applicant: See Claimant and Job applicant
Tribunal proceedings:
　Submission of claim form: 9510+
　Effect of conduct: 9573
See also Job applicant

Application:
Tribunal claim: 9510
See also Job application

Appointment:
Main entry: 710+
Of director: 2112

Appraisal:
Main entry: 6465+
To prevent poor performance issues: 6660
To identify training needs: 6310
During probation period:
　As implied contract term: 946, 1202
End of probation period: 950

Apprentice:
Main entry: 6351+
Government-backed programmes: 6375+
National minimum wage: 2868, 2869
Non-renewal of apprenticeship:
　Whether redundancy dismissal: 8778
Recovery of fee/premium paid by:
　On insolvency of employer: 9053+
See also Young person

Appropriate representative:
Consultation requirement:
　Collective redundancies: 8925+
　TUPE transfer: 8063

Approved company share option plan:
Tax: 3345

Arbitration: 9360+

ARD: See TUPE

Area covenants: See Restrictive covenants

Arrears of pay:
Recovery of: 1730+
Unlawful deduction of wages: 3050+

Asbestos exposure:
Liability for: 5110+

Assertion of statutory right: 8394+

Assessable benefit: See Benefits

Assets:
Made available:
　Tax of benefit: 3215+
Transfer/sale of:
　Whether TUPE applies: 7923

Assignment:
Employee: 2200+
Agency worker: 2048
Within EEA:
　Effect on NICs: 7025+
Overseas: 7035+ (reciprocal agreement country), 7040+ (other country)
EU and UK Governmental support: 6390
See also Overseas work

Associated employer:
For unfair dismissal purposes: 8682
For redundancy purposes:
　General: 8741
　Collective: 8922
Employee move to:
　Effect on continuity of employment: 1035

Associative and perceptive discrimination:
On the grounds of:
　Sex/sexual orientation: 5263
　Racial/religion or belief: 5385
　Disability: 5453

Asylum seekers/refugees:
Permission to work: 777, 750+

Attachment of earnings: 3017+

Attendance:
Absence (discipline): 6650+
Absence (sickness): 4210+
Failure to attend tribunal hearing: 9648+

Attendance record:
Whether fair redundancy selection criterion: 8836

Auditor:
Union duty to appoint: 7148

Automatic enrolment (pensions): 3402

Automatic recognition: 7227

Automatic termination: 8270+

Automatic unfair dismissal:
Main entry: 8390+
Due to right to be accompanied to discipline or grievance meeting: 6793

Average weekly working time: 3680+

Award (unfair dismissal):
Basic:
　Main entry: 8575+
　No overlap with wrongful dismissal award: 8177
　Impact of failure to follow dismissal and disciplinary procedure: 6514
　Insolvency of employer: 9053+
　Reduction due to re-engagement offer: 1657
Compensatory:
　Main entry: 8585+
　Overlap with wrongful dismissal award: 8177
　Impact of failure to follow dismissal and disciplinary procedure: 6514
　Impact of failure to meet requirements of written particulars: 6526
　Reduction due to failure to use internal appeal: 6705
　Reduction due to re-engagement offer: 1657
Additional:
　Main entry: 8689
　No overlap with wrongful dismissal award: 8177

B

Ballot:
Industrial action: 7443+, 7455+, 7485+, 7490, 7492+
Recognition: 7227
Derecognition: 7341
Endorsement (domestic information and consultation): 7685+
EWC employee representative: 7804
Information and consultation representatives: 7734, 7735+
Negotiated agreement: 7725+
See also Election

Bank holidays:
Effect on statutory annual leave: 4009+
Part-time worker entitlement: 1899

Bankrupt employee:
Effect on unfair dismissal claim: 8562

Bankruptcy: See Insolvency

Bargaining unit: See Recognition/derecognition

Basic award: See Award

Behavioural guidelines: 6455
See also Disciplinary rules

Benchmarking: 6470+

Benefits:
Main entry: 2837+
List of non-taxable benefits: 3155
List of taxable benefits: 3190
Tax: 3150+
Reporting requirements to HMRC: 6895, 6897, 6898, 6899
Service agreement: 2119
PAYE settlement agreement: 6902+
Settlement/compromise agreement: 9268
On assignment: 2218
Part-time worker:
　Right to equal treatment: 1887, 1889+, 1893
Fixed term employee:
　Right to equal treatment: 1965, 1966+
Best practice to avoid discrimination: 5819
Suspension/continuance during:
　Maternity leave/Adoption leave: 4439/4530
Loss of:
　Wrongful dismissal damages: 8162+, 8355
　Compensatory award: 8593+
　Reinstatement award: 8681

Betting employee:
Sunday trading rules: 3800+
Definition: 3880+

Bias:
Right to a fair trial: 9612+
As ground for appeal: 9753

Binding contract: See Contract

Birth:
Automatic commencement of maternity leave: 4430+
Requirement to take compulsory maternity leave after birth: 4433
See also Maternity rights

Blacklists: 7565

Blue pencil test:
Enforceability of restrictive covenants: 2633+

Body corporate employer:
Employee move to another:
　Effect on continuity of employment: 1035

Bonus:
Main entry: 2828+
Effect of maternity leave/adoption leave: 4435/4530
Loss of:
 Compensatory award: 8594
Service agreement: 2119

Breach:
Director duties: 2160+
See also Breach of contract

Breach of contract:
Remedies: 1700+
Amounting to constructive dismissal: 8230+
Tribunal claim: 9425+
 Time limit: 9463, 9490
Civil claim: 9442+
 Time limit: 1711
Damages set off against:
 Compensatory award (unfair dismissal): 8619
 Protective award: 8953
Due to unilateral variation: 1650+
Effect on restrictive covenants: 2616+
Qualification as protected disclosure: 2711
Resignation due to: 8106
Settlement agreement regarding: 9276, 9320
Trust and confidence: 1245+, 8232

Breaks (work): See Rest periods

Bribery: 2175+
See also Account for profits

British citizen:
Right to work in the UK: 750+

Buddy system/training: 6313

Bullying: 5040+, 5247
See also Harassment, Victimisation

Bumping/transferred redundancy: 8784+

Burchell test: 8505

Business efficacy: 1174, 1630

Business expenses: See Expenses

Business for own account:
Test for employee/self-employed: 50+

Business reorganisation:
Whether fair reason for dismissal: 8532

Business transfer:
Effect on continuity of employment: 1035
Employer statement (reasonable care): 1243
See also TUPE

Business visit:
To UK:
 Restrictions on working: 776

C

CAC: See Central Arbitration Committee

Canteen meals:
Tax of benefit: 3157

Capability: See Incapability

Capacity:
Of contracting parties:
 Essential element of contract: 1111

Car:
Tax of benefit: 3221+
Use of employee's own car:
 As a deductible expense: 3303+
Loss of:
 Compensatory award: 8595
Monitoring usage: 6237

Care of dependants:
Right to time off: 4740+
Right to request flexible working: 4690+, 4694, 4695
Remedies (specific): 4780+

Carers: See Care of dependants

Casual worker:
Whether mutuality/personal performance: 36+

CCTV:
Usage in workplace: 6233+

Central Arbitration Committee: 7225

Certainty:
Contract terms: 1120

Certificate of independence:
Evidence of independence: 7160
Requirement for statutory recognition: 7225+
Withdrawal leading to derecognition: 7340

Certification officer: 7160+

Chancery Division: See High Court

Change of employer:
Identity/name:
 Duty to notify in writing: 1450
Effect on continuity of employment: 1035
See also TUPE

Change of workplace: See Mobility clause

Changes to contract: See Variation of terms

Childcare:
Right to take PL: 4620+
Time off to care for dependants: 4740+
Right to request flexible working: 1813+, 4690+
Child maintenance support:
 Attachment of earnings: 3017+
Employer provided (whether taxable): 3169+
Whether subject to Class 1A NIC: 6980

Children:
Capacity to enter into contract: 1111
Restrictions and duties regarding: 4970+
Specific risk assessment: 4976+
See also Young person

Choice of law: See Applicable law

Civil claims: 9850+

Civil partnership status: 5325+
Paternity leave: 4574
Right to request flexible working: 4694, 4695

CJEU: See Court of Justice of the European Union

Claim form: See ET1 Form

Claimant:
Tribunal proceedings:
 Submission of claim form: 9510+
 Effect of conduct: 9573

Claims:
Main entry: 9400+
In EU: 2261+
In EFTA states: 2266
Outside EU/EFTA: 2268+
Recognition of judgments:
 In EU: 2265
 Outside EU: 2273

Class 1 NIC: 6940+

Class 1A NIC: 6980+

Class 1B NIC: 6990

Closed shop: See Exclusion/expulsion

CML: See Leave

Code:
PAYE: 6825+

Codes of conduct: 1480
Behavioural guidelines: 6455
Disciplinary rules: 6534+
Details given at induction stage: 926
See also Disciplinary procedure

Collective agreement:
Main entry: 7363+
Incorporation into contract: 1270
Requirement for written particulars: 1420
Effect of terms:
 Duty to consult on collective redundancy: 8916
 Night workers: 3699
 PL procedure: 4650
 Statutory redundancy scheme: 8993
 Working time rules: 3660
Effect on terms:
 Of TUPE transfer: 7985

Collective bargaining:
Main entry: 7360+
In statutory recognition: 7383+
On pay: 2982, 2818

Collective redundancy: See Redundancy

Commencement of claim/appeal:
Tribunal claim: 9510+
EAT appeal: 9755+
Supreme Court appeal: 9831
Civil claim: 9851+

Commission: 2828

Commonwealth citizen:
Right to work in the UK: 762+

Community-scale undertaking: See European works councils

Commuting:
Whether deductible expense: 3285+
Whether partially exclusion from working time rules: 3652

Company car: See Car

Company handbook manual: See Staff handbook

Company property:
Return of:
On termination: 8302
As part of settlement/compromise agreement: 9272

Comparator:
Sex/sexual orientation discrimination: 5273+
Racial/religion or belief discrimination: 5393
Disability discrimination: 5505+
Equal pay claims: 5667+
Of part-time worker: 1882, 1884+
Of fixed-term employee: 1964
Victimisation:
Sex/sexual orientation: 5353
Racial/religion or belief: 5428

Compassionate leave: 3900

Compensation:
Main entry: 9700+
Dismissal:
Unfair: 8570+
Wrongful: 8156, 8160+
Constructive: 8248+
Discrimination: 5740+
Equal pay: 5770+
Breach of contract:
Pre-agreed award: 1703
Maximum tribunal award: 9428
Statement of by tribunal: 9691
In respect of patents: 2343

Compensatory award: See Award

Competence:
Implied term: 1202+
Statements: 6460+

Competition:
Duty not to compete: 1215, 2510
Duty not to work for competitor:
Express term: 2522+
Implied term: 2511+
Refusal to agree new terms: 8537+
See also Restrictive covenants

Complaints: See Grievance procedure

Compromise agreement:
Main entry: 9315+
Waiver:
Statutory redundancy pay: 8995
Statutory rights: 9259+, 8412
With regard to references: 8326, 9270
With regard to restrictive covenants: 3140, 9276
Effect of TUPE transfer before agreement: 8039

Compromise agreement *(continued)*
Continuity of employment (reinstatement/re-engagement): 1027

Compulsory online filing: 6850+, 6875+

Compulsory maternity leave (CML): 4433

Computer equipment:
Tax of benefit: 3165

Conciliation:
Negotiating/settling disputes:
Main entry: 9215+
Alternative to tribunal proceedings: 9200+
Settlement documentation: 9300+
Tribunal claims: 9515

Conduct:
Of parties:
Effect of illegality: 1305+
Effect on contract terms: 1176
Of employer:
Whether requirement to act reasonably: 1241+
Of employee:
On variation of contract: 1640+
Effect on basic award: 8582
Effect on compensatory award: 8635+
Effect on reinstatement award: 8687
Unreasonable during tribunal proceedings:
Leading to strike out of claim: 9573
Effect on recovery of costs: 9702+

Confidence:
Breach of: 2661, 6285+, 6540+

Confidential advice service: 5030

Confidential information:
Main entry: 2400+
Legitimate business interest:
Whether protectable: 2560+
Protectable interest:
Whether enforceable: 2573
Duration of enforceability:
Factors affecting: 2581
Relevant in grant of injunction: 2648
Care when transmitting/disclosing: 6010, 6165, 6264

Confidentiality:
Main entry: 2400+
Home-worker duty: 1845
Director duty: 2139+
Employee duty: 1223
Breach of:
Use of email: 6264

Confidentiality (continued)
Employee representative duty: 8938
Of health questionnaire: 625, 626
Of employee grievance records: 6771
As part of settlement/compromise agreement: 9276
Tribunal claim:
Disclosure and inspection of documents: 9549+

Consent:
Mutual agreement to vary terms: 1635+
Processing of personal/sensitive data: 5950+, 5969 (transfer abroad)
For verification of qualifications:
During recruitment: 680

Consideration:
Contractual requirement: 1116
To vary terms: 1636
Settlement/compromise agreement requirement: 9250+

Construction:
General principles: 1118

Constructive dismissal:
Main entry: 8230+, 1715+
Resignation with notice:
Effect on date of termination: 8347
Resignation without notice:
Effect on date of termination: 8352
Effect of TUPE: 8035, 8038
See also Dismissal

Consultation:
Redundancy dismissal:
Main entry: 8900+
On TUPE transfer:
Main entry: 8060+
Liability for non-compliance:
Whether transfers under TUPE: 8087
Domestic information: 7655+
European works councils: 7785+
As a relevant factor:
In determining fairness of dismissal: 4258+, 8440
Failure to comply with duty of:
Effect on compensatory award: 8631
For health and safety management: 4861, 4912

Continuation order:
Main entry: 8704
Effect on relevant end date regarding continuity of employment: 1058

Continuity of employment:
Main entry: 1000+
Contractual start date:
Requirement for written particulars: 1420
Effect of:
Assignment: 2210
Dismissal and re-engagement: 1656, 1676
Illegality: 1314
Maternity suspension: 4953
Medical suspension: 4985
Maternity leave/Adoption leave: 4436/4530
Parental leave: 4639
Probation: 945
Re-engagement: 8682
Reinstatement: 8681
Renewal/re-engagement: 8863
Effect on:
TUPE transfer: 7974

Continuity of service/production:
Whether results in partial exclusion from working time rules: 3654

Contract:
Of employment:
Definition: 11
Model: 9910
Comparison with contract for services: 30+
Of service: 13
Formation: 1110+
Evidence of:
Written statement of particulars: 1402
See also under specific topics (e.g. variation, termination)

Contracting in:
Of in-house services:
Whether TUPE applies: 7914

Contracting out:
Of in-house services:
Whether TUPE applies: 7914
Of statutory provisions:
Unenforceable term: 1335
See also TUPE

Contractor/sub-contractor:
Status: 15+

Contractual retiring age: 8203+
See also Retirement

Contractual terms: See Terms

Control:
As requirement for employment: 40+

Controlling shareholder:
As employee:
Determining factors: 43

Copyright issues: 2311+, 6276

Corporate manslaughter: 5187, 5192+

Costs:
Award of:
  In tribunal proceedings: 9702+
  On appeal to EAT: 9800+, 9802
  In civil claim: 9857
Order:
  Effect on deposit paid in hopeless/vexatious cases: 9570+
  For failure to attend hearing: 9649+
  On extension for entering response: 9524
  On granting request for postponement of hearing: 9626
  Civil court: 9857
Employer's payment of employee's legal costs on termination:
  Exemption from tax: 3144
Of arbitration: 9378
Of recruitment:
  Government assistance: 535, 6370+
Of training:
  Recovery of: 6327
See also Wasted costs order

Costs order: See Costs

COT3 form: 9306

Council tax:
Attachment of earnings: 3017+

Counselling services:
Tax of benefit: 3155
Tax on outplacement counselling on redundancy: 3141
Confidential advice service:
  To help give reasonable support: 5030

Counter notice: See Notice

County court:
Jurisdiction to hear claims: 9443
Forum to bring enforcement proceedings of tribunal award: 9715
Procedure: 9850+
Injunctions: 1771+, 2645+

Court of Appeal:
Jurisdiction to hear appeals: 9820+
Decision:
  Whether binding on EAT: 9798

Court of Justice of the European Union:
Referrals to: 9840+

Covert monitoring: 6250+

Credit reference agencies:
Employer use of to monitor workers: 6240

Credit token:
Tax of benefit: 3208

Crime:
Use of covert monitoring to prevent/detect: 6250+

Criminal convictions:
Whether disclosure: 612+
Data protection compliance: 685

Criminal liability:
Of employer:
  Whether transfers under TUPE: 8002
As result of unlawful industrial action: 7550+

Criminal offence:
Disciplinary procedure: 6588, 6671+
Health and safety: 5180+
Non-compliance with national minimum wage rules: 2906
Non-compliance with working time rules: 3755
Of corporate manslaughter: 5192+
Of employing illegal worker: 780 (memo point)
Of fraudulent/wrongful trading: 2168
Of gross negligence manslaughter: 5190
Of supplying and using of drugs: 5051
As result of unlawful industrial action: 7550+
Protected disclosure: 2711

Cross appeal/contest of appeal: 9770+

Curriculum vitae:
Use of: 600+

Custom and practice:
Implied term: 1178, 1180
Incorporation of collective agreement terms by: 7371
Absence by:
  Effect on continuity of employment: 1019

Cycles and safety equipment:
Tax of benefit: 3155

D

Daily average agreement: 2896

Damages:
Employer breach of contract: 1725+
Employee breach of contract: 1760+

Damages *(continued)*
Breach of implied term/express term/restrictive covenants: 2660+
Breach of duty of care for health and safety: 5130+
Aggravated: 5754
Stigma: 5746, 8167
As alternative to injunction: 2646
For unfair dismissal: 8570+
For wrongful dismissal: 8160+
See also Award

Dangerous occurrences:
Reporting duties: 4880+

Data controller: 5922

Data processor: 5931

Data protection:
Main entry: 5910+
Remedies: 6040+
During recruitment process: 676+
Good practice recommendations on monitoring: 6167, 6190, 6200+
In relation to discipline and grievance: 6504
In relation to information about workers' health: 4940+
In relation to pension schemes: 3445+
Information gathering for tribunal claim: 9140+
Monitoring equal opportunities: 5845
References: 8328+, 705
Sickness records: 4224
With regard to OSP: 4175
With regard to PHI: 4206

Data protection commissioner: See Information commissioner

Data subjects: 5920

Database rights (IPR): 2315

Date of termination:
Main entry: 8340+
Impact of internal appeal hearing: 6680
Relevance in identifying start of tribunal time limits: 9457+
Effect on relevant end date for continuous employment: 1055+

De facto director: 2101

Death:
Of employee:
  Company liability for: 5192+
  Automatic termination of employment: 8276

Death *(continued)*
  During notice period: 8348
  Impact on unfair dismissal claim: 8561
  Effect on entitlement to redundancy payment: 9014+
  Effect on entitlement to redundancy payment for lay-off/short-time working: 7893
  Effect on protective award: 8954
Of employer:
  Effect on continuity of employment: 1035
  Effect on contract of employment: 8276
  Effect on entitlement to redundancy payment: 9015+
  Effect on entitlement to redundancy payment for lay-off/short-time working: 7892
  Effect on outstanding claims: 8276
  Effect on suitable alternative employment offer: 9015

Death in service
Benefit: 3411, 3126

Death, injury or disability:
Tax of lump sum payments: 3126

Debts:
Director's personal liability: 2160
Owed by insolvent transferor: 7998
On insolvency of employer: 9053+

Decision:
Disciplinary hearing: 6625+
Internal appeal hearing: 6695+
Tribunal: 9690+, 9700+, 9702+, 9715+, 9718+
Tribunal's review: 9725
EAT: 9794
Court of Appeal: 9823
Supreme Court: 9833+
Court of Justice of the European Union: 9841
Civil courts: 9855

Deduction of pay:
Main entry: 3000+
Itemised pay statement: 2985
Standing statement of fixed deductions: 2986+
Tribunal claim:
  Time limit: 9462, 9490

Deductions:
PAYE: 6820+
NIC: 6925+

Defamation:
Email contents: 6268

Default judgment:
Main entry: 9526+
Review of: 9726+

Defence to tribunal claim: 9519+

Delivery up:
Recovery of confidential information: 2642

Demotion: 6633, 6664
As alternative to dismissal: 6633

Dependant:
Time off for care of: 4740+

Deposit:
To continue tribunal proceedings: 9570+

Derecognition: See Recognition/derecognition

Design rights: 2314+

Detrimental treatment:
Right not to suffer: 8394+
Best practice to avoid discrimination: 5830

Direct discrimination:
Racial/religion or belief: 5390+,
Sex/sexual orientation: 5265+
Disability: 5500+
Age: 5605+
Marital status: 5327+
Civil partnership status: 5327+

Directions (claim):
For further and better particulars: 9542+
In tribunal proceedings:
 Main entry: 9560+
In EAT: 9762+
Civil claim: 9853

Director:
Main entry: 2100+
Duties: 2133+
Personal liability: 2160+,
 Employment of illegal worker: 780
 Bribery: 2175+
 Health and safety: 5185+
NIC: 6967+
Reasonable notice of dismissal: 8129
Resignation as part of settlement/compromise agreement: 9274
Tax of benefits: 3148
Tax of earnings: 3114

Disability:
Application form: 611
Car benefit:
 Exemption from tax: 3223
Disciplinary issues: 6651
Dismissal due to incapacity: 4248
Health questionnaire: 625
Ill health dismissal: 8477
Induction: 933
Job adverts: 590
Medical testing: 706+
Offer of employment: 713
Recruitment interview: 662
Selection testing: 647
Short-listing procedures: 634

Disability discrimination:
Main entry: 5450+
See also Discrimination

Disciplinary hearing:
Main entry: 6610+
Right to be accompanied: 6780+
Relevance in determining fairness of dismissal: 8501

Disciplinary procedure:
Main entry: 6555+
Avoiding victimisation: 5829
Best practice to avoid discrimination: 5829
Employee resignation during: 8183
Failure to follow: 6514, 8630+ (effect on compensation in unfair dismissal)
 Effect on wrongful dismissal damages: 8165
Relevance in dispute: 9151
Requirement for written particulars: 1420

Disciplinary rules:
Main entry: 6534+
Requirement for written particulars: 1420

Discipline:
Of employees: 6530+
Of union members: 7142+
Misconduct:
 As fair reason for dismissal: 8490+
Record:
 Whether fair redundancy selection criterion: 8836
Disciplinary warning:
 Relevance in dispute: 9152
With regard to sickness: 4230+

Disclosure:

Of personal/sensitive data: 5970+

Of information:
    Official requests for information: 5979
    For access arrangements during recognition/derecognition: 7352
    Regarding selection for redundancy dismissals: 8840

As part of tribunal proceedings: 9545+, 9185

Service agreement: 2120, 2122

Of director's interests: 2155

Discrimination:

Main entry: 5200+

Dismissal due to: 8111

Constructive dismissal: 8249

Disciplinary procedures: 6579

Special grievance procedures: 6761

Redundancy selection criteria: 8838

Agencies, by: 2066

Bonuses, incentive payments and commission: 2830

During recruitment process: 540+, 591+, 607, 611, 630+, 707

Ending employment during maternity leave: 4450

Extended statement of reasons for tribunal: 9691

Failure to train: 6320

Family-friendly rights: 4765

Home workers: 1850

Less favourable treatment of fixed-term employee: 1964+

Less favourable treatment of part-time worker: 1887+

Pension schemes: 3435+

References on termination: 8322

Request for flexible working: 1816

Trade union duties: 7146

Trade union membership/non-membership: 7563

Tribunal claim:
    Time limits: 9460, 9490

See also Equal pay and specific types (e.g. Sex discrimination, Racial discrimination, Disability discrimination, Age discrimination, Marital status discrimination, Civil partnership status discrimination, Religion or belief discrimination, Sexual orientation discrimination etc.)

Dishonesty:

Establishing employee's:
    Requirements in fair disciplinary procedure: 6588

Dishonesty (continued)

Resulting in breakdown of trust and confidence:
    SOSR dismissal: 8541

See also Honesty

Dismissal:

Main entry: 8100+, 8105+, 8380+

Requirement for fair reason: 8420+

Requirement for fair procedure: 8435+

Statement of reasons for dismissal: 8310+

With notice:
    Main entry: 8120+
    Effect on date of termination: 8343+

Without notice:
    Main entry: 8155+
    Determining date of termination: 8349+

Constructive: 8230+

As final disciplinary sanction: 6634+

Best practice to avoid discrimination: 5830

Due to long-term illness: 4245+

Due to variation of terms: 1655

During probation: 953

Effect on PHI: 4203

Effect on trust and confidence: 1247

Effect of TUPE: 8030+

Employee with persistent short-term absences: 4280+

Executive director: 2125+

Issues relating to disciplinary matters: 6500+

Redundancy: 8730+

Retirement: 8200+

Dispensation:

Expenses: 6900

Dispute resolution:

Main entry: 9100+

Disciplinary procedure as means of: 6555+

Grievance procedure as means of: 6730+

Disqualification order:

Director: 2111

Doctor:

Working time rules: 3640

Documents:

In disciplinary hearing: 6607

In tribunal proceedings: 9634, 9780+
    Disclosure of: 9545+, 2642

EAT appeal: 9780

Delivery up: 2642

Domestic information and consultation: 7655+

Domicile:
Tax concept: 3377

Double Contributions Conventions:
Accrual of social benefit in UK: 7021

Dress code: 5826
Sex discrimination: 5261

Drug/alcohol misuse: 5050+
As disciplinary matter: 6652

Drug screening: See Screening/medical testing

Due diligence and care:
Duty of: 1205+

Duration:
Of restrictive covenants (generally):
  Effect on reasonableness of restrictive covenants: 2567
Of non-compete covenants:
  Effect on enforceability of covenant: 2580
Of non-solicitation covenants (customers):
  Effect on enforceability of covenant: 2589
Of non-solicitation covenants (employees):
  Effect on enforceability of covenant: 2604
Of illegality:
  Effect on enforceability of contract: 1311
Period of illegality:
  Effect on employment rights: 1314
Temporary/fixed term/work abroad:
  Requirement for written particulars: 1420

Duties:
Of director: 2133+
Of employee:
  Implied by common law: 1200+, 1202+, 1205+, 1208+, 1213+, 1223+, 1226
Of employer:
  Implied by common law: 1230+, 1233+, 1237, 1239, 1241+, 1255, 1257, 1260
Of office-holder: 2134

Duty of care:
Employer: 1237, 4810+
Employee: 1205+
Director: 2141+
Providing references: 1257, 8325+
Statements in context with transfer: 1243

Duty of fidelity:
Main entry: 1213+

Duty of fidelity *(continued)*
Breach of:
  Damages: 1760
Confidential information and trade secrets:
  During employment: 2410+
  Post employment: 2417
Not to compete: 2510
On garden leave: 2532
Employee withholding goodwill:
  Effect on pay: 3009

Duty to mitigate: See Mitigation of loss

E

Early retirement:
Main entry: 8228+
Pension options: 3413+
Whether benefits transfer under TUPE: 7994
Whether dismissal: 8260
Whether redundancy dismissal: 8776, 8835, 8106
See also Retirement

Earnings:
Tax of: 3100+
See also Pay

EAT: See Employment Appeal Tribunal

Economic entity:
Relevant in identifying TUPE transfer: 7932

EDT: See Effective date of termination

Educational body member:
Right to time off: 3920

EEA citizen:
Right to work in the UK: 765

Effective date of termination: 8340+

Election:
Of employee representatives: 8928+
Of union representatives: 7148
Of negotiating representatives: 7702+
Of information and consultation representatives: 7722
Of EWC representatives: 7804

Electronic communications:
Monitoring: 6190+

Electronic payments: 6864+

Email and internet:
Main entry: 6260+

Email and internet *(continued)*
Monitoring: 6190+
Legality of interception: 6220+
Access to workers during recognition/derecognition: 7356
See also Social media issues

Emergency procedures:
Health and safety: 4860
Requirement for appointed persons and first aiders: 4905+

Emoluments: See Earnings

Employee:
Main definition: 11
Summary of main rights: 12
Main implied statutory rights: 1185+
Common law duties: 1200, 1202+, 1205+, 1208+, 1213+, 1223+, 1226
Comparison with self-employed: 30+
As agency worker: 2042+
As controlling shareholder: 43
As director: 2100+, 2110+
As employed earner: 6800+
As lower paid employee: 3146
As preferential creditor: 9080+
As relevant employee:
  In relation to tax of benefits/expenses: 3146, 3194
See also under specific types

Employee information (required under TUPE): 8090+

Employee representative:
Duties of:
  In relation to domestic information and consultation procedure: 7705
Collective consultation on TUPE: 8062+
Collective consultation on redundancies:
  Main entry: 8915+
  Right to receive copy of notification to BIS: 8972
Consultation with:
  When compiling staff handbook: 1489
Paid time off: 3910
Health and safety: 4910+
Involvement with discipline and grievance procedures: 6535, 6574, 6757, 6764

Employee share schemes: See Share scheme

Employee support: See Training

Employer:
Implied duties:
  Statutory: 1185+
  Common law: 1230+
Control:
  As requirement for employment: 40
Same employer, different employments:
  Effect on continuity of employment: 1010+, 1013+
Change of:
  Where no break of continuity of employment: 1035
Small:
  Additional relief on SMP/SAP/SPP and ASPP: 4495/4563/4608

Employment agencies: See Agencies

Employment Appeal Tribunal (EAT):
Right to bring appeal: 9745+
Acas conciliation: 9216

Employment judge: 9605+

Employment status:
Whether employed/self-employed: 30+
Right to work: 750+

Employment tribunal: See Tribunal

Enforcement:
Of tribunal award: 9715+
See also Criminal offence

Enforcement notice:
Health and safety/fire precautions: 5165+

Enterprise management incentive share scheme (EMI):
Tax: 3350

Entertainment (staff):
Whether taxable: 3175

Enticement: See Restrictive covenants

Environmental body member:
Right to time off: 3920

Equal opportunities:
Best practice: 5800+
Contractual retiring age: 8204
During recruitment process: 540+
In selection process: 630+
Job advertisement: 595

Equal pay: 5650+
During recruitment process: 591

Equal treatment:
Main entry: 5200+
Job advertisement: 591+
Part-time worker: 1887+
Fixed-term employees: 1964+
Home worker: 1850

Equality and Human Rights Commission (EHRC): 5205, 5790+
Copy of claim form to be sent to: 9516

Equality at work: 5200+

Establishment:
Definition for purpose of collective redundancies: 8921

Estoppel: 9631+

ET1 form:
Main entry: 9511+
Amendments to: 9530+

ET3 form:
Main entry: 9520+
Amendments: 9530+

ETO reason: 8016

EU law claims:
Whether tribunal jurisdiction to hear: 9432

European Convention on Human Rights: See Human rights

European Court of Justice: See Court of Justice of the European Union

European Economic Area (EEA):
National:
  Right to work: 765
Moving within:
  Effect on NICs: 7025+

European works councils: 7785+

Evidence:
Of contract:
  Written statement of particulars: 1402
Of incapacity: 4251+
Of employment relationship: 31+
Of entitlement to: 4427 (ML); 4487 (SMP); 4527 (AL); 4559 (SAP); 4581 (PAL); 4603 (SPP); 4604 (ASPP); 4662 (PL – fallback scheme)
Of medical condition (sickness absence): 4211
Of right to work in UK: 781+
At disciplinary hearing: 6610+
At internal appeal: 6691+

Evidence *(continued)*
At tribunal hearing: 9660+
At EAT: 9752, 9782
Handling disputes: 9140+
See also under specific types (e.g. Medical, Witness etc)

EWC: See European works councils

Ex gratia payment: See Lump sum payment

Ex parte application: See Injunction

Exact percentage method: 6957

Exclusion/expulsion:
From union: 7140

Executive director: See Director

Expenses:
General: 2847
Tax of: 3265+
  In relation to duties performed abroad: 3392
  Non-UK domiciled employees: 3394+
Employer duty:
  Implied by common law: 1255
Business:
  Whether PAYE: 6814
PAYE reporting requirements: 6895+
Payments made in relation to:
  Not protected by unauthorised deduction rules: 3056
Loss of:
  Wrongful dismissal damages: 8164
  Compensatory award damages: 8608
For attending tribunal proceedings: 9712

Experiential learning:
As informal training: 6313

Expert evidence:
In relation to health and safety matters: 5030
In relation to discrimination matters: 5462, 5524, 5721, 5745
In tribunal proceedings: 9563+
In civil claims: 9853

Express agreement:
To vary terms: 1638

Express incorporation:
Of collective agreement terms: 7369+

Express terms:
Main entry: 1155+

Express terms (continued)
During maternity leave/adoption leave: 4435/4530
During parental leave: 4639

Extension:
Of time limits in tribunal proceedings: 9452, 9465+

F

Factory work:
Health and safety: 4870
Children/young persons: 4971+
Compulsory maternity leave: 4433

Fair trial:
Right to: 6558, 6780, 9435, 9612+, 9648, 9663, 9669, 9693

Family Division: See High Court

Family member:
Foreign travel expenses: 3312

Family worker:
No entitlement to minimum wage: 2868
Exclusion from working time rules: 3625

Family-friendly rights: 4400+, 4410+, 4520+, 4570+, 4620+, 4690+, 4740+

Fast track cases (on appeal): 9765+

Fidelity: See Duty of fidelity

Fiduciary duties:
Of employees: 1217
Breach of duties:
    Account for profits: 2665
Of directors: 2139+, 2510, 2550

Final salary scheme: 3410

Finance sector:
Special regulations covering recruitment: 578

Financial dealings:
Director's duty to observe restrictions: 2155

Fire safety/precautions:
Specific duties: 4870
Requirement for appointed advisers: 4903

First aid:
Specific duties: 4870
Specific risk assessment: 4867
Requirement for appointed persons and first aiders: 4905+

Fixed-term working:
Main entry: 1950+
Whether non-renewal of contract is redundancy: 8778
Expiry date:
    Requirement for written particulars: 1420
Reasonableness of duration of garden leave: 2531
Duty to consult in collective redundancy situation: 8919
Redundancy selection discrimination: 8838

Flexibility clause:
Main entry: 1618+
Impact of with regard to redundancy situation: 8762
See also Mobility clause

Flexible working:
Main entry: 1800+
Right to request: 4690+
    Remedies (specific): 4780
Best practice to avoid discrimination: 5820+

Foreign service:
Lump sum payments made in relation to:
    Tax of: 3128

Foreign travel: See Overseas work, Assignment

Foreign worker:
Right to work:
    Main entry: 750+
Liability for NICs: 7000+

Form:
Of contract of employment: 1125+
Of tribunal hearing: 9645+

Formation:
Of contract of employment: 1110+

Forum non conveniens: 2271

Fraudulent trading:
By director of insolvent company: 2168

Frustration:
Main entry: 8285+
Due to incapacity of employee: 4270+
Due to employee's imprisonment: 6674

Fuel:
Tax of benefit: 3229+

Fundamental breach:
Main entry: 8230+
Remedies for: 1750+

Further and better particulars: See Additional information

G

Garden leave:
Main entry: 2529+
Injunctions: 2651+
Effect on validity of restrictive covenants: 2619
Tax during: 3137
Effect on date of termination: 8343+

Gas incidents:
Reporting duties: 4880

Gender reassignment discrimination: 5335+

Golden handshake:
As compensation for loss of office: 2131

Good faith: See Fiduciary duties

Goodwill:
Whether protectable: 2560+
Withholding of:
 Right to deduct pay: 3009

Gratuities:
Main entry: 2846
Whether liable for NICs: 6946

Grievance procedure:
Main entry: 6730+
Right to be accompanied: 6780+
Common law duty: 1239
Requirement for written particulars: 1420
Best practice to avoid discrimination: 5829
Relevance in determining fairness of dismissal: 8501

Gross misconduct:
Summary dismissal: 8155, 6640
As fair reason for dismissal: 8491
Disciplinary rules: 6540
Suspension with pay during investigation of: 6595
Effect on entitlement to SRP: 9001
See also Misconduct

Grounds of appeal: See Appeal

Group performance review: 6467

Guarantee payment: See Statutory guarantee payment

H

Harassment:
On grounds of:
 Sex and sexual orientation: 5360+
 Racial and religion or belief: 5430
 Disability: 5570
 Age: 5645
Email and internet issues: 6272+
Liability under Protection from Harassment Act: 4827, 5045+
Special grievance procedures: 6761
See also Victimisation

Hazardous materials:
Specific duties: 4870

Hazardous work:
Night workers:
 Special working time rules: 3699

Health and safety:
Main entry: 4800+, 4810+, 4860+, 5010+
Remedies: 5130+
Home worker issues: 1840+
Employer duty: 1237

Health assessment:
Use of health questionnaires: 625+
Night worker: 3701+
Young night worker: 3725
Records (working time): 3742
See also Risk assessment

Health questionnaire:
At recruitment stage: 625+

Health service employer:
Employee move to another health service employer:
 Effect on continuity of employment: 1035

Healthcare:
Cover during posting: 2245+
Medical insurance/treatment fees/screening:
 Tax of benefit: 3155, 3211

Hearing:
Discipline: 6610+
Grievance: 6766+

Hearing *(continued)*
Internal appeal: 6690+
Pre-hearing tribunal review: 9580+
Tribunal main hearing: 9600+
EAT appeal: 9788+
Preliminary hearing/directions by EAT: 9762+
Civil claim: 9854

Hearsay: See Evidence

High Court:
Jurisdiction: 9440+
Procedure: 9850+
Injunction: 1771+, 2645+

HMRC: 3100+
PAYE/NIC year end routine: 6875+
Benefits and expenses reporting obligations: 6895+
Student loan deductions: 6911
Issue of PAYE codes: 6825+
Recovery of SSP: 4112
Recovery of SMP/SAP/SPP and ASPP: 4495/4563/4608

Holiday: See Leave

Home worker:
Main entry: 1820+, 1825+, 1835+, 1845+
Use of home for business (tax): 3326+

Home working: See Home worker

Honesty:
Duty of: 1216

House of Lords: See Supreme Court

HRP: See Human resource planning

Human resource planning (HRP): 525+

Human rights:
Right to privacy: 6287
Monitoring/surveillance: 6160+
Impact on breach of confidence: 6286
Impact on disciplinary hearing: 6560
Impact on unfair dismissal (misconduct): 8490
Impact on conduct/make up of tribunal proceedings: 9612, 9435+
Effect of dress code on: 5826
Medical insurance/treatment fees/screening: 706

I

Identity of employer and employee:
Requirement for written particulars: 1420, 1407

Ill health:
Absence: 4100+
Early retirement due to: 8229
See also Sickness

Illegal terms:
Effect on continuity of employment: 1010
Effect on contract: 1305+

Illegality:
Effect on continuity of employment: 1010

Illness: See Sickness

Immigration:
Status: 750+

Impairment: 5457+
See also Disability discrimination

Implied term:
By the courts: 1170+
By statute: 1185+
By common law: 1195+, 1200+, 1230+
See also Terms

Imprisonment:
Frustration of contract: 8290
Whether potentially fair reason for dismissal: 8544

Incapability:
Whether potentially fair reason for dismissal: 8450+
Whether fair redundancy selection criterion: 8836

Incapacity:
Due to sickness or injury: 4100+

Incentive payments: 2829

Income:
Liability under PAYE: 6814+
Liability for NICs: 6944+

Income support:
If not entitled to MA: 4483 (memo point)
Effect on protective award: 8953
Main social benefits: 9920

Incompetence:
As fair reason for dismissal: 8452+
See also Incapability

Indemnity:
For director liability: 2172
Settlement adviser: 9340

Indirect control:
Whether sufficient for employment relationship: 40

Indirect discrimination:
Age: 5605+
Disability: 5509
Marital/civil partnership status: 5330
Sex/sexual orientation: 5300+
Racial/religion or belief: 5410+

Inducement (unlawful): 7573, 7582, 7593

Induction:
New employee: 910+

Industrial action:
Main entry: 7400+
Term restricting right to: 1360
Whether affects duty to work: 1200
Deduction of pay as a result of:
    Not protected by unauthorised deduction rules: 3065
No entitlement to guarantee payment: 7864
Effect on entitlement to SSP: 4132
Effect on entitlement to lay-off/short-time redundancy payment: 7864
Effect on entitlement to SRP: 9001

Inform, duty to:
For collective bargaining purposes: 7395
    Personal/sensitive data: 5976
Under TUPE: 8060+, 8062+, 8090+
    Personal/sensitive data: 5977
Under collective redundancy consultation requirements: 8935+
Of opt-out:
    With regard to shop and betting employees: 3833
Health and safety: 4875
Under domestic information and consultation requirements: 7658+, 7750+
    Pensions: 3448
Under EWC rules: 7785, 7794

Information and consultation representatives: 7733+

Information Commissioner:
Role: 5911
Notification requirements: 5990+
Applications to: 6043+

Injunction:
Breach of contract: 1732, 1771+
Breach of restrictive covenant/implied term/express term: 2645+
Unprotected industrial action: 7534
Discrimination cases: 5790
Freezing: 9590

Injury at work: See Sickness

Injury to feelings:
Damages for wrongful dismissal: 8166
Compensatory award: 8610
Whether damages for breach of contract: 1726
See also Damages

Inland Revenue: See HMRC

Insolvency:
Whether terminates employment: 8277+
Employee rights on: 9040+
Director liability: 2168
Duty to consult on collective redundancies: 8923
TUPE transfers: 7998, 8023

Inspection: See Disclosure

Insurance against liability: 4990
See also Indemnity

Intellectual property rights (IPR): 2310+
Email and computer use: 6276

Intention:
Of employer:
    Relevance in claim for constructive dismissal: 8235
Of parties:
    Incorporation of collective agreement into terms: 7372
    Regarding legality of contract: 1307
    Relevance in determining employment status: 53
    Requirement for legally binding contract: 1117+

Interest:
On tribunal awards: 9716+

Interim orders:
Tribunal: 9501

Interim orders (continued)
Appeal against: 9754
EAT: 9775+

Interim relief:
Unfair dismissal proceedings: 8700+

Interlocutory application: See Interim orders

Interlocutory injunction: See Injunction

Internet: See Email and internet and Social media issues

Interview:
During recruitment: 630, 643+
Data protection issues: 683
Best practice to avoid discrimination: 5816

Invention:
Registered IPR: 2316, 2340+

Investigation:
During disciplinary proceedings: 6585+, 6625+
Effect on fairness of dismissal: 8439, 8501+

IPR: See Intellectual property rights

Itemised pay statement: 2985+

J

Job advertisement:
Main entry: 590+
Best practice to avoid discrimination: 5807+
Data protection requirements: 678
Requirement of union membership: 592

Job applicant:
Recruitment and selection: 510+
Data protection issues: 676+
Discrimination: 5218
Equal opportunities: 540+

Job application:
Main entry: 600+
Data protection issues: 679+

Job banding: 6451+

Job description: 575, 577

Job evaluation: 6451+

Job offer: See Offer of employment

Job shadowing:
As informal training: 6313

Job title:
Requirement for written particulars: 1420, 1407

Jobseeker:
Work programme assistance: 6380+
Allowance:
  Effect on protective award: 8953

Jobsharing:
As flexible working: 1811
Part-time worker: 1907

Joint negotiating body: See Collective bargaining

Jurisdiction:
Tribunal: 9420+
High Court: 9440+
County court: 9443
Over international employment disputes: 2260+
Stated in settlement/compromise agreement: 9284

L

Last in first out:
Whether fair redundancy selection criterion: 8838

Last straw doctrine: 8234

Lay members tribunal: 9605+

Lay-off/short-time working: 7858+

Leave:
Time off during working hours: 3910+
Annual:
  Main entry: 4000+
  Calculation of a week's pay: 2920+
  Effect of other leave: 4442 (ML); 4530 (AL); 4102 (sick leave)
  On insolvency of employer: 9053+
  Part-time workers: 1897
  Written particulars: 1420, 1407
Sickness: 4100+
Maternity: 4420+
  Protection from discrimination: 5320
Adoption: 4520+
Paternity: 4570+
Parental: 4620+

Leave to enter/remain in UK: 750+

Legal aid:
Tribunal claims: 9131
Appeal to EAT: 9791

Legal aid *(continued)*
Referral to Court of Justice of the European Union: 9841
Arbitration: 9373

Legal professional privilege:
Tribunal proceedings: 9185, 9551

Legal representation: See Representation

Legitimate business interests:
As subject of restrictive covenant: 2560+

Less favourable treatment:
On the ground of a person's disability: 5500
For a reason connected with a disability: 5510
Disabled job applicant: 546+, 548+
Sex/sexual orientation discrimination: 5276
Racial/religion or belief discrimination: 5395
Age discrimination: 5610
Fixed-time employee: 1964+
Part-time worker: 1887+

Liability insurance:
Director: 2173

Libel:
References on termination: 8323

Liquidated damages clause: 1703

Liquidation:
Whether TUPE applies: 7919, 8023
See also Insolvency

Listed company:
Director duties: 2134 (memo point)

Listing:
Tribunal case: 9623
EAT appeal: 9760

Litigant in person: See Representation

Litigation: See Tribunal (claim)

Living accommodation: See Accommodation

Loan:
Main entry: 2848+
Deduction from pay:
  Contractual: 3005+
  Statutory: 3030
Tax of benefit: 3238+

Local councillor:
Right to time off: 3920

Long service award:
Tax of benefit: 3180

Lump sum payment:
Main entry: 2845
Tax of: 3115+

Luncheon voucher:
Tax of benefit: 3155

M

Magistrate:
Right to time off: 3920

Management of health and safety: 4860+

Manslaughter:
Liability for: 5187

Marital status discrimination: 5325+

MAT B1 form: 4487

Matching certificate: 4559

Maternity allowance: 4483 (memo point)

Maternity pay: See Statutory maternity pay (SMP)

Maternity rights:
Main entry: 4410+
Health and safety: 4950+
Risk assessment: 4956+
Whether pregnant employee qualifies for SSP: 4127+
See also Maternity leave (under Leave)

Mean hourly output rate: 2889

Medical:
Examination:
  During recruitment: 706
  With regard to managing sickness: 4213+
Evidence:
  Entitlement to SMP: 4487
  Relevance in employment disputes: 9156
  Required for pension on early retirement: 3414
  As factor in early retirement due to ill health: 8229
Data protection issues: 4940+
Investigation:
  Persistent short-term absence: 4280
Insurance/treatment:
  Tax of benefit: 3211, 3155

Member: See specific types of member (e.g. Union member, Tribunal member, Police authority member etc)

Mental impairment:
Capacity to enter into contract: 1111

Minimum wage: See National minimum wage

Misconduct:
As fair reason for dismissal: 8490+
Disciplinary rules: 6540+
Fair procedure: 8501+
Admission of: 6588
During redundancy situation: 8780
Effect of on compensatory award: 8585
Informal procedures: 6601
Sexual:
  Restricted reporting orders in tribunal proceedings: 9583+
Warning: 6631

Misrepresentation:
Job application form: 603

Mitigation of loss:
Wrongful dismissal damages: 8171
Compensatory award: 8620+
Evidence in employment disputes: 9158
Relevance in tribunal remedies: 9701

Mobile phones:
Tax of benefit: 3167
Loss of:
  Compensatory award: 8595

Mobile workers:
Whether covered by working time rules: 3644

Mobility clause:
Express: 1618+
Implied: 1631
Effect on redundancy: 8751
Effect when exercising right to return after maternity leave: 4472
See also Flexibility clause

Money purchase scheme: 3410

Monitoring and surveillance:
Main entry: 6150+, 6230+
Performance standards:
  For job evaluation purposes: 6450+
  For disciplinary purposes: 6660+
Equal opportunities: 5835+

Monitoring and surveillance *(continued)*
Recruitment process: 675
Sickness levels: 4210+
Absence levels: 6650

Mutuality of obligation:
As requirement for employment: 35+

N

Name and shame policy (health and safety): 5161

National minimum wage: 2865+
Effect on unfair dismissal award: 8571

Natural justice: 9610+

Naturalisation:
British citizenship: 760

Negligent misstatement:
Due to information on TUPE transfer: 8069

Negotiated agreement (domestic information and consultation): 7665+

Negotiating representatives: 7702+

New mother:
Specific health and safety duties: 4950+
Specific risk assessment: 4956+

NIC:
Main entry: 6925+, 6940+
Effect on calculation of average hourly rate: 2881
Working abroad: 2238+

Night work:
Whether partial exclusion from working time rules:
  Due to flexibility, continuity or special reason: 3650+
Special requirements regarding young persons: 3725
Special working time limits on normal hours: 3695
New/expectant mother: 4954

No case to answer: 9675+

Non-compete covenants: See Restrictive covenants

Non-dealing covenants: See Restrictive covenants

Non-discrimination notices: 5790

Non-executive director: See Director

Non-solicitation covenants: See Restrictive covenants

Non-taxable benefits: 3155

Normal retiring age: 8206+

Notice:
Requirements for annual leave: 4015+
Requirements for maternity leave: 4423+
Requirements for adoption leave: 4524
Requirements for paternity leave/additional paternity leave: 4576+, 4585, 4587
Requirements for SMP/SAP/SPP/ASPP: 4485/4557/4602/4604
Requirements for early return to work after ML/AL:
 (employee): 4459 (ML); 4530 (AL)
 (employer): 4457 (ML); 4530 (AL)
Requirements with regard to parental leave fall-back scheme: 4660
Requirements for time off to care for dependants: 4744
Enforcement:
 Health and safety/fire precautions: 5160+
For redundancy payment due to lay-off/short-time working: 7884+, 7887+
Requirements before industrial action: 7490
Of opt-in:
 With regard to shop and betting employees: 3845
Of opt-out:
 With regard to shop and betting employees: 3831+
Of tribunal hearing: 9625
See also Notice of termination

Notice of appearance: See ET3 Form

Notice of termination:
Dismissal with: 8120+
Dismissal without: 8155+, 1755+
Employer duty to provide: 1260
Statutory minimum notice: 8131
Reasonable notice: 1226, 8129
For redundancy payment due to lay-off/short-time working: 7886
Garden leave during: 2529+, 8150
Insolvency of employer (recovery of statutory minimum notice on): 9053+
Mutual agreement to terminate: 8181
On resignation: 8181+

Notice of termination *(continued)*
Relevance of:
 At recruitment stage: 666
Requirement for written particulars: 1420
When possible to bring tribunal claim: 9458+
Whether required in redundancy dismissal: 8802
Under service agreements: 2118

Notification:
To take maternity leave/adoption leave (employee): 4423/4524
Of end of maternity leave/adoption leave (employer): 4428/4528
To change start of maternity leave/adoption leave (employee): 4426/4526
Of early return from maternity leave/adoption leave (employee): 4459/4530
Of pregnancy/new mother/breast-feeding:
 For health and safety specific duties to apply: 4952
To Information Commissioner: 5990+
Requirements with regard to ballots on industrial action: 7463+
Employer's (domestic information and consultation): 7695+
Requirements with regard to redundancy: 8900+
To BIS:
 With regard to collective redundancies: 8970+

NRA: See Normal retiring age

O

Obedience:
Employee duty of: 1208+

Occupational diseases:
Reporting duties: 4880+

Occupational pension scheme: 3405+

Occupational requirement:
Recruitment: 580
Sex/sexual orientation discrimination: 5290
Gender reassignment discrimination: 5340
Marital/civil partnership discrimination: 5328
Racial discrimination: 5404
Religion or belief discrimination: 5405+
Age discrimination: 5620

Occupational sick pay (OSP): 4170+

Off-shore workers:
Whether exclusion from working time rules: 3640+

Offer and acceptance:
Requirement for binding contract: 1113+

Offer of employment:
Main entry: 700+

Office-holder: See Director

OML: See Leave

Online filing: 6850+, 6853+, 6856, 6877, 6895

Opt-in:
Of Sunday working:
  For shop and betting employees: 3845+

Opt-out:
Of average weekly working time limit: 3688
Of Sunday working:
  For shop and betting employees: 3831+

Order:
For directions: 9560+
For disclosure: 9545+
For additional information: 9537, 9539+
EAT: 9795+
See also specific types (e.g. Costs order, Continuation order, Witness order, Restricted reporting order, Search order)

Ordinary adoption leave (OAL): See Leave

Ordinary maternity leave (OML): See Leave

Originating application: See ET1 Form

Output worker: 2889+

Overpayment:
Whether right to deduct: 3010+, 3065
Recovery of:
  Effect on calculation of average hourly rate: 2881

Overseas transfer of data: 5967+

Overseas work:
Applicable law: 2255+
Applicable jurisdiction: 2260+
Foreign travel expenses as deductible expense: 3310+
NIC obligations: 7000+

Overseas work *(continued)*
Posted worker's statutory employment rights: 2275+
Requirement for written particulars: 1420
Union member's right to vote in industrial action ballot: 7452
Whether TUPE applies: 7943+

Overtime:
Main entry: 2825+
Payments:
  Effect on calculation of average hourly rate: 2880

P

P9D form: 6895+

P11 form:
Reporting requirements: 6842+
Leaving employees: 6853
SSP, SMP, SAP, and SPP payments: 6907
Student loan deductions: 6911

P11D form: 6895+

P11D(b) form: 6895+, 6984

P11DX form: 6901

P14 form: 6880
Reporting requirements: 6877+

P35 form: 6878
Reporting requirements: 6877+

P38A form: 6879, 6877

P45 form:
Main entry: 6850+
No effect on date of termination: 8350

P46 form: 6851

P46 (Car) form: 6898

P46 (Pen) form: 6853

P60 form: 6877, 6880

PAL: See Leave

Parental leave (PL): 4620+
Remedies (specific): 4780

Parents:
Rights of: 4400+

Parking:
Tax of benefit: 3155

Part-performance: See Refusal to work

Part-time work:
Main entry: 1870+
Calculation of pay during time off: 3942
Protection from discrimination: 5323

Part-time worker: See Part-time work

Patents: 2340+

Paternity leave: See Leave

Pay:
Main entry: 2800+
As consideration: 1116
Directors: 2119+
During statutory notice of dismissal: 8135
Fixed-term employees:
  Right to equal treatment: 1966
For time off: 3930+
For annual leave: 4012+
Loss of:
  Effect on wrongful dismissal damages: 8162
Loss/future loss of:
  Effect on compensatory damages: 8593+
Part-time workers:
  Right to equal treatment: 1893
Recovery of arrears:
  On insolvency of employer: 9053+
Requirement for written particulars: 1420, 1407
Suspension/continuance of:
  During maternity leave/adoption leave: 4438, 4530
  During parental leave: 4639
  During disciplinary procedure: 6595+
Withholding:
  Refusal to work/industrial action: 3007+, 7515+
Working abroad: 2236
See also Statutory maternity pay, Statutory sick pay, Statutory redundancy pay, Statutory guarantee payment, Unlawful deduction

Pay as you earn: See PAYE

Pay in lieu of notice (PILON):
Main entry: 8145+
Effect on:
  Compensatory award: 8616
  Date of termination: 8345, 8351
  Restrictive covenants: 2618
Taxation of: 3134
Whether wrongful dismissal: 8155
Where employee resigns: 8180

PAYE:
Main entry: 6810+

PAYE *(continued)*
Paid for directors:
  Tax of benefit: 3247
Settlement agreements: 6902+
  Liability for Class 1B NIC: 6990

Payment:
In kind:
  Whether liable for PAYE: 6815
Settlement: 9251+
To employer:
  As unauthorised deduction: 3050+
See also Lump sum payment

Payroll:
Processing of data by third party: 5931
Requirement for system: 6820+
Use in calculating NICs: 6957
Giving to charities: 3328

Penalties:
Short of dismissal: 6633
SSP non-compliance: 4118
SMP/SAP/SPP and ASPP non-compliance: 4498/4563/4608
Working time rules non-compliance: 3750+
Attachment of earnings order non-compliance: 3026
Returns: 6881, 6899
Online filing: 6856, 6881
Share scheme: 3344
Health and safety/fire precautions: 5180+
Against workers for unlawful industrial action: 7550+

Penalty clause: See Liquidated damages clause

Pension:
Main entry: 3400+
Effect of maternity leave: 4440
Exclusion of accrued rights from waiver of rights:
  In settlement/compromise agreement: 9261
Impact of early retirement on: 8228
Information and consultation requirements: 3448
Loss of:
  Compensatory award: 8601+
Payment:
  Excluded in calculation of average hourly rate: 2875
  Not protected by unauthorised deduction rules: 3056
Recovery of unpaid pension contributions:
  Insolvency of employer: 9056+

Pension *(continued)*
Requirement for written particulars: 1420
State pensionable age:
  Effect on liability to pay NICs: 6928+
Whether rights and liabilities transfer under TUPE: 7992+
Working abroad: 2250

Pensions Ombudsman: 3463

Pensions Regulator: 3460

Performance:
Assessment: 6465+
As disciplinary matter: 6660+
Dealing with dismissals relating to: 8471
Poor/incomplete leading to deduction of wages: 3005+
Whether fair redundancy selection criterion: 8836

Permanent health insurance (PHI):
Main entry: 4200+
Data protection issues: 4206
Tax issues: 3211

Personal allowance:
Effect on PAYE code: 6825+

Personal/sensitive data: 5925+, 5945+, 5975+
Handling data during recruitment: 680+

Personal injury:
Whether liability transfers under TUPE: 7981
Exclusion from waiver of rights:
  In settlement/compromise agreement: 9261

Personal liability:
Director: 2160+

Personal performance:
As requirement for employment: 45
Director's duties: 2137

Personnel file:
Data protection issues: 5925+
Disciplinary proceedings: 6645
Duty of confidentiality: 2410
Employment dispute: 9150

Picketing: 7495+

PILON: See Pay in lieu of notice

PIW: 4142

Place of work: See Workplace

Police:
Involvement in disciplinary procedure: 6673

Police authority member:
Right to time off: 3920

Policies and procedures:
Main entry: 1480+
Data protection: 6000+
Disciplinary: 6555+
Dress and appearance: 5826
Drugs and alcohol: 5055+
Email and internet: 6260+
Equal opportunities: 5800+
Grievance: 6739
Monitoring/surveillance: 6163+, 6205
Sickness absence: 4220+
Smoking: 5100+
Social media: 6282
Recruitment: 520, 525+, 535
Redundancy: 8810
Retirement: 8205
Whistleblowing: 2730

Political objects:
Of union: 7120

Political party:
Effect of carrying out activities: 7140

Polkey reduction: 8445, 8630+

Pool car:
Tax of benefit: 3222

Poor performance: See Performance

Pornography:
Use of email/internet: 6272+

Positive action: See Preferential treatment

Post termination obligations: See Restrictive covenants

Posted worker rights:
EU postings: 2282

Posting abroad: See Assignment and Overseas work

Postponement:
Tribunal hearing: 9625+

Preferential creditor: See Insolvency

Preferential treatment: 5243
Sex/sexual orientation discrimination: 5282, 5288
Racial/religion or belief discrimination: 5399+
Age discrimination: 5623
Best practice to avoid discrimination: 5831
During recruitment: 549

Pregnant employee/new mother:
Time off for antenatal care: 4411+
Entitlement to maternity leave: 4420+
Whether entitled to SMP: 4480+
Whether qualifies for statutory sick pay (SSP): 4127+
Right not to be discriminated against/suffer detriment: 4765+
Specific health and safety considerations: 4950+
Whether fair redundancy selection criterion: 8836

Pre-hearing reviews: 9567+

Preliminary hearing/directions:
EAT appeal: 9762+
Tribunal proceedings: 9580+

Premises:
Duty of care: 4815, 4840, 4841

Preparation time order: 9702+

Primary contributions: See Class 1 NIC

Prison independent monitoring board member:
Right to time off: 3920

Privacy:
Main entry: 6285+
Disclosure of information: 5970+
Monitoring/surveillance issues: 6160+, 6252

Private health insurance (PHI):
Loss of:
    Compensatory award: 8595

Privilege: See Legal professional privilege

Probation:
Main entry: 940+
Disciplinary issues: 6660

Professional privilege: See Legal professional privilege

Profiling:
Role in recruitment process: 575, 577+

Promotion:
Best practice to avoid discrimination: 5818

Protected disclosure:
Main entry: 2715
See also Whistleblowing

Protective award:
Failure to consult on collective redundancies: 8951+
Recovery:
    On insolvency of employer: 9053+

PSA: See PAYE, Settlement agreement

Psychiatric damage:
Main entry: 5010+
Wrongful dismissal damages: 8166
Discrimination compensation: 5753

Psychiatric illness: See Psychiatric damage

Psychological/psychometric tests:
In selection process: 650

Public authority:
Whistleblowing disclosure: 2735
Human rights issues: 6287
Transfers involving public authorities: 7928

Public company:
Director duties: 2134 (memo point)

Public hearings: 9619+, 9793

Public holidays:
Effect on statutory entitlement to annual leave: 4009+
Part-time worker entitlement: 1899

Public official:
Right to time off: 3920+

Public register:
Of tribunal cases: 9517, 9698

Publication:
Of personal/sensitive data: 5975

Q

Qualifications:
Recruitment: 579
Obtaining as part of formal training: 6312
As potentially fair reason for dismissal: 8461+

Qualified independent person: See Recognition/derecognition

Qualifying days:
For the purposes of SSP: 4147

Qualifying disclosure:
Under whistleblowing rules: 2711

Qualifying period: 1080

Quality assurance: 6470+

Queen's Bench Division: See High Court

Questionnaires:
Discrimination and equal pay: 548, 5711+

R

Race discrimination:
Main entry: 5375+
Disciplinary procedures: 6579
Redundancy selection criteria: 8838
Composition of tribunal:
    In tribunal proceedings: 9605

Rate:
National minimum wage: 2869
SMP/SAP/SPP and ASPP: 4492+/4563/4608
SSP: 4165

Reasonable adjustments:
Disabled individuals:
    Main entry: 5530+
    Interview stage: 662
    Disciplinary hearing: 6607

Reasonable care:
Regarding health and safety: 4815+

Receiver: See Insolvency

Reciprocal agreements:
Accrual of social benefit in UK: 7021
NIC obligations: 7035

Recognition: See Recognition/derecognition

Recognition/derecognition:
Main entry: 7200+
Effect of TUPE on recognition: 7987

Recognition of judgment:
Within EU countries: 2265
Outside EU countries: 2273

Records:
Data protection compliance: 5910+
    Collecting and handling records: 6003+
For compliance with working time rules: 3740
For compliance with minimum wage rules: 2900+
Health and safety accident reports: 4884
    Obtaining records: 4254
Health questionnaire: 625
Of disciplinary decisions: 6645
Of employee grievances: 6771
Of personal or sensitive data: 5945+
Of poor performance: 6666
Annual leave: 4030
SSP: 4115
Sickness absence: 6650
SMP/SAP/SPP and ASPP: 4496+/4563+/4608
Payroll giving: 3328
PAYE/NIC: 6875+, 6842
Checks on criminal records: 619+
Union's duty to permit inspection by members: 7148
Director's duty to maintain: 2155

Recoupment notice: 8646

Recruitment:
Main entry: 500+
Best practice to avoid discrimination: 5807+
Fixed-term employees:
    Right to equal treatment: 1967
Part-time workers:
    Right to equal treatment: 1901+

Redundancy:
Main entry: 8730+
As fair reason for dismissal: 8510+
Effect of TUPE: 8042
During maternity leave/adoption leave:
    Special protection against: 4453/4530
Mobility clause: 1627
Outplacement counselling:
    Exemption from tax: 3141
Paid time off/statutory payment:
    Maximum limit: 2923
Re-employment within four weeks:
    Effect on continuity of employment: 1024+
Re-training:
    Exemption from tax: 3160
Selection:
    Best practice to avoid discrimination: 5830
    Effect of unfair selection on compensatory award: 8631

Redundancy (continued)
Selection for inadmissible reason:
Automatic unfair dismissal claim: 8391
Statutory redundancy pay: 8990+
Tax of payments: 3132
Tribunal claims:
Time limits: 9458, 9490
Voluntary:
Dismissal/no dismissal: 8106, 8260
Warning of:
Whether amounts to anticipatory breach of contract: 8233

Redundancy pay:
Contractual terms: 8823
Effect on basic award: 8583
Effect on compensatory award: 8618
Not protected by unauthorised deduction rules: 3056
Presumption of redundancy situation: 8767+
Suitable alternative employment/statutory trial period: 8865+
See also Statutory redundancy pay

Redundancy selection: See Selection

Reference (tribunal):
Written statement of particulars: 1460

References:
Recruitment: 704+
Employer duty of care: 1257
Termination of employment: 8320+
Agreed as part of settlement/compromise agreement: 9270

Refusal to work:
Right to deduct pay as a result of: 3007+

Register:
Unions: 7121
Union members: 7148
Tribunal decision: 9698

Registered intellectual property rights: 2316+, 2340+

Registered pension schemes: 3420+

Reinstatement/re-engagement:
Unfair dismissal:
Main entry: 8680+
When order awarded: 8684+
Refusal of offer of
Effect on basic award: 8581
Employer's failure to comply with order: 8710
Effect on continuity of employment: 1027

Relevant agreement: 4000+

Relevant date of termination: 8340+

Religion or belief discrimination:
Main entry: 5375+
Employee's religious needs:
Best practice to avoid discrimination: 5822
See also Discrimination

Relocation:
Expenses:
Tax of benefit: 3177+
Costs:
On assignment: 2218
Whether employee refusal a fair reason to dismiss: 8534

Remedies:
Main tribunal remedies: 9700+
Civil claim: 9856
See also under specific causes of action

Remuneration See Pay

Reportable injury:
Reporting duties: 4880+

Reporting duties:
Benefits and expense payments: 6895, 6897, 6898, 6899
Health and safety: 4880+
Settlement considerations: 9280
Share schemes: 3343+
State imposed payments and deductions: 6905+
Year end routine: 6875+

Reporting order:
Tribunal proceedings: 9583+

Representation:
Tribunal hearing: 9640+
Effect on costs: 9702 (tribunal); 9801 (EAT)
EAT appeal: 9791

Representative:
Appropriate:
TUPE consultation: 8063
Health and safety: 4910+
Union:
Election requirements: 7148
Workforce agreements: 4650 (memo point)
See also Employee representative

Repudiatory breach: See Breach of contract

Reputation:
Loss of:
  Wrongful dismissal damages: 8167

Res judicata: See Estoppel

Reservist (Armed forces) (time off): 3926+

Residency:
Effect on income tax: 3370+
Effect on NIC obligations: 7005+

Resignation:
Main entry: 8180+
When constructive dismissal: 8238+
Employer repudiatory breach:
  Effect on restrictive covenants: 2616+
During statutory notice of dismissal: 8139
Under notice of redundancy:
  Entitlement to/effect of: 9000
  Effect on date of termination: 8346
Director: 2130

Respondent:
Tribunal proceedings:
  Adding to/substituting: 9535+
  Conduct: 9573, 9704

Response form: See ET3 Form

Rest periods:
Main entry: 3710+
Claim for breach of working time rules: 3761+
For young worker: 3727
Whether exclusion from working time rules:
  Due to flexibility, continuity or special reason: 3650+
Whether requirement for records: 3741

Restraint of trade:
Main entry: 2551+, 1355
Effect on garden leave: 2531
See also Restrictive covenants

Restraints: 2500+
See also Restrictive covenants

Restricted reporting order:
Tribunal proceedings: 9583+

Restrictive covenants:
Main entry: 2500+
Tax of payments made in relation to: 3140
As part of settlement/compromise agreement: 9276
Effect of TUPE transfer: 7975

Retail employment:
Deductions of wages:
  Special rules: 3070+

Retirement:
Main entry: 8199+
Normal retirement date: 3412+, 8206+
Contractual retiring age: 8203+
Tax of lump sum payment on: 3138
Pension options on retirement due to ill health: 3414
PAYE obligations: 6853+
Whether dismissal: 8106

Retirement benefit scheme:
Lump sum payments made in relation to:
  Taxation of: 3127

Return to work, right to: 4450+, 4465 (ML); 4530 (AL); 4583 (PAL); 4596+ (APAL); 4621 (PL)

Revenue and Customs: See HMRC

Review:
Appraisals and performance management reviews: 6465+
Tribunal decision: 9718+
EAT decision: 9805+
Internal decision: 6690+

Right to return to work: See Return to work, right to

Right to work: 750+
Proof of: 780+

Risk assessment:
Main entry: 4865+
Identifying what is hazardous work with regard to night workers: 3699

Road accidents:
Reporting duties: 4880

Rule 3(7) cases: 9761

S

SAP: See Statutory adoption pay

Safe Harbor Agreement:
Transfer of personal data to USA: 5967

Safe workplace and equipment:
Specific duties: 4870
Specific risk assessment: 4867

Safety adviser: 4900+

Safety committee: 4913

Safety representative: See Employee representative

Safety requirements: 4800+

Salaried-hours worker: 2886

Salary: See Pay

Sanction:
Disciplinary offence: 6630+
Failure to comply:
 Witness order: 9556
 Restricted reporting order: 9586

SAYE option scheme:
Tax: 3360

Scholarships:
Tax of benefit: 3162+

School governor:
Right to time off: 3920+

Screening/medical testing:
Drug and alcohol policy: 5060+

Scrutineer:
Industrial action ballots: 7445+

Search:
Order: 2642

Secondary contributions: See Class 1A NIC

Section 401 (chargeable under): 3124+

Securities:
Restriction on executive's holdings: 2528

Segregation: 5395

Selection:
Recruitment:
 General issues: 630+
 Best practice to avoid discrimination: 5811+
Redundancy:
 General issues: 8830+
 Best practice to avoid discrimination: 5830

Self-assessment review: 6467

Self-employed:
Comparison with employee: 30+
Worker or in business on own account: 14+, 50+

Semi-voluntary recognition: 7290+

Sensitive data: 5927, 5945+

Service agreement:
Main entry: 2115+
Confidentiality provisions: 2450+
IPR: 2350
Restrictive covenants: 2520+, 2565+

Service provision change: 7914+, 7936+

Settlement:
As alternative to tribunal/court action: 9210+

Settlement agreement:
Main entry: 9315+, 9350+, 9353
PAYE: 6902+
 Liability for Class 1B NIC: 6990
See also Compromise agreement

Severance agreement:
See Compromise agreement and Settlement agreement

Sex discrimination:
Main entry: 5260+
Mobility clause: 1625
Part-time workers: 1909+
Contractual retiring age: 8204
Composition of tribunal:
 Tribunal proceedings: 9605
See also Discrimination

Sexual orientation discrimination:
Main entry: 5260+
See also Discrimination

Shadow director: 2101

Share incentive plan:
Tax: 3355

Share options:
Whether transfer under TUPE: 7990

Share sale:
Whether TUPE applies: 7923

Shares, options or other securities:
Purchase of:
 Effect on calculation of average hourly rate: 2881
Tax of share schemes: 3340+
Loss of rights under:
 Compensatory award: 8595
Whether TUPE applies: 7923, 7990

Shift worker:
Partial exclusion from working time rules: 3635

Shop employee:
Sunday trading rules: 3800+
Definition: 3810+

Short-listing:
Recruitment:
  General issues: 630+
Data protection issues: 682
  Best practice to avoid discrimination: 5816+

Short-time working: See Lay-off/short-time working

Sick pay: 4100+
See also Statutory sick pay (SSP), Occupational sick pay (OSP) and Permanent health insurance (PHI)

Sickness:
Absence due to: 4100+
Policies and procedures: 4220+
Requirement for written particulars: 1420
Effect of sickness during annual leave: 4008
Special protection for pregnant employees and those on maternity leave: 4765, 5320+
Whether pregnancy sickness automatically commences maternity leave: 4430+
Disabled employees: 4248
Long term:
  Main entry: 4240+
  Effect on annual leave: 4007
  Whether fair reason for dismissal: 8458
  Leading to early retirement: 8229
Persistent short term:
  Consequences of: 4280+
  Whether fair reason for dismissal: 8458
Handling sickness issues: 4210+, 8475+
Health problems due to night work: 3702
During gap between contracts same employer – greater than one week:
  Effect on continuity of employment: 1021
Early retirement: 8229
See also Statutory sick pay (SSP), Occupational sick pay (OSP) and Permanent health insurance (PHI)

Skeleton arguments: 9786+

SMP: See Statutory maternity pay

Smoking ban: 5080+

SNB: See Special negotiating body

Social media issues: 6282

Social security benefits:
Main entry: 9920
Entitlement to: 6931

Social security benefits (continued)
Working abroad: 2238+
Maternity: 4483 (memo point)
Effect on:
  Wrongful dismissal damages: 8172
  Compensatory award: 8643+

Some other substantial reason (SOSR):
Main entry: 8530+
On TUPE dismissal: 8042

Special negotiating body: 7802+

Specific purpose contract:
Termination issues: 8106, 8155
Collective redundancy consultation requirements: 8919

Sports facilities:
Tax of benefit: 3155

SPP: See Statutory paternity pay

SRP: See Statutory redundancy pay

SSP: See Statutory sick pay

Staff handbook:
Main entry: 1480+
Written particulars reference to handbook: 1408

Staff suggestion schemes:
Tax of benefit: 3182

Stakeholder pension: 3400 (memo point)

Start date:
Requirement for written particulars: 1420

Starting employment: 900+
PAYE obligations: 6850+

State benefits: See Social security benefits

State guaranteed payments: See Insolvency

State pensionable age: 6929

Statement of general policy:
Health and safety: 4862

Statement of particulars: See Written particulars

Statement of reasons:
Main entry: 8310+
As evidence in tribunal proceedings: 8421
Of tribunal: 9691

Statement of written particulars: See Written particulars

Statutory adoption pay (SAP): 4554+, 4401

Statutory claims:
Tribunal: 9424
High Court: 9441

Statutory guarantee payment:
Main entry: 7860+
Maximum limit: 2923
Protected by unauthorised deduction rules: 3056

Statutory maternity pay (SMP):
Main entry: 4480+, 4401
Protected by unauthorised deduction rules: 3056
Recovery on insolvency of employer: 9045

Statutory minimum notice:
See also Notice

Statutory paternity pay (SPP): 4600+, 4401
Additional statutory paternity pay (ASPP): 4600+, 4401

Statutory recognition: 7225+

Statutory redundancy pay (SRP):
Main entry: 8990+
Claim for payment: 9010+
Statement of entitlement: 9017
Suitable alternative employment:
　Effect on entitlement to SRP: 8856
Payment for lay-off/short-time working: 7875+
On insolvency of employer: 9049+

Statutory rights:
Summary of main employee rights: 12
Summary of main worker rights: 17
Contracting out of: 1335
Loss of:
　Wrongful dismissal damages: 8165
　Compensatory award: 8609

Statutory sick pay (SSP):
Main entry: 4110+
Effect on compensatory award: 8647+
Protected by unauthorised deduction rules: 3056

Stigma damages: See Damages, Reputation

Stress: 5010+

Strike: See Industrial action

Strike out:
Tribunal claim: 9562, 9571, 9573+, 9675, 9709, 9776
Complaint to Certification Office: 7163

Student loan deductions: 3030
Collecting via PAYE: 6911

Subcontracting:
Whether TUPE applies: 7914

Subject access:
Data protection compliance: 5980+
Job applicant's right of access: 676

Subject to contract: 9243, 9920

Successive contracts:
Fixed-term: 1980+
Gaps between:
　Effect on continuity of employment: 1013+

Suggestion schemes:
Award: 3182
　Excluded in calculation of average hourly rate: 2875

Suitable alternative employment:
See Alternative employment (option of)

Suitable alternative work:
As alternative to medical suspension (new or expectant mothers): 4953

Summary dismissal:
Main entry: 8155+
Effect on date of termination: 8349+
Under notice of redundancy:
　Effect on reason for dismissal: 8772

Sunday trading: 3800+

Supervening event:
Leading to automatic termination of employment: 8275+

Supreme Court: 9830+
Whether binding on EAT: 9798

Surveillance: See Monitoring and surveillance

Suspension:
Maternity reasons: 3056, 4953
Medical, pay during: 4985+
During disciplinary procedure: 6595+
Disciplinary sanction: 6633

T

Tax:
Pay: 3100+
Share scheme: 3340+
Expenses: 3265+
PAYE scheme: 6800+
Period: 6817
Incorrect deductions: 6846+
Tables:
    Use of: 6840
Unfair dismissal awards: 8570
Wrongful dismissal damages: 8173
Unfair dismissal damages: 8570
On settlement/compromise agreements: 9265+
Working abroad: 3370+, 2237

Tax credits: 9920, 6862 (memo point)

Taxable benefits: 3190+

Telephone:
Monitoring: 6190+, 6233

Teleworking: See Home worker

Temporary worker:
Whether non-renewal of contract is redundancy: 8778
Dismissal due to return of permanent staff: 8539+

Termination date: See Date of termination

Termination of employment:
Main entry: 8100+
Mutual agreement: 8260+
Agreed (effect on settlement): 9247+
Of fixed-term contract: 1990+
Effect on office-holder: 2125+
Effect on statutory entitlement to annual leave: 4025+
Lump sum payment:
    As a golden handshake: 2131
    Tax of: 3123, 3124+, 3131
PAYE obligations: 6853+
Pre-agreed compensation clause: 1703
References on: 8320+

Terms:
Main entry: 1150+
Variation of: 1600+
Discriminatory: 1330
Best practice to avoid discrimination: 5819

Terms *(continued)*
Job advertisement: 596
See also Implied term

Third party gifts and entertaining:
Tax of benefit: 3184

Time at work: See Working time

Time limit:
Main entry: 9450+
Extension of: 9465+
For main tribunal claims: 9490
Breach of contract claims in tribunal and civil courts: 1711, 1751, 9463
Impact of internal appeal procedure: 6700 (disciplinary), 6777 (grievance)
For tribunal proceedings:
    Response: 9521, 9524
    Amendments to claim/response: 9531
    Review of decision: 9722
For EAT proceedings:
    Lodging appeal: 9756+
For CA proceedings:
    Lodging appeal: 9821
For SC proceedings:
    Lodging appeal: 9831
For complaints to certification officer: 7162
For claims on insolvency of employer: 9072, 9073

Time off:
Main entry: 3900+
In lieu of overtime: 2826
Statutory pay for:
    Protected by unauthorised deduction rules: 3056
See also Leave

Time off to train requests: 6400+

Time worker: 2886+

Tips: See Gratuities

Trade dispute: 7417

Trade secrets: 2400+

Trade union:
Main entry: 7115+
Employee health and safety representatives: 4912+
Employer failure to give time off to member/official: 3961
Whether recognition transfers on TUPE transfer: 7987

Trade union *(continued)*

Discrimination:
During recruitment process: 551

Member:
Main entry: 7128
Rights as against union: 7138+
General rights: 7560+
Time off: 7152
As relevant independent adviser: 9339

Non-member:
General rights: 7578

Official:
Right to attend picket: 7496
As companion at disciplinary hearing: 6782
Disciplinary proceedings: 6670

Representative:
Election requirements: 7148
Time off: 7153

Subscriptions:
Main entry: 3035+
Right not to pay: 7563, 7578

See also Collective agreement, Collective bargaining, Recognition/derecognition, Union learning representative

Trademarks:
Registered IPR: 2310

Trainee:
Main entry: 6350
National traineeships: 6375+
Whether entitled to minimum wage: 2868
Whether covered by whistleblowing legislation: 2710
Whether covered by working time rules: 3615, 3673
Whether non-renewal of training contract is redundancy: 8778

Training:
Main entry: 6310+
Right to request time off to train or study: 6400
Right of young persons to take time off: 6330+
To remedy poor performance: 6660+
Whether working time: 3673, 3615
Health and safety: 4877
First aiders: 4906
Representatives of employee safety: 4919+
Best practice to avoid discrimination: 5818
Part-time workers:
Right to equal treatment: 1905
Relating to disciplinary procedures: 6574
Independent recognised union representative right to time off: 7153

Training *(continued)*

Employer duty to consult independent recognised union: 7388
Repayment of training costs: 2849, 2850
Union Learning Representative right to time off: 7155

Training contract:
Whether non-renewal of contract is redundancy: 8778
Other than under a contract of employment:
Persons covered by working time rules: 3615

Training course:
Tax of benefit: 3159+

Transfer of undertaking: See TUPE

Transferee:
Duties on TUPE transfer: 7970+

Transferor:
Duty to provide employee information: 8060, 8061, 8062+, 8090+

Transport facilities (disabled employees, works bus etc.):
Tax of benefit: 3155

Transport worker:
Whether exclusion from working time rules: 3640+

Travel (and subsistence):
To work:
Whether working time: 3673
Expenses:
Working abroad: 2218
Attendance at interview: 660
Tax of expenses: 3285+

Trial period:
Statutory: 8872+
Common law: 8876
Effect of employee leaving during: 8357

Tribunal:
Jurisdiction: 9420+
Claim: 9500+
Member:
Right to time off: 3920+

Troncmaster:
PAYE: 6812
NIC: 6946

Trust and confidence:
Main entry: 1241+
Whether breach repudiatory: 8232, 1716, 1717
Whether down is fair reason for dismissal: 8541
Duty to pension members: 3430+
Duty to take care: 4835

Trustee:
Duty to transfers of pension scheme: 3432+

TUPE:
Main entry: 7900+
No dismissal due to: 8107
Effect on collective agreement: 7380
Effect on restrictive covenants: 2622
Dismissal: 8380, 8531

U

UCTA: 1340

Umbrella contract: See Global contract

Unauthorised deductions: 3050+

Undertaking: See TUPE

Unfair dismissal:
Main entry: 8380+
Due to unilateral variation of contract: 1665+
Of employees shortly before TUPE transfer: 7960
Redundancy dismissal: 8790, 8804, 8853+
Remedies: 9700
  Whether overlap with wrongful dismissal damages: 8177
  Maximum limits for awards: 2923
Tax of awards made in relation to: 3143
Tribunal claim:
  Time limits: 9458, 9465+, 9490
See also Dismissal

Union: See Trade union

Union learning representative:
Time off: 7155

Unlawful deduction: 3000, 3001, 3050+, 6665

Unlawful instruction:
Effect on implied duty of obedience: 1210

Unmeasured time worker: 2895

Unregistered intellectual property rights: 2311, 2335

Unregistered pension scheme: 3425+

V

Van:
Tax of benefit: 3233+

Variation of terms:
Contract of employment:
  Main entry: 1600+
Tax of lump sum payment: 3121+
On return from maternity leave/adoption leave: 4465+ /4530+
Requirement for consideration: 1116
PHI clause: 4202
During probationary period: 940+
Working abroad: 2215+
Collective agreement: 7376+
Constructive dismissal: 8232
TUPE transfer: 8010+
  In insolvency proceedings: 8023
Leading to redundancy: 8757

Vehicle: See Car, Van

Vexatious/hopeless claims: 9566+, 9703

Vicarious liability:
Main entry: 4825+, 5047
Employee negligence: 1205+
Constructive dismissal liability: 8236

Victimisation:
Due to:
  Candidature/membership of SNB/EWC: 7852+
  Disability: 5565+, 5570+
  Employee grievance: 6759
  Racial/religion or belief: 5425+
  Recognition/derecognition: 7586+
  Sex/sexual orientation: 5350+
  Union membership/activities or non-membership: 7560+
  Whistleblowing: 2761
Employer's vicarious liability for employee acts: 4829

Visa (entry clearance): 768+

Voluntary recognition: 7214+

Voluntary redundancy:
Whether a dismissal: 8776, 8917
As redundancy selection criterion: 8834

Volunteers:
Whether employees/workers: 39, 5216

Vouchers and credit cards:
Tax of benefit: 3208+

W

Wages: See Pay

Waiver:
Statutory redundancy pay:
  Collective agreement: 8993
Contractual and statutory rights:
  Settlement/compromise agreement: 9259+
Contractual rights:
  Settlement agreement: 9320
Statutory rights:
  Compromise agreement: 9322+
Tribunal time limits: 9452

Warning:
As disciplinary sanction: 6631+
Poor performance: 6662
Relevance in employment dispute: 9152
Whether previous warning relevant in determining disciplinary sanction: 6627

Wasted costs order: 9641, 9711, 9802

Week 53 payments: 6817

Week's pay:
Main entry: 2920+
Minimum entitlement: 2921
Maximum limits: 2923+
Statutory redundancy pay: 9005
Guarantee payment: 7866
Basic award: 8575
Additional award: 8689
Protective award: 8952

Whistleblowing:
Main entry: 2700+
Special grievance procedure: 6762
Appropriate authorities: 2735

Winding up:
Whether TUPE applies: 7998, 8023

Without prejudice:
Settlement negotiations: 9230+
Admissibility of communications at tribunal hearing: 9670

Witness:
Evidence:
  Disciplinary proceedings: 6607, 6618
  Tribunal proceedings: 9170+, 9553+, 9661+

Witness *(continued)*
Order:
  Tribunal proceedings: 9553+
Statement: 6607, 6618, 9501, 9561, 9635+, 9662

Women:
Specific health and safety protections: 4950+
Specific risk assessment: 4956+
See also Sex discrimination

Work abroad: See Overseas work

Work experience: 6300

Work permit:
Whether requirement for: 760+

Work pressures:
Whether liability for stress: 4950+

Work programme (Government scheme): 6380+

Work rules: 1295

Worker:
Definition: 13
Summary of main statutory rights: 17
Comparison to employee: 30+
Comparison to self-employed person: 14
See also under specific types

Workforce agreement: 1293
To partially exclude working time rules: 3660
Reference period in relation to calculation of average weekly working time: 3681
Defining what is hazardous work with regard to night workers: 3699
Impact on procedure regarding parental leave: 4650
Impact on procedure regarding annual leave: 4000
To extend validity of fixed-term contracts beyond 4 years: 1985

Working conditions:
General duties: 4810+
Specific duties: 4870
General risk assessment: 4865
Specific risk assessment: 4867

Working from home: See Home working

Working tax credit: 6862 (memo point)

Working time:
Main entry: 3605+
Summary of application of rules: 3608

Working time *(continued)*
Time worked for second employer: 2524
Requirement for written particulars: 1420
Whether duty of care regarding: 5030 (memo point)
See also Leave, Time off, Sunday trading

Work-life balance: See Flexible working

Workplace:
Requirement for written particulars: 1420
Travel to and from:
 Whether deductible expense: 3287, 3288, 3292+
 Whether working time: 3673
Whether closure leads to redundancy situation: 8749+

Written answers (claims):
Tribunal: 9541
EAT: 9771

Written particulars:
Main entry: 1400+
Model: 9900
Amendment: 1605
Award for infringement of right:
 Calculation of a week's pay: 2920+
Requirement in respect of disciplinary rules and procedures: 6525+

Written particulars *(continued)*
Offer of alternative employment: 8851
TUPE transfer (informing transferee): 8091+

Written representations: 9637

Written statements:
Fixed-term employee requesting: 1977+, 1987+
Part-time worker requesting: 1891+
Reasons for dismissal: 8310+

Wrongful dismissal:
Main entry: 8155+
Damages:
 Main entry: 8160+
 Effect on compensatory award: 8619

Wrongful trading:
By director of insolvent company: 2168

Y

Young person:
National minimum wage: 2869
Working time rules: 3720+
Health and safety restrictions: 4970+
Specific risk assessment: 4976+
Time off for training: 6330+
See also Apprentice and Trainee

Typeset by NORD COMPO
Printed February 2013 by L.E.G.O. S.p.A, Lavis (TN)

Achevé d'imprimer en février 2013
sur les presses de L.E.G.O. S.p.A, Lavis (TN)